BEING AND BECOMING

BEING AND BECOMING

An Introduction to Literature

Anne Mills King

Sandra Kurtinitis
Prince George's Community College

Random House New York

Library of Congress Cataloging-in-Publication Data

Being and becoming.

Includes indexes.
1. Literature—Collections.   I. King, Anne
Mills, 1921–   II. Kurtinitis, Sandra, 1943–
PN6014.B43   1987   808.8   86-26064
ISBN 0-394-36345-0
Manufactured in the United States of America

COVER ART: Hans Hofman's *Memoria in Aeternum,* 1962. Painting, courtesy of The Museum of Modern Art, New York. Gift of the artist.

Cover Design: Glen M. Edelstein
Book Design: Karin Batten

Additional acknowledgments and credits appear on pp. 1117–1125.

ACKNOWLEDGMENTS

"The Man Who Was Almost a Man," copyright © 1961 by Richard Wright from *Eight Men* by Richard Wright © 1940 by T. Y. Crowell Co. Reprinted by permission of John Hawkins & Associates, Inc.

"Raymond's Run," copyright © 1970 by Toni Cade Bambara. Reprinted from *Gorilla, My Love,* by Toni Cade Bambara, by permission of Random House, Inc.

"I Stand Here Ironing" excerpted from the book *Tell Me a Riddle* by Tillie Olsen. Copyright © 1956 by Tillie Olsen. Reprinted by permission of Delacorte Press/Seymour Lawrence.

"Angelina Sandoval," from *Chicano* by Richard Vasquez. Reprinted by permission of Richard Vasquez.

"The Spinoza of Market Street" from *The Collected Stories of Isaac Bashevis Singer.* Copyright © 1961, 1982 by Isaac Bashevis Singer. Reprinted by permission of Farrar, Straus and Giroux, Inc.

"A Worn Path," copyright 1941, 1969 by Eudora Welty. Reprinted from her volume *A Curtain of Green and Other Stories* by permission of Harcourt Brace Jovanovich, Inc.

PREFACE

To Those Who Will Use This Book: To Students and Their Instructors

To the Students

You who read this book are the "new college students." You may be recent high school graduates, seventy-year-old retirees, women, men, blacks, whites, orientals, Hispanic or Arabic. Your lifestyles include more variety than was dreamed of when courses like "Introduction to Literature" were first planned. Attending college, for you, is no longer just a rite of passage from high school to adulthood; it becomes a lifelong learning process for people of all social, cultural, and professional ties.

We have organized the book to reflect this variety. It is arranged thematically because we think a collection holds more interest that way. Its first section "Youth to Age," explores the experiences all human beings go through from early childhood to old age: the basic time-scheme of life. Section two, "City and Country," emphasizes the environments in which people live, and how these places influence their lives. The next section, "Human Relationships," tells of the connections that bind people together. After this comes a section entitled "Choices and Conflicts" which explores choices individuals make to solve the conflicts that life presents to them. Finally, in the closing section of the book, "Dreams and Realizations," we have gathered selections that reflect how dreams and realizations determine people's destiny. Some achieve their dreams; others are frustrated, but all of humanity's dreams become subjects for creative fiction, plays, and poems. Therefore our book centers on human existence, the human psyche, and human fate in works of literature—some immortal, some transitory, but all showing creativity.

Each of the five sections begins with a story that derives in some way from a myth or from the folklore of humanity. "Youth to Age" starts with Washington Irving's "Rip Van Winkle"—the myth of a sleeper who sees his world change from its youth to its maturity while he dreams his lazy dream. The section on "City and Country" begins with Stephen Crane's story of the Old West giving place to the new, "The Bride Comes to Yellow Sky." James Thurber's fable for our times, "The Unicorn in the Garden," calls on a mythical beast to satirize the relationship between two people. In "Choices and Conflicts," Nathaniel Hawthorne's "Young Goodman Brown" evokes the conflict of Puritan morality and its connection with witchcraft, while finally, in "Dreams and Realizations," Doris Betts' "The Ugliest Pilgrim" puts the old story of a religious pilgrimage in very modern clothes.

Within each of the five sections, the three genres—stories, poems, and plays—are presented in that order. Within each of these divisions the organization reflects a process, a "becoming," rather than a chronology. Within sections, for example, the progression is from youth to age, from country to city, from love to its contradictory opposites, from easy to difficult choices, and from simple to complex dreams and their realizations.

Our book, then, tries to show the ways that writers across the ages have dealt with human life and its passages, environments, relationships, conflicts, and dreams. Regardless of the order in which you read the book, we hope you will make it your own and enjoy it as much as we have.

To the Instructors

For many students, Introduction to Literature will be their only literature course, necessitating that this course speak to the student through accessible, involving, and appealing literary works. These students, and those who will continue literary study, will profit from the solid introduction to literary concepts included in the Appendix.

Although the primary table of contents in this book is thematic, a second one—organized by genre—supports a more traditional approach to the course. The book's wide range of readings and ample questions for discussion and writing expand its flexibility. The purpose of the Appendix is to offer practical advice on poetry, fiction, drama, as well as suggestions on how to write about literature. Included too are biographies of the writers, with short bibliographies of works by them and about them.

Neither headnotes nor study questions appear in the text itself. These are reserved for a substantial Instructor's Manual which supplies general background material, interpretive questions and analyses, and useful critical and media bibliographies where appropriate.

This book would not have been possible without the collaboration of a host of colleagues, students, friends, and editors. Most of all we wish to express our debt of gratitude to Betty Renshaw and Bill Fry, colleagues who started this book. Some of the other people whose mark it bears are: Margaret Warner and Charmaine Boyd of the Prince George's Community College Library, and Barbara Mowat of the Folger Shakespeare Library. Help and encouragement came from Stewart King; Jerry, Ian, Sara, and Jenny Kurtinitis; and Basil Karmazyn. Students who field-tested the material in a succession of classes were especially helpful, among them Carol Sheffler Calvery, Damien Brennan, Shahbaz Aulakh, Hyang Pak, Phong Tran, Brian Prigg, Sallie Smith, Cecilia Zampelli, Denise Ho, Shan-te Yu, Donald Graham, Sang Nahm, and Sarah Elliott. Our mentor at Random House was Steve Pensinger, English Editor, who, along with Cynthia Ward, Eleanor Castellano, and Andrea Haight nursed our book through all its stages. In addition, we wish to express our gratitude to our reviewers at various stages of manuscript preparation: Jennifer Banks, Michigan State University; Patrick Brostowin, Nassau Community College; Jon Burton, North Virginia Community College; Donald Fay, Kennesaw College; Gary Hall, North Harris County College; Beverly Head, Atlanta Jr. College; Rosemary Palms, Pratt Institute; and Carolyn Simonson, Tacoma Community College.

Anne Mills King
Sandra Kurtinitis

TABLE OF
CONTENTS I
(Arranged by theme)

Preface   v

YOUTH TO AGE   1

Epigraph: From "Ulysses"—Alfred, Lord Tennyson

Fiction   4

Poetry   65

Drama   87

CITY AND COUNTRY   213

Epigraph: Dust of Snow—Robert Frost

Fiction   216

Poetry   274

Drama   305

HUMAN RELATIONSHIPS   363

Epigraph: Western Wind—Anonymous

Fiction   366

Poetry   489

Drama   528

CHOICES AND CONFLICTS   589

Epigraph: The Road Not Taken—Robert Frost

APPENDIXES

TABLE OF CONTENTS II

(Arranged by genre)

FICTION

Poetry

Drama

Memoir

Oration

Appendixes

BEING AND BECOMING

Katie and Anne, 1955, by Fairfield Porter. (Hirshhorn Museum and Sculpture Garden, Smithsonian Institution.)

YOUTH
TO
AGE

I am a part of all that I have met;
Yet all experience is an arch wherethrough
Gleams that untraveled world whose margin fades
Forever and forever when I move.

from "Ulysses" by Alfred, Lord Tennyson

Who are we and what are we becoming? This first section of *Being and Becoming* chronicles, in different kinds of literature from many centuries, the passage of the human being from childhood to old age and death. It presents, in stories, plays, and poems, the shifting, never-ending movement of experience as one grows up, matures, and grows older. As the elderly Ulysses points out, in the epigraph to this section, one never stops growing and learning. The selections that follow reflect different stages of life: youth, adolescence, maturity, old age.

Washington Irving's "Rip Van Winkle," the first selection, sets parameters of the theme—reflecting, on the one hand, the youth of our country, America, and on the other, Rip's own careless youth and his rude awakening from it. In addition, Irving's story is a very early example of American fiction and so can be said to come from the youth, or beginnings, of modern fiction. In the middle of life comes a shock of recognition, as it did to Rip; in old age come acceptance and adaptation. Rip's old age was spent adapting—that is, storytelling about the exploits of his youth. Using a traditional element from myth and fairy tale—the long enchanted sleep—Irving created a tale of America's youth beloved by generations of readers.

The stories and poems that follow tell of both the joys and traumas of being young. Poems such as those by William Butler Yeats, Robert Louis Stevenson, and e. e. cummings capture the fanciful world of childhood, while Dylan Thomas's "Fern Hill" sings of both its lyricism and its quick flight.

The more complex dimension of adolescence unfolds with poems by Lawrence Ferlinghetti, A. E. Housman, and Robert Herrick that echo the adolescent wonder of sexuality. Other works show the darker side. Some of the stories and poems feature the pains of growing up and rebelling against the past. Richard Wright's "The Man Who Was Almost a Man" shows a young boy running away from the pressures that surround him. "Raymond's Run," by Toni Cade Bambara, captures an important moment in the emotional maturing of a young girl athlete. Tillie Olsen's "I Stand Here Ironing" probes a mother's thoughts about her daughter's deprived childhood, while Richard Vasquez's "Angelina Sandoval" shows how Angelina becomes strong enough to defy both tradition and parents to make her own way in the world.

In the middle portion of life comes a transition between rebellion and acceptance, between growing up and slowing down. As Rip Van Winkle is startled to recognize old friends in changed states, so many of our literary characters experience a shock of recognition, realizing that youth is over. Poems like Langston Hughes's "Mother to Son," Millay's Sonnet #57 ("Time, that renews the tissues of this frame"), and Gerard Manley Hopkins's "Spring and Fall: To a Young Child" show reflection and a desire to pass on wisdom to another generation. Shakespeare's King Lear tries this transition of power and fails, because of his own limitations and his false sense of kingliness.

At the other extreme of the spectrum of life stand old age and death. Some, like John Donne, Ruth Whitman, and Po Chu-i, write of noble and dignified acceptance of death. On the other hand, Keats and Tennyson, like Thomas, "rage against the dying of the light." Isaac Bashevis Singer's Dr. Fischelson reconciles philosophy and sex in a late marriage in "The Spinoza of Market Street." Eudora Welty's Phoenix Jackson, in "A Worn Path," portrays noble dignity in poverty and old age, while Arna Bontemps's Jeff and Jennie Patton, in "A Summer Tragedy," demonstrate a courageous solution to the shabby treatment of the elderly by modern society. Edward

Albee's "The Sandbox" dramatizes with satiric coldness the cruelty inherent in treating old people like children. Sylvia Plath looks to the horrible side of death, while Yeats longs for a kind of immortality.

These two extremes of life, youth and age, stand appropriately at the beginning of this anthology. The literary works in the remainder of our book show how these two extremes affect the "middle of life"—its human relationships, its environments, its choices and conflicts, and finally, its dreams and their realizations.

Fiction

RIP VAN WINKLE

Washington Irving

(1783–1859)

Biography p. 1079

[The following Tale was found among the papers of the late Diedrich Knickerbocker, an old gentleman of New York, who was very curious in the Dutch history of the province, and the manners of the descendants from its primitive settlers. His historical researches, however, did not lie so much among books as among men; for the former are lamentably scanty on his favorite topics; whereas he found the old burghers, and still more their wives, rich in that legendary lore so invaluable to true history. Whenever, therefore, he happened upon a genuine Dutch family, snugly up in its low-roofed farmhouse, under a spreading sycamore, he looked upon it as a little clasped volume of black-letter, and studied it with the zeal of a book-worm.

The result of all these researches was a history of the province during the reign of the Dutch governors, which he published some years since. There have been various opinions as to the literary character of his work, and, to tell the truth, it is not a whit better than it should be. Its chief merit is its scrupulous accuracy, which indeed was a little questioned on its first appearance, but has since been completely established; and it is now admitted into all historical collections as a book of unquestionable authority.]

WHOEVER has made a voyage up the Hudson must remember the Kaatskill mountains. They are a dismembered branch of the great Appalachian family, and are seen away to the west of the river, swelling up to a noble height, and lording it over the surrounding country. Every change of season, every change of weather, indeed, every hour of the day, produces some change in the magical hues and shapes of these mountains, and they are regarded by all the good wives, far and near, as perfect barometers. When the weather is fair and settled, they are clothed in blue and purple, and print their bold outlines on the clear evening sky; but sometimes, when the rest of the landscape is cloudless, they will gather a hood of gray vapors about their summits, which, in the last rays of the setting sun, will glow and light up like a crown of glory.

At the foot of these fairy mountains, the voyager may have descried the light smoke curling up from a village, whose shingle-roofs gleam among the trees, just where the blue tints of the upland melt away into the fresh green of the nearer landscape. It is a little village, of great antiquity, having been founded by some of the Dutch colonists in the early times of the province, just about the beginning of the government of the good Peter Stuyvesant, (may he rest in peace!) and there were some of the houses of the original settlers standing within a few years, built of small yellow bricks brought from Holland, having latticed windows and gable fronts, surmounted with weather-cocks.

In that same village, and in one of these very houses (which, to tell the precise truth, was sadly time-worn and weather-beaten), there lived, many years since, while the country was yet a province of Great Britain, a simple, good-natured fellow, of the name of Rip Van Winkle. He was a descendant of the Van Winkles who figured so gallantly in the chivalrous days of Peter Stuyvesant, and accompanied him to the siege of Fort Christina. He inherited, however, but little of the martial character of his ancestors. I have observed that he was a simple, good-natured man; he was, moreover, a kind neighbor, and an obedient, hen-pecked husband. Indeed, to the latter circumstance might be owing that meekness of spirit which gained him such universal popularity; for those men are most apt to be obsequious and conciliating abroad, who are under the discipline of shrews at home. Their tempers, doubtless, are rendered pliant and malleable in the fiery furnace of domestic tribulation; and a curtain-lecture is worth all the sermons in the world for teaching the virtues of patience and long-suffering. A termagant wife may, therefore, in some respects, be considered a tolerable blessing; and if so, Rip Van Winkle was thrice blessed.

Certain it is, that he was a great favorite among all the good wives of the village, who, as usual with the amiable sex, took his part in all family squabbles; and never failed, whenever they talked those matters over in their evening gossipings, to lay all the blame on Dame Van Winkle. The children of the village, too, would shout with joy whenever he approached. He assisted at their sports, made their playthings, taught them to fly kites and shoot marbles, and told them long stories of ghosts, witches, and Indians. Whenever he went dodging about the village, he was surrounded by a troop of them, hanging on his skirts, clambering on his back, and playing a thousand tricks on him with impunity; and not a dog would bark at him throughout the neighborhood.

The great error in Rip's composition was an insuperable aversion to all kinds of profitable labor. It could not be from the want of assiduity or perseverance; for he would sit on a wet rock, with a rod as long and heavy as a Tartar's lance, and fish all day without a murmur, even though he should not be encouraged by a single nibble. He would carry a fowling-piece on his shoulder for hours together, trudging through woods and swamps, and up hill and down dale, to shoot a few squirrels or wild pigeons. He would never refuse to assist a neighbor even in the roughest toil, and was a foremost man at all country frolics for husking Indian corn, or building stone fences; the women of the village, too, used to employ him to run their errands, and to do such little odd jobs as their less obliging husbands would not do for them. In a word, Rip was ready to attend to anybody's business but his own; but as to doing family duty, and keeping his farm in order, he found it impossible.

In fact, he declared it was of no use to work on his farm; it was the most pestilent little piece of ground in the whole country; everything about it went wrong, and would go wrong, in spite of him. His fences were continually falling to pieces; his cow would either go astray, or get among the cabbages; weeds were sure to grow quicker in his fields than anywhere else; the rain always made a point of setting in just as he had some out-door work to do; so that though his patrimonial estate had dwindled away under his management, acre by acre, until there was little more left than a mere patch of Indian corn and potatoes, yet it was the worst conditioned farm in the neighborhood.

His children, too, were as ragged and wild as if they belonged to nobody. His son Rip, an urchin begotten in his own likeness, promised to inherit the habits, with the old clothes, of his father. He was generally seen trooping like a colt at his mother's heels, equipped in a pair of his father's cast-off galligaskins, which he had much ado to hold up with one hand, as a fine lady does her train in bad weather.

Rip Van Winkle, however, was one of those happy mortals, of foolish, well-oiled dispositions, who take the world easy, eat white bread or brown, whichever can be got with least thought or trouble, and would rather starve on a penny than work for a pound. If left to himself, he would have whistled life away in perfect contentment; but his wife kept continually dinning in his ears about his idleness, his carelessness, and the ruin he was bringing on his family. Morning, noon, and night, her tongue was incessantly going, and everything he said or did was sure to produce a torrent of household eloquence. Rip had but one way of replying to all lectures of the kind, and that, by frequent use, had grown into a habit. He shrugged his shoulders, shook his head, cast up his eyes, but said nothing. This, however, always provoked a fresh volley from his wife; so that he was fain to draw off his forces, and take to the outside of the house—the only side which, in truth, belongs to a hen-pecked husband.

Rip's sole domestic adherent was his dog Wolf, who was as much hen-pecked as his master; for Dame Van Winkle regarded them as companions in idleness, and even looked upon Wolf with an evil eye, as the cause of his master's going so often astray. True it is, in all points of spirit befitting an honorable dog, he was as courageous an animal as ever scoured the woods; but what courage can withstand the ever-during and all-besetting terrors of a woman's tongue? The moment Wolf entered the house his crest fell, his tail drooped to the ground, or curled between his legs, he sneaked about with a gallows air, casting many a sidelong glance at Dame Van Winkle, and at the least flourish of a broomstick or ladle he would fly to the door with yelping precipitation.

Times grew worse and worse with Rip Van Winkle as years of matrimony rolled on; a tart temper never mellows with age, and a sharp tongue is the only edged tool that grows keener with constant use. For a long while he used to console himself, when driven from home, by frequenting a kind of perpetual club of the sages, philosophers, and other idle personages of the village, which held its sessions on a bench before a small inn, designated by a rubicund portrait of His Majesty George the Third. Here they used to sit in the shade through a long, lazy summer's day, talking listlessly over village gossip, or telling endless sleepy stories about nothing. But it would have been worth any statesman's money to have heard the profound discussions that sometimes took place, when by chance an old newspaper fell into their hands from some passing traveller. How solemnly they would listen to the contents, as drawled out by Derrick Van Bummel, the schoolmaster, a dapper learned little man, who was not to be daunted by the most gigantic word in the dictionary; and how sagely they would deliberate upon public events some months after they had taken place.

The opinions of this junto were completely controlled by Nicholas Vedder, a patriarch of the village, and landlord of the inn, at the door of which he took his seat from morning till night, just moving sufficiently to avoid the sun and keep in the shade of a large tree; so that the neighbors could tell the hour by his movements as accurately as by a sun-dial. It is true he was rarely heard to speak, but smoked his pipe inces- santly. His adherents, however (for every great man has his adherents), perfectly understood him, and knew how to gather his opinions. When anything that was read or related displeased him, he was observed to smoke his pipe vehemently, and to send forth short, frequent, and angry puffs; but when pleased, he would inhale the smoke slowly and tranquilly, and emit it in light and placid clouds; and sometimes, taking the pipe from his mouth, and letting the fragrant vapor curl about his nose, would gravely nod his head in token of perfect approbation.

From even this stronghold the unlucky Rip was at length routed by his termagant wife, who would suddenly break in upon the tranquillity of the assemblage and call the members all to naught; nor was that august personage, Nicholas Vedder himself, sacred from the daring tongue of this terrible virago, who charged him outright with encouraging her husband in habits of idleness.

Poor Rip was at last reduced almost to despair; and his only alternative, to escape from the labor of the farm and clamor of his wife, was to take gun in hand and stroll away into the woods. Here he would sometimes seat himself at the foot of a tree, and share the contents of his wallet with Wolf, with whom he sympathized as a fellow-sufferer in persecution. "Poor Wolf," he would say, "thy mistress leads thee a dog's life of it; but never mind, my lad, whilst I live thou shalt never want a friend to stand by thee!" Wolf would wag his tail, look wistfully in his master's face; and if dogs can feel pity, I verily believe he reciprocated the sentiment with all his heart.

In a long ramble of the kind on a fine autumnal day, Rip had unconsciously scrambled to one of the highest parts of the Kaatskill mountains. He was after his favorite sport of squirrel-shooting, and the still solitudes had echoed and re-echoed with the reports of his gun. Panting and fatigued, he threw himself, late in the afternoon, on a green knoll, covered with mountain herbage, that crowned the brow of a precipice. From an opening between the trees he could overlook all the lower country for many a mile of rich woodland. He saw at a distance the lordly Hudson, far, far below him, moving on its silent but majestic course, with the reflection of a purple cloud, or the sail of a lagging bark, here and there sleeping on its glassy bosom, and at last losing itself in the blue highlands.

On the other side he looked down into a deep mountain glen, wild, lonely, and shagged, the bottom filled with fragments from the impending cliffs, and scarcely lighted by the reflected rays of the setting sun. For some time Rip lay musing on this scene; evening was gradually advancing; the mountains began to throw their long blue shadows over the valleys; he saw that it would be dark long before he could reach the village, and he heaved a heavy sigh when he thought of encountering the terrors of Dame Van Winkle.

As he was about to descend, he heard a voice from a distance, hallooing, "Rip Van Winkle! Rip Van Winkle!" He looked round, but could see nothing but a crow winging its solitary flight across the mountain. He thought his fancy must have deceived him, and turned again to descend, when he heard the same cry ring through the still evening air: "Rip Van Winkle! Rip Van Winkle!"—at the same time Wolf bristled up his back, and giving a low growl, skulked to his master's side, looking fearfully down into the glen. Rip now felt a vague apprehension stealing over him; he looked anxiously in the same direction, and perceived a strange figure slowly toiling up the rocks, and bending under the weight of something he carried on his back. He was surprised to see any human being in this lonely and unfrequented place; but supposing it to be some one of the neighborhood in need of his assistance, he hastened down to yield it.

On nearer approach he was still more surprised at the singularity of the stranger's appearance. He was a short, square-built old fellow, with thick bushy hair, and a grizzled beard. His dress was of the antique Dutch fashion,—a cloth jerkin strapped round the waist—several pair of breeches, the outer one of ample volume, decorated with rows of buttons down the sides, and bunches at the knees. He bore on his shoulder a stout keg, that seemed full of liquor, and made signs for Rip to approach and assist him with the load. Though rather shy and distrustful of this new acquaintance, Rip complied with his usual alacrity; and mutually relieving one another, they clambered up a narrow gully, apparently the dry bed of a mountain torrent. As they ascended, Rip every now and then heard long, rolling peals, like distant thunder, that seemed to issue out of a deep ravine, or rather cleft, between lofty rocks, toward which their rugged path conducted. He paused for an instant, but supposing it to be the muttering of one of those transient thundershowers which often take place in mountain heights, he proceeded. Passing through the ravine, they came to a hollow, like a small amphitheatre, surrounded by perpendicular precipices, over the brinks of which impending trees shot their branches, so that you only caught glimpses of the azure sky and the bright evening cloud. During the whole time Rip and his companion had labored on in silence; for though the former marvelled greatly what could be the object of carrying a keg of liquor up this wild mountain, yet there was something strange and incomprehensible about the unknown, that inspired awe and checked familiarity.

On entering the amphitheatre, new objects of wonder presented themselves. On a level spot in the centre was a company of odd-looking personages playing at ninepins. They were dressed in a quaint, outlandish fashion; some wore short doublets, others jerkins, with long knives in their belts, and most of them had enormous breeches, of similar style with that of the guide's. Their visages, too, were peculiar: one had a large beard, broad face, and small piggish eyes; the face of another seemed to consist entirely of nose, and was surmounted by a white sugar-loaf hat, set off with a little red cock's tail. They all had beards, of various shapes and colors. There was one who seemed to be the commander. He was a stout old gentleman, with a weather-beaten countenance; he wore a laced doublet, broad belt and hanger, high crowned hat and feather, red stockings, and high-heeled shoes, with roses in them. The whole group reminded Rip of the figures in an old Flemish painting, in the parlor of Dominie Van Shaick, the village parson, and which had been brought over from Holland at the time of the settlement.

What seemed particularly odd to Rip was, that, though these folks were evidently amusing themselves, yet they maintained the gravest faces, the most mysterious silence, and were, withal, the most melancholy party of pleasure he had ever witnessed. Nothing interrupted the stillness of the scene but the noise of the balls, which, whenever they were rolled, echoed along the mountains like rumbling peals of thunder.

As Rip and his companion approached them, they suddenly desisted from their play, and stared at him with such fixed, statue-like gaze, and such strange, uncouth, lack-lustre countenances, that his heart turned within him, and his knees smote together. His companion now emptied the contents of the keg into large flagons, and made signs to him to wait upon the company. He obeyed with fear and trembling; they quaffed the liquor in profound silence, and then returned to their game.

By degrees Rip's awe and apprehension subsided. He even ventured, when no eye was fixed upon him, to taste the beverage, which he found had much of the flavor of excellent Hollands. He was naturally a thirsty soul, and was soon tempted to repeat the draught. One taste provoked another; and he reiterated his visits to the flagon so often that at length his senses were overpowered, his eyes swam in his head, his head gradually declined, and he fell into a deep sleep.

On waking, he found himself on the green knoll whence he had first seen the old man of the glen. He rubbed his eyes—it was a bright sunny morning. The birds were hopping and twittering among the bushes, and the eagle was wheeling aloft, and breasting the pure mountain breeze. "Surely," thought Rip, "I have not slept here all night." He recalled the occurrences before he fell asleep. The strange man with a keg of liquor—the mountain ravine—the wild retreat among the rocks—the woe-begone party at ninepins—the flagon—"Oh! that flagon! that wicked flagon!" thought Rip, —"what excuse shall I make to Dame Van Winkle?"

He looked round for his gun, but in place of the clean, well-oiled fowling-piece, he found an old fire-lock lying by him, the barrel incrusted with rust, the lock falling off, and the stock worm-eaten. He now suspected that the grave roisters of the mountain had put a trick upon him, and, having dosed him with liquor, had robbed him of his gun. Wolf, too, had disappeared but he might have strayed away after a squirrel or partridge. He whistled after him, and shouted his name, but all in vain; the echoes repeated his whistle and shout, but no dog was to be seen.

He determined to revisit the scene of the last evening's gambol, and if he met with any of the party, to demand his dog and gun. As he rose to walk, he found himself stiff in the joints, and wanting in his usual activity. "These mountain beds do not agree with me," thought Rip, "and if this frolic should lay me up with a fit of the rheumatism, I shall have a blessed time with Dame Van Winkle." With some difficulty he got down into the glen: he found the gully up which he and his companion had ascended the preceding evening; but to his astonishment a mountain stream was now foaming down it, leaping from rock to rock, and filling the glen with babbling murmurs. He, however, made shift to scramble up its sides, working his toilsome way through thickets of birch, sassafras, and witch-hazel, and sometimes tripped up or entangled by the wild grape-vines that twisted their coils or tendrils from tree to tree, and spread a kind of network in his path.

At length he reached to where the ravine had opened through the clifts to the amphitheatre; but no traces of such opening remained. The rocks presented a high, impenetrable wall, over which the torrent came tumbling in a sheet of feathery foam, and fell into a broad deep basin, black from the shadows of the surrounding forest. Here, then, poor Rip was brought to a stand. He again called and whistled after his dog; he was only answered by the cawing of a flock of idle crows, sporting high in air about a dry tree that overhung a sunny precipice; and who, secure in their elevation, seemed to look down and scoff at the poor man's perplexities. What was to be done? the morning was passing away, and Rip felt famished for want of his breakfast. He grieved to give up his dog and gun; he dreaded to meet his wife; but it would not do to starve among the mountains. He shook his head, shouldered the rusty firelock, and, with a heart full of trouble and anxiety, turned his steps homeward.

As he approached the village he met a number of people, but none whom he knew, which somewhat surprised him, for he had thought himself acquainted with every one in the country round. Their dress, too, was of a different fashion from that to which he was accustomed. They all stared at him with equal marks of surprise, and whenever they cast their eyes upon him, invariably stroked their chins. The constant recurrence of this gesture induced Rip, involuntarily, to do the same, when, to his astonishment, he found his beard had grown a foot long!

He had now entered the skirts of the village. A troop of strange children ran at his heels, hooting after him, and pointing at his gray beard. The dogs, too, not one of which he recognized for an old acquaintance, barked at him as he passed. The very village was altered; it was larger and more populous. There were rows of houses which he had never seen before, and those which had been his familiar haunts had disappeared. Strange names were over the doors—strange faces at the windows—everything was strange. His mind now misgave him; he began to doubt whether both he and the world around him were not bewitched. Surely this was his native village, which he had left but the day before. There stood the Kaatskill mountains—there ran the silver Hudson at a distance—there was every hill and dale precisely as it had always been. Rip was sorely perplexed. "That flagon last night," thought he, "has addled my poor head sadly!"

It was with some difficulty that he found the way to his own house, which he approached with silent awe, expecting every moment to hear the shrill voice of Dame Van Winkle. He found the house gone to decay—the roof fallen in, the windows shattered, and the doors off the hinges. A half-starved dog that looked like Wolf was skulking about it. Rip called him by name, but the cur snarled, showed his teeth, and passed on. This was an unkind cut indeed. "My very dog," sighed poor Rip, "has forgotten me!"

He entered the house, which, to tell the truth, Dame Van Winkle had always kept in neat order. It was empty, forlorn, and apparently abandoned. This desolateness overcame all his connubial fears—he called loudly for his wife and children—the lonely chambers rang for a moment with his voice, and then all again was silence.

He now hurried forth, and hastened to his old resort, the village inn—but it too was gone. A large rickety wooden building stood in its place, with great gaping windows, some of them broken and mended with old hats and petticoats, and over the door was painted, "The Union Hotel, by Jonathan Doolittle." Instead of the great tree that used to shelter the quiet little Dutch inn of yore, there now was reared a tall naked pole, with something on the top that looked like a red nightcap, and from it was fluttering a flag, on which was a singular assemblage of stars and stripes;—all this was strange and incomprehensible. He recognized on the sign, however, the ruby face of King George, under which he had smoked so many a peaceful pipe; but even this was singularly metamorphosed. The red coat was changed for one of blue and buff, a sword was held in the hand instead of a sceptre, the head was decorated with a cocked hat, and underneath was painted in large characters, GENERAL WASHINGTON.

There was, as usual, a crowd of folk about the door, but none that Rip recollected. The very character of the people seemed changed. There was a busy, bustling, disputatious tone about it, instead of the accustomed phlegm and drowsy tranquillity. He looked in vain for the sage Nicholas Vedder, with his broad face, double chin, and fair long pipe, uttering clouds of tobacco-smoke instead of idle speeches; or Van

Bummel, the schoolmaster, doling forth the contents of an ancient newspaper. In place of these, a lean, bilious-looking fellow, with his pockets full of hand-bills, was haranguing vehemently about rights of citizens—elections—members of Congress—liberty—Bunker's Hill—heroes of seventy-six—and other words, which were a perfect Babylonish jargon to the bewildered Van Winkle.

The appearance of Rip, with his long, grizzled beard, his rusty fowling-piece, his uncouth dress, and an army of women and children at his heels, soon attracted the attention of the tavern-politicians. They crowded round him, eying him from head to foot with great curiosity. The orator bustled up to him, and, drawing him partly aside, inquired, "On which side he voted?" Rip stared in vacant stupidity. Another short but busy little fellow pulled him by the arm, and, rising on tiptoe, inquired in his ear, "Whether he was Federal or Democrat?" Rip was equally at a loss to comprehend the question; when a knowing, self-important old gentleman, in a sharp cocked hat, made his way through the crowd, putting them to the right and left with his elbows as he passed, and planting himself before Van Winkle, with one arm akimbo, the other resting on his cane, his keen eyes and sharp hat penetrating, as it were, into his very soul, demanded in an austere tone, "What brought him to the election with a gun on his shoulder, and a mob at his heels; and whether he meant to breed a riot in the village?"—"Alas! gentlemen," cried Rip, somewhat dismayed, "I am a poor quiet man, a native of the place, and a loyal subject of the King, God bless him!"

Here a general shout burst from the by-standers—"A tory! a tory! a spy! a refugee! hustle him! away with him!" It was with great difficulty that the self-important man in the cocked hat restored order; and, having assumed a tenfold austerity of brow, demanded again of the unknown culprit, what he came there for, and whom he was seeking? The poor man humbly assured him that he meant no harm, but merely came there in search of some of his neighbors, who used to keep about the tavern.

"Well—who are they?—name them."

Rip bethought himself a moment, and inquired, "Where's Nicholas Vedder?"

There was a silence for a little while, when an old man replied, in a thin piping voice, "Nicholas Vedder! why, he is dead and gone these eighteen years! There was a wooden tombstone in the churchyard that used to tell all about him, but that's rotten and gone too."

"Where's Brom Dutcher?"

"Oh, he went off to the army in the beginning of the war; some say he was killed at the storming of Stony Point—others say he was drowned in a squall at the foot of Antony's Nose. I don't know—he never came back again."

"Where's Van Bummel, the schoolmaster?"

"He went off to the wars too, was a great militia general, and is now in Congress."

Rip's heart died away at hearing of these sad changes in his home and friends, and finding himself thus alone in the world. Every answer puzzled him too, by treating of such enormous lapses of time, and of matters which he could not understand: war—congress—Stony Point—he had no courage to ask after any more friends, but cried out in despair, "Does nobody here know Rip Van Winkle?"

"Oh, Rip Van Winkle!" exclaimed two or three, "oh, to be sure! that's Rip Van Winkle yonder, leaning against the tree."

Rip looked, and beheld a precise counterpart of himself, as he went up the mountain; apparently as lazy, and certainly as ragged. The poor fellow was now completely confounded. He doubted his own identity, and whether he was himself or another man. In the midst of his bewilderment, the man in the cocked hat demanded who he was, and what was his name.

"God knows," exclaimed he, at his wit's end; "I'm not myself—I'm somebody else —that's me yonder—no—that's somebody else got into my shoes—I was myself last night, but I fell asleep on the mountain, and they've changed my gun, and everything's changed, and I'm changed, and I can't tell what's my name, or who I am!"

The by-standers began now to look at each other, nod, wink significantly, and tap their fingers against their foreheads. There was a whisper, also, about securing the gun, and keeping the old fellow from doing mischief, at the very suggestion of which the self-important man in the cocked hat retired with some precipitation. At this critical moment a fresh, comely woman pressed through the throng to get a peep at the gray-bearded man. She had a chubby child in her arms, which, frightened at his looks, began to cry. "Hush, Rip," cried she, "hush, you little fool; the old man won't hurt you." The name of the child, the air of the mother, the tone of her voice, all awakened a train of recollections in his mind. "What is your name, my good woman?" asked he.

"Judith Gardenier."

"And your father's name?"

"Ah, poor man, Rip Van Winkle was his name, but it's twenty years since he went away from home with his gun, and never has been heard of since,—his dog came home without him; but whether he shot himself, or was carried away by the Indians, nobody can tell. I was then but a little girl."

Rip had but one question more to ask; but he put it with a faltering voice:

"Where's your mother?"

"Oh, she too had died but a short time since; she broke a bloodvessel in a fit of passion at a New-England pedler."

There was a drop of comfort, at least, in this intelligence. The honest man could contain himself no longer. He caught his daughter and her child in his arms. "I am your father!" cried he—"Young Rip Van Winkle once—old Rip Van Winkle now!— Does nobody know poor Rip Van Winkle?"

All stood amazed, until an old woman, tottering out from among the crowd, put her hand to her brow, and peering under it in his face for a moment, exclaimed, "Sure enough! it is Rip Van Winkle—it is himself! Welcome home again, old neighbor. Why, where have you been these twenty long years?"

Rip's story was soon told, for the whole twenty years had been to him but as one night. The neighbors stared when they heard it; some were seen to wink at each other, and put their tongues in their cheeks; and the self-important man in the cocked hat, who, when the alarm was over, had returned to the field, screwed down the corners of his mouth, and shook his head—upon which there was a general shaking of the head throughout the assemblage.

It was determined, however, to take the opinion of old Peter Vanderdonk, who was seen slowly advancing up the road. He was a descendant of the historian of that name, who wrote one of the earliest accounts of the province. Peter was the most ancient inhabitant of the village, and well versed in all the wonderful events and traditions of the neighborhood. He recollected Rip at once, and corroborated his story in the most satisfactory manner. He assured the company that it was a fact, handed down from his ancestor the historian, that the Kaatskill mountains had always been haunted by strange beings. That it was affirmed that the great Hendrick Hudson, the first discoverer of the river and country, kept a kind of vigil there every twenty years, with his crew of the Half-moon; being permitted in this way to revisit the scenes of his enterprise, and keep a guardian eye upon the river and the great city called by his name. That his father had once seen them in their old Dutch dresses playing at ninepins in a hollow of the mountain; and that he himself had heard, one summer afternoon, the sound of their balls, like distant peals of thunder.

To make a long story short, the company broke up and returned to the more important concerns of the election. Rip's daughter took him home to live with her; she had a snug, well-furnished house, and a stout, cheery farmer for a husband, whom Rip recollected for one of the urchins that used to climb upon his back. As to Rip's son and heir, who was the ditto of himself, seen leaning against the tree, he was employed to work on the farm; but evinced an hereditary disposition to attend to anything else but his business.

Rip now resumed his old walks and habits; he soon found many of his former cronies, though all rather the worse for the wear and tear of time; and preferred making friends among the rising generation, with whom he soon grew into great favor.

Having nothing to do at home, and being arrived at that happy age when a man can be idle with impunity, he took his place once more on the bench at the inn-door, and was reverenced as one of the patriarchs of the village, and a chronicle of the old times "before the war." It was some time before he could get into the regular track of gossip, or could be made to comprehend the strange events that had taken place during his torpor. How that there had been a revolutionary war,—that the country had thrown off the yoke of old England,—and that, instead of being a subject of his Majesty George the third, he was now a free citizen of the United States. Rip, in fact, was no politician; the changes of states and empires made but little impression on him; but there was one species of despotism under which he had long groaned, and that was—petticoat government. Happily that was at an end; he had got his neck out of the yoke of matrimony, and could go in and out whenever he pleased, without dreading the tyranny of Dame Van Winkle. Whenever her name was mentioned, however, he shook his head, shrugged his shoulders, and cast up his eyes; which might pass either for an expression of resignation to his fate, or joy at his deliverance.

He used to tell his story to every stranger that arrived at Mr. Doolittle's hotel. He was observed, at first, to vary on some points every time he told it, which was, doubtless, owing to his having so recently awaked. It at last settled down precisely to the tale I have related, and not a man, woman, or child in the neighborhood but knew it by heart. Some always pretended to doubt the reality of it, and insisted that Rip had been out of his head, and that this was one point on which he always remained flighty. The old Dutch inhabitants, however, almost universally gave it full credit. Even to this day they never hear a thunderstorm of a summer afternoon about the Kaatskill, but they say Hendrick Hudson and his crew are at their game of ninepins; and it is a common wish of all hen-pecked husbands in the neighborhood, when life hangs heavy on their hands, that they might have a quieting draught out of Rip Van Winkle's flagon.

THE MAN WHO WAS ALMOST A MAN

Richard Wright
(1908–1960)

Biography p. 1109

Dave struck out across the fields, looking homeward through paling light. Whuts the usa talkin wid em niggers in the field? Anyhow, his mother was putting supper on the table. Them niggers can't understand *nothing*. One of these days he was going to get a gun and practice shooting, then they can't talk to him as though he were a little boy. He slowed, looking at the ground. Shucks, Ah ain scareda them even ef they are biggern me! Aw, Ah know what Ahma do. . . . Ahm going by ol Joe's sto n git that Sears Roebuck catlog n look at them guns. Mabbe Ma will lemme buy one when she gits mah pay from ol man Hawkins. Ahma beg her t gimme some money. Ahm ol ernough to hava gun. Ahm seventeen. Almos a man. He strode, feeling his long, loose-jointed limbs. Shucks, a man oughta hava little gun aftah he done worked hard all day. . . .

He came in sight of Joe's store. A yellow lantern glowed on the front porch. He mounted steps and went through the screen door, hearing it bang behind him. There was a strong smell of coal oil and mackerel fish. He felt very confident until he saw fat Joe walk in through the rear door, then his courage began to ooze.

'Howdy, Dave! Whutcha want?'

'How yuh, Mistah Joe? Aw, Ah don wanna buy nothing. Ah jus wanted t see ef yuhd lemme look at tha ol catlog erwhile.'

'Sure! You wanna see it here?'

'Nawsuh. Ah wans t take it home wid me. Ahll bring it back termorrow when Ah come in from the fiels.'

'You plannin on buyin something?'

'Yessuh.'

'Your ma letting you have your own money now?'

'Shucks. Mistah Joe, Ahm gittin t be a man like anybody else!'

Joe laughed and wiped his greasy white face with a red bandanna.

'Whut you plannin on buyin?'

Dave looked at the floor, scratched his head, scratched his thigh, and smiled. Then he looked up shyly.

'Ahll tell yuh, Mistah Joe, ef yuh promise yuh won't tell.'

'I promise.'

'Waal, Ahma buy a gun.'

'A gun? Whut you want with a gun?'

'Ah wanna keep it.'

'You ain't nothing but a boy. You don't need a gun.'

'Aw, lemme have the catlog, Mistah Joe. Ahll bring it back.'

Joe walked through the rear door. Dave was elated. He looked around at barrels of sugar and flour. He heard Joe coming back. He craned his neck to see if he were bringing the book. Yeah, he's got it! Gawddog, he's got it!

'Here; but be sure you bring it back. It's the only one I got.'

'Sho, Mistah Joe.'

'Say, if you wanna buy a gun, why don't you buy one from me. I gotta gun to sell.'

'Will it shoot?'

'Sure it'll shoot.'

'Whut kind is it?'

'Oh, it's kinda old. . . . A Lefthand Wheeler. A pistol. A big one.'

'Is it got bullets in it?'

'It's loaded.'

'Kin Ah see it?'

'Where's your money?'

'Whut yuh wan fer it?'

'I'll let you have it for two dollars.'

'Just *two* dollahs? Shucks, Ah could buy tha when Ah git mah pay.'

'I'll have it here when you want it.'

'Awright, suh. Ah be in fer it.'

He went through the door, hearing it slam again behind him. Ahma git some money from Ma n buy me a gun! Only *two* dollahs! He tucked the thick catalogue under his arm and hurried.

'Where yuh been, boy?' His mother held a steaming dish of black-eyed peas.

'Aw, Ma, Ah jus stopped down the road t talk wid th boys.'

'Yuh know bettah than t keep suppah waitin.'

He sat down, resting the catalogue on the edge of the table.

'Yuh git up from there and git to the well n wash yosef! Ah ain feedin no hogs in mah house!'

She grabbed his shoulder and pushed him. He stumbled out of the room, then came back to get the catalogue.

'Whut this?'

'Aw, Ma, it's jusa catlog.'

'Who yuh git it from?'

'From Joe, down at the sto.'

'Waal, thas good. We kin use it around the house.'

'Naw, Ma.' He grabbed for it. 'Gimme mah catlog, Ma.'

She held onto it and glared at him.

'Quit hollerin at me! Whuts wrong wid yuh? Yuh crazy?'

'But Ma, please. It ain mine! It's Joe's! He tol me t bring it back t im termorrow.'

She gave up the book. He stumbled down the back steps, hugging the thick book under his arm. When he had splashed water on his face and hands, he groped back to the kitchen and fumbled in a corner for the towel. He bumped into a chair; it clattered to the floor. The catalogue sprawled at his feet. When he had dried his eyes he snatched up the book and held it again under his arm. His mother stood watching him.

'Now, ef yuh gonna acka fool over that ol book, Ahll take it n burn it up.'

'Naw, Ma, please.'

'Waal, set down n be still!'

He sat and drew the oil lamp close. He thumbed page after page, unaware of the food his mother set on the table. His father came in. Then his small brother.

'Whutcha got there, Dave?' his father asked.

'Jusa catlog,' he answered, not looking up.

'Ywah, here they is!' His eyes glowed at blue and black revolvers. He glanced up, feeling sudden guilt. His father was watching him. He eased the book under the table and rested it on his knees. After the blessing was asked, he ate. He scooped up peas and swallowed fat meat without chewing. Buttermilk helped to wash it down. He did not want to mention money before his father. He would do much better by cornering his mother when she was alone. He looked at his father uneasily out of the edge of his eye.

'Boy, how come yuh don quit foolin wid tha book n eat yo suppah?'

'Yessuh.'

'How yuh n ol man Hawkins gittin erlong?'

'Suh?'

'Can't yuh hear? Why don yuh lissen? Ah ast yuh how wuz yuh n ol man Hawkins gittin erlong?'

'Oh, swell, Pa. Ah plows mo lan than anybody over there.'

'Waal, yuh oughta keep yo min on whut yuh doin.'

'Yessuh.'

He poured his plate full of molasses and sopped at it slowly with a chunk of cornbread. When all but his mother had left the kitchen, he still sat and looked again at the guns in the catalogue. Lawd, ef Ah only had tha pretty one! He could almost feel the slickness of the weapon with his fingers. If he had a gun like that he would polish it and keep it shining so it would never rust. N Ahd keep it loaded, by Gawd!

'Ma?'

'Hunh?'

'Ol man Hawkins give yuh mah money yit?'

'Yeah, but ain no usa yuh thinkin bout thowin nona it erway. Ahm keepin tha money sos yuh kin have cloes t go to school this winter.'

He rose and went to her side with the open catalogue in his palms. She was washing dishes, her head bent low over a pan. Shyly he raised the open book. When he spoke his voice was husky, faint.

'Ma, Gawd knows Ah wans one of these.'

'One of whut?' she asked, not raising her eyes.

'One of *these*,' he said again, not daring even to point. She glanced up at the page, then at him with wide eyes.

'Nigger is yuh gone plum crazy?'

'Ah, Ma———'

'Git outta here! Don yuh talk t me bout no gun! Yuh a fool!'

'Ma, Ah kin buy one fer *two* dollahs.'

'Not ef Ah knows it yuh ain!'

'But yuh promised me one———'

'Ah don care whut Ah promised! Yuh ain nothing but a boy yit!'

'Ma, ef yuh lemme buy one Ahll *never* ast yuh fer nothing no mo.'

'Ah tol yuh t git outta here! Yuh ain gonna toucha penny of tha money fer no gun! Thas how come Ah has Mistah Hawkins t pay yo wages t me, cause Ah knows yuh ain got no sense.'

'But Ma, we needa gun. Pa ain got no gun. We needa gun in the house. Yuh kin never tell whut might happen.'

'Now don yuh try to maka fool outta me, boy! Ef we did hava gun yuh wouldn't have it!'

He laid the catalogue down and slipped his arm around her waist.

'Aw, Ma, Ah done worked hard alla summer n ain ast yuh fer nothin, is Ah, now?'

'Thas whut yuh spose t do!'

'But Ma, Ah wans a gun. Yuh kin lemme have two dollahs outta mah money. Please, Ma. I kin give it to Pa . . . Please, Ma! Ah loves yuh, Ma.'

When she spoke her voice came soft and low.

'Whut yuh wan wida gun, Dave? Yuh don need no gun. Yuhll git in trouble. N ef yo Pa jus *thought* Ah let yuh have money t buy a gun he'd hava fit.'

'Ahll hide it, Ma, it ain but two dollahs.'

'Lawd, chil, whuts wrong wid yuh?'

'Ain nothing wrong, Ma. Ahm almos a man now. Ah wans a gun.'

'Who gonna sell yuh a gun?'

'Ol Joe at the sto.'

'N it don cos but two dollahs?'

'Thas all, Ma. Just two dollahs. Please, Ma.'

She was stacking the plates away; her hands moved slowly, reflectively. Dave kept an anxious silence. Finally, she turned to him.

'Ahll let yuh git tha gun ef yuh promise me one thing.'

'Whuts tha, Ma?'

'Yuh bring it straight back t *me,* yuh hear? Itll be fer Pa.'

'Yessum! Lemme go now, Ma.'

She stooped, turned slightly to one side, raised the hem of her dress, rolled down the top of her stocking, and came up with a slender wad of bills.

'Here,' she said. 'Lawd knows yuh don need no gun. But yer Pa does. Yuh bring it right back t *me,* yuh hear? Ahma put it up. Now ef yuh don, Ahma have yuh Pa lick yuh so hard yuh won ferget it.'

'Yessum.'

He took the money, ran down the steps, and across the yard.

'Dave! Yuuuuuh Daaaaave!'

He heard, but he was not going to stop now. 'Naw, Lawd!'

The first movement he made the following morning was to reach under his pillow for the gun. In the gray light of dawn he held it loosely, feeling a sense of power. Could killa man wida gun like this. Kill anybody, black er white. And if he were holding his gun in his hand nobody could run over him; they would have to respect him. It was a big gun, with a long barrel and a heavy handle. He raised and lowered it in his hand, marveling at its weight.

He had not come straight home with it as his mother had asked; instead he had stayed out in the fields, holding the weapon in his hand, aiming it now and then at some imaginary foe. But he had not fired it; he had been afraid that his father might hear. Also he was not sure he knew how to fire it.

To avoid surrendering the pistol he had not come into the house until he knew that all were asleep. When his mother had tiptoed to his bedside late that night and demanded the gun, he had first played 'possum; then he had told her that the gun was hidden outdoors, that he would bring it to her in the morning. Now he lay turning it slowly in his hands. He broke it, took out the cartridges, felt them, and then put them back.

He slid out of bed, got a long strip of old flannel from a trunk, wrapped the gun in it, and tied it to his naked thigh while it was still loaded. He did not go in to breakfast. Even though it was not yet daylight, he started for Jim Hawkins' plantation. Just as the sun was rising he reached the barns where the mules and plows were kept.

'Hey! That you, Dave?'

He turned. Jim Hawkins stood eying him suspiciously.

'Whatre yuh doing here so early?'

'Ah didn't know Ah wuz gittin up so early, Mistah Hawkins. Ah wuz fixin t hitch up ol Jenny n take her t the fiels.'

'Good. Since you're here so early, how about plowing that stretch down by the woods?'

'Suits me. Mistah Hawkins.'

'O.K. Go to it!'

He hitched Jenny to a plow and started across the fields. Hot dog! This was just what he wanted. If he could get down by the woods, he could shoot his gun and nobody would hear. He walked behind the plow, hearing the traces creaking, feeling the gun tied tight to his thigh.

When he reached the woods, he plowed two whole rows before he decided to take out the gun. Finally, he stopped, looked in all directions, then untied the gun and held it in his hand. He turned to the mule and smiled.

'Know whut this is, Jenny? Naw, yuh wouldn't know! Yuhs jusa ol mule! Anyhow, this is a gun, n it kin shoot, by Gawd!'

He held the gun at arm's length. Whut t hell, Ahma shoot this thing! He looked at Jenny again.

'Lissen here, Jenny! When Ah pull this ol trigger Ah don wan yuh t run n acka fool now.'

Jenny stood with head down, her short ears pricked straight. Dave walked off about twenty feet, held the gun far out from him, at arm's length, and turned his head. Hell, he told himself, Ah ain afraid. The gun felt loose in his fingers; he waved it wildly for a moment. Then he shut his eyes and tightened his forefinger. *Blooom!* A report half-deafened him and he thought his right hand was torn from his arm. He heard Jenny whinnying and galloping over the field, and he found himself on his knees, squeezing his fingers hard between his legs. His hand was numb; he jammed it into his mouth, trying to warm it, trying to stop the pain. The gun lay at his feet. He did not quite know what had happened. He stood up and stared at the gun as though it were a live thing. He gritted his teeth and kicked the gun. Yuh almos broke mah arm! He turned to look for Jenny; she was far over the fields, tossing her head and kicking wildly.

'Hol on there, ol mule!'

When he caught up with her she stood trembling, walling her big white eyes at him. The plow was far away; the traces had broken. Then Dave stopped short, looking, not believing. Jenny was bleeding. Her left side was red and wet with blood. He went closer. Lawd have mercy! Wondah did Ah shoot this mule? He grabbed for Jenny's mane. She flinched, snorted, whirled, tossing her head.

'Hol on now! Hol on.'

Then he saw the hole in Jenny's side, right between the ribs. It was round, wet, red. A crimson stream streaked down the front leg, flowing fast. Good Gawd! Ah wuznt shootin at tha mule. . . . He felt panic. He knew he had to stop that blood, or Jenny would bleed to death. He had never seen so much blood in all his life. He ran the mule for half a mile, trying to catch her. Finally she stopped, breathing hard, stumpy tail half arched. He caught her mane and led her back to where the plow and gun lay. Then he stopped and grabbed handfuls of damp black earth and tried to plug the bullet hole. Jenny shuddered, whinnied, and broke from him.

'Hol on! Hol on now!'

He tried to plug it again, but blood came anyhow. His fingers were hot and sticky. He rubbed dirt hard into his palms, trying to dry them. Then again he attempted to plug the bullet hole, but Jenny shied away, kicking her heels high. He stood helpless. He had to do something. He ran at Jenny; she dodged him. He watched a red stream of blood flow down Jenny's leg and form a bright pool at her feet.

'Jenny . . . Jenny . . .' he called weakly.

His lips trembled. She's bleeding t death! He looked in the direction of home, wanting to go back, wanting to get help. But he saw the pistol lying in the damp black clay. He had a queer feeling that if he only did something, this would not be; Jenny would not be there bleeding to death.

When he went to her this time, she did not move. She stood with sleepy, dreamy eyes; and when he touched her she gave a low-pitched whinny and knelt to the ground, her front knees slopping in blood.

'Jenny . . . Jenny . . .' he whispered.

For a long time she held her neck erect; then her head sank, slowly. Her ribs swelled with a mighty heave and she went over.

Dave's stomach felt empty, very empty. He picked up the gun and held it gingerly between his thumb and forefinger. He buried it at the foot of a tree. He took a stick and tried to cover the pool of blood with dirt—but what was the use? There was Jenny lying with her mouth open and her eyes walled and glassy. He could not tell Jim Hawkins he had shot his mule. But he had to tell something. Yeah, Ahll tell em Jenny started gittin wil n fell on the joint of the plow. . . . But that would hardly happen to a mule. He walked across the field slowly, head down.

It was sunset. Two of Jim Hawkins' men were over near the edge of the woods digging a hole in which to bury Jenny. Dave was surrounded by a knot of people; all of them were looking down at the dead mule.

'I don't see how in the world it happened,' said Jim Hawkins for the tenth time.

The crowd parted and Dave's mother, father, and small brother pushed into the center.

'Where Dave?' his mother called.

'There he is,' said Jim Hawkins.

His mother grabbed him.

'Whut happened, Dave? Whut yuh done?'

'Nothing.'

'C'mon, boy, talk,' his father said.

Dave took a deep breath and told the story he knew nobody believed.

'Waal,' he drawled. 'Ah brung ol Jenny down here sos Ah could do mah plowin. Ah plowed bout two rows, just like yuh see.' He stopped and pointed at the long rows of upturned earth. 'Then something musta been wrong wid ol Jenny. She wouldn't ack right atall. She started snortin n kickin her heels. Ah tried to hol her, but she pulled erway, rearin n goin on. Then when the point of the plow was stickin up in the air, she swung erroun n twisted hersef back on it. . . . She stuck hersef n started t bleed. N fo Ah could do anything, she wuz dead.'

'Did you ever hear of anything like that in all your life?' asked Jim Hawkins.

There were white and black standing in the crowd. They murmured. Dave's mother came close to him and looked hard into his face.

'Tell the truth, Dave,' she said.

'Looks like a bullet hole ter me,' said one man.

'Dave, whut yuh do wid tha gun?' his mother asked.

The crowd surged in, looking at him. He jammed his hands into his pockets, shook his head slowly from left to right, and backed away. His eyes were wide and painful.

'Did he hava gun?' asked Jim Hawkins.

'By Gawd, Ah tol yuh tha wuz a *gun* wound,' said a man, slapping his thigh.

His father caught his shoulders and shook him till his teeth rattled.

'Tell whut happened, yuh rascal! Tell whut . . .'

Dave looked at Jenny's stiff legs and began to cry.

'Whut yuh do wid tha gun?' his mother asked.

'Whut wuz he doin wida gun?' his father asked.

'Come on and tell the truth,' said Hawkins. 'Ain't nobody going to hurt you . . .'

His mother crowded close to him.

'Did yuh shoot tha mule, Dave?'

Dave cried, seeing blurred white and black faces.

'Ahh ddinnt gggo tt sshoooot hher. . . . Ah ssswear off Gawd Ahh ddint. . . . Ah wuz a-tryin t sssee ef the ol gggun would sshoot———'

'Where yuh git the gun from?' his father asked.

'Ah got it from Joe, at the sto.'

'Where yuh git the money?'

'Ma give it t me.'

'He kept worryin me, Bob. . . . Ah had t. . . . Ah tol im t bring the gun right back to me. . . . It was fer yuh, the gun.'

'But how yuh happen to shoot that mule?' asked Jim Hawkins.

'Ah wuznt shootin at the mule, Mistah Hawkins. The gun jumped when Ah pulled the trigger . . . N fo Ah knowed anything Jenny wuz there a-bleedin.'

Somebody in the crowd laughed. Jim Hawkins walked close to Dave and looked into his face.

'Well, looks like you have bought you a mule, Dave.'

'Ah swear fo Gawd, Ah didn't go t kill the mule, Mistah Hawkins!'

'But you killed her!'

All the crowd was laughing now. They stood on tiptoe and poked heads over one another's shoulders.

'Well, boy, looks like yuh done bought a dead mule! Hahaha!'

'Ain tha ershame.'

'Hohohohoho.'

Dave stood head down, twisting his feet in the dirt.

'Well, you needn't worry about it, Bob,' said Jim Hawkins to Dave's father. 'Just let the boy keep on working and pay me two dollars a month.'

'Whut yuh wan fer yo mule, Mistah Hawkins?'

Jim Hawkins screwed up his eyes.

'Fifty dollars.'

'Whut yuh do wid tha gun?' Dave's father demanded.

Dave said nothing.

'Yuh wan me t take a tree lim n beat yuh till yuh talk!'

'Nawsuh!'

'Whut yuh do wid it?'

'Ah thowed it erway.'

'Where?'

'Ah . . . Ah thowed it in the creek.'

'Waal, c mon home. N firs thing in the mawnin git to tha creek n fin tha gun.'

'Yessuh.'

'Whut yuh pay fer it?'

'Two dollahs.'

'Take tha gun n git yo money back n carry it t Mistah Hawkins, yuh hear? N don fergit Ahma lam yo black bottom good fer this! Now march yosef on home, suh!'

Dave turned and walked slowly. He heard people laughing. Dave glared, his eyes welling with tears. Hot anger bubbled in him. Then he swallowed and stumbled on.

That night Dave did not sleep. He was glad that he had gotten out of killing the mule so easily, but he was hurt. Something hot seemed to turn over inside him each time he remembered how they had laughed. He tossed on his bed, feeling his hard pillow. N Pa says he's gonna beat me. . . . He remembered other beatings, and his back quivered. Naw, naw, Ah sho don wan im t beat me tha way no mo. . . . Dam em *all!* Nobody ever gave him anything. All he did was work. They treat me lika mule. . . . N then they beat me. . . . He gritted his teeth. N Ma had t tell on me.

Well, if he had to, he would take old man Hawkins that two dollars. But that meant selling the gun. And he wanted to keep that gun. Fifty dollahs fer a dead mule.

He turned over, thinking of how he had fired the gun. he had an itch to fire it again. Ef other men kin shoota gun, by Gawd, Ah kin! He was still listening. Mebbe they all sleepin now. . . . The house was still. He heard the soft breathing of his brother. Yes, now! He would go down and get that gun and see if he could fire it! He eased out of bed and slipped into overalls.

The moon was bright. He ran almost all the way to the edge of the woods. He stumbled over the ground, looking for the spot where he had buried the gun. Yeah, here it is. Like a hungry dog scratching for a bone he pawed it up. He puffed his black cheeks and blew dirt from the trigger and barrel. He broke it and found four cartridges unshot. He looked around; the fields were filled with silence and moonlight. He clutched the gun stiff and hard in his fingers. But as soon as he wanted to pull the trigger, he shut his eyes and turned his head. Naw, Ah can't shoot wid mah eyes closed n mah head turned. With effort he held his eyes open; then he squeezed. *Blooooom!* He was stiff, not breathing. The gun was still in his hands. Dammit, he'd done it! He fired again. *Bloooom!* He smiled. *Bloooom! Bloooom! Click, click.* There! It was empty. If anybody could shoot a gun, he could. He put the gun into his hip pocket and started across the fields.

When he reached the top of a ridge he stood straight and proud in the moonlight, looking at Jim Hawkins' big white house, feeling the gun sagging in his pocket. Lawd, ef Ah had jus one mo bullet Ahd taka shot at tha house. Ahd like t scare ol man Hawkins jusa little. . . . Jussa enough t let im know Dave Sanders is a man.

To his left the road curved, running to the tracks of the Illinois Central. He jerked his head, listening. From far off came a faint *hoooof-hoooof; hoooof-hoooof; hoooof-hoooof* . . . Tha's number eight. He took a swift look at Jim Hawkins' white house; he thought of pa, of ma, of his little brother, and the boys. He thought of the dead mule and heard *hoooof-hoooof; hoooof-hoooof; hoooof-hoooof* . . . He stood rigid. Two dollahs a mont. Les see now. . . . Tha means itll take bout two years. Shucks! Ahll be dam!

He started down the road, toward the tracks. Yeah, here she comes! He stood beside the track and held himself stiffly. Here she comes, erroun the ben. . . . C mon, yuh slow poke! C mon! He had his hand on his gun; something quivered in his stomach. Then the train thundered past, the gray and brown box cars rumbling and clinking. He gripped the gun tightly; then he jerked his hand out of his pocket. Ah betcha Bill wouldn't do it! Ah betcha. . . . The cars slid past, steel grinding upon steel. Ahm riding yuh ternight so hep me Gawd! He was hot all over. He hesitated just a moment; then he grabbed, pulled atop of a car, and lay flat. He felt his pocket; the gun was still there. Ahead the long rails were glinting in the moonlight, stretching away, away to somewhere, somewhere where he could be a man. . . .

RAYMOND'S RUN

Toni Cade Bambara
(b. 1939)

Biography p. 1061

I don't have much work to do around the house like some girls. My mother does that. And I don't have to earn my pocket money by hustling; George runs errands for the big boys and sells Christmas cards. And anything else that's got to get done, my father does. All I have to do in life is mind my brother Raymond, which is enough.

Sometimes I slip and say my little brother Raymond. But as any fool can see he's much bigger and he's older too. But a lot of people call him my little brother cause he needs looking after cause he's not quite right. And a lot of smart mouths got lots to say about that too, especially when George was minding him. But now, if anybody has anything to say to Raymond, anything to say about his big head, they have to come by me. And I don't play the dozens or believe in standing around with somebody in my face doing a lot of talking. I much rather just knock you down and take my chances even if I am a little girl with skinny arms and a squeaky voice, which is how I got the name Squeaky. And if things get too rough, I run. And as anybody can tell you, I'm the fastest thing on two feet.

There is no track meet that I don't win the first place medal. I used to win the twenty-yard dash when I was a little kid in kindergarten. Nowadays, it's the fifty-yard dash. And tomorrow I'm subject to run the quarter-meter relay all by myself and come in first, second, and third. The big kids call me Mercury cause I'm the swiftest thing in the neighborhood. Everybody knows that—except two people who know better, my father and me. He can beat me to Amsterdam Avenue with me having a two fire-hydrant headstart and him running with his hands in his pockets and whistling. But that's private information. Cause can you imagine some thirty-five-year-old man stuffing himself into PAL shorts to race little kids? So as far as everyone's concerned, I'm the fastest and that goes for Gretchen, too, who has put out the tale that she is going to win the first-place medal this year. Ridiculous. In the second place, she's got short legs. In the third place, she's got freckles. In the first place, no one can beat me and that's all there is to it.

I'm standing on the corner admiring the weather and about to take a stroll down Broadway so I can practice my breathing exercises, and I've got Raymond walking on the inside close to the buildings, cause he's subject to fits of fantasy and starts thinking he's a circus performer and that the curb is a tightrope strung high in the air. And sometimes after a rain he likes to step down off his tightrope right into the gutter and slosh around getting his shoes and cuffs wet. Then I get hit when I get home. Or sometimes if you don't watch him he'll dash across traffic to the island in the middle of Broadway and give the pigeons a fit. Then I have to go behind him apologizing to all the old people sitting around trying to get some sun and getting all upset with the pigeons fluttering around them, scattering their newspapers and upsetting the waxpaper lunches in their laps. So I keep Raymond on the inside of me, and he plays like he's driving a stage coach which is O.K. by me so long as he doesn't run me over or interrupt my breathing exercises, which I have to do on account of I'm serious about my running, and I don't care who knows it.

Now some people like to act like things come easy to them, won't let on that they practice. Not me. I'll high-prance down 34th Street like a rodeo pony to keep my knees strong even if it does get my mother uptight so that she walks ahead like she's not with me, don't know me, is all by herself on a shopping trip, and I am somebody else's crazy child. Now you take Cynthia Procter for instance. She's just the opposite. If there's a test tomorrow, she'll say something like, "Oh, I guess I'll play handball this afternoon and watch television tonight," just to let you know she ain't thinking about the test. Or like last week when she won the spelling bee for the millionth time, "A good thing you got 'receive,' Squeaky, cause I would have got it wrong. I completely forgot about the spelling bee." And she'll clutch the lace on her blouse like it was a narrow escape. Oh, brother. But of course when I pass her house on my early morning trots around the block, she is practicing the scales on the piano over and over and over and over. Then in music class she always lets herself get bumped around so she falls accidently on purpose onto the piano stool and is so surprised to find herself sitting there that she decides just for fun to try out the ole keys. And what do you know—Chopin's waltzes just spring out of her fingertips and she's the most surprised thing in the world. A regular prodigy. I could kill people like that. I stay up all night studying the words for the spelling bee. And you can see me any time of day practicing running. I never walk if I can trot, and shame on Raymond if he can't keep up. But of course he does, cause if he hangs back someone's liable to walk up to him and get smart, or take his allowance from him, or ask him where he got that great big pumpkin head. People are so stupid sometimes.

So I'm strolling down Broadway breathing out and breathing in on counts of seven, which is my lucky number, and here comes Gretchen and her sidekicks: Mary Louise, who used to be a friend of mine when she first moved to Harlem from Baltimore and got beat up by everybody till I took up for her on account of her mother and my mother used to sing in the same choir when they were young girls, but people ain't grateful, so now she hangs out with the new girl Gretchen and talks about me like a dog; and Rosie, who is as fat as I am skinny and has a big mouth where Raymond is concerned and is too stupid to know that there is not a big deal of difference between herself and Raymond and that she can't afford to throw stones. So they are steady coming up Broadway and I see right away that it's going to be one of those Dodge City scenes cause the street ain't that big and they're close to the buildings just as we are. First I think I'll step into the candy store and look over the new comics and let them pass. But that's chicken and I've got a reputation to consider. So then I think I'll just walk straight on through them or even over them if necessary. But as they get to me, they slow down. I'm ready to fight, cause like I said I don't feature a whole lot of chit-chat, I much prefer to just knock you down right from the jump and save everybody a lotta precious time.

"You signing up for the May Day races?" smiles Mary Louise, only it's not a smile at all. A dumb question like that doesn't deserve an answer. Besides, there's just me and Gretchen standing there really, so no use wasting my breath talking to shadows.

"I don't think you're going to win this time," says Rosie, trying to signify with her hands on her hips all salty, completely forgetting that I have whupped her behind many times for less salt than that.

"I always win cause I'm the best," I say straight at Gretchen who is, as far as I'm concerned, the only one talking in this ventriloquist-dummy routine. Gretchen smiles, but it's not a smile, and I'm thinking that girls never really smile at each other because they don't know how and don't want to know how and there's probably no one to teach us how, cause grown-up girls don't know either. Then they all look at Raymond who has just brought his mule team to a standstill. And they're about to see what trouble they can get into through him.

"What grade you in now, Raymond?"

"You got anything to say to my brother, you say it to me, Mary Louise Williams of Raggedy Town, Baltimore."

"What are you, his mother?" sasses Rosie.

"That's right, Fatso. And the next word out of anybody and I'll be *their* mother too." So they just stand there and Gretchen shifts from one leg to the other and so do they. Then Gretchen puts her hands on her hips and is about to say something with her freckle-face self but doesn't. Then she walks around me looking me up and down but keeps walking up Broadway, and her sidekicks follow her. So me and Raymond smile at each other and he says, "Gidyap" to his team and I continue with my breathing exercises, strolling down Broadway toward the ice man on 145th with not a care in the world cause I am Miss Quicksilver herself.

I take my time getting to the park on May Day because the track meet is the last thing on the program. The biggest thing on the program is the May Pole dancing, which I can do without, thank you, even if my mother thinks it's a shame I don't take part and act like a girl for a change. You'd think my mother'd be grateful not to have to make me a white organdy dress with a big satin sash and buy me new white baby-doll shoes that can't be taken out of the box till the big day. You'd think she'd be glad her daughter ain't out there prancing around a May Pole getting the new clothes all dirty and sweaty and trying to act like a fairy or a flower or whatever you're supposed to be when you should be trying to be yourself, whatever that is, which is, as far as I am concerned, a poor Black girl who really can't afford to buy shoes and a new dress you only wear once a lifetime cause it won't fit next year.

I was once a strawberry in a Hansel and Gretel pageant when I was in nursery school and didn't have no better sense than to dance on tiptoe with my arms in a circle over my head doing umbrella steps and being a perfect fool just so my mother and father could come dressed up and clap. You'd think they'd know better than to encourage that kind of nonsense. I am not a strawberry. I do not dance on my toes. I run. That is what I am all about. So I always come late to the May Day program, just in time to get my number pinned on and lay in the grass till they announce the fifty-yard dash.

I put Raymond in the little swings, which is a tight squeeze this year and will be impossible next year. Then I look around for Mr. Pearson, who pins the numbers on. I'm really looking for Gretchen if you want to know the truth, but she's not around. The park is jam-packed. Parents in hats and corsages and breast-pocket handkerchiefs peeking up. Kids in white dresses and light-blue suits. The parkees unfolding chairs and chasing the rowdy kids from Lenox as if they had no right to be there. The big guys with their caps on backwards, leaning against the fence swirling the basketballs on the tips of their fingers, waiting for all these crazy people to clear out the park so they can play. Most of the kids in my class are carrying bass drums and glockenspiels and flutes. You'd think they'd put in a few bongos or something for real like that.

Then here comes Mr. Pearson with his clipboard and his cards and pencils and whistles and safety pins and fifty million other things he's always dropping all over the place with his clumsy self. He sticks out in a crowd because he's on stilts. We used to call him Jack and the Beanstalk to get him mad. But I'm the only one that can outrun him and get away, and I'm too grown for that silliness now.

"Well, Squeaky," he says, checking my name off the list and handing me number seven and two pins. And I'm thinking he's got no right to call me Squeaky, if I can't call him Beanstalk.

"Hazel Elizabeth Deborah Parker," I correct him and tell him to write it down on his board.

"Well, Hazel Elizabeth Deborah Parker, going to give someone else a break this year?" I squint at him real hard to see if he is seriously thinking I should lose the race on purpose just to give someone else a break. "Only six girls running this time," he continues, shaking his head sadly like it's my fault all of New York didn't turn out in sneakers. "That new girl should give you a run for your money." He looks around the park for Gretchen like a periscope in a submarine movie. "Wouldn't it be a nice gesture if you were . . . to ahhh . . ."

I give him such a look he couldn't finish putting that idea into words. Grownups got a lot of nerve sometimes. I pin number seven to myself and stomp away, I'm so burnt. And I go straight for the track and stretch out on the grass while the band winds up with "Oh, the Monkey Wrapped His Tail Around the Flag Pole," which my teacher calls by some other name. The man on the loudspeaker is calling everyone over to the track and I'm on my back looking at the sky, trying to pretend I'm in the country, but I can't, because even grass in the city feels hard as sidewalk, and there's just no pretending you are anywhere but in a "concrete jungle" as my grandfather says.

The twenty-yard dash takes all of two minutes cause most of the little kids don't know no better than to run off the track or run the wrong way or run smack into the fence and fall down and cry. One little kid, though, has got the good sense to run straight for the white ribbon up ahead so he wins. Then the second-graders line up for the thirty-yard dash and I don't even bother to turn my head to watch cause Raphael Perez always wins. He wins before he even begins by psyching the runners, telling them they're going to trip on their shoelaces and fall on their faces or lose their shorts or something, which he doesn't really have to do since he is very fast, almost as fast as I am. After that is the forty-yard dash which I use to run when I was in first grade. Raymond is hollering from the swings cause he knows I'm about to do my thing cause the man on the loudspeaker has just announced the fifty-yard dash, although he might just as well be giving a recipe for angel food cake cause you can hardly make out what he's sayin for the static. I get up and slip off my sweat pants and then I see Gretchen standing at the starting line, kicking her legs out like a pro. Then as I get into place I see that ole Raymond is on line on the other side of the fence, bending down with his fingers on the ground just like he knew what he was doing. I was going to yell at him but then I didn't. It burns up your energy to holler.

Every time, just before I take off in a race, I always feel like I'm in a dream, the kind of dream you have when you're sick with fever and feel all hot and weightless. I dream I'm flying over a sandy beach in the early morning sun, kissing the leaves of the trees as I fly by. And there's always the smell of apples, just like in the country when I was little and used to think I was a choo-choo train, running through the fields of corn and chugging up the hill to the orchard. And all the time I'm dreaming this, I get lighter and lighter until I'm flying over the beach again, getting blown through the sky like a feather that weighs nothing at all. But once I spread my fingers in the dirt and crouch over the Get on Your Mark, the dream goes and I am solid again and am telling myself, Squeaky you must win, you must win, you are the fastest thing in the world, you can even beat your father up Amsterdam if you really try. And then I feel my weight coming back just behind my knees then down to my feet then into the earth and the pistol shot explodes in my blood and I am off and weightless again, flying past the other runners, my arms pumping up and down and the whole world is quiet except for the crunch as I zoom over the gravel in the track. I glance to my left and there is no one. To the right, a blurred Gretchen, who's got her chin jutting out as if it would win the race all by itself. And on the other side of the fence is Raymond with his arms down to his side and the palms tucked up behind him, running in his very own style, and it's the first time I ever saw that and I almost stop to watch my brother Raymond on his first run. But the white ribbon is bouncing toward me and I tear past it, racing into the distance till my feet with a mind of their own start digging up footfuls of dirt and brake me short. Then all the kids standing on the side pile on me, banging me on the back and slapping my head with their May Day programs, for I have won again and everybody on 151st Street can walk tall for another year.

"In first place . . ." the man on the loudspeaker is clear as a bell now. But then he pauses and the loudspeaker starts to whine. Then static. And I lean down to catch my breath and here comes Gretchen walking back, for she's overshot the finish line too, huffing and puffing with her hands on her hips taking it slow, breathing in steady time like a real pro and I sort of like her a little for the first time. "In first place . . ." and then three or four voices get all mixed up on the loudspeaker and I dig my sneaker into the grass and stare at Gretchen who's staring back, we both wondering just who did win. I can hear old Beanstalk arguing with the man on the loudspeaker and then a few others running their mouths about what the stopwatches say. Then I hear Raymond yanking at the fence to call me and I wave to shush him, but he keeps rattling the fence like a gorilla in a cage like in them gorilla movies, but then like a dancer or something he starts climbing up nice and easy but very fast. And it occurs to me, watching how smoothly he climbs hand over hand and remembering how he looked running with his arms down to his side and with the wind pulling his mouth back and his teeth showing and all, it occurred to me that Raymond would make a very fine runner. Doesn't he always keep up with me on my trots? And he surely knows how to breathe in counts of seven cause he's always doing it at the dinner table, which drives my brother George up the wall. And I'm smiling to beat the band cause if I've lost this race, or if me and Gretchen tied, or even if I've won, I can always retire as a runner and begin a whole new career as a coach with Raymond as my champion. After all, with a little more study I can beat Cynthia and her phony self at the spelling bee. And if I bugged my mother, I could get piano lessons and become a star. And I have a big rep as the baddest thing around. And I've got a roomful of ribbons and medals and awards. But what has Raymond got to call his own?

So I stand there with my new plans, laughing out loud by this time as Raymond jumps down from the fence and runs over with his teeth showing and his arms down to the side, which no one before him has quite mastered as a running style. And by the time he comes over I'm jumping up and down so glad to see him—my brother Raymond, a great runner in the family tradition. But of course everyone thinks I'm jumping up and down because the men on the loudspeaker have finally gotten themselves together and compared notes and are announcing "In first place—Miss Hazel Elizabeth Deborah Parker." (Dig that.) "In second place—Miss Gretchen P. Lewis." And I look over at Gretchen wondering what the "P" stands for. And I smile. Cause she's good, no doubt about it. Maybe she'd like to help me coach Raymond; she obviously is serious about running, as any fool can see. And she nods to congratulate me and then she smiles. And I smile. We stand there with this big smile of respect between us. It's about as real a smile as girls can do for each other, considering we don't practice real smiling every day, you know, cause maybe we too busy being flowers or fairies or strawberries instead of something honest and worthy of respect . . . you know . . . like being people.

I STAND HERE IRONING

Tillie Olsen

(b. 1913)

Biography p. 1090

I stand here ironing, and what you asked me moves tormented back and forth with the iron.

"I wish you would manage the time to come in and talk with me about your daughter. I'm sure you can help me understand her. She's a youngster who needs help and whom I'm deeply interested in helping."

"Who needs help." . . . Even if I came, what good would it do? You think because I am her mother I have a key, or that in some way you could use me as a key? She has lived for nineteen years. There is all that life that has happened outside of me, beyond me.

And when is there time to remember, to sift, to weigh, to estimate, to total? I will start and there will be an interruption and I will have to gather it all together again. Or I will become engulfed with all I did or did not do, with what should have been and what cannot be helped.

She was a beautiful baby. The first and only one of our five that was beautiful at birth. You do not guess how new and uneasy her tenancy in her now-loveliness. You did not know her all those years she was thought homely, or see her poring over her baby pictures, making me tell her over and over how beautiful she had been—and would be, I would tell her—and was now, to the seeing eye. But the seeing eyes were few or nonexistent. Including mine.

I nursed her. They feel that's important nowadays. I nursed all the children, but with her, with all the fierce rigidity of first motherhood, I did like the books then said. Though her cries battered me to trembling and my breasts ached with swollenness, I waited till the clock decreed.

Why do I put that first? I do not even know if it matters, or if it explains anything.

She was a beautiful baby. She blew shining bubbles of sound. She loved motion, loved light, loved color and music and textures. She would lie on the floor in her blue overalls patting the surface so hard in ecstasy her hands and feet would blur. She was a miracle to me, but when she was eight months old I had to leave her daytimes with the woman downstairs to whom she was no miracle at all, for I worked or looked for work and for Emily's father, who "could no longer endure" (he wrote in his good-bye note) "sharing want with us."

I was nineteen. It was the pre-relief, pre-WPA world of the depression. I would start running as soon as I got off the streetcar, running up the stairs, the place smelling sour, and awake or asleep to startle awake, when she saw me she would break into a clogged weeping that could not be comforted, a weeping I can hear yet.

After a while I found a job hashing at night so I could be with her days, and it was better. But it came to where I had to bring her to his family and leave her.

It took a long time to raise the money for her fare back. Then she got chicken pox and I had to wait longer. When she finally came, I hardly knew her, walking quick and nervous like her father, looking like her father, thin, and dressed in a shoddy red that yellowed her skin and glared at the pockmarks. All the baby loveliness gone.

She was two. Old enough for nursery school they said, and I did not know then what I know now—the fatigue of the long day, and the lacerations of group life in the kinds of nurseries that are only parking places for children.

Except that it would have made no difference if I had known. It was the only place there was. It was the only way we could be together, the only way I could hold a job.

And even without knowing, I knew. I knew the teacher that was evil because all these years it has curdled into my memory, the little boy hunched in the corner, her rasp, "why aren't you outside, because Alvin hits you? that's no reason, go out, scaredy." I knew Emily hated it even if she did not clutch and implore "don't go Mommy" like the other children, mornings.

She always had a reason why we should stay home. Momma, you look sick. Momma, I feel sick. Momma, the teachers aren't there today, they're sick. Momma, we can't go, there was a fire there last night. Momma, it's a holiday today, no school, they told me.

But never a direct protest, never rebellion. I think of our others in their three-, four-year-oldness—the explosions, the tempers, the denunciations, the demands—and I feel suddenly ill. I put the iron down. What in me demanded that goodness in her? And what was the cost, the cost to her of such goodness?

The old man living in the back once said in his gentle way: "You should smile at Emily more when you look at her." What *was* in my face when I looked at her? I loved her. There were all the acts of love.

It was only with the others I remembered what he said, and it was the face of joy, and not of care or tightness or worry I turned to them—too late for Emily. She does not smile easily, let alone almost always as her brothers and sisters do. Her face is closed and sombre, but when she wants, how fluid. You must have seen it in her pantomimes, you spoke of her rare gift for comedy on the stage that rouses a laughter out of the audience so dear they applaud and applaud and do not want to let her go.

Where does it come from, that comedy? There was none of it in her when she came back to me that second time, after I had had to send her away again. She had a new daddy now to learn to love, and I think perhaps it was a better time.

Except when we left her alone nights, telling ourselves she was old enough.

"Can't you go some other time, Mommy, like tomorrow?" she would ask. "Will it be just a little while you'll be gone? Do you promise?"

The time we came back, the front door open, the clock on the floor in the hall. She rigid awake. "It wasn't just a little while. I didn't cry. Three times I called you, just three times, and then I ran downstairs to open the door so you could come faster. The clock talked loud. I threw it away, it scared me what it talked."

She said the clock talked loud again that night I went to the hospital to have Susan. She was delirious with the fever that comes before red measles, but she was fully conscious all the week I was gone and the week after we were home when she could not come near the new baby or me.

She did not get well. She stayed skeleton thin, not wanting to eat, and night after night she had nightmares. She would call for me, and I would rouse from exhaustion to sleepily call back: "You're all right, darling, go to sleep, it's just a dream," and if she still called, in a sterner voice, "now go to sleep, Emily, there's nothing to hurt you." Twice, only twice, when I had to get up for Susan anyhow, I went in to sit with her.

Now when it is too late (as if she would let me hold and comfort her like I do the others) I get up and go to her at once at her moan or restless stirring. "Are you awake, Emily? Can I get you something?" And the answer is always the same: "No, I'm all right, go back to sleep, Mother."

They persuaded me at the clinic to send her away to a convalescent home in the country where "she can have the kind of food and care you can't manage for her, and you'll be free to concentrate on the new baby." They still send children to that place. I see pictures on the society page of sleek young women planning affairs to raise money for it, or dancing at the affairs, or decorating Easter eggs or filling Christmas stockings for the children.

They never have a picture of the children so I do not know if the girls still wear those gigantic red bows and the ravaged looks on the every other Sunday when parents can come to visit "unless otherwise notified"—as we were notified the first six weeks.

Oh it is a handsome place, green lawns and tall trees and fluted flower beds. High up on the balconies of each cottage the children stand, the girls in their red bows and white dresses, the boys in white suits and giant red ties. The parents stand below shrieking up to be heard and the children shriek down to be heard, and between them the invisible wall "Not To Be Contaminated by Parental Germs or Physical Affection."

There was a tiny girl who always stood hand in hand with Emily. Her parents never came. One visit she was gone. "They moved her to Rose Cottage" Emily shouted in explanation. "They don't like you to love anybody here."

She wrote once a week, the labored writing of a seven-year-old. "I am fine. How is the baby. If I write my leter nicly I will have a star. Love." There never was a star. We wrote every other day, letters she could never hold or keep but only hear read —once. "We simply do not have room for children to keep any personal possessions," they patiently explained when we pieced one Sunday's shrieking together to plead how much it would mean to Emily, who loved so to keep things, to be allowed to keep her letters and cards.

Each visit she looked frailer. "She isn't eating," they told us.

(They had runny eggs for breakfast or mush with lumps, Emily said later, I'd hold it in my mouth and not swallow. Nothing ever tasted good, just when they had chicken.)

It took us eight months to get her released home, and only the fact that she gained back so little of her seven lost pounds convinced the social worker.

I used to try to hold and love her after she came back, but her body would stay stiff, and after a while she'd push away. She ate little. Food sickened her, and I think much of life too. Oh she had physical lightness and brightness, twinkling by on skates, bouncing like a ball up and down up and down over the jump rope, skimming over the hill; but these were momentary.

She fretted about her appearance, thin and dark and foreign-looking at a time when every little girl was supposed to look or thought she should look a chubby blonde replica of Shirley Temple. The doorbell sometimes rang for her, but no one seemed to come and play in the house or be a best friend. Maybe because we moved so much.

There was a boy she loved painfully through two school semesters. Months later she told me how she had taken pennies from my purse to buy him candy. "Licorice was his favorite and I brought him some every day, but he still liked Jennifer better'n me. Why, Mommy?" The kind of question for which there is no answer.

School was a worry to her. She was not glib or quick in a world where glibness and quickness were easily confused with ability to learn. To her overworked and exasperated teachers she was an overconscientious "slow learner" who kept trying to catch up and was absent entirely too often.

I let her be absent, though sometimes the illness was imaginary. How different from my now-strictness about attendance with the others. I wasn't working. We had a new baby, I was home anyhow. Sometimes, after Susan grew old enough, I would keep her home from school, too, to have them all together.

Mostly Emily had asthma, and her breathing, harsh and labored, would fill the house with a curiously tranquil sound. I would bring the two old dresser mirrors and her boxes of collections to her bed. She would select beads and single earrings, bottle tops and shells, dried flowers and pebbles, old postcards and scraps, all sorts of oddments; then she and Susan would play Kingdom, setting up landscapes and furniture, peopling them with action.

Those were the only times of peaceful companionship between her and Susan. I have edged away from it, that poisonous feeling between them, that terrible balancing of hurts and needs I had to do between the two, and did so badly, those earlier years.

Oh there are conflicts between the others too, each one human, needing, demanding, hurting, taking—but only between Emily and Susan, no, Emily toward Susan that corroding resentment. It seems so obvious on the surface, yet it is not obvious. Susan, the second child, Susan, golden- and curly-haired and chubby, quick and articulate and assured, everything in appearance and manner Emily was not; Susan, not able to resist Emily's precious things, losing or sometimes clumsily breaking them; Susan telling jokes and riddles to company for applause while Emily sat silent (to say to me later: that was *my* riddle, Mother, I told it to Susan); Susan, who for all the five years' difference in age was just a year behind Emily in developing physically.

I am glad for that slow physical development that widened the difference between her and her contemporaries, though she suffered over it. She was too vulnerable for that terrible world of youthful competition, of preening and parading, of constant measuring of yourself against every other, of envy, "If I had that copper hair," "If I had that skin. . . ." She tormented herself enough about not looking like the others, there was enough of the unsureness, the having to be conscious of words before you speak, the constant caring—what are they thinking of me? without having it all magnified by the merciless physical drives.

Ronnie is calling. He is wet and I change him. It is rare there is such a cry now. That time of motherhood is almost behind me when the ear is not one's own but must always be racked and listening for the child cry, the child call. We sit for a while and I hold him, looking out over the city spread in charcoal with its soft aisles of light. *"Shoogily,"* he breathes and curls closer. I carry him back to bed, asleep. *Shoogily.* A funny word, a family word, inherited from Emily, invented by her to say: *comfort.*

In this and other ways she leaves her seal, I say aloud. And startle at my saying it. What do I mean? What did I start to gather together, to try and make coherent?

I was at the terrible, growing years. War years. I do not remember them well. I was working, there were four smaller ones now, there was not time for her. She had to help be a mother, and housekeeper, and shopper. She had to set her seal. Mornings of crisis and near hysteria trying to get lunches packed, hair combed, coats and shoes found, everyone to school or Child Care on time, the baby ready for transportation. And always the paper scribbled on by a smaller one, the book looked at by Susan then mislaid, the homework not done. Running out to that huge school where she was one, she was lost, she was a drop; suffering over the unpreparedness, stammering and unsure in her classes.

There was so little time left at night after the kids were bedded down. She would struggle over books, always eating (it was in those years she developed her enormous appetite that is legendary in our family) and I would be ironing, or preparing food for the next day, or writing V-mail to Bill, or tending the baby. Sometimes, to make me laugh, or out of her despair, she would imitate happenings or types at school.

I think I said once: "Why don't you do something like this in the school amateur show?" One morning she phoned me at work, hardly understandable through the weeping: "Mother, I did it. I won, I won; they gave me first prize; they clapped and clapped and wouldn't let me go."

Now suddenly she was Somebody, and as imprisoned in her difference as she had been in anonymity.

She began to be asked to perform at other high schools, even in colleges, then at city and statewide affairs. The first one we went to, I only recognized her that first moment when thin, shy, she almost drowned herself into the curtains. Then: Was this Emily? The control, the command, the convulsing and deadly clowning, the spell, then the roaring, stamping audience, unwilling to let this rare and precious laughter out of their lives.

Afterwards: You ought to do something about her with a gift like that—but without money or knowing how, what does one do? We have left it all to her, and the gift has as often eddied inside, clogged and clotted, as been used and growing.

She is coming. She runs up the stairs two at a time with her light graceful step, and I know she is happy tonight. Whatever it was that occasioned your call did not happen today.

"Aren't you ever going to finish the ironing, Mother? Whistler painted his mother in a rocker. I'd have to paint mine standing over an ironing board." This is one of her communicative nights and she tells me everything and nothing as she fixes herself a plate of food out of the icebox.

She is so lovely. Why did you want me to come in at all? Why were you concerned? She will find her way.

She starts up the stairs to bed. "Don't get me up with the rest in the morning." "But I thought you were having midterms." "Oh, those," she comes back in, kisses me, and says quite lightly, "in a couple of years when we'll all be atom-dead they won't matter a bit."

She has said it before. She *believes* it. But because I have been dredging the past, and all that compounds a human being is so heavy and meaningful in me, I cannot endure it tonight.

I will never total it all. I will never come in to say: She was a child seldom smiled at. Her father left me before she was a year old. I had to work her first six years when there was work, or I sent her home and to his relatives. There were years she had care she hated. She was dark and thin and foreign-looking in a world where the prestige went to blondeness and curly hair and dimples, she was slow where glibness was prized. She was a child of anxious, not proud, love. We were poor and could not afford for her the soil of easy growth. I was a young mother, I was a distracted mother. There were the other children pushing up, demanding. Her younger sister seemed all that she was not. There were years she did not want me to touch her. She kept too much in herself, her life was such she had to keep too much in herself. My wisdom came too late. She has much to her and probably little will come of it. She is a child of her age, of depression, of war, of fear.

Let her be. So all that is in her will not bloom—but in how many does it? There is still enough left to live by. Only help her to know—help make it so there is cause for her to know—that she is more than this dress on the ironing board, helpless before the iron.

ANGELINA SANDOVAL

Richard Vasquez

Biography p. 1105

Angelina Sandoval was the eldest offspring of Don Neftali and Doña Alicia Sandoval. Her first impression of the world around her had been negative. When she was a toddler her parents made no attempt to hide their disappointment at her being born a girl. The oldest child, she came to realize, should always be a boy. When the first born was a girl, a little awkwardness was involved in overlooking her and bypassing her in favor of the first boy to be born in the family. Thank God, Don Neftali and Doña Alicia thought when their second child was a boy. Now, regardless of the sex or number of subsequent progeny, the family pattern could commence. The eldest son would be second in command in the family. He would be consulted (and only he) concerning any plans regarding building, moving or the acquisition of anything material. He would inherit, regardless of the needs of any of the other siblings. If the family could afford only one education, or only one of anything advantageous, it would be his. This was a custom, a way of life which the family accepted without question—except when a girl was born first. Then the family accepted this way of life and this custom with a tiny bit of question.

Augmenting the awkwardness of the situation were several things. First, Angelina was a very bright child, and had to go to school in the nearby Anglo community. Within a few years she was speaking and reading English, and she learned that the rest of the world didn't feel about first-born sons and daughters the way her parents felt. Her first reaction was that she had been cheated by being a girl. Her second was that the subsequent children had been cheated by having an elder brother. Another reaction was that her younger brother, who was the older brother, was extremely selfish in thinking that things were fine just as they were.

One morning when Angelina was about eight years old, and Gregorio was seven, and Victorio was six, and Luisa was five, and Orlando was four, and little Pedro was three, and Roberto, Rita, and Delores were not born yet, the family was seated at the table having breakfast.

On the large stove, which had little silica windows through which could be seen red flames eating at chunks of wood, cooked four big, round tortillas made of flour. The old wooden table, covered by a stained, torn oilcloth, supported plates of fried rabbit—Don Neftali had shot the rabbits in the back yard that very morning while the family slept—the inevitable pot of beans, and fried potatoes. The children all talked or hollered at one another, while their father occasionally raised his voice, threatening corporal punishment as the alternative to silence. In a thread-bare sweater, with nothing underneath, and cotton trousers and ankle-high heavy shoes, he dished out portions of food according to the size of the individual child. He allowed only four-year-old Orlando and three-year-old Pedro to eat with their hands. The others ate with metal utensils.

When the first four tortillas were cooked to a spotted brown and white, Alicia

Sandoval took two and handed them to her husband. The other two were divided up among the grasping little hands, and four more tortillas were set to cook on the near red-hot stove top. Alicia wore an old and ragged cotton print dress and hand-stitched leather slippers. Nothing more. She wore her jet-black hair in a bun at the back. She was now heavy and solid, and commanded her children's respect in more ways than one. All who knew her were aware of her unwavering, immense mother love, which motivated her life far more than anything else, which influenced her every movement, even as her strong hand flicked out to crack sharply against a little cheek or bottom.

Several goats, kept in a pen attached to the rear of the stone house, supplied the Sandoval children with fresh milk daily and with cheese occasionally. The pen was next to the kitchen-front room-dining room in which the family ate, cooked and lived most of the time, and a small window, left open in the warm months, blocked off in the winter, looked out at the pen. A larger goat, by standing on its hind legs, could thrust its head partway through the window in the thick stone wall and bleat, begging for food, until another goat, overcome by jealousy, shoved it aside to take its place.

"Do not feed the goats while we are eating," Don Neftali had ordered many times. And while he wasn't watching, the children tossed little morsels of tortillas or potato to the goat at the window, and the goat would either snap them up or plaintively watch them fall back to the stone floor out of reach. The little window not only provided an outlook post for keeping an eye on the animals, but also solved the Sandovals' garbage problem.

The goats had had a problem too. When the leftovers were dumped into their pen through the window, the family dog, a large mongrel, would crawl under the fence and intimidate the herd, while taking his pick of the garbage. Then a young billy goat started to mature. At first there were terrific fights between the young billy and the dog. The children would shriek, fearing one would be hurt.

"Let them alone," papa Sandoval would say. "They will settle it." And sure enough. The dog soon found that at best he was taking a terrible battering for such a small reward. And then as the billy continued to mature, the battering became even more severe, and the dog was completely outclassed by the sharp hoofs and ram's horns. The dog withdrew to the other side of the house to be content with bones, fat, gristle and sour milk.

Now the dog lay at the doorstep of the front room, peering through the slats that formed a coarse screen on a door frame, anticipating the rabbit bones and entrails that would soon be his when the family finished eating.

Little Pedro squealed in delight as he shoved a handful of beans into his mouth. Angelina took a large square white cloth that had been a flour sack, now used as a napkin by all the children in turn, and wiped the bean-and-potato-streaked face of her youngest brother. Through eating, Papa Sandoval sat finishing his coffee, rolling a cigarette, regarding first Angelina and then the family pride, the oldest son, Gregorio.

"Too bad," he said to his wife for the hundredth time, "that she had to be so light and he so dark."

Doña Alicia looked for the ten millionth time at the dark, homely, Indian-like face of her oldest son. It almost seemed to her that Gregorio's face became a shade darker at hearing his father's words. The boy was looking intently at Angelina.

"Yes," the mother said as she had so many times before, "had he been born first, he would have had the light skin."

Angelina found herself returning Gregorio's stare. She knew the parents' words did not hurt him, only remind him. It was at school. The Anglo kids. How they taunted him, left him out. There were many other Mexican children at the school, but only a few were as dark, squat-featured and . . . non-Anglo looking—she realized—as her brother. She had many times examined herself in the piece of broken mirror above the stone sink. Her olive skin—lighter, actually—black hair, black eyes with a tiny bit of what looked like smoke in the whites, her features, all combined to make her look, Mexican to be sure, but very unlike Gregorio. The other Sandoval children varied in appearance between the relative extremes of Angelina and Gregorio.

Now the other children looked at the two older ones, then began screaming at their mother, "Mama! How light am I?" "I'm lighter than you!" "Look here, Mama," said Victorio, showing the untanned underside of his arm.

By virtue of the futility of the situation, Angelina felt but little sympathy for Gregorio. She remembered his severe rebuff when, in the unintentionally cruel way of children, the Anglo kids let Gregorio know his being the oldest son meant nothing to them. Well she could understand his dislike at leaving this little community whenever it was necessary, where being the eldest son entitled him to accompany his father on adult business to other homes where his position in the family was recognized as an important one. But Angelina had heard even the friendliest, most well-intentioned of neighbors in Irwindale say, "Too bad he's so dark. Poor thing."

At the age of sixteen Angelina was told by her father to stay out of school and work in a nearby packinghouse to help support the family. Gregorio, a year younger, stayed in school. "It's necessary that he prepare himself," the old man said, but Angelina never did quite understand what he was to prepare himself for. Then when Victorio was sixteen, he also went to work beside his father in the fields, and the following year when Rosita was sixteen, she too went to work.

Don Neftali's plan was to get Gregorio started in a little cobbler shop. While modernization had defeated Neftali on different occasions in the past, "People will always need shoes," he told his family. And it was necessary that Gregorio get all the schooling he can, so that he might be a successful businessman. There was an old, old man, so old he could remember the gringos arriving around Rabbit Town in covered wagons, and he had been a zapatero, a cobbler. Neftali invited him to the house, and the three of them, Neftali, the old man and Gregorio, made plans. They would build a little shop next to the house. With the money the older children earned, Neftali would buy the necessary equipment and pay the old man—Pelón, Baldy, he was called—to teach Gregorio the cobbling trade. And within a few months Gregorio drove a large stake into the ground in front of the house and nailed a hand-lettered sign reading ZAPATERO across it.

But the year was 1941. The family for years had had delivered a daily English language newspaper. Now the children read to Neftali, translating into Spanish the news, and explaining why all the boys over eighteen had to register for the draft. Pedro was just eighteen and Gregorio was twenty-two years old, and Victorio and Orlando were in between. Together, Gregorio assuming leadership, they went to the nearest town to register, and within weeks they were all told to report for induction, except for Orlando, who was retarded. Neftali and Alicia had recognized his affliction and taken him out of school early, dubbed him Poca Luz, and had him work in the fields. To them he could be as useful as anyone else, even if the gringo schools didn't want him.

The war dragged on. The three boys came home several times, rarely together. Neftali noticed they were changing. With the exception of Gregorio, they seemed only to tolerate the family system and traditions of Neftali and their mother Alicia. "I bought a stitching machine," Neftali proudly told them. "When Gregorio returns for good, he'll have a fine business."

On a hot, dusty afternoon as Angelina arrived home from the packing plant she found a Western Union messenger trying to make her mother and father understand they were to accept and sign for a telegram. She signed and thanked the messenger, then turned to her wide-eyed parents. She had already seen it was from the War Department. A chilling lump formed in her stomach as she kept her face calm and opened the envelope. *Which one?*

She read the brief sentences with hardly more than a glance and then said softly, "It's a death notice, Papa."

Neftali's face grew taunt and white, and Alicia's head began shaking as her face screwed up. "Which one?" Neftali asked, trembling, "Not Gregorio, I know."

Angelina knew there was no kind, pleasant way.

"Yes, Gregorio has been killed." She felt as though she was in a trance as she saw her father stiffen, and her mother begin tearing her hair and screaming. It was more than an hour later before Neftali and Alicia could ask for further details, and Angelina gave them what meager information the telegram contained, that Gregorio was buried on a little island in the Pacific, that his belongings would be coming soon. She left them clutching one another and set about to inform her other Army brothers so they might be home for the services.

Pedro and Victorio came home and the family walked to the little stone church a quarter mile away. After the services, the family walked slowly back, through the fields of cactus and sand and boulders, to the stone house Neftali had built himself.

They sat around the kitchen-living room, the Sandoval family, now reduced to ten members. Pedro and Victorio, still in their immaculate Army uniforms, said nothing. The younger children began warily to play and drift into the added stone rooms. Neftali and Alicia sat at the dinner table, palms to their foreheads, stifling sobs.

Victorio, now the eldest son, broke the silence.

"Papa, I can take over the cobbler shop. Perhaps not as well as Gregorio could have, but I can turn it into a thriving business, once I'm out of the Army. I know I can . . ."

Neftali shook his head. "No. It wasn't meant to be. There won't be a cobbler shop. I have already made arrangements with Pelón to buy the equipment and supplies. None of you has had the training or preparation to begin a business." And he continued to brood over the death of his eldest son.

They sat. Soon all the younger children were in the other rooms, away from the despair and depression. The older offspring sat self-consciously, occasionally glancing at one another, knowing sooner or later the mood would have to change. The soldiers found themselves looking at Angelina. Somehow, her face was different from what it should be. She wore a black dress, almost tight, showing off her well-shaped figure. Her long black hair was smooth and shiny. Her expression was one now of anger and impatience instead of grief. Suddenly she arose, standing straight and tall.

She spoke English, as they all did when they preferred that their parents not understand the conversation. "Well, I've had enough." She said it simply, with conviction, hands on hips as she faced her brothers. They looked puzzled. The old man looked up from the table, a little annoyed.

"What do you mean?" Victorio asked, his voice low, his attitude still one of remorse.

Angelina looked at each one a moment before continuing.

"I mean, when you guys get out of the Army you can come back here and spend the rest of your life picking oranges and using an outside open toilet, but you won't find me here."

Pedro was looking at her evenly, but Victorio seemed angered. "Angie! What are you talking about?"

Neftali Sandoval raised his voice above the others.

"Now listen! I won't have you speaking English in front of your mother and me. We have the right to know . . ."

Angelina turned to him, speaking politely but firmly.

"Please, papa. Stay out of this. We have something to discuss. When we work it out we'll tell you about it."

Rarely had a son or daughter talked back to him, but Neftali knew this was one of the changes coming about in the younger generation raised away from the old country. He remained silent.

Angelina continued. "You, Victorio, are a gutless wonder. You won't say a word about papa not letting you run a shop. He'd rather give it away than let one of you take Gregorio's place. Well, listen to me. I paid for half that Goddamn stuff there, and helped support Gregorio while he sat on his ass learning to drive tacks into soles. Christ, I'm twenty-three years old, and you know how many dates I've had? Not one real one, that's how many. Every time a boy came to see me papa would interview him. Or worse yet—and I truthfully couldn't stand it another time—if papa wasn't going to be here he'd appoint Gregorio to look him over. And if he looked like a good prospect for me"—she jerked her thumb—"out he'd go. Because I'm needed to help bring in money.

Victorio was looking shocked. Orlando sat uncertainly, as usual, taking it all in. Pedro, however, was listening intently.

Victorio said, "Angie, all this was for your own good. Dad was raised in the old country. We shouldn't be talking like this about the old traditions . . ."

"Oh, crap. I'll tell you how sacred the old traditions are. If things had been really tough, he'd have married me off to the first cholo that came along when I was fifteen. But I was able to work all the time. So that makes him extremely selective in my behalf. Now there's not a guy within ten miles who'll come near me, because he'll have to give a personal history to Dad or my brother. I've had it and I'm getting the hell out of here, and if you guys are smart, you won't come back."

Victorio persisted. "But the folks. They need money. Dad makes very little and there's still the younger kids . . ."

"Good grief, Victor. I could get a factory job in the city, support myself and still send mama and papa more money than I make packing fruit."

"But . . . living by yourself in a city . . . it's not proper for a girl . . ."

"*Girl!* I'm practically an old maid."

"There'd be none of us to look after you and see that you meet the right boy . . ."

Angelina gave a huge shrug and turned her back. "It's hopeless. The way you're talking, I'm more than ever convinced I've got to get out of here. Now. Immediately."

Pedro stood up and spoke for the first time. "She's right, Vic. That's the way I feel, too." He spoke with more of a Spanish accent than the others, and now his voice cracked, as though he was ready to cry. "I'm tired of this way. All my life, I've had the feeling I don't matter to mama and papa. I helped pay for Gregorio's shop also. I'm good enough to work hard in the fields from age sixteen, but not good enough to learn to use the tools I sweated to help buy. Since I've been in the Army I've learned other people don't live like we do. Not even the mejicanos in the cities. They laugh and say we're Mexican hillbillies."

Orlando sat listening, squinting, concentrating, trying to understand. He remained silent. Neftali sat glaring, impatiently waiting to be told what the heated conversation was about. Alicia looked bewildered. She too had not understood a word.

Victorio stared at Angelina a few moments, then said. "All right. What do you plan to do?"

She faced him squarely. "Get out of here. Now. Today, quickly, so there's not the slightest chance I'll lose my nerve and reconsider for even a week."

"Where'll you go?"

"The Ornelas family. They live in East Los Angeles. Olivia Ornelas invited me to come and stay there. There's plenty of defense plant work. And I'm going."

They all looked at one another. Neftali cleared his throat.

"Okay, now tell *them* about it," Victorio said, indicating their parents. Angelina waited a long moment, sighed, then turned to her mother and father still seated at the dinner table.

"Papa, mama, please try to understand . . ."

"I don't understand," Neftali said when she'd finished. "Why? We have it good here. We've always had plenty to eat. So we all do have to work hard. The Bible says . . ."

"Don't try, papa," Angelina said softly. "My mind's made up. I'm going to get my things together now."

Neftali's eyes were watering. "I know, this never would have happened in Mexico. It's because you see all the gringos, who have no sense of proper behavior. No one looks after the gringas to see that every man that happens by doesn't take advantage of them. It's because you've seen them in their loose way, that you no longer want to have propriety . . ."

Angelina pressed her forefinger to his lips gently to shut off the conversation. There were tears in her eyes too as she said, "You're right, papa."

Pedro coughed once and came to stand in front of his father.

"I have to be getting back to camp," he said, a little nervously. "I'll walk with Angelina to the bus stop and leave from there. I'd better be going. The Army is hard on you when you're late." He paused, obviously wanting to say more. Neftali waited. "And papa, when I get out in a year or so, I'll come to see you. But don't make plans for me. I have plans of my own."

Neftali looked at him hard for nearly a minute. Then he slumped a little. "All right, son," he said. He looked at Victorio. "And you? Are you wanting to leave your family, too?"

Victorio looked at the stone floor. "No, papa. I'll come back to stay."

Neftali regarded Orlando, still sitting silently on the couch. "And my son with the small light in his brain," he said fondly, "he'll always be with me."

THE SPINOZA OF MARKET STREET

Isaac Bashevis Singer

(b. 1904)

Biography p. 1101

I

Dr. Nahum Fischelson paced back and forth in his garret room in Market Street, Warsaw. Dr. Fischelson was a short, hunched man with a grayish beard, and was quite bald except for a few wisps of hair remaining at the nape of the neck. His nose was as crooked as a beak and his eyes were large, dark, and fluttering like those of some huge bird. It was a hot summer evening, but Dr. Fischelson wore a black coat which reached to his knees, and he had on a stiff collar and a bow tie. From the door he paced slowly to the dormer window set high in the slanting room and back again. One had to mount several steps to look out. A candle in a brass holder was burning on the table and a variety of insects buzzed around the flame. Now and again one of the creatures would fly too close to the fire and sear its wings, or one would ignite and glow on the wick for an instant. At such moments Dr. Fischelson grimaced. His wrinkled face would twitch and beneath his disheveled moustache he would bite his lips. Finally he took a handkerchief from his pocket and waved it at the insects.

"Away from there, fools and imbeciles," he scolded. "You won't get warm here; you'll only burn yourself."

The insects scattered but a second later returned and once more circled the trembling flame. Dr. Fischelson wiped the sweat from his wrinkled forehead and sighed, "Like men they desire nothing but the pleasure of the moment." On the table lay an open book written in Latin, and on its broad-margined pages were notes and comments printed in small letters by Dr. Fischelson. The book was Spinoza's *Ethics* and Dr. Fischelson had been studying it for the last thirty years. He knew every proposition, every proof, every corollary, every note by heart. When he wanted to find a particular passage, he generally opened to the place immediately without having to search for it. But, nevertheless, he continued to study the *Ethics* for hours every day with a magnifying glass in his bony hand, murmuring and nodding his head in agreement. The truth was that the more Dr. Fischelson studied, the more puzzling sentences, unclear passages, and cryptic remarks he found. Each sentence contained hints unfathomed by any of the students of Spinoza. Actually the philosopher had anticipated all of the criticisms of pure reason made by Kant and his followers. Dr. Fischelson was writing a commentary on the *Ethics.* He had drawers full of notes and drafts, but it didn't seem that he would ever be able to complete his work. The stomach ailment which had plagued him for years was growing worse from day to day. Now he would get pains in his stomach after only a few mouthfuls of oatmeal. "God in Heaven, it's difficult, very difficult," he would say to himself using the same intonation as had his father, the late Rabbi of Tishevitz. "It's very, very hard."

Dr. Fischelson was not afraid of dying. To begin with, he was no longer a young man. Secondly, it is stated in the fourth part of the *Ethics* that "a free man thinks of nothing less than of death and his wisdom is a meditation not of death, but of life." Thirdly, it is also said that "the human mind cannot be absolutely destroyed with the human body but there is some part of it that remains eternal." And yet Dr. Fischelson's ulcer (or perhaps it was a cancer) continued to bother him. His tongue was always coated. He belched frequently and emitted a different foul-smelling gas each time. He suffered from heartburn and cramps. At times he felt like vomiting and at other times he was hungry for garlic, onions, and fried foods. He had long ago discarded the medicines prescribed for him by the doctors and had sought his own remedies. He found it beneficial to take grated radish after meals and lie on his bed, belly down, with his head hanging over the side. But these home remedies offered only temporary relief. Some of the doctors he consulted insisted there was nothing the matter with him. "It's just nerves," they told him. "You could live to be a hundred."

But on this particular hot summer night, Dr. Fischelson felt his strength ebbing. His knees were shaky, his pulse weak. He sat down to read and his vision blurred. The letters on the page turned from green to gold. The lines became waved and jumped over each other, leaving white gaps as if the text had disappeared in some mysterious way. The heat was unbearable, flowing down directly from the tin roof; Dr. Fischelson felt he was inside of an oven. Several times he climbed the four steps to the window and thrust his head out into the cool of the evening breeze. He would remain in that position for so long his knees would become wobbly. "Oh it's a fine breeze," he would murmur, "really delightful," and he would recall that according to Spinoza, morality and happiness were identical, and that the most moral deed a man could perform was to indulge in some pleasure which was not contrary to reason.

II

Dr. Fischelson, standing on the top step at the window and looking out, could see into two worlds. Above him were the heavens, thickly strewn with stars. Dr. Fischelson had never seriously studied astronomy but he could differentiate between the planets, those bodies which like the earth, revolve around the sun, and the fixed stars, themselves distant suns, whose light reaches us a hundred or even a thousand years later. He recognized the constellations which mark the path of the earth in space and that nebulous sash, the Milky Way. Dr. Fischelson owned a small telescope he had bought in Switzerland where he had studied and he particularly enjoyed looking at the moon through it. He could clearly make out on the moon's surface the volcanoes bathed in sunlight and the dark, shadowy craters. He never wearied of gazing at these cracks and crevasses. To him they seemed both near and distant, both substantial and insubstantial. Now and then he would see a shooting star trace a wide arc across the sky and disappear, leaving a fiery trail behind it. Dr. Fischelson would know then that a meteorite had reached our atmosphere, and perhaps some unburned fragment of it had fallen into the ocean or had landed in the desert or perhaps even in some inhabited region. Slowly the stars which had appeared from behind Dr. Fischelson's roof rose until they were shining above the house across the street. Yes, when Dr. Fischelson looked up into the heavens, he became aware of that infinite extension which is, according to Spinoza, one of God's attributes. It comforted Dr. Fischelson to think that although he was only a weak, puny man, a changing mode of the absolutely infinite Substance, he was nevertheless a part of the cosmos, made of the same matter as the celestial bodies; to the extent that he was a part of the Godhead, he knew he could not be destroyed. In such moments, Dr. Fischelson experienced the *Amor Dei Intellectualis* which is, according to the philosopher of Amsterdam, the highest perfection of the mind. Dr. Fischelson breathed deeply, lifted his head as high as his stiff collar permitted and actually felt he was whirling in company with the earth, the sun, the stars of the Milky Way, and the infinite host of galaxies known only to infinite thought. His legs became light and weightless and he grasped the window frame with both hands as if afraid he would lose his footing and fly out into eternity.

When Dr. Fischelson tired of observing the sky, his glance dropped to Market Street below. He could see a long strip extending from Yanash's market to Iron Street with the gas lamps lining it merged into a string of fiery dots. Smoke was issuing from the chimneys on the black, tin roofs; the bakers were heating their ovens, and here and there sparks mingled with the black smoke. The street never looked so noisy and crowded as on a summer evening. Thieves, prostitutes, gamblers, and fences loafed in the square which looked from above like a pretzel covered with poppy seeds. The young men laughed coarsely and the girls shrieked. A peddler with a keg of lemonade on his back pierced the general din with his intermittent cries. A watermelon vendor shouted in a savage voice, and the long knife which he used for cutting the fruit dripped with the blood-like juice. Now and again the street became even more agitated. Fire engines, their heavy wheels clanging, sped by; they were drawn by sturdy black horses which had to be tightly curbed to prevent them from running wild. Next came an ambulance, its siren screaming. Then some thugs had a fight among themselves and the police had to be called. A passerby was robbed and ran about shouting for help. Some wagons loaded with firewood sought to get through into the courtyards where the bakeries were located but the horses could not lift the wheels over the steep curbs and the drivers berated the animals and lashed them with their whips. Sparks rose from the clanging hoofs. It was now long after seven, which was the prescribed closing time for stores, but actually business had only begun. Customers were led in stealthily through back doors. The Russian policemen on the street, having been paid off, noticed nothing of this. Merchants continued to hawk their wares, each seeking to outshout the others.

"Gold, gold, gold," a woman who dealt in rotten oranges shrieked.

"Sugar, sugar, sugar," croaked a dealer of overripe plums.

"Heads, heads, heads," a boy who sold fishheads roared.

Through the window of a *Chassidic* study house across the way, Dr. Fischelson could see boys with long sidelocks swaying over holy volumes, grimacing and studying aloud in sing-song voices. Butchers, porters, and fruit dealers were drinking beer in the tavern below. Vapor drifted from the tavern's open door like steam from a bathhouse, and there was the sound of loud music. Outside of the tavern, streetwalkers snatched at drunken soldiers and at workers on their way home from the factories. Some of the men carried bundles of wood on their shoulders, reminding Dr. Fischelson of the wicked who are condemned to kindle their own fires in Hell. Husky record players poured out their raspings through open windows. The liturgy of the high holidays alternated with vulgar vaudeville songs.

Dr. Fischelson peered into the half-lit bedlam and cocked his ears. He knew that the behavior of this rabble was the very antithesis of reason. These people were immersed in the vainest of passions, were drunk with emotions, and, according to

Spinoza, emotion was never good. Instead of the pleasure they ran after, all they succeeded in obtaining was disease and prison, shame and the suffering that resulted from ignorance. Even the cats which loitered on the roofs here seemed more savage and passionate than those in other parts of the town. They caterwauled with the voices of women in labor, and like demons scampered up walls and leaped onto eaves and balconies. One of the toms paused at Dr. Fischelson's window and let out a howl which made Dr. Fischelson shudder. The doctor stepped from the window and, picking up a broom, brandished it in front of the black beast's glowing, green eyes. "Scat, begone, you ignorant savage!"—and he rapped the broom handle against the roof until the tom ran off.

III

When Dr. Fischelson had returned to Warsaw from Zurich, where he had studied philosophy, a great future had been predicted for him. His friends had known that he was writing an important book on Spinoza. A Jewish Polish journal had invited him to be a contributor; he had been a frequent guest at several wealthy households and he had been made head librarian at the Warsaw synagogue. Although even then he had been considered an old bachelor, the matchmakers had proposed several rich girls for him. But Dr. Fischelson had not taken advantage of these opportunities. He had wanted to be as independent as Spinoza himself. And he had been. But because of his heretical ideas he had come into conflict with the rabbi and had had to resign his post as librarian. For years after that, he had supported himself by giving private lessons in Hebrew and German. Then, when he had become sick, the Berlin Jewish community had voted him a subsidy of five hundred marks a year. This had been made possible through the intervention of the famous Dr. Hildesheimer with whom he corresponded about philosophy. In order to get by on so small a pension, Dr. Fischelson had moved into the attic room and had begun cooking his own meals on a kerosene stove. He had a cupboard which had many drawers, and each drawer was labelled with the food it contained—buckwheat, rice, barley, onions, carrots, potatoes, mushrooms. Once a week Dr. Fischelson put on his widebrimmed black hat, took a basket in one hand and Spinoza's *Ethics* in the other, and went off to the market for his provisions. While he was waiting to be served, he would open the *Ethics*. The merchants knew him and would motion him to their stalls.

"A fine piece of cheese, Doctor—just melts in your mouth."

"Fresh mushrooms, Doctor, straight from the woods."

"Make way for the Doctor, ladies," the butcher would shout. "Please don't block the entrance."

During the early years of his sickness, Dr. Fischelson had still gone in the evening to a café which was frequented by Hebrew teachers and other intellectuals. It had been his habit to sit there and play chess while drinking a half a glass of black coffee. Sometimes he would stop at the bookstores on Holy Cross Street where all sorts of old books and magazines could be purchased cheap. On one occasion a former pupil of his had arranged to meet him at a restaurant one evening. When Dr. Fischelson arrived, he had been surprised to find a group of friends and admirers who forced him to sit at the head of the table while they made speeches about him. But these were things that had happened long ago. Now people were no longer interested in him. He had isolated himself completely and had become a forgotten man. The events of 1905 when the boys of Market Street had begun to organize strikes, throw bombs at police stations, and shoot strike breakers so that the stores were closed even on weekdays had greatly increased his isolation. He began to despise everything associated with the modern Jew—Zionism, socialism, anarchism. The young men in question seemed to him nothing but an ignorant rabble intent on destroying society, society without which no reasonable existence was possible. He still read a Hebrew magazine occasionally, but he felt contempt for modern Hebrew which had no roots in the Bible or the Mishnah. The spelling of Polish words had changed also. Dr. Fischelson concluded that even the so-called spiritual men had abandoned reason and were doing their utmost to pander to the mob. Now and again he still visited a library and browsed through some of the modern histories of philosophy, but he found that the professors did not understand Spinoza, quoted him incorrectly, attributed their own muddled ideas to the philosopher. Although Dr. Fischelson was well aware that anger was an emotion unworthy of those who walk the path of reason, he would become furious, and would quickly close the book and push it from him. "Idiots," he would mutter, "asses, upstarts." And he would vow never again to look at modern philosophy.

IV

Every three months a special mailman who only delivered money orders brought Dr. Fischelson eighty rubles. He expected his quarterly allotment at the beginning of July but as day after day passed and the tall man with the blond moustache and the shiny buttons did not appear, the Doctor grew anxious. He had scarcely a groshen left. Who knows—possibly the Berlin Community had rescinded his subsidy; perhaps Dr. Hildesheimer had died, God forbid; the post office might have made a mistake. Every event has its cause, Dr. Fischelson knew. All was determined, all necessary, and a man of reason had no right to worry. Nevertheless, worry invaded his brain, and buzzed about like the flies. If the worst came to the worst, it occurred to him, he could commit suicide, but then he remembered that Spinoza did not approve of suicide and compared those who took their own lives to the insane.

One day when Dr. Fischelson went out to a store to purchase a composition book, he heard people talking about war. In Serbia somewhere, an Austrian Prince had been shot and the Austrians had delivered an ultimatum to the Serbs. The owner of the store, a young man with a yellow beard and shifty yellow eyes, announced, "We are about to have a small war," and he advised Dr. Fischelson to store up food because in the near future there was likely to be a shortage.

Everything happened so quickly. Dr. Fischelson had not even decided whether it was worthwhile to spend four groshen on a newspaper, and already posters had been hung up announcing mobilization. Men were to be seen walking on the street with round, metal tags on their lapels, a sign that they were being drafted. They were followed by their crying wives. One Monday when Dr. Fischelson descended to the street to buy some food with his last kopecks, he found the stores closed. The owners and their wives stood outside and explained that merchandise was unobtainable. But certain special customers were pulled to one side and let in through back doors. On the street all was confusion. Policemen with swords unsheathed could be seen riding on horseback. A large crowd had gathered around the tavern where, at the command of the Tsar, the tavern's stock of whiskey was being poured into the gutter.

Dr. Fischelson went to his old café. Perhaps he would find some acquaintances there who would advise him. But he did not come across a single person he knew. He decided, then, to visit the rabbi of the synagogue where he had once been librarian, but the sexton with the six-sided skull cap informed him that the rabbi and his family had gone off to the spas. Dr. Fischelson had other old friends in town but he found no one at home. His feet ached from so much walking; black and green spots appeared before his eyes and he felt faint. He stopped and waited for the giddiness to pass. The passers-by jostled him. A dark-eyed high school girl tried to give him a coin. Although the war had just started, soldiers eight abreast were marching in full battle dress— the men were covered with dust and were sunburnt. Canteens were strapped to their sides and they wore rows of bullets across their chests. The bayonets on their rifles gleamed with a cold, green light. They sang with mournful voices. Along with the men came cannons, each pulled by eight horses; their blind muzzles breathed gloomy terror. Dr. Fischelson felt nauseous. His stomach ached; his intestines seemed about to turn themselves inside out. Cold sweat appeared on his face.

"I'm dying," he thought. "This is the end." Nevertheless, he did manage to drag himself home where he lay down on the iron cot and remained, panting and gasping. He must have dozed off because he imagined that he was in his home town, Tishvitz. He had a sore throat and his mother was busy wrapping a stocking stuffed with hot salt around his neck. He could hear talk going on in the house; something about a candle and about how a frog had bitten him. He wanted to go out into the street but they wouldn't let him because a Catholic procession was passing by. Men in long robes, holding double edged axes in their hands, were intoning in Latin as they sprinkled holy water. Crosses gleamed; sacred pictures waved in the air. There was an odor of incense and corpses. Suddenly the sky turned a burning red and the whole world started to burn. Bells were ringing; people rushed madly about. Flocks of birds flew overhead, screeching. Dr. Fischelson awoke with a start. His body was covered with sweat and his throat was now actually sore. He tried to meditate about his extraordinary dream, to find its rational connection with what was happening to him and to comprehend it *sub specie eternitatis,* but none of it made sense. "Alas, the brain is a receptacle for nonsense," Dr. Fischelson thought. "This earth belongs to the mad."

And he once more closed his eyes; once more he dozed; once more he dreamed.

#

The eternal laws, apparently, had not yet ordained Dr. Fischelson's end.

There was a door to the left of Dr. Fischelson's attic room which opened off a dark corridor, cluttered with boxes and baskets, in which the odor of fried onions and laundry soap was always present. Behind this door lived a spinster whom the neighbors called Black Dobbe. Dobbe was tall and lean, and as black as a baker's shovel. She had a broken nose and there was a mustache on her upper lip. She spoke with the hoarse voice of a man and she wore men's shoes. For years Black Dobbe had sold breads, rolls, and bagels which she had bought from the baker at the gate of the house. But one day she and the baker had quarreled and she had moved her business to the market place and now she dealt in what were called "wrinklers," which was a synonym for cracked eggs. Black Dobbe had no luck with men. Twice she had been engaged to baker's apprentices but in both instances they had returned the engagement contract to her. Some time afterwards she had received an engagement contract from an old man, a glazier who claimed that he was divorced, but it had later come to light that he still had a wife. Black Dobbe had a cousin in America, a shoemaker, and repeatedly she boasted that this cousin was sending her passage, but she remained in Warsaw. She was constantly being teased by the women who would say, "There's no hope for you, Dobbe. You're fated to die an old maid." Dobbe always answered, "I don't intend to be a slave for any man. Let them all rot."

That afternoon Dobbe received a letter from America. Generally she would go to Leizer the Tailor and have him read it to her. However, that day Leizer was out and so Dobbe thought of Dr. Fischelson whom the other tenants considered a convert since he never went to prayer. She knocked on the door of the doctor's room but there was no answer. "The heretic is probably out," Dobbe thought but, nevertheless, she knocked once more, and this time the door moved slightly. She pushed her way in and stood there frightened. Dr. Fischelson lay fully clothed on his bed; his face was as yellow as wax; his Adam's apple stuck out prominently; his beard pointed upward. Dobbe screamed; she was certain that he was dead, but—no—his body moved. Dobbe picked up a glass which stood on the table, ran into the corridor, filled the glass with water from the faucet, hurried back, and threw the water into the face of the unconscious man. Dr. Fischelson shook his head and opened his eyes.

"What's wrong with you?" Dobbe asked. "Are you sick?"

"Thank you very much. No."

"Have you a family? I'll call them."

"No family," Dr. Fischelson said.

Dobbe wanted to fetch the barber from across the street but Dr. Fischelson signified that he didn't wish the barber's assistance. Since Dobbe was not going to the market that day, no "wrinklers" being available, she decided to do a good deed. She assisted the sick man to get off the bed and smoothed down the blanket. Then she undressed Dr. Fischelson and prepared some soup for him on the kerosene stove. The sun never entered Dobbe's room, but here squares of sunlight shimmered on the faded walls. The floor was painted red. Over the bed hung a picture of a man who was wearing a broad frill around his neck and had long hair. "Such an old fellow and yet he keeps his place so nice and clean," Dobbe thought approvingly. Dr. Fischelson asked for the *Ethics,* and she gave it to him disapprovingly. She was certain it was a gentile prayer book. Then she began bustling about, brought in a pail of water, swept the floor. Dr. Fischelson ate; after he had finished, he was much stronger and Dobbe asked him to read her the letter.

He read it slowly, the paper trembling in his hands. It came from New York, from Dobbe's cousin. Once more he wrote that he was about to send her a "really important letter" and a ticket to America. By now, Dobbe knew the story by heart and she helped the old man decipher her cousin's scrawl. "He's lying," Dobbe said. "He forgot about me a long time ago." In the evening, Dobbe came again. A candle in a brass holder was burning on the chair next to the bed. Reddish shadows trembled on the walls and ceiling. Dr. Fischelson sat propped up in bed, reading a book. The candle threw a golden light on his forehead which seemed as if cleft in two. A bird had flown in through the window and was perched on the table. For a moment Dobbe was frightened. This man made her think of witches, of black mirrors and corpses wandering around at night and terrifying women. Nevertheless, she took a few steps toward him and inquired, "How are you? Any better?"

"A little, thank you."

"Are you really a convert?" she asked although she wasn't quite sure what the word meant.

"Me, a convert? No, I'm a Jew like any other Jew," Dr. Fischelson answered.

The doctor's assurances made Dobbe feel more at home. She found the bottle of kerosene and lit the stove, and after that she fetched a glass of milk from her room and began cooking kasha. Dr. Fischelson continued to study the *Ethics,* but that evening he could make no sense of the theorems and proofs with their many references to axioms and definitions and other theorems. With trembling hand he raised the book to his eyes and read, "The idea of each modification of the human body does not involve adequate knowledge of the human body itself. . . . The idea of the idea of each modification of the human mind does not involve adequate knowledge of the human mind."

VI

Dr. Fischelson was certain he would die any day now. He made out his will, leaving all of his books and manuscripts to the synagogue library. His clothing and furniture would go to Dobbe since she had taken care of him. But death did not come. Rather his health improved. Dobbe returned to her business in the market, but she visited the old man several times a day, prepared soup for him, left him a glass of tea, and told him news of the war. The Germans had occupied Kalish, Bendin, and Cestechow, and they were marching on Warsaw. People said that on a quiet morning one could hear the rumblings of the cannon. Dobbe reported that the casualties were heavy. "They're falling like flies," she said. "What a terrible misfortune for the women."

She couldn't explain why, but the old man's attic room attracted her. She liked to remove the gold-rimmed books from the bookcase, dust them, and then air them on the window sill. She would climb the few steps to the window and look out through the telescope. She also enjoyed talking to Dr. Fischelson. He told her about Switzerland where he had studied, of the great cities he had passed through, of the high mountains that were covered with snow even in the summer. His father had been a rabbi, he said, and before he, Dr. Fischelson, had become a student, he had attended a yeshiva. She asked him how many languages he knew and it turned out that he could speak and write Hebrew, Russian, German, and French, in addition to Yiddish. He also knew Latin. Dobbe was astonished that such an educated man should live in an attic room on Market Street. But what amazed her most of all was that although he had the title "Doctor," he couldn't write prescriptions. "Why don't you become a real doctor?" she would ask him. "I am a doctor," he would answer. "I'm just not a physician." "What kind of a doctor?" "A doctor of philosophy." Although she had no idea of what this meant, she felt it must be very important. "Oh my blessed mother," she would say, "where did you get such a brain?"

Then one evening after Dobbe had given him his crackers and his glass of tea with milk, he began questioning her about where she came from, who her parents were, and why she had not married. Dobbe was surprised. No one had ever asked her such questions. She told him her story in a quiet voice and stayed until eleven o'clock. Her father had been a porter at the kosher butcher shops. Her mother had plucked chickens in the slaughterhouse. The family had lived in a cellar at No. 19 Market Street. When she had been ten, she had become a maid. The man she had worked for had been a fence who bought stolen goods from thieves on the square. Dobbe had had a brother who had gone into the Russian army and had never returned. Her sister had married a coachman in Praga and had died in childbirth. Dobbe told of the battles between the underworld and the revolutionaries in 1905, of blind Itche and his gang and how they collected protection money from the stores, of the thugs who attacked young boys and girls out on Saturday afternoon strolls if they were not paid money for security. She also spoke of the pimps who drove about in carriages and abducted women to be sold in Buenos Aires. Dobbe swore that some men had even sought to inveigle her into a brothel, but that she had run away. She complained of a thousand evils done to her. She had been robbed; her boy friend had been stolen; a competitor had once poured a pint of kerosene into her basket of bagels; her own cousin, the shoemaker, had cheated her out of a hundred rubles before he had left for America. Dr. Fischelson listened to her attentively. He asked her questions, shook his head, and grunted.

"Well, do you believe in God?" he finally asked her.

"I don't know," she answered. "Do you?"

"Yes, I believe."

"Then why don't you go to synagogue?" she asked.

"God is everywhere," he replied. "In the synagogue. In the marketplace. In this very room. We ourselves are parts of God."

"Don't say such things," Dobbe said. "You frighten me."

She left the room and Dr. Fischelson was certain she had gone to bed. But he wondered why she had not said "good night." "I probably drove her away with my philosophy," he thought. The very next moment he heard her footsteps. She came in carrying a pile of clothing like a peddler.

"I wanted to show you these," she said. "They're my trousseau." And she began to spread out, on the chair, dresses—woolen, silk, velvet. Taking each dress up in turn, she held it to her body. She gave him an account of every item in her trousseau— underwear, shoes, stockings.

"I'm not wasteful, she said. "I'm a saver. I have enough money to go to America."

Then she was silent and her face turned brick-red. She looked at Dr. Fischelson out of the corner of her eyes, timidly, inquisitively. Dr. Fischelson's body suddenly began to shake as if he had the chills. He said, "Very nice, beautiful things." His brow furrowed and he pulled at his beard with two fingers. A sad smile appeared on his toothless mouth and his large fluttering eyes, gazing into the distance through the attic window, also smiled sadly.

VII

The day that Black Dobbe came to the rabbi's chambers and announced that she was to marry Dr. Fischelson, the rabbi's wife thought she had gone mad. But the news had already reached Leizer the Tailor, and had spread to the bakery, as well as to other shops. There were those who thought that the "old maid" was very lucky; the doctor, they said, had a vast hoard of money. But there were others who took the view that he was a run-down degenerate who would give her syphilis. Although Dr. Fischelson had insisted that the wedding be a small, quiet one, a host of guests assembled in the rabbi's rooms. The baker's apprentices who generally went about barefoot, and in their underwear, with paper bags on the tops of their heads, now put on light-colored suits, straw hats, yellow shoes, gaudy ties, and they brought with them huge cakes and pans filled with cookies. They had even managed to find a bottle of vodka although liquor was forbidden in wartime. When the bride and groom entered the rabbi's chamber, a murmur arose from the crowd. The women could not believe their eyes. The woman that they saw was not the one they had known. Dobbe wore a wide-brimmed hat which was amply adorned with cherries, grapes, and plumes, and the dress that she had on was of white silk and was equipped with a train; on her feet were high-heeled shoes, gold in color, and from her thin neck hung a string of imitation pearls. Nor was this all: her fingers sparkled with rings and glittering stones. Her face was veiled. She looked almost like one of those rich brides who were married in the Vienna Hall. The bakers' apprentices whistled mockingly. As for Dr. Fischelson, he was wearing his black coat and broad-toed shoes. He was scarcely able to walk; he was leaning on Dobbe. When he saw the crowd from the doorway, he became frightened and began to retreat, but Dobbe's former employer approached him saying, "Come in, come in, bridegroom. Don't be bashful. We are all brethren now."

The ceremony proceeded according to the law. The rabbi, in a worn satin gabardine, wrote the marriage contract and then had the bride and groom touch his handkerchief as a token of agreement; the rabbi wiped the point of the pen on his skullcap. Several porters who had been called from the street to make up the quorum supported the canopy. Dr. Fischelson put on a white robe as a reminder of the day of his death and Dobbe walked around him seven times as custom required. The light from the braided candles flickered on the walls. The shadows wavered. Having poured wine into a goblet, the rabbi chanted the benedictions in a sad melody. Dobbe uttered only a single cry. As for the other women, they took out their lace handkerchiefs and stood with them in their hands, grimacing. When the baker's boys began to whisper wisecracks to each other, the rabbi put a finger to his lips and murmured, *"Eh nu oh,"* as a sign that talking was forbidden. The moment came to slip the wedding ring on the bride's finger, but the bridegroom's hand started to tremble and he had trouble locating Dobbe's index finger. The next thing, according to custom, was the smashing of the glass, but though Dr. Fischelson kicked the goblet several times, it remained unbroken. The girls lowered their heads, pinched each other gleefully, and giggled. Finally one of the apprentices struck the goblet with his heel and it shattered. Even the rabbi could not restrain a smile. After the ceremony the guests drank vodka and ate cookies. Dobbe's former employer came up to Dr. Fischelson and said, *"Mazel tov,* bridegroom. Your luck should be as good as your wife." "Thank you, thank you," Dr. Fischelson murmured, "but I don't look forward to any luck." He was anxious to return as quickly as possible to his attic room. He felt a pressure in his stomach and his chest ached. His face had become greenish. Dobbe had suddenly become angry. She pulled back her veil and called out to the crowd, "What are you laughing at? This isn't a show." And without picking up the cushion-cover in which the gifts were wrapped, she returned with her husband to their rooms on the fifth floor.

Dr. Fischelson lay down on the freshly made bed in his room and began reading the *Ethics*. Dobbe had gone back to her own room. The doctor had explained to her that he was an old man, that he was sick and without strength. He had promised her nothing. Nevertheless she returned wearing a silk nightgown, slippers with pompoms, and with her hair hanging down over her shoulders. There was a smile on her face, and she was bashful and hesitant. Dr. Fischelson trembled and the *Ethics* dropped from his hands. The candle went out. Dobbe groped for Dr. Fischelson in the dark and kissed his mouth. "My dear husband," she whispered to him, *"Mazel tov."*

What happened that night could be called a miracle. If Dr. Fischelson hadn't been convinced that every occurrence is in accordance with the laws of nature, he would have thought that Black Dobbe had bewitched him. Powers long dormant awakened in him. Although he had had only a sip of the benediction wine, he was as if intoxicated. He kissed Dobbe and spoke to her of love. Long forgotten quotations from Klopfstock, Lessing, Goethe, rose to his lips. The pressures and aches stopped. He embraced Dobbe, pressed her to himself, was again a man as in his youth. Dobbe was faint with delight; crying, she murmured things to him in a Warsaw slang which he did not understand. Later, Dr. Fischelson slipped off into the deep sleep young men know. He dreamed that he was in Switzerland and that he was climbing mountains —running, falling, flying. At dawn he opened his eyes; it seemed to him that someone had blown into his ears. Dobbe was snoring. Dr. Fischelson quietly got out of bed. In his long nightshirt he approached the window, walked up the steps and looked out in wonder. Market Street was asleep, breathing with a deep stillness. The gas lamps were flickering. The black shutters on the stores were fastened with iron bars. A cool breeze was blowing. Dr. Fischelson looked up at the sky. The black arch was thickly sown with stars—there were green, red, yellow, blue stars; there were large ones and small ones, winking and steady ones. There were those that were clustered in dense groups and those that were alone. In the higher sphere, apparently, little notice was taken of the fact that a certain Dr. Fischelson had in his declining days married someone called Black Dobbe. Seen from above even the Great War was nothing but a temporary play of the modes. The myriads of fixed stars continued to travel their destined courses in unbounded space. The comets, planets, satellites, asteroids kept circling these shining centers. Worlds were born and died in cosmic upheavals. In the chaos of nebulae, primeval matter was being formed. Now and again a star tore loose, and swept across the sky, leaving behind it a fiery streak. It was the month of August when there are showers of meteors. Yes, the divine substance was extended and had neither beginning nor end; it was absolute, indivisible, eternal, without duration, infinite in its attributes. Its waves and bubbles danced in the universal cauldron, seething with change, following the unbroken chain of causes and effects, and he, Dr. Fischelson, with his unavoidable fate, was part of this. The doctor closed his eyelids and allowed the breeze to cool the sweat on his forehead and stir the hair of his beard. He breathed deeply of the midnight air, supported his shaky hands on the window sill and murmured, "Divine Spinoza, forgive me. I have become a fool."

Translated by
Martha Glicklich and
Cecil Hemley

A WORN PATH

Eudora Welty

(b. 1909)

Biography p. 1106

It was December—a bright frozen day in the early morning. Far out in the country there was an old Negro woman with her head tied in a red rag, coming along a path through the pinewoods. Her name was Phoenix Jackson. She was very old and small and she walked slowly in the dark pine shadows, moving a little from side to side in her steps, with the balanced heaviness and lightness of a pendulum in a grandfather clock. She carried a thin, small cane made from an umbrella, and with this she kept tapping the frozen earth in front of her. This made a grave and persistent noise in the still air, that seemed meditative like the chirping of a solitary little bird.

She wore a dark striped dress reaching down to her shoe tops, and an equally long apron of bleached sugar sacks, with a full pocket: all neat and tidy, but every time she took a step she might have fallen over her shoelaces, which dragged from her unlaced shoes. She looked straight ahead. Her eyes were blue with age. Her skin had a pattern all its own of numberless branching wrinkles and as though a whole little tree stood in the middle of her forehead, but a golden color ran underneath, and the two knobs of her cheeks were illumined by a yellow burning under the dark. Under the red rag her hair came down on her neck in the frailest of ringlets, still black, and with an odor like copper.

Now and then there was a quivering in the thicket. Old Phoenix said, "Out of my way, all you foxes, owls, beetles, jack rabbits, coons and wild animals! . . . Keep out from under these feet, little bob-whites. . . . Keep the big wild hogs out of my path. Don't let none of those come running my direction. I got a long way." Under her small black-freckled hand her cane, limber as a buggy whip, would switch at the brush as if to rouse up any hiding things.

On she went. The woods were deep and still. The sun made the pine needles almost too bright to look at, up where the wind rocked. The cones dropped as light as feathers. Down in the hollow was the mourning dove—it was not too late for him.

The path ran up a hill. "Seem like there is chains about my feet, time I get this far," she said, in the voice of argument old people keep to use with themselves. "Something always take a hold of me on this hill—pleads I should stay."

After she got to the top she turned and gave a full, severe look behind her where she had come. "Up through pines," she said at length. "Now down through oaks."

Her eyes opened their widest, and she started down gently. But before she got to the bottom of the hill a bush caught her dress.

Her fingers were busy and intent, but her skirts were full and long, so that before she could pull them free in one place they were caught in another. It was not possible to allow the dress to tear. "I in the thorny bush," she said. "Thorns, you doing your appointed work. Never want to let folks pass, no sir. Old eyes thought you was a pretty little *green* bush."

Finally, trembling all over, she stood free, and after a moment dared to stoop for her cane.

"Sun so high!" she cried, leaning back and looking, while the thick tears went over her eyes. "The time getting all gone here."

At the foot of this hill was a place where a log was laid across the creek.

"Now comes the trial," said Phoenix.

Putting her right foot out, she mounted the log and shut her eyes. Lifting her skirt, leveling her cane fiercely before her, like a festival figure in some parade, she began to march across. Then she opened her eyes and she was safe on the other side.

"I wasn't as old as I thought," she said.

But she sat down to rest. She spread her skirts on the bank around her and folded her hands over her knees. Up above her was a tree in a pearly cloud of mistletoe. She did not dare to close her eyes, and when a little boy brought her a plate with a slice of marble-cake on it she spoke to him. "That would be acceptable," she said. But when she went to take it there was just her own hand in the air.

So she left that tree, and had to go through a barbed-wire fence. There she had to creep and crawl, spreading her knees and stretching her fingers like a baby trying to climb the steps. But she talked loudly to herself: she could not let her dress be torn now, so late in the day, and she could not pay for having her arm or her leg sawed off if she got caught fast where she was.

At last she was safe through the fence and risen up out in the clearing. Big dead trees, like black men with one arm, were standing in the purple stalks of the withered cotton field. There sat a buzzard.

"Who you watching?"

In the furrow she made her way along.

"Glad this not the season for bulls," she said, looking sideways, "and the good Lord made his snakes to curl up and sleep in the winter. A pleasure I don't see no two-headed snake coming around that tree, where it come once. It took a while to get by him, back in the summer."

She passed through the old cotton and went into a field of dead corn. It whispered and shook and was taller than her head. "Through the maze now," she said, for there was no path.

Then there was something tall, black, and skinny there, moving before her.

At first she took it for a man. It could have been a man dancing in the field. But she stood still and listened, and it did not make a sound. It was as silent as a ghost.

"Ghost," she said sharply, "who be you the ghost of? For I have heard of nary death close by."

But there was no answer—only the ragged dancing in the wind.

She shut her eyes, reached out her hand, and touched a sleeve. She found a coat and inside that an emptiness, cold as ice.

"You scarecrow," she said. Her face lighted. "I ought to be shut up for good," she said with laughter. "My senses is gone. I too old. I the oldest people I ever know. Dance, old scarecrow," she said, "while I dancing with you."

She kicked her foot over the furrow, and with mouth drawn down, shook her head once or twice in a little strutting way. Some husks blew down and whirled in streamers about her skirts.

Then she went on, parting her way from side to side with the cane, through the whispering field. At last she came to the end, to a wagon track where the silver grass blew between the red ruts. The quail were walking around like pullets, seeming all dainty and unseen.

"Walk pretty," she said. "This the easy place. This the easy going."

She followed the track, swaying through the quiet bare fields, through the little strings of trees silver in their dead leaves, past cabins silver from weather, with the doors and windows boarded shut, all like old women under a spell sitting there. "I walking in their sleep," she said, nodding her head vigorously.

In a ravine she went where a spring was silently flowing through a hollow log. Old Phoenix bent and drank. "Sweet-gum makes the water sweet," she said, and drank more. "Nobody know who made this well, for it was here when I was born."

The track crossed a swampy part where the moss hung as white as lace from every limb. "Sleep on, alligators, and blow your bubbles." Then the track went into the road.

Deep, deep the road went down between the high green-colored banks. Overhead the live-oaks met, and it was as dark as a cave.

A black dog with a lolling tongue came up out of the weeds by the ditch. She was meditating, and not ready, and when he came at her she only hit him a little with her cane. Over she went in the ditch, like a little puff of milkweed.

Down there, her senses drifted away. A dream visited her, and she reached her hand up, but nothing reached down and gave her a pull. So she lay there and presently went to talking. "Old woman," she said to herself, "that black dog come up out of the weeds to stall you off, and now there he sitting on his fine tail, smiling at you."

A white man finally came along and found her—a hunter, a young man, with his dog on a chain.

"Well, Granny!" he laughed. "What are you doing there?"

"Lying on my back like a June-bug waiting to be turned over, mister," she said, reaching up her hand.

He lifted her up, gave her a swing in the air, and set her down. "Anything broken, Granny?"

"No sir, them old dead weeds is springy enough," said Phoenix, when she had got her breath. "I thank you for your trouble."

"Where do you live, Granny?" he asked, while the two dogs were growling at each other.

"Away back yonder, sir, behind the ridge. You can't even see it from here."

"On your way home?"

"No sir, I going to town."

"Why, that's too far! That's as far as I walk when I come out myself, and I get something for my trouble." He patted the stuffed bag he carried, and there hung down a little closed claw. It was one of the bob-whites, with its beak hooked bitterly to show it was dead. "Now you go on home, Granny!"

"I bound to go to town, mister," said Phoenix. "The time come around."

He gave another laugh, filling the whole landscape. "I know you old colored people! Wouldn't miss going to town to see Santa Claus!"

But something held old Phoenix very still. The deep lines in her face went into a fierce and different radiation. Without warning, she had seen with her own eyes a flashing nickel fall out of the man's pocket onto the ground.

"How old are you, Granny?" he was saying.

"There is no telling, mister," she said, "no telling."

Then she gave a little cry and clapped her hands and said, "Git on away from here, dog! Look! Look at that dog!" She laughed as if in admiration. "He ain't scared of nobody. He a big black dog." She whispered, "Sic him!"

"Watch me get rid of that cur," said the man. "Sic him, Pete! Sic him!"

Phoenix heard the dogs fighting, and heard the man running and throwing sticks. She even heard a gunshot. But she was slowly bending forward by that time, further and further forward, the lids stretched down over her eyes, as if she were doing this in her sleep. Her chin was lowered almost to her knees. The yellow palm of her hand came out from the fold of her apron. Her fingers slid down and along the ground under the piece of money with the grace and care they would have in lifting an egg from under a setting hen. Then she slowly straightened up, she stood erect, and the nickel was in her apron pocket. A bird flew by. Her lips moved. "God watching me the whole time. I come to stealing."

The man came back, and his own dog panted about them. "Well, I scared him off that time," he said, and then he laughed and lifted his gun and pointed it at Phoenix.

She stood straight and faced him.

"Doesn't the gun scare you?" he said, still pointing it.

"No, sir, I seen plenty go off closer by, in my day, and for less than what I done," she said, holding utterly still.

He smiled, and shouldered the gun. "Well, Granny," he said, "you must be a hundred years old, and scared of nothing. I'd give you a dime if I had any money with me. But you take my advice and stay home, and nothing will happen to you."

"I bound to go on my way, mister," said Phoenix. She inclined her head in the red rag. Then they went in different directions, but she could hear the gun shooting again and again over the hill.

She walked on. The shadows hung from the oak trees to the road like curtains. Then she smelled wood-smoke, and smelled the river, and she saw a steeple and the cabins on their steep steps. Dozens of little black children whirled around her. There ahead was Natchez shining. Bells were ringing. She walked on.

In the paved city it was Christmas time. There were red and green electric lights strung and crisscrossed everywhere, and all turned on in the daytime. Old Phoenix would have been lost if she had not distrusted her eyesight and depended on her feet to know where to take her.

She paused quietly on the sidewalk where people were passing by. A lady came along in the crowd, carrying an armful of red-, green- and silver-wrapped presents; she gave off perfume like the red roses in hot summer, and Phoenix stopped her.

"Please, missy, will you lace up my shoe?" She held up her foot.

"What do you want, Grandma?"

"See my shoe," said Phoenix. "Do all right for out in the country, but wouldn't look right to go in a big building."

"Stand still then, Grandma," said the lady. She put her packages down on the sidewalk beside her and laced and tied both shoes tightly.

"Can't lace 'em with a cane," said Phoenix. "Thank you, missy. I doesn't mind asking a nice lady to tie up my shoe, when I gets out on the street."

Moving slowly and from side to side, she went into the big building, and into a tower of steps, where she walked up and around and around until her feet knew to stop.

She entered a door, and there she saw nailed up on the wall the document that had been stamped with the gold seal and framed in the gold frame, which matched the dream that was hung up in her head.

"Here I be," she said. There was a fixed and ceremonial stiffness over her body.

"A charity case, I suppose," said an attendant who sat at the desk before her.

But Phoenix only looked above her head. There was sweat on her face, the wrinkles in her skin shone like a bright net.

"Speak up, Grandma," the woman said. "What's your name? We must have your history, you know. Have you been here before? What seems to be the trouble with you?"

Old Phoenix only gave a twitch to her face as if a fly were bothering her.

"Are you deaf?" cried the attendant.

But then the nurse came in.

"Oh, that's just old Aunt Phoenix," she said. "She doesn't come for herself—she has a little grandson. She makes these trips just as regular as clockwork. She lives away back off the Old Natchez Trace." She bent down. "Well, Aunt Phoenix, why don't you just take a seat? We won't keep you standing after your long trip." She pointed.

The old woman sat down, bolt upright in the chair.

"Now, how is the boy?" asked the nurse.

Old Phoenix did not speak.

"I said, how is the boy?"

But Phoenix only waited and stared straight ahead, her face very solemn and withdrawn into rigidity.

"Is his throat any better?" asked the nurse. "Aunt Phoenix, don't you hear me? Is your grandson's throat any better since the last time you came for the medicine?"

With her hands on her knees, the old woman waited, silent, erect and motionless, just as if she were in armor.

"You mustn't take up our time this way, Aunt Phoenix," the nurse said. "Tell us quickly about your grandson, and get it over. He isn't dead, is he?"

At last there came a flicker and then a flame of comprehension across her face, and she spoke.

"My grandson. It was my memory had left me. There I sat and forgot why I made my long trip."

"Forgot?" The nurse frowned. "After you came so far?"

Then Phoenix was like an old woman begging a dignified forgiveness for waking up frightened in the night. "I never did go to school, I was too old at the Surrender," she said in a soft voice. "I'm an old woman without an education. It was my memory fail me. My little grandson, he is just the same, and I forgot it in the coming."

"Throat never heals, does it?" said the nurse, speaking in a loud, sure voice to old Phoenix. By now she had a card with something written on it, a little list. "Yes. Swallowed lye. When was it?—January—two, three years ago—"

Phoenix spoke unasked now. "No, missy, he not dead, he just the same. Every little while his throat begin to close up again, and he not able to swallow. He not get his breath. He not able to help himself. So the time come around, and I go on another trip for the soothing medicine."

"All right. The doctor said as long as you came to get it, you could have it," said the nurse. "But it's an obstinate case."

"My little grandson, he sit up there in the house all wrapped up, waiting by himself," Phoenix went on. "We is the only two left in the world. He suffer and it don't seem to put him back at all. He got a sweet look. He going to last. He wear a little patch quilt and peep out holding his mouth open like a little bird. I remembers so plain now. I not going to forget him again, no, the whole enduring time. I could tell him from all the others in creation."

"All right." The nurse was trying to hush her now. She brought her a bottle of medicine. "Charity," she said, making a check mark in a book.

Old Phoenix held the bottle close to her eyes, and then carefully put it into her pocket.

"I thank you," she said.

"It's Christmas time, Grandma," said the attendant. "Could I give you a few pennies out of my purse?"

"Five pennies is a nickel," said Phoenix stiffly.

"Here's a nickel," said the attendant.

Phoenix rose carefully and held out her hand. She received the nickel and then fished the other nickel out of her pocket and laid it beside the new one. She stared at her palm closely, with her head on one side.

Then she gave a tap with her cane on the floor.

"This is what come to me to do," she said. "I going to the store and buy my child a little windmill they sells, made out of paper. He going to find it hard to believe there such a thing in the world. I'll march myself back where he waiting, holding it straight up in this hand."

She lifted her free hand, gave a little nod, turned around, and walked out of the doctor's office. Then her slow step began on the stairs, going down.

A SUMMER TRAGEDY

Arna Bontemps

(b. 1902)

Biography p. 1063

Old Jeff Patton, the black share farmer, fumbled with his bow tie. His fingers trembled, and the high, stiff collar pinched his throat. A fellow loses his hand for such vanities after thirty or forty years of simple life. Once a year, or maybe twice if there's a wedding among his kin-folks, he may spruce up; but generally fancy clothes do nothing but adorn the wall of the big room and feed the moths. That had been Jeff Patton's experience. He had not worn his stiff-bosomed shirt more than a dozen times in all his married life. His swallowtailed coat lay on the bed beside him, freshly brushed and pressed, but it was as full of holes as the overalls in which he worked on week days. The moths had used it badly. Jeff twisted his mouth into a hideous toothless grimace as he contended with the obstinate bow. He stamped his good foot and decided to give up the struggle.

"Jennie," he called.

"What's that, Jeff?" His wife's shrunken voice came out of the adjoining room like an echo. It was hardly bigger than a whisper.

"I reckon you'll have to he'p me wid this heah bow tie, baby," he said meekly. "Dog if I can hitch it up."

Her answer was not strong enough to reach him, but presently the old woman came to the door, feeling her way with a stick. She had a wasted, dead-leaf appearance. Her body, as scrawny and gnarled as a stringbean, seemed less than nothing in the ocean of frayed and faded petticoats that surrounded her. These hung an inch or two above the tops of her heavy, unlaced shoes and showed little grotesque piles where the stockings had fallen down from her negligible legs.

"You oughta could do a heap mo' wid a thing like that 'n me—beingst as you got yo' good sight."

"Looks like I *oughta* could," he admitted. "But ma fingers is gone democrat on me. I get all mixed up in the looking glass an' can't tell whicha way to twist the devilish thing."

Jennie sat on the side of the bed and old Jeff Patton got down on one knee while she tied the bow knot. It was a slow and painful ordeal for each of them in this position. Jeff's bones cracked, his knee ached, and it was only after a half dozen attempts that Jennie worked a semblance of a bow into the tie.

"I got to dress maself now," the old woman whispered. "These is ma old shoes an' stockings, and I ain't so much as unwrapped ma dress."

"Well, don't worry 'bout me no mo', baby," Jeff said. "That 'bout finishes me. All I gotta do now is slip on that old coat 'n ves' an' I'll be fixed to leave."

Jennie disappeared again through the dim passage into the shed room. Being blind was no handicap to her in that black hole. Jeff heard the cane placed against the wall beside the door and knew that his wife was on easy ground. He put on his coat, took a battered top hat from the bed post, and hobbled to the front door. He was ready to travel. As soon as Jennie could get on her Sunday shoes and her old black silk dress, they would start.

Outside the tiny log house the day was warm and mellow with sunshine. A host of wasps was humming with busy excitement in the trunk of a dead sycamore. Grey squirrels were searching through the grass for hickory nuts and blue jays were in the trees, hopping from branch to branch. Pine woods stretched away to the left like a black sea. Among them were scattered scores of log houses like Jeff's, houses of black share farmers. Cows and pigs wandered freely among the trees. There was no danger of loss. Each farmer knew his own stock and knew his neighbor's as well as he knew his neighbor's children.

Down the slope to the right were the cultivated acres on which the colored folks worked. They extended to the river, more than two miles away, and they were today green with the unmade cotton crop. A tiny thread of a road, which passed directly in front of Jeff's place, ran through these green fields like a pencil mark.

Jeff, standing outside the door with his absurd hat in his left hand, surveyed the wide scene tenderly. He had been forty-five years on these acres. He loved them with the unexplained affection that others have for the countries to which they belong.

The sun was hot on his head, his collar still pinched his throat, and the Sunday clothes were intolerably hot. Jeff transferred the hat to his right hand and began fanning with it. Suddenly the whisper that was Jennie's voice came out of the shed room.

"You can bring the car round front whilst you's waitin'," it said feebly. There was a tired pause; then it added, "I'll soon be fixed to go."

"A'right, baby," Jeff answered. "I'll get it in a minute."

But he didn't move. A thought struck him that made his mouth fall open. The mention of the car brought to his mind, with new intensity, the trip he and Jennie were about to take. Fear came into his eyes; excitement took his breath. Lord, Jesus!

"Jeff . . . Oh Jeff," the old woman's whisper called.

He awakened with a jolt. "Hunh, baby?"

"What you doin'?"

"Nuthin. Jes studyin'. I jes been turnin' things round 'n round in ma mind."

"You could be gettin' the car," she said.

"Oh yes, right away, baby."

He started round to the shed, limping heavily on his bad leg. There were three frizzly chickens in the yard. All his other chickens had been killed or stolen recently. But the frizzly chickens had been saved somehow. That was fortunate indeed, for these curious creatures had a way of devouring "poison" from the yard and in that way protecting against conjure and bad luck and spells. But even the frizzly chickens seemed now to be in a stupor. Jeff thought they had some ailment; he expected all three of them to die shortly.

The shed in which the old model-T Ford stood was only a grass roof held up by four corner poles. It had been built by tremulous hands at a time when the little rattletrap car had been regarded as a peculiar treasure. And, miraculously, despite wind and downpour, it still stood.

Jeff adjusted the crank and put his weight on it. The engine came to life with a sputter and bang that rattled the old car from radiator to tail light. Jeff hopped into the seat and put his foot on the accelerator. The sputtering and banging increased. The rattling became more violent. That was good. It was good banging, good sputtering and rattling, and it meant that the aged car was still in running condition. She could be depended on for this trip.

Again Jeff's thought halted as if paralyzed. The suggestion of the trip fell into the machinery of his mind like a wrench. He felt dazed and weak. He swung the car out into the yard, made a half turn, and drove around to the front door. When he took his hands off the wheel, he noticed that he was trembling violently. He cut off the motor and climbed to the ground to wait for Jennie.

A few moments later she was at the window, her voice rattling against the pane like a broken shutter.

"I'm ready, Jeff."

He did not answer, but limped into the house and took her by the arm. He led her slowly through the big room, down the step, and across the yard.

"You reckon I'd oughta lock the do'?" he asked softly.

They stopped and Jennie weighed the question. Finally she shook her head.

"Ne' mind the do'," she said. "I don't see no cause to lock up things."

"You right," Jeff agreed. "No cause to lock up."

Jeff opened the door and helped his wife into the car. A quick shudder passed over him. Jesus! Again he trembled.

"How come you shaking so?" Jennie whispered.

"I don't know," he said.

"You mus' be scairt, Jeff."

"No, baby, I ain't scairt."

He slammed the door after her and went around to crank up again. The motor started easily. Jeff wished that it had not been so responsive. He would have liked a few more minutes in which to turn things around in his head. As it was, with Jennie chiding him about being afraid, he had to keep going. He swung the car into the little pencil-mark road and started off toward the river, driving very slowly, very cautiously.

Chugging across the green countryside, the small, battered Ford seemed tiny indeed. Jeff felt a familiar excitement, a thrill, as they came down the first slope to the immense levels on which the cotton was growing. He could not help reflecting that the crops were good. He knew what that meant, too; he had made forty-five of them with his own hands. It was true that he had worn out nearly a dozen mules, but that was the fault of old man Stevenson, the owner of the land. Major Stevenson had the odd notion that one mule was all a share farmer needed to work a thirty-acre plot. It was an expensive notion, the way it killed mules from overwork, but the old man held to it. Jeff thought it killed a good many share farmers as well as mules, but he had no sympathy for them. He had always been strong, and he had been taught to have no patience with weakness in men. Women or children might be tolerated if they were puny, but a weak man was a curse. Of course, his own children—

Jeff's thought halted there. He and Jennie never mentioned their dead children any more. And naturally he did not wish to dwell upon them in his mind. Before he knew it, some remark would slip out of his mouth and that would make Jennie feel blue. Perhaps she would cry. A woman like Jennie could not easily throw off the grief that comes from losing five grown children within two years. Even Jeff was still staggered by the blow. His memory had not been much good recently. He frequently talked to himself. And, although he had kept it a secret, he knew that his courage had left him. He was terrified by the least unfamiliar sound at night. He was reluctant to venture far from home in the daytime. And that habit of trembling when he felt fearful was now far beyond his control. Sometimes he became afraid and trembled without knowing what had frightened him. The feeling would just come over him like a chill.

The car rattled slowly over the dusty road. Jennie sat erect and silent, with a little absurd hat pinned to her hair. Her useless eyes seemed very large and very white in their deep sockets. Suddenly Jeff heard her voice, and he inclined his head to catch the words.

"Is we passed Delia Moore's house yet?" she asked.

"Not yet," he said.

"You must be drivin' mighty slow, Jeff."

"We jes as well take our time, baby."

There was a pause. A little puff of steam was coming out of the radiator of the car. Heat wavered above the hood. Delia Moore's house was nearly half a mile away. After a moment Jennie spoke again.

"You ain't really scairt, is you, Jeff?"

"Nah, baby, I ain't scairt."

"You know how we agreed—we gotta keep on goin'."

Jewels of perspiration appeared on Jeff's forehead. His eyes rounded, blinked, became fixed on the road.

"I don't know," he said with a shiver. "I reckon it's the only thing to do."

"Hm."

A flock of guinea fowls, pecking in the road, were scattered by the passing car. Some of them took to their wings; others hid under bushes. A blue jay, swaying on a leafy twig, was annoying a roadside squirrel. Jeff held an even speed till he came near Delia's place. Then he slowed down noticeably.

Delia's house was really no house at all, but an abandoned store building converted into a dwelling. It sat near a crossroads, beneath a single black cedar tree. There Delia, a catlike old creature of Jennie's age, lived alone. She had been there more years than anybody could remember, and long ago had won the disfavor of such women as Jennie. For in her young days Delia had been gayer, yellower, and saucier than seemed proper in those parts. Her ways with menfolks had been dark and suspicious. And the fact that she had had as many husbands as children did not help her reputation.

"Yonder's old Delia," Jeff said as they passed.

"What she doin'?"

"Jes sittin' in the do'," he said.

"She see us?"

"Hm," Jeff said. "Musta did."

That relieved Jennie. It strengthened her to know that her old enemy had seen her pass in her best clothes. That would give the old she-devil something to chew her gums and fret about, Jennie thought. Wouldn't she have a fit if she didn't find out? Old evil Delia! This would be just the thing for her. It would pay her back for being so evil. It would also pay her, Jennie thought, for the way she used to grin at Jeff—long ago when her teeth were good.

The road became smooth and red, and Jeff could tell by the smell of the air that they were nearing the river. He could see the rise where the road turned and ran along parallel to the stream. The car chugged on monotonously. After a long silent spell, Jennie leaned against Jeff and spoke.

"How many bale o' cotton you think we got standin'?" she said.

Jeff wrinkled his forehead as he calculated.

"'Bout twenty-five, I reckon."

"How many you make las' year?"

"Twenty-eight," he said. "How come you ask that?"

"I's jes thinkin'," Jennie said quietly.

"It don't make a speck o' diff'ence though," Jeff reflected. "If we get much or if we get little, we still gonna be in debt to old man Stevenson when he gets through counting up agin us. It's took us a long time to learn that."

Jennie was not listening to these words. She had fallen into a trance-like meditation. Her lips twitched. She chewed her gums and rubbed her old gnarled hands nervously. Suddenly, she leaned forward, buried her face in the nervous hands, and burst into tears. She cried aloud in a dry, cracked voice that suggested the rattle of fodder on dead stalks. She cried aloud like a child, for she had never learned to suppress a genuine sob. Her slight old frame shook heavily and seemed hardly able to sustain such violent grief.

"What's the matter, baby?" Jeff asked awkwardly. "Why you cryin' like all that?"

"I's jes thinkin'," she said.

"So you the one what's scairt now, hunh?"

"I ain't scairt, Jeff. I's jes thinkin' 'bout leavin' eve'thing like this—eve'thing we been used to. It's right sad-like."

Jeff did not answer, and presently Jennie buried her face again and continued crying.

The sun was almost overhead. It beat down furiously on the dusty wagon path road, on the parched roadside grass, and the tiny battered car. Jeff's hands, gripping the wheel, became wet with perspiration; his forehead sparkled. Jeff's lips parted and his mouth shaped a hideous grimace. His face suggested the face of a man being burned. But the torture passed and his expression softened again.

"You mustn't cry, baby," he said to his wife. "We gotta be strong. We can't break down."

Jennie waited a few seconds, then said, "You reckon we oughta do it, Jeff? You reckon we oughta go 'head an' do it really?"

Jeff's voice choked; his eyes blurred. He was terrified to hear Jennie say the thing that had been in his mind all morning. She had egged him on when he had wanted more than anything in the world to wait, to reconsider, to think things over a little longer. Now *she* was getting cold feet. Actually, there was no need of thinking the question through again. It would only end in making the same painful decision once more. Jeff knew that. There was no need of fooling around longer.

"We jes as well to do like we planned," he said. "They ain't nuthin else for us now —it's the bes' thing."

Jeff thought of the handicaps, the near impossibility, of making another crop with his leg bothering him more and more each week. Then there was always the chance that he would have another stroke, like the one that had made him lame. Another one might kill him. The least it could do would be to leave him helpless. Jeff gasped . . . Lord, Jesus! He could not bear to think of being helpless, like a baby, on Jennie's hands. Frail, blind Jennie.

The little pounding motor of the car worked harder and harder. The puff of steam from the cracked radiator became larger. Jeff realized that they were climbing a little rise. A moment later the road turned abruptly and he looked down upon the face of the river.

"Jeff."

"Hunh?"

"Is that the water I hear?"

"Hm. Tha's it."

"Well, which way you goin' now?"

"Down this-a way," he answered. "The road runs 'longside o' the water a lil piece."

She waited a while calmly. Then she said, "Drive faster."

"A'right, baby," Jeff said.

The water roared in the bed of the river. It was fifty or sixty feet below the level of the road. Between the road and the water there was a long smooth slope, sharply inclined. The slope was dry; the clay had been hardened by prolonged summer heat. The water below, roaring in a narrow channel, was noisy and wild.

"Jeff."

"Hunh?"

"How far you goin'?"

"Jes a lil piece down the road."

"You ain't scairt is you, Jeff?"

"Nah, baby," he said trembling. "I ain't scairt."

"Remember how we planned it, Jeff. We gotta do it like we said. Brave-like."

"Hm."

Jeff's brain darkened. Things suddenly seemed unreal, like figures in a dream. Thoughts swam in his mind foolishly, hysterically, like little blind fish in a pool within a dense cave. They rushed, crossed one another, jostled, collided, retreated, and rushed again. Jeff soon became dizzy. He shuddered violently and turned to his wife.

"Jennie, I can't do it. I can't." His voice broke pitifully.

She did not appear to be listening. All the grief had gone from her face. She sat erect, her unseeing eyes wide open, strained and frightful. Her glossy black skin had become dull. She seemed as thin and as sharp and bony as a starved bird. Now, having suffered and endured the sadness of tearing herself away from beloved things, she showed no anguish. She was absorbed with her own thoughts, and she didn't even hear Jeff's voice shouting in her ear.

Jeff said nothing more. For an instant there was light in his cavernous brain. That chamber was, for less than a second, peopled by characters he knew and loved. They were simple, healthy creatures, and they behaved in a manner that he could understand. They had quality. But since he had already taken leave of them long ago, the remembrance did not break his heart again. Young Jeff Patton was among them, the Jeff Patton of fifty years ago who went down to New Orleans with a crowd of country boys to the Mardi Gras doings. The gay young crowd—boys with candy-striped shirts and rouged brown girls in noisy silks—was like a picture in his head. Yet it did not make him sad. On that very trip Slim Burns had killed Joe Beasley—the crowd had been broken up. Since then Jeff Patton's world had been the Greenbrier Plantation.

If there had been other Mardi Gras carnivals, he had not heard of them. Since then there had been no time; the years had fallen on him like waves. Now he was old, worn out. Another paralytic stroke like the one he had already suffered would put him on his back for keeps. In that condition, with a frail blind woman to look after him, he would be worse off than if he were dead.

Suddenly Jeff's hands became steady. He actually felt brave. He slowed down the motor of the car and carefully pulled off the road. Below, the water of the stream boomed, a soft thunder in the deep channel. Jeff ran the car onto the clay slope, pointed it directly toward the stream, and put his foot heavily on the accelerator. The little car leaped furiously down the steep incline toward the water. The movement was nearly as swift and direct as a fall. The two old black folks, sitting quietly side by side, showed no excitement. In another instant the car hit the water and dropped immediately out of sight.

A little later it lodged in the mud of a shallow place. One wheel of the crushed and upturned little Ford became visible above the rushing water.

Poetry

A CRADLE SONG

William Butler Yeats
(1865–1939)

Biography p. 1109

The angels are stooping
Above your bed;
They weary of trooping
With the whimpering dead.

God's laughing in Heaven 5
To see you so good;
The Sailing Seven
Are gay with His mood.

I sigh that kiss you,
For I must own 10
That I shall miss you
When you have grown.

FIRST LESSON

Philip Booth
(b. 1925)

Biography p. 1063

Lie back, daughter, let your head
be tipped back in the cup of my hand.
Gently, and I will hold you. Spread
your arms wide, lie out on the stream
and look high at the gulls. A dead- 5
man's-float is face down. You will dive
and swim soon enough where this tidewater
ebbs to the sea. Daughter, believe
me, when you tire on the long thrash

to your island, lie up, and survive.   10
As you float now, where I held you
and let go, remember when fear
cramps your heart what I told you:
lie gently and wide to the light-year
stars, lie back, and the sea will hold you.   15

THE LAND OF COUNTERPANE

Robert Louis Stevenson
(1850–1894)

Biography p. 1103

When I was sick and lay a-bed,
I had two pillows at my head,
And all my toys beside me lay
To keep me happy all the day.

And sometimes for an hour or so   5
I watched my leaden soldiers go,
With different uniforms and drills,
Among the bed-clothes, through the hills;

And sometimes sent my ships in fleets
All up and down among the sheets;   10
Or brought my trees and houses out,
And planted cities all about.

I was the giant great and still
That sits upon the pillow-hill,
And sees before him, dale and plain,   15
The pleasant land of counterpane.

DOMINIC HAS A DOLL

E. E. Cummings
(1894–1962)

Biography p. 1068

dominic has

a doll wired
to the radiator of his
ZOOM DOOM

icecoalwood truck a   5

wistful little
clown
whom somebody buried

upsidedown in an ashbarrel so

of course dominic   10
took him
home

& mrs dominic washed his sweet

dirty
face & mended   15
his bright torn trousers(quite

as if he were really her &

she
but)& so
that   20

's how dominic has a doll

& every now & then my
wonderful
friend dominic depaola

gives me a most tremendous hug   25

knowing
i feel
that

we & worlds

are   30
less alive
than dolls &

dream

EUCLID

Vachel Lindsay
(1879–1931)

Biography p. 1085

Old Euclid drew a circle
On a sand-beach long ago.
He bounded and enclosed it
With angles thus and so.
His set of solemn graybeards   5
Nodded and argued much
Of arc and of circumference,
Diameter and such.
A silent child stood by them
From morning until noon   10
Because they drew such charming
Round pictures of the moon.

OFFSPRING

Naomi Long Madgett
(b. 1923)

Biography p. 1087

I tried to tell her:
    This way the twig is bent.
    Born of my trunk and strengthened by my roots,
    You must stretch newgrown branches
    Closer to the sun   5
    Than I can reach.
I wanted to say:
    Extend my self to that far atmosphere
    Only my dreams allow.

But the twig broke,   10
And yesterday I saw her
Walking down an unfamiliar street,
    Feet confident,
    Face slanted upward toward a threatening sky,
And   15
    She was smiling
    And she was
    Her very free,
    Her very individual,
    Unpliable   20
    Own.

THE PENNYCANDYSTORE BEYOND THE EL

Lawrence Ferlinghetti
(b. 1919)

Biography p. 1072

The pennycandystore beyond the El
is where I first
        fell in love
            with unreality

Jellybeans glowed in the semi-gloom   5
of that september afternoon
A cat upon the counter moved among
                              the licorice sticks
                and tootsie rolls
        and Oh Boy Gum   10

Outside the leaves were falling as they died

A wind had blown away the sun

A girl ran in
Her hair was rainy
Her breasts were breathless in the little room   15

Outside the leaves were falling
                and they cried
                        Too soon! too soon!

FERN HILL

Dylan Thomas
(1914–1953)

Biography p. 1104

Now as I was young and easy under the apple boughs
About the lilting house and happy as the grass was green,
    The night above the dingle starry,
        Time let me hail and climb
    Golden in the heydays of his eyes,   5
And honoured among wagons I was prince of the apple towns
And once below a time I lordly had the trees and leaves
        Trail with daisies and barley
    Down the rivers of the windfall light.

And as I was green and carefree, famous among the barns   10
About the happy yard and singing as the farm was home,
    In the sun that is young once only,
        Time let me play and be
    Golden in the mercy of his means,
And green and golden I was huntsman and herdsman, the calves   15
Sang to my horn, the foxes on the hills barked clear and cold,

And the sabbath rang slowly
In the pebbles of the holy streams.

All the sun long it was running, it was lovely, the hay
Fields high as the house, the tunes from the chimneys, it was air   20
    And playing, lovely and watery
        And fire green as grass.
    And nightly under the simple stars
As I rode to sleep the owls were bearing the farm away,
All the moon long I heard, blessed among stables, the night
        jars   25
    Flying with the ricks, and the horses
        Flashing into the dark.

And then to awake, and the farm, like a wanderer white
With the dew, come back, the cock on his shoulder: it was all
    Shining, it was Adam and maiden,   30
        The sky gathered again
    And the sun grew round that very day.
So it must have been after the birth of the simple light
In the first, spinning place, the spellbound horses walking
        warm
    Out of the whinnying green stable   35
        On to the fields of praise.

And honoured among foxes and pheasants by the gay house
Under the new made clouds and happy as the heart was long,
    In the sun born over and over,
        I ran my heedless ways,   40
    My wishes raced through the house high hay
And nothing I cared, at my sky blue trades, that time allows
In all his tuneful turning so few and such morning songs
    Before the children green and golden
        Follow him out of grace,   45

Nothing I cared, in the lamb white days, that time would take me
Up to the swallow thronged loft by the shadow of my hand,
    In the moon that is always rising,
        Nor that riding to sleep
    I should hear him fly with the high fields   50
And wake to the farm forever fled from the childless land.
Oh as I was young and easy in the mercy of his means,
        Time held me green and dying
    Though I sang in my chains like the sea.

WHEN I WAS ONE AND TWENTY

A. E. Housman

(1859–1936)

Biography p. 1078

When I was one-and-twenty
  I heard a wise man say,
'Give crowns and pounds and guineas
  But not your heart away;
Give pearls away and rubies   5
  But keep your fancy free.'
But I was one-and-twenty,
  No use to talk to me.

When I was one-and-twenty
  I heard him say again,   10
'The heart out of the bosom
  Was never given in vain;
'Tis paid with sighs a plenty
  And sold for endless rue.'
And I am two-and-twenty,   15
  And oh, 'tis true, 'tis true.

TO THE VIRGINS, TO MAKE MUCH OF TIME

Robert Herrick

(1591–1674)

Biography p. 1077

Gather ye Rose-buds while ye may,
  Old Time is still a flying:
And this same flower that smiles to day,
  To morrow will be dying.

The glorious Lamp of Heaven, the Sun,   5
  The higher he's a getting;
The sooner will his Race be run,
  And neerer he's to Setting.

That Age is best, which is the first,
    When Youth and Blood are warmer;   10
But being spent, the worse, and worst
    Times, still succeed the former.

Then be not coy, but use your time;
    And while ye may, goe marry:
For having lost but once your prime,   15
    You may for ever tarry.

JABBERWOCKY

Lewis Carroll

(1832–1898)

Biography p. 1065

'Twas brillig, and the slithy toves
    Did gyre and gimble in the wabe;
All mimsy were the borogoves,
    And the mome raths outgrabe.

"Beware the Jabberwock, my son!   5
    The jaws that bite, the claws that catch!
Beware the Jubjub bird, and shun
    The frumious Bandersnatch!"

He took his vorpal sword in hand:
    Long time the manxome foe he sought—   10
So rested he by the Tumtum tree,
    And stood awhile in thought.

And as in uffish thought he stood,
    The Jabberwock, with eyes of flame,
Came whiffling through the tulgey wood,   15
    And burbled as it came!

One, two! One, two! And through and through
    The vorpal blade went snicker-snack!
He left it dead, and with its head
    He went galumphing back.   20

"And hast thou slain the Jabberwock?
    Come to my arms, my beamish boy!

O frabjous day! Callooh! Callay!"
   He chortled in his joy.

'Twas brillig, and the slithy toves   25
   Did gyre and gimble in the wabe;
All mimsy were the borogoves,
   And the mome raths outgrabe.

SPRING AND FALL: TO A YOUNG CHILD

Gerard Manley Hopkins
(1844–1889)

Biography p. 1077

Márgarét, áre you gríeving
Over Goldengrove unleaving?
Leáves, líke the things of man, you
With your fresh thoughts care for, can you?
Áh! ás the heart grows older   5
It will come to such sights colder
By and by, nor spare a sigh
Though worlds of wanwood leafmeal lie;
And yet you *will* weep and know why.
Now no matter, child, the name: 10
Sórrow's spríngs áre the same.
Nor mouth had, no nor mind, expressed
What heart heard of, ghost guessed:
It ís the blight man was born for,
It is Margaret you mourn for.   15

SONNET #57

Edna St. Vincent Millay
(1892–1950)

Biography p. 1088

Time, that renews the tissues of this frame,
That built the child and hardened the soft bone,
Taught him to wail, to blink, to walk alone,
Stare, question, wonder, give the world a name,
Forget the watery darkness whence he came,   5
Attends no less the boy to manhood grown,
Brings him new raiment, strips him of his own;
All skins are shed at length, remorse, even shame.
Such hope is mine, if this indeed be true,
I dread no more the first white in my hair,   10
Or even age itself, the easy shoe,
The cane, the wrinkled hands, the special chair:
Time, doing this to me, may alter too
My sorrow, into something I can bear.

LADY LAZARUS

Sylvia Plath
(1932–1963)

Biography p. 1092

I have done it again.
One year in every ten
I manage it——

A sort of walking miracle, my skin
Bright as a Nazi lampshade,   5
My right foot

A paperweight,
My face a featureless, fine
Jew linen.

Peel off the napkin   10
O my enemy.
Do I terrify?————

The nose, the eye pits, the full set of teeth?
The sour breath
Will vanish in a day.   15

Soon, soon the flesh
The grave cave ate will be
At home on me

And I a smiling woman.
I am only thirty.   20
And like the cat I have nine times to die.

This is Number Three.
What a trash
To annihilate each decade.

What a million filaments.   25
The peanut-crunching crowd
Shoves in to see

Them unwrap me hand and foot————
The big strip tease.
Gentlemen, ladies   30

These are my hands
My knees.
I may be skin and bone,

Nevertheless, I am the same, identical woman.
The first time it happened I was ten.   35
It was an accident.

The second time I meant
To last it out and not come back at all.
I rocked shut

As a seashell.   40
They had to call and call
And pick the worms off me like sticky pearls.

Dying
Is an art, like everything else.
I do it exceptionally well.   45

I do it so it feels like hell.
I do it so it feels real.
I guess you could say I've a call.

It's easy enough to do it in a cell.
It's easy enough to do it and stay put.   50
It's the theatrical

Comeback in broad day
To the same place, the same face, the same brute
Amused shout:

'A miracle!'   55
That knocks me out.
There is a charge

For the eyeing of my scars, there is a charge
For the hearing of my heart——
It really goes.   60

And there is a charge, a very large charge
For a word or a touch
Or a bit of blood

Or a piece of my hair or my clothes.
So, so, Herr Doktor.   65
So, Herr Enemy.

I am your opus,
I am your valuable,
The pure gold baby

That melts to a shriek.   70
I turn and burn.
Do not think I underestimate your great concern.

Ash, ash—
You poke and stir.
Flesh, bone, there is nothing there——   75

A cake of soap,
A wedding ring,
A gold filling.

Herr God, Herr Lucifer
Beware   80
Beware.

Out of the ash
I rise with my red hair
And I eat men like air.

MR. FLOOD'S PARTY

Edwin Arlington Robinson
(1869–1935)

Biography p. 1095

Old Eben Flood, climbing alone one night
Over the hill between the town below
And the forsaken upland hermitage
That held as much as he should ever know
On earth again of home, paused warily.   5
The road was his with not a native near;
And Eben, having leisure, said aloud,
For no man else in Tilbury Town to hear:

"Well, Mr. Flood, we have the harvest moon
Again, and we may not have many more;   10
The bird is on the wing, the poet says,
And you and I have said it here before.
Drink to the bird." He raised up to the light
The jug that he had gone so far to fill,
And answered huskily: "Well, Mr. Flood,   15
Since you propose it, I believe I will."

Alone, as if enduring to the end
A valiant armor of scarred hopes outworn,
He stood there in the middle of the road
Like Roland's ghost winding a silent horn.   20
Below him, in the town among the trees,
Where friends of other days had honored him,
A phantom salutation of the dead
Rang thinly till old Eben's eyes were dim.

Then, as a mother lays her sleeping child   25
Down tenderly, fearing it may awake,
He set the jug down slowly at his feet
With trembling care, knowing that most things break;
And only when assured that on firm earth
It stood, as the uncertain lives of men   30
Assuredly did not, he paced away,
And with his hand extended paused again:

"Well, Mr. Flood, we have not met like this
In a long time; and many a change has come
To both of us, I fear, since last it was   35
We had a drop together. Welcome home!"
Convivially returning with himself,

Again he raised the jug up to the light;
And with an acquiescent quaver said:
"Well, Mr. Flood, if you insist, I might.   40

"Only a very little, Mr. Flood—
For auld lang syne. No more, sir; that will do."
So, for the time, apparently it did,
And Eben evidently thought so too;
For soon amid the silver loneliness   45
Of night he lifted up his voice and sang,
Secure, with only two moons listening,
Until the whole harmonious landscape rang—

"For auld lang syne." The weary throat gave out,
The last word wavered, and the song was done.   50
He raised again the jug regretfully
And shook his head, and was again alone.
There was not much that was ahead of him,
And there was nothing in the town below—
Where strangers would have shut the many doors   55
That many friends had opened long ago.

ON BEING SIXTY

Po Chu-i

(772–846)

Biography p. 1092

Between thirty and forty, one is distracted by the Five Lusts;
Between seventy and eighty, one is a prey to a hundred diseases.
But from fifty to sixty one is free from all ills;
Calm and still—the heart enjoys rest.
I have put behind me Love and Greed; I have done with Profit and Fame;   5
I am still short of illness and decay and far from decrepit age.
Strength of limb I still possess to seek the rivers and hills;
Still my heart has spirit enough to listen to flutes and strings.
At leisure I open new wine and taste several cups;
Drunken I recall old poems and sing a whole volume.   10
Mêng-tê has asked for a poem and herewith I exhort him
Not to complain of three-score, "the time of obedient ears."

Translated by Arthur Waley

OLD AGE

(Addressed to Liu Yü-hsi, who was born in the same year)

(A.D. 835)

We are growing old together, you and I;
Let us ask ourselves, what is age like?
The dull eye is closed ere night comes;
The idle head, still uncombed at noon.
Propped on a staff, sometimes a walk abroad;   5
Or all day sitting with closed doors.
One dares not look in the mirror's polished face;
One cannot read small-letter books.
Deeper and deeper, one's love of old friends;
Fewer and fewer, one's dealings with young men.   10
One thing only, the pleasure of idle talk,
Is great as ever, when you and I meet.

Translated by Arthur Waley

CASTOFF SKIN

Ruth Whitman

(b. 1922)

Biography p. 1106

She lay in her girlish sleep at ninety-six,
small as a twig.
Pretty good figure

for an old lady, she said to me once.
Then she crawled away, leaving   5
a tiny stretched transparence

behind her. When I kissed her paper cheek
I thought of the snake,
of his quick motion.

ULYSSES

Alfred, Lord Tennyson
(1809–1892)

Biography p. 1104

It little profits that an idle king,
By this still hearth, among these barren crags,
Matched with an aged wife, I mete and dole
Unequal laws unto a savage race
That hoard, and sleep, and feed, and know not me.   5
I cannot rest from travel; I will drink
Life to the lees. All times I have enjoyed
Greatly, have suffered greatly, both with those
That loved me, and alone; on shore, and when
Through scudding drifts the rainy Hyades   10
Vexed the dim sea. I am become a name;
For always roaming with a hungry heart
Much have I seen and known—cities of men
And manners, climates, councils, governments,
Myself not least, but honored of them all—   15
And drunk delight of battle with my peers,
Far on the ringing plains of windy Troy.
I am a part of all that I have met;
Yet all experience is an arch wherethrough
Gleams that untraveled world whose margin fades   20
Forever and forever when I move.
How dull it is to pause, to make an end,
To rust unburnished, not to shine in use!
As though to breathe were life! Life piled on life
Were all too little, and of one to me   25
Little remains; but every hour is saved
From that eternal silence, something more,
A bringer of new things; and vile it were
For some three suns to store and hoard myself,
And this grey spirit yearning in desire   30
To follow knowledge like a sinking star,
Beyond the utmost bound of human thought.
    This is my son, mine own Telemachus,
To whom I leave the scepter and the isle—
Well-loved of me, discerning to fulfill   35
This labor, by slow prudence to make mild
A rugged people, and through soft degrees
Subdue them to the useful and the good.
Most blameless is he, centered in the sphere
Of common duties, decent not to fail   40
In offices of tenderness, and pay

Meet adoration to my household gods,
When I am gone. He works his work, I mine.
  There lies the port; the vessel puffs her sail;
There gloom the dark, broad seas. My mariners,   45
Souls that have toiled, and wrought, and thought with me—
That ever with a frolic welcome took
The thunder and the sunshine, and opposed
Free hearts, free foreheads—you and I are old;
Old age hath yet his honor and his toil.   50
Death closes all; but something ere the end,
Some work of noble note, may yet be done,
Not unbecoming men that strove with Gods.
The lights begin to twinkle from the rocks;
The long day wanes; the slow moon climbs; the deep   55
Moans round with many voices. Come, my friends,
'Tis not too late to seek a newer world.
Push off, and sitting well in order smite
The sounding furrows; for my purpose holds
To sail beyond the sunset, and the baths   60
Of all the western stars, until I die.
It may be that the gulfs will wash us down;
It may be we shall touch the Happy Isles,
And see the great Achilles, whom we knew.
Though much is taken, much abides; and though   65
We are not now that strength which in old days
Moved earth and heaven, that which we are, we are—
One equal temper of heroic hearts,
Made weak by time and fate, but strong in will
To strive, to seek, to find, and not to yield.   70

WHEN I HAVE FEARS THAT I MAY CEASE TO BE

John Keats

(1795–1821)

Biography p. 1080

When I have fears that I may cease to be
  Before my pen has gleaned my teeming brain,
Before high-piled books, in charactery,
  Hold like rich garners the full ripened grain;

When I behold, upon the night's starred face,   5
  Huge cloudy symbols of a high romance,
And think that I may never live to trace
  Their shadows, with the magic hand of chance;
And when I feel, fair creature of an hour,
  That I shall never look upon thee more,   10
Never have relish in the faery power
  Of unreflecting love;—then on the shore
Of the wide world I stand alone, and think
Till love and fame to nothingness do sink.

THE EMPEROR OF ICE CREAM

Wallace Stevens
(1879–1955)

Biography p. 1103

Call the roller of big cigars,
The muscular one, and bid him whip
In kitchen cups concupiscent curds.
Let the wenches dawdle in such dress
As they are used to wear, and let the boys   5
Bring flowers in last month's newspapers.
Let be be finale of seem.
The only emperor is the emperor of ice-cream.

Take from the dresser of deal,
Lacking the three glass knobs, that sheet   10
On which she embroidered fantails once
And spread it so as to cover her face.
If her horny feet protrude, they come
To show how cold she is, and dumb.
Let the lamp affix its beam.   15
The only emperor is the emperor of ice-cream.

SAILING TO BYZANTIUM

William Butler Yeats
(1865–1939)

Biography p. 1109

I

That is no country for old men. The young
In one another's arms, birds in the trees
—Those dying generations—at their song,
The salmon-falls, the mackerel-crowded seas,
Fish, flesh, or fowl, commend all summer long   5
Whatever is begotten, born, and dies.
Caught in that sensual music all neglect
Monuments of unageing intellect.

II

An aged man is but a paltry thing,
A tattered coat upon a stick, unless   10
Soul clap its hands and sing, and louder sing
For every tatter in its mortal dress,
Nor is there singing school but studying
Monuments of its own magnificence;
And therefore I have sailed the seas and come   15
To the holy city of Byzantium.

III

O sages standing in God's holy fire
As in the gold mosaic of a wall,
Come from the holy fire, perne in a gyre,
And be the singing-masters of my soul.   20
Consume my heart away; sick with desire
And fastened to a dying animal
It knows not what it is; and gather me
Into the artifice of eternity.

IV

Once out of nature I shall never take   25
My bodily form from any natural thing,
But such a form as Grecian goldsmiths make
Of hammered gold and gold enamelling
To keep a drowsy Emperor awake;
Or set upon a golden bough to sing   30

To lords and ladies of Byzantium
Of what is past, or passing, or to come.

DEATH BE NOT PROUD

John Donne

(1572–1631)

Biography p. 1070

Death be not proud, though some have called thee
Mighty and dreadfull, for, thou art not soe,
For, those, whom thou think'st, thou dost overthrow,
Die not, poore death, nor yet canst thou kill mee;
From rest and sleepe, which but thy pictures bee,   5
Much pleasure, then from thee, much more must flow,
And soonest our best men with thee doe goe,
Rest of their bones, and soules deliverie.
Thou art slave to Fate, Chance, kings, and desperate men,
And doth with poyson, warre, and sicknesse dwell,   10
And poppie, or charmes can make us sleepe as well,
And better then thy stroake; why swell'st thou then?
One short sleepe past, wee wake eternally,
And death shall be no more, death, thou shalt die.

DO NOT GO GENTLE INTO THAT GOOD NIGHT

Dylan Thomas

(1914–1953)

Biography p. 1104

Do not go gentle into that good night,
Old age should burn and rave at close of day;
Rage, rage against the dying of the light.

Though wise men at their end know dark is right,
Because their words had forked no lightning they   5
Do not go gentle into that good night.

Good men, the last wave by, crying how bright
Their frail deeds might have danced in a green bay,
Rage, rage against the dying of the light.

Wild men who caught and sang the sun in flight,   10
And learn, too late, they grieved it on its way,
Do not go gentle into that good night.

Grave men, near death, who see with blinding sight
Blind eyes could blaze like meteors and be gay,
Rage, rage against the dying of the light.   15

And you, my father, there on the sad height,
Curse, bless, me now with your fierce tears, I pray.
Do not go gentle into that good night.
Rage, rage against the dying of the light.

Drama

THE SANDBOX
Edward Albee
(b. 1928)

Biography p. 1059

The Players

THE YOUNG MAN,	25.	A good-looking, well-built boy in a bathing suit.
MOMMY,	55.	A well-dressed, imposing woman.
DADDY,	60.	A small man; gray, thin.
GRANDMA,	86.	A tiny, wizened woman with bright eyes.
THE MUSICIAN.		No particular age, but young would be nice.

Note. When, in the course of the play, MOMMY and DADDY call each other by these names, there should be no suggestion of regionalism. These names are empty of affection and point up the pre-senility and vacuity of their characters.

The Scene. A bare stage, with only the following: Near the footlights, far stage-right, two simple chairs set side by side, facing the audience; near the footlights, far stage-left, a chair facing stage-right with a music stand before it; farther back, and stage-center, slightly elevated and raked, a large child's sandbox with a toy pail and shovel; the background is the sky, which alters from brightest day to deepest night.

At the beginning, it is brightest day; the YOUNG MAN is alone on stage, to the rear of the sandbox, and to one side. He is doing calesthenics; he does calesthenics until quite at the very end of the play. These calesthenics, employing the arms only, should suggest the beating and fluttering of wings. The YOUNG MAN is, after all, the Angel of Death.

MOMMY *and* DADDY *enter from stage-left,* MOMMY *first.*

MOMMY (*motioning to* DADDY).   Well, here we are; this is the beach.
DADDY (*whining*).   I'm cold.
MOMMY (*dismissing him with a little laugh*).   Don't be silly; it's as warm as toast.

Look at that nice young man over there: *he* doesn't think it's cold. (*Waves to the* YOUNG MAN) Hello.

YOUNG MAN *(with an endearing smile).*   Hi!

MOMMY *(looking about).*   This will do perfectly . . . don't you think so, Daddy? There's sand there . . . and the water beyond. What do you think, Daddy?

DADDY *(vaguely).*   Whatever you say, Mommy.

MOMMY *(with the same little laugh).*   Well, of course . . . whatever I say. Then, it's settled, is it?

DADDY *(shrugs).*   She's *your* mother, not mine.

MOMMY.   *I* know she's my mother. What do you take me for? *(A pause)* All right, now; let's get on with it. *(She shouts into the wings, stage-left)* You! Out there! You can come in now.

(The MUSICIAN *enters, seats himself in the chair, stage-left, places music on the music stand, is ready to play.* MOMMY *nods approvingly.)*

MOMMY.   Very nice; very nice. Are you ready, Daddy? Let's go get Grandma.

DADDY.   Whatever you say, Mommy.

MOMMY *(leading the way out, stage-left).*   Of course, whatever I say. (*To the* MUSICIAN) You can begin now.

(The MUSICIAN *begins playing;* MOMMY *and* DADDY *exit; the* MUSICIAN, *all the while playing, nods to the* YOUNG MAN.)

YOUNG MAN *(with the same endearing smile).*   Hi!

(After a moment, MOMMY *and* DADDY *re-enter, carrying* GRANDMA. *She is borne in by their hands under her armpits; she is quite rigid; her legs are drawn up; her feet do not touch the ground; the expression on her ancient face is that of puzzlement and fear.)*

DADDY.   Where do we put her?

MOMMY. *(the same little laugh).*   Wherever I say, of course. Let me see . . . well . . . all right, over there . . . in the sandbox. *(Pause)* Well, what are you waiting for, Daddy? . . . The sandbox!

(Together they carry GRANDMA *over to the sandbox and more or less dump her in.)*

GRANDMA *(righting herself to a sitting position; her voice a cross between a baby's laugh and cry).*   Ahhhhhh! Graaaaa!

DADDY *(dusting himself).*   What do we do now?

MOMMY *(to the* MUSICIAN).   You can stop now.

(The MUSICIAN *stops.)*

(*Back to* DADDY) What do you mean, what do we do now? We go over there and sit down, of course. (*To the* YOUNG MAN) Hello there.

YOUNG MAN *(again smiling).*   Hi!

*(*MOMMY *and* DADDY *move to the chairs, stage-right, and sit down. A pause.)*

GRANDMA *(same as before).*   Ahhhhhh! Ah-haaaaaa! Graaaaaa!

DADDY.   Do you think . . . do you think she's . . . comfortable?

MOMMY *(impatiently).*   How would I know?

DADDY. *(Pause.)*   What do we do now?

MOMMY *(as if remembering).*   We . . . wait. We . . . sit here . . . and we wait. . . . that's what we do.

DADDY *(after a pause).*   Shall we talk to each other?

MOMMY *(with that little laugh; picking something off her dress).*   Well, *you* can talk, if you want to . . . if you can think of anything to *say* . . . if you can think of anything *new.*

DADDY. *(Thinks.)*   No . . . I suppose not.

MOMMY *(with a triumphant laugh).*   Of course not!

GRANDMA *(banging the toy shovel against the pail).*   Haaaaaa! Ah-haaaaaa!

MOMMY *(out over the audience).*   Be quiet, Grandma . . . just be quiet, and wait.

(GRANDMA *throws a shovelful of sand at* MOMMY.)

MOMMY *(still out over the audience).*   She's throwing sand at me! You stop that, Grandma; you stop throwing sand at Mommy! *(To* DADDY) She's throwing sand at me.

(DADDY *looks around at* GRANDMA, *who screams at him.*)

GRANDMA.   GRAAAAAA!

MOMMY.   Don't look at her. Just . . . sit here . . . be very still . . . and wait. *(To the* MUSICIAN) You . . . uh . . . you go ahead and do whatever it is you do.

(The MUSICIAN *plays.)*

(MOMMY *and* DADDY *are fixed, staring out beyond the audience.* GRANDMA *looks at them, looks at the* MUSICIAN, *looks at the sandbox, throws down the shovel.*)

GRANDMA.   Ah-haaaaaa! Graaaaaa! *(Looks for reaction; gets none. Now . . . directly to the audience)* Honestly! What a way to treat an old woman! Drag her out of the house . . . stick her in a car . . . bring her out here from the city . . . dump her in a pile of sand . . . and leave her here to set. I'm eighty-six years old! I was married when I was seventeen. To a farmer. He died when I was thirty. *(To the* MUSICIAN) Will you stop that, please?

(The MUSICIAN *stops playing.)*

I'm a feeble old woman . . . how do you expect anybody to hear me over that peep! peep! peep! *(To herself)* There's no respect around here. *(To the* YOUNG MAN) There's no respect around here!

YOUNG MAN. *(same smile).*   Hi!

GRANDMA. *(After a pause, a mild double-take, continues, to the audience.)*   My husband died when I was thirty *(indicates* MOMMY), and I had to raise that big cow over there all by my lonesome. You can imagine what *that* was like. Lordy! *(To the* YOUNG MAN) Where'd they get *you?*

YOUNG MAN.   Oh . . . I've been around for a while.

GRANDMA.   I'll bet you have! Heh, heh, heh. Will you look at you!

YOUNG MAN *(flexing his muscles).*   Isn't that something? *(Continues his calesthen-ics.)*

GRANDMA.   Boy, oh boy; I'll say. Pretty good.

YOUNG MAN *(sweetly).*   I'll say.

GRANDMA.   Where ya from?

YOUNG MAN.   Southern California.

GRANDMA *(nodding).*   Figgers; figgers. What's your name, honey?

YOUNG MAN.   I don't know. . . .

GRANDMA *(to the audience).*   Bright, too!

YOUNG MAN.   I mean . . . I mean, they haven't given me one yet . . . the studio . . .

GRANDMA *(giving him the once-over).*   You don't say . . . you don't say. Well . . . uh, I've got to talk some more . . . don't you go 'way.

YOUNG MAN.   Oh, no.

GRANDMA *(turning her attention back to the audience).*   Fine; fine. *(Then, once more, back to the* YOUNG MAN) You're . . . you're an actor, hunh?

YOUNG MAN *(beaming).*   Yes. I am.

GRANDMA *(to the audience again; shrugs).*   I'm smart that way. *Anyhow,* I had to raise. . . *that* over there all by my lonesome; and what's next to her there . . . that's what she married. Rich? I tell you . . . money, money, money. They took me off the *farm* . . . which was real decent of them . . . and they moved me into the big town house with *them* . . . fixed a nice place for me under the stove . . . gave me an army blanket . . . and my own dish . . . my very own dish! So, what have I got to complain about? Nothing, of course. I'm not complaining. *(She looks up at the sky, shouts to someone off stage)* Shouldn't it be getting dark now, dear?

(The lights dim; night comes on. The MUSICIAN *begins to play; it becomes deepest night. There are spots on all the players, including the* YOUNG MAN, *who is, of course, continuing his calisthenics.)*

DADDY *(stirring).*   It's nighttime.

MOMMY.   Shhhh. Be still . . . wait.

DADDY *(whining).*   It's so hot.

MOMMY.   Shhhhhh. Be still . . . wait.

GRANDMA *(to herself).*   That's better. Night. *(To the* MUSICIAN) Honey, do you play all through this part?

(The MUSICIAN *nods.)*

Well, keep it nice and soft; that's a good boy.

(The MUSICIAN *nods again; plays softly.)*

That's nice.

(There is an off-stage rumble.)

DADDY *(starting).*   What was that?

MOMMY *(beginning to weep).*   It was nothing.

DADDY.   It was . . . it was . . . thunder . . . or a wave breaking . . . or something.

MOMMY *(whispering, through her tears).*   It was an off-stage rumble . . . and you know what *that* means. . . .

DADDY.   I forget. . . .

MOMMY *(barely able to talk).*   It means the time has come for poor Grandma . . . and I can't bear it!

DADDY *(vacantly).*   I . . . I suppose you've got to be brave.

GRANDMA *(mocking).*   That's right, kid; be brave. You'll bear up; you'll get over it.

(Another off-stage rumble . . . louder.)

MOMMY.   Ohhhhhhhhhhh . . . poor Grandma . . . poor Grandma. . . .

GRANDMA *(to* MOMMY).   I'm fine! I'm all right! It hasn't happened yet!

(A violent off-stage rumble. All the lights go out, save the spot on the YOUNG MAN; *the* MUSICIAN *stops playing.)*

MOMMY.   Ohhhhhhhhhh. . . . Ohhhhhhhhhh. . . .

(Silence)

GRANDMA.   Don't put the lights up yet . . . I'm not ready; I'm not quite ready. *(Silence)* All right, dear . . . I'm about done.

(The lights come up again, to brightest day; the MUSICIAN *begins to play.* GRANDMA *is discovered, still in the sandbox, lying on her side, propped up on an elbow, half covered, busily shoveling sand over herself.)*

GRANDMA *(muttering).*   I don't know how I'm supposed to do anything with this goddam toy shovel. . . .

DADDY.   Mommy! It's daylight!

MOMMY *(brightly).*   So it is! Well! Our long night is over. We must put away our tears, take off our mourning . . . and face the future. It's our duty.

GRANDMA *(still shoveling; mimicking).*   . . . take off our mourning . . . face the future. . . . Lordy!

*(*MOMMY *and* DADDY *rise, stretch.* MOMMY *waves to the* YOUNG MAN.*)*

YOUNG MAN. *(with that smile).*   Hi!

*(*GRANDMA *plays dead. (!)* MOMMY *and* DADDY *go over to look at her; she is a little more than half buried in the sand; the toy shovel is in her hands, which are crossed on her breast.*)*

MOMMY *(before the sandbox; shaking her head).*   Lovely! It's . . . it's hard to be sad . . . she looks . . . so happy. *(With pride and conviction)* It pays to do things well. *(To the* MUSICIAN*)* All right, you can stop now, if you want to. I mean, stay around for a swim, or something; it's all right with us. *(She sighs heavily.)* Well, Daddy . . . off we go.

DADDY.   Brave Mommy!

MOMMY.   Brave Daddy!

(They exit, stage-left.)

GRANDMA *(after they leave; lying quite still).*   It pays to do things well. . . . Boy, oh boy! *(She tries to sit up)* . . . well, kids . . . *(but she finds she can't).* . . I . . . I can't get up. I . . . I can't move. . . .

(The YOUNG MAN *stops his calisthenics, nods to the* MUSICIAN, *walks over to* GRANDMA, *kneels down by the sandbox.)*

GRANDMA.   I . . . can't move. . . .

YOUNG MAN.   Shhhhh . . . be very still. . . .

GRANDMA.   I . . . I can't move. . . .

YOUNG MAN.   Uh . . . ma'am; I . . . I have a line here.

GRANDMA.   Oh, I'm sorry, sweetie; you go right ahead.

YOUNG MAN.   I am . . . uh . . .

GRANDMA.   Take your time, dear.

YOUNG MAN. *(Prepares; delivers the line like a real amateur.)*   I am the Angel of Death. I am . . . uh . . . I am come for you.

GRANDMA.   What . . . wha . . . *(Then, with resignation)* . . . ohhhh . . . ohhhh, I see.

(The YOUNG MAN *bends over, kisses* GRANDMA *gently on the forehead.)*

GRANDMA *(her eyes closed, her hands folded on her breast again, the shovel between her hands, a sweet smile on her face).*   Well . . . that was very nice, dear. . . .

YOUNG MAN *(still kneeling).*   Shhhhhh . . . be still. . . .

GRANDMA.   What I meant was . . . you did that very well, dear. . . .

YOUNG MAN *(blushing).*   . . . oh . . .

GRANDMA.   No; I mean it. You've got that . . . you've got a quality.

YOUNG MAN *(with his endearing smile).*   Oh . . . thank you; thank you very much . . . ma'am.

GRANDMA *(slowly; softly—as the* YOUNG MAN *puts his hands on top of* GRANDMA's*).*   You're . . . you're welcome . . . dear.

(Tableau. The MUSICIAN *continues to play as the curtain slowly comes down.)*

THE TRAGEDY OF KING LEAR

William Shakespeare
(1564–1616)

Biography p. 1098

Characters

Lear, King of Britain
King of France
Duke of Burgundy
Duke of Cornwall, husband to Regan
Duke of Albany, husband to Goneril
Earl of Kent
Earl of Gloucester
Edgar, son to Gloucester
Edmund, bastard son to Gloucester
Curan, a courtier
Oswald, steward to Goneril
Old Man, tenant to Gloucester
Doctor
Lear's Fool
A Captain, subordinate to Edmund
Gentlemen, attending on Cordelia
A Herald
Servants to Cornwall
Goneril
Regan   daughters to Lear
Cordelia
Knights attending on Lear, Officers,
    Messengers, Soldiers, Attendants

    [*Scene: Britain*]

ACT I

Scene I. [*King Lear's palace.*]

Enter KENT, GLOUCESTER, *and* EDMUND.

KENT.   I thought the King had more affected°¹ the Duke of Albany° than Cornwall.

GLOUCESTER.   It did always seem so to us; but now, in the division of the kingdom, it appears not which of the dukes he values most, for equalities are so weighed that curiosity in neither can make choice of   5 either's moiety.°

KENT.   Is not this your son, my lord?

GLOUCESTER.   His breeding,° sir, hath been at my charge. I have so often blushed to acknowledge him that now I am brazed° to't.

KENT.   I cannot conceive° you.   10

GLOUCESTER.   Sir, this young fellow's mother could; whereupon she grew round-wombed, and had indeed, sir, a son for her cradle ere she had a husband for her bed. Do you smell a fault?

KENT.   I cannot wish the fault undone, the issue° of it being so proper.°

GLOUCESTER.   But I have a son, sir, by order of law, some year elder   15 than this, who yet is no dearer in my account:° though this knave° came something saucily° to the world before he was sent for, yet was his mother fair, there was good sport at his making, and the whoreson° must be acknowledged. Do you know this noble gentleman, Edmund?

EDMUND.   No, my lord.   20

GLOUCESTER.   My Lord of Kent. Remember him hereafter as my honorable friend.

EDMUND.   My services to your lordship.

KENT.   I must love you, and sue° to know you better.

Footnotes are from Signet Classic Shakespeare *The Tragedy of King Lear,* edited by Russell Fraser, General Editor: Sylvan Barnet, New York: New American Library, 1963.

¹The degree sign (°) indicates a footnote, which is keyed to the text by line number. Text references are printed in *italic* type; the annotation follows in roman type.

I.i. ¹*affected* loved

²*Albany* Albanacte, whose domain extended "from the river Humber to the point of Caithness" (Holinshed)

⁶*equalities . . . moiety* i.e., shares are so balanced against one another that careful examination by neither can make him wish the other's portion

⁸*breeding* upbringing

⁹*brazed* made brazen, hardened

¹⁰*conceive* understand (pun follows)

¹⁴*issue* result (child)

¹⁴*proper* handsome

¹⁶*account* estimation

¹⁶*knave* fellow (without disapproval)

¹⁷*saucily* (1) insolently (2) lasciviously

¹⁸*whoreson* fellow (lit., son of a whore)

²⁴*sue* entreat

EDMUND.   Sir, I shall study deserving.   25
GLOUCESTER.   He hath been out° nine years, and away he shall again.
    The King is coming.

    Sound a sennet.° Enter one bearing a coronet,° then KING LEAR,
    then the Dukes of CORNWALL *and* ALBANY, *next* GONERIL,
    REGAN, CORDELIA, *and* ATTENDANTS.

LEAR.   Attend the lords of France and Burgundy, Gloucester.
GLOUCESTER.   I shall, my lord.

                                          Exit [*with* EDMUND].

                                                                                        30

LEAR.   Meantime we shall express our darker purpose.°
    Give me the map there. Know that we have divided
    In three our kingdom; and 'tis our fast° intent
    To shake all cares and business from our age,
    Conferring them on younger strengths, while we
    Unburthened crawl toward death. Our son of Cornwall,   35
    And you our no less loving son of Albany,
    We have this hour a constant will to publish°
    Our daughters' several° dowers, that future strife
    May be prevented° now. The Princes, France and Burgundy,
    Great rivals in our youngest daughter's love,   40
    Long in our court have made their amorous sojourn,
    And here are to be answered. Tell me, my daughters
    (Since now we will divest us both of rule,
    Interest° of territory, cares of state),
    Which of you shall we say doth love us most,   45
    That we our largest bounty may extend
    Where nature doth with merit challenge.° Goneril,
    Our eldest-born, speak first.
GONERIL.   Sir, I love you more than word can wield° the matter;
    Dearer than eyesight, space° and liberty;   50
    Beyond what can be valued, rich or rare;

---

²⁶*out* away, abroad
²⁷s.d. *sennet* set of notes played on a trumpet, signalizing the entrance or departure of a procession
²⁷s.d. *coronet* small crown, intended for Cordelia
³⁰*darker purpose* hidden intention
³²*fast* fixed
³⁷*constant will to publish* fixed intention to proclaim
³⁸*several* separate
³⁹*prevented* forestalled
⁴⁴*Interest* legal right
⁴⁷*nature . . . challenge* i.e., natural affection contends with desert for (or lays claim to) bounty
⁴⁹*wield* handle
⁵⁰*space* scope

No less than life, with grace, health, beauty, honor;
As much as child e'er loved, or father found;
A love that makes breath° poor, and speech unable:°
Beyond all manner of so much° I love you.   55
CORDELIA.   [*Aside*] What shall Cordelia speak? Love, and be silent.
LEAR.   Of all these bounds, even from this line to this,
With shadowy forests, and with champains riched,°
With plenteous rivers, and wide-skirted meads,°
We make thee lady. To thine and Albany's issues°   60
Be this perpetual.° What says our second daughter,
Our dearest Regan, wife of Cornwall? Speak.
REGAN.   I am made of that self mettle° as my sister,
And prize me at her worth.° In my true heart
I find she names my very deed of love;°   65
Only she comes too short, that° I profess
Myself an enemy to all other joys
Which the most precious square of sense professes,°
And find I am alone felicitate°
In your dear Highness' love.
CORDELIA.   [*Aside*] Then poor Cordelia!   70
And yet not so, since I am sure my love's
More ponderous° than my tongue.
LEAR.   To thee and thine hereditary ever
Remain this ample third of our fair kingdom,
No less in space, validity,° and pleasure   75
Than that conferred on Goneril. Now, our joy,
Although our last and least;° to whose young love
The vines of France and milk° of Burgundy
Strive to be interest;° what can you say to draw
A third more opulent than your sisters? Speak.   80
CORDELIA.   Nothing, my lord.

---

^{54}*breath* language; *unable* impotent
^{55}*Beyond . . . much* beyond all these comparisons
^{58}*champains riched* enriched plains
^{59}*wide-skirted meads* extensive grasslands
^{60}*issues* descendants
^{61}*perpetual* in perpetuity
^{63}*self mettle* same material or temperament
^{64}*prize . . . worth* value me the same (imperative)
^{65}*my . . . love* what my love really is (a legalism)
^{66}*that* in that
^{68}*Which . . . professes* which the choicest estimate of sense avows
^{69}*felicitate* made happy
^{72}*ponderous* weighty
^{75}*validity* value
^{77}*least* youngest, smallest
^{78}*milk* i.e., pastures
^{79}*interest* closely connected, as interested parties

LEAR.   Nothing?

CORDELIA.   Nothing.

LEAR.   Nothing will come of nothing. Speak again.

CORDELIA.   Unhappy that I am, I cannot heave   85
  My heart into my mouth. I love your Majesty
  According to my bond,° no more nor less.

LEAR.   How, how, Cordelia? Mend your speech a little,
  Lest you may mar your fortunes.

CORDELIA.   Good my lord,
  You have begot me, bred me, loved me. I   90
  Return those duties back as are right fit,°
  Obey you, love you, and most honor you.
  Why have my sisters husbands, if they say
  They love you all? Haply,° when I shall wed,
  That lord whose hand must take my plight° shall carry   95
  Half my love with him, half my care and duty.
  Sure I shall never marry like my sisters,
  To love my father all.

LEAR.   But goes thy heart with this?

CORDELIA.   Ay, my good lord.

LEAR.   So young, and so untender?   100

CORDELIA.   So young, my lord, and true.

LEAR.   Let it be so, thy truth then be thy dower!
  For, by the sacred radiance of the sun,
  The mysteries of Hecate° and the night,
  By all the operation of the orbs°   105
  From whom we do exist and cease to be,
  Here I disclaim all my paternal care,
  Propinquity and property of blood,°
  And as a stranger to my heart and me
  Hold thee from this for ever. The barbarous Scythian,°   110
  Or he that makes his generation messes°
  To gorge his appetite, shall to my bosom
  Be as well neighbored, pitied, and relieved,
  As thou my sometime° daughter.

KENT.   Good my liege———

[87] *bond* i.e., filial obligation

[91] *Return . . . fit* i.e., am correspondingly dutiful

[94] *Haply* perhaps

[95] *plight* troth plight

[104] *mysteries of Hecate* secret rites of Hecate (goddess of the infernal world, and of witchcraft)

[105] *operation of the orbs* astrological influence

[108] *Propinquity and property of blood* relationship and common blood

[110] *Scythian* (type of the savage)

[111] *makes his generation messes* eats his own offspring

[114] *sometime* former

LEAR.   Peace, Kent!   115
    Come not between the Dragon° and his wrath.
    I loved her most, and thought to set my rest°
    On her kind nursery.° Hence and avoid my sight!
.   So be my grave my peace, as here I give
    Her father's heart from her! Call France. Who stirs?   120
    Call Burgundy. Cornwall and Albany,
    With my two daughters' dowers digest° the third;
    Let pride, which she calls plainness, marry her.°
    I do invest you jointly with my power,
    Pre-eminence, and all the large effects   125
    That troop with majesty.° Ourself,° by monthly course,
    With reservation° of an hundred knights,
    By you to be sustained, shall our abode
    Make with you by due turn. Only we shall retain
    The name, and all th' addition° to a king. The sway,   130
    Revènue, execution of the rest,
    Belovèd sons, be yours; which to confirm,
    This coronet° part between you.
KENT.   Royal Lear,
    Whom I have ever honored as my king,
    Loved as my father, as my master followed,   135
    As my great patron thought on in my prayers————
LEAR.   The bow is bent and drawn; make from the shaft.°
KENT.   Let it fall° rather, though the fork° invade
    The region of my heart. Be Kent unmannerly
    When Lear is mad. What wouldst thou do, old man?   140
    Think'st thou that duty shall have dread to speak
    When power to flattery bows? To plainness honor's bound
    When majesty falls to folly. Reserve thy state,°
    And in thy best consideration° check
    This hideous rashness. Answer my life my judgment,°   145
    Thy youngest daughter does not love thee least,

[116]*Dragon* (1) heraldic device of Britain (2) emblem of ferocity
[117]*set my rest* (1) stake my all (a term from the card game of primero) (2) find my rest
[118]*nursery* care, nursing
[122]*digest* absorb
[123]*Let . . . her* i.e., let her pride be her dowry and gain her a husband
[126]*effects/That troop with majesty* accompaniments that go with kingship
[126]*Ourself* (the royal "we")
[127]*reservation* the action of reserving a privilege (a legalism)
[130]*addition* titles and honors
[133]*coronet* (the crown which was to have been Cordelia's)
[137]*make from the shaft* avoid the arrow
[138]*fall* strike
[138]*fork* forked head of the arrow
[143]*Reserve thy state* retain your kingly authority
[144]*best consideration* most careful reflection
[145]*Answer . . . judgment* I will stake my life on my opinion

Nor are those empty-hearted whose low sounds
Reverb° no hollowness.°

LEAR.   Kent, on thy life, no more!

KENT.   My life I never held but as a pawn°
To wage° against thine enemies; nor fear to lose it,   150
Thy safety being motive.°

LEAR.   Out of my sight!

KENT.   See better, Lear, and let me still° remain
The true blank° of thine eye.

LEAR.   Now by Apollo———

KENT.   Now by Apollo, King,
Thou swear'st thy gods in vain.

LEAR.   O vassal! Miscreant!°   155

[*Laying his hand on his sword.*]

ALBANY, CORNWALL.   Dear sir, forbear!

KENT.   Kill thy physician, and the fee bestow
Upon the foul disease. Revoke thy gift,
Or, whilst I can vent clamor° from my throat,
I'll tell thee thou dost evil.

LEAR.   Hear me, recreant!°   160
On thine allegiance,° hear me!
That thou hast sought to make us break our vows,
Which we durst never yet, and with strained° pride
To come betwixt our sentence° and our power,
Which nor our nature nor our place can bear,   165
Our potency made good,° take thy reward.
Five days we do allot thee for provision°
To shield thee from diseases° of the world,
And on the sixth to turn thy hated back
Upon our kingdom. If, on the tenth day following,   170

148*Reverb* reverberate
148*hollowness* (1) emptiness (2) insincerity
149*pawn* stake in a wager
150*wage* (1) wager (2) carry on war
151*motive* moving cause
152*still* always
153*blank* the white spot in the center of the target (at which Lear should aim)
155*vassal! Miscreant!* base wretch! Misbeliever!
159*vent clamor* utter a cry
160*recreant* traitor
161*On thine allegiance* (to forswear, which is to commit high treason)
163*strained* forced (and so excessive)
164*sentence* judgment, decree
166*Our potency made good* my royal authority being now asserted
167*for provision* for making preparation
168*diseases* troubles

Thy banished trunk° be found in our dominions,
The moment is thy death. Away! By Jupiter,
This shall not be revoked.
KENT.   Fare thee well, King. Sith° thus thou wilt appear,
Freedom lives hence, and banishment is here.   175
[*To* CORDELIA] The gods to their dear shelter take thee, maid,
That justly think'st, and hast most rightly said.
[*To* REGAN *and* GONERIL] And your large speeches may your deeds
       approve,°
That good effects° may spring from words of love.
Thus Kent, O Princes, bids you all adieu;   180
He'll shape his old course° in a country new.

                                                    Exit.

     Flourish.° *Enter* GLOUCESTER, *with* FRANCE *and* BURGUNDY;
                    ATTENDANTS.

GLOUCESTER.   Here's France and Burgundy, my noble lord.
LEAR.   My Lord of Burgundy,
We first address toward you, who with this king
Hath rivaled for our daughter. What in the least   185
Will you require in present° dower with her,
Or cease your quest of love?
BURGUNDY.   Most royal Majesty,
I crave no more than hath your Highness offered,
Nor will you tender° less.
LEAR.   Right noble Burgundy,
When she was dear° to us, we did hold her so;   190
But now her price is fallen. Sir, there she stands.
If aught within that little seeming substance,°
Or all of it, with our displeasure pieced,°
And nothing more, may fitly like° your Grace,
She's there, and she is yours.
BURGUNDY.   I know no answer.   195
LEAR.   Will you, with those infirmities she owes,°

---

[171]*trunk* body
[174]*Sith* since
[178]*approve* prove true
[179]*effects* results
[181]*shape . . . course* pursue his customary way
[181]s.d. *Flourish* trumpet fanfare
[186]*present* immediate
[189]*tender* offer
[190]*dear* (1) beloved (2) valued at a high price
[192]*little seeming substance* person who is (1) inconsiderable (2) outspoken
[193]*pieced* added to it
[194]*fitly like* please by its fitness
[196]*owes* possesses

Unfriended, new adopted to our hate,
Dow'red with our curse, and strangered° with our oath,
Take her, or leave her?
BURGUNDY.   Pardon me, royal sir.
Election makes not up° on such conditions.   200
LEAR.   Then leave her, sir; for, by the pow'r that made me,
I tell you all her wealth. [*To* FRANCE] For you, great King,
I would not from your love make such a stray
To° match you where I hate; therefore beseech° you
T' avert your liking a more worthier way°   205
Than on a wretch whom nature is ashamed
Almost t' acknowledge hers.
FRANCE.   This is most strange,
That she whom even but now was your best object,°
The argument° of your praise, balm of your age,
The best, the dearest, should in this trice of time   210
Commit a thing so monstrous to dismantle°
So many folds of favor. Sure her offense
Must be of such unnatural degree
That monsters it,° or your fore-vouched° affection
Fall into taint;° which to believe of her   215
Must be a faith that reason without miracle
Should never plant in me.°
CORDELIA.   I yet beseech your Majesty,
If for° I want that glib and oily art
To speak and purpose not,° since what I well intend
I'll do't before I speak, that you make known   220
It is no vicious blot, murder, or foulness,
No unchaste action or dishonored step,
That hath deprived me of your grace and favor;

198*strangered* made a stranger
200*Election makes not up* no one can choose
204*make such a stray/To* stray so far as to
204*beseech* I beseech
205*avert . . . way* turn your affections from her and bestow them on a better person
208*best object* i.e., the one you loved most
209*argument* subject
211*dismantle* strip off
214*That monsters it* as makes it monstrous, unnatural
214*forevouched* previously sworn
215*Fall into taint* must be taken as having been unjustified all along i.e., Cordelia was unworthy of your love from the first
216*reason . . . me* my reason would have to be supported by a miracle to make me believe
218*for* because
219*purpose not* not mean to do what I promise

But even for want of that for which I am richer,
A still-soliciting° eye, and such a tongue   225
That I am glad I have not, though not to have it
Hath lost° me in your liking.
LEAR.   Better thou
Hadst not been born than not t' have pleased me better.
FRANCE.   Is it but this? A tardiness in nature°
Which often leaves the history unspoke°   230
That it intends to do. My Lord of Burgundy,
What say you° to the lady? Love's not love
When it is mingled with regards° that stands
Aloof from th' entire point.° Will you have her?
She is herself a dowry.
BURGUNDY.   Royal King,   235
Give but that portion which yourself proposed,
And here I take Cordelia by the hand,
Duchess of Burgundy.
LEAR.   Nothing. I have sworn. I am firm.
BURGUNDY.   I am sorry then you have so lost a father   240
That you must lose a husband.
CORDELIA.   Peace be with Burgundy.
Since that respects of fortune° are his love,
I shall not be his wife.
FRANCE.   Fairest Cordelia, that art most rich being poor,
Most choice forsaken, and most loved despised,   245
Thee and thy virtues here I seize upon.
Be it lawful I take up what's cast away.
Gods, gods! 'Tis strange that from their cold'st neglect
My love should kindle to inflamed respect.°
Thy dow'rless daughter, King, thrown to my chance,°   250
Is Queen of us, of ours, and our fair France.
Not all the dukes of wat'rish° Burgundy
Can buy this unprized precious° maid of me.
Bid them farewell, Cordelia, though unkind.
Thou losest here, a better where° to find.   255

---

[225]*still-soliciting* always begging
[227]*lost* ruined
[229]*tardiness in nature* natural reticence
[230]*leaves the history unspoke* does not announce the action
[232]*What say you* i.e., will you have
[233]*regards* considerations (the dowry)
[234]*stands . . . point* have nothing to do with the essential question (love)
[242]*respects of fortune* mercenary considerations
[249]*inflamed respect* more ardent affection
[250]*chance* lot
[252]*wat'rish* (1) with many rivers (2) weak, diluted
[253]*unprized precious* unappreciated by others, and yet precious
[255]*here . . . where* in this place, in another place

LEAR.   Thou hast her, France; let her be thine, for we
          Have no such daughter, nor shall ever see
          That face of hers again. Therefore be gone,
          Without our grace, our love, our benison.°
          Come, noble Burgundy.   260

          Flourish. Exeunt [LEAR, BURGUNDY, CORNWALL, ALBANY,
                   GLOUCESTER, *and* ATTENDANTS].

FRANCE.   Bid farewell to your sisters.
CORDELIA.   The jewels of our father,° with washed° eyes
          Cordelia leaves you. I know you what you are,
          And, like a sister,° am most loath to call
          Your faults as they are named.° Love well our father.   265
          To your professèd° bosoms I commit him.
          But yet, alas, stood I within his grace,
          I would prefer° him to a better place.
          So farewell to you both.
REGAN.   Prescribe not us our duty.
GONERIL.   Let your study   270
          Be to content your lord, who hath received you
          At Fortune's alms.° You have obedience scanted,°
          And well are worth the want that you have wanted.°
CORDELIA.   Time shall unfold what plighted° cunning hides,
          Who covers faults, at last shame them derides.°   275
          Well may you prosper.
FRANCE.   Come, my fair Cordelia.

                            Exit FRANCE *and* CORDELIA.

GONERIL.   Sister, it is not little I have to say of what most nearly
          appertains to us both. I think our father will hence tonight.
REGAN.   That's most certain, and with you; next month with us.
GONERIL.   You see how full of changes his age is. The observation we   280
          have made of it hath not been little. He always loved our sister most,

---

259*benison* blessing
262*The jewels of our father* you creatures prized by our father
262*washed* (1) weeping (2) clear-sighted
264*like a sister* because I am a sister i.e., loyal, affectionate
265*as they are named* i.e., by their right and ugly names
266*professèd* pretending to love
268*prefer* recommend
272*At Fortune's alms* as a charitable bequest from Fortune (and so, by extension, as one
beggared or cast down by Fortune)
272*scanted* stinted
273*worth . . . wanted* deserve to be denied, even as you have denied
274*plighted* pleated, enfolded
275*Who . . . derides* those who hide their evil are finally exposed and shamed ("He that
hideth his sins, shall not prosper")

and with what poor judgment he hath now cast her off appears too
grossly.°

REGAN.   'Tis the infirmity of his age; yet he hath ever but slenderly
known himself.   285

GONERIL.   The best and soundest of his time° hath been but rash; then
must we look from his age to receive not alone the imperfections of
long-in-grafted° condition,° but therewithal° the unruly waywardness
that infirm and choleric years bring with them.

REGAN.   Such unconstant starts° are we like to have from him as this   290
of Kent's banishment.

GONERIL.   There is further compliment° of leave-taking between
France and him. Pray you, let's hit° together; if our father carry
authority with such disposition as he bears,° this last surrender° of his
will but offend° us.   295

REGAN.   We shall further think of it.

GONERIL.   We must do something, and i' th' heat.°

                                                                                    Exeunt.

Scene II. [*The Earl of Gloucester's castle*]

Enter EDMUND [*with a letter*].

EDMUND.   Thou, Nature,° art my goddess; to thy law
My services are bound. Wherefore should I
Stand in the plague of custom,° and permit
The curiosity° of nations to deprive me,
For that° I am some twelve or fourteen moonshines°   5
Lag of° a brother? Why bastard? Wherefore base?
When my dimensions are as well compact,°

283*grossly* obviously
286*of his time* period of his life up to now
288*long-ingrafted* implanted for a long time
288*condition* disposition
288*therewithal* with them
290*unconstant starts* impulsive whims
292*compliment* formal courtesy
293*hit* agree
294*carry . . . bears* continues, and in such frame of mind, to wield the sovereign power
294*last surrender* recent abdication
295*offend* vex
297*i' th' heat* while the iron is hot I.ii.
1*Nature* (Edmund's conception of Nature accords with our description of a bastard as a
natural child)
3*Stand . . . custom* respect hateful convention
4*curiosity* nice distinctions
5*For that* because
5*moonshines* months
6*Lag of* short of being (in age)
7*compact* framed

My mind as generous,° and my shape as true,
As honest° madam's issue? Why brand they us
With base? With baseness? Bastardy? Base? Base?   10
Who, in the lusty stealth of nature, take
More composition° and fierce° quality
Than doth, within a dull, stale, tired bed,
Go to th' creating a whole tribe of fops°
Got° 'tween asleep and wake? Well then,   15
Legitimate Edgar, I must have your land.
Our father's love is to the bastard Edmund
As to th' legitimate. Fine word, "legitimate."
Well, my legitimate, if this letter speed,°
And my invention° thrive, Edmund the base   20
Shall top th' legitimate. I grow, I prosper.
Now, gods, stand up for bastards.

Enter GLOUCESTER.

GLOUCESTER.   Kent banished thus? and France in choler parted?
And the King gone tonight? prescribed° his pow'r?
Confined to exhibition?° All this done   25
Upon the gad?° Edmund, how now? What news?
EDMUND.   So please your lordship, none.
GLOUCESTER.   Why so earnestly seek you to put up° that letter?
EDMUND.   I know no news, my lord.
GLOUCESTER.   What paper were you reading?   30
EDMUND.   Nothing, my lord.
GLOUCESTER.   No? What needed then that terrible dispatch° of it into
your pocket? The quality of nothing hath not such need to hide itself.
Let's see. Come, if it be nothing, I shall not need spectacles.
EDMUND.   I beseech you, sir, pardon me. It is a letter from my brother   35
that I have not all o'er-read; and for so much as I have perused, I find
it not fit for your o'erlooking.°

---

[8] *generous* gallant
[9] *honest* chaste
[12] *composition* completeness
[12] *fierce* energetic
[14] *fops* fools
[15] *Got* begot
[19] *speed* prosper
[20] *invention* plan
[24] *prescribed* limited
[25] *exhibition* an allowance or pension
[26] *Upon the gad* on the spur of the moment (as if pricked by a gad or goad)
[28] *put up* put away, conceal
[32] *terrible dispatch* hasty putting away
[37] *o'erlooking* inspection

GLOUCESTER.   Give me the letter, sir.

EDMUND.   I shall offend, either to detain or give it. The contents, as
in part I understand them, are to blame.°   40

GLOUCESTER.   Let's see, let's see.

EDMUND.   I hope, for my brother's justification, he wrote this but as
an essay or taste° of my virtue.

GLOUCESTER.   *(Reads.)* "This policy and reverence° of age makes the
world bitter to the best of our times;° keeps our fortunes from us till   45
our oldness cannot relish° them. I begin to find an idle and fond°
bondage in the oppression of aged tyranny, who sways, not as it hath
power, but as it is suffered.° Come to me, that of this I may speak
more. If our father would sleep till I waked him, you should enjoy
half his revenue° for ever, and live the beloved of your brother,   50
Edgar." Hum! Conspiracy? "Sleep till I waked him, you should enjoy
half his revenue." My son Edgar! Had he a hand to write this? A heart
and brain to breed it in? When came you to this? Who brought it?

EDMUND.   It was not brought me, my lord; there's the cunning of it.
I found it thrown in at the casement of my closet.°   55

GLOUCESTER.   You know the character° to be your brother's?

EDMUND.   If the matter were good, my lord, I durst swear it were his;
but in respect of that,° I would fain° think it were not.

GLOUCESTER.   It is his.

EDMUND.   It is his hand, my lord; but I hope his heart is not in the   60
contents.

GLOUCESTER.   Has he never before sounded° you in this business?

EDMUND.   Never, my lord. But I have heard him oft maintain it to be
fit that, sons at perfect° age, and fathers declined, the father should
be as ward to the son, and the son manage his revenue.   65

GLOUCESTER.   O villain, villain! His very opinion in the letter. Abhorred villain, unnatural, detested,° brutish villain; worse than brutish! Go, sirrah,° seek him. I'll apprehend him. Abominable villain!
Where is he?

EDMUND.   I do not well know, my lord. If it shall please you to   70

---

[40]*to blame* blameworthy
[43]*essay or taste* test
[44]*policy and reverence* policy of reverencing (hendiadys)
[45]*best of our times* best years of our lives (i.e., our youth)
[46]*relish* enjoy
[46]*idle and fond* foolish
[48]*who . . . suffered* which rules, not from its own strength, but from our allowance
[50]*revenue* income
[55]*casement of my closet* window of my room
[56]*character* handwriting
[58]*in respect of that* in view of what it is
[58]*fain* prefer to
[62]*sounded* sounded you out
[64]*perfect* mature
[67]*detested* detestable
[68]*sirrah* sir (familiar form of address)

suspend your indignation against my brother till you can derive from
him better testimony of his intent, you should run a certain
course;° where, if you violently proceed against him, mistaking his
purpose, it would make a great gap° in your own honor and shake in
pieces the heart of his obedience. I dare pawn down° my life for him   75
that he hath writ this to feel° my affection to your honor, and to no
other pretense of danger.°

GLOUCESTER.   Think you so?

EDMUND.   If your honor judge it meet,° I will place you where you
shall hear us confer of this, and by an auricular assurance° have your   80
satisfaction, and that without any further delay than this very evening.

GLOUCESTER.   He cannot be such a monster.

EDMUND.   Nor is not, sure.

GLOUCESTER.   To his father, that so tenderly and entirely loves him.   85
Heaven and earth! Edmund, seek him out; wind me into him,° I pray
you; frame° the business after your own wisdom. I would unstate
myself to be in a due resolution.°

EDMUND.   I will seek him, sir, presently;° convey° the business as I
shall find means, and acquaint you withal.°   90

GLOUCESTER.   These late° eclipses in the sun and moon portend no
good to us. Though the wisdom of Nature° can reason° it thus and
thus, yet Nature finds itself scourged by the sequent effects.° Love
cools, friendship falls off,° brothers divide. In cities, mutinies;° in
countries, discord; in palaces, treason; and the bond cracked 'twixt   95
son and father. This villain of mine comes under the prediction,°
there's son against father; the King falls from bias of nature,° there's

[73]*run a certain course* i.e., proceed safely, know where you are going
[74]*gap* breach
[75]*pawn down* stake
[76]*feel* test
[77]*pretense of danger* dangerous purpose
[79]*meet* fit
[80]*auricular assurance* proof heard with your own ears
[86]*wind me into him* insinuate yourself into his confidence for me
[87]*frame* manage
[88]*unstate . . . resolution* forfeit my earldom to know the truth
[89]*presently* at once
[89]*convey* manage
[90]*withal* with it
[91]*late* recent
[92]*wisdom of Nature* scientific learning
[92]*reason* explain
[93]*yet . . . effects* nonetheless our world is punished with subsequent disasters
[94]*falls off* revolts
[94]*mutinies* riots
[96]*This . . . prediction* i.e., my son's villainous behavior is included in these portents, and
bears them out
[97]*bias of nature* natural inclination (the metaphor is from the game of bowls)

father against child. We have seen the best of our time.° Machina-
tions, hollowness,° treachery, and all ruinous disorders follow us   100
disquietly° to our graves. Find out this villain, Edmund; it shall lose
thee nothing.° Do it carefully. And the noble and true-hearted Kent
banished; his offense, honesty. 'Tis strange.

Exit.

EDMUND.   This is the excellent foppery° of the world, that when we
are sick in fortune, often the surfeits of our own behavior,° we make   105
guilty of our disasters the sun, the moon, and stars; as if we were
villains on° necessity; fools by heavenly compulsion; knaves, thieves,
and treachers by spherical predominance;° drunkards, liars, and
adulterers by an enforced obedience of planetary influence;° and all
that we are evil in, by a divine thrusting on.° An admirable evasion   110
of whoremaster° man, to lay his goatish° disposition on the charge
of a star. My father compounded° with my mother under the Dragon's Tail,° and my nativity° was under Ursa Major,° so that it follows I am rough and lecherous. Fut!° I should have been that° I am,
had the maidenliest star in the firmament twinkled on my bastardiz-   115
ing. Edgar———

Enter EDGAR.

and pat he comes, like the catastrophe° of the old comedy. My cue
is villainous melancholy, with a sigh like Tom o' Bedlam.°—O,
these eclipses do portend these divisions. Fa, sol, la, mi.°
EDGAR.   How now, brother Edmund; what serious contemplation are
you in?   120

[99]*best of our time* our best days
[100]*hollowness* insincerity
[101]*disquietly* unquietly
[102]*it . . . nothing* you will not lose by it
[104]*foppery* folly
[105]*often . . . behavior* often caused by our own excesses
[107]*on* of
[108]*treachers . . . predominance* traitors because of the ascendancy of a particular star at
our birth
[109]*by . . . influence* because we had to submit to the influence of our star
[110]*divine thrusting on* supernatural compulsion
[111]*whoremaster* lecherous
[111]*goatish* lascivious
[112]*compounded* (1) made terms (2) formed (a child)
[113]*Dragon's Tail* the constellation Draco
[113]*nativity* birthday
[113]*Ursa Major* the Great Bear
[114]*Fut!*'s foot (an impatient oath)
[114]*that* what
[117]*catastrophe* conclusion
[117]*My . . . Bedlam* I must be doleful, like a lunatic beggar out of Bethlehem (Bedlam)
Hospital, the London madhouse
[118]*Fa, sol, la, mi* (Edmund's humming of the musical notes is perhaps prompted by his
use of the word "division," which describes a musical variation.)

EDMUND.   I am thinking, brother, of a prediction I read this other day, what should follow these eclipses.

EDGAR.   Do you busy yourself with that?

EDMUND.   I promise you, the effects he writes of succeed° unhappily: as of unnaturalness° between the child and the parent, death, dearth,   125 dissolutions of ancient amities,° divisions in state, menaces and maledictions against King and nobles, needless diffidences,° banishment of friends, dissipation of cohorts,° nuptial breaches, and I know not what.

EDGAR.   How long have you been a sectary astronomical?°   130

EDMUND.   Come, come, when saw you my father last?

EDGAR.   Why, the night gone by.

EDMUND.   Spake you with him?

EDGAR.   Ay, two hours together.

EDMUND.   Parted you in good terms? Found you no displeasure in him   135 by word nor countenance?°

EDGAR.   None at all.

EDMUND.   Bethink yourself wherein you may have offended him; and at my entreaty forbear his presence° until some little time hath qualified° the heat of his displeasure, which at this instant so rageth   140 in him that with the mischief of your person it would scarcely allay.°

EDGAR.   Some villain hath done me wrong.

EDMUND.   That's my fear, brother I pray you have a continent forbearance° till the speed of his rage goes slower; and, as I say, retire   145 with me to my lodging, from whence I will fitly° bring you to hear my lord speak. Pray ye, go; there's my key. If you do stir abroad, go armed.

EDGAR.   Armed, brother?

EDMUND.   Brother, I advise you to the best. Go armed. I am no honest   150 man if there be any good meaning toward you. I have told you what I have seen and heard; but faintly, nothing like the image and horror° of it. Pray you, away.

EDGAR.   Shall I hear from you anon?°

EDMUND.   I do serve you in this business.   155

---

[124]*succeed* follow
[125]*unnaturalness* unkindness
[126]*amities* friendships
[127]*diffidences* distrusts
[128]*dissipation of cohorts* falling away of supporters
[130]*sectary astronomical* believer in astrology
[136]*countenance* expression
[139]*forbear his presence* keep away from him
[140]*qualified* lessened
[142]*with . . . allay* even an injury to you would not appease his anger
[145]*have a continent forbearance* be restrained and keep yourself withdrawn
[146]*fitly* at a fit time
[153]*image and horror* true horrible picture
[154]*anon* in a little while

Exit EDGAR.

A credulous father, and a brother noble,
Whose nature is so far from doing harms   155
That he suspects none; on whose foolish honesty
My practices° ride easy. I see the business.
Let me, if not by birth, have lands by wit.
All with me's meet° that I can fashion fit.°

Exit.

Scene III. [*The Duke of Albany's palace.*]

Enter GONERIL, *and* [OSWALD, *her*] *Steward.*

GONERIL.   Did my father strike my gentleman for chiding of his Fool?°
OSWALD.   Ay, madam.
GONERIL.   By day and night he wrongs me. Every hour
He flashes into one gross crime° or other
That sets us all at odds. I'll not endure it.   5
His knights grow riotous,° and himself upbraids us
On every trifle. When he returns from hunting,
I will not speak with him. Say I am sick.
If you come slack of former services,°
You shall do well; the fault of it I'll answer.°   10

[*Horns within.*]

OSWALD.   He's coming, madam; I hear him.
GONERIL.   Put on what weary negligence you please,
You and your fellows. I'd have it come to question.°
If he distaste° it, let him to my sister,
Whose mind and mine I know in that are one,   15
Not to be overruled. Idle° old man,
That still would manage those authorities
That he hath given away. Now, by my life,
Old fools are babes again, and must be used
With checks as flatteries, when they are seen abused.°   20
Remember what I have said.

---

¹⁵⁷*practices* plots
¹⁵⁹*meet* proper
¹⁵⁹*fashion fit* shape to my purpose
I.iii. ¹*Fool* court jester
⁴*crime* offense
⁶*riotous* dissolute
⁹*come . . . services* are less serviceable to him than formerly
¹⁰*answer* answer for
¹³*come to question* be discussed openly
¹⁴*distaste* dislike
¹⁶*Idle* foolish
²⁰*With . . . abused* with restraints as well as soothing words when they are misguided

OSWALD.   Well, madam.
GONERIL.   And let his knights have colder looks among you.
What grows of it, no matter; advise your fellows so.
I would breed from hence occasions, and I shall,
That I may speak.° I'll write straight° to my sister   25
To hold my course. Go, prepare for dinner.

                                                        Exeunt.

                    Scene IV. [*A hall in the same*]

                    Enter KENT [*disguised*].

KENT.   If but as well I other accents borrow
That can my speech defuse,° my good intent
May carry through itself to that full issue°
For which I razed my likeness.° Now, banished Kent,
If thou canst serve where thou dost stand condemned,   5
So may it come,° thy master whom thou lov'st
Shall find thee full of labors.

        Horns within.° Enter LEAR, [KNIGHTS] *and* ATTENDANTS.

LEAR.   Let me not stay° a jot for dinner; go, get it ready. [*Exit an*
        ATTENDANT.] How now, what art thou?
KENT.   A man, sir.   10
LEAR.   What dost thou profess?° What wouldst thou with us?
KENT.   I do profess° to be no less than I seem, to serve him truly that
        will put me in trust, to love him that is honest, to converse with him
        that is wise and says little, to fear judgment,° to fight when I cannot
        choose, and to eat no fish.°   15
LEAR.   What art thou?
KENT.   A very honest-hearted fellow, and as poor as the King.
LEAR.   If thou be'st as poor for a subject as he's for a king, thou art
        poor enough. What wouldst thou?
KENT.   Service.   20
LEAR.   Who wouldst thou serve?

---

^{25}*breed . . . speak* find in this opportunities for speaking out
^{25}*straight* at once
I.iv. ^{2}*defuse* disguise
^{3}*full issue* perfect result
^{4}*razed my likeness* shaved off, disguised my natural appearance
^{6}*So may it come* so may it fall out
^{7}s.d. *within* offstage
^{8}*stay* wait
^{11}*What dost thou profess* what do you do
^{12}*profess* claim
^{14}*judgment* (by a heavenly or earthly judge)
^{15}*eat no fish* i.e., (1) I am no Catholic, but a loyal Protestant (2) I am no weakling (3) I
use no prostitutes

KENT.   You.

LEAR.   Dost thou know me, fellow?

KENT.   No, sir, but you have that in your countenance° which I would
fain° call master.   25

LEAR.   What's that?

KENT.   Authority.

LEAR.   What services canst thou do?

KENT.   I can keep honest counsel,° ride, run, mar a curious tale in
telling it,° and deliver a plain message bluntly. That which ordinary   30
men are fit for, I am qualified in, and the best of me is diligence.

LEAR.   How old art thou?

KENT.   Not so young, sir, to love a woman for singing, nor so old to
dote on her for anything. I have years on my back forty-eight.

LEAR.   Follow me; thou shalt serve me. If I like thee no worse after   35
dinner, I will not part from thee yet. Dinner, ho, dinner! Where's my
knave?° my Fool? Go you and call my Fool hither.

                                  [*Exit an* ATTENDANT.]

                            Enter OSWALD.

                You, you, sirrah, where's my daughter?

OSWALD.   So please you——

                                                              Exit.

LEAR.   What says the fellow there? Call the clotpoll° back. [*Exit a*   40
KNIGHT.] Where's my Fool? Ho, I think the world's asleep.

                      [*Re-enter* KNIGHT.]

How now? Where's that mongrel?

KNIGHT.   He says, my lord, your daughter is not well.

LEAR.   Why came not the slave back to me when I called him?

KNIGHT.   Sir, he answered me in the roundest° manner, he would not.   45

LEAR.   He would not?

KNIGHT.   My lord, I know not what the matter is; but to my judgment
your Highness is not entertained° with that ceremonious affection as
you were wont. There's a great abatement of kindness appears as well
in the general dependants° as in the Duke himself also and your   50
daughter.

²⁴*countenance* bearing
²⁵*fain* like to
²⁹*honest counsel* honorable secrets
³⁰*mar . . . it* i.e., I cannot speak like an affected courtier ("curious" = "elaborate," as
against "plain")
³⁷*knave* boy
⁴⁰*clotpoll* clodpoll, blockhead
⁴⁵*roundest* rudest
⁴⁸*entertained* treated
⁵⁰*dependants* servants

LEAR.   Ha? Say'st thou so?

KNIGHT.   I beseech you pardon me, my lord, if I be mistaken; for my
duty cannot be silent when I think your Highness wronged.

LEAR.   Thou but rememb'rest° me of mine own conception.° I have   55
perceived a most faint neglect° of late, which I have rather blamed
as mine own jealous curiosity° than as a very pretense° and purpose
of unkindness. I will look further into't. But where's my Fool? I have
not seen him this two days.

KNIGHT.   Since my young lady's going into France, sir, the Fool hath   60
much pined away.

LEAR.   No more of that; I have noted it well. Go you and tell my
daughter I would speak with her. Go you, call hither my Fool.

[Exit an ATTENDANT.]

Enter OSWALD.

O, you, sir, you! Come you hither, sir. Who am I, sir?

OSWALD.   My lady's father.   65

LEAR.   "My lady's father"? My lord's knave, you whoreson dog, you
slave, you cur!

OSWALD.   I am none of these, my lord; I beseech your pardon.

LEAR.   Do you bandy° looks with me, you rascal?

[Striking him.]

OSWALD.   I'll not be strucken,° my lord.   70

KENT.   Nor tripped neither, you base football° player.

[Tripping up his heels.]

LEAR.   I thank thee, fellow. Thou serv'st me, and I'll love thee.

KENT.   Come, sir, arise, away. I'll teach you differences.° Away, away.
If you will measure your lubber's° length again, tarry; but away. Go
to!° Have you wisdom?° So.°   75

[Pushes OSWALD *out.]*

---

⁵⁵*rememb'rest* remindest
⁵⁵*conception* idea
⁵⁶*faint neglect* i.e., "weary negligence" (I.iii.10)
⁵⁷*mine own jealous curiosity* suspicious concern for my own dignity
⁵⁷*very pretense* actual intention
⁶⁹*bandy* exchange insolently (metaphor from tennis)
⁷⁰*strucken* struck
⁷¹*football* (a low game played by idle boys to the scandal of sensible men)
⁷³*differences* (of rank)
⁷⁴*lubber's* lout's
⁷⁵*Go to* (expression of derisive incredulity)
⁷⁵*Have you wisdom* i.e., do you know what's good for you
⁷⁵*So* good

LEAR.   Now, my friendly knave, I thank thee. There's earnest° of thy
service.

[Giving KENT *money.*]*

Enter FOOL.

FOOL.   Let me hire him too. Here's my coxcomb.°

[Offering KENT *his cap.*]*

LEAR.   How now, my pretty knave? How dost thou?

FOOL.   Sirrah, you were best° take my coxcomb.   80

KENT.   Why, Fool?

FOOL.   Why? For taking one's part that's out of favor. Nay, an° thou
canst not smile as the wind sits,° thou'lt catch cold shortly. There,
take my coxcomb. Why, this fellow has banished° two on's daughters,
and did the third a blessing against his will. If thou follow him, thou   85
must needs wear my coxcomb.—How now, Nuncle?° Would I had
two coxcombs and two daughters.

LEAR.   Why, my boy?

FOOL.   If I gave them all my living,° I'd keep my coxcombs myself.
There's mine; beg another of thy daughters.   90

LEAR.   Take heed, sirrah—the whip.

FOOL.   Truth's a dog must to kennel; he must be whipped out, when
Lady the Brach° may stand by th' fire and stink.

LEAR.   A pestilent gall° to me.

FOOL.   Sirrah, I'll teach thee a speech.   95

LEAR.   Do.

FOOL.   Mark it, Nuncle.
        Have more than thou showest,
        Speak less than thou knowest,
        Lend less than thou owest,°   100
        Ride more than thou goest,°
        Learn more than thou trowest,°
        Set less than thou throwest:°
        Leave thy drink and thy whore,
        And keep in-a-door,   105

---

[76]*earnest* money for services rendered
[78]*coxcomb* professional fool's cap, shaped like a coxcomb
[80]*you were best* you had better
[82]*an* if
[83]*smile . . . sits* ingratiate yourself with those in power
[84]*banished* alienated (by making them independent)
[86]*Nuncle* (contraction of "mine uncle")
[89]*living* property
[93]*Brach* bitch
[94]*gall* sore
[100]*owest* ownest
[101]*goest* walkest
[102]*trowest* knowest
[103]*Set . . . throwest* bet less than you play for (get odds from your opponent)

And thou shalt have more
Than two tens to a score.°

KENT.   This is nothing, Fool.

FOOL.   Then 'tis like the breath of an unfeed° lawyer—you gave me
nothing for't. Can you make no use of nothing, Nuncle?   110

LEAR.   Why, no, boy. Nothing can be made out of nothing.

FOOL.   [*To* KENT] Prithee tell him, so much the rent of his land comes
to; he will not believe a Fool.

LEAR.   A bitter° Fool.

FOOL.   Dost thou know the difference, my boy, between a bitter Fool   115
and a sweet one?

LEAR.   No, lad; teach me.

FOOL.
That lord that counseled thee
To give away thy land,
Come place him here by me,   120
Do thou for him stand.
The sweet and bitter fool
Will presently appear;
The one in motley° here,
The other found out° there.°   125

LEAR.   Dost thou call me fool, boy?

FOOL.   All thy other titles thou hast given away; that thou wast born
with.

KENT.   This is not altogether fool, my lord.

FOOL.   No, faith; lords and great men will not let me.° If I had a   130
monopoly° out, they would have part on't. And ladies too, they will
not let me have all the fool to myself; they'll be snatching. Nuncle,
give me an egg, and I'll give thee two crowns.

LEAR.   What two crowns shall they be?

FOOL.   Why, after I have cut the egg i' th' middle and eat up the meat, 135
the two crowns of the egg. When thou clovest thy crown i' th' middle
and gav'st away both parts, thou bor'st thine ass on thy back o'er the
dirt.° Thou hadst little wit in thy bald crown when thou gav'st thy
golden one away. If I speak like myself° in this, let him be
whipped° that first finds it so.   140

107*have . . . score* i.e., come away with more than you had (two tens, or twenty shillings,
make a score, or one pound)

109*unfeed* unpaid for

114*bitter* satirical

124*motley* the drab costume of the professional jester

125*found out* revealed

125*there* (the Fool points at Lear, as a fool in the grain)

130*let me* (have all the folly to myself)

131*monopoly* (James I gave great scandal by granting to his "snatching" courtiers royal
patents to deal exclusively in some commodity)

138*bor'st . . . dirt* (like the foolish and unnatural countryman in Aesop's fable)

139*like myself* like a Fool

140*let him be whipped* i.e., let the man be whipped for a Fool who thinks my true saying
to be foolish

[*Singing*]   Fools had ne'er less grace in a year,
              For wise men are grown foppish,
              And know not how their wits to wear,
              Their manners are so apish.°

LEAR.   When were you wont to be so full of songs, sirrah?   145

FOOL.   I have used° it, Nuncle, e'er since thou mad'st thy daughters thy
            mothers; for when thou gav'st them the rod, and put'st down thine
            own breeches,

[*Singing*]   Then they for sudden joy did weep,
              And I for sorrow sung,   150
              That such a king should play bo-peep°
              And go the fools among.

Prithee, Nuncle, keep a schoolmaster that can teach thy Fool to lie.
I would fain learn to lie.

LEAR.   And° you lie, sirrah, we'll have you whipped.   155

FOOL.   I marvel what kin thou and thy daughters are. They'll have me
            whipped for speaking true; thou'lt have me whipped for lying; and
            sometimes I am whipped for holding my peace. I had rather be any
            kind o' thing than a Fool, and yet I would not be thee, Nuncle: thou
            hast pared thy wit o' both sides and left nothing i' th' middle. Here   160
            comes one o' the parings.

                        Enter GONERIL.

LEAR.   How now, daughter? What makes that frontlet° on? Methinks
            you are too much of late i' th' frown.

FOOL.   Thou wast a pretty fellow when thou hadst no need to care for
            her frowning. Now thou art an O without a figure.° I am better than   165
            thou art now: I am a Fool, thou art nothing. [*To* GONERIL] Yes,
            forsooth, I will hold my tongue. So your face bids me, though you
            say nothing. Mum, mum,
                        He that keeps nor crust nor crum,°
                        Weary of all, shall want° some.   170

[*Pointing to* LEAR] That's a shealed peascod.°

GONERIL.   Not only, sir, this your all-licensed° Fool,
            But other° of your insolent retinue

---

[144]*Fools . . . apish* i.e., fools were never in less favor than now, and the reason is that
wise men, turning foolish, and not knowing how to use their intelligence, imitate the
professional fools and so make them unnecessary
[146]*used* practiced
[151]*play bo-peep* (1) act like a child (2) blind himself
[155]*And* if
[162]*frontlet* frown (lit., ornamental band)
[165]*figure* digit, to give value to the cipher (Lear is a nought)
[169]*crum* soft bread inside the loaf
[170]*want* lack
[171]*shealed peascod* empty pea pod
[172]*all-licensed* privileged to take any liberties
[173]*other* others

Do hourly carp and quarrel, breaking forth
In rank° and not-to-be-endurèd riots. Sir,   175
I had thought by making this well known unto you
To have found a safe° redress, but now grow fearful,
By what yourself too late° have spoke and done,
That you protect this course, and put it on
By your allowance;° which if you should, the fault   180
Would not 'scape censure, nor the redresses sleep,°
Which, in the tender of° a wholesome weal,°
Might in their working do you that offense,
Which else were shame, that then necessity
Will call discreet proceeding.°   185

FOOL.   For you know, Nuncle,
The hedge-sparrow fed the cuckoo° so long
That it had it head bit off by it° young.
So out went the candle, and we were left darkling.°

LEAR.   Are you our daughter?   190

GONERIL.   Come, sir,
I would you would make use of your good wisdom
Whereof I know you are fraught° and put away
These dispositions° which of late transport you
From what you rightly are.   195

FOOL.   May not an ass know when the cart draws the horse? Whoop,
Jug,° I love thee!

LEAR.   Does any here know me? This is not Lear.
Does Lear walk thus? Speak thus? Where are his eyes?
Either his notion° weakens, or his discernings°   200
Are lethargied°—Ha! Waking? 'Tis not so.
Who is it that can tell me who I am?

---

[175]*rank* gross
[177]*safe* sure
[178]*too late* lately
[180]*put . . . allowance* promote it by your approval
[180]*allowance* approval
[181]*redresses sleep* correction fail to follow
[182]*tender of* desire for
[182]*weal* state
[185]*Might . . . proceeding* as I apply it, the correction might humiliate you; but the need
to take action cancels what would otherwise be unfilial conduct in me
[187]*cuckoo* (who lays its eggs in the nests of other birds)
[188]*it* its
[189]*darkling* in the dark
[193]*fraught* endowed
[194]*dispositions* moods
[197]*Jug* Joan (? a quotation from a popular song)
[200]*notion* understanding
[200]*discernings* faculties
[201]*lethargied* paralyzed

FOOL.   Lear's shadow.

LEAR.   I would learn that; for, by the marks of sovereignty,° knowl-
           edge, and reason, I should be false° persuaded I had daughters.   205

FOOL.   Which° they will make an obedient father.

LEAR.   Your name, fair gentlewoman?

GONERIL.   This admiration,° sir, is much o' th' savor°
           Of other your° new pranks. I do beseech you
           To understand my purposes aright.   210
           As you are old and reverend, should be wise.
           Here do you keep a hundred knights and squires,
           Men so disordered, so deboshed,° and bold,
           That this our court, infected with their manners,
           Shows° like a riotous inn. Epicurism° and lust   215
           Makes it more like a tavern or a brothel
           Than a graced° palace. The shame itself doth speak
           For instant remedy. Be then desired°
           By her, that else will take the thing she begs,
           A little to disquantity your train,°   220
           And the remainders° that shall still depend,°
           To be such men as may besort° your age,
           Which know themselves, and you.

LEAR.   Darkness and devils!
           Saddle my horses; call my train together.
           Degenerate° bastard, I'll not trouble thee: 225
           Yet have I left a daughter.

GONERIL.   You strike my people, and your disordered rabble
           Make servants of their betters.

                        Enter ALBANY.

LEAR.   Woe, that too late repents. O, sir, are you come?
           Is it your will? Speak, sir. Prepare my horses.   230
           Ingratitude! thou marble-hearted fiend,

---

²⁰⁴*marks of sovereignty* i.e., tokens that Lear is king, and hence father to his daughters
²⁰⁵*false* falsely
²⁰⁶*Which* whom (Lear)
²⁰⁸*admiration* (affected) wonderment
²⁰⁸*is much o' th' savor* smacks much
²⁰⁹*other your* others of your
²¹³*deboshed* debauched
²¹⁵*Shows* appears
²¹⁵*Epicurism* riotous living
²¹⁷*graced* dignified
²¹⁸*desired* requested
²²⁰*disquantity your train* reduce the number of your dependents
²²¹*remainders* those who remain
²²¹*depend* attend on you
²²²*besort* befit
²²⁵*Degenerate* unnatural

More hideous when thou show'st thee in a child
Than the sea-monster.
ALBANY.   Pray, sir, be patient
LEAR.   Detested kite,° thou liest.
My train are men of choice and rarest parts,°   235
That all particulars of duty know,
And, in the most exact regard,° support
The worships° of their name. O most small fault,
How ugly didst thou in Cordelia show!
Which, like an engine,° wrenched my frame of nature   240
From the fixed place;° drew from my heart all love,
And added to the gall.° O Lear, Lear, Lear!
Beat at this gate that let thy folly in [*Striking his head*]
And thy dear judgment out. Go, go, my people.
ALBANY.   My lord, I am guiltless, as I am ignorant   245
Of what hath moved you.
LEAR.   It may be so, my lord.
Hear, Nature, hear; dear Goddess, hear:
Suspend thy purpose if thou didst intend
To make this creature fruitful.
Into her womb convey sterility,   250
Dry up in her the organs of increase,°
And from her derogate° body never spring
A babe to honor her. If she must teem,°
Create her child of spleen,° that it may live
And be a thwart disnatured° torment to her.   255
Let it stamp wrinkles in her brow of youth,
With cadent° tears fret° channels in her cheeks,
Turn all her mother's pains and benefits°
To laughter and contempt, that she may feel
How sharper than a serpent's tooth it is   260
To have a thankless child. Away, away!

                                                           Exit.

[234]*kite* scavenging bird of prey
[235]*parts* accomplishments
[237]*exact regard* strict attention to detail
[238]*worships* honor
[240]*engine* destructive contrivance
[241]*wrenched . . . place* i.e., disordered my natural self
[242]*gall* bitterness
[251]*increase* childbearing
[252]*derogate* degraded
[253]*teem* conceive
[254]*spleen* ill humor
[255]*thwart disnatured* perverse unnatural
[257]*cadent* falling
[257]*fret* wear
[258]*benefits* the mother's beneficent care of her child

ALBANY.   Now, gods that we adore, whereof comes this?
GONERIL.   Never afflict yourself to know the cause,
    But let his disposition° have that scope
    As° dotage gives it.   265

Enter LEAR.

LEAR.   What, fifty of my followers at a clap?°
    Within a fortnight?
ALBANY.   What's the matter, sir?
LEAR.   I'll tell thee. [*To* GONERIL] Life and death, I am ashamed
    That thou hast power to shake my manhood° thus!
    That these hot tears, which break from me perforce,°   270
    Should make thee worth them. Blasts and fogs upon thee!
    Th' untented woundings° of a father's curse
    Pierce every sense about thee! Old fond° eyes,
    Beweep° this cause again, I'll pluck ye out
    And cast you, with the waters that you loose,°   275
    To temper° clay. Yea, is it come to this?
    Ha! Let it be so. I have another daughter,
    Who I am sure is kind and comfortable.°
    When she shall hear this of thee, with her nails
    She'll flay thy wolvish visage. Thou shalt find   280
    That I'll resume the shape° which thou dost think
    I have cast off for ever.

Exit [*Lear with Kent and Attendants*].

GONERIL.   Do you mark that?
ALBANY.   I cannot be so partial, Goneril,
    To the great love I bear you°———
GONERIL.   Pray you, content. What, Oswald, ho!   285
    [*To the Fool*] You, sir, more knave than fool, after your master!
FOOL.   Nuncle Lear, Nuncle Lear, tarry. Take the Fool° with thee.
    A fox, when one has caught her,
    And such a daughter,

---

[264] *disposition* mood
[265] *As* that
[266] *at a clap* at one stroke
[269] *shake my manhood* i.e., with tears
[270] *perforce* involuntarily, against my will
[272] *untented woundings* wounds too deep to be probed with a tent (a roll of lint)
[273] *fond* foolish
[274] *Beweep* if you weep over
[275] *loose* (1) let loose (2) lose, as of no avail
[276] *temper* mix with and soften
[278] *comfortable* ready to comfort
[281] *shape* i.e., kingly role
[284] *I cannot . . . you* i.e., even though my love inclines me to you, I must protest
[287] *Fool* (1) the Fool himself (2) the epithet or character of "fool"

Should sure to the slaughter,   290
If my cap would buy a halter.°
So the Fool follows after.°

Exit.

GONERIL.   This man hath had good counsel. A hundred knights!
'Tis politic° and safe to let him keep
At point° a hundred knights: yes, that on every dream,   295
Each buzz,° each fancy, each complaint, dislike,
He may enguard° his dotage with their pow'rs
And hold our lives in mercy.° Oswald, I say!
ALBANY.   Well, you may fear too far.
GONERIL.   Safer than trust too far.   300
Let me still take away the harms I fear,
Not fear still to be taken.° I know his heart.
What he hath uttered I have writ my sister.
If she sustain him and his hundred knights,
When I have showed th' unfitness———   305

Enter OSWALD.

How now, Oswald?
What, have you writ that letter to my sister?
OSWALD.   Ay, madam.
GONERIL.   Take you some company,° and away to horse.
Inform her full of my particular° fear,
And thereto add such reasons of your own   310
As may compact° it more. Get you gone,
And hasten your return. [*Exit* OSWALD.] No, no, my lord,
This milky gentleness and course° of yours,
Though I condemn not,° yet under pardon,
You are much more attasked° for want of wisdom   315
Than praised for harmful mildness.°
ALBANY.   How far your eyes may pierce I cannot tell; Striving to
better, oft we mar what's well.

291, 292*halter, after* pronounced "hauter," "auter"
294*politic* good policy
295*At point* armed
296*buzz* rumor
297*enguard* protect
298*in mercy* at his mercy
302*Not . . . taken* rather than remain fearful of being overtaken by them
308*company* escort
309*particular* own
311*compact* strengthen
313*milky . . . course* mild and gentle way (hendiadys)
314*condemn not* condemn it not
315*attasked* taken to task, blamed
316*harmful mildness* dangerous indulgence

GONERIL.   Nay then————
ALBANY.   Well, well, th' event.°   320

Exeunt.

Scene V. [*Court before the same.*]

Enter LEAR, KENT, *and* FOOL.

LEAR.   Go you before to Gloucester with these letters. Acquaint my
daughter no further with anything you know than comes from her
demand out of the letter.° If your diligence be not speedy, I shall be
there afore you.

KENT.   I will not sleep, my lord, till I have delivered your letter.   5

Exit.

FOOL.   If a man's brains were in's heels, were't° not in danger of
kibes?°
LEAR.   Ay, boy.
FOOL.   Then I prithee be merry. Thy wit shall not go slipshod.°
LEAR.   Ha, ha, ha.   10
FOOL.   Shalt° see thy other daughter will use thee kindly;° for though
she's as like this as a crab's° like an apple, yet I can tell what I can
tell.
LEAR.   Why, what canst thou tell, my boy?
FOOL.   She will taste as like this as a crab does to a crab. Thou canst   15
tell why one's nose stands i' th' middle on's° face?
LEAR.   No.
FOOL.   Why, to keep one's eyes of° either side's nose, that what a man
cannot smell out, he may spy into.
LEAR.   I did her wrong.   20
FOOL.   Canst tell how an oyster makes his shell?
LEAR.   No.
FOOL.   Nor I neither; but I can tell why a snail has a house.
LEAR.   Why?
FOOL.   Why, to put 's head in; not to give it away to his daughters, and   25
leave his horns° without a case.

[320]*th' event* i.e., we'll see what happens
[3]*than . . . letter* than her reading of the letter brings her to ask
[6]*were't* i.e., the brains
[7]*kibes* chilblains
[9]*Thy . . . slipshod* your brains shall not go in slippers (because you have no brains to be
protected from chilblains)
[11]*Shalt* thou shalt
[11]*kindly* (1) affectionately (2) after her kind or nature
[12]*crab* crab apple
[16]*on's* of his
[18]*of* on
[26]*horns* (1) snail's horns (2) cuckold's horns

LEAR.　　I will forget my nature.° So kind a father! Be my horses ready?

FOOL.　　Thy asses are gone about 'em. The reason why the seven stars° are no moe° than seven is a pretty° reason.　　　　30

LEAR.　　Because they are not eight.

FOOL.　　Yes indeed. Thou wouldst make a good Fool.

LEAR.　　To take't again perforce!° Monster ingratitude!

FOOL.　　If thou wert my Fool, Nuncle, I'd have thee beaten for being old before thy time.　　　　35

LEAR.　　How's that?

FOOL.　　Thou shouldst not have been old till thou hadst been wise.

LEAR.　　O, let me not be mad, not mad, sweet heaven! Keep me in temper;° I would not be mad!

[Enter GENTLEMAN.]

How now, are the horses ready?

GENTLEMAN.　　Ready, my lord.　　　　40

LEAR.　　Come, boy.

FOOL.　　She that's a maid now, and laughs at my departure, Shall not be a maid long, unless things be cut shorter.°

Exeunt.

ACT II

Scene I. [*The Earl of Gloucester's castle.*]

Enter EDMUND *and* CURAN, *severally.*°

EDMUND.　　Save° thee, Curan.

CURAN.　　And you, sir. I have been with your father, and given him notice that the Duke of Cornwall and Regan his duchess will be here with him this night.

EDMUND.　　How comes that?　　　　5

CURAN.　　Nay, I know not. You have heard of the news abroad? I mean the whispered ones, for they are yet but ear-kissing arguments.°

27*nature* paternal instincts
30*seven stars* the Pleiades
30*moe* more
30*pretty* apt
33*To . . . perforce* (1) of Goneril, who has forcibly taken away Lear's privileges; or (2) of Lear, who meditates a forcible resumption of authority
39*in temper* sane
43*She . . . shorter* the maid who laughs, missing the tragic implications of this quarrel, will not have sense enough to preserve her virginity ("things" = penises)
II.i. ¹s.d. *severally* separately (from different entrances on stage)
1*Save* God save
7*ear-kissing arguments* subjects whispered in the ear

EDMUND.   Not I. Pray you, what are they?
CURAN.   Have you heard of no likely° wars toward,° 'twixt the Dukes
of Cornwall and Albany?   10
EDMUND.   Not a word.
CURAN.   You may do, then, in time. Fare you well, sir.

                                                                 Exit.

EDMUND.   The Duke be here tonight? The better!° best!
This weaves itself perforce° into my business.
My father hath set guard to take my brother,   15
And I have one thing of a queasy question°
Which I must act. Briefness° and Fortune, work!
Brother, a word; descend. Brother, I say!

                         Enter EDGAR.

                 My father watches. O sir, fly this place.
Intelligence° is given where you are hid.   20
You have now the good advantage of the night.
Have you not spoken 'gainst the Duke of Cornwall?
He's coming hither, now i' th' night, i' th' haste,°
And Regan with him. Have you nothing said
Upon his party° 'gainst the Duke of Albany?   25
Advise yourself.°
EDGAR.   I am sure on't,° not a word.
EDMUND.   I hear my father coming. Pardon me:
In cunning° I must draw my sword upon you.
Draw, seem to defend yourself; now quit you° well.
Yield! Come before my father! Light ho, here!   30
Fly, brother. Torches, torches!—So farewell.

                                                   Exit EDGAR.

Some blood drawn on me would beget opinion°

                                    [*Wounds his arm.*]

⁹*likely* probable
⁹*toward* impending
¹³*The better* so much the better
¹⁴*perforce* necessarily
¹⁶*of a queasy question* that requires delicate handling (to be "queasy" is to be on the
point of vomiting)
¹⁷*Briefness* speed
²⁰*Intelligence* information
²³*i' th' haste* in great haste
²⁵*Upon his party* censuring his enmity
²⁶*Advise yourself* reflect
²⁶*on't* of it
²⁸*In cunning* as a pretense
²⁹*quit you* acquit yourself
³²*beget opinion* create the impression

Of my more fierce endeavor. I have seen drunkards
Do more than this in sport. Father, father!
Stop, stop! No help?   35

     Enter GLOUCESTER, *and* SERVANTS *with torches.*

GLOUCESTER.   Now, Edmund, where's the villain?
EDMUND.   Here stood he in the dark, his sharp sword out,
    Mumbling of wicked charms, conjuring the moon
    To stand auspicious mistress.
GLOUCESTER.   But where is he?
EDMUND.   Look, sir, I bleed.   40
GLOUCESTER.   Where is the villain, Edmund?
EDMUND.   Fled this way, sir, when by no means he could———
GLOUCESTER.   Pursue him, ho! Go after.

                [*Exeunt some* SERVANTS.]

    By no means what?
EDMUND.   Persuade me to the murder of your lordship;   45
    But that I told him the revenging gods
    'Gainst parricides did all the thunder bend;°
    Spoke with how manifold and strong a bond
    The child was bound to th' father. Sir, in fine,°
    Seeing how loathly opposite° I stood   50
    To his unnatural purpose, in fell° motion°
    With his preparèd sword he charges home
    My unprovided° body, latched° mine arm;
    But when he saw my best alarumed° spirits
    Bold in the quarrel's right,° roused to th' encounter,   55
    Or whether gasted° by the noise I made,
    Full suddenly he fled.
GLOUCESTER.   Let him fly far.
    Not in this land shall he remain uncaught;
    And found—dispatch.° The noble Duke my master,
    My worthy arch° and patron, comes tonight.   60
    By his authority I will proclaim it,
    That he which finds him shall deserve our thanks,

[47] *bend* aim
[49] *in fine* finally
[50] *loathly opposite* bitterly opposed
[51] *fell* deadly
[51] *motion* thrust (a term from fencing)
[53] *unprovided* unprotected
[53] *latched* wounded (lanced)
[54] *best alarumed* wholly aroused
[55] *Bold . . . right* confident in the rightness of my cause
[56] *gasted* struck aghast
[59] *dispatch* i.e., he will be killed
[60] *arch* chief

Bringing the murderous coward to the stake.
He that conceals him, death.°
EDMUND.   When I dissuaded him from his intent,   65
And found him pight° to do it, with curst° speech
I threatened to discover° him. He replied,
"Thou unpossessing° bastard, dost thou think,
If I would stand against thee, would the reposal°
Of any trust, virtue, or worth in thee   70
Make thy words faithed?° No. What I should deny—
As this I would, ay, though thou didst produce
My very character°—I'd turn it all
To thy suggestion,° plot, and damnèd practice.°
And thou must make a dullard of the world,°   75
If they not thought° the profits of my death
Were very pregnant° and potential spirits°
To make thee seek it."
GLOUCESTER.   O strange and fastened° villain!
Would he deny his letter, said he? I never got° him.

                                        Tucket° within.

Hark, the Duke's trumpets. I know not why he comes.   80
All ports° I'll bar; the villain shall not 'scape;
The Duke must grant me that. Besides, his picture
I will send far and near, that all the kingdom
May have due note of him; and of my land,
Loyal and natural° boy, I'll work the means   85
To make thee capable.°

                    Enter CORNWALL, REGAN, *and* ATTENDANTS.

[64]*death* (the same elliptical form that characterizes "dispatch,")
[66]*pight* determined
[66]*curst* angry
[67]*discover* expose
[68]*unpossessing* beggarly (landless)
[69]*reposal* placing
[71]*faithed* believed
[73]*character* handwriting
[74]*suggestion* instigation
[74]*practice* device
[75]*make . . . world* think everyone stupid
[76]*not thought* did not think
[77]*pregnant* teeming with incitement
[77]*potential spirits* powerful evil spirits
[78]*fastened* hardened
[79]*got* begot
[79]s.d. *Tucket* (Cornwall's special trumpet call)
[81]*ports* exits, of whatever sort
[85]*natural* (1) kind (filial) (2) illegitimate
[86]*capable* able to inherit

CORNWALL.   How now, my noble friend! Since I came hither,
    Which I can call but now, I have heard strange news.
REGAN.   If it be true, all vengeance comes too short
    Which can pursue th' offender. How dost, my lord?   90
GLOUCESTER.   O madam, my old heart is cracked, it's cracked.
REGAN.   What, did my father's godson seek your life?
    He whom my father named, your Edgar?
GLOUCESTER.   O lady, lady, shame would have it hid.
REGAN.   Was he not companion with the riotous knights   95
    That tended upon my father?
GLOUCESTER.   I know not, madam. 'Tis too bad, too bad.
EDMUND.   Yes, madam, he was of that consort.°
REGAN.   No marvel then, though he were ill affected.°
    'Tis they have put° him on the old man's death,   100
    To have th' expense and waste° of his revenues.
    I have this present evening from my sister
    Been well informed of them, and with such cautions
    That, if they come to sojourn at my house,
    I'll not be there.
CORNWALL.   Nor I, assure thee, Regan.   105
    Edmund, I hear that you have shown your father
    A childlike° office.
EDMUND.   It was my duty, sir.
GLOUCESTER.   He did bewray his practice,° and received
    This hurt you see, striving to apprehend him.
CORNWALL.   Is he pursued?
GLOUCESTER.   Ay, my good lord.   110
CORNWALL.   If he be taken, he shall never more
    Be feared of doing° harm. Make your own purpose,
    How in my strength you please.° For you, Edmund,
    Whose virtue and obedience° doth this instant
    So much commend itself, you shall be ours.   115
    Natures of such deep trust we shall much need;
    You we first seize on.
EDMUND.   I shall serve you, sir,
    Truly, however else.
GLOUCESTER.   For him I thank your Grace.
CORNWALL.   You know not why we came to visit you?

---

⁹⁸*consort* company
⁹⁹*ill affected* disposed to evil
¹⁰⁰*put* set
¹⁰¹*expense and waste* squandering
¹⁰⁷*childlike* filial
¹⁰⁸*bewray his practice* disclose his plot
¹¹²*of doing* because he might do
¹¹³*Make . . . please* use my power freely, in carrying out your plans for his capture
¹¹⁴*virtue and obedience* virtuous obedience

REGAN.   Thus out of season, threading dark-eyed night.   120
Occasions, noble Gloucester, of some prize,°
Wherein we must have use of your advice.
Our father he hath writ, so hath our sister,
Of differences,° which° I best thought it fit
To answer from° our home. The several messengers   125
From hence attend dispatch.° Our good old friend,
Lay comforts to your bosom,° and bestow
Your needful° counsel to our businesses,
Which craves the instant use.°
GLOUCESTER.   I serve you, madam.
Your Graces are right welcome.   130

Exeunt. Flourish.

Scene II. [Before Gloucester's castle.]

Enter KENT and OSWALD, severally.

OSWALD.   Good dawning° to thee, friend. Art of this house?°
KENT.   Ay.
OSWALD.   Where may we set our horses?
KENT.   I' th' mire.
OSWALD.   Prithee, if thou lov'st me, tell me.   5
KENT.   I love thee not.
OSWALD.   Why then, I care not for thee.
KENT.   If I had thee in Lipsbury Pinfold,° I would make thee care for
     me.
OSWALD.   Why dost thou use me thus? I know thee not.   10
KENT.   Fellow, I know thee.
OSWALD.   What dost thou know me for?
KENT.   A knave, a rascal, an eater of broken meats;° a base, proud,
     shallow, beggarly, three-suited,° hundred-pound,° filthy worsted-

---

[121]*prize* importance
[124]*differences* quarrels
[124]*which* (referring not to "differences," but to the letter Lear has written)
[125]*from* away from
[126]*attend dispatch* are waiting to be sent off
[127]*Lay . . . bosom* console yourself (about Edgar's supposed treason)
[128]*needful* needed
[129]*craves the instant use* demands immediate transaction
[1]*dawning* (dawn is impending, but not yet arrived)
[1]*Art of this house* i.e., do you live here
[8]*Lipsbury Pinfold* a pound or pen in which strayed animals are enclosed ("Lipsbury"
may denote a particular place, or may be slang for "between my teeth")
[13]*broken meats* scraps of food
[14]*three-suited* (the wardrobe permitted to a servant or "knave")
[14]*hundred-pound* (the extent of Oswald's wealth, and thus a sneer at his aspiring to
gentility)

stocking° knave; a lily-livered, action-taking,° whoreson, glass-gazing,° superserviceable,° finical° rogue; one-trunk-inheriting° slave; one
that wouldst be a bawd in way of good service,° and art nothing but
the composition° of a knave, beggar, coward, pander, and the son and
heir of a mongrel bitch; one whom I will beat into clamorous whining
if thou deniest the least syllable of thy addition.°   20

OSWALD.   Why, what a monstrous fellow art thou, thus to rail on one
that is neither known of thee nor knows thee!

KENT.   What a brazen-faced varlet art thou to deny thou knowest me!
Is it two days since I tripped up thy heels and beat thee before the
King? [*Drawing his sword*] Draw, you rogue, for though it be night,   25
yet the moon shines. I'll make a sop o' th' moonshine° of you. You
whoreson cullionly barbermonger,° draw!

OSWALD.   Away, I have nothing to do with thee.

KENT.   Draw, you rascal. You come with letters against the King, and
take Vanity the puppet's° part against the royalty of her father. Draw,   30
you rogue, or I'll so carbonado° your shanks. Draw, you rascal. Come
your ways!°

OSWALD.   Help, ho! Murder! Help!

KENT.   Strike, you slave! Stand, rogue! Stand, you neat° slave! Strike!
[*Beating him*]   35

OSWALD.   Help, ho! Murder, murder!

Enter EDMUND, *with his rapier drawn*, CORNWALL, REGAN, GLOUCES-
TER, SERVANTS.

EDMUND.   How now? What's the matter? Part!

KENT.   With you,° goodman boy,° if you please! Come, I'll flesh° ye,
come on, young master.

GLOUCESTER.   Weapons? Arms? What's the matter here?   40

---

¹⁵*worsted-stocking* (worn by servants)
¹⁵*action-taking* one who refuses a fight and goes to law instead
¹⁶*glass-gazing* conceited
¹⁶*superserviceable* sycophantic, serving without principle.
¹⁶*finical* overfastidious
¹⁶*one-trunk-inheriting* possessing only a trunkful of goods
¹⁷*bawd . . . service* pimp, to please his master
¹⁸*composition* compound
²⁰*addition* titles
²⁶*sop o' th' moonshine* i.e., Oswald will admit the moonlight, and so sop it up, through
the open wounds Kent is preparing to give him
²⁷*cullionly barbermonger* base patron of hairdressers (effeminate man)
³⁰*Vanity the puppet's* Goneril, here identified with one of the personified characters in
the morality plays, which were sometimes put on as puppet shows
³¹*carbonado* cut across, like a piece of meat before cooking
³²*Come your ways* get along
³⁴*neat* (1) foppish (2) unmixed, as in "neat wine"
³⁸*With you* i.e., the quarrel is with you
³⁸*goodman boy* young man (peasants are "goodmen"; "boy" is a term of
contempt)
³⁸*flesh* introduce to blood (term from hunting)

CORNWALL.   Keep peace, upon your lives.
   He dies that strikes again. What is the matter?
REGAN.   The messengers from our sister and the King.
CORNWALL.   What is your difference?° Speak.
OSWALD.   I am scarce in breath, my lord.   45
KENT.   No marvel, you have so bestirred° your valor. You cowardly
   rascal, nature disclaims in thee.° A tailor made thee.°
CORNWALL.   Thou art a strange fellow. A tailor make a man?
KENT.   A tailor, sir. A stonecutter or a painter could not have made
   him so ill, though they had been but two years o' th' trade.   50
CORNWALL.   Speak yet, how grew your quarrel?
OSWALD.   This ancient ruffian, sir, whose life I have spared at suit of°
   his gray beard———
KENT.   Thou whoreson zed,° thou unnecessary letter! My lord, if you
   will give me leave, I will tread this unbolted° villain into mortar and   55
   daub the wall of a jakes° with him. Spare my gray beard, you
   wagtail!°
CORNWALL.   Peace, sirrah!
   You beastly° knave, know you no reverence?
KENT.   Yes, sir, but anger hath a privilege.   60
CORNWALL.   Why art thou angry?
KENT.   That such a slave as this should wear a sword,
   Who wears no honesty. Such smiling rogues as these,
   Like rats, oft bite the holy cords° atwain
   Which are too intrince° t' unloose; smooth° every passion   65
   That in the natures of their lords rebel,
   Being oil to fire, snow to the colder moods;
   Renege,° affirm, and turn their halcyon beaks°
   With every gale and vary° of their masters,
   Knowing naught, like dogs, but following.   70

---

[44]*difference* quarrel
[46]*bestirred* exercised
[47]*nature disclaims in thee* nature renounces any part in you
[47]*A tailor made thee* (from the proverb "The tailor makes the man")
[52]*at suit of* out of pity for
[54]*zed* the letter *Z,* generally omitted in contemporary dictionaries
[55]*unbolted* unsifted, i.e., altogether a villain
[56]*jakes* privy
[57]*wagtail* a bird that bobs its tail up and down, and thus suggests obsequiousness
[59]*beastly* irrational
[64]*holy cords* sacred bonds of affection (as between husbands and wives, parents and children)
[65]*intrince* entangled, intricate
[65]*smooth* appease
[68]*Renege* deny
[68]*halcyon beaks* (the halcyon or kingfisher serves here as a type of the opportunist because, when hung up by the tail or neck, it was supposed to turn with the wind, like a weathervane)
[69]*gale and vary* varying gale (hendiadys)

A plague upon your epileptic° visage!
Smile you° my speeches, as I were a fool?
Goose, if I had you upon Sarum Plain,°
I'd drive ye cackling home to Camelot.°

CORNWALL.   What, art thou mad, old fellow?   75

GLOUCESTER.   How fell you out? Say that.

KENT.   No contraries° hold more antipathy
Than I and such a knave.

CORNWALL.   Why dost thou call him knave? What is his fault?

KENT.   His countenance likes° me not.   80

CORNWALL.   No more perchance does mine, nor his, nor hers.

KENT.   Sir, 'tis my occupation to be plain:
I have seen better faces in my time
Than stands on any shoulder that I see
Before me at this instant.

CORNWALL.   This is some fellow   85
Who, having been praised for bluntness, doth affect
A saucy roughness, and constrains the garb
Quite from his nature.° He cannot flatter, he;
An honest mind and plain, he must speak truth.
And° they will take it, so; if not, he's plain.   90
These kind of knaves I know, which in this plainness
Harbor more craft and more corrupter ends
Than twenty silly-ducking observants°
That stretch their duties nicely.°

KENT.   Sir, in good faith, in sincere verity,   95
Under th' allowance° of your great aspect,°
Whose influence,° like the wreath of radiant fire
On flick'ring Phoebus' front°————

CORNWALL.   What mean'st by this?

KENT.   To go out of my dialect,° which you discommend so much. I

---

⁷¹*epileptic* distorted by grinning
⁷²*Smile you* do you smile at
⁷³*Sarum Plain* Salisbury Plain
⁷⁴*Camelot* the residence of King Arthur (presumably a particular point, now lost, is intended here)
⁷⁷*contraries* opposites
⁸⁰*likes* pleases
⁸⁸*constrains . . . nature* forces the manner of candid speech to be a cloak, not for candor but for craft
⁹⁰*And* if
⁹³*silly-ducking observants* ridiculously obsequious attendants
⁹⁴*nicely* punctiliously
⁹⁶*allowance* approval
⁹⁶*aspect* (1) appearance (2) position of the heavenly bodies
⁹⁷*influence* astrological power
⁹⁸*Phoebus' front* forehead of the sun
⁹⁹*dialect* customary manner of speaking

know, sir, I am no flatterer. He° that beguiled you in a plain accent   100
was a plain knave, which, for my part, I will not be, though I should
win your displeasure to entreat me to't.°
CORNWALL.   What was th' offense you gave him?
OSWALD.   I never gave him any.
It pleased the King his master very late°   105
To strike at me, upon his misconstruction;°
When he, compact,° and flattering his displeasure,
Tripped me behind; being down, insulted, railed,
And put upon him such a deal of man°
That worthied him,° got praises of the King   110
For him attempting who was self-subdued;°
And, in the fleshment° of this dread exploit,
Drew on me here again.
KENT.   None of these rogues and cowards
But Ajax is their fool.°
CORNWALL.   Fetch forth the stocks!
You stubborn° ancient knave, you reverent° braggart,   115
We'll teach you.
KENT.   Sir, I am too old to learn.
Call not your stocks for me, I serve the King,
On whose employment I was sent to you.
You shall do small respect, show too bold malice
Against the grace and person° of my master,   120
Stocking his messenger.
CORNWALL.   Fetch forth the stocks. As I have life and honor,
There shall he sit till noon.
REAGAN.   Till noon? Till night, my lord, and all night too.
KENT.   Why, madam, if I were your father's dog,   125
You should not use me so.
REGAN.   Sir, being his knave, I will.

100*He* i.e., the sort of candid-crafty man Cornwall has been describing
102*though . . . to't* even if I were to succeed in bringing your graceless person
("displeasure" personified, and in lieu of the expected form, "your grace") to beg
me to be a plain knave
105*very late* recently
106*misconstruction* misunderstanding
107*compact* in league with the king
109*put . . . man* pretended such manly behavior
110*worthied him* made him seem heroic
111*For . . . self-subdued* for attacking a man (Oswald) who offered no resistance
112*fleshment* the bloodthirstiness excited by his first success or "fleshing"
114*None . . . fool* i.e., cowardly rogues like Oswald always impose on fools like
Cornwall (who is likened to Ajax: [1] the braggart Greek warrior [2] a jakes or
privy)
115*stubborn* rude
115*reverent* old
120*grace and person* i.e., Lear as sovereign and in his personal character

CORNWALL.   This is a fellow of the selfsame color°
Our sister speaks of. Come, bring away° the stocks.

Stocks brought out.

GLOUCESTER.   Let me beseech your Grace not to do so.
His fault is much, and the good King his master   130
Will check° him for't. Your purposed° low correction
Is such as basest and contemnèd'st° wretches
For pilf'rings and most common trespasses
Are punished with.
The King his master needs must take it ill   135
That he, so slightly valued in° his messenger,
Should have him thus restrained.
CORNWALL.   I'll answer° that.
REGAN.   My sister may receive it much more worse,
To have her gentleman abused, assaulted,
For following her affairs. Put in his legs.   140

[KENT *is put in the stocks.*]

Come, my good lord, away!

[*Exeunt all but* GLOUCESTER *and* KENT.]

GLOUCESTER.   I am sorry for thee, friend. 'Tis the Duke's pleasure,
Whose disposition° all the world well knows
Will not be rubbed° nor stopped. I'll entreat for thee.
KENT.   Pray do not, sir. I have watched° and traveled hard.   145
Some time I shall sleep out, the rest I'll whistle.
A good man's fortune may grow out at heels.°
Give° you good morrow.
GLOUCESTER.   The Duke's to blame in this. 'Twill be ill taken.°

Exit.

KENT.   Good King, that must approve° the common saw,°   150

127*color* kind
128*away* out
131*check* correct
131*purposed* intended
132*contemnèd'st* most despised
136*slightly valued in* little honored in the person of
137*answer* answer for
143*disposition* inclination
144*rubbed* diverted (metaphor from the game of bowls)
145*watched* gone without sleep
147*A . . . heels* even a good man may have bad fortune
148*Give* God give
149*taken* received
150*approve* confirm
150*saw* proverb

Thou out of Heaven's benediction com'st
To the warm sun.°
Approach, thou beacon to this under globe,°
That by thy comfortable° beams I may
Peruse this letter. Nothing almost sees miracles   155
But misery.° I know 'tis from Cordelia,
Who hath most fortunately been informed
Of my obscurèd° course. And shall find time
From this enormous state, seeking to give
Losses their remedies.° All weary and o'erwatched,   160
Take vantage,° heavy eyes, not to behold
This shameful lodging. Fortune, good night;
Smile once more, turn thy wheel.°

                                                        Sleeps.

Scene III. [*A wood.*]

Enter EDGAR.

EDGAR.   I heard myself proclaimed,
And by the happy° hollow of a tree
Escaped the hunt. No port is free, no place
That guard and most unusual vigilance
Does not attend my taking.° Whiles I may 'scape,   5
I will preserve myself; and am bethought°
To take the basest and most poorest shape
That ever penury, in contempt of man,
Brought near to beast;° my face I'll grime with filth,
Blanket° my loins, elf° all my hairs in knots,   10
And with presented° nakedness outface°

---

¹⁵²*Thou . . . sun* i.e., Lear goes from better to worse, from Heaven's blessing or shelter
to lack of shelter
¹⁵³*beacon . . . globe* i.e., the sun, whose rising Kent anticipates
¹⁵⁴*comfortable* comforting
¹⁵⁶*Nothing . . . misery* i.e., true perception belongs only to the wretched
¹⁵⁸*obscurèd* disguised
¹⁶⁰*shall . . . remedies* (a possible reading: Cordelia, away from this monstrous state of
things, will find occasion to right the wrongs we suffer)
¹⁶¹*vantage* advantage (of sleep)
¹⁶³*turn thy wheel* i.e., so that Kent, who is at the bottom, may climb upward
II.iii.²*happy* lucky
⁵*attend my taking* watch to capture me
⁶*am bethought* have decided
⁹*penury . . . beast* poverty, to show how contemptible man is, reduced to the level of a
beast
¹⁰*Blanket* cover only with a blanket
¹⁰*elf* tangle (into "elflocks," supposed to be caused by elves)
¹¹*presented* the show of
¹¹*outface* brave

The winds and persecutions of the sky.
The country gives me proof° and precedent
Of Bedlam° beggars, who, with roaring voices,
Strike° in their numbed and mortified° bare arms   15
Pins, wooden pricks,° nails, sprigs of rosemary;
And with this horrible object,° from low° farms,
Poor pelting° villages, sheepcotes, and mills,
Sometimes with lunatic bans,° sometime with prayers,
Enforce their charity. Poor Turlygod, Poor Tom,°   20
That's something yet: Edgar I nothing am.°

Exit.

Scene IV. [*Before Gloucester's castle.* KENT *in the stocks.*]

Enter LEAR, FOOL, *and* GENTLEMAN.

LEAR.   'Tis strange that they should so depart from home,
   And not send back my messenger.
GENTLEMAN.   As I learned,
   The night before there was no purpose° in them
   Of this remove.°
KENT.   Hail to thee, noble master.
LEAR.   Ha!   5
   Mak'st thou this shame thy pastime?°
KENT.   No, my lord.
FOOL.   Ha, ha, he wears cruel° garters. Horses are tied by the heads,
   dogs and bears by th' neck, monkeys by th' loins, and men by th'
   legs. When a man's over-lusty at legs,° then he wears wooden ne-
   therstocks.°   10
LEAR.   What's he that hath so much thy place mistook
   To set thee here?

13*proof* example
14*Bedlam* (see I.ii.r.[117])
15*strike* stick
15*mortified* not alive to pain
16*pricks* skewers
17*object* spectacle
17*low* humble
18*pelting* paltry
19*bans* curses
20*Poor . . . Tom* (Edgar recites the names a Bedlam beggar gives himself)
21*That's . . . am* there's a chance for me in that I am no longer known for myself
3*purpose* intention
4*remove* removal
6*Mak'st . . . pastime* i.e., are you doing this to amuse yourself
7*cruel* (1) painful (2) "crewel," a worsted yarn used in garters
9*overlusty at legs* (1) a vagabond (2) ? sexually promiscuous
10*netherstocks* stockings (as opposed to knee breeches or upperstocks)

KENT.   It is both he and she,
  Your son and daughter.
LEAR.   No.
KENT.   Yes.   15
LEAR.   No, I say.
KENT.   I say yea.
LEAR.   No, no, they would not.
KENT.   Yes, they have.
LEAR.   By Jupiter, I swear no!   20
KENT.   By Juno, I swear ay!
LEAR.   They durst not do't;
  They could not, would not do't. 'Tis worse than murder
  To do upon respect° such violent outrage.
  Resolve° me with all modest° haste which way
  Thou mightst deserve or they impose this usage,   25
  Coming from us.
KENT.   My lord, when at their home
  I did commend° your Highness' letters to them,
  Ere I was risen from the place that showed
  My duty kneeling, came there a reeking post,°
  Stewed° in his haste, half breathless, panting forth   30
  From Goneril his mistress salutations,
  Delivered letters, spite of intermission,°
  Which presently° they read; on° whose contents
  They summoned up their meiny,° straight took horse,
  Commanded me to follow and attend   35
  The leisure of their answer, gave me cold looks,
  And meeting here the other messenger,
  Whose welcome I perceived had poisoned mine,
  Being the very fellow which of late
  Displayed° so saucily against your Highness,   40
  Having more man than wit° about me, drew;
  He raised° the house, with loud and coward cries.
  Your son and daughter found this trespass worth°
  The shame which here it suffers.

---

²³*upon respect* (1) on the respect due to the King (2) deliberately
²⁴*Resolve* inform
²⁴*modest* becoming
²⁷*commend* deliver
²⁹*reeking post* sweating messenger
³⁰*stewed* steaming
³²*spite of intermission* in spite of the interrupting of my business
³³*presently* at once
³³*on* on the strength of
³⁴*meiny* retinue
⁴⁰*Displayed* showed off
⁴¹*more man than wit* more manhood than sense
⁴²*raised* aroused
⁴³*worth* deserving

FOOL.   Winter's not gone yet, if the wild geese fly that   45
way.°
> Fathers that wear rags
>   Do make their children blind,°
> But fathers that bear bags°
>   Shall see their children kind.   50
> Fortune, that arrant whore,
>   Ne'er turns the key° to th' poor.

But for all this, thou shalt have as many dolors° for thy daughters as
thou canst tell° in a year.

LEAR.   O, how this mother° swells up toward my heart!   55
Hysterica passio,° down, thou climbing sorrow,
Thy element's° below. Where is this daughter?

KENT.   With the Earl, sir, here within.

LEAR.   Follow me not;
Stay here.

Exit.

GENTLEMAN.   Made you no more offense but what you speak of?

KENT.   None.   60
How chance° the King comes with so small a number?

FOOL.   And° thou hadst been set i' th' stocks for that question, thou'dst
well deserved it.

KENT.   Why, Fool?

FOOL.   We'll set thee to school to an ant, to teach thee there's no   65
laboring i' th' winter.° All that follow their noses are led by their eyes
but blind men, and there's not a nose among twenty but can smell
him that's stinking.° Let go thy hold when a great wheel runs down
a hill, lest it break thy neck with following. But the great one that
goes upward, let him draw thee after. When a wise man gives thee   70
better counsel, give me mine again. I would have none but knaves
follow it since a Fool gives it.

---

[46]*Winter's . . . way* i.e., more trouble is to come, since Cornwall and Regan act so
("geese" is used contemptuously, as in Kent's quarrel with Oswald, II.ii. 74–75)
[48]*blind* i.e., indifferent
[49]*bags* moneybags
[52]*turns the key* i.e., opens the door
[53]*dolors* (1) sorrows (2) dollars (English name for Spanish and German coins)
[54]*tell* (1) tell about (2) count
[55–56]*mother . . . Hysterica passio* hysteria, causing suffocation or choking
[57]*element* proper place
[61]*How chance* how does it happen that
[62]*And* if
[66]*We'll . . . winter* (in the popular fable the ant, unlike the improvident grasshopper,
anticipates the winter when none can labor by laying up provisions in the summer. Lear,
trusting foolishly to summer days, finds himself unprovided for, and unable to provide,
now that "winter" has come.)
[68]*All . . . stinking* i.e., all can smell out the decay of Lear's fortunes

That sir, which serves and seeks for gain,
    And follows but for form,°
Will pack,° when it begins to rain,   75
    And leave thee in the storm.
But I will tarry; the Fool will stay,
    And let the wise man fly.
The knave turns Fool that runs away,
    The Fool no knave,° perdy.°   80

KENT.   Where learned you this, Fool?
FOOL.   Not i' th' stocks, fool.

Enter LEAR *and* GLOUCESTER.

LEAR.   Deny° to speak with me? They are sick, they are weary,
    They have traveled all the night? Mere fetches,°
    The images° of revolt and flying off!°   85
    Fetch me a better answer.
GLOUCESTER.   My dear lord,
    You know the fiery quality° of the Duke,
    How unremovable and fixed he is
    In his own course.
LEAR.   Vengeance, plague, death, confusion!
    Fiery? What quality? Why, Gloucester, Gloucester,   90
    I'd speak with the Duke of Cornwall and his wife.
GLOUCESTER.   Well, my good lord, I have informed them so.
LEAR.   Informed them? Dost thou understand me, man?
GLOUCESTER.   Ay, my good lord.
LEAR.   The King would speak with Cornwall. The dear father   95
    Would with his daughter speak, commands—tends°—service.
    Are they informed of this? My breath and blood!
    Fiery? The fiery Duke, tell the hot Duke that—
    No, but not yet. May be he is not well.
    Infirmity doth still neglect all office   100
    Whereto our health is bound.° We are not ourselves
    When nature, being oppressed, commands the mind
    To suffer with the body. I'll forbear;

74*form* show
75*pack* be off
80*The . . . knave* i.e., the faithless man is the true fool, for wisdom requires fidelity.
Lear's Fool, who remains faithful, is at least no knave
80*perdy* by God (Fr. *par Dieu*)
83*Deny* refuse
84*fetches* subterfuges, acts of tacking (nautical metaphor)
85*images* exact likenesses
85*flying off* desertion
87*quality* temperament
96*tends* attends (i.e., awaits); with, possibly, an ironic second meaning, "tenders," or
"offers"
101*Whereto . . . bound* duties which we are required to perform, when in health

And am fallen out° with my more headier will°
To take the indisposed and sickly fit   105
For the sound man. [*Looking on Kent*] Death on my state!° Wherefore
Should he sit here? This act persuades me
That this remotion° of the Duke and her
Is practice° only. Give me my servant forth.°
Go tell the Duke and's wife I'd speak with them!   110
Now, presently!° Bid them come forth and hear me,
Or at their chamber door I'll beat the drum
Till it cry sleep to death.°

GLOUCESTER.   I would have all well betwixt you.

Exit.

LEAR.   O me, my heart, my rising heart! But down!   115
FOOL.   Cry to it, Nuncle, as the cockney° did to the eels when she put
'em i' th' paste° alive. She knapped° 'em o' th' coxcombs° with a stick
and cried, "Down, wantons,° down!" 'Twas her brother that, in pure
kindness to his horse, buttered his hay.°

        Enter CORNWALL, REGAN, GLOUCESTER, SERVANTS.

LEAR.   Good morrow to you both.
CORNWALL.   Hail to your Grace.   120

                              KENT *here set at liberty.*

REGAN.   I am glad to see your Highness.
LEAR.   Regan, I think you are. I know what reason
I have to think so. If thou shouldst not be glad,
I would divorce me from thy mother's tomb,
Sepulchring an adultress.° [*To* KENT] O, are you free?   125
Some other time for that. Beloved Regan,
Thy sister's naught.° O Regan, she hath tied
Sharp-toothed unkindness, like a vulture, here.

                              [*Points to his heart.*]

104*fallen out* angry
104*headier will* headlong inclination
106*state* royal condition
108*remotion* (1) removal (2) remaining aloof
109*practice* pretense
109*forth* i.e., out of the stocks
111*presently* at once
113*cry . . . death* follow sleep, like a cry or pack of hounds, until it kills it
116*cockney* Londoner (ignorant city dweller)
117*paste* pastry pie
117*knapped* rapped
117*coxcombs* heads
118*wantons* i.e., playful things (with a sexual implication)
119*buttered his hay* i.e., the city dweller does from ignorance what the dishonest ostler
does from craft: greases the hay the traveler has paid for, so that the horse will not eat
125*divorce . . . adultress* i.e., repudiate your dead mother as having conceived you by
another man
127*naught* wicked

I can scarce speak to thee. Thou'lt not believe
With how depraved a quality°—O Regan!   130
REGAN.   I pray you, sir, take patience. I have hope
      You less know how to value her desert
      Than she to scant her duty.°
LEAR.   Say? how is that?
REGAN.   I cannot think my sister in the least   135
      Would fail her obligation. If, sir, perchance
      She have restrained the riots of your followers,
      'Tis on such ground, and to such wholesome end,
      As clears her from all blame.
LEAR.   My curses on her!
REGAN.   O, sir, you are old,
      Nature in you stands on the very verge   140
      Of his confine.° You should be ruled, and led
      By some discretion that discerns your state
      Better than you yourself.° Therefore I pray you
      That to our sister you do make return,
      Say you have wronged her.
LEAR.   Ask her forgiveness?   145
      Do you but mark how this becomes the house:°
      "Dear daughter, I confess that I am old.

                                                    [*Kneeling.*]

      Age is unnecessary. On my knees I beg
      That you'll vouchsafe me raiment, bed, and food."
REGAN.   Good sir, no more. These are unsightly tricks.   150
      Return you to my sister.
LEAR.   [*Rising*] Never, Regan.
      She hath abated° me of half my train,
      Looked black upon me, struck me with her tongue,
      Most serpentlike, upon the very heart.
      All the stored vengeances of heaven fall   155
      On her ingrateful top!° Strike her young bones,°
      You taking° airs, with lameness.
CORNWALL.   Fie, sir, fie!

---

¹³⁰*quality* nature
¹³³*I . . . duty* (despite the double negative, the passage means, "I believe that you fail to
give Goneril her due, rather than that she fails to fulfill her duty")
¹⁴¹*Nature . . . confine* i.e., you are nearing the end of your life
¹⁴³*some . . . yourself* some discreet person who understands your condition more than
you do
¹⁴⁶*becomes the house* suits my royal and paternal position
¹⁵²*abated* curtailed
¹⁵⁶*top* head
¹⁵⁶*young bones* (the reference may be to unborn children, rather than to Goneril herself)
¹⁵⁷*taking* infecting

LEAR.   You nimble lightnings, dart your blinding flames
             Into her scornful eyes! Infect her beauty,
             You fen-sucked° fogs, drawn by the pow'rful sun,   160
             To fall and blister° her pride.
REGAN.   O the blest gods!
             So will you wish on me when the rash mood is on.
LEAR.   No, Regan, thou shalt never have my curse.
             Thy tender-hefted° nature shall not give
             Thee o'er to harshness. Her eyes are fierce, but thine   165
             Do comfort, and not burn. 'Tis not in thee
             To grudge my pleasures, to cut off my train,
             To bandy° hasty words, to scant my sizes,°
             And, in conclusion, to oppose the bolt°
             Against my coming in. Thou better know'st   170
             The offices of nature, bond of childhood,°
             Effects° of courtesy, dues of gratitude.
             Thy half o' th' kingdom hast thou not forgot,
             Wherein I thee endowed.
REGAN.   Good sir, to th' purpose.°

                                        Tucket within.

LEAR.   Who put my man i' th' stocks?
CORNWALL.   What trumpet's that?   175
REGAN.   I know't—my sister's. This approves° her letter,
             That she would soon be here.

                        Enter Oswald.

                           Is your lady come?
LEAR.   This is a slave, whose easy borrowed° pride
             Dwells in the fickle grace° of her he follows.
             Out, varlet,° from my sight.
CORNWALL.   What means your Grace?
LEAR.   Who stocked my servant? Regan, I have good hope   180
             Thou didst not know on't.

¹⁶⁰*fen-sucked* drawn up from swamps by the sun
¹⁶¹*fall and blister* fall upon and raise blisters
¹⁶⁴*tender-hefted* gently framed
¹⁶⁸*bandy* volley (metaphor from tennis)
¹⁶⁸*scant my sizes* reduce my allowances
¹⁶⁹*oppose the bolt* i.e., bar the door
¹⁷¹*offices . . . childhood* natural duties, a child's duty to its parent
¹⁷²*Effects* manifestations
¹⁷⁴*to th' purpose* come to the point
¹⁷⁶*approves* confirms
¹⁷⁷*easy borrowed* (1) facile and taken from another (2) acquired without anything to
back it up (like money borrowed without security)
¹⁷⁸*grace* favor
¹⁷⁹*varlet* base fellow

Enter GONERIL.

        Who comes here? O heavens!
If you do love old men, if your sweet sway
Allow° obedience, if you yourselves are old,
Make it° your cause. Send down, and take my part.
[*To* GONERIL] Art not ashamed to look upon this beard?
O Regan, will you take her by the hand?   185
GONERIL. Why not by th' hand, sir? How have I offended?
All's not offense that indiscretion finds°
And dotage terms so.
LEAR.   O sides,° you are too tough!
Will you yet hold? How came my man i' th' stocks?
CORNWALL. I set him there, sir; but his own disorders° 190
Deserved much less advancement.°
LEAR.   You? Did you?
REGAN. I pray you, father, being weak, seem so.°
If till the expiration of your month
You will return and sojourn with my sister,
Dismissing half your train, come then to me.   195
I am now from home, and out of that provision
Which shall be needful for your entertainment.°
LEAR. Return to her, and fifty men dismissed?
No, rather I abjure all roofs, and choose
To wage° against the enmity o' th' air,   200
To be a comrade with the wolf and owl,
Necessity's sharp pinch.° Return with her?
Why, the hot-blooded° France, that dowerless took
Our youngest born, I could as well be brought
To knee° his throne, and squirelike,° pension beg   205
To keep base life afoot. Return with her?
Persuade me rather to be slave and sumpter°
To this detested groom. [*Pointing at* OSWALD]
GONERIL.   At your choice, sir.
LEAR. I prithee, daughter, do not make me mad.   210

---

[182]*Allow* approve of
[183]*it* i.e., my cause
[187]*finds* judges
[188]*sides* breast
[190]*disorders* misconduct
[191]*advancement* promotion
[192]*seem so* i.e., act weak
[197]*entertainment* maintenance
[200]*wage* fight
[202]*Necessity's sharp pinch* (a summing up of the hard choice he has just announced)
[203]*hot-blooded* passionate
[205]*knee* kneel before
[205]*squirelike* like a retainer
[207]*sumpter* pack horse

I will not trouble thee, my child; farewell.
We'll no more meet, no more see one another.
But yet thou art my flesh, my blood, my daughter,
Or rather a disease that's in my flesh,
Which I must needs call mine. Thou art a boil,   215
A plague-sore, or embossèd carbuncle°
In my corrupted blood. But I'll not chide thee.
Let shame come when it will, I do not call it.
I do not bid the Thunder-bearer° shoot,
Nor tell tales of thee to high-judging° Jove.   220
Mend when thou canst, be better at thy leisure,
I can be patient, I can stay with Regan,
I and my hundred knights.

REGAN.   Not altogether so.
I looked not for you yet, nor am provided
For your fit welcome. Give ear, sir, to my sister,   225
For those that mingle reason with your passion°
Must be content to think you old, and so—
But she knows what she does.

LEAR.   Is this well spoken?

REGAN.   I dare avouch° it, sir. What, fifty followers?
Is it not well? What should you need of more?   230
Yea, or so many, sith that° both charge° and danger
Speak 'gainst so great a number? How in one house
Should many people, under two commands,
Hold° amity? 'Tis hard, almost impossible.

GONERIL.   Why might not you, my lord, receive attendance   235
From those that she calls servants, or from mine?

REGAN.   Why not, my lord? If then they chanced to slack° ye,
We could control them. If you will come to me
(For now I spy a danger), I entreat you
To bring but five-and-twenty. To no more   240
Will I give place or notice.°

LEAR.   I gave you all.

REGAN.   And in good time you gave it.

LEAR.   Made you my guardians, my depositaries,°
But kept a reservation° to be followed

---

216 *embossèd carbuncle* swollen boil
219 *Thunder-bearer* i.e., Jupiter
220 *high-judging* (1) supreme (2) judging from heaven
226 *mingle . . . passion* i.e., consider your turbulent behavior coolly and reasonably
229 *avouch* swear by
231 *sith that* since
231 *charge* expense
234 *hold* preserve
237 *slack* neglect
241 *notice* recognition
243 *depositaries* trustees
244 *reservation* condition

With such a number. What, must I come to you   245
With five-and-twenty? Regan, said you so?
REGAN.   And speak't again, my lord. No more with me.
LEAR.   Those wicked creatures yet do look well-favored°
When others are more wicked; not being the worst
Stands in some rank of praise.° [*To* GONERIL] I'll go with thee.   250
Thy fifty yet doth double five-and-twenty,
And thou art twice her love.°
GONERIL.   Hear me, my lord.
What need you five-and-twenty? ten? or five?
To follow° in a house where twice so many
Have a command to tend you?
REGAN.   What need one?   255
LEAR.   O reason° not the need! Our basest beggars
Are in the poorest thing superfluous.°
Allow not nature more than nature needs,°
Man's life is cheap as beast's. Thou art a lady:
If only to go warm were gorgeous,   260
Why, nature needs not what thou gorgeous wear'st,
Which scarcely keeps thee warm.° But, for true need—
You heavens, give me that patience, patience I need.
You see me here, you gods, a poor old man,
As full of grief as age, wretched in both.   265
If it be you that stirs these daughters' hearts
Against their father, fool° me not so much
To bear° it tamely; touch me with noble anger,
And let not women's weapons, water drops,
Stain my man's cheeks. No, you unnatural hags!   270
I will have such revenges on you both
That all the world shall—I will do such things—
What they are, yet I know not; but they shall be
The terrors of the earth. You think I'll weep.
No, I'll not weep.   275

                              Storm and tempest.

I have full cause of weeping, but this heart

[248]*well-favored* handsome
[250]*not . . . praise* i.e., that Goneril is not so bad as Regan is one thing in her
favor
[252]*her love* i.e., as loving as she
[254]*follow* attend on you
[256]*reason* scrutinize
[257]*Are . . . superfluous* i.e., have some trifle not absolutely necessary
[258]*needs* i.e., to sustain life
[262]*If . . . warm* i.e., if to satisfy the need for warmth were to be gorgeous, you would
not need the clothing you wear, which is worn more for beauty than warmth
[267]*fool* humiliate
[268]*To bear* as to make me bear

Shall break into a hundred thousand flaws°
Or ere° I'll weep. O Fool, I shall go mad!

         Exeunt LEAR, GLOUCESTER, KENT, *and* FOOL.

CORNWALL.   Let us withdraw, 'twill be a storm.
REGAN.   This house is little the old man and's people   280
    Cannot be well bestowed.°
GONERIL.   'Tis his own blame; hath° put himself from rest°
    And must needs taste his folly.
REGAN.   For his particular,° I'll receive him gladly,
    But not one follower.
GONERIL.   So am I purposed.°
    Where is my Lord of Gloucester?   285
CORNWALL.   Followed the old man forth.

Enter GLOUCESTER.

    He is returned.
GLOUCESTER.   The King is in high rage.
CORNWALL.   Whither is he going?
GLOUCESTER.   He calls to horse, but will I know not whither.
CORNWALL.   'Tis best to give him way, he leads himself.°
GONERIL.   My lord, entreat him by no means to stay.   290
GLOUCESTER.   Alack, the night comes on, and the high winds
    Do sorely ruffle.° For many miles about
    There's scarce a bush.
REGAN.   O, sir, to willful men
    The injuries that they themselves procure
    Must be their schoolmasters. Shut up your doors.   295
    He is attended with a desperate train,
    And what they may incense° him to, being apt
    To have his ear abused,° wisdom bids fear.
CORNWALL.   Shut up your doors, my lord; 'tis a wild night.
    My Regan counsels well. Come out o' th' storm.   300

                              Exeunt.

---

[277]*flaws* (1) pieces (2) cracks (3) gusts of passion
[278]*Or ere* before
[280]*bestowed* lodged
[281]*hath* he hath
[281]*rest* (1) place of residence (2) repose of mind
[283]*his particular* himself personally
[284]*purposed* determined
[289]*give . . . himself* let him go; he insists on his own way
[292]*ruffle* rage
[297]*incense* incite
[298]*being . . . abused* he being inclined to harken to bad counsel

ACT III

Scene I. [*A heath.*]

Storm still.° Enter KENT *and a* GENTLEMAN *severally.*

KENT.   Who's there besides foul weather?

GENTLEMAN.   One minded like the weather most unquietly.°

KENT.   I know you. Where's the King?

GENTLEMAN.   Contending with the fretful elements;
Bids the wind blow the earth into the sea,   5
Or swell the curlèd waters 'bove the main,°
That things might change,° or cease; tears his white hair,
Which the impetuous blasts, with eyeless° rage,
Catch in their fury, and make nothing of;
Strives in his little world of man° to outscorn   10
The to-and-fro-conflicting wind and rain.
This night, wherein the cub-drawn° bear would couch,°
The lion, and the belly-pinchèd° wolf
Keep their fur dry, unbonneted° he runs,
And bids what will take all.°

KENT.   But who is with him?   15

GENTLEMAN.   None but the Fool, who labors to outjest
His heart-struck injuries.

KENT.   Sir, I do know you,
And dare upon the warrant of my note°
Commend a dear thing° to you. There is division,
Although as yet the face of it is covered   20
With mutual cunning, 'twixt Albany and Cornwall;
Who have—as who have not, that° their great stars
Thronèd° and set high?—servants, who seem no less,°

III.i.s.d. *still* continually
[2]*minded . . . unquietly* disturbed in mind, like the weather
[6]*main* land
[7]*change* (1) be destroyed (2) be exchanged (i.e., turned upside down) (3) change for the better
[8]*eyeless* (1) blind (2) invisible
[10]*little world of man* (the microcosm, as opposed to the universe or macrocosm, which it copies in little)
[12]*cub-drawn* sucked dry by her cubs, and so ravenously hungry
[12]*couch* take shelter in its lair
[13]*belly-pinchèd* starved
[14]*unbonneted* hatless
[15]*take all* (like the reckless gambler, staking all he has left)
[18]*warrant of my note* strength of what I have taken note (of you)
[19]*Commend . . . thing* entrust important business
[22]*that* whom
[23]*stars/Thronèd* destinies have throned
[23]*seem no less* seem to be so

Which are to France the spies and speculations
Intelligent° of our state. What hath been seen,   25
Either in snuffs and packings° of the Dukes,
Or the hard rein which both of them hath borne°
Against the old kind King, or something deeper,
Whereof, perchance, these are but furnishings°—
But, true it is, from France there comes a power°   30
Into this scattered° kingdom, who already,
Wise in our negligence, have secret feet
In some of our best ports, and are at point°
To show their open banner. Now to you:
If on my credit you dare build° so far   35
To° make your speed to Dover, you shall find
Some that will thank you, making° just° report
Of how unnatural and bemadding° sorrow
The King hath cause to plain.°
I am a gentleman of blood and breeding,°   40
And from some knowledge and assurance° offer
This office° to you.
GENTLEMAN.   I will talk further with you.
KENT.   No, do not.
For confirmation that I am much more
Than my out-wall,° open this purse and take   45
What it contains. If you shall see Cordelia,
As fear not but you shall, show her this ring,
And she will tell you who that fellow° is
That yet you do not know. Fie on this storm!
I will go seek the King.   50
GENTLEMAN.   Give me your hand. Have you no more to say?
KENT.   Few words, but, to effect,° more than all yet:

25*speculations/Intelligent* giving intelligence
26*snuffs and packings* quarrels and plots
27*hard . . . borne* close and cruel control they have exercised
29*furnishings* excuses
30*power* army
31*scattered* disunited
33*at point* ready
35*If . . . build* if you can trust me, proceed
36*To* as to
37*making* for making
37*just* accurate
38*bemadding* maddening
39*plain* complain of
40*blood and breeding* noble family
41*knowledge and assurance* sure and trustworthy information
42*office* service (i.e., the trip to Dover)
45*out-wall* superficial appearance
48*fellow* companion
52*to effect* in their importance

That when we have found the King—in which your pain°
That way, I'll this—he that first lights on him,
Holla the other.   55

Exeunt [*severally*].

Scene II. [*Another part of the heath.*]

Storm still.

Enter Lear and Fool.

LEAR.   Blow, winds, and crack your cheeks. Rage, blow!
You cataracts and hurricanoes,° spout
Till you have drenched our steeples, drowned the cocks.°
You sulph'rous and thought-executing° fires,
Vaunt-couriers° of oak-cleaving thunderbolts,   5
Singe my white head. And thou, all-shaking thunder,
Strike flat the thick rotundity° o' th' world,
Crack Nature's molds,° all germains spill° at once,
That makes ingrateful° man.
FOOL.   O Nuncle, court holy-water° in a dry house is   10
better than this rain water out o' door. Good Nuncle, in; ask thy
daughters blessing. Here's a night pities neither wise man nor
fools.
LEAR.   Rumble thy bellyful. Spit, fire. Spout, rain!
Nor rain, wind, thunder, fire are my daughters.
I tax° not you, you elements, with unkindness.
I never gave you kingdom, called you children,   15
You owe me no subscription.° Then let fall
Your horrible pleasure.° Here I stand your slave,
A poor, infirm, weak, and despised old man.
But yet I call you servile ministers,°
That will with two pernicious daughters join   20

---

[53]*pain* labor
III.ii.[2]*hurricanoes* waterspouts
[3]*cocks* weathercocks
[4]*thought-executing* (1) doing execution as quick as thought (2) executing or carrying out
the thought of him who hurls the lightning
[5]*Vaunt-couriers* heralds, scouts who range before the main body of the army
[7]*rotundity* i.e., not only the sphere of the globe, but the roundness of gestation (Delius)
[8]*Nature's molds* the molds or forms in which men are made
[8]*all germains spill* destroy the basic seeds of life
[9]*ingrateful* ungrateful
[10]*court holy-water* flattery
[14]*tax* accuse
[16]*subscription* allegiance, submission
[17]*pleasure* will
[19]*ministers* agents

Your high-engendered battles° 'gainst a head
So old and white as this. O, ho! 'tis foul.

FOOL.   He that has a house to put 's head in has a good head-
piece.°

         The codpiece° that will house   25
           Before the head has any,
         The head and he° shall louse:
           So beggars marry many.°
         The man that makes his toe
           What he his heart should make   30
         Shall of a corn cry woe,
           And turn his sleep to wake.°

For there was never yet fair woman but she made mouths in a
glass.°

Enter KENT.

LEAR.   No, I will be the pattern of all patience,   35
I will say nothing.

KENT.   Who's there?

FOOL.   Marry,° here's grace and a codpiece; that's a wise man and a
fool.°

KENT.   Alas, sir, are you here? Things that love night   40
Love not such nights as these. The wrathful skies
Gallow° the very wanderers of the dark
And make them keep° their caves. Since I was man,
Such sheets of fire, such bursts of horrid° thunder,
Such groans of roaring wind and rain, I never   45
Remember to have heard. Man's nature cannot carry°
Th' affliction nor the fear.

[21]*high-engendered battles* armies formed in the heavens
[24]*headpiece* (1) helmet (2) brain
[25]*codpiece* penis (lit., padding worn at the crotch of a man's hose)
[27]*he* it
[28]*many* i.e., lice
[28]*The . . . many* i.e., the man who gratifies his sexual appetites before he has a roof
over his head will end up a lousy beggar
[32]*The . . . wake* i.e., the man who, ignoring the fit order of things, elevates what is base
above what is noble, will suffer for it as Lear has, in banishing Cordelia and enriching
her sisters
[34]*made mouths in a glass* posed before a mirror (irrelevant nonsense, except that it calls
to mind the general theme of vanity and folly)
[38]*Marry* by the Virgin Mary
[39]*here's . . . fool* (Kent's question is answered: The King ("grace") is here, and the
Fool—who customarily wears an exaggerated codpiece. But which is which is left
ambiguous, since Lear has previously been called a codpiece)
[42]*Gallow* frighten
[43]*keep* remain inside
[44]*horrid* horrible
[46]*carry* endure

LEAR.   Let the great gods
    That keep this dreadful pudder° o'er our heads
    Find out their enemies now.° Tremble, thou wretch,
    That hast within thee undivulgèd crimes   50
    Unwhipped of justice. Hide thee, thou bloody hand,
    Thou perjured,° and thou simular° of virtue
    That art incestuous. Caitiff,° to pieces shake,
    That under covert and convenient seeming°
    Has practiced on° man's life. Close° pent-up guilts,   55
    Rive° your concealing continents° and cry
    These dreadful summoners grace.° I am a man
    More sinned against than sinning.
KENT.   Alack, bareheaded?
    Gracious my lord,° hard by here is a hovel;
    Some friendship will it lend you 'gainst the tempest.   60
    Repose you there, while I to this hard house
    (More harder than the stones whereof 'tis raised,
    Which even but now, demanding after° you,
    Denied me to come in) return, and force
    Their scanted° courtesy.
LEAR.   My wits begin to turn.   65
    Come on, my boy. How dost, my boy? Art cold?
    I am cold myself. Where is this straw, my fellow?
    The art° of our necessities is strange,
    That can make vile things precious. Come, your hovel.
    Poor Fool and knave, I have one part in my heart   70
    That's sorry yet for thee.
FOOL.   [Singing]
    He that has and a little tiny wit,
      With heigh-ho, the wind and the rain,
    Must make content with his fortunes fit,°   75
      Though the rain it raineth every day.

[48]*pudder* turmoil
[49]*Find . . . now* i.e., discover sinners by the terror they reveal
[52]*perjured* perjurer
[52]*simular* counterfeiter
[53]*Caitiff* wretch
[54]*seeming* hypocrisy
[55]*practiced on* plotted against
[55]*Close* hidden
[56]*Rive* split open
[56]*continents* containers
[57]*cry . . . grace* beg mercy from the vengeful gods (here figured as officers who summoned a man charged with immorality before the ecclesiastical court)
[59]*Gracious my lord* my gracious lord
[63]*demanding after* asking for
[65]*scanted* stinted
[68]*art* magic powers of the alchemists, who sought to transmute base metals into precious
[75]*Must . . . fit* must be satisfied with a fortune as tiny as his wit

LEAR.   True, my good boy. Come, bring us to this hovel.

Exit [*with* KENT].

FOOL.   This is a brave° night to cool a courtesan. I'll speak a prophecy
  ere I go:
  When priests are more in word than matter;
  When brewers mar their malt with water;   80
  When nobles are their tailors' tutors,
  No heretics burned, but wenches' suitors;°
  When every case in law is right,
  No squire in debt nor no poor knight;
  When slanders do not live in tongues;   85
  Nor cutpurses come not to throngs;
  When usurers tell their gold i' th' field,°
  And bawds and whores do churches build,°
  Then shall the realm of Albion°
  Come to great confusion.   90
  Then comes the time, who lives to see't,
  That going shall be used with feet.°

This prophecy Merlin° shall make, for I live before his time.

                   Exit.

Scene III. [*Gloucester's castle.*]

Enter GLOUCESTER *and* EDMUND.

GLOUCESTER.   Alack, alack, Edmund, I like not this unnatural dealing. When I desired their leave that I might pity° him, they took from
me the use of mine own house, charged me on pain of perpetual
displeasure neither to speak of him, entreat for him, or any way
sustain° him.   5

EDMUND.   Most savage and unnatural.

GLOUCESTER.   Go to; say you nothing. There is division° between the

---

[78]*brave* fine

[82]*When . . . suitors* (the first four prophecies are fulfilled already, and hence "confusion"
has come to England. The priest does not suit his action to his words. The brewer
adulterates his beer. The nobleman is subservient to his tailor [i.e., cares only for
fashion]. Religious heretics escape, and only those burn [i.e., suffer] who are afflicted
with venereal disease)

[87]*tell . . . field* count their money in the open

[88]*When . . . build* (the last six prophecies, as they are Utopian, are meant ironically.
They will never be fulfilled)

[89]*Albion* England

[92]*going . . . feet* people will walk on their feet

[93]*Merlin* King Arthur's great magician who, according to Holinshed's *Chronicles*, lived
later than Lear

III.iii. [2]*pity* show pity to

[5]*sustain* care for

[7]*division* falling out

Dukes, and a worse° matter than that. I have received a letter this
night—'tis dangerous to be spoken°—I have locked the letter in my
closet.° These injuries the King now bears will be revenged   10
home;° there is part of a power° already footed;° we must incline
to° the King. I will look° him and privily° relieve him. Go you and
maintain talk with the Duke, that my charity be not of° him perceived. If he ask for me, I am ill and gone to bed. If I die for it, as
no less is threatened me, the King my old master must be relieved.   15
There is strange things toward,° Edmund; pray you be careful.

                                                              Exit.

EDMUND.   This courtesy forbid° thee shall the Duke
Instantly know, and of that letter too.
This seems a fair deserving,° and must draw me
That which my father loses—no less than all.   20
The younger rises when the old doth fall.

                                                              Exit.

            Scene IV. [*The heath. Before a hovel.*]

                Enter LEAR, KENT, *and* FOOL.

KENT.   Here is the place, my lord. Good my lord, enter.
The tyranny of the open night's too rough
For nature to endure.

                                                        Storm still.

LEAR.   Let me alone.
KENT.   Good my lord, enter here.
LEAR.   Wilt break my heart?°
KENT.   I had rather break mine own. Good my lord, enter.   5
LEAR.   Thou think'st 'tis much that this contentious storm
Invades us to the skin: so 'tis to thee;
But where the greater malady is fixed,°

[8]*worse* more serious (i.e., the French invasion)
[9]*spoken* spoken of
[10]*closet* room
[11]*home* to the utmost
[11]*power* army
[11]*footed* landed
[12]*incline to* take the side of
[12]*look* search for
[12]*privily* secretly
[13]*of* by
[16]*toward* impending
[17]*courtesy forbid* kindness forbidden (i.e., to Lear)
[19]*fair deserving* an action deserving reward
III.iv. [4]*break my heart* i.e., by shutting out the storm which distracts me from thinking
[8]*fixed* lodged (in the mind)

The lesser is scarce felt. Thou'dst shun a bear;
But if thy flight lay toward the roaring sea,   10
Thou'dst meet the bear i' th' mouth.° When the mind's free,°
The body's delicate. The tempest in my mind
Doth from my senses take all feeling else,
Save what beats there. Filial ingratitude,
Is it not as° this mouth should tear this hand   15
For lifting food to't? But I will punish home.°
No, I will weep no more. In such a night
To shut me out! Pour on, I will endure.
In such a night as this! O Regan, Goneril,
Your old kind father, whose frank° heart gave all—   20
O, that way madness lies; let me shun that.
No more of that.

KENT.   Good my lord, enter here.
LEAR.   Prithee go in thyself; seek thine own ease.
This tempest will not give me leave to ponder
On things would hurt me more, but I'll go in.   25
[*To the* FOOL] In, boy; go first. You houseless poverty°—
Nay, get thee in. I'll pray, and then I'll sleep.

                                        Exit [FOOL].

                    Poor naked wretches, wheresoe'er you are,
                    That bide° the pelting of this pitiless storm,
How shall your houseless heads and unfed sides,   30
Your looped and windowed° raggedness, defend you
From seasons such as these? O, I have ta'en
Too little care of this! Take physic, pomp;°
Expose thyself to feel what wretches feel,
That thou mayst shake the superflux° to them,   35
And show the heavens more just.

EDGAR.   [*Within*] Fathom and half, fathom and half!°
Poor Tom!

                    Enter FOOL.

FOOL.   Come not in here, Nuncle, here's a spirit. Help me, help me!
KENT.   Give me thy hand. Who's there?   40

<hr>

[11]*i' th' mouth* in the teeth
[11]*free* i.e., from care
[15]*as* as if
[16]*home* to the utmost
[20]*frank* liberal (magnanimous)
[26]*houseless poverty* (the unsheltered poor, abstracted)
[29]*bide* endure
[31]*looped and windowed* full of holes
[33]*Take physic, pomp* take medicine to cure yourselves, you great men
[35]*superflux* superfluity
[37]*Fathom and half* (Edgar, because of the downpour, pretends to take soundings)

FOOL.   A spirit, a spirit. He says his name's Poor Tom.
KENT.   What art thou that dost grumble there i' th' straw?
Come forth.

Enter EDGAR [*disguised as a madman*].

EDGAR.   Away! the foul fiend follows me. Through the sharp hawthorn
blows the cold wind.° Humh! Go to thy cold bed, and warm   45
thee.°
LEAR.   Didst thou give all to thy daughters? And art thou come to
this?
EDGAR.   Who gives anything to Poor Tom? Whom the foul fiend hath
led through fire and through flame, through ford and whirlpool, o'er   50
bog and quagmire; that hath laid knives under his pillow and halters
in his pew,° set ratsbane° by his porridge,° made him proud of heart,
to ride on a bay trotting horse over four-inched bridges,° to
course° his own shadow for° a traitor. Bless thy five wits,° Tom's
a-cold. O, do, de, do, de, do, de. Bless thee from whirlwinds,   55
star-blasting,° and taking.° Do Poor Tom some charity, whom the
foul fiend vexes. There could I have him now—and there—and
there again—and there.

Storm still.

LEAR.   What, has his daughters brought him to this pass?°
Couldst thou save nothing? Wouldst thou give 'em all?   60
FOOL.   Nay, he reserved a blanket,° else we had been all shamed.
LEAR.   Now all the plagues that in the pendulous° air
Hang fated o'er° men's faults light on thy daughters!
KENT.   He hath no daughters, sir.
LEAR.   Death, traitor; nothing could have subdued° nature   65
To such a lowness but his unkind daughters.
Is it the fashion that discarded fathers

[45]*Through . . . wind* (a line from the ballad of "The Friar of Orders Gray")
[46]*go . . . thee* (a reminiscence of *The Taming of the Shrew,* Induction, 1.10)
[52]*knives . . . halters . . . ratsbane* (the fiend tempts Poor Tom to suicide)
[52]*pew* gallery or balcony outside a window
[52]*porridge* broth
[53]*ride . . . bridges* i.e., risk his life
[54]*course* chase
[54]*for* as
[54]*five wits* i.e., common wit, imagination, fantasy, estimation, memory
[56]*star-blasting* the evil caused by malignant stars
[56]*taking* pernicious influences
[59]*pass* wretched condition
[61]*blanket* i.e., to cover his nakedness
[62]*pendulous* overhanging
[63]*fated o'er* destined to punish
[65]*subdued* reduced

Should have thus little mercy on° their flesh?
Judicious punishment—'twas this flesh begot
Those pelican° daughters.   70

EDGAR.   Pillicock sat on Pillicock Hill.° Alow, alow, loo, loo!°

FOOL.   This cold night will turn us all to fools and madmen.

EDGAR.   Take heed o' th' foul fiend; obey thy parents; keep thy word's
justice;° swear not; commit not° with man's sworn spouse; set not
thy sweet heart on proud array. Tom's a-cold.   75

LEAR.   What hast thou been?

EDGAR.   A servingman, proud in heart and mind; that curled my hair,
wore gloves in my cap;° served the lust of my mistress' heart, and
did the act of darkness with her; swore as many oaths as I spake
words, and broke them in the sweet face of heaven. One that slept   80
in the contriving of lust, and waked to do it. Wine loved I deeply,
dice dearly; and in woman out-paramoured the Turk.° False of
heart, light of ear,° bloody of hand; hog in sloth, fox in stealth, wolf
in greediness, dog in madness, lion in prey.° Let not the creak-
ing° of shoes nor the rustling of silks betray thy poor heart to   85
woman. Keep thy foot out of brothels, thy hand out of plackets,°
thy pen from lenders' books,° and defy the foul fiend. Still through
the hawthorn blows the cold wind; says suum, mun, nonny.° Dol-
phin° my boy, boy, sessa!° let him trot by.

Storm still.

LEAR.   Thou wert better in a grave than to answer° with thy uncov-   90
ered body this extremity° of the skies. Is man no more than this?
Consider him well. Thou ow'st° the worm no silk, the beast no hide,

---

68*on* i.e., shown to
70*pelican* (supposed to feed on its parent's blood)
71*Pillicock . . . Hill* (probably quoted from a nursery rhyme, and suggested by
"pelican." *Pillicock* is a term of endearment and the phallus)
71*Alow . . . loo* (? a hunting call, or the refrain of the song)
74*keep . . . justice* i.e., do not break thy word
74*commit not* i.e., adultery
78*gloves in my cap* i.e., as a pledge from his mistress
82*out-paramoured the Turk* had more concubines than the Sultan
83*light of ear* ready to hear flattery and slander
84*prey* preying
85*creaking* (deliberately cultivated, as fashionable)
86*plackets* openings in skirts
87*pen . . . books* i.e., do not enter your name in the moneylender's account
book
88*suum, mun, nonny* the noise of the wind
89*Dolphin* the French Dauphin (identified by the English with the devil.
Poor Tom is presumably quoting from a ballad)
89*sessa* an interjection: "Go on!"
90*answer* confront, bear the brunt of
91*extremity* extreme severity
92*ow'st* have taken from

the sheep no wool, the cat° no perfume. Ha! here's three on's° are
sophisticated.° Thou art the thing itself; unaccommodated° man is
no more but such a poor, bare, forked° animal as thou art. Off, off,   95
you lendings!° Come, unbutton here.

[Tearing off his clothes.]

FOOL.   Prithee, Nuncle, be contented, 'tis a naughty° night to swim
in. Now a little fire in a wild° field were like an old lecher's heart—
a small spark, all the rest on's body, cold. Look, here comes a walking fire.   100

Enter GLOUCESTER, *with a torch.*

EDGAR.   This is the foul fiend Flibbertigibbet.° He begins at curfew,° and walks till the first cock.° He gives the web and the
pin,° squints° the eye, and makes the harelip; mildews the white°
wheat, and hurts the poor creature of earth.
    Swithold footed thrice the old;°   105
    He met the nightmare,° and her nine fold;°
      Bid her alight°
      And her troth plight,°
    And aroint° thee, witch, aroint thee!
KENT.   How fares your Grace?   110
LEAR.   What's he?
KENT.   Who's there? What is't you seek?
GLOUCESTER.   What are you there? Your names?
EDGAR.   Poor Tom, that eats the swimming frog, the toad, the todpole,
the wall-newt and the water;° that in the fury of his heart, when the foul   115

---

[93]*cat* civet cat, whose glands yield perfume
[93]*on's* of us
[94]*sophisticated* adulterated, made artificial
[94]*unaccommodated* uncivilized
[95]*forked* i.e., two-legged
[96]*lendings* borrowed garments
[97]*naughty* wicked
[98]*wild* barren
[101]*Flibbertigibbet* (a figure from Elizabethan demonology)
[102]*curfew:* 9 P.M.
[102]*first cock* midnight
[103]*web and the pin* cataract
[103]*squints* crosses
[103]*white* ripening
[105]*Swithold . . . old* Withold (an Anglo-Saxon saint who subdued demons) walked three
times across the open country
[106]*nightmare* demon
[106]*fold* offspring
[107]*alight* i.e., from the horse she had possessed
[108]*her troth plight* pledge her word
[109]*aroint* be gone
[115]*todpole . . . water* tadpole, wall lizard, water newt

fiend rages, eats cow-dung for sallets,° swallows the old rat and the
ditch-dog,° drinks the green mantle° of the standing° pool; who is
whipped from tithing° to tithing, and stocked, punished, and imprisoned; who hath had three suits to his back, six shirts to his body,

> Horse to ride, and weapon to wear,   120
> But mice and rats, and such small deer,°
> Have been Tom's food for seven long year.°

Beware my follower!° Peace, Smulkin,° peace, thou fiend!

GLOUCESTER.   What, hath your Grace no better company?

EDGAR.   The Prince of Darkness is a gentleman.   125
Modo° he's called, and Mahu.°

GLOUCESTER.   Our flesh and blood, my Lord, is grown so vile
That it doth hate what gets° it.

EDGAR.   Poor Tom's a-cold.

GLOUCESTER.   Go in with me. My duty cannot suffer°   130
T' obey in all your daughters' hard commands.
Though their injunction be to bar my doors
And let this tyrannous night take hold upon you,
Yet have I ventured to come seek you out
And bring you where both fire and food is ready.   135

LEAR.   First let me talk with this philosopher.
What is the cause of thunder?

KENT.   Good my lord, take his offer; go into th' house.

LEAR.   I'll talk a word with this same learnèd Theban.°
What is your study?°   140

EDGAR.   How to prevent° the fiend, and to kill vermin.

LEAR.   Let me ask you one word in private.

KENT.   Importune him once more to go, my lord.
His wits begin t' unsettle.

GLOUCESTER.   Canst thou blame him?

                                             Storm still.

His daughters seek his death. Ah, that good Kent,

---

¹¹⁶*sallets* salads
¹¹⁷*ditch-dog* dead dog in a ditch
¹¹⁷*mantle* scum
¹¹⁷*standing* stagnant
¹¹⁸*tithing* a district comprising ten families
¹²¹⁻¹²²*But . . . year* (adapted from a popular romance, "Bevis of Hampton")
¹²¹*deer* game
¹²³*follower* familiar
¹²³, ¹²⁶*Smulkin, Modo, Mahu* (Elizabethan devils, from Samuel Harsnett's *Declaration* of
1603)
¹²⁸*gets* begets
¹³⁰*suffer* permit me
¹³⁹*Theban* i.e., Greek philosopher
¹⁴⁰*study* particular scientific study
¹⁴¹*prevent* balk

He said it would be thus, poor banished man!
Thou say'st the King grows mad—I'll tell thee, friend,   145
I am almost mad myself. I had a son,
Now outlawed from my blood;° he sought my life
But lately, very late.° I loved him, friend,
No father his son dearer. True to tell thee,
The grief hath crazed my wits. What a night's this!   150
I do beseech your Grace———

LEAR.   O, cry you mercy,° sir.
Noble philosopher, your company.

EDGAR.   Tom's a-cold.

GLOUCESTER.   In, fellow, there, into th' hovel; keep thee warm.

LEAR.   Come, let's in all.

KENT.   This way, my lord.

LEAR.   With him!   155
I will keep still with my philosopher.

KENT.   Good my lord, soothe° him; let him take the fellow.

GLOUCESTER.   Take him you on.°

KENT.   Sirrah, come on; go along with us.

LEAR.   Come, good Athenian.°   160

GLOUCESTER.   No words, no words! Hush.

EDGAR.   Child Rowland to the dark tower came;°
His word was still,° "Fie, foh, and fum,
I smell the blood of a British man."°

Exeunt.

Scene V. [*Gloucester's castle.*]

Enter CORNWALL *and* EDMUND.

CORNWALL.   I will have my revenge ere I depart his house.

EDMUND.   How, my lord, I may be censured,° that nature thus gives
way to loyalty, something fears° me to think of.

---

[147]*outlawed from my blood* disowned and tainted, like a carbuncle in the corrupted
blood
[148]*late* recently
[151]*cry you mercy* I beg your pardon
[157]*soothe* humor
[158]*you on* with you
[160]*Athenian* i.e., philosopher (like "Theban")
[162]*Child . . . came* (? from a lost ballad; "child" = a candidate for knighthood;
Rowland was Charlemagne's nephew, the hero of *The Song of Roland*)
[163]*His . . . still* his motto was always
[164]*Fie . . . man* (a deliberately absurd linking of the chivalric hero with the nursery tale
of Jack the Giant-Killer)
II.v. [2]*censured* judged
[3]*something fears* somewhat frightens

CORNWALL.   I now perceive it was not altogether your brother's evil
  disposition made him seek his death; but a provoking merit, set   5
  a-work by a reprovable badness in himself.°
EDMUND.   How malicious is my fortune that I must repent to be just!
  This is the letter which he spoke of, which approves° him an intelligent party° to the advantages° of France. O heavens, that his treason
  were not! or not I the detector!   10
CORNWALL.   Go with me to the Duchess.
EDMUND.   If the matter of this paper be certain, you have mighty
  business in hand.
CORNWALL.   True or false, it hath made thee Earl of Gloucester. Seek
  out where thy father is, that he may be ready for our apprehension.°   15
EDMUND.   [Aside] If I find him comforting° the King, it will stuff his
  suspicion more fully.—I will persever° in my course of loyalty,
  though the conflict be sore between that and my blood.°
CORNWALL.   I will lay trust upon° thee, and thou shalt find a dearer
  father in my love.   20

                                                      Exeunt.

Scene VI. [*A chamber in a farmhouse adjoining the castle.*]

                    Enter KENT *and* GLOUCESTER.

GLOUCESTER.   Here is better than the open air; take it thankfully. I
  will piece out the comfort with what addition I can. I will not be long
  from you.
KENT.   All the power of his wits have given way to his impatience.° The gods reward your kindness.   5

                        Exit [GLOUCESTER].

                Enter LEAR, EDGAR, *and* FOOL.

EDGAR.   Frateretto° calls me, and tells me Nero° is an angler in the lake
  of darkness. Pray, innocent,° and beware the foul fiend.

⁶*a provoking . . . himself* a stimulating goodness in Edgar, brought into play by a
blamable badness in Gloucester
⁸*approves* proves
⁹*intelligent party* (1) spy (2) well-informed person
⁹*to the advantages* on behalf of
¹⁵*apprehension* arrest
¹⁶*comforting* supporting (a legalism)
¹⁷*persever* persevere
¹⁸*blood* natural feelings
¹⁹*lay trust upon* (1) trust (2) advance
III.vi. ⁵*impatience* raging
⁶*Frateretto* Elizabethan devil, from Harsnett's *Declaration*
⁶*Nero* (who is mentioned by Harsnett, and whose angling is reported by Chaucer in
"The Monk's Tale")
⁷*innocent* fool

FOOL.   Prithee, Nuncle, tell me whether a madman be a gentleman or
a yeoman.°
LEAR.   A king, a king.   10
FOOL.   No, he's a yeoman that has a gentleman to his son; for he's a
mad yeoman that sees his son a gentleman before him.
LEAR.   To have a thousand with red burning spits
Come hizzing° in upon 'em————
EDGAR.   The foul fiend bites my back.   15
FOOL.   He's mad that trusts in the tameness of a wolf, a horse's health,
a boy's love, or a whore's oath.
LEAR.   It shall be done; I will arraign° them straight.°
[To EDGAR] Come, sit thou here, most learned justice.°
[To the FOOL] Thou, sapient° sir, sit here. Now, you she-foxes————   20
EDGAR.   Look, where he° stands and glares. Want'st thou eyes at trial,
madam?°
Come o'er the bourn,° Bessy, to me.
FOOL.   Her boat hath a leak,
And she must not speak
Why she dares not come over to thee.°   25
EDGAR.   The foul fiend haunts Poor Tom in the voice of a nightin-
gale.° Hoppedance° cries in Tom's belly for two white herring.°
Croak° not, black angel; I have no food for thee.
KENT.   How do you, sir? Stand you not so amazed.°
Will you lie down and rest upon the cushions?   30
LEAR.   I'll see their trial first. Bring in their evidence.°
[To EDGAR] Thou, robèd man of justice, take thy place.
[To the FOOL] And thou, his yokefellow of equity,°
Bench° by his side. [To KENT] You are o' th' commission;°
Sit you too.   35

⁹yeoman farmer (just below a gentleman in rank. The Fool asks what class of man has
most indulged his children, and thus been driven mad)
¹⁴hizzing hissing
¹⁸arraign bring to trial
¹⁸straight straightaway
¹⁹justice justicer, judge
²⁰sapient wise
²¹he i.e., a fiend
²¹Want'st . . . madam (to Goneril) i.e., do you want eyes to look at you during your
trial? The fiend serves that purpose
²²bourn brook (Edgar quotes from a popular ballad)
²⁵Her . . . thee (the Fool parodies the ballad)
²⁷nightingale i.e., the Fool's singing
²⁷Hoppedance Hoberdidance (another devil from Harsnett's Declaration)
²⁷white herring unsmoked (? as against the black and sulfurous devil)
²⁸Croak rumble (because his belly is empty)
²⁹amazed astonished
³¹evidence the evidence of witnesses against them
³³yokefellow of equity partner in justice
³⁴Bench sit on the bench
³⁴commission those commissioned as king's justices

EDGAR.   Let us deal justly.
               Sleepest or wakest thou, jolly shepherd?
               Thy sheep be in the corn;°
               And for one blast of thy minikin° mouth   40
               Thy sheep shall take no harm.°
          Purr, the cat is gray.°
LEAR.   Arraign her first. 'Tis Goneril, I here take my oath before this
          honorable assembly, she kicked the poor King her father.
FOOL.   Come hither, mistress. Is your name Goneril?   45
LEAR.   She cannot deny it.
FOOL.   Cry you mercy, I took you for a joint stool.°
LEAR.   And here's another, whose warped looks proclaim
          What store° her heart is made on. Stop her there!
          Arms, arms, sword, fire! Corruption in the place!°   50
          False justicer, why hast thou let her 'scape?
EDGAR.   Bless thy five wits!
KENT.   O pity! Sir, where is the patience now
          That you so oft have boasted to retain?
EDGAR.   [Aside] My tears begin to take his part so much   55
          They mar my counterfeiting.°
LEAR.   The little dogs and all,
          Tray, Blanch, and Sweetheart—see, they bark at me.
EDGAR.   Tom will throw his head at them. Avaunt, you curs.
               Be thy mouth or black or° white,   60
               Tooth that poisons if it bite;
               Mastiff, greyhound, mongrel grim,
               Hound or spaniel, brach° or lym,°
               Or bobtail tike, or trundle-tail°———
               Tom will make him weep and wail;   65
               For, with throwing° thus my head,
               Dogs leaped the hatch,° and all are fled.

³⁹Sleepest . . . harm (probably quoted or adapted from an Elizabethan song)
³⁹corn wheat
⁴⁰minikin shrill
⁴²gray (devils were thought to assume the shape of a gray cat)
⁴⁷Cry . . . joint stool (proverbial and deliberately impudent apology for overlooking a
person. A joint stool was a low stool made by a joiner, perhaps here a stage property to
represent Goneril and in line 47, Regan. "Joint stool" can also suggest the judicial
bench; hence Goneril may be identified by the Fool, ironically, with those in power, who
judge)
⁴⁹store stuff
⁵⁰Corruption . . . place bribery in the court
⁵⁶counterfeiting i.e., feigned madness
⁶⁰or . . . or either . . . or
⁶³brach bitch
⁶³lym bloodhound (from the liam or leash with which he was led)
⁶⁴bobtail . . . trundle-tail short-tailed or long-tailed cur
⁶⁶throwing jerking (as a hound lifts its head from the ground, the scent having been
lost)
⁶⁷leaped the hatch leaped over the lower half of a divided door (i.e., left in a hurry)

Do, de, de, de. Sessa!° Come, march to wakes° and fairs and market
towns. Poor Tom, thy horn° is dry.

LEAR.   Then let them anatomize Regan. See what breeds about her   70
heart.° Is there any cause in nature that make° these hard hearts?
[*To* EDGAR] You, sir, I entertain° for one of my hundred;° only I do
not like the fashion of your garments. You will say they are Persian;° but let them be changed.

KENT.   Now, good my lord, lie here and rest awhile.   75

LEAR.   Make no noise, make no noise; draw the curtains.°
So, so. We'll go to supper i' th' morning.

FOOL.   And I'll go to bed at noon.°

Enter GLOUCESTER.

GLOUCESTER.   Come hither, friend. Where is the King my master?

KENT.   Here, sir, but trouble him not; his wits are gone.   80

GLOUCESTER.   Good friend, I prithee take him in thy arms.
I have o'erheard a plot of death upon him.
There is a litter ready; lay him in't
And drive toward Dover, friend, where thou shalt meet
Both welcome and protection. Take up thy master.   85
If thou shouldst dally half an hour, his life,
With thine and all that offer to defend him,
Stand in assurèd loss. Take up, take up,
And follow me, that will to some provision°
Give thee quick conduct.°

KENT.   Oppressèd nature sleeps.   90
This rest might yet have balmed thy broken sinews,°
Which, if convenience° will not allow,
Stand in hard cure.° [*To the Fool*] Come, help to bear thy master.
Thou must not stay behind.

GLOUCESTER.   Come, come, away!

[68]*Sessa* be off
[68]*wakes* feasts attending the dedication of a church
[69]*horn* horn bottle which the Bedlam used in begging a drink (Edgar is suggesting that
he is unable to play his role any longer)
[71]*Then . . . heart* i.e., if the Bedlam's horn is dry, let Regan, whose heart has become as
hard as horn, be dissected
[71]*make* (subjunctive)
[72]*entertain* engage
[72]*hundred* i.e., Lear's hundred knights
[74]*Persian* gorgeous (ironically of Edgar's rags)
[76]*curtains* (Lear imagines himself in bed)
[78]*And . . . noon* (the Fool's last words)
[89]*provision* maintenance
[90]*conduct* direction
[91]*balmed thy broken sinews* soothed thy racked nerves
[92]*convenience* fortunate occasion
[93]*Stand . . . cure* will be hard to cure

Exeunt [all but EDGAR].

EDGAR.   When we our betters see bearing our woes,   95
          We scarcely think our miseries our foes.°
          Who alone suffers suffers most i' th' mind,
          Leaving free° things and happy shows° behind;
          But then the mind much sufferance° doth o'erskip
          When grief hath mates, and bearing fellowship.°   100
          How light and portable° my pain seems now,
          When that which makes me bend makes the King bow.
          He childed as I fathered. Tom, away.
          Mark the high noises,° and thyself bewray°
          When false opinion, whose wrong thoughts° defile thee,   105
          In thy just proof repeals and reconciles thee.°
          What will hap more° tonight, safe 'scape the King!
          Lurk,° lurk.

                                                        [*Exit.*]

              Scene VII. [*Gloucester's castle.*]

     Enter CORNWALL, REGAN, GONERIL, EDMUND, *and* SERVANTS.

CORNWALL.   [*To* GONERIL] Post speedily to my Lord your husband;
     show him this letter. The army of France is landed. [*To* SERVANTS]
     Seek out the traitor Gloucester.

                              [*Exeunt some of the* SERVANTS.]

REGAN.   Hang him instantly.
GONERIL.   Pluck out his eyes.   5
CORNWALL.   Leave him to my displeasure. Edmund, keep you our
     sister company. The revenges we are bound° to take upon your trai-
     torous father are not fit for your beholding. Advise the Duke where
     you are going, to a most festinate° preparation. We are bound to the

---

⁹⁶*our foes* enemies peculiar to ourselves
⁹⁸*free* carefree
⁹⁸*shows* scenes
⁹⁹*sufferance* suffering
¹⁰⁰*bearing fellowship* suffering has company
¹⁰¹*portable* able to be supported or endured
¹⁰⁴*Mark the high noises* observe the rumors of strife among those in power
¹⁰⁴*bewray* reveal
¹⁰⁵*wrong thoughts* misconceptions
¹⁰⁶*In . . . thee* on the manifesting of your innocence recalls you from outlawry and
restores amity between you and your father
¹⁰⁷*What . . . more* whatever else happens
¹⁰⁸*Lurk* hide
III.vii. °*bound* (1) forced (2) purposing to
⁹*festinate* speedy

like. Our posts° shall be swift and intelligent° betwixt us. Farewell,   10
dear sister; farewell, my Lord of Gloucester.°

Enter OSWALD.

         How now? Where's the King?
OSWALD.   My Lord of Gloucester hath conveyed him hence.
    Some five or six and thirty of his knights,
    Hot questrists° after him, met him at gate;   15
    Who, with some other of the lords dependants,°
    Are gone with him toward Dover, where they boast
    To have well-armèd friends.
CORNWALL.   Get horses for your mistress.

                               [*Exit* OSWALD.]

GONERIL.   Farewell, sweet lord, and sister.   20
CORNWALL.   Edmund, farewell.

                    [*Exeunt* GONERIL *and* EDMUND.]

              Go seek the traitor Gloucester,
    Pinion him like a thief, bring him before us.

                  [*Exeunt other* SERVANTS.]

    Though well we may not pass upon° his life
    Without the form of justice, yet our power
    Shall do a court'sy to° our wrath, which men   25
    May blame, but not control.

    Enter GLOUCESTER, *brought in by two or three.*

              Who's there, the traitor?
REGAN.   Ingrateful fox, 'tis he.
CORNWALL.   Bind fast his corky° arms.
GLOUCESTER.   What means your Graces? Good my friends, consider
    You are my guests. Do me no foul play, friends.   30
CORNWALL.   Bind him, I say.

                        [*Servants bind him.*]

REGAN.   Hard, hard! O filthy traitor.
GLOUCESTER.   Unmerciful lady as you are, I'm none.
CORNWALL.   To this chair bind him. Villain, thou shalt find———

¹⁰*posts* messengers
¹⁰*intelligent* full of information
¹¹*Lord of Gloucester* i.e., Edmund, now elevated to the title
¹⁵*questrists* searchers
¹⁶*lords dependants* attendant lords (members of Lear's retinue)
²³*pass upon* pass judgment on
²⁵*do a court'sy to* indulge
²⁸*corky* sapless (because old)

[*Regan plucks his beard.°*]

GLOUCESTER.   By the kind gods, 'tis mostly ignobly done
 To pluck me by the beard.   35
REGAN.   So white, and such a traitor?
GLOUCESTER.   Naughty° lady,
 These hairs which thou dost ravish from my chin
 Will quicken° and accuse thee. I am your host.
 With robber's hands my hospitable favors°
 You should not ruffle° thus. What will you do?   40
CORNWALL.   Come, sir, what letters had you late° from France?
REGAN.   Be simple-answered,° for we know the truth.
CORNWALL.   And what confederacy have you with the traitors
 Late footed in the kingdom?
REGAN.   To whose hands you have sent the lunatic King: 45
 Speak.
GLOUCESTER.   I have a letter guessingly° set down,
 Which came from one that's of a neutral heart,
 And not from one opposed.
CORNWALL.   Cunning.
REGAN.   And false.
CORNWALL.   Where hast thou sent the King?   50
GLOUCESTER.   To Dover.
REGAN.   Wherefore to Dover? Wast thou not charged at peril°———
CORNWALL.   Wherefore to Dover? Let him answer that.
GLOUCESTER.   I am tied to th' stake, and I must stand the course.°
REGAN.   Wherefore to Dover?   55
GLOUCESTER.   Because I would not see thy cruel nails
 Pluck out his poor old eyes; nor thy fierce sister
 In his anointed° flesh rash° boarish fangs.
 The sea, with such a storm as his bare head
 In hell-black night endured, would have buoyed° up   60
 And quenched the stellèd° fires.

<hr>

[33]s.d. *plucks his beard* (a deadly insult)
[36]*Naughty* wicked
[38]*quicken* come to life
[39]*hospitable favors* face of your host
[40]*ruffle* tear at violently
[41]*late* recently
[42]*simple-answered* straightforward in answering
[47]*guessingly* without certain knowledge
[52]*charged at peril* ordered under penalty
[54]*course* coursing (in which a relay of dogs baits a bull or bear tied in the pit)
[58]*anointed* holy (because king)
[58]*rash* strike with the tusk, like a boar
[60]*buoyed* risen
[61]*stellèd* (1) fixed (as opposed to the planets or wandering stars) (2) starry

Yet, poor old heart, he holp° the heavens to rain.
If wolves had at thy gate howled that dearn° time,
Thou shouldst have said, "Good porter, turn the key."°
All cruels else subscribe.° But I shall see   65
The wingèd° vengeance overtake such children.
CORNWALL.   See't shalt thou never. Fellows, hold the chair.
Upon these eyes of thine I'll set my foot.
GLOUCESTER.   He that will think° to live till he be old,
Give me some help.—O cruel! O you gods!   70
REGAN.   One side will mock° another. Th' other too.
CORNWALL.   If you see vengeance————
FIRST SERVANT.   Hold your hand, my lord!
I have served you ever since I was a child;
But better service have I never done you   75
Than now to bid you hold.
REGAN.   How now, you dog?
FIRST SERVANT. If you did wear a beard upon your chin,
I'd shake it° on this quarrel. What do you mean!°
CORNWALL.   My villain!°

Draw and fight.

FIRST SERVANT.   Nay, then, come on, and take the chance of anger.   80
REGAN.   Give me thy sword. A peasant stand up thus?

She takes a sword and runs at him behind, kills him.

FIRST SERVANT.   O, I am slain! my lord, you have one eye left
To see some mischief° on him. O!
CORNWALL.   Lest it see more, prevent it. Out, vile jelly.
Where is thy luster now?   85
GLOUCESTER.   All dark and comfortless. Where's my son Edmund?
Edmund, enkindle all the sparks of nature°
To quit° this horrid act.
REGAN.   Out, treacherous villain,
Thou call'st on him that hates thee. It was he

[62] *holp* helped
[63] *dearn* dread
[64] *turn the key* i.e., unlock the gate
[65] *All cruels else subscribe* all cruel creatures but man are compassionate
[66] *wingèd* (1) heavenly (2) swift
[69] *will think* expects
[71] *mock* make ridiculous (because of the contrast)
[78] *shake it* (an insult comparable to Regan's plucking of Gloucester's beard)
[78] *What . . . mean* i.e., what terrible thing are you doing
[79] *villain* serf (with a suggestion of the modern meaning)
[83] *mischief* injury
[87] *enkindle . . . nature* fan your natural feeling into flame
[88] *quit* requite

That made the overture° of thy treasons to us;   90
Who is too good to pity thee.
GLOUCESTER.   O my follies! Then Edgar was abused.°
Kind gods, forgive me that, and prosper him.
REGAN.   Go thrust him out at gates, and let him smell
His way to Dover.   95

Exit [one] with Gloucester.

How is't, my lord? How look you?°

CORNWALL.   I have received a hurt. Follow me, lady.
Turn out that eyeless villain. Throw this slave
Upon the dunghill. Regan, I bleed apace.
Untimely comes this hurt. Give me your arm.

Exeunt.

SECOND SERVANT.   I'll never care what wickedness I do,   100
If this man come to good.
THIRD SERVANT.   If she live long,
And in the end meet the old course of death,°
Women will all turn monsters.
SECOND SERVANT.   Let's follow the old Earl, and get the Bedlam
To lead him where he would. His roguish madness   105
Allows itself to anything.°
THIRD SERVANT.   Go thou. I'll fetch some flax and whites of eggs
To apply to his bleeding face. Now heaven help him.

[Exeunt severally.]

ACT IV

Scene I. [*The heath.*]

Enter EDGAR.

EDGAR.   Yet better thus, and known to be contemned,°
Than still contemned and flattered. To be worst,
The lowest and most dejected° thing of fortune,
Stands still in esperance,° lives not in fear:

⁹⁰*overture* disclosure
⁹²*abused* wronged
⁹⁵*How look you* how are you
¹⁰²*meet . . . death* die the customary death of old age
¹⁰⁶*His . . . anything* his lack of all self-control leaves him open to any suggestion
IV.i. ¹*known to be contemned* conscious of being despised
³*dejected* abased
⁴*esperance* hope

The lamentable change is from the best,   5
The worst returns to laughter.° Welcome then,
Thou unsubstantial air that I embrace!
The wretch that thou hast blown unto the worst
Owes° nothing to thy blasts.

Enter GLOUCESTER, led by an OLD MAN.

                         But who comes here?
My father, poorly led?° World, world, O world!
But that thy strange mutations make us hate thee,   10
Life would not yield to age.°
OLD MAN.   O, my good lord, I have been your tenant, and your father's
    tenant, these fourscore years.
GLOUCESTER.   Away, get thee away; good friend, be gone:
Thy comforts° can do me no good at all;   15
Thee they may hurt.°
OLD MAN.   You cannot see your way.
GLOUCESTER.   I have no way and therefore want° no eyes;
I stumbled when I saw. Full oft 'tis seen,
Our means secure us, and our mere defects
Prove our commodities.° Oh, dear son Edgar,   20
The food° of thy abusèd° father's wrath!
Might I but live to see thee in° my touch,
I'd say I had eyes again!
OLD MAN.   How now! Who's there?
EDGAR.   [*Aside*] O gods! Who is 't can say "I am at the worst"?
I am worse than e'er I was.
OLD MAN.   'Tis poor mad Tom.   25
EDGAR.   [*Aside*] And worse I may be yet: the worst is not
So long as we can say "This is the worst."°
OLD MAN.   Fellow, where goest?
GLOUCESTER.   Is it a beggar-man?
OLD MAN.   Madman and beggar too.

---

[6]*returns to laughter* changes for the better
[9]*Owes* is in debt for
[9]*poorly led* (1) led like a poor man, with only one attendant (2) led by a poor man
[11]*But . . . age* we should not agree to grow old and hence die, except for the hateful
mutability of life
[15]*comforts* ministrations
[16]*hurt* injure
[17]*want* require
[20]*Our . . . commodities* our resources make us overconfident, while our afflictions make
for our advantage
[21]*food* i.e., the object on which Gloucester's anger fed
[21]*abusèd* deceived
[22]*in* i.e., with, by means of
[27]*the . . . worst* so long as a man continues to suffer (i.e., is still alive), even greater
suffering may await him

GLOUCESTER.   He has some reason,° else he could not beg.   30
I' th' last night's storm I such a fellow saw,
Which made me think a man a worm. My son
Came then into my mind, and yet my mind
Was then scarce friends with him. I have heard more since.
As flies to wanton° boys, are we to th' gods,   35
They kill us for their sport.
EDGAR.   [*Aside*]   How should this be?°
Bad is the trade that must play fool to sorrow,
Ang'ring° itself and others. Bless thee, master!
GLOUCESTER.   Is that the naked fellow?
OLD MAN.   Ay, my lord.
GLOUCESTER.   Then, prithee, get thee gone: if for my sake   40
Thou wilt o'ertake us hence a mile or twain
I' th' way toward Dover, do it for ancient° love,
And bring some covering for this naked soul,
Which I'll entreat to lead me.
OLD MAN.   Alack, sir, he is mad.
GLOUCESTER.   'Tis the times' plague,° when madmen lead the blind.   45
Do as I bid thee, or rather do thy pleasure;°
Above the rest,° be gone.
OLD MAN. I'll bring him the best 'parel° that I have,
Come on 't what will.

Exit.

GLOUCESTER.   Sirrah, naked fellow——   50
EDGAR.   Poor Tom's a-cold. [*Aside*] I cannot daub it° further.
GLOUCESTER.   Come hither, fellow.
EDGAR.   [*Aside*] And yet I must.—Bless thy sweet eyes, they bleed.
GLOUCESTER.   Know'st thou the way to Dover?
EDGAR.   Both stile and gate, horse-way and footpath. Poor Tom hath   55
been scared out of his good wits. Bless thee, good man's son, from
the foul fiend! Five fiends have been in Poor Tom at once; of lust, as
Obidicut;° Hobbididence, prince of dumbness;° Mahu, of stealing;

³⁰*reason* faculty of reasoning
³⁵*wanton* (1) playful (2) reckless
³⁶*How should this be* i.e., how can this horror be?
³⁸*Ang'ring* offending
⁴²*ancient* (1) the love the Old Man feels, by virtue of his long tenancy (2) the love that
formerly obtained between master and man
⁴⁵*times' plague* characteristic disorder of this time
⁴⁶*thy pleasure* as you like
⁴⁷*the rest* all
⁴⁸*'parel* apparel
⁵¹*daub it* lay it on (figure from plastering mortar)
⁵⁸*Obidicut* Hoberdicut, a devil (like the four that follow, from Harsnett's *Declaration*)
⁵⁸*dumbness* muteness (like the crimes and afflictions in the next lines, the result of
diabolic possession)

Modo, of murder; Flibbertigibbet, of mopping and mowing;° who   60
since possesses chambermaids and waiting-women. So, bless thee,
master!

GLOUCESTER.   Here, take this purse, thou whom the heavens' plagues
Have humbled to all strokes:° that I am wretched
Makes thee the happier. Heavens, deal so still!
Let the superfluous° and lust-dieted° man,   65
That slaves° your ordinance,° that will not see
Because he does not feel, feel your pow'r quickly;
So distribution should undo excess,°
And each man have enough. Dost thou know Dover?

EDGAR.   Ay, master.   70

GLOUCESTER.   There is a cliff whose high and bending° head
Looks fearfully° in the confinèd deep:°
Bring me but to the very brim of it,
And I'll repair the misery thou dost bear
With something rich about me: from that place   75
I shall no leading need.

EDGAR.   Give me thy arm:
Poor Tom shall lead thee.

Exeunt.

Scene II. [*Before the Duke of Albany's palace.*]

Enter GONERIL *and* EDMUND.

GONERIL.   Welcome, my lord: I marvel our mild husband
Not met° us on the way.

Enter OSWALD.

                    Now, where's your master?

OSWALD.   Madam, within; but never man so changed.
I told him of the army that was landed:
He smiled at it. I told him you were coming;
His answer was, "The worse." Of Gloucester's treachery,   5
And of the loyal service of his son

---

⁵⁹*mopping and mowing* grimacing and making faces
⁶³*humbled to all strokes* brought so low as to bear anything humbly
⁶⁵*superfluous* possessed of superfluities
⁶⁵*lust-dieted* whose lust is gratified (like Gloucester's)
⁶⁶*slaves* (1) tramples, spurns like a slave (2) ? tears, rends (Old English *slaefan*)
⁶⁶*ordinance* law
⁶⁸*So . . . excess* then the man with too much wealth would distribute it among those with too little
⁷¹*bending* overhanging
⁷²*fearfully* occasioning fear
⁷²*confinèd deep* the sea, hemmed in below
IV.ii. ²*Not met* did not meet

When I informed him, then he called me sot,°
And told me I had turned the wrong side out:
What most he should dislike seems pleasant to him;
What like,° offensive.   10
GONERIL.   [*To* EDMUND] Then shall you go no further.
It is the cowish° terror of his spirit,
That dares not undertake:° he'll not feel wrongs,
Which tie him to an answer.° Our wishes on the way
May prove effects.° Back, Edmund, to my brother;   15
Hasten his musters° and conduct his pow'rs.°
I must change names° at home and give the distaff°
Into my husband's hands. This trusty servant
Shall pass between us: ere long you are like to hear,
If you dare venture in your own behalf,   20
A mistress's° command. Wear this; spare speech;

[*Giving a favor.*]

Decline your head.° This kiss, if it durst speak,
Would stretch thy spirits up into the air:
Conceive,° and fare thee well.
EDMUND.   Yours in the ranks of death.   25
GONERIL.

My most dear Gloucester!

Exit [EDMUND].

O, the difference of man and man!
To thee a woman's services are due:
My fool usurps my body.°
OSWALD.   Madam, here comes my lord.   30

Exit.

Enter ALBANY.

7*sot* fool
10*What like* what he should like
12*cowish* cowardly
13*undertake* venture
14*tie him to an answer* oblige him to retaliate
15*Our . . . effects* our desires (that you might be my husband), as we journeyed here,
may be fulfilled
16*musters* collecting of troops
16*conduct his pow'rs* lead his army
17*change names* i.e., exchange the name of "mistress" for that of "master"
17*distaff* spinning stick (wifely symbol)
21*mistress's* lover's (and also, Albany having been disposed of, lady's or wife's)
22*Decline your head* i.e., that Goneril may kiss him
24*Conceive* understand (with a sexual implication, that includes "stretch thy spirits," l.
23; and "death," l. 25: "to die," meaning "to experience sexual intercourse")
29*My fool usurps body* my husband wrongfully enjoys me

GONERIL.   I have been worth the whistle.°
ALBANY.   O Goneril!
  You are not worth the dust which the rude wind
  Blows in your face. I fear your disposition:°
  That nature which contemns° its origin
  Cannot be bordered certain in itself;°   35
  She that herself will sliver and disbranch°
  From her material sap,° perforce must wither
  And come to deadly use.°
GONERIL.   No more; the text° is foolish.
ALBANY.   Wisdom and goodness to the vile seem vile: 40
  Filths savor but themselves.° What have you done?
  Tigers, not daughters, what have you performed?
  A father, and a gracious agèd man,
  Whose reverence even the head-lugged bear° would lick,
  Most barbarous, most degenerate, have you madded.°   45
  Could my good brother suffer you to do it?
  A man, a prince, by him so benefited!
  If that the heavens do not their visible spirits°
  Send quickly down to tame these vile offenses,
  It will come,   50
  Humanity must perforce prey on itself,
  Like monsters of the deep.
GONERIL.   Milk-livered° man!
  That bear'st a cheek for blows, a head for wrongs;
  Who hast not in thy brows an eye discerning
  Thine honor from thy suffering;° that not know'st   55
  Fools do those villains pity who are punished
  Ere they have done their mischief.° Where's thy drum?
  France spreads his banners in our noiseless° land,

---

[31]*I . . . whistle* i.e., once you valued me (the proverb is implied, "It is a poor dog that is not worth the whistling")
[33]*disposition* nature
[34]*contemns* despises
[35]*bordered . . . itself* kept within its normal bounds
[36]*sliver and disbranch* cut off
[37]*material sap* essential and life-giving sustenance
[38]*come to deadly use* i.e., be as a dead branch for the burning
[39]*text* i.e., on which your sermon is based
[41]*Filths savor but themselves* the filthy relish only the taste of filth
[44]*head-lugged bear* bear-baited by the dogs, and hence enraged
[45]*madded* made mad
[48]*visible spirits* avenging spirits in material form
[52]*Milk-livered* lily-livered (hence cowardly, the liver being regarded as the seat of courage)
[55]*discerning . . . suffering* able to distinguish between insults that ought to be resented, and ordinary pain that is to be borne
[57]*Fools . . . mischief* only fools are sorry for criminals whose intended criminality is prevented by punishment
[58]*noiseless* i.e., the drum, signifying preparation for war, is silent

With plumèd helm° thy state begins to threat,°
Whilst thou, a moral° fool, sits still and cries
"Alack, why does he so?"

ALBANY.   See thyself, devil!
Proper° deformity seems not in the fiend
So horrid as in woman.

GONERIL.   O vain fool!

ALBANY.   Thou changèd and self-covered° thing, for shame,
Be-monster not thy feature.° Were 't my fitness°
To let these hands obey my blood,°
They are apt enough to dislocate and tear
Thy flesh and bones: howe'er° thou art a fiend,
A woman's shape doth shield thee.

GONERIL.   Marry,° your manhood mew°———   70

Enter a MESSENGER.

ALBANY.   What news?

MESSENGER.   O, my good lord, the Duke of Cornwall's dead,
Slain by his servant, going to° put out
The other eye of Gloucester.

ALBANY.   Gloucester's eyes!

MESSENGER.   A servant that he bred,° thrilled with remorse,°   75
Opposed against the act, bending his sword
To his great master, who thereat enraged
Flew on him, and amongst them felled° him dead,
But not without that harmful stroke which since
Hath plucked him after.°

ALBANY.   This shows you are above,   80
You justicers,° that these our nether° crimes

60 *helm* helmet
59 *thy . . . threat* France begins to threaten Albany's realm
60 *moral* moralizing; but also with the implication that morality and folly are one
62 *Proper* (1) natural (to a fiend) (2) fair-appearing
64 *changèd and self-covered* i.e., transformed, by the contorting of her woman's face, on which appears the fiendish behavior she has allowed herself. (Goneril has disguised nature by wickedness)
65 *Be-monster not thy feature* do not change your appearance into a fiend's
65 *my fitness* appropriate for me
66 *blood* passion
68 *howe'er* but even if
70 *Marry* by the Virgin Mary
70 *your manhood mew* (1) coop up or confine your (pretended) manhood (2) molt or shed it, if that is what is supposed to "shield" me from you
73 *going to* as he was about to
75 *bred* reared
75 *thrilled with remorse* pierced by compassion
78 *amongst them felled* others assisting, they felled
80 *plucked him after* i.e., brought Cornwall to death with his servant
81 *justicers* judges
81 *nether* committed below (on earth)

So speedily can venge.° But, O poor Gloucester!
Lost he his other eye?
MESSENGER.   Both, both, my lord.
This letter, madam, craves° a speedy answer;
'Tis from your sister.
GONERIL.   [*Aside*]   One way I like this well;   85
But being widow, and my Gloucester with her,
May all the building in my fancy pluck
Upon my hateful life.° Another way,°
The news is not so tart.°—I'll read, and answer.

                                                    Exit.

ALBANY.   Where was his son when they did take his eyes?   90
MESSENGER.   Come with my lady hither.
ALBANY.   He is not here.
MESSENGER.   No, my good lord; I met him back° again.
ALBANY.   Knows he the wickedness?
MESSENGER.   Ay, my good lord; 'twas he informed against him,
And quit the house on purpose, that their punishment   95
Might have the freer course.
ALBANY.   Gloucester, I live
To thank thee for the love thou showed'st the King,
And to revenge thine eyes. Come hither, friend:
Tell me what more thou know'st.

                                                    Exeunt.

Scene III. [*The French camp near Dover.*]

Enter KENT *and a* GENTLEMAN.

KENT.   Why the King of France is so suddenly gone back, know you
    no reason?
GENTLEMAN.   Something he left imperfect in the state,° which since
    his coming forth is thought of, which imports° to the kingdom so
    much fear and danger that his personal return was most required and   5
    necessary.
KENT.   Who hath he left behind him general?

---

⁸²*venge* avenge
⁸⁴*craves* demands
⁸⁸*May . . . life* these things (1.84) may send my future hopes, my castles in air, crashing
down upon the hateful (married) life I lead now
⁸⁸*Another way* looked at another way
⁸⁹*tart* sour
⁹²*back* going back
IV.iii. ³*imperfect in the state* unsettled in his own kingdom
⁴*imports* portends

GENTLEMAN.   The Marshal of France, Monsieur La Far.

KENT.   Did your letters pierce° the queen to any dem-
onstration of grief?   10

GENTLEMAN.   Ay, sir; she took them, read them in my presence,
And now and then an ample tear trilled° down
Her delicate cheek: it seemed she was a queen
Over her passion, who most rebel-like
Sought to be king o'er her.

KENT.   O, then it moved her.   15

GENTLEMAN.   Not to a rage: patience and sorrow strove
Who should express her goodliest.° You have seen
Sunshine and rain at once: her smiles and tears
Were like a better way:° those happy smilets°
That played on her ripe lip seemed not to know   20
What guests were in her eyes, which parted thence
As pearls from diamonds dropped. In brief,
Sorrow would be a rarity most belovèd,
If all could so become it.°

KENT.   Made she no verbal question?

GENTLEMAN.   Faith, once or twice she heaved° the name of "father"   25
Pantingly forth, as if it pressed her heart;
Cried "Sisters! Sisters! Shame of ladies! Sisters!
Kent! Father! Sisters! What, i' th' storm? i' th' night?
Let pity not be believed!"° There she shook   30
The holy water from her heavenly eyes,
And clamor moistened:° then away she started
To deal with grief alone.

KENT.   It is the stars,
The stars above us, govern our conditions;°
Else one self mate and make could not beget   35
Such different issues.° You spoke not with her since?

GENTLEMAN.   No.

KENT.   Was this before the King returned?

GENTLEMAN.   No, since.

KENT.   Well, sir, the poor distressèd Lear's i' th' town;

---

⁹*pierce* impel
¹²*trilled* trickled
¹⁷*Who . . . goodliest* which should give her the most becoming expression
¹⁹*Were like a better way* i.e., improved on that spectacle
¹⁹*smilets* little smiles
²⁴*Sorrow . . . it* sorrow would be a coveted jewel if it became others as it does her
²⁵*heaved* expressed with difficulty
³⁰*Let pity not be believed* let it not be believed for pity
³²*clamor moistened* moistened clamor, i.e., mixed (and perhaps assuaged) her outcries with tears
³⁴*govern our conditions* determine what we are
³⁶*Else . . . issues* otherwise the same husband and wife could not produce such different children

Who sometime in his better tune° remembers   40
What we are come about, and by no means
Will yield to see his daughter.
GENTLEMAN.   Why, good sir?
KENT.   A sovereign° shame so elbows° him: his own unkindness
That stripped her from his benediction, turned her
To foreign casualties,° gave her dear rights   45
To his dog-hearted daughters: these things sting
His mind so venomously that burning shame
Detains him from Cordelia.
GENTLEMAN.   Alack, poor gentleman!
KENT.   Of Albany's and Cornwall's powers you heard not?
GENTLEMAN.   'Tis so;° they are afoot.   50
KENT.   Well, sir, I'll bring you to our master Lear,
And leave you to attend him: some dear cause°
Will in concealment wrap me up awhile;
When I am known aright, you shall not grieve
Lending me this acquaintance. I pray you, go   55
Along with me.

                                        [*Exeunt.*]

                Scene IV. [*The same. A tent.*]

    Enter, with drum and colors, CORDELIA, DOCTOR, *and* SOLDIERS.

CORDELIA.   Alack, 'tis he: why, he was met even now
As mad as the vexed sea; singing aloud;
Crowned with rank femiter and furrow-weeds,
With hardocks, hemlock, nettles, cuckoo-flow'rs,
Darnel,° and all the idle weeds that grow   5
In our sustaining corn.° A century° send forth;
Search every acre in the high-grown field,
And bring him to our eye [*Exit an* OFFICER.] What can man's
    wisdom°

---

⁴⁰*better tune* composed, less jangled intervals
⁴³*sovereign* overpowering
⁴³*elbows* jogs his elbow i.e., reminds him
⁴⁵*casualties* chances
⁵⁰*'Tis so* i.e., I have heard of them
⁵²*dear cause* important reason
IV.iv. ³⁻⁵*femiter . . . Darnel: femiter* fumitory, whose leaves and juice are bitter;
furrow-weeds weeds that grow in the furrow; or plowed land; *hardocks* ? hoar or white
docks, burdocks, harlocks; *hemlock* a poison; *nettles* plants which sting and burn;
cuckoo-flow'rs identified with a plant employed to remedy diseases of the brain; *Darnel*
tares, noisome weeds
⁶*sustaining corn* life-maintaining wheat
⁶*century* ? sentry; troop of a hundred soldiers
⁸*What can man's wisdom* what can science accomplish

In the restoring his bereavèd° sense?
He that helps him take all my outward° worth.   10
DOCTOR.   There is means, madam:
   Our foster-nurse° of nature is repose,
   The which he lacks: that to provoke° in him,
   Are many simples operative,° whose power
   Will close the eye of anguish.
CORDELIA.   All blest secrets,   15
   All you unpublished virtues° of the earth,
   Spring with my tears! be aidant and remediate°
   In the good man's distress! Seek, seek for him,
   Lest his ungoverned rage dissolve the life
   That wants the means to lead it.°

Enter MESSENGER.

MESSENGER.   News, madam;   20
   The British pow'rs are marching hitherward.
CORDELIA.   'Tis known before. Our preparation stands
   In expectation of them. O dear father,
   It is thy business that I go about;
   Therefore° great France   25
   My mourning and importuned° tears hath pitied.
   No blown° ambition doth our arms incite,
   But love, dear love, and our aged father's right:
   Soon may I hear and see him!

Exeunt.

Scene V. [*Gloucester's castle.*]

Enter REGAN *and* OSWALD.

REGAN.   But are my brother's pow'rs set forth?
OSWALD.   Ay, madam.
REGAN.   Himself in person there?
OSWALD.   Madam, with much ado:°
   Your sister is the better soldier.

⁹*bereavèd* impaired
¹⁰*outward* material
¹²*foster-nurse* fostering nurse
¹³*provoke* induce
¹⁴*simples operative* efficacious medicinal herbs
¹⁶*unpublished virtues* i.e., secret remedial herbs
¹⁷*remediate* remedial
²⁰*wants . . . it* i.e., lacks the reason to control the rage
²⁵*Therefore* because of that
²⁶*importuned* importunate
²⁷*blown* puffed up
IV.v. ²*ado* bother and persuasion

REGAN.   Lord Edmund spake not with your lord at home?
OSWALD.   No, madam.   5
REGAN.   What might import° my sister's letter to him?
OSWALD.   I know not, lady.
REGAN.   Faith, he is posted° hence on serious matter.
      It was great ignorance,° Gloucester's eyes being out,
      To let him live. Where he arrives he moves   10
      All hearts against us: Edmund, I think, is gone,
      In pity of his misery, to dispatch
      His nighted° life; moreover, to descry
      The strength o' th' enemy.
OSWALD.   I must needs after him, madam, with my letter.   15
REGAN.   Our troops set forth tomorrow: stay with us;
      The ways are dangerous.
OSWALD.   I may not, madam:
      My lady charged my duty° in this business.
REGAN.   Why should she write to Edmund? Might not you
      Transport her purposes° by word? Belike,°   20
      Some things I know not what. I'll love thee much,
      Let me unseal the letter.
OSWALD.   Madam, I had rather———
REGAN.   I know your lady does not love her husband;
      I am sure of that: and at her late° being here
      She gave strange eliads° and most speaking looks   25
      To noble Edmund. I know you are of her bosom.°
OSWALD.   I, madam?
REGAN.   I speak in understanding: y'are; I know 't:
      Therefore I do advise you, take this note:°
      My lord is dead; Edmund and I have talked;   30
      And more convenient° is he for my hand
      Than for your lady's: you may gather more.°
      If you do find him, pray you, give him this;°
      And when your mistress hears thus much from you,

---

⁶*import* purport, carry as its message
⁸*is posted* has ridden speedily
⁹*ignorance* folly
¹³*nighted* (1) darkened, because blinded (2) benighted
¹⁸*charged my duty* ordered me as a solemn duty
²⁰*Transport her purposes* convey her intentions
²⁰*Belike* probably
²⁴*late* recently
²⁵*eliads* amorous looks
²⁶*of her bosom* in her confidence
²⁹*take this note* take note of this
³¹*convenient* fitting
³²*gather more* surmise more yourself
³³*this* this advice

I pray, desire her call° her wisdom to her.   35
So, fare you well.
If you do chance to hear of that blind traitor,
Preferment° falls on him that cuts him off.
OSWALD.   Would I could meet him, madam! I should show
   What party I do follow.
REGAN.   Fare thee well.   40

Exeunt.

Scene VI. [*Fields near Dover.*]

Enter GLOUCESTER *and* EDGAR.

GLOUCESTER.   When shall I come to th' top of that same hill?
EDGAR.   You do climb up it now. Look, how we labor.
GLOUCESTER.   Methinks the ground is even.
EDGAR.   Horrible steep.
   Hark, do you hear the sea?
GLOUCESTER.   No, truly.
EDGAR.   Why then your other senses grow imperfect   5
   By your eyes' anguish.°
GLOUCESTER.   So may it be indeed.
   Methinks thy voice is altered, and thou speak'st
   In better phrase and matter than thou didst.
EDGAR.   Y'are much deceived: in nothing am I changed
   But in my garments.
GLOUCESTER.   Methinks y'are better spoken.   10
EDGAR.   Come on, sir; here's the place: stand still. How fearful
   And dizzy 'tis to cast one's eyes so low!
   The crows and choughs° that wing the midway air°
   Show scarce so gross° as beetles. Half way down
   Hangs one that gathers sampire,° dreadful trade!   15
   Methinks he seems no bigger than his head.
   The fishermen that walk upon the beach
   Appear like mice; and yond tall anchoring° bark
   Diminished to her cock;° her cock, a buoy
   Almost too small for sight. The murmuring surge   20

___

35*call* recall
38*Preferment* promotion
IV.vi. °*anguish* pain
13*choughs* a kind of crow
13*midway air* i.e., halfway down the cliff
14*gross* large
15*sampire* samphire, an aromatic herb associated with Dover Cliffs
18*anchoring* anchored
19*cock* cockboat, a small boat usually towed behind the ship

That on th' unnumb'red idle pebble° chafes
Cannot be heard so high. I'll look no more,
Lest my brain turn and the deficient sight
Topple° down headlong.

GLOUCESTER.   Set me where you stand.

EDGAR.   Give me your hand: you are now within a foot   25
Of th' extreme verge: for all beneath the moon
Would I not leap upright.°

GLOUCESTER.   Let go my hand.
Here, friend, 's another purse; in it a jewel
Well worth a poor man's taking. Fairies° and gods
Prosper it with thee! Go thou further off;   30
Bid me farewell, and let me hear thee going.

EDGAR.   Now fare ye well, good sir.

GLOUCESTER.   With all my heart.

EDGAR.   [Aside] Why I do trifle thus with his despair
Is done to cure it.°

GLOUCESTER.   O you mighty gods!

He kneels.

This world I do renounce, and in your sights   35
Shake patiently my great affliction off:
If I could bear it longer and not fall
To quarrel° with your great opposeless° wills,
My snuff° and loathèd part of nature should
Burn itself out. If Edgar live, O bless him!   40
Now, fellow, fare thee well.

He falls.

EDGAR.   Gone, sir, farewell.
And yet I know not how° conceit° may rob
The treasury of life, when life itself
Yields to° the theft. Had he been where he thought,
By this had thought been past. Alive or dead?   45
Ho, you sir! friend! Hear you, sir! speak!

---

[21]*unnumb'red idle pebble* innumerable pebbles, moved to and fro by the waves to no purpose
[24]*the deficient sight/Topple* my failing sight topple me
[27]*upright* i.e., even up in the air, to say nothing of forward, over the cliff
[29]*Fairies* (who are supposed to guard and multiply hidden treasure)
[34]*Why . . . it* I play on his despair in order to cure it
[38]*fall/To quarrel with* rebel against
[38]*opposeless* not to be, and not capable of being, opposed
[39]*snuff* the guttering (and stinking) wick of a burnt-out candle
[42]*how* but what
[42]*conceit* imagination
[44]*Yields to* allows

    Thus might he pass° indeed: yet he revives.
    What are you, sir?
GLOUCESTER.   Away, and let me die.
EDGAR.   Hadst thou been aught but gossamer, feathers, air,
    So many fathom down precipitating,°   50
    Thou'dst shivered like an egg: but thou dost breathe;
    Hast heavy substance; bleed'st not; speak'st; art sound.
    Ten masts at each° make not the altitude
    Which thou hast perpendicularly fell:
    Thy life's° a miracle. Speak yet again.   55
GLOUCESTER.   But have I fall'n, or no?
EDGAR.   From the dread summit of this chalky bourn.°
    Look up a-height;° the shrill-gorged° lark so far
    Cannot be seen or heard: do but look up.
GLOUCESTER.   Alack, I have no eyes.   60
    Is wretchedness deprived that benefit,
    To end itself by death? 'Twas yet some comfort,
    When misery could beguile° the tyrant's rage
    And frustrate his proud will.
EDGAR.   Give me your arm.
    Up, so. How is 't? Feel you° your legs? You stand.   65
GLOUCESTER.   Too well, too well.
EDGAR.   This is above all strangeness.
    Upon the crown o' th' cliff, what thing was that
    Which parted from you?
GLOUCESTER.   A poor unfortunate beggar.
EDGAR.   As I stood here below, me thought his eyes
    Were two full moons; he had a thousand noses,   70
    Horns whelked° and waved like the enridgèd° sea:
    It was some fiend; therefore, thou happy father,°
    Think that the clearest° gods, who make them honors
    Of men's impossibilities,° have preserved thee.

---

[47]*pass* die
[50]*precipitating* falling
[53]*at each* one on top of the other
[55]*life's* survival
[57]*bourn* boundary
[58]*a-height* on high
[58]*gorged* throated, voiced
[63]*beguile* cheat (i.e., by suicide)
[65]*Feel you* have you any feeling in
[71]*whelked* twisted
[71]*enridgèd* i.e., furrowed into waves
[72]*happy father* fortunate old man
[73]*clearest* purest
[74]*who . . . impossibilities* who cause themselves to be honored and revered by performing miracles of which men are incapable

GLOUCESTER.   I do remember now: henceforth I'll bear   75
    Affliction till it do cry out itself
    "Enough, enough," and die. That thing you speak of,
    I took it for a man; often 'twould say
    "The fiend, the fiend"—he led me to that place.

EDGAR.   Bear free° and patient thoughts.   80

        Enter LEAR [*fantastically dressed with wild flowers*].

                             But who comes here?
    The safer° sense will ne'er accommodate°
    His master thus.

LEAR.   No, they cannot touch me for coining;° I am the King himself.

EDGAR.   O thou side-piercing sight!

LEAR.   Nature's above art in that respect.° There's your press-
    money.° That fellow handles his bow like a crow-keeper;° draw me a   85
    clothier's yard.° Look, look, a mouse! Peace, peace; this piece of
    toasted cheese will do 't. There's my gauntlet;° I'll prove it on° a giant.
    Bring up the brown bills.° O, well flown,° bird! i' th' clout, i' th'
    clout:° hewgh!° Give the word.°

EDGAR.   Sweet marjoram.°   90

LEAR.   Pass.

GLOUCESTER.   I know that voice.

LEAR.   Ha! Goneril, with a white beard! They flattered me like a
    dog,° and told me I had white hairs in my beard ere the black ones
    were there.° To say "ay" and "no" to everything that I said! "Ay"   95
    and "no" too was no good divinity.° When the rain came to wet me

---

[80] *free* i.e., emancipated from grief and despair, which fetter the soul
[80] *safer* sounder, saner
[80] *accommodate* dress, adorn
[82] *touch me for coining* arrest me for minting coins (the king's prerogative)
[84] *Nature's . . . respect* i.e., a born king is superior to legal (and hence artificial)
inhibition. There is also a glance here at the popular Renaissance debate, concerning the
relative importance of nature (inspiration) and art (training)
[85] *press-money* (paid to conscripted soldiers)
[85] *crow-keeper* a farmer scaring away crows
[86] *clothier's yard* (the standard English arrow was a cloth-yard long. Here the injunction
is to draw the arrow back, like a powerful archer, a full yard to the ear)
[87] *gauntlet* armored glove, thrown down as a challenge
[87] *prove it on* maintain my challenge even against
[88] *brown bills* halberds varnished to prevent rust (here the reference is to the soldiers
who carry them)
[88] *well flown* (falconer's cry; and perhaps a reference to the flight of the arrow)
[89] *clout* the target shot at
[89] *hewgh* ? imitating the whizzing of the arrow
[89] *word* password
[90] *Sweet marjoram* herb, used as a remedy for brain disease
[94] *like a dog* as a dog flatters
[94-95] *I . . . there* I was wise before I had even grown a beard
[96] *no good divinity* (bad theology, because contrary to the Biblical saying
[II Corinthians 1:18], "Our word toward you was not yea and nay." See also James 5:12

once and the wind to make me chatter; when the thunder would not
peace at my bidding; there I found 'em, there I smelt 'em out. Go to,
they are not men o' their words: they told me I was everything; 'tis
a lie, I am not ague-proof.°   100

GLOUCESTER.   The trick° of that voice I do well remember:
Is't not the king?

LEAR.   Ay, every inch a king.
When I do stare, see how the subject quakes.
I pardon that man's life. What was thy cause?°
Adultery?   105
Thou shalt not die: die for adultery! No:
The wren goes to 't, and the small gilded fly
Does lecher° in my sight.
Let copulation thrive; for Gloucester's bastard son
Was kinder to his father than my daughters   110
Got° 'tween the lawful sheets.
To 't, luxury,° pell-mell! for I lack soldiers.°
Behold yond simp'ring dame,
Whose face between her forks presages snow,°
That minces° virtue and does shake the head   115
To hear of pleasure's name.°
The fitchew,° nor the soilèd° horse, goes to 't
With a more riotous appetite.
Down from the waist they are Centaurs,°
Though women all above: 120
But to the girdle° do the gods inherit,°
Beneath is all the fiend's.
There's hell, there's darkness, there is the sulphurous pit,
Burning, scalding, stench, consumption; fie, fie, fie! pah, pah! Give me

---

"But let your yea be yea, and your nay, nay; lest ye fall into condemnation"; and
Matthew 5:36–37)
100*ague-proof* secure against fever
101*trick* intonation
104*cause* offense
108*lecher* copulate
111*Got* begot
112*luxury* lechery
112*for . . . soldiers* i.e., ? (1) whom copulation will supply (2) and am therefore
powerless
114*Whose . . . snow* whose cold demeanor seems to promise chaste behavior ("forks":
legs)
115*minces* squeamishly pretends to
116*pleasure's name* the very name of sexual pleasure
117*fitchew* polecat (and slang for "prostitute")
117*soilèd* put to pasture, and hence wanton with feeding
119*Centaurs* lustful creatures, half man and half horse
121*girdle* waist
121*inherit* possess

an ounce of civet;° good apothecary, sweeten my imagination: there's
money for thee.

GLOUCESTER.   O, let me kiss that hand!   125

LEAR.   Let me wipe it first; it smells of mortality.°

GLOUCESTER.   O ruined piece of nature! This great world
Shall so wear out to nought.° Dost thou know me?

LEAR.   I remember thine eyes well enough. Dost thou squiny° at me?
No, do thy worst, blind Cupid;° I'll not love. Read thou this chal-   130
lenge;° mark but the penning of it.

GLOUCESTER.   Were all thy letters suns, I could not see.

EDGAR.   I would not take° this from report: it is,
And my heart breaks at it.

LEAR.   Read.   135

GLOUCESTER.   What, with the case° of eyes?

LEAR.   O, ho, are you there with me?° No eyes in your head, nor no
money in your purse? Your eyes are in a heavy case,° your purse in
a light,° yet you see how this world goes.

GLOUCESTER.   I see it feelingly.°   140

LEAR.   What, art mad? A man may see how this world goes with no
eyes. Look with thine ears: see how yond justice rails upon yond
simple° thief. Hark, in thine ear: change places, and, handy-
dandy,° which is the justice, which is the thief? Thou hast seen a
farmer's dog bark at a beggar?   145

GLOUCESTER.   Ay, sir.

LEAR.   And the creature run from the cur? There thou mightst behold
the great image of authority:° a dog's obeyed in office.°
Thou rascal beadle,° hold thy bloody hand!
Why dost thou lash that whore? Strip thy own back;   150
Thou hotly lusts to use her in that kind°

---

[124]*civet* perfume
[126]*mortality* (1) death (2) existence
[128]*This . . . nought* i.e., the universe (macrocosm) will decay to nothing in the same way
as the little world of man (microcosm)
[129]*squiny* squint, look sideways, like a prostitute
[130]*blind Cupid* the sign hung before a brothel
[131]*challenge* a reminiscence of ll. 89–90
[133]*take* believe
[136]*case* empty sockets
[137]*are . . . me* is that what you tell me
[138]*heavy case* sad plight (pun on l. 136)
[139]*light* i.e., empty
[140]*feelingly* (1) by touch (2) by feeling pain (3) with emotion
[143]*simple* common, of low estate
[144]*handy-dandy* i.e., choose, guess (after the children's game—"Handy-dandy, prickly
prandy"—of choosing the right hand)
[148]*image of authority* symbol revealing the true meaning of authority
[148]*a . . . office* i.e., whoever has power is obeyed
[149]*beadle* parish constable
[151]*kind* i.e., sexual act

For which thou whip'st her. The usurer hangs the cozener.°
Through tattered clothes small vices do appear;
Robes and furred gowns° hide all. Plate sin with gold,
And the strong lance of justice hurtless° breaks;   155
Arm it in rags, a pygmy's straw does pierce it.
None does offend, none, I say, none; I'll able° 'em:
Take that° of me, my friend, who have the power
To seal th' accuser's lips. Get thee glass eyes,°
And, like a scurvy politician,° seem   160
To see the things thou dost not. Now, now, now, now.
Pull off my boots: harder, harder: so.
EDGAR.   O, matter and impertinency° mixed!
  Reason in madness!
LEAR.   If thou wilt weep my fortunes, take my eyes.   165
  I know thee well enough; thy name is Gloucester:
  Thou must be patient; we came crying hither:
  Thou know'st, the first time that we smell the air
  We wawl and cry. I will preach to thee: mark.
GLOUCESTER.   Alack, alack the day!   170
LEAR.   When we are born, we cry that we are come
  To this great stage of fools. This'° a good block.°
  It were a delicate° stratagem, to shoe
  A troop of horse with felt: I'll put 't in proof;°
  And when I have stol'n upon these son-in-laws,   175
  Then, kill, kill, kill, kill, kill, kill!

Enter a GENTLEMAN [*with* ATTENDANTS].

GENTLEMAN.   O, here he is: lay hand upon him. Sir,
  Your most dear daughter————
LEAR.   No rescue? What, a prisoner? I am even

---

¹⁵²*The usurer . . . cozener* i.e., the powerful moneylender, in his role as judge, puts to
death the petty cheat
¹⁵⁴*Robes and furred gowns* (worn by a judge)
¹⁵⁵*hurtless* i.e., without hurting the sinner
¹⁵⁷*able* vouch for
¹⁵⁸*that* (the immunity just conferred) (l. 154)
¹⁵⁹*glass eyes* spectacles
¹⁶⁰*scurvy politician* vile politic man
¹⁶³*matter and impertinency* sense and nonsense
¹⁷²*This'* this is
¹⁷²*block* (various meanings have been suggested, for example, the stump of a tree, on
which Lear is supposed to climb; a mounting-block, which suggests "horse" 1. 174; a
hat [which Lear or another must be made to wear], from the block on which a felt hat
is molded, and which would suggest a "felt" 1. 174. The proposal here is that "block"
be taken to denote the quintain, whose function is to bear blows, . . . an object shaped
like a man and used for tilting practice.
¹⁷³*delicate* subtle
¹⁷⁴*put 't in proof* test it

The natural fool° of fortune. Use me well;   180
You shall have ransom. Let me have surgeons;
I am cut° to th' brains.

GENTLEMAN.   You shall have anything.

LEAR.   No seconds?° all myself?
Why, this would make a man a man of salt,°
To use his eyes for garden water-pots,   185
Ay, and laying autumn's dust.

GENTLEMAN.   Good sir———

LEAR.   I will die bravely,° like a smug° bridegroom.° What!
I will be jovial: come, come; I am a king;
Masters, know you that?   190

GENTLEMAN.   You are a royal one, and we obey you.

LEAR.   Then there's life in 't.° Come, and you get it, you shall get it
by running. Sa, sa, sa, sa.°

Exit [*running;* ATTENDANTS *follow*].

GENTLEMAN.   A sight most pitiful in the meanest wretch,
Past speaking of in a king! Thou hast one daughter   195
Who redeems nature from the general curse
Which twain have brought her to.°

EDGAR.   Hail, gentle° sir.

GENTLEMAN.   Sir, speed° you: what's your will?

EDGAR.   Do you hear aught, sir, of a battle toward?°

GENTLEMAN.   Most sure and vulgar:° every one hears that,   200
Which can distinguish sound.

EDGAR.   But, by your favor,
How near's the other army?

GENTLEMAN.   Near and on speedy foot; the main descry
Stands on the hourly thought.°

EDGAR.   I thank you, sir: that's all.

¹⁸⁰*natural fool* born sport (with pun on "natural": "imbecile")
¹⁸²*cut* wounded
¹⁸³*seconds* supporters
¹⁸⁴*man of salt* i.e., all (salt) tears
¹⁸⁸*bravely* (1) smartly attired (2) courageously
¹⁸⁸*smug* spick and span
¹⁸⁸*bridegroom* whose "brave" sexual feats are picked up in the pun on "die"
¹⁹²*there's life in 't* there's still hope
¹⁹³*Sa . . . sa* hunting and rallying cry; also an interjection of defiance
¹⁹⁷*general . . . to* (1) universal condemnation which Goneril and Regan have made for
(2) damnation incurred by the original sin of Adam and Eve
¹⁹⁸*gentle* noble
¹⁹⁸*speed* God speed
¹⁹⁹*toward* impending
²⁰⁰*vulgar* common knowledge
²⁰⁴*the . . . thought* we expect to see the main body of the army any
hour

GENTLEMAN.   Though that the Queen on special cause is here,   205
    Her army is moved on.
EDGAR.   I thank you, sir.

                                     Exit [GENTLEMAN].

GLOUCESTER.   You ever-gentle gods, take my breath from me;
    Let not my worser spirit° tempt me again
    To die before you please.
EDGAR.   Well pray you, father.
GLOUCESTER.   Now, good sir, what are you?   210
EDGAR.   A most poor man, made tame° to fortune's blows;
    Who, by the art of known and feeling sorrows,°
    Am pregnant° to good pity. Give me your hand,
    I'll lead you to some biding.°
GLOUCESTER.   Hearty thanks;
    The bounty and the benison° of heaven   215
    To boot, and boot.°

                Enter OSWALD.

OSWALD.   A proclaimed prize°! Most happy!°
    That eyeless head of thine was first framed° flesh
    To raise my fortunes. Thou old unhappy traitor,
    Briefly thyself remember:° the sword is out
    That must destroy thee.   220
GLOUCESTER.   Now let thy friendly° hand   220
    Put strength enough to 't.

                [EDGAR *interposes.*]

OSWALD.   Wherefore, bold peasant,
    Dar'st thou support a published° traitor? Hence!
    Lest that th' infection of his fortune take
    Like hold on thee. Let go his arm.
EDGAR.   Chill° not let go, zir, without vurther 'casion.°   225
OSWALD.   Let go, slave, or thou diest!

208*worser spirit* bad angel, evil side of my nature
211*tame* submissive
212*art . . . sorrows* instruction of sorrows painfully experienced
213*pregnant* disposed
214*biding* place of refuge
215*benison* blessing
216*To boot, and boot* also, and in the highest degree
216*proclaimed prize* i.e., one with a price on his head
216*happy* fortunate (for Oswald)
217*framed* created
219*thyself remember* i.e., pray, think of your sins
220*friendly* i.e., because it offers the death Gloucester covets
222*published* proclaimed
225*Chill . . .* (Edgar speaks in rustic dialect)
225*vurther 'casion* further occasion

EDGAR.   Good gentleman, go your gait,° and let poor volk° pass. And
    chud ha' bin zwaggered° out of my life, 'twould not ha' bin zo long
    as 'tis by a vortnight. Nay, come not near th' old man; keep out, che
    vor' ye,° or I'se° try whether your costard° or my ballow° be the   230
    harder: chill be plain with you.
OSWALD.   Out, dunghill!

                                                        They fight.

EDGAR.   Chill pick your teeth,° zir: come; no matter vor your
    foins.°

                                                        [OSWALD *falls.*]

OSWALD.   Slave, thou hast slain me. Villain, take my purse: 235
    If ever thou wilt thrive, bury my body,
    And give the letters which thou find'st about° me
    To Edmund Earl of Gloucester; seek him out
    Upon the English party.° O, untimely death!
    Death!   240

                                                        He dies.

EDGAR.   I know thee well. A serviceable° villain,
    As duteous° to the vices of thy mistress
    As badness would desire.
GLOUCESTER.   What, is he dead?
EDGAR.   Sit you down, father; rest you.
    Let's see these pockets: the letters that he speaks of   245
    May be my friends. He's dead; I am only sorry
    He had no other deathsman.° Let us see:
    Leave,° gentle wax;° and, manners, blame us not:
    To know our enemies' minds, we rip their hearts;
    Their papers° is more lawful.   250

227*gait* way
227*volk* folk
228*And chud ha' bin zwaggered* if I could have been swaggered
230*Che vor' ye* I warrant you
230*I'se* I shall
230*costard* head (literally, "apple")
230*ballow* cudgel
233*Chill pick your teeth* I will knock your teeth out
234*foins* thrusts
237*about* upon
239*party* side
241*serviceable* ready to be used
242*duteous* obedient
247*deathsman* executioner
248*Leave* by your leave
248*wax* (with which the letter is sealed)
250*Their papers* i.e., to rip their papers

Reads the letter.

"Let our reciprocal vows be remembered. You have many
opportunities to cut him off: if your will want not,° time and
place will be fruitfully offered. There is nothing done, if he
return the conqueror: then am I the prisoner, and his bed my
jail; from the loathed warmth whereof deliver me, and supply the   255
place for your labor.
"Your—wife, so I would° say—affectionate servant, and for you
her own for venture,°

                                              'Goneril.' "

O indistinguished space of woman's will!°
A plot upon her virtuous husband's life;
And the exchange° my brother! Here in the sands   260
Thee I'll rake up,° the post unsanctified°
Of murderous lechers; and in the mature° time,
With this ungracious paper° strike° the sight
Of the death-practiced° Duke: for him 'tis well
That of thy death and business I can tell.   265
GLOUCESTER.   The King is mad: how stiff° is my vile sense,°
That I stand up, and have ingenious° feeling
Of my huge sorrows! Better I were distract:°
So should my thoughts be severed from my griefs,
And woes by wrong imaginations° lose   270
The knowledge of themselves.

                                              Drum afar off.

EDGAR.   Give me your hand:
Far off, methinks, I hear the beaten drum.
Come, father, I'll bestow° you with a friend.

                                              Exeunt.

252*if . . . not* if your desire (and lust) be not lacking
257*would* would like to
257*and . . . venture* i.e., and one who holds you her own for venturing (Edmund had
earlier been promised union by Goneril, "If you dare venture in your own behalf,"
IV.ii.20).
258*indistinguished . . . will* unlimited range of woman's lust
260*exchange* substitute
261*rake up* cover up, bury
261*post unsanctified* unholy messenger
262*mature* ripe
263*ungracious paper* wicked letter
263*strike* blast
264*death-practiced* whose death is plotted
266*stiff* unbending
266*vile sense* hateful capacity for feeling
267*ingenious* conscious
268*distract* distracted, mad
270*wrong imaginations* delusions
274*bestow* lodge

Scene VII. [*A tent in the French camp.*]

Enter CORDELIA, KENT, DOCTOR, *and* GENTLEMAN.

CORDELIA.   O thou good Kent, how shall I live and work,
  To match thy goodness? My life will be too short,
  And every measure fail me.
KENT.   To be acknowledged, madam, is o'erpaid.
  All my reports go° with the modest truth,   5
  Nor more nor clipped,° but so.
CORDELIA.   Be better suited:°
  These weeds° are memories° of those worser hours:
  I prithee, put them off.
KENT.   Pardon, dear madam;
  Yet to be known shortens my made intent:°
  My boon I make it,° that you know me not   10
  Till time and I think meet.°
CORDELIA.   Then be 't so, my good lord. [*To the* DOCTOR] How does
  the King?
DOCTOR.   Madam, sleeps still.
CORDELIA.   O you kind gods!   15
  Cure this great breach in his abusèd° nature.
  Th' untuned and jarring senses, O, wind up°
  Of this child-changèd° father.
DOCTOR.   So please your Majesty
  That we may wake the King: he hath slept long.
CORDELIA.   Be governed by your knowledge, and proceed   20
  I' th' sway of° your own will. Is he arrayed?

Enter LEAR *in a chair carried by* SERVANTS.

GENTLEMAN.   Ay, madam; in the heaviness of sleep
  We put fresh garments on him.
DOCTOR.   Be by, good madam, when we do awake him;
  I doubt not of his temperance.°   25

---

[5]IV.vii. *go* conform
[6]*clipped* curtailed
[6]*suited* attired
[7]*weeds* clothes
[7]*memories* reminders
[9]*Yet . . . intent* to reveal myself just yet interferes with the plan I have made
[10]*My boon I make it* I ask this reward
[11]*meet* fitting
[16]*abusèd* disturbed
[17]*wind up* tune
[18]*child-changèd* changed, deranged (and also, reduced to a child) by the cruelty of his
children
[21]*I' th' sway of* according to
[25]*temperance* sanity

CORDELIA.   Very well.   25

DOCTOR.   Please you, draw near. Louder the music there!

CORDELIA.   O my dear father, restoration hang
    Thy medicine on my lips, and let this kiss
    Repair those violent harms that my two sisters
    Have in thy reverence° made.

KENT.   Kind and dear Princess.   30

CORDELIA.   Had you not been their father, these white flakes°
    Did challenge° pity of them. Was this a face
    To be opposed against the warring winds?
    To stand against the deep dread-bolted° thunder?
    In the most terrible and nimble stroke   35
    Of quick, cross° lightning to watch—poor perdu!°—
    With this thin helm?° Mine enemy's dog,
    Though he had bit me, should have stood that night
    Against my fire; and wast thou fain,° poor father,
    To hovel thee with swine and rogues° forlorn,   40
    In short° and musty straw? Alack, alack!
    'Tis wonder that thy life and wits at once
    Had not concluded all.° He wakes; speak to him.

DOCTOR.   Madam, do you; 'tis fittest.

CORDELIA.   How does my royal lord? How fares your Majesty?   45

LEAR.   You do me wrong to take me out o' th' grave:
    Thou art a soul in bliss; but I am bound
    Upon a wheel of fire,° that mine own tears
    Do scald like molten lead.

CORDELIA.   Sir, do you know me?

LEAR.   You are a spirit, I know. Where did you die?   50

CORDELIA.   Still, still, far wide.°

DOCTOR.   He's scarce awake: let him alone awhile.

LEAR.   Where have I been? Where am I? Fair daylight?

---

[30]*reverence* revered person
[31]*flakes* hairs (in long strands)
[32]*challenge* claim
[34]*deep dread-bolted* deep-voiced and furnished with the dreadful thunderbolt
[36]*cross* zigzag
[36]*perdu* (1) sentry in a forlorn position (2) lost one
[37]*helm* helmet (his scanty hair)
[39]*fain* pleased
[40]*rogues* vagabonds
[41]*short* (when straw is freshly cut, it is long, and suitable for bedding, given its flexibility and crispness. As it is used, it becomes musty, shreds into pieces, is "short." In contemporary Maine usage, "short manure" refers to dung mixed with straw that has been broken up; "long manure" to dung mixed with coarse new straw)
[43]*concluded all* come to a complete end
[48]*wheel of fire* (torment associated by the Middle Ages with Hell, where Lear thinks he is)
[51]*wide* i.e., of the mark (of sanity)

I am mightily abused.° I should ev'n die with pity,
To see another thus. I know not what to say.   55
I will not swear these are my hands: let's see;
I feel this pin prick. Would I were assured
Of my condition.
CORDELIA.   O, look upon me, sir,
And hold your hand in benediction o'er me.
You must not kneel.
LEAR.   Pray, do not mock me: 60
I am a very foolish fond° old man,
Fourscore and upward, not an hour more nor less;
And, to deal plainly,
I fear I am not in my perfect mind.
Methinks I should know you and know this man,   65
Yet I am doubtful; for I am mainly° ignorant
What place this is, and all the skill I have
Remembers not these garments, nor I know not
Where I did lodge last night. Do not laugh at me,
For, as I am a man, I think this lady   70
To be my child Cordelia.
CORDELIA.   And so I am, I am.
LEAR.   Be your tears wet? Yes, faith. I pray, weep not.
If you have poison for me, I will drink it.
I know you do not love me; for your sisters
Have, as I do remember, done me wrong.   75
You have some cause, they have not.
CORDELIA.   No cause, no cause.
LEAR.   Am I in France?
KENT.   In your own kingdom, sir.
LEAR.   Do not abuse° me.
DOCTOR.   Be comforted, good madam: the great rage,°
You see, is killed in him: and yet it is danger   80
To make him even o'er° the time he has lost.
Desire him to go in; trouble him no more
Till further settling.°
CORDELIA.   Will't please your Highness walk?°
LEAR.   You must bear with me. Pray you now, forget and forgive. I
am old and foolish.   85

⁵⁴*abused* deluded
⁶¹*fond* in dotage
⁶⁶*mainly* entirely
⁷⁸*abuse* deceive
⁷⁹*rage* frenzy
⁸¹*even o'er* smooth over by filling in; and hence, "recollect"
⁸³*settling* calming
⁸³*walk* (perhaps in the sense of "withdraw")

Exeunt. Mane[n]t° KENT *and* GENTLEMAN.

GENTLEMAN.   Holds it true, sir, that the Duke of Cornwall was so
slain?
KENT.   Most certain, sir.
GENTLEMAN.   Who is conductor of his people?
KENT.   As 'tis said, the bastard son of Gloucester.   90
GENTLEMAN.   They say Edgar, his banished son, is with the Earl of
Kent in Germany.
KENT.   Report is changeable.° 'Tis time to look about; the powers° of
the kingdom approach apace.
GENTLEMAN.   The arbitrement° is like to be bloody. Fare you well, sir.   95

[*Exit.*]

KENT.   My point and period will be throughly wrought,°
Or well or ill, as this day's battle's fought.

Exit.

ACT V

Scene I. [*The British camp near Dover.*]

Enter, with drum and colors, EDMUND, REGAN, GENTLEMEN, *and*
SOLDIERS.

EDMUND.   Know° of the Duke if his last purpose hold,°
Or whether since he is advised° by aught
To change the course: he's full of alteration
And self-reproving: bring his constant pleasure.°

[*To a* GENTLEMAN, *who goes out.*]

REGAN.   Our sister's man is certainly miscarried.°   5
EDMUND.   'Tis to be doubted,° madam.
REGAN.   Now, sweet lord,
You know the goodness I intend upon you:

[85]s.d. *Mane[n]t* remain
[93]*Report is changeable* rumors are unreliable
[93]*powers* armies
[95]*arbitrement* deciding encounter
[97]*My . . . wrought* the aim and end, the close of my life will be completely worked out
V.i. [1]*Know* learn
[1]*last purpose hold* most recent intention (to fight) be maintained
[2]*advised* induced
[4]*constant pleasure* fixed (final) decision
[5]*miscarried* come to grief
[6]*doubted* feared

Tell me, but truly, but then speak the truth,
Do you not love my sister?
EDMUND.   In honored° love.
REGAN.   But have you never found my brother's way   10
To the forfended° place?
EDMUND.   That thought abuses° you.
REGAN.   I am doubtful that you have been conjunct
And bosomed with her, as far as we call hers.°
EDMUND.   No, by mine honor, madam.
REGAN.   I shall never endure her: dear my lord,   15
Be not familiar with her.
EDMUND.   Fear° me not.—
She and the Duke her husband!

Enter, with drum and colors, ALBANY, GONERIL [*and*] SOLDIERS.

GONERIL.   [*Aside*] I had rather lose the battle than that sister
Should loosen° him and me.
ALBANY.   Our very loving sister, well be-met.°   20
Sir, this I heard, the King is come to his daughter,
With others whom the rigor of our state°
Forced to cry out. Where I could not be honest,°
I never yet was valiant: for this business,
It touches us, as° France invades our land,   25
Not bolds the King, with others, whom, I fear,
Most just and heavy causes make oppose.°
EDMUND.   Sir, you speak nobly.
REGAN.   Why is this reasoned?°
GONERIL.   Combine together 'gainst the enemy;
For these domestic and particular broils°   30
Are not the question° here.
ALBANY.   Let's then determine
With th' ancient of war° on our proceeding.

---

[9] *honored* honorable
[11] *forfended* forbidden
[11] *abuses* (1) deceives (2) demeans, is unworthy of
[13] *I . . . hers* I fear that you have united with her intimately, in the fullest possible way
[16] *Fear* distrust
[19] *loosen* separate
[20] *be-met* met
[22] *rigor . . . state* tyranny of our government
[23] *honest* honorable
[25] *touches us, as* concerns me, only in that
[27] *Not . . . oppose* and not in that France emboldens the King and others, who have been led, by real and serious grievances, to take up arms against us
[28] *reasoned* argued
[30] *particular broils* private quarrels
[31] *question* issue
[32] *th' ancient of war* experienced commanders

EDMUND.	I shall attend you presently at your tent.	
REGAN.	Sister, you'll go with us?°	
GONERIL.	No.	35
REGAN.	'Tis most convenient;° pray you, go with us.	
GONERIL.	[*Aside*] O, ho, I know the riddle.°—I will go.	

Exeunt both the Armies.

Enter Edgar [disguised].

EDGAR.   If e'er your Grace had speech with man so poor,
    Hear me one word.

ALBANY.   [*To those going out*] I'll overtake you. [*To Edgar*] Speak.   40

Exeunt [all but Albany and Edgar].

EDGAR.   Before you fight the battle, ope this letter.
    If you have victory, let the trumpet sound
    For° him that brought it: wretched though I seem,
    I can produce a champion that will prove°
    What is avouchèd° there. If you miscarry,   45
    Your business of° the world hath so an end,
    And machination° ceases. Fortune love you.

ALBANY.   Stay till I have read the letter.

EDGAR.   I was forbid it.
    When time shall serve, let but the herald cry,
    And I'll appear again.   50

ALBANY.   Why, fare thee well: I will o'erlook° thy paper.

Exit [EDGAR].

Enter EDMUND.

EDMUND.   The enemy's in view: draw up your powers.
    Here is the guess° of their true strength and forces
    By diligent discovery;° but your haste
    Is now urged on you.

ALBANY.   We will greet° the time.   55

Exit.

---

[34]*us* me (rather than Edmund)
[36]*convenient* fitting, desirable
[37]*riddle* real reason (for Regan's curious request)
[43]*sound/For* summon
[44]*prove* i.e., by trial of combat
[45]*avouchèd* maintained
[46]*of* in
[47]*machination* plotting
[51]*o'erlook* read over
[53]*guess* estimate
[54]*By diligent discovery* obtained by careful reconnoitering
[55]*greet* i.e., meet the demands of

EDMUND.   To both these sisters have I sworn my love;
    Each jealous° of the other, as the stung
    Are of the adder. Which of them shall I take?
    Both? One? Or neither? Neither can be enjoyed,
    If both remain alive: to take the widow   60
    Exasperates, makes mad her sister Goneril;
    And hardly° shall I carry out my side,°
    Her husband being alive. Now then, we'll use
    His countenance° for the battle; which being done,
    Let her who would be rid of him devise   65
    His speedy taking off. As for the mercy
    Which he intends to Lear and to Cordelia,
    The battle done, and they within our power,
    Shall never see his pardon; for my state
    Stands on me to defend, not to debate.°   70

Exit.

Scene II. [*A field between the two camps.*]

Alarum° within. Enter, with drum and colors

LEAR, CORDELIA, *and* SOLDIERS, *over the stage;*
and exeunt.

Enter EDGAR *and* GLOUCESTER.

EDGAR.   Here, father,° take the shadow of this tree
    For your good host; pray that the right may thrive.
    If ever I return to you again,
    I'll bring you comfort.
GLOUCESTER.   Grace go with you, sir.

Exit [Edgar].

Alarum and retreat° within. [Re-]enter Edgar.

EDGAR.   Away, old man; give me thy hand; away!   5
    King Lear hath lost, he and his daughter ta'en:°
    Give me thy hand; come on.
GLOUCESTER.   No further, sir; a man may rot even here.
EDGAR.   What, in ill thoughts again? Men must endure

57*jealous* suspicious
62*hardly* with difficulty
62*carry . . . side* (1) satisfy my ambition (2) fulfill my bargain (with Goneril)
64*countenance* authority
70*for . . . debate* my position requires me to act, not to reason about right and wrong
V.ii. s.d. *Alarum* a trumpet call to battle
1*father* i.e., venerable old man (Edgar has not yet revealed his identity)
4s.d. *retreat* (signaled by a trumpet)
6*ta'en* captured

Their going hence, even as their coming hither: 10
  Ripeness° is all. Come on.
GLOUCESTER.   And that's true too.

                                        Exeunt.

                Scene III. [*The British camp near Dover.*]

        Enter, in conquest, with drum and colors, EDMUND;

            LEAR *and* CORDELIA, *as prisoners;*
                SOLDIERS, CAPTAIN.

EDMUND.   Some officers take them away: good guard,°
  Until their greater pleasures° first be known
  That are to censure° them.
CORDELIA.   We are not the first
  Who with best meaning° have incurred the worst.
  For thee, oppressèd King, I am cast down;   5
  Myself could else out-frown false fortune's frown.
  Shall we not see these daughters and these sisters?
LEAR.   No, no, no, no! Come, let's away to prison:
  We two alone will sing like birds i' th' cage:
  When thou dost ask me blessing, I'll kneel down   10
  And ask of thee forgiveness: so we'll live,
  And pray, and sing, and tell old tales, and laugh
  At gilded butterflies,° and hear poor rogues
  Talk of court news; and we'll talk with them too,
  Who loses and who wins, who's in, who's out;   15
  And take upon's the mystery of things,
  As if we were God's spies:° and we'll wear out,°
  In a walled prison, packs and sects of great ones
  That ebb and flow by th' moon.°
EDMUND.   Take them away.
LEAR.   Upon such sacrifices, my Cordelia,   20
  The gods themselves throw incense.° Have I caught thee?
  He that parts us shall bring a brand from heaven,

---

[11]*Ripeness* maturity, as of fruit that is ready to fall
V.iii. [1]*good guard* let there be good guard
[2]*their greater pleasures* the will of those in command, the great ones
[3]*censure* pass judgment on
[4]*meaning* intentions
[13]*gilded butterflies* i.e., gorgeously attired courtiers, fluttering after nothing
[17]*take . . . spies* profess to read the riddle of existence, as if endowed with divine
omniscience
[17]*wear out* outlast
[19]*packs . . . moon* intriguing and partisan cliques of those in high station, whose
fortunes change every month
[21]*Upon . . . incense* i.e., the gods approve our renunciation of the world

And fire us hence like foxes.° Wipe thine eyes;
The good years° shall devour them,° flesh and fell,°
Ere they shall make us weep. We'll see 'em starved first.   25
Come.

                    [*Exeunt* LEAR *and* CORDELIA, *guarded.*]

EDMUND.   Come hither, captain; hark.
Take thou this note: go follow them to prison:
One step I have advanced thee; if thou dost
As this instructs thee, thou dost make thy way   30
To noble fortunes: know thou this, that men
Are as the time is:° to be tender-minded
Does not become a sword:° thy great employment
Will not bear question;° either say thou'lt do 't,
Or thrive by other means.
CAPTAIN.   I'll do 't, my lord.   35
EDMUND.   About it; and write happy° when th' hast done.
Mark; I say, instantly, and carry it so°
As I have set it down.
CAPTAIN.   I cannot draw a cart, nor eat dried oats;
If it be man's work, I'll do 't.   40

                                        Exit CAPTAIN.

Flourish. Enter ALBANY, GONERIL, REGAN [*another* CAPTAIN, *and*]
                    SOLDIERS.

ALBANY.   Sir, you have showed today your valiant strain,°
And fortune led you well: you have the captives
Who were the opposites of° this day's strife:
I do require them of you, so to use them
As we shall find their merits° and our safety   45
May equally determine.
EDMUND.   Sir, I thought it fit
To send the old and miserable King

---

²³*He . . . foxes* no human agency can separate us, but only divine interposition, as of a
heavenly torch parting us like foxes who are driven from their place of refuge by fire
and smoke
²⁴*good years* plague and pestilence ("undefined malefic power or agency," *N.E.D.*)
²⁴*them* i.e., the enemies of Lear and Cordelia
²⁴*fell* skin
³²*as the time is* i.e., absolutely determined by the exigencies of the moment
³³*become a sword* befit a soldier
³⁴*bear question* admit of discussion
³⁶*write happy* style yourself fortunate
³⁷*carry it so* manage the affair in exactly that manner (as if Cordelia had taken her own
life)
⁴¹*strain* (1) stock (2) character
⁴³*opposites of* opponents in
⁴⁵*merits* deserts

To some retention and appointed guard;°
Whose° age had charms in it, whose title more,
To pluck the common bosom on his side,°   50
And turn our impressed lances in our eyes°
Which do command them. With him I sent the Queen:
My reason all the same; and they are ready
Tomorrow, or at further space,° t' appear
Where you shall hold your session.° At this time   55
We sweat and bleed: the friend hath lost his friend;
And the best quarrels, in the heat, are cursed
By those that feel their sharpness.°
The question of Cordelia and her father
Requires a fitter place.   60
ALBANY.   Sir, by your patience,   60
I hold you but a subject of° this war,
Not as a brother.
REGAN.   That's as we list to grace° him.
Methinks our pleasure might have been demanded,
Ere you had spoke so far. He led our powers,
Bore the commission of my place and person;   65
The which immediacy may well stand up
And call itself your brother.°
GONERIL.   Not so hot:
In his own grace he doth exalt himself
More than in your addition.°
REGAN.   In my rights,
By me invested, he compeers° the best.   70
GONERIL.   That were the most,° if he should husband you.°
REGAN.   Jesters do oft prove prophets.
GONERIL.   Holla, holla!
That eye that told you so looked but a-squint.°

48*retention . . . guard* confinement under duly appointed guard
49*Whose* i.e., Lear's
50*pluck . . . side* win the sympathy of the people to himself
51*turn . . . eyes* turn our conscripted lancers against us
54*further space* a later time
55*session* trial
58*the . . . sharpness* the worthiest causes may be judged badly by those who have been affected painfully by them, and whose passion has not yet cooled
61*subject of* subordinate in
62*list to grace* wish to honor
67*Bore . . . brother* was authorized, as my deputy, to take command; his present status, as my immediate representative, entitles him to be considered your equal
69*your addition* honors you have bestowed on him
70*compeers* equals
71*most* most complete investing in your rights
71*husband you* become your husband
73*a-squint* cross-eyed

REGAN.   Lady, I am not well; else I should answer
     From a full-flowing stomach.° General,   75
     Take thou my soldiers, prisoners, patrimony;°
     Dispose of them, of me; the walls is thine:°
     Witness the world, that I create thee here
     My lord, and master.
GONERIL.   Mean you to enjoy him?
ALBANY.   The let-alone° lies not in your good will.   80
EDMUND.   Nor in thine, lord.
ALBANY.   Half-blooded° fellow, yes.
REGAN.   [*To* EDMUND] Let the drum strike, and prove my title
     thine.°
ALBANY.   Stay yet; hear reason. Edmund, I arrest thee
     On capital treason; and in thy attaint°   85
     This gilded serpent [*pointing to* GONERIL]. For your claim, fair sister,
     I bar it in the interest of my wife.
     'Tis she is subcontracted° to this lord,
     And I, her husband, contradict your banes.°
     If you will marry, make your loves° to me;   90
     My lady is bespoke.°
GONERIL.   An interlude!°
ALBANY.   Thou art armed, Gloucester: let the trumpet sound:
     If none appear to prove upon thy person
     Thy heinous, manifest, and many treasons,
     There is my pledge° [*throwing down a glove*]: I'll make° it on thy heart,   95
     Ere I taste bread, thou art in nothing less
     Than I have here proclaimed thee.
REGAN.   Sick, O, sick!
GONERIL.   [*Aside*] If not, I'll ne'er trust medicine.°
EDMUND.   [*Throwing down a glove*] There's my exchange:° what in the
     world he is   100

[75]*From . . . stomach* angrily
[76]*patrimony* inheritance
[77]*walls is thine* i.e., Regan's person, which Edmund has stormed and won
[80]*let-alone* power to prevent
[81]*Half-blooded* bastard, and so only half noble
[83]*prove . . . thine* prove by combat your entitlement to my rights
[85]*in thy attaint* as a sharer in the treason for which you are impeached
[88]*subcontracted* pledged by a contract which is called into question by the existence of a
previous contract (Goneril's marriage)
[89]*contradict your banes* forbid your announced intention to marry (by citing the
precontract)
[90]*loves* love-suits
[91]*bespoke* already pledged
[91]*interlude* play
[95]*pledge* gage
[95]*make* prove
[98]*medicine* poison
[99]*exchange* (technical term, denoting the glove Edmund throws down)

That names me traitor, villain-like he lies:°
Call by the trumpet:° he that dares approach,
On him, on you—who not?—I will maintain
My truth and honor firmly.
ALBANY.   A herald, ho!
EDMUND.   A herald, ho, a herald!   105
ALBANY.   Trust to thy single virtue;° for thy soldiers,
All levied in my name, have in my name
Took their discharge.
REGAN.   My sickness grows upon me.
ALBANY.   She is not well; convey her to my tent.

[*Exit* REGAN, *led.*]

Enter a HERALD.

Come hither, herald. Let the trumpet sound—   110
And read out this.
CAPTAIN.   Sound, trumpet!

A trumpet sounds.

HERALD.   (*Reads.*) "If any man of quality or degree° within the
lists° of the army will maintain upon Edmund, supposed Earl of
Gloucester, that he is a manifold traitor, let him appear by the third   115
sound of the trumpet: he is bold in his defense."
EDMUND.   Sound!

First trumpet.

HERALD.   Again!

Second trumpet.

HERALD.   Again!

Third trumpet.

Trumpet answers within. Enter EDGAR, *at the*   120
third sound, armed, a trumpet before him.°
ALBANY.   Ask him his purposes, why he appears
Upon this call o' th' trumpet.
HERALD.   What are you?
Your name, your quality,° and why you answer
This present summons?   125

---

[101]*villain-like he lies* (the lie direct, a challenge to mortal combat)
[102]*trumpet* trumpeter
[106]*single virtue* unaided valor
[113]*quality or degree* rank or position
[114]*lists* rolls
[121]s.d. *trumpet before him* trumpeter preceding him
[124]*quality* rank

EDGAR.   Know, my name is lost;   125
    By treason's tooth bare-gnawn and canker-bit:°
    Yet am I noble as the adversary
    I come to cope.°
ALBANY.   Which is that adversary?
EDGAR.   What's he that speaks for Edmund, Earl of Gloucester?
EDMUND.   Himself: what say'st thou to him?
EDGAR.   Draw thy sword,   130
    That if my speech offend a noble heart,
    Thy arm may do thee justice: here is mine.
    Behold it is my privilege,
    The privilege of mine honors,
    My oath, and my profession.° I protest,   135
    Maugre° thy strength, place, youth, and eminence,
    Despite thy victor sword and fire-new° fortune,
    Thy valor and thy heart,° thou art a traitor,
    False to thy gods, thy brother, and thy father,
    Conspirant° 'gainst this high illustrious prince,   140
    And from th' extremest upward° of thy head
    To the descent and dust below thy foot,°
    A most toad-spotted traitor.° Say thou "No,"
    This sword, this arm and my best spirits are bent°
    To prove upon thy heart, whereto I speak,°   145
    Thou liest.
EDMUND.   In wisdom° I should ask thy name,
    But since thy outside looks so fair and warlike,
    And that thy tongue some say° of breeding breathes,
    What safe and nicely° I might well delay°
    By rule of knighthood, I disdain and spurn: 150
    Back do I toss these treasons° to thy head;

126 *canker-bit* eaten by the caterpillar
128 *cope* encounter
135 *it . . . profession* my knighthood entitles me to challenge you, and to have my
challenge accepted
136 *Maugre* despite
137 *fire-new* fresh from the forge or mint
138 *heart* courage
140 *Conspirant* conspiring, a conspirator
141 *extremest upward* the very top
142 *the . . . foot* your lowest part (sole) and the dust beneath it
143 *toad-spotted traitor* spotted with treason (and hence venomous, as the toad is
allegedly marked with spots that exude venom)
144 *bent* directed
145 *whereto I speak* (Edgar speaks from the heart, and speaks to the heart of Edmund)
146 *wisdom* prudence (since he is not obliged to fight with one of lesser rank)
148 *say* assay (i.e., touch, sign)
149 *safe and nicely* cautiously and punctiliously
149 *delay* i.e., avoid
151 *treasons* accusations of treason

With the hell-hated° lie o'erwhelm thy heart;
Which for they yet glance by and scarcely bruise,
This sword of mine shall give them instant way,
Where they shall rest for ever.° Trumpets, speak!   155

     Alarums. [*They*] *fight.* [EDMUND *falls.*]

ALBANY.   Save° him, save him!
GONERIL.   This is practice,° Gloucester:
By th' law of war thou wast not bound to answer
An unknown opposite;° thou art not vanquished,
But cozened and beguiled.
ALBANY.   Shut your mouth, dame,
Or with this paper shall I stop it. Hold, sir;°   160
Thou° worse than any name, read thine own evil.
No tearing, lady; I perceive you know it.
GONERIL.   Say, if I do, the laws are mine, not thine:
Who can arraign me for 't?
ALBANY.   Most monstrous! O!
Know'st thou this paper?
GONERIL.   Ask me not what I know.   165

                       Exit.

ALBANY.   Go after her; she's desperate; govern° her.
EDMUND.   What you have charged me with, that have I done;
And more, much more; the time will bring it out.
'Tis past, and so am I. But what art thou
That hast this fortune on° me? If thou 'rt noble,   170
I do forgive thee.
EDGAR.   Let's exchange charity.°
I am no less in blood° than thou art, Edmund;
If more,° the more th' hast wronged me.
My name is Edgar, and thy father's son.
The gods are just, and of our pleasant° vices   175
Make instruments to plague us:

---

[152] *hell-hated* hated like hell
[155] *Which . . . ever* which accusations of treason, since as yet they do no harm, even though I have hurled them back, I now thrust upon you still more forcibly, with my sword, so that they may remain with you permanently
[156] *Save* spare
[156] *practice* trickery
[158] *opposite* opponent
[160] *Hold, sir* (to Edmund: "Just a moment!")
[161] *Thou* (probably Goneril)
[166] *govern* control
[170] *fortune on* victory over
[171] *charity* forgiveness and love
[172] *blood* lineage
[173] *If more* if I am more noble (since legitimate)
[175] *of our pleasant* out of our pleasurable

The dark and vicious place° where thee he got°
Cost him his eyes.
EDMUND.   Th' hast spoken right, 'tis true;
The wheel is come full circle; I am here.°
ALBANY.   Methought thy very gait did prophesy°   180
A royal nobleness: I must embrace thee:
Let sorrow split my heart, if ever I
Did hate thee or thy father!
EDGAR.   Worthy° Prince, I know 't.
ALBANY.   Where have you hid yourself?
How have you known the miseries of your father?   185
EDGAR.   By nursing them, my lord. List a brief tale;
And when 'tis told, O, that my heart would burst!
The bloody proclamation to escape°
That followed me so near—O, our lives' sweetness,
That we the pain of death would hourly die   190
Rather than die at once!°—taught me to shift
Into a madman's rags, t' assume a semblance
That very dogs disdained: and in this habit°
Met I my father with his bleeding rings,°
Their precious stones new lost; became his guide,   195
Led him, begged for him, saved him from despair;
Never—O fault!—revealed myself unto him,
Until some half-hour past, when I was armed,
Not sure, though hoping, of this good success,
I asked his blessing, and from first to last   200
Told him our pilgrimage.° But his flawed° heart—
Alack, too weak the conflict to support—
'Twixt two extremes of passion, joy and grief,
Burst smilingly.
EDMUND.   This speech of yours hath moved me,
And shall perchance do good: but speak you on;   205
You look as you had something more to say.
ALBANY.   If there be more, more woeful, hold it in;

---

[177]*place* i.e., the adulterous bed
[177]*got* begot
[179]*Wheel . . . here* i.e., Fortune's wheel, on which Edmund ascended, has now, in its downward turning, deposited him at the bottom, whence he began
[180]*gait did prophesy* carriage did promise
[183]*Worthy* honorable
[188]*to escape* (my wish) to escape the sentence of death
[191]*O . . . once* how sweet is life, that we choose to suffer death every hour rather than make an end at once
[193]*habit* attire
[194]*rings* sockets
[201]*our pilgrimage* of our (purgatorial) journey
[201]*flawed* cracked

For I am almost ready to dissolve,°
Hearing of this.
EDGAR.   This would have seemed a period°
To such as love not sorrow; but another,   210
To amplify too much, would make much more,
And top extremity.°
Whilst I was big in clamor,° came there in a man,
Who, having seen me in my worst estate,°
Shunned my abhorred° society; but then, finding   215
Who 'twas that so endured, with his strong arms
He fastened on my neck, and bellowed out
As he'd burst heaven; threw him on my father;
Told the most piteous tale of Lear and him
That ever ear received: which in recounting   220
His grief grew puissant,° and the strings of life
Began to crack: twice then the trumpets sounded,
And there I left him tranced.°
ALBANY.   But who was this?
EDGAR.   Kent, sir, the banished Kent; who in disguise
Followed his enemy° king, and did him service   225
Improper for a slave.

Enter a GENTLEMAN, *with a bloody knife.*

GENTLEMAN.   Help, help, O, help!
EDGAR.   What kind of help?
ALBANY.   Speak, man.
EDGAR.   What means this bloody knife?
GENTLEMAN.   'Tis hot, it smokes;°
It came even from the heart of—O, she's dead!
ALBANY.   Who dead? Speak, man.   230
GENTLEMAN.   Your lady, sir, your lady: and her sister
By her is poisoned; she confesses it.
EDMUND.   I was contracted° to them both: all three
Now marry° in an instant.
EDGAR.   Here comes Kent.

208*dissolve* i.e., into tears
209*period* limit
212*but . . . extremity* just one woe more, described too fully, would go beyond the
extreme limit
213*big in clamor* loud in lamentation
214*estate* condition
215*abhorred* abhorrent
221*puissant* overmastering
223*tranced* insensible
225*enemy* hostile
228*smokes* steams
233*contracted* betrothed
234*marry* i.e., unite in death

ALBANY.   Produce the bodies, be they alive or dead.   235

[Exit GENTLEMAN.]

This judgment of the heavens, that makes us tremble,
Touches us not with pity.

Enter KENT.

                              O, is this he?
The time will not allow the compliment°
Which very manners° urges.
KENT.   I am come
To bid my king and master aye° good night: 240
Is he not here?
ALBANY.   Great thing of° us forgot!
Speak, Edmund, where's the King? and where's Cordelia?
Seest thou this object,° Kent?

The bodies of GONERIL *and* REGAN *are brought in.*
KENT.   Alack, why thus?
EDMUND.   Yet° Edmund was beloved:
The one the other poisoned for my sake,   245
And after slew herself.
ALBANY.   Even so. Cover their faces.
EDMUND.   I pant for life:° some good I mean to do,
Despite of mine own nature. Quickly send,
Be brief in it, to th' castle; for my writ°   250
Is on the life of Lear and on Cordelia:
Nay, send in time.
ALBANY.   Run, run, O, run!
EDGAR.   To who, my lord? Who has the office?° Send
Thy token of reprieve.°
EDMUND.   Well thought on: take my sword,   255
Give it the captain.
EDGAR.   Haste thee, for thy life.

[Exit MESSENGER.]

²³⁸*compliment* ceremony
²³⁹*very manners* ordinary civility
²⁴⁰*aye* forever
²⁴¹*thing of* matter by
²⁴³*object* sight (the bodies of Goneril and Regan)
²⁴⁴*Yet* in spite of all
²⁴⁸*pant for life* gasp for breath
²⁵⁰*writ* command (ordering the execution)
²⁵³*office* commission
²⁵⁴*token of reprieve* sign that they are reprieved

EDMUND.   He hath commission from thy wife and me
    To hang Cordelia in the prison, and
    To lay the blame upon her own despair,
    That she fordid° herself.   260
ALBANY.   The gods defend her! Bear him hence awhile.

                [EDMUND *is borne off.*]

Enter LEAR, *with* CORDELIA *in his arms* [GENTLEMAN, *and others*
following].

LEAR.   Howl, howl, howl, howl! O, you are men of stones:
    Had I your tongues and eyes, I'd use them so
    That heaven's vault should crack. She's gone for ever.
    I know when one is dead and when one lives;   265
    She's dead as earth. Lend me a looking-glass;
    If that her breath will mist or stain the stone,°
    Why, then she lives.
KENT.   Is this the promised end?°
EDGAR.   Or image° of that horror?
ALBANY.   Fall and cease.°
LEAR.   This feather stirs; she lives. If it be so,   270
    It is a chance which does redeem° all sorrows
    That ever I have felt.
KENT.   O my good master.
LEAR.   Prithee, away.
EDGAR.   'Tis noble Kent, your friend.
LEAR.   A plague upon you, murderers, traitors all!
    I might have saved her; now she's gone for ever.   275
    Cordelia, Cordelia, stay a little. Ha,
    What is 't thou say'st? Her voice was ever soft,
    Gentle and low, an excellent thing in woman.
    I killed the slave that was a-hanging thee.
GENTLEMAN.   'Tis true, my lords, he did.
LEAR.   Did I not, fellow?   280
    I have seen the day, with my good biting falchion°
    I would have made them skip: I am old now,
    And these same crosses° spoil me.° Who are you?
    Mine eyes are not o' th' best: I'll tell you straight.°

---

[260]*fordid* destroyed
[267]*stone* i.e., the surface of the crystal looking glass
[268]*promised end* Doomsday
[269]*image* exact likeness
[269]*Fall and cease* i.e., let the heavens fall, and all things finish
[271]*redeem* make good
[281]*falchion* small curved sword
[283]*crosses* troubles
[283]*spoil me* i.e., my prowess as a swordsman
[284]*tell you straight* recognize you straightway

KENT.   If Fortune brag of two° she loved and hated,   285
     One of them we behold.

LEAR.   This is a dull sight.° Are you not Kent?

KENT.   The same,
     Your servant Kent. Where is your servant Caius?°

LEAR.   He's a good fellow, I can tell you that;
     He'll strike, and quickly too: he's dead and rotten.   290

KENT.   No, my good lord; I am the very man.

LEAR.   I'll see that straight.°

KENT.   That from your first of difference and decay°
     Have followed your sad steps.

LEAR.   You are welcome hither.

KENT.   Nor no man else:° all's cheerless, dark and deadly.   295
     Your eldest daughters have fordone° themselves,
     And desperately° are dead.

LEAR.   Ay, so I think.

ALBANY.   He knows not what he says, and vain is it
     That we present us to him.

EDGAR.   Very bootless.°

Enter a MESSENGER.

MESSENGER.   Edmund is dead, my lord.

ALBANY.   That's but a trifle here.   300
     You lords and noble friends, know our intent.
     What comfort to this great decay may come°
     Shall be applied. For us, we° will resign,
     During the life of this old majesty,
     To him our absolute power: [*To* EDGAR *and* KENT] you, to your   305
     rights;
     With boot,° and such addition° as your honors
     Have more than merited. All friends shall taste
     The wages of their virtue, and all foes
     The cup of their deservings. O, see, see!

[285] *two* i.e., Lear, and some hypothetical second, who is also a prime example of Fortune's inconstancy ("loved and hated")
[287] *dull sight* (1) melancholy spectacle (2) faulty eyesight (Lear's own, clouded by weeping)
[288] *Caius* (Kent's name, in disguise)
[292] *see that straight* attend to that in a moment
[293] *your . . . decay* beginning of your decline in fortune
[295] *Nor no man else* no, I am not welcome, nor is anyone else
[296] *fordone* destroyed
[297] *desperately* in despair
[299] *bootless* fruitless
[302] *What . . . come* whatever aid may present itself to this great ruined man
[303] *us, we* (the royal "we")
[306] *boot* good measure
[306] *addition* additional titles and rights

LEAR.   And my poor fool° is hanged: no, no, no life?   310
Why should a dog, a horse, a rat, have life,
And thou no breath at all? Thou'lt come no more,
Never, never, never, never, never.
Pray you, undo this button.° Thank you, sir.
Do you see this? Look on her. Look, her lips,   315
Look there, look there.

                                                  He dies.

EDGAR.   He faints. My lord, my lord!
KENT.   Break, heart; I prithee, break.
EDGAR.   Look up, my lord.
KENT.   Vex not his ghost:° O, let him pass! He hates him
That would upon the rack° of this tough world
Stretch him out longer.°
EDGAR.   He is gone indeed.   320
KENT.   The wonder is he hath endured so long:
He but usurped° his life.
ALBANY.   Bear them from hence. Our present business
Is general woe. [*To* KENT *and* EDGAR] Friends of my soul, you twain,
Rule in this realm and the gored state sustain.   325
KENT.   I have a journey, sir, shortly to go;
My master calls me, I must not say no.
EDGAR.   The weight of this sad time we must obey,°
Speak what we feel, not what we ought to say.
The oldest hath borne most: we that are young   330
Shall never see so much, nor live so long.

                                Exeunt, with a dead march.

---

[310]*fool* Cordelia ("fool" being a term of endearment. But it is perfectly possible to take the word as referring also to the Fool)
[314]*undo this button* i.e., to ease the suffocation Lear feels
[318]*Vex . . . ghost* do not trouble his departing spirit
[319]*rack* instrument of torture, stretching the victim's joints to dislocation
[320]*longer* (1) in time (2) in bodily length
[322]*usurped* possessed beyond the allotted term
[328]*obey* submit to

YOUTH TO AGE

TOPICS FOR SHORT PAPERS, JOURNALS, OR DISCUSSION:

1. Select two protagonists (main characters; see page 1011 for discussion of this term) from any of the selections in "Youth to Age," perhaps two young people, two old people, or one old and one young. Compare and/or contrast the two characters: their stations in life, their life-styles, the lessons they learned or did not learn—anything that shows their similarities or makes them unique and distinctive. Some possibilities are Rip Van Winkle and Eben Flood; Dave Saunders from "The Man Who Was Almost a Man" and Angelina Sandoval; Phoenix Jackson from "A Worn Path" and Jeff and Jennie Patton from "A Summer Tragedy"; the speakers in "I Stand Here Ironing" and "First Lesson."

2. Choose one or two poems in this section that seem to make a statement on the contrast between youth and age, and discuss the way in which the poet expresses the contrast (through ideas, language, and structure).

3. The point of view of the narrator or main character in a story is not the only one a reader may need to think about. Consider the perspectives of these characters from stories in this section:

- The daughter in Tillie Olsen's "I Stand Here Ironing"
- The brother in Toni Cade Bambara's "Raymond's Run"
- Victor, one of Angelina's brothers, in "Angelina Sandoval"
- The grandson in Welty's "A Worn Path"

In each case, tell how you would feel if you were in the place of that character. What would you do if you were that character? How would this distinctive point of view change the story as it is now written?

4. Write to a friend who has been absent from class during the discussion of one of the plays, poems, or stories in this section. In your communication, explain what happened in class in detail, including some confidential information on how the class reacted to whatever was going on, and what seemed to be the interpretations of the instructor and the various class members about the selections discussed.

LONGER PAPERS OR RESEARCH PROJECTS

5. Select a group of poems relating to one phase of life, from this section or others. For example, you might pick poems about childhood from Yeats's "Cradle Song" through Naomi Long Madgett's "Offspring." Discuss the poets' sense of the essence of that age by drawing on specific imagery, rhythmic effects, and thematic strains from the poems. You might refer to the section "On Reading Poetry: Limericks to Lyrics" on pages 1014–1028 to help you in your analyses.

6. Several of the selections in this section discuss a refinement of the issue of youth and age: the relationships of parents and children (e.g., *King Lear, The Sandbox,* "I Stand Here Ironing," "dominic has a doll"). Synthesize a central idea about relationships between parents and children as seen in several of the short stories, plays, and

poems. Then support your central idea by selecting and discussing specific examples of language or plot that reveal these relationships.

CREATIVE PROJECTS

7. If you were planning a program for a discussion group at a nursing home or retirement home, which selections would you make from this section and why? Give specific selections and explain how they would relate to your audience.

8. Write your own future biography or autobiography, as you would like to have it read ten or twenty years from now. You can be fantastic, romantic, or pragmatic, but you need to pretend to look back from years hence and see what you have become. Use present or future tense—whatever seems to fit best.

9. How do other media treat the theme of "Youth to Age"? Give examples from sculpture, painting, and dance. Collect photographs or postcards of these art forms and discuss the ways in which these different arts develop the same ideas expressed in this section in plays, poems, and stories.

Corner Apartments (Down 18th Street), 1980, by Wayne Thiebaud. (Hirshhorn Museum and Sculpture Garden, Smithsonian Institute. Museum purchase with funds donated by Edward R. Downe, Jr., 1980.)

CITY AND COUNTRY

DUST OF SNOW

The way a crow
Shook down on me
The dust of snow
From a hemlock tree

Has given my heart
A change of mood
And saved some part
Of a day I had rued.

Robert Frost

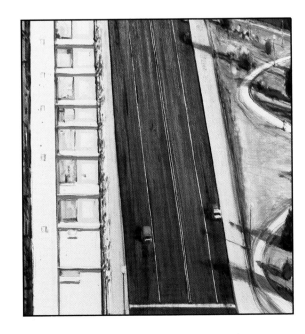

In "Dust of Snow"—this section's epigraph—the poet feels a cold sprinkle of snow shaken down on him from a tree as a crow flies off. This simple contact with nature revives the poet's spirits, although he had been depressed until then. Like Robert Frost, other writers often use environment—the surroundings people live in—as metaphors to express thoughts or feelings about other aspects of life. The theme of this section insists that mountains and skyscrapers—and snow—are more than scenery; they have the power to form our lives and to symbolize our struggles, joys, and traumas.

Some of the stories and poems in this section focus on the impact city and country have on one another. As we do in each section, we start with a myth: in this case, the myth of the Old West. In the story "The Bride Comes to Yellow Sky," city economy and customs from the East gradually change the Old West of legend. In "Chrysanthemums," John Steinbeck contrasts the lushness of the valley and of the chrysanthemums with the sterility of Elisa's life and marriage. Her starved feelings draw her to growing plants, and her repressed sexuality draws her to the traveling pot mender.

A traditional yet powerful metaphor emerges in stories and poems, such as Katherine Anne Porter's "The Grave," Alice Walker's "Everyday Use," Philip Booth's "Great Farm," and several Frost poems, that let the country represent the simpler, more honest life. The city, except perhaps for Carl Sandburg's "bustling, brawling city of big shoulders," is the harlot; the country is the virgin. The city—and the brutal forces it houses—seems generally the image of evil; the country that of innocence. From William Blake's "London" to Paul Simon's "The Sound of Silence"; from Pietro Di Donato's "Christ in Concrete" to John Rechy's "Pete: A Quarter Ahead" and Ann Petry's "Like a Winding Sheet," writers have chronicled the destructive forces that prey upon the people of the cities. Images emerge, among others, of pathetic hustlers hovering on Times Square, of tenants unable to get their broken stairs or leaky pipes fixed, as well as of unlikable commuters like Donald Wryson who routinely flee to the modern suburbs, where city and country meet. Henrik Ibsen's play *An Enemy of the People* makes a metaphor of the impact of a water pollution problem on human lives and politics in a small town, by showing the self-serving and corrupt attitudes of most of the inhabitants.

Some nature poems, on the other hand, show the idealized countryside as a simple object of beauty: Robert Browning's "Home Thoughts from Abroad," Housman's "Loveliest of Trees," and Norman MacCaig's "Frogs" are among these. This mythical, almost stereotyped view of the redemptive qualities of nature is also found in a group of poems that illuminate the contrast between city and country: William Wordworth's "The Daffodils" and "The World Is Too Much with Us," along with Maxine Kumin's "Morning Swim."

Poems by Benjamin Durazo and Leonard Adamé, in contrast to these idyllic views of the country, tell about the migratory farm workers' barren lives. The cityworker's pitiful lot is portrayed in Carolyn Rodgers's "Portrait" as well as Di Donato's "Christ in Concrete." Walt Whitman, however, finds beauty and inspiration in the city in "Crossing Brooklyn Ferry."

The factual, pragmatic details of life and work on this planet are raw materials from which writers develop fictional ideas. From these otherwise ordinary objects and events, ideas and forms emerge as works of art. Many of the poems and stories in this section use aspects of the cityscape or country landscape as symbols. Ibsen turns the townspeople's conspiracy to keep the pollution of their mineral springs a secret into a symbolic dramatization of the evils of mob rule. For Yeats, in "The Lake Isle of Innisfree," landscape represents quiet and contemplation, while in "Sailing to Byzantium" he turns his back on nature and embraces the immortality of art. Robert Frost uses a simple winter landscape in "Stopping By Woods on a Snowy Evening" to discuss themes of commitment to life, a wish for death, and the demands of responsibility.

The importance of the poems, stories, and plays in this section lies in their graphic illustration of the power of place to evoke strong images. We cannot entirely explain or excuse human failings by blaming environment as the cause of evil or good. But the impact of place on human thought and action remains important for creative writing.

Fiction

THE BRIDE COMES TO YELLOW SKY

Stephen Crane

(1871–1900)

Biography p. 1067

I

The great Pullman was whirling onward with such dignity of motion that a glance from the window seemed simply to prove that the plains of Texas were pouring eastward. Vast flats of green grass, dull-hued spaces of mesquite and cactus, little groups of frame houses, woods of light and tender trees, all were sweeping into the east, sweeping over the horizon, a precipice.

A newly married pair had boarded this coach at San Antonio. The man's face was reddened from many days in the wind and sun, and a direct result of his new black clothes was that his brick-colored hands were constantly performing in a most conscious fashion. From time to time he looked down respectfully at his attire. He sat with a hand on each knee, like a man waiting in a barber's shop. The glances he devoted to other passengers were furtive and shy.

The bride was not pretty, nor was she very young. She wore a dress of blue cashmere, with small reservations of velvet here and there, and with steel buttons abounding. She continually twisted her head to regard her puff sleeves, very stiff, straight, and high. They embarrassed her. It was quite apparent that she had cooked, and that she expected to cook, dutifully. The blushes caused by the careless scrutiny of some passengers as she had entered the car were strange to see upon this plain, underclass countenance, which was drawn in placid, almost emotionless lines.

They were evidently very happy. "Ever been in a parlor car before?" he asked, smiling with delight.

"No," she answered. "I never was. It's fine, ain't it?"

"Great! And then after a while we'll go forward to the diner, and get a big layout. Finest meal in the world. Charge a dollar."

"Oh, do they?" cried the bride. "Charge a dollar? Why, that's too much—for us—ain't it, Jack?"

"Not this trip, anyhow," he answered bravely. "We're going to go the whole thing."

Later, he explained to her about the trains. "You see, it's a thousand miles from one end of Texas to the other; and this train runs right across it, and never stops but four times." He had the pride of an owner. He pointed out to her the dazzling fittings of the coach; and in truth her eyes opened wider as she contemplated the sea-green figured velvet, the shining brass, silver, and glass, the wood that gleamed as darkly brilliant as the surface of a pool of oil. At one end a bronze figure sturdily held a support for a separated chamber, and at convenient places on the ceiling were frescoes in olive and silver.

To the minds of the pair, their surroundings reflected the glory of their marriage that morning in San Antonio. This was the environment of their new estate, and the man's face in particular beamed with an elation that made him appear ridiculous to the negro porter. This individual at times surveyed them from afar with an amused and superior grin. On other occasions he bullied them with skill in ways that did not make it exactly plain to them that they were being bullied. He subtly used all the manners of the most unconquerable kind of snobbery. He oppressed them; but of this oppression they had small knowledge, and they speedily forgot that infrequently a number of travelers covered them with stares of derisive enjoyment. Historically there was supposed to be something infinitely humorous in their situation.

"We are due in Yellow Sky at 3:42," he said, looking tenderly into her eyes.

"Oh, are we?" she said, as if she had not been aware of it. To evince surprise at her husband's statement was part of her wifely amiability. She took from a pocket a little silver watch; and as she held it before her, and stared at it with a frown of attention, the new husband's face shone.

"I bought it in San Anton' from a friend of mine," he told her gleefully.

"It's seventeen minutes past twelve," she said, looking up at him with a kind of shy and clumsy coquetry. A passenger, noting this play, grew excessively sardonic, and winked at himself in one of the numerous mirrors.

At last they went to the dining car. Two rows of negro waiters, in glowing white suits, surveyed their entrance with the interest, and also the equanimity, of men who had been forewarned. The pair fell to the lot of a waiter who happened to feel pleasure in steering them through their meal. He viewed them with the manner of a fatherly pilot, his countenance radiant with benevolence. The patronage, entwined with the ordinary deference, was not plain to them. And yet, as they returned to their coach, they showed in their faces a sense of escape.

To the left, miles down a long purple slope, was a little ribbon of mist where moved the keening Rio Grande. The train was approaching it at an angle, and the apex was Yellow Sky. Presently it was apparent that, as the distance from Yellow Sky grew shorter, the husband became commensurately restless. His brick-red hands were more insistent in their prominence. Occasionally he was even rather absent-minded and faraway when the bride leaned forward and addressed him.

As a matter of truth, Jack Potter was beginning to find the shadow of a deed weigh upon him like a leaden slab. He, the town marshal of Yellow Sky, a man known, liked, and feared in his corner, a prominent person, had gone to San Antonio to meet a girl he believed he loved, and there, after the usual prayers, had actually induced her to marry him, without consulting Yellow Sky for any part of the transaction. He was now bringing his bride before an innocent and unsuspecting community.

Of course people in Yellow Sky married as it pleased them, in accordance with a general custom; but such was Potter's thought of his duty to his friends, or of their idea of his duty, or of an unspoken form which does not control men in these matters, that he felt he was heinous. He had committed an extraordinary crime. Face to face with this girl in San Antonio, and spurred by his sharp impulse, he had gone headlong over all the social hedges. At San Antonio he was like a man hidden in the dark. A knife to sever any friendly duty, any form, was easy to his hand in that remote city. But the hour of Yellow Sky—the hour of daylight—was approaching.

He knew full well that his marriage was an important thing to his town. It could only be exceeded by the burning of the new hotel. His friends could not forgive him. Frequently he had reflected on the advisability of telling them by telegraph, but a new cowardice had been upon him. He feared to do it. And now the train was hurrying him toward a scene of amazement, glee, and reproach. He glanced out of the window at the line of haze swinging slowly in toward the train.

Yellow Sky had a kind of brass band, which played painfully, to the delight of the populace. He laughed without heart as he thought of it. If the citizens could dream of his prospective arrival with his bride, they would parade the band at the station and escort them, amid cheers and laughing congratulations, to his adobe home.

He resolved that he would use all the devices of speed and plains-craft in making the journey from the station to his house. Once within that safe citadel, he could issue some sort of a vocal bulletin, and then not go among the citizens until they had time to wear off a little of their enthusiasm.

The bride looked anxiously at him. "What's worrying you, Jack?"

He laughed again. "I'm not worrying, girl. I'm only thinking of Yellow Sky."

She flushed in comprehension.

A sense of mutual guilt invaded their minds and developed a finer tenderness. They looked at each other with eyes softly aglow. But Potter often laughed the same nervous laugh. The flush upon the bride's face seemed quite permanent.

The traitor to the feelings of Yellow Sky narrowly watched the speeding landscape. "We're nearly there," he said.

Presently the porter came and announced the proximity of Potter's home. He held a brush in his hand, and, with all his airy superiority gone, he brushed Potter's new clothes as the latter slowly turned this way and that way. Potter fumbled out a coin and gave it to the porter, as he had seen others do. It was a heavy and muscle-bound business, as that of a man shoeing his first horse.

The porter took their bag, and as the train began to slow they moved forward to the hooded platform of the car. Presently the two engines and their long string of coaches rushed into the station of Yellow Sky.

"They have to take water here," said Potter, from a constricted throat and in mournful cadence, as one announcing death. Before the train stopped, his eye had swept the length of the platform, and he was glad and astonished to see there was none upon it but the station-agent, who, with a slightly hurried and anxious air, was walking toward the water tanks. When the train had halted, the porter alighted first, and placed in position a little temporary step.

"Come on, girl," said Potter, hoarsely. As he helped her down they each laughed on a false note. He took the bag from the negro, and bade his wife cling to his arm. As they slunk rapidly away, his hangdog glance perceived that they were unloading the two trunks, and also that the station-agent, far ahead near the baggage car, had turned and was running toward him, making gestures. He laughed, and groaned as he laughed, when he noted the first effect of his marital bliss upon Yellow Sky. He gripped his wife's arm firmly to his side, and they fled. Behind them the porter stood, chuckling fatuously.

II

The California express on the Southern Railway was due at Yellow Sky in twenty-one minutes. There were six men at the bar of the Weary Gentleman saloon. One was a drummer who talked a great deal and rapidly; three were Texans who did not care to talk at that time; and two were Mexican sheepherders, who did not talk as a general practice in the Weary Gentleman saloon. The barkeeper's dog lay on the boardwalk that crossed in front of the door. His head was on his paws, and he glanced drowsily here and there with the constant vigilance of a dog that is kicked on occasion. Across the sandy street were some vivid green grass-plots, so wonderful in appearance, amid the sands that burned near them in a blazing sun, that they caused a doubt in the mind. They exactly resembled the grass mats used to represent lawns on the stage. At the cooler end of the railway station, a man without a coat sat in a tilted chair and smoked his pipe. The fresh-cut bank of the Rio Grande circled near the town, and there could be seen beyond it a great plum-colored plain of mesquite.

Save for the busy drummer and his companions in the saloon, Yellow Sky was dozing. The newcomer leaned gracefully upon the bar, and recited many tales with the confidence of a bard who has come upon a new field.

"—and at the moment that the old man fell downstairs with the bureau in his arms, the old woman was coming up with two scuttles of coal, and of course—"

The drummer's tale was interrupted by a young man who suddenly appeared in the open door. He cried: "Scratchy Wilson's drunk, and has turned loose with both hands." The two Mexicans at once set down their glasses and faded out of the rear entrance of the saloon.

The drummer, innocent and jocular, answered: "All right, old man. S'pose he has? Come in and have a drink, anyhow."

But the information had made such an obvious cleft in every skull in the room that the drummer was obliged to see its importance. All had become instantly solemn. "Say," said he, mystified, "what is this?" His three companions made the introductory gesture of eloquent speech, but the young man at the door forestalled them.

"It means, my friend," he answered, as he came into the saloon, "that for the next two hours this town won't be a health resort."

The barkeeper went to the door and locked and barred it. Reaching out of the window, he pulled in heavy wooden shutters and barred them. Immediately a solemn, chapel-like gloom was upon the place. The drummer was looking from one to another.

"But say," he cried, "what is this, anyhow? You don't mean there is going to be a gunfight?"

"Don't know whether there'll be a fight or not," answered one man, grimly. "But there'll be some shootin'—some good shootin'."

The young man who had warned them waved his hand. "Oh, there'll be a fight fast enough, if any one wants it. Anybody can get a fight out there in the street. There's a fight just waiting."

The drummer seemed to be swayed between the interest of a foreigner and a perception of personal danger.

"What did you say his name was?" he asked.

"Scratchy Wilson," they answered in chorus.

"And will he kill anybody? What are you going to do? Does this happen often? Does he rampage around like this once a week or so? Can he break in that door?"

"No; he can't break down that door," replied the barkeeper. "He's tried it three times. But when he comes you'd better lay down on the floor, stranger. He's dead sure to shoot at it, and a bullet may come through."

Thereafter the drummer kept a strict eye upon the door. The time had not yet been called for him to hug the floor, but, as a minor precaution, he sidled near to the wall. "Will he kill anybody?" he said again.

The men laughed low and scornfully at the question.

"He's out to shoot, and he's out for trouble. Don't see any good in experimentin' with him."

"But what do you do in a case like this? What do you do?"

A man responded: "Why, he and Jack Potter—"

"But," in chorus the other men interrupted, "Jack Potter's in San Anton'."

"Well, who is he? What's he got to do with it?"

"Oh, he's the town marshal. He goes out and fights Scratchy when he gets on one of these tears."

"Wow!" said the drummer, mopping his brow. "Nice job he's got."

The voices had toned away to mere whisperings. The drummer wished to ask further questions, which were born of an increasing anxiety and bewilderment; but when he attempted them, the men merely looked at him in irritation and motioned him to remain silent. A tense waiting hush was upon them. In the deep shadows of the room their eyes shone as they listened for sounds from the street. One man made three gestures at the barkeeper; and the latter, moving like a ghost, handed him a glass and a bottle. The man poured a full glass of whiskey, and set down the bottle noiselessly. He gulped the whiskey in a swallow, and turned again toward the door in immovable silence. The drummer saw that the barkeeper, without a sound, had taken a Winchester from beneath the bar. Later he saw this individual beckoning to him, so he tiptoed across the room.

"You better come with me back of the bar."

"No, thanks," said the drummer, perspiring. "I'd rather be where I can make a break for the back door."

Whereupon the man of bottles made a kindly but peremptory gesture. The drummer obeyed it, and, finding himself seated on a box with his head below the level of the bar, balm was laid upon his soul at sight of various zinc and copper fittings that bore a resemblance to armor plate. The barkeeper took a seat comfortably upon an adjacent box.

"You see," he whispered, "this here Scratchy Wilson is a wonder with a gun—a perfect wonder—and when he goes on the war trail, we hunt our holes—naturally. He's about the last one of the old gang that used to hang out along the river here. He's a terror when he's drunk. When he's sober he's all right—kind of simple—wouldn't hurt a fly—nicest fellow in town. But when he's drunk—whoo!"

There were periods of stillness. "I wish Jack Potter was back from San Anton'," said the barkeeper. "He shot Wilson up once—in the leg—and he would sail in and pull out the kinks in this thing."

Presently they heard from a distance the sound of a shot, followed by three wild yowls. It instantly removed a bond from the men in the darkened saloon. There was a shuffling of feet. They looked at each other. "Here he comes," they said.

III

A man in a maroon-colored flannel shirt, which had been purchased for purposes of decoration, and made principally by some Jewish women on the East Side of New York, rounded a corner and walked into the middle of the main street of Yellow Sky. In either hand the man held a long, heavy, blue-black revolver. Often he yelled, and these cries rang through a semblance of a deserted village, shrilly flying over the roofs in a volume that seemed to have no relation to the ordinary vocal strength of a man. It was as if the surrounding stillness formed the arch of a tomb over him. These cries of ferocious challenge rang against walls of silence. And his boots had red tops with gilded imprints, of the kind beloved in winter by little sledding boys on the hillsides of New England.

The man's face flamed in a rage begot of whiskey. His eyes, rolling, and yet keen for ambush, hunted the still doorways and windows. He walked with the creeping movement of the midnight cat. As it occurred to him, he roared menacing information. The long revolvers in his hands were as easy as straws; they were moved with an electric swiftness. The little fingers of each hand played sometimes in a musician's way. Plain from the low collar of the shirt, the cords of his neck straightened and sank, straightened and sank, as passion moved him. The only sounds were his terrible invitations. The calm adobes preserved their demeanor at the passing of this small thing in the middle of the street.

There was no offer of fight—no offer of fight. The man called to the sky. There were no attractions. He bellowed and fumed and swayed his revolvers here and everywhere.

The dog of the barkeeper of the Weary Gentleman saloon had not appreciated the advance of events. He yet lay dozing in front of his master's door. At sight of the dog, the man paused and raised his revolver humorously. At sight of the man, the dog sprang up and walked diagonally away, with a sullen head, and growling. The man yelled, and the dog broke into a gallop. As it was about to enter an alley, there was a loud noise, a whistling, and something spat the ground directly before it. The dog screamed, and, wheeling in terror, galloped headlong in a new direction. Again there was a noise, a whistling, and sand was kicked viciously before it. Fear-stricken, the dog turned and flurried like an animal in a pen. The man stood laughing, his weapons at his hips.

Ultimately the man was attracted by the closed door of the Weary Gentleman saloon. He went to it and, hammering with a revolver, demanded drink.

The door remaining imperturbable, he picked a bit of paper from the walk, and nailed it to the framework with a knife. He then turned his back contemptuously upon this popular resort and, walking to the opposite side of the street and spinning there on his heel quickly and lithely, fired at the bit of paper. He missed it by a half-inch. He swore at himself, and went away. Later, he comfortably fusilladed the windows of his most intimate friend. The man was playing with this town. It was a toy for him.

But still there was no offer of fight. The name of Jack Potter, his ancient antagonist, entered his mind, and he concluded that it would be a glad thing if he should go to Potter's house, and by bombardment induce him to come out and fight. He moved in the direction of his desire, chanting Apache scalp-music.

When he arrived at it, Potter's house presented the same still front as had the other adobes. Taking up a strategic position, the man howled a challenge. But this house regarded him as might a great stone god. It gave no sign. After a decent wait, the man howled further challenges, mingling with them wonderful epithets.

Presently there came the spectacle of a man churning himself into deepest rage over the immobility of a house. He fumed at it as the winter wind attacks a prairie cabin in the North. To the distance there should have gone the sound of a tumult like the fighting of two hundred Mexicans. As necessity bade him, he paused for breath or to reload his revolvers.

IV

Potter and his bride walked sheepishly and with speed. Sometimes they laughed together shamefacedly and low.

"Next corner, dear," he said finally.

They put forth the efforts of a pair walking bowed against a strong wind. Potter was about to raise a finger to point the first appearance of the new home when, as they circled the corner, they came face to face with a man in a maroon-colored shirt, who was feverishly pushing cartridges into a large revolver. Upon the instant the man dropped his revolver to the ground, and, like lightning, whipped another from its holster. The second weapon was aimed at the bridegroom's chest.

There was a silence. Potter's mouth seemed to be merely a grave for his tongue. He exhibited an instinct to at once loosen his arm from the woman's grip, and he dropped the bag to the sand. As for the bride, her face had gone as yellow as old cloth. She was a slave to hideous rites, gazing at the apparitional snake.

The two men faced each other at a distance of three paces. He of the revolver smiled with a new and quiet ferocity.

"Tried to sneak up on me," he said. "Tried to sneak up on me!" His eyes grew more baleful. As Potter made a slight movement, the man thrust his revolver venomously forward. "No; don't you do it, Jack Potter. Don't you move a finger toward a gun just yet. Don't you move an eyelash. The time has come for me to settle with you, and I'm goin' to do it my own way, and loaf along with no interferin'. So if you don't want a gun bent on you, just mind what I tell you."

Potter looked at his enemy. "I ain't got a gun on me, Scratchy," he said. "Honest, I ain't." He was stiffening and steadying, but yet somewhere at the back of his mind a vision of the Pullman floated: the sea-green figured velvet, the shining brass, silver, and glass, the wood that gleamed as darkly brilliant as the surface of a pool of oil—all the glory of the marriage, the environment of the new estate. "You know I fight when it comes to fighting, Scratchy Wilson; but I ain't got a gun on me. You'll have to do all the shootin' yourself."

His enemy's face went livid. He stepped forward, and lashed his weapon to and fro before Potter's chest. "Don't you tell me you ain't got no gun on you, you whelp. Don't tell me no lie like that. There ain't a man in Texas ever seen you without no gun. Don't take me for no kid." His eyes blazed with light, and his throat worked like a pump.

"I ain't takin' you for no kid," answered Potter. His heels had not moved an inch backward. "I'm takin' you for a damn fool. I tell you I ain't got a gun, and I ain't. If you're goin' to shoot me up, you better begin now. You'll never get a chance like this again."

So much enforced reasoning had told on Wilson's rage. He was calmer. "If you ain't got a gun, why ain't you got a gun?" he sneered. "Been to Sunday school?"

"I ain't got a gun because I've just come from San Anton' with my wife. I'm married," said Potter. "And if I'd thought there was going to be any galoots like you prowling around when I brought my wife home, I'd had a gun, and don't you forget it."

"Married!" said Scratchy, not at all comprehending.

"Yes, married. I'm married," said Potter, distinctly.

"Married?" said Scratchy. Seemingly for the first time, he saw the drooping, drowning woman at the other man's side. "No!" he said. He was like a creature allowed a glimpse of another world. He moved a pace backward, and his arm, with the revolver, dropped to his side. "Is this the lady?" he asked.

"Yes; this is the lady," answered Potter.

There was another period of silence.

"Well," said Wilson at last, slowly, "I s'pose it's all off now."

"It's all off if you say so, Scratchy. You know I didn't make the trouble." Potter lifted his valise.

"Well, I low it's off, Jack," said Wilson. He was looking at the ground. "Married!" He was not a student of chivalry; it was merely that in the presence of this foreign condition he was a simple child of the earlier plains. He picked up his starboard revolver, and, placing both weapons in their holsters, he went away. His feet made funnel-shaped tracks in the heavy sand.

THE CHRYSANTHEMUMS

John Steinbeck

(1902–1968)

Biography p. 1102

The high grey-flannel fog of winter closed off the Salinas Valley from the sky and from all the rest of the world. On every side it sat like a lid on the mountains and made of the great valley a closed pot. On the broad, level land floor the gang plows bit deep and left the black earth shining like metal where the shares had cut. On the foothill ranches across the Salinas River, the yellow stubble fields seemed to be bathed in pale cold sunshine, but there was no sunshine in the valley now in December. The thick willow scrub along the river flamed with sharp and positive yellow leaves.

It was a time of quiet and of waiting. The air was cold and tender. A light wind blew up from the southwest so that the farmers were mildly hopeful of a good rain before long; but fog and rain do not go together.

Across the river, on Henry Allen's foothill ranch there was little work to be done, for the hay was cut and stored and the orchards were plowed up to receive the rain deeply when it should come. The cattle on the higher slopes were becoming shaggy and rough-coated.

Elisa Allen, working in her flower garden, looked down across the yard and saw Henry, her husband, talking to two men in business suits. The three of them stood by the tractor shed, each man with one foot on the side of the little Fordson. They smoked cigarettes and studied the machine as they talked.

Elisa watched them for a moment and then went back to her work. She was thirty-five. Her face was lean and strong and her eyes were as clear as water. Her figure looked blocked and heavy in her gardening costume, a man's black hat pulled low down over her eyes, clodhopper shoes, a figured print dress almost completely covered by a big corduroy apron with four big pockets to hold the snips, the trowel and scratcher, the seeds and the knife she worked with. She wore heavy leather gloves to protect her hands while she worked.

She was cutting down the old year's chrysanthemum stalks with a pair of short and powerful scissors. She looked down toward the men by the tractor shed now and then. Her face was eager and mature and handsome; even her work with the scissors was over-eager, over-powerful. The chrysanthemum stems seemed too small and easy for her energy.

She brushed a cloud of hair out of her eyes with the back of her glove, and left a smudge of earth on her cheek in doing it. Behind her stood the neat white farm house with red geraniums close-banked around it as high as the windows. It was a hard-swept looking little house, with hard-polished windows, and a clean mud-mat on the front steps.

Elisa cast another glance toward the tractor shed. The strangers were getting into their Ford coupe. She took off a glove and put her strong fingers down into the forest of new green chrysanthemum sprouts that were growing around the old roots. She spread the leaves and looked down among the close-growing stems. No aphids were there, no sowbugs or snails or cutworms. Her terrier fingers destroyed such pests before they could get started.

Elisa started at the sound of her husband's voice. He had come near quietly, and he leaned over the wire fence that protected her flower garden from cattle and dogs and chickens.

"At it again," he said. "You've got a strong new crop coming."

Elisa straightened her back and pulled on the gardening glove again. "Yes. They'll be strong this coming year." In her tone and on her face there was a little smugness.

"You've got a gift with things," Henry observed. "Some of those yellow chrysanthemums you had this year were ten inches across. I wish you'd work out in the orchard and raise some apples that big."

Her eyes sharpened. "Maybe I could do it, too. I've a gift with things, all right. My mother had it. She could stick anything in the ground and make it grow. She said it was having planters' hands that knew how to do it."

"Well, it sure works with flowers," he said.

"Henry, who were those men you were talking to?"

"Why, sure, that's what I came to tell you. They were from the Western Meat Company. I sold those thirty head of three-year-old steers. Got nearly my own price, too."

"Good," she said. "Good for you."

"And I thought," he continued, "I thought how it's Saturday afternoon, and we might go into Salinas for dinner at a restaurant, and then to a picture show—to celebrate, you see."

"Good," she repeated. "Oh, yes. That will be good."

Henry put on his joking tone. "There's fights tonight. How'd you like to go to the fights?"

"Oh, no," she said breathlessly. "No, I wouldn't like fights."

"Just fooling, Elisa. We'll go to a movie. Let's see. It's two now. I'm going to take Scotty and bring down those steers from the hill. It'll take us maybe two hours. We'll go in town about five and have dinner at the Cominos Hotel. Like that?"

"Of course I'll like it. It's good to eat away from home."

"All right, then. I'll go get up a couple of horses."

She said, "I'll have plenty of time to transplant some of these sets, I guess."

She heard her husband calling Scotty down by the barn. And a little later she saw the two men ride up the pale yellow hillside in search of the steers.

There was a little square sandy bed kept for rooting the chrysanthemums. With her trowel she turned the soil over and over, and smoothed it and patted it firm. Then she dug ten parallel trenches to receive the sets. Back at the chrysanthemum bed she pulled out the little crisp shoots, trimmed off the leaves of each one with her scissors and laid it on a small orderly pile.

A squeak of wheels and plod of hoofs came from the road. Elisa looked up. The country road ran along the dense bank of willows and cottonwoods that bordered the river, and up this road came a curious vehicle, curiously drawn. It was an old spring-wagon, with a round canvas top on it like the cover of a prairie schooner. It was drawn by an old bay horse and a little grey-and-white burro. A big stubble-bearded man sat between the cover flaps and drove the crawling team. Underneath the wagon, between the hind wheels, a lean and rangy mongrel dog walked sedately. Words were painted on the canvas, in clumsy, crooked letters. "Pots, pans, knives, sisors, lawn mores, Fixed." Two rows of articles, and the triumphantly definitive "Fixed" below. The black paint had run down in little sharp points beneath each letter.

Elisa, squatting on the ground, watched to see the crazy, loose-jointed wagon pass by. But it didn't pass. It turned into the farm road in front of her house, crooked old wheels skirling and squeaking. The rangy dog darted from between the wheels and ran ahead. Instantly the two ranch shepherds flew out at him. Then all three stopped, and with stiff and quivering tails, with taut straight legs, with ambassadorial dignity, they slowly circled, sniffing daintily. The caravan pulled up to Elisa's wire fence and stopped. Now the newcomer dog, feeling out-numbered, lowered his tail and retired under the wagon with raised hackles and bared teeth.

The man on the wagon seat called out, "That's a bad dog in a fight when he gets started."

Elisa laughed. "I see he is. How soon does he generally get started?"

The man caught up her laughter and echoed it heartily. "Sometimes not for weeks and weeks," he said. He climbed stiffly down, over the wheel. The horse and the donkey drooped like unwatered flowers.

Elisa saw that he was a very big man. Although his hair and beard were greying, he did not look old. His worn black suit was wrinkled and spotted with grease. The laughter had disappeared from his face and eyes the moment his laughing voice ceased. His eyes were dark, and they were full of the brooding that gets in the eyes of teamsters and of sailors. The calloused hands he rested on the wire fence were cracked, and every crack was a black line. He took off his battered hat.

"I'm off my general road, ma'am," he said. "Does this dirt road cut over across the river to the Los Angeles highway?"

Elisa stood up and shoved the thick scissors in her apron pocket. "Well, yes, it does, but it winds around and then fords the river. I don't think your team could pull through the sand."

He replied with some asperity. "It might surprise you what them beasts can pull through."

"When they get started?" she asked.

He smiled for a second. "Yes. When they get started."

"Well," said Elisa, "I think you'll save time if you go back to the Salinas road and pick up the highway there."

He drew a big finger down the chicken wire and made it sing. "I ain't in any hurry, ma'am. I go from Seattle to San Diego and back every year. Takes all my time. About six months each way. I aim to follow nice weather."

Elisa took off her gloves and stuffed them in the apron pocket with the scissors. She touched the under edge of her man's hat, searching for fugitive hairs. "That sounds like a nice kind of a way to live," she said.

He leaned confidentially over the fence. "Maybe you noticed the writing on my wagon. I mend pots and sharpen knives and scissors. You got any of them things to do?"

"Oh, no," she said quickly. "Nothing like that." Her eyes hardened with resistance.

"Scissors is the worst thing," he explained. "Most people just ruin scissors trying to sharpen 'em, but I know how. I got a special tool. It's a little bobbit kind of thing, and patented. But it sure does the trick."

"No. My scissors are all sharp."

"All right, then. Take a pot," he continued earnestly, "a bent pot, or a pot with a hole. I can make it like new so you don't have to buy no new ones. That's a saving for you."

"No," she said shortly. "I tell you I have nothing like that for you to do."

His face fell to an exaggerated sadness. His voice took on a whining undertone. "I ain't had a thing to do today. Maybe I won't have no supper tonight. You see I'm off my regular road. I know folks on the highway clear from Seattle to San Diego. They save their things for me to sharpen up because they know I do it so good and save them money."

"I'm sorry," Elisa said irritably. "I haven't anything for you to do."

His eyes left her face and fell to searching the ground. They roamed about until they came to the chrysanthemum bed where she had been working. "What's them plants, ma'am?"

The irritation and resistance melted from Elisa's face. "Oh, those are chrysanthemums, giant whites and yellows. I raise them every year, bigger than anybody around here."

"Kind of a long-stemmed flower? Looks like a quick puff of colored smoke?" he asked.

"That's it. What a nice way to describe them."

"They smell kind of nasty till you get used to them," he said.

"It's a good bitter smell," she retorted, "not nasty at all."

He changed his tone quickly. "I like the smell myself."

"I had ten-inch blooms this year," she said.

The man leaned farther over the fence. "Look. I know a lady down the road a piece, has got the nicest garden you ever seen. Got nearly every kind of flower but no chrysantheums. Last time I was mending a copper-bottom washtub for her (that's a hard job but I do it good), she said to me, 'If you ever run acrost some nice chrysantheums I wish you'd try to get me a few seeds.' That's what she told me."

Elisa's eyes grew alert and eager. "She couldn't have known much about chrysanthemums. You *can* raise them from seed, but it's much easier to root the little sprouts you see there."

"Oh," he said. "I s'pose I can't take none to her, then."

"Why yes you can," Elisa cried. "I can put some in damp sand, and you can carry them right along with you. They'll take root in the pot if you keep them damp. And then she can transplant them."

"She'd sure like to have some, ma'am. You say they're nice ones?"

"Beautiful," she said. "Oh, beautiful." Her eyes shone. She tore off the battered hat and shook out her dark pretty hair. "I'll put them in a flower pot, and you can take them right with you. Come into the yard."

While the man came through the picket gate Elisa ran excitedly along the geranium-bordered path to the back of the house. And she returned carrying a big red flower pot. The gloves were forgotten now. She kneeled on the ground by the starting bed and dug up the sandy soil with her fingers and scooped it into the bright new flower pot. Then she picked up the little pile of shoots she had prepared. With her strong fingers she pressed them into the sand and tamped around them with her knuckles. The man stood over her. "I'll tell you what to do," she said. "You remember so you can tell the lady."

"Yes, I'll try to remember."

"Well, look. These will take root in about a month. Then she must set them out, about a foot apart in good rich earth like this, see?" She lifted a handful of dark soil for him to look at. "They'll grow fast and tall. Now remember this: In July tell her to cut them down, about eight inches from the ground."

"Before they bloom?" he asked.

"Yes, before they bloom." Her face was tight with eagerness. "They'll grow right up again. About the last of September the buds will start."

She stopped and seemed perplexed. "It's the budding that takes the most care," she said hesitantly. "I don't know how to tell you." She looked deep into his eyes, searchingly. Her mouth opened a little, and she seemed to be listening. "I'll try to tell you," she said. "Did you ever hear of planting hands?"

"Can't say I have, ma'am."

"Well, I can only tell you what it feels like. It's when you're picking off the buds you don't want. Everything goes right down into your fingertips. You watch your fingers work. They do it themselves. You can feel how it is. They pick and pick the buds. They never make a mistake. They're with the plant. Do you see? Your fingers and the plant. You can feel that, right up your arm. They know. They never make a mistake. You can feel it. When you're like that you can't do anything wrong. Do you see that? Can you understand that?"

She was kneeling on the ground looking up at him. Her breast swelled passionately.

The man's eyes narrowed. He looked away self-consciously. "Maybe I know," he said. "Sometimes in the night in the wagon there——"

Elisa's voice grew husky. She broke in on him, "I've never lived as you do, but I know what you mean. When the night is dark—why, the stars are sharp-pointed, and there's quiet. Why, you rise up and up! Every pointed star gets driven into your body. It's like that. Hot and sharp and—lovely."

Kneeling there, her hand went out toward his legs in the greasy black trousers. Her hesitant fingers almost touched the cloth. Then her hand dropped to the ground. She crouched low like a fawning dog.

He said, "It's nice, just like you say. Only when you don't have no dinner, it ain't."

She stood up then, very straight, and her face was ashamed. She held the flower pot out to him and placed it gently in his arms. "Here. Put it in your wagon, on the seat, where you can watch it. Maybe I can find something for you to do."

At the back of the house she dug in the can pile and found two old and battered aluminum saucepans. She carried them back and gave them to him. "Here, maybe you can fix these."

His manner changed. He became professional. "Good as new I can fix them." At the back of his wagon he set a little anvil, and out of an oily tool box dug a small machine hammer. Elisa came through the gate to watch him while he pounded out the dents in the kettles. His mouth grew sure and knowing. At a difficult part of the work he sucked his under-lip.

"You sleep right in the wagon?" Elisa asked.

"Right in the wagon, ma'am. Rain or shine I'm dry as a cow in there."

"It must be nice," she said. "It must be very nice. I wish women could do such things."

"It ain't the right kind of life for a woman."

Her upper lip raised a little, showing her teeth. "How do you know? How can you tell?" she said.

"I don't know, ma'am," he protested. "Of course I don't know. Now here's your kettles, done. You don't have to buy no new ones."

"How much?"

"Oh, fifty cents'll do. I keep my prices down and my work good. That's why I have all them satisfied customers up and down the highway."

Elisa brought him a fifty-cent piece from the house and dropped it in his hand. "You might be surprised to have a rival some time. I can sharpen scissors, too. And I can beat the dents out of little pots. I could show you what a woman might do."

He put his hammer back in the oily box and shoved the little anvil out of sight. "It would be a lonely life for a woman, ma'am, and a scarey life, too, with animals creeping under the wagon all night." He climbed over the singletree, steadying himself with a hand on the burro's white rump. He settled himself in the seat, picked up the lines. "Thank you kindly, ma'am," he said. "I'll do like you told me; I'll go back and catch the Salinas road."

"Mind," she called, "if you're long in getting there, keep the sand damp."

"Sand, ma'am? . . . Sand? Oh, sure. You mean around the chrysantheums. Sure I will." He clucked his tongue. The beasts leaned luxuriously into their collars. The mongrel dog took his place between the back wheels. The wagon turned and crawled out the entrance road and back the way it had come, along the river.

Elisa stood in front of her wire fence watching the slow progress of the caravan. Her shoulders were straight, her head thrown back, her eyes half-closed, so that the scene came vaguely into them. Her lips moved silently, forming the words "Good-bye —good-bye." Then she whispered, "That's a bright direction. There's a glowing there." The sound of her whisper startled her. She shook herself free and looked about to see whether anyone had been listening. Only the dogs had heard. They lifted their heads toward her from their sleeping in the dust, and then stretched out their chins and settled asleep again. Elisa turned and ran hurriedly into the house.

In the kitchen she reached behind the stove and felt the water tank. It was full of hot water from the noonday cooking. In the bathroom she tore off her soiled clothes and flung them into the corner. And then she scrubbed herself with a little block of pumice, legs and thighs, loins and chest and arms, until her skin was scratched and red. When she had dried herself she stood in front of a mirror in her bedroom and looked at her body. She tightened her stomach and threw out her chest. She turned and looked over her shoulder at her back.

After a while she began to dress, slowly. She put on her newest underclothing and her nicest stockings and the dress which was the symbol of her prettiness. She worked carefully on her hair, penciled her eyebrows and rouged her lips.

Before she was finished she heard the little thunder of hoofs and the shouts of Henry and his helper as they drove the red steers into the corral. She heard the gate bang shut and set herself for Henry's arrival.

His step sounded on the porch. He entered the house calling, "Elisa, where are you?"

"In my room, dressing. I'm not ready. There's hot water for your bath. Hurry up. It's getting late."

When she heard him splashing in the tub, Elisa laid his dark suit on the bed, and shirt and socks and tie beside it. She stood his polished shoes on the floor beside the bed. Then she went to the porch and sat primly and stiffly down. She looked toward the river road where the willow-line was still yellow with frosted leaves so that under the high grey fog they seemed a thin band of sunshine. This was the only color in the grey afternoon. She sat unmoving for a long time. Her eyes blinked rarely.

Henry came banging out of the door, shoving his tie inside his vest as he came. Elisa stiffened and her face grew tight. Henry stopped short and looked at her. "Why— why, Elisa. You look so nice!"

"Nice? You think I look nice? What do you mean by 'nice'?"

Henry blundered on. "I don't know. I mean you look different, strong and happy."

"I am strong? Yes, strong. What do you mean 'strong'?"

He looked bewildered. "You're playing some kind of a game," he said helplessly. "It's a kind of a play. You look strong enough to break a calf over your knee, happy enough to eat it like a watermelon."

For a second she lost her rigidity. "Henry! Don't talk like that. You didn't know what you said." She grew complete again. "I'm strong," she boasted. "I never knew before how strong."

Henry looked down toward the tractor shed, and when he brought his eyes back to her, they were his own again. "I'll get out the car. You can put on your coat while I'm starting."

Elisa went into the house. She heard him drive to the gate and idle down his motor, and then she took a long time to put on her hat. She pulled it here and pressed it there. When Henry turned the motor off she slipped into her coat and went out.

The little roadster bounced along on the dirt road by the river, raising the birds and driving the rabbits into the brush. Two cranes flapped heavily over the willow-line and dropped into the river-bed.

Far ahead on the road Elisa saw a dark speck. She knew.

She tried not to look as they passed it, but her eyes would not obey. She whispered to herself sadly, "He might have thrown them off the road. That wouldn't have been much trouble, not very much. But he kept the pot," she explained. "He had to keep the pot. That's why he couldn't get them off the road."

The roadster turned a bend and she saw the caravan ahead. She swung full around toward her husband so she could not see the little covered wagon and the mismatched team as the car passed them.

In a moment it was over. The thing was done. She did not look back.

She said loudly, to be heard above the motor, "It will be good, tonight, a good dinner."

"Now you're changed again," Henry complained. He took one hand from the wheel and patted her knee. "I ought to take you in to dinner oftener. It would be good for both of us. We get so heavy out on the ranch."

"Henry," she asked, "could we have wine at dinner?"

"Sure we could. Say! That will be fine."

She was silent for a while; then she said, "Henry, at those prize fights, do the men hurt each other very much?"

"Sometimes a little, not often. Why?"

"Well, I've read how they break noses, and blood runs down their chests. I've read how the fighting gloves get heavy and soggy with blood."

He looked around at her. "What's the matter, Elisa? I didn't know you read things like that." He brought the car to a stop, then turned to the right over the Salinas River bridge.

"Do any women ever go to the fights?" she asked.

"Oh, sure, some. What's the matter, Elisa? Do you want to go? I don't think you'd like it, but I'll take you if you really want to go."

She relaxed limply in the seat. "Oh, no. No. I don't want to go. I'm sure I don't." Her face was turned away from him. "It will be enough if we can have wine. It will be plenty." She turned up her coat collar so he could not see that she was crying weakly—like an old woman.

THE GRAVE

Katherine Anne Porter

(1890–1980)

Biography p. 1094

The grandfather, dead for more than thirty years, had been twice disturbed in his long repose by the constancy and possessiveness of his widow. She removed his bones first to Louisiana and then to Texas as if she had set out to find her own burial place, knowing well she would never return to the places she had left. In Texas she set up a small cemetery in a corner of her first farm, and as the family connection grew, and oddments of relations came over from Kentucky to settle, it contained at last about twenty graves. After the grandmother's death, part of her land was to be sold for the benefit of certain of her children, and the cemetery happened to lie in the part set aside for sale. It was necessary to take up the bodies and bury them again in the family plot in the big new public cemetery, where the grandmother had been buried. At last her husband was to lie beside her for eternity, as she had planned.

The family cemetery had been a pleasant small neglected garden of tangled rose bushes and ragged cedar trees and cypress, the simple flat stones rising out of un-cropped sweet-smelling wild grass. The graves were lying open and empty one burning day when Miranda and her brother Paul, who often went together to hunt rabbits and doves, propped their twenty-two Winchester rifles carefully against the rail fence, climbed over and explored among the graves. She was nine years old and he was twelve.

They peered into the pits all shaped alike with such purposeful accuracy, and looking at each other with pleased adventurous eyes, they said in solemn tones: "These were graves!" trying by words to shape a special, suitable emotion in their minds, but they felt nothing except an agreeable thrill of wonder: they were seeing a new sight, doing something they had not done before. In them both there was also a small disappointment at the entire commonplaceness of the actual spectacle. Even if it had once contained a coffin for years upon years, when the coffin was gone a grave was just a hole in the ground. Miranda leaped into the pit that had held her grandfather's bones. Scratching around aimlessly and pleasurably as any young animal, she scooped up a lump of earth and weighed it in her palm. It had a pleasantly sweet, corrupt smell, being mixed with cedar needles and small leaves, and as the crumbs fell apart, she saw a silver dove no larger than a hazel nut, with spread wings and a neat fan-shaped tail. The breast had a deep round hollow in it. Turning it up to the fierce sunlight, she saw that the inside of the hollow was cut in little whorls. She scrambled out, over the pile of loose earth that had fallen back into one end of the grave, calling to Paul that she had found something, he must guess what . . . His head appeared smiling over the rim of another grave. He waved a closed hand at her. "I've got something too!" They ran to compare treasures, making a game of it, so many guesses each, all wrong, and a final showdown with opened palms. Paul had found a thin wide gold ring carved with intricate flowers and leaves. Miranda was smitten at sight of the ring and wished to have it. Paul seemed more impressed by the dove. They made a trade, with some little bickering. After he had got the dove in his hand, Paul said, "Don't you know what this is? This is a screw head for a *coffin!* . . . I'll bet nobody else in the world has one like this!"

Miranda glanced at it without covetousness. She had the gold ring on her thumb; it fitted perfectly. "Maybe we ought to go now," she said, "maybe one of the niggers 'll see us and tell somebody." They knew the land had been sold, the cemetery was no longer theirs, and they felt like trespassers. They climbed back over the fence, slung their rifles loosely under their arms—they had been shooting at targets with various kinds of firearms since they were seven years old—and set out to look for the rabbits and doves or whatever small game might happen along. On these expeditions Miranda always followed at Paul's heels along the path, obeying instructions about handling her gun when going through fences; learning how to stand it up properly so it would not slip and fire unexpectedly; how to wait her time for a shot and not just bang away in the air without looking, spoiling shots for Paul, who really could hit things if given a chance. Now and then, in her excitement at seeing birds whizz up suddenly before her face, or a rabbit leap across her very toes, she lost her head, and almost without sighting she flung her rifle up and pulled the trigger. She hardly ever hit any sort of mark. She had no proper sense of hunting at all. Her brother would be often completely disgusted with her. "You don't care whether you get your bird or not," he said. "That's no way to hunt." Miranda could not understand his indignation. She had seen him smash his hat and yell with fury when he had missed his aim. "What I like about shooting," said Miranda, with exasperating inconsequence, "is pulling the trigger and hearing the noise."

"Then, by golly," said Paul, "whyn't you go back to the range and shoot at bulls-eyes?"

"I'd just as soon," said Miranda, "only like this, we walk around more."

"Well, you just stay behind and stop spoiling my shots," said Paul, who, when he made a kill, wanted to be certain he had made it. Miranda, who alone brought down a bird once in twenty rounds, always claimed as her own any game they got when they fired at the same moment. It was tiresome and unfair and her brother was sick of it.

"Now, the first dove we see, or the first rabbit, is mine," he told her. "And the next will be yours. Remember that and don't get smarty."

"What about snakes?" asked Miranda idly. "Can I have the first snake?"

Waving her thumb gently and watching her gold ring glitter, Miranda lost interest in shooting. She was wearing her summer roughing outfit: dark blue overalls, a light blue shirt, a hired-man's straw hat, and thick brown sandals. Her brother had the same outfit except his was a sober hickorynut color. Ordinarily Miranda preferred her overalls to any other dress, though it was making rather a scandal in the countryside, for the year was 1903, and in the back country the law of female decorum had teeth in it. Her father had been criticized for letting his girls dress like boys and go careering around astride barebacked horses. Big sister Maria, the really independent and fearless one, in spite of her rather affected ways, rode at a dead run with only a rope knotted around her horse's nose. It was said the motherless family was running down, with the Grandmother no longer there to hold it together. It was known that she had discriminated against her son Harry in her will, and that he was in straits about money. Some of his old neighbors reflected with vicious satisfaction that now he would probably not be so stiffnecked, nor have any more high-stepping horses either. Miranda knew this, though she could not say how. She had met along the road old women of the kind who smoked corn-cob pipes, who had treated her grandmother with most sincere respect. They slanted their gummy old eyes side-ways at the granddaughter and said, "Ain't you ashamed of yoself, Missy? It's against the Scriptures to dress like that. Whut yo Pappy thinkin about?" Miranda, with her powerful social sense, which was like a fine set of antennae radiating from every pore of her skin, would feel ashamed because she knew well it was rude and ill-bred to shock anybody, even bad-tempered old crones, though she had faith in her father's judgment and was perfectly comfortable in the clothes. Her father had said, "They're just what you need, and they'll save your dresses for school . . ." This sounded quite simple and natural to her. She had been brought up in rigorous economy. Wastefulness was vulgar. It was also a sin. These were truths; she had heard them repeated many times and never once disputed.

Now the ring, shining with the serene purity of fine gold on her rather grubby thumb, turned her feelings against her overalls and sockless feet, toes sticking through the thick brown leather straps. She wanted to go back to the farmhouse, take a good cold bath, dust herself with plenty of Maria's violet talcum powder—provided Maria was not present to object, of course—put on the thinnest, most becoming dress she owned, with a big sash, and sit in a wicker chair under the trees . . . These things were not all she wanted, of course; she had vague stirrings of desire for luxury and a grand way of living which could not take precise form in her imagination but were founded on family legend of past wealth and leisure. These immediate comforts were what she could have, and she wanted them at once. She lagged rather far behind Paul, and once she thought of just turning back without a word and going home. She stopped, thinking that Paul would never do that to her, and so she would have to tell him. When a rabbit leaped, she let Paul have it without dispute. He killed it with one shot.

When she came up with him, he was already kneeling, examining the wound, the rabbit trailing from his hands. "Right through the head," he said complacently, as if he had aimed for it. He took out his sharp, competent bowie knife and started to skin the body. He did it very cleanly and quickly. Uncle Jimbilly knew how to prepare the skins so that Miranda always had fur coats for her dolls, for though she never cared much for her dolls she liked seeing them in fur coats. The children knelt facing each other over the dead animal. Miranda watched admiringly while her brother stripped the skin away as if he were taking off a glove. The flayed flesh emerged dark scarlet, sleek, firm; Miranda with thumb and finger felt the long fine muscles with the silvery flat strips binding them to the joints. Brother lifted the oddly bloated belly. "Look," he said, in a low amazed voice. "It was going to have young ones."

Very carefully he slit the thin flesh from the center ribs to the flanks, and a scarlet bag appeared. He slit again and pulled the bag open, and there lay a bundle of tiny rabbits, each wrapped in a thin scarlet veil. The brother pulled these off and there they were, dark gray, their sleek wet down lying in minute even ripples, like a baby's head just washed, their unbelievably small delicate ears folded close, their little blind faces almost featureless.

Miranda said, "Oh, I want to *see*," under her breath. She looked and looked—excited but not frightened, for she was accustomed to the sight of animals killed in hunting—filled with pity and astonishment and a kind of shocked delight in the wonderful little creatures for their own sakes, they were so pretty. She touched one of them ever so carefully, "Ah, there's blood running over them," she said and began to tremble without knowing why. Yet she wanted most deeply to see and to know. Having seen, she felt at once as if she had known all along. The very memory of her former ignorance faded, she had always known just this. No one had ever told her anything outright, she had been rather unobservant of the animal life around her because she was so accustomed to animals. They seemed simply disorderly and unaccountably rude in their habits, but altogether natural and not very interesting. Her brother had spoken as if he had known about everything all along. He may have seen all this before. He had never said a word to her, but she knew now a part at least of what he knew. She understood a little of the secret, formless intuitions in her own mind and body, which had been clearing up, taking form, so gradually and so steadily she had not realized that she was learning what she had to know. Paul said cautiously, as if he were talking about something forbidden: "They were just about ready to be born." His voice dropped on the last word. "I know," said Miranda, "like kittens. I know, like babies." She was quietly and terribly agitated, standing again with her rifle under her arm, looking down at the bloody heap. "I don't want the skin," she said, "I won't have it." Paul buried the young rabbits again in their mother's body, wrapped the skin around her, carried her to a clump of sage bushes, and hid her away. He came out again at once and said to Miranda, with an eager friendliness, a confidential tone quite unusual in him, as if he were taking her into an important secret on equal terms: "Listen now. Now you listen to me, and don't ever forget. Don't you ever tell a living soul that you saw this. Don't tell a soul. Don't tell Dad because I'll get into trouble. He'll say I'm leading you into things you ought not to do. He's always saying that. So now don't you go and forget and blab out sometime the way you're always doing . . . Now, that's a secret. Don't you tell."

Miranda never told, she did not even wish to tell anybody. She thought about the whole worrisome affair with confused unhappiness for a few days. Then it sank quietly into her mind and was heaped over by accumulated thousands of impressions, for nearly twenty years. One day she was picking her path among the puddles and crushed refuse of a market street in a strange city of a strange country, when without warning, plain and clear in its true colors as if she looked through a frame upon a scene that had not stirred nor changed since the moment it happened, the episode of that far-off day leaped from its burial place before her mind's eye. She was so reasonlessly horrified she halted suddenly staring, the scene before her eyes dimmed by the vision back of them. An Indian vendor had held up before her a tray of dyed sugar sweets, in the shapes of all kinds of small creatures: birds, baby chicks, baby rabbits, lambs, baby pigs. They were in gay colors and smelled of vanilla, maybe. . . . It was a very hot day and the smell in the market, with its piles of raw flesh and wilting flowers, was like the mingled sweetness and corruption she had smelled that other day in the empty cemetery at home: the day she had remembered always until now vaguely as the time she and her brother had found treasure in the opened graves. Instantly upon this thought the dreadful vision faded, and she saw clearly her brother, whose childhood face she had forgotten, standing again in the blazing sunshine, again twelve years old, a pleased sober smile in his eyes, turning the silver dove over and over in his hands.

LIKE A WINDING SHEET

Ann Petry

(b. 1911)

Biography p. 1091

He had planned to get up before Mae did and surprise her by fixing breakfast. Instead he went back to sleep and she got out of bed so quietly he didn't know she wasn't there beside him until he woke up and heard the queer soft gurgle of water running out of the sink in the bathroom.

He knew he ought to get up but instead he put his arms across his forehead to shut the afternoon sunlight out of his eyes, pulled his legs up close to his body, testing them to see if the ache was still in them.

Mae had finished in the bathroom. He could tell because she never closed the door when she was in there and now the sweet smell of talcum powder was drifting down the hall and into the bedroom. Then he heard her coming down the hall.

"Hi, babe," she said affectionately.

"Hum," he grunted, and moved his arms away from his head, opened one eye.

"It's a nice morning."

"Yeah." He rolled over and the sheet twisted around him, outlining his thighs, his chest. "You mean afternoon, don't ya?"

Mae looked at the twisted sheet and giggled. "Looks like a winding sheet," she said. "A shroud—" Laughter tangled with her words and she had to pause for a moment before she could continue. "You look like a huckleberry—in a winding sheet—"

"That's no way to talk. Early in the day like this," he protested.

He looked at his arms silhouetted against the white of the sheets. They were inky black by contrast and he had to smile in spite of himself and he lay there smiling and savoring the sweet sound of Mae's giggling.

"Early?" She pointed a finger at the alarm clock on the table near the bed and giggled again. "It's almost four o'clock. And if you don't spring up out of there, you're going to be late again."

"What do you mean 'again'?"

"Twice last week. Three times the week before. And once the week before and—"

"I can't get used to sleeping in the daytime," he said fretfully. He pushed his legs out from under the covers experimentally. Some of the ache had gone out of them but they weren't really rested yet. "It's too light for good sleeping. And all that standing beats the hell out of my legs."

"After two years you oughta be used to it," Mae said.

He watched her as she fixed her hair, powdered her face, slipped into a pair of blue denim overalls. She moved quickly and yet she didn't seem to hurry.

"You look like you'd had plenty of sleep," he said lazily. He had to get up but he kept putting the moment off, not wanting to move, yet he didn't dare let his legs go completely limp because if he did he'd go back to sleep. It was getting later and later but the thought of putting his weight on his legs kept him lying there.

When he finally got up he had to hurry, and he gulped his breakfast so fast that he wondered if his stomach could possibly use food thrown at it at such a rate of speed. He was still wondering about it as he and Mae were putting their coats on in the hall.

Mae paused to look at the calendar. "It's the thirteenth," she said. Then a faint excitement in her voice, "Why, it's Friday the thirteenth." She had one arm in her coat sleeve and she held it there while she stared at the calendar. "I oughta stay home," she said. "I shouldn't go outa the house."

"Aw, don't be a fool," he said. "Today's payday. And payday is a good luck day everywhere, any way you look at it." And as she stood hesitating he said, "Aw, come on."

And he was late for work again because they spent fifteen minutes arguing before he could convince her she ought to go to work just the same. He had to talk persuasively, urging her gently, and it took time. But he couldn't bring himself to talk to her roughly or threaten to strike her like a lot of men might have done. He wasn't made that way.

So when he reached the plant he was late and he had to wait to punch the time clock because the day-shift workers were streaming out in long lines, in groups and bunches that impeded his progress.

Even now just starting his workday his legs ached. He had to force himself to struggle past the outgoing workers, punch the time clock, and get the little cart he pushed around all night, because he kept toying with the idea of going home and getting back in bed.

He pushed the cart out on the concrete floor, thinking that if this was his plant he'd make a lot of changes in it. There were too many standing-up jobs for one thing. He'd figure out some way most of 'em could be done sitting down and he'd put a lot more benches around. And this job he had—this job that forced him to walk ten hours a night, pushing this little cart, well, he'd turn it into a sitting-down job. One of those little trucks they used around railroad stations would be good for a job like this. Guys sat on a seat and the thing moved easily, taking up little room and turning in hardly any space at all, like on a dime.

He pushed the cart near the foreman. He never could remember to refer to her as the forelady even in his mind. It was funny to have a white woman for a boss in a plant like this one.

She was sore about something. He could tell by the way her face was red and her eyes were half-shut until they were slits. Probably been out late and didn't get enough sleep. He avoided looking at her and hurried a little, head down, as he passed her though he couldn't resist stealing a glance at her out of the corner of his eyes. He saw the edge of the light-colored slacks she wore and the tip end of a big tan shoe.

"Hey, Johnson!" the woman said.

The machines had started full blast. The whirr and the grinding made the building shake, made it impossible to hear conversations. The men and women at the machines talked to each other but looking at them from just a little distance away, they appeared to be simply moving their lips because you couldn't hear what they were saying. Yet the woman's voice cut across the machine sounds—harsh, angry.

He turned his head slowly. "Good evenin', Mrs. Scott," he said, and waited.

"You're late again."

"That's right. My legs were bothering me."

The woman's face grew redder, angrier looking. "Half this shift comes in late," she said. "And you're the worst one of all. You're always late. Whatsa matter with ya?"

"It's my legs," he said. "Somehow they don't ever get rested. I don't seem to get used to sleeping days. And I just can't get started."

"Excuses. You guys always got excuses," her anger grew and spread. "Every guy comes in here late always has an excuse. His wife's sick or his grandmother died or somebody in the family had to go to the hospital," she paused, drew a deep breath. "And the niggers is the worse. I don't care what's wrong with your legs. You get in here on time. I'm sick of you niggers—"

"You got the right to get mad," he interrupted softly. "You got the right to cuss me four ways to Sunday but I ain't letting nobody call me a nigger."

He stepped closer to her. His fists were doubled. His lips were drawn back in a thin narrow line. A vein in his forehead stood out swollen, thick.

And the woman backed away from him, not hurriedly but slowly—two, three steps back.

"Aw, forget it," she said. "I didn't mean nothing by it. It slipped out. It was an accident." The red of her face deepened until the small blood vessels in her cheeks were purple. "Go on and get back to work," she urged. And she took three more slow backward steps.

He stood motionless for a moment and then turned away from the sight of the red lipstick on her mouth that made him remember that the foreman was a woman. And he couldn't bring himself to hit a woman. He felt a curious tingling in his fingers and he looked down at his hands. They were clenched tight, hard, ready to smash some of those small purple veins in her face.

He pushed the cart ahead of him, walking slowly. When he turned his head, she was staring in his direction, mopping her forehead with a dark blue handkerchief. Their eyes met and then they both looked away.

He didn't glance in her direction again but moved past the long work benches, carefully collecting the finished parts, going slowly and steadily up and down, back and forth the length of the building, and as he walked he forced himself to swallow his anger, get rid of it.

And he succeeded so that he was able to think about what had happened without getting upset about it. An hour went by but the tension stayed in his hands. They were clenched and knotted on the handles of the cart as though ready to aim a blow.

And he thought he should have hit her anyway, smacked her hard in the face, felt the soft flesh of her face give under the hardness of his hands. He tried to make his hands relax by offering them a description of what it would have been like to strike her because he had the queer feeling that his hands were not exactly a part of him anymore—they had developed a separate life of their own over which he had no control. So he dwelt on the pleasure his hands would have felt—both of them cracking at her, first one and then the other. If he had done that his hands would have felt good now—relaxed, rested.

And he decided that even if he'd lost his job for it, he should have let her have it and it would have been a long time, maybe the rest of her life, before she called anybody else a nigger.

The only trouble was he couldn't hit a woman. A woman couldn't hit back the same way a man did. But it would have been a deeply satisfying thing to have cracked her

narrow lips wide open with just one blow, beautifully timed and with all his weight
in back of it. That way he would have gotten rid of all the energy and tension his anger
had created in him. He kept remembering how his heart had started pumping blood
so fast he had felt it tingle even in the tips of his fingers.

With the approach of night, fatigue nibbled at him. The corners of his mouth
drooped, the frown between his eyes deepened, his shoulders sagged; but his hands
stayed tight and tense. As the hours dragged by he noticed that the women workers
had started to snap and snarl at each other. He couldn't hear what they said because
of the sound of machines but he could see the quick lip movements that sent words
tumbling from the sides of their mouths. They gestured irritably with their hands and
scowled as their mouths moved.

Their violent jerky motions told him that it was getting close on to quitting time
but somehow he felt that the night still stretched ahead of him, composed of endless
hours of steady walking on his aching legs. When the whistle finally blew he went on
pushing the cart, unable to believe that it had sounded. The whirring of the machines
died away to a murmur and he knew then that he'd really heard the whistle. He stood
still for a moment, filled with a relief that made him sigh.

Then he moved briskly, putting the cart in the storeroom, hurrying to take his place
in the line forming before the paymaster. That was another thing he'd change, he
thought. He'd have the pay envelopes handed to the people right at their benches so
there wouldn't be ten or fifteen minutes lost waiting for the pay. He always got home
about fifteen minutes late on payday. They did it better in the plant where Mae
worked, brought the money right to them at their benches.

He stuck his pay envelope in his pants' pocket and followed the line of workers
heading for the subway in a slow-moving stream. He glanced up at the sky. It was
a nice night, the sky looked packed full to running over with stars. And he thought
if he and Mae would go right to bed when they got home from work they'd catch a
few hours of darkness for sleeping. But they never did. They fooled around—cooking
and eating and listening to the radio and he always stayed in a big chair in the living
room and went almost but not quite to sleep and when they finally got to bed it was
five or six in the morning and daylight was already seeping around the edges of the
sky.

He walked slowly, putting off the moment when he would have to plunge into the
crowd hurrying toward the subway. It was a long ride to Harlem and tonight the
thought of it appalled him. He paused outside an all-night restaurant to kill time, so
that some of the first rush of workers would be gone when he reached the subway.

The lights in the restaurant were brilliant, enticing. There was life and motion
inside. And as he looked through the window he thought that everything within range
of his eyes gleamed—the long imitation marble counter, the tall stools, the white
porcelain-topped tables and especially the big metal coffee urn right near the window.
Steam issued from its top and a gas flame flickered under it—a lively, dancing, blue
flame.

A lot of the workers from his shift—men and women—were lining up near the
coffee urn. He watched them walk to the porcelain-topped tables carrying steaming
cups of coffee and he saw that just the smell of the coffee lessened the fatigue lines
in their faces. After the first sip their faces softened, they smiled, they began to talk
and laugh.

On a sudden impulse he shoved the door open and joined the line in front of the coffee urn. The line moved slowly. And as he stood there the smell of the coffee, the sound of the laughter and of the voices, helped dull the sharp ache in his legs.

He didn't pay any attention to the white girl who was serving the coffee at the urn. He kept looking at the cups in the hands of the men who had been ahead of him. Each time a man stepped out of the line with one of the thick white cups the fragrant steam got in his nostrils. He saw that they walked carefully so as not to spill a single drop. There was a froth of bubbles at the top of each cup and he thought about how he would let the bubbles break against his lips before he actually took a big deep swallow.

Then it was his turn. "A cup of coffee," he said, just as he had heard the others say.

The white girl looked past him, put her hands up to her head and gently lifted her hair away from the back of her neck, tossing her head back a little. "No more coffee for a while," she said.

He wasn't certain he'd heard her correctly and he said, "What?" blankly.

"No more coffee for a while," she repeated.

There was silence behind him and then uneasy movement. He thought someone would say something, ask why or protest, but there was only silence and then a faint shuffling sound as though the men standing behind him had simultaneously shifted their weight from one foot to the other.

He looked at the girl without saying anything. He felt his hands begin to tingle and the tingling went all the way down to his finger tips so that he glanced down at them. They were clenched tight, hard, into fists. Then he looked at the girl again. What he wanted to do was hit her so hard that the scarlet lipstick on her mouth would smear and spread over her nose, her chin, out toward her cheeks, so hard that she would never toss her head again and refuse a man a cup of coffee because he was black.

He estimated the distance across the counter and reached forward, balancing his weight on the balls of his feet, ready to let the blow go. And then his hands fell back down to his sides because he forced himself to lower them, to unclench them and make them dangle loose. The effort took his breath away because his hands fought against him. But he couldn't hit her. He couldn't even now bring himself to hit a woman, not even this one, who had refused him a cup of coffee with a toss of her head. He kept seeing the gesture with which she had lifted the length of her blond hair from the back of her neck as expressive of her contempt for him.

When he went out the door he didn't look back. If he had he would have seen the flickering blue flame under the shiny coffee urn being extinguished. The line of men who had stood behind him lingered a moment to watch the people drinking coffee at the tables and then they left just as he had without having had the coffee they wanted so badly. The girl behind the counter poured water in the urn and swabbed it out and as she waited for the water to run out, she lifted her hair gently from the back of her neck and tossed her head before she began making a fresh lot of coffee.

But he had walked away without a backward look, his head down, his hands in his pockets, raging at himself and whatever it was inside of him that had forced him to stand quiet and still when he wanted to strike out.

The subway was crowded and he had to stand. He tried grasping an overhead strap and his hands were too tense to grip it. So he moved near the train door and stood there swaying back and forth with the rocking of the train. The roar of the train beat inside his head, making it ache and throb, and the pain in his legs clawed up into his groin so that he seemed to be bursting with pain and he told himself that it was due to all that anger-born energy that had piled up in him and not been used and so it had spread through him like a poison—from his feet and legs all the way up to his head.

Mae was in the house before he was. He knew she was home before he put the key in the door of the apartment. The radio was going. She had it tuned up loud and she was singing along with it.

"Hello, babe," she called out, as soon as he opened the door.

He tried to say 'hello' and it came out half grunt and half sigh.

"You sure sound cheerful," she said.

She was in the bedroom and he went and leaned against the doorjamb. The denim overalls she wore to work were carefully draped over the back of a chair by the bed. She was standing in front of the dresser, tying the sash of a yellow housecoat around her waist and chewing gum vigorously as she admired her reflection in the mirror over the dresser.

"Whatsa matter?" she said. "You get bawled out by the boss or somep'n?"

"Just tired," he said slowly. "For God's sake, do you have to crack that gum like that?"

"You don't have to lissen to me," she said complacently. She patted a curl in place near the side of her head and then lifted her hair away from the back of her neck, ducking her head forward and then back.

He winced away from the gesture. "What you got to be always fooling with your hair for?" he protested.

"Say, what's the matter with you anyway?" She turned away from the mirror to face him, put her hands on her hips. "You ain't been in the house two minutes and you're picking on me."

He didn't answer her because her eyes were angry and he didn't want to quarrel with her. They'd been married too long and got along too well and so he walked all the way into the room and sat down in the chair by the bed and stretched his legs out in front of him, putting his weight on the heels of his shoes, leaning way back in the chair, not saying anything.

"Lissen," she said sharply. "I've got to wear those overalls again tomorrow. "You're going to get them all wrinkled up leaning against them like that."

He didn't move. He was too tired and his legs were throbbing now that he had sat down. Besides the overalls were already wrinkled and dirty, he thought. They couldn't help but be for she'd worn them all week. He leaned farther back in the chair.

"Come on, get up," she ordered.

"Oh, what the hell," he said wearily, and got up from the chair. "I'd just as soon live in a subway. There'd be just as much place to sit down."

He saw that her sense of humor was struggling with her anger. But her sense of humor won because she giggled.

"Aw, come on and eat," she said. There was a coaxing note in her voice. "You're nothing but an old hungry nigger trying to act tough and—" she paused to giggle and then continued, "You—"

He had always found her giggling pleasant and deliberately said things that might amuse her and then waited, listening for the delicate sound to emerge from her throat. This time he didn't even hear the giggle. He didn't let her finish what she was saying. She was standing close to him and that funny tingling started in his finger tips, went fast up his arms and sent his fist shooting straight for her face.

There was the smacking sound of soft flesh being struck by a hard object and it wasn't until she screamed that he realized he had hit her in the mouth—so hard that the dark red lipstick had blurred and spread over her full lips, reaching up toward the tip of her nose, down toward her chin, out toward her cheeks.

The knowledge that he had struck her seeped through him slowly and he was appalled but he couldn't drag his hands away from her face. He kept striking her and he thought with horror that something inside him was holding him, binding him to this act, wrapping and twisting about him so that he had to continue it. He had lost all control over his hands. And he groped for a phrase, a word, something to describe what this thing was like that was happening to him and he thought it was like being enmeshed in a winding sheet—that was it—like a winding sheet. And even as the thought formed in his mind, his hands reached for her face again and yet again.

EVERYDAY USE

Alice Walker
(b. 1944)

Biography p. 1105

for your grandmama

I will wait for her in the yard that Maggie and I made so clean and wavy yesterday afternoon. A yard like this is more comfortable than most people know. It is not just a yard. It is like an extended living room. When the hard clay is swept clean as a floor and the fine sand around the edges lined with tiny, irregular grooves, anyone can come and sit and look up into the elm tree and wait for the breezes that never come inside the house.

Maggie will be nervous until after her sister goes: she will stand hopelessly in corners, homely and ashamed of the burn scars down her arms and legs, eying her sister with a mixture of envy and awe. She thinks her sister has held life always in the palm of one hand, that "no" is a word the world never learned to say to her.

You've no doubt seen those TV shows where the child who has "made it" is confronted, as a surprise, by her own mother and father, tottering in weakly from backstage. (A pleasant surprise, of course: What would they do if parent and child came on the show only to curse out and insult each other?) On TV mother and child embrace and smile into each other's faces. Sometimes the mother and father weep, the child wraps them in her arms and leans across the table to tell how she would not have made it without their help. I have seen these programs.

Sometimes I dream a dream in which Dee and I are suddenly brought together on a TV program of this sort. Out of a dark and soft-seated limousine I am ushered into a bright room filled with many people. There I meet a smiling, gray, sporty man like Johnny Carson who shakes my hand and tells me what a fine girl I have. Then we are on the stage and Dee is embracing me with tears in her eyes. She pins on my dress a large orchid, even though she has told me once that she thinks orchids are tacky flowers.

In real life I am a large, big-boned woman with rough, man-working hands. In the winter I wear flannel nightgowns to bed and overalls during the day. I can kill and clean a hog as mercilessly as a man. My fat keeps me hot in zero weather. I can work outside all day, breaking ice to get water for washing; I can eat pork liver cooked over the open fire minutes after it comes steaming from the hog. One winter I knocked a bull calf straight in the brain between the eyes with a sledge hammer and had the meat hung up to chill before nightfall. But of course all this does not show on television. I am the way my daughter would want me to be: a hundred pounds lighter, my skin like an uncooked barley pancake. My hair glistens in the hot bright lights. Johnny Carson has much to do to keep up with my quick and witty tongue.

But that is a mistake. I know even before I wake up. Who ever knew a Johnson with a quick tongue? Who can even imagine me looking a strange white man in the eye? It seems to me I have talked to them always with one foot raised in flight, with my head turned in whichever way is farthest from them. Dee, though. She would always look anyone in the eye. Hesitation was no part of her nature.

"How do I look, Mama?" Maggie says, showing just enough of her thin body enveloped in pink skirt and red blouse for me to know she's there, almost hidden by the door.

"Come out into the yard," I say.

Have you ever seen a lame animal, perhaps a dog run over by some careless person rich enough to own a car, sidle up to someone who is ignorant enough to be kind to him? That is the way my Maggie walks. She has been like this, chin on chest, eyes on ground, feet in shuffle, ever since the fire that burned the other house to the ground.

Dee is lighter than Maggie, with nicer hair and a fuller figure. She's a woman now, though sometimes I forget. How long ago was it that the other house burned? Ten, twelve years? Sometimes I can still hear the flames and feel Maggie's arms sticking to me, her hair smoking and her dress falling off her in little black papery flakes. Her eyes seemed stretched open, blazed open by the flames reflected in them. And Dee. I see her standing off under the sweet gum tree she used to dig gum out of; a look of concentration on her face as she watched the last dingy gray board of the house fall in toward the red-hot brick chimney. Why don't you do a dance around the ashes? I'd wanted to ask her. She had hated the house that much.

I used to think she hated Maggie, too. But that was before we raised the money, the church and me, to send her to Augusta to school. She used to read to us without pity; forcing words, lies, other folks' habits, whole lives upon us two, sitting trapped and ignorant underneath her voice. She washed us in a river of make-believe, burned us with a lot of knowledge we didn't necessarily need to know. Pressed us to her with the serious way she read, to shove us away at just the moment, like dimwits, we seemed about to understand.

Dee wanted nice things. A yellow organdy dress to wear to her graduation from high school; black pumps to match a green suit she'd made from an old suit somebody gave me. She was determined to stare down any disaster in her efforts. Her eyelids would not flicker for minutes at a time. Often I fought off the temptation to shake her. At sixteen she had a style of her own: and knew what style was.

I never had an education myself. After second grade the school was closed down. Don't ask my why: in 1927 colored asked fewer questions than they do now. Sometimes Maggie reads to me. She stumbles along good-naturedly but can't see well. She knows she is not bright. Like good looks and money, quickness passed her by. She will marry John Thomas (who has mossy teeth in an earnest face) and then I'll be free to sit here and I guess just sing church songs to myself. Although I never was a good singer. Never could carry a tune. I was always better at a man's job. I used to love to milk till I was hooked in the side in '49. Cows are soothing and slow and don't bother you, unless you try to milk them the wrong way.

I have deliberately turned my back on the house. It is three rooms, just like the one that burned, except the roof is tin; they don't make shingle roofs any more. There are no real windows, just some holes cut in the sides, like the portholes in a ship, but not round and not square, with rawhide holding the shutters up on the outside. This house is in a pasture, too, like the other one. No doubt when Dee sees it she will want to tear it down. She wrote me once that no matter where we "choose" to live, she will manage to come see us. But she will never bring her friends. Maggie and I thought about this and Maggie asked me, "Mama, when did Dee ever *have* any friends?"

She had a few. Furtive boys in pink shirts hanging about on washday after school. Nervous girls who never laughed. Impressed with her they worshiped the well-turned phrase, the cute shape, the scalding humor that erupted like bubbles in lye. She read to them.

When she was courting Jimmy T she didn't have much time to pay to us, but turned all her faultfinding power on him. He *flew* to marry a cheap city girl from a family of ignorant flashy people. She hardly had time to recompose herself.

When she comes I will meet—but there they are!

Maggie attempts to make a dash for the house, in her shuffling way, but I stay her with my hand. "Come back here," I say. And she stops and tries to dig a well in the sand with her toe.

It is hard to see them clearly through the strong sun. But even the first glimpse of leg out of the car tells me it is Dee. Her feet were always neat-looking, as if God himself had shaped them with a certain style. From the other side of the car comes a short, stocky man. Hair is all over his head a foot long and hanging from his chin like a kinky mule tail. I hear Maggie suck in her breath. "Uhnnnh," is what it sounds like. Like when you see the wriggling end of a snake just in front of your foot on the road. "Uhnnnh."

Dee next. A dress down to the ground, in this hot weather. A dress so loud it hurts my eyes. There are yellows and oranges enough to throw back the light of the sun. I feel my whole face warming from the heat waves it throws out. Earrings gold, too, and hanging down to her shoulders. Bracelets dangling and making noises when she moves her arm up to shake the folds of the dress out of her armpits. The dress is loose and flows, and as she walks closer, I like it. I hear Maggie go "Uhnnnh" again. It is her sister's hair. It stands straight up like the wool on a sheep. It is black as night and around the edges are two long pigtails that rope about like small lizards disappearing behind her ears.

"Wa-su-zo-Tean-o!" she says, coming on in that gliding way the dress makes her move. The short stocky fellow with the hair to his navel is all grinning and he follows up with "Asalamalakim, my mother and sister!" He moves to hug Maggie but she falls back, right up against the back of my chair. I feel her trembling there and when I look up I see the perspiration falling off her chin.

"Don't get up," says Dee. Since I am stout it takes something of a push. You can see me trying to move a second or two before I make it. She turns, showing white heels through her sandals, and goes back to the car. Out she peeks next with a Polaroid. She stoops down quickly and lines up picture after picture of me sitting there in front of the house with Maggie cowering behind me. She never takes a shot without making sure the house is included. When a cow comes nibbling around the edge of the yard she snaps it and me and Maggie *and* the house. Then she puts the Polaroid in the back seat of the car, and comes up and kisses me on the forehead.

Meanwhile Asalamalakim is going through motions with Maggie's hand. Maggie's hand is as limp as a fish, and probably as cold, despite the sweat, and she keeps trying to pull it back. It looks like Asalamalakim wants to shake hands but wants to do it fancy. Or maybe he don't know how people shake hands. Anyhow, he soon gives up on Maggie.

"Well," I say. "Dee."

"No, Mama," she says. "Not 'Dee,' Wangero Leewanika Kemanjo!"

"What happened to 'Dee'?" I wanted to know.

"She's dead," Wangero said. "I couldn't bear it any longer, being named after the people who oppress me."

"You know as well as me you was named after your aunt Dicie," I said. Dicie is my sister. She named Dee. We called her "Big Dee" after Dee was born.

"But who was *she* named after?" asked Wangero.

"I guess after Grandma Dee," I said.

"And who was she named after?" asked Wangero.

"Her mother," I said, and saw Wangero was getting tired. "That's about as far back as I can trace it," I said. Though, in fact, I probably could have carried it back beyond the Civil War through the branches.

"Well," said Asalamalakim, "there you are."

"Uhnnnh," I heard Maggie say.

"There I was not," I said, "before 'Dicie' cropped up in our family, so why should I try to trace it that far back?"

He just stood there grinning, looking down on me like somebody inspecting a Model A car. Every once in a while he and Wangero sent eye signals over my head.

"How do you pronounce this name?" I asked.

"You don't have to call me by it if you don't want to," said Wangero.

"Why shouldn't I?" I asked. "If that's what you want us to call you, we'll call you."

"I know it might sound awkward at first," said Wangero.

"I'll get used to it," I said. "Ream it out again."

Well, soon we got the name out of the way. Asalamalakim had a name twice as long and three times as hard. After I tripped over it two or three times he told me to just call him Hakim-a-barber. I wanted to ask him was he a barber, but I didn't really think he was, so I didn't ask.

"You must belong to those beef-cattle peoples down the road," I said. They said "Asalamalakim" when they met you, too, but they didn't shake hands. Always too busy: feeding the cattle, fixing the fences, putting up salt-lick shelters, throwing down hay. When the white folks poisoned some of the herd the men stayed up all night with rifles in their hands. I walked a mile and a half just to see the sight.

Hakim-a-barber said, "I accept some of their doctrines, but farming and raising cattle is not my style." (They didn't tell me, and I didn't ask, whether Wangero (Dee) had really gone and married him.)

We sat down to eat and right away he said he didn't eat collards and pork was unclean. Wangero, though, went on through the chitlins and corn bread, the greens and everything else. She talked a blue streak over the sweet potatoes. Everything delighted her. Even the fact that we still used the benches her daddy made for the table when we couldn't afford to buy chairs.

"Oh, Mama!" she cried. Then turned to Hakim-a-barber. "I never knew how lovely these benches are. You can feel the rump prints," she said, running her hands underneath her and along the bench. Then she gave a sigh and her hand closed over

Grandma Dee's butter dish. "That's it!" she said. "I knew there was something I wanted to ask you if I could have." She jumped up from the table and went over in the corner where the churn stood, the milk in it clabber by now. She looked at the churn and looked at it.

"This churn top is what I need," she said. "Didn't Uncle Buddy whittle it out of a tree you all used to have?"

"Yes," I said.

"Uh huh," she said happily. "And I want the dasher, too."

"Uncle Buddy whittle that, too?" asked the barber.

Dee (Wangero) looked up at me.

"Aunt Dee's first husband whittled the dash," said Maggie so low you almost couldn't hear her. "His name was Henry, but they called him Stash."

"Maggie's brain is like an elephant's," Wangero said, laughing. "I can use the churn top as a centerpiece for the alcove table," she said, sliding a plate over the churn, "and I'll think of something artistic to do with the dasher."

When she finished wrapping the dasher the handle stuck out. I took it for a moment in my hands. You didn't even have to look close to see where hands pushing the dasher up and down to make butter had left a kind of sink in the wood. In fact, there were a lot of small sinks; you could see where thumbs and fingers had sunk into the wood. It was beautiful light yellow wood, from a tree that grew in the yard where Big Dee and Stash had lived.

After dinner Dee (Wangero) went to the trunk at the foot of my bed and started rifling through it. Maggie hung back in the kitchen over the dishpan. Out came Wangero with two quilts. They had been pieced by Grandma Dee and then Big Dee and me had hung them on the quilt frames on the front porch and quilted them. One was in the Lone Star pattern. The other was Walk Around the Mountain. In both of them were scraps of dresses Grandma Dee had worn fifty and more years ago. Bits and pieces of Grandpa Jarrell's Paisley shirts. And one teeny faded blue piece, about the size of a penny matchbox, that was from Great Grandpa Ezra's uniform that he wore in the Civil War.

"Mama," Wangero said sweet as a bird. "Can I have these old quilts?"

I heard something fall in the kitchen, and a minute later the kitchen door slammed.

"Why don't you take one or two of the others?" I asked. "These old things was just done by me and Big Dee from some tops your grandma pieced before she died."

"No," said Wangero. "I don't want those. They are stitched around the borders by machine."

"That'll make them last better," I said.

"That's not the point," said Wangero. "These are all pieces of dresses Grandma used to wear. She did all this stitching by hand. Imagine!" She held the quilts securely in her arms, stroking them.

"Some of the pieces, like those lavender ones, come from old clothes her mother handed down to her," I said, moving up to touch the quilts. Dee (Wangero) moved back just enough so that I couldn't reach the quilts. They already belonged to her.

"Imagine!" she breathed again, clutching them closely to her bosom.

"The truth is," I said, "I promised to give them quilts to Maggie, for when she marries John Thomas."

She gasped like a bee had stung her.

"Maggie can't appreciate these quilts!" she said. "She'd probably be backward enough to put them to everyday use."

"I reckon she would," I said. "God knows I been saving 'em for long enough with nobody using 'em. I hope she will!" I didn't want to bring up how I had offered Dee (Wangero) a quilt when she went away to college. Then she had told me they were old-fashioned, out of style.

"But they're *priceless!*" she was saying now, furiously; for she has a temper. "Maggie would put them on the bed and in five years they'd be in rags. Less than that!"

"She can always make some more," I said. "Maggie knows how to quilt."

Dee (Wangero) looked at me with hatred. "You just will not understand. The point is these quilts, *these* quilts!"

"Well," I said, stumped. "What would *you* do with them?"

"Hang them," she said. As if that was the only thing you *could* do with quilts.

Maggie by now was standing in the door. I could almost hear the sound her feet made as they scraped over each other.

"She can have them, Mama," she said, like somebody used to never winning anything, or having anything reserved for her. "I can 'member Grandma Dee without the quilts."

I looked at her hard. She had filled her bottom lip with checkerberry snuff and it gave her face a kind of dopey, hangdog look. It was Grandma Dee and Big Dee who taught her how to quilt herself. She stood there with her scarred hands hidden in the folds of her skirt. She looked at her sister with something like fear but she wasn't mad at her. This was Maggie's portion. This was the way she knew God to work.

When I looked at her like that something hit me in the top of my head and ran down to the soles of my feet. Just like when I'm in church and the spirit of God touches me and I get happy and shout. I did something I never had done before: hugged Maggie to me, then dragged her on into the room, snatched the quilts out of Miss Wangero's hands and dumped them into Maggie's lap. Maggie just sat there on my bed with her mouth open.

"Take one or two of the others," I said to Dee.

But she turned without a word and went out to Hakim-a-barber.

"You just don't understand," she said, as Maggie and I came out to the car.

"What don't I understand?" I wanted to know.

"Your heritage," she said. And then she turned to Maggie, kissed her, and said, "You ought to try to make something of yourself, too, Maggie. It's really a new day for us. But from the way you and Mama still live you'd never know it."

She put on some sunglasses that hid everything above the tip of her nose and her chin.

Maggie smiled; maybe at the sunglasses. But a real smile, not scared. After we watched the car dust settle I asked Maggie to bring me a dip of snuff. And then the two of us sat there just enjoying, until it was time to go in the house and go to bed.

CHRIST IN CONCRETE

Pietro Di Donato

(b. 1911)

Biography p. 1069

1

March whistled stinging snow against the brick walls and up the gaunt girders. Geremio, the foreman, swung his arms about, and gaffed the men on.

Old Nick, the "Lean," stood up from over a dust-flying brick pile, tapped the side of his nose and sent an oyster directly to the ground. "Master Geremio, the Devil himself could not break his tail any harder than we here."

Burly Julio of the walrus mustache and known as the "Snoutnose" let fall the chute door of the concrete hopper and sang over in the Lean's direction: "Mari-Annina's belly and the burning night will make of me once more a milk-mouthed stripling lad . . ."

The Lean loaded his wheelbarrow and spat furiously. "Sons of two-legged dogs . . . despised of even the Devil himself! Work! Sure! For America beautiful will eat you and spit your bones into the earth's hole! Work!" And with that his wiry frame pitched the barrow violently over the rough floor.

Snoutnose waved his head to and fro and with mock pathos wailed, "Sing on, O guitar of mine . . ."

Short, cheery-faced Tomas, the scaffoldman, paused with hatchet in hand and tenpenny spike sticking out from small dicelike teeth to tell the Lean as he went by, in a voice that all could hear, "Ah, father of countless chicks, the old age is a carrion!"

Geremio chuckled and called to him. "Hey, little Tomas, who are you to talk? You and big-titted Cola can't even hatch an egg, whereas the Lean has just to turn the doorknob of his bedroom and old Philomena becomes a balloon!"

Coarse throats tickled and mouths opened wide in laughter.

The Lean pushed his barrow on, his face cruelly furrowed with time and struggle. Sirupy sweat seeped from beneath his cap, down his bony nose and turned icy at its end. He muttered to himself. "Saints up, down, sideways and inside out! How many more stones must I carry before I'm over-stuffed with the light of day! I don't understand . . . blood of the Virgin, I don't understand!"

Mike the "Barrel-mouth" pretended he was talking to himself and yelled out in his best English . . . he was always speaking English while the rest carried on in their native Italian. "I don't know myself, but somebodys whose gotta bigga buncha keeds and he alla times talka from somebodys elsa!"

Geremio knew it was meant for him and he laughed. "On the tomb of Saint Pimple-legs, this little boy my wife is giving me next week shall be the last! Eight hungry little Christians to feed is enough for any man."

Tomas nodded to the rest. "Sure, Master Geremio had a telephone call from the next bambino. Yes, it told him it had a little bell between instead of a rose bush. . . . It even told him its name!"

"Laugh, laugh all of you," returned Geremio, "but I tell you that all my kids must be boys so that they someday will be big American builders. And then I'll help them to put the gold away in the basements!"

A great din of riveting shattered the talk among the fast-moving men. Geremio added a handful of Honest tobacco to his corncob, puffed strongly, and cupped his hands around the bowl for a bit of warmth. The chill day caused him to shiver, and he thought to himself: Yes, the day is cold, cold . . . but who am I to complain when the good Christ Himself was crucified?

Pushing the job is all right (when has it been otherwise in my life?), but this job frightens me. I feel the building wants to tell me something; just as one Christian to another. Or perhaps the Easter week is making of me a spirit-seeing pregnant woman. I don't like this. Mr. Murdin tells me, Push it up! That's all he knows. I keep telling him that the underpinning should be doubled and the old material removed from the floors, but he keeps the inspector drunk and . . . "Hey, Ashes-ass! Get away from under that pilaster! Don't pull the old work. Push it away from you or you'll have a nice present for Easter if the wall falls on you!" . . . Well, with the help of God I'll see this job through. It's not my first, nor the . . . "Hey, Patsy number two! Put more cement in that concrete; we're putting up a building, not an Easter cake!"

Patsy hurled his shovel to the floor and gesticulated madly. "The padrone Murdinsa tells me, 'Too much, too much! Lil' bit is plenty!' And you tell me I'm stingy! The rotten building can fall after I leave!"

Six floors below, the contractor called. "Hey, Geremio! Is your gang of dagos dead?"

Geremio cautioned the men. "On your toes, boys. If he writes out slips, someone won't have big eels on the Easter table."

The Lean cursed that the padrone could take the job and all the Saints for that matter and shove it . . . !

Curly-headed Lazarene, the roguish, pigeon-toed scaffoldman, spat a cloud of tobacco juice and hummed to his own music . . . "Yes, certainly yes to your face, master padrone . . . and behind, This to you and all your kind!"

The day, like all days came to an end. Calloused and bruised bodies sighed, and numb legs shuffled toward shabby railroad flats . . .

"Ah, bella casa mio. Where my little freshets of blood and my good woman await me. Home where my broken back will not ache so. Home where midst the monkey chatter of my piccolinos I will float off to blessed slumber with my feet on the chair and the head on the wife's soft full breast."

These great child-hearted ones leave one another without words or ceremony, and as they ride and walk home, a great pride swells the breast . . .

"Blessings to Thee, O Jesus. I have fought winds and cold. Hand to hand I have locked dumb stones in place and the great building rises. I have earned a bit of bread for me and mine."

The mad day's brutal conflict is forgiven, and strained limbs prostrate themselves so that swollen veins can send the yearning blood coursing and pulsating deliciously as though the body mountained leaping streams.

The job alone remained behind . . . and yet, they also, having left the bigger part of their lives with it. The cold ghastly beast, the Job, stood stark, the eerie March wind wrapping it in sharp shadows of falling dusk.

That night was a crowning point in the life of Geremio. He bought a house! Twenty years he had helped to mold the New World. And now he was to have a house of his own! What mattered that it was no more than a wooden shack? It was his own!

He had proudly signed his name and helped Annunziata to make her X on the wonderful contract that proved them owners. And she was happy to think that her next child, soon to come, would be born under their own rooftree. She heard the church chimes, and cried to the children, "Children, to bed! It is near midnight. And remember, shut-mouth to the paesanos! Or they will send the evil eye to our new home even before we put foot."

The children scampered off to the icy yellow bedroom where three slept in one bed and three in the other. Coltishly and friskily they kicked about under the covers; their black iron-cotton stockings not removed . . . what! and freeze the peanut-little toes?

Said Annunziata, "The children are so happy, Geremio; let them be, for even I would dance a Tarantella." And with that she turned blushing. He wanted to take her on her word. She patted his hands, kissed them, and whispered. "Our children will dance for us . . . in the American style someday."

Geremio cleared his throat and wanted to sing. "Yes, with joy I could sing in a richer feeling than the great Caruso." He babbled little old-country couplets and circled the room until the tenant below tapped the ceiling.

Annunziata whispered, "Geremio, to bed and rest. Tomorrow is a day for great things . . . and the day on which our Lord died for us."

The children were now hard asleep. Heads under the cover, over . . . snotty noses whistling, and little damp legs entwined.

In bed Geremio and Annunziata clung closely to each other. They mumbled figures and dates until fatigue stilled their thoughts. And with chubby Johnny clutching fast his bottle and warmed between them . . . life breathed heavily, and dreams entertained in far, far worlds, the nation-builder's brood.

But Geremio and Annunziata remained for a long while staring into the darkness . . . silently.

At last Annunziata spoke. "Geremio?"

"Yes?"

"This job you are now working . . ."

"So?"

"You used always to tell me about what happened on the jobs . . . who was jealous, and who praised . . ."

"You should know by now that all work is the same . . ."

"Geremio. The month you have been on this job, you have not spoken a word about the work . . . And I have felt that I am walking into a dream. Is the work dangerous? Why don't you answer . . . ?"

2

Job loomed up damp, shivery gray. Its giant members waiting.

Builders donned their coarse robes, and waited.

Geremio's whistle rolled back into his pocket and the symphony of struggle began.

Trowel rang through brick and slashed mortar rivets were machine-gunned fast with angry grind Patsy number one check Patsy number two check the Lean three check Julio four steel bellowed back at hammer donkey engines coughed purple Ashes-ass Pietro fifteen chisel point intoned stone thin steel whirred and wailed through wood liquid stone flowed with dull rasp through iron veins and hoist screamed through space Rosario the Fat twenty-four and Giacomo Sangini check . . . The multitudinous voices of a civilization rose from the surroundings and melted with the efforts of the Job.

The Lean as he fought his burden on looked forward to only one goal, the end. The barrow he pushed, he did not love. The stones that brutalized his palms, he did not love. The great God Job, he did not love. He felt a searing bitterness and a fathomless consternation at the queer consciousness that inflicted the ever mounting weight of structures that he *had to! had to!* raise above his shoulders! When, when and where would the last stone be? Never . . . did he bear his toil with the rhythm of song! Never . . . did his gasping heart knead the heavy mortar with lilting melody! A voice within him spoke in wordless language.

The language of worn oppression and the despair of realizing that his life had been left on brick piles. And always, there had been hunger and her bastard, the fear of hunger.

Murdin bore down upon Geremio from behind and shouted:

"Goddammit, Geremio, if you're givin' the men two hours off today with pay, why the hell are they draggin' their tails? And why don't you turn that skinny old Nick loose, and put a young wop in his place?"

"Now listen-a to me, Mister Murdin—"

"Don't give me that! And bear in mind that there are plenty of good barefoot men in the streets who'll jump for a day's pay!"

"Padrone—padrone, the underpinning gotta be make safe and . . ."

"Lissenyawopbastard! if you don't like it, you know what you can do!" And with that he swung swaggering away.

The men had heard, and those who hadn't knew instinctively.

The new home, the coming baby, and his whole background, kept the fire from Geremio's mouth and bowed his head. "Annunziata speaks of scouring the ashcans for the children's bread in case I didn't want to work on a job where. . . . But am I not a man, to feed my own with these hands? Ah, but day will end and no boss in the world can then rob me the joy of my home!"

Murdin paused for a moment before descending the ladder.

Geremio caught his meaning and jumped to, nervously directing the rush of work. . . . No longer Geremio, but a machinelike entity.

The men were transformed into single, silent beasts. Snoutnose steamed through ragged mustache whip-lashing sand into mixer Ashes-ass dragged under four-by-twelve beam Lean clawed wall knots jumping in jaws masonry crumbled dust billowed thundered choked . . .

At noon, dripping noses were blown, old coats thrown over shoulders, and foot-long sandwiches were toasted at the end of wire over the flames. Shadows were once again personalities. Laughter added warmth.

Geremio drank his wine from an old-fashioned magnesia bottle and munched a great pepper sandwich . . . no meat on Good Friday.

Said one, "Are some of us to be laid off? Easter is upon us and communion dresses are needed and . . ."

That, while Geremio was dreaming of the new house and the joys he could almost taste. Said he, "Worry not. You should know Geremio." It then all came out. He regaled them with his wonderful joy of the new house. He praised his wife and children one by one. They listened respectfully and returned him well wishes and blessings. He went on and on. . . . "Paul made a radio—all by himself, mind you! One can hear *Barney Google* and many American songs!"

"A radio!"

"An electric machine like magic—yes."

"With music and Christian voices?"

"That is nothing to what he shall someday accomplish!"

"Who knows," suggested Giacomo amazed, "but that Dio has deigned to gift you with a Marconi . . ."

"I tell you, son of Geremio shall never never lay bricks! Paulie mine will study from books—he will be the great builder! This very moment I can see him . . . How proud he!"

Said they in turn: "Master Geremio, in my province it is told that for good luck in a new home, one is to sprinkle well with salt . . . especially the corners, and on moving day sweep with a new broom to the center and pick all up—but do not sweep it out over the threshold!"

"That may be, Pietro. But, Master Geremio, it would be better in my mind that holy water should bless. And also a holy picture of Saint Joseph guarding the door."

"The Americans use the shoe of a horse . . . there must be something in that. One may try . . ."

Snoutnose knew a better way. "You know, you know." He ogled his eyes and smacked his lips. Then, reaching out his hands over the hot embers . . . "To embrace a goose-fat breast and bless the house with the fresh milk. And one that does not belong to the wife . . . that is the way!"

Acid-smelling di Nobilis were lit. Geremio preferred his corncob. And Lazarene "tobacco-eater" proudly chawed his quid . . . in the American style.

The ascent to labor was made, and as they trod the ladder, heads turned and eyes communed with the mute flames of the brazier whose warmth they were leaving, not with willing heart, and in that fleeting moment the breast wanted much to speak of hungers that never reached the tongue.

About an hour later, Geremio called over to Pietro, "Pietro, see if Mister Murdin is in the shanty and tell him I must see him! I will convince him that the work must not go on like this . . . just for the sake of a little more profit!"

Pietro came up soon. "The padrone is not coming up. He was drinking from a large bottle of whisky and cursed in American words that if you did not carry out his orders—"

Geremio turned away disconcerted, stared dumbly at the structure and mechanically listed in his mind's eye the various violations of construction safety. An uneasy sensation hollowed him. The Lean brought down an old piece of wall and the structure palsied. Geremio's heart broke loose and out-thumped the floor's vibrations, a rapid wave of heat swept him and left a chill touch in its wake. He looked about to the men, a bit frightened. They seemed usual, life-size, and moved about with the methodical deftness that made the moment then appear no different than the task of toil had ever been.

Snoutnose's voice boomed into him. "Master Geremio, the concrete is re-ady!"

"Oh yes, yes, Julio." And he walked gingerly toward the chute, but not without leaving behind some part of his strength, sending out his soul to wrestle with the limbs of Job, who threatened in stiff silence. He talked and joked with Snoutnose. Nothing said anything, nor seemed wrong. Yet a vague uneasiness was to him as certain as the foggy murk that floated about Job's stone and steel.

"Shall I let the concrete down now, Master Geremio?"

"Well, let me see—no, hold it a minute. Hey, Lazarene! Tighten the chute cables!"

Snoutnose straightened, looked about, and instinctively rubbed the sore small of his spine. "Ah," sighed he, "all the men feel as I—yes, I can tell. They are tired but happy that today is Good Friday and we quit at three o'clock—" And he swelled in human ecstasy at the anticipation of food, drink and the hairy flesh-tingling warmth of wife, and then, extravagant rest.

Geremio gazed about and was conscious of seeming to understand many things. He marveled at the strange feeling which permitted him to sense the familiarity of life. And yet—all appeared unreal, a dream pungent and nostalgic.

Life, dream, reality, unreality, spiraling ever about each other. "Ha," he chuckled, "how and from where do these thoughts come?"

Snoutnose had his hand on the hopper latch and was awaiting the word from Geremio. "Did you say something, Master Geremio?"

"Why yes, Julio, I was thinking—funny! A—yes, what is the time—yes, that is what I was thinking."

"My American can of tomatoes says ten minutes from two o'clock. It won't be long now, Master Geremio."

Geremio smiled. "No, about an hour . . . and then, home."

"Oh, but first we stop at Mulberry Street, to buy their biggest eels, and the other finger-licking stuffs."

Geremio was looking far off, and for a moment happiness came to his heart without words, a warm hand stealing over. Snoutnose's words sang to him pleasantly, and he nodded.

"And Master Geremio, we ought really to buy the sea-fruits with the shells—you know, for the much needed steam they put into the—"

He flushed despite himself and continued, "It is true, I know it—especially the juicy clams . . . uhmn, my mouth waters like a pump."

Geremio drew on his unlit pipe and smiled acquiescence. The men around him were moving to their tasks silently, feeling of their fatigue, but absorbed in contemplations the very same as Snoutnose's. The noise of labor seemed not to be noise, and as Geremio looked about, life settled over him a gray concert—gray forms, atmosphere and gray notes. . . . Yet his off-tone world felt so near, and familiar.

"Five minutes from two," swished through Snoutnose's mustache.

Geremio automatically took out his watch, rewound and set it. Lazarene had done with the cables. The tone and movement of the scene seemed to Geremio strange, differently strange, and yet, a dream familiar from a timeless date. His hand went up in motion to Julio. The molten stone gurgled low, and then with heightening rasp. His eyes followed the stone-cementy pudding, and to his ears there was no other sound than its flow. From over the roofs somewhere, the tinny voice of *Barney Google* whined its way, hooked into his consciousness and kept itself a revolving record beneath his skullplate.

"Ah, yes, *Barney Google,* my son's wonderful radio machine . . . wonderful Paul."
His train of thought quickly took in his family, home and hopes. And with hope came
fear. Something within asked, "Is it not possible to breathe God's air without fear
dominating with the pall of unemployment? And the terror of production for Boss,
Boss and Job? To rebel is to lose all of the very little. To be obedient is to choke. O
dear Lord, guide my path."

Just then, the floor lurched and swayed under his feet. The slipping of the underpinning below rumbled up through the undetermined floors.

Was he faint or dizzy? Was it part of the dreamy afternoon? He put his hands in
front of him and stepped back, and looked up wildly. "No! No!"

The men poised stricken. Their throats wanted to cry out and scream but didn't
dare. For a moment they were a petrified and straining pageant. Then the bottom of
their world gave way. The building shuddered violently, her supports burst with the
crackling slap of wooden gunfire. The floor vomited upward. Geremio clutched at the
air and shrieked agonizingly. "Brothers, what have we done? Ahhh-h, children of
ours!" With the speed of light, balance went sickeningly awry and frozen men went
flying explosively. Job tore down upon them madly. Walls, floors, beams became
whirling, solid, splintering waves crashing with detonations that ground man and
material in bonds of death.

The strongly shaped body that slept with Annunziata nights and was perfect in all
the limitless physical quantities thudded as a worthless sack amongst the giant débris
that crushed fragile flesh and bone with centrifugal intensity.

Darkness blotted out his terror and the resistless form twisted, catapulted insanely
in its directionless flight, and shot down neatly and deliberately between the empty
wooden forms of a foundation wall pilaster in upright position, his blue swollen face
pressed against the form and his arms outstretched, caught securely through the meat
by the thin round bars of reinforcing steel.

The huge concrete hopper that was sustained by an independent structure of thick
timber wavered a breath or so, its heavy concrete rolling uneasily until a great
sixteen-inch wall caught it squarely with all the terrific verdict of its dead weight and
impelled it downward through joists, beams and masonry until it stopped short,
arrested by two girders, an arm's length above Geremio's head; the gray concrete
gushing from the hopper mouth, and sealing up the mute figure.

Giacomo had been thrown clear of the building and dropped six floors to the street
gutter, where he lay writhing.

The Lean had evinced no emotion. When the walls descended, he did not move.
He lowered his head. One minute later he was hanging in mid-air, his chin on his
chest, his eyes tearing loose from their sockets, a green foam bubbling from his mouth
and his body spasming, suspended by the shreds left of his mashed arms, pinned
between a wall and a girder.

A two-by-four hooked little Tomas up under the back of his jumper and swung him
around in a circle to meet a careening I-beam. In the flash that he lifted his frozen
cherubic face, its shearing edge sliced through the top of his skull.

When Snoutnose cried beseechingly, "Saint Michael!" blackness enveloped him. He
came to in a world of horror. A steady stream, warm, thick, and sickening as hot wine,
bathed his face and clogged his nose, mouth, and eyes. The nauseous sirup that
pumped over his face clotted his mustache red and drained into his mouth. He gulped
for air, and swallowed blood. As he breathed, the pain shocked him to oppressive

semiconsciousness. The air was wormingly alive with cries, screams, moans, and dust, and his crushed chest seared him with a thousand fires. He couldn't see, nor breathe enough to cry. His right hand moved to his face and wiped at the gelatinizing substance, but it kept coming on, and a heartbreaking moan wavered about him, not far. He wiped his eyes in subconscious despair. Where was he? What kind of a dream was he having? Perhaps he wouldn't wake up in time for work, and then what? But how queer; his stomach beating him, his chest on fire, he sees nothing but dull red, only one hand moving about, and a moaning in his face!

The sound and clamor of the rescue squads called to him from far off.

Ah, yes, he's dreaming in bed, and, far out in the streets, engines are going to a fire. Oh, poor devils! Suppose his house were on fire? With the children scattered about in the rooms he could not remember! He must do his utmost to break out of this dream! He's swimming under water, not able to raise his head and get to the air. He must get back to consciousness to save his children!

He swam frantically with his one right hand, and then felt a face beneath its touch. A face! It's Angelina alongside of him! Thank God, he's awake! He tapped her face. It moved. It felt cold, bristly, and wet. "It moves so. What is this?" His fingers slithered about grisly sharp bones and in a gluey, stringy, hollow mass, yielding as wet macaroni. Gray light brought sight, and hysteria punctured his heart. A girder lay across his chest, his right hand clutched a grotesque human mask, and suspended almost on top of him was the twitching, faceless body of Tomas. Julio fainted with an inarticulate sigh. His fingers loosed and the bodiless headless face dropped and fitted to the side of his face while the drippings above came slower and slower.

The rescue men cleaved grimly with pick and ax.

Geremio came to with a start . . . far from their efforts. His brain told him instantly what had happened and where he was. He shouted wildly. "Save me! Save me! I'm being buried alive!"

He paused exhausted. His genitals convulsed. The cold steel rod upon which they were impaled froze his spine. He shouted louder and louder. "Save me! I am hurt badly! I can be saved I can—save me before it's too late!" But the cries went no farther than his own ears. The icy wet concrete reached his chin. His heart appalled. "In a few seconds I will be entombed. If I can only breathe, they will reach me. Surely, they will!" His face was quickly covered, its flesh yielding to the solid sharp-cut stones. "Air! Air!" screamed his lungs as he was completely sealed. Savagely he bit into the wooden form pressed upon his mouth. An eighth of an inch of its surface splintered off. Oh, if he could only hold out long enough to bite even the smallest hole through to air! He must! There can be no other way! He must! There can be no other way! He is responsible for his family! He cannot leave them like this! He didn't want to die! This could not be the answer to life! He had bitten halfway through when his teeth snapped off to the gums in the uneven conflict. The pressure of the concrete was such, and its effectiveness so thorough, that the wooden splinters, stumps of teeth, and blood never left the choking mouth.

Why couldn't he go any farther?

Air! Quick! He dug his lower jaw into the little hollowed space and gnashed in choking agonized fury. Why doesn't it go through! Mother of Christ, why doesn't it give? Can there be a notch, or two-by-four stud behind it? Sweet Jesu! No! No! Make it give . . . Air! Air!

He pushed the bone-bare jaw maniacally; it splintered, cracked, and a jagged fleshless edge cut through the form, opening a small hole to air. With a desperate burst the lung-prisoned air blew an opening through the shredded mouth and whistled back greedily a gasp of fresh air. He tried to breathe, but it was impossible. The heavy concrete was settling immutably and its rich cement-laden grout ran into his pierced face. His lungs would not expand and were crushing in tighter and tighter under the settling concrete.

"Mother mine—mother of Jesu—Annunziata—children of mine—dear, dear, for mercy, Jesu-Giuseppe e' Mari," his blue foamed tongue called. It then distorted in a shuddering coil and mad blood vomited forth. Chills and fire played through him and his tortured tongue stuttered, "Mercy, blessed Father—salvation, most kind Father—Saviour—Saviour of His children, help me—adored Saviour—I kiss your feet eternally—you are my Lord—there is but one God—you are my God of infinite mercy—Hail Mary divine Virgin—our Father who art in heaven hallowed be thy—name—our Father—my Father," and the agony excruciated with never-ending mount, "our Father—Jesu, Jesu, soon Jesu, hurry dear Jesu Jesu! Je-sssu . . . !" His mangled voice trebled hideously, and hung in jerky whimperings. Blood vessels burst like mashed flower stems. He screamed. "Show yourself now, Jesu! Now is the time! Save me! Why don't you come! Are you there! I cannot stand it—ohhh, why do you let it happen—where are you? Hurry hurry hurry!"

His bones cracked mutely and his sanity went sailing distorted in the limbo of the subconscious. With the throbbing tones of an organ in the hollow background, the fighting brain disintegrated and the memories of a baffled lifetime sought outlet.

He moaned the simple songs of barefoot childhood, scenes flashed desperately on and off, and words and parts of words came pitifully high and low from his inaudible lips.

Paul's crystal-set earphones pressed the sides of his head tighter and tighter, the organ boomed the mad dance of the Tarentella, and the hysterical mind sang cringingly and breathlessly, "Jesu my Lord my God my all Jesu my Lord my God my all Jesu my Lord my God my all Jesu my Lord my God my all."

PETE: A QUARTER AHEAD

John Rechy

(b. 1934)

Biography p. 1094

1

There was a Youngman I had seen often around Times Square. Like me, he was there almost every night; and like me, too, he was, I knew, hustling. I would learn later his name is Pete. Although each of us had noticed the other—and it was obvious—we avoided pointedly more than glancing at each other whenever we met: He was very cocky, a wiseass; and, I figured, I struck him much the same way.

One night I saw him by the subway entrance on 42nd Street talking to an older man dressed in black. It was a warm night. After a series of wintry ones, the warmth returned miraculously and the street is crowded tonight, each person clutching for one last taste of a springlike night. . . . Theyre glancing at me, Pete and the older man. They talk some more, the older man nods yes, and Pete swaggers up to me. He said: "That score digs you, spote—" (He said sport like that: "spote.") "—he'll lay ten bucks on you—and itll be like cuhrazy," rolling his eyes. Pete's in his early 20s, not tall, very well built, dark; knowing eyes, sometimes moody, dreamy. Hes wearing an army fatigue cap rakishly almost over his eyes, so that he has to hold his chin up to look at you. . . . I turned and looked at the black-dressed man, and he smiled broadly at me, walked toward us. If he had worn a white collar, he would have looked like a priest. Pete says to me: "This is Al," indicating the older man, pats my shoulder —"Later, spote"—and disappears jauntily into the street, almost bouncing into the crowd.

"I havent seen you before—youre new?" the man in black was saying. He didnt wait for an answer: If he asks too many questions, he exposes himself to the possibility that he will get an entirely different answer from the one he wants to hear and it will shatter his sexdream.

I went around the corner with the black-dressed Al, down from 42nd Street— wordlessly—to a large room in an apartment house. "I dont live here," he explained as he opened the door into an almost-bare room: a bed, a table, two chairs. "I just keep this place—well—as a Convenience." He asked me to take my clothes off, but, "Not the pants, theyll do," he tells me. He went to a large closet, and brought out some clothes. Theres a black leather jacket with stars like a general, eagled motorcycle cap, engineer boots with gleaming polished buckles. He left the closet door open, and I could see, hanging neatly, other similar clothes—different sizes, I knew. On the floor were at least seven pairs of engineer boots, all different sizes. "Ive reached the point," Al said, "where I can tell the exact size by just glancing at the person, on the street. . . . Here, put these on." I did, and they fitted. "Fine!" he said. "Now lets go." Im startled. "Where?" I asked him. "Outside," the man says, then noticing me hesitating suspiciously: "I just want us to take a little walk. Dont worry—I'll pay you."

That night, for about an hour, I walked with him through Times Square, from block to block in that area, into the park, silently—just walked. A couple of times I was tempted to leave, walk away with his clothes—but Im curious and I need the money. At the end of the hour we returned to the room, I removed the clothes. He didnt touch me once. He hands me $10.00. I looked at him surprised. I thought somehow I had disappointed him, and I felt grossly rejected. "Thats all," he said; he smiles. "You were fine, just fine," he says, sensing whats troubling me. "But, you see," he said, rather wistfully, "thats *all* I want; to be seen along Times Square with a youngman in those clothes."

A few minutes later, I was back on 42nd Street, and Pete was still there, slouched outside the spaghetti place. He smiled at me. "Some scene, huh?" he said.

"Did he give you anything for it?" I ask him.

"What do *you* think, spote? He gives me five bucks for everyone I get him. I meet him once every two, three weeks. He spots someone he digs, I introduce him. Hes too shy to talk to anyone, so I do it for him, and he lays some bread on me—and I dont have to do nothing," he says smartly.

"Did you ever go with him—*spote?*" I said.

"Oh, sure!" He laughed. "And thats all he digs, spote. He dresses everyone he goes with in that motorcycle drag—and it bugs him for me to call it that. Then he walks around with them. Hardly anybody ever walks away with his clothes—theyre too curious. Hes hung up on that drag, thats how he gets his Kicks. . . . Oh, sure, I been with him." Then proudly—his gaze shifting back and forth from me to the street, pegging people—he adds. "Im the only cat he walked around with *two* nights—in a row!"

2

Pete was a familiar figure in that world of Times Square. With his slouched army fatigue cap and his thick shaggy army jacket which he had dyed brown, his bouncing walk—it was easy to spot him in any crowd.

After that first night, I would meet him often, never by arrangement, but always at about the same time, around the same place. We would hang around together for a while, and then, compulsively, we'd split. Often, minutes later, we would meet again standing in the same place.

Although he wasn't much older than I—but because, as he told me, he'd been hustling the streets since he was 16—Pete liked to play the jaded, all-knowing street hustler, explaining to me how to make out. He had a series of rules: Walk up to people, dont wait to be asked; if you do, you may wait all day. Forget about the vice squad, and you'll never get caught. A quick score in a toilet for a few bucks can be worth more than a big one that takes all day. Stand at the urinal long after youre through pissing. At the slightest indication of interest from someone in one of the cubicles, go up to him quickly before he gets any free ideas and say. "I'll make it with you for twenty." But go for much less if you have to.

As we sat in Bickford's in the cold light, he told me without embarrassment that once he'd gone for 75¢. "It was a slow day, he explained, "and I had only four bits, just enough to make the flix. I thought, Do I buy a Hotdog or make the flix and try to score? It was raining—no one on the streets. So I made the flix. No scores. Then someone wants to give me 75¢, and Im in the balcony anyway, so I let him. Hell, man," he adds pragmatically, "I was a quarter ahead—I could still have that Hot-dog." And he goes on: "Youll learn; sometimes youll stand around all day and wait for a 15-buck score, a 10-buck score, even a deuce—all day—so, hell, take what comes, spote—so long as it dont louse up all your time—but always ask for the highest. Ask for Twenty. That way they think they got a Bargain."

Part of Pete's technique as a hustler was to tell the men he'd been with that he knew other youngmen like himself, and, if they wanted, he would fix them up. Like a social secretary, he kept mental dates when he'd meet certain people. If he still didnt have someone for the score, they would walk around Times Square until the man spotted someone he wanted. Pete would make the introductions—as he had that night with me and the black-dressed Al—and would get a few bucks for it. . . . There was one problem, Pete explained: As the score got to know more and more people, he'd dispense with Pete's services.

Occasionally, we sat in the automat, talking for a long time, Bragging, exaggerating last night's Big Score. Soon it would turn bitter cold, he warned me (and, already, the wind raked the streets savagely), and the hustling would become more difficult; the competition on the streets keener. "You can shack up with someone permanent, though," he told me, looking at me curiously as if he were trying to find out something about me; "but me," he added hurriedly, "I dont dig that scene—I guess Im too Restless."

He made it, instead, from place to place, week to week, night to night. Or, he told me, he'd stay in one of the all-night movies. Sometimes he would rent a room off Seventh Avenue where they knew him. "And if you aint got a pad any time, spote," he said, "you can pad there too." Then he changed the subject quickly. "I dig feeling Free all the time," he said suddenly, stretching his arms.

And I could understand those feelings. Alone, I, too, felt that Enormous freedom. Yet . . . there was always a persistent sensation of guilt: a strong compulsion to spend immediately whatever money I had scored.

I still lived in that building on 34th Street, its mirrored lobby a ghost of its former elegance.

I paid $8.50 a week for the room. Opposite my window, in another wing of the same building, lived an old man who coughed all night. Sometimes he kept me awake. Sometimes it was the old, old woman who staggered up and down the hallway whistling, checking to see that no one had left the water running in the bathrooms or the gas burning in the community kitchen. At times it was Gene de Lancey—the woman with the demented eyes I had met the first day in the hallway—who kept me up. Once she had been Beautiful—she had sighingly shown me pictures of herself, then!—now she was sadly faded, and her eyes burned with the knowledge. She seldom went out, although I did see her on the street one late afternoon, shielding her face with her hand. She'd knock on my door sometimes early in the morning, often as I had just walked in: I would wonder if she listened for me to come in. I would open the door, and shes standing there in a Japanese kimono. "Lambie-pie," she'd say in a childish whimper, "I just couldn't sleep, I just gotta have a cigarette and talk—Steve's asleep—" That was her present husband. "—and I knew you wouldnt mind, sweetie." She would sit and talk into the morning, with such passion, such lonesome-ness, that I couldnt bring myself to ask her to leave. She would tell me about how everyone she had ever loved had left her: her mother, dead—her father, constantly sending her to boarding schools as a girl—her two previous husbands, Gone—her son, disappeared. "There's no love in this harsh world," she lamented. "Everybody's hunting for Something—but what?" When, finally, she would get up, she would kiss me on the cheek and leave quickly. . . .

I mentioned her to Pete, and he says: "Great, man, she sounds like a swinging nympho—lets make it with her together sometime!"

Like the rest of us on that street—who played the male role with other men—Pete was touchy about one subject: his masculinity. In Bickford's one afternoon, a good-looking masculine youngman walked in, looked at us, walked out again hurriedly. "That cat's queer," Pete says, glaring at him. "I used to see him and I thought he was hustling, and one day he tried to put the make on me in the flix. It bugged me, him thinking I was queer or something. I told him fuck off, I wasnt gonna make it for free." He was moodily silent for a long while, and then he said almost belligerently. "Whatever a guy does with other guys, if he does it for money, that dont make him queer. Youre still straight. It's when you start doing it for free, with other young guys, that you start growing wings." . . .

And because this is such a big thing in That life, youll hear untrue stories from almost everyone whos paid someone about the person hes paid. It's a kind of petty vindication, to put down the hustler's masculinity—whether correctly or not—at the same time that they seek it out.

Standing on the street, Pete would always come on about the young girls that would breeze by like flowers, the wind lapping at their skirts coyly. . . .

I found out Pete can be vengeful. I saw him in Bryant Park and he was fuming. The manager of a moviehouse one block away had refused to let him in. (I had seen the manager—a skinny, tall, nervous, gaunt, pale-faced man. The theater is one of the gayest in New York. Late at night men stand leaning along the stairways, waiting.) "Hes a queer," Pete said angrily, "he dont give a fuck what goes on so long as it dont go on for money—thats why he wouldnt let me in." Later, Pete tells everyone the place is *crawling* with plainclothes, vice squad, ready to raid it: Stay Away! And the theater balcony was almost empty for weeks.

He also told me that another hustler had taken a score from right under his nose in the park, and Pete went around telling people the other hustler had the clap. . . . "Make it anyway you can," he said when he finished telling me that, "and when you cant make it, get even."

He knew almost everyone on the street who paid. He would point them out to me. "See that blond pale kid? He pimps for this old guy: real swank pad, too. And, man, what a weirdo that old guy is. Dig: he pays by the hour, and talks, talks, talks!—hes a teacher or something—laid up in bed from an accident. I used to fall asleep—I'd wear sunglasses—and he never knew the difference, just kept on talking. . . ."

At least once I regretted not listening to Pete's advice.

"See that one over there?" he said, pointing to a harmless-looking middle-aged man in a raincoat. "Stay away from him, spote, hes psycho."

But remembering what he had told everyone about the theater whose manager wouldnt let him in, and remembering what he'd done to the hustler whod taken his score in the park, I figured this may be some kind of revenge on the man for whatever reason. The man looked entirely harmless, and I went with him.

After we had made a very ordinary scene—and I still hadnt got any money from

him—his composure changed suddenly into savage rage. Before I knew it, he had
pulled a knife on me. I dashed out, down the creaking steps. Like a demon—his
shadow flung grotesquely down the stairs—he stands at the landing shouting:
"God! Damn! You! *God damn all of you!*"

3

I also learned not always to trust Pete.

One sharply cold windy Sunday afternoon—the clouds sweeping the newyork sky
like sheets—I saw him coming toward me where I was standing. "You wanna score?"
he says. "See that old cat over there?" He points to a small mousy man a few feet
away. "He wants us both to come over to his house. Hes only good for five," he
explained, adding quickly when he saw me hesitating: "but most of the time he'll lay
more if he digs you. . . . Cummon, man," he coaxed me. "Lets go with him. It's a
draggy day anyhow. And anyway, we get to eat there real good." He adds, smiling
secretly. "And we dont have to do much. Oh, hes Special!" Remembering the man
I had walked around Times Square with, wearing a jacket and cap, I began to laugh.
"Not that," Pete says, "we wont be walking around Times Square in leather."

Without going to him, Pete motions yes to the man, who goes down the steps, into
the subway. Pete and I follow. I was walking fast, to catch up with the man. "Cool
it," Pete explains. "I know where we get off." Without glancing back, the man gets
in one of the cars, and we got in another. "He doesnt want anyone to see him leaving
with guys," Pete said. I had been through this before: Unlike the black-dressed Al,
who walked you around for an hour through Times Square, some scores dont want
to be seen leaving the street with a younger man. "He lives in—hold on—*Queens!*"
Pete laughed. "And dig this, spote: I think he teaches at Queens College. They even
got a school now," he says, shaking his head.

We got off at Queens Plaza, and followed the man to a large apartment house. We
waited at the corner for a few minutes, and then we walked into the lobby. It's a
moderate-priced apartment house, very quiet, softly lighted. We reached the second
floor, and along the hallway, a door was open slightly. There stood the little man
beaming at us sweetly. He had taken off his coat, and he was wearing a gayly colored
apron now.

"Hello, hello, hello!" he chirped merrily. "Im so glad you boys could come. I was
hardly expecting—"

Pete whispered to me (I couldnt see how the man could help but hear him, but
possibly neither cared): "Play it Cool and go along with it." At times Pete seemed
to have an enormous tolerance for the quirks of the people he knew: a tolerance which
could instantly turn into intolerance when he felt he'd been had.

"Itll be just a few minutes, boys," the old man announced, "and then we'll have
a Lovely dinner. You boys must be famished, and I just happen to have some Very
Nice Steaks. Now," he says, and his voice trembles slightly, "you boys get-uh-
Comfortable." He stood watching us intently. I glanced at Pete, and he had begun
to unbutton his shirt.

"Do what I do," he told me, but I was strangely embarrassed suddenly, because
by then Pete was taking off all his clothes. "Come on, man," he says to me, annoyed.

"You wanna score or dont you?" (Again, I knew the man, his gaze nailed on us, could hear him, and I realized conclusively this didnt matter.) "This cat's pretty swinging people if he digs you," Pete goes on, "and we can come back and have 'dinner.' " He laughed again. "Come on."

I finally did. Pete sat on the couch, glancing at a comic book. He was completely unembarrassed. I sat on a chair looking at a magazine. The man returned to the kitchen, humming gayly. "Itll be just a few more minutes, now boys—" He turned at the door and looks fondly at Pete. "Petey-boy," he said, "I do believe youve been gaining a few pounds—you should have more salads, less starches. . . . You boys dont know how to care for yourselves, but we'll fix that. . . . And you, my boy—" turning now to me like a doting mother "—you could stand a bit more weight—just a few more pounds, not much—and we'll fix that too." He disappeared into the kitchen, and I could hear dishes rattle.

I glanced up abruptly, and Pete is looking at me over the comic book. He smiles broadly.

Soon, the meal was served, on a small, carefully set table in the dining room. We were summoned by a tinkling little bell which the man jingled. I had never eaten like this before, and I start to put my pants on. Pete said no, emphatically, reminding me we're in the presence of "cool people" and I should play along. We sat at the table —just Pete and myself, facing each other. The man flutters in and out of the kitchen like a butterfly, returning, serving us lovingly, rearranging the silver, the glasses— standing back to see that they were Just Right. There was no place for him. He brought a chair and set it away from the table. He sat there, staring raptly as we ate. Completely unself-consciously Pete ate his food. I dropped my fork a couple of times, and the man rushed into the kitchen to get me a clean one. Finally we had finished, and the man places a cake before us, gives us a large portion. "And there's ice cream!" he announced joyously. "Vanilla?" he asked. Pete said, "Chocolate." I took vanilla. "All boys love cake and ice cream," the man said knowingly, and by then I was enjoying it. I even ate more cake.

"Now a nice rest," the man said. His voice shook slightly, as when he asked us to get "Comfortable." We went into the bedroom, where there were twin beds. Pete lay in one, I lay in the other. The man came in with a chair, which he stations between the two beds. "Now take a long rest," he said. Pete is looking at me steadily, as if to remind me to play along; winks—then pretends to fall asleep immediately. He even snored a couple of times. I lay in bed, my eyes supposedly closed, but I was glancing at the man: He sat on the chair, his chin propped on his hands: staring fixedly from one to the other; occasionally his face would brighten up benevolently like a mother watching over her adored children. . . .

After about 15 minutes, he "woke" us, and we sat in the bedroom, on one bed, Pete and I, and played checkers, while the man watched us with the fascinated attention of a child enjoying a cartoon. Pete couldnt play checkers, and we sat there merely moving them back and forth.

"We'll have to go now, Mom," Pete said finally. I looked at him startled. Had he called him "Mom"? Pete nods at me, indicating I must do the same. I couldnt bring myself to call him "Mom." The old man looked at me with a hurt look.

"We'll have to go now, Mom," Pete repeated. He gives me an exasperated look.

"Oh, must you?" the man said. "Im so sorry you cant stay longer." He removed the apron, rubbed his hands on it, folded it neatly, and he went into the kitchen. Pete follows him. I can hear voices. Then Pete returns, hands me $5.00. "You fucked up, spote," he told me, shaking his head. "You didnt call him Mom. Just five bucks. When hes real happy, he lays ten." He shook his head regretfully. "But we can come again, and if youre cool, we'll score more. Why—didnya—call—him—Mom?"

A week later, alone, I ran into the same man. This time he knew me and he came and talked to me. "Do you have a young friend whod like to come up and have dinner with us?" he asked me. "I havent seen Petey-boy here today," he said, glancing around for him. "If you find another nice youngman, we'll have a lovely dinner, and youll each be $10.00 richer." "Ten?" I said. "Why, child," he said somewhat indignantly, "I *always* give ten." From my expression, he understood what had happened. "That Pete!" he said, and I thought he was going to stamp his foot. "Hes done it to me again. Why, I bet he only gave you five." I felt embarrassed to admit I'd been taken, and I said, no, he'd given me ten. "Well, Im relieved!" the man said. "Hes done that before, you know—gives his young friend only five, and keeps fifteen. But what can I do? It embarrasses me so, when Ive first met a youngman, to give him the money. Idont reallyknow whattodo." Then he smiles Tolerantly. "But Petey is a lovely youngman —only—only—"He frowns slightly. "—only I wish he wouldnt call me Mom."

When I saw Pete again, one night in Bryant Park, I mentioned the money to him. He looked at his feet, pretending—I was sure he was pretending—embarrassment. "You gotta learn not to trust no one too much," he mumbled. Then he reached for his wallet, brought out three dollars. "Thats all I got now," he said, sighing ("What Am I Going To Do Now?!"). "Here, take em," he said. I did, and he stared at me in surprise. "Youre learning, spote," he said.

A few days later I got even with him.

I told him I knew a girl who wanted to be a stripper. I had met her not too long ago in the lobby of an apartment house I had just scored in. Her name was Flip, and she asked me to come up with her—just like that. She shows me sexy pictures of herself, turning me on. She was very pretty, very young. To the groaning sounds of "Night Train" she began to do a strip—then stopped coquettishly; tells me poutingly shes sorry, she cant go all the way: "You see, zoll—" (Thats how she said doll.) "—little Flip's got the mean rag on." Suddenly I realized without doubt that Flip was a man. She was the first dragqueen I had ever been with. I didnt let her know I had found out, and she went ahead and did what she told me she liked anyway. . . . When it was over, she says: "If you know any other cute zolls, tell them about me. Im always Ready, zoll."

When I told Pete about Flip (leaving out that she was actually a dragqueen), she too sounded like a nympho to him. "I gotta meet that chick," he told me—and later, I took him to her apartment. "We'll all three make it together," he said enthusiastically, "it's Sexier that way." And although he kept insisting as we stood outside Flip's door that I should stay, I said I had something else to do.

"Just ring the bell," I told him. "She wont even ask who you are. She'll just let you in."

I waited on the steps until I saw him ring the bell. The door opened. I heard Flip squeal: "Ooo, you are a zoll!"

That night I expected perversely to see an indignant Pete. But when I saw him, he said: "Man!—what a great Lay that chick is!" . . .

I felt very smug—and very surprised.

4

Then, one day—in the midst of that cold bitter winter, when the snow cut across the streets like an icy knife and the wind shrieked like something from Hell—one day, the memory of my Mother—accentuated by the long painfully written three-times-a-week letters without punctuation asking when I would be Back, asking me to promise not to get into trouble—that memory seized me with a racking violence—and I decided to put down Times Square again—a pattern of guilt which would recur periodically. I got a job, with a Foundation dedicated to Spreading The Greatness of The American Way of Life. And I kept away from The Streets. At night I would stay home or go to the movies—but not on 42nd Street or The Others. But—again—that job lasted only briefly, and impulsively, I quit. The cold air outside struck me like my lost freedom, regained. That very night I was back on Times Square.

"Where you been, spote?" Pete said. "I thought you got busted or something, I looked around for you. Dont split like that again, hear?" For the first time since I had known him, we shook hands.

After that, I saw him more and more often. Sometimes—having scored—we would meet afterwards and sit in the automat at 42nd and Park Avenue (this appealed to him as Classier). He told me he was staying in the room which the black-dressed Al rented to keep his motorcycle clothes in. "He dont dig anyone staying there," Pete told me, "but I finally conned him into letting me."

Yet, although I saw Pete at least once a day now, there was still the urgency, on both our parts, to split abruptly—to get away from each other.

Occasionally, we would go to see "Mom." And the initial embarrassment I had felt was completely gone: It was always the same scene, the man never touched either of us, he merely sat staring. Once he even took a picture of us at the table.

By now Pete had learned how to play checkers. And one afternoon, strangely—as Pete and I sat on the bed playing checkers for much longer than we ever had before, as if there had been no third party, no "performance," actually enjoying it—with startling suddenness "Mom" abandoned his role as watcher, as doting mother, and nervously, claiming A Huge Headache, he asked us to leave. He folded the board hurriedly and abruptly dumped the checkers into their box.

As we left, he almost slammed the door.

"What bugged him?" Pete asked; then, shrugging, dismissing it, "I guess he did have a bad headache—shes kinda weird, anyway. . . . Fuck-im."

We didnt go back.

5

Now the nights began to warm up. It's that magnificent interlude in New York between winter and spring, when you feel the warmth stirring, and you remember that the dreadful naked trees will inevitably sprout tiny green buds, soon. Everyone rushes into the parks, the streets—and you even forget that, very soon, summer will come scorchingly, dropping from the sky like a blanket of steam. . . .

"I dont feel like fuckin around today," Pete told me one afternoon. He seemed pensive. "Lets just make the flix, spote—and forget all about trying to score."

We saw a double feature—one, a French movie about Lesbians in a girls' school. When we got outside, it was dark, the sky beaded wondrously with spring stars. "You really believe two chicks could dig each other that tough?" Pete asked me. I answer, "Sure." I was wondering what had prompted such amazing, for him, naïveté. "It sure seems strange," he went on. "Dig: I can see guys making it with each other—sure—for money—but— . . . Well, it sure seems strange, just digging each other like that —and those two chicks, man, they were both beautiful." We were standing outside. Even the lights on the signs seemed livelier in the warm air.

I didnt have any place to go, but I said, "Later," to Pete. This is how it had always been before. "No, wait," he says, "dont split—unless you got something to do." "Nothing," I said. "Lets stick together," he said. "I just dont feel like fuckin around tonight," he said moodily.

We went to a cafeteria on the same block and ate. The drifting youngmen were in there, sitting at the tables sipping coffee, staring at the older men who walked in. "Sometimes this whole scene bugs me," Pete said. "I guess maybe I should split— leave New York—go somewhere else: L.A., maybe. You wanna know something? I been in the East all my life—New Jersey—New York. . . ." He stared dreamily out the window. "Lets go to Washington Square!" he said abruptly.

In a few minutes, by subway, we were there.

In Washington Square there were many people. In the center, around the fountain, the young painters and their girlfriends clustered; some had baby carriages. They seemed very happy. And I felt the same. I was sure it was the approaching warm weather. . . . One youngman with a beard played a guitar and sang softly in Spanish. Pete and I sat by the fountain, listening. Soon, we got up, walked around the west side—toward the "meat rack"—the gay part of the park. There, it was as if someone had hung a line of marionettes on the railing: the lonesome young homosexuals, legs dangling, looking, waiting for that one-night's sexual connection. . . . "This wouldnt be a good place for scoring tonight anyway," Pete says, "theres too many out for free fun." But we sit there too, silently.

Next to us, a Negro queen has nervously stationed herself—a screamingly effemi- nate youngman in a candy-striped shirt: twisting her neck haughtily, looking around her in pretended disdain. Soon a couple of her white "sisters" swish by, two equally effeminate youngmen. They stand talking to the Negro queen, gossiping breathlessly. Now theyre talking about gowns. "It was Fabulous!" said the Negro queen, "I dressed like the Queen of Sheba, and honey, I Mean To Tell You, I looked *Real!*"

"Wasnt thuh Queen of Shayba white?" says one of the white queens, a fiercely blond one, affecting a thick Southern accent.

The Negro queen's eyes open Wide. "Are you trying to dish me, Mary?" she says angrily.

"Honey," said the blond one, "all Ah asked was a simple question. Wasnt thuh Queen of Shayba White? For all Ah know, you *painted* youhself White."

"Mary," says the Negro queen, ready to spring from the railing, "I may not be the Queen of Sheba, *exactly,* but I am The Queen of This Meat Rack—and I'll prove it to any nelly-assed queen that wants to try me."

"Youretoomuch," says the blond one airily. "Why! whoevuh heard of a nigguh *Queen?*"

In one instant, the Negro queen jumps off the railing, grabs the blond one by her thin shoulders and shakes her back and forth until she begins to sob, trying tearfully to tear herself away from the Negro queen. Finally, the Negro queen lets go, and the blond one rushes off wailing:

"Mothuh-fuckuh, if we wuz in The South, Ahd show you whos Queen of thuh Meat Rack!" . . .

Pete said moodily: "She shoudnuh called her a nigger."

A fat zero-policeman comes by swinging his stick like a baton: "Move on, move on," he says. "Yes, sir, officer, sir," Pete says, raising his middle finger up at the cop as he passes by. . . . We move on, and it was beginning to get cool—the hint of spring withdrawing teasingly. We walk again through Washington Square. The guitarist with the beard has left, and we sit on a bench.

Sitting there with Pete, a great Loneliness overwhelmed me. Was it the sky? So like a Texas sky at night—the stars flung prodigiously in the expansive blackness. Or the sudden breathtaking memory of my Mother miles away? Her love radiates that great distance toward me stifling me. . . . Or was it the sudden change in the park?

The youngmen and girls had left—the older people were gone from the benches too. Now there remain only the hunting young homosexuals looking for a partner. They sit momentarily on benches, move away, stand restlessly. One sat near us. "You figure he thinks we're queer?" Pete asked me indignantly—and then he stared him away. . . . I wondered if the franticness of their search was overwhelming Pete as it was me; he was strangely silent. . . . Two youngmen walked by. Previously I had seen them standing a few feet apart, on the walk, moving slowly closer to each other. Then they had talked briefly—now they walked away together, speaking softly. They were both young, both goodlooking. I saw them smile at each other: For them, this night's search was over—not for money—but for a mutual, if fleeting, sharing. Staring after them, Pete says: "They couda fooled me, even. They look like hustlers, dont they? And I bet theyre gonna make it with each other."

We move along Fifth Avenue, past a dimlit bar in a hotel. Through the windows we see a woman playing the piano. A man is leaning over her, her lips move in a song, she slides closer to him. . . . We pause for a while, and then we continue walking—into Union Square now, were we stand listening to a man in a tight suit heatedly hollering about what a blight Union Square is. "Perverts and tramps!" he yells. And a little old tramp staggers up to him, he reeks of wine, his nose like a red lightbulb —and he shakes his old finger unsteadily at the man yelling out damnation and says: clearly: "Listenere, you—you jes listenere: Theres gonna be hobos! homos! and momos! in Our Park long after youve grown deaf and dumb!"

"Hey, spote," says Pete to me, "whats a momo?"

"I dont know, I guess he just made it up."

"That's cute," says Pete. "Homos, hobos and—and—what?"

"Momos," I said.

"Yeah: Momos. Hey! Maybe *we're* momos!" he laughs.

Weve reached the 34th Street, the corner of the Armory on Park Avenue.

"Heres where I live," I told Pete now.

"Can I come up and talk for a while?" he asked me, rushing the words together.

"Im tired," I said quickly.

"Cummon," he insisted, "its early yet—or you can come up with me Im still staying at Al's with all the motorcycle jackets. Come up there, I got a pint of juice, we'll kill it."

"It's too far," I told him.

He looked hurt.

"Okay. Lets go to my place," I said hurriedly.

There is still a doorman in the building where I lived: a Negro from Jamaica: a clinging relic, like the mirrored lobby, of its sadly gone elegance: Beyond the lobby and the doorman—who sits in a little room, nodding asleep through the night—the building is seedy two-room apartments and gray rooms—layers of wallpaper make the walls soft like quilts; the plumbing rattles; steam gives out on the coldest days. . . . We went up in the complaining elevator, into the apartment, broken up, in turn, into smaller apartments, tiny rooms. I turned on the light.

"This is nice," Pete said, looking at the dingy room. One thing was colorful: a Mexican blanket which my mother had sent me. . . . "I wish I had a place of my own," Pete says. "You know, I actually been thinking of getting a small apartment—with someone, maybe—you know, split the rent—it wouldnt be much that way. . . . You like living alone, spote?"

I pretended I hadnt heard him. . . . But long before that night when I had resolved to explore this world not with one person but with many, I had become aware that there was something about someone getting too close to me which suffocated me. . . .

"Maybe," Pete says, going on, "maybe—you know—I was just thinking—shacking up with another guy for a while—we could hustle together, really make the scores. It wouldnt be hard: I know lots of scores. Theyd stop digging me; dig you; so on— I mean, whoever it was, we would keep going like that. . . . I was even thinking— Christ—well—that fuckin street—it bugs me—sometimes I get nightmares about those toilets—I mean, all those fags—and—well, if I got a job, even—and split the rent with someone—well—"

"It's past midnight," I said interrupting him.

For a long while there seems to be nothing to say. Im aware of a smothering self-consciousness between us. I wanted him to leave. It was the first time anyone other than the curious men and women in the other rooms had been in this room with me.

"Can I stay here tonight?" I heard him ask clearly.

In a kind of panic, I want to say no. "Yes," I answered.

The lights are out now. The darkness seems very real, like a third person waiting. I lay on the very edge of one side of the bed, and he lay on the very edge of the other. A long time passed. Hours.

"Are you asleep?" he asked me.

"No—I cant sleep."

"Me neither," he says. "Maybe I should go." But he didnt move.

More silence.

And then I felt his hand, lightly, on mine.

Neither of us moved. Moments passed like that. And now his hand closes over mine, tightly.

And that was all that happened.

The man in the other wing of the building, on the other side of my window, began to cough very early, and I got up hurriedly and dressed. "I have to go out," I told Pete.

"Me, too," he said. "I have to see someone."

We avoided looking at each other. "I'll see you around The Street," he said at the door. "Man," he says—but his voice was forced, as mine was, "I got a real tough score lined up today—hes worth Twenty."

"Later," I said.

"Later—spote," he said.

I saw him again, many times—in the movie theaters, in Bryant Park, on Times Square. We would say hello to each other, stop, talk casually: He would exaggerate his scores, I would exaggerate mine. But we were never together for long any more. "I have to score," one of us would say, and we'd split.

Soon we wouldnt stop to talk to each other when we met. We would say hello, rush on. . . . And then one day, one stifling summer day, I saw him bouncing along the street in my direction. I turned sharply, pretended to be looking at some movie posters; and glancing back once, briefly, I noticed that he—for the same reason I had turned away, to avoid meeting—had crossed to the other side of the street.

THE WRYSONS

John Cheever

(1912–1982)

Biography p. 1066

The Wrysons wanted things in the suburb of Shady Hill to remain exactly as they were. Their dread of change—of irregularity of any sort—was acute, and when the Larkin estate was sold for an old people's rest home, the Wrysons went to the Village Council meeting and demanded to know what sort of old people these old people were going to be. The Wrysons' civic activities were confined to upzoning, but they were very active in this field, and if you were invited to their house for cocktails, the chances were that you would be asked to sign an upzoning petition before you got away. This was something more than a natural desire to preserve the character of the community. They seemed to sense that there was a stranger at the gates—unwashed, tirelessly scheming, foreign, the father of disorderly children who would ruin their rose garden and depreciate their real-estate investment, a man with a beard, a garlic breath, and a book. The Wrysons took no part in the intellectual life of the community. There was hardly a book in their house, and, in a place where even cooks were known to have Picasso reproductions hanging above their washstands, the Wrysons' taste in painting stopped at marine sunsets and bowls of flowers. Donald Wryson was a large man with thinning fair hair and the cheerful air of a bully, but he was a bully only in the defense of rectitude, class distinctions, and the orderly appearance of things. Irene Wryson was not a totally unattractive woman, but she was both shy and contentious—especially contentious on the subject of upzoning. They had one child, a little girl named Dolly, and they lived in a pleasant house on Alewives Lane, and they went in for gardening. This was another way of keeping up the appearance of things, and Donald Wryson was very critical of a neighbor who had ragged syringa bushes and a bare spot on her front lawn. They led a limited social life; they seemed to have no ambitions or needs in this direction, although at Christmas each year they sent out about six hundred cards. The preparation and addressing of these must have occupied their evenings for at least two weeks. Donald had a laugh like a jackass, and people who did not like him were careful not to sit in the same train coach with him. The Wrysons were stiff; they were inflexible. They seemed to experience not distaste but alarm when they found quack grass in their lawn or heard of a contemplated divorce among their neighbors. They were odd, of course. They were not as odd as poor, dizzy Flossie Dolmetch, who was caught forging drug prescriptions and was discovered to have been under the influence of morphine for three years. They were not as odd as Caruthers Mason, with his collection of two thousand lewd photographs, or as odd as Mrs. Temon, who, with those two lovely children in the next room— But why go on? They were odd.

Irene Wryson's oddness centered on a dream. She dreamed once or twice a month that someone—some enemy or hapless American pilot—had exploded a hydrogen bomb. In the light of day, her dream was inadmissible, for she could not relate it to her garden, her interest in upzoning, or her comfortable way of life. She could not bring herself to tell her husband at breakfast that she had dreamed about the hydrogen bomb. Faced with the pleasant table and its view of the garden—faced even with rain and snow—she could not find it in herself to explain what had troubled her sleep. The dream cost her much in energy and composure, and often left her deeply depressed. Its sequence of events varied, but it usually went like this.

The dream was set in Shady Hill—she dreamed that she woke in her own bed. Donald was always gone. She was at once aware of the fact that the bomb had exploded. Mattress stuffing and a trickle of brown water were coming through a big hole in the ceiling. The sky was gray—lightless—although there were in the west a few threads of red light, like those charming vapor trails we see in the air after the sun has set. She didn't know if these were vapor trails or some part of that force that would destroy the marrow in her bones. The gray air seemed final. The sky would never shine with light again. From her window she could see a river, and now, as she watched, boats began to come upstream. At first, there were only two or three. Then there were tens, and then there were hundreds. There were outboards, excursion boats, yachts, schooners with auxiliary motors; there were even rowboats. The number of boats grew until the water was covered with them, and the noise of motors rose to a loud din. The jockeying for position in this retreat up the river became aggressive and then savage. She saw men firing pistols at one another, and a rowboat, in which there was a family with little children, smashed and sunk by a cruiser. She cried, in her dream, to see this inhumanity as the world was ending. She cried, and she went on watching, as if some truth was being revealed to her—as if she had always known this to be the human condition, as if she had always known the world to be dangerous and the comforts of her life in Shady Hill to be the merest palliative.

Then in her dream she turned away from the window and went through the bathroom that connected their room and Dolly's. Her daughter was sleeping sweetly, and she woke her. At this point, her emotions were at their strongest. The force and purity of the love that she felt toward this fragrant child was an agony. She dressed the little girl and put a snowsuit on her and led her into the bathroom. She opened the medicine cabinet, the one place in the house that the Wrysons, in their passion for neatness, had not put in order. It was crowded with leftover medicines from Dolly's trifling illnesses—cough syrups, calamine lotion for poison ivy, aspirin, and physics. And the mild perfume of these remnants and the tenderness she had felt for her daughter when she was ill—as if the door of the medicine cabinet had been a window opening onto some dazzling summer of the emotions—made her cry again. Among the bottles was one that said "Poison," and she reached for this and unscrewed the top, and shook into her left hand a pill for herself and one for the girl. She told the trusting child some gentle lie, and was about to put the pill between her lips when the ceiling of the bathroom collapsed and they stood knee deep in plaster and dirty water. She groped around in the water for the poison, but it was lost, and the dream usually ended in this way. And how could she lean across the breakfast table and explain her pallor to her husky husband with this detailed vision of the end of the world? He would have laughed his jackass laugh.

Donald Wryson's oddness could be traced easily enough to his childhood. He had been raised in a small town in the Middle West that couldn't have had much to recommend it, and his father, an old-fashioned commercial traveler, with a hothouse rose in his buttonhole and buff-colored spats, had abandoned his wife and his son when the boy was young. Mrs. Wryson had few friends and no family. With her husband gone, she got a job as a clerk in an insurance office, and took up, with her son, a life of unmitigated melancholy and need. She never forgot the horror of her abandonment, and she leaned so heavily for support on her son that she seemed to threaten his animal spirits. Her life was a Calvary, as she often said, and the most she could do was to keep body and soul together.

She had been young and fair and happy once, and the only way she had of evoking these lost times was by giving her son baking lessons. When the nights were long and cold and the wind whistled around the four-family house where they lived, she would light a fire in the kitchen range and drop an apple peel onto the stove lid for the fragrance. Then Donald would put on an apron and scurry around, getting out the necessary bowls and pans, measuring out flour and sugar, separating eggs. He learned the contents of every cupboard. He knew where the spices and the sugar were kept, the nutmeats and the citron, and when the work was done, he enjoyed washing the bowls and pans and putting them back where they belonged. Donald loved these hours himself, mostly because they seemed to dispel the oppression that stood unlifted over those years of his mother's life—and was there any reason why a lonely boy should rebel against the feeling of security that he found in the kitchen on a stormy night? She taught him how to make cookies and muffins and banana bread and, finally, a Lady Baltimore cake. It was sometimes after eleven o'clock when their work was done. "We do have a good time together, don't we, son?" Mrs. Wryson would ask. "We have a lovely time together, don't we, you and me? Oh, hear that wind howling! Think of the poor sailors at sea." Then she would embrace him, she would run her fingers through his light hair, and sometimes, although he was much too big, she would draw him onto her lap.

All of that was long ago. Mrs. Wryson was dead, and when Donald stood at the edge of her grave he had not felt any very great grief. She had been reconciled to dying years before she did die, and her conversation had been full of gallant references to the grave. Years later, when Donald was living alone in New York, he had been overtaken suddenly, one spring evening, by a depression as keen as any in his adolescence. He did not drink, he did not enjoy books or movies or the theatre, and, like his mother, he had few friends. Searching desperately for some way to take himself out of this misery, he hit on the idea of baking a Lady Baltimore cake. He went out and bought the ingredients—deeply ashamed of himself—and sifted the flour and chopped the nuts and citron in the kitchen of the little walk-up apartment where he lived. As he stirred the cake batter, he felt his depression vanish. It was not until he had put the cake in the oven and sat down to wipe his hands on his apron that he realized how successful he had been in summoning the ghost of his mother and the sense of security he had experienced as a child in her kitchen on stormy nights. When the cake was done he iced it, ate a slice, and dumped the rest into the garbage.

The next time he felt troubled, he resisted the temptation to bake a cake, but he was not always able to do this, and during the eight or nine years he had been married to Irene he must have baked eight or nine cakes. He took extraordinary precautions, and she knew nothing of this. She believed him to be a complete stranger to the kitchen. And how could he at the breakfast table—all two hundred and sixteen pounds of him—explain that he looked sleepy because he had been up until three baking a Lady Baltimore cake, which he had hidden in the garbage?

Given these unpleasant facts, then, about these not attractive people, we can dispatch them brightly enough, and who but Dolly would ever miss them? Donald Wryson, in his crusading zeal for upzoning, was out in all kinds of weather, and let's say that one night, when he was returning from a referendum in an ice storm, his car skidded down Hill Street, struck the big elm at the corner, and was demolished. Finis. His poor widow, either through love or dependence, was inconsolable. Getting out of bed one morning, a month or so after the loss of her husband, she got her feet caught in the dust ruffle and fell and broke her hip. Weakened by a long convalescence, she contracted pneumonia and departed this life. This leaves us with Dolly to account for, and what a sad tale we can write for this little girl. During the months in which her parents' will is in probate, she lives first on the charity and then on the forbearance of her neighbors. Finally, she is sent to live with her only relative, a cousin of her mother's, who is a schoolteacher in Los Angeles. How many hundreds of nights will she cry herself to sleep in bewilderment and loneliness. How strange and cold the world will seem. There is little to remind her of her parents except at Christmas, when, forwarded from Shady Hill, will come Greetings from Mrs. Sallust Trevor, who has been living in Paris and does not know about the accident; Salutations from the Parkers, who live in Mexico and never did get their lists straight; Season's Greetings from Meyers' Drugstore; Merry Christmas from the Perry Browns; Santissimas from the Oak Tree Italian Restaurant; A Joyeux Noël from Dodie Smith. Year after year, it will be this little girl's responsibility to throw into the wastebasket these cheerful holiday greetings that have followed her parents to and beyond the grave. . . . But this did not happen, and if it had, it would have thrown no light on what we know.

What happened was this: Irene Wryson had her dream one night. When she woke, she saw that her husband was not in bed. The air smelled sweet. Sweating suddenly, the beating of her heart strained with terror, she realized that the end had come. What could that sweetness in the air be but atomic ash? She ran to the window, but the river was empty. Half asleep and feeling cruelly lost as she was, she was kept from waking Dolly only by a healthy curiosity. There was smoke in the hallway, but it was not the smoke of any common fire. The sweetness made her feel sure that this was lethal ash. Led on by the smell, she went on down the stairs and through the dining room into the lighted kitchen. Donald was asleep with his head on the table and the room was full of smoke. "Oh, my darling," she cried, and woke him.

"I burned it," he said when he saw the smoke pouring from the oven. "I burned the damned thing."

"I thought it was the hydrogen bomb," she said.

"It's a cake," he said. "I burned it. What made you think it was the hydrogen bomb?"

"If you wanted something to eat, you should have waked me," she said.

She turned off the oven, and opened the window to let out the smell of smoke and let in the smell of nicotiana and other night flowers. She may have hesitated for a moment, for what would the stranger at the gates—that intruder with his beard and his book—have made of this couple, in their nightclothes, in the smoke-filled kitchen at half past four in the morning? Some comprehension—perhaps momentary—of the complexity of life must have come to them, but it was only momentary. There were no further explanations. He threw the cake, which was burned to a cinder, into the garbage, and they turned out the lights and climbed the stairs, more mystified by life than ever, and more interested than ever in a good appearance.

Poetry

Robert Frost
(1874–1963)

Biography p. 1073

STOPPING BY WOODS ON A SNOWY EVENING

Whose woods these are I think I know.
His house is in the village though;
He will not see me stopping here
To watch his woods fill up with snow.

My little horse must think it queer   5
To stop without a farmhouse near
Between the woods and frozen lake
The darkest evening of the year.

He gives his harness bells a shake
To ask if there is some mistake   10
The only other sound's the sweep
Of easy wind and downy flake.

The woods are lovely, dark and deep.
But I have promises to keep,
And miles to go before I sleep,   15
And miles to go before I sleep.

BIRCHES

When I see birches bend to left and right
Across the lines of straighter darker trees,
I like to think some boy's been swinging them.
But swinging doesn't bend them down to stay
As ice storms do. Often you must have seen them   5
Loaded with ice a sunny winter morning
After a rain. They click upon themselves
As the breeze rises, and turn many-colored
As the stir cracks and crazes their enamel.

Soon the sun's warmth makes them shed crystal shells   10
Shattering and avalanching on the snow crust—
Such heaps of broken glass to sweep away
You'd think the inner dome of heaven had fallen.
They are dragged to the withered bracken by the load,
And they seem not to break; though once they are bowed   15
So low for long, they never right themselves:
You may see their trunks arching in the woods
Years afterwards, trailing their leaves on the ground
Like girls on hands and knees that throw their hair
Before them over their heads to dry in the sun.   20
But I was going to say when Truth broke in
With all her matter of fact about the ice storm,
I should prefer to have some boy bend them
As he went out and in to fetch the cows—
Some boy too far from town to learn baseball,   25
Whose only play was what he found himself,
Summer or winter, and could play alone.
One by one he subdued his father's trees
By riding them down over and over again
Until he took the stiffness out of them,   30
And not one but hung limp, not one was left
For him to conquer. He learned all there was
To learn about not launching out too soon
And so not carrying the tree away
Clear to the ground. He always kept his poise   35
To the top branches, climbing carefully
With the same pains you use to fill a cup
Up to the brim, and even above the brim.
Then he flung outward, feet first, with a swish,
Kicking his way down through the air to the ground.   40
So was I once myself a swinger of birches.
And so I dream of going back to be.
It's when I'm weary of considerations,
And life is too much like a pathless wood
Where your face burns and tickles with the cobwebs   45
Broken across it, and one eye is weeping
From a twig's having lashed across it open.
I'd like to get away from earth awhile
And then come back to it and begin over.
May no fate willfully misunderstand me   50
And half grant what I wish and snatch me away
Not to return. Earth's the right place for love:
I don't know where it's likely to go better.
I'd like to go by climbing a birch tree,
And climb black branches up a snow-white trunk   55
Toward heaven, till the tree could bear no more,
But dipped its top and set me down again.
That would be good both going and coming back.
One could do worse than be a swinger of birches.

MENDING WALL

Something there is that doesn't love a wall,
That sends the frozen-ground-swell under it,
And spills the upper boulders in the sun;
And makes gaps even two can pass abreast.
The work of hunters is another thing: 5
I have come after them and made repair
Where they have left not one stone on a stone,
But they would have the rabbit out of hiding,
To please the yelping dogs. The gaps I mean,
No one has seen them made or heard them made,   10
But at spring mending-time we find them there.
I let my neighbour know beyond the hill;
And on a day we meet to walk the line
And set the wall between us once again.
We keep the wall between us as we go.   15
To each the boulders that have fallen to each.
And some are loaves and some so nearly balls
We have to use a spell to make them balance:
"Stay where you are until our backs are turned!"
We wear our fingers rough with handling them.   20
Oh, just another kind of out-door game,
One on a side. It comes to little more:
There where it is we do not need the wall:
He is all pine and I am apple orchard.
My apple trees will never get across   25
And eat the cones under his pines, I tell him.
He only says, "Good fences make good neighbours."
Spring is the mischief in me, and I wonder
If I could put a notion in his head:
"Why do they make good neighbours? Isn't it   30
Where there are cows? But here there are no cows.
Before I built a wall I'd ask to know
What I was walling in or walling out,
And to whom I was like to give offence.
Something there is that doesn't love a wall,   35
That wants it down." I could say "Elves" to him,
But it's not elves exactly, and I'd rather
He said it for himself. I see him there
Bringing a stone grasped firmly by the top
In each hand, like an old-stone savage armed.   40
He moves in darkness as it seems to me,
Not of woods only and the shade of trees.
He will not go behind his father's saying,
And he likes having thought of it so well
He says again, "Good fences make good neighbours."   45

William Wordsworth
(1770–1850)

Biography p. 1108

THE DAFFODILS

I wandered lonely as a cloud
That floats on high o'er vales and hills,
When all at once I saw a crowd,
A host, of golden daffodils;
Beside the lake, beneath the trees,   5
Fluttering and dancing in the breeze.

Continuous as the stars that shine
And twinkle on the Milky Way,
They stretched in never-ending line
Along the margin of a bay: 10
Ten thousand saw I at a glance,
Tossing their heads in sprightly dance.

The waves beside them danced; but they
Outdid the sparkling waves in glee;
A poet could not but be gay   15
In such a jocund company;
I gazed—and gazed—but little thought
What wealth the show to me had brought:

For oft, when on my couch I lie
In vacant or in pensive mood,   20
They flash upon that inward eye
Which is the bliss of solitude;
And then my heart with pleasure fills,
And dances with the daffodils.

THE WORLD IS TOO MUCH WITH US

The world is too much with us; late and soon,
Getting and spending, we lay waste our powers;
Little we see in Nature that is ours;
We have given our hearts away, a sordid boon!
This Sea that bares her bosom to the moon,   5
The winds that will be howling at all hours,
And are up-gathered now like sleeping flowers,
For this, for everything, we are out of tune;

It moves us not.—Great God! I'd rather be
A Pagan suckled in a creed outworn;   10
So might I, standing on this pleasant lea,
Have glimpses that would make me less forlorn;
Have sight of Proteus rising from the sea;
Or hear Old Triton blow his wreathèd horn.

MORNING SWIM

Maxine Kumin
(b. 1925)

Biography p. 1082

Into my empty head there come
a cotton beach, a dock wherefrom

I set out, oily and nude
through mist, in chilly solitude.

There was no line, no roof or floor   5
to tell the water from the air.

Night fog thick as terry cloth
closed me in its fuzzy growth.

I hung my bathrobe on two pegs.
I took the lake between my legs.   10

Invaded and invader, I
went overhand on that flat sky.

Fish twitched beneath me, quick and tame.
in their green zone they sang my name

and in the rhythm of the swim   15
I hummed a two-four-time slow hymn.

I hummed *Abide with Me.* The beat
rose in the fine thrash of my feet,

rose in the bubbles I put out
slantwise, trailing through my mouth.   20

My bones drank water; water fell
through all my doors. I was the well

that fed the lake that met my sea
in which I sang *Abide with Me.*

HOME-THOUGHTS FROM ABROAD

Robert Browning

(1812–1882)

Biography p. 1064

1

Oh, to be in England
Now that April's there,
And whoever wakes in England
Sees, some morning, unaware,
That the lowest boughs and the brushwood sheaf   5
Round the elm-tree bole are in tiny leaf.
While the chaffinch sings on the orchard bough
In England—now!

2

And after April, when May follows,
And the whitethroat builds, and all the swallows!   10
Hark, where my blossomed pear-tree in the hedge
Leans to the field and scatters on the clover
Blossoms and dewdrops—at the bent spray's edge—
That's the wise thrush; he sings each song twice over,

Lest you should think he never could recapture   15
The first fine careless rapture!
And though the fields look rough with hoary dew
All will be gay when noontide wakes anew
The buttercups, the little children's dower
—Far brighter than this gaudy melon-flower!   20

LOVELIEST OF TREES

A. E. Housman
(1859–1936)

Biography p. 1078

Loveliest of trees, the cherry now
Is hung with bloom along the bough,
And stands about the woodland ride
Wearing white for Eastertide.

Now, of my threescore years and ten,   5
Twenty will not come again,
And take from seventy springs a score,
It only leaves me fifty more.

And since to look at things in bloom
Fifty springs are little room,   10
About the woodlands I will go
To see the cherry hung with snow.

FROGS

Norman MacCaig
(b. 1910)

Biography p. 1086

Frogs sit more solid
Than anything sits. In mid-leap they are
Parachutists falling
In a free fall. They die on roads
With arms across their chests and   5
Heads high.

I love frogs that sit
Like Buddha, that fall without
Parachutes, that die
Like Italian tenors.   10

Above all, I love them because,
Pursued in water, they never
Panic so much that they fail
To make stylish triangles
With their ballet dancer's   15
Legs.

WINDOW-PANE WITH FORMS

Josephine Jacobsen

(b. 1908)

Biography p. 1080

In flight
sun-feathered, they let
earth drop
through blue
air,   5
fly up up
alight high
as angels.

Here into
the feeder   10
come twitch, jerk, dart;
saurian claw,
seed-black look
sharp as a
beak.   15

They through
strange glass
see
some
bird's eye   20
me.

GREAT FARM

Philip Booth
(b. 1925)

Biography p. 1063

In April, when raining is sunlight,
when dawn is a coarse young crow,
as willows bend to feather
the Great Farm springs to grow.

The orchard is loud: bees   5
and blossoms claim the bough;
a meadow of frogs, a sky
of swallows, flood the air now.

Two girls ride two white horses
(the world is green to plow!)   10
and sideways a big man with buckets
sets hugely to milk a big cow.

THE LAKE ISLE OF INNISFREE

William Butler Yeats
(1865–1939)

Biography p. 1109

I will arise and go now, and go to Innisfree,
And a small cabin build there, of clay and wattles made:
Nine bean-rows will I have there, a hive for the honeybee,
And live alone in the bee-loud glade.

And I shall have some peace there, for peace comes dropping slow,   5
Dropping from the veils of the morning to where the cricket sings;
There midnight's all a glimmer, and noon a purple glow,
And evening full of the linnet's wings.

I will arise and go now, for always night and day
I hear lake water lapping with low sounds by the shore;   10
While I stand on the roadway, or on the pavements grey,
I hear it in the deep heart's core.

GRAPEFIELDS AS A CHILD

Benjamin Durazo
(1915–1971)

Biography p. 1071

Great clouds wired to the ground
            confer and tremble
when a boy, loaded with water, passes
pulling his feet quickly from the smoldering earth.
    His family has sent him, the youngest,   5
        for the gallon jugs, that were of wine,
            now covered with soaked burlap.

    The brown skin blotches with the dust
            that is everywhere
His father, who is grey, has spotted him but keeps working.   10
        And there are people now, everywhere,
            bobbing in and out of the leaves
        eating from the clouds
            that tug at the ground.

ON SIDES OF TRACTOR PATHS

Leonard Adamé
(b. 1947)

Biography p. 1059

In the shed
showing me
nailing, stacking
of cherry tomato lugs.

Talking softly,   5
only of nailing,
hearing you through
the hum of machine noise.

Your eyes wide,
stepping on the pedal   10
releasing 300 pounds
of pressure

hundreds of times,
every day,
eyes unchanging,   15
wide and quiet and brown.

Lunch alone by
the nailer, tacos
dripping chile colorado
from a grease-stained   20
lunch bag.

At 5:00 waiting,
your wife in the field,
children asleep in
the new rusty '50 Chevy.   25

June, then suddenly August,
sweat and overripe fruit
rotting on sides
of tractor paths.

One day, another at   30
the machine,
familiar rhythm broken.

When I asked, someone said
in the field

while they irrigated   35
you shot your rifle
at the foreman, your eyes wide,
he running through vines
screaming.

Then, your wife looking,   40
the barrel to your mouth,
you shot again.

In the payroll line
they put $1.65 in
mud-stained pockets   45
and did not stay
to laugh and talk
as on other days.

A NARROW FELLOW IN THE GRASS

Emily Dickinson

(1830–1886)

Biography p. 1069

A narrow Fellow in the Grass
Occasionally rides—
You may have met Him—did you not
His notice sudden is—

The Grass divides as with a Comb—   5
A spotted shaft is seen—
And then it closes at your feet
And opens further on—

He likes a Boggy Acre
A Floor too cool for Corn—   10
Yet when a Boy, and Barefoot—
I more than once at Noon
Have passed, I thought, a Whip lash
Unbraiding in the Sun
When stooping to secure it   15
It wrinkled, and was gone—

Several of Nature's People
I know, and they know me—

I feel for them a transport
Of cordiality—   20

But never met this Fellow
Attended, or alone
Without a tighter breathing
And Zero at the Bone—

SNAKE

D. H. Lawrence

(1885–1930)

Biography p. 1083

A snake came to my water-trough
On a hot, hot day, and I in pyjamas for the heat,
To drink there.

In the deep, strange-scented shade of the great dark carob-tree
I came down the steps with my pitcher   5
And must wait, must stand and wait, for there he was at the trough before me.

He reached down from a fissure in the earth-wall in the gloom
And trailed his yellow-brown slackness soft-bellied down, over the edge of the
     stone trough
And rested his throat upon the stone bottom,
And where the water had dripped from the tap, in a small clearness,   10
He sipped with his straight mouth,
Softly drank through his straight gums, into his slack long body,
Silently.

Someone was before me at my water-trough,
And I, like a second comer, waiting.   15

He lifted his head from his drinking, as cattle do,
And looked at me vaguely, as drinking cattle do,
And flickered his two-forked tongue from his lips, and mused a moment,
And stooped and drank a little more,
Being earth-brown, earth-golden from the burning bowels of the earth   20
On the day of Sicilian July, with Etna smoking.

The voice of my education said to me
He must be killed,
For in Sicily the black, black snakes are innocent, the gold are venomous.

And voices in me said, If you were a man   25
You would take a stick and break him now, and finish him off.

But must I confess how I liked him,
How glad I was he had come like a guest in quiet, to drink at my water-trough
And depart peaceful, pacified, and thankless,
Into the burning bowels of this earth?   30

Was it cowardice, that I dared not kill him?
Was it perversity, that I longed to talk to him?
Was it humility, to feel so honoured?
I felt so honoured.

And yet those voices: 35
If you were not afraid, you would kill him!

And truly I was afraid, I was most afraid,
But even so, honoured still more
That he should seek my hospitality
From out the dark door of the secret earth.   40

He drank enough
And lifted his head, dreamily, as one who has drunken,
And flickered his tongue like a forked night on the air, so black,
Seeming to lick his lips,
And looked around like a god, unseeing, into the air,   45
And slowly turned his head,
And slowly, very slowly, as if thrice adream,
Proceeded to draw his slow length curving round
And climb again the broken bank of my wall-face.

And as he put his head into that dreadful hole,   50
And as he slowly drew up, snake-easing his shoulders, and entered farther,
A sort of horror, a sort of protest against his withdrawing into that horrid black
    hole,
Deliberately going into the blackness, and slowly drawing himself after,
Overcame me now his back was turned.

I looked round, I put down my pitcher,   55
I picked up a clumsy log
And threw it at the water-trough with a clatter.

I think it did not hit him,
But suddenly that part of him that was left behind convulsed in undignified haste,
Writhed like lightning, and was gone   60

Into the black hole, the earth-lipped fissure in the wall-front,
At which, in the intense still noon, I stared with fascination.

And immediately I regretted it.
I thought how paltry, how vulgar, what a mean act!
I despised myself and the voices of my accursed human education.   65
And I thought of the albatross,
And I wished he would come back, my snake.

For he seemed to me again like a king,
Like a king in exile, uncrowned in the underworld,
Now due to be crowned again.   70

And so, I missed my chance with one of the lords
Of life.
And I have something to expiate;
A pettiness.

THE FISH

Elizabeth Bishop
(1911–1979)

Biography p. 1062

I caught a tremendous fish
and held him beside the boat
half out of water, with my hook
fast in a corner of his mouth.
He didn't fight.   5
He hadn't fought at all.
He hung a grunting weight,
battered and venerable
and homely. Here and there
his brown skin hung in strips   10
like ancient wallpaper,
and its pattern of darker brown
was like wallpaper:
shapes like full-blown roses
stained and lost through age.   15
He was speckled with barnacles,
fine rosettes of lime,
and infested
with tiny white sea-lice,

and underneath two 'or three   20
rags of green weed hung down.
While his gills were breathing in
the terrible oxygen
—the frightening gills,
fresh and crisp with blood,   25
that can cut so badly—
I thought of the coarse white flesh
packed in like feathers,
the big bones and the little bones,
the dramatic reds and blacks   30
of his shiny entrails,
and the pink swim-bladder
like a big peony.
I looked into his eyes
which were far larger than mine   35
but shallower, and yellowed,
the irises backed and packed
with tarnished tinfoil
seen through the lenses
of old scratched isinglass.   40
They shifted a little, but not
to return my stare.
—It was more like the tipping
of an object toward the light.
I admired his sullen face,   45
the mechanism of his jaw,
and then I saw
that from his lower lip
—if you could call it a lip—
grim, wet, and weaponlike,   50
hung five old pieces of fish-line,
or four and a wire leader
with the swivel still attached,
with all their five big hooks
grown firmly in his mouth.   55
A green line, frayed at the end
where he broke it, two heavier lines,
and a fine black thread
still crimped from the strain and snap
when it broke and he got away.   60
Like medals with their ribbons
frayed and wavering,
a five-haired beard of wisdom
trailing from his aching jaw.
I stared and stared   65
and victory filled up
the little rented boat,
from the pool of bilge
where oil had spread a rainbow
around the rusted engine   70

to the bailer rusted orange,
the sun-cracked thwarts,
the oarlocks on their strings,
the gunnels—until everything
was rainbow, rainbow, rainbow!   75
And I let the fish go.

Carl Sandburg
(1878–1967)

Biography p. 1096

GRASS

Pile the bodies high at Austerlitz and Waterloo.
Shovel them under and let me work—
      I am the grass; I cover all.

And pile them high at Gettysburg
And pile them high at Ypres and Verdun.   5
Shovel them under and let me work.
Two years, ten years, and passengers ask the conductor:
      What place is this?
      Where are we now?

      I am the grass.   10
      Let me work.

CHICAGO

Hog Butcher for the World,
Tool Maker, Stacker of Wheat,
Player with Railroads and the Nation's Freight Handler;
Stormy, husky, brawling,
City of the Big Shoulders: 5

They tell me you are wicked and I believe them, for I have seen your painted
    women under the gas lamps luring the farm boys.
And they tell me you are crooked and I answer: Yes, it is true I have seen the
    gunman kill and go free to kill again.
And they tell me you are brutal and my reply is: On the faces of women and
    children I have seen the marks of wanton hunger.

And having answered so I turn once more to those who sneer at this my city,
    and I give them back the sneer and say to them:
Come and show me another city with lifted head singing so proud to be alive and
    coarse and strong and cunning.   10
Flinging magnetic curses amid the toil of piling job on job, here is a tall bold
    slugger set vivid against the little soft cities;

Fierce as a dog with tongue lapping for action, cunning
    as a savage pitted against the wilderness,
        Bareheaded,
        Shoveling,
        Wrecking,   15
        Planning,
        Building, breaking, rebuilding,
Under the smoke, dust all over his mouth, laughing with white teeth,
Under the terrible burden of destiny laughing as a young man laughs,
Laughing even as an ignorant fighter laughs who has never lost a battle,   20
Bragging and laughing that under his wrist is the pulse, and under his ribs the
    heart of the people,
                        Laughing!
Laughing the stormy, husky, brawling laughter of
    Youth, half-naked, sweating, proud to be Hog
    Butcher, Tool Maker, Stacker of Wheat, Player with
    Railroads and Freight Handler to the Nation.

STREET WINDOW

    The pawn-shop man knows hunger,
    And how far hunger has eaten the heart
    Of one who comes with an old keepsake.
    Here are wedding rings and baby bracelets,
    Scarf pins and shoe buckles, jeweled garters,   5
    Old-fashioned knives with inlaid handles,
    Watches of old gold and silver,
    Old coins worn with finger-marks.
    They tell stories.

SKYSCRAPER

By day the skyscraper looms in the smoke and sun and has a soul.
Prairie and valley, streets of the city, pour people into it and they mingle among
    its twenty floors and are poured out again back to the streets, prairies and
    valleys.
It is the men and women, boys and girls so poured in and out all day that give

the building a soul of dreams and thoughts and memories.
(Dumped in the sea or fixed in a desert, who would care for the building or
    speak its name or ask a policeman the way to it?)

Elevators slide on their cables and tubes catch letters and parcels and iron pipes
    carry gas and water in and sewage out.   5
Wires climb with secrets, carry light and carry words, and tell terrors and profits
    and loves—curses of men grappling plans of business and questions of women
    in plots of love.

Hour by hour the caissons reach down to the rock of the
    earth and hold the building to a turning planet.
Hour by hour the girders play as ribs and reach out and
    hold together the stone walls and floors.
Hour by hour the hand of the mason and the stuff of the mortar clinch the pieces
    and parts to the shape an architect voted.
Hour by hour the sun and the rain, the air and the rust, and the press of time
    running into centuries, play on the building inside and out and use it.   10

Men who sunk the pilings and mixed the mortar are laid in graves where the
    wind whistles a wild song without words
And so are men who strung the wires and fixed the pipes and tubes and those
    who saw it rise floor by floor.
Souls of them all are here, even the hod carrier begging at the back doors
    hundreds of miles away and the bricklayer who went to state's prison for
    shooting another man while drunk.
(One man fell from a girder and broke his neck at the end of a straight plunge—
    he is here—his soul has gone into the stones of the building.)

On the office doors from tier to tier—hundreds of names and each name standing
    for a face written across with a dead child, a passionate lover, a driving
    ambition for a million dollar business or a lobster's ease of life.   15

Behind the signs on the doors they work and the walls tell nothing from room to
    room.
Ten-dollar-a-week stenographers take letters from corporation officers, lawyers,
    efficiency engineers, and tons of letters go bundled from the building to all
    ends of the earth.
Smiles and tears of each office girl go into the soul of the building just the same
    as the master-men who rule the building.

Hands of clocks turn to noon hours and each floor empties its men and women
    who go away and eat and come back to work.
Toward the end of the afternoon all work slackens and all jobs go slower as the
    people feel day closing on them.   20
One by one the floors are emptied . . . The uniformed elevator men are gone.
    Pails clang . . . Scrubbers work, talking in foreign tongues. Broom and water
    and mop clean from the floors human dust and spit, and machine grime of
    the day.
Spelled in electric fire on the roof are words telling miles of houses and people
    where to buy a thing for money. The sign speaks till midnight.

Darkness on the hallways. Voices echo. Silence holds . . . Watchmen walk slow
    from floor to floor and try the doors. Revolvers bulge from their hip pockets
    . . . Steel safes stand in corners. Money is stacked in them.
A young watchman leans at a window and sees the lights of barges butting their
    way across a harbor, nets of red and white lanterns in a railroad yard, and a
    span of glooms splashed with lines of white and blurs of crosses and clusters
    over the sleeping city.
By night the skyscraper looms in the smoke and the stars and has a soul.   25

PRAYERS OF STEEL

Lay me on an anvil, O God.
Beat me and hammer me into a crowbar.
Let me pry loose old walls.
Let me lift and loosen old foundations.

Lay me on an anvil, O God.   5
Beat me and hammer me into a steel spike.
Drive me into the girders that hold a skyscraper together.
Take red-hot rivets and fasten me into the central girders.
Let me be the great nail holding a skyscraper through blue nights into white
    stars.   10

LONDON

William Blake

(1757–1827)

Biography p. 1062

I wander thro' each charter'd street,
Near where the charter'd Thames does flow
And mark in every face I meet
Marks of weakness, marks of woe.

In every cry of every Man,   5
In every Infant's cry of fear,
In every voice, in every ban,
The mind-forg'd manacles I hear.

How the Chimney-sweeper's cry
Every blackning Church appalls,   10
And the hapless Soldier's sigh
Runs in blood down Palace walls.

But most thro' midnight streets I hear
How the youthful Harlot's curse
Blasts the new-born Infant's tear   15
And blights with plagues the Marriage hearse.

SPARKLING ALLEYS

José Rendon

Biography p. 1094

Sparkling alleys have long
    been my school
here my blood-red
    puffed eyes
have seen the wonders   5
    of the inside
    of heads
opened with meat cleavers
    and
    garages   10
giving comfort to
    fat smelly women
with 12 men
here the power of government
    is felt   15
coming from both sides
    with piercing lights
        and leather-covered
            pieces of steel
and here also   20
    our
    identity crisis
is solved

THINGS

Jane Cooper
(b. 1924)

Biography p. 1067

Things have their own lives here. The hall chairs
count me as I climb the steps. The piano
is playing at will from behind three potted plants,
while the photograph of the dead girl in the luminescent hat
glows pink since the lamp lighted itself at four.　　　　　5

We are very humane here. Of course people
go off course sometimes, radio to the outside world
only through typewriter noise or the bathwater running.
And then the empty glasses, the books on health food left around. . . .
But the things have been here longer than we have.　　　　　10

And the trees are older even than furniture.
They were here to witness the original drownings
(because I always think the children drowned, no matter what you say).
Last night a voice called me from outside my door.
It was no one's voice, perhaps it came from the umbrella stand.　　　　　15

JUNK

Richard Wilbur
(b. 1921)

Biography p. 1107

Huru Welandes
　　　　　worc ne geswiceœ
monna œnigum

ðara ðe Mimming can
heardne gehealdan.[1]

waldere

An axe angles
                    from my neighbor's ashcan;
It is hell's handiwork,
                    the wood not hickory,
The flow of the grain   5
                    not faithfully followed.
The shivered shaft
                    rises from a shellheap
Of plastic playthings,
                    paper plates,   10
And the sheer shards
                    of shattered tumblers
That were not annealed
                    for the time needful.
At the same curbside,   15
                    a cast-off cabinet
Of wavily-warped
                    unseasoned wood
Waits to be trundled
                    in the trash-man's truck.   20
Haul them off! Hide them!
                    The heart winces
For junk and gimcrack,
                    for jerrybuilt things
And the men who make them   25
                    for a little money,
Bartering pride
                    like the bought boxer
Who pulls his punches,
                    or the paid-off jockey   30
Who in the home stretch
                    holds in his horse.
Yet the things themselves
                    in thoughtless honor
Have kept composure,   35
                    like captives who would not
Talk under torture.
                    Tossed from a tailgate
Where the dump displays
                    its random dolmens,   40
Its black barrows
                    and blazing valleys,
They shall waste in the weather
                    toward what they were.

[1]A fragment of an old Anglo-Saxon poem on the mythical smith Wayland. It reads: "Wayland's work—the sword Mimming—will not fail any man able to wield it bravely."

The sun shall glory   45
                    in the glitter of glass-chips,
Foreseeing the salvage
                    of the prisoned sand,
And the blistering paint
                    peel off in patches,   50
That the good grain
                    be discovered again.
Then burnt, bulldozed,
                    they shall all be buried
To the depth of diamonds,   55
                    in the making dark
Where halt Hephaestus
                    keeps his hammer
And Wayland's work
                    is worn away.   60

PORTRAIT

Carolyn Rodgers

Biography p. 1096

mama spent pennies
in uh gallon milk jug
saved pennies
fuh four babies
college educashuns   5

and when the babies
got bigger they would
secretly "borrow" mama's
pennies to buy candy

and pop cause mama   10
saved extras
fuh college educashuns
and pop and candy

was uh non-credit in bad teeth
mama pooled pennies   15
in uh gallon milk jug
Borden's by the way

and the babies went
to school cause mama saved
and spent and paid   20

fuh four babies
college educashuns
mama spent pennies

and nickels
and quarters   25
and dollars

and one life.
mama spent her life
in uh gallon milk jug
fuh four Black babies   30
college educashuns.

CROSSING BROOKLYN FERRY.

Walt Whitman
(1829–1892)

Biography p. 1106

1

Flood-tide below me! I see you face to face!
Clouds of the west—sun there half an hour high—I see you also face to face.

Crowds of men and women attired in the usual costumes, how curious you are to
    me!
On the ferry-boats the hundreds and hundreds that cross, returning home, are
    more curious to me than you suppose,
And you that shall cross from shore to shore years hence are more to me, and
    more in my meditations, than you might suppose.   5

2

The impalpable sustenance of me from all things at all hours of the day,
The simple, compact, well-join'd scheme, myself disintegrated, every one
    disintegrated yet part of the scheme,
The similitudes of the past and those of the future,
The glories strung like beads on my smallest sights and hearings, on the walk in
    the street and the passage over the river,
The current rushing so swiftly and swimming with me far away,   10
The others that are to follow me, the ties between me and them,
The certainty of others, the life, love, sight, hearing of others.

Others will enter the gates of the ferry and cross from shore to shore,
Others will watch the run of the flood-tide,
Others will see the shipping of Manhattan north and west, and the heights of
    Brooklyn to the south and east,   15
Others will see the islands large and small;
Fifty years hence, others will see them as they cross, the sun half an hour high,
A hundred years hence, or ever so many hundred years hence, others will see
    them,
Will enjoy the sunset, the pouring-in of the flood-tide, the falling-back to the sea
    of the ebb-tide.

3

It avails not, time nor place—distance avails not,   20
I am with you, you men and women of a generation, or ever so many generations
    hence,
Just as you feel when you look on the river and sky, so I felt,
Just as any of you is one of a living crowd, I was one of a crowd,
Just as you are refresh'd by the gladness of the river and the bright flow, I was
    refresh'd,
Just as you stand and lean on the rail, yet hurry with the swift current, I stood
    yet was hurried,   25
Just as you look on the numberless masts of ships and the thick-stemm'd pipes of
    steamboats, I look'd.

I too many and many a time cross'd the river of old,
Watched the Twelfth-month sea-gulls, saw them high in the air floating with
    motionless wings, oscillating their bodies,
Saw how the glistening yellow lit up parts of their bodies and left the rest in
    strong shadow,
Saw the slow-wheeling circles and the gradual edging toward the south,   30
Saw the reflection of the summer sky in the water,
Had my eyes dazzled by the shimmering track of beams,
Look'd at the fine centrifugal spokes of light round the shape of my head in the
    sunlit water,
Look'd on the haze on the hills southward and south-westward,
Look'd on the vapor as it flew in fleeces tinged with violet,   35
Look'd toward the lower bay to notice the vessels arriving,
Saw their approach, saw aboard those that were near me,
Saw the white sails of schooners and sloops, saw the ships at anchor,
The sailors at work in the rigging or out astride the spars,
The round masts, the swinging motion of the hulls, the slender serpentine
    pennants,   40
The large and small steamers in motion, the pilots in their pilot-houses,
The white wake left by the passage, the quick tremulous whirl of the wheels,
The flags of all nations, the falling of them at sunset,
The scallop-edged waves in the twilight, the ladled cups, the frolicsome crests and
    glistening,

The stretch afar growing dimmer and dimmer, the gray walls of the granite
    storehouses by the docks,   45
On the river the shadowy group, the big steam-tug closely flank'd on each side by
    the barges, the hay-boat, the belated lighter,
On the neighboring shore the fires from the foundry chimneys burning high and
    glaringly into the night,
Casting their flicker of black contrasted with wild red and yellow light over the
    tops of houses, and down into the clefts of streets.

4

These and all else were to me the same as they are to you,
I loved well those cities, loved well the stately and rapid river,   50
The men and women I saw were all near to me,
Others the same—others who look back on me because I look'd forward to them,
(The time will come, though I stop here to-day and to-night.)

5

What is it then between us?
What is the count of the scores or hundreds of years between us?   55

Whatever it is, it avails not—distance avails not, and place avails not,
I too lived, Brooklyn of ample hills was mine,
I too walk'd the streets of Manhattan island, and bathed in the waters around it,
I too felt the curious abrupt questionings stir within me,
In the day among crowds of people sometimes they came upon me,   60
In my walks home late at night or as I lay in my bed they came upon me,
I too had been struck from the float forever held in solution,
I too had receiv'd identity by my body,
That I was I knew was of my body, and what I should be I knew I should be of
    my body.

6

It is not upon you alone the dark patches fall,   65
The dark threw its patches down upon me also,
The best I had done seem'd to me blank and suspicious,
My great thoughts as I supposed them, were they not in reality meagre?
Nor is it you alone who know what it is to be evil,
I am he who knew what it was to be evil,   70
I too knitted the old knot of contrariety,
Blabb'd, blush'd, resented, lied, stole, grudg'd,
Had guile, anger, lust, hot wishes I dared not speak,
Was wayward, vain, greedy, shallow, sly, cowardly, malignant,
The wolf, the snake, the hog, not wanting in me,   75
The cheating look, the frivolous word, the adulterous wish, not wanting,
Refusals, hates, postponements, meanness, laziness, none of these wanting,
Was one with the rest, the days and haps of the rest,

Was call'd by my nightest name by clear loud voices of young men as they saw
    me approaching or passing,
Felt their arms on my neck as I stood, or the negligent leaning of their flesh
    against me as I sat,   80
Saw many I loved in the street or ferry-boat or public assembly, yet never told
    them a word,
Lived the same life with the rest, the same old laughing, gnawing, sleeping,
Play'd the part that still looks back on the actor or actress,
The same old role, the role that is what we make it, as great as we like,
Or as small as we like, or both great and small.   85

7

Closer yet I approach you,
What thought you have of me now, I had as much of you—I laid in my stores in
    advance,
I consider'd long and seriously of you before you were born.

Who was to know what should come home to me?
Who knows but I am enjoying this?   90
Who knows, for all the distance, but I am as good as looking at you now, for all
    you cannot see me?

8

Ah, what can ever be more stately and admirable to me than mast-hemm'd
    Manhattan?
River and sunset and scallop-edg'd waves of flood-tide?
The sea-gulls oscillating their bodies, the hay-boat in the twilight, and the belated
    lighter?
What gods can exceed these that clasp me by the hand, and with voices I love
    call me promptly and loudly by my nighest name as I approach?   95
What is more subtle than this which ties me to the woman or man that looks in
    my face?
Which fuses me into you now, and pours my meaning into you?

We understand then do we not?
What I promis'd without mentioning it, have you not accepted?
What the study could not teach—what the preaching could not accomplish is
    accomplish'd, is it not?   100

9

Flow on, river! flow with the flood-tide, and ebb with the ebb-tide!
Frolic on, crested and scallop-edg'd waves!
Gorgeous clouds of the sunset! drench with your splendor me, or the men and
    women generations after me!
Cross from shore to shore, countless crowds of passengers!
Stand up, tall masts of Mannahatta! stand up, beautiful hills of Brooklyn!   105
Throb, baffled and curious brain! throw out questions and answers!

Suspend here and everywhere, eternal float of solution!
Gaze, loving and thirsting eyes, in the house or street or public assembly!
Sound out, voices of young men! loudly and musically call me by my nighest
    name!
Live, old life! play the part that looks back on the actor or actress!   110
Play the old role, the role that is great or small according as one makes it!
Consider, you who peruse me, whether I may not in unknown ways be looking
    upon you;
Be firm, rail over the river, to support those who lean idly, yet haste with the
    hasting current;
Fly on, sea-birds! fly sideways, or wheel in large circles high in the air;
Receive the summer sky, you water, and faithfully hold it till all downcast eyes
    have time to take it from you!   115
Diverge, fine spokes of light, from the shape of my head, or any one's head, in
    the sunlit water!
Come on, ships from the lower bay! pass up or down, white-sail'd schooners,
    sloops, lighters!
Flaunt away, flags of all nations! be duly lower'd at sunset!
Burn high your fires, foundry chimneys! cast black shadows at nightfall! cast red
    and yellow light over the tops of the houses!
Appearances, now or henceforth, indicate what you are,   120
You necessary film, continue to envelop the soul,
About my body for me, and your body for you, be hung our divinest aromas,
Thrive, cities—bring your freight, bring your shows, ample and sufficient rivers,
Expand, being than which none else is perhaps more spiritual,
Keep your places, objects than which none else is more lasting.   125

You have waited, you always wait, you dumb, beautiful ministers,
We receive you with free sense at last, and are insatiate henceforward,
Not you any more shall be able to foil us, or withhold yourselves from us,
We use you, and do not cast you aside—we plant you permanently within us,
We fathom you not—we love you—there is perfection in you also,   130
You furnish your parts toward eternity,
Great or small, you furnish your parts toward the soul.

PITY THIS BUSY MONSTER, MANUNKIND

E. E. Cummings
(1894–1962)

Biography p. 1068

pity this busy monster,manunkind,

not. Progress is a comfortable disease:
your victim(death and life safely beyond)

plays with the bigness of his littleness
—electrons deify one razorblade   5
into a mountainrange;lenses extend

unwish through curving wherewhen till unwish
returns on its unself.
                    A world of made
is not a world of born—pity poor flesh

and trees,poor stars and stones,but never this   10
fine specimen of hypermagical

ultraomnipotence. We doctors know

a hopeless case if—listen: there's a hell
of a good universe next door;let's go

THE SOUND OF SILENCE

Paul Simon
Biography p. 1100

Hello darkness my old friend,
I've come to talk with you again,
Because a vision softly creeping,
Left its seeds while I was sleeping,

And the vision that was planted in my brain   5
Still remains within the sound of silence.

In restless dreams I walked alone
Narrow streets of cobble-stone,
'Neath the halo of a street lamp,
I turned my collar to the cold and damp   10
When my eyes were stabbed by the flash of a neon light
That split the night and touched the sound of silence.

And in the naked light I saw
Ten thousand people maybe more.
People talking without speaking,   15
People hearing without listening,
People writing songs that voices never share
And no one dare disturb the sound of silence.
"Fools!" said I, "You do not know
Silence like a cancer grows.   20
Hear my words that I might teach you,
Take my arms that I might reach you."
But my words like silent raindrops fell,
And echoed in the wells of silence.

And the people bowed and prayed   25
To the neon god they made.
And the sign flashed out its warning
In the words that it was forming,
And the sign said:
          "The words of the prophets are written   30
          on the subway walls and tenement halls"
And whispered in the sounds of silence.

Drama

AN ENEMY OF THE PEOPLE

Henrik Ibsen

(1828–1906)

Biography p. 1079

Adapted by Arthur Miller

Characters

MORTEN KIIL
BILLING
MRS. STOCKMANN
PETER STOCKMANN
HOVSTAD
DR. STOCKMANN
MORTEN
EJLIF
CAPTAIN HORSTER
PETRA
ASLAKSEN
THE DRUNK
TOWNSPEOPLE

Synopsis of Scenes

THE ACTION TAKES PLACE IN A NORWEGIAN TOWN

ACT ONE

Scene 1: Dr. Stockmann's living room.
Scene 2: The same, the following morning.

ACT TWO

Scene 1: Editorial office of the *People's Daily Messenger.*
Scene 2: A room in Captain Horster's house.

ACT THREE

Scene: Dr. Stockmann's living room the following morning.

Throughout, in the stage directions, right and left mean stage right and stage left.

ACT ONE: SCENE 1

It is evening. DR. STOCKMANN's *living room is simply but cheerfully furnished. A doorway, upstage right, leads into the entrance hall, which extends from the front door to the dining room, running unseen behind the living room. At the left is another door, which leads to the Doctor's study and other rooms. In the upstage left corner is a stove. Toward the left foreground is a sofa with a table behind it. In the right foreground are two chairs, a small table between them, on which stand a lamp and a bowl of apples. At the back, to the left, an open doorway leads to the dining room, part of which is seen. The windows are in the right wall, a bench in front of them.*

As the curtain rises, BILLING *and* MORTEN KIIL *are eating in the dining room.* BILLING *is junior editor of the People's Daily Messenger.* KIIL *is a slovenly old man who is feeding himself in a great hurry. He gulps his last bite and comes into the living room, where he puts on his coat and ratty fur hat.* BILLING *comes in to help him.*

BILLING.   You sure eat fast, Mr. Kiil. (BILLING *is an enthusiast to the point of foolishness.*)

KIIL.   Eating don't get you anywhere, boy. Tell my daughter I went home.

(KIIL *starts across to the front door.* BILLING *returns to his food in the dining room.* KIIL *halts at the bowl of apples; he takes one, tastes it, likes it, takes another and puts it in his pocket, then continues on toward the door. Again he stops, returns, and takes another apple for his pocket. Then he sees a tobacco can on the table. He covers his action from Billing's possible glance, opens the can, smells it, pours some into his side pocket. He is just closing the can when* CATHERINE STOCKMANN *enters from the dining room.*)

MRS. STOCKMANN.   Father! You're not going, are you?

KIIL.   Got business to tend to.

MRS. STOCKMANN.   Oh, you're only going back to your room and you know it. Stay! Mr. Billing's here, and Hovstad's coming. It'll be interesting for you.

KIIL.   Got all kinds of business. The only reason I came over was the butcher told me you bought roast beef today. Very tasty, dear.

MRS. STOCKMANN.   Why don't you wait for Tom? He only went for a little walk.

KIIL *(taking out his pipe).*   You think he'd mind if I filled my pipe?

MRS. STOCKMANN.   No, go ahead. And here—take some apples. You should always have some fruit in your room.

KIIL.   No, no, wouldn't think of it.

(The doorbell rings.)

MRS. STOCKMANN.   That must be Hovstad. *(She goes to the door and opens it.)*

(PETER STOCKMANN, *the Mayor, enters. He is a bachelor, nearing sixty. He has always been one of those men who make it their life work to stand in the center of the ship to keep it from overturning. He probably envies the family life and warmth of this house, but when he comes he never wants to admit he came and often sits with his coat on.)*

MRS. STOCKMANN.   Peter! Well, this is a surprise!

PETER STOCKMANN.   I was just passing by . . . *(He sees* KIIL *and smiles, amused.)* Mr. Kiil!

KIIL *(sarcastically).*   Your Honor! *(He bites into his apple and exits.)*

MRS. STOCKMANN.   You musn't mind him, Peter, he's getting terribly old. Would you like a bite to eat?

PETER STOCKMANN.   No, no thanks. *(He sees* BILLING *now, and* BILLING *nods to him from the dining room.)*

MRS. STOCKMANN *(embarrassed).*   He just happened to drop in.

PETER STOCKMANN.   That's all right. I can't take hot food in the evening. Not with my stomach.

MRS. STOCKMANN.   Can't I ever get you to eat anything in this house?

PETER STOCKMANN.   Bless you, I stick to my tea and toast. Much healthier and more economical.

MRS. STOCKMANN *(smiling).*   You sound as though Tom and I throw money out the window.

PETER STOCKMANN.   Not you, Catherine. He wouldn't be home, would he?

MRS. STOCKMANN.   He went for a little walk with the boys.

PETER STOCKMANN.   You don't think that's dangerous, right after dinner? *(There is a loud knocking on the front door.) That* sounds like my brother.

MRS. STOCKMANN.   I doubt it, so soon. Come in, please.

(HOVSTAD *enters. He is in his early thirties, a graduate of the peasantry struggling with a terrible conflict. For while he hates authority and wealth, he cannot bring himself to cast off a certain desire to partake of them. Perhaps he is dangerous because he wants more than anything to belong, and in a radical that is a withering wish, not easily to be borne.)*

MRS. STOCKMANN.   Mr. Hovstad—

HOVSTAD.   Sorry I'm late. I was held up at the printing shop. *(Surprised:)* Good evening, Your Honor.

PETER STOCKMANN *(rather stiffly).*   Hovstad. On business, no doubt.

HOVSTAD.   Partly. It's about an article for the paper—

PETER STOCKMANN *(sarcastically).*   Ha! I don't doubt it. I understand my brother has become a prolific contributor to—what do you call it?—the *People's Daily Liberator?*

HOVSTAD *(laughing, but holding his ground).*   The *People's Daily Messenger,* sir. The Doctor sometimes honors the *Messenger* when he wants to uncover the real truth of some subject.

PETER STOCKMANN.   The truth! Oh, yes, I see.

MRS. STOCKMANN *(nervously to* HOVSTAD*).*   Would you like to . . . *(She points to dining room.)*

PETER STOCKMANN.   I don't want you to think I blame the Doctor for using your paper. After all, every performer goes for the audience that applauds him most. It's really not your paper I have anything against, Mr. Hovstad.

HOVSTAD.   I really didn't think so, Your Honor.

PETER STOCKMANN.   As a matter of fact, I happen to admire the spirit of tolerance in our town. It's magnificent. Just don't forget that we have it because we all believe in the same thing; it brings us together.

HOVSTAD.   Kirsten Springs, you mean.

PETER STOCKMANN.   The springs, Mr. Hovstad, our wonderful new springs. They've changed the soul of this town. Mark my words, Kirsten Springs are going to put us on the map, and there is no question about it.

MRS. STOCKMANN.   That's what Tom says too.

PETER STOCKMANN.   Everything is shooting ahead—real estate going up, money changing hands every hour, business humming—

HOVSTAD.   And no more unemployment.

PETER STOCKMANN.   Right. Give us a really good summer, and sick people will be coming here in carloads. The springs will turn into a regular fad, a new Carlsbad. And for once the well-to-do people won't be the only ones paying taxes in this town.

HOVSTAD.   I hear reservations are really starting to come in?

PETER STOCKMANN.   Coming in every day. Looks very promising, very promising.

HOVSTAD.   That's fine. *(To* MRS. STOCKMANN*)* Then the Doctor's article will come in handy.

PETER STOCKMANN.   He's written something again?

HOVSTAD.   No, it's a piece he wrote at the beginning of the winter, recommending the water. But at the time I let the article lie.

PETER STOCKMANN.   Why, some hitch in it?

HOVSTAD.   Oh, no, I just thought it would have a bigger effect in the spring, when people start planning for the summer.

PETER STOCKMANN.   That's smart, Mr. Hovstad, very smart.

MRS. STOCKMANN.   Tom is always so full of ideas about the springs; every day he—

PETER STOCKMANN.   Well, he ought to be, he gets his salary from the springs, my dear.

HOVSTAD.   Oh, I think it's more than that, don't you? After all, Doctor Stockmann *created* Kirsten Springs.

PETER STOCKMANN.   You don't say! I've been hearing that lately, but I did think I had a certain modest part—

MRS. STOCKMANN.   Oh, Tom always says—

HOVSTAD.   I only meant the original idea was—

PETER STOCKMANN.   My good brother is never at a loss for ideas. All sorts of ideas. But when it comes to putting them into action you need another kind of man, and I did think that at least people in this house would—

MRS. STOCKMANN.   But Peter, dear—we didn't mean to—Go get yourself a bite, Mr. Hovstad, my husband will be here any minute.

HOVSTAD.   Thank you, maybe just a little something. *(He goes into the dining room and joins Billing at the table.)*

PETER STOCKMANN *(lowering his voice).*   Isn't it remarkable? Why is it that people without background can never learn tact?

MRS. STOCKMANN.   Why let it bother you? Can't you and Thomas share the honor like good brothers?

PETER STOCKMANN.   The trouble is that certain men are never satisfied to share, Catherine.

MRS. STOCKMANN.   Nonsense. You've always gotten along beautifully with Tom —That must be him now.

(She goes to the front door, opens it. DR. STOCKMANN *is laughing and talking outside. He is in the prime of his life. He might be called the eternal amateur—a lover of things, of people, of sheer living, a man for whom the days are too short, and the future fabulous with discoverable joys. And for all this most people will not like him—he will not compromise for less than God's own share of the world while they have settled for less than Man's.)*

DR. STOCKMANN *(in the entrance hall).*   Hey, Catherine! Here's another guest for you! Here's a hanger for your coat, Captain. Oh, that's right, you don't wear overcoats! Go on in, boys. You kids must be hungry all over again. Come here, Captain Horster, I want you to get a look at this roast. *(He pushes Captain Horster along the hallway to the dining room. Ejlif and Morten also go to the dining room.)*

MRS. STOCKMANN.   Tom, dear . . . *(She motions toward Peter in the living room.)*

DR. STOCKMANN *(turns around in the doorway to the living room and sees Peter).* Oh, Peter . . . *(He walks across and stretches out his hand.)* Say now, this is really nice.

PETER STOCKMANN.   I'll have to go in a minute.

DR. STOCKMANN.   Oh, nonsense, not with the toddy on the table. You haven't forgotten the toddy, have you, Catherine?

MRS. STOCKMANN.   Of course not, I've got the water boiling. *(She goes into the dining room.)*

PETER STOCKMANN.   Toddy too?

DR. STOCKMANN.   Sure, just sit down and make yourself at home.

PETER STOCKMANN.   No, thanks, I don't go in for drinking parties.

DR. STOCKMANN.   But this is no party.

PETER STOCKMANN.   What else do you call it? *(He looks toward the dining room.)* It's extraordinary how you people can consume all this food and live.

DR. STOCKMANN *(rubbing his hands).*   Why? What's finer than to watch young people eat? Peter, those are the fellows who are going to stir up the whole future.

PETER STOCKMANN *(a little alarmed).*   Is that so! What's there to stir up? *(He sits in a chair to the left.)*

DR. STOCKMANN *(walking around).*   Don't worry, they'll let us know when the time comes. Old idiots like you and me, we'll be left behind like—

PETER STOCKMANN.   I've never been called *that* before.

DR. STOCKMANN.   Oh, Peter, don't jump on me every minute! You know your trouble, Peter? Your impressions are blunted. You ought to sit up there in that crooked corner of the north for five years, the way I did, and then come back here. It's like watching the first seven days of creation!

PETER STOCKMANN.   Here!

DR. STOCKMANN.   Things to work and fight for, Peter! Without that you're dead. Catherine, you sure the mailman came today?

MRS. STOCKMANN *(from the dining room).*   There wasn't any mail today.

DR. STOCKMANN.   And another thing, Peter—a good income; *that's* something you learn to value after you've lived on a starvation diet.

PETER STOCKMANN.   When did you starve?

DR. STOCKMANN.   Damned near! It was pretty tough going a lot of the time up there. And now, to be able to live like a prince! Tonight, for instance, we had roast beef for dinner, and, by God, there was enough left for supper too. Please have a piece—come here.

PETER STOCKMANN.   Oh, no, no—please, certainly not.

DR. STOCKMANN.   At least let me show it to you! Come in here—we even have a tablecloth. *(He pulls his brother toward the dining room.)*

PETER STOCKMANN.   I saw it.

DR. STOCKMANN.   Live to the hilt! that's my motto. Anyway, Catherine says I'm earning almost as much as we spend.

PETER STOCKMANN *(refusing an apple).*   Well, you are improving.

DR. STOCKMANN.   Peter, that was a joke! You're supposed to laugh! *(He sits in the other chair to the left.)*

PETER STOCKMANN.   Roast beef twice a day is no joke.

DR. STOCKMANN.   Why can't I give myself the pleasure of having people around me? It's a necessity for me to see young, lively, happy people, free people burning with a desire to do something. You'll see. When Hovstad comes in we'll talk and—

PETER STOCKMANN.   Oh, yes, Hovstad. That reminds me. He told me he was going to print one of your articles.

DR. STOCKMANN.   One of my articles?

PETER STOCKMANN.   Yes, about the springs—an article you wrote during the winter?

DR. STOCKMANN.   Oh, that one! In the first place, I don't want that one printed right now.

PETER STOCKMANN.   No? It sounded to me like it would be very timely.

DR. STOCKMANN.   Under normal conditions, maybe so. *(He gets up and walks across the floor.)*

PETER STOCKMANN *(looking after him).*   Well, what is abnormal about the conditions now?

DR. STOCKMANN *(stopping.)*   I can't say for the moment, Peter—at least not tonight. There could be a great deal abnormal about conditions; then again, there could be nothing at all.

PETER STOCKMANN.   Well, you've managed to sound mysterious. Is there anything wrong? Something you're keeping from me? Because I wish once in a while you'd remind yourself that I am chairman of the board for the springs.

DR. STOCKMANN.   And I would like *you* to remember that, Peter. Look, let's not get into each other's hair.

PETER STOCKMANN.   I don't make a habit of getting into people's hair! But I'd like to underline that everything concerning Kirsten Springs must be treated in a businesslike manner, through the proper channels, and dealt with by the legally constituted authorities. I can't allow anything done behind my back in a roundabout way.

DR. STOCKMANN.   When did I ever go behind your back, Peter?

PETER STOCKMANN.   You have an ingrained tendency to go your own way, Thomas, and that simply can't go on in a well-organized society. The individual really must subordinate himself to the over-all, or—*(groping for words, he points to himself)*—to the authorities who are in charge of the general welfare. *(He gets up.)*

DR. STOCKMANN.   Well, that's probably so. But how the hell does that concern me, Peter?

PETER STOCKMANN.   My dear Thomas, this is exactly what you will never learn. But you had better watch out because someday you might pay dearly for it. Now I've said it. Good-by.

DR. STOCKMANN.   Are you out of your mind? You're absolutely on the wrong track.

PETER STOCKMANN.   I am usually not. Anyway, may I be excused? *(He nods toward the dining room.)* Good-by, Catherine. Good evening, gentlemen. *(He leaves.)*

MRS. STOCKMANN *(entering the living room).*   He left?

DR. STOCKMANN.   And burned up!

MRS. STOCKMANN.   What did you do to him now?

DR. STOCKMANN.   What does he want from me? He can't expect me to give him an accounting of every move I make, every thought I think, until I am ready to do it.

MRS. STOCKMANN.   Why? What should you give him an accounting of?

DR. STOCKMANN *(hesitantly).*   Just leave that to me, Catherine. Peculiar the mail-man didn't come today.

(HOVSTAD, BILLING, and CAPTAIN HORSTER have gotten up from the dining-room table and enter the living room. EJLIF and MORTEN come in a little later. CATHERINE exits.)

BILLING *(stretching out his arms).*   After a meal like that, by God, I feel like a new man. This house is so—

HOVSTAD *(cutting him off).*   The Mayor certainly wasn't in a glowing mood tonight.

DR. STOCKMANN.   It's his stomach. He has a lousy digestion.

HOVSTAD.   I think two editors from the *People's Daily Messenger* didn't help either.

DR. STOCKMANN.   No, it's just that Peter is a lonely man. Poor fellow, all he knows is official business and duties, and then all that damn weak tea that he pours into himself. Catherine, may we have the toddy?

MRS. STOCKMANN *(calling from the dining room).*   I'm just getting it.

DR. STOCKMANN.   Sit down here on the couch with me, Captain Horster—a rare guest like you—sit here. Sit down, friends.

HORSTER.   This used to be such an ugly house. Suddenly it's beautiful!

(BILLING and HOVSTAD sit down at the right. MRS. STOCKMANN brings a tray with pot, glasses, bottles, etc. on it, and puts it on the table behind the couch.)

BILLING *(to HORSTER, intimately, indicating STOCKMANN).*   Great man!

MRS. STOCKMANN.   Here you are. Help yourselves.

DR. STOCKMANN *(taking a glass).*   We sure will. *(He mixes the toddy.)* And the cigars, Ejlif—you know where the box is. And Morten, get my pipe. *(The boys go out to the left.)* I have a sneaking suspicion that Ejlif is snitching a cigar now and then, but I don't pay any attention. Catherine, you know where I put it? Oh, he's got it. Good boys! *(The boys bring the various things in.)* Help yourselves, fellows. I'll stick to the pipe. This one's gone through plenty of blizzards with me up in the north. Skol! *(He looks around.)* Home! What an invention, heh?

(The boys sit down on the bench near the windows.)

MRS. STOCKMANN *(who has sat down and is now knitting).*   Are you sailing soon, Captain Horster?

HORSTER.   I expect to be ready next week.

MRS. STOCKMANN.   And then to America, Captain?

HORSTER.   Yes, that's the plan.

BILLING.   Oh, then you won't be home for the new election?

HORSTER.   Is there going to be another election?

BILLING.   Didn't you know?

HORSTER.   No, I don't get mixed up in those things.

BILLING.   But you are interested in public affairs, aren't you?

HORSTER.   Frankly, I don't understand a thing about it.

(He does, really, although not very much. Captain Horster is one of the longest silent roles in dramatic literature, but he is not to be thought of as characterless therefor. It is not a bad thing to have a courageous, quiet man for a friend, even if it has gone out of fashion.)

MRS. STOCKMANN *(sympathetically).*   Neither do I, Captain. Maybe that's why I'm always so glad to see you.

BILLING.   Just the same, you ought to vote, Captain.

HORSTER.   Even if I don't understand anything about it?

BILLING.   Understand! What do you mean by that? Society, Captain, is like a ship —every man should do something to help navigate the ship.

HORSTER.   That may be all right on shore, but on board a ship it doesn't work out so well.

(PETRA in hat and coat and with textbooks and notebooks under her arm comes into the entrance hall. She is Ibsen's clear-eyed hope for the future—and probably ours. She is forthright, determined, and knows the meaning of work, which to her is the creation of good on the earth.)

PETRA *(from the hall).*   Good evening.
DR. STOCKMANN *(warmly).*   Good evening, Petra!
BILLING *(to* HORSTER*).*   Great young woman!

(There are mutual greetings. PETRA *removes her coat and hat and places the books on a chair in the entrance hall.)*

PETRA *(entering the living room).*   And here you are, lying around like lizards while I'm out slaving.
DR. STOCKMANN.   Well, you come and be a lizard too. Come here, Petra, sit with me. I look at her and say to myself, "How did I do it?"

*(*PETRA *goes over to her father and kisses him.)*

BILLING.   Shall I mix a toddy for you?
PETRA *(coming up to the table).*   No, thanks, I had better do it myself—you always mix it too strong. Oh, Father, I forgot—I have a letter for you. *(She goes to the chair where her books are.)*
DR. STOCKMANN *(alerted).*   Who's it from?
PETRA.   I met the mailman on the way to school this morning and he gave me your mail too, and I just didn't have time to run back.
DR. STOCKMANN *(getting up and walking toward her).*   And you don't give it to me until now!
PETRA.   I really didn't have time to run back, Father.
MRS. STOCKMANN.   If she didn't have time . . .
DR. STOCKMANN.   Let's see it—come on, child! *(He takes the letter and looks at the envelope.)* Yes, indeed.
MRS. STOCKMANN.   Is that the one you've been waiting for?
DR. STOCKMANN.   I'll be right back. There wouldn't be a light on in my room, would there?
MRS. STOCKMANN.   The lamp is on the desk, burning away.
DR. STOCKMANN.   Please excuse me for a moment. *(He goes into his study and quickly returns.* MRS. STOCKMANN *hands him his glasses. He goes out again.)*
PETRA.   What is that, Mother?
MRS. STOCKMANN.   I don't know. The last couple of days he's been asking again and again about the mailman.
BILLING.   Probably an out-of-town patient of his.
PETRA.   Poor Father, he's got much too much to do. *(She mixes her drink.)* This ought to taste good.
HOVSTAD.   By the way, what happened to that English novel you were going to translate for us?
PETRA.   I started it, but I've gotten so busy—
HOVSTAD.   Oh, teaching evening school again?
PETRA.   Two hours a night.
BILLING.   Plus the high school every day?
PETRA *(sitting down on the couch).*   Yes, five hours, and every night a pile of lessons to correct!
MRS. STOCKMANN.   She never stops going.
HOVSTAD.   Maybe that's why I always think of you as kind of breathless and—well, breathless.

PETRA.   I love it. I get so wonderfully tired.

BILLING (*to* HORSTER).   She looks tired.

MORTEN.   You must be a wicked woman, Petra.

PETRA (*laughing*).   Wicked?

MORTEN.   You work so much. My teacher says that work is a punishment for our sins.

EJLIF.   And you believe that?

MRS. STOCKMANN.   Ejlif! Of course he believes his teacher!

BILLING (*smiling*).   Don't stop him . . .

HOVSTAD.   Don't you like to work, Morten?

MORTEN.   Work? No.

HOVSTAD.   Then what will you ever amount to in this world?

MORTEN.   Me? I'm going to be a Viking.

EJLIF.   You can't! You'd have to be a heathen!

MORTEN.   So I'll be a heathen.

MRS. STOCKMANN.   I think it's getting late, boys.

BILLING.   I agree with you, Morten. I think—

MRS. STOCKMANN (*making signs to* BILLING).   You certainly don't, Mr. Billing.

BILLING.   Yes, by God, I do. I am a real heathen and proud of it. You'll see, pretty soon we're all going to be heathens!

MORTEN.   And then we can do anything we want!

BILLING.   Right! You see, Morten—

MRS. STOCKMANN (*interrupting*).   Don't you have any homework for tomorrow, boys? Better go in and do it.

EJLIF.   Oh, can't we stay in here a while?

MRS. STOCKMANN.   No, neither of you. Now run along.

(The boys say good night and go off at the left.)

HOVSTAD.   You really think it hurts them to listen to such talk?

MRS. STOCKMANN.   I don't know, but I don't like it.

(DR. STOCKMANN enters from his study, an open letter in his hand. He is like a sleepwalker, astonished, engrossed. He walks toward the front door.)

MRS. STOCKMANN.   Tom!

(He turns, suddenly aware of them.)

DR. STOCKMANN.   Boys, there is going to be news in this town!

BILLING.   News?

MRS. STOCKMANN.   What kind of news?

DR. STOCKMANN.   A terrific discovery, Catherine.

HOVSTAD.   Really?

MRS. STOCKMANN.   That you made?

DR. STOCKMANN.   That I made. *(He walks back and forth.)* Now let the baboons running this town call me a lunatic! Now they'd better watch out. Oh, how the mighty have fallen!

PETRA.   What is it, Father?

DR. STOCKMANN.   Oh, if Peter were only here! Now you'll see how human beings can walk around and make judgments like blind rats.

HOVSTAD.   What in the world's happened, Doctor? .

DR. STOCKMANN *(stopping at the table).*   It's the general opinion, isn't it, that our town is a sound and healthy spot?

HOVSTAD.   Of course.

MRS. STOCKMANN.   What happened?

DR. STOCKMANN.   Even a rather unusually healthy spot! Oh, God, a place that can be recommended not only to all people but to sick people!

MRS. STOCKMANN.   But, Tom, what are you—

DR. STOCKMANN.   And we certainly have recommended it. I myself have written and written, in the *People's Messenger,* pamphlets—

HOVSTAD.   Yes, yes, but—

DR. STOCKMANN.   The miraculous springs that cost such a fortune to build, the whole Health Institute, is a pesthole!

PETRA.   Father! The springs?

MRS. STOCKMANN *(simultaneously).*   Our springs?

BILLING.   That's unbelievable!

DR. STOCKMANN.   You know the filth up in Windmill Valley? That stuff that has such a stinking smell? It comes down from the tannery up there, and the same damn poisonous mess comes right out into the blessed, miraculous water we're supposed to *cure* people with!

HORSTER.   You mean actually where our beaches are?

DR. STOCKMANN.   Exactly.

HOVSTAD.   How are you so sure about this, Doctor?

DR. STOCKMANN.   I had a suspicion about it a long time ago—last year there were too many sick cases among the visitors, typhoid and gastric disturbances.

MRS. STOCKMANN.   That did happen. I remember Mrs. Svensen's niece—

DR. STOCKMANN.   Yes, dear. At the time we thought that the visitors brought the bug, but later this winter I got a new idea and I started investigating the water.

MRS. STOCKMANN.   So that's what you've been working on!

DR. STOCKMANN.   I sent samples of the water to the University for an exact chemical analysis.

HOVSTAD.   And that's what you have just received?

DR. STOCKMANN *(waving the letter again).*   This is it. It proves the existence of infectious organic matter in the water.

MRS. STOCKMANN.   Well, thank God you discovered it in time.

DR. STOCKMANN.   I think we can say that, Catherine.

MRS. STOCKMANN.   Isn't it wonderful!

HOVSTAD.   And what do you intend to do now, Doctor?

DR. STOCKMANN.   Put the thing right, of course.

HOVSTAD.   Do you think that can be done?

DR. STOCKMANN.   Maybe. If not, the whole Institute is useless. But there's nothing to worry about—I am quite clear on what has to be done.

MRS. STOCKMANN.   But, Tom, why did you keep it so secret?

DR. STOCKMANN.   What did you want me to do? Go out and shoot my mouth off before I really knew? *(He walks around, rubbing his hands.)* You don't realize what this means, Catherine—the whole water system has got to be changed.

MRS. STOCKMANN.   The *whole* water system?

DR. STOCKMANN.   The whole water system. The intake is too low, it's got to be raised to a much higher spot. The whole construction's got to be ripped out!

PETRA.   Well, Father, at last you can prove they should have listened to you!

DR. STOCKMANN.   Ha, she remembers!

MRS. STOCKMANN.   That's right, you did warn them—

DR. STOCKMANN.   Of course I warned them. When they started the damned thing I told them not to build it down there! But who am I, a mere scientist, to tell politicians where to build a health institute! Well, now they're going to get it, both barrels!

BILLING.   This is tremendous! (*To* HORSTER) He's a great man!

DR. STOCKMANN.   It's bigger than tremendous. (*He starts toward his study.*) Wait'll they see this! (*He stops.*) Petra, my report is on my desk . . . (PETRA *goes into his study.*) An envelope, Catherine! (*She goes for it.*) Gentlemen, this final proof from the University (PETRA *comes out with the report, which he takes*) and my report (*he flicks the pages—five solid, explosive pages . . .*)

MRS. STOCKMANN (*handing him an envelope*).   Is this big enough?

DR. STOCKMANN.   Fine. Right to the Board of Directors! (*He inserts the report, seals the envelope, and hands it to* CATHERINE.) Will you give this to the maid —what's her name again?

MRS. STOCKMANN.   Randine, dear, Randine.

DR. STOCKMANN.   Tell our darling Randine to wipe her nose and run over to the Mayor right now.

(MRS. STOCKMANN *just stands there looking at him.*)

DR. STOCKMANN.   What's the matter, dear?

MRS. STOCKMANN.   I don't know . . .

PETRA.   What's Uncle Peter going to say about this?

MRS. STOCKMANN.   That's what I'm wondering.

DR. STOCKMANN.   What can he say! He ought to be damn glad that such an important fact is brought out before we start an epidemic! Hurry, dear!

(CATHERINE *exits at the left.*)

HOVSTAD.   I would like to put a brief item about this discovery in the *Messenger.*

DR. STOCKMANN.   Go ahead. I'd really be grateful for that now.

HOVSTAD.   Because the public ought to know soon.

DR. STOCKMANN.   Right away.

BILLING.   By God, you'll be the leading man in this town, Doctor.

DR. STOCKMANN (*walking around with an air of satisfaction*).   Oh, there was nothing to it. Every detective gets a lucky break once in his life. But just the same I—

BILLING.   Hovstad, don't you think the town ought to pay Dr. Stockmann some tribute?

DR. STOCKMANN.   Oh, no, no . . .

HOVSTAD.   Sure, let's all put in a word for—

BILLING.   I'll talk to Aslaksen about it!

(CATHERINE *enters.*)

DR. STOCKMANN.   No, no, fellows, no fooling around! I won't put up with any commotion. Even if the Board of Directors wants to give me an increase I won't take it—I just won't take it, Catherine.

MRS. STOCKMANN *(dutifully).*   That's right, Tom.

PETRA *(lifting her glass).*   Skol, Father!

EVERYBODY.   Skol, Doctor!

HORSTER.   Doctor, I hope this will bring you great honor and pleasure.

DR. STOCKMANN.   Thanks, friends, thanks. There's one blessing above all others. To have earned the respect of one's neighbors is—is—Catherine, I'm going to dance!

He grabs his wife and whirls her around. There are shouts and struggles, general commotion. The boys in nightgowns stick their heads through the doorway at the right, wondering what is going on. MRS. STOCKMANN, *seeing them, breaks away and chases them upstairs as*

The Curtain Falls.

ACT ONE: SCENE 2

Dr. Stockmann's living room the following morning. As the curtain rises, MRS. STOCKMANN *comes in from the dining room, a sealed letter in her hand. She goes to the study door and peeks in.*

MRS. STOCKMANN.   Are you there, Tom?

DR. STOCKMANN *(from within).*   I just got in. *(He enters the living room.)* What's up?

MRS. STOCKMANN.   From Peter. It just came. *(She hands him the envelope.)*

DR. STOCKMANN.   Oh, let's see. *(He opens the letter and reads.)* "I am returning herewith the report you submitted . . ." *(He continues to read, mumbling to himself.)*

MRS. STOCKMANN.   Well, what does he say? Don't stand there!

DR. STOCKMANN *(putting the letter in his pocket).*   He just says he'll come around this afternoon.

MRS. STOCKMANN.   Oh. Well, maybe you ought to try to remember to be home then.

DR. STOCKMANN.   Oh, I sure will. I'm through with my morning visits anyway.

MRS. STOCKMANN.   I'm dying to see how he's going to take it.

DR. STOCKMANN.   Why, is there any doubt? He'll probably make it look like he made the discovery, not I.

MRS. STOCKMANN.   But aren't you a little bit afraid of that?

DR. STOCKMANN.   Oh, underneath he'll be happy, Catherine. It's just that Peter is so afraid that somebody else is going to do something good for this town.

MRS. STOCKMANN.   I wish you'd go out of your way and share the honors with him. Couldn't we say that he put you on the right track or something?

DR. STOCKMANN.   Oh, I don't mind—as long as it makes everybody happy.

(MORTEN KIIL *sticks his head through the doorway. He looks around searchingly and chuckles. He will continue chuckling until he leaves the house. He is the archetype of the little twinkle-eyed man who sneaks into so much of Ibsen's work. He will chuckle you right over the precipice. He is the dealer, the man with the rat's finely tuned brain. But he is sometimes likable because he is without morals and announces the fact by laughing.*)

KIIL *(slyly).*   Is it really true?

MRS. STOCKMANN *(walking toward him).*   Father!

DR. STOCKMANN.   Well, good morning!

MRS. STOCKMANN.   Come on in.

KIIL.   It better be true or I'm going.

DR. STOCKMANN.   What had better be true?

KIIL.   This crazy story about the water system. Is it true?

MRS. STOCKMANN.   Of course it's true! How did you find out about it?

KIIL.   Petra came flying by on her way to school this morning.

DR. STOCKMANN.   Oh, she did?

KIIL.   Ya. I thought she was trying to make a fool out of me—

MRS. STOCKMANN.   Now why would she do that?

KIIL.   Nothing gives more pleasure to young people than to make fools out of old people. But this is true, eh?

DR. STOCKMANN.   Of course it's true. Sit down here. It's pretty lucky for the town, eh?

KIIL *(fighting his laughter).*   Lucky for the town!

DR. STOCKMANN.   I mean, that I made the discovery before it was too late.

KIIL.   Tom, I never thought you had the imagination to pull your own brother's leg like this.

DR. STOCKMANN.   Pull his leg?

MRS. STOCKMANN.   But, Father, he's not—

KIIL.   How does it go now, let me get it straight. There's some kind of—like cockroaches in the waterpipes—

DR. STOCKMANN *(laughing).*   No, not cockroaches.

KIIL.   Well, some kind of little animals.

MRS. STOCKMANN.   Bacteria, Father.

KIIL *(who can barely speak through his laughter).*   Ah, but a whole mess of them, eh?

DR. STOCKMANN.   Oh, there'd be millions and millions.

KIIL.   And nobody can see them but you, is that it?

DR. STOCKMANN.   Yes, that's—well, of course anybody with a micro—*(He breaks off.)* What are you laughing at?

MRS. STOCKMANN *(smiling at Kiil).*   You don't understand, Father. Nobody can actually see bacteria, but that doesn't mean they're not there.

KIIL.   Good girl, you stick with him! By God, this is the best thing I ever heard in my life!

DR. STOCKMANN *(smiling).*   What do you mean?

KIIL.   But tell me, you think you are actually going to get your brother to believe this?

DR. STOCKMANN.   Well, we'll see soon enough!

KIIL.   You really think he's that crazy?

DR. STOCKMANN.   I hope the whole town will be that crazy, Morten.

KIIL.   Ya, they probably are, and it'll serve them right too—they think they're so much smarter than us old-timers. Your good brother ordered them to bounce me out of the council, so they chased me out like a dog! Make jackasses out of all of them, Stockmann!

DR. STOCKMANN.   Yes, but, Morten—

KIIL.   Long-eared, short-tailed jackasses! *(He gets up.)* Stockmann, if you can make the Mayor and his elegant friends grab at this bait, I will give a couple of hundred crowns to charity, and right now, right on the spot.

DR. STOCKMANN.   Well, that would be very kind of you, but I'm—

KIIL.   I haven't got much to play around with, but if you can pull the rug out from under him with this cockroach business, I'll give at least fifty crowns to some poor people on Christmas Eve. Maybe this'll teach them to put some brains back in Town Hall!

(Hovstad enters from the hall.)

HOVSTAD.   Good morning! Oh, pardon me . . .

KIIL *(enjoying this proof immensely).*   Oh, this one is in on it, too?

HOVSTAD.   What's that, sir?

DR. STOCKMANN.   Of course he's in on it.

KIIL.   Couldn't I have guessed that! And it's going to be in the papers, I suppose. You're sure tying down the corners, aren't you? Well, lay it on thick. I've got to go.

DR. STOCKMANN.   Oh, no, stay a while, let me explain it to you!

KIIL.   Oh, I get it, don't worry! Only you can see them, heh? That's the best idea I've ever—damn it, you shouldn't do this for nothing! *(He goes toward the hall.)*

MRS. STOCKMANN *(following him out, laughing).*   But, Father, you don't understand about bacteria.

DR. STOCKMANN *(laughing).*   The old badger doesn't believe a word of it.

HOVSTAD.   What does he think you're doing?

DR. STOCKMANN.   Making an idiot out of my brother—imagine that?

HOVSTAD.   You got a few minutes?

DR. STOCKMANN.   Sure, as long as you like.

HOVSTAD.   Have you heard from the Mayor?

DR. STOCKMANN.   Only that he's coming over later.

HOVSTAD.   I've been thinking about this since last night—

DR. STOCKMANN.   Don't say?

HOVSTAD.   For you as a medical man, a scientist, this is a really rare opportunity. But I've been wondering if you realize that it ties in with a lot of other things.

DR. STOCKMANN.   How do you mean? Sit down. *(They sit at the right.)* What are you driving at?

HOVSTAD.   You said last night that the pollution comes from impurities in the ground—

DR. STOCKMANN.   It comes from the poisonous dump up in Windmill Valley.

HOVSTAD.   Doctor, I think it comes from an entirely different dump.

DR. STOCKMANN.   What do you mean?

HOVSTAD *(with growing zeal)*.   The same dump that is poisoning and polluting our whole social life in this town.

DR. STOCKMANN.   For God's sake, Hovstad, what are you babbling about?

HOVSTAD.   Everything that matters in this town has fallen into the hands of a few bureaucrats.

DR. STOCKMANN.   Well, they're not all bureaucrats—

HOVSTAD.   They're all rich, all with old reputable names, and they've got everything in the palm of their hands.

DR. STOCKMANN.   Yes, but they happen to have ability and knowledge.

HOVSTAD.   Did they show ability and knowledge when they built the water system where they did?

DR. STOCKMANN.   No, of course not, but that happened to be a blunder, and we'll clear it up now.

HOVSTAD.   You really imagine it's going to be as easy as all that?

DR. STOCKMANN.   Easy or not easy, it's got to be done.

HOVSTAD.   Doctor, I've made up my mind to give this whole scandal very special treatment.

DR. STOCKMANN.   Now wait. You can't call it a scandal yet.

HOVSTAD.   Doctor, when I took over the *People's Messenger* I swore I'd blow that smug cabal of old, stubborn, self-satisfied fogies to bits. This is the story that can do it.

DR. STOCKMANN.   But I still think we owe them a deep debt of gratitude for building the springs.

HOVSTAD.   The Mayor being your brother, I wouldn't ordinarily want to touch it, but I know you'd never let that kind of thing obstruct the truth.

DR. STOCKMANN.   Of course not, but . . .

HOVSTAD.   I want you to understand me. I don't have to tell you I come from a simple family. I know in my bones what the underdog needs—he's got to have a say in the government of society. That's what brings out ability, intelligence, and self-respect in people.

DR. STOCKMANN.   I understand that, but . . .

HOVSTAD.   I think a newspaperman who turns down any chance to give the underdog a lift is taking on a responsibility that I don't want. I know perfectly well that in fancy circles they call it agitation, and they can call it anything they like if it makes them happy, but I have my own conscience—

DR. STOCKMANN *(interrupting)*.   I agree with you, Hovstad, but this is just the water supply and—*(There is a knock on the door.)* Damn it! Come in!

(MR. ASLAKSEN, *the publisher, enters from the hall. He is simply but neatly dressed. He wears gloves and carries a hat and an umbrella in his hand. He is so utterly drawn it is unnecessary to say anything at all about him.*)

ASLAKSEN.   I beg your pardon, Doctor, if I intrude . . .

HOVSTAD *(standing up)*.   Are you looking for me, Aslaksen?

ASLAKSEN.   No, I didn't know you were here. I want to see the Doctor.

DR. STOCKMANN.   What can I do for you?

ASLAKSEN.   Is it true, Doctor, what I hear from Mr. Billing, that you intend to campaign for a better water system?

DR. STOCKMANN.   Yes, for the Institute. But it's not a campaign.

ASLAKSEN.   I just wanted to call and tell you that we are behind you a hundred per cent.

HOVSTAD (*to* DR. STOCKMANN).   There, you see!

DR. STOCKMANN.   Mr. Aslaksen, I thank you with all my heart. But you see—

ASLAKSEN.   We can be important, Doctor. When the little businessman wants to push something through, he turns out to be the majority, you know, and it's always good to have the majority on your side.

DR. STOCKMANN.   That's certainly true, but I don't understand what this is all about. It seems to me it's a simple, straightforward business. The water—

ASLAKSEN.   Of course we intend to behave with moderation, Doctor. I always try to be a moderate and careful man.

DR. STOCKMANN.   You are known for that, Mr. Aslaksen, but—

ASLAKSEN.   The water system is very important to us little businessmen, Doctor. Kirsten Springs are becoming a gold mine for this town, especially for the property owners, and that is why, in my capacity as chairman of the Property Owners Association—

DR. STOCKMANN.   Yes.

ASLAKSEN.   And furthermore, as a representative of the Temperance Society— You probably know, Doctor, that I am active for prohibition.

DR. STOCKMANN.   So I have heard.

ASLAKSEN.   As a result, I come into contact with all kinds of people, and since I am known to be a law-abiding and solid citizen, I have a certain influence in this town—you might even call it a little power.

DR. STOCKMANN.   I know that very well, Mr. Aslaksen.

ASLAKSEN.   That's why you can see that it would be practically nothing for me to arrange a demonstration.

DR. STOCKMANN.   Demonstration! What are you going to demonstrate about?

ASLAKSEN.   The citizens of the town complimenting you for bringing this important matter to everybody's attention. Obviously it would have to be done with the utmost moderation so as not to hurt the authorities.

HOVSTAD.   This could knock the big-bellies right into the garbage can!

ASLAKSEN.   No indiscretion or extreme aggressiveness toward the authorities, Mr. Hovstad! I don't want any wild-eyed radicalism on this thing. I've had enough of that in my time, and no good ever comes of it. But for a good solid citizen to express his calm, frank, and free opinion is something nobody can deny.

DR. STOCKMANN (*shaking the publisher's hand*).   My dear Aslaksen, I can't tell you how it heartens me to hear this kind of support. I am happy—I really am —I'm happy. Listen! Wouldn't you like a glass of sherry?

ASLAKSEN.   I am a member of the Temperance Society. I—

DR. STOCKMANN.   Well, how about a glass of beer?

ASLAKSEN. *(Considers, then)*   I don't think I can go quite that far, Doctor. I never take anything. Well, good day, and I want you to remember that the little man is behind you like a wall.

DR. STOCKMANN.   Thank you.

ASLAKSEN.   You have the solid majority on your side, because when the little—

DR. STOCKMANN *(trying to stop Aslaksen's talk).*   Thanks for that, Mr. Aslaksen, and good day.

ASLAKSEN.   Are you going back to the printing shop, Mr. Hovstad?

HOVSTAD.   I just have a thing or two to attend to here.

ASLAKSEN.   Very well. *(He leaves.)*

HOVSTAD.   Well, what do you say to a little hypodermic for these fence-sitting deadheads?

DR. STOCKMANN *(surprised).*   Why? I think Aslaksen is a very sincere man.

HOVSTAD.   Isn't it time we pumped some guts into these well-intentioned men of good will? Under all their liberal talk they still idolize authority, and that's got to be rooted out of this town. This blunder of the water system has to be made clear to every voter. Let me print your report.

DR. STOCKMANN.   Not until I talk to my brother.

HOVSTAD.   I'll write an editorial in the meantime, and if the Mayor won't go along with us—

DR. STOCKMANN.   I don't see how you can imagine such a thing!

HOVSTAD.   Believe me, Doctor, it's possible, and then—

DR. STOCKMANN.   Listen, I promise you: he will go along, and then you can print my report, every word of it.

HOVSTAD.   On your word of honor?

DR. STOCKMANN *(giving* HOVSTAD *the manuscript).*   Here it is. Take it. It can't do any harm for you to read it. Return it to me later.

HOVSTAD.   Good day, Doctor.

DR. STOCKMANN.   Good day. You'll see, it's going to be easier than you think, Hovstad!

HOVSTAD.   I hope so, Doctor. Sincerely. Let me know as soon as you hear from His Honor. *(He leaves.)*

DR. STOCKMANN *(goes to dining room and looks in).*   Catherine! Oh, you're home already, Petra!

PETRA *(coming in).*   I just got back from school.

MRS. STOCKMANN *(entering).*   Hasn't he been here yet?

DR. STOCKMANN.   Peter? No, but I just had a long chat with Hovstad. He's really fascinated with my discovery, and you know, it has more implications that I thought at first. Do you know what I have backing me up?

MRS. STOCKMANN.   What in heaven's name have you got backing you up?

DR. STOCKMANN.   The solid majority.

MRS. STOCKMANN.   Is that good?

DR. STOCKMANN.   Good? It's wonderful. You can't imagine the feeling, Catherine, to know that your own town feels like a brother to you. I have never felt so at home in this town since I was a boy. *(A noise is heard.)*

MRS. STOCKMANN.   That must be the front door.

DR. STOCKMANN.   Oh, it's Peter then. Come in.

PETER STOCKMANN *(entering from the hall).*   Good morning!

DR. STOCKMANN.   It's nice to see you, Peter.

MRS. STOCKMANN.   Good morning. How are you today?

PETER STOCKMANN.   Well, so so. *(To* DR. STOCKMANN*)* I received your thesis about the condition of the springs yesterday.

DR. STOCKMANN.   I got your note. Did you read it?

PETER STOCKMANN.   I read it.

DR. STOCKMANN.   Well, what do you have to say?

(PETER STOCKMANN *clears his throat and glances at the women.*)

MRS. STOCKMANN.   Come on, Petra. *(She and* PETRA *leave the room at the left.)*

PETER STOCKMANN *(after a moment).*   Thomas, was it really necessary to go into this investigation behind my back?

DR. STOCKMANN.   Yes. Until I was convinced myself, there was no point in—

PETER STOCKMANN.   And now you are convinced?

DR. STOCKMANN.   Well, certainly. Aren't you too, Peter? *(Pause.)* The University chemists corroborated . . .

PETER STOCKMANN.   You intend to present this document to the Board of Directors, officially, as the medical officer of the springs?

DR. STOCKMANN.   Of course, something's got to be done, and quick.

PETER STOCKMANN.   You always use such strong expressions, Thomas. Among other things, in your report you say that we *guarantee* our guests and visitors a permanent case of poisoning.

DR. STOCKMANN.   But, Peter, how can you describe it any other way? Imagine! Poisoned internally and externally!

PETER STOCKMANN.   So you merrily conclude that we must build a waste-disposal plant—and reconstruct a brand-new water system from the bottom up!

DR. STOCKMANN.   Well, do you know some other way out? I don't.

PETER STOCKMANN.   I took a little walk over to the city engineer this morning and in the course of conversation I sort of jokingly mentioned these changes —as something we might consider for the future, you know.

DR. STOCKMANN.   The future won't be soon enough, Peter.

PETER STOCKMANN.   The engineer kind of smiled at my extravagance and gave me a few facts. I don't suppose you have taken the trouble to consider what your proposed changes would cost?

DR. STOCKMANN.   No, I never thought of that.

PETER STOCKMANN.   Naturally. Your little project would come to at least three hundred thousand crowns.

DR. STOCKMANN *(astonished).*   That expensive!

PETER STOCKMANN.   Oh, don't look so upset—it's only money. The worst thing is that it would take some two years.

DR. STOCKMANN.   Two years?

PETER STOCKMANN.   At the least. And what do you propose we do about the springs in the meantime? Shut them up, no doubt! Because we would have to, you know. As soon as the rumor gets around that the water is dangerous, we won't have a visitor left. So that's the picture, Thomas. You have it in your power literally to ruin your own town.

DR. STOCKMANN.   Now look, Peter! I don't want to ruin anything.

PETER STOCKMANN.   Kirsten Springs are the blood supply of this town, Thomas —the only future we've got here. Now will you stop and think?

DR. STOCKMANN.   Good God! Well, what do you think we ought to do?

PETER STOCKMANN.   Your report has not convinced me that the conditions are as dangerous as you try to make them.

DR. STOCKMANN.   Now listen; they are even worse than the report makes them out to be. Remember, summer is coming, and the warm weather!

PETER STOCKMANN.   I think you're exaggerating. A capable physician ought to know what precautions to take.

DR. STOCKMANN.   And what then?

PETER STOCKMANN.   The existing water supply for the springs is a fact, Thomas, and has got to be treated as a fact. If you are reasonable and act with discretion, the directors of the Institute will be inclined to take under consideration any means to make possible improvements, reasonably and without financial sacrifices.

DR. STOCKMANN.   Peter, do you imagine that I would ever agree to such trickery?

PETER STOCKMANN.   Trickery?

DR. STOCKMANN.   Yes, a trick, a fraud, a lie! A treachery, a downright crime, against the public and against the whole community!

PETER STOCKMANN.   I said before that I am not convinced that there is any actual danger.

DR. STOCKMANN.   Oh, you aren't? Anything else is impossible! My report is an absolute fact. The only trouble is that you and your administration were the ones who insisted that the water supply be built where it is, and now you're afraid to admit the blunder you committed. Damn it! Don't you think I can see through it all?

PETER STOCKMANN.   All right, let's suppose that's true. Maybe I do care a little about my reputation. I still say I do it for the good of the town—without moral authority there can be no government. And that is why, Thomas, it is my duty to prevent your report from reaching the Board. Some time later I will bring up the matter for discussion. In the meantime, not a single word is to reach the public.

DR. STOCKMANN.   Oh, my dear Peter, do you imagine you can prevent that!

PETER STOCKMANN.   It will be prevented.

DR. STOCKMANN.   It can't be. There are too many people who already know about it.

PETER STOCKMANN (angered).   Who? It can't possibly be those people from the *Daily Messenger* who—

DR. STOCKMANN.   Exactly. The liberal, free, and independent press will stand up and do its duty!

PETER STOCKMANN.   You are an unbelievably irresponsible man, Thomas! Can't you imagine what consequences that is going to have for you?

DR. STOCKMANN.   For me?

PETER STOCKMANN.   Yes, for you and your family.

DR. STOCKMANN.   What the hell are you saying now!

PETER STOCKMANN.   I believe I have the right to think of myself as a helpful brother, Thomas.

DR. STOCKMANN.   You have been, and I thank you deeply for it.

PETER STOCKMANN.   Don't mention it. I often couldn't help myself. I had hoped that by improving your finances I would be able to keep you from running completely hog wild.

DR. STOCKMANN.   You mean it was only for your own sake?

PETER STOCKMANN.   Partly, yes. What do you imagine people think of an official whose closest relatives get themselves into trouble time and time again?

DR. STOCKMANN.   And that's what I have done?

PETER STOCKMANN.   You do it without knowing it. You're like a man with an automatic brain—as soon as an idea breaks into your head, no matter how idiotic it may be, you get up like a sleepwalker and start writing a pamphlet about it.

DR. STOCKMANN.   Peter, don't you think it's a citizen's duty to share a new idea with the public?

PETER STOCKMANN.   The public doesn't need new ideas—the public is much better off with old ideas.

DR. STOCKMANN.   You're not even embarrassed to say that?

PETER STOCKMANN.   Now look, I'm going to lay this out once and for all. You're always barking about authority. If a man gives you an order he's persecuting you. Nothing is important enough to respect once you decide to revolt against your superiors. All right then, I give up. I'm not going to try to change you any more. I told you the stakes you are playing for here, and now I am going to give you an order. And I warn you, you had better obey it if you value your career.

DR. STOCKMANN.   What kind of an order?

PETER STOCKMANN.   You are going to deny these rumors officially.

DR. STOCKMANN.   How?

PETER STOCKMANN.   You simply say that you went into the examination of the water more thoroughly and you find that you overestimated the danger.

DR. STOCKMANN.   I see.

PETER STOCKMANN.   And that you have complete confidence that whatever improvements are needed, the management will certainly take care of them.

DR. STOCKMANN *(after a pause)*.   My convictions come from the condition of the water. My convictions will change when the water changes, and for no other reason.

PETER STOCKMANN.   What are you talking about convictions? You're an official, you keep your convictions to yourself!

DR. STOCKMANN.   To myself?

PETER STOCKMANN.   As an official, I said. God knows, as a private person that's something else, but as a subordinate employee of the Institute, you have no right to express any convictions or personal opinions about anything connected with policy.

DR. STOCKMANN.   Now you listen to me. I am a doctor and a scientist—

PETER STOCKMANN.   This has nothing to do with science!

DR. STOCKMANN.   Peter, I have the right to express my opinion on anything in the world!

PETER STOCKMANN.   Not about the Institute—that I forbid.

DR. STOCKMANN.   You forbid!

PETER STOCKMANN.   I forbid you as your superior, and when I give orders you obey.

DR. STOCKMANN.   Peter, if you weren't my brother—

PETRA *(throwing the door at the left open).*   Father! You aren't going to stand for this! *(She enters.)*

MRS. STOCKMANN *(coming in after her).*   Petra, Petra!

PETER STOCKMANN.   What have you two been doing, eavesdropping?

MRS. STOCKMANN.   You were talking so loud we couldn't help . . .

PETRA.   Yes, I was eavesdropping!

PETER STOCKMANN.   That makes me very happy.

DR. STOCKMANN *(approaching his brother).*   You said something to me about forbidding—

PETER STOCKMANN.   You forced me to.

DR. STOCKMANN.   So you want me to spit in my own face officially—is that it?

PETER STOCKMANN.   Why must you always be so colorful?

DR. STOCKMANN.   And if I don't obey?

PETER STOCKMANN.   Then we will publish our own statement, to calm the public.

DR. STOCKMANN.   Good enough! And I will write against you. I will stick to what I said, and I will prove that I am right and that you are wrong, and what will you do then?

PETER STOCKMANN.   Then I simply won't be able to prevent your dismissal.

DR. STOCKMANN.   What!

PETRA.   Father!

PETER STOCKMANN.   Dismissed from the Institute is what I said. If you want to make war on Kirsten Springs, you have no right to be on the Board of Directors.

DR. STOCKMANN *(after a pause).*   You'd dare to do that?

PETER STOCKMANN.   Oh, no, you're the daring man.

PETRA.   Uncle, this is a rotten way to treat a man like Father!

MRS. STOCKMANN.   Will you be quiet, Petra!

PETER STOCKMANN.   So young and you've got opinions already—but that's natural. *(To Mrs. Stockmann)* Catherine dear, you're probably the only sane person in this house. Knock some sense into his head, will you? Make him realize what he's driving his whole family into.

DR. STOCKMANN.   My family concerns nobody but myself.

PETER STOCKMANN.   His family and his own town.

DR. STOCKMANN.   I'm going to show you who loves his town. The people are going to get the full stink of this corruption, Peter, and then we will see who loves his town!

PETER STOCKMANN.   You love your town when you blindly, spitefully, stubbornly go ahead trying to cut off our most important industry?

DR. STOCKMANN.   That source is poisoned, man. We are getting fat by peddling filth and corruption to innocent people!

PETER STOCKMANN.   I think this has gone beyond opinions and convictions, Thomas. A man who can throw that kind of insinuation around is nothing but a traitor to society!

DR. STOCKMANN *(starting toward his brother in a fury).*   How dare you to—

MRS. STOCKMANN *(stepping between them).*   Tom!

PETRA *(grabbing her father's arm).*   Be careful, Father!

PETER STOCKMANN *(with dignity).* I won't expose myself to violence. You have been warned. Consider what you owe yourself and your family! Good day! *(He exits.)*

DR. STOCKMANN *(walking up and down).* He's insulted. *He's* insulted!

MRS. STOCKMANN. It's shameful, Tom.

PETRA. Oh, I would love to give him a piece of my mind!

DR. STOCKMANN. It was my own fault! I should have shown my teeth right from the beginning. He called me a traitor to society. Me! Damn it all, that's not going to stick!

MRS. STOCKMANN. Please, think! He's got all the power on his side.

DR. STOCKMANN. Yes, but I have the truth on mine.

MRS. STOCKMANN. Without power, what good is the truth?

PETRA. Mother, how can you say such a thing?

DR. STOCKMANN. That's ridiculous, Catherine. I have the liberal press with me, and the majority. If that isn't power, what is?

MRS. STOCKMANN. But, for heaven's sake, Tom, you aren't going to—

DR. STOCKMANN. What am I not going to do?

MRS. STOCKMANN. You aren't going to fight it out in public with your brother!

DR. STOCKMANN. What the hell else do you want me to do?

MRS. STOCKMANN. But it won't do you any earthly good. If they won't do it, they won't. All you'll get out of it is a notice that you're fired.

DR. STOCKMANN. I am going to do my duty, Catherine. Me, the man he calls a traitor to society!

MRS. STOCKMANN. And how about your duty toward your family—the people you're supposed to provide for?

PETRA. Don't always think of us first, Mother.

MRS. STOCKMANN *(to Petra).* You can talk! If worst comes to worst, you can manage for yourself. But what about the boys, Tom, and you and me?

DR. STOCKMANN. What about you? You want me to be the miserable animal who'd crawl up the boots of that damn gang? Will you be happy if I can't face myself the rest of my life?

MRS. STOCKMANN. Tom, Tom, there's so much injustice in the world! You've simply got to learn to live with it. If you go on this way, God help us, we'll have no money again. Is it so long since the north that you've forgotten what it was to live like we lived? Haven't we had enough of that for one lifetime? *(The boys enter.)* What will happen to them? We've got nothing if you're fired!

DR. STOCKMANN. Stop it! *(He looks at the boys.)* Well, boys, did you learn anything in school today?

MORTEN *(looking at them, puzzled).* We learned what an insect is.

DR. STOCKMANN. You don't say!

MORTEN. What happened here? Why is everybody—

DR. STOCKMANN. Nothing, nothing. You know what I'm going to do, boys? From now on I'm going to teach you what a man is. *(He looks at Mrs. Stockman.)* She cries as

The Curtain Falls.

ACT TWO: SCENE 1

The editorial office of the People's Daily Messenger. *At the back of the room, to the left, is a door leading to the printing room. Near it, in the left wall, is another door. At the right of the stage is the entrance door. In the middle of the room there is a large table covered with papers, newspapers, and books. Around it are a few chairs. A writing desk stands against the right wall. The room is dingy and cheerless, the furniture shabby.*

As the curtain rises, BILLING *is sitting at the desk, reading the manuscript.* HOVSTAD *comes in after a moment from the printing room.* BILLING *looks up.*

BILLING.   The Doctor not come yet?

HOVSTAD.   No, not yet. You finish it?

(BILLING *holds up a hand to signal "just a moment." He reads on, the last paragraph of the manuscript.* HOVSTAD *comes and stands over him, reading with him. Now* BILLING *closes the manuscript, glances up at Hovstad with some trepidation, then looks off.* HOVSTAD, *looking at Billing, walks a few steps away.*)

HOVSTAD.   Well? What do you think of it?

BILLING *(with some hesitation).*   It's devastating. The Doctor is a brilliant man. I swear, I myself never really understood how incompetent those fat fellows are, on top. *(He picks up the manuscript and waves it a little.)* I hear the rumble of revolution in this.

HOVSTAD *(looking toward the door).*   Sssh! Aslaksen's inside.

BILLING.   Aslaksen's a coward. With all that moderation talk, all he's saying is, he's yellow. You're going to print this, aren't you?

HOVSTAD.   Sure, I'm just waiting for the Doctor to give the word. If his brother hasn't given in, we put it on the press anyway.

BILLING.   Yes, but if the Mayor's against this it's going to get pretty rough. You know that, don't you?

HOVSTAD.   Just let him try to block the reconstruction—the little businessmen and the whole town'll be screaming for his head. Aslaksen'll see to that.

BILLING *(ecstatically).*   The stockholders'll have to lay out a fortune of money if this goes through!

HOVSTAD.   My boy, I think it's going to bust them. And when the springs go busted, the people are finally going to understand the level of genius that's been running this town. Those five sheets of paper are going to put in a liberal administration once and for all.

BILLING.   It's a revolution. You know that? *(With hope and fear)* I mean it, we're on the edge of a real revolution!

DR. STOCKMANN *(entering).*   Put it on the press!

HOVSTAD *(excited).*   Wonderful! What did the Mayor say?

DR. STOCKMANN.   The Mayor has declared war, so war is what it's going to be! *(He takes the manuscript from Billing.)* And this is only the beginning! You know what he tried to do?

BILLING *(calling into the printing room).*   Mr. Aslaksen, the Doctor's here!

DR. STOCKMANN *(continuing).*   He actually tried to blackmail me! He's got the nerve to tell me that I'm not allowed to speak my mind without his permission! Imagine the shameless effrontery!

HOVSTAD.   He actually said it right out?

DR. STOCKMANN.   Right to my face! The trouble with me was I kept giving them credit for being our kind of people, but they're dictators! They're people who'll try to hold power even if they have to poison the town to do it.

(Toward the last part of Dr. Stockmann's speech ASLAKSEN *enters.)*

ASLAKSEN.   Now take it easy, Doctor, you—you mustn't always be throwing accusations. I'm with you, you understand, but moderation—

DR. STOCKMANN *(cutting him off).*   What'd you think of the article, Hovstad?

HOVSTAD.   It's a masterpiece. In one blow you've managed to prove beyond any doubt what kind of men are running us.

ASLAKSEN.   May we print it now, then?

DR. STOCKMANN.   I should say *so!*

HOVSTAD.   We'll have it ready for tomorrow's paper.

DR. STOCKMANN.   And listen, Mr. Aslaksen, do me a favor, will you? You run a fine paper, but supervise the printing personally, eh? I'd hate to see the weather report stuck into the middle of my article.

ASLAKSEN *(laughing).*   Don't worry, that won't happen this time!

DR. STOCKMANN.   Make it perfect, eh? Like you were printing money. You can't imagine how I'm dying to see it in print. After all the lies in the papers, the half-lies, the quarter-lies—to finally see the absolute, unvarnished truth about something important. And this is only the beginning. We'll go on to other subjects and blow up every lie we live by! What do you say, Aslaksen?

ASLAKSEN *(nodding in agreement:)*   But just remember . . .

BILLING *and* HOVSTAD *together with* ASLAKSEN.   Moderation!

ASLAKSEN *(to* BILLING *and* HOVSTAD).   I don't know what's so funny about that!

BILLING *(enthralled).*   Doctor Stockmann, I feel as though I were standing in some historic painting. Goddammit, this is a historic day! Someday this scene'll be in a museum, entitled, "The Day the Truth Was Born."

DR. STOCKMANN *(suddenly).*   Oh! I've got a patient half-bandaged down the street. *(He leaves.)*

HOVSTAD *(to* ASLAKSEN).   I hope you realize how useful he could be to us.

ASLAKSEN.   I don't like that business about "this is only the beginning." Let him stick to the springs.

BILLING.   What makes you so scared all the time?

ASLAKSEN.   I have to live here. It'd be different if he were attacking the national government or something, but if he thinks I'm going to start going after the whole town administration—

BILLING.   What's the difference? Bad is bad!

ASLAKSEN.   Yes, but there is a difference. You attack the national government, what's going to happen? Nothing. They go right on. But a town administration —they're liable to be overthrown or something! I represent the small property owners in this town—

BILLING.　　Ha! It's always the same. Give a man a little property and the truth can go to hell!

ASLAKSEN.　　Mr. Billing, I'm older than you are. I've seen fireeaters before. You know who used to work at that desk before you? Councilman Stensford—*councilman!*

BILLING.　　Just because I work at a renegade's desk, does that mean—

ASLAKSEN.　　You're a politician. A politician never knows where he's going to end up. And besides you applied for a job as secretary to the Magistrate, didn't you?

HOVSTAD *(surprised, laughs).*　　Billing!

BILLING *(to Hovstad).*　　Well, why not? If I get it I'll have a chance to put across some good things. I could put plenty of big boys on the spot with a job like that!

ASLAKSEN.　　All right, I'm just saying. *(He goes to the printing-room door.)* People change. Just remember when you call me a coward—I may not have made the hot speeches, but I never went back on my beliefs either. Unlike some of the big radicals around here, I didn't change. Of course, I *am* a little more moderate, but moderation is—

HOVSTAD.　　Oh, God!

ASLAKSEN.　　I don't see what's so funny about that! *(He glares at* HOVSTAD *and goes out.)*

BILLING.　　If we could get rid of him we—

HOVSTAD.　　Take it easy—he pays the printing bill, he's not that bad. *(He picks up the manuscript.)* I'll get the printer on this. *He starts out.*

BILLING.　　Say, Hovstad, how about asking Stockmann to back us? Then we could really put out a paper!

HOVSTAD.　　What would he do for money?

BILLING.　　His father-in-law.

HOVSTAD.　　Kiil? Since when has he got money?

BILLING.　　I think he's loaded with it.

HOVSTAD.　　No! Why, as long as I've known him he's worn the same overcoat, the same suit—

BILLING.　　Yeah, and the same ring on his right hand. You ever get a look at that boulder? *(He points to his finger.)*

HOVSTAD.　　No, I never—

BILLING.　　All year he wears the diamond inside, but on New Year's Eve he turns it around. Figure it out—when a man has no visible means of support, what is he living on? Money, right?

(PETRA *enters, carrying a book.*)

PETRA.　　Hello.

HOVSTAD.　　Well, fancy seeing you here. Sit down. What—

PETRA *(walking slowly up to* HOVSTAD).　　I want to ask you a question. *(She starts to open the book.)*

BILLING.　　What's that?

PETRA.　　The English novel you wanted translated.

HOVSTAD.   Aren't you going to do it?

PETRA *(with deadly seriousness and curiosity).*   I don't get this.

HOVSTAD.   You don't get what?

PETRA.   This book is absolutely against everything you people believe.

HOVSTAD.   Oh, it isn't that bad.

PETRA.   But, Mr. Hovstad, it says if you're good there's a supernatural force that'll fix it so you end up happy. And if you're bad you'll be punished. Since when does the world work that way?

HOVSTAD.   Yes, Petra, but this is a newspaper, people like to read that kind of thing. They buy the paper for that and then we slip in our political stuff. A newspaper can't buck the public—

PETRA *(astonished, beginning to be angry).*   You don't say! *(She starts to go.)*

HOVSTAD *(hurrying after her).*   Now, wait a minute, I don't want you to go feeling that way. *(He holds the manuscript out to Billing.)* Here, take this to the printer, will you?

BILLING *(taking the manuscript).*   Sure. *(He goes.)*

HOVSTAD.   I just want you to understand something: I never even read that book. It was Billing's idea.

PETRA *(trying to penetrate his eyes).*   I thought he was a radical.

HOVSTAD.   He is. But he's also a—

PETRA *(testily).*   A newspaperman.

HOVSTAD.   Well, that too, but I was going to say that Billing is trying to get the job as secretary to the Magistrate.

PETRA.   What?

HOVSTAD.   People are—people, Miss Stockmann.

PETRA.   But the Magistrate! He's been fighting everything progressive in this town for thirty years.

HOVSTAD.   Let's not argue about it, I just didn't want you to go out of here with a wrong idea of me. I guess you know that I—I happen to admire women like you. I've never had a chance to tell you, but I—well, I want you to know it. Do you mind? *(He smiles.)*

PETRA.   No, I don't mind, but—reading that book upset me. I really don't understand. Will you tell me why you're supporting my father?

HOVSTAD.   What's the mystery? It's a matter of principle.

PETRA.   But a paper that'll print a book like this has no principle.

HOVSTAD.   Why do you jump to such extremes? You're just like . . .

PETRA.   Like what?

HOVSTAD.   I simply mean that . . .

PETRA *(moving away from him).*   Like my father, you mean. You really have no use for him, do you?

HOVSTAD.   Now wait a minute!

PETRA.   What's behind this? Are you just trying to hold my hand or something?

HOVSTAD.   I happen to agree with your father, and that's why I'm printing his stuff.

PETRA.   You're trying to put something over, I think. Why are you in this?

HOVSTAD.   Who're you accusing? Billing gave you that book, not me!

PETRA.   But you don't mind printing it, do you? What are you trying to do with my father? You have no principles—what are you up to here?

(ASLAKSEN *hurriedly enters from the printing shop, Stockmann's manuscript in his hand.*)

ASLAKSEN.   My God! Hovstad! (*He sees Petra.*) Miss Stockmann.

PETRA (*looking at* HOVSTAD). I don't think I've been so frightened in my life. (*She goes out.*)

HOVSTAD (*starting after her*).   Please, you mustn't think I—

ASLAKSEN (*stopping him*).   Where are you going? The Mayor's out there.

HOVSTAD.   The Mayor!

ASLAKSEN.   He wants to speak to you. He came in the back door. He doesn't want to be seen.

HOVSTAD.   What does he want? (*He goes to the printing-room door, opens it, calls out with a certain edge of servility.*) Come in, Your Honor!

PETER STOCKMANN (*entering*).   Thank you.

(*Hovstad carefully closes the door.*)

PETER STOCKMANN (*walking around*).   It's clean! I always imagined this place would look dirty. But it's clean. (*Commendingly*) Very nice, Mr. Aslaksen. (*He puts his hat on the desk.*)

ASLAKSEN.   Not at all, Your Honor—I mean to say, I always . . .

HOVSTAD.   What can I do for you, Your Honor? Sit down?

PETER STOCKMANN. (*Sits, placing his cane on the table.*)   I had a very annoying thing happen today, Mr. Hovstad.

HOVSTAD.   That so?

PETER STOCKMANN.   It seems my brother has written some sort of—memorandum. About the springs.

HOVSTAD.   You don't say.

PETER STOCKMANN (*looking at* HOVSTAD *now*).   He mentioned it . . . to you?

HOVSTAD.   Yes. I think he said something about it.

ASLAKSEN. (*nervously starts to go out, attempting to hide the manuscript.*)   Will you excuse me, gentlemen . . .

PETER STOCKMANN (*pointing to the manuscript*).   That's it, isn't it?

ASLAKSEN.   This? I don't know, I haven't had a chance to look at it, the printer just handed it to me . . .

HOVSTAD.   Isn't that the thing the printer wanted the spelling checked?

ASLAKSEN.   That's it. It's only a question of spelling. I'll be right back.

PETER STOCKMANN.   I'm very good at spelling. (*He holds out his hand.*) Maybe I can help you.

HOVSTAD.   No, Your Honor, there's some Latin in it. You wouldn't know Latin, would you?

PETER STOCKMANN.   Oh, yes. I used to help my brother with his Latin all the time. Let me have it.

(ASLAKSEN *gives him the manuscript.* PETER STOCKMANN *looks at the title on the first page, then glances up sarcastically at* HOVSTAD, *who avoids his eyes.*)

PETER STOCKMANN. You're going to print this?

HOVSTAD. I can't very well refuse a signed article. A signed article is the author's responsibility.

PETER STOCKMANN. Mr. Aslaksen, you're going to allow this?

ASLAKSEN. I'm the publisher, not the editor, Your Honor. My policy is freedom for the editor.

PETER STOCKMANN. You have a point—I can see that.

ASLAKSEN *(reaching for the manuscript).* So if you don't mind . . .

PETER STOCKMANN. Not at all. *(But he holds on to the manuscript. After a pause)* This reconstruction of the springs—

ASLAKSEN. I realize, Your Honor—it does mean tremendous sacrifices for the stockholders.

PETER STOCKMANN. Don't upset yourself. The first thing a Mayor learns is that the less wealthy can always be prevailed upon to demand a spirit of sacrifice for the public good.

ASLAKSEN. I'm glad you see that.

PETER STOCKMANN. Oh, yes. Especially when it's the wealthy who are going to do the sacrificing. What you don't seem to understand, Mr. Aslaksen, is that so long as I am Mayor, any changes in those springs are going to be paid for by a municipal loan.

ASLAKSEN. A municipal—you mean you're going to tax the people for this?

PETER STOCKMANN. Exactly.

HOVSTAD. But the springs are a private corporation!

PETER STOCKMANN. The corporation built Kirsten Springs out of its own money. If the people want them changed, the people naturally must pay the bill. The corporation is in no position to put out any more money. It simply can't do it.

ASLAKSEN *(to* HOVSTAD). That's impossible! People will never stand for a new tax. *(To the* MAYOR) Is this a fact or your opinion?

PETER STOCKMANN. It happens to be a fact. Plus another fact—you'll forgive me for talking about facts in a newspaper office—but don't forget that the springs will take two years to make over. Two years without income for your small businessmen, Mr. Aslaksen, and a heavy new tax besides. And all because— *(his private emotion comes to the surface; he throttles the manuscript in his hand)*—because of this dream, this hallucination, that we live in a pesthole!

HOVSTAD. That's based on science.

PETER STOCKMANN *(raising the manuscript and throwing it down on the table).* This is based on vindictiveness, on his hatred of authority and nothing else. *(He pounds on the manuscript.)* This is the mad dream of a man who is trying to blow up our way of life! It has nothing to do with reform or science or anything else, but pure and simple destruction! And I intend to see to it that the people understand it exactly so!

ASLAKSEN *(hit by this).* My God! *(To* HOVSTAD). Maybe . . . You sure you want to support this thing, Hovstad?

HOVSTAD *(nervously).* Frankly I'd never thought of it in quite that way. I mean . . . *(To the Mayor)* When you think of it psychologically it's completely possible, of course, that the man is simply out to—I don't know what to say,

Your Honor. I'd hate to hurt the town in any way. I never imagined we'd have to have a new tax.

PETER STOCKMANN.   You should have imagined it because you're going to have to advocate it. Unless, of course, liberal and radical newspaper readers enjoy high taxes. But you'd know that better than I. I happen to have here a brief story of the actual facts. It proves that, with a little care, nobody need be harmed at all by the water. *(He takes out a long envelope.)* Of course, in time we'd have to make a few minor structural changes and we'd pay for those.

HOVSTAD.   May I see that?

PETER STOCKMANN.   I want you to *study* it, Mr. Hovstad, and see if you don't agree that—

BILLING *(entering quickly).*   Are you expecting the Doctor?

PETER STOCKMANN *(alarmed).*   He's here?

BILLING.   Just coming across the street.

PETER STOCKMANN.   I'd rather not run into him here. How can I . . .

BILLING.   Right this way, sir, hurry up!

ASLAKSEN *(at the entrance door, peeking).*   Hurry up!

PETER STOCKMANN *(going with* BILLING *through the door at the left)* Get him out of here right away! *(They exit.)*

HOVSTAD.   Do something, do something!

(ASLAKSEN *pokes among some papers on the table.* HOVSTAD *sits at the desk, starts to "write."* DR. STOCKMANN *enters.)*

DR. STOCKMANN.   Any proofs yet? *(He sees they hardly turn to him.)* I guess not, eh?

ASLAKSEN *(without turning).*   No, you can't expect them for some time.

DR. STOCKMANN.   You mind if I wait?

HOVSTAD.   No sense in that, Doctor, it'll be quite a while yet.

DR. STOCKMANN *(laughing, places his hand on Hovstad's back).*   Bear with me, Hovstad, I just can't wait to see it in print.

HOVSTAD.   We're pretty busy, Doctor, so . . .

DR. STOCKMANN *(starting toward the door).*   Don't let me hold you up. That's the way to be, busy, busy. We'll make this town shine like a jewel! *(He has opened the door, now he comes back.)* Just one thing. I—

HOVSTAD.   Couldn't we talk some other time? We're very—

DR. STOCKMANN.   Two words. Just walking down the street now, I looked at the people, in the stores, driving the wagons, and suddenly I was—well, touched, you know? By their innocence, I mean. What I'm driving at is, when this exposé breaks they're liable to start making a saint out of me or something, and I—Aslaksen, I want you to promise me that you're not going to try to get up any dinner for me or—

ASLAKSEN *(turning toward the Doctor).*   Doctor, there's no use concealing—

DR. STOCKMANN.   I knew it. Now look, I will simply not attend a dinner in my honor.

HOVSTAD *(getting up).*   Doctor, I think it's time we—

(MRS. STOCKMANN *enters.)*

MRS. STOCKMANN.   I thought so. Thomas, I want you home. Now come. I want you to talk to Petra.

DR. STOCKMANN.   What happened? What are you doing here?

HOVSTAD.   Something wrong, Mrs. Stockmann?

MRS. STOCKMANN (*leveling a look of accusation at* HOVSTAD).   Doctor Stockmann is the father of three children, Mr. Hovstad.

DR. STOCKMANN.   Now look, dear, everybody knows that. What's the—

MRS. STOCKMANN (*restraining an outburst at her husband*).   Nobody would *believe* it from the way you're dragging us into this disaster!

DR. STOCKMANN.   What disaster?

MRS. STOCKMANN (*to Hovstad*).   He treated you like a son, now you make a fool of him?

HOVSTAD.   *I'm* not making a—

DR. STOCKMANN.   Catherine! (*He indicates* HOVSTAD.) How can you accuse—

MRS. STOCKMANN (*to* HOVSTAD).   He'll lose his job at the springs, do you realize that? You print the article, and they'll grind him up like a piece of flesh!

DR. STOCKMANN.   Catherine, you're embarrassing me! I beg your pardon, gentlemen . . .

MRS. STOCKMANN.   Mr. Hovstad, what are you up to?

DR. STOCKMANN.   I won't have you jumping at Hovstad, Catherine!

MRS. STOCKMANN.   I want you home! This man is not your friend!

DR. STOCKMANN.   He is my friend! Any man who shares my risk is my friend! You simply don't understand that as soon as this breaks everybody in this town is going to come out in the streets and drive that gang of—(*He picks up the* MAYOR'S *cane from the table, notices what it is, and stops. He looks from it to* HOVSTAD *and* ASLAKSEN.) What's this? (*They don't reply. Now he notices the hat on the desk and picks it up with the tip of the cane. He looks at them again. He is angry, incredulous.*) What the hell is he doing here?

ASLAKSEN.   All right, Doctor, now let's be calm and—

DR. STOCKMANN (*starting to move*).   Where is he? What'd he do, talk you out of it? Hovstad! (HOVSTAD *remains immobile.*) He won't get away with it! Where'd you hide him? (*He opens the door at the left.*)

ASLAKSEN.   Be careful, Doctor!

(PETER STOCKMANN *enters with Billing through the door Dr. Stockmann opened.* PETER STOCKMANN *tries to hide his embarrassment.*)

DR. STOCKMANN.   Well, Peter, poisoning the water was not enough! You're working on the press now, eh? (*He crosses to the entrance door.*)

PETER STOCKMANN.   My hat, please. And my stick. (DR. STOCKMANN *puts on the Mayor's hat.*) Now what's *this* nonsense! Take that off, that's official insignia!

DR. STOCKMANN.   I just wanted you to realize, Peter—(*he takes off the hat and looks at it*)—that anyone may wear this hat in a democracy, and that a free citizen is not afraid to touch it. (*He hands him the hat.*) And as for the baton of command, Your Honor, it can pass from hand to hand. (*He hands the cane to* PETER STOCKMANN.) So don't gloat yet. The people haven't spoken.

(*He turns to* HOVSTAD *and* ASLAKSEN.) And I have the people because I have the truth, my friends!

ASLAKSEN.   Doctor, we're not scientists. We can't judge whether your article is really true.

DR. STOCKMANN.   Then print it under my name. Let *me* defend it!

HOVSTAD.   I'm not printing it. I'm not going to sacrifice this newspaper. When the whole story gets out the public is not going to stand for any changes in the springs.

ASLAKSEN.   His Honor just told us, Doctor—you see, there will have to be a new tax—

DR. STOCKMANN.   Ahhhhh! Yes. I see. That's why you're not scientists suddenly and can't decide if I'm telling the truth. Well. So!

HOVSTAD.   Don't take that attitude. The point is—

DR. STOCKMANN.   The point, the point, oh, the point is going to fly through this town like an arrow, and I am going to fire it! (*To* ASLAKSEN) Will you print this article as a pamphlet? I'll pay for it.

ASLAKSEN.   I'm not going to ruin this paper and this town. Doctor, for the sake of your family—

MRS. STOCKMANN.   You can leave his family out of this, Mr. Aslaksen. God help me, I think you people are horrible!

DR. STOCKMANN.   My article, if you don't mind.

ASLAKSEN (*giving it to him*).   Doctor, you won't get it printed in this town.

PETER STOCKMANN.   Can't you forget it? (*He indicates* HOVSTAD *and* AS-LAKSEN.) Can't you see now that everybody—

DR. STOCKMANN.   Your Honor, I can't forget it, and you will never forget it as long as you live. I am going to call a mass meeting, and I—

PETER STOCKMANN.   And who is going to rent you a hall?

DR. STOCKMANN.   Then I will take a drum and go from street to street, proclaiming that the springs are befouled and poison is rotting the body politic! (*He starts for the door.*)

PETER STOCKMANN.   And I believe you really are that mad!

DR. STOCKMANN.   Mad? Oh, my brother, you haven't even heard me raise my voice yet. Catherine? (*He holds out his hand, she gives him her elbow. They go stiffly out.*)

PETER STOCKMANN *looks regretfully toward the exit, then takes out his manuscript and hands it to* HOVSTAD, *who in turn gives it to* BILLING, *who hands it to* ASLAKSEN, *who takes it and exits.* PETER STOCKMANN *puts his hat on and moves toward the door. Blackout.*

The Curtain Falls.

ACT TWO: SCENE 2

A room in Captain Horster's house. The room is bare, as though unused for a long time. A large doorway is at the left, two shuttered windows at the back, and another door at the right. Upstage right, packing cases have been set together, form-

ing a platform, on which are a chair and a small table. There are two chairs next to the platform at the right. One chair stands downstage left.

The room is angled, thus making possible the illusion of a large crowd off in the wing to the left. The platform faces the audience at an angle, thus giving the speakers the chance to speak straight out front and creating the illusion of a large crowd by addressing "people" in the audience.

As the curtain rises the room is empty. CAPTAIN HORSTER *enters, carrying a pitcher of water, a glass, and a bell. He is putting these on the table when* BILLING *enters. A crowd is heard talking outside in the street.*

BILLING.   Captain Horster?

HORSTER *(turning).*   Oh, come in. I don't have enough chairs for a lot of people so I decided not to have chairs at all.

BILLING.   My name is Billing. Don't you remember, at the Doctor's house?

HORSTER *(a little coldly).*   Oh, yes, sure. I've been so busy I didn't recognize you. *(He goes to a window and looks out.)* Why don't those people come inside?

BILLING.   I don't know, I guess they're waiting for the Mayor or somebody important so they can be sure it's respectable in here. I wanted to ask you a question before it begins, Captain. Why are you lending your house for this? I never heard of you connected with anything political.

HORSTER *(standing still).*   I'll answer that. I travel most of the year and—did you ever travel?

BILLING.   Not abroad, no.

HORSTER.   Well, I've been in a lot of places where people aren't allowed to say unpopular things. Did you know that?

BILLING.   Sure, I've read about it.

HORSTER *(simply).*   Well, I don't like it. *(He starts to go out.)*

BILLING.   One more question. What's your opinion about the Doctor's proposition to rebuild the springs?

HORSTER *(turning, thinks, then):*   Don't understand a thing about it.

(Three citizens enter.)

HORSTER.   Come in, come in. I don't have enough chairs so you'll just have to stand. *(He goes out.)*

FIRST CITIZEN.   Try the horn.

SECOND CITIZEN.   No, let him start to talk first.

THIRD CITIZEN *(a big beef of a man, takes out a horn).*   Wait'll they hear this! I could blow your mustache off with this!

(HORSTER returns. He sees the horn and stops abruptly.)

HORSTER.   I don't want any roughhouse, you hear me?

(MRS. STOCKMANN and PETRA enter.)

HORSTER.   Come in. I've got chairs just for you.

MRS. STOCKMANN *(nervously).*   There's quite a crowd on the sidewalk. Why don't they come in?

HORSTER.   I suppose they're waiting for the Mayor.

PETRA.   Are all those people on his side?

HORSTER.   Who knows? People are bashful, and it's so unusual to come to a meeting like this, I suppose they—

BILLING *(going over to this group).*   Good evening, ladies. *(They simply look at him.)* I don't blame you for not speaking. I just wanted to say I don't think this is going to be a place for ladies tonight.

MRS. STOCKMANN.   I don't remember asking your advice, Mr. Billing.

BILLING.   I'm not as bad as you think, Mrs. Stockmann.

MRS. STOCKMANN.   Then why did you print the Mayor's statement and not a word about my husband's report? Nobody's had a chance to find out what he really stands for. Why, everybody on the street there is against him already!

BILLING.   If we printed his report it only would have hurt your husband.

MRS. STOCKMANN.   Mr. Billing, I've never said this to anyone in my life, but I think you're a liar.

(Suddenly the THIRD CITIZEN *lets out a blast on his horn. The women jump,* BILLING *and* HORSTER *turn around quickly.)*

HORSTER.   You do that once more and I'll throw you out of here!

*(*PETER STOCKMANN *enters. Behind him comes the crowd. He pretends to be unconnected with them. He goes straight to* MRS. STOCKMANN, *bows.)*

PETER STOCKMANN.   Catherine? Petra?

PETRA.   Good evening.

PETER STOCKMANN.   Why so coldly? He wanted a meeting and he's got it. *(To* HORSTER*)* Isn't he here?

HORSTER.   The Doctor is going around town to be sure there's a good attendance.

PETER STOCKMANN.   Fair enough. By the way, Petra, did you paint that poster? The one somebody stuck on the Town Hall?

PETRA.   If you can call it painting, yes.

PETER STOCKMANN.   You know I could arrest you? It's against the law to deface the Town Hall.

PETRA.   Well, here I am. *(She holds out her hands for the handcuffs.)*

MRS. STOCKMANN *(taking it seriously).*   If you arrest her, Peter, I'll never speak to you!

PETER STOCKMANN *(laughing).*   Catherine, you have no sense of humor!

(He crosses and sits down at the left. They sit right. A drunk comes out of the crowd.)

DRUNK.   Say, Billy, who's runnin'? Who's the candidate?

HORSTER.   You're drunk, Mister, now get out of here!

DRUNK.   There's no law says a man who's drunk can't vote!

HORSTER *(pushing the drunk toward the door as the crowd laughs).*   Get out of here! Get out!

DRUNK.   I wanna vote! I got a right to vote!

(Aslaksen enters hurriedly, sees Peter Stockmann, and rushes to him.)

ASLAKSEN.   Your Honor . . . (*He points to the door.*) He's . . .

DR. STOCKMANN. (*offstage:*)   Right this way, gentlemen! In you go, come on, fellows!

(HOVSTAD *enters, glances at* PETER STOCKMANN *and* ASLAKSEN, *then at* DR. STOCKMANN *and another crowd behind him, who enter.*)

DR. STOCKMANN.   Sorry, no chairs, gentlemen, but we couldn't get a hall, y'know, so just relax. It won't take long anyway. (*He goes to the platform, sees* PETER STOCKMANN.) Glad you're here, Peter!

PETER STOCKMANN.   Wouldn't miss it for the world.

DR. STOCKMANN.   How do you feel, Catherine?

MRS. STOCKMANN (*nervously*).   Just promise me, don't lose your temper . . .

HORSTER (*seeing the drunk pop in through the door*).   Did I tell you to get out of here!

DRUNK.   Look, if you ain't votin', what the hell's going on here? (HORSTER *starts after him.*) Don't push!

PETER STOCKMANN (*to the* DRUNK).   I order you to get out of here and stay out!

DRUNK.   I don't like the tone of your voice! And if you don't watch your step I'm gonna tell the Mayor right now, and he'll throw yiz all in the jug! (*To all*) What're you, a revolution here?

(*The crowd bursts out laughing; the drunk laughs with them, and they push him out.* DR. STOCKMANN *mounts the platform.*)

DR. STOCKMANN (*quieting the crowd*).   All right, gentlemen, we might as well begin. Quiet down, please. (*He clears his throat.*) The issue is very simple—

ASLAKSEN.   We haven't elected a chairman, Doctor.

DR. STOCKMANN.   I'm sorry, Mr. Aslaksen, this isn't a meeting. I advertised a lecture and I—

A CITIZEN.   I came to a meeting, Doctor. There's got to be some kind of control here.

DR. STOCKMANN.   What do you mean, control? What is there to control?

SECOND CITIZEN.   Sure, let him speak, this is no meeting!

THIRD CITIZEN.   Your Honor, why don't you take charge of this—

DR. STOCKMANN.   Just a minute now!

THIRD CITIZEN.   Somebody responsible has got to take charge. There's a big difference of opinion here—

DR. STOCKMANN.   What makes you so sure? You don't even know yet what I'm going to say.

THIRD CITIZEN.   I've got a pretty good idea what you're going to say, and I don't like it! If a man doesn't like it here, let him go where it suits him better. We don't want any troublemakers here!

(*There is assent from much of the crowd.* DR. STOCKMANN *looks at them with new surprise.*)

DR. STOCKMANN.   Now look, friend, you don't know anything about me—

FOURTH CITIZEN.   We know plenty about you, Stockmann!

DR. STOCKMANN.   From what? From the newspapers? How do you know I don't like this town? *(He picks up his manuscript.)* I'm here to save the life of this town!

PETER STOCKMANN *(quickly)*.   Now just a minute, Doctor, I think the democratic thing to do is to elect a chairman.

FIFTH CITIZEN.   I nominate the Mayor!

(Seconds are heard.)

PETER STOCKMANN.   No, no, no! That wouldn't be fair. We want a neutral person. I suggest Mr. Aslaksen—

SECOND CITIZEN.   I came to a lecture, I didn't—

THIRD CITIZEN *(to* SECOND CITIZEN*)*.   What're you afraid of, a fair fight? *(To the Mayor)* Second Mr. Aslaksen!

(The crowd assents.)

DR. STOCKMANN.   All right, if that's your pleasure. I just want to remind you that the reason I called this meeting was that I have a very important message for you people and I couldn't get it into the press, and nobody would rent me a hall. *(To Peter Stockmann:)* I just hope I'll be given time to speak here. Mr. Aslaksen?

(As ASLAKSEN *mounts the platform and* DR. STOCKMANN *steps down,* KIIL *enters, looks shrewdly around.)*

ASLAKSEN.   I just have one word before we start. Whatever is said tonight, please remember, the highest civic virtue is moderation. *(He can't help turning to Dr. Stockmann, then back to the crowd.)* Now if anybody wants to speak—

(The DRUNK *enters suddenly.)*

DRUNK *(pointing at* ASLAKSEN*)*.   I heard that! Since when you allowed to electioneer at the poles? *(CITIZENS push him toward the door amid laughter.)* I'm gonna report this to the Mayor, goddammit! *(They push him out and close the door.)*

ASLAKSEN.   Quiet, please, quiet. Does anybody want the floor?

*(*DR. STOCKMANN *starts to come forward, raising his hand, but* PETER STOCKMANN *also has his hand raised.)*

PETER STOCKMANN.   Mr. Chairman!

ASLAKSEN *(quickly recognizing Peter Stockmann)*.   His Honor the Mayor will address the meeting.

*(*DR. STOCKMANN *stops, looks at* PETER STOCKMANN, *and, suppressing a remark, returns to his place. The* MAYOR *mounts the platform.)*

PETER STOCKMANN.   Gentlemen, there's no reason to take very long to settle this tonight and return to our ordinary, calm, and peaceful life. Here's the issue: Doctor Stockmann, my brother—and believe me, it is not easy to say this— has decided to destroy Kirsten Springs, our Health Institute—

DR. STOCKMANN.   Peter!

ASLAKSEN *(ringing his bell).*   Let the Mayor continue, please. There mustn't be any interruptions.

PETER STOCKMANN.   He has a long and very involved way of going about it, but that's the brunt of it, believe me.

THIRD CITIZEN.   Then what're we wasting time for? Run him out of town!

(Others join in the cry.)

PETER STOCKMANN.   Now wait a minute. I want no violence here. I want you to understand his motives. He is a man, always has been, who is never happy unless he is badgering authority, ridiculing authority, destroying authority. He wants to attack the springs so he can prove that the administration blundered in the construction.

DR. STOCKMANN *(to* ASLAKSEN*).*   May I speak? I—

ASLAKSEN.   The Mayor's not finished.

PETER STOCKMANN.   Thank you. Now there are a number of people here who seem to feel that the Doctor has a right to say anything he pleases. After all, we are a democratic country. Now, God knows, in ordinary times I'd agree a hundred per cent with anybody's right to say anything. But these are not ordinary times. Nations have crises, and so do towns. There are ruins of nations, and there are ruins of towns all over the world, and they were wrecked by people who, in the guise of reform, and pleading for justice, and so on, broke down all authority and left only revolution and chaos.

DR. STOCKMANN.   What the hell are you talking about!

ASLAKSEN.   I'll have to insist, Doctor—

DR. STOCKMANN.   I called a lecture! I didn't invite him to attack me. He's got the press and every hall in town to attack me, and I've got nothing but this room tonight!

ASLAKSEN.   I don't think you're making a very good impression, Doctor.

(Assenting laughter and catcalls. Again DR. STOCKMANN *is taken aback by this reaction.)*

ASLAKSEN.   Please continue, Your Honor.

PETER STOCKMANN.   Now this is our crisis. We know what this town was without our Institute. We could barely afford to keep the streets in condition. It was a dead, third-rate hamlet. Today we're just on the verge of becoming internationally known as a resort. I predict that within five years the income of every man in this room will be immensely greater. I predict that our schools will be bigger and better. And in time this town will be crowded with fine carriages; great homes will be built here; first-class stores will open all along Main Street. I predict that if we are not defamed and maliciously attacked we will someday be one of the richest and most beautiful resort towns in the world. There are your choices. Now all you've got to do is ask yourselves a simple question: Has any one of us the right, the "democratic right," as they like to call it, to pick at minor flaws in the springs, to exaggerate the most picayune faults? *(Cries of No, No!)* And to attempt to publish these defamations for the whole world to see? We live or die on what the outside world thinks of us. I believe there is a line that must be drawn, and if a man decides to cross that line, we the people must finally take him by the collar and declare, "You cannot say that!"

(There is an uproar of assent. ASLAKSEN *rings the bell.)*

PETER STOCKMANN *(continuing).*   All right then. I think we all understand each other. Mr. Aslaksen, I move that Doctor Stockmann be prohibited from reading his report at this meeting! *(He goes back to his chair, which meanwhile* KIIL *has occupied.)*

*(*ASLAKSEN *rings the bell to quiet the enthusiasm.* DR. STOCKMANN *is jumping to get up on the platform, the report in his hand.)*

ASLAKSEN.   Quiet, please. Please now. I think we can proceed to the vote.
DR. STOCKMANN.   Well, aren't you going to let me speak at all?
ASLAKSEN.   Doctor, we are just about to vote on that question.
DR. STOCKMANN.   But damn it, man, I've got a right to—
PETRA *(standing up).*   Point of order, Father!
DR. STOCKMANN *(picking up the cue).*   Yes, point of order!
ASLAKSEN *(turning to him now).*   Yes, Doctor.

*(*DR. STOCKMANN, *at a loss, turns to* PETRA *for further instructions.)*

PETRA.   You want to discuss the motion.
DR. STOCKMANN.   That's right, damn it, I want to discuss the motion!
ASLAKSEN.   Ah . . . *(He glances at Peter Stockmann.)* All right, go ahead.
DR. STOCKMANN *(to the crowd).*   Now, listen. *(He points at* PETER STOCK-MANN.*)* He talks and he talks and he talks, but not a word about the facts! *(He holds up the manuscript.)*
THIRD CITIZEN.   We don't want to hear any more about the water!
FOURTH CITIZEN.   You're just trying to blow up everything!
DR. STOCKMANN.   Well, judge for yourselves, let me read—

(Cries of No, No, No! The man with the horn blows it. ASLAKSEN *rings the bell. DR. STOCKMANN is utterly shaken. Astonished, he looks at the maddened faces. He lowers the hand holding the manuscript and steps back, defeated.)*

ASLAKSEN.   Please, please now, quiet. We can't have this uproar! *Quiet returns.* I think, Doctor, that the majority wants to take the vote before you start to speak. If they so will, you can speak. Otherwise, majority rules. You won't deny that.
DR. STOCKMANN. *(Turns, tosses the manuscript on the floor, turns back to Aslaksen.)* Don't bother voting. I understand everything now. Can I have a few minutes—
PETER STOCKMANN.   Mr. Chairman!
DR. STOCKMANN *(to his brother).*   I won't mention the Institute. I have a new discovery that's a thousand times more important than all the Institutes in the world. *(To* ASLAKSEN*)* May I have the platform.
ASLAKSEN *(to the crowd).*   I don't see how we can deny him that, as long as he confines himself to—

DR. STOCKMANN.   The springs are not the subject. *(He mounts the platform, looks at the crowd.)* Before I go into my subject I want to congratulate the liberals and radicals among us, like Mr. Hovstad—

HOVSTAD.   What do you mean, radical! Where's your evidence to call me a radical!

DR. STOCKMANN.   You've got me there. There isn't any evidence. I guess there never really was. I just wanted to congratulate you on your self-control tonight —you who have fought in every parlor for the principle of free speech these many years.

HOVSTAD.   I believe in democracy. When my readers are overwhelmingly against something, I'm not going to impose my will on the majority.

DR. STOCKMANN.   You have begun my remarks, Mr. Hovstad. *(He turns to the crowd.)* Gentlemen, Mrs. Stockmann, Miss Stockmann. Tonight I was struck by a sudden flash of light, a discovery second to none. But before I tell it to you—a little story. I put in a good many years in the north of our country. Up there the rulers of the world are the great seal and the gigantic squadrons of duck. Man lives on ice, huddled together in little piles of stones. His whole life consists of grubbing for food. Nothing more. He can barely speak his own language. And it came to me one day that it was romantic and sentimental for a man of my education to be tending these people. They had not yet reached the stage where they needed a doctor. If the truth were to be told, a veterinary would be more in order.

BILLING.   Is that the way you refer to decent hard-working people!

DR. STOCKMANN.   I expected that, my friend, but don't think you can fog up my brain with that magic word—the People! Not any more! Just because there is a mass of organisms with the human shape, they do not automatically become a People. That honor has to be earned! Nor does one automatically become a Man by having human shape, and living in a house, and feeding one's face —and agreeing with one's neighbors. That name *also* has to be earned. Now, when I came to my conclusions about the springs—

PETER STOCKMANN.   You have no right to—

DR. STOCKMANN.   That's a picayune thing, to catch me on a word, Peter. I am not going into the springs. *(To the crowd)* When I became convinced of my theory about the water, the authorities moved in at once, and I said to myself, I will fight them to the death, because—

THIRD CITIZEN.   What're you trying to do, make a revolution here? He's a revolutionist!

DR. STOCKMANN.   Let me finish. I thought to myself: The majority, I have the majority! And let me tell you, friends, it was a grand feeling. Because that's the reason I came back to this place of my birth. I wanted to give my education to this town. I loved it so, I spent months without pay or encouragement and dreamed up the whole project of the springs. And why? Not as my brother says, so that fine carriages could crowd our streets, but so that we might cure the sick, so that we might meet people from all over the world and learn from them, and become broader and more civilized. In other words, more like Men, more like A People.

A CITIZEN.   You don't like anything about this town, do you?

ANOTHER CITIZEN.   Admit it, you're a revolutionist, aren't you? Admit it!

DR. STOCKMANN.   I don't admit it! I proclaim it now! I am a revolutionist! I am
    in revolt against the age-old lie that the majority is always right!

HOVSTAD.   He's an aristocrat all of a sudden!

DR. STOCKMANN.   And more! I tell you now that the majority is always wrong,
    and in this way!

PETER STOCKMANN.   Have you lost your mind! Stop talking before—

DR. STOCKMANN.   Was the majority right when they stood by while Jesus was
    crucified? *(Silence.)* Was the majority right when they refused to believe that
    the earth moved around the sun and let Galileo be driven to his knees like a
    dog? It takes fifty years for the majority to be right. The majority is never right
    until it *does* right.

HOVSTAD.   I want to state right now, that although I've been this man's friend,
    and I've eaten at his table many times, I now cut myself off from him abso-
    lutely.

DR. STOCKMANN.   Answer me this! Please, one more moment! A platoon of sol-
    diers is walking down a road toward the enemy. Every one of them is con-
    vinced he is on the right road, the safe road. But two miles ahead stands one
    lonely man, the outpost. He sees that this road is dangerous, that his comrades
    are walking into a trap. He runs back, he finds the platoon. Isn't it clear that
    this man must have the right to warn the majority, to argue with the majority,
    to fight with the majority if he believes he has the truth? Before many can know
    something, *one* must know it! *(His passion has silenced the crowd.)* It's always
    the same. Rights are sacred until it hurts for somebody to use them. I beg you
    now—I realize the cost is great, the inconvenience is great, the risk is great
    that other towns will get the jump on us while we're rebuilding—

PETER STOCKMANN.   Aslaksen, he's not allowed to—

DR. STOCKMANN.   Let me prove it to you! The water is poisoned!

THIRD CITIZEN. *(Steps up on the platform, waves his fist in* DR. STOCKMANN's *face.)*
    One more word about poison and I'm gonna take you outside!

(The crowd is roaring; some try to charge the platform. The horn is blowing.
ASLAKSEN *rings his bell.* PETER STOCKMANN *steps forward, raising his hands.* KIIL
quietly exits.)

PETER STOCKMANN.   That's enough. Now stop it! Quiet! There is not going to be
    any violence here! *(There is silence. He turns to* DR. STOCKMANN.*)* Doctor,
    come down and give Mr. Aslaksen the platform.

DR. STOCKMANN *(staring down at the crowd with new eyes).*   I'm not through yet.

PETER STOCKMANN.   Come down or I will not be responsible for what happens.

MRS. STOCKMANN.   I'd like to go home. Come on, Tom.

PETER STOCKMANN.   I move the chairman order the speaker to leave the platform.

VOICES.   Sit down! Get off that platform!

DR. STOCKMANN.   All right. Then I'll take this to out-of-town newspapers until
    the whole country is warned!

PETER STOCKMANN.   You wouldn't dare!

HOVSTAD.   You're trying to ruin this town—that's all; trying to ruin it.

DR. STOCKMANN.   You're trying to build a town on a morality so rotten that it
    will infect the country and the world! If the only way you can prosper is this

murder of freedom and truth, then I say with all my heart, "Let it be destroyed! Let the people perish!"

(He leaves the platform.)

FIRST CITIZEN *(to the* MAYOR*).*   Arrest him! Arrest him!
SECOND CITIZEN.   He's a traitor!

(Cries of "Enemy! Traitor! Revolution!")

ASLAKSEN *(ringing for quiet).*   I would like to submit the following resolution: The people assembled here tonight, decent and patriotic citizens, in defense of their town and their country, declare that Doctor Stockmann, medical officer of Kirsten Springs, is an enemy of the people and of his community.

(An uproar of assent starts.)

MRS. STOCKMANN *(getting up).*   That's not true! He loves this town!
DR. STOCKMANN.   You damned fools, you fools!

(The Doctor and his family are all standing together, at the right, in a close group.)

ASLAKSEN *(shouting over the din).*   Is there anyone against this motion! Anyone against!
HORSTER *(raising his hand).*   I am.
ASLAKSEN.   One? *(He looks around.)*
DRUNK *(who has returned, raising his hand).*   Me too! You can't do without a doctor! Anybody'll . . . tell you . . .
ASLAKSEN.   Anyone else? With all votes against two, this assembly formally declares Doctor Thomas Stockmann to be the people's enemy. In the future, all dealings with him by decent, patriotic citizens will be on that basis. The meeting is adjourned.

(Shouts and applause. People start leaving. DR. STOCKMANN *goes over to* HORSTER.*)*

DR. STOCKMANN.   Captain, do you have room for us on your ship to America?
HORSTER.   Any time you say, Doctor.
DR. STOCKMANN.   Catherine? Petra?

(The three start for the door, but a gantlet has formed, dangerous and silent, except for)

THIRD CITIZEN.   You'd better get aboard soon, Doctor!
MRS. STOCKMANN.   Let's go out the back door.
HORSTER.   Right this way.
DR. STOCKMANN.   No, no. No back doors. *To the crowd:* I don't want to mislead anybody—the enemy of the people is not finished in this town—not quite yet. And if anybody thinks—

The horn blasts, cutting him off. The crowd starts yelling hysterically: "Enemy! Traitor! Throw him in the river! Come on, throw him in the river! Enemy! Enemy!

Enemy!" The STOCKMANNS, *erect, move out through the crowd, with* HORSTER. *Some of the crowd follow them out, yelling.*

Downstage, watching, are PETER STOCKMANN, BILLING, ASLAKSEN, *and* HOVSTAD. *The stage is throbbing with the chant, "Enemy, Enemy, Enemy!" as*

The Curtain Falls.

ACT THREE

Dr. Stockmann's living room the following morning. The windows are broken. There is great disorder. As the curtain rises, DR. STOCKMANN *enters, a robe over shirt and trousers—it's cold in the house. He picks up a stone from the floor, lays it on the table.*

DR. STOCKMANN.   Catherine! Tell what's-her-name there are still some rocks to pick up in here.

MRS. STOCKMANN *(from inside).*   She's not finished sweeping up the glass.

(As DR. STOCKMANN *bends down to get at another stone under a chair a rock comes through one of the last remaining panes. He rushes to the window, looks out.* MRS. STOCKMANN *rushes in.)*

MRS. STOCKMANN *(frightened).*   You all right?

DR. STOCKMANN *(looking out).*   A little boy. Look at him run! *(He picks up the stone.)* How fast the poison spreads—even to the children!

MRS. STOCKMANN *(looking out the window).*   It's hard to believe this is the same town.

DR. STOCKMANN *(adding this rock to the pile on the table).*   I'm going to keep these like sacred relics. I'll put them in my will. I want the boys to have them in their homes to look at every day. *(He shudders.)* Cold in here. Why hasn't what's-her-name got the glazier here?

MRS. STOCKMANN.   She's getting him . . .

DR. STOCKMANN.   She's been getting him for two hours! We'll freeze to death in here.

MRS. STOCKMANN *(unwillingly).*   He won't come here, Tom.

DR. STOCKMANN *(stops moving).*   No! The glazier's afraid to fix my windows?

MRS. STOCKMANN.   You don't realize—people don't like to be pointed out. He's got neighbors, I suppose, and— *(She hears something.)* Is that someone at the door, Randine?

(She goes to front door. He continues picking up stones. She comes back.)

MRS. STOCKMANN.   Letter for you.

DR. STOCKMANN *(taking and opening it).*   What's this now?

MRS. STOCKMANN *(continuing his pick-up for him).*   I don't know how we're going to do any shopping with everybody ready to bite my head off and—

DR. STOCKMANN.   Well, what do you know? We're evicted.

MRS. STOCKMANN.   Oh, no!

DR. STOCKMANN.   He hates to do it, but with public opinion what it is . . .

MRS. STOCKMANN *(frightened).*   Maybe we shouldn't have let the boys go to school today.

DR. STOCKMANN.   Now don't get all frazzled again.

MRS. STOCKMANN.   But the landlord is such a nice man. If he's got to throw us out, the town must be ready to murder us!

DR. STOCKMANN.   Just calm down, will you? We'll go to America, and the whole thing'll be like a dream.

MRS. STOCKMANN.   But I don't want to go to America—*(She notices his pants.)* When did this get torn?

DR. STOCKMANN *(examining the tear).*   Must've been last night.

MRS. STOCKMANN.   Your best pants!

DR. STOCKMANN.   Well, it just shows you, that's all—when a man goes out to fight for the truth he should never wear his best pants. *(He calms her.)* Stop worrying, will you? You'll sew them up, and in no time at all we'll be three thousand miles away.

MRS. STOCKMANN.   But how do you know it'll be any different there?

DR. STOCKMANN.   I don't know. It just seems to me, in a big country like that, the spirit must be bigger. Still, I suppose they must have the solid majority there too. I don't know, at least there must be more room to hide there.

MRS. STOCKMANN.   Think about it more, will you? I'd hate to go half around the world and find out we're in the same place.

DR. STOCKMANN.   You know, Catherine, I don't think I'm ever going to forget the face of that crowd last night.

MRS. STOCKMANN.   Don't think about it.

DR. STOCKMANN.   Some of them had their teeth bared, like animals in a pack. And who leads them? Men who call themselves liberals! Radicals! *(She starts looking around at the furniture, figuring.)* The crowd lets out one roar, and where are they, my liberal friends? I bet if I walked down the street now not one of them would admit he ever met me! Are you listening to me?

MRS. STOCKMANN.   I was just wondering what we'll ever do with this furniture if we go to America.

DR. STOCKMANN.   Don't you ever listen when I talk, dear?

MRS. STOCKMANN.   Why must I listen? I know you're right.

(PETRA *enters.*)

MRS. STOCKMANN.   Petra! Why aren't you in school?

DR. STOCKMANN.   What's the matter?

PETRA *(with deep emotion, looks at Dr. Stockmann, goes up and kisses him).*   I'm fired.

MRS. STOCKMANN.   They wouldn't!

PETRA.   As of two weeks from now. But I couldn't bear to stay there.

DR. STOCKMANN *(shocked).*   Mrs. Busk fired you?

MRS. STOCKMANN.   Who'd ever imagine she could do such a thing!

PETRA.   It hurt her. I could see it, because we've always agreed so about things. But she didn't dare do anything else.

DR. STOCKMANN.   The glazier doesn't dare fix the windows, the landlord doesn't dare let us stay on—

PETRA.   The landlord!

DR. STOCKMANN.   Evicted, darling! Oh, God, on the wreckage of all the civilizations in the world there ought to be a big sign: "They Didn't Dare!"

PETRA.   I really can't blame her, Father. She showed me three letters she got this morning—

DR. STOCKMANN.   From whom?

PETRA.   They weren't signed.

DR. STOCKMANN.   Oh, naturally. The big patriots with their anonymous indignation, scrawling out the darkness of their minds onto dirty little slips of paper —that's morality, and *I'm* the traitor! What did the letters say?

PETRA.   Well, one of them was from somebody who said that he'd heard at the club that somebody who visits this house said that I had radical opinions about certain things.

DR. STOCKMANN.   Oh, wonderful! Somebody heard that somebody heard that she heard, that he heard . . . ! Catherine, pack as soon as you can. I feel as though vermin were crawling all over me.

(HORSTER *enters.*)

HORSTER.   Good morning.

DR. STOCKMANN.   Captain! You're just the man I want to see.

HORSTER.   I thought I'd see how you all were.

MRS. STOCKMANN.   That's awfully nice of you, Captain, and I want to thank you for seeing us through the crowd last night.

PETRA.   Did you get home all right? We hated to leave you alone with that mob.

HORSTER.   Oh, nothing to it. In a storm there's just one thing to remember: it will pass.

DR. STOCKMANN.   Unless it kills you.

HORSTER.   You mustn't let yourself get too bitter.

DR. STOCKMANN.   I'm trying, I'm trying. But I don't guarantee how I'll feel when I try to walk down the street with "Traitor" branded on my forehead.

MRS. STOCKMANN.   Don't think about it.

HORSTER.   Ah, what's a word?

DR. STOCKMANN.   A word can be like a needle sticking in your heart, Captain. It can dig and corrode like an acid, until you become what they want you to be—really an enemy of the people.

HORSTER.   You mustn't ever let that happen, Doctor.

DR. STOCKMANN.   Frankly, I don't give a damn any more. Let summer come, let an epidemic break out, then they'll know whom they drove into exile. When are you sailing?

PETRA.   You really decided to go, Father?

DR. STOCKMANN.   Absolutely. When do you sail, Captain?

HORSTER.   That's really what I came to talk to you about.

DR. STOCKMANN.   Why? Something happen to the ship?

MRS. STOCKMANN (*happily, to* DR. STOCKMANN).   You see! We can't go!

HORSTER.   No, the ship will sail. But I won't be aboard.

DR. STOCKMANN.   No!

PETRA.   You fired too? 'Cause I was this morning.

MRS. STOCKMANN.   Oh, Captain, you shouldn't have given us your house.

HORSTER.   Oh, I'll get another ship. It's just that the owner, Mr. Vik, happens to belong to the same party as the Mayor, and I suppose when you belong to a party, and the party takes a certain position . . . Because Mr. Vik himself is a very decent man.

DR. STOCKMANN.   Oh, they're all decent men!

HORSTER.   No, really, he's not like the others.

DR. STOCKMANN.   He doesn't have to be. A party is like a sausage grinder: it mashes up clearheads, longheads, fatheads, blockheads—and what comes out? Meatheads!

(There is a knock on the hall door. PETRA *goes to answer.)*

MRS. STOCKMANN.   Maybe that's the glazier!

DR. STOCKMANN.   Imagine, Captain! *(He points to the window.)* Refused to come all morning!

*(*PETER STOCKMANN *enters, his hat in his hand. Silence.)*

PETER STOCKMANN.   If you're busy . . .

DR. STOCKMANN.   Just picking up broken glass. Come in, Peter. What can I do for you this fine, brisk morning? *(He demonstratively pulls his robe tighter around his throat.)*

MRS. STOCKMANN.   Come inside, won't you, Captain?

HORSTER.   Yes, I'd like to finish our talk, Doctor.

DR. STOCKMANN.   Be with you in a minute, Captain.

*(*HORSTER *follows* PETRA *and* CATHERINE *out through the dining-room doorway.* PETER STOCKMANN *says nothing, looking at the damage.)*

DR. STOCKMANN.   Keep your hat on if you like, it's a little drafty in here today.

PETER STOCKMANN.   Thanks, I believe I will. *(He puts his hat on.)* I think I caught cold last night—that house was freezing.

DR. STOCKMANN.   I thought it was kind of warm—suffocating, as a matter of fact. What do you want?

PETER STOCKMANN.   May I sit down? *(He indicates a chair near the window.)*

DR. STOCKMANN.   Not there. A piece of the solid majority is liable to open your skull. Here.

(They sit on the couch. PETER STOCKMANN *takes out a large envelope.)*

DR. STOCKMANN.   Now don't tell me.

PETER STOCKMANN.   Yes. *(He hands the Doctor the envelope.)*

DR. STOCKMANN.   I'm fired.

PETER STOCKMANN.   The Board met this morning. There was nothing else to do, considering the state of public opinion.

DR. STOCKMANN *(after a pause).*   You look scared, Peter.

PETER STOCKMANN.   I—I haven't completely forgotten that you're still my brother.

DR. STOCKMANN.   I doubt that.

PETER STOCKMANN.   You have no practice left in this town, Thomas.

DR. STOCKMANN.   Oh, people always need a doctor.

PETER STOCKMANN.   A petition is going from house to house. Everybody is signing it. A pledge not to call you any more. I don't think a single family will dare refuse to sign it.

DR. STOCKMANN.   You started that, didn't you?

PETER STOCKMANN.   No. As a matter of fact, I think it's all gone a little too far. I never wanted to see you ruined, Thomas. This will ruin you.

DR. STOCKMANN.   No, it won't.

PETER STOCKMANN.   For once in your life, will you act like a responsible man?

DR. STOCKMANN.   Why don't you say it, Peter? You're afraid I'm going out of town to start publishing about the springs, aren't you?

PETER STOCKMANN.   I don't deny that. Thomas, if you really have the good of the town at heart, you can accomplish everything without damaging anybody, including yourself.

DR. STOCKMANN.   What's this now?

PETER STOCKMANN.   Let me have a signed statement saying that in your zeal to help the town you went overboard and exaggerated. Put it any way you like, just so you calm anybody who might feel nervous about the water. If you'll give me that, you've got your job. And I give you my word, you can gradually make all the improvements you feel are necessary. Now, that gives you what you want . . .

DR. STOCKMANN.   You're nervous, Peter.

PETER STOCKMANN (*nervously*).   I am not nervous!

DR. STOCKMANN.   You expect me to remain in charge while people are being poisoned? (*He gets up.*)

PETER STOCKMANN.   In time you can make your changes.

DR. STOCKMANN.   When, five years, ten years? You know your trouble, Peter? You just don't grasp—even now—that there are certain men you can't buy.

PETER STOCKMANN.   I'm quite capable of understanding that. But you don't happen to be one of those men.

DR. STOCKMANN (*after a slight pause*).   What do you mean by that now?

PETER STOCKMANN.   You know damned well what I mean by that. Morten Kiil is what I mean by that.

DR. STOCKMANN.   Morten Kiil?

PETER STOCKMANN.   Your father-in-law, Morten Kiil.

DR. STOCKMANN.   I swear, Peter, one of us is out of his mind! What are you talking about?

PETER STOCKMANN.   Now don't try to charm me with that professional innocence!

DR. STOCKMANN.   What are you talking about?

PETER STOCKMANN.   You don't know that your father-in-law has been running around all morning buying up stock in Kirsten Springs?

DR. STOCKMANN (*perplexed*).   Buying up stock?

PETER STOCKMANN.   Buying up stock, every share he can lay his hands on!

DR. STOCKMANN.   Well, I don't understand, Peter. What's that got to do with—

PETER STOCKMANN *(walking around agitatedly).*   Oh, come now, come now, come now!

DR. STOCKMANN.   I hate you when you do that! Don't just walk around gabbling "Come now, come now!" What the hell are you talking about?

PETER STOCKMANN.   Very well, if you insist on being dense. A man wages a relentless campaign to destroy confidence in a corporation. He even goes so far as to call a mass meeting against it. The very next morning, when people are still in a state of shock about it all, his father-in-law runs all over town, picking up shares at half their value.

DR. STOCKMANN *(realizing, turns away).*   My God!

PETER STOCKMANN.   And you have the nerve to speak to me about principles!

DR. STOCKMANN.   You mean you actually believe that I . . . ?

PETER STOCKMANN.   I'm not interested in psychology! I believe what I see! And what I see is nothing but a man doing a dirty, filthy job for Morten Kiil. And let me tell you—by tonight every man in this town'll see the same thing!

DR. STOCKMANN.   Peter, you, you . . .

PETER STOCKMANN.   Now go to your desk and write me a statement denying everything you've been saying, or . . .

DR. STOCKMANN.   Peter, you're a low creature!

PETER STOCKMANN.   All right then, you'd better get this one straight, Thomas. If you're figuring on opening another attack from out of town, keep this in mind: the morning it's published I'll send out a subpoena for you and begin a prosecution for conspiracy. I've been trying to make you respectable all my life; now if you want to make the big jump there'll be nobody there to hold you back. Now do we understand each other?

DR. STOCKMANN.   Oh, we do, Peter! *(PETER STOCKMANN starts for the door.)* Get the girl—what the hell is her name—scrub the floors, wash down the walls, a pestilence has been here!

(KIIL enters. PETER STOCKMANN almost runs into him. PETER turns to his brother.)

PETER STOCKMANN *(pointing to KIIL).*   Ha! *(He turns and goes out.)*

(KIIL, humming quietly, goes to a chair.)

DR. STOCKMANN.   Morten! What have you done? What's the matter with you? Do you realize what this makes me look like?

(KIIL has started taking some papers out of his pocket. DR. STOCKMANN breaks off on seeing them. KIIL places them on the table.)

DR. STOCKMANN.   Is that—them?

KIIL.   That's them, yes. Kirsten Springs shares. And very easy to get this morning.

DR. STOCKMANN.   Morten, don't play with me—what is this all about?

KIIL.   What are you so nervous about? Can't a man buy some stock without . . . ?

DR. STOCKMANN.   I want an explanation, Morten.

KIIL *(nodding).*   Thomas, they hated you last night—

DR. STOCKMANN.   You don't have to tell me that.

KIIL.   But they also believed you. They'd love to murder you, but they believe you. *(Slight pause.)* The way they say it, the pollution is coming down the river from Windmill Valley.

DR. STOCKMANN.   That's exactly where it's coming from.

KIIL.   Yes. And that's exactly where my tannery is.

(Pause. DR. STOCKMANN *sits down slowly.)*

DR. STOCKMANN.   Well, Morten, I never made a secret to you that the pollution was tannery waste.

KIIL.   I'm not blaming you. It's my fault. I didn't take you seriously. But it's very serious now. Thomas, I got that tannery from my father; he got it from his father; and his father got it from my great-grandfather. I do not intend to allow my family's name to stand for the three generations of murdering angels who poisoned this town.

DR. STOCKMANN.   I've waited a long time for this talk, Morten. I don't think you can stop that from happening.

KIIL.   No, but you can.

DR. STOCKMANN.   I?

KIIL *(nudging the shares).*   I've bought these shares because—

DR. STOCKMANN.   Morten, you've thrown your money away. The springs are doomed.

KIIL.   I never throw my money away, Thomas. These were bought with your money.

DR. STOCKMANN.   My money? What . . . ?

KIIL.   You've probably suspected that I might leave a little something for Catherine and the boys?

DR. STOCKMANN.   Well, naturally, I'd hoped you'd . . .

KIIL *(touching the shares).*   I decided this morning to invest that money in some stock.

DR. STOCKMANN *(slowly getting up).*   You bought that junk with Catherine's money!

KIIL.   People call me "badger," and that's an animal that roots out things, but it's also some kind of a pig, I understand. I've lived a clean man and I'm going to die clean. You're going to clean my name for me.

DR. STOCKMANN.   Morten . . .

KIIL.   Now I want to see if you really belong in a strait jacket.

DR. STOCKMANN.   How could you do such a thing? What's the matter with you!

KIIL.   Now don't get excited, it's very simple. If you should make another investigation of the water—

DR. STOCKMANN.   I don't *need* another investigation, I—

KIIL.   If you think it over and decide that you ought to change your opinion about the water—

DR. STOCKMANN.   But the water is poisoned! It is poisoned!

KIIL.   If you simply go on insisting the water is poisoned—*(he holds up the shares)* —with these in your house, then there's only one explanation for you—you're absolutely crazy. *(He puts the shares down on the table again.)*

DR. STOCKMANN.   You're right! I'm mad! I'm insane!

KIIL *(with more force).*   You're stripping the skin off your family's back! Only a madman would do a thing like that!

DR. STOCKMANN.   Morten, Morten, I'm a penniless man! Why didn't you tell me before you bought this junk?

KIIL.   Because you would understand it better if I told you after. *(He goes up to* DR. STOCKMANN, *holds him by the lapels. With terrific force, and the twinkle still in his eye)* And, goddammit, I think you do understand it now, don't you? Millions of tons of water come down that river. How do you know the day you made your tests there wasn't something unusual about the water?

DR. STOCKMANN *(not looking at* KIIL).   Yes, but I . . .

KIIL.   How do you know? Why couldn't those little animals have clotted up only the patch of water you souped out of the river? How do you know the rest of it wasn't pure?

DR. STOCKMANN.   It's not probable. People were getting sick last summer . . .

KIIL.   They were sick when they came here or they wouldn't have come!

DR. STOCKMANN *(breaking away).*   Not intestinal diseases, skin diseases . . .

KIIL *(following him).*   The only place anybody gets a bellyache is here! There are no carbuncles in Norway? Maybe the food was bad. Did you ever think of the food?

DR. STOCKMANN *(with the desire to agree with him).*   No, I didn't look into the food . . .

KIIL.   Then what makes you so sure it's the water?

DR. STOCKMANN.   Because I tested the water and—

KIIL *(taking hold of him again).*   Admit it! We're all alone here. You have some doubt.

DR. STOCKMANN.   Well, there's always a possible . . .

KIIL.   Then part of it's imaginary.

DR. STOCKMANN.   Well, nothing is a hundred per cent on this earth, but—

KIIL.   Then you have a perfect right to doubt the other way! You have a scientific right! And did you ever think of some disinfectant? I bet you never even thought of that.

DR. STOCKMANN.   Not for a mass of water like that, you can't . . .

KIIL.   Everything can be killed. That's science! Thomas, I never liked your brother either, you have a perfect right to hate him.

DR. STOCKMANN.   I didn't do it because I hate my brother.

KIIL.   Part of it, part of it, don't deny it! You admit there's some doubt in your mind about the water, you admit there may be ways to disinfect it, and yet you went after your brother as though these doubts didn't exist; as though the only way to cure the thing was to blow up the whole Institute! There's hatred in that, boy, don't forget it. *(He points to the shares.)* These can belong to you now, so be sure, be sure! Tear the hatred out of your heart, stand naked in front of yourself—*are you sure?*

DR. STOCKMANN.   What right have you to gamble my family's future on the strength of my convictions?

KIIL.   Aha! Then the convictions are not really that strong!

DR. STOCKMANN.   I am ready to hang for my convictions! But no man has a right to make martyrs of others; my family is innocent. Sell back those shares, give her what belongs to her. I'm a penniless man!

KIIL.   Nobody is going to say Morten Kiil wrecked this town. *(He gathers up the shares.)* You retract your convictions—or these go to my charity.

DR. STOCKMANN.   Everything?

KIIL.   There'll be a little something for Catherine, but not much. I want my good name. It's exceedingly important to me.

DR. STOCKMANN *(bitterly).*   And charity . . .

KIIL.   Charity will do it, or you will do it. It's a serious thing to destroy a town.

DR. STOCKMANN.   Morten, when I look at you, I swear to God I see the devil!

(The door opens, and before we see who is there . . .)

DR. STOCKMANN.   You!

(ASLAKSEN enters, holding up his hand defensively.)

ASLAKSEN.   Now don't get excited! Please!

(HOVSTAD enters. He and ASLAKSEN stop short and smile on seeing KIIL.)

KIIL.   Too many intellectuals here: I'd better go.

ASLAKSEN *(apologetically).*   Doctor, can we have five minutes of—

DR. STOCKMANN.   I've got nothing to say to you.

KIIL *(going to the door).*   I want an answer right away. You hear? I'm waiting. *(He leaves.)*

DR. STOCKMANN.   All right, say it quick, what do you want?

HOVSTAD.   We don't expect you to forgive our attitude at the meeting, but . . .

DR. STOCKMANN *(groping for the word).*   Your attitude was prone . . . prostrated . . . prostituted!

HOVSTAD.   All right, call it whatever you—

DR. STOCKMANN.   I've got a lot on my mind, so get to the point. What do you want?

ASLAKSEN.   Doctor, you should have told us what was in back of it all. You could have had the *Messenger* behind you all the way.

HOVSTAD.   You'd have had public opinion with you now. Why didn't you tell us?

DR. STOCKMANN.   Look, I'm very tired, let's not beat around the bush!

HOVSTAD *(gesturing toward the door where KIIL went out).*   He's been all over town buying up stock in the springs. It's no secret any more.

DR. STOCKMANN *(after a slight pause).*   Well, what about it?

HOVSTAD *(in a friendly way).*   You don't want me to spell it out, do you?

DR. STOCKMANN.   I certainly wish you would. I—

HOVSTAD.   All right, let's lay it on the table. Aslaksen, you want to . . . ?

ASLAKSEN.   No, no, go ahead.

HOVSTAD.   Doctor, in the beginning we supported you. But it quickly became clear that if we kept on supporting you in the face of public hysteria—

DR. STOCKMANN.   Your paper created the hysteria.

HOVSTAD.   One thing at a time, all right? *(Slowly, to drive it into Dr. Stockmann's head)* We couldn't go on supporting you because, in simple language, we didn't have the money to withstand the loss in circulation. You're boycotted now? Well, the paper would have been boycotted too, if we'd stuck with you.

ASLAKSEN.   You can see that, Doctor.

DR. STOCKMANN.   Oh, yes. But what do you want?

HOVSTAD.   *The People's Messenger* can put on such a campaign that in two months you will be hailed as a hero in this town.

ASLAKSEN.   We're ready to go.

HOVSTAD.   We will prove to the public that you had to buy up the stock because the management would not make the changes required for public health. In other words, you did it for absolutely scientific, public-spirited reasons. Now what do you say, Doctor?

DR. STOCKMANN.   You want money from me, is that it?

ASLAKSEN.   Well, now, Doctor . . .

HOVSTAD *(to* ASLAKSEN*)*.   No, don't walk around it. *(To Dr. Stockmann)* If we started to support you again, Doctor, we'd lose circulation for a while. We'd like you—or Mr. Kiil rather—to make up the deficit. *(Quickly)* Now that's open and above-board, and I don't see anything wrong with it. Do you?

(Pause. DR. STOCKMANN *looks at him, then turns and walks to the windows, deep in thought.)*

ASLAKSEN.   Remember, Doctor, you need the paper, you need it desperately.

DR. STOCKMANN *(returning)*.   No, there's nothing wrong with it at all. I—I'm not at all averse to cleaning up my name—although for myself it never was dirty. But I don't *enjoy* being hated, if you know what I mean.

ASLAKSEN.   Exactly.

HOVSTAD.   Aslaksen, will you show him the budget . . .

*(*ASLAKSEN *reaches into his pocket.)*

DR. STOCKMANN.   Just a minute. There is one point. I hate to keep repeating the same thing, but the water is poisoned.

HOVSTAD.   Now, Doctor . . .

DR. STOCKMANN.   Just a minute. The Mayor says that he will levy a tax on everybody to pay for the reconstruction. I assume you are ready to support that tax at the same time you're supporting me.

ASLAKSEN.   That tax would be extremely unpopular.

HOVSTAD.   Doctor, with you back in charge of the baths, I have absolutely no fear that anything can go wrong.

DR. STOCKMANN.   In other words, you will clean up my name—so that I can be in charge of the corruption.

HOVSTAD.   But we can't tackle everything at once. A new tax—there'd be an uproar!

ASLAKSEN.   It would ruin the paper!

DR. STOCKMANN.   Then you don't intend to do anything about the water?

HOVSTAD.   We have faith you won't let anyone get sick.

DR. STOCKMANN.   In other words, gentlemen, you are looking for someone to blackmail into paying your printing bill.

HOVSTAD (*indignantly*).   We are trying to clear your name, Doctor Stockmann! And if you refuse to cooperate, if that's going to be your attitude . . .

DR. STOCKMANN.   Yes? Go on. What will you do?

HOVSTAD (*to* ASLAKSEN).   I think we'd better go.

DR. STOCKMANN (*stepping in their way*).   What will you do? I would like you to tell me. Me, the man two minutes ago you were going to make into a hero— what will you do now that I won't pay you?

ASLAKSEN.   Doctor, the public is almost hysterical . . .

DR. STOCKMANN.   To my face, tell me what you are going to do!

HOVSTAD.   The Mayor will prosecute you for conspiracy to destroy a corporation, and without a paper behind you, you will end up in prison.

DR. STOCKMANN.   And you'll support him, won't you? I want it from your mouth, Hovstad. This little victory you will not deny me. (HOVSTAD *starts for the door.* DR. STOCKMANN *steps into his way.*) Tell the hero, Hovstad. You're going to go on crucifying the hero, are you not? Say it to me! You will not leave here until I get this from your mouth!

HOVSTAD (*looking directly at* DR. STOCKMANN).   You are a madman. You are insane with egotism. And don't excuse it with humanitarian slogans, because a man who'll drag his family through a lifetime of disgrace is a demon in his heart! (*He advances on* DR. STOCKMANN.) You hear me? A demon who cares more for the purity of a public bath than the lives of his wife and children. Doctor Stockmann, you deserve everything you're going to get!

(DR. STOCKMANN *is struck by Hovstad's ferocious conviction.* ASLAKSEN *comes toward him, taking the budget out of his pocket.*)

ASLAKSEN (*nervously*).   Doctor, please consider it. It won't take much money, and in two months' time I promise you your whole life will change and . . .

(*Offstage* MRS. STOCKMANN *is heard calling in a frightened voice,* "What happened? My God, what's the matter?" *She runs to the front door.* DR. STOCKMANN, *alarmed, goes quickly to the hallway.* EJLIF *and* MORTEN *enter. Morten's head is bruised.* PETRA *and* CAPTAIN HORSTER *enter from the left.*)

MRS. STOCKMANN.   Something happened! Look at him!

MORTEN.   I'm all right, they just . . .

DR. STOCKMANN (*looking at the bruise*).   What happened here?

MORTEN.   Nothing, Papa, I swear . . .

DR. STOCKMANN (*to* EJLIF).   What happened? Why aren't you in school?

EJLIF.   The teacher said we better stay home the rest of the week.

DR. STOCKMANN.   The boys hit him?

EJLIF.   They started calling you names, so he got sore and began to fight with one kid, and all of a sudden the whole bunch of them . . .

MRS. STOCKMANN (*to* MORTEN).   Why did you answer!

MORTEN (*indignantly*).   They called him a traitor! My father is no traitor!

EJLIF.   But you didn't have to answer!

MRS. STOCKMANN.   You should've known they'd all jump on you! They could have killed you!

MORTEN.   I don't care!

DR. STOCKMANN *(to quiet him—and his own heart).*   Morten . . .

MORTEN *(pulling away from his father).*   I'll kill them! I'll take a rock and the next time I see one of them I'll kill him!

(DR. STOCKMANN reaches for MORTEN, who, thinking his father will chastise him, starts to run. DR. STOCKMANN catches him and grips him by the arm.)

MORTEN.   Let me go! Let me . . . !

DR. STOCKMANN.   Morten . . . Morten . . .

MORTEN *(crying in his father's arms).*   They called you traitor, an enemy . . . *(He sobs.)*

DR. STOCKMANN.   Sssh. That's all. Wash your face.

(MRS. STOCKMANN takes MORTEN. DR. STOCKMANN stands erect, faces ASLAKSEN and HOVSTAD.)

DR. STOCKMANN.   Good day, gentlemen.

HOVSTAD.   Let us know what you decide and we'll—

DR. STOCKMANN.   I've decided. I am an enemy of the people.

MRS. STOCKMANN.   Tom, what are you . . . ?

DR. STOCKMANN.   To such people, who teach their own children to think with their fists—to them I'm an enemy! And my boy . . . my boys . . . my family . . . I think you can count us all enemies.

ASLAKSEN.   Doctor, you could have everything you want!

DR. STOCKMANN.   Except the truth. I could have everything but that—that the water is poisoned!

HOVSTAD.   But you'll be in charge.

DR. STOCKMANN.   But the children are poisoned, the people are poisoned! If the only way I can be a friend of the people is to take charge of that corruption, then I am an enemy! The water is poisoned, poisoned, poisoned! That's the beginning of it and that's the end of it! Now get out of here!

HOVSTAD.   You know where you're going to end?

DR. STOCKMANN.   I said get out of here! *(He grabs ASLAKSEN's umbrella out of his hand.)*

MRS. STOCKMANN.   What are you doing?

(ASLAKSEN and HOVSTAD back toward the door as DR. STOCKMANN starts to swing.)

ASLAKSEN.   You're a fanatic, you're out of your mind!

MRS. STOCKMANN *(grabbing DR. STOCKMANN to take the umbrella).*   What are you doing?

DR. STOCKMANN.   They want me to buy the paper, the public, the pollution of the springs, buy the whole pollution of this town! They'll make a hero out of me for that! *(Furiously, to ASLAKSEN and HOVSTAD)* But I'm not a hero, I'm the enemy—and now you're first going to find out what kind of enemy I am! I will sharpen my pen like a dagger—you, all you friends of the people, are going to bleed before I'm done! Go, tell them to sign the petitions! Warn them not to call me when they're sick! Beat up my children! And never let her *(he points to PETRA)* in the school again or she'll destroy the immaculate purity of the vacuum there! See to all the barricades—the truth is coming! Ring the bells, sound the alarm! The truth, the truth is out, and soon it will be prowling like a lion in the streets!

HOVSTAD.   Doctor, you're out of your mind.

(He and ASLAKSEN *turn to go. They are in the doorway.)*

EJLIF *(rushing at them).*   Don't you say that to him!

DR. STOCKMANN *(as* MRS. STOCKMANN *cries out, rushes them with the umbrella).* Out of here!

(They rush out. DR. STOCKMANN *throws the umbrella after them, then slams the door. Silence. He has his back pressed against the door, facing his family.)*

DR. STOCKMANN.   I've had all the ambassadors of hell today, but there'll be no more. Now, now listen, Catherine! Children, listen. Now we're besieged. They'll call for blood now, they'll whip the people like oxen—*(A rock comes through a remaining pane. The boys start for the window.)* Stay away from there!

MRS. STOCKMANN.   The Captain knows where we can get a ship.

DR. STOCKMANN.   No ships.

PETRA.   We're staying?

MRS. STOCKMANN.   But they can't go back to school! I won't let them out of the house!

DR. STOCKMANN.   We're staying.

PETRA.   Good!

DR. STOCKMANN.   We must be careful now. We must live through this. Boys, no more school. I'm going to teach you, and Petra will. Do you know any kids, street louts, hookey-players—

EJLIF.   Oh, sure, we—

DR. STOCKMANN.   We'll want about twelve of them to start. But I want them good and ignorant, absolutely uncivilized. Can we use your house, Captain?

HORSTER.   Sure, I'm never there.

DR. STOCKMANN.   Fine. We'll begin, Petra, and we'll turn out not taxpayers and newspaper subscribers, but free and independent people, hungry for the truth. Oh, I forgot! Petra, run to Grandpa and and tell him—tell him as follows: NO!

MRS. STOCKMANN *(puzzled).*   What do you mean?

DR. STOCKMANN *(going over to Mrs. Stockmann).*   It means, my dear, that we are all alone. And there'll be a long night before it's day—

(A rock comes through a paneless window. HORSTER *goes to the window. A crowd is heard approaching.)*

HORSTER.   Half the town is out!

MRS. STOCKMANN.   What's going to happen? Tom! What's going to happen?

DR. STOCKMANN *(holding his hands up to quiet her, and with a trembling mixture of trepidation and courageous insistence).*   I don't know. But remember now, everybody. You are fighting for the truth, and that's why you're alone. And that makes you strong. We're the strongest people in the world . . .

(The crowd is heard angrily calling outside. Another rock comes through a window.)

DR. STOCKMANN.   . . . and the strong must learn to be lonely!

The crowd noise gets louder. He walks upstage toward the windows as a wind rises and the curtains start to billow out toward him.

The Curtain Falls.

CITY AND COUNTRY

TOPICS FOR SHORT PAPERS, JOURNALS, OR DISCUSSION

1. In several of the stories and plays in this section, the emphasis is on ecology—relations between living organisms and their environment. Choose examples from some of the stories and poems that seem to you to relate to how we treat our environment, to discuss this topic. Possibilities include "Snake," "Christ in Concrete," or "pity this busy monster,manunkind."

2. In much literature and discussion, the country is portrayed as idyllic and the city as sordid. Choose some of the selections from this section to develop this theme. Can you find, in some of the reading here, any examples that would allow you to refute this premise? If so, expand them into an essay.

3. How do "environments" affect your life, whether you live in the city or the country or in between, in the suburbs? Jot down your thoughts. From your jottings, pick one aspect to discuss in class, or to develop in a short paper.

LONGER PAPERS OR RESEARCH PROJECTS

4. Nature is often made the subject of mythical narrative. In the library, check a dictionary of mythology or one of the standard texts of mythology, legend, and folklore for myths relating to nature. The forces of nature are often personified in these stories in the form of an Earth Mother, Father Time, or the gods of wind, war, and weather. Using stories like "The Grave," "The Chrysanthemums," or "The Unicorn in the Garden," or some scenes from *King Lear,* explain how one of these bio-myths is used to enhance a narrative or underscore a meaning.

5. Human lives are warped or shaped by the environment in which they exist. With direct references, explain how some stories like "Christ in Concrete" and "Everyday Use," or a play like *An Enemy of the People,* or poems like those of Durazo, Simon, or Adamé, illustrate this idea. Relate the concept of the environment as metaphor to courses in sociology or psychology that you have taken, and the principles you learned in them.

6. Today, there is renewed interest in country things and simple artifacts. How do such writings as "Everyday Use," "The Chrysanthemums," "The Grave," and the poems in this section by Robert Frost and Josephine Jacobsen, D. H. Lawrence and Philip Booth parallel or anticipate this interest? You may find other examples in other sections of the book as well. As background material, read some of the *Foxfire* books, student writing collected by Eliot Wigginton, a teacher in the Blue Ridge Mountains, who involved his students in the history and folklore of their region. You might also examine some issues of magazines like *The Old House Journal* and *Antiques.*

CREATIVE PROJECTS.

7. Go to an antique store or auction, choose a piece of furniture, a dish, a quilt, or any other object, and write a story or poem in which the object is of central significance.

8. Using a newspaper story about the environment (such as acid rain, erosion of the ozone layer, effects of strip mining), show how you could treat the subject as a play or story. Outline your treatment as a proposal to send to a magazine.

The Conquest of the Air, 1913, by Roger de La Fresnaye. (The Museum of Modern Art, New York. Mrs. Simon Guggenheim Fund.)

HUMAN RELATIONSHIPS

Western Wind, when wilt thou blow
The small rain down can rain?
Christ, if my love were in my arms
And I in my bed again!

Anonymous

Passion in its many forms provides the center, the turning point, of the series of themes in this book. Who we are, where we live, would be meaningless without the emotions that drive us. Fiction writers have long provided vicarious looks at all kinds of human emotions. The anonymous fifteenth-century author of the epigraph for this section cries out for the comfort of love, a theme echoed by writers of every century. Whether in the form of rock song or Harlequin Romance, the realm of emotions between lovers occupies great popular attention. Not surprisingly, then, writers of every era from the fifth century B.C. to the twentieth century make of that subject a common theme. The stories, plays, and poems collected here emphasize several types of these relationships, beginning with the heartfelt longing of the anonymous author, possibly a Crusader, in "Western Wind."

The section begins with a modern fable by James Thurber, "The Unicorn in the Garden," which endows the battle of the sexes with a humorous twist. The Thurber piece introduces a series of short stories, plays, and poems telling of human passions. These passionate relationships include relationships between husbands and wives, parents and children, lovers, friends, and enemies. Some of these relationships are conventional; others are less so. Some are fruitful; others have failed.

Fierce physical passion mirrors an abrupt thunderstorm in Kate Chopin's "The Storm," while a mother's possessive love for her baby forces her husband and best friend together in Doris Lessing's "A Man and Two Women." Troubled or failed marriages are seen in Ernest Hemingway's "The Short, Happy Life of Francis Macomber," Robert Browning's "My Last Duchess," or Susan Fromberg Schaeffer's short poem, "Housewife." But just as often, a theme of mutual love and respect sounds, as in Anne Bradstreet's "To My Dear and Loving Husband," or in John Donne's "A Valediction Forbidding Mourning." Love poetry has even acquired a traditional association with one special form: the sonnet. (See page 1017 for an ample discussion of this form.) Examples are Elizabeth Barrett Browning's "How Do I Love Thee?" and Louise Labé's "I Live and Die." An unconventional pair of lovers appears in Anne McCaffrey's "The Ship Who Sang": a space-ship "brain" and her human pilot. Troubled relationships appear in works like Adrienene Rich's "Living in Sin," Dorothy Parker's "Chant for Dark Hours," and the ballad "Frankie and Johnny." No less familiar is the racy "time's a-wastin' " or *carpe diem* philosophy of the impetuous lover in Christopher Marlowe's "The Passionate Shepherd to His Love."

Another source of intense human relationships is the bond between parent and child. The strong rendition of parenting in a story such as Juanita Platero and Siyowin Miller's "Chee's Daughter" is violently contrasted by the guilt and regret of Anne Sexton's "The Abortion," or by the compassionate lament of Sylvia Plath's "For a Fatherless Son." Other elements of the tension of love and anger in parent-child relationships emerge in poems such as Susan Griffin's "The Awful Mother" or James Wright's "Mutterings over the Crib of a Deaf Child."

An important element of human relationships is the connection between people who are not allied by bonds of family or even of love. Karl Shapiro's poem "Auto Wreck" uses analogy to depict the failed connections between people, and in "Paul's Case" Willa Cather writes the tragic story of a boy who is driven to suicide because he substitutes fantasies for real human relationships.

Finally, the two plays in this section restate the topic of human relationships in the context of more universal values. Both Sophocles and Bernard Pomerance focus their plays, 2500 years apart, on characters whose relationships with others suffer because of their own human failings, their "tragic flaws." Antigone proudly and fearlessly puts loyalty to gods and family ahead of loyalty to the State and its laws, but her uncle Creon is unbending. Pomerance's John Merrick, hideously deformed, paradoxically represents natural, unspoiled man. The people who surround him, with perhaps one exception, are selfishly motivated, and, in the end, literally crush him. In both *Antigone* and *The Elephant Man,* the protagonists' humanity and nobility in their relationships with others finally become their undoing.

Fiction

THE UNICORN IN THE GARDEN
James Thurber
(1894–1961)

Biography p. 1104

Once upon a sunny morning a man who sat in a breakfast nook looked up from his scrambled eggs to see a white unicorn with a golden horn quietly cropping the roses in the garden. The man went up to the bedroom where his wife was still asleep and woke her. "There's a unicorn in the garden," he said. "Eating roses." She opened one unfriendly eye and looked at him. "The unicorn is a mythical beast," she said, and turned her back on him. The man walked slowly downstairs and out into the garden. The unicorn was still there; he was now browsing among the tulips. "Here, unicorn," said the man, and he pulled up a lily and gave it to him. The unicorn ate it gravely. With a high heart, because there was a unicorn in his garden, the man went upstairs and roused his wife again. "The unicorn," he said, "ate a lily." His wife sat up in bed and looked at him, coldly. "You are a booby," she said, "and I am going to have you put in the booby-hatch," The man, who had never liked the words "booby" and "booby-hatch," and who liked them even less on a shining morning when there was a unicorn in the garden, thought for a moment. "We'll see about that," he said. He walked over to the door. "He has a golden horn in the middle of his forehead," he told her. Then he went back to the garden to watch the unicorn; but the unicorn had gone away. The man sat down among the roses and went to sleep.

As soon as the husband had gone out of the house, the wife got up and dressed as fast as she could. She was very excited and there was a gloat in her eye. She telephoned the police and she telephoned a psychiatrist; she told them to hurry to her house and bring a strait-jacket. When the police and the psychiatrist arrived they sat down in chairs and looked at her, with great interest. "My husband," she said, "saw a unicorn this morning." The police looked at the psychiatrist and the psychiatrist looked at the police. "He told me it ate a lily," she said. The psychiatrist looked at the police and the police looked at the psychiatrist. "He told me it had a golden horn in the middle of its forehead," she said. At a solemn signal from the psychiatrist, the police leaped from their chairs and seized the wife. They had a hard time subduing her, for she put up a terrific struggle, but they finally subdued her. Just as they got her into the strait-jacket, the husband came back into the house.

"Did you tell your wife you saw a unicorn?" asked the police. "Of course not," said the husband. "The unicorn is a mythical beast." "That's all I wanted to know," said the psychiatrist. "Take her away. I'm sorry, sir, but your wife is as crazy as a jay bird." So they took her away, cursing and screaming, and shut her up in an institution. The husband lived happily ever after.

Moral: Don't count your boobies until they are hatched.

THE STORM

Kate Chopin

(1851–1904)

Biography p. 1066

I

The leaves were so still that even Bibi thought it was going to rain. Bobinôt, who was accustomed to converse on terms of perfect equality with his little son, called the child's attention to certain sombre clouds that were rolling with sinister intention from the west, accompanied by a sullen, threatening roar. They were at Friedheimer's store and decided to remain there till the storm had passed. They sat within the door on two empty kegs. Bibi was four years old and looked very wise.

"Mama'll be 'fraid, yes," he suggested with blinking eyes.

"She'll shut the house. Maybe she got Sylvie helpin' her this evenin'," Bobinôt responded reassuringly.

"No; she ent got Sylvie. Sylvie was helpin' her yistiday," piped Bib.

Bobinôt arose and going across to the counter purchased a can of shrimps, of which Calixta was very fond. Then he returned to his perch on the keg and sat stolidly holding the can of shrimps while the storm burst. It shook the wooden store and seemed to be ripping great furrows in the distant field. Bibi laid his little hand on his father's knee and was not afraid.

II

Calixta, at home, felt no uneasiness for their safety. She sat at a side window sewing furiously on a sewing machine. She was greatly occupied and did not notice the approaching storm. But she felt very warm and often stopped to mop her face on which the perspiration gathered in beads. She unfastened her white sacque at the throat. It began to grow dark, and suddenly, realizing the situation she got up hurriedly and went about closing windows and doors.

Out on the small front gallery she had hung Bobinôt's Sunday clothes to air and she hastened out to gather them before the rain fell. As she stepped outside, Alcée Laballière rode in at the gate. She had not seen him very often since her marriage, and never alone. She stood there with Bobinôt's coat in her hands, and the big rain drops began to fall. Alcée rode his horse under the shelter of a side projection where the chickens had huddled and there were plows and a harrow piled up in the corner.

"May I come and wait on your gallery till the storm is over, Calixta?" he asked.

"Come 'long in, M'sieur Alcée."

His voice and her own startled her as if from a trance, and she seized Bobinôt's vest. Alcée, mounting to the porch, grabbed the trousers and snatched Bibi's braided jacket that was about to be carried away by a sudden gust of wind. He expressed an intention to remain outside, but it was soon apparent that he might as well have been out in the open: the water beat in upon the boards in driving sheets, and he went inside, closing the door after him. It was even necessary to put something beneath the door to keep the water out.

"My! what a rain! It's good two years sence it rain' like that," exclaimed Calixta as she rolled up a piece of bagging and Alcée helped her to thrust it beneath the crack.

She was a little fuller of figure than five years before when she married; but she had lost nothing of her vivacity. Her blue eyes still retained their melting quality; and her yellow hair, dishevelled by the wind and rain, kinked more stubbornly than ever about her ears and temples.

The rain beat upon the low, shingled roof with a force and clatter that threatened to break an entrance and deluge them there. They were in the dinning room—the sitting room—the general utility room. Adjoining was her bed room, with Bibi's couch along side her own. The door stood open, and the room with its white, monumental bed, its closed shutters, looked dim and mysterious.

Alcée flung himself into a rocker and Calixta nervously began to gather up from the floor the lengths of a cotton sheet which she had been sewing.

"If this keeps up, *Dieu sait* if the levees goin' to stan' it!" she exclaimed.

"What have you got to do with the levees?"

"I got enough to do! An' there's Bobinôt with Bibi out in that storm—if he only didn' left Friedheimer's!"

"Let us hope, Calixta, that Bobinôt's got sense enough to come in out of a cyclone."

She went and stood at the window with a greatly disturbed look on her face. She wiped the frame that was clouded with moisture. It was stiflingly hot. Alcée got up and joined her at the window, looking over her shoulder. The rain was coming down in sheets obscuring the view of far-off cabins and enveloping the distant wood in a gray mist. The playing of the lightning was incessant. A bolt struck a tall chinaberry tree at the edge of the field. It filled all visible space with a blinding glare and the crash seemed to invade the very boards they stood upon.

Calixta put her hands to her eyes, and with a cry, staggered backward. Alcée's arm encircled her, and for an instant he drew her close and spasmodically to him.

"*Bonté!*" she cried, releasing herself from his encircling arm and retreating from the window, "the house'll go next! If I only knew w'ere Bibi was!" She would not compose herself; she would not be seated. Alcée clasped her shoulders and looked into her face. The contact of her warm, palpitating body when he had unthinkingly drawn her into his arms, had aroused all the old-time infatuation and desire for her flesh.

"Calixta," he said, "don't be frightened. Nothing can happen. The house is too low to be struck, with so many tall trees standing about. There! aren't you going to be quiet? say, aren't you?" He pushed her hair back from her face that was warm and steaming. Her lips were as red and moist as pomegranate seed. Her white neck and a glimpse of her full, firm bosom disturbed him powerfully. As she glanced up at him the fear in her liquid blue eyes had given place to a drowsy gleam that unconsciously betrayed a senuous desire. He looked down into her eyes and there was nothing for him to do but to gather her lips in a kiss. It reminded him of Assumption.

"Do you remember—in Assumption, Calixta?" He asked in a low voice broken by passion. Oh! she remembered; for in Assumption he had kissed her and kissed and kissed her; until his senses would well nigh fail, and to save her he would resort to a desperate flight. If she was not an immaculate dove in those days, she was still inviolate; a passionate creature whose very defenselessness had made her defense, against which his honor forbade him to prevail. Now—well, now—her lips seemed in a manner free to be tasted, as well as her round, white throat and her whiter breasts.

They did not heed the crashing torrents, and the roar of the elements made her laugh as she lay in his arms. She was a revelation in that dim, mysterious chamber; as white as the couch she lay upon. Her firm, elastic flesh that was knowing for the first time its birthright, was like a creamy lily that the sun invites to contribute its breath and perfume to the undying life of the world.

The generous abundance of her passion, without guile or trickery, was like a white flame which penetrated and found response in depths of his own sensuous nature that had never yet been reached.

When he touched her breasts they gave themselves up in quivering ecstasy, inviting his lips. Her mouth was a fountain of delight. And when he possessed her, they seemed to swoon together at the very borderland of life's mystery.

He stayed cushioned upon her, breathless, dazed, enervated, with his heart beating like a hammer upon her. With one hand she clasped his head, her lips lightly touching his forehead. The other hand stroked with a soothing rhythm his muscular shoulders.

The growl of the thunder was distant and passing away. The rain beat softly upon the shingles, inviting them to drowsiness and sleep. But they dared not yield.

The rain was over; and the sun was turning the glistening green world into a palace of gems. Calixta, on the gallery, watched Alcée ride away. He turned and smiled at her with a beaming face; and she lifted her pretty chin in the air and laughed aloud.

III

Bobinôt and Bibi, trudging home, stopped without at the cistern to make themselves presentable.

"My! Bibi, w'at will yo' mama say! You ought to be ashame'. You oughtn' put on those good pants. Look at 'em! an' that mud on yo' collar! How you got that mud on yo' collar, Bibi? I never saw such a boy!" Bibi was the picture of pathetic resignation. Bobinôt was the embodiment of serious solicitude as he strove to remove from his own person and his son's the signs of their tramp over heavy roads and through wet fields. He scraped the mud off Bibi's bare legs and feet with a stick and carefully removed all traces from his heavy brogans. Then, prepared for the worst—the meeting with an over-scrupulous housewife, they entered cautiously at the back door.

Calixta was preparing supper. She had set the table and was dripping coffee at the hearth. She sprang up as they came in.

"Oh, Bobinôt! You back! My! but I was uneasy. W'ere you been during the rain? An' Bibi? he ain't wet? he ain't hurt?" She had clasped Bibi and was kissing him effusively. Bobinôt's explanations and apologies which he had been composing all along the way, died on his lips as Calixta felt him to see if he were dry, and seemed to express nothing but satisfaction at their safe return.

"I brought you some shrimps, Calixta," offered Bobinôt, hauling the can from his ample side pocket and laying it on the table.

"Shrimps! Oh, Bobinôt! you too good fo' anything! and she gave him a smacking kiss on the cheek that resounded. "*J'vous réponds,* we'll have a feas' to night! umph-umph!"

Bobinôt and Bibi began to relax and enjoy themselves, and when the three seated themselves at table they laughed much and so loud that anyone might have heard them as far away as Laballière's.

IV

Alcée Laballière wrote to his wife, Clarisse, that night. It was a loving letter, full of tender solicitude. He told her not to hurry back, but if she and the babies liked it at Biloxi, to stay a month longer. He was getting on nicely; and though he missed them, he was willing to bear the separation a while longer—realizing that their health and pleasure were the first things to be considered.

V

As for Clarisse, she was charmed upon receiving her husband's letter. She and the babies were doing well. The society was agreeable; many of her old friends and acquaintances were at the bay. And the first free breath since her marriage seemed to restore the pleasant liberty of her maiden days. Devoted as she was to her husband, their intimate conjugal life was something which she was more than willing to forego for a while.

So the storm passed and every one was happy.

A MAN AND TWO WOMEN

Doris Lessing

(b. 1919)

Biography p. 1084

Stella's friends the Bradfords had taken a cheap cottage in Essex for the summer, and she was going down to visit them. She wanted to see them, but there was no doubt there was something of a letdown (and for them too) in the English cottage. Last summer Stella had been wandering with her husband around Italy; had seen the English couple at a café table, and found them sympathetic. They all liked each other, and the four went about for some weeks, sharing meals, hotels, trips. Back in London the friendship had not, as might have been expected, fallen off. Then Stella's husband departed abroad, as he often did, and Stella saw Jack and Dorothy by herself. There were a great many people she might have seen, but it was the Bradfords she saw most often, two or three times a week, at their flat or hers. They were at ease with each other. Why were they? Well, for one thing they were all artists—in different ways. Stella designed wallpapers and materials; she had a name for it.

The Bradfords were real artists. He painted, she drew. They had lived mostly out of England in cheap places around the Mediterranean. Both from the North of England, they had met at art school, married at twenty, had taken flight from England, then returned to it, needing it, then off again; and so on, for years, in the rhythm of so many of their kind, needing, hating, loving England. There had been seasons of real poverty, while they lived on *pasta* or bread or rice, and wine and fruit and sunshine, in Majorca, southern Spain, Italy, North Africa.

A French critic had seen Jack's work, and suddenly he was successful. His show in Paris, then one in London, made money; and now he charged in the hundreds where a year or so ago he charged ten or twenty guineas. This had deepened his contempt for the values of the markets. For a while Stella thought that this was the bond between the Bradfords and herself. They were so very much, as she was, of the new generation of artists (and poets and playwrights and novelists) who had one thing in common, a cool derision about the racket. They were so very unlike (they felt) the older generation with their Societies and their Lunches and their salons and their cliques: their atmosphere of connivance with the snobberies of success. Stella, too, had been successful by a fluke. Not that she did not consider herself talented; it was that others as talented were unfêted, and unbought. When she was with the Bradfords and other fellow spirits, they would talk about the racket, using each other as yardsticks or fellow consciences about how much to give in, what to give, how to use without being used, how to enjoy without becoming dependent on enjoyment.

Of course Dorothy Bradford was not able to talk in quite the same way, since she had not yet been "discovered"; she had not "broken through." A few people with discrimination bought her unusual delicate drawings, which had a strength that was hard to understand unless one knew Dorothy herself. But she was not at all, as Jack was, a great success. There was a strain here, in the marriage, nothing much; it was kept in check by their scorn for their arbitrary rewards of "the racket." But it was there, nevertheless.

Stella's husband had said: "Well, I can understand that, it's like me and you— you're creative, whatever that may mean, I'm just a bloody TV journalist." There was no bitterness in this. He was a good journalist, and besides he sometimes got the chance to make a good small film. All the same, there was that between him and Stella, just as there was between Jack and his wife.

After a time Stella saw something else in her kinship with the couple. It was that the Bradfords had a close bond, bred of having spent so many years together in foreign places, dependent on each other because of their poverty. It had been a real love marriage, one could see it by looking at them. It was now. And Stella's marriage was a real marriage. She understood she enjoyed being with the Bradfords because the two couples were equal in this. Both marriages were those of strong, passionate, talented individuals; they shared a battling quality that strengthened them, not weakened them.

The reason why it had taken Stella so long to understand this was that the Bradfords had made her think about her own marriage, which she was beginning to take for granted, sometimes even found exhausting. She had understood, through them, how lucky she was in her husband; how lucky they all were. No marital miseries; nothing of (what they saw so often in friends) one partner in a marriage victim to the other, resenting the other; no claiming of outsiders as sympathisers or allies in an unequal battle.

There had been a plan for these four people to go off again to Italy or Spain, but then Stella's husband departed, and Dorothy got pregnant. So there was the cottage in Essex instead, a bad second choice, but better, they all felt, to deal with a new baby on home ground, at least for the first year. Stella, telephoned by Jack (on Dorothy's particular insistence, he said), offered and received commiserations on its being only Essex and not Majorca or Italy. She also received sympathy because her husband had been expected back this weekend, but had wired to say he wouldn't be back for another month, probably—there was trouble in Venezuela. Stella wasn't really forlorn; she didn't mind living alone, since she was always supported by knowing her man would be back. Besides, if she herself were offered the chance of a month's "trouble" in Venezuela, she wouldn't hesitate, so it wasn't fair . . . fairness characterised their relationship. All the same, it was nice that she could drop down (or up) to the Bradfords, people with whom she could always be herself, neither more nor less.

She left London at midday by train, armed with food unobtainable in Essex: salamis, cheeses, spices, wine. The sun shone, but it wasn't particularly warm. She hoped there would be heating in the cottage, July or not.

The train was empty. The little station seemed stranded in a green nowhere. She got out, cumbered by bags full of food. A porter and a stationmaster examined, then came to succour her. She was a tallish, fair woman, rather ample; her soft hair, drawn back, escaped in tendrils, and she had great helpless-looking blue eyes. She wore a dress made in one of the materials she had designed. Enormous green leaves laid hands all over her body, and fluttered about her knees. She stood smiling, accustomed to men running to wait on her, enjoying them enjoying her. She walked with them to the barrier where Jack waited, appreciating the scene. He was a smallish man, compact, dark. He wore a blue-green summer shirt, and smoked a pipe and smiled, watching. The two men delivered her into the hands of the third, and departed, whistling, to their duties.

Jack and Stella kissed, then pressed their cheeks together.

"Food," he said, "food," relieving her of the parcels.

"What's it like here, shopping?"

"Vegetables all right, I suppose."

Jack was still Northern in this: he seemed brusque, to strangers; he wasn't shy, he simply hadn't been brought up to enjoy words. Now he put his arm briefly around Stella's waist, and said: "Marvellous, Stell, marvellous." They walked on, pleased with each other. Stella had with Jack, her husband had with Dorothy, these moments, when they said to each other wordlessly: If I were not married to my husband, if you were not married to your wife, how delightful it would be to be married to you. These moments were not the least of the pleasures of this four-sided friendship.

"Are you liking it down here?"

"It's what we bargained for."

There was more than his usual shortness in this, and she glanced at him to find him frowning. They were walking to the car, parked under a tree.

"How's the baby?"

"Little bleeder never sleeps, he's wearing us out, but he's fine."

The baby was six weeks old. Having the baby was a definite achievement: getting it safely conceived and born had taken a couple of years. Dorothy, like most independent women, had had divided thoughts about a baby. Besides, she was over thirty and complained she was set in her ways. All this—the difficulties, Dorothy's hesitations—had added up to an atmosphere which Dorothy herself described as "like wondering if some damned horse is going to take the fence." Dorothy would talk, while she was pregnant, in a soft staccato voice: "Perhaps I don't really want a baby at all? Perhaps I'm not fitted to be a mother? Perhaps . . . and if so . . . and how . . . ?"

She said: "Until recently Jack and I were always with people who took it for granted that getting pregnant was a disaster, and now suddenly all the people we know have young children and baby-sitters and . . . perhaps . . . if . . ."

Jack said: "You'll feel better when it's born."

Once Stella had heard him say, after one of Dorothy's long troubled dialogues with herself: "Now that's enough, that's enough, Dorothy." He had silenced her, taking the responsibility.

They reached the car, got in. It was a second-hand job recently bought. "They" (being the press, the enemy generally) "wait for us" (being artists or writers who have made money) "to buy flashy cars." They had discussed it, decided that *not* to buy an expensive car if they felt like it would be allowing themselves to be bullied, but bought a second-hand one after all. Jack wasn't going to give *them* so much satisfaction, apparently.

"Actually we could have walked," he said, as they shot down a narrow lane, "but with these groceries, it's just as well."

"If the baby's giving you a tough time, there can't be much time for cooking." Dorothy was a wonderful cook. But now again there was something in the air as he said: "Food's definitely not too good just now. You can cook supper, Stell, we could do with a good feed."

Now Dorothy hated anyone in her kitchen, except, for certain specified jobs, her husband; and this was surprising.

"The truth is, Dorothy's worn out," he went on, and now Stella understood he was warning her.

"Well, it is tiring," said Stella soothingly.

"You were like that?"

Like that was saying a good deal more than just worn out, or tired, and Stella understood that Jack was really uneasy. She said, plaintively humorous: "You two always expect me to remember things that happened a hundred years ago. Let me think. . . ."

She had been married when she was eighteen, got pregnant at once. Her husband had left her. Soon she had married Philip, who also had a small child from a former marriage. These two children, her daughter, seventeen, his son, twenty, had grown up together.

She remembered herself at nineteen, alone, with a small baby. "Well, I was alone," she said. "That makes a difference. I remember I was exhausted. Yes, I was definitely irritable and unreasonable."

"Yes," said Jack, with a brief reluctant look at her.

"All right, don't worry," she said, replying aloud as she often did to things that Jack had not said aloud.

"Good," he said.

Stella thought of how she had seen Dorothy, in the hospital room, with the new baby. She had sat up in bed, in a pretty bed jacket, the baby beside her in a basket. He was restless. Jack stood between basket and bed, one large hand on his son's stomach. "Now, you just shut up, little bleeder," he had said, as he grumbled. Then he had picked him up, as if he'd been doing it always, held him against his shoulder, and, as Dorothy held her arms out, had put the baby into them. "Want your mother, then? Don't blame you."

That scene, the case of it, the way the two parents were together, had, for Stella, made nonsense of all the months of Dorothy's self-questioning. As for Dorothy, she had said, parodying the expected words but meaning them: "He's the most beautiful baby ever born. I can't imagine why I didn't have him before."

"There's the cottage," said Jack. Ahead of them was a small labourer's cottage, among full green trees, surrounded by green grass. It was painted white, had four sparkling windows. Next to it a long shed or structure that turned out to be a greenhouse.

"The man grew tomatoes," said Jack. "Fine studio now."

The car came to rest under another tree.

"Can I just drop in to the studio?"

"Help yourself." Stella walked into the long, glass-roofed shed. In London Jack and Dorothy shared a studio. They had shared huts, sheds, any suitable building, all around the Mediterranean. They always worked side by side. Dorothy's end was tidy, exquisite, Jack's lumbered with great canvases, and he worked in a clutter. Now Stella looked to see if this friendly arrangement continued, but as Jack came in behind her he said: "Dorothy's not set herself up yet. I miss her, I can tell you."

The greenhouse was still partly one: trestles with plants stood along the ends. It was lush and warm.

"As hot as hell when the sun's really going, it makes up. And Dorothy brings Paul in sometimes, so he can get used to a decent climate young."

Dorothy came in, at the far end, without the baby. She had recovered her figure. She was a small dark woman, with neat, delicate limbs. Her face was white, with scarlet rather irregular lips, and black glossy brows, a little crooked. So while she was not pretty, she was lively and dramatic-looking. She and Stella had their moments together, when they got pleasure from contrasting their differences, one woman so big and soft and blond, the other so dark and vivacious.

Dorothy came forward through shafts of sunlight, stopped, and said: "Stella, I'm glad you've come." Then forward again, to a few steps off, where she stood looking at them. "You two look good together," she said, frowning. There was something heavy and overemphasised about both statements, and Stella said: "I was wondering what Jack had been up to."

"Very good, I think," said Dorothy, coming to look at the new canvas on the easel. It was of sunlit rocks, brown and smooth, with blue sky, blue water, and people swimming in spangles of light. When Jack was in the South he painted pictures that his wife described as "dirt and grime and misery"—which was how they both described their joint childhood background. When he was in England he painted scenes like these.

"Like it? It's good, isn't it?" said Dorothy.

"Very much," said Stella. She always took pleasure from the contrast between Jack's outward self—the small, self-contained little man who could have vanished in a moment into a crowd of factory workers in, perhaps Manchester, and the sensuous bright pictures like these.

"And you?" asked Stella.

"Having a baby's killed everything creative in me—quite different from being pregnant," said Dorothy, but not complaining of it. She had worked like a demon while she was pregnant.

"Have a heart," said Jack, "he's only just got himself born."

"Well, I don't care," said Dorothy. "That's the funny thing, I *don't* care." She said this flat, indifferent. She seemed to be looking at them both again from a small troubled distance. "You two look good together," she said, and again there was the small jar.

"Well, how about some tea?" said Jack, and Dorothy said at once: "I made it when I heard the car. I thought better inside, it's not really hot in the sun." She led the way out of the greenhouse, her white linen dress dissolving in lozenges of yellow light from the glass panes above, so that Stella was reminded of the white limbs of Jack's swimmers disintegrating under sunlight in his new picture. The work of these two people was always reminding one of each other, or each other's work, and in all kinds of ways: they were so much married, so close.

The time it took to cross the space of rough grass to the door of the little house was enough to show Dorothy was right: it was really chilly in the sun. Inside two electric heaters made up for it. There had been two little rooms downstairs, but they had been knocked into one fine low-ceilinged room, stone-floored, whitewashed. A tea table, covered with a purple checked cloth, stood waiting near a window where flowering bushes and trees showed through clean panes. Charming. They adjusted the heaters and arranged themselves so they could admire the English countryside through glass. Stella looked for the baby; Dorothy said: "In the pram at the back." Then she asked: "Did yours cry a lot?"

Stella laughed and said again: "I'll try to remember."

"We expect you to guide and direct, with all your experience," said Jack.

"As far as I can remember, she was a little demon for about three months, for no reason I could see, then suddenly she became civilised."

"Roll on the three months," said Jack.

"Six weeks to go," said Dorothy, handling teacups in a languid indifferent manner Stella found new in her.

"Finding it tough going?"

"I've never felt better in my life," said Dorothy at once, as if being accused.

"You look fine."

She looked a bit tired, nothing much; Stella couldn't see what reason there was for Jack to warn her. Unless he meant the languor, a look of self-absorption? Her vivacity, a friendly aggressiveness that was the expression of her lively intelligence, was dimmed. She sat leaning back in a deep airchair, letting Jack manage things, smiling vaguely.

"I'll bring him in in a minute," she remarked, listening to the silence from the sunlit garden at the back.

"Leave him," said Jack. "He's quiet seldom enough. Relax, woman, and have a cigarette."

He lit a cigarette for her, and she took it in the same vague way, and sat breathing out smoke, her eyes half closed.

"Have you heard from Philip?" she asked, not from politeness, but with sudden insistence.

"Of course she has, she got a wire," said Jack.

"I want to know how she feels," said Dorothy. "How do you feel, Stell?" She was listening for the baby all the time.

"Feel about what?"

"About his not coming back."

"But he is coming back, it's only a month," said Stella, and heard, with surprise, that her voice sounded edgy.

"You see?" said Dorothy to Jack, meaning the words, not the edge on them.

At this evidence that she and Philip had been discussed, Stella felt, first, pleasure: because it was pleasurable to be understood by two such good friends; then she felt discomfort, remembering Jack's warning.

"See what?" she asked Dorothy, smiling.

"That's enough now," said Jack to his wife in a flash of stubborn anger, which continued the conversation that had taken place.

Dorothy took direction from her husband, and kept quiet a moment, then seemed impelled to continue: "I've been thinking it must be nice, having your husband go off, then come back. Do you realise Jack and I haven't been separated since we married? That's over ten years. Don't you think there's something awful in two grown people stuck together all the time like Siamese twins?" This ended in a wail of genuine appeal to Stella.

"No, I think it's marvellous."

"But you don't mind being alone so much?"

"It's not *so* much, it's two or three months in a year. Well of course I mind. But I enjoy being alone, really. But I'd enjoy it too if we were together all the time. I envy you two." Stella was surprised to find her eyes wet with self-pity because she had to be without her husband another month.

"And what does he think?" demanded Dorothy. "What does Philip think?"

Stella said: "Well, I think he likes getting away from time to time—yes. He likes intimacy, he enjoys it, but it doesn't come as easily to him as it does to me." She had never said this before because she had never thought about it. She was annoyed with herself that she had had to wait for Dorothy to prompt her. Yet she knew that getting annoyed was what she must not do, with the state Dorothy was in, whatever it was. She glanced at Jack for guidance, but he was determinedly busy on his pipe.

"Well, I'm like Philip," announced Dorothy. "Yes, I'd love it if Jack went off sometimes. I think I'm being stifled being shut up with Jack day and night, year in year out."

"Thanks," said Jack, short but good-humoured.

"No, but I mean it. There's something humiliating about two adult people never for one second out of each other's sight."

"Well," said Jack, "when Paul's a bit bigger, you buzz off for a month or so and you'll appreciate me when you get back."

"It's not that I don't appreciate you, it's not that at all," said Dorothy, insistent, almost strident, apparently fevered with restlessness. Her languor had quite gone, and her limbs jerked and moved. And now the baby, as if he had been prompted by his father's mentioning him, let out a cry. Jack got up, forestalling his wife, saying: "I'll get him."

Dorothy sat, listening for her husband's movements with the baby, until he came back, which he did, supporting the infant sprawled against his shoulder with a competent hand. He sat down, let his son slide onto his chest, and said: "There now, you shut up and leave us in peace a bit longer." The baby was looking up into his face with the astonished expression of the newly born, and Dorothy sat smiling at both of them. Stella understood that her restlessness, her repeated curtailed movements, meant that she longed—more, needed—to have the child in her arms, have its body against hers. And Jack seemed to feel this, because Stella could have sworn it was not a conscious decision that made him rise and slide the infant into his wife's arms. Her flesh, her needs, had spoken direct to him without words, and he had risen at once to give her what she wanted. This silent instinctive conversation between husband and wife made Stella miss her own husband violently, and with resentment against fate that kept them apart so often. She ached for Philip.

Meanwhile Dorothy, now the baby was sprawled softly against her chest, the small feet in her hand, seemed to have lapsed into good humour. And Stella, watching, remembered something she really had forgotten: the close, fierce physical tie between herself and her daughter when she had been a tiny baby. She saw this bond in the way Dorothy stroked the small head that trembled on its neck as the baby looked up into his mother's face. Why, she remembered it was like being in love, having a new baby. All kinds of forgotten or unused instincts woke in Stella. She lit a cigarette, took herself in hand; set herself to enjoy the other woman's love affair with her baby instead of envying her.

The sun, dropping into the trees, struck the windowpanes; and there was a dazzle and a flashing of yellow and white light into the room, particularly over Dorothy in her white dress and the baby. Again Stella was reminded of Jack's picture of the white-limbed swimmers in sun-dissolving water. Dorothy shielded the baby's eyes with her hand and remarked dreamily: "This is better than any man, isn't it, Stell? Isn't it better than any man?"

"Well—no," said Stella laughing. "No, not for long."

"If you say so, you should know . . . but I can't imagine ever . . . tell me, Stell, does your Philip have affairs when he's away?"

"For God's sake!" said Jack, angry. But he checked himself.

"Yes, I am sure he does."

"Do you mind?" asked Dorothy, loving the baby's feet with her enclosing palm.

And now Stella was forced to remember, to think about having minded, minding, coming to terms, and the ways in which she now did not mind.

"I don't think about it," she said.

"Well, I don't think I'd mind," said Dorothy.

"Thanks for letting me know," said Jack, short despite himself. Then he made himself laugh.

"And you, do you have affairs while Phillip's away?"

"Sometimes. Not really."

"Do you know, Jack was unfaithful to me this week," remarked Dorothy, smiling at the baby.

"That's *enough,*" said Jack, really angry.

"No it isn't enough, it isn't. Because what's awful is, I don't care."

"Well why should you care, in the circumstances?" Jack turned to Stella. "There's a silly bitch Lady Edith lives across that field. She got all excited, real live artists living down her lane. Well Dorothy was lucky, she had an excuse in the baby, but I had to go to her silly party. Booze flowing in rivers, and the most incredible people—you know. If you read about them in a novel you'd never believe . . . but I can't remember much after about twelve."

"Do you know what happened?" said Dorothy. "I was feeding the baby, it was terribly early. Jack sat straight up in bed and said: 'Jesus, Dorothy, I've just remembered, I screwed that silly bitch Lady Edith on her brocade sofa.' "

Stella laughed. Jack let out a snort of laughter. Dorothy laughed, an unscrupulous chuckle of appreciation. Then she said seriously: "But that's the point, Stella—the thing is, I don't care a tuppenny damn."

"But why should you?" asked Stella.

"But it's the first time he ever has, and surely I should have minded?"

"Don't you be too sure of that," said Jack, energetically puffing his pipe. "Don't be too sure." But it was only for form's sake, and Dorothy knew it, and said: "Surely I should have cared, Stell?"

"No. You'd have cared if you and Jack weren't so marvellous together. Just as I'd care if Philip and I weren't. . . ." Tears came running down her face. She let them. These were her good friends; and besides, instinct told her tears weren't a bad thing, with Dorothy in this mood. She said, sniffling: "When Philip gets home, we always have a flaming bloody row in the first day or two, about something unimportant, but what it's really about, and we know it, is that I'm jealous of any affair he's had and vice versa. Then we go to bed and make up." She wept, bitterly, thinking of his happiness, postponed for a month, to be succeeded by the delightful battle of their day to day living.

"Oh Stella," said Jack. "Stell . . ." He got up, fished out a handkerchief, dabbed her eyes for her. "There, love, he'll be back soon."

"Yes, I know. It's just that you two are so good together and whenever I'm with you I miss Philip."

"Well, I suppose we're good together?" said Dorothy, sounding surprised. Jack, bending over Stella with his back to his wife, made a warning grimace, then stood up and turned, commanding the situation. "It's nearly six. You'd better feed Paul. Stella's going to cook supper."

"Is she? How nice," said Dorothy. "There's everything in the kitchen, Stella. How lovely to be looked after."

"I'll show you our mansion," said Jack.

Upstairs were two small white rooms. One was the bedroom, with their things and the baby's in it. The other was an overflow room, jammed with stuff. Jack picked up a large leather folder off the spare bed and said: "Look at these, Stell." He stood at the window, back to her, his thumb at work in his pipe bowl, looking into the garden. Stella sat on the bed, opened the folder and at once exclaimed: "When did she do these?"

"The last three months she was pregnant. Never seen anything like it, she just turned them out one after the other."

There were a couple of hundred pencil drawings, all of two bodies in every kind of balance, tension, relationship. The two bodies were Jack's and Dorothy's, mostly unclothed, but not all. The drawings startled, not only because they marked a real jump forward in Dorothy's achievement, but because of their bold sensuousness. They were a kind of chant, or exaltation about the marriage. The instinctive closeness, the harmony of Jack and Dorothy, visible in every movement they made towards or away from each other, visible even when they were not together, was celebrated here with a frank, calm triumph.

"Some of them are pretty strong," said Jack, the Northern working-class boy reviving in him for a moment's puritanism.

But Stella laughed, because the prudishness masked pride: some of the drawings were indecent.

In the last few of the series the woman's body was swollen in pregnancy. They showed her trust in her husband, whose body, commanding hers, stood or lay in positions of strength and confidence. In the very last Dorothy stood turned away from her husband, her two hands supporting her big belly, and Jack's hands were protective on her shoulders.

"They are marvellous," said Stella.

"They are, aren't they."

Stella looked, laughing, and with love, towards Jack; for she saw that his showing her the drawings was not only pride in his wife's talent; but that he was using this way of telling Stella not to take Dorothy's mood too seriously. And to cheer himself up. She said, impulsively: "Well that's all right then, isn't it?"

"What? Oh yes, I see what you mean, yes, I think it's all right."

"Do you know what?" said Stella, lowering her voice. "I think Dorothy's guilty because she feels unfaithful to you."

"*What?*"

"No, I mean, with the baby, and that's what it's all about."

He turned to face her, troubled, then slowly smiling. There was the same rich unscrupulous quality of appreciation in that smile as there had been in Dorothy's laugh over her husband and Lady Edith. "You think so?" They laughed together, irrepressibly and loudly.

"What's the joke?" shouted Dorothy.

"I'm laughing because your drawings are so good," shouted Stella.

"Yes, they are, aren't they?" But Dorothy's voice changed to flat incredulity: "The trouble is, I can't imagine how I ever did them, I can't imagine ever being able to do it again."

"Downstairs," said Jack to Stella, and they went down to find Dorothy nursing the baby. He nursed with his whole being, all of him in movement. He was wrestling with the breast, thumping Dorothy's plump pretty breast with his fists. Jack stood looking down at the two of them, grinning. Dorothy reminded Stella of a cat, half closing her yellow eyes to stare over her kittens at work on her side, while she stretched out a paw where claws sheathed and unsheathed themselves, making a small rip-rip-rip on the carpet she lay on.

"You're a savage creature," said Stella, laughing.

Dorothy raised her small vivid face and smiled. "Yes, I am," she said, and looked at the two of them calm, and from a distance, over the head of her energetic baby.

Stella cooked supper in a stone kitchen, with a heater brought by Jack to make it tolerable. She used the good food she had brought with her, taking trouble. It took some time, then the three ate slowly over a big wooden table. The baby was not asleep. He grumbled for some minutes on a cushion on the floor, then his father held him briefly, before passing him over, as he had done earlier, in response to his mother's need to have him close.

"I'm supposed to let him cry," remarked Dorothy. "But why should he? If he were an Arab or an African baby he'd be plastered to my back."

"And very nice too," said Jack. "I think they come out too soon into the light of day, they should just stay inside for about eighteen months, much better all around."

"Have a heart," said Dorothy and Stella together, and they all laughed; but Dorothy added, quite serious: "Yes, I've been thinking so too."

This good nature lasted through the long meal. The light went cool and then outside; and inside they let the summer dusk deepen, without lamps.

"I've got to go quite soon," said Stella, with regret.

"Oh, no, you've got to stay!" said Dorothy, strident. It was sudden, the return of the woman who made Jack and Dorothy tense themselves to take strain.

"We all thought Philip was coming. The children will be back tomorrow night, they've been on holiday."

"Then stay till tomorrow, I *want* you," said Dorothy, petulant.

"But I can't," said Stella.

"I never thought I'd want another woman around, cooking in my kitchen, looking after me, but I do," said Dorothy, apparently about to cry.

"Well, love, you'll have to put up with me," said Jack.

"Would you mind, Stell?"

"Mind *what?*" asked Stella, cautious.

"Do you find Jack attractive?"

"Very."

"Well I know you do. Jack, do you find Stella attractive?"

"Try me," said Jack, grinning; but at the same time signalling warnings to Stella.

"Well, then!" said Dorothy.

"A *ménage à trois?*" asked Stella laughing. "And how about my Philip? Where does he fit in?"

"Well, if it comes to that, I wouldn't mind Philip myself," said Dorothy, knitting her sharp black brows and frowning.

"I don't blame you," said Stella, thinking of her handsome husband.

"Just for a month, till he comes back," said Dorothy. "I tell you what, we'll abandon this silly cottage, we must have been mad to stick ourselves away in England in the first place. The three of us'll just pack up and go off to Spain or Italy with the baby."

"And what else?" enquired Jack, good-natured at all costs, using his pipe as a safety valve.

"Yes, I've decided I approve of polygamy," announced Dorothy. She had opened her dress and the baby was nursing again, quietly this time, relaxed against her. She stroked his head, softly, softly, while her voice rose and insisted at the other two people: "I never understood it before, but I do now. I'll be the senior wife, and you two can look after me."

"Any other plans?" enquired Jack, angry now. "You just drop in from time to time to watch Stella and me have a go, is that it? Or are you going to tell us when we can go off and do it, give us your gracious permission?"

"Oh I don't care what you do, that's the point," said Dorothy, sighing, sounding forlorn, however.

Jack and Stella, careful not to look at each other, sat waiting.

"I read something in the newspaper yesterday, it struck me," said Dorothy, conversational. "A man and two women living together—here, in England. They are both his wives, they consider themselves his wives. The senior wife has a baby, and the younger wife sleeps with him—well, that's what it looked like, reading between the lines."

"You'd better stop reading between lines," said Jack. "It's not doing you any good."

"No, I'd like it," insisted Dorothy. "I think our marriages are silly. Africans and people like that, they know better, they've got some sense."

"I can just see you if I did make love to Stella," said Jack.

"Yes!" said Stella, with a short laugh which, against her will, was resentful.

"But I wouldn't mind," said Dorothy, and burst into tears.

"Now, Dorothy, that's enough," said Jack. He got up, took the baby, whose sucking was mechanical now, and said: "Now listen, you're going right upstairs and you're going to sleep. This little stinker's full as a tick, he'll be asleep for hours, that's my bet."

"I don't feel sleepy," said Dorothy, sobbing.

"I'll give you a sleeping pill, then."

Then started a search for sleeping pills. None to be found.

"That's just like us," wailed Dorothy, "we don't even have a sleeping pill in the place. . . . Stella, I wish you'd stay, I really do. Why can't you?"

"Stella's going in just a minute, I'm taking her to the station," said Jack. He poured some Scotch into a glass, handed it to his wife and said: "Now drink that, love, and let's have an end of it. I'm getting fed-up." He sounded fed-up.

Dorothy obediently drank the Scotch, got unsteadily from her chair and went slowly upstairs. "Don't let him cry," she demanded, as she disappeared.

"Oh you silly bitch," he shouted after her. "When have I let him cry? Here, you hold on a minute," he said to Stella, handing her the baby. He ran upstairs.

Stella held the baby. This was almost for the first time, since she sensed how much another woman's holding her child made Dorothy's fierce new possessiveness uneasy. She looked down at the small, sleepy, red face and said softly: "Well, you're causing a lot of trouble, aren't you?"

Jack shouted from upstairs: "Come up a minute, Stell." She went up, with the baby. Dorothy was tucked up in bed, drowsy from the Scotch, the bedside light turned away from her. She looked at the baby, but Jack took it from Stella.

"Jack says I'm a silly bitch," said Dorothy, apologetic, to Stella.

"Well, never mind, you'll feel different soon."

"I suppose so, if you say so. All right, I *am* going to sleep," said Dorothy, in a stubborn, sad little voice. She turned over, away from them. In the last flare of her hysteria she said: "Why don't you two walk to the station together? It's a lovely night."

"We're going to," said Jack, "don't worry."

She let out a weak giggle, but did not turn. Jack carefully deposited the now sleeping baby in the bed, about a foot from Dorothy. Who suddenly wriggled over until her small, defiant white back was in contact with the blanketed bundle that was her son.

Jack raised his eyebrows at Stella: but Stella was looking at mother and baby, the nerves of her memory filling her with sweet warmth. What right had this woman, who was in possession of such delight, to torment her husband, to torment her friend, as she had been doing—what right had she to rely on their decency as she did?

Surprised by these thoughts, she walked away downstairs, and stood at the door into the garden, her eyes shut, holding herself rigid against tears.

She felt a warmth on her bare arm—Jack's hand. She opened her eyes to see him bending towards her, concerned.

"It'd serve Dorothy right if I did drag you off into the bushes. . . ."

"Wouldn't have to drag me," he said; and while the words had the measure of facetiousness the situation demanded, she felt his seriousness envelop them both in danger.

The warmth of his hand slid across her back, and she turned towards him under its pressure. They stood together, cheeks touching, scents of skin and hair mixing with the smells of warmed grass and leaves.

She thought: What is going to happen now will blow Dorothy and Jack and that baby sky-high; it's the end of my marriage; I'm going to blow everything to bits. There was almost uncontrollable pleasure in it.

She saw Dorothy, Jack, the baby, her husband, the two half-grown children, all dispersed, all spinning downwards through the sky like bits of debris after an explosion.

Jack's mouth was moving along her cheek towards her mouth, dissolving her whole self in delight. She saw, against closed lids, the bundled baby upstairs, and pulled back from the situation, exclaiming energetically: "Damn Dorothy, damn her, damn her, I'd like to kill her. . . ."

And he, exploding into reaction, said in a low furious rage: "Damn you both! I'd like to wring both your bloody necks. . . ."

Their faces were at a foot's distance from each other, their eyes staring hostility. She thought that if she had not had the vision of the helpless baby they would now be in each other's arms—generating tenderness and desire like a couple of dynamos, she said to herself, trembling with dry anger.

"I'm going to miss my train if I don't go," she said.

"I'll get your coat," he said, and went in, leaving her defenceless against the emptiness of the garden.

When he came out, he slid the coat around her without touching her, and said: "Come on, I'll take you by car." He walked away in front of her to the car, and she followed meekly over rough lawn. It really was a lovely night.

CECILIA ROSAS

Amado Muro (Chester Seltzer)

(1915–1971)

Biography p. 1089

When I was in the ninth grade at Bowie High School in El Paso, I got a job hanging up women's coats at La Feria Department Store on Saturdays. It wasn't the kind of a job that had much appeal for a Mexican boy or for boys of any other nationality either. But the work wasn't hard, only boring. Wearing a smock, I stood around the Ladies' Wear Department all day long waiting for women customers to finish trying on coats so I could hang them up.

Having to wear a smock was worse than the work itself. It was an agonizing ordeal. To me it was a loathsome stigma of unmanly toil that made an already degrading job even more so. The work itself I looked on as onerous and effeminate for a boy from a family of miners, shepherds, and ditchdiggers. But working in Ladies' Wear had two compensations: earning three dollars every Saturday was one; being close to the Señorita Cecilia Rosas was the other.

This alluring young woman, the most beautiful I had ever seen, more than made up for my mollycoddle labor and the smock that symbolized it. My chances of looking at her were almost limitless. And like a good Mexican, I made the most of them. But I was only too painfully aware that I wasn't the only one who thought this saleslady gorgeous.

La Feria had water fountains on every one of its eight floors. But men liked best the one on the floor where Miss Rosas worked. So they made special trips to Ladies' Wear all day long to drink water and look at her.

Since I was only fourteen and in love for the first time, I looked at her more chastely than most. The way her romantic lashes fringed her obsidian eyes was especially enthralling to me. Then, too, I never tired of admiring her shining raven hair, her Cupid's-bow lips, the warmth of her gleaming white smile. Her rich olive skin was almost as dark as mine. Sometimes she wore a San Juan rose in her hair. When she did, she looked so very lovely I forgot all about what La Feria was paying me to do and stood gaping at her instead. My admiration was decorous but complete. I admired her hourglass figure as well as her wonderfully radiant face.

Other men admired her too. They inspected her from the water fountain. Some stared at her boldly, watching her trimly rhythmic hips sway. Others, less frank and open, gazed furtively at her swelling bosom or her shapely calves. Their effrontery made me indignant. I, too, looked at these details of Miss Rosas. But I prided myself on doing so more romantically, far more poetically than they did, with much more love than desire.

Then, too, Miss Rosas was the friendliest as well as the most beautiful saleslady in Ladies' Wear. But the other salesladies, Mexican girls all, didn't like her. She was so nice to them all they were hard put to justify their dislike. They couldn't very well admit they disliked her because she was pretty. So they all said she was haughty and imperious. Their claim was partly true. Her beauty was Miss Rosas' only obvious vanity. But she had still another. She prided herself on being more American than Mexican because she was born in El Paso. And she did her best to act, dress, and talk the way Americans do. She hated to speak Spanish, disliked her Mexican name. She called herself Cecile Roses instead of Cecilia Rosas. This made the other salesladies smile derisively. They called her La Americana or the Gringa from Xochimilco every time they mentioned her name.

Looking at this beautiful girl was more important than money to me. It was my greatest compensation for doing work that I hated. She was so lovely that a glance at her sweetly expressive face was enough to make me forget my shame at wearing a smock and my dislike for my job with its eternal waiting around.

Miss Rosas was an exemplary saleslady. She could be frivolous, serious or demure, primly efficient too, molding herself to each customer's personality. Her voice matched her exotically mysterious eyes. It was the richest, the softest I had ever heard. Her husky whisper, gentle as a rain breeze, was like a tender caress. Hearing it made me want to dream and I did. Romantic thoughts burgeoned up in my mind like rosy billows of hope scented with Miss Rosas' perfume. These thoughts made me so languid at my work that the floor manager, Joe Apple, warned me to show some enthusiasm for it or else suffer the consequences.

But my dreams sapped my will to struggle, making me oblivious to admonitions. I had neither the desire nor the energy to respond to Joe Apple's warnings. Looking at Miss Rosas used up so much of my energy that I had little left for my work. Miss Rosas was twenty, much too old for me, everyone said. But what everyone said didn't matter. So I soldiered on the job and watched her, entranced by her beauty, her grace. While I watched I dreamed of being a hero. It hurt me to have her see me doing menial work. But there was no escape from it. I needed the job to stay in school. So more and more I took refuge in dreams.

When I had watched her as much, if not more, than I could safely do without attracting the attention of other alert Mexican salesladies, I slipped out of Ladies' Wear and walked up the stairs to the top floor. There I sat on a window ledge smoking Faro cigarettes, looking down at the city's canyons, and best of all, thinking about Miss Rosas and myself.

They say Chihuahua Mexicans are good at dreaming because the mountains are so gigantic and the horizons so vast in Mexico's biggest state that men don't think pygmy thoughts there. I was no exception. Lolling on the ledge, I became what I wanted to be. And what I wanted to be was a handsome American Miss Rosas could love and marry. The dreams I dreamed were imaginative masterpieces, or so I thought. They transcended the insipid realities of a casual relationship, making it vibrantly thrilling and infinitely more romantic. They transformed me from a colorless Mexican boy who put women's coats away into the debonair American, handsome, dashing and worldly, that I longed to be for her sake. For the first time in my life I revelled in the magic of fantasy. It brought happiness. Reality didn't.

But my window ledge reveries left me bewildered and shaken. They had a narcotic quality. The more thrillingly romantic fantasies I created, the more I needed to create. It got so I couldn't get enough dreaming time in Ladies' Wear. My kind of dreaming demanded disciplined concentration. And there was just too much hubbub, too much gossiping, too many coats to be put away there.

So I spent less time in Ladies' Wear. My flights to the window ledge became more recklessly frequent. Sometimes I got tired sitting there. When I did, I took the freight elevator down to the street floor and brazenly walked out of the store without so much as punching a time clock. Walking the streets quickened my imagination, gave form and color to my thoughts. It made my brain glow with impossible hopes that seemed incredibly easy to realize. So absorbed was I in thoughts of Miss Rosas and myself that I bumped into Americans, apologizing mechanically in Spanish instead of English, and wandered down South El Paso Street like a somnambulist, without really seeing its street vendors, cafes and arcades, tattoo shops, and shooting galleries at all.

But if there was confusion in these walks there was some serenity too. Something good did come from the dreams that prompted them. I found I could tramp the streets with a newly won tranquillity, no longer troubled by, or even aware of, girls in tight skirts, overflowing blouses, and drop-stitch stockings. My love for Miss Rosas was my shield against the furtive thoughts and indiscriminate desires that had made me so uneasy for a year or more before I met her.

Then, too, because of her, I no longer looked at the pictures of voluptuous women in the *Vea* and *Vodevil* magazines at Zamora's newsstand. The piquant thoughts Mexicans call *malos deseos* were gone from my mind. I no longer thought about women as I did before I fell in love with Miss Rosas. Instead, I thought about a woman, only one. This clear-cut objective and the serenity that went with it made me understand something of one of the nicest things about love.

I treasured the walks, the window-ledge sittings, and the dreams that I had then. I clung to them just as long as I could. Drab realities closed in on me chokingly just as soon as I gave them up. My future was a time clock with an American Mister telling me what to do and this I knew only too well. A career as an ice-dock laborer stretched ahead of me. Better said, it dangled over me like a Veracruz machete. My uncle Rodolfo Avitia, a straw boss on the ice docks, was already training me for it. Every night he took me to the mile-long docks overhanging the Southern Pacific freight yards. There he handed me tongs and made me practice tripping three-hundred-pound ice blocks so I could learn how to unload an entire boxcar of ice blocks myself.

Thinking of this bleak future drove me back into my fantasies, made me want to prolong them forever. My imagination was taxed to the breaking point by the heavy strain I put on it.

I thought about every word Miss Rosas had ever said to me, making myself believe she looked at me with unmistakable tenderness when she said them. When she said: "Amado, please hang up this fur coat," I found special meaning in her tone. It was as though she had said: "Amadito, I love you."

When she gave these orders, I pushed into action like a man blazing with a desire to perform epically heroic feats. At such times I felt capable of putting away not one but a thousand fur coats, and would have done so joyously.

Sometimes on the street I caught myself murmuring: "Cecilia, *linda amorcita,* I love you." When these surges swept over me, I walked down empty streets so I could whisper: "Cecilia, *'te quiero con toda mi alma"* as much as I wanted to and mumble everything else that I felt. And so I emptied my heart on the streets and window ledge while women's coats piled up in Ladies' Wear.

But my absences didn't go unnoticed. Once an executive-looking man, portly, gray, and efficiently brusque, confronted me while I sat on the window ledge with a Faro cigarette pasted to my lips, a cloud of tobacco smoke hanging over my head, and many perfumed dreams inside it. He had a no-nonsense approach that jibed with his austere mine. He asked me what my name was, jotted down my work number, and went off to make a report on what he called "sordid malingering."

Other reports followed this. Gruff warnings, stern admonitions, and blustery tirades developed from them. They came from both major and minor executives. These I was already inured to. They didn't matter anyway. My condition was far too advanced, already much too complex to be cleared up by mere lectures, fatherly or otherwise. All the threats and rebukes in the world couldn't have made me give up my window-ledge reveries or kept me from roaming city streets with Cecilia Rosas' name on my lips like a prayer.

The reports merely made me more cunning, more doggedly determined to city-slick La Feria out of work hours I owed it. The net result was that I timed my absences more precisely and contrived better lies to explain them. Sometimes I went to the men's room and looked at myself in the mirror for as long as ten minutes at a time. Such self-studies filled me with gloom. The mirror reflected an ordinary Mexican face, more homely than comely. Only my hair gave me hope. It was thick and wavy, deserving a better face to go with it. So I did the best I could with what I had, and combed it over my temples in ringlets just like the poets back in my hometown of Parral, Chihuahua, used to do.

My inefficiency, my dreams, my general lassitude could have gone on indefinitely, it seemed. My life at the store wavered between bright hope and leaden despair, unrelieved by Miss Rosas' acceptance or rejection of me. Then one day something happened that almost made my overstrained heart stop beating.

It happened on the day Miss Rosas stood behind me while I put a fur coat away. Her heady perfume, the fragrance of her warm healthy body, made me feel faint. She was so close to me I thought about putting my hands around her lissome waist and hugging her as hard as I could. But thoughts of subsequent disgrace deterred me, so instead of hugging her I smiled wanly and asked her in Spanish how she was feeling.

"Amado, speak English," she told me. "And pronounce the words slowly and carefully so you won't sound like a country Mexican."

Then she looked at me in a way that made me the happiest employee who ever punched La Feria's time clock.

"Amadito," she whispered the way I had always dreamed she would.

"Yes, Señorita Cecilia," I said expectantly.

Her smile was warmly intimate. "Amadito, when are you going to take me to the movies?" she asked.

Other salesladies watched us, all smiling. They made me so nervous I couldn't answer.

"Amadito, you haven't answered me," Miss Rosas said teasingly. "Either you're bashful as a village sweetheart or else you don't like me at all."

In voluble Spanish, I quickly assured her the latter wasn't the case. I was just getting ready to say "Señorita Cecilia, I more than like you, I love you" when she frowned and told me to speak English. So I slowed down and tried to smooth out my ruffled thoughts.

"Señorita Cecilia," I said. "I'd love to take you to the movies any time."

Miss Rosas smiled and patted my cheek. "Will you buy me candy and popcorn?" she said.

I nodded, putting my hand against the imprint her warm palm had left on my face. "And hold my hand?"

I said "yes" so enthusiastically it made her laugh. Other salesladies laughed too. Dazed and numb with happiness, I watched Miss Rosas walk away. How proud and confident she was, how wholesomely clean and feminine. Other salesladies were poking at me and laughing.

Miss Sandoval came over to me. *"Ay papacito,"* she said. "With women you're the divine tortilla."

Miss de la Rosa came over too. "When you take the Americana to the movies, remember not to speak Christian," she said. "And be sure you wear the pants that don't have any patches on them."

What they said made me blush and wonder how they knew what we had been talking about. Miss Arroyo came over to join them. So did Miss Torres.

"Amado, remember women are weak and men aren't made of sweet bread," Miss Arroyo said.

This embarrassed me but it wasn't altogether unpleasant. Miss Sandoval winked at Miss de la Rosa, then looked back at me.

"Don't go too fast with the Americana, Amado," she said. "Remember the procession is long and the candles are small."

They laughed and slapped me on the back. They all wanted to know when I was going to take Miss Rosas to the movies. "She didn't say," I blurted out without thinking.

This brought another burst of laughter. It drove me back up to the window ledge where I got out my package of Faros and thought about the wonderful thing that had happened. But I was too nervous to stay there. So I went to the men's room and looked at myself in the mirror again, wondering why Miss Rosas liked me so well. The mirror made it brutally clear that my looks hadn't influenced her. So it must have been something else, perhaps character. But that didn't seem likely either. Joe Apple had told me I didn't have much of that. And other store officials had bulwarked his opinion. Still, I had seen homely men walking the streets of El Paso's Little Chihuahua quarter with beautiful Mexican women and no one could explain that either. Anyway it was time for another walk. So I took one.

This time I trudged through Little Chihuahua, where both Miss Rosas and I lived. Little Chihuahua looked different to me that day. It was a broken-down Mexican quarter honeycombed with tenements, Mom and Pop groceries, herb shops, cafes, and spindly salt-cedar trees; with howling children running its streets and old Mexican revolutionaries sunning themselves on its curbs like iguanas. But on that clear frosty day it was the world's most romantic place because Cecilia Rosas lived there.

While walking, I reasoned that Miss Rosas might want to go dancing after the movies. So I went to Professor Toribio Ortega's dance studio and made arrangements to take my first lesson. Some neighborhood boys saw me when I came out. They howled *"Mariquita"* and made flutteringly effeminate motions, all vulgar if not obscene. It didn't matter. On my lunch hour I went back and took my first lesson anyway. Professor Ortega danced with me. Softened by weeks of dreaming, I went limp in his arms imagining he was Miss Rosas.

The rest of the day was the same as many others before it. As usual I spent most of it stealing glances at Miss Rosas and hopping up to the window ledge. She looked busy, efficient, not like a woman in love. Her many other admirers trooped to the water fountain to look at the way her black silk dress fitted her calves. Their profane admiration made me scowl even more than I usually did at such times.

When the day's work was done, I plodded home from the store just as dreamily as I had gone to it. Since I had no one else to confide in, I invited my oldest sister, Dulce Nombre de María, to go to the movies with me. They were showing Jorge Negrete and Maria Felix in *El Rapto* at the Colon Theater. It was a romantic movie, just the kind I wanted to see.

After it was over, I bought Dulce Nombre *churros* and hot *impurrado* at the Golden Taco Cafe. And I told my sister all about what had happened to me. She looked at me thoughtfully, then combed my hair back with her fingertips as though trying to soothe me. "Manito," she said, softly. "I wouldn't . . . " Then she looked away and shrugged her shoulders.

On Monday I borrowed three dollars from my Uncle Rodolfo without telling him what it was for. Miss Rosas hadn't told me what night she wanted me to take her to the movies. But the way she had looked at me made me think that almost any night would do. So I decided on Friday. Waiting for it to come was hard. But I had to keep my mind occupied. So I went to Zamora's news stand to get the Alma Nortena songbook. Pouring through it for the most romantic song I could find, I decided on *La Cecilia.*

All week long I practiced singing it on my way to school and in the shower after basketball practice with the Little Chihuahua Tigers at the Sagrado Corazón gym. But, except for singing this song, I tried not to speak Spanish at all. At home I made my mother mad by saying in English, "Please pass the sugar."

My mother looked at me as though she couldn't believe what she had heard. Since my Uncle Rodolfo couldn't say anything more than "hello" and "goodbye" in English, he couldn't tell what I had said. So my sister Consuelo did.

"May the Dark Virgin with the benign look make this boy well enough to speak Christian again," my mother whispered.

This I refused to do. I went on speaking English even though my mother and uncle didn't understand it. This shocked my sisters as well. When they asked me to explain my behavior, I parroted Miss Rosas, saying, "We're living in the United States now."

My rebellion against being a Mexican created an uproar. Such conduct was unorthodox, if not scandalous, in a neighborhood where names like Burgiaga, Rodriguez, and Castillo predominated. But it wasn't only the Spanish language that I lashed out against.

"Mother, why do we always have to eat *sopa, frijoles, refritos, mondongo,* and *pozole?*" I complained. "Can't we ever eat roast beef or ham and eggs like Americans do?"

My mother didn't speak to me for two days after that. My Uncle Rodolfo grimaced and mumbled something about renegade Mexicans who want to eat ham and eggs even though the Montes Packing Company turned out the best *chorizo* this side of

Toluca. My sister Consuelo giggled and called me a Rio Grande Irishman, an American Mister, a gringo, and a *bolillo*. Dulce Nombre looked at me worriedly.

Life at home was almost intolerable. Cruel jokes and mocking laughter made it so. I moped around looking sad as a day without bread. My sister Consuelo suggested I go to the courthouse and change my name to Beloved Wall which is English for Amado Muro. My mother didn't agree. "If *Nuestro Señor* had meant for Amadito to be an American he would have given him a name like Smeeth or Jonesy," she said. My family was unsympathetic. With a family like mine, how could I ever hope to become an American and win Miss Rosas?

Friday came at last. I put on my only suit, slicked my hair down with liquid vaseline, and doused myself with Dulce Nombre's perfume.

"Amado's going to serenade that pretty girl everyone calls La Americana," my sister Consuelo told my mother and uncle when I sat down to eat. "Then he's going to take her to the movies."

This made my uncle laugh and my mother scowl.

"*Qué pantalones tiene* (what nerve that boy's got)," my uncle said, "to serenade a twenty-year-old woman."

"La Americana," my mother said derisively. "That one's Mexican as pulque cured with celery."

They made me so nervous I forgot to take off my cap when I sat down to eat.

"Amado, take off your cap," my mother said. "You're not in La Lagunilla Market."

My uncle frowned. "All this boy thinks about is kissing girls," he said gruffly.

"But my boy's never kissed one," my mother said proudly.

My sister Consuelo laughed. "That's because they won't let him," she said.

This wasn't true. But I couldn't say so in front of my mother. I had already kissed Emalina Uribe from Porfirio Díaz Street not once but twice. Both times I'd kissed her in a darkened doorway less than a block from her home. But the kisses were over so soon we hardly had time to enjoy them. This was because Ema was afraid of her big brother, the husky one nicknamed Toro, would see us. But if we'd had more time it would have been better, I knew.

Along about six o'clock the three musicians who called themselves the Mariachis of Tecalitlán came by and whistled for me, just as they had said they would. They never looked better than they did on that night. They had on black and silver charro uniforms and big, black, Zapata sombreros.

My mother shook her head when she saw them. "Son, who ever heard of serenading a girl at six o'clock in the evening," she said. "When your father had the mariachis sing for me it was always two o'clock in the morning—the only proper time for a six-song *galio*."

But I got out my Ramirez guitar anyway. I put on my cap and rushed out to give the mariachis the money without even kissing my mother's hand or waiting for her to bless me. Then we headed for Miss Rosas' home. Some boys and girls I knew were out in the street. This made me uncomfortable. They looked at me wonderingly as I led the mariachi band to Miss Rosas' home.

A block away from Miss Rosas' home I could see her father, a grizzled veteran who fought for Pancho Villa, sitting on the curb reading the Juarez newspaper, *El Fronterizo*.

The sight of him made me slow down for a moment. But I got back in stride when I saw Miss Rosas herself.

She smiled and waved at me. "Hello, Amadito," she said.

"Hello, Señorita Cecilia," I said.

She looked at the mariachis, then back to me.

"Ay, Amado, you're going to serenade your girl," she said. I didn't reply right away. Then when I was getting ready to say "Señorita Cecilia, I came to serenade you," I saw the American man sitting in the sports roadster at the curb.

Miss Rosas turned to him. "I'll be right there, Johnny," she said.

She patted my cheek. "I've got to run now, Amado," she said. "Have a real nice time, darling."

I looked at her silken legs as she got into the car. Everything had happened so fast I was dazed. Broken dreams made my head spin. The contrast between myself and the poised American in the sports roadster was so cruel it made me wince.

She was happy with him. That was obvious. She was smiling and laughing, looking forward to a good time. Why had she asked me to take her to the movies if she already had a boyfriend? Then I remembered how the other salesladies had laughed, how I had wondered why they were laughing when they couldn't even hear what we were saying. And I realized it had all been a joke, everyone had known it but me. Neither Miss Rosas nor the other salesladies had ever dreamed I would think she was serious about wanting me to take her to the movies.

The American and Miss Rosas drove off. Gloomy thoughts oppressed me. They made me want to cry. To get rid of them I thought of going to one of the "bad death" cantinas in Juarez where tequila starts fights and knives finish them to one of the cantinas where the panders, whom Mexicans call *burros*, stand outside shouting "It's just like Paris, only not so many people" was where I wanted to go. There I could forget her in Jalisco-state style with mariachis, tequila, and night-life women. Then I remembered I was so young that night-life women would shun me and *cantineros* wouldn't serve me tequila.

So I thought some more. Emalina Uribe was the only other alternative. If we went over to Porfirio Díaz Street and serenaded her I could go back to being a Mexican again. She was just as Mexican as I was, Mexican as *chicharrones*. I thought about smiling, freckle-faced Ema.

Ema wasn't like the Americana at all. She wore wash dresses that fitted loosely and even ate the *melcocha* candies Mexicans liked so well on the street. On Sundays she wore a Zamora shawl to church and her mother wouldn't let her use lipstick or let her put on high heels.

But with a brother like Toro who didn't like me anyway, such a serenade might be more dangerous than romantic. Besides that, my faith in my looks, my character, or whatever it was that made women fall in love with men, was so undermined I could already picture her getting into a car with a handsome American just like Miss Rosas had done.

The Mariachis of Tecalitlán were getting impatient. They had been paid to sing six songs and they wanted to sing them. But they were all sympathetic. None of them laughed at me.

"Amado, don't look sad as I did the day I learned I'd never be a millionare," the mariachi captain said, putting his arm around me. "If not that girl, then another."

But without Miss Rosas there was no one we could sing *La Cecilia* to. The street seemed bleak and empty now that she was gone. And I didn't want to serenade Ema Uribe even though she hadn't been faithless as Miss Rosas had been. It was true she hadn't been faithless, but only lack of opportunity would keep her from getting into a car with an American, I reasoned cynically.

Just about then Miss Rosas' father looked up from his newspaper. He asked the mariachis if they knew how to sing *Cananea Jail.* They told him they did. Then they looked at me. I thought it over for a moment. Then I nodded and started strumming the bass strings of my guitar. What had happened made it only too plain I could never trust Miss Rosas again. So we serenaded her father instead.

THE SHORT HAPPY LIFE OF FRANCIS MACOMBER

Ernest Hemingway

(1898–1961)

Biography p. 1076

It was now lunch time and they were all sitting under the double green fly of the dining tent pretending that nothing had happened.

"Will you have lime juice or lemon squash?" Macomber asked.

"I'll have a gimlet," Robert Wilson told him.

"I'll have a gimlet too. I need something," Macomber's wife said.

"I suppose it's the thing to do," Macomber agreed. "Tell him to make three gimlets."

The mess boy had started them already, lifting the bottles out of the canvas cooling bags that sweated wet in the wind that blew through the trees that shaded the tents.

"What had I ought to give them?" Macomber asked.

"A quid would be plenty," Wilson told him. "You don't want to spoil them."

"Will the headman distribute it?"

"Absolutely."

Francis Macomber had, half an hour before, been carried to his tent from the edge of the camp in triumph on the arms and shoulders of the cook, the personal boys, the skinner and the porters. The gun-bearers had taken no part in the demonstration. When the native boys put him down at the door of his tent, he had shaken all their hands, received their congratulations, and then gone into the tent and sat on the bed until his wife came in. She did not speak to him when she came in and he left the tent at once to wash his face and hands in the portable wash basin outside and go over to the dining tent to sit in a comfortable canvas chair in the breeze and the shade.

"You've got your lion," Robert Wilson said to him, "and a damned fine one too."

Mrs. Macomber looked at Wilson quickly. She was an extremely handsome and well-kept woman of the beauty and social position which had, five years before, commanded five thousand dollars as the price of endorsing, with photographs, a beauty product which she had never used. She had been married to Francis Macomber for eleven years.

"He is a good lion, isn't he?" Macomber said. His wife looked at him now. She looked at both these men as though she had never seen them before.

One, Wilson, the white hunter, she knew she had never truly seen before. He was about middle height with sandy hair, a stubby mustache, a very red face and extremely cold blue eyes with faint white wrinkles at the corners that grooved merrily when he smiled. He smiled at her now and she looked away from his face at the way his shoulders sloped in the loose tunic he wore with the four big cartridges held in loops where the left breast pocket should have been, at his big brown hands, his old slacks, his very dirty boots and back to his red face again. She noticed where the baked red of his face stopped in a white line that marked the circle left by his Stetson hat that hung now from one of the pegs of the tent pole.

"Well, here's to the lion," Robert Wilson said. He smiled at her again and, not smiling, she looked curiously at her husband.

Francis Macomber was very tall, very well built if you did not mind that length of bone, dark, his hair cropped like an oarsman, rather thin-lipped, and was considered handsome. He was dressed in the same sort of safari clothes that Wilson wore except that his were new, he was thirty-five years old, kept himself very fit, was good at court games, had a number of big-game fishing records, and had just shown himself, very publicly, to be a coward.

"Here's to the lion," he said. "I can't ever thank you for what you did."

Margaret, his wife, looked away from him and back to Wilson.

"Let's not talk about the lion," she said.

Wilson looked over at her without smiling and now she smiled at him.

"It's been a very strange day," she said. "Hadn't you ought to put your hat on even under the canvas at noon? You told me that, you know."

"Might put it on," said Wilson.

"You know you have a very red face, Mr. Wilson," she told him and smiled again.

"Drink," said Wilson.

"I don't think so," she said. "Francis drinks a great deal, but his face is never red."

"It's red today," Macomber tried a joke.

"No," said Margaret. "It's mine that's red today. But Mr. Wilson's is always red."

"Must be racial," said Wilson. "I say, you wouldn't like to drop my beauty as a topic, would you?"

"I've just started on it."

"Let's chuck it," said Wilson.

"Conversation is going to be so difficult," Margaret said.

"Don't be silly, Margot," her husband said.

"No difficulty," Wilson said. "Got a damn fine lion."

Margot looked at them both and they both saw that she was going to cry. Wilson had seen it coming for a long time and he dreaded it. Macomber was past dreading it.

"I wish it hadn't happened. Oh, I wish it hadn't happened," she said and started for her tent. She made no noise of crying but they could see that her shoulders were shaking under the rose-colored, sun-proofed shirt she wore.

"Women upset," said Wilson to the tall man. "Amounts to nothing. Strain on the nerves and one thing'n another."

"No," said Macomber. "I suppose that I rate that for the rest of my life now."

"Nonsense. Let's have a spot of the giant killer," said Wilson. "Forget the whole thing. Nothing to it anyway."

"We might try," said Macomber. "I won't forget what you did for me though."

"Nothing," said Wilson. "All nonsense."

So they sat there in the shade where the camp was pitched under some wide-topped acacia trees with a boulder-strewn cliff behind them, and a stretch of grass that ran to the bank of a boulder-filled stream in front with forest beyond it, and drank their just-cool lime drinks and avoided one another's eyes while the boys set the table for lunch. Wilson could tell that the boys all knew about it now and when he saw Macomber's personal boy looking curiously at his master while he was putting dishes on the table he snapped at him in Swahili. The boy turned away with his face blank.

"What were you telling him?" Macomber asked.

"Nothing. Told him to look alive or I'd see he got about fifteen of the best."

"What's that? Lashes?"

"It's quite illegal," Wilson said. "You're supposed to fine them."

"Do you still have them whipped?"

"Oh, yes. They could raise a row if they chose to complain. But they don't. They prefer it to the fines."

"How strange!" said Macomber.

"Not strange, really," Wilson said. "Which would you rather do? Take a good birching or lose your pay?"

Then he felt embarrassed at asking it and before Macomber could answer he went on, "We all take a beating every day, you know, one way or another."

This was no better. "Good God," he thought. "I am a diplomat, aren't I?"

"Yes, we take a beating," said Macomber, still not looking at him. "I'm awfully sorry about that lion business. It doesn't have to go any further, does it? I mean no one will hear about it, will they?"

"You mean will I tell it at the Mathaiga Club?" Wilson looked at him now coldly. He had not expected this. So he's a bloody four-letter man as well as a bloody coward, he thought. I rather liked him too until today. But how is one to know about an American?

"No," said Wilson. "I'm a professional hunter. We never talk about our clients. You can be quite easy on that. It's supposed to be bad form to ask us not to talk though."

He had decided now that to break would be much easier. He would eat, then, by himself and could read a book with his meals. They would eat by themselves. He would see them through the safari on a very formal basis—what was it the French called it? Distinguished consideration—and it would be a damn sight easier than having to go through this emotional trash. He'd insult him and make a good clean break. Then he could read a book with his meals and he'd still be drinking their whisky. That was the phrase for it when a safari went bad. You ran into another white hunter and you asked, "How is everything going?" and he answered, "Oh, I'm still drinking their whisky," and you knew everything had gone to pot.

"I'm sorry," Macomber said and looked at him with his American face that would stay adolescent until it became middle-aged, and Wilson noted his crew-cropped hair, fine eyes only faintly shifty, good nose, thin lips and handsome jaw. "I'm sorry I didn't realize that. There are lots of things I don't know."

So what could he do, Wilson thought. He was all ready to break it off quickly and neatly and here the beggar was apologizing after he had just insulted him. He made one more attempt. "Don't worry about me talking," he said. "I have a living to make. You know in Africa no woman ever misses her lion and no white man ever bolts."

"I bolted like a rabbit," Macomber said.

Now what in hell were you going to do about a man who talked like that, Wilson wondered.

Wilson looked at Macomber with his flat, blue, machine-gunner's eyes and the other smiled back at him. He had a pleasant smile if you did not notice how his eyes showed when he was hurt.

"Maybe I can fix it up on buffalo," he said. "We're after them next, aren't we?"

"In the morning if you like," Wilson told him. Perhaps he had been wrong. This was certainly the way to take it. You most certainly could not tell a damned thing about an American. He was all for Macomber again. If you could forget the morning. But, of course, you couldn't. The morning had been about as bad as they come.

"Here comes the Memsahib," he said. She was walking over from her tent looking refreshed and cheerful and quite lovely. She had a very perfect oval face, so perfect that you expected her to be stupid. But she wasn't stupid, Wilson thought, no, not stupid.

"How is the beautiful red-faced Mr. Wilson? Are you feeling better, Francis, my pearl?"

"Oh, much," said Macomber.

"I've dropped the whole thing," she said, sitting down at the table. "What importance is there to whether Francis is any good at killing lions? That's not his trade. That's Mr. Wilson's trade. Mr. Wilson is really very impressive killing anything. You do kill anything, don't you?"

"Oh, anything," said Wilson. "Simply anything." They are, he thought, the hardest in the world; the hardest, the cruelest, the most predatory and the most attractive and their men have softened or gone to pieces nervously as they have hardened. Or is it that they pick men they can handle? They can't know that much at the age they marry, he thought. He was grateful that he had gone through his education on American women before now because this was a very attractive one.

"We're going after buff in the morning," he told her.

"I'm coming," she said.

"No, you're not."

"Oh, yes, I am. Mayn't I, Francis?"

"Why not stay in camp?"

"Not for anything," she said. "I wouldn't miss something like today for anything."

When she left, Wilson was thinking, when she went off to cry, she seemed a hell of a fine woman. She seemed to understand, to realize, to be hurt for him and for herself and to know how things really stood. She is away for twenty minutes and now she is back, simply enamelled in that American female cruelty. They are the damnedest women. Really the damnedest.

"We'll put on another show for you tomorrow," Francis Macomber said.

"You're not coming," Wilson said.

"You're very mistaken," she told him. "And I want so to see you perform again. You were lovely this morning. That is if blowing things' heads off is lovely."

"Here's the lunch," said Wilson. "You're very merry, aren't you?"

"Why not? I didn't come out here to be dull."

"Well, it hasn't been dull," Wilson said. He could see the boulders in the river and the high bank beyond with the trees and he remembered the morning.

"Oh, no," she said. "It's been charming. And tomorrow. You don't know how I look forward to tomorrow."

"That's eland he's offering you," Wilson said.

"They're the big cowy things that jump like hares, aren't they?"

"I suppose that describes them," Wilson said.

"It's very good meat," Macomber said.

"Did you shoot it, Francis?" she asked.

"Yes."

"They're not dangerous, are they?"

"Only if they fall on you," Wilson told her.

"I'm so glad."

"Why not let up on the bitchery just a little, Margot," Macomber said, cutting the eland steak and putting some mashed potato, gravy and carrot on the down-turned fork that tined through the piece of meat.

"I suppose I could," she said, "since you put it so prettily."

"Tonight we'll have champagne for the lion," Wilson said. "It's a bit too hot at noon."

"Oh, the lion," Margot said. "I'd forgotten the lion!"

So, Robert Wilson thought to himself, she *is* giving him a ride, isn't she? Or do you suppose that's her idea of putting up a good show? How should a woman act when she discovers her husband is a bloody coward? She's damn cruel but they're all cruel. They govern, of course, and to govern one has to be cruel sometimes. Still, I've seen enough of their damn terrorism.

"Have some more eland," he said to her politely.

That afternoon, late, Wilson and Macomber went out in the motor car with the native driver and the two gun-bearers. Mrs. Macomber stayed in the camp. It was too hot to go out, she said, and she was going with them in the early morning. As they drove off Wilson saw her standing under the big tree, looking pretty rather than beautiful in her faintly rosy kahki, her dark hair drawn back off her forehead and gathered in a knot low on her neck, her face as fresh, he thought, as though she were in England. She waved to them as the car went off through the swale of high grass and curved around through the trees into the small hills of orchard bush.

In the orchard bush they found a herd of impala, and leaving the car they stalked one old ram with long, wide-spread horns and Macomber killed it with a very creditable shot that knocked the buck down at a good two hundred yards and sent the herd off bounding wildly and leaping over one another's backs in long, leg-drawn-up leaps as unbelievable and as floating as those one makes sometimes in dreams.

"That was a good shot," Wilson said. "They're a small target."

"Is it worth-while head?" Macomber asked.

"It's excellent," Wilson told him. "You shoot like that and you'll have no trouble."

"Do you think we'll find buffalo tomorrow?"

"There's a good chance of it. They feed out early in the morning and with luck we may catch them in the open."

"I'd like to clear away that lion business," Macomber said. "It's not very pleasant to have your wife see you do something like that."

I should think it would be even more unpleasant to do it, Wilson thought, wife or no wife, or to talk about it having done it. But he said, "I wouldn't think about that any more. Any one could be upset by his first lion. That's all over."

But that night after dinner and a whisky and soda by the fire before going to bed, as Francis Macomber lay on his cot with the mosquito bar over him and listened to the night noises it was not all over. It was neither all over nor was it beginning. It was there exactly as it happened with some parts of it indelibly emphasized and he was miserably ashamed at it. But more than shame he felt cold, hollow fear in him. The fear was still there like a cold slimy hollow in all the emptiness where once his confidence had been and it made him feel sick. It was still there with him now.

It had started the night before when he had wakened and heard the lion roaring somewhere up along the river. It was a deep sound and at the end there were sort of coughing grunts that made him seem just outside the tent, and when Francis Macomber woke in the night to hear it he was afraid. He could hear his wife breathing quietly, asleep. There was no one to tell he was afraid, nor to be afraid with him, and, lying alone, he did not know the Somali proverb that says a brave man is always frightened three times by a lion; when he first sees his track, when he first hears him roar and when he first confronts him. Then while they were eating breakfast by lantern light out in the dining tent, before the sun was up, the lion roared again and Francis thought he was just at the edge of camp.

"Sounds like an old-timer," Robert Wilson said, looking up from his kippers and coffee. "Listen to him cough."

"Is he very close?"

"A mile or so up the stream."

"Will we see him?"

"We'll have a look."

"Does his roaring carry that far? It sounds as though he were right in camp."

"Carries a hell of a long way," said Robert Wilson. "It's strange the way it carries. Hope he's a shootable cat. The boys said there was a very big one about here."

"If I get a shot, where should I hit him," Macomber asked, "to stop him?"

"In the shoulders," Wilson said. "In the neck if you can make it. Shoot for bone. Break him down."

"I hope I can place it properly," Macomber said.

"You shoot very well," Wilson told him. "Take your time. Make sure of him. The first one in is the one that counts."

"What range will it be?"

"Can't tell. Lion has something to say about that. Won't shoot unless it's close enough so you can make sure."

"At under a hundred yards?" Macomber asked.

Wilson looked at him quickly.

"Hundred's about right. Might have to take him a bit under. Shouldn't chance a shot at much over that. A hundred's a decent range. You can hit him wherever you want at that. Here comes the Memsahib."

"Good morning," she said. "Are we going after that lion?"

"As soon as you deal with your breakfast," Wilson said. "How are you feeling?"

"Marvellous," she said. "I'm very excited."

"I'll just go and see that everything is ready." Wilson went off. As he left the lion roared again.

"Noisy beggar," Wilson said. "We'll put a stop to that."

"What's the matter, Francis?" his wife asked him.

"Nothing," Macomber said.

"Yes, there is," she said. "What are you upset about?"

"Nothing," he said.

"Tell me," she looked at him. "Don't you feel well?"

"It's that damned roaring," he said. "It's been going on all night, you know."

"Why didn't you wake me," she said. "I'd love to have heard it."

"I've got to kill the damned thing," Macomber said, miserably.

"Well, that's what you're out here for, isn't it?"

"Yes. But I'm nervous. Hearing the thing roar gets on my nerves."

"Well then, as Wilson said, kill him and stop his roaring."

"Yes, darling," said Francis Macomber. "It sounds easy, doesn't it?"

"You're not afraid, are you?"

"Of course not. But I'm nervous from hearing him roar all night."

"You'll kill him marvellously," she said. "I know you will. I'm awfully anxious to see it."

"Finish your breakfast and we'll be starting."

"It's not light yet," she said. "This is a ridiculous hour."

Just then the lion roared in a deep-chested moaning, suddenly guttural, ascending vibration that seemed to shake the air and ended in a sigh and a heavy, deep-chested grunt.

"He sounds almost here," Macomber's wife said.

"My God," said Macomber. "I hate that damned noise."

"It's very impressive."

"Impressive. It's frightful."

Robert Wilson came up then carrying his short, ugly, shockingly big-bored .505 Gibbs and grinning.

"Come on," he said. "Your gun-bearer has your Springfield and the big gun. Everything's in the car. Have you solids?"

"Yes."

"I'm ready," Mrs. Macomber said.

"Must make him stop that racket," Wilson said. "You get in front. The Memsahib can sit back here with me."

They climbed into the motor car and, in the gray first daylight, moved off up the river through the trees. Macomber opened the breech of his rifle and saw he had metal-cased bullets, shut the bolt and put the rifle on safety. He saw his hand was trembling. He felt in his pocket for more cartridges and moved his fingers over the cartridges in the loops of his tunic front. He turned back to where Wilson sat in the rear seat of the doorless, box-bodied motor car beside his wife, them both grinning with excitement, and Wilson leaned forward and whispered,

"See the birds dropping. Means the old boy has left his kill."

On the far bank of the stream Macomber could see, above the trees, vultures circling and plummeting down.

"Chances are he'll come to drink along here," Wilson whispered. "Before he goes to lay up. Keep an eye out."

They were driving slowly along the high bank of the stream which here cut deeply to its boulder-filled bed, and they wound in and out through big trees as they drove. Macomber was watching the opposite bank when he felt Wilson take hold of his arm. The car stopped.

"There he is," he heard the whisper. "Ahead and to the right. Get out and take him. He's a marvellous lion."

Macomber saw the lion now. He was standing almost broadside, his great head up and turned toward them. The early morning breeze that blew toward them was just stirring his dark mane, and the lion looked huge, silhouetted on the rise of bank in the gray morning light, his shoulders heavy, his barrel of a body bulking smoothly.

"How far is he?" asked Macomber, raising his rifle.

"About seventy-five. Get out and take him."

"Why not shoot from where I am?"

"You don't shoot them from cars," he heard Wilson saying in his ear. "Get out. He's not going to stay there all day."

Macomber stepped out of the curved opening at the side of the front seat, onto the step and down onto the ground. The lion still stood looking majestically and coolly toward this object that his eyes only showed in silhouette, bulking like some super-rhino. There was no man smell carried toward him and he watched the object, moving his great head a little from side to side. Then watching the object, not afraid, but hesitating before going down the bank to drink with such a thing opposite him, he saw a man figure detach itself from it and he turned his heavy head and swung away toward the cover of the trees as he heard a cracking crash and felt the slam of a .30–06 220-grain solid bullet that bit his flank and ripped in sudden hot scalding nausea through his stomach. He trotted, heavy, big-footed, swinging wounded full-bellied, through the trees toward the tall grass and cover, and the crash came again to go past him ripping the air apart. Then it crashed again and he felt the blow as it hit his lower ribs and ripped on through, blood sudden hot and frothy in his mouth, and he galloped toward the high grass where he could crouch and not be seen and make them bring the crashing thing close enough so he could make a rush and get the man that held it.

Macomber had not thought how the lion felt as he got out of the car. He only knew his hands were shaking and as he walked away from the car it was almost impossible for him to make his legs move. They were stiff in the thighs, but he could feel the muscles fluttering. He raised the rifle, sighted on the junction of the lion's head and shoulders and pulled the trigger. Nothing happened though he pulled until he thought his finger would break. Then he knew he had the safety on and as he lowered the rifle to move the safety over he moved another frozen pace forward, and the lion seeing his silhouette now clear of the silhouette of the car, turned and started off at a trot, and, as Macomber fired, he heard a whunk that meant that the bullet was home; but the lion kept on going. Macomber shot again and every one saw the bullet throw a spout of dirt beyond the trotting lion. He shot again, remembering to lower his aim, and they all heard the bullet hit, and the lion went into a gallop and was in the tall grass before he had the bolt pushed forward.

Macomber stood there feeling sick at his stomach, his hands that held the Springfield still cocked, shaking, and his wife and Robert Wilson were standing by him. Beside him too were the two gun-bearers chattering in Wakamba.

"I hit him," Macomber said. "I hit him twice."

"You gut-shot him and you hit him somewhere forward," Wilson said without enthusiasm. The gun-bearers looked very grave. They were silent now.

"You may have killed him," Wilson went on. "We'll have to wait a while before we go in to find out."

"What do you mean?"

"Let him get sick before we follow him up."

"Oh," said Macomber.

"He's a hell of a fine lion," Wilson said cheerfully. "He's gotten into a bad place though."

"Why is it bad?"

"Can't see him until you're on him."

"Oh," said Macomber.

"Come on," said Wilson. "The Memsahib can stay here in the car. We'll go to have a look at the blood spoor."

"Stay here, Margot," Macomber said to his wife. His mouth was very dry and it was hard for him to talk.

"Why?" she asked.

"Wilson says to."

"We're going to have a look," Wilson said. "You stay here. You can see even better from here."

"All right."

Wilson spoke in Swahili to the driver. He nodded and said, "Yes, Bwana."

Then they went down the steep bank and across the stream, climbing over and around the boulders and up the other bank, pulling up by some projecting roots, and along it until they found where the lion had been trotting when Macomber first shot. There was dark blood on the short grass that the gun-bearers pointed out with grass stems, and that ran away behind the river bank trees.

"What do we do?" asked Macomber.

"Not much choice," said Wilson. "We can't bring the car over. Bank's too steep. We'll let him stiffen up a bit and then you and I'll go in and have a look for him."

"Can't we set the grass on fire?" Macomber asked.

"Too green."

"Can't we send beaters?"

Wilson looked at him appraisingly. "Of course we can," he said. "But it's just a touch murderous. You see we know the lion's wounded. You can drive an unwounded lion—he'll move on ahead of a noise—but a wounded lion's going to charge. You can't see him until you're right on him. He'll make himself perfectly flat in cover you wouldn't think would hide a hare. You can't very well send boys in there to that sort of a show. Somebody bound to get mauled."

"What about the gun-bearers?"

"Oh, they'll go with us. It's their *shauri*. You see, they signed on for it. They don't look too happy though, do they?"

"I don't want to go in there," said Macomber. It was out before he knew he'd said it.

"Neither do I," said Wilson very cheerily. "Really no choice though." Then, as an afterthought, he glanced at Macomber and saw suddenly how he was trembling and the pitiful look on his face.

"You don't have to go in, of course," he said. "That's what I'm hired for, you know. That's why I'm so expensive."

"You mean you'd go in by yourself? Why not leave him there?"

Robert Wilson, whose entire occupation had been with the lion and the problem he presented, and who had not been thinking about Macomber except to note that he was rather windy, suddenly felt as though he had opened the wrong door in a hotel and seen something shameful.

"What do you mean?"

"Why not just leave him?"

"You mean pretend to ourselves he hasn't been hit?"

"No. Just drop it."

"It isn't done."

"Why not?"

"For one thing, he's certain to be suffering. For another, some one else might run onto him."

"I see."

"But you don't have to have anything to do with it."

"I'd like to," Macomber said. "I'm just scared, you know."

"I'll go ahead when we go in," Wilson said, "with Kongoni tracking. You keep behind me and a little to one side. Chances are we'll hear him growl. If we see him we'll both shoot. Don't worry about anything. I'll keep you backed up. As a matter of fact, you know, perhaps you'd better not go. It might be much better. Why don't you go over and join the Memsahib while I just get it over with?"

"No, I want to go."

"All right," said Wilson. "But don't go in if you don't want to. This is my *shauri* now, you know."

"I want to go," said Macomber.

They sat under a tree and smoked.

"Want to go back and speak to the Memsahib while we're waiting?" Wilson asked.

"No."

"I'll just step back and tell her to be patient."

"Good," said Macomber. He sat there, sweating under his arms, his mouth dry, his stomach hollow feeling, wanting to find courage to tell Wilson to go on and finish off the lion without him. He could not know that Wilson was furious because he had not noticed the state he was in earlier and sent him back to his wife. While he sat there Wilson came up. "I have your big gun," he said. "Take it. We've given him time, I think. Come on."

Macomber took the big gun and Wilson said:

"Keep behind me and about five yards to the right and do exactly as I tell you." Then he spoke in Swahili to the two gun-bearers who looked the picture of gloom.

"Let's go," he said.

"Could I have a drink of water?" Macomber asked. Wilson spoke to the older gun-bearer, who wore a canteen on his belt, and the man unbuckled it, unscrewed the top and handed it to Macomber, who took it noticing how heavy it seemed and how hairy and shoddy the felt covering was in his hand. He raised it to drink and looked ahead at the high grass with the flat-topped trees behind it. A breeze was blowing toward them and the grass rippled gently in the wind. He looked at the gun-bearer and he could see the gun-bearer was suffering too with fear.

Thirty-five yards into the grass the big lion lay flattened out along the ground. His ears were back and his only movement was a slight twitching up and down of his long, black-tufted tail. He had turned at bay as soon as he had reached this cover and he was sick with the wound through his full belly, and weakening with the wound through his lungs that brought a thin foamy red to his mouth each time he breathed. His flanks were wet and hot and flies were on the little openings the solid bullets had made in his tawny hide, and his big yellow eyes, narrowed with hate, looked straight ahead, only blinking when the pain came as he breathed, and his claws dug in the soft baked earth. All of him, pain, sickness, hatred and all of his remaining strength, was tightening into an absolute concentration for a rush. He could hear the men talking and he waited, gathering all of himself into this preparation for a charge as soon as the men would come into the grass. As he heard their voices his tail stiffened to twitch up and down, and, as they came into the edge of the grass, he made a coughing grunt and charged.

Kongoni, the old gun-bearer, in the lead watching the blood spoor, Wilson watching the grass for any movement, his big gun ready, the second gun-bearer looking ahead and listening, Macomber close to Wilson, his rifle cocked, they had just moved into the grass when Macomber heard the blood-choked coughing grunt, and saw the swishing rush in the grass. The next thing he knew he was running; running wildly, in panic in the open, running toward the stream.

He heard the *ca-ra-wong!* of Wilson's big rifle, and again in a second crashing *carawong!* and turning saw the lion, horrible-looking now, with half his head seeming to be gone, crawling toward Wilson in the edge of the tall grass while the red-faced man worked the bolt on the short ugly rifle and aimed carefully as another blasting *carawong!* came from the muzzle, and the crawling, heavy, yellow bulk of the lion stiffened and the huge, mutilated head slid forward and Macomber, standing by himself in the clearing where he had run, holding a loaded rifle, while two black men and a white man looked back at him in contempt, knew the lion was dead. He came toward Wilson, his tallness all seeming a naked reproach, and Wilson looked at him and said:

"Want to take pictures?"

"No," he said.

That was all any one had said until they reached the motor car. Then Wilson had said:

"Hell of a fine lion. Boys will skin him out. We might as well stay here in the shade."

Macomber's wife had not looked at him nor he at her and he had sat by her in the back seat with Wilson sitting in the front seat. Once he had reached over and taken his wife's hand without looking at her and she had removed her hand from his. Looking across the stream to where the gun-bearers were skinning out the lion he could see that she had been able to see the whole thing. While they sat there his wife had reached forward and put her hand on Wilson's shoulder. He turned and she had leaned forward over the low seat and kissed him on the mouth.

"Oh, I say," said Wilson, going redder than his natural baked color.

"Mr. Robert Wilson," she said. "The beautiful red-faced Mr. Robert Wilson."

Then she sat down beside Macomber again and looked away across the stream to where the lion lay, with uplifted, white-muscled, tendon-marked naked forearms, and white bloating belly, as the black men fleshed away the skin. Finally the gun-bearers brought the skin over, wet and heavy, and climbed in behind with it, rolling it up before they got in, and the motor car started. No one had said anything more until they were back in camp.

That was the story of the lion. Macomber did not know how the lion had felt before he started his rush, nor during it when the unbelievable smash of the .505 with a muzzle velocity of two tons had hit him in the mouth, nor what kept him coming after that, when the second ripping crash had smashed his hind quarters and he had come crawling on toward the crashing, blasting thing that had destroyed him. Wilson knew something about it and only expressed it by saying, "Damned fine lion," but Macomber did not know how Wilson felt about things either. He did not know how his wife felt except that she was through with him.

His wife had been through with him before but it never lasted. He was very wealthy, and would be much wealthier, and he knew she would not leave him ever now. That was one of the few things that he really knew. He knew about that, about motor cycles—that was earliest—about motor cars, about duck-shooting, about fishing, trout, salmon and big-sea, about sex in books, many books, too many books, about all court games, about dogs, not much about horses, about hanging on to his money, about most of the other things his world dealt in, and about his wife not leaving him. His wife had been a great beauty and she was still a great beauty in Africa, but she was not a great enough beauty any more at home to be able to leave him and better herself and she knew it and he knew it. She had missed the chance to leave him and he knew it. If he had been better with women she would probably have started to worry about him getting another new, beautiful wife; but she knew too much about him to worry about him either. Also, he had always had a great tolerance which seemed the nicest thing about him if it were not the most sinister.

All in all they were known as a comparatively happily married couple, one of those whose disruption is often rumored but never occurs, and as the society columnist put it, they were adding more than a spice of *adventure* to their much envied and ever-enduring *Romance* by a *Safari* in what was known as *Darkest Africa* until the Martin Johnsons lighted it on so many silver screens where they were pursuing *Old Simba* the lion, the buffalo, *Tembo* the elephant and as well collecting specimens for the Museum of Natural History. This same columnist had reported them *on the verge* as least three times in the past and they had been. But they always made it up. They had a sound basis of union. Margot was too beautiful for Macomber to divorce her and Macomber had too much money for Margot ever to leave him.

It was now about three o'clock in the morning and Francis Macomber, who had been asleep a little while after he had stopped thinking about the lion, wakened and then slept again, woke suddenly, frightened in a dream of the bloody-headed lion standing over him, and listening while his heart pounded, he realized that his wife was not in the other cot in the tent. He lay awake with that knowledge for two hours.

At the end of that time his wife came into the tent, lifted her mosquito bar and crawled cozily into bed.

"Where have you been?" Macomber asked in the darkness.

"Hello," she said. "Are you awake?"

"Where have you been?"

"I just went out to get a breath of air."

"You did, like hell."

"What do you want me to say, darling?"

"Where have you been?"

"Out to get a breath of air."

"That's a new name for it. You *are* a bitch."

"Well, you're a coward."

"All right," he said. "What of it?"

"Nothing as far as I'm concerned. But please let's not talk, darling, because I'm very sleepy."

"You think that I'll take anything."

"I know you will, sweet."

"Well, I won't."

"Please, darling, let's not talk. I'm so very sleepy."

"There wasn't going to be any of that. You promised there wouldn't be."

"Well, there is now," she said sweetly.

"You said if we made this trip that there would be none of that. You promised."

"Yes, darling. That's the way I meant it to be. But the trip was spoiled yesterday. We don't have to talk about it, do we?"

"You don't wait long when you have an advantage, do you?"

"Please let's not talk. I'm so sleeply, darling."

"I'm going to talk."

"Don't mind me then, because I'm going to sleep." And she did.

At breakfast they were all three at the table before daylight and Francis Macomber found that, of all the many men that he had hated, he hated Robert Wilson the most.

"Sleep well?" Wilson asked in his throaty voice, filling a pipe.

"Did you?"

"Topping," the white hunter told him.

You bastard, thought Macomber, you insolent bastard.

So she woke him when she came in, Wilson thought, looking at them both with his flat, cold eyes. Well, why doesn't he keep his wife where she belongs? What does he think I am, a bloody plaster saint? Let him keep her where she belongs. It's his own fault.

"Do you think we'll find buffalo?" Margot asked, pushing away a dish of apricots.

"Chance of it," Wilson said and smiled at her. "Why don't you stay in camp?"

"Not for anything," she told him.

"Why not order her to stay in camp?" Wilson said to Macomber.

"You order her," said Macomber coldly.

"Let's not have any ordering, nor," turning to Macomber, "any silliness, Francis," Margot said quite pleasantly.

"Are you ready to start?" Macomber asked.

"Any time," Wilson told him. "Do you want the Memsahib to go?"

"Does it make any difference whether I do or not?"

The hell with it, thought Robert Wilson. The utter complete hell with it. So this is what it's going to be like. Well, this is what it's going to be like, then.

"Makes no difference," he said.

"You're sure you wouldn't like to stay in camp with her yourself and let me go out and hunt the buffalo?" Macomber asked.

"Can't do that," said Wilson. "Wouldn't talk rot if I were you."

"I'm not talking rot. I'm disgusted."

"Bad word, disgusted."

"Francis, will you please try to speak sensibly!" his wife said.

"I speak too damned sensibly," Macomber said. "Did you ever eat such filthy food?"

"Something wrong with the food?" asked Wilson quietly.

"No more than with everything else."

"I'd pull yourself together, laddybuck," Wilson said very quietly. "There's a boy waits at table that understands a little English."

"The hell with him."

Wilson stood up and puffing on his pipe strolled away, speaking a few words in Swahili to one of the gun-bearers who was standing waiting for him. Macomber and his wife sat on at the table. He was staring at his coffee cup.

"If you make a scene I'll leave you, darling," Margot said quietly.

"No, you won't."

"You can try it and see."

"You won't leave me."

"No," she said. "I won't leave you and you'll behave yourself."

"Behave myself? That's a way to talk. Behave myself."

"Yes. Behave yourself."

"Why don't *you* try behaving?"

"I've tried it so long. So very long."

"I hate that red-faced swine," Macomber said. "I loathe the sight of him."

"He's really *very* nice."

"Oh, *shut up,*" Macomber almost shouted. Just then the car came up and stopped in front of the dining tent and the driver and the two gun-bearers got out. Wilson walked over and looked at the husband and wife sitting there at the table.

"Going shooting?" he asked.

"Yes," said Macomber, standing up. "Yes."

"Better bring a woolly. It will be cool in the car," Wilson said.

"I'll get my leather jacket," Margot said.

"The boy has it," Wilson told her. He climbed into the front with the driver and Francis Macomber and his wife sat, not speaking, in the back seat.

Hope the silly beggar doesn't take a notion to blow the back of my head off, Wilson thought to himself. Women *are* a nuisance on safari.

The car was grinding down to cross the river at a pebbly ford in the gray daylight and then climbed, angling up the steep bank, where Wilson had ordered a way shovelled out the day before so they could reach the parklike wooded rolling country on the far side.

It was a good morning, Wilson thought. There was a heavy dew and as the wheels went through the grass and low bushes he could smell the odor of the crushed fronds. It was an odor like verbena and he liked this early morning smell of the dew, the crushed bracken and the look of the tree trunks showing black through the early morning mist, as the car made its way through the untracked, parklike country. He had put the two in the back seat out of his mind now and was thinking about buffalo. The buffalo that he was after stayed in the daytime in a thick swamp where it was impossible to get a shot, but in the night they fed out into an open stretch of country and if he could come between them and their swamp with the car, Macomber would have a good chance at them in the open. He did not want to hunt buff with Macomber in thick cover. He did not want to hunt buff or anything else with Macomber at all, but he was a professional hunter and he had hunted with some rare ones in his time. If they got buff today there would only be rhino to come and the poor man would have gone through his dangerous game and things might pick up. He'd have nothing more to do with the woman and Macomber would get over that too. He must have gone through plenty of that before by the look of things. Poor beggar. He must have a way of getting over it. Well, it was the poor sod's own bloody fault.

He, Robert Wilson, carried a double size cot on safari to accommodate any windfalls he might receive. He had hunted for a certain clientele, the international, fast, sporting set, where the women did not feel they were getting their money's worth unless they had shared that cot with the white hunter. He despised them when he was away from them although he liked some of them well enough at the time, but he made his living by them; and their standards were his standards as long as they were hiring him.

They were his standards in all except the shooting. He had his own standards about the killing and they could live up to them or get some one else to hunt them. He knew, too, that they all respected him for this. This Macomber was an odd one though. Damned if he wasn't. Now the wife. Well, the wife. Yes, the wife. Hm, the wife. Well he'd dropped all that. He looked around at them. Macomber sat grim and furious. Margot smiled at him. She looked younger today, more innocent and fresher and not so professionally beautiful. What's in her heart God knows, Wilson thought. She hadn't talked much last night. At that it was a pleasure to see her.

The motor car climbed up a slight rise and went on through the trees and then out into a grassy prairie-like opening and kept in the shelter of the trees along the edge, the driver going slowly and Wilson looking carefully out across the prairie and all along its far side. He stopped the car and studied the opening with his field glasses. Then he motioned to the driver to go on and the car moved slowly along, the driver avoiding wart-hog holes and driving around the mud castles ants had built. Then, looking across the opening, Wilson suddenly turned and said,

"By God, there they are!"

And looking where he pointed, while the car jumped forward and Wilson spoke in rapid Swahili to the driver, Macomber saw three huge, black animals looking almost cylindrical in their long heaviness, like big black tank cars, moving at a gallop across the far edge of the open prairie. They moved at a stiff-necked, stiff bodied gallop and he could see the upswept wide black horns on their heads as they galloped heads out; the heads not moving.

"They're three old bulls," Wilson said. "We'll cut them off before they get to the swamp."

The car was going a wild forty-five miles an hour across the open and as Macomber watched, the buffalo got bigger and bigger until he could see the gray, hairless, scabby look of one huge bull and how his neck was a part of his shoulders and the shiny black of his horns as he galloped a little behind the others that were strung out in that steady plunging gait; and then, the car swaying as though it had just jumped a road, they drew up close and he could see the plunging hugeness of the bull, and the dust in his sparsely haired hide, the wide boss of horn and his outstretched, wide-nostrilled muzzle, and he was raising his rifle when Wilson shouted, "Not from the car, you fool!" and he had no fear, only hatred of Wilson, while the brakes clamped on and the car skidded, plowing sideways to an almost stop and Wilson was out on one side and he on the other, stumbling as his feet hit the still speeding-by of the earth, and then he was shooting at the bull as he moved away, hearing the bullets whunk into him, emptying his rifle at him as he moved steadily away, finally remembering to get his shots forward into the shoulder, and as he fumbled to re-load, he saw the bull was down. Down on his knees, his big head tossing, and seeing the other two still galloping he shot at the leader and hit him. He shot again and missed and he heard the *carawonging* roar as Wilson shot and saw the leading bull slide forward onto his nose.

"Get that other," Wilson said. "Now you're shooting!"

But the other bull was moving steadily at the same gallop and he missed, throwing a spout of dirt, and Wilson missed and the dust rose in a cloud and Wilson shouted, "Come on. He's too far!" and grabbed his arm and they were in the car again, Macomber and Wilson hanging on the sides and rocketing swayingly over the uneven ground, drawing up on the steady, plunging, heavy-necked, straight-moving gallop of the bull.

They were behind him and Macomber was filling his rifle, dropping shells onto the ground, jamming it, clearing the jam, then they were almost up with the bull when Wilson yelled "Stop," and the car skidded so that it almost swung over and Macomber fell forward onto his feet, slammed his bolt forward and fired as far forward as he could aim into the galloping, rounded black back, aimed and shot again, then again, then again, and the bullets, all of them hitting, had no effect on the buffalo that he could see. Then Wilson shot, the roar deafening him, and he could see the bull stagger. Macomber shot again, aiming carefully, and down he came, onto his knees.

"All right," Wilson said. "Nice work. That's the three."

Macomber felt a drunken elation.

"How many times did you shoot?" he asked.

"Just three," Wilson said. "You killed the first bull. The biggest one. I helped you finish the other two. Afraid they might have got into cover. You had them killed. I was just mopping up a little. You shot damn well."

"Let's go to the car," said Macomber. "I want a drink."

"Got to finish off that buff first," Wilson told him. The buffalo was on his knees and he jerked his head furiously and bellowed in pig-eyed, roaring rage as they came toward him.

"Watch he doesn't get up," Wilson said. Then, "Get a little broadside and take him in the neck just behind the ear."

Macomber aimed carefully at the center of the huge, jerking, rage-driven neck and shot. At the shot the head dropped forward.

"That does it," said Wilson. "Got the spine. They're a hell of a looking thing, aren't they?"

"Let's get the drink," said Macomber. In his life he had never felt so good.

In the car Macomber's wife sat very white faced. "You were marvelous, darling," she said to Macomber. "What a ride."

"Was it rough?" Wilson asked.

"It was frightful. I've never been more frightened in my life."

"Let's all have a drink," Macomber said.

"By all means," said Wilson. "Give it to the Memsahib." She drank the neat whisky from the flask and shuddered a little when she swallowed. She handed the flask to Macomber who handed it to Wilson.

"It was frightfully exciting," she said. "It's given me a dreadful headache. I didn't know you were allowed to shoot them from cars though."

"No one shot from cars," said Wilson coldly.

"I mean chase them from cars."

"Wouldn't ordinarily," Wilson said. "Seemed sporting enough to me though while we were doing it. Taking more chance driving that way across the plain full of holes and one thing and another than hunting on foot. Buffalo could have charged us each time we shot if he liked. Gave him every chance. Wouldn't mention it to any one though. It's illegal if that's what you mean."

"It seemed very unfair to me," Margot said, "chasing those big helpless things in a motor car."

"Did it?" said Wilson

"What would happen if they heard about it in Nairobi?"

"I'd lose my licence for one thing. Other unpleasantnesses," Wilson said, taking a drink from the flask. "I'd be out of business."

"Really?"

"Yes, really."

"Well," said Macomber, and he smiled for the first time all day. "Now she has something on you."

"You have such a pretty way of putting things, Francis," Margot Macomber said. Wilson looked at them both. If a four-letter man marries a five-letter woman, he was thinking, what number of letters would their children be? What he said was, "We lost a gun-bearer. Did you notice it?"

"My God, no," Macomber said.

"Here he comes," Wilson said. "He's all right. He must have fallen off when we left the first bull."

Approaching them was the middle-aged gun-bearer, limping along in his knitted cap, khaki tunic, shorts and rubber sandals, gloomy-faced and disgusted looking. As he came up he called out to Wilson in Swahili and they all saw the change in the white hunter's face.

"What does he say?" asked Margot.

"He says the first bull got up and went into the bush," Wilson said with no expression in his voice.

"Oh," said Macomber blankly.

"Then it's going to be just like the lion," said Margot, full of anticipation.

"It's not going to be a damned bit like the lion," Wilson told her. "Did you want another drink, Macomber?"

"Thanks, yes," Macomber said. He expected the feeling he had had about the lion to come back but it did not. For the first time in his life he really felt wholly without fear. Instead of fear he had a feeling of definite elation.

"We'll go and have a look at the second bull," Wilson said. "I'll tell the driver to put the car in the shade."

"What are you going to do?" asked Margaret Macomber.

"Take a look at the buff," Wilson said.

"I'll come."

"Come along."

The three of them walked over to where the second buffalo bulked blackly in the open, head forward on the grass, the massive horns swung wide.

"He's a very good head," Wilson said. "That's close to a fifty-inch spread."

Macomber was looking at him with delight.

"He's hateful looking," said Margot. "Can't we go into the shade?"

"Of course," Wilson said. "Look," he said to Macomber, and pointed. "See that patch of bush?"

"Yes."

"That's where the first bull went in. The gun-bearer said when he fell off the bull was down. He was watching us helling along and the other two buff galloping. When he looked up there was the bull up and looking at him. Gun-bearer ran like hell and the bull went off slowly into that bush."

"Can we go in after him now?" asked Macomber eagerly.

Wilson looked at him appraisingly. Damned if this isn't a strange one, he thought. Yesterday he's scared sick and today he's a ruddy fire eater.

"No, we'll give him a while."

"Let's please go into the shade," Margot said. Her face was white and she looked ill.

They made their way to the car where it stood under a single, wide-spreading tree and all climbed in.

"Chances are he's dead in there," Wilson remarked. "After a little we'll have a look."

Macomber felt a wild unreasonable happiness that he had never known before.

"By God, that was a chase," he said. "I've never felt any such feeling. Wasn't it marvellous, Margot?"

"I hated it."

"Why?"

"I hated it," she said bitterly. "I loathed it."

"You know I don't think I'd ever be afraid of anything again," Macomber said to Wilson. "Something happened in me after we first saw the buff and started after him. Like a dam bursting. It was pure excitement."

"Cleans out your liver," said Wilson. "Damn funny things happen to people."

Macomber's face was shining. "You know something did happen to me," he said. "I feel absolutely different."

His wife said nothing and eyed him strangely. She was sitting far back in the seat and Macomber was sitting forward talking to Wilson who turned sideways talking over the back of the front seat.

"You know, I'd like to try another lion," Macomber said. "I'm really not afraid of them now. After all, what can they do to you?"

"That's it," said Wilson. "Worst one can do is kill you. How does it go? Shakespeare. Damned good. See if I can remember. Oh, damned good. Used to quote it to myself at one time. Let's see. 'By my troth, I care not; a man can die but once; we owe God a death and let it go which way it will, he that dies this year is quit for the next.' Damned fine, eh?"

He was very embarrassed, having brought out this thing he had lived by, but he had seen men come of age before and it always moved him. It was not a matter of their twenty-first birthday.

It had taken a strange chance of hunting, a sudden precipitation into action without opportunity for worrying beforehand, to bring this about with Macomber, but regardless of how it had happened it had most certainly happened. Look at the beggar now, Wilson thought. It's that some of them stay little boys so long, Wilson thought. Sometimes all their lives. Their figures stay boyish when they're fifty. The great American boy-men. Damned strange people. But he liked this Macomber now. Damned strange fellow. Probably meant the end of cuckoldry too. Well, that would be a damned good thing. Damned good thing. Beggar had probably been afraid all his life. Don't know what started it. But over now. Hadn't had time to be afraid with the buff. That and being angry too. Motor car too. Motor cars made it familiar. Be a damn fire eater now. He'd seen it in the war work the same way. More of a change than any loss of virginity. Fear gone like an operation. Something else grew in its place. Main thing a man had. Made him into a man. Women knew it too. No bloody fear.

From the far corner of the seat Margaret Macomber looked at the two of them. There was no change in Wilson. She saw Wilson as she had seen him the day before when she had first realized what his great talent was. But she saw the change in Francis Macomber now.

"Do you have that feeling of happiness about what's going to happen?" Macomber asked, still exploring his new wealth.

"You're not supposed to mention it," Wilson said, looking in the other's face. "Much more fashionable to say you're scared. Mind you, you'll be scared too, plenty of times."

"But you *have* a feeling of happiness about action to come?"

"Yes," said Wilson. "There's that. Doesn't do to talk too much about all this. Talk the whole thing away. No pleasure in anything if you mouth it up too much."

"You're both talking rot," said Margot. "Just because you've chased some helpless animals in a motor car you talk like heroes."

"Sorry," said Wilson. "I have been gassing too much." She's worried about it already, he thought.

"If you don't know what we're talking about why not keep out of it?" Macomber asked his wife.

"You've gotten awfully brave, awfully suddenly," his wife said contemptuously, but her contempt was not secure. She was very afraid of something.

Macomber laughed, a very natural hearty laugh. "You know I *have*," he said. "I really have."

"Isn't it sort of late?" Margot said bitterly. Because she had done the best she could for many years back and the way they were together now was no one person's fault.

"Not for me," said Macomber.

Margot said nothing but sat back in the corner of the seat.

"Do you think we've given him time enough?" Macomber asked Wilson cheerfully.

"We might have a look," Wilson said. "Have you any solids left?"

"The gun-bearer has some."

Wilson called in Swahili and the older gun-bearer, who was skinning out one of the heads, straightened up, pulled a box of solids out of his pocket and brought them over to Macomber, who filled his magazine and put the remaining shells in his pocket.

"You might as well shoot the Springfield," Wilson said. "You're used to it. We'll leave the Mannlicher in the car with the Memsahib. Your gun-bearer can carry your heavy gun. I've this damned cannon. Now let me tell you about them." He had saved this until the last because he did not want to worry Macomber. "When a buff comes he comes with his head high and thrust straight out. The boss of the horns covers any sort of a brain shot. The only shot is straight into the nose. The only other shot is into his chest or, if you're to one side, into the neck or the shoulders. After they've been hit once they take a hell of a lot of killing. Don't try anything fancy. Take the easiest shot there is. They've finished skinning out that head now. Should we get started?"

He called to the gun-bearers, who came up wiping their hands, and the older one got into the back.

"I'll only take Kongoni," Wilson said. "The other can watch to keep the birds away."

As the car moved slowly across the open space toward the island of brushy trees that ran in a tongue of foliage along a dry water course that cut the open swale, Macomber felt his heart pounding and his mouth was dry again, but it was excitement, not fear.

"Here's where he went in," Wilson said. Then to the gun-bearer in Swahili, "Take the blood spoor."

The car was parallel to the patch of bush. Macomber, Wilson and the gun-bearer got down. Macomber, looking back, saw his wife, with the rifle by her side, looking at him. He waved to her and she did not wave back.

The brush was very thick ahead and the ground was dry. The middle-aged gun-bearer was sweating heavily and Wilson had his hat down over his eyes and his red neck showed just ahead of Macomber. Suddenly the gun-bearer said something in Swahili to Wilson and ran forward.

"He's dead in there," Wilson said. "Good work," and he turned to grip Macomber's hand and as they shook hands, grinning at each other, the gun-bearer shouted wildly and they saw him coming out of the bush sideways, fast as a crab, and the bull coming, nose out, mouth tight closed, blood dripping, massive head straight out, coming in a charge, his little pig eyes bloodshot as he looked at them. Wilson, who was ahead was kneeling shooting, and Macomber, as he fired, unhearing his shot in the roaring of Wilson's gun, saw fragments like slate burst from the huge boss of the horns, and the head jerked, he shot again at the wide nostrils and saw the horns jolt again and fragments fly, and he did not see Wilson now and, aiming carefully, shot again with the buffalo's huge bulk almost on him and his rifle almost level with the on-coming head, nose out, and he could see the little wicked eyes and the head started to lower and he felt a sudden white-hot, blinding flash explode inside his head and that was all he ever felt.

Wilson had ducked to one side to get in a shoulder shot. Macomber had stood solid and shot for the nose, shooting a touch high each time and hitting the heavy horns, splintering and chipping them like hitting a slate roof, and Mrs. Macomber, in the car, had shot at the buffalo with the 6.5 Mannlicher as it seemed about to gore Macomber and had hit her husband about two inches up and a little to one side of the base of his skull.

Francis Macomber lay now, face down, not two yards from where the buffalo lay on his side and his wife knelt over him with Wilson beside her.

"I wouldn't turn him over," Wilson said.

The woman was crying hysterically.

"I'd get back in the car," Wilson said. "Where's the rifle?"

She shook her head, her face contorted. The gun-bearer picked up the rifle.

"Leave it as it is," said Wilson. Then, "Go get Abdulla so that he may witness the manner of the accident."

He knelt down, took a handkerchief from his pocket, and spread it over Francis Macomber's crew-cropped head where it lay. The blood sank into the dry, loose earth.

Wilson stood up and saw the buffalo on his side, his legs out, his thinly-haired belly crawling with ticks. "Hell of a good bull," his brain registered automatically. "A good fifty inches, or better. Better." He called to the driver and told him to spread a blanket over the body and stay by it. Then he walked over to the motor car where the woman sat crying in the corner.

"That was a pretty thing to do," he said in a toneless voice. "He *would* have left you too."

"Stop it," she said.

"Of course it's an accident," he said. "I know that."

"Stop it," she said.

"Don't worry," he said. "There will be a certain amount of unpleasantness but I will have some photographs taken that will be very useful at the inquest. There's the testimony of the gun-bearers and the driver too. You're perfectly all right."

"Stop it," she said.

"There's a hell of a lot to be done," he said. "And I'll have to send a truck off to the lake to wireless for a plane to take the three of us into Nairobi. Why didn't you poison him? That's what they do in England."

"Stop it. Stop it. Stop it," the woman cried.

Wilson looked at her with his flat blue eyes.

"I'm through now," he said. "I was a little angry. I'd begun to like your husband."

"Oh, please stop it," she said. "Please, please stop it."

"That's better," Wilson said. "Please is much better. Now I'll stop."

A DOMESTIC DILEMMA

Carson McCullers

(1917–1967)

Biography p. 1087

On Thursday Martin Meadows left the office early enough to make the first express bus home. It was the hour when the evening lilac glow was fading in the slushy streets, but by the time the bus had left the Mid-town terminal the bright city night had come. On Thursdays the maid had a half-day off and Martin liked to get home as soon as possible, since for the past year his wife had not been—well. This Thursday he was very tired and, hoping that no regular commuter would single him out for conversation, he fastened his attention to the newspaper until the bus had crossed the George Washington Bridge. Once on 9-W Highway Martin always felt that the trip was halfway done, he breathed deeply, even in cold weather when only ribbons of draught cut through the smoky air of the bus, confident that he was breathing country air. It used to be that at this point he would relax and begin to think with pleasure of his home. But in this last year nearness brought only a sense of tension and he did not anticipate the journey's end. This evening Martin kept his face close to the window and watched the barren fields and lonely lights of passing townships. There was a moon, pale on the dark earth and areas of late, porous snow; to Martin the countryside seemed vast and somehow desolate that evening. He took his hat from the rack and put his folded newspaper in the pocket of his overcoat a few minutes before time to pull the cord.

The cottage was a block from the bus stop, near the river but not directly on the shore; from the living-room window you could look across the street and opposite yard and see the Hudson. The cottage was modern, almost too white and new on the narrow plot of yard. In summer the grass was soft and bright and Martin carefully tended a flower border and a rose trellis. But during the cold, fallow months the yard was bleak and the cottage seemed naked. Lights were on that evening in all the rooms in the little house and Martin hurried up the front walk. Before the steps he stopped to move a wagon out of the way.

The children were in the living room, so intent on play that the opening of the front door was at first unnoticed. Martin stood looking at his safe, lovely children. They had opened the bottom drawer of the secretary and taken out the Christmas decorations. Andy had managed to plug in the Christmas tree lights and the green and red bulbs glowed with out-of-season festivity on the rug of the living room. At the moment he was trying to trail the bright cord over Marianne's rocking horse. Marianne sat on the floor pulling off an angel's wings. The children wailed a startling welcome. Martin swung the fat little baby girl up to his shoulder and Andy threw himself against his father's legs.

'Daddy, Daddy, Daddy!'

Martin set down the little girl carefully and swung Andy a few times like a pendulum. Then he picked up the Christmas tree cord.

'What's all this stuff doing out? Help me put it back in the drawer. You're not to fool with the light socket. Remember I told you that before. I mean it, Andy.'

The six-year-old child nodded and shut the secretary drawer. Martin stroked his fair soft hair and his hand lingered tenderly on the nape of the child's frail neck.

'Had supper yet, Bumpkin?'

'It hurt. The toast was hot.'

The baby girl stumbled on the rug and, after the first surprise of the fall, began to cry; Martin picked her up and carried her in his arms back to the kitchen.

'See, Daddy,' said Andy. 'The toast——'

Emily had laid the childrens' supper on the uncovered porcelain table. There were two plates with the remains of cream-of-wheat and eggs and silver mugs that had held milk. There was also a platter of cinnamon toast, untouched except for one tooth-marked bite. Martin sniffed the bitten piece and nibbled gingerly. Then he put the toast into the garbage pail.

'Hoo—phui—What on earth!'

Emily had mistaken the tin of cayenne for the cinnamon.

'I like to have burnt up,' Andy said. 'Drank water and ran outdoors and opened my mouth. Marianne didn't eat none.'

'Any,' corrected Martin. He stood helpless, looking around the walls of the kitchen. 'Well, that's that, I guess,' he said finally. 'Where is your mother now?'

'She's up in you all's room.'

Martin left the children in the kitchen and went up to his wife. Outside the door he waited for a moment to still his anger. He did not knock and once inside the room he closed the door behind him.

Emily sat in the rocking chair by the window of the pleasant room. She had been drinking something from a tumbler and as he entered she put the glass hurriedly on the floor behind the chair. In her attitude there was confusion and guilt which she tried to hide by a show of spurious vivacity.

'Oh, Marty! You home already? The time slipped up on me. I was just going down——' She lurched to him and her kiss was strong with sherry. When he stood unresponsive she stepped back a pace and giggled nervously.

'What's the matter with you? Standing there like a barber pole. Is anything wrong with you?'

'Wrong with *me?*' Martin bent over the rocking chair and picked up the tumbler from the floor. 'If you could only realize how sick I am—how bad it is for all of us.'

Emily spoke in a false, airy voice that had become too familiar to him. Often at such times she affected a slight English accent, copying perhaps some actress she admired. 'I haven't the vaguest idea what you mean. Unless you are referring to the glass I used for a spot of sherry. I had a finger of sherry——maybe two. But what is the crime in that, pray tell me? I'm quite all right. Quite all right.'

'So anyone can see.'

As she went into the bathroom Emily walked with careful gravity. She turned on the cold water and dashed some on her face with her cupped hands, then patted herself dry with the corner of a bath towel. Her face was delicately featured and young, unblemished.

'I was just going down to make dinner.' She tottered and balanced herself by holding to the door frame.

'I'll take care of dinner. You stay up here. I'll bring it up.'

'I'll do nothing of the sort. Why, whoever heard of such a thing?'

'Please,' Martin said.

'Leave me alone. I'm quite all right. I was just on the way down——'

'Mind what I say.'

'Mind your grandmother.'

She lurched toward the door, but Martin caught her by the arm. 'I don't want the children to see you in this condition. Be reasonable.'

'Condition!' Emily jerked her arm. Her voice rose angrily. 'Why, because I drink a couple of sherries in the afternoon you're trying to make me out a drunkard. Condition! Why, I don't even touch whiskey. As well you know. *I* don't swill liquor at bars. And that's more than you can say. I don't even have a cocktail at dinner time. I only sometimes have a glass of sherry. What, I ask you, is the disgrace of that? Condition!'

Martin sought words to calm his wife. 'We'll have a quiet supper by ourselves up here. That's a good girl.' Emily sat on the side of the bed and he opened the door for a quick departure.

'I'll be back in a jiffy.'

As he busied himself with the dinner downstairs he was lost in the familiar question as to how this problem had come upon his home. He himself had always enjoyed a good drink. When they were still living in Alabama they had served long drinks or cocktails as a matter of course. For years they had drunk one or two—possibly three drinks before dinner, and at bedtime a long nightcap. Evenings before holidays they might get a buzz on, might even become a little tight. But alcohol had never seemed a problem to him, only a bothersome expense that with the increase in the family they could scarcely afford. It was only after his company had transferred him to New York that Martin was aware that certainly his wife was drinking too much. She was tippling, he noticed, during the day.

The problem acknowledged, he tried to analyze the source. The change from Alabama to New York had somehow disturbed her; accustomed to the idle warmth of a small Southern town, the matrix of the family and cousinship and childhood friends, she had failed to accommodate herself to the stricter, lonelier mores of the North. The duties of motherhood and housekeeping were onerous to her. Homesick for Paris City, she had made no friends in the suburban town. She read only magazines and murder books. Her interior life was insufficient without the artifice of alcohol.

The revelations of incontinence insidiously undermined his previous conceptions of his wife. There were times of unexplainable malevolence, times when the alcoholic fuse caused an explosion of unseemly anger. He encountered a latent coarseness in Emily, inconsistent with her natural simplicity. She lied about drinking and deceived him with unsuspected stratagems.

Then there was an accident. Coming home from work one evening about a year ago, he was greeted with screams from the children's room. He found Emily holding the baby, wet and naked from her bath. The baby had been dropped, her frail, frail skull striking the table edge, so that a thread of blood was soaking into the gossamer hair. Emily was sobbing and intoxicated. As Martin cradled the hurt child, so infinitely precious at that moment, he had an affrighted vision of the future.

The next day Marianne was all right. Emily vowed that never again would she touch liquor, and for a few weeks she was sober, cold and downcast. Then gradually she began—not whiskey or gin—but quantities of beer or sherry, or outlandish liqueurs; once he had come across a hatbox of empty crème de menthe bottles. Martin found a dependable maid who managed the household competently. Virgie was also from Alabama and Martin had never dared tell Emily the wage scale customary in New York. Emily's drinking was entirely secret now, done before he reached the house. Usually the effects were almost imperceptible—a looseness of movement or the heavy-lidded eyes. The times of irresponsibilities, such as the cayenne-pepper toast, were rare, and Martin could dismiss his worries when Virgie was at the house. But, nevertheless, anxiety was always latent, a threat of indefined disaster that underlaid his days.

'Marianne!' Martin called, for even the recollection of that time brought the need for reassurance. The baby girl, no longer hurt, but no less precious to her father, came into the kitchen with her brother. Martin went on with the preparations for the meal. He opened a can of soup and put two chops in the frying pan. Then he sat down by the table and took his Marianne on his knees for a pony ride. Andy watched them, his fingers wobbling the tooth that had been loose all that week.

'Andy-the-candyman!' Martin said. 'Is that old critter still in your mouth? Come closer, let Daddy have a look.'

'I got a string to pull it with.' The child brought from his pocket a tangled thread. 'Virgie said to tie it to the tooth and tie the other end to the doorknob and shut the door real suddenly.'

Martin took out a clean handkerchief and felt the loose tooth carefully. 'That tooth is coming out of my Andy's mouth tonight. Otherwise I'm awfully afraid we'll have a tooth tree in the family.'

'A what?'

'A tooth tree,' Martin said. 'You'll bite into something and swallow that tooth. And the tooth will take root in poor Andy's stomach and grow into a tooth tree with sharp little teeth instead of leaves.'

'Shoo, Daddy,' Andy said. But he held the tooth firmly between his grimy little thumb and forefinger. 'There ain't any tree like that. I never seen one.'

'There *isn't* any tree like that and I never *saw* one.'

Martin tensed suddenly. Emily was coming down the stairs. He listened to her fumbling footsteps, his arm embracing the little boy with dread. When Emily came into the room he saw from her movements and her sullen face that she had again been at the sherry bottle. She began to yank open drawers and set the table.

'Condition!' she said in a furry voice. 'You talk to me like that. Don't think I'll forget. I remember every dirty lie you say to me. Don't you think for a minute that I forget.'

'Emily!' he begged. 'The children——'

'The children—yes! Don't think I don't see through your dirty plots and schemes. Down here trying to turn my own children against me. Don't think I don't see and understand.'

'Emily! I beg you—please go upstairs.'

'So you can turn my children—my very own children——' Two large tears coursed rapidly down her cheeks. 'Trying to turn my little boy, my Andy, against his own mother.'

With drunken impulsiveness Emily knelt on the floor before the startled child. Her hands on his shoulders balanced her. 'Listen, my Andy—you wouldn't listen to any lies your father tells you? You wouldn't believe what he says? Listen, Andy, what was your father telling you before I came downstairs?' Uncertain, the child sought his father's face. 'Tell me. Mama wants to know.'

'About the tooth tree.'

'What?'

The child repeated the words and she echoed them with unbelieving terror. 'The tooth tree!' She swayed and renewed her grasp on the child's shoulder. 'I don't know what you're talking about. But listen, Andy, Mama is all right, isn't she?' The tears were spilling down her face and Andy drew back from her, for he was afraid. Grasping the table edge, Emily stood up.

'See! You have turned my child against me.'

Marianne began to cry, and Martin took her in his arms.

'That's all right, you can take *your* child. You have always shown partiality from the very first. I don't mind, but at least you can leave me my little boy.'

Andy edged close to his father and touched his leg. 'Daddy,' he wailed.

Martin took the children to the foot of the stairs. 'Andy, you take up Marianne and Daddy will follow you in a minute.'

'But Mama?' the child asked, whispering.

'Mama will be all right. Don't worry.'

Emily was sobbing at the kitchen table, her face buried in the crook of her arm. Martin poured a cup of soup and set it before her. Her rasping sobs unnerved him; the vehemence of her emotion, irrespective of the source, touched in him a strain of tenderness. Unwillingly he laid his hand on her dark hair. 'Sit up and drink the soup.' Her face as she looked up at him was chastened and imploring. The boy's withdrawal or the touch of Martin's hand had turned the tenor of her mood.

'Ma-Martin,' she sobbed. 'I'm so ashamed.'

'Drink the soup.'

Obeying him, she drank between gasping breaths. After a second cup she allowed him to lead her up to their room. She was docile now and more restrained. He laid her nightgown on the bed and was about to leave the room when a fresh round of grief, the alcoholic tumult, came again.

'He turned away. My Andy looked at me and turned away.'

Impatience and fatigue hardened his voice, but he spoke warily. 'You forget that Andy is still a little child—he can't comprehend the meaning of such scenes.'

'Did I make a scene? Oh, Martin, did I make a scene before the children?'

Her horrified face touched and amused him against his will. 'Forget it. Put on your nightgown and go to sleep.'

'My child turned away from me. Andy looked at his mother and turned away. The children——'

She was caught in the rhythmic sorrow of alcohol. Martin withdrew from the room saying: 'For God's sake go to sleep. The children will forget by tomorrow.'

As he said this he wondered if it was true. Would the scene glide so easily from memory—or would it root in the unconscious to fester in the after-years? Martin did not know, and the last alternative sickened him. He thought of Emily, forsaw the morning-after humiliation: the shards of memory, the lucidities that glared from the obliterating darkness of shame. She would call the New York office twice—possibly three or four times. Martin anticipated his own embarrassment, wondering if the others at the office could possibly suspect. He felt that his secretary had divined the trouble long ago and that she pitied him. He suffered a moment of rebellion against his fate; he hated his wife.

Once in the children's room he closed the door and felt secure for the first time that evening. Marianne fell down on the floor, picked herself up and calling: 'Daddy, watch me,' fell again, got up, and continued the falling-calling routine. Andy sat in the child's low chair, wobbling the tooth. Martin ran the water in the tub, washed his own hands in the lavatory, and called the boy into the bathroom.

'Let's have another look at that tooth.' Martin sat on the toilet, holding Andy between his knees. The child's mouth gaped and Martin grasped the tooth. A wobble, a quick twist and the nacreous milk tooth was free. Andy's face was for the first moment split between terror, astonishment, and delight. He mouthed a swallow of water and spat into the lavatory.

'Look, Daddy! It's blood. Marianne!'

Martin loved to bathe his children, loved inexpressibly the tender, naked bodies as they stood in the water so exposed. It was not fair of Emily to say that he showed partiality. As Martin soaped the delicate boy-body of his son he felt that further love would be impossible. Yet he admitted the difference in the quality of his emotions for the two children. His love for his daughter was graver, touched with a strain of melancholy, a gentleness that was akin to pain. His pet names for the little boy were the absurdities of daily inspiration—he called the little girl always Marianne, and his voice as he spoke it was a caress. Martin patted dry the fat baby stomach and the sweet little genital fold. Then washed child faces were radiant as flower petals, equally loved.

'I'm putting the tooth under my pillow. I'm supposed to get a quarter.'

'What for?'

'*You* know, Daddy. Johnny got a quarter for his tooth.'

'Who puts the quarter there?' asked Martin. 'I used to think the fairies left it in the night. It was a dime in my day, though.'

'That's what they say in kindergarten.'

'Who does put it there?'

'Your parents,' Andy said. 'You!'

Martin was pinning the cover on Marianne's bed. His daughter was already asleep. Scarcely breathing, Martin bent over and kissed her forehead, kissed again the tiny hand that lay palm-upward, flung in slumber beside her head.

'Good night, Andy-man.'

The answer was only a drowsy murmur. After a minute Martin took out his change and slid a quarter underneath the pillow. He left a night light in the room.

As Martin prowled about the kitchen making a late meal, it occurred to him that the children had not once mentioned their mother or the scene that must have seemed to them incomprehensible. Absorbed in the instant—the tooth, the bath, the quarter—the fluid passage of child-time had borne these weightless episodes like leaves in the swift current of a shallow stream while the adult enigma was beached and forgotten on the shore. Martin thanked the Lord for that.

But his own anger, repressed and lurking, arose again. His youth was being frittered by a drunkard's waste, his very manhood subtly undermined. And the children, once the immunity of incomprehension passed—what would it be like in a year or so? With his elbows on the table he ate his food brutishly, untasting. There was no hiding the truth—soon there would be gossip in the office and in the town; his wife was a dissolute woman. Dissolute. And he and his children were bound to a future of degradation and slow ruin.

Martin pushed away from the table and stalked into the living room. He followed the lines of a book with his eyes but his mind conjured miserable images: he saw his children drowned in the river, his wife a disgrace on the public street. By bedtime the dull, hard anger was like a weight upon his chest and his feet dragged as he climbed the stairs.

The room was dark except for the shafting light from the half-opened bathroom door. Martin undressed quietly. Little by little, mysteriously, there came in him a change. His wife was asleep, her peaceful respiration sounding gently in the room. Her high-heeled shoes with the carelessly dropped stockings made to him a mute appeal. Her underclothes were flung in disorder on the chair. Martin picked up the girdle and the soft, silk brassière and stood for a moment with them in his hands. For the first time that evening he looked at his wife. His eyes rested on the sweet forehead, the arch of the fine brow. The brow had descended to Marianne, and the tilt at the end of the delicate nose. In his son he could trace the high cheekbones and pointed chin. Her body was full-bosomed, slender and undulant. As Martin watched the tranquil slumber of his wife the ghost of the old anger vanished. All thoughts of blame or blemish were distant from him now. Martin put out the bathroom light and raised the window. Careful not to awaken Emily he slid into the bed. By moonlight he watched his wife for the last time. His hand sought the adjacent flesh and sorrow paralleled desire in the immense complexity of love.

THE FALL OF THE HOUSE OF USHER

Edgar Allan Poe

(1809–1849)

Biography p. 1093

Son coeur est un luth suspendu;
Sitôt qu'on le touche il résonne.*
De Béranger

During the whole of a dull, dark, and soundless day in the autumn of the year, when the clouds hung oppressively low in the heavens, I had been passing alone, on horseback, through a singularly dreary tract of country; and at length found myself, as the shades of the evening drew on, within view of the melancholy House of Usher. I know not how it was—but, with the first glimpse of the building, a sense of insufferable gloom pervaded my spirit. I say insufferable; for the feeling was unrelieved by any of that half-pleasurable, because poetic, sentiment, with which the mind usually receives even the sternest natural images of the desolate or terrible. I looked upon the scene before me—upon the mere house, and the simple landscape features of the domain—upon the bleak walls—upon the vacant eye-like windows—upon a few rank sedges—and upon a few white trunks of decayed trees—with an utter depression of soul which I can compare to no earthly sensation more properly than to the after-dream of the reveller upon opium—the bitter lapse into everyday life—the hideous dropping off of the veil. There was an iciness, a sinking, a sickening of the heart—an unredeemed dreariness of thought which no goading of the imagination could torture into aught of the sublime. What was it—I paused to think—what was it that so unnerved me in the contemplation of the House of Usher? It was a mystery all insoluble; nor could I grapple with the shadowy fancies that crowded upon me as I pondered. I was forced to fall back upon the unsatisfactory conclusion, that while, beyond doubt, there *are* combinations of very simple natural objects which have the power of thus affecting us, still the analysis of this power lies among considerations beyond our depth. It was possible, I reflected, that a mere different arrangement of the particulars of the scene, of the details of the picture, would be sufficient to modify, or perhaps to annihilate its capacity for sorrowful impression; and, acting upon this idea, I reined my horse to the precipitous brink of a black and lurid tarn that lay in unruffled lustre by the dwelling, and gazed down—but with a shudder even more thrilling than before—upon the remodelled and inverted images of the gray sedge, and the ghastly tree-stems, and the vacant and eye-like windows.

Nevertheless, in this mansion of gloom I now proposed to myself a sojourn of some weeks. Its proprietor, Roderick Usher, had been one of my boon companions in boyhood; but many years had elapsed since our last meeting. A letter, however, had

*His heart is a hanging lute; As soon as one touches it, it reverberates.

lately reached me in a distant part of the country—a letter from him—which, in its wildly importunate nature, had admitted of no other than a personal reply. The MS. gave evidence of nervous agitation. The writer spoke of acute bodily illness—of a mental disorder which oppressed him—and of an earnest desire to see me, as his best, and indeed his only personal friend, with a view of attempting, by the cheerfulness of my society, some alleviation of his malady. It was the manner in which all this, and much more, was said—it was the apparent *heart* that went with his request— which allowed me no room for hesitation; and I accordingly obeyed forthwith what I still considered a very singular summons.

Although, as boys, we had been even intimate associates, yet I really knew little of my friend. His reserve had been always excessive and habitual. I was aware, however, that his very ancient family had been noted, time out of mind, for a peculiar sensibility of temperament, displaying itself, through long ages, in many works of exalted art, and manifested, of late, in repeated deeds of munificent yet unobtrusive charity, as well as in a passionate devotion to the intricacies, perhaps even more than to the orthodox and easily recognisable beauties, of musical science. I had learned, too, the very remarkable fact, that the stem of the Usher race, all time-honoured as it was, had put forth, at no period, any enduring branch; in other words, that the entire family lay in the direct line of descent, and had always, with very trifling and very temporary variation, so lain. It was this deficiency, I considered, while running over in thought the perfect keeping of the character of the premises with the accredited character of the people, and while speculating upon the possible influence which the one, in the long lapse of centuries, might have exercised upon the other—it was this deficiency, perhaps, of collateral issue, and the consequent undeviating transmission, from sire to son, of the patrimony with the name, which had, at length, so identified the two as to merge the original title of the estate in the quaint and equivocal appellation of the "House of Usher"—an appellation which seemed to include, in the minds of the peasantry who used it, both the family and the family mansion.

I have said that the sole effect of my somewhat childish experiment—that of looking down within the tarn—had been to deepen the first singular impression. There can be no doubt that the consciousness of the rapid increase of my superstition—for why should I not so term it?—served mainly to accelerate the increase itself. Such, I have long known, is the paradoxical law of all sentiments having terror as a basis. And it might have been for this reason only, that, when I again uplifted my eyes to the house itself, from its image in the pool, there grew in my mind a strange fancy—a fancy so ridiculous, indeed, that I but mention it to show the vivid force of the sensations which oppressed me. I had so worked upon my imagination as really to believe that about the whole mansion and domain there hung an atmosphere peculiar to themselves and their immediate vicinity—an atmosphere which had no affinity with the air of heaven, but which had reeked up from the decayed trees, and the gray wall, and the silent tarn—a pestilent and mystic vapour, dull, sluggish, faintly discernible, and leaden-hued.

Shaking off from my spirit what *must* have been a dream, I scanned more narrowly the real aspect of the building. Its principal feature seemed to be that of an excessive antiquity. The discoloration of ages had been great. Minute fungi overspread the whole exterior, hanging in a fine tangled web-work from the eaves. Yet all this was apart from any extraordinary dilapidation. No portion of the masonry had fallen; and there appeared to be a wild inconsistency between its still perfect adaptation of parts, and the crumbling condition of the individual stones. In this there was much that reminded me of the specious totality of old wood-work which has rotted for long years in some neglected vault, with no disturbance from the breath of the external air. Beyond this indication of extensive decay, however, the fabric gave little token of instability. Perhaps the eye of a scrutinising observer might have discovered a barely perceptible fissure, which, extending from the roof of the building in front, made its way down the wall in a zigzag direction, until it became lost in the sullen waters of the tarn.

Noticing these things, I rode over a short causeway to the house. A servant in waiting took my horse, and I entered the Gothic archway of the hall. A valet, of stealthy step, thence conducted me, in silence, through many dark and intricate passages in my progress to the *studio* of his master. Much that I encountered on the way contributed, I know not how, to heighten the vague sentiments of which I have already spoken. While the objects around me—while the carvings of the ceilings, the sombre tapestries of the walls, the ebon blackness of the floors, and the phantasma-goric armorial trophies which rattled as I strode, were but matters to which, or to such as which, I had been accustomed from my infancy—while I hesitated not to acknowledge how familiar was all this—I still wondered to find how unfamiliar were the fancies which ordinary images were stirring up. On one of the staircases, I met the physician of the family. His countenance, I thought, wore a mingled expression of low cunning and perplexity. He accosted me with trepidation and passed on. The valet now threw open a door and ushered me into the presence of his master.

The room in which I found myself was very large and lofty. The windows were long, narrow, and pointed, and at so vast a distance from the black oaken floor as to be altogether inaccessible from within. Feeble gleams of encrimsoned light made their way through the trellised panes, and served to render sufficiently distinct the more prominent objects around; the eye, however, struggled in vain to reach the remoter angles of the chamber, or the recesses of the vaulted and fretted ceiling. Dark drap-eries hung upon the walls. The general furniture was profuse, comfortless, antique, and tattered. Many books and musical instruments lay scattered about, but failed to give any vitality to the scene. I felt that I breathed an atmosphere of sorrow. An air of stern, deep, and irredeemable gloom hung over and pervaded all.

Upon my entrance, Usher arose from a sofa on which he had been lying at full length, and greeted me with a vivacious warmth which had much in it, I at first thought, of an overdone cordiality—of the constrained effort of the *ennuyé* man of the world. A glance, however, at his countenance, convinced me of his perfect sincer-ity. We sat down; and for some moments, while he spoke not, I gazed upon him with a feeling half of pity, half of awe. Surely, man had never before so terribly altered, in so brief a period, as had Roderick Usher! It was with difficulty that I could bring myself to admit the identity of the wan being before me with the companion of my early boyhood. Yet the character of his face had been at all times remarkable. A cadaverousness of complexion; an eye large, liquid, and luminous beyond comparison; lips somewhat thin and very pallid, but of a surpassingly beautiful curve; a nose of a delicate Hebrew model, but with a breadth of nostril unusual in similar formations; a finely moulded chin, speaking, in its want of prominence, of a want of moral energy; hair of a more than web-like softness and tenuity; these features, with an inordinate expansion above the regions of the temple, made up altogether a countenance not easily to be forgotten. And now in the mere exaggeration of the prevailing character of these features, and of the expression they were wont to convey, lay so much of change that I doubted to whom I spoke. The now ghastly pallor of the skin, and the now miraculous lustre of the eye, above all things startled and even awed me. The silken hair, too, had been suffered to grow all unheeded, and as, in its wild gossamer texture, it floated rather than fell about the face, I could not, even with effort, connect its Arabesque expression with any idea of simple humanity.

In the manner of my friend I was at once struck with an incoherence—an inconsistency; and I soon found this to arise from a series of feeble and futile struggles to overcome an habitual trepidancy—an excessive nervous agitation. For something of this nature I had indeed been prepared, no less by his letter, than by reminiscences of certain boyish traits, and by conclusions deduced from his peculiar physical conformation and temperament. His action was alternately vivacious and sullen. His voice varied rapidly from a tremulous indecision (when the animal spirits seemed utterly in abeyance) to that species of energetic concision—that abrupt, weighty, unhurried, and hollow-sounding enunciation—that leaden, self-balanced and perfectly modulated guttural utterance, which may be observed in the lost drunkard, or the irreclaimable eater of opium, during the periods of his most intense excitement.

It was thus that he spoke of the object of my visit, of his earnest desire to see me, and of the solace he expected me to afford him. He entered, at some length, into what he conceived to be the nature of his malady. It was, he said, a constitutional and a family evil, and one for which he despaired to find a remedy—a mere nervous affection, he immediately added, which would undoubtedly soon pass off. It displayed itself in a host of unnatural sensations. Some of these, as he detailed them, interested and bewildered me; although, perhaps, the terms, and the general manner of the narration had their weight. He suffered much from a morbid acuteness of the senses; the most insipid food was alone endurable; he could wear only garments of certain texture; the odours of all flowers were oppressive; his eyes were tortured by even a faint light; and there were but peculiar sounds, and these from stringed instruments, which did not inspire him with horror.

To an anomalous species of terror I found him a bounden slave. "I shall perish," said he, "I *must* perish in this deplorable folly. Thus, thus, and not otherwise, shall I be lost. I dread the events of the future, not in themselves, but in their results. I shudder at the thought of any, even the most trivial, incident, which may operate upon this intolerable agitation of soul. I have, indeed, no abhorrence of danger, except in its absolute effect—in terror. In this unnerved—in this pitiable condition—I feel that the period will sooner or later arrive when I must abandon life and reason together, in some struggle with the grim phantasm, FEAR."

I learned, moreover, at intervals, and through broken and equivocal hints, another singular feature of his mental condition. He was enchained by certain superstitious impressions in regard to the dwelling which he tenanted, and whence, for many years, he had never ventured forth—in regard to an influence whose suppositious force was conveyed in terms too shadowy here to be re-stated—an influence which some peculiarities in the mere form and substance of his family mansion, had, by dint of long sufferance, he said, obtained over his spirit—an effect which the *physique* of the gray walls and turrets, and of the dim tarn into which they all looked down, had, at length, brought about upon the *morale* of his existence.

He admitted, however, although with hesitation, that much of the peculiar gloom which thus afflicted him could be traced to a more natural and far more palpable origin—to the severe and long-continued illness—indeed to the evidently approaching dissolution—of a tenderly beloved sister—his sole companion for long years—his last and only relative on earth. "Her decease," he said, with a bitterness which I can never forget, "would leave him (him the hopeless and the frail) the last of the ancient race of the Ushers." While he spoke, the lady Madeline (for so was she called) passed slowly through a remote portion of the apartment, and, without having noticed my presence, disappeared. I regarded her with an utter astonishment not unmingled with dread—and yet I found it impossible to account for such feelings. A sensation of stupor oppressed me, as my eyes followed her retreating steps. When a door, at length, closed upon her, my glance sought instinctively and eagerly the countenance of the brother—but he had buried his face in his hands, and I could only perceive that a far more than ordinary wanness had overspread the emaciated fingers through which trickled many passionate tears.

The disease of the lady Madeline had long baffled the skill of her physicians. A settled apathy, a gradual wasting away of the person, and frequent although transient affections of a partially cataleptical character, were the unusual diagnosis. Hitherto she had steadily borne up against the pressure of her malady, and had not betaken herself finally to bed; but, on the closing in of the evening of my arrival at the house, she succumbed (as her brother told me at night with inexpressible agitation) to the prostrating power of the destroyer; and I learned that the glimpse I had obtained of her person would thus probably be the last I should obtain—that the lady, at least while living, would be seen by me no more.

For several days ensuing, her name was unmentioned by either Usher or myself: and during this period I was busied in earnest endeavours to alleviate the melancholy of my friend. We painted and read together; or I listened, as if in a dream, to the wild improvisations of his speaking guitar. And thus, as a closer and still closer intimacy admitted me more unreservedly into the recesses of his spirit, the more bitterly did I perceive the futility of all attempt at cheering a mind from which darkness, as if an inherent positive quality, poured forth upon all objects of the moral and physical universe, in one unceasing radiation of gloom.

I shall ever bear about me a memory of the many solemn hours I thus spent alone with the master of the House of Usher. Yet I should fail in any attempt to convey an idea of the exact character of the studies, or of the occupations, in which he involved me, or led me the way. An excited and highly distempered ideality threw a sulphureous lustre over all. His long improvised dirges will ring forever in my ears. Among other things, I hold painfully in mind a certain singular perversion and amplification of the wild air of the last waltz of Von Weber. From the paintings over which his elaborate fancy brooded, and which grew, touch by touch, into vaguenesses at which I shuddered the more thrillingly, because I shuddered knowing not why;—from these paintings (vivid as their images now are before me) I would in vain endeavour to educe more than a small portion which should lie within the compass of merely written words. By the utter simplicity, by the nakedness of his designs, he arrested and overawed attention. If ever mortal painted an idea, that mortal was

Roderick Usher. For me at least—in the circumstances then surrounding me—there arose out of the pure abstractions which the hypochondriac contrived to throw upon his canvas, an intensity of intolerable awe, no shadow of which felt I ever yet in the contemplation of the certainly glowing yet too concrete reveries of Fuseli.

One of the phantasmagoric conceptions of my friend, partaking not so rigidly of the spirit of abstraction, may be shadowed forth, although feebly, in words. A small picture presented the interior of an immensely long and rectangular vault or tunnel, with low walls, smooth, white, and without interruption or device. Certain accessory points of the design served well to convey the idea that this excavation lay at an exceeding depth below the surface of the earth. No outlet was observed in any portion of its vast extent, and no torch, or other artificial source of light was discernible; yet a flood of intense rays rolled throughout, and bathed the whole in a ghastly and inappropriate splendour.

I have just spoken of that morbid condition of the auditory nerve which rendered all music intolerable to the sufferer, with the exception of certain effects of stringed instruments. It was, perhaps, the narrow limits to which he thus confined himself upon the guitar, which gave birth, in great measure, to the fantastic character of his performances. But the fervid *facility* of his *impromptus* could not be so accounted for. They must have been, and were, in the notes, as well as in the words of his wild fantasias (for he not unfrequently accompanied himself with rhymed verbal improvisations), the result of that intense mental collectedness and concentration to which I have previously alluded as observable only in particular moments of the highest artificial excitement. The words of one of these rhapsodies I have easily remembered. I was, perhaps, the more forcibly impressed with it, as he gave it, because, in the under or mystic current of its meaning, I fancied that I perceived, and for the first time, a full consciousness on the part of Usher, of the tottering of his lofty reason upon her throne. The verses, which were entitled "The Haunted Palace," ran very nearly, if not accurately, thus:

I.

In the greenest of our valleys,
    By good angels tenanted,
Once a fair and stately palace—
    Radiant palace—reared its head.
In the monarch Thought's dominion—
    It stood there!
Never seraph spread a pinion
    Over fabric half so fair.

II.

Banners yellow, glorious, golden,
    On its roof did float and flow;
(This—all this—was in the olden
    Time long ago)
And every gentle air that dallied,
    In that sweet day,
Along the ramparts plumed and pallid,
    A winged odour went away.

III.

Wanderers in that happy valley
    Through two luminous windows saw
Spirits moving musically
    To a lute's well-tunèd law,
Round about a throne, where sitting
    (Porphyrogene!)
In state his glory well befitting,
    The ruler of the realm was seen.

IV.

And all with pearl and ruby glowing
    Was the fair palace door,
Through which came flowing, flowing, flowing
    And sparkling evermore,
A troop of Echoes whose sweet duty
    Was but to sing,
In voices of surpassing beauty,
    The wit and wisdom of their king.

V.

But evil things, in robes of sorrow,
    Assailed the monarch's high estate;
(Ah, let us mourn, for never morrow
    Shall dawn upon him, desolate!)
And, round about his home, the glory
    That blushed and bloomed
Is but a dim-remembered story
    Of the old time entombed.

VI.

And travellers now within that valley,
    Through the red-litten windows, see
Vast forms that move fantastically
    To a discordant melody;
While, like a rapid ghastly river,
    Through the pale door,
A hideous throng rush out forever,
    And laugh—but smile no more.

I well remember that suggestions arising from this ballad, led us into a train of thought wherein there became manifest an opinion of Usher's which I mention not so much on account of its novelty, (for other men have thought thus,) as on account of the pertinacity with which he maintained it. This opinion, in its general form, was that of the sentience of all vegetable things. But, in his disordered fancy, the idea had assumed a more daring character, and trespassed, under certain conditions, upon the kingdom of inorganization. I lack words to express the full extent, or the earnest *abandon* of his persuasion. The belief, however, was connected (as I have previously hinted) with the gray stones of the home of his forefathers. The conditions of the sentience had been here, he imagined, fulfilled in the method of collocation of these stones—in the order of their arrangement, as well as in that of the many *fungi* which overspread them, and of the decayed trees which stood around—above all, in the long undisturbed endurance of this arrangement, and in its reduplication in the still waters of the tarn. Its evidence—the evidence of the sentience—was to be seen, he said, (and I here started as he spoke,) in the gradual yet certain condensation of an atmosphere of their own about the waters and the walls. The result was discoverable, he added, in that silent, yet importunate and terrible influence which for centuries had moulded the destinies of his family, and which made *him* what I now saw him—what he was. Such opinions need no comment, and I will make none.

Our books—the books which, for years, had formed no small portion of the mental existence of the invalid—were, as might be supposed, in strict keeping with this character of phantasm. We pored together over such works as the Ververt et Chartreuse of Gresset; the Belphegor of Machiavelli; the Heaven and Hell of Swedenborg; the Subterranean Voyage of Nicholas Klimm by Holberg; the Chiromancy of Robert Flud, of Jean D'Indaginé, and of De la Chambre; the Journey into the Blue Distance of Tieck; and the City of the Sun of Campanella. One favourite volume was a small octavo edition of the *Directorium Inquisitorum,* by the Dominican Eymeric de Gironne; and there were passages in Pomponius Mela, about the old African Satyrs and Ægipans, over which Usher would sit dreaming for hours. His chief delight, however, was found in the perusal of an exceedingly rare and curious book in quarto Gothic— the manual of a forgotten church—the *Vigiliæ Mortuorum secundum Chorum Ecclesiæ Maguntinæ.*

I could not help thinking of the wild ritual of this work, and of its probable influence upon the hypochondriac, when, one evening, having informed me abruptly that the lady Madeline was no more, he stated his intention of preserving her corpse for a fortnight, (previously to its final internment,) in one of the numerous vaults within the main walls of the building. The worldly reason, however, assigned for this singular proceeding, was one which I did not feel at liberty to dispute. The brother had been led to his resolution (so he told me) by consideration of the unusual character of the malady of the deceased, of certain obtrusive and eager inquiries on the part of her medical men, and of the remote and exposed situation of the burial-ground of the family. I will not deny that when I called to mind the sinister countenance of the person whom I met upon the staircase, on the day of my arrival at the house, I had no desire to oppose what I regarded as at best but a harmless, and by no means an unnatural, precaution.

At the request of Usher, I personally aided him in the arrangements for the temporary entombment. The body having been encoffined, we two alone bore it to its rest. The vault in which we placed it (and which had been so long unopened that our torches, half smothered in its oppressive atmosphere, gave us little opportunity for investigation) was small, damp, and entirely without means of admission for light; lying, at great depth, immediately beneath that portion of the building in which was my own sleeping apartment. It had been used, apparently, in remote feudal times, for the worst purposes of a donjon-keep, and, in later days, as a place of deposit for powder, or some other highly combustible substance, as a portion of its floor, and the whole interior of a long archway through which we reached it, were carefully sheathed with copper. The door, of massive iron, had been, also, similarly protected. Its immense weight caused an unusually sharp grating sound, as it moved upon its hinges.

Having deposited our mournful burden upon tressels within this region of horror, we partially turned aside the yet unscrewed lid of the coffin, and looked upon the face of the tenant. A striking similitude between the brother and sister now first arrested my attention; and Usher, divining, perhaps, my thoughts, murmured out some few words from which I learned that the deceased and himself had been twins, and that sympathies of a scarcely intelligible nature had always existed between them. Our glances, however, rested not long upon the dead—for we could not regard her unawed. The disease which had thus entombed the lady in the maturity of youth, had left, as usual in all maladies of a strictly cataleptical character, the mockery of a faint blush upon the bosom and the face, and that suspiciously lingering smile upon the lip which is so terrible in death. We replaced and screwed down the lid, and, having secured the door of iron, made our way, with toil, into the scarcely less gloomy apartments of the upper portion of the house.

And now, some days of bitter grief having elapsed, an observable change came over the features of the mental disorder of my friend. His ordinary manner had vanished. His ordinary occupations were neglected or forgotten. He roamed from chamber to chamber with hurried, unequal, and objectless step. The pallor of his countenance had assumed, if possible, a more ghastly hue—but the luminousness of his eye had utterly gone out. The once occasional huskiness of his tone was heard no more; and a tremulous quaver, as if of extreme terror, habitually characterized his utterance. There were times, indeed, when I thought his unceasingly agitated mind was labouring with some oppressive secret, to divulge which he struggled for the necessary courage. At times, again, I was obliged to resolve all into the mere inexplicable vagaries of madness, for I beheld him gazing upon vacancy for long hours, in an attitude of the profoundest attention, as if listening to some imaginary sound. It was no wonder that his condition terrified—that it infected me. I felt creeping upon me, by slow yet certain degrees, the wild influences of his own fantastic yet impressive superstitions.

It was, especially, upon retiring to bed late in the night of the seventh or eighth day after the placing of the lady Madeline within the donjon, that I experienced the full power of such feelings. Sleep came not near my couch—while the hours waned and waned away. I struggled to reason off the nervousness which had dominion over me. I endeavoured to believe that much, if not all of what I felt, was due to the bewildering influence of the gloomy furniture of the room—of the dark and tattered draperies, which, tortured into motion by the breath of a rising tempest, swayed fitfully to and fro upon the walls, and rustled uneasily about the decorations of the bed. But my efforts were fruitless. An irrepressible tremour gradually pervaded my frame; and, at length, there sat upon my very heart an incubus of utterly causeless alarm. Shaking this off with a gasp and a struggle, I uplifted myself upon the pillows, and, peering earnestly within the intense darkness of the chamber, hearkened—I know not why, except that an instinctive spirit prompted me—to certain low and indefinite sounds which came, through the pauses of the storm, at long intervals, I knew not whence. Overpowered by an intense sentiment of horror, unaccountable yet unendurable, I threw on my clothes with haste (for I felt that I should sleep no more during the night), and endeavored to arouse myself from the pitiable condition into which I had fallen, by pacing rapidly to and fro through the apartment.

I had taken but few turns in this manner, when a light step on an adjoining staircase arrested my attention. I presently recognised it as that of Usher. In an instant afterward he rapped, with a gentle touch, at my door, and entered, bearing a lamp. His countenance was, as usual, cadaverously wan—but, moreover, there was a species of mad hilarity in his eyes—an evidently restrained *hysteria* in his whole demeanour. His air appalled me—but anything was preferable to the solitude which I had so long endured, and I even welcomed his presence as a relief.

"And you have not seen it?" he said abruptly, after having stared about him for some moments in silence—"you have not then seen it?—but, stay! you shall." Thus speaking, and having carefully shaded his lamp, he hurried to one of the casements, and threw it freely open to the storm.

The impetuous fury of the entering gust nearly lifted us from our feet. It was, indeed, a tempestuous yet sternly beautiful night, and one wildly singular in its terror and its beauty. A whirlwind had apparently collected its force in our vicinity; for there were frequent and violent alterations in the direction of the wind; and the exceeding density of the clouds (which hung so low as to press upon the turrets of the house) did not prevent our perceiving the life-like velocity with which they flew careering from all points against each other, without passing away into the distance. I say that even their exceeding density did not prevent our perceiving this—yet we had no glimpse of the moon or stars—nor was there any flashing forth of the lightning. But the under surfaces of the huge masses of agitated vapour, as well as all terrestrial objects immediately around us, were glowing in the unnatural light of a faintly luminous and distinctly visible gaseous exhalation which hung about and enshrouded the mansion.

"You must not—you shall not behold this!" said I, shudderingly, to Usher, as I led him, with a gentle violence, from the window to a seat. "These appearances, which bewilder you, are merely electrical phenomena not uncommon—or it may be that they have their ghastly origin in the rank miasma of the tarn. Let us close this casement; —the air is chilling and dangerous to your frame. Here is one of your favourite romances. I will read, and you shall listen;—and so we will pass away this terrible night together."

The antique volume which I had taken up was the "Mad Trist" of Sir Launcelot Canning; but I had called it a favourite of Usher's more in sad jest than in earnest; for, in truth, there is little in its uncouth and unimaginative prolixity which could have had interest for the lofty and spiritual ideality of my friend. It was, however, the only book immediately at hand; and I indulged a vague hope that the excitement which now agitated the hypochondriac, might find relief (for the history of mental disorder is full of similar anomalies) even in the extremeness of the folly which I should read. Could I have judged, indeed, by the wild overstrained air of vivacity with which he hearkened, or apparently hearkened, to the words of the tale, I might well have congratulated myself upon the success of my design.

I had arrived at that well-known portion of the story where Ethelred, the hero of the Trist, having sought in vain for peaceable admission into the dwelling of the hermit, proceeds to make good an entrance by force. Here, it will be remembered, the words of the narrative run thus:

"And Ethelred, who was by nature of a doughty heart, and who was now mighty withal, on account of the powerfulness of the wine which he had drunken, waited no longer to hold parley with the hermit, who, in sooth, was of an obstinate and maliceful turn, but, feeling the rain upon his shoulders, and fearing the rising of the tempest, uplifted his mace outright, and, with blows, made quickly room in the plankings of the door for his gauntleted hand; and now pulling therewith sturdily, he so cracked, and ripped, and tore all asunder, that the noise of the dry and hollow-sounding wood alarumed and reverberated throughout the forest."

At the termination of this sentence I started, and for a moment, paused; for it appeared to me (although I at once concluded that my excited fancy had deceived me)—it appeared to me that, from some very remote portion of the mansion, there came, indistinctly, to my ears, what might have been, in its exact similarity of charac- ter, the echo (but a stifled and dull one certainly) of the very cracking and ripping sound which Sir Launcelot had so particularly described. It was, beyond doubt, the coincidence alone which had arrested my attention; for, amid the rattling of the sashes of the casements, and the ordinary commingled noises of the still increasing storm, the sound, in itself, had nothing, surely, which should have interested or disturbed me. I continued the story:

"But the good champion Ethelred, now entering within the door, was sore enraged and amazed to perceive no signal of the maliceful hermit; but, in the stead thereof, a dragon of a scaly and prodigious demeanour, and of a fiery tongue, which sate in guard before a palace of gold, with a floor of silver; and upon the wall there hung a shield of shining brass with this legend enwritten—

Who entereth herein, a conqueror hath bin;
Who slayeth the dragon, the shield he shall win;

And Ethelred uplifted his mace, and struck upon the head of the dragon, which fell before him, and gave up his pesty breath, with a shriek so horrid and harsh, and withal so piercing, that Ethelred had fain to close his ears with his hands against the dreadful noise of it, the like whereof was never before heard."

Here again I paused abruptly, and now with a feeling of wild amazement—for there could be no doubt whatever that, in this instance, I did actually hear (although from what direction it proceeded I found it impossible to say) a low and apparently distant, but harsh, protracted, and most unusual screaming or grating sound—the exact counterpart of what my fancy had already conjured up for the dragon's unnatural shriek as described by the romancer.

Oppressed, as I certainly was, upon the occurrence of the second and most extraor- dinary coincidence, by a thousand conflicting sensations, in which wonder and ex- treme terror were predominant, I still retained sufficient presence of mind to avoid exciting, by any observation, the sensitive nervousness of my companion. I was by no means certain that he had noticed the sounds in question; although, assuredly, a strange alteration had, during the last few minutes, taken place in his demeanour. From a position fronting my own, he had gradually brought round his chair, so as to sit with his face to the door of the chamber; and thus I could but partially perceive his features, although I saw that his lips trembled as if he were murmuring inaudibly. His head had dropped upon his breast—yet I knew that he was not asleep, from the wide and rigid opening of the eye as I caught a glance of it in profile. The motion of his body, too, was at variance with this idea—for he rocked from side to side with a gentle yet constant and uniform sway. Having rapidly taken notice of all this, I resumed the narrative of Sir Launcelot, which thus proceeded:

"And now, the champion, having escaped from the terrible fury of the dragon, bethinking himself of the brazen shield, and of the breaking up of the enchantment which was upon it, removed the carcass from out of the way before him, and approached valorously over the silver pavement of the castle to where the shield was upon the wall; which in sooth tarried not for his full coming, but fell down at his feet upon the silver floor, with a mighty great and terrible ringing sound."

No sooner had these syllables passed my lips, than—as if a shield of brass had indeed, at the moment, fallen heavily upon a floor of silver—I became aware of a distinct, hollow, metallic, and clangorous, yet apparently muffled reverberation. Completely unnerved, I leaped to my feet; but the measured rocking movement of Usher was undisturbed. I rushed to the chair in which he sat. His eyes were bent fixedly before him, and throughout his whole countenance there reigned a stony rigidity. But, as I placed my hand upon his shoulder, there came a strong shudder over his whole person; a sickly smile quivered about his lips; and I saw that he spoke in a low, hurried, and gibbering murmur, as if unconscious of my presence. Bending closely over him, I at length drank in the hideous import of his words.

"Not hear it?—yes, I hear it, and *have* heard it. Long—long—long—many minutes, many hours, many days, have I heard it—yet I dared not—oh, pity me, miserable wretch that I am!—I dared not—I *dared* not speak! *We have put her living in the tomb!* Said I not that my senses were acute? I *now* tell you that I heard her first feeble movements in the hollow coffin. I heard them—many, many days ago—yet I dared not—*I dared not speak!* And now—to-night—Ethelred—ha! ha!—the breaking of the hermit's door, and the death-cry of the dragon, and the clangour of the shield!—say, rather, the rending of her coffin, and the grating of the iron hinges of her prison, and her struggles within the coppered archway of the vault! Oh whither shall I fly? Will she not be here anon? Is she not hurrying to upbraid me for my haste? Have I not heard her footstep on the stair? Do I not distinguish that heavy and horrible beating of her heart? MADMAN!" here he sprang furiously to his feet, and shrieked out his syllables, as if in the effort he were giving up his soul—"MADMAN! I TELL YOU THAT SHE NOW STANDS WITHOUT THE DOOR!"

As if in the superhuman energy of his utterance there had been found the potency of a spell—the huge antique panels to which the speaker pointed, threw slowly back, upon the instant, their ponderous and ebony jaws. It was the work of the rushing gust—but then without those doors there DID stand the lofty and enshrouded figure of the lady Madeline of Usher. There was blood upon her white robes, and the evidence of some bitter struggle upon every portion of her emaciated frame. For a moment she remained trembling and reeling to and fro upon the threshold, then, with a low moaning cry, fell heavily inward upon the person of her brother, and in her violent and now final death-agonies, bore him to the floor a corpse, and a victim to the terrors he had anticipated.

From that chamber, and from that mansion, I fled aghast. The storm was still abroad in all its wrath as I found myself crossing the old causeway. Suddenly there shot along the path a wild light, and I turned to see whence a gleam so unusual could have issued; for the vast house and its shadows were alone behind me. The radiance was that of the full, setting, and blood-red moon which now shone vividly through that once barely-discernible fissure of which I have before spoken as extending from the roof of the building, in a zigzag direction, to the base. While I gazed, this fissure rapidly widened—there came a fierce breath of the whirlwind—the entire orb of the satellite burst at once upon my sight—my brain reeled as I saw the mighty walls rushing asunder—there was a long tumultuous shouting sound like the voice of a thousand waters—and the deep and dank tarn at my feet closed sullenly and silently over the fragments of the "House of Usher."

MRS. BAGLEY GOES TO MARS

Kate Wilhelm

(b. 1928)

Biography p. 1108

On a dreary Tuesday in March, Mrs. Bagley told her family she was going to Mars. It was a day exactly like all others—she always got up first, shook her husband, put on her robe, went to the kitchen to make coffee, pounded on Joey's door until he grunted, and then went to shower and dress, passing her husband who by then was finished with the bathroom. While she dressed and did her hair, Mr. Bagley and Joey had breakfast: cold cereal, juice she had made the night before, toast.

When she returned to the kitchen the air was smoky; a piece of burned toast lay soaking up spilled milk on the counter.

"Better take that toaster to the shop," her husband said, not looking up.

"Mom," Joey said, "you got that ten dollars?"

"What ten dollars?"

Mr. Bagley didn't look up.

"I told you. After school we get measured for caps and gowns. I gotta put ten down . . ."

Somewhere water was falling. A silver trickle kissed mossy rocks, a thundering cascade ripped house-sized boulders loose from the cliffs, crashed them down. . . .

". . . by six, I hope. Oh, yeah, can you spare a couple of bucks for gas?"

That was when she said, "I'm going to Mars."

Mr. Bagley, like a well-bred visitor who didn't overhear family matters, didn't look up.

Somewhere a star was going nova, a black hole was vacuuming space, a comet was combing its hair.

Mr. Bagley finished his cereal and pushed his bowl back. He had been talking. ". . . seven calls, at least. You won't be late if we leave now. Come on. You can eat at the cafeteria, can't you?"

"I haven't even had coffee yet!"

"You can drink it on the way to the bus. Come on or we'll both be late."

Her supervisor, Bentsen, said, "Mrs. Bagley, this is the third time in two weeks. Why?"

"It's rained three times these two weeks."

"We don't want to have to let you go, Mrs. Bagley, but . . ."

Somewhere a giraffe stretched out a purple tongue toward bright green leaves at the top of a tree. Somewhere a wound-down kitten slept on a pillow, like a fuzzy pom-pom.

At her machine she pressed a knee lever and green plastic flowed toward her. They were making tank covers, or bus covers; she was not certain just what they were making. Across from her Dolores was talking.

"Ellie and me, we're walking to catch our bus and it's warm in the terminal, you know. We're carrying our coats. And here comes this black dude, big, not really black, but like coffee that's half milk, and he's staring at Ellie's. You know? Me, I'm invisible when I'm with Ellie, like a star when the sun comes up, still there, but invisible. We're talking about killing Bentsen, that's all we ever talk about any more. And this dude is staring and grinning and making sucking faces. Ellie slows down and starts to stare too, right at his dingus, and he likes that fine, you can tell. Then Ellie starts to laugh and she laughs like she's going to bust something. And she tries to keep her eyes on him, but she can't, she's laughing too hard, and she puts her arm around me and puts her head on my shoulder, like one of *them.* You know? And that cat, he just vanishes, melts right into the floor. Never fails! That Ellie!"

Somewhere a father was holding up a little girl so she could glimpse a shiny train sliding silently through the silver night. Somewhere a spotted dog quivered as it listened to a school bus long before it came into sight.

"You don't feel so hot or something?" Dolores was leaning forward, looking at her.

"I'm okay. I'm going to Mars, you know."

"Like that place over in Jersey? I heard they keep you a week and do exams no one else even heard of yet. Same exams they give the astronauts, I heard. You'll be okay. It's not to worry." She glanced up and pressed her knee lever hard, causing a tidal wave of plastic to flow. Bentsen passed and Dolores said, "Tell you about this guy I met last night? Ellie and me was in this place . . ."

Somewhere a pink bird picked out the pink stones on a beach and laid a wall. Somewhere red sands sifted moonlight and starlight and rose hues bathed the land.

It rained on Wednesday, too.

"Mrs. Bagley, is there a problem?" The personnel supervisor was very young and pretty. She wore her hair down her back and when she put on her glasses to glance at the file before her, she looked like a child playing grown-up.

"I have sick leave coming, don't I?" Mrs. Bagley asked.

The girl ran her finger down the paper before her. She had silver polish on her long nails. "You haven't had time off for six years!"

"There are examinations, like they give the astronauts, I understand, and they keep you at least a week. A place over in Jersey."

"Oh dear! I do hope it isn't serious. There's a form here somewhere you should have them fill out for us. Just routine." She rummaged in her desk, got up and opened a file drawer and extracted a paper. "Here we are. Now, let's just go over this together, shall we? You have to fill out this part, see? Your name, address, where you live at present . . ."

Somewhere rising smoke became a column that supported a gray sky over a gray land. Somewhere a golden fish floated among lily pads carelessly splashed with violet flowers.

"Mom, I told you! We have to pay today! It's for our graduation party, over at the shore!"

Joey held out his hand and Mrs. Bagley walked around it, carrying dishes to the sink.

"I got seven calls today," Mr. Bagley said, dipping his doughnut into his coffee. "I can't make them all by bus."

Mrs. Bagley went to the bedroom to get her purse. Joey followed, his hand still out, jiggling the car keys with his other hand. She caught the keys and dropped them into her pocket. "Ask your father," she said.

"He ain't got no money."

"I get paid today. I have to go to the bank after work."

"Hey! How'm I supposed to get to school?"

"Walk."

Mr. Bagley read the paper and dunked his doughnut. Joey turned toward him, shrugged, and left the house, slamming the door. "I ain't going to school today!"

"Why'd you take his keys?"

"They aren't his. They are mine. I'm paying for the car, insurance, everything, and I'm the one who rides the bus. Not today."

"What are you mad about anyway? Because I got all them calls to make? That make you mad?"

Mrs. Bagley returned to the bedroom and took off her coat; she began to throw things out of her drawer onto the bed. She would need all her underwear, all her knee hose, no curlers. They didn't curl their hair on Mars.

"What in hell are you doing?"

"I'm going to Mars," Mrs. Bagley said. "I told you."

"You're crazy. Put that stuff away. You'll be late."

"Goodbye," Mrs. Bagley said. "I don't know how long I'll be away."

"You hear me? Put that stuff away."

Mrs. Bagley sat on the edge of the bed and presently Mr. Bagley said, "I've got to go. You sick or something? Call in sick. You got the time coming to you."

She didn't answer and after a moment he left for work. Mrs. Bagley finished packing, turned off the lights and the stove and left also.

At the plant she parked in the visitor section when she picked up her check. She went to the bank and withdrew a hundred dollars and cashed her check. Altogether she now had a little over two hundred dollars, enough, she hoped, to permit her to buy a little souvenir or two. In order not to be a burden on the flight people, she went to a supermarket and bought a few provisions for the trip—canned apple juice, some instant coffee, cheese, crackers and several candy bars. Satisfied, she drove toward Lincoln Tunnel and New Jersey.

It was almost dark when she pulled off the interstate and ate her crackers and cheese. She should have asked directions, she realized, but she had been so certain that she knew the way. As if she had glimpsed a map, or had gone before, she recognized the route as she reached various turns, but it would be comforting to have a map. She drank the apple juice, and with the food and drink, her certainty returned and she started to drive again.

Somewhere a ship was standing in moonlight, waiting. Somewhere the flight attendants were glancing at their watches, hoping she would not delay them too much.

She turned at Kittatinny Mountain and there on the side of the road was her guide, waving to her. When he opened the car door, the overhead light came on and he hesitated, glanced in the back seat, then back down the road she had just driven.

"It's all right," she said. "I've been expecting you." Not really *him,* she told herself, someone. "You do know the way, don't you?"

He got in, but kept very close to the door, pressing against it with his back in such a way that he could look at her, out the back window, back to her. "Way to where?"

"To the ship."

She hoped he wouldn't sense her disappointment in his appearance. But of course, they would look like everyone else, or their lives would be endangered.

"I've always known I'd get to go," Mrs. Bagley said. "I used to read about space and Mars, all that, when I was a girl, and once I stood out on the sidewalk and crossed my arms and tried wishing myself up, but nothing happened." The road was narrow and unmarked and she was driving slowly, braking for curves, pulling over as far as she could whenever a car approached. There was little traffic. Woods grew close to the road on both sides here, and the farm house lights were far apart. The road started to climb and she slowed more.

"You turn right up there," the guide said. He had stopped looking out the rear window, was watching her. This road was even narrower and no light at all showed.

"I suppose you were excited when you found that you were coming to Earth," Mrs. Bagley said. "It is a surprise, in a way, but not really. It's like finding something you lost a long time ago, but always felt would turn up again."

"You turn again soon," he said. "Left." He leaned forward, watching the road. "Now."

This was hardly more than a trail. Mrs. Bagley concentrated on driving. There were water-filled holes that reflected her headlights and she couldn't guess how deep they were.

"Stop," her guide said, and his voice seemed changed, deeper and thicker.

Mrs. Bagley stopped and turned off the engine, switched off the lights. She could see nothing beyond the car, could only see the outline of the man against the darkness outside, could see something gleam briefly.

"Now don't you start yelling or nothing . . ."

But she wasn't listening to him. "Look!" she cried. "Look at it! It's beautiful. Come on! They're waiting." She pushed the door open and jumped out, ran toward the ship.

On Mars they allowed her to rest several minutes before they began tests to see what occupation would be suitable for her. She soon found herself installed before a machine that heat-seamed plastic to make covers for tanks, or buses, or something. The plastic was red; she operated the machine with her elbow, and the operator across from her was not Dolores.

She listened to the tongue-twisting monologue of not/Dolores until the coffee break, and then she told her supervisor she was returning to Earth.

They were sorry to lose her, they said sibilantly, but they understood. It must be very difficult to be the only Earthman on Mars. They never did understand she was a female: all Earth persons looked alike to them. "You are born," they said. "You ingest food, defecate, mature, reproduce, grow old and die. All of you alike."

Mrs. Bagley shook her head. "Your sources are wrong," she said. "Women, females, ladies, one half the population or even a little bit more don't defecate. You won't find that in your sources. They go to the little girls' room, or the powder room, or ladies room. They freshen up, or wash their hands, or fix their make-up, but they never shit."

The Martians, hissing with bewilderment over this incomprehensible difference between the male and female organisms of the Earth species, returned to their sources. They saw Mrs. Bagley off regretfully, she thought, but did not attempt to detain her. They even returned the price of her ticket since she had not stayed the seventy-two-hour trial period.

The ship landed on the spot where she had embarked, and she stood for a short time looking at the discarded body of her former guide. It was clever of them to assume a human form and then abandon it this way, making it look like a dreadful accident, or even a homicide. No one would bother to probe deeply into the death of a bum found with a knife in his heart.

She backed out the lane carefully, made her turn and retracted her drive back home. Mr. Bagley was reading the Sunday papers when she entered the apartment.

"How's your sister?" he asked, not looking up.

"I haven't seen her."

"You ain't kidding me. You think I don't know where you been? Where else would you go?" He folded the paper and started on the comics.

"Did you call her?"

"And give you that satisfaction? You kidding?"

"Where's Joey?"

"Out somewhere."

Mrs. Bagley unpacked her suitcase and put away her things, then she started dinner.

On Monday a light drizzle was falling.

"Look, Mom, it ain't fair! I gotta pick up Suzanne and Eddie and take them to the jewelry store for their rings, and we gotta . . ."

Somewhere a dragon, breathing heavily, seared a shishkabob for its beloved. Somewhere a butterfly squirmed from its sleeping bag and stretched first one then the other emerald wing, and yawned.

"When you go to the store, get me some shaving cream, will you? And we're out of toothpaste, and my tan suit needs to go to the cleaners. And get that damn toaster fixed." Mr. Bagley spoke with his mouth full and didn't look at her, but marked his place in the newspaper with one finger, then resumed reading. Joey left, slamming the door.

"You got some change? I'm going to be in the Bronx all day, can't get to the bank."

She handed him a ten-dollar bill and he grunted and turned the page to the sports section.

"You better have a talk with Joey when he gets home. Out all night Saturday. To be expected when his old lady stays out all weekend. I don't like it, though, telling you." He scanned the scores, talking, eating, dripping coffee.

Somewhere rainbow-colored clouds swirled gently, thick enough to float on, to ride to earth. Somewhere a new flower opened and stared at the sun wide-eyed.

". . . the hell you do, but you could let us know. . . ."

She went to the living room and started to gather dirty clothes, Joey's sweater and socks, an ashtray filled with candy wrappers, beer cans. . . .

When she heard the door close, she dropped the dirty clothes and sat on the couch. She picked up the classified section of the paper and, at first idly, then with more attention, began to read the Help Wanted column.

It was still drizzling when Mrs. Bagley left the apartment and took the bus to the station where she could catch a train to Long Island. Ganymede, she thought, that was the answer. Mars had been too close, too like Earth, but Ganymede was different.

On Ganymede they showed her an efficiency that was to be hers, and a native explained her duties to her, wished her luck and left her alone. Here they lived in immense apartments, with plush carpeting and futuristic furniture, and they spoke another language so they could not jabber at her. She was to clean the apartments for them.

She sat down and turned on her own nine-inch television set and leaned back. Somewhere, she thought, dirty clothes were rising to the ceiling, and smoke was curling up from the bottom of the heap. Somewhere dishes were growing strange molds—gray, green, blue. Somewhere a man in an undershirt was jamming a coffee-soaked doughnut into his ear.

Later, when the building was silent and dark, she went to the street and checked one more time, and it was still there: Ganymede Arms. She went back to her room and to bed knowing they would never find her on Ganymede.

REVELATION

Flannery O'Connor

(1925–1964)

Biography p. 1090

The doctor's waiting room, which was very small, was almost full when the Turpins entered and Mrs. Turpin, who was very large, made it look even smaller by her presence. She stood looming at the head of the magazine table set in the center of it, a living demonstration that the room was inadequate and ridiculous. Her little bright black eyes took in all the patients as she sized up the seating situation. There was one vacant chair and a place on the sofa occupied by a blond child in a dirty blue romper who should have been told to move over and make room for the lady. He was five or six, but Mrs. Turpin saw at once that no one was going to tell him to move over. He was slumped down in the seat, his arms idle at his sides and his eyes idle in his head; his nose ran unchecked.

Mrs. Turpin put a firm hand on Claud's shoulder and said in a voice that included anyone who wanted to listen, "Claud, you sit in that chair there," and gave him a push down into the vacant one. Claud was florid and bald and sturdy, somewhat shorter than Mrs. Turpin, but he sat down as if he were accustomed to doing what she told him to.

Mrs. Turpin remained standing. The only man in the room besides Claud was a lean stringy old fellow with a rusty hand spread out on each knee, whose eyes were closed as if he were asleep or dead or pretending to be so as not to get up and offer her his seat. Her gaze settled agreeably on a well-dressed grey-haired lady whose eyes met hers and whose expression said: if that child belonged to me, he would have some manners and move over—there's plenty of room there for you and him too.

Claud looked up with a sigh and made as if to rise.

"Sit down," Mrs. Turpin said. "You know you're not supposed to stand on that leg. He has an ulcer on his leg," she explained.

Claud lifted his foot onto the magazine table and rolled his trouser leg up to reveal a purple swelling on a plump marble-white calf.

"My!" the pleasant lady said. "How did you do that?"

"A cow kicked him," Mrs. Turpin said.

"Goodness!" said the lady.

Claud rolled his trouser leg down.

"Maybe the little boy would move over," the lady suggested, but the child did not stir.

"Somebody will be leaving in a minute," Mrs. Turpin said. She could not understand why a doctor—with as much money as they made charging five dollars a day to just stick their head in the hospital door and look at you—couldn't afford a decent-sized waiting room. This one was hardly bigger than a garage. The table was cluttered with limp-looking magazines and at one end of it there was a big green glass ash tray full of cigaret butts and cotton wads with little blood spots on them. If she had had anything to do with the running of the place, that would have been emptied every so often. There were no chairs against the wall at the head of the room. It had a rectangular-shaped panel in it that permitted a view of the office where the nurse came and went and the secretary listened to the radio. A plastic fern in a gold pot sat in the opening and trailed its fronds down almost to the floor. The radio was softly playing gospel music.

Just then the inner door opened and a nurse with the highest stack of yellow hair Mrs. Turpin had ever seen put her face in the crack and called for the next patient. The woman sitting beside Claud grasped the two arms of her chair and hoisted herself up; she pulled her dress free from her legs and lumbered through the door where the nurse had disappeared.

Mrs. Turpin eased into the vacant chair, which held her tight as a corset. "I wish I could reduce," she said, and rolled her eyes and gave a comic sigh.

"Oh, *you* aren't fat," the stylish lady said.

"Ooooo I am too," Mrs. Turpin said. "Claud he eats all he wants to and never weighs over one hundred and seventy-five pounds, but me I just look at something good to eat and I gain some weight," and her stomach and shoulders shook with laughter. "You can eat all you want to, can't you, Claud?" she asked, turning to him.

Claud only grinned.

"Well, as long as you have such a good disposition," the stylish lady said, "I don't think it makes a bit of difference what size you are. You just can't beat a good disposition."

Next to her was a fat girl of eighteen or nineteen, scowling into a thick blue book which Mrs. Turpin saw was entitled *Human Development.* The girl raised her head and directed her scowl at Mrs. Turpin as if she did not like her looks. She appeared annoyed that anyone should speak while she tried to read. The poor girl's face was blue with acne and Mrs. Turpin thought how pitiful it was to have a face like that at that age. She gave the girl a friendly smile but the girl only scowled the harder. Mrs. Turpin herself was fat but she had always had good skin, and, though she was forty-seven years old, there was not a wrinkle in her face except around her eyes from laughing too much.

Next to the ugly girl was the child, still in exactly the same position, and next to him was a thin leathery old woman in a cotton print dress. She and Claud had three sacks of chicken feed in their pump house that was in the same print. She had seen from the first that the child belonged with the old woman. She could tell by the way they sat—kind of vacant and white-trashy, as if they would sit there until Doomsday if nobody called and told them to get up. And at right angles but next to the well-dressed pleasant lady was a lank-faced woman who was certainly the child's mother. She had on a yellow sweat shirt and wine-colored slacks, both gritty-looking, and the rims of her lips were stained with snuff. Her dirty yellow hair was tied behind with a little piece of red paper ribbon. Worse than niggers any day, Mrs. Turpin thought.

The gospel hymn playing was, "When I looked up and He looked down," and Mrs. Turpin, who knew it, supplied the last line mentally, "And wona these days I know I'll we-eara crown."

Without appearing to, Mrs. Turpin always noticed people's feet. The well-dressed lady had on red and grey suede shoes to match her dress. Mrs. Turpin had on her good black patent leather pumps. The ugly girl had on Girl Scout shoes and heavy socks. The old woman had on tennis shoes and the white-trashy mother had on what appeared to be bedroom slippers, black straw with gold braid threaded through them—exactly what you would have expected her to have on.

Sometimes at night when she couldn't go to sleep, Mrs. Turpin would occupy herself with the question of who she would have chosen to be if she couldn't have been herself. If Jesus had said to her before he made her, "There's only two places available for you. You can either be a nigger or white-trash," what would she have said? "Please, Jesus, please," she would have said, "just let me wait until there's another place available," and he would have said, "No, you have to go right now and I have only those two places so make up your mind." She would have wiggled and squirmed and begged and pleaded but it would have been no use and finally she would have said, "All right, make me a nigger then—but that don't mean a trashy one." And he would have made her a neat clean respectable Negro woman, herself but black.

Next to the child's mother was a red-headed youngish woman, reading one of the magazines and working a piece of chewing gum, hell for leather, as Claud would say. Mrs. Turpin could not see the woman's feet. She was not white-trash, just common. Sometimes Mrs. Turpin occupied herself at night naming the classes of people. On the bottom of the heap were most colored people, not the kind she would have been if she had been one, but most of them; then next to them—not above, just away from—were the white-trash; then above them were the home-owners, and above them the home-and-land owners, to which she and Claud belonged. Above she and Claud were people with a lot of money and much bigger houses and much more land. But here the complexity of it would begin to bear in on her, for some of the people with a lot of money were common and ought to be below she and Claud and some of the people who had good blood had lost their money and had to rent and then there were colored people who owned their homes and land as well. There was a colored dentist in town who had two red Lincolns and a swimming pool and a farm with registered white-face cattle on it. Usually by the time she had fallen asleep all the classes of people were moiling and roiling around in her head, and she would dream they were all crammed in together in a box car, being ridden off to be put in a gas oven.

"That's a beautiful clock," she said and nodded to her right. It was a big wall clock, the face encased in a brass sunburst.

"Yes, it's very pretty," the stylish lady said agreeably. "And right on the dot too," she added, glancing at her watch.

The ugly girl beside her cast an eye upward at the clock, smirked, then looked directly at Mrs. Turpin and smirked again. Then she returned her eyes to her book. She was obviously the lady's daughter because, although they didn't look anything alike as to disposition, they both had the same shape of face and the same blue eyes. On the lady they sparkled pleasantly but in the girl's seared face they appeared alternately to smolder and to blaze.

What if Jesus had said, "All right, you can be white-trash or a nigger or ugly"!

Mrs. Turpin felt an awful pity for the girl, though she thought it was one thing to be ugly and another to act ugly.

The woman with the snuff-stained lips turned around in her chair and looked up at the clock. Then she turned back and appeared to look a little to the side of Mrs.

Turpin. There was a cast in one of her eyes. "You want to know wher you can get you one of themther clocks?" she asked in a loud voice.

"No, I already have a nice clock," Mrs. Turpin said. Once somebody like her got a leg in the conversation, she would be all over it.

"You can get you one with green stamps," the woman said. "That's most likely wher he got hisn. Save you up enough, you can get you most anythang. I got me some joo'ry."

Ought to have got you a wash rag and some soap, Mrs. Turpin thought.

"I get contour sheets with mine," the pleasant lady said.

The daughter slammed her book shut. She looked straight in front of her, directly through Mrs. Turpin and on through the yellow curtain and the plate glass window which made the wall behind her. The girl's eyes seemed lit all of a sudden with a peculiar light, an unnatural light like night road signs give. Mrs. Turpin turned her head to see if there was anything going on outside that she should see, but she could not see anything. Figures passing cast only a pale shadow through the curtain. There was no reason the girl should single her out for her ugly looks.

"Miss Finley," the nurse said, cracking the door. The gum-chewing woman got up and passed in front of her and Claud and went into the office. She had on red high-heeled shoes.

Directly across the table, the ugly girl's eyes were fixed on Mrs. Turpin as if she had some very special reason for disliking her.

"This is wonderful weather, isn't it?" the girl's mother said.

"It's good weather for cotton if you can get the niggers to pick it," Mrs. Turpin said, "but niggers don't want to pick cotton any more. You can't get the white folks to pick it and now you can't get the niggers—because they got to be right up there with the white folks."

"They gonna *try* anyways," the white-trash woman said, leaning forward.

"Do you have one of those cotton-picking machines?" the pleasant lady asked.

"No," Mrs. Turpin said, "they leave half the cotton in the field. We don't have much cotton anyway. If you want to make it farming now, you have to have a little of everything. We got a couple of acres of cotton and a few hogs and chickens and just enough white-face that Claud can look after them himself."

"One thang I don't want," the white-trash woman said, wiping her mouth with the back of her hand. "Hogs. Nasty stinking things, a-gruntin and a-rootin all over the place."

Mrs. Turpin gave her the merest edge of her attention. "Our hogs are not dirty and they don't stink," she said. "They're cleaner than some children I've seen. Their feet never touch the ground. We have a pig-parlor—that's where you raise them on concrete," she explained to the pleasant lady, "and Claud scoots them down with the hose every afternoon and washes off the floor." Cleaner by far than that child right there, she thought. Poor nasty little thing. He had not moved except to put the thumb of his dirty hand into his mouth.

The woman turned her face away from Mrs. Turpin. "I know I wouldn't scoot down no hog with no hose," she said to the wall.

You wouldn't have no hog to scoot down, Mrs. Turpin said to herself.

"A-gruntin and a-rootin and a-groanin," the woman muttered.

"We got a little of everything," Mrs. Turpin said to the pleasant lady. "It's no use in having more than you can handle yourself with help like it is. We found enough niggers to pick our cotton this year but Claud he has to go after them and take them home again in the evening. They can't walk that half a mile. No they can't. I tell you," she said and laughed merrily, "I sure am tired of buttering up niggers, but you got to love em if you want em to work for you. When they come in the morning, I run out and I say, 'Hi yawl this morning?' and when Claud drives them off to the field I just wave to beat the band and they just wave back." And she waved her hand rapidly to illustrate.

"Like you read out of the same book," the lady said, showing she understood perfectly.

"Child, yes," Mrs. Turpin said. "And when they come in from the field, I run out with a bucket of icewater. That's the way it's going to be from now on," she said. "You may as well face it."

"One thang I know," the white-trash woman said. "Two thangs I ain't going to do: love no niggers or scoot down no hog with no hose." And she let out a bark of contempt.

The look that Mrs. Turpin and the pleasant lady exchanged indicated they both understood that you had to *have* certain things before you could *know* certain things. But every time Mrs. Turpin exchanged a look with the lady, she was aware that the ugly girl's peculiar eyes were still on her, and she had trouble bringing her attention back to the conversation.

"When you got something," she said, "you got to look after it." And when you ain't got a thing but breath and britches, she added to herself, you can afford to come to town every morning and just sit on the Court House coping and spit.

A grotesque revolving shadow passed across the curtain behind her and was thrown palely on the opposite wall. Then a bicycle clattered down against the outside of the building. The door opened and a colored boy glided in with a tray from the drug store. It had two large red and white paper cups on it with tops on them. He was a tall, very black boy in discolored white pants and a green nylon shirt. He was chewing gum slowly, as if to music. He set the tray down in the office opening next to the fern and stuck his head through to look for the secretary. She was not in there. He rested his arms on the ledge and waited, his narrow bottom stuck out, swaying slowly to the left and right. He raised a hand over his head and scratched the base of his skull.

"You see that button there, boy?" Mrs. Turpin said. "You can punch that and she'll come. She's probably in the back somewhere."

"Is thas right?" the boy said agreeably, as if he had never seen the button before. He leaned to the right and put his finger on it. "She sometime out," he said and twisted around to face his audience, his elbows behind him on the counter. The nurse appeared and he twisted back again. She handed him a dollar and he rooted in his pocket and made the change and counted it out to her. She gave him fifteen cents for a tip and he went out with the empty tray. The heavy door swung to slowly and closed at length with the sound of suction. For a moment no one spoke.

"They ought to send all them niggers back to Africa," the white-trash woman said. "That's wher they come from in the first place."

"Oh, I couldn't do without my good colored friends," the pleasant lady said.

"There's a heap of things worse than a nigger," Mrs. Turpin agreed. "It's all kinds of them just like it's all kinds of us."

"Yes, and it takes all kinds to make the world go round," the lady said in her musical voice.

As she said it, the raw-complexioned girl snapped her teeth together. Her lower lip turned downwards and inside out, revealing the pale pink inside of her mouth. After a second it rolled back up. It was the ugliest face Mrs. Turpin had ever seen anyone make and for a moment she was certain that the girl had made it at her. She was looking at her as if she had known and disliked her all her life—all of Mrs. Turpin's life, it seemed too, not just all the girl's life. Why, girl, I don't even know you, Mrs. Turpin said silently.

She forced her attention back to the discussion. "It wouldn't be practical to send them back to Africa," she said. "They wouldn't want to go. They got it too good here."

"Wouldn't be what they wanted—if I had anythang to do with it," the woman said.

"It wouldn't be a way in the world you could get all the niggers back over there," Mrs. Turpin said. "They'd be hiding out and lying down and turning sick on you and wailing and hollering and raring and pitching. It wouldn't be a way in the world to get them over there."

"They got over here," the trashy woman said. "Get back like they got over."

"It wasn't so many of them then," Mrs. Turpin explained.

The woman looked at Mrs. Turpin as if here was an idiot indeed but Mrs. Turpin was not bothered by the look, considering where it came from.

"Nooo," she said, "they're going to stay here where they can go to New York and marry white folks and improve their color. That's what they all want to do, every one of them, improve their color."

"You know what comes of that, don't you?" Claud asked.

"No, Claud, what?" Mrs. Turpin said.

Claud's eyes twinkled. "White-faced niggers," he said with never a smile.

Everybody in the office laughed except the white-trash and the ugly girl. The girl gripped the book in her lap with white fingers. The trashy woman looked around her from face to face as if she thought they were all idiots. The old woman in the feed sack dress continued to gaze expressionless across the floor at the high-top shoes of the man opposite her, the one who had been pretending to be asleep when the Turpins came in. He was laughing heartily, his hands still spread out on his knees. The child had fallen to the side and was lying now almost face down in the old woman's lap.

While they recovered from their laughter, the nasal chorus on the radio kept the room from silence.

> *"You go to blank blank*
> *And I'll go to mine*
> *But we'll all blank along*
> *To-geth-ther,*
> *And all along the blank*
> *We'll hep eachother out*
> *Smile-ling in any kind of*
> *Weath-ther!"*

Mrs. Turpin didn't catch every word but she caught enough to agree with the spirit of the song and it turned her thoughts sober. To help anybody out that needed it was her philosophy of life. She never spared herself when she found somebody in need, whether they were white or black, trash or decent. And of all she had to be thankful for, she was most thankful that this was so. If Jesus had said, "You can be high society and have all the money you want and be thin and svelte-like, but you can't be a good woman with it," she would have had to say, "Well don't make me that then. Make me a good woman and it don't matter what else, how fat or how ugly or how poor!" Her heart rose. He had not made her a nigger or white-trash or ugly! He had made her herself and given her a little of everything. Jesus, thank you! she said. Thank you thank you thank you! Whenever she counted her blessings she felt as buoyant as if she weighed one hundred and twenty-five pounds instead of one hundred and eighty.

"What's wrong with your little boy?" the pleasant lady asked the white-trashy woman.

"He has a ulcer," the woman said proudly. "He ain't give me a minute's peace since he was born. Him and her are just alike," she said, nodding at the old woman, who was running her leathery fingers through the child's pale hair. "Look like I can't get nothing down them two but Co'Cola and candy."

That's all you try to get down em, Mrs. Turpin said to herself. Too lazy to light the fire. There was nothing you could tell her about people like them that she didn't know already. And it was not just that they didn't have anything. Because if you gave them everything, in two weeks it would all be broken or filthy or they would have chopped it up for lightwood. She knew all this from her own experience. Help them you must, but help them you couldn't.

All at once the ugly girl turned her lips inside out again. Her eyes were fixed like two drills on Mrs. Turpin. This time there was no mistaking that there was something urgent behind them.

Girl, Mrs. Turpin exclaimed silently, I haven't done a thing to you! The girl might be confusing her with somebody else. There was no need to sit by and let herself be intimidated. "You must be in college," she said boldly, looking directly at the girl. "I see you reading a book there."

The girl continued to stare and pointedly did not answer.

Her mother blushed at this rudeness. "The lady asked you a question, Mary Grace," she said under her breath.

"I have ears," Mary Grace said.

The poor mother blushed again. "Mary Grace goes to Wellesley College," she explained. She twisted one of the buttons on her dress. "In Massachusetts," she added with a grimace. "And in the summer she just keeps right on studying. Just reads all the time, a real book worm. She's done real well at Wellesley; she's taking English and Math and History and Psychology and Social Studies," she rattled on, "and I think it's too much. I think she ought to get out and have fun."

The girl looked as if she would like to hurl them all through the plate glass window.

"Way up north," Mrs. Turpin murmured and thought, well, it hasn't done much for her manners.

"I'd almost rather to have him sick," the white-trash woman said, wrenching the attention back to herself. "He's so mean when he ain't. Look like some children just take natural to meanness. It's some gets bad when they get sick but he was the opposite. Took sick and turned good. He don't give me no trouble now. It's me waitin to see the doctor," she said.

If I was going to send anybody back to Africa, Mrs. Turpin thought, it would be your kind, woman. "Yes, indeed," she said aloud, but looking up at the ceiling, "it's a heap of things worse than a nigger." And dirtier than a hog, she added to herself.

"I think people with bad dispositions are more to be pitied than anyone on earth," the pleasant lady said in a voice that was decidedly thin.

"I thank the Lord he has blessed me with a good one," Mrs. Turpin said. "The day has never dawned that I couldn't find something to laugh at."

"Not since she married me anyways," Claud said with a comical straight face.

Everybody laughed except the girl and the white-trash.

Mrs. Turpin's stomach shook. "He's such a caution," she said, "that I can't help but laugh at him."

The girl made a loud ugly noise through her teeth.

Her mother's mouth grew thin and tight. "I think the worst thing in the world," she said, "is an ungrateful person. To have everything and not appreciate it. I know a girl," she said, "who has parents who would give her anything, a little brother who loves her dearly, who is getting a good education, who wears the best clothes, but who can never say a kind word to anyone, who never smiles, who just criticizes and complains all day long."

"Is she too old to paddle?" Claud asked.

The girl's face was almost purple.

"Yes," the lady said, "I'm afraid there's nothing to do but leave her to her folly. Some day she'll wake up and it'll be too late."

"It never hurt anyone to smile," Mrs. Turpin said. "It just makes you feel better all over."

"Of course," the lady said sadly, "but there are just some people you can't tell anything to. They can't take criticism."

"If it's one thing I am," Mrs. Turpin said with feeling, "it's grateful. When I think who all I could have been besides myself and what all I got, a little of everything, and a good disposition besides, I just feel like shouting, "Thank you, Jesus, for making everything the way it is!' It could have been different!" For one thing, somebody else could have got Claud. At the thought of this, she was flooded with gratitude and a terrible pang of joy ran through her. "Oh thank you, Jesus, Jesus, thank you!" she cried aloud.

The book struck her directly over her left eye. It struck almost at the same instant that she realized the girl was about to hurl it. Before she could utter a sound, the raw face came crashing across the table toward her, howling. The girl's fingers sank like clamps into the soft flesh of her neck. She heard the mother cry out and Claud shout, "Whoa!" There was an instant when she was certain that she was about to be in an earthquake.

All at once her vision narrowed and she saw everything as if it were happening in a small room far away, or as if she were looking at it through the wrong end of a telescope. Claud's face crumpled and fell out of sight. The nurse ran in, then out, then in again. Then the gangling figure of the doctor rushed out of the inner door. Magazines flew this way and that as the table turned over. The girl fell with a thud and Mrs. Turpin's vision suddenly reversed itself and she saw everything large instead of small. The eyes of the white-trashy woman were staring hugely at the floor. There the girl, held down on one side by the nurse and on the other by her mother, was wrenching and turning in their grasp. The doctor was kneeling astride her, trying to hold her arm down. He managed after a second to sink a long needle into it.

Mrs. Turpin felt entirely hollow except for her heart which swung from side to side as if it were agitated in a great empty drum of flesh.

"Somebody that's not busy call for the ambulance," the doctor said in the off-hand voice young doctors adopt for terrible occasions.

Mrs. Turpin could not have moved a finger. The old man who had been sitting next to her skipped nimbly into the office and made the call, for the secretary still seemed to be gone.

"Claud!" Mrs. Turpin called.

He was not in his chair. She knew she must jump up and find him but she felt like some one trying to catch a train in a dream, when everything moves in slow motion and the faster you try to run the slower you go.

"Here I am," a suffocated voice, very unlike Claud's, said.

He was doubled up in the corner on the floor, pale as paper, holding his leg. She wanted to get up and go to him but she could not move. Instead, her gaze was drawn slowly downward to the churning face on the floor, which she could see over the doctor's shoulder.

The girl's eyes stopped rolling and focused on her. They seemed a much lighter blue than before, as if a door that had been tightly closed behind them was now open to admit light and air.

Mrs. Turpin's head cleared and her power of motion returned. She leaned forward until she was looking directly into the fierce brilliant eyes. There was no doubt in her mind that the girl did know her, knew her in some intense and personal way, beyond time and place and condition. "What you got to say to me?" she asked hoarsely and held her breath, waiting, as for a revelation.

The girl raised her head. Her gaze locked with Mrs. Turpin's. "Go back to hell where you came from, you old wart hog," she whispered. Her voice was low but clear. Her eyes burned for a moment as if she saw with pleasure that her message had struck its target.

Mrs. Turpin sank back in her chair.

After a moment the girl's eyes closed and she turned her head wearily to the side.

The doctor rose and handed the nurse the empty syringe. He leaned over and put both hands for a moment on the mother's shoulders, which were shaking. She was sitting on the floor, her lips pressed together, holding Mary Grace's hand in her lap. The girl's fingers were gripped like a baby's around her thumb. "Go on to the hospital," he said. "I'll call and make the arrangements."

"Now let's see that neck," he said in a jovial voice to Mrs. Turpin. He began to inspect her neck with his first two fingers. Two little moon-shaped lines like pink fish bones were indented over her windpipe. There was the beginning of an angry red swelling above her eye. His fingers passed over this also.

"Lea' me be," she said thickly and shook him off. "See about Claud. She kicked him."

"I'll see about him in a minute," he said and felt her pulse. He was a thin grey-haired man, given to pleasantries. "Go home and have yourself a vacation the rest of the day," he said and patted her on the shoulder.

Quit your pattin me, Mrs. Turpin growled to herself.

"And put an ice pack over that eye," he said. Then he went and squatted down beside Claud and looked at his leg. After a moment he pulled him up and Claud limped after him into the office.

Until the ambulance came, the only sounds in the room were the tremulous moans of the girl's mother, who continued to sit on the floor. The white-trash woman did not take her eyes off the girl. Mrs. Turpin looked straight ahead at nothing. Presently the ambulance drew up, a long dark shadow, behind the curtain. The attendants came in and set the stretcher down beside the girl and lifted her expertly onto it and carried her out. The nurse helped the mother gather up her things. The shadow of the ambulance moved silently away and the nurse came back in the office.

"That ther girl is going to be a lunatic, ain't she?" the white-trash woman asked the nurse, but the nurse kept on to the back and never answered her.

"Yes, she's going to be a lunatic," the white-trash woman said to the rest of them.

"Po' critter," the old woman murmured. The child's face was still in her lap. His eyes looked idly out over her knees. He had not moved during the disturbance except to draw one leg up under him.

"I thank Gawd," the white-trash woman said fervently, "I ain't a lunatic."

Claud came limping out and the Turpins went home.

As their pick-up truck turned into their own dirt road and made the crest of the hill, Mrs. Turpin gripped the window ledge and looked out suspiciously. The land sloped gracefully down through a field dotted with lavender weeds and at the start of the rise their small yellow frame house, with its little flower beds spread out around it like a fancy apron, sat primly in its accustomed place between two giant hickory trees. She would not have been startled to see a burnt wound between two blackened chimneys.

Neither of them felt like eating so they put on their house clothes and lowered the shade in the bedroom and lay down, Claud with his leg on a pillow and herself with a damp washcloth over her eye. The instant she was flat on her back, the image of a razor-backed hog with warts on its face and horns coming out behind its ears snorted into her head. She moaned, a low quiet moan.

"I am not," she said tearfully, "a wart hog. From hell." But the denial had no force. The girl's eyes and her words, even the tone of her voice, low but clear, directed only to her, brooked no repudiation. She had been singled out for the message, though there was trash in the room to whom it might justly have been applied. The full force of this fact struck her only now. There was a woman there who was neglecting her own child but she had been overlooked. The message had been given to Ruby Turpin, a respectable, hard-working, church-going woman. The tears dried. Her eyes began to burn instead with wrath.

She rose on her elbow and the washcloth fell into her hand. Claud was lying on his back, snoring. She wanted to tell him what the girl had said. At the same time, she did not wish to put the image of herself as a wart hog from hell into his mind.

"Hey, Claud," she muttered and pushed his shoulder.

Claud opened one pale baby blue eye.

She looked into it warily. He did not think about anything. He just went his way.

"Wha, whasit?" he said and closed the eye again.

"Nothing," she said. "Does your leg pain you?"

"Hurts like hell," Claud said.

"It'll quit terreckly," she said and lay back down. In a moment Claud was snoring again. For the rest of the afternoon they lay there. Claud slept. She scowled at the ceiling. Occasionally she raised her fist and made a small stabbing motion over her chest as if she was defending her innocence to invisible guests who were like the comforters of Job, reasonable-seeming but wrong.

About five-thirty Claud stirred. "Got to go after those niggers," he sighed, not moving.

She was looking straight up as if there were unintelligible handwriting on the ceiling. The protuberance over her eye had turned a greenish-blue. "Listen here," she said.

"What?"

"Kiss me."

Claud leaned over and kissed her loudly on the mouth. He pinched her side and their hands interlocked. Her expression of ferocious concentration did not change. Claud got up, groaning and growling, and limped off. She continued to study the ceiling.

She did not get up until she heard the pick-up truck coming back with the Negroes. Then she rose and thrust her feet in her brown oxfords, which she did not bother to lace, and stumped out onto the back porch and got her red plastic bucket. She emptied a tray of ice cubes into in and filled it half full of water and went out into the back yard. Every afternoon after Claud brought the hands in, one of the boys helped him put out hay and the rest waited in the back of the truck until he was ready to take them home. The truck was parked in the shade under one of the hickory trees.

"Hi yawl this evening?" Mrs. Turpin asked grimly, appearing with the bucket and the dipper. There were three women and a boy in the truck.

"Us doin nicely," the oldest woman said. "Hi you doin?" and her gaze stuck immediately on the dark lump on Mrs. Turpin's forehead. "You done fell down, ain't you?" she asked in a solicitous voice. The old woman was dark and almost toothless. She had on an old felt hat of Claud's set back on her head. The other two women were younger and lighter and they both had new bright green sun hats. One of them had hers on her head; the other had taken hers off and the boy was grinning beneath it.

Mrs. Turpin set the bucket down on the floor of the truck. "Yawl hep yourselves," she said. She looked around to make sure Claud had gone. "No. I didn't fall down," she said, folding her arms. "It was something worse than that."

"Ain't nothing bad happen to you!" the old woman said. She said it as if they all knew that Mrs. Turpin was protected in some special way by Divine Providence. "You just had you a little fall."

"We were in town at the doctor's office for where the cow kicked Mr. Turpin," Mrs. Turpin said in a flat tone that indicated they could leave off their foolishness. "And there was this girl there. A big fat girl with her face all broke out. I could look at that girl and tell she was peculiar but I couldn't tell how. And me and her mama were just talking and going along and all of a sudden WHAM! She throws this big book she was reading at me and . . ."

"Naw!" the old woman cried out.

"And then she jumps over the table and commences to choke me."

"Naw!" they all exclaimed, "naw!"

"Hi come she do that?" the old woman asked. "What ail her?"

Mrs. Turpin only glared in front of her.

"Somethin ail her," the old woman said.

"They carried her off in an ambulance," Mrs. Turpin continued, "but before she went she was rolling on the floor and they were trying to hold her down to give her a shot and she said something to me." She paused. "You know what she said to me?"

"What she say?" they asked.

"She said," Mrs. Turpin began, and stopped, her face very dark and heavy. The sun was getting whiter and whiter, blanching the sky overhead so that the leaves of the hickory tree were black in the face of it. She could not bring forth the words. "Something real ugly," she muttered.

"She sho shouldn't said nothin ugly to you," the old woman said. "You so sweet. You the sweetest lady I know."

"She pretty too," the one with the hat on said.

"And stout," the other one said. "I never knowed no sweeter white lady."

"That's the truth befo' Jesus," the old woman said. "Amen! You des as sweet and pretty as you can be."

Mrs. Turpin knew just exactly how much Negro flattery was worth and it added to her rage. "She said," she began again and finished this time with a fierce rush of breath, "that I was an old wart hog from hell."

There was an astounded silence.

"Where she at?" the youngest woman cried in a piercing voice.

"Lemme see her. I'll kill her!"

"I'll kill her with you!" the other one cried.

"She b'long in the sylum," the old woman said emphatically. "You the sweetest white lady I know."

"She pretty too," the other two said. "Stout as she can be and sweet. Jesus satisfied with her!"

"Deed he is," the old woman declared.

Idiots! Mrs. Turpin growled to herself. You could never say anything intelligent to a nigger. You could talk at them but not with them. "Yawl ain't drunk your water," she said shortly. "Leave the bucket in the truck when you're finished with it. I got more to do than just stand around and pass the time of day," and she moved off and into the house.

She stood for a moment in the middle of the kitchen. The dark protuberance over her eye looked like a miniature tornado cloud which might any moment sweep across the horizon of her brow. Her lower lip protruded dangerously. She squared her massive shoulders. Then she marched into the front of the house and out the side door and started down the road to the pig parlor. She had the look of a woman going single-handed, weaponless, into battle.

The sun was a deep yellow now like a harvest moon and was riding westward very fast over the far tree line as if it meant to reach the hogs before she did. The road was rutted and she kicked several good-sized stones out of her path as she strode along. The pig parlor was on a little knoll at the end of a lane that ran off from the side of the barn. It was a square of concrete as large as a small room, with a board fence about four feet high around it. The concrete floor sloped slightly so that the hog wash could drain off into a trench where it was carried to the field for fertilizer. Claud was standing on the outside, on the edge of the concrete, hanging onto the top board, hosing down the floor inside. The hose was connected to the faucet of a water trough nearby.

Mrs. Turpin climbed up beside him and glowered down at the hogs inside. There were seven long-snouted bristly shoats in it—tan with liver-colored spots—and an old sow a few weeks off from farrowing. She was lying on her side grunting. The shoats were running about shaking themselves like idiot children, their little slit pig eyes searching the floor for anything left. She had read that pigs were the most intelligent animal. She doubted it. They were supposed to be smarter than dogs. There had even been a pig astronaut. He had performed his assignment perfectly but died of a heart attack afterwards because they left him in his electric suit, sitting upright throughout his examination when naturally a hog should be on all fours.

A-gruntin and a-rootin and a-groanin.

"Gimme that hose," she said, yanking it away from Claud. "Go on and carry them niggers home and then get off that leg."

"You look like you might have swallowed a mad dog," Claud observed, but he got down and limped off. He paid no attention to her humors.

Until he was out of earshot, Mrs. Turpin stood on the side of the pen, holding the hose and pointing the stream of water at the hind quarters of any shoat that looked as if it might try to lie down. When he had had time to get over the hill, she turned her head slightly and her wrathful eyes scanned the path. He was nowhere in sight. She turned back again and seemed to gather herself up. Her shoulders rose and she drew in her breath.

"What do you send me a message like that for?" she said in a low fierce voice, barely above a whisper but with the force of a shout in its concentrated fury. "How am I a hog and me both? How am I saved and from hell too?" Her free fist was knotted and with the other she gripped the hose, blindly pointing the stream of water in and out of the eye of the old sow whose outraged squeal she did not hear.

The pig parlor commanded a view of the back pasture where their twenty beef cows were gathered around the hay-bales Claud and the boy had put out. The freshly cut pasture sloped down to the highway. Across it was their cotton field and beyond that a dark green dusty wood which they owned as well. The sun was behind the wood, very red, looking over the paling of trees like a farmer inspecting his own hogs.

"Why me?" she rumbled. "It's no trash around here, black or white, that I haven't given to. And break my back to the bone every day working. And do for the church."

She appeared to be the right size woman to command the arena before her. "How am I a hog?" she demanded. "Exactly how am I like them?" and she jabbed the stream of water at the shoats. "There was plenty of trash there. It didn't have to be me.

"If you like trash better, go get yourself some trash then," she railed. "You could have made me trash. Or a nigger. If trash is what you wanted why didn't you make me trash?" She shook her fist with the hose in it and a watery snake appeared momentarily in the air. "I could quit working and take it easy and be filthy," she growled. "Lounge about the sidewalks all day drinking root beer. Dip snuff and spit in every puddle and have it all over my face. I could be nasty.

"Or you could have made me a nigger. It's too late for me to be a nigger," she said with deep sarcasm, "but I could act like one. Lay down in the middle of the road and stop traffic. Roll on the ground."

In the deepening light everything was taking on a mysterious hue. The pasture was growing a peculiar glassy green and the streak of highway had turned lavender. She braced herself for a final assault and this time her voice rolled out over the pasture. "Go on," she yelled, "call me a hog! Call me a hog again. From hell. Call me a wart hog from hell. Put that bottom rail on top. There'll still be a top and bottom!"

A garbled echo returned to her.

A final surge of fury shook her and she roared, "Who do you think you are?"

The color of everything, field and crimson sky, burned for a moment with a transparent intensity. The question carried over the pasture and across the highway and the cotton field and returned to her clearly like an answer from beyond the wood.

She opened her mouth but no sound came out of it.

A tiny truck, Claud's, appeared on the highway, heading rapidly out of sight. Its gears scraped thinly. It looked like a child's toy. At any moment a bigger truck might smash into it and scatter Claud's and the niggers' brains all over the road.

Mrs. Turpin stood there, her gaze fixed on the highway, all her muscles rigid, until in five or six minutes the truck reappeared, returning. She waited until it had had time to turn into their own road. Then like a monumental statue coming to life, she bent her head slowly and gazed, as if through the very heart of mystery, down into the pig parlor at the hogs. They had settled all in one corner around the old sow who was grunting softly. A red glow suffused them. They appeared to pant with a secret life.

Until the sun slipped finally behind the tree line, Mrs. Turpin remained there with her gaze bent to them as if she were absorbing some abysmal life-giving knowledge. At last she lifted her head. There was only a purple streak in the sky, cutting through a field of crimson and leading, like an extension of the highway, into the descending dusk. She raised her hands from the side of the pen in a gesture hieratic and profound. A visionary light settled in her eyes. She saw the streak as a vast swinging bridge extending upward from the earth through a field of living fire. Upon it a vast horde of souls were rumbling toward heaven. There were whole companies of white-trash, clean for the first time in their lives, and bands of black niggers in white robes, and battalions of freaks and lunatics shouting and clapping and leaping like frogs. And bringing up the end of the procession was a tribe of people whom she recognized at once as those who, like herself and Claud, had always had a little of everything and the God-given wit to use it right. She leaned forward to observe them closer. They were marching behind the others with great dignity, accountable as they had always been for good order and common sense and respectable behavior. They alone were on key. Yet she could see by their shocked and altered faces that even their virtues were being burned away. She lowered her hands and gripped the rail of the hog pen, her eyes small but fixed unblinkingly on what lay ahead. In a moment the vision faded but she remained where she was, immobile.

At length she got down and turned off the faucet and made her slow way on the darkening path to the house. In the woods around her the invisible cricket choruses had struck up, but what she heard were the voices of the souls climbing upward into the starry field and shouting hallelujah.

PAUL'S CASE

Willa Cather

(1873–1947)

Biography p. 1066

It was Paul's afternoon to appear before the faculty of the Pittsburgh High School to account for his various misdemeanours. He had been suspended a week ago, and his father had called at the Principal's office and confessed his perplexity about his son. Paul entered the faculty room suave and smiling. His clothes were a trifle outgrown, and the tan velvet on the collar of his open overcoat was frayed and worn; but for all that there was something of the dandy about him, and he wore an opal pin in his neatly knotted black four-in-hand, and a red carnation in his button-hole. This latter adornment the faculty somehow felt was not properly significant of the contrite spirit befitting a boy under the ban of suspension.

Paul was tall for his age and very thin, with high, cramped shoulders and a narrow chest. His eyes were remarkable for a certain hysterical brilliancy, and he continually used them in a conscious, theatrical sort of way, peculiarly offensive in a boy. The pupils were abnormally large, as though he were addicted to belladonna, but there was a glassy glitter about them which that drug does not produce.

When questioned by the Principal as to why he was there, Paul stated, politely enough, that he wanted to come back to school. This was a lie, but Paul was quite accustomed to lying; found it, indeed, indispensable for overcoming friction. His teachers were asked to state their respective charges against him, which they did with such a rancour and aggrievedness as evinced that this was not a usual case. Disorder and impertinence were among the offences named, yet each of his instructors felt that it was scarcely possible to put into words the real cause of the trouble, which lay in a sort of hysterically defiant manner of the boy's; in the contempt which they all knew he felt for them, and which he seemingly made not the least effort to conceal. Once, when he had been making a synopsis of a paragraph at the blackboard, his English teacher had stepped to his side and attempted to guide his hand. Paul had started back with a shudder and thrust his hands violently behind him. The astonished woman could scarcely have been more hurt and embarrassed had he struck at her. The insult was so involuntary and definitely personal as to be unforgettable. In one way and another, he had made all his teachers, men and women alike, conscious of the same feeling of physical aversion. In one class he habitually sat with his hand shading his eyes; in another he always looked out of the window during the recitation; in another he made a running commentary on the lecture, with humorous intent.

His teachers felt this afternoon that his whole attitude was symbolized by his shrug and his flippantly red carnation flower, and they fell upon him without mercy, his English teacher leading the pack. He stood through it smiling, his pale lips parted over his white teeth. (His lips were continually twitching, and he had a habit of raising his eyebrows that was contemptuous and irritating to the last degree.) Older boys than Paul had broken down and shed tears under that ordeal, but his set smile did not once desert him, and his only sign of discomfort was the nervous trembling of the fingers that toyed with the buttons of his overcoat, and an occasional jerking of the other hand which held his hat. Paul was always smiling, always glancing about him, seeming to feel that people might be watching him and trying to detect something. This conscious expression, since it was as far as possible from boyish mirthfulness, was usually attributed to insolence or "smartness."

As the inquisition proceeded, one of his instructors repeated an impertinent remark of the boy's, and the Principal asked him whether he thought that a courteous speech to make to a woman. Paul shrugged his shoulders slightly and his eyebrows twitched.

"I don't know," he replied. "I didn't mean to be polite or impolite, either. I guess it's a sort of way I have, of saying things regardless."

The Principal asked him whether he didn't think that a way it would be well to get rid of. Paul grinned and said he guessed so. When he was told that he could go, he bowed gracefully and went out. His bow was like a repetition of the scandalous red carnation.

His teachers were in despair, and his drawing master voiced the feeling of them all when he declared there was something about the boy which none of them understood. He added: "I don't really believe that smile of his comes altogether from insolence; there's something sort of haunted about it. The boy is not strong, for one thing. There is something wrong about the fellow."

The drawing master had come to realize that, in looking at Paul, one saw only his white teeth and the forced animation of his eyes. One warm afternoon the boy had gone to sleep at his drawing-board, and his master had noted with amazement what a white, blue-veined face it was; drawn and wrinkled like an old man's about the eyes, the lips twitching even in his sleep.

His teachers left the building dissatisfied and unhappy; humiliated to have felt so vindictive toward a mere boy, to have uttered this feeling in cutting terms, and to have set each other on, as it were, in the grewsome game of intemperate reproach. One of them remembered having seen a miserable street cat set at bay by a ring of tormentors.

As for Paul, he ran down the hill whistling the Soldiers' Chorus from *Faust,* looking wildly behind him now and then to see whether some of his teachers were not there to witness his light-heartedness. As it was now late in the afternoon and Paul was on duty that evening as usher at Carnegie Hall, he decided that he would not go home to supper.

When he reached the concert hall the doors were not yet open. It was chilly outside, and he decided to go up into the picture gallery—always deserted at this hour—where there were some of Raffelli's gay studies of Paris streets and an airy blue Venetian scene or two that always exhilarated him. He was delighted to find no one in the gallery but the old guard, who sat in the corner, a newspaper on his knee, a black patch over one eye and the other closed. Paul possessed himself of the place and walked confidently up and down, whistling under his breath. After a while he sat down before a blue Rico and lost himself. When he bethought him to look at his watch, it was after seven o'clock, and he rose with a start and ran downstairs making a face at Augustus Cæsar, peering out from the cast-room, and an evil gesture at the Venus of Milo as he passed her on the stairway.

When Paul reached the ushers' dressing-room half-a-dozen boys were there already, and he began excitedly to tumble into his uniform. It was one of the few that at all approached fitting, and Paul thought it very becoming—though he knew the tight, straight coat accentuated his narrow chest, about which he was exceedingly sensitive. He was always excited while he dressed, twanging all over to the tuning of the strings and the preliminary flourishes of the horns in the music-room; but tonight he seemed quite beside himself, and he teased and plagued the boys until, telling him that he was crazy, they put him down on the floor and sat on him.

Somewhat calmed by his suppression, Paul dashed out to the front of the house to seat the early comers. He was a model usher. Gracious and smiling he ran up and down the aisles. Nothing was too much trouble for him; he carried messages and brought programs as though it were his greatest pleasure in life, and all the people in his section thought him a charming boy, feeling that he remembered and admired them. As the house filled, he grew more and more vivacious and animated, and the colour came to his cheeks and lips. It was very much as though this were a great reception and Paul were the host. Just as the musicians came out to take their places, his English teacher arrived with checks for the seats which a prominent manufacturer had taken for the season. She betrayed some embarrassment when she handed Paul the tickets, and a *hauteur* which subsequently made her feel very foolish. Paul was startled for a moment, and had the feeling of wanting to put her out; what business had she here among all these fine people and gay colours? He looked her over and decided that she was not appropriately dressed and must be a fool to sit downstairs in such togs. The tickets had probably been sent her out of kindness, he reflected, as he put down a seat for her, and she had about as much right to sit there as he had.

When the symphony began Paul sank into one of the rear seats with a long sigh of relief, and lost himself as he had done before the Rico. It was not that symphonies, as such, meant anything in particular to Paul, but the first sigh of the instruments seemed to free some hilarious spirit within him; something that struggled there like the Genius in the bottle found by the Arab fisherman. He felt a sudden zest of life; the lights danced before his eyes and the concert hall blazed into unimaginable splendour. When the soprano soloist came on, Paul forgot even the nastiness of his teacher's being there, and gave himself up to the peculiar intoxication such personages always had for him. The soloist chanced to be a German woman, by no means in her first youth, and the mother of many children; but she wore a satin gown and a tiara, and she had that indefinable air of achievement, that world-shine upon her, which always blinded Paul to any possible defects.

After a concert was over, Paul was often irritable and wretched until he got to sleep,—and tonight he was even more than usually restless. He had the feeling of not being able to let down; of its being impossible to give up this delicious excitement which was the only thing that could be called living at all. During the last number he withdrew and, after hastily changing his clothes in the dressing-room, slipped out to the side door where the singer's carriage stood. Here he began pacing rapidly up and down the walk, waiting to see her come out.

Over yonder the Schenley, in its vacant stretch, loomed big and square through the fine rain, the windows of its twelve stories glowing like those of a lighted card-board house under a Christmas tree. All the actors and singers of any importance stayed there when they were in the city, and a number of the big manufacturers of the place lived there in the winter. Paul had often hung about the hotel, watching the people go in and out, longing to enter and leave school-masters and dull care behind him for ever.

At last the singer came out, accompanied by the conductor, who helped her into her carriage and closed the door with a cordial *auf wiedersehen,*—which set Paul to wondering whether she were not an old sweetheart of his. Paul followed the carriage over to the hotel, walking so rapidly as not to be far from the entrance when the singer alighted and disappeared behind the swinging glass doors which were opened by a negro in a tall hat and a long coat. In the moment that the door was ajar, it seemed to Paul that he, too, entered. He seemed to feel himself go after her up the steps, into the warm, lighted building, into an exotic, a tropical world of shiny, glistening surfaces and basking ease. He reflected upon the mysterious dishes that were brought into the dining-room, the green bottles in buckets of ice, as he had seen them in the supper party pictures of the Sunday supplement. A quick gust of wind brought the rain down with sudden vehemence, and Paul was startled to find that he was still outside in the slush of the gravel driveway; that his boots were letting in the water and his scanty overcoat was clinging wet about him; that the lights in front of the concert hall were out, and that the rain was driving in sheets between him and the orange glow of the windows above him. There it was, what he wanted—tangibly before him, like the fairy world of a Christmas pantomime; as the rain beat in his face, Paul wondered whether he were destined always to shiver in the black night outside, looking up at it.

He turned and walked reluctantly toward the car tracks. The end had to come sometime; his father in his nightclothes at the top of the stairs, explanations that did not explain, hastily improvised fictions that were forever tripping him up, his upstairs room and its horrible yellow wallpaper, the creaking bureau with the greasy plush collar-box, and over his painted wooden bed the pictures of George Washington and John Calvin, and the framed motto, "Feed my Lambs," which had been worked in red worsted by his mother, whom Paul could not remember.

Half an hour later, Paul alighted from the Negley Avenue car and went slowly down one of the side streets off the main thoroughfare. It was a highly respectable street, where all the houses were exactly alike, and where business men of moderate means begot and reared large families of children, all of whom went to Sabbath-school and learned the shorter catechism, and were interested in arithmetic; all of whom were as exactly alike as their homes, and of a piece with the monotony in which they lived. Paul never went up Cordelia Street without a shudder of loathing. His home was next the house of the Cumberland minister. He approached it tonight with the nerveless sense of defeat, the hopeless feeling of sinking back forever into ugliness and common-ness that he had always had when he came home. The moment he turned into Cordelia Street he felt the waters close above his head. After each of these orgies of living, he experienced all the physical depression which follows a debauch; the loathing of respectable beds, of common food, of a house permeated by kitchen odours; a shud-dering repulsion for the flavourless, colourless mass of every-day existence; a morbid desire for cool things and soft lights and fresh flowers.

The nearer he approached the house, the more absolutely unequal Paul felt to the sight of it all; his ugly sleeping chamber; the cold bath-room with the grimy zinc tub, the cracked mirror, the dripping spiggots; his father, at the top of the stairs, his hairy legs sticking out from his nightshirt, his feet thrust into carpet slippers. He was so much later than usual that there would certainly be inquiries and reproaches. Paul stopped short before the door. He felt that he could not be accosted by his father tonight; that he could not toss again on that miserable bed. He would not go in. He would tell his father that he had no car fare, and it was raining so hard he had gone home with one of the boys and stayed all night.

Meanwhile, he was wet and cold. He went around to the back of the house and tried one of the basement windows, found it open, raised it cautiously, and scrambled down the cellar wall to the floor. There he stood, holding his breath, terrified by the noise he had made; but the floor above him was silent, and there was no creak on the stairs. He found a soap-box, and carried it over to the soft ring of light that streamed from the furnace door, and sat down. He was horribly afraid of rats, so he did not try to sleep, but sat looking distrustfully at the dark, still terrified lest he might have awakened his father. In such reactions, after one of the experiences which made days and nights out of the dreary blanks of the calendar, when his senses were deadened, Paul's head was always singularly clear. Suppose his father had heard him getting in at the window and had come down and shot him for a burglar? Then, again, suppose his father had come down, pistol in hand, and he had cried out in time to save himself, and his father had been horrified to think how nearly he had killed him? Then, again, suppose a day should come when his father would remember that night, and wish there had been no warning cry to stay his hand? With this last supposition Paul entertained himself until daybreak.

The following Sunday was fine; the sodden November chill was broken by the last flash of autumnal summer. In the morning Paul had to go to church and Sabbath-school, as always. On seasonable Sunday afternoons the burghers of Cordelia Street usually sat out on their front "stoops," and talked to their neighbours on the next stoop, or called to those across the street in neighbourly fashion. The men sat placidly on gay cushions placed upon the steps that led down to the sidewalk, while the women, in their Sunday "waists," sat in rockers on the cramped porches, pretending to be greatly at their ease. The children played in the streets; there were so many of them that the place resembled the recreation grounds of a kindergarten. The men on the steps—all in their shirt sleeves, their vests unbuttoned—sat with their legs well apart, their stomachs comfortably protruding, and talked of the prices of things, or told anecdotes of the sagacity of their various chiefs and overlords. They occasionally looked over the multitude of squabbling children, listened affectionately to their high-pitched, nasal voices, smiling to see their own proclivities reproduced in their offspring, and interspersed their legends of the iron kings with remarks about their sons' progress at school, their grades in arithmetic, and the amounts they had saved in their toy banks.

On this last Sunday of November, Paul sat all the afternoon on the lowest step of his "stoop," staring into the street, while his sisters, in their rockers, were talking to the minister's daughters next door about how many shirt-waists they had made in the last week, and how many waffles some one had eaten at the last church supper. When the weather was warm, and his father was in a particularly jovial frame of mind, the girls made lemonade, which was always brought out in a red-glass pitcher, ornamented with forget-me-nots in blue enamel. This the girls thought very fine, and the neighbours joked about the suspicious colour of the pitcher.

Today Paul's father, on the top step, was talking to a young man who shifted a restless baby from knee to knee. He happened to be the young man who was daily held up to Paul as a model, and after whom it was his father's dearest hope that he would pattern. This young man was of a ruddy complexion, with a compressed, red mouth, and faded, near-sighted eyes, over which he wore thick spectacles, with gold bows that curved about his ears. He was clerk to one of the magnates of a great steel corporation, and was looked upon in Cordelia Street as a young man with a future. There was a story that, some five years ago—he was now barely twenty-six—he had been a trifle "dissipated," but in order to curb his appetites and save the loss of time and strength that a sowing of wild oats might have entailed, he had taken his chief's advice, oft reiterated to his employés, and at twenty-one had married the first woman whom he could persuade to share his fortunes. She happened to be an angular school-mistress, much older than he, who also wore thick glasses, and who had now borne him four children, all near-sighted, like herself.

The young man was relating how his chief, now cruising in the Mediterranean, kept in touch with all the details of the business, arranging his office hours on his yacht just as though he were at home, and "knocking off work enough to keep two stenographers busy." His father told, in turn, the plan his corporation was considering, of putting in an electric railway plant at Cairo. Paul snapped his teeth; he had an awful apprehension that they might spoil it all before he got there. Yet he rather liked to hear these legends of the iron kings, that were told and retold on Sundays and holidays; these stories of palaces in Venice, yachts on the Mediterranean, and high play at Monte Carlo appealed to his fancy, and he was interested in the triumphs of cash boys who had become famous, though he had no mind for the cash-boy stage.

After supper was over, and he had helped to dry the dishes, Paul nervously asked his father whether he could go to George's to get some help in his geometry, and still more nervously asked for car-fare. This latter request he had to repeat, as his father, on principle, did not like to hear requests for money, whether much or little. He asked Paul whether he could not go to some boy who lived nearer, and told him that he ought not to leave his school work until Sunday; but he gave him the dime. He was not a poor man, but he had a worthy ambition to come up in the world. His only reason for allowing Paul to usher was that he thought a boy ought to be earning a little.

Paul bounded upstairs, scrubbed the greasy odour of the dish-water from his hands with the ill-smelling soap he hated, and then shook over his fingers a few drops of violet water from the bottle he kept hidden in his drawer. He left the house with his geometry conspicuously under his arm, and the moment he got out of Cordelia Street and boarded a downtown car, he shook off the lethargy of two deadening days, and began to live again.

The leading juvenile of the permanent stock company which played at one of the downtown theatres was an acquaintance of Paul's, and the boy had been invited to drop in at the Sunday-night rehearsals whenever he could. For more than a year Paul had spent every available moment loitering about Charley Edwards's dressing-room. He had won a place among Edwards's following not only because the young actor, who could not afford to employ a dresser, often found him useful, but because he recognized in Paul something akin to what churchmen term "vocation."

It was at the theatre and at Carnegie Hall that Paul really lived; the rest was but a sleep and a forgetting. This was Paul's fairy tale, and it had for him all the allurement of a secret love. The moment he inhaled the gassy, painty, dusty odour behind the scenes, he breathed like a prisoner set free, and felt within him the possibility of doing or saying splendid, brilliant things. The moment the cracked orchestra beat out the overture from *Martha,* or jerked at the serenade from *Rigoletto,* all stupid and ugly things slid from him, and his senses were deliciously, yet delicately fired.

Perhaps it was because, in Paul's world, the natural nearly always wore the guise of ugliness, that a certain element of artificiality seemed to him necessary in beauty. Perhaps it was because his experience of life elsewhere was so full of Sabbath-school picnics, petty economies, wholesome advice as to how to succeed in life, and the unescapable odours of cooking, that he found this existence so alluring, these smartly-clad men and women so attractive, that he was so moved by these starry apple orchards that bloomed perennially under the lime-light.

It would be difficult to put it strongly enough how convincingly the stage entrance of that theatre was for Paul the actual portal of Romance. Certainly none of the company ever suspected it, least of all Charley Edwards. It was very like the old stories that used to float about London of fabulously rich Jews, who had subterranean halls, with palms, and fountains, and soft lamps and richly apparelled women who never saw the disenchanting light of London day. So, in the midst of that smoke-palled city, enamoured of figures and grimy toil, Paul had his secret temple, his wishing-carpet, his bit of blue-and-white Mediterranean shore bathed in perpetual sunshine.

Several of Paul's teachers had a theory that his imagination had been perverted by garish fiction; but the truth was, he scarcely ever read at all. The books at home were not such as would either tempt or corrupt a youthful mind, and as for reading the novels that some of his friends urged upon him—well, he got what he wanted much more quickly from music; any sort of music, from an orchestra to a barrel organ. He needed only the spark, the indescribable thrill that made his imagination master of his senses, and he could make plots and pictures enough of his own. It was equally true that he was not stage-struck—not, at any rate, in the usual acceptation of that expression. He had no desire to become an actor, any more than he had to become a musician. He felt no necessity to do any of these things; what he wanted was to see, to be in the atmosphere, float on the wave of it, to be carried out, blue league after blue league, away from everything.

After a night behind the scenes, Paul found the school-room more than ever repulsive; the bare floors and naked walls; the prosy men who never wore frock coats, or violets in their buttonholes; the women with their dull gowns, shrill voices, and pitiful seriousness about prepositions that govern the dative. He could not bear to have the other pupils think, for a moment, that he took these people seriously; he must convey to them that he considered it all trivial, and was there only by way of a joke, anyway. He had autograph pictures of all the members of the stock company which he showed his classmates, telling them the most incredible stories of his familiarity with these people, of his acquaintance with the soloists who came to Carnegie Hall, his suppers with them and the flowers he sent them. When these stories lost their effect, and his audience grew listless, he would bid all the boys good-bye, announcing that he was going to travel for awhile; going to Naples, to California, to Egypt. Then, next Monday, he would slip back, conscious and nervously smiling; his sister was ill, and he would have to defer his voyage until spring.

Matters went steadily worse with Paul at school. In the itch to let his instructors know how heartily he despised them, and how thoroughly he was appreciated else-where, he mentioned once or twice that he had no time to fool with theorems; adding—with a twitch of the eyebrows and a touch of that nervous bravado which so perplexed them—that he was helping the people down at the stock company; they were old friends of his.

The upshot of the matter was, that the Principal went to Paul's father, and Paul was taken out of school and put to work. The manager at Carnegie Hall was told to get another usher in his stead; the doorkeeper at the theatre was warned not to admit him to the house; and Charley Edwards remorsefully promised the boy's father not to see him again.

The members of the stock company were vastly amused when some of Paul's stories reached them—especially the women. They were hard-working women, most of them supporting indolent husbands or brothers, and they laughed rather bitterly at having stirred the boy to such fervid and florid inventions. They agreed with the faculty and with his father, that Paul's was a bad case.

The east-bound train was ploughing through a January snow-storm; the dull dawn was beginning to show grey when the engine whistled a mile out of Newark. Paul started up from the seat where he had lain curled in uneasy slumber, rubbed the breath-misted window glass with his hand, and peered out. The snow was whirling in curling eddies above the white bottom lands, and the drifts lay already deep in the fields and along the fences, while here and there the long dead grass and dried weed stalks protruded black above it. Lights shone from the scattered houses, and a gang of labourers who stood beside the track waved their lanterns.

Paul had slept very little, and he felt grimy and uncomfortable. He had made the all-night journey in a day coach because he was afraid if he took a Pullman he might be seen by some Pittsburgh business man who had noticed him in Denny & Carson's office. When the whistle woke him, he clutched quickly at his breast pocket, glancing about him with an uncertain smile. But the little, clay-bespattered Italians were still sleeping, the slatternly women across the aisle were in open-mouthed oblivion, and even the crumby, crying babies were for the nonce stilled. Paul settled back to struggle with his impatience as best he could.

When he arrived at the Jersey City station, he hurried through his breakfast, manifestly ill at ease and keeping a sharp eye about him. After he reached the Twenty-third Street station, he consulted a cabman, and had himself driven to a men's furnishing establishment which was just opening for the day. He spent upward of two hours there, buying with endless reconsidering and great care. His new street suit he put on in the fitting-room; the frock coat and dress clothes he had bundled into the cab with his new shirts. Then he drove to a hatter's and a shoe house. His next errand was at Tiffany's, where he selected silver mounted brushes and a scarf-pin. He would not wait to have his silver marked, he said. Lastly, he stopped at a trunk shop on Broadway, and had his purchases packed into various travelling bags.

It was a little after one o'clock when he drove up to the Waldorf, and, after settling with the cabman, went into the office. He registered from Washington; said his mother and father had been abroad, and that he had come down to await the arrival of their steamer. He told his story plausibly and had no trouble, since he offered to pay for them in advance, in engaging his rooms; a sleeping-room, sitting-room and bath.

Not once, but a hundred times Paul had planned this entry into New York. He had gone over every detail of it with Charley Edwards, and in his scrap book at home there were pages of description about New York hotels, cut from the Sunday papers.

When he was shown to his sitting-room on the eighth floor, he saw at a glance that everything was as it should be; there was but one detail in his mental picture that the place did not realize, so he rang for the bell boy and sent him down for flowers. He moved about nervously until the boy returned, putting away his new linen and fingering it delightedly as he did so. When the flowers came, he put them hastily into water, and then tumbled into a hot bath. Presently he came out of his white bathroom, resplendent in his new silk underwear, and playing with the tassels of his red robe. The snow was whirling so fiercely outside his windows that he could scarcely see across the street; but within, the air was deliciously soft and fragrant. He put the violets and jonquils on the tabouret beside the couch, and threw himself down with a long sigh, covering himself with a Roman blanket. He was throughly tired; he had been in such haste, he had stood up to such a strain, covered so much ground in the last twenty-four hours, that he wanted to think how it had all come about. Lulled by the sound of the wind, the warm air, and the cool fragrance of the flowers, he sank into deep, drowsy retrospection.

It had been wonderfully simple; when they had shut him out of the theatre and concert hall, when they had taken away his bone, the whole thing was virtually determined. The rest was a mere matter of opportunity. The only thing that at all surprised him was his own courage—for he realized well enough that he had always been tormented by fear, a sort of apprehensive dread that, of late years, as the meshes of the lies he had told closed about him, had been pulling the muscles of his body tighter and tighter. Until now, he could not remember a time when he had not been dreading something. Even when he was a little boy, it was always there—behind him, or before, or on either side. There had always been the shadowed corner, the dark place into which he dared not look, but from which something seemed always to be watching him—and Paul had done things that were not pretty to watch, he knew.

But now he had a curious sense of relief, as though he had at last thrown down the gauntlet to the thing in the corner.

Yet it was but a day since he had been sulking in the traces; but yesterday afternoon that he had been sent to the bank with Denny & Carson's deposit, as usual—but this time he was instructed to leave the book to be balanced. There was above two thousand dollars in checks, and nearly a thousand in the bank notes which he had taken from the book and quietly transferred to his pocket. At the bank he had made out a new deposit slip. His nerves had been steady enough to permit of his returning to the office, where he had finished his work and asked for a full day's holiday tomorrow, Saturday, giving a perfectly reasonable pretext. The bank book, he knew, would not be returned before Monday or Tuesday, and his father would be out of town for the next week. From the time he slipped the bank notes into his pocket until he boarded the night train for New York, he had not known a moment's hesitation.

How astonishingly easy it had all been; here he was, the thing done; and this time there would be no awakening, no figure at the top of the stairs. He watched the snow flakes whirling by his window until he fell asleep.

When he awoke, it was four o'clock in the afternoon. He bounded up with a start; one of his precious days gone already! He spent nearly an hour in dressing, watching every stage of his toilet carefully in the mirror. Everything was quite perfect; he was exactly the kind of boy he had always wanted to be.

When he went downstairs, Paul took a carriage and drove up Fifth avenue toward the Park. The snow had somewhat abated; carriages and tradesmen's wagons were hurrying soundlessly to and fro in the winter twilight; boys in woollen mufflers were shovelling off the door-steps; the avenue stages made fine spots of colour against the white street. Here and there on the corners whole flower gardens blooming behind glass windows, against which the snow flakes stuck and melted; violets, roses, carnations, lilies of the valley—somehow vastly more lovely and alluring that they blossomed thus unnaturally in the snow. The Park itself was a wonderful stage winter-piece.

When he returned, the pause of the twilight had ceased, and the tune of the streets had changed. The snow was falling faster, lights streamed from the hotels that reared their many stories fearlessly up into the storm, defying the raging Atlantic winds. A long, black stream of carriages poured down the avenue, intersected here and there by other streams, tending horizontally. There were a score of cabs about the entrance of his hotel, and his driver had to wait. Boys in livery were running in and out of the awning stretched across the sidewalk, up and down the red velvet carpet laid from the door to the street. Above, about, within it all, was the rumble and roar, the hurry and toss of thousands of human beings as hot for pleasure as himself, and on every side of him towered the glaring affirmation of the omnipotence of wealth.

The boy set his teeth and drew his shoulders together in a spasm of realization; the plot of all dramas, the text of all romances, the nerve-stuff of all sensations was whirling about him like the snow flakes. He burnt like a faggot in a tempest.

When Paul came down to dinner, the music of the orchestra floated up the elevator shaft to greet him. As he stepped into the thronged corridor, he sank back into one of the chairs against the wall to get his breath. The lights, the chatter, the perfumes, the bewildering medley of colour—he had, for a moment, the feeling of not being able to stand it. But only for a moment; these were his own people, he told himself. He went slowly about the corridors, through the writing-rooms, smoking-rooms, reception-rooms, as though he were exploring the chambers of an enchanted palace, built and peopled for him alone.

When he reached the dining-room he sat down at a table near a window. The flowers, the white linen, the many-coloured wine glasses, the gay toilettes of the women, the low popping of corks, the undulating repetitions of the *Blue Danube* from the orchestra, all flooded Paul's dream with bewildering radiance. When the roseate tinge of his champagne was added—that cold, precious, bubbling stuff that creamed and foamed in his glass—Paul wondered that there were honest men in the world at all. This was what all the world was fighting for, he reflected; this was what all the struggle was about. He doubted the reality of his past. Had he ever known a place called Cordelia Street, a place where fagged looking business men boarded the early car? Mere rivets in a machine they seemed to Paul,—sickening men, with combings of children's hair always hanging to their coats, and the smell of cooking in their clothes. Cordelia Street—Ah, that belonged to another time and country! Had he not always been thus, had he not sat here night after night, from as far back as he could remember, looking pensively over just such shimmering textures, and slowly twirling the stem of a glass like this one between his thumb and middle finger? He rather thought he had.

He was not in the least abashed or lonely. He had no especial desire to meet or to know any of these people; all he demanded was the right to look on and conjecture, to watch the pageant. The mere stage properties were all he contended for. Nor was he lonely later in the evening, in his loge at the Opera. He was entirely rid of his nervous misgivings, of his forced aggressiveness, of the imperative desire to show himself different from his surroundings. He felt now that his surroundings explained him. Nobody questioned the purple; he had only to wear it passively. He had only to glance down at his dress coat to reassure himself that here it would be impossible for anyone to humiliate him.

He found it hard to leave his beautiful sitting-room to go to bed that night, and sat long watching the raging storm from his turret window. When he went to sleep, it was with the lights turned on in his bedroom; partly because of his old timidity, and partly so that, if he should wake in the night, there would be no wretched moment of doubt, no horrible suspicion of yellow wall-paper, or of Washington and Calvin above his bed.

On Sunday morning the city was practically snow-bound. Paul breakfasted late, and in the afternoon he fell in with a wild San Francisco boy, a freshman at Yale, who said he had run down for a "little flyer" over Sunday. The young man offered to show Paul the night side of the town, and the two boys went off together after dinner, not returning to the hotel until seven o'clock the next morning. They had started out in the confiding warmth of a champagne friendship, but their parting in the elevator was singularly cool. The freshman pulled himself together to make his train, and Paul went to bed. He awoke at two o'clock in the afternoon, very thirsty and dizzy, and rang for ice-water, coffee, and the Pittsburgh papers.

On the part of the hotel management, Paul excited no suspicion. There was this to be said for him, that he wore his spoils with dignity and in no way made himself conspicuous. His chief greediness lay in his ears and eyes, and his excesses were not offensive ones. His dearest pleasures were the grey winter twilights in his sitting-room; his quiet enjoyment of his flowers, his clothes, his wide divan, his cigarette and his sense of power. He could not remember a time when he had felt so at peace with himself. The mere release from the necessity of petty lying, lying every day and every day, restored his self-respect. He had never lied for pleasure, even at school; but to make himself noticed and admired, to assert his difference from other Cordelia Street boys; and he felt a good deal more manly, more honest, even, now that he had no need for boastful pretensions, now that he could, as his actor friends used to say, "dress the part." It was characteristic that remorse did not occur to him. His golden days went by without a shadow, and he made each as perfect as he could.

On the eighth day after his arrival in New York, he found the whole affair exploited in the Pittsburgh papers, exploited with a wealth of detail which indicated that local news of a sensational nature was at a low ebb. The firm of Denny & Carson announced that the boy's father had refunded the full amount of his theft, and that they had no intention of prosecuting. The Cumberland minister had been interviewed, and expressed his hope of yet reclaiming the motherless lad, and Paul's Sabbath-school teacher declared that she would spare no effort to that end. The rumour had reached Pittsburgh that the boy had been seen in a New York hotel, and his father had gone East to find him and bring him home.

Paul had just come in to dress for dinner; he sank into a chair, weak in the knees, and clasped his head in his hands. It was to be worse than jail, even; the tepid waters of Cordelia Street were to close over him finally and forever. The grey monotony stretched before him in hopeless, unrelieved years; Sabbath-school, Young People's Meeting, the yellow-papered room, the damp dish-towels; it all rushed back upon him with sickening vividness. He had the old feeling that the orchestra had suddenly stopped, the sinking sensation that the play was over. The sweat broke out on his face, and he sprang to his feet, looked about him with his white, conscious smile, and winked at himself in the mirror. With something of the childish belief in miracles with which he had so often gone to class, all his lessons unlearned, Paul dressed and dashed whistling down the corridor to the elevator.

He had no sooner entered the dining-room and caught the measure of the music, than his remembrance was lightened by his old elastic power of claiming the moment, mounting with it, and finding it all sufficient. The glare and glitter about him, the mere scenic accessories had again, and for the last time, their old potency. He would show himself that he was game, he would finish the thing splendidly. He doubted, more than ever, the existence of Cordelia Street, and for the first time he drank his wine recklessly. Was he not, after all, one of these fortunate beings? Was he not still himself, and in his own place? He drummed a nervous accompaniment to the music and looked about him, telling himself over and over that it had paid.

He reflected drowsily, to the swell of the violin and the chill sweetness of his wine, that he might have done it more wisely. He might have caught an outbound steamer and been well out of their clutches before now. But the other side of the world had seemed too far away and too uncertain then; he could not have waited for it; his need had been too sharp. If he had to choose over again, he would do the same thing tomorrow. He looked affectionately about the dining-room, now gilded with a soft mist. Ah, it had paid indeed!

Paul was awakened next morning by a painful throbbing in his head and feet. He had thrown himself across the bed without undressing, and had slept with his shoes on. His limbs and hands were lead heavy, and his tongue and throat were parched. There came upon him one of those fateful attacks of clear-headedness that never occurred except when he was physically exhausted and his nerves hung loose. He lay still and closed his eyes and let the tide of realities wash over him.

His father was in New York; "stopping at some joint or other," he told himself. The memory of successive summers on the front stoop fell upon him like a weight of black water. He had not a hundred dollars left; and he knew now, more than ever, that money was everything, the wall that stood between all he loathed and all he wanted. The thing was winding itself up; he had thought of that on his first glorious day in New York, and had even provided a way to snap the thread. It lay on his dressing-table now; he had got it out last night when he came blindly up from dinner,—but the shiny metal hurt his eyes, and he disliked the look of it, anyway.

He rose and moved about with a painful effort, succumbing now and again to attacks of nausea. It was the old depression exaggerated; all the world had become Cordelia Street. Yet somehow he was not afraid of anything, was absolutely calm; perhaps because he had looked into the dark corner at last, and knew. It was bad enough, what he saw there; but somehow not so bad as his long fear of it had been. He saw everything clearly now. He had a feeling that he had made the best of it, that he had lived the sort of life he was meant to live, and for half an hour he sat staring at the revolver. But he told himself that was not the way, so he went downstairs and took a cab to the ferry.

When Paul arrived at Newark, he got off the train and took another cab, directing the driver to follow the Pennsylvania tracks out of the town. The snow lay heavy on the roadways and had drifted deep in the open fields. Only here and there the dead grass or dried weed stalks projected, singularly black, above it. Once well into the country, Paul dismissed the carriage and walked, floundering along the tracks, his mind a medley of irrelevant things. He seemed to hold in his brain an actual picture of everything he had seen that morning. He remembered every feature of both his drivers, the toothless old woman from whom he had bought the red flowers in his coat, the agent from whom he had got his ticket, and all of his fellow-passengers on the ferry. His mind, unable to cope with vital matters near at hand, worked feverishly and deftly at sorting and grouping these images. They made for him a part of the ugliness of the world, of the ache in his head, and the bitter burning on his tongue. He stooped and put a handful of snow into his mouth as he walked, but that, too, seemed hot. When he reached a little hillside, where the tracks ran through a cut some twenty feet below him, he stopped and sat down.

The carnations in his coat were drooping with the cold, he noticed; all their red glory over. It occurred to him that all the flowers he had seen in the show windows that first night must have gone the same way, long before this. It was only one splendid breath they had, in spite of their brave mockery at the winter outside the glass. It was a losing game in the end, it seemed, this revolt against the homilies by which the world is run. Paul took one of the blossoms carefully from his coat and scooped a little hole in the snow, where he covered it up. Then he dozed a while, from his weak condition, seeming insensible to the cold.

The sound of an approaching train woke him, and he started to his feet, remembering only his resolution, and afraid lest he should be too late. He stood watching the approaching locomotive, his teeth chattering, his lips drawn away from them in a frightened smile; once or twice he glanced nervously sidewise, as though he were being watched. When the right moment came, he jumped. As he fell, the folly of his haste occurred to him with merciless clearness, the vastness of what he had left undone. There flashed through his brain, clearer than ever before, the blue of Adriatic water, the yellow of Algerian sands.

He felt something strike his chest,—his body was being thrown swiftly through the air, on and on, immeasurably far and fast, while his limbs gently relaxed. Then, because the picture making mechanism was crushed, the disturbing visions flashed into black, and Paul dropped back into the immense design of things.

THE SHIP WHO SANG

Anne McCaffrey

(b. 1926)

Biography p. 1086

She was born a thing and as such would be condemned if she failed to pass the encephalograph test required of all newborn babies. There was always the possibility that though the limbs were twisted, the mind was not, that though the ears would hear only dimly, the eyes see vaguely, the mind behind them was receptive and alert.

The electro-encephalogram was entirely favorable, unexpectedly so, and the news was brought to the waiting, grieving parents. There was the final, harsh decision: to give their child euthanasia or permit it to become an encapsulated "brain," a guiding mechanism in any one of a number of curious professions. As such, their offspring would suffer no pain, live a comfortable existence in a metal shell for several centuries, performing unusual service to Central Worlds.

She lived and was given a name, Helva. For her first 3 vegetable months she waved her crabbed claws, kicked weakly with her clubbed feet and enjoyed the usual routine of the infant. She was not alone, for there were three other such children in the big city's special nursery. Soon they all were removed to Central Laboratory School, where their delicate transformation began.

One of the babies died in the initial transferral, but of Helva's 'class,' 17 thrived in the metal shells. Instead of kicking feet, Helva's neural responses started her wheels; instead of grabbing with hands, she manipulated mechanical extensions. As she matured, more and more neural synapses would be adjusted to operate other mechanisms that went into the maintenance and running of a space ship. For Helva was destined to be the "brain" half of a scout ship, partnered with a man or a woman, whichever she chose, as the mobile half. She would be among the elite of her kind. Her initial intelligence tests registered above normal and her adaptation index was unusually high. As long as her development within her shell lived up to expectations, and there were no side-effects from the pituitary tinkering, Helva would live a rewarding, rich and unusual life, a far cry from what she would have faced as an ordinary, "normal" being.

However, no diagram of her brain patterns, no early I.Q. tests recorded certain essential facts about Helva that Central must eventually learn. They would have to bide their official time and see, trusting that the massive doses of shell-psychology would suffice her, too, as the necessary bulwark against her unusual confinement and the pressures of her profession. A ship run by a human brain could not run rogue or insane with the power and resources Central had to build into their scout ships. Brain ships were, of course, long past the experimental stages. Most babies survived the perfected techniques of pituitary manipulation that kept their bodies small, eliminating the necessity of transfers from smaller to larger shells. And very, very few were lost when the final connection was made to the control panels of ship or industrial combine. Shell-people resembled mature dwarfs in size whatever their natal deformities were, but the well-oriented brain would not have changed places with the most perfect body in the Universe.

So, for happy years, Helva scooted around in her shell with her classmates, playing such games as Stall, Power-Seek, studying her lessons in trajectory, propulsion techniques, computation, logistics, mental hygiene, basic alien psychology, philology, space history, law, traffic, codes: all the et ceteras that eventually became compounded into a reasoning, logical, informed citizen. Not so obvious to her, but of more importance to her teachers, Helva ingested the precepts of her conditioning as easily as she absorbed her nutrient fluid. She would one day be grateful to the patient drone of the subconscious-level instruction.

Helva's civilization was not without busy, do-good associations, exploring possible inhumanities to terrestrial as well as extraterrestrial citizens. One such group— Society for the Preservation of the Rights of Intelligent Minorities—got all incensed over shelled "children" when Helva was just turning 14. When they were forced to, Central Worlds shrugged its shoulders, arranged a tour of the Laboratory Schools and set the tour off to a big start by showing the members case histories, complete with photographs. Very few committees ever looked past the first few photos. Most of their original objections about "shells" were overriden by the relief that these hideous (to them) bodies *were* mercifully concealed.

Helva's class was doing fine arts, a selective subject in her crowded program. She had activated one of her microscopic tools which she would later use for minute repairs to various parts of her control panel. Her subject was large—a copy of the Last Supper—and her canvas, small—the head of a tiny screw. She had tuned her sight to the proper degree. As she worked she absentmindedly crooned, producing a curious sound. Shell-people used their own vocal chords and diaphragms, but sound issued through microphones rather than mouths. Helva's hum, then, had a curious vibrancy, a warm, dulcet quality even in its aimless chromatic wanderings.

"Why, what a lovely voice you have," said one of the female visitors.

Helva "looked" up and caught a fascinating panorama of regular, dirty craters on a flaky pink surface. Her hum became a gurgle of surprise. She instinctively regulated her "sight" until the skin lost its cratered look and the pores assumed normal proportions.

"Yes, we have quite a few years of voice training, madam," remarked Helva calmly. "Vocal peculiarities often become excessively irritating during prolonged intrastellar distances and must be eliminated. I enjoyed my lessons."

Although this was the first time that Helva had seen unshelled people, she took this experience calmly. Any other reaction would have been reported instantly.

"I meant that you have a nice singing voice . . . dear," the lady said.

"Thank you. Would you like to see my work?" Helva asked, politely. She instinctively sheered away from personal discussions, but she filed the comment away for further meditation.

"Work?" asked the lady.

"I am currently reproducing the Last Supper on the head of a screw."

"O, I say," the lady twittered.

Helva turned her vision back to magnification and surveyed her copy critically.

"Of course, some of my color values do not match the old Master's and the perspective is faulty, but I believe it to be a fair copy."

The lady's eyes, unmagnified, bugged out.

"Oh, I forget," and Helva's voice was really contrite. If she could have blushed, she would have. "You people don't have adjustable vision."

The monitor of this discourse grinned with pride and amusement as Helva's tone indicated pity for the unfortunate.

"Here, this will help," said Helva, substituting a magnifying device in one extension and holding it over the picture.

In a kind of shock, the ladies and gentlemen of the committee bent to observe the incredibly copied and brilliantly executed Last Supper on the head of a screw.

"Well," remarked one gentleman who had been forced to accompany his wife, "the good Lord can eat where angels fear to tread."

"Are you referring, sir," asked Helva politely, "to the Dark Age discussions of the number of angels who could stand on the head of a pin?"

"I had that in mind."

"If you substitute 'atom' for 'angel,' the problem is not insoluble, given the metallic content of the pin in question."

"Which you are programmed to compute?"

"Of course."

"Did they remember to program a sense of humor, as well, young lady?"

"We are directed to develop a sense of proportion, sir, which contributes the same effect."

The good man chortled appreciatively and decided the trip was worth his time.

If the investigation committee spent months digesting the thoughtful food served them at the Laboratory School, they left Helva with a morsel as well.

"Singing" as applicable to herself required research. She had, of course, been exposed to and enjoyed a music appreciation course that had included the better known classical works such as "Tristan und Isolde," "Candide," "Oklahoma," and "Le Nozze di Figaro," along with the atomic age singers, Birgit Nilsson, Bob Dylan, and Geraldine Todd, as well as the curious rhythmic progressions of the Venusians, Capellan visual chromatics, the sonic concerti of the Altairians and Reticulan croons. But "singing" for any shell-person posed considerable technical difficulties. Shell-people were schooled to examine every aspect of a problem or situation before making a prognosis. Balanced properly between optimism and practicality, the nondefeatist attitude of the shell-people led them to extricate themselves, their ships, and personnel from bizarre situations. Therefore, to Helva, the problem that she couldn't open her mouth to sing, among other restrictions, did not bother her. She would work out a method, by-passing her limitations, whereby she could sing.

She approached the problem by investigating the methods of sound reproduction through the centuries, human and instrumental. Her own sound production equipment was essentially more instrumental than vocal. Breath control and the proper enunciation of vowel sounds within the oral cavity appeared to require the most development and practice. Shell-people did not, strictly speaking, breathe. For their purposes, oxygen and other gases were not drawn from the surrounding atmosphere through the medium of lungs but sustained artificially by solution in their shells. After experimentation, Helva discovered that she could manipulate her diaphragmic unit to sustain tone. By relaxing the throat muscles and expanding the oral cavity well into the frontal sinuses, she could direct the vowel sounds into the most felicitous position for proper reproduction through her throat microphone. She compared the results with tape recordings of modern singers and was not unpleased, although her own tapes had a peculiar quality about them, not at all unharmonious, merely unique. Acquiring a repertoire from the Laboratory library was no problem to one trained to perfect recall. She found herself able to sing any role and any song which struck her fancy. It would not have occurred to her that it was curious for a female to sing bass, baritone, tenor, mezzo, soprano, and coloratura as she pleased. It was, to Helva, only a matter of the correct reproduction and diaphragmic control required by the music attempted.

If the authorities remarked on her curious avocation, they did so among themselves. Shell-people were encouraged to develop a hobby so long as they maintained proficiency in their technical work.

On the anniversary of her 16th year, Helva was unconditionally graduated and installed in her ship, the XH-834. Her permanent titanium shell was recessed behind an even more indestructible barrier in the central shaft of the scout ship. The neural, audio, visual, and sensory connections were made and sealed. Her extendibles were diverted, connected or augmented and the final, delicate-beyond-description brain taps were completed while Helva remained anesthetically unaware of the proceedings. When she woke, she *was* the ship. Her brain and intelligence controlled every function from navigation to such loading as a scout ship of her class needed. She could take care of herself, and her ambulatory half, in any situation already recorded in the annals of Central Worlds and any situation its most fertile minds could imagine.

Her first actual flight, for she and her kind had made mock flights on dummy panels since she was 8, showed her to be a complete master of the techniques of her profession. She was ready for her great adventures and the arrival of her mobile partner.

There were nine qualified scouts sitting around collecting base pay the day Helva reported for active duty. There were several missions that demanded instant attention, but Helva had been of interest to several department heads in Central for some time and each bureau chief was determined to have her assigned to *his* section. No one had remembered to introduce Helva to the prospective partners. The ship always chose its own partner. Had there been another brain ship at the base at the moment, Helva would have been guided to make the first move. As it was, while Central wrangled among itself, Robert Tanner sneaked out of the pilots' barracks, out to the field and over to Helva's slim metal hull.

"Hello, anyone at home?" Tanner said.

"Of course," replied Helva, activating her outside scanners. "Are you my partner?" she asked hopefully, as she recognized the Scout Service uniform.

"All you have to do is ask," he retorted in a wistful tone.

"No one has come. I thought perhaps there were no partners available and I've had no directives from Central."

Even to herself Helva sounded a little self-pitying, but the truth was she was lonely, sitting on the darkened field. She had always had the company of other shells and, more recently, technicians by the score. The sudden solitude had lost its momentary charm and become oppressive.

"No directives from Central is scarcely a cause for regret, but there happen to be eight other guys biting their fingernails to the quick just waiting for an invitation to board you, you beautiful thing."

Tanner was inside the central cabin as he said this, running appreciative fingers over her panel, the scout's gravity-chair, poking his head into the cabins, the galley, the head, the pressured-storage compartments.

"Now, if you want to goose Central and do *us* a favor all in one, call up the barracks and let's have a ship-warming partner-picking party. Hmmmm?"

Helva chuckled to herself. He was so completely different from the occasional visitors or the various Laboratory technicians she had encountered. He was so gay, so assured, and she was delighted by his suggestion of a partner-picking party. Certainly it was not against anything in her understanding of regulations.

"Cencom, this is XH-834. Connect me with Pilot Barracks."

"Visual?"

"Please."

A picture of lounging men in various attitudes of boredom came on her screen.

"This is XH-834. Would the unassigned scouts do me the favor of coming aboard?"

Eight figures galvanized into action, grabbing pieces of wearing apparel, disengaging tape mechanisms, disentangling themselves from bedsheets and towels.

Helva dissolved the connection while Tanner chuckled gleefully and settled down to await their arrival.

Helva was engulfed in an unshell-like flurry of anticipation. No actress on her opening night could have been more apprehensive, fearful or breathless. Unlike the actress, she could throw no hysterics, china objets d'art or grease-paint to relieve her tension. She could, of course, check her stores for edibles and drinks, which she did, serving Tanner from the virgin selection of her commissary.

Scouts were colloquially known as "brawns" as opposed to their ship "brains." They had to pass as rigorous a training program as the brains and only the top 1 percent of each contributory world's highest scholars were admitted to Central Worlds Scout Training Program. Consequently the eight young men who came pounding up the gantry into Helva's hospitable lock were unusually fine-looking, intelligent, well-coordinated and adjusted young men, looking forward to a slightly drunken evening, Helva permitting, and all quite willing to do each other dirt to get possession of her.

Such a human invasion left Helva mentally breathless, a luxury she thoroughly enjoyed for the brief time she felt she should permit it.

She sorted out the young men. Tanner's opportunism amused but did not specifically attract her; the blond Nordsen seemed too simple; dark-haired Al-atpay had a kind of obstinacy with which she felt no compassion: Mir-Ahnin's bitterness hinted an inner darkness she did not wish to lighten, although he made the biggest outward play for her attention. Hers was a curious courtship—this would be only the first of several marriages for her, for brawns retired after 75 years of service, or earlier if they were unlucky. Brains, their bodies safe from any deterioration, were indestructible. In theory, once a shell-person had paid off the massive debt of early care, surgical adaptation and maintenance charges, he or she was free to seek employment elsewhere. In practice, shell-people remained in the service until they chose to self-destruct or died in line of duty. Helva had actually spoken to one shell-person 322 years old. She had been so awed by the contact she hadn't presumed to ask the personal questions she had wanted to.

Her choice of a brawn did not stand out from the others until Tanner started to sing a scout ditty, recounting the misadventures of the bold, dense, painfully inept Billy Brawn. An attempt at harmony resulted in cacophony and Tanner wagged his arms wildly for silence.

"What we need is a roaring good lead tenor. Jennan, besides palming aces, what do you sing?"

"Sharp," Jennan replied with easy good humor.

"If a tenor is absolutely necessary, I'll attempt it," Helva volunteered.

"My good *woman*," Tanner protested.

"Sound your 'A'," laughed Jennan.

Into the stunned silence that followed the rich, clear, high 'A,' Jennan remarked quietly, "Such an A Caruso would have given the rest of his notes to sing."

It did not take them long to discover her full range.

"All Tanner asked for was one roaring good lead tenor," Jennan said jokingly, "and our sweet mistress supplied us an entire repertory company. The boy who gets this ship will go far, far, far."

"To the Horsehead Nebula?" asked Nordsen, quoting an old Central saw.

"To the Horsehead Nebula and back, we shall make beautiful music," said Helva, chuckling.

"Together," Jennan said. "Only you'd better make the music and, with my voice, I'd better listen."

"I rather imagined it would be I who listened," suggested Helva.

Jennan executed a stately bow with an intricate flourish of his crush-brimmed hat. He directed his bow toward the central control pillar where Helva *was*. Her own personal preference crystallized at that precise moment and for that particular reason: Jennan, alone of the men, had addressed his remarks directly at her physical presence, regardless of the fact that he knew she could pick up his image wherever he was in the ship and regardless of the fact that her body was behind massive metal walls. Throughout their partnership, Jennan never failed to turn his head in her direction no matter where he was in relation to her. In response to this personalization, Helva at that moment and from then on always spoke to Jennan only through her central mike, even though that was not always the most efficient method.

Helva didn't know that she fell in love with Jennan that evening. As she had never been exposed to love or affection, only the drier cousins, respect and admiration, she could scarcely have recognized her reaction to the warmth of his personality and thoughtfulness. As a shell-person, she considered herself remote from emotions largely connected with physical desires.

"Well, Helva, it's been swell meeting you," said Tanner suddenly as she and Jennan were arguing about the baroque quality of "Come All Ye Sons of Art." "See you in space some time, you lucky dog, Jennan. Thanks for the party, Helva."

"You don't have to go so soon?" asked Helva, realizing belatedly that she and Jennan had been excluding the others from this discussion.

"Best man won," Tanner said, wryly. "Guess I'd better go get a tape on love ditties. Might need 'em for the next ship, if there're any more at home like you."

Helva and Jennan watched them leave, both a little confused.

"Perhaps Tanner's jumping to conclusions?" Jennan asked.

Helva regarded him as he slouched against the console, facing her shell directly. His arms were crossed on his chest and the glass he held had been empty for some time. He was handsome, they all were; but his watchful eyes were unwary, his mouth assumed a smile easily, his voice (to which Helva was particularly drawn) was resonant, deep, and without unpleasant overtones or accent.

"Sleep on it, at any rate, Helva. Call me in the morning if it's your opt."

She called him at breakfast, after she had checked her choice through Central. Jennan moved his things aboard, received their joint commission, had his personality and experience file locked into her reviewer, gave her the coordinates of their first mission. The XH-834 officially became the JH-834.

Their first mission was a dull but necessary crash priority (Medical got Helva), rushing a vaccine to a distant system plagued with a virulent spore disease. They had only to get to Spica as fast as possible.

After the initial, thrilling forward surge at her maximum speed, Helva realized her muscles were to be given less of a workout than her brawn on this tedious mission. But they did have plenty of time for exploring each other's personalities. Jennan, of course, knew what Helva was capable of as a ship and partner, just as she knew what she could expect from him. But these were only facts and Helva looked forward eagerly to learning that human side of her partner which could not be reduced to a series of symbols. Nor could the give and take of two personalities be learned from a book. It had to be experienced.

"My father was a scout, too, or is that programmed?" began Jennan their third day out.

"Naturally."

"Unfair, you know. You've got all my family history and I don't know one blamed thing about yours."

"I've never known either," Helva said. "Until I read yours, it hadn't occurred to me I must have one, too, someplace in Central's files."

Jennan snorted. "Shell psychology!"

Helva laughed. "Yes, and I'm even programmed against curiosity about it. You'd better be, too."

Jennan ordered a drink, slouched into the gravity couch opposite her, put his feet on the bumpers, turning himself idly from side to side on the gimbals.

"Helva—a made-up name . . ."

"With a Scandinavian sound."

"You aren't blonde," Jennan said positively.

"Well, then, there're dark Swedes."

"And blonde Turks and this one's harem is limited to one."

"Your woman in purdah, yes, but you can comb the pleasure houses—" Helva found herself aghast at the edge to her carefully trained voice.

"You know," Jennan interrupted her, deep in some thought of his own, "my father gave me the impression he was a lot more married to his ship, the Silvia, than to my mother. I know I used to think Silvia was my grandmother. She was a low number so she must have been a great-great-grandmother at least. I used to talk to her for hours."

"Her registry?" asked Helva, unwittingly jealous of everyone and anyone who had shared his hours.

"422. I think she's TS now. I ran into Tom Burgess once."

Jennan's father had died of a planetary disease, the vaccine for which his ship had used up in curing the local citizens.

"Tom said she'd got mighty tough and salty. You lose your sweetness and I'll come back and haunt you, girl," Jennan threatened.

Helva laughed. He startled her by stamping up to the column panel, touching it with light, tender fingers.

"I *wonder* what you look like," he said softly, wistfully.

Helva had been briefed about this natural curiosity of scouts. She didn't know anything about herself and neither of them ever would or could.

"Pick any form, shape, and shade and I'll be yours obliging," she countered, as training suggested.

"Iron Maiden, I fancy blondes with long tresses," and Jennan pantomined Lady Godiva-like tresses. "Since you're immolated in titanium, I'll call you Brunehilde, my dear," and he made his bow.

With a chortle, Helva launched into the appropriate aria just as Spica made contact.

"What'n'ell's that yelling about? Who are you? And unless you're Central Worlds Medical go away. We've got a plague. No visiting privileges."

"My ship is singing, we're the JH-834 of Worlds and we've got your vaccine. What are our landing coordinates?"

"Your *ship* is singing?"

"The greatest S.A.T.B. in organized space. Any request?"

The JH-834 delivered the vaccine but no more arias and received immediate orders to proceed to Leviticus IV. By the time they got there, Jennan found a reputation awaiting him and was forced to defend the 834's virgin honor.

"I'll stop singing," murmured Helva contritely as she ordered up poultices for this third black eye in a week.

"You will not," Jennan said through gritted teeth. "If I have to black eyes from here to the Horsehead to keep the snicker out of the title, we'll be the ship who sings."

After the "ship who sings" tangled with a minor but vicious narcotic ring in the Lesser Magellanics, the title became definitely respectful. Central was aware of each episode and punched out a "special interest" key on JH-834's file. A first-rate team was shaking down well.

Jennan and Helva considered themselves a first-rate team, too, after their tidy arrest.

"Of all the vices in the universe, I *hate* drug addiction," Jennan remarked as they headed back to Central Base. "People can go to hell quick enough without that kind of help."

"Is that why you volunteered for Scout Service? To redirect traffic?"

"I'll bet my official answer's on your review."

"In far too flowery wording. 'Carrying on the traditions of my family, which has been proud of four generations in Service', if I may quote you your own words."

Jennan groaned. "I was *very* young when I wrote that. I certainly hadn't been through Final Training. And once I was in Final Training, my pride wouldn't let me fail. . . .

"As I mentioned, I used to visit Dad on board the Silvia and I've a very good idea she might have had her eye on me as a replacement for my father because I had had massive doses of scout-oriented propaganda. It took. From the time I was 7, I was going to be a scout or else." He shrugged as if deprecating a youthful determination that had taken a great deal of mature application to bring to fruition.

"Ah, so? Scout Sahir Silan on the JS-44 penetrating into the Horsehead Nebulae?" Jennan chose to ignore her sarcasm.

"With *you,* I may even get that far. But even with Silvia's nudging *I* never daydreamed myself *that* kind of glory in my wildest flights of fancy. I'll leave the whoppers to your agile brain henceforth. I have in mind a smaller contribution to space history."

"So modest?"

"No. Practical. We also serve, et cetera." He placed a dramatic hand on his heart.

"Glory hound!" scoffed Helva.

"Look who's talking, my Nebula-bound friend. At least I'm not greedy. There'll only be one hero like my dad at Parsaea, but I *would* like to be remembered for some kudo. Everyone does. Why else do or die?"

"Your father died on his way back from Parsaea, if I may point out a few cogent facts. So he could never have known he was a hero for damming the flood with his ship. Which kept Parsaean colony from being abandoned. Which gave them a chance to discover the antiparalytic qualities of Parsaea. Which *he* never knew."

"I know," said Jennan softly.

Helva was immediately sorry for the tone of her rebuttal. She knew very well how deep Jennan's attachment to his father had been. On his review a note was made that he had rationalized his father's loss with the unexpected and welcome outcome of the Affair at Parsaea.

"Facts are not human, Helva. My father was and so am I. And *basically,* so are you. Check over your dial, 834. Amid all the wires attached to you is a heart, an underdeveloped human heart. Obviously!"

"I apologize, Jennan," she said.

Jennan hesitated a moment, threw out his hands in acceptance and then tapped her shell affectionately.

"If they ever take us off the milkruns, we'll make a stab at the Nebula, huh?"

As so frequently happened in the Scout Service, within the next hour they had orders to change course, not to the Nebula, but to a recently colonized system with two habitable planets, one tropical, one glacial. The sun, named Ravel, had become unstable; the spectrum was that of a rapidly expanding shell, with absorption lines rapidly displacing toward violet. The augmented heat of the primary had already forced evacuation of the nearer world, Daphnis. The pattern of spectral emissions gave indication that the sun would sear Chloe as well. All ships in the immediate spatial vicinity were to report to Disaster Headquarters on Chloe to effect removal of the remaining colonists.

The JH-834 obediently presented itself and was sent to outlying areas on Chloe to pick up scattered settlers who did not appear to appreciate the urgency of the situation. Chloe, indeed, was enjoying the first temperatures above freezing since it had been flung out of its parent. Since many of the colonists were religious fanatics who had settled on rigorous Chloe to fit themselves for a life of pious reflection, Chloe's abrupt thaw was attributed to sources other than a rampaging sun.

Jennan had to spend so much time countering specious arguments that he and Helva were behind schedule on their way to the fourth and last settlement.

Helva jumped over the high range of jagged peaks that surrounded and sheltered the valley from the former raging snows as well as the present heat. The violent sun with its flaring corona was just beginning to brighten the deep valley as Helva dropped down to a landing.

"They'd better grab their toothbrushes and hop aboard," Helva said. "HQ says speed it up."

"All women," remarked Jennan in surprise as he walked down to meet them. "Unless the men on Chloe wear furred skirts."

"Charm 'em but pare the routine to the bare essentials. And turn on your two-way private."

Jennan advanced smiling, but his explanation of his mission was met with absolute incredulity and considerable doubt as to his authenticity. He groaned inwardly as the matriarch paraphrased previous explanations of the warming sun.

"Revered mother, there's been an overload on that prayer circuit and the sun is blowing itself up in one obliging burst. I'm here to take you to the spaceport at Rosary—"

"That Sodom?" The worthy woman glowered and shuddered disdainfully at his suggestion. "We thank you for your warning but we have no wish to leave our cloister for the rude world. We must go about our morning meditation which has been interrupted—"

"It'll be permanently interrupted when that sun starts broiling you. You must come now," Jennan said firmly.

"Madame," said Helva, realizing that perhaps a female voice might carry more weight in this instance than Jennan's very masculine charm.

"Who spoke?" cried the nun, startled by the bodiless voice.

"I, Helva, the ship. Under my protection you and your sisters-in-faith may enter safely and be unprofaned by association with a male. I will guard you and take you safely to a place prepared for you."

The matriarch peered cautiously into the ship's open port.

"Since only Central Worlds is permitted the use of such ships, I acknowledge that you are not trifling with us, young man. However, we are in no danger here."

"The temperature at Rosary is now 99°," said Helva. "As soon as the sun's rays penetrate directly into this valley, it will also be 99°, and it is due to climb to approximately 180° today. I notice your buildings are made of wood with moss chinking. Dry moss. It should fire around noontime."

The sunlight was beginning to slant into the valley through the peaks and the fierce rays warmed the restless group behind the matriarch. Several opened the throats of their furry parkas.

"Jennan," said Helva privately to him, "our time is very short."

"I can't leave them, Helva. Some of those girls are barely out of their teens."

"Pretty, too. No wonder the matriarch doesn't want to get in."

"Helva."

"It will be the Lord's will," said the matriarch stoutly and turned her back squarely on rescue.

"To burn to death?" shouted Jennan as she threaded her way through her murmuring disciples.

"They want to be martyrs? Their opt, Jennan," said Helva dispassionately, "We must leave and that is no longer a matter of option."

"How can I leave, Helva?"

"Parsaea?" Helva asked tauntingly as he stepped forward to grab one of the women. "You can't drag them *all* aboard and we don't have time to fight it out. Get on board, Jennan, or I'll have you on report."

"They'll die," muttered Jennan dejectedly as he reluctantly turned to climb on board.

"You can risk only so much," Helva said sympathetically. "As it is we'll just have time to make a rendezvous. Lab reports a critical speedup in spectral evolution."

Jennan was already in the airlock when one of the younger women, screaming, rushed to squeeze in the closing port. Her action set off the others. They stampeded through the narrow-opening. Even crammed back to breast, there was not enough room inside for all the women. Jennan broke out spacesuits to the three who would have to remain with him in the airlock. He wasted valuable time explaining to the matriarch that she must put on the suit because the airlock had no independent oxygen or cooling units.

"We'll be caught," said Helva in a grim tone to Jennan on their private connection. "We've lost 18 minutes in this last-minute rush. I am now overloaded for maximum speed and I must attain maximum speed to outrun the heat wave."

"Can you lift? We're suited."

"Lift? Yes," she said, doing so. "Run? I stagger."

Jennan, bracing himself and the women, could feel her sluggishness as she blasted upward. Heartlessly, Helva applied thrust as long as she could, despite the fact that the gravitational force mashed her cabin passengers brutally and crushed two fatally. It was a question of saving as many as possible. The only one for whom she had any concern was Jennan and she was in desperate terror about his safety. Airless and uncooled, protected by only one layer of metal, not three, the airlock was not going to be safe for the four trapped there, despite their spacesuits. These were only the standard models, not built to withstand the excessive heat to which the ship would be subjected.

Helva ran as fast as she could but the incredible wave of heat from the explosive sun caught them halfway to cold safety.

She paid no heed to the cries, moans, pleas, and prayers in her cabin. She listened only to Jennan's tortured breathing, to the missing throb in his suit's purifying system and the sucking of the overloaded cooling unit. Helpless, she heard the hysterical screams of his three companions as they writhed in the awful heat. Vainly, Jennan tried to calm them, tried to explain they would soon be safe and cool if they could be still and endure the heat. Undisciplined by their terror and torment, they tried to strike out at him despite the close quarters. One flailing arm became entangled in the leads to his power pack and the damage was quickly done. A connection, weakened by heat and the dead weight of the arm, broke.

For all the power at her disposal, Helva was helpless. She watched as Jennan fought for his breath, as he turned his head beseechingly toward *her,* and died.

Only the iron conditioning of her training prevented Helva from swinging around and plunging back into the cleansing heart of the exploding sun. Numbly she made rendezvous with the refugee convoy. She obediently transferred her burned, heat-prostrated passengers to the assigned transport.

"I will retain the body of my scout and proceed to the nearest base for burial," she informed Central dully.

"You will be provided escort," was the reply.

"I have no need of escort."

"Escort is provided, XH-834," she was told curtly. The shock of hearing Jennan's initial severed from her call number cut off her half-formed protest. Stunned, she waited by the transport until her screens showed the arrival of two other slim brain ships. The cortege proceeded homeward at unfunereal speeds.

"834? The ship who sings?"

"I have no more songs."

"Your scout was Jennan."

"I do not wish to communicate."

"I'm 422."

"Silvia?"

"Silvia died a long time ago. I'm 422. Currently MS," the ship rejoined curtly. "AH-640 is our other friend, but Henry's not listening in. Just as well—he wouldn't understand it if you wanted to turn rogue. But I'd stop *him* if he tried to deter you."

"Rogue?" The term snapped Helva out of her apathy.

"Sure. You're young. You've got power for years. Skip. Others have done it. 732 went rogue 20 years ago after she lost her scout on a mission to that white dwarf. Hasn't been seen since."

"I never heard about rogues."

"As it's exactly the thing we're conditioned against, you sure wouldn't hear about it in school, my dear," 422 said.

"Break conditioning?" cried Helva, anguished, thinking longingly of the white, white furious hot heart of the sun she had just left.

"For you I don't think it would be hard at the moment," 422 said quietly, her voice devoid of her earlier cynicism. "The stars are out there, winking."

"Alone?" cried Helva from her heart.

"Alone!" 422 confirmed bleakly.

Alone with all of space and time. Even the Horsehead Nebula would not be far enough away to daunt her. Alone with a hundred years to live with her memories and nothing . . . nothing more.

"Was Parsaea worth it?" she asked 422 softly.

"Parsaea?" 422 repeated, surprised. "With his father? Yes. We were there, at Parsaea when we were needed. Just as you . . . and his son . . . were at Chloe. When you were needed. The crime is not knowing where need is and not being there."

"But *I* need *him*. Who will supply my need?" said Helva bitterly. . . .

"834," said 422 after a day's silent speeding, "Central wishes your report. A replacement awaits your opt at Regulus Base. Change course accordingly."

"A replacement?" That was certainly not what she needed . . . a reminder inadequately filling the void Jennan left. Why, her hull was barely cool of Chloe's heat. Atavistically, Helva wanted time to mourn Jennan.

"Oh, none of them are impossible if *you're* a good ship," 422 remarked philosophically. "And it is just what you need. The sooner the better."

"You told them I wouldn't go rogue, didn't you?" Helva said.

"The moment passed you even as it passed me after Parsaea, and before that, after Glen Arhur, and Betelgeuse."

"We're conditioned to go on, aren't we? We *can't* go rogue. You were testing."

"Had to. Orders. Not even Psych knows why a rogue occurs. Central's very worried, and so, daughter, are your sister ships. I asked to be your escort. I . . . don't want to lose you both."

In her emotional nadir, Helva could feel a flood of gratitude for Silvia's rough sympathy.

"We've all known this grief, Helva. It's no consolation, but if we couldn't feel with our scouts, we'd only be machines wired for sound."

Helva looked at Jennan's still form stretched before her in its shroud and heard the echo of his rich voice in the quiet cabin.

"Silvia! I *couldn't* help him," she cried from her soul.

"Yes, dear, I know," 422 murmured gently and then was quiet.

The three ships sped on, wordless, to the great Central Worlds base at Regulus. Helva broke silence to acknowledge landing instructions and the officially tendered regrets.

The three ships set down simultaneously at the wooded edge where Regulus' gigantic blue trees stood sentinel over the sleeping dead in the small Service cemetery. The entire Base complement approached with measured step and formed an aisle from Helva to the burial ground. The honor detail, out of step, walked slowly into her cabin. Reverently they placed the body of her dead love on the wheeled bier, covered it honorably with the deep blue, star-splashed flag of the Service. She watched as it was driven slowly down the living aisle which closed in behind the bier in last escort.

Then, as the simple words of interment were spoken, as the atmosphere planes dipped in tribute over the open grave, Helva found voice for her lonely farewell.

Softly, barely audible at first, the strains of the ancient song of evening and requiem swelled to the final poignant measure until black space itself echoed back the sound of the song the ship sang.

CHEE'S DAUGHTER

Juanita Platero and Siyowin Miller

Biography p. 1092

The hat told the story, the big, black, drooping Stetson. It was not at the proper angle, the proper rakish angle for so young a Navaho. There was no song, and that was not in keeping either. There should have been at least a humming, a faint, all-to-himself "he he he heya," for it was a good horse he was riding, a slender-legged, high-stepping buckskin that would race the wind with light knee-urging. This was a day for singing, a warm winter day, when the touch of the sun upon the back belied the snow high on distant mountains.

Wind warmed by the sun touched his high-boned cheeks like flicker feathers, and still he rode on silently, deeper into Little Canyon, until the red rock walls rose straight upward from the stream bed and only a narrow piece of blue sky hung above. Abruptly the sky widened where the canyon walls were pushed back to make a wide place, as though in ancient times an angry stream had tried to go all ways at once.

This was home—this wide place in the canyon—levels of jagged rock and levels of rich red earth. This was home to Chee, the rider of the buckskin, as it had been to many generations before him.

He stopped his horse at the stream and sat looking across the narrow ribbon of water to the bare-branched peach trees. He was seeing them each springtime with their age-gnarled limbs transfigured beneath veils of blossom pink; he was seeing them in autumn laden with their yellow fruit, small and sweet. Then his eyes searched out the indistinct furrows of the fields beside the stream, where each year the corn and beans and squash drank thirstily of the overflow from summer rains. Chee was trying to outweigh today's bitter betrayal of hope by gathering to himself these reminders of the integrity of the land. Land did not cheat! His mind lingered deliberately on all the days spent here in the sun caring for the young plants, his songs to the earth and to the life springing from it— ". . . In the middle of the wide field . . . Yellow Corn Boy . . . He has started both ways . . . ," then the harvest and repayment in full measure. Here was the old feeling of wholeness and of oneness with the sun and earth and growing things.

Chee urged the buckskin toward the family compound where, secure in a recess of overhanging rock, was his mother's dome-shaped hogan, red rock and red adobe like the ground on which it nestled. Not far from the hogan was the half-circle of brush like a dark shadow against the canyon wall—corral for sheep and goats. Farther from the hogan, in full circle, stood the horse corral made of heavy cedar branches sternly interlocked. Chee's long thin lips curved into a smile as he passed his daughter's tiny hogan squatted like a round Pueblo oven beside the corral. He remembered the summer day when together they sat back on their heels and plastered wet adobe all about the circling wall of rock and the woven dome of piñon twigs. How his family laughed when the Little One herded the bewildered chickens into her tiny hogan as the first snow fell.

Then the smile faded from Chee's lips and his eyes darkened as he tied his horse to a corral post and turned to the strangely empty compound. "Someone has told them," he thought, "and they are inside weeping." He passed his mother's deserted loom on the south side of the hogan and pulled the rude wooden door toward him, bowing his head, hunching his shoulders to get inside.

His mother sat sideways by the center fire, her feet drawn up under her full skirts. Her hands were busy kneading dough in the chipped white basin. With her head down, her voice was muffled when she said, "The meal will soon be ready, son."

Chee passed his father sitting against the wall, hat over his eyes as though asleep. He passed his older sister who sat turning mutton ribs on a crude wire grill over the coals, noticed tears dropping on her hands. "She cared more for my wife than I realized," he thought.

Then because something must be said sometime, he tossed the black Stetson upon a bulging sack of wool and said, "You have heard, then." He could not shut from his mind how confidently he had set the handsome new hat on his head that very morning, slanting the wide brim over one eye: he was going to see his wife and today he would ask the doctors about bringing her home; last week she had looked so much better.

His sister nodded but did not speak. His mother sniffled and passed her velveteen sleeve beneath her nose. Chee sat down, leaning against the wall. "I suppose I was a fool for hoping all the time. I should have expected this. Few of our people get well from the coughing sickness. But *she* seemed to be getting better."

His mother was crying aloud now and blowing her nose noisily on her skirt. His father sat up, speaking gently to her.

Chee shifted his position and started a cigarette. His mind turned back to the Little One. At least she was too small to understand what had happened, the Little One who had been born three years before in the sanitarium where his wife was being treated for the coughing sickness, the Little One he had brought home to his mother's hogan to be nursed by his sister whose baby was a few months older. As she grew fat-cheeked and sturdy-legged, she followed him about like a shadow; somehow her baby mind had grasped that of all those at the hogan who cared for her and played with her, he—Chee—belonged most to her. She sat cross-legged at his elbow when he worked silver at the forge; she rode before him in the saddle when he drove the horses to water; often she lay wakeful on her sheep-pelts until he stretched out for the night in the darkened hogan and she could snuggle warm against him.

Chee blew smoke slowly and some of the sadness left his dark eyes as he said, "It is not as bad as it might be. It is not as though we are left with nothing."

Chee's sister arose, sobs catching in her throat, and rushed past him out the doorway. Chee sat upright, a terrible fear possessing him. For a moment his mouth could make no sound. Then: "The Little One! Mother, where is she?"

His mother turned her stricken face to him. "Your wife's people came after her this morning. They heard yesterday of their daughter's death through the trader at Red Sands."

Chee started to protest but his mother shook her head slowly. "I didn't expect they would want the Little One either. But there is nothing you can do. She is a girl child and belongs to her mother's people; it is custom."

Frowning, Chee got to his feet, grinding his cigarette into the dirt floor. "Custom!

When did my wife's parents begin thinking about custom? Why, the hogan where they live doesn't even face the East!" He started toward the door. "Perhaps I can overtake them. Perhaps they don't realize how much we want her with us. I'll ask them to give my daughter back to me. Surely they won't refuse."

His mother stopped him gently with her outstretched hand. "You couldn't overtake them now. They were in the trader's car. Eat and rest, and think more about this."

"Have you forgotten how things have always been between you and your wife's people?" his father said.

That night, Chee's thoughts were troubled—half-forgotten incidents became disturbingly vivid—but early the next morning he saddled the buckskin and set out for the settlement of Red Sands. Even though his father-in-law, Old Man Fat, might laugh, Chee knew that he must talk to him. There were some things to which Old Man Fat might listen.

Chee rode the first part of the fifteen miles to Red Sands expectantly. The sight of sandstone buttes near Cottonwood Spring reddening in the morning sun brought a song almost to his lips. He twirled his reins in salute to the small boy herding sheep toward many-colored Butterfly Mountain, watched with pleasure the feathers of smoke rising against tree-darkened western mesas from the hogans sheltered there. But as he approached the familiar settlement sprawled in mushroom growth along the highway, he began to feel as though a scene from a bad dream was becoming real.

Several cars were parked around the trading store which was built like two log hogans side by side, with red gas pumps in front and a sign across the tarpaper roofs: *Red Sands Trading Post—Groceries Gasoline Cold Drinks Sandwiches Indian Curios.* Back of the trading post an unpainted frame house and outbuildings squatted on the drab, treeless land. Chee and the Little One's mother had lived there when they stayed with his wife's people. That was according to custom—living with one's wife's people—but Chee had never been convinced that it was custom alone which prompted Old Man Fat and his wife to insist that their daughter bring her husband to live at the trading post.

Beside the Post was a large hogan of logs, with brightly painted pseudo-Navaho designs on the roof—a hogan with smoke-smudged windows and a garish blue door which faced north to the highway. Old Man Fat had offered Chee a hogan like this one. The trader would build it if he and his wife would live there and Chee would work at his forge making silver jewelry where tourists could watch him. But Chee had asked instead for a piece of land for a cornfield and help in building a hogan far back from the highway and a corral for the sheep he had brought to this marriage.

A cold wind blowing down from the mountains began to whistle about Chee's ears. It flapped the gaudy Navaho rugs which were hung in one long bright line to attract tourists. It swayed the sign *Navaho Weaver at Work* beside the loom where Old Man Fat's wife sat hunched in her striped blanket, patting the colored thread of a design into place with a wooden comb. Tourists stood watching the weaver. More tourists stood in a knot before the hogan where the sign said: *See Inside a Real Navaho Home 25¢.*

Then the knot seemed to unravel as a few people returned to their cars; some had cameras; and there against the blue door Chee saw the Little One standing uncertainly. The wind was plucking at her new purple blouse and wide green skirt; it freed truant strands of soft dark hair from the meager queue into which it had been tied with white yarn.

"Isn't she cunning!" one of the women tourists was saying as she turned away.

Chee's lips tightened as he began to look around for Old Man Fat. Finally he saw him passing among the tourists collecting coins.

Then the Little One saw Chee. The uncertainty left her face and she darted through the crowd as her father swung down from his horse. Chee lifted her in his arms, hugging her tight. While he listened to her breathless chatter, he watched Old Man Fat bearing down on them, scowling.

As his father-in-law walked heavily across the gravelled lot, Chee was reminded of a statement his mother sometimes made: "When you see a fat Navaho, you see one who hasn't worked for what he has."

Old Man Fat was fattest in the middle. There was indolence in his walk even though he seemed to hurry, indolence in his cheeks so plump they made his eyes squint, eyes now smoldering with anger.

Some of the tourists were getting into their cars and driving away. The old man said belligerently to Chee, "Why do you come here? To spoil our business? To drive people away?"

"I came to talk with you," Chee answered, trying to keep his voice steady as he faced the old man.

"We have nothing to talk about," Old Man Fat blustered and did not offer to touch Chee's extended hand.

"It's about the Little One." Chee settled his daughter more comfortably against his hip as he weighed carefully all the words he had planned to say. "We are going to miss her very much. It wouldn't be so bad if we knew that *part* of each year she could be with us. That might help you too. You and your wife are no longer young people and you have no young ones here to depend upon." Chee chose his next words remembering the thriftlessness of his wife's parents, and their greed. "Perhaps we could share the care of this little one. Things are good with us. So much snow this year will make lots of grass for the sheep. We have good land for corn and melons."

Chee's words did not have the expected effect. Old Man Fat was enraged. "Farmers, all of you! Long-haired farmers! Do you think everyone must bend his back over the short-handled hoe in order to have food to eat?" His tone changed as he began to brag a little. "We not only have all the things from cans at the trader's, but when the Pueblos come past here on their way to town we buy their salty jerked mutton, young corn for roasting, dried sweet peaches."

Chee's dark eyes surveyed the land along the highway as the old man continued to brag about being "progressive." *He* no longer was tied to the land. He and his wife made money easily and could *buy* all the things they wanted. Chee realized too late that he had stumbled into the old argument between himself and his wife's parents. They had never understood his feeling about the land—that a man took care of his land and it in turn took care of him. Old Man Fat and his wife scoffed at him, called him a Pueblo farmer, all during that summer when he planted and weeded and harvested. Yet they ate the green corn in their mutton stews, and the chili paste from the fresh ripe chilis, and the tortillas from the cornmeal his wife ground. None of this working and sweating in the sun for Old Man Fat, who talked proudly of his easy way of living—collecting money from the trader who rented this strip of land beside the highway, collecting money from the tourists.

Yet Chee had once won that argument. His wife had shared his belief in the integrity of the earth, that jobs and people might fail one but the earth never would. After that first year she had turned from her own people and gone with Chee to Little Canyon.

Old Man Fat was reaching for the Little One. "Don't be coming here with plans for my daughter's daughter," he warned. "If you try to make trouble, I'll take the case to the government man in town."

The impulse was strong in Chee to turn and ride off while he still had the Little One in his arms. But he knew his time of victory would be short. His own family would uphold the old custom of children, especially girl children, belonging to the mother's people. He would have to give his daughter up if the case were brought before the Headman of Little Canyon, and certainly he would have no better chance before a strange white man in town.

He handed the bewildered Little One to her grandfather who stood watching every movement suspiciously. Chee asked, "If I brought you a few things for the Little One, would that be making trouble? Some velvet for a blouse, or some of the jerky she likes so well . . . this summer's melon?"

Old Man Fat backed away from him. "Well," he hesitated, as some of the anger disappeared from his face and beads of greed shone in his eyes. "Well," he repeated. Then as the Little One began to squirm in his arms and cry, he said, "No! No! Stay away from here, you and all your family."

The sense of his failure deepened as Chee rode back to Little Canyon. But it was not until he sat with his family that evening in the hogan, while the familiar bustle of meal preparing went on about him, that he began to doubt the wisdom of the things he'd always believed. He smelled the coffee boiling and the oily fragrance of chili powder dusted into the bubbling pot of stew; he watched his mother turning round crusty fried bread in the small black skillet. All around him was plenty—a half of mutton hanging near the door, bright strings of chili drying, corn hanging by the braided husks, cloth bags of dried peaches. Yet in his heart was nothing.

He heard the familiar sounds of the sheep outside the hogan, the splash of water as his father filled the long drinking trough from the water barrel. When his father came in, Chee could not bring himself to tell a second time of the day's happenings. He watched his wiry, soft-spoken father while his mother told the story, saw his father's queue of graying hair quiver as he nodded his head with sympathetic exclamations.

Chee's doubting, acrid thoughts kept forming: Was it wisdom his father had passed on to him or was his inheritance only the stubbornness of a long-haired Navaho resisting change? Take care of the land and it will take care of you. True, the land had always given him food, but now food was not enough. Perhaps if he had gone to school he would have learned a different kind of wisdom, something to help him now. A schoolboy might even be able to speak convincingly to this government man whom Old Man Fat threatened to call, instead of sitting here like a clod of earth itself—Pueblo farmer indeed. What had the land to give that would restore his daughter?

In the days that followed, Chee herded sheep. He got up in the half-light, drank the hot coffee his mother had ready, then started the flock moving. It was necessary to drive the sheep a long way from the hogan to find good winter forage. Sometimes Chee met friends or relatives who were on their way to town or to the road camp where they hoped to get work; then there was friendly banter and an exchange of news. But most of the days seemed endless; he could not walk far enough or fast enough from his memories of the Little One or from his bitter thoughts. Sometimes it seemed his daughter trudged beside him, so real he could almost hear her foot-steps—the muffled pad-pad of little feet clad in deerhide. In the glare of a snow bank he would see her vivid face, brown eyes sparkling. Mingling with the tinkle of sheep bells he heard her laughter.

When, weary of following the small sharp hoof marks that crossed and recrossed in the snow, he sat down in the shelter of a rock, it was only to be reminded that in his thoughts he had forsaken his brotherhood with the earth and sun and growing things. If he remembered times when he had flung himself against the earth to rest, to lie there in the sun until he could no longer feel where he left off and the earth began, it was to remember also that now he sat like an alien against the same earth; the belonging-together was gone. The earth was one thing and he was another.

It was during the days when he herded sheep that Chee decided he must leave Little Canyon. Perhaps he would take a job silversmithing for one of the traders in town. Perhaps, even though he spoke little English, he could get a job at the road camp with his cousins; he would ask them about it.

Springtime transformed the mesas. The peach trees in the canyon were shedding fragrance and pink blossoms on the gentled wind. The sheep no longer foraged for the yellow seeds of chamiso but ranged near the hogan with the long-legged new lambs, eating tender young grass.

Chee was near the hogan on the day his cousins rode up with the message for which he waited. He had been watching with mixed emotions while his father and his sister's husband cleared the fields beside the stream.

"The boss at the camp says he needs an extra hand, but he wants to know if you'll be willing to go with the camp when they move it to the other side of the town?" The tall cousin shifted his weight in the saddle.

The other cousin took up the explanation. "The work near here will last only until the new cut-off beyond Red Sands is finished. After that, the work will be too far away for you to get back here often."

That was what Chee had wanted—to get away from Little Canyon—yet he found himself not so interested in the job beyond town as in this new cut-off which was almost finished. He pulled a blade of grass, split it thoughtfully down the center as he asked questions of his cousins. Finally he said: "I need to think more about this. If I decide on this job I'll ride over."

Before his cousins were out of sight down the canyon Chee was walking toward the fields, a bold plan shaping in his mind. As the plan began to flourish, wild and hardy as young tumbleweed, Chee added his own voice softly to the song his father was singing: ". . . In the middle of the wide field . . . Yellow Corn Boy . . . I wish to put in."

Chee walked slowly around the field, the rich red earth yielding to his footsteps. His plan depended upon this land and upon the things he remembered most about his wife's people.

Through planting time Chee worked zealously and tirelessly. He spoke little of the large new field he was planting because he felt so strongly that just now this was something between himself and the land. The first days he was ever stooping, piercing the ground with the pointed stick, placing the corn kernels there, walking around the field and through it, singing, ". . . His track leads into the ground . . . Yellow Corn Boy . . . his track leads into the ground." After that, each day Chee walked through his field watching for the tips of green to break through; first a few spikes in the center and then more and more until the corn in all parts of the field was above ground. Surely, Chee thought, if he sang the proper songs, if he cared for this land faithfully, it would not forsake him now, even though through the lonely days of winter he had betrayed the goodness of the earth in his thoughts.

Through the summer Chee worked long days, the sun hot upon his back, pulling weeds from around young corn plants; he planted squash and pumpkin; he terraced a small piece of land near his mother's hogan and planted carrots and onions and the moisture-loving chili. He was increasingly restless. Finally he told his family what he hoped the harvest from this land would bring him. Then the whole family waited with him, watching the corn: the slender graceful plants that waved green arms and bent to embrace each other as young winds wandered through the field, the maturing plants flaunting their pollen-laden tassels in the sun, the tall and sturdy parent corn with new-formed ears and a froth of purple, red and yellow corn-beards against the dusty emerald of broad leaves.

Summer was almost over when Chee slung the bulging packs across two pack ponies. His mother helped him tie the heavy rolled pack behind the saddle of the buckskin. Chee knotted the new yellow kerchief about his neck a little tighter, gave the broad black hat brim an extra tug, but these were only gestures of assurance and he knew it. The land had not failed him. That part was done. But this he was riding into? Who could tell?

When Chee arrived at Red Sands, it was as he had expected to find it—no cars on the highway. His cousins had told him that even the Pueblo farmers were using the new cut-off to town. The barren gravel around the Red Sands Trading Post was deserted. A sign banged against the dismantled gas pumps *Closed until further notice*.

Old Man Fat came from the crude summer shelter built beside the log hogan from a few branches of scrub cedar and the sides of wooden crates. He seemed almost friendly when he saw Chee.

"Get down, my son," he said, eyeing the bulging packs. There was no bluster in his voice today and his face sagged, looking somewhat saddened; perhaps because his cheeks were no longer quite full enough to push his eyes upward at the corners. "You are going on a journey?"

Chee shook his head. "Our fields gave us so much this year, I thought to sell or trade this to the trader. I didn't know he was no longer here."

Old Man Fat sighed, his voice dropping to an injured tone. "He says he and his wife are going to rest this winter; then after that he'll build a place up on the new highway."

Chee moved as though to be traveling on, then jerked his head toward the pack ponies. "Anything you need?"

"I'll ask my wife," Old Man Fat said as he led the way to the shelter. "Maybe she has a little money. Things have not been too good with us since the trader closed. Only a few tourists come this way." He shrugged his shoulders. "And with the trader gone—no credit."

Chee was not deceived by his father-in-law's unexpected confidences. He recognized them as a hopeful bid for sympathy and, if possible, something for nothing. Chee made no answer. He was thinking that so far he had been right about his wife's parents: their thriftlessness had left them with no resources to last until Old Man Fat found another easy way of making a living.

Old Man Fat's Wife was in the shelter working at her loom. She turned rather wearily when her husband asked with noticeable deference if she would give him money to buy supplies. Chee surmised that the only income here was from his mother-in-law's weaving.

She peered around the corner of the shelter at the laden ponies, and then she looked at Chee. "What do you have there, my son?"

Chee smiled to himself as he turned to pull the pack from one of the ponies, dragged it to the shelter where he untied the ropes. Pumpkins and hardshelled squash tumbled out, and the ears of corn—pale yellow husks fitting firmly over plump ripe kernels, blue corn, red corn, yellow corn, many-colored corn, ears and ears of it—tumbled into every corner of the shelter.

"Yooooh," Old Man Fat's Wife exclaimed as she took some of the ears in her hands. Then she glanced up at her son-in-law. "But we have no money for all this. We have sold almost everything we own—even the brass bed that stood in the hogan."

Old Man Fat's brass bed. Chee concealed his amusement as he started back for another pack. That must have been a hard parting. Then he stopped, for, coming from the cool darkness of the hogan was the Little One, rubbing her eyes as though she had been asleep. She stood for a moment in the doorway and Chee saw that she was dirty, barefoot, her hair uncombed, her little blouse shorn of all its silver buttons. Then she ran toward Chee, her arms outstretched. Heedless of Old Man Fat and his wife, her father caught her in his arms, her hair falling in a dark cloud across his face, the sweetness of her laughter warm against his shoulder.

It was the haste within him to get this slow waiting game played through to the finish that made Chee speak unwisely. It was the desire to swing her before him in the saddle and ride fast to Little Canyon that prompted his words. "The money doesn't matter. You still have something. . . ."

Chee knew immediately that he had overspoken. The old woman looked from him to the corn spread before her. Unfriendliness began to harden in his father-in-law's face. All the old arguments between himself and his wife's people came pushing and crowding in between them now.

Old Man Fat began kicking the ears of corn back onto the canvas as he eyed Chee angrily. "And you rode all the way over here thinking that for a little food we would give up our daughter's daughter?"

Chee did not wait for the old man to reach for the Little One. He walked dazedly to the shelter, rubbing his cheek against her soft dark hair and put her gently into her grandmother's lap. Then he turned back to the horses. He had failed. By his own haste he had failed. He swung into the saddle, his hand touching the roll behind it. Should he ride on into town?

Then he dismounted, scarcely glancing at Old Man Fat, who stood uncertainly at the corner of the shelter, listening to his wife. "Give me a hand with this other pack of corn, Grandfather," Chee said, carefully keeping the small bit of hope from his voice.

Puzzled, but willing, Old Man Fat helped carry the other pack to the shelter, opening it to find more corn as well as carrots and round pale yellow onions. Chee went back for the roll behind the buckskin's saddle and carried it to the entrance of the shelter where he cut the ropes and gave the canvas a nudge with his toe. Tins of coffee rolled out, small plump cloth bags; jerked meat from several butcherings spilled from a flour sack, and bright red chilis splashed like flames against the dust.

"I will leave all this anyhow," Chee told them. "I would not want my daughter nor even you old people to go hungry."

Old Man Fat picked up a shiny tin of coffee, then put it down. With trembling hands he began to untie one of the cloth bags—dried sweet peaches.

The Little One had wriggled from her grandmother's lap, unheeded, and was on her knees, digging her hands into the jerked meat.

"There is almost enough food here to last all winter," Old Man Fat's Wife sought the eyes of her husband.

Chee said, "I meant it to be enough. But that was when I thought you might send the Little One back with me." He looked down at his daughter noisily sucking jerky. Her mouth, both fists were full of it. "I am sorry that you feel you cannot bear to part with her."

Old Man Fat's Wife brushed a straggly wisp of gray hair from her forehead as she turned to look at the Little One. Old Man Fat was looking too. And it was not a thing to see. For in that moment the Little One ceased to be their daughter's daughter and became just another mouth to feed.

"And why not?" the old woman asked wearily.

Chee was settled in the saddle, the barefooted Little One before him. He urged the buckskin faster, and his daughter clutched his shirtfront. The purpling mesas fling back the echo: ". . . My corn embrace each other. In the middle of the wide field . . . Yellow Corn Boy embrace each other."

Poetry

BARBARA ALLEN

(A traditional British-American ballad)

In scarlet town, where I was born,
   There was a fair maid dwellin',
Made every youth cry *Well-a-way!*
   Her name was Barbara Allen.

All in the merry month of May   5
   When green buds they were swellin',
Young Jemmy Grove on his death-bed lay,
   For love of Barbara Allen.

He sent his man in to her then,
   To the town where she was dwellin',   10
"O haste and come to my master dear,
   If your name be Barbara Allen."

So slowly, slowly rose she up,
   And slowly she came nigh him,
And when she drew the curtain by—   15
   "Young man, I think you're dyin'."

"O it's I'm sick and very very sick,
   And it's all for Barbara Allen."
"O the better for me ye'se never be,
   Tho' your heart's blood were a-spillin'!   20

"O dinna ye mind, young man," says she,
   "When the red wine ye were fillin',
That ye made the healths go round and round,
   And slighted Barbara Allen?"

He turn'd his face unto the wall,   25
   And death was with him dealin':
"Adieu, adieu, my dear friends all,
   And be kind to Barbara Allen!"

As she was walking o'er the fields,
   She heard the dead-bell knellin';   30
And every jow the dead-bell gave,
   Cried "Woe to Barbara Allen."

"O mother, mother, make my bed,
　　O make it saft and narrow:
My love has died for me today,
　　I'll die for him tomorrow.   35

"Farewell," she said, "ye virgins all,
　　And shun the fault I fell in;
Henceforth take warning by the fall
　　Of cruel Barbara Allen."   40

SIR PATRICK SPENS

(A Scottish popular ballad)

The king sits in Dumfermline town,
　　Drinking the blude-red wine;
"O whare will I get a skeely skipper,
　　To sail this new ship of mine?"

O up and spake an eldern knight,   5
　　Sat at the king's right knee,—
"Sir Patrick Spens is the best sailor
　　That ever sailed the sea,"

Our king has written a braid letter,
　　And seal'd it with his hand,   10
And sent it to Sir Patrick Spens,
　　Was walking on the strand.

"To Noroway, to Noroway,
　　To Noroway o'er the faem;
The king's daughter of Noroway   15
　　'Tis thou maun bring her hame."

The first word that Sir Patrick read,
　　Sae loud, loud laughed he;
The neist word that Sir Patrick read,
　　The tear blinded his e'e.   20

"O wha is this has done this deed,
　　And tauld the king o' me,
To send us out, at this time of the year,
　　To sail upon the sea?

"Be it wind, be it weet, be it hail, be it sleet,   25
    Our ship must sail the faem;
The king's daughter of Noroway,
    'Tis we must fetch her hame."

They hoysed their sails on Monenday morn,
    Wi' a' the speed they may;   30
They hae landed in Noroway,
    Upon a Wodensday.

They hadna been a week, a week
    In Noroway but twae,
When that the lords o' Noroway   35
    Began aloud to say,—

"Ye Scottishmen spend a' our king's goud,
    And a' our queenis fee."
"Ye lie, ye lie, ye liars loud!
    Fu' loud I hear ye lie.   40

"For I brought as much white monie
    As gane my men and me,
And I brought a half-fou o' gude red goud
    Out o'er the sea wi' me.

"Make ready, make ready, my merrymen a'!   45
    Our gude ship sails the morn."
"Now, ever alake, my master dear,
    I fear a deadly storm!

"I saw the new moon, late yestreen,
    Wi' the auld moon in her arm;   50
And if we gang to sea, master,
    I fear we'll come to harm."

They hadna sailed a league, a league,
    A league but barely three,
When the lift grew dark, and the wind blew loud,   55
    And gurly grew the sea.

The ankers brak, and the topmasts lap,
    It was sic a deadly storm;
And the waves came o'er the broken ship,
    Till a' her sides were torn.   60

"O where will I get a gude sailor,
    To take my helm in hand,
Till I get up to the tall top-mast,
    To see if I can spy land?"

"O here am I, a sailor gude,   65
   To take the helm in hand,
Till you go up to the tall top-mast;
   But I fear you'll ne'er spy land."

He hadna gane a step, a step,
   A step but barely ane,   70
When a bout flew out of our goodly ship,
   And the salt sea it came in.

"Gae, fetch a web o' the silken claith,
   Another o' the twine,
And wrap them into our ship's side,   75
   And letna the sea come in."

They fetched a web o' the silken claith,
   Another of the twine,
And they wrapped them roun' that gude ship's side,
   But still the sea came in.   80

O laith, laith, were our gude Scots lords
   To weet their cork-heel'd shoon!
But lang or a' the play was play'd,
   They wat their hats aboon.

And mony was the feather-bed   85
   That fluttered on the faem;
And mony was the gude lord's son
   That never mair cam home.

The ladyes wrang their fingers white,
   The maidens tore their hair,   90
A' for the sake of their true loves;
   For them they'll see na mair.

O lang, lang, may the ladyes sit,
   Wi' their fans into their hand,
Before they see Sir Patrick Spens   95
   Come sailing to the strand!

And lang, lang may the maidens sit,
   Wi' their goud kaims in their hair,
A' waiting for their own dear loves!
   For them they'll see na mair.   100

O forty miles off Aberdeen
   'Tis fifty fathoms deep,
And there lies gude Sir Patrick Spens,
   Wi' the Scots lords at his feet.

FRANKIE AND JOHNNIE

(American ballad, early twentieth century)

Frankie and Johnnie were lovers,
Oh, Lordy, how they could love;
Swore to be true to each other,
Just as true as the stars above.
    He was her man,   5
    But he done her wrong.

Frankie, she was a good woman,
Just like everyone knows,
She'd give her man a hundred dollars,
Just to buy himself some clothes.   10
    He was her man,
    But he done her wrong.

Frankie went to Memphis—
She went on the morning train—
She paid a hundred dollars   15
For Johnnie a watch and chain.
    He was her man,
    But he done her wrong.

Frankie lived down in a crib-house,
Crib-house with only one door,   20
Gave all her money to Johnnie,
To throw on the parlor-girls' floor.
    He was her man,
    But he done her wrong.

Johnnie went down to the corner saloon,   25
He called for a glass of beer;
Frankie went down in an hour or so,
And said, "Has Johnnie Dean been here?"
    He was her man,
    But he done her wrong.   30

"I'll not tell you any stories,
I'll not tell you a lie,
Johnnie left here about an hour ago
With a girl called Ella Bly."
    He was her man,   35
    But he done her wrong.

Frankie went down to the pawn-shop,
She bought herself a little forty-four,
She aimed it at the ceiling,

And shot a big hole in the floor.   40
   He was her man,
   But he done her wrong.

Frankie went down to the hotel,
She rang that hotel bell,
"Stand back, all you floozies,   45
Or I'll blow you all to hell!"
   He was her man,
   But he done her wrong.

Frankie looked over the transom,
And there before her eye,   50
Yes, there on the chair sat Johnnie,
Makin' love to Ella Bly.
   He was her man,
   But he done her wrong.

Frankie threw back her kimono,   55
She took out her bright forty-four,
Root-a-toot-toot, three times she shot,
Right through that hardwood door.
   She shot her man,
   But he done her wrong.   60

Johnnie he grabbed off his Stetson,
"O-my-gawd, Frankie, don't shoot!"
But Frankie put her finger on the trigger,
And again it went root-a-toot-toot.
   For he was her man,   65
   But he done her wrong.

"Roll me over once, doctor,
Roll me over slow,
Roll me onto my right side,
For those bullets hurt me so!"   70
   She finished her man,
   But he done her wrong.

"Bring on your rubber-tired carriages,
Bring on your rubber-tired hack,
Take my daddy to the cemetery,   75
But bring his suit and wrist-watch back.
   Best part of my man,
   That has done me wrong."

Thirteen girls dressed in mourning,
Thirteen men dressed in black,   80
They all went out to the cemetery,
But only twelve of the men came back.
   They left her man,
   That had done her wrong.

"Oh, bring 'round a thousand policemen,   85
Bring 'em around today,
To lock me in the dungeon,
And throw the key away.
    I shot my man,
    But he done me wrong.   90

"Yes, put me in that dungeon,
Oh, put me in that cell,
Put me where the north wind blows
From the southeast corner of hell.
    I shot my man,   95
    When he done me wrong."

Frankie then said to the warden,
"What are they goin' to do?"
The warden said to Frankie,
"It's a pardon, my girl, for you.   100
    You shot your man,
    But he done you wrong."

The sheriff came 'round in the morning,
And said it was all for the best,
He said her lover, Johnnie,   105
Was nothin' but a gawdam pest.
    He was her man,
    But he done her wrong.

Now it wasn't any kind of murder,
In either the second or third,   110
This woman simply dropped her lover,
Like a hunter drops a bird.
    He was her man,
    But he done her wrong.

Frankie now sits in the parlor,   115
Underneath an electric fan,
Telling her little sisters
To beware of the gawdam man.
    They'll do you wrong,
    Yes, they'll do you wrong.   120

The last time I saw pretty Frankie,
She surely was looking fine,
Diamonds as big as horse birds,
The owner of a big silver mine.
    She was minus her man,   125
    That had done her wrong.

This story has no moral,
This story has no end,
This story only goes to show

That there ain't no good in men.   130
   He was her man,
   But he done her wrong.

THE PASSIONATE SHEPHERD TO HIS LOVE

Christopher Marlowe
(1564–1593)

Come live with me and be my love,
And we will all the pleasures prove
That valleys, groves, hills, and fields,
Woods, or steepy mountain yields.

And we will sit upon the rocks,   5
Seeing the shepherds feed their flocks,
By shallow rivers to whose falls
Melodious birds sing madrigals.

And I will make thee beds of roses
And a thousand fragrant posies,   10
A cap of flowers, and a kirtle
Embroidered all with leaves of myrtle;

A gown made of the finest wool
Which from our pretty lambs we pull;
Fair lined slippers for the cold,   15
With buckles of the purest gold;

A belt of straw and ivy buds,
With coral clasps and amber studs:
And if these pleasures may thee move,
Come live with me, and be my love.   20

The shepherds' swains shall dance and sing
For thy delight each May morning:
If these delights thy mind may move,
Then live with me and be my love.

THE NYMPH'S REPLY TO THE SHEPHERD

Sir Walter Ralegh
(1552–1618)

Biography p. 1094

If all the world and love were young,
And truth in every shepherd's tongue,
These pretty pleasures might me move
To live with thee and be thy love.

Time drives the flocks from field to fold   5
When rivers rage and rocks grow cold,
And Philomel becometh dumb;
The rest complains of cares to come.

The flowers do fade, and wanton fields
To wayward winter reckoning yields;   10
A honey tongue, a heart of gall,
Is fancy's spring, but sorrow's fall.

Thy gowns, thy shoes, thy beds of roses,
Thy cap, thy kirtle, and thy posies
Soon break, soon wither, soon forgotten—   15
In folly ripe, in reason rotten.

Thy belt of straw and ivy buds,
Thy coral clasps and amber studs,
All these in me no means can move
To come to thee and be thy love.   20

But could youth last and love still breed,
Had joys no date nor age no need,
Then these delights my mind might move
To live with thee and be thy love.

SUZANNE

Leonard Cohen
(b. 1934)

Biography p. 1067

Suzanne takes you down
To her place near the river
You can hear the boats go by
You can spend the night beside her.
And you know that she's half crazy   5
But that's why you want to be there
And she feeds you tea and oranges
That come all the way from China.
And just when you mean to tell her
That you have no love to give her   10
Then she gets you on her wavelength
And she lets the river answer
That you've always been her lover
And you want to travel with her
And you want to travel blind   15
And you know that she will trust you
For you've touched her perfect body
    with your mind.

And Jesus was a sailor
When he walked upon the water   20
And he spent a long time watching
From his lonely wooden tower.
And when he knew for certain
Only drowning men could see him
He said, "All men will be sailors then   25
Until the sea shall free them."
But he himself was broken
Long before the sky would open
Forsaken, almost human,
He sank beneath your wisdom like a stone.   30
And you want to travel with him
And you want to travel blind
And you think maybe you'll trust him
For he's touched your perfect body
    with his mind.   35

Now Suzanne takes your hand
And she leads you to the river
She is wearing rags and feathers
From Salvation Army counters.

And the sun pours down like honey   40
On our lady of the harbour;
And she shows you where to look
Among the garbage and the flowers.
There are heroes in the seaweed,
There are children in the morning,   45
They are leaning out for love
And they will lean that way forever.
While Suzanne holds the mirror
And you want to travel with her
And you want to travel blind   50
And you know that you can trust her
For she's touched your perfect body
   with her mind.

ELEANOR RIGBY

John Lennon   Paul McCartney
(1940–1980)   (b. 1942)

Biography p. 1084   *Biography p. 1086*

Ah look at all the lonely people!
Ah look at all the lonely people!

Eleanor Rigby, picks up the rice in the church where a wedding has been,
lives in a dream.
Waits at the window wearing the face that she keeps in a jar by the door,
who is it for?

All the lonely people, where do they all come from?   5
All the lonely people, where do they all belong?

Father McKenzie writing the words of a sermon that no one will hear,
no one comes near.
Look at him working, darning his socks in the night when there's nobody there,
what does he care?

All the lonely people, where do they all come from?
All the lonely people, where do they all belong?   10

Eleanor Rigby, died in the church and was buried along with her name,
nobody came.

Father McKenzie, wiping the dirt from his hands as he walks from the grave,
no one was saved.

All the lonely people, where do they all come from?
All the lonely people, where do they all belong?   20

SONNET #8: I LIVE AND DIE

Louise Labé
(1520–1566)

Biography p. 1082

I live and die; drowning I burn to death,
Seared by the ice and frozen by the fire;
Life is as hard as iron, as soft as breath;
My joy and trouble dance on the same wire.

In the same sudden breath I laugh and weep,   5
My torment pleasure where my pleasure grieves;
My treasure's lost which I for all time keep,
At once I wither and put out new leaves.

Thus constant Love is my inconstant guide;
And when I am to pain's refinement brought,   10
Beyond all hope, he grants me a reprieve.

And when I think joy cannot be denied,
And scaled the peak of happiness I sought,
He casts me down into my former grief.

WILLIAM SHAKESPEARE
(1564–1616)

Biography p. 1098

SONNET 18

Shall I compare thee to a summer's day?
Thou art more lovely and more temperate.
Rough winds do shake the darling buds of May,
And summer's lease hath all too short a date.
Sometime too hot the eye of heaven shines,   5
And often is his gold complexion dimmed;
And every fair from fair sometime declines,
By chance, or nature's changing course, untrimmed;
But thy eternal summer shall not fade
Nor lose possession of that fair thou ow'st,   10
Nor shall Death brag thou wand'rest in his shade
When in eternal lines to time thou grow'st.
   So long as men can breathe or eyes can see,
   So long lives this, and this gives life to thee.

SONNET 29

When, in disgrace with Fortune and men's eyes,
I all alone beweep my outcast state,
And trouble deaf heaven with my bootless cries,
And look upon myself and curse my fate,
Wishing me like to one more rich in hope,   5
Featured like him, like him with friends possessed,
Desiring this man's art, and that man's scope,
With what I most enjoy contented least;
Yet in these thoughts myself almost despising,
Haply I think on thee, and then my state,   10
Like to the lark at break of day arising
From sullen earth, sings hymns at heaven's gate;
   For thy sweet love rememb'red such wealth brings
   That then I scorn to change my state with kings.

SONNET 130

My mistress' eyes are nothing like the sun;
Coral is far more red than her lips' red;
If snow be white, why then her breasts are dun;
If hairs be wires, black wires grow on her head.
I have seen roses damasked, red and white,   5
But no such roses see I in her cheeks;
And in some perfumes is there more delight
Than in the breath that from my mistress reeks.
I love to hear her speak, yet well I know
That music hath a far more pleasing sound;   10
I grant I never saw a goddess go;
My mistress, when she walks, treads on the ground.
    And yet, by heaven, I think my love as rare
    As any she belied with false compare.

SONNET #43: HOW DO I LOVE THEE?

Elizabeth Barrett Browning

(1806–1861)

Biography p. 1064

How do I love thee? Let me count the ways.
I love thee to the depth and breadth and height
My soul can reach, when feeling out of sight
For the ends of Being and ideal Grace.
I love thee to the level of every day's   5
Most quiet need, by sun and candlelight.
I love thee freely, as men strive for Right;
I love thee purely, as they turn from Praise.
I love thee with the passion put to use
In my old griefs, and with my childhood's faith.   10
I love thee with a love I seemed to lose
With my lost saints,—I love thee with the breath,
Smiles, tears, of all my life!—and, if God choose,
I shall but love thee better after death.

SONNET #30: LOVE IS NOT ALL

Edna St. Vincent Millay

(1892–1950)

Biography p. 1088

Love is not all: it is not meat nor drink
Nor slumber nor a roof against the rain;
Nor yet a floating spar to men that sink
And rise and sink and rise and sink again;
Love can not fill the thickened lung with breath,   5
Nor clean the blood, nor set the fractured bone;
Yet many a man is making friends with death
Even as I speak, for lack of love alone.
It well may be that in a difficult hour,
Pinned down by pain and moaning for release,   10
Or nagged by want past resolution's power,
I might be driven to sell your love for peace,
Or trade the memory of this night for food.
It well may be. I do not think I would.

ANGEL OF BEACH HOUSES AND PICNICS

Anne Sexton

(1928–1974)

Biography p. 1098

Angel of beach houses and picnics, do you know solitaire?
Fifty-two reds and blacks and only myself to blame.
My blood buzzes like a hornet's nest. I sit in a kitchen chair
at a table set for one. The silverware is the same
and the glass and the sugar bowl. I hear my lungs fill and expel   5
as in an operation. But I have no one left to tell.

Once I was a couple. I was my own king and queen
with cheese and bread and rosé on the rocks of Rockport.
Once I sunbathed in the buff, all brown and lean,
watching the toy sloops go by, holding court   10

for busloads of tourists. Once I called breakfast the sexiest
meal of the day. Once I invited arrest

at the peace march in Washington. Once I was young and bold
and left hundreds of unmatched people out in the cold.

LIVING IN SIN

Adrienne Rich

(b. 1929)

Biography p. 1095

She had thought the studio would keep itself;
No dust upon the furniture of love.
Half heresy, to wish the taps less vocal,
The panes relieved of grime. A plate of pears,
A piano with a Persian shawl, a cat
Stalking the picturesque amusing mouse   5
Had been her vision when he pleaded "Come."
Not that at five each separate stair would writhe
Under the milkman's tramp; that morning light
So coldly would delineate the scraps
Of last night's cheese and blank sepulchral bottles;   10
That on the kitchen shelf among the saucers
A pair of beetle-eyes would fix her own—
Envoy from some black village in the mouldings . . .
Meanwhile her night's companion, with a yawn
Sounded a dozen notes upon the keyboard,   15
Declared it out of tune, inspected whistling
A twelve hours' beard, went out for cigarettes;
While she, contending with a woman's demons,
Pulled back the sheets and made the bed and found
A fallen towel to dust the table-top,   20
And wondered how it was a man could wake
From night to day and take the day for granted.
By evening she was back in love again,
Though not so wholly but throughout the night
She woke sometimes to feel the daylight coming   25
Like a relentless milkman up the stairs.

TO HIS COY MISTRESS

Andrew Marvell
(1621–1678)

Biography p. 1088

    Had we but world enough, and time,
This coyness, Lady, were no crime.
We would sit down, and think which way
To walk, and pass our long love's day.
Thou by the Indian Ganges' side   5
Shouldst rubies find; I by the tide
Of Humber would complain. I would
Love you ten years before the flood,
And you should, if you please, refuse
Till the conversion of the Jews.   10
My vegetable love should grow
Vaster than empires and more slow;
An hundred years should go to praise
Thine eyes, and on thy forehead gaze;
Two hundred to adore each breast,   15
But thirty thousand to the rest;
An age at least to every part,
And the last age should show your heart.
For, lady, you deserve this state,
Nor would I love at lower rate.   20
    But at my back I always hear
Time's wingèd chariot hurrying near;
And yonder all before us lie
Deserts of vast eternity.
Thy beauty shall no more be found,   25
Nor, in thy marble vault, shall sound
My echoing song; then worms shall try
That long-preserved virginity,
And your quaint honour turn to dust,
And into ashes all my lust: 30
The grave's a fine and private place,
But none, I think, do there embrace.
    Now therefore, while the youthful hue
Sits on thy skin like morning dew,
And while thy willing soul transpires   35
At every pore with instant fires,
Now let us sport us while we may,
And now, like amorous birds of prey,
Rather at once our time devour
Than languish in his slow-chapt power.   40
Let us roll all our strength and all

Our sweetness up into one ball,
And tear our pleasures with rough strife
Thorough the iron gates of life;
Thus, though we cannot make our sun   45
Stand still, yet we will make him run.

TO MY DEAR AND LOVING HUSBAND

Anne Bradstreet

(1612–1672)

Biography p. 1063

If ever two were one, then surely we.
If ever man were loved by wife, then thee;
If ever wife was happy in a man,
Compare with me ye women if you can.
I prize thy love more than whole mines of gold.   5
Or all the riches that the East doth hold.
My love is such that rivers cannot quench,
Nor ought but love from thee give recompense.
Thy love is such I can no way repay;
The heavens reward thee manifold, I pray.   10
Then while we live, in love let's so persever,
That when we live no more we may live ever.

A VALEDICTION FORBIDDING MOURNING

John Donne

(1572–1631)

Biography p. 1070

As virtuous men pass mildly away,
    And whisper to their souls to go,
Whilst some of their sad friends do say,
    "The breath goes now," and some say, "No."

So let us melt and make no noise,   5
   No tear-floods nor sigh-tempests move;
'Twere profanation of our joys
   To tell the laity our love.

Moving of the earth brings harms and fears;
   Men reckon what it did and meant   10
But trepidation of the spheres,
   Though greater far, is innocent.

Dull sublunary lovers' love,
   Whose soul is sense, cannot admit
Absence because it doth remove   15
   Those things which elemented it.

But we by love so much refined
   That ourselves know not what it is,
Inter-assured of the mind,
   Care less eyes, lips, and hands to miss.   20

Our two souls, therefore, which are one,
   Though I must go, endure not yet
A breach, but an expansion,
   Like gold to airy thinness beat.

If they be two, they are two so   25
   As stiff twin compasses are two;
Thy soul, the fixed foot, makes no show
   To move, but doth if th' other do.

And though it in the center sit,
   Yet when the other far doth roam,   30
It leans and harkens after it,
   And grows erect as that comes home.

Such wilt thou be to me, who must,
   Like th' other foot, obliquely run;
Thy firmness makes my circle just,   35
   And makes me end where I begun.

JANUARY 25TH

Maxine Kumin

(b. 1925)

Biography p. 1082

All night in the flue like a trapped thing,
like a broken bird,
the wind knocked unanswered.
Snow fell down the chimney, making
the forked logs spit   5
ashes of resurrected crickets.
By 3 A.M. both stoves were dead.
A ball of steel wool
froze to the kitchen window sill,
while we lay back to back in bed,   10

two thin survivors. Somewhere in a small dream,
a chipmunk uncorked from his hole
and dodged along the wall.
My love, we live at such extremes
that when, in the leftover spite of the storm,   15
we touch and grow warm,
I can believe I saw
the ground release
that brown and orange commonplace
sign of thaw.   20

Now daylight the color of buttermilk
tunnels through the coated glass.
Lie still; lie close.
Watch the sun pick
splinters from the window flowers.   25
Now under the ice, under twelve knee-deep layers
of mud in last summer's pond
the packed hearts of peepers are beating
barely, barely repeating
themselves enough to hang on.   30

LOVE POEM

Leslie Marmon Silko
(b. 1948)

Biography p. 1100

Rain smell comes with the wind
            out of the southwest.
Smell of the sand dunes
        tall grass glistening
              in the rain.   5
Warm raindrops that fall easy
           (this woman)
The summer is born.
Smell of her breathing new life
           small gray toads on damp sand.   10
(this woman)
      whispering to dark wide leaves
      white moon blossoms dripping
            tracks in the sand.
Rain smell   15
    I am full of hunger
    deep and longing to touch
wet tall grass, green and strong beneath.
This woman loved a man
and she breathed to him   20
        her damp earth song.
I am haunted by this story
I remember it in cottonwood leaves
        their fragrance in the shade.
I remember it in the wide blue sky   25
when the rain smell comes with the wind.

WHEN YOU ARE OLD

William Butler Yeats
(1865–1939)

Biography p. 1109

When you are old and grey and full of sleep,
And nodding by the fire, take down this book,
And slowly read, and dream of the soft look
Your eyes had once, and of their shadows deep;

How many loved your moments of glad grace,   5
And loved your beauty with love false or true,
But one man loved the pilgrim soul in you,
And loved the sorrows of your changing face;

And bending down beside the glowing bars,
Murmur, a little sadly, how Love fled   10
And paced upon the mountains overhead
And hid his face amid a crowd of stars.

MY LAST DUCHESS

Robert Browning
(1812–1882)

Biography p. 1064

That's my last Duchess painted on the wall,
Looking as if she were alive. I call
That piece a wonder, now: Fra Pandolf's hands
Worked busily a day, and there she stands.
Will't please you sit and look at her? I said   5
"Fra Pandolf" by design, for never read
Strangers like you that pictured countenance,
The depth and passion of its earnest glance,
But to myself they turned (since none puts by
The curtain I have drawn for you, but I)   10
And seemed as they would ask me, if they durst,
How such a glance came there; so, not the first

Are you to turn and ask thus. Sir, 't was not
Her husband's presence only, called that spot
Of joy into the Duchess' cheek: perhaps   15
Fra Pandolf chanced to say, "Her mantel laps
Over my lady's wrist too much," or "Paint
Must never hope to reproduce the faint
Half-flush that dies along her throat": such stuff
Was courtesy, she thought, and cause enough   20
For calling up that spot of joy. She had
A heart—how shall I say?—too soon made glad,
Too easily impressed; she liked whate'er
She looked on, and her looks went everywhere.
Sir, 't was all one! My favor at her breast,   25
The dropping of the daylight in the West,
The bough of cherries some officious fool
Broke in the orchard for her, the white mule
She rode with round the terrace—all and each
Would draw from her alike the approving speech,   30
Or blush, at least. She thanked men,—good! but thanked
Somehow—I know not how—as if she ranked
My gift of a nine-hundred-years-old name
With anybody's gift. Who'd stoop to blame
This sort of trifling? Even had you skill   35
In speech—(which I have not)—to make your will
Quite clear to such an one, and say, "Just this
Or that in you disgusts me; here you miss,
Or there exceed the mark"—and if she let
Herself be lessoned so, nor plainly set   40
Her wits to yours, forsooth, and made excuse,
—E'en then would be some stooping; and I choose
Never to stoop. Oh sir, she smiled, no doubt,
Whene'er I passed her; but who passed without
Much the same smile? This grew; I gave commands: 45
Then all smiles stopped together. There she stands
As if alive. Will 't please you rise? We'll meet
The company below, then. I repeat,
The Count your master's known munificence
Is ample warrant that no just pretence   50
Of mine for dowry will be disallowed;
Though his fair daughter's self, as I avowed
At starting, is my object. Nay, we'll go
Together down, sir. Notice Neptune, though,
Taming a sea-horse, thought a rarity,   55
Which Claus of Innsbruck cast in bronze for me!

THE LOVE SONG OF J. ALFRED PRUFROCK

T. S. Eliot

(1888–1965)

Biography p. 1071

S'io credesse che mia risposta fosse
A persona che mai tornasse al mondo,
Questa fiamma staria senza piu scosse.
Ma perciocche giammai di questo fondo
Non torno vivo alcun, s'i'odo il vero,
Senza tema d'infamia it rispondo.[1]

Let us go then, you and I,
When the evening is spread out against the sky
Like a patient etherised upon a table;
Let us go, through certain half-deserted streets,
The muttering retreats   5
Of restless nights in one-night cheap hotels
And sawdust restaurants with oyster-shells:
Streets that follow like a tedious argument
Of insidious intent
To lead you to an overwhelming question . . .   10
Oh, do not ask, "What is it?"
Let us go and make our visit.

    In the room the women come and go
Talking of Michelangelo.

    The yellow fog that rubs its back upon the window-panes,   15
The yellow smoke that rubs its muzzle on the window-panes
Licked its tongue into the corners of the evening,
Lingered upon the pools that stand in drains,
Let fall upon its back the soot that falls from chimneys,
Slipped by the terrace, made a sudden leap,   20
And seeing that it was a soft October night,
Curled once about the house, and fell asleep.

[1]"If I thought that my reply was to one who would return to the world, this flame would stay without moving a bit, but since none has ever returned alive from this depth, if I hear truly, without fear of infamy I answer you" (Dante, *The Inferno,* XXVII, 61–66). In the *Inferno,* the Latin poet Virgil leads Dante to the underworld, where they meet various sinners. Here, Guido da Montefeltro, shut up in a flame as punishment for having been a false counselor in life, tells his story truthfully to Dante because he believes Dante will never return to Earth to tell it.

And indeed there will be time
For the yellow smoke that slides along the street,
Rubbing its back upon the window-panes;   25
There will be time, there will be time
To prepare a face to meet the faces that you meet;
There will be time to murder and create,
And time for all the works and days of hands
That lift and drop a question on your plate;   30
Time for you and time for me,
And time yet for a hundred indecisions,
And for a hundred visions and revisions,
Before the taking of a toast and tea.

    In the room the women come and go   35
Talking of Michelangelo.

    And indeed there will be time
To wonder, "Do I dare?" and, "Do I dare?"
Time to turn back and descend the stair,
With a bald spot in the middle of my hair—   40
(They will say: "How his hair is growing thin!")
My morning coat, my collar mounting firmly to the chin,
My necktie rich and modest, but asserted by a simple pin—
(They will say: "But how his arms and legs are thin!")
Do I dare   45
Disturb the universe?
In a minute there is time
For decisions and revisions which a minute will reverse.

    For I have known them all already, known them all:—
Have known the evenings, mornings, afternoons,   50
I have measured out my life with coffee spoons;
I know the voices dying with a dying fall
Beneath the music from a farther room.
    So how should I presume?

    And I have known the eyes already, known them all—   55
The eyes that fix you in a formulated phrase,
And when I am formulated, sprawling on a pin,
When I am pinned and wriggling on the wall,
Then how should I begin
To spit out all the butt-ends of my days and ways?   60
    And how should I presume?

    And I have known the arms already, known them all—
Arms that are braceleted and white and bare
(But in the lamplight, downed with light brown hair!)
Is it perfume from a dress   65
That makes me so digress?

Arms that lie along a table, or wrap about a shawl.
    And should I then presume?
    And how should I begin?

                        .   .   .   .   .

Shall I say, I have gone at dusk through narrow streets   70
And watched the smoke that rises from the pipes
Of lonely men in shirt-sleeves, leaning out of windows? . . .

    I should have been a pair of ragged claws
Scuttling across the floors of silent seas.

                        .   .   .   .   .

And the afternoon, the evening, sleeps so peacefully!   75
Smoothed by long fingers,
Asleep . . . tired . . . or it malingers,
Stretched on the floor, here beside you and me.
Should I, after tea and cakes and ices,
Have the strength to force the moment to its crisis?   80
But though I have wept and fasted, wept and prayed,
Though I have seen my head (grown slightly bald) brought in upon a platter,
I am no prophet—and here's no great matter;
I have seen the moment of my greatness flicker,
And I have seen the eternal Footman hold my coat, and snicker,   85
And in short, I was afraid.

    And would it have been worth it, after all,
After the cups, the marmalade, the tea,
Among the procelain, among some talk of you and me,
Would it have been worth while,   90
To have bitten off the matter with a smile,
To have squeezed the universe into a ball
To roll it toward some overwhelming question,
To say: "I am Lazarus, come from the dead,
Come back to tell you all, I shall tell you all"—   95
If one, settling a pillow by her head,
    Should say: "That is not what I meant at all.
    That is not it, at all."

    And would it have been worth it, after all,
Would it have been worth while,   100
After the sunsets and the dooryards and the sprinkled streets,
After the novels, after the teacups, after the skirts that trail along the floor—
And this, and so much more?—
It is impossible to say just what I mean!
But as if a magic lantern threw the nerves in patterns on a screen: 105
Would it have been worth while
If one, settling a pillow or throwing off a shawl,
And turning toward the window, should say:

"That is not it at all,
That is not what I meant, at all."   110

. . . . .

No! I am not Prince Hamlet, nor was meant to be;
Am an attendant lord, one that will do
To swell a progress, start a scene or two,
Advise the prince; no doubt, an easy tool,
Deferential, glad to be of use,   115
Politic, cautious, and meticulous;
Full of high sentence, but a bit obtuse;
At times, indeed, almost ridiculous—
Almost, at times, the Fool.

    I grow old . . . I grow old . . .   120
I shall wear the bottoms of my trousers rolled.

    Shall I part my hair behind? Do I dare to eat a peach?
I shall wear white flannel trousers, and walk upon the beach.
I have heard the mermaids singing, each to each.

    I do not think that they will sing to me.   125

    I have seen them riding seaward on the waves
Combing the white hair of the waves blown back
When the wind blows the water white and black.

    We have lingered in the chambers of the sea
By sea-girls wreathed with seaweed red and brown   130
Till human voices wake us, and we drown.

THE ABORTION

Anne Sexton

(1928–1974)

Biography p. 1098

Somebody who should have been born is gone.

Just as the earth puckered its mouth,
each bud puffing out from its knot,
I changed my shoes, and then drove south.   5

Up past the Blue Mountains, where
Pennsylvania humps on endlessly,
wearing, like a crayoned cat, its green hair,

its roads sunken in like a gray washboard;
where, in truth, the ground cracks evilly,   10
a dark socket from which the coal has poured,

Somebody who should have been born is gone.

the grass as bristly and stout as chives,
and me wondering when the ground would break,   15
and me wondering how anything fragile survives;

up in Pennsylvania, I met a little man,
not Rumpelstiltskin, at all, at all . . .
he took the fullness that love began.

Returning north, even the sky grew thin   20
like a high window looking nowhere.
The road was as flat as a sheet of tin.

Somebody who should have been born is gone.

Yes, woman, such logic will lead   25
to loss without death. Or say what you meant,
you coward . . . this baby that I bleed.

HOUSEWIFE

Susan Fromberg Schaeffer

(b. 1941)

Biography p. 1098

What can be wrong
That some days I hug this house
About me like a shawl, and feel
Each window like a tatter in its skin,
Or worse, bright eyes I must not look through?   5

Now my husband stands above me
High as ever my father did

And I in that house of dolls, which,
When young I could not shrink to.

I feel the shrinkage in each bone.   10
No matter what I do, my two girls
Spoil like fruit. Already they push us back
Like too-full plates. They play with us
Like dolls.

The road before the house is like a wish   15
That stretches out and out and will not
Stop, and the smallest hills are built
Like steps to the slippery moon,
But I
Circle this lit house like any moth   20
And see each day open its fingers
To disclose the stone,—which hand, which hand?
And the stone in both.

Once, I drove my car into a tree.
The bottles in the back   25
Burst like bombs, tubular glass beasts,
Giving up the ghost. My husband
Thought it was the road. It was.
In the rearview mirror, it curved and curled,
Longer and stronger than the road ahead,   30
A question of perspective, I thought then.
I watched it until it turned, and I did not.
I sucked in pain like air,
As if, I, the rib, had cracked.

I did not feel this pain, not then,   35
Almost in my mouth. I wiggle this life
And find it loose. Like my girls,
I would pull it out, would watch
Something new and white
Push like mushrooms from the rich red soil.   40
But there is just this hole, this bone.

So I live inside my wedding ring,
Beneath its arch,
Multiplying the tables of my days,
Rehearsing the lessons of this dish, that sleeve,   45
Wanting the book that no one wrote,
Loving my husband, my children, my house,
With this pain in my jaw,
Wanting to go.

Do others feel like this? Where do they go?   50

CHANT FOR DARK HOURS

Dorothy Parker
(1893–1967)

Biography p. 1091

Some men, some men
Cannot pass a
Book shop.
(Lady, make your mind up, and wait your life away.)

Some men, some men   5
Cannot pass a
Crap game.
(He said he'd come at moonrise, and here's another day!)

Some men, some men
Cannot pass a   10
Bar-room.
(Wait about, and hang about, and that's the way it goes.)

Some men, some men
Cannot pass a
Woman.   15
(Heaven never send me another one of those!)

Some men, some men
Cannot pass a
Golf course.
(Read a book, and sew a seam, and slumber if you can.)   20

Some men, some men
Cannot pass a
Haberdasher's.
(All your life you wait around for some damn man!)

THE AWFUL MOTHER

Susan Griffin

(b. 1943)

Biography p. 1075

The whole weight of history bears down
on the awful mother's shoulders.
Hiroshima, the Holocaust, the Inquisition
each massacre of innocents
her own childhood   5
and the childhood of her mother
and the childhood of her child.
What can she do?
She remembers.
The child's drawing, the lost   10
mittens, the child
cold, the awful mother shouting
the child's story of shadows
in her room, the child waiting
the awful mother   15
waiting, and *her* mother
waiting, already asleep
and the awful mother
knowing too late
the howling of children   20
in cattle cars and fires.
The wind blows so hard
it is as if the earth had fallen
on its side.
But nobody wakes up.   25
Only the awful mother stirs stricken
with grief.

MOTHER TO SON

Langston Hughes

(1902–1967)

Biography p. 1078

Well, son, I'll tell you:
Life for me ain't been no crystal stair.
It's had tacks in it,
And splinters,
And boards torn up,   5
And places with no carpet on the floor—
Bare.
But all the time
I'se been a-climbin' on,
And reachin' landin's,   10
And turnin' corners,
And sometimes goin' in the dark
Where there ain't been no light.
So boy, don't you turn back.
Don't you set down on the steps   15
'Cause you finds it's kinder hard.
Don't you fall now—
For I'se still goin', honey,
I'se still climbin',
And life for me ain't been no crystal stair.   20

SEDUCTION

Nikki Giovanni

(b. 1943)

Biography p. 1074

one day
you gonna walk in this house
and i'm gonna have on a long African
gown
you'll sit down and say "The Black . . ."   5
and i'm gonna take one arm out

then you—not noticing me at all—will say "What about
this brother . . ."
and i'm going to be slipping it over my head
and you'll rapp on about "The revolution . . ."   10
while i rest your hand against my stomach
you'll go on—as you always do—saying
"I just can't dig . . ."
while i'm moving your hand up and down
and i'll be taking your dashiki off   15
then you'll say "What we really need . . ."
and i'll be licking your arm
and "The way I see it we ought to . . ."
and unbuckling your pants
"And what about the situation . . ."   20
and taking your shorts off
then you'll notice
your state of undress
and knowing you you'll just say
"Nikki,   25
isn't this counterrevolutionary . . . ?"

THE BLINDED SOLDIER TO HIS LOVE

Alfred Noyes

(1880–1937)

Biography p. 1089

I did not know you then
    I cannot see you now;
But let my hands again
    Feel your sweet hair and brow.
Your eyes are grey, I am told,   5
Your hair a tawny gold.

Yet, if of these I tire,
    I shall not need to stray.
Your eyes shall feed my fire
    With brown or blue for grey;   10
And your deep hair shall be
As mutable as the sea.

Let forms and colours flow
    Like clouds around a star.

I clasp the soul and know   15
   How vain those day-dreams are;
Dreams, from these eyes withdrawn
Beyond all thought of dawn.

But what is dawn to me?
   In Love's Arabian night,   20
What lover cares to see
   The unwelcome morning light?
With you, O sweetest friend,
My night shall never end.

MUTTERINGS OVER THE CRIB OF A DEAF CHILD

James Wright

(b. 1927)

Biography p. 1109

"How will he hear the bell at school
Arrange the broken afternoon,
And know to run across the cool
Grasses where the starlings cry,
Or understand the day is gone?"   5

Well, someone lifting curious brows
Will take the measure of the clock.
And he will see the birchen boughs
Outside sagging dark from the sky,
And the shade crawling upon the rock.   10

"And how will he know to rise at morning?
His mother has other sons to waken,
She has the stove she must build to burning
Before the coals of the nighttime die;
And he never stirs when he is shaken."   15

I take it the air affects the skin,
And you remember, when you were young,
Sometimes you could feel the dawn begin,
And the fire would call you, by and by,
Out of the bed and bring you along.   20

"Well, good enough. To serve his needs
All kinds of arrangements can be made.
But what will you do if his finger bleeds?
Or a bobwhite whistles invisibly
And flutes like an angel off in the shade?"   25

He will learn pain. And, as for the bird,
It is always darkening when that comes out.
I will putter as though I had not heard,
And lift him into my arms and sing
Whether he hears my song or not.   30

SUNDAY AT THE STATE HOSPITAL

David Ignatow

(b. 1914)

Biography p. 1079

I am sitting across the table
eating my visit sandwich.
The one I brought him stays suspended
near his mouth; his eyes focus
on the table and seem to think,   5
his shoulders hunched forward.
I chew methodically,
pretending to take him
as a matter of course.
The sandwich tastes mad   10
and I keep chewing.
My past is sitting in front of me
filled with itself
and trying with almost no success
to bring the present to its mouth.   15

FOR A FATHERLESS SON

Sylvia Plath

(1932–1963)

Biography p. 1092

You will be aware of an absence, presently,
Growing beside you, like a tree,
A death tree, color gone, an Australian gum tree—
Balding, gelded by lightning—an illusion,
And a sky like a pig's backside, an utter lack of attention.   5

But right now you are dumb.
And I love your stupidity,
The blind mirror of it. I look in
And find no face but my own, and you think that's funny.
It is good for me   10

To have you grab my nose, a ladder rung.
One day you may touch what's wrong
The small skulls, the smashed blue hills, the godawful hush.
Till then your smiles are found money.

ELEGY FOR JANE

My Student, Thrown by a Horse

Theodore Roethke

(1908–1963)

Biography p. 1096

I remember the neckcurls, limp and damp as tendrils;
And her quick look, a sidelong pickerel smile;
And how, once startled into talk, the light syllables leaped for
    her,
And she balanced in the delight of her thought,
A wren, happy, tail into the wind,   5
Her song trembling the twigs and small branches.
The shade sang with her;

The leaves, their whispers turned to kissing;
And the mold sang in the bleached valleys under the rose.

Oh, when she was sad, she cast herself down into such a pure depth,   10
Even a father could not find her:
Scraping her cheek against straw;
Stirring the clearest water.

My sparrow, you are not here,
Waiting like a fern, making a spiny shadow.   15
The sides of wet stones cannot console me,
Nor the moss, wound with the last light.

If only I could nudge you from this sleep,
My maimed darling, my skittery pigeon.
Over this damp grave I speak the words of my love: 20
I, with no rights in this matter,
Neither father nor lover.

AUTO WRECK

Karl Shapiro

(b. 1913)

Biography p. 1099

Its quick soft silver bell beating, beating,
And down the dark one ruby flare
Pulsing out red light like an artery,
The ambulance at top speed floating down
Past beacons and illuminated clocks   5
Wings in a heavy curve, dips down,
And brakes speed, entering the crowd.
The doors leap open, emptying light;
Stretchers are laid out, the mangled lifted
And stowed into the little hospital.   10
Then the bell, breaking the hush, tolls once,
And the ambulance with its terrible cargo
Rocking, slightly rocking, moves away,
As the doors, an afterthought, are closed.

We are deranged, walking among the cops   15
Who sweep glass and are large and composed.
One is still making notes under the light.

One with a bucket douches ponds of blood
Into the street and gutter.
One hangs lanterns on the wrecks that cling,   20
Empty husks of locusts, to iron poles.

Our throats were tight as tourniquets,
Our feet were bound with splints, but now,
Like convalescents intimate and gauche,
We speak through sickly smiles and warn   25
With the stubborn saw of common sense,
The grim joke and the banal resolution.
The traffic moves around with care,
But we remain, touching a wound
That opens to our richest horror.   30
Already old, the question Who shall die?
Becomes unspoken Who is innocent?
For death in war is done by hands;
Suicide has cause and stillbirth, logic;
And cancer, simple as a flower, blooms.   35
But this invites the occult mind,
Cancels our physics with a sneer,
And spatters all we knew of denouement
Across the expedient and wicked stones.

SINCE FEELING IS FIRST

E. E. Cummings

(1894–1962)

Biography p. 1068

since feeling is first
who pays any attention
to the syntax of things
will never wholly kiss you;

wholly to be a fool   5
while Spring is in the world
my blood approves,
and kisses are a better fate
than wisdom

lady i swear by all flowers. Don't cry 10
—the best gesture of my brain is less than
your eyelids' flutter which says

we are for each other: then
laugh, leaning back in my arms
for life's not a paragraph 15

And death i think is no parenthesis

Drama

ANTIGONE

Sophocles

(496–406 B.C.)

Biography p. 1011

Persons Represented

ANTIGONE
ISMENE
EURYDICE
CREON
HAIMON
TEIRESIAS
A SENTRY
A MESSENGER
CHORUS

SCENE: *Before the palace of Creon, King of Thebes. A central double door, and two lateral doors. A platform extends the length of the façade, and from this platform three steps lead down into the "orchestra," or chorus-ground.* TIME: *dawn of the day after the repulse of the Argive army from the assault on Thebes.*

PROLOGUE

(ANTIGONE *and* ISMENE *enter from the central door of the Palace.*)

ANTIGONE.   Ismenê, dear sister,
  You would think that we had already suffered enough
  For the curse on Oedipus:
  I cannot imagine any grief
  That you and I have not gone through. And now—
  Have they told you of the new decree of our King Creon?
ISMENE.   I have heard nothing: I know
  That two sisters lost two brothers, a double death

In a single hour; and I know that the Argive army
Fled in the night; but beyond this, nothing.

ANTIGONE.   I thought so. And that is why I wanted you
To come out here with me. There is something we must do.

ISMENE.   Why do you speak so strangely?

ANTIGONE.   Listen, Ismenê:
Creon buried our brother Eteoclês
With military honors, gave him a soldier's funeral,
And it was right that he should; but Polyneicês,
Who fought as bravely and died as miserably,—
They say that Creon has sworn
No one shall bury him, no one mourn for him,
But his body must lie in the fields, a sweet treasure
For carrion birds to find as they search for food.
That is what they say, and our good Creon is coming here
To announce it publicly; and the penalty—
Stoning to death in the public square!

                              There it is,
And now you can prove what you are:
A true sister, or a traitor to your family.

ISMENE.   Antigonê, you are mad! What could I possibly do?

ANTIGONE.   You must decide whether you will help me or not.

ISMENE.   I do not understand you. Help you in what?

ANTIGONE.   Ismenê, I am going to bury him. Will you come?

ISMENE.   Bury him! You have just said the new law forbids it.

ANTIGONE.   He is my brother. And he is your brother, too.

ISMENE.   But think of the danger! Think what Creon will do!

ANTIGONE.   Creon is not strong enough to stand in my way.

ISMENE.   Ah sister!
Oedipus died, everyone hating him
For what his own search brought to light, his eyes
Ripped out by his own hand; and Iocastê died,
His mother and wife at once: she twisted the cords
That strangled her life; and our two brothers died,
Each killed by the other's sword. And we are left:
But oh, Antigonê,
Think how much more terrible than these
Our own death would be if we should go against Creon
And do what he has forbidden! We are only women,
We cannot fight with men, Antigonê!
The law is strong, we must give in to the law
In this thing, and in worse. I beg the Dead
To forgive me, but I am helpless: I must yield
To those in authority. And I think it is dangerous business
To be always meddling.

ANTIGONE.   If that is what you think,
I should not want you, even if you asked to come.

You have made your choice, you can be what you want to be.
But I will bury him; and if I must die,
I say that this crime is holy: I shall lie down
With him in death, and I shall be as dear
To him as he to me.
                   It is the dead,
Not the living, who make the longest demands:
We die for ever . . .
                        You may do as you like,
Since apparently the laws of the gods mean nothing to you.

ISMENE.   They mean a great deal to me; but I have no strength
To break laws that were made for the public good.

ANTIGONE.   That must be your excuse, I suppose. But as for me,
I will bury the brother I love.

ISMENE.   Antigonê,
I am so afraid for you!

ANTIGONE.   You need not be:
You have yourself to consider, after all.

ISMENE.   But no one must hear of this, you must tell no one!
I will keep it a secret, I promise!

ANTIGONE.   Oh tell it! Tell everyone!
Think how they'll hate you when it all comes out
If they learn that you knew about it all the time!

ISMENE.   So fiery! You should be cold with fear.

ANTIGONE.   Perhaps. But I am doing only what I must.

ISMENE.   But can you do it? I say that you cannot.

ANTIGONE.   Very well: when my strength gives out, I shall do no more.

ISMENE.   Impossible things should not be tried at all.

ANTIGONE.   Go away, Ismenê:
I shall be hating you soon, and the dead will too,
For your words are hateful. Leave me my foolish plan:
I am not afraid of the danger; if it means death,
It will not be the worst of deaths—death without honor.

ISMENE.   Go then, if you feel that you must.
You are unwise,
But a loyal friend indeed to those who love you.

(Exit into the Palace. ANTIGONE goes off,

                       L. Enter the CHORUS.)

PARODOS

CHORUS.

                                   [STROPHE 1]

Now the long blade of the sun, lying
Level east to west, touches with glory

Thebes of the Seven Gates. Open, unlidded
Eye of golden day! O marching light
Across the eddy and rush of Dircê's stream,
Striking the white shields of the enemy
Thrown headlong backward from the blaze of morning!
CHORAGOS.   Polyneicês their commander
Roused them with windy phrases,
He the wild eagle screaming
Insults above our land,
His wings their shields of snow,
His crest their marshalled helms.
CHORUS.

[ANTISTROPHE 1]

Against our seven gates in a yawning ring
The famished spears came onward in the night;
But before his jaws were sated with our blood,
Or pinefire took the garland of our towers,
He was thrown back; and as he turned, great Thebes—
No tender victim for his noisy power—
Rose like a-dragon behind him, shouting war.
CHORAGOS.   For God hates utterly
The bray of bragging tongues;
And when he beheld their smiling,
Their swagger of golden helms,
The frown of his thunder blasted
Their first man from our walls.
CHORUS.

[STROPHE 2]

We heard his shout of triumph high in the air
Turn to a scream; far out in a flaming arc
He fell with his windy torch, and the earth struck him.
And others storming in fury no less than his
Found shock of death in the dusty joy of battle.
CHORAGOS.   Seven captains at seven gates
Yielded their clanging arms to the god
That bends the battle-line and breaks it.
These two only, brothers in blood,
Face to face in matchless rage,
Mirroring each the other's death,
Clashed in long combat.
CHORUS.

[ANTISTROPHE 2]

But now in the beautiful morning of victory
Let Thebes of the many chariots sing for joy!

With hearts for dancing we'll take leave of war:
Our temples shall be sweet with hymns of praise,
And the long night shall echo with our chorus.

SCENE I

CHORAGOS.   But now at last our new King is coming:
Creon of Thebes, Menoikeus' son.
In this auspicious dawn of his reign
What are the new complexities
That shifting Fate has woven for him?
What is his counsel? Why has he summoned
The old men to hear him?

(Enter CREON *from the Palace, center. He*
addresses the CHORUS *from the top step.)*

CREON.   Gentlemen: I have the honor to inform you that our Ship of State, which recent storms have threatened to destroy, has come safely to harbor at last, guided by the merciful wisdom of Heaven. I have summoned you here this morning because I know that I can depend upon you: your devotion to King Laïos was absolute; you never hesitated in your duty to our late ruler Oedipus; and when Oedipus died, your loyalty was transferred to his children. Unfortunately, as you know, his two sons, the princes Eteoclês and Polyneicês, have killed each other in battle; and I, as the next in blood, have succeeded to the full power of the throne.

I am aware, of course, that no Ruler can expect complete loyalty from his subjects until he has been tested in office. Nevertheless, I say to you at the very outset that I have nothing but contempt for the kind of Governor who is afraid, for whatever reason, to follow the course that he knows is best for the State; and as for the man who sets private friendship above the public welfare,—I have no use for him, either.

I call God to witness that if I saw my country headed for ruin, I should not be afraid to speak out plainly; and I need hardly remind you that I would never have any dealings with an enemy of the people. No one values friendship more highly than I; but we must remember that friends made at the risk of wrecking our Ship are not real friends at all.

These are my principles, at any rate, and that is why I have made the following decision concerning the sons of Oedipus: Eteoclês, who died as a man should die, fighting for his country, is to be buried with full military honors, with all the ceremony that is usual when the greatest heroes die; but his brother Polyneicês, who broke his exile to come back with fire and sword against his native city and the shrines of his fathers' gods, whose one idea was to spill the blood of his blood and sell his own people into slavery—Polyneicês, I say, is to have no burial: no man is to touch him or say the least prayer for him; he shall lie on the plain, unburied; and the birds and the scavenging dogs can do with him whatever they like.

This is my command, and you can see the wisdom behind it. As long as I am
King, no traitor is going to be honored with the loyal man. But whoever shows
by word and deed that he is on the side of the State,—he shall have my respect
while he is living, and my reverence when he is dead.

CHORAGOS.   If that is your will, Creon son of Menoikeus,
You have the right to enforce it: we are yours.

CREON.   That is my will. Take care that you do your part.

CHORAGOS.   We are old men: let the younger ones carry it out.

CREON.   I do not mean that: the sentries have been appointed.

CHORAGOS.   Then what is it that you would have us do?

CREON.   You will give no support to whoever breaks this law.

CHORAGOS.   Only a crazy man is in love with death!

CREON.   And death it is; yet money talks, and the wisest
Have sometimes been known to count a few coins too many.

(Enter SENTRY *from left.)*

SENTRY.   I'll not say that I'm out of breath from running, King, because every
time I stopped to think about what I have to tell you, I felt like going back. And
all the time a voice kept saying, "You fool, don't you know you're walking
straight into trouble?"; and then another voice: "Yes, but if you let somebody
else get the news to Creon first, it will be even worse than that for you!" But good
sense won out, at least I hope it was good sense, and here I am with a story that
makes no sense at all; but I'll tell it anyhow, because, as they say, what's going
to happen's going to happen, and—

CREON.   Come to the point. What have you to say?

SENTRY.   I did not do it. I did not see who did it. You must not punish me for
what someone else has done.

CREON.   A comprehensive defense! More effective, perhaps,
If I knew its purpose. Come: what is it?

SENTRY.   A dreadful thing . . . I don't know how to put it—

CREON.   Out with it!

SENTRY.   Well, then;
The dead man—
          Polyneicês—

(Pause. The SENTRY *is overcome, fumbles*
     for words. CREON *waits impassively.)*

                              out there—
                                        someone,—
New dust on the slimy flesh!

(Pause. No sign from CREON.*)*

Someone has given it burial that way, and
     Gone . . .

(Long pause. CREON *finally speaks with*
     deadly control.)

CREON.   And the man who dared do this?
SENTRY.   I swear I
Do not know! You must believe me!
                                  Listen:
The ground was dry, not a sign of digging, no,
Not a wheeltrack in the dust, no trace of anyone.
It was when they relieved us this morning: and one of them,
The corporal, pointed to it.
                            There it was,
The strangest—
            Look:
The body, just mounded over with light dust: you see?
Not buried really, but as if they'd covered it
Just enough for the ghost's peace. And no sign
Of dogs or any wild animal that had been there.

And then what a scene there was! Every man of us
Accusing the other: we all proved the other man did it,
We all had proof that we could not have done it.
We were ready to take hot iron in our hands,
Walk through fire, swear by all the gods,
It was not I!
I do not know who it was, but it was not I!

                (CREON's rage has been mounting steadily,
                but the SENTRY *is too intent upon his story*
                                        to notice it.)

And then, when this came to nothing, someone said
A thing that silenced us and made us stare
Down at the ground: you had to be told the news,
And one of us had to do it! We threw the dice,
And the bad luck fell to me. So here I am,
No happier to be here than you are to have me:
Nobody likes the man who brings bad news.
CHORAGOS.   I have been wondering, King: can it be that the gods have done
    this?
CREON   *(furiously)*. Stop!
Must you doddering wrecks
Go out of your heads entirely? "The gods!"
Intolerable!
The gods favor this corpse? Why? How had he served them?
Tried to loot their temples, burn their images,
Yes, and the whole State, and its laws with it!
Is it your senile opinion that the gods love to honor bad men?
A pious thought!—
                    No, from the very beginning
There have been those who have whispered together,
Stiff-necked anarchists, putting their heads together,

Scheming against me in alleys. These are the men,
And they have bribed my own guard to do this thing.

Money!

(Sententiously)

There's nothing in the world so demoralizing as money.
Down go your cities,
Homes gone, men gone, honest hearts corrupted,
Crookedness of all kinds, and all for money!

(To SENTRY*)* But you—!

I swear by God and by the throne of God,
The man who has done this thing shall pay for it!
Find that man, bring him here to me, or your death
Will be the least of your problems: I'll string you up
Alive, and there will be certain ways to make you
Discover your employer before you die;
And the process may teach you a lesson you seem to have missed:
The dearest profit is sometimes all too dear:
That depends on the source. Do you understand me?
A fortune won is often misfortune.

SENTRY.   King, may I speak?
CREON.   Your very voice distresses me.
SENTRY.   Are you sure that it is my voice, and not your conscience?
CREON.   By God, he wants to analyze me now!
SENTRY.   It is not what I say, but what has been done, that hurts you.
CREON.   You talk too much.
SENTRY.   Maybe; but I've done nothing.
CREON.   Sold your soul for some silver: that's all you've done.
SENTRY.   How dreadful it is when the right judge judges wrong!
CREON.   Your figures of speech
May entertain you now; but unless you bring me the man,
You will get little profit from them in the end.

(Exit CREON *into the Palace.)*

SENTRY.   "Bring me the man"—!
I'd like nothing better than bringing him the man!
But bring him or not, you have seen the last of me here.
At any rate, I am safe!   *(Exit* SENTRY.*)*

ODE I

CHORUS.

[STROPHE 1]

Numberless are the world's wonders, but none
More wonderful than man; the stormgray sea
Yields to his prows, the huge crests bear him high;

Earth, holy and inexhaustible, is graven
With shining furrows where his plows have gone
Year after year, the timeless labor of stallions.

[ANTISTROPHE 1]

The lightboned birds and beasts that cling to cover,
The lithe fish lighting their reaches of dim water,
All are taken, tamed in the net of his mind;
The lion on the hill, the wild horse windy-maned,
Resign to him; and his blunt yoke has broken
The sultry shoulders of the mountain bull.

[STROPHE 2]

Words also, and thought as rapid as air,
He fashions to his good use; statecraft is his,
And his the skill that deflects the arrows of snow,
The spears of winter rain: from every wind
He has made himself secure—from all but one:
In the late wind of death he cannot stand.

[ANTISTROPHE 2]

O clear intelligence, force beyond all measure!
O fate of man, working both good and evil!
When the laws are kept, how proudly his city stands!
When the laws are broken, what of his city then?
Never may the anárchic man find rest at my hearth,
Never be it said that my thoughts are his thoughts.

SCENE II

(Re-enter SENTRY *leading* ANTIGONE.*)*

CHORAGOS.   What does this mean? Surely this captive woman
    Is the Princess, Antigonê. Why should she be taken?
SENTRY.   Here is the one who did it! We caught her
    In the very act of burying him.—Where is Creon?
CHORAGOS.   Just coming from the house.

(Enter CREON, *center.)*

CREON.   What has happened?
    Why have you come back so soon?
SENTRY   *(expansively).*   O King,
    A man should never be too sure of anything:
    I would have sworn
    That you'd not see me here again: your anger

Frightened me so, and the things you threatened me with;
But how could I tell then
That I'd be able to solve the case so soon?

No dice-throwing this time: I was only too glad to come!

Here is this woman. She is the guilty one:
We found her trying to bury him.
Take her, then; question her; judge her as you will.
I am through with the whole thing now, and glad of it.

CREON.   But this is Antigonê! Why have you brought her here?

SENTRY.   She was burying him, I tell you!

CREON   *(severely).* Is this the truth?

SENTRY.   I saw her with my own eyes. Can I say more?

CREON.   The details: come, tell me quickly!

SENTRY.   It was like this:
After those terrible threats of yours, King,
We went back and brushed the dust away from the body.
The flesh was soft by now, and stinking,
So we sat on a hill to windward and kept guard.
No napping this time! We kept each other awake.
But nothing happened until the white round sun
Whirled in the center of the round sky over us:
Then, suddenly,
A storm of dust roared up from the earth, and the sky
Went out, the plain vanished with all its trees
In the stinging dark. We closed our eyes and endured it.
The whirlwind lasted a long time, but it passed;
And then we looked, and there was Antigonê!
I have seen
A mother bird come back to a stripped nest, heard
Her crying bitterly a broken note or two
For the young ones stolen. Just so, when this girl
Found the bare corpse, and all her love's work wasted,
She wept, and cried on heaven to damn the hands
That had done this thing.
                              And then she brought more dust
And sprinkled wine three times for her brother's ghost.
We ran and took her at once. She was not afraid,
Not even when we charged her with what she had done.
She denied nothing.
                        And this was a comfort to me,
And some uneasiness: for it is a good thing
To escape from death, but it is no great pleasure
To bring death to a friend.
                              Yet I always say
There is nothing so comfortable as your own safe skin!

CREON   *(slowly, dangerously).* And you, Antigonê,
    You with your head hanging,—do you confess this thing?
ANTIGONE.   I do. I deny nothing.
CREON   *(to* SENTRY*).* You may go.

                                                (Exit SENTRY.*)*

(To ANTIGONE*)* Tell me, tell me briefly:
    Had you heard my proclamation touching this matter?
ANTIGONE.   It was public. Could I help hearing it?
CREON.   And yet you dared defy the law.
ANTIGONE.   I dared.

    It was not God's proclamation. That final Justice
    That rules the world below makes no such laws.

    Your edict, King, was strong,
    But all your strength is weakness itself against
    The immortal unrecorded laws of God.
    They are not merely now: they were, and shall be,
    Operative for ever, beyond man utterly.

    I knew I must die, even without your decree:
    I am only mortal. And if I must die
    Now, before it is my time to die,
    Surely this is no hardship: can anyone
    Living, as I live, with evil all about me,
    Think Death less than a friend? This death of mine
    Is of no importance; but if I had left my brother
    Lying in death unburied, I should have suffered.
    Now I do not.
                        You smile at me. Ah Creon,
    Think me a fool, if you like; but it may well be
    That a fool convicts me of folly.
CHORAGOS.   Like father, like daughter: both headstrong, deaf to reason!
    She has never learned to yield.
CREON.   She has much to learn.
    The inflexible heart breaks first, the toughest iron
    Cracks first, and the wildest horses bend their necks
    At the pull of the smallest curb.
                                    Pride? In a slave?
    This girl is guilty of a double insolence,
    Breaking the given laws and boasting of it.
    Who is the man here,
    She or I, if this crime goes unpunished?
    Sister's child, or more than sister's child,
    Or closer yet in blood—she and her sister
    Win bitter death for this!

(To servants) Go, some of you,
Arrest Ismenê. I accuse her equally.
Bring her: you will find her sniffling in the house there.

Her mind's a traitor: crimes kept in the dark
Cry for light, and the guardian brain shudders;
But how much worse than this
Is brazen boasting of barefaced anarchy!

ANTIGONE.   Creon, what more do you want than my death?
CREON.   Nothing.
That gives me everything.
ANTIGONE.   Then I beg you: kill me.
This talking is a great weariness: your words
Are distasteful to me, and I am sure that mine
Seem so to you. And yet they should not seem so:
I should have praise and honor for what I have done.
All these men here would praise me
Were their lips not frozen shut with fear of you.
(Bitterly) Ah the good fortune of kings,
Licensed to say and do whatever they please!
CREON.   You are alone here in that opinion.
ANTIGONE.   No, they are with me. But they keep their tongues in leash.
CREON.   Maybe. But you are guilty, and they are not.
ANTIGONE.   There is no guilt in reverence for the dead.
CREON.   But Eteoclês—was he not your brother too?
ANTIGONE.   My brother too.
CREON.   And you insult his memory?
ANTIGONE   *(softly).* The dead man would not say that I insult it.
CREON.   He would: for you honor a traitor as much as him.
ANTIGONE.   His own brother, traitor or not, and equal in blood.
CREON.   He made war on his country. Eteoclês defended it.
ANTIGONE.   Nevertheless, there are honors due all the dead.
CREON.   But not the same for the wicked as for the just.
ANTIGONE.   Ah Creon, Creon,
Which of us can say what the gods hold wicked?
CREON.   An enemy is an enemy, even dead.
ANTIGONE.   It is my nature to join in love, not hate.
CREON   *(finally losing patience).* Go join them, then; if you must have your love,
Find it in hell!
CHORAGOS.   But see, Ismenê comes:

(Enter ISMENE, *guarded.)*

Those tears are sisterly, the cloud
That shadows her eyes rains down gentle sorrow.
CREON.   You too, Ismenê,
Snake in my ordered house, sucking my blood
Stealthily—and all the time I never knew

That these two sisters were aiming at my throne!

                                        Ismenê,

Do you confess your share in this crime, or deny it?

Answer me.

ISMENE.   Yes, if she will let me say so. I am guilty.

ANTIGONE   *(coldly)*. No, Ismenê. You have no right to say so.

You would not help me, and I will not have you help me.

ISMENE.   But now I know what you meant; and I am here

To join you, to take my share of punishment.

ANTIGONE.   The dead man and the gods who rule the dead

Know whose act this was. Words are not friends.

ISMENE.   Do you refuse me, Antigonê? I want to die with you:

I too have a duty that I must discharge to the dead.

ANTIGONE.   You shall not lessen my death by sharing it.

ISMENE.   What do I care for life when you are dead?

ANTIGONE.   Ask Creon. You're always hanging on his opinions.

ISMENE.   You are laughing at me. Why, Antigonê?

ANTIGONE.   It's a joyless laughter, Ismenê.

ISMENE.   But can I do nothing?

ANTIGONE.   Yes. Save yourself. I shall not envy you.

There are those who will praise you; I shall have honor, too.

ISMENE.   But we are equally guilty!

ANTIGONE.   No more, Ismenê.

You are alive, but I belong to Death.

CREON   *(to the* CHORUS*)*. Gentlemen, I beg you to observe these girls:

One has just now lost her mind; the other,

It seems, has never had a mind at all.

ISMENE.   Grief teaches the steadiest minds to waver, King.

CREON.   Yours certainly did, when you assumed guilt with the guilty!

ISMENE.   But how could I go on living without her?

CREON.   You are.

She is already dead.

ISMENE.   But your own son's bride!

CREON.   There are places enough for him to push his plow.

I want no wicked women for my sons!

ISMENE.   O dearest Haimon, how your father wrongs you!

CREON.   I've had enough of your childish talk of marriage!

CHORAGOS.   Do you really intend to steal this girl from your son?

CREON.   No; Death will do that for me.

CHORAGOS.   Then she must die?

CREON   *(ironically)*. You dazzle me.

                    —But enough of this talk!

(To GUARDS*)* You, there, take them away and guard them well:

For they are but women, and even brave men run

When they see Death coming.

               (Exeunt ISMENE, ANTIGONE, *and* GUARDS.*)*

ODE II

CHORUS.

Fortunate is the man who has never tasted God's vengeance!
Where once the anger of heaven has struck, that house is shaken
For ever: damnation rises behind each child
Like a wave cresting out of the black northeast,
When the long darkness under sea roars up
And bursts drumming death upon the windwhipped sand.

I have seen this gathering sorrow from time long past
Loom upon Oedipus' children: generation from generation
Takes the compulsive rage of the enemy god.
So lately this last flower of Oedipus' line
Drank the sunlight! but now a passionate word
And a handful of dust have closed up all its beauty.

What mortal arrogance
Transcends the wrath of Zeus?
Sleep cannot lull him, nor the effortless long months
Of the timeless gods: but he is young for ever,
And his house is the shining day of high Olympos.
All that is and shall be,
And all the past, is his.
No pride on earth is free of the curse of heaven.

The straying dreams of men
May bring them ghosts of joy:
But as they drowse, the waking embers burn them;
Or they walk with fixed éyes, as blind men walk.
But the ancient wisdom speaks for our own time:
Fate works most for woe
With Folly's fairest show.
Man's little pleasure is the spring of sorrow.

SCENE III

CHORAGOS.   But here is Haimon, King, the last of all your sons.
Is it grief for Antigonê that brings him here,
And bitterness at being robbed of his bride?

(Enter HAIMON.*)*

CREON.   We shall soon see, and no need of diviners.

                                          —Son,

    You have heard my final judgment on that girl:
    Have you come here hating me, or have you come
    With deference and with love, whatever I do?

HAIMON.   I am your son, father. You are my guide.
    You make things clear for me, and I obey you.
    No marriage means more to me than your continuing wisdom.

CREON.   Good. That is the way to behave: subordinate
    Everything else, my son, to your father's will.
    This is what a man prays for, that he may get
    Sons attentive and dutiful in his house,
    Each one hating his father's enemies,
    Honoring his father's friends. But if his sons
    Fail him, if they turn out unprofitably,
    What has he fathered but trouble for himself
    And amusement for the malicious?

                            So you are right
    Not to lose your head over this woman.
    Your pleasure with her would soon grow cold, Haimon,
    And then you'd have a hellcat in bed and elsewhere.
    Let her find her husband in Hell!
    Of all the people in this city, only she
    Has had contempt for my law and broken it.

    Do you want me to show myself weak before the people?
    Or to break my sworn word? No, and I will not.
    The woman dies.

    I suppose she'll plead "family ties." Well, let her.
    If I permit my own family to rebel,
    How shall I earn the world's obedience?
    Show me the man who keeps his house in hand,
    He's fit for public authority.

                    I'll have no dealings
    With law-breakers, critics of the government:
    Whoever is chosen to govern should be obeyed—
    Must be obeyed, in all things, great and small,
    Just and unjust! O Haimon,
    The man who knows how to obey, and that man only,
    Knows how to give commands when the time comes.
    You can depend on him, no matter how fast
    The spears come: he's a good soldier, he'll stick it out.

    Anarchy, anarchy! Show me a greater evil!
    This is why cities tumble and the great houses rain down,
    This is what scatters armies!

No, no: good lives are made so by discipline.
We keep the laws then, and the lawmakers,
And no woman shall seduce us. If we must lose,
Let's lose to a man, at least! Is a woman stronger than we?

CHORAGOS.   Unless time has rusted my wits,
What you say, King, is said with point and dignity.

HAIMON   *(boyishly earnest).* Father:
Reason is God's crowning gift to man, and you are right
To warn me against losing mine. I cannot say—
I hope that I shall never want to say!—that you
Have reasoned badly. Yet there are other men
Who can reason, too; and their opinions might be helpful.
You are not in a position to know everything
That people say or do, or what they feel:
Your temper terrifies them—everyone
Will tell you only what you like to hear.
But I, at any rate, can listen; and I have heard them
Muttering and whispering in the dark about this girl.
They say no woman has ever, so unreasonably,
Died so shameful a death for a generous act:
"She covered her brother's body. Is this indecent?
She kept him from dogs and vultures. Is this a crime?
Death?—She should have all the honor that we can give her!"

This is the way they talk out there in the city.

You must believe me:
Nothing is closer to me than your happiness.
What could be closer? Must not any son
Value his father's fortune as his father does his?
I beg you, do not be unchangeable:
Do not believe that you alone can be right.
The man who thinks that,
The man who maintains that only he has the power
To reason correctly, the gift to speak, the soul—
A man like that, when you know him, turns out empty.

It is not reason never to yield to reason!

In flood time you can see how some trees bend,
And because they bend, even their twigs are safe,
While stubborn trees are torn up, roots and all.
And the same thing happens in sailing:
Make your sheet fast, never slacken,—and over you go,
Head over heels and under: and there's your voyage.

Forget you are angry! Let yourself be moved!
I know I am young; but please let me say this:
The ideal condition
Would be, I admit, that men should be right by instinct;
But since we are all too likely to go astray,
The reasonable thing is to learn from those who can teach.

CHORAGOS.   You will do well to listen to him, King,
If what he says is sensible. And you, Haimon,
Must listen to your father.—Both speak well.

CREON.   You consider it right for a man of my years and experience
To go to school to a boy?

HAIMON.   It is not right
If I am wrong. But if I am young, and right,
What does my age matter?

CREON.   You think it right to stand up for an anarchist?

HAIMON.   Not at all. I pay no respect to criminals.

CREON.   Then she is not a criminal?

HAIMON.   The City would deny it, to a man.

CREON.   And the City proposes to teach me how to rule?

HAIMON.   Ah. Who is it that's talking like a boy now?

CREON.   My voice is the one voice giving orders in this City!

HAIMON.   It is no City if it takes orders from one voice.

CREON.   The State is the King!

HAIMON.   Yes, if the State is a desert.

(Pause.)

CREON.   This boy, it seems, has sold out to a woman.

HAIMON.   If you are a woman: my concern is only for you.

CREON.   So? Your "concern"! In a public brawl with your father!

HAIMON.   How about you, in a public brawl with justice?

CREON.   With justice, when all that I do is within my rights?

HAIMON.   You have no right to trample on God's right.

CREON   *(completely out of control)*. Fool, adolescent fool! Taken in by a woman!

HAIMON.   You'll never see me taken in by anything vile.

CREON.   Every word you say is for her!

HAIMON   *(quietly, darkly)*.   And for you.
And for me. And for the gods under the earth.

CREON.   You'll never marry her while she lives.

HAIMON.   Then she must die.—But her death will cause another.

CREON.   Another?
Have you lost your senses? Is this an open threat?

HAIMON.   There is no threat in speaking to emptiness.

CREON.   I swear you'll regret this superior tone of yours!
You are the empty one!

HAIMON.   If you were not my father,
I'd say you were perverse.

CREON.   You girlstruck fool, don't play at words with me!

HAIMON.   I am sorry. You prefer silence.
CREON.   Now, by God—!

I swear, by all the gods in heaven above us,
You'll watch it, I swear you shall!
                    (To the SERVANTS) Bring her out!
Bring the woman out! Let her die before his eyes!
Here, this instant, with her bridegroom beside her!
HAIMON.   Not here, no; she will not die here, King.
And you will never see my face again.
Go on raving as long as you've a friend to endure you.

(Exit HAIMON.*)*

CHORAGOS.   Gone, gone.
Creon, a young man in a rage is dangerous!
CREON.   Let him do, or dream to do, more than a man can.
He shall not save these girls from death.
CHORAGOS.   These girls?

You have sentenced them both?
CREON.   No, you are right.
I will not kill the one whose hands are clean.
CHORAGOS.   But Antigonê?
CREON   *(somberly).* I will carry her far away
Out there in the wilderness, and lock her
Living in a vault of stone. She shall have food,
As the custom is, to absolve the State of her death.
And there let her pray to the gods of hell:
They are her only gods:
Perhaps they will show her an escape from death,
Or she may learn,
                    though late,
That piety shown the dead is pity in vain.

(Exit CREON.*)*

ODE III

CHORUS.   Love, unconquerable   [STROPHE]
Waster of rich men, keeper
Of warm lights and all-night vigil
In the soft face of a girl:
Sea-wanderer, forest-visitor!
Even the pure Immortals cannot escape you,
And mortal man, in his one day's dusk,
Trembles before your glory.

Surely you swerve upon ruin   [ANTISTROPHE]
The just man's consenting heart,
As here you have made bright anger
Strike between father and son—
And none has conquered but Love!
A girl's glánce wórking the will of heaven:
Pleasure to her alone who mocks us,
Merciless Aphroditê.

SCENE IV

CHORAGOS.

(As ANTIGONE *enters guarded.)*

But I can no longer stand in awe of this,
Nor, seeing what I see, keep back my tears.
Here is Antigonê, passing to that chamber
Where all find sleep at last.

ANTIGONE.   Look upon me, friends, and pity me   [STROPHE 1]
Turning back at the night's edge to say
Good-by to the sun that shines for me no longer;
Now sleepy Death
Summons me down to Acheron, that cold shore:
There is no bridesong there, nor any music.

CHORUS.   Yet not unpraised, not without a kind of honor,
You walk at last into the underworld;
Untouched by sickness, broken by no sword.
What woman has ever found your way to death?

ANTIGONE.   [ANTISTROPHE 1]

How often I have heard the story of Niobê,
Tantalos' wretched daughter, how the stone
Clung fast about her, ivy-close: and they say
The rain falls endlessly
And sifting soft snow; her tears are never done.
I feel the loneliness of her death in mine.

CHORUS.   But she was born of heaven, and you
Are woman, woman-born. If her death is yours,
A mortal woman's, is this not for you
Glory in our world and in the world beyond?

ANTIGONE.   You laugh at me. Ah, friends, friends,   [STROPHE 2]
Can you not wait until I am dead? O Thebes,
O men many-charioted, in love with Fortune,
Dear springs of Dircê, sacred Theban grove,
Be witnesses for me, denied all pity,
Unjustly judged! and think a word of love

For her whose path turns
Under dark earth, where there are no more tears.

CHORUS. You have passed beyond human daring and come at last
Into a place of stone where Justice sits.
I cannot tell
What shape of your father's guilt appears in this.

ANTIGONE. [ANTISTROPHE 2]

You have touched it at last: that bridal bed
Unspeakable, horror of son and mother mingling:
Their crime, infection of all our family!
O Oedipus, father and brother!
Your marriage strikes from the grave to murder mine.
I have been a stranger here in my own land:
All my life
The blasphemy of my birth has followed me.

CHORUS. Reverence is a virtue, but strength
Lives in established law: that must prevail.
You have made your choice,
Your death is the doing of your conscious hand.

ANTIGONE. [EPODE]

Then let me go, since all your words are bitter,
And the very light of the sun is cold to me.
Lead me to my vigil, where I must have
Neither love nor lamentation; no song, but silence.

(CREON *interrupts impatiently.*)

CREON. If dirges and planned lamentations could put off death,
Men would be singing for ever.
(To the SERVANTS)
Take her, go!
You know your orders: take her to the vault
And leave her alone there. And if she lives or dies,
That's her affair, not ours: our hands are clean.

ANTIGONE. O tomb, vaulted bride-bed in eternal rock,
Soon I shall be with my own again
Where Persephonê welcomes the thin ghosts underground:
And I shall see my father again, and you, mother,
And dearest Polyneicês—
dearest indeed
To me, since it was my hand
That washed him clean and poured the ritual wine:
And my reward is death before my time!

And yet, as men's hearts know, I have done no wrong,
I have not sinned before God. Or if I have,
I shall know the truth in death. But if the guilt

Lies upon Creon who judged me, then, I pray,
May his punishment equal my own.

CHORAGOS.   O passionate heart,
Unyielding, tormented still by the same winds!

CREON.   Her guards shall have good cause to regret their delaying.

ANTIGONE.   Ah! That voice is like the voice of death!

CREON.   I can give you no reason to think you are mistaken.

ANTIGONE.   Thebes, and you my fathers' gods,
And rulers of Thebes, you see me now, the last
Unhappy daughter of a line of kings,
Your kings, led away to death. You will remember
What things I suffer, and at what men's hands,
Because I would not transgress the laws of heaven.

(To the GUARDS, *simply)*

Come: let us wait no longer.

(Exit ANTIGONE, *left, guarded.)*

ODE IV

CHORUS.

[STROPHE 1]

All Danaê's beauty was locked away
In a brazen cell where the sunlight could not come:
A small room, still as any grave, enclosed her.
Yet she was a princess too,
And Zeus in a rain of gold poured love upon her.
O child, child,
No power in wealth or war
Or tough sea-blackened ships
Can prevail against untiring Destiny!

[ANTISTROPHE 1]

And Dryas' son also, that furious king,
Bore the god's prisoning anger for his pride:
Sealed up by Dionysos in deaf stone,
His madness died among echoes.
So at the last he learned what dreadful power
His tongue had mocked:
For he had profaned the revels,
And fired the wrath of the nine
Implacable Sisters that love the sound of the flute.

[STROPHE 2]

And old men tell a half-remembered tale
Of horror done where a dark ledge splits the sea
And a double surf beats on the gráy shóres:

How a king's new woman, sick
With hatred for the queen he had imprisoned,
Ripped out his two sons' eyes with her bloody hands
While grinning Arês watched the shuttle plunge
Four times: four blind wounds crying for revenge,

                                                          [ANTISTROPHE 2]

Crying, tears and blood mingled.—Piteously born,
Those sons whose mother was of heavenly birth!
Her father was the god of the North Wind
And she was cradled by gales,
She raced with young colts on the glittering hills
And walked untrammeled in the open light:
But in her marriage deathless Fate found means
To build a tomb like yours for all her joy.

SCENE V

> (Enter blind TEIRESIAS, led by a boy. The
> opening speeches of TEIRESIAS should be
> in singsong contrast to the realistic lines of
> CREON.)

TEIRESIAS.   This is the way the blind man comes, Princes, Princes,
    Lock-step, two heads lit by the eyes of one.
CREON.   What new thing have you to tell us, old Teiresias?
TEIRESIAS.   I have much to tell you: listen to the prophet, Creon.
CREON.   I am not aware that I have ever failed to listen.
TEIRESIAS.   Then you have done wisely, King, and ruled well.
CREON.   I admit my debt to you. But what have you to say?
TEIRESIAS.   This, Creon: you stand once more on the edge of fate.
CREON.   What do you mean? Your words are a kind of dread.
TEIRESIAS.   Listen, Creon:
    I was sitting in my chair of augury, at the place
    Where the birds gather about me. They were all a-chatter.
    As is their habit, when suddenly I heard
    A strange note in their jangling, a scream, a
    Whirring fury; I knew that they were fighting,
    Tearing each other, dying
    In a whirlwind of wings clashing. And I was afraid.
    I began the rites of burnt-offering at the altar,
    But Hephaistos failed me: instead of bright flame,
    There was only the sputtering slime of the fat thigh-flesh
    Melting: the entrails dissolved in gray smoke,
    The bare bone burst from the welter. And no blaze!

    This was a sign from heaven. My boy described it,
    Seeing for me as I see for others.

I tell you, Creon, you yourself have brought
This new calamity upon us. Our hearths and altars
Are stained with the corruption of dogs and carrion birds
That glut themselves on the corpse of Oedipus' son.
The gods are deaf when we pray to them, their fire
Recoils from our offering, their birds of omen
Have no cry of comfort, for they are gorged
With the thick blood of the dead.

        O my son,
These are no trifles! Think: all men make mistakes,
But a good man yields when he knows his course is wrong,
And repairs the evil. The only crime is pride.

Give in to the dead man, then: do not fight with a corpse—
What glory is it to kill a man who is dead?
Think, I beg you:
It is for your own good that I speak as I do.
You should be able to yield for your own good.

CREON.   It seems that prophets have made me their especial province.
All my life long
I have been a kind of butt for the dull arrows
Of doddering fortune-tellers!

       No, Teiresias:
If your birds—if the great eagles of God himself
Should carry him stinking bit by bit to heaven,
I would not yield. I am not afraid of pollution:
No man can defile the gods.

       Do what you will,
Go into business, make money, speculate
In India gold or that synthetic gold from Sardis,
Get rich otherwise than by my consent to bury him.
Teiresias, it is a sorry thing when a wise man
Sells his wisdom, lets out his words for hire!

TEIRESIAS.   Ah Creon! Is there no man left in the world—

CREON.   To do what?—Come, let's have the aphorism!

TEIRESIAS.   No man who knows that wisdom outweighs any wealth?

CREON.   As surely as bribes are baser than any baseness.

TEIRESIAS.   You are sick, Creon! You are deathly sick!

CREON.   As you say: it is not my place to challenge a prophet.

TEIRESIAS.   Yet you have said my prophecy is for sale.

CREON.   The generation of prophets has always loved gold.

TEIRESIAS.   The generation of kings has always loved brass.

CREON.   You forget yourself! You are speaking to your King.

TEIRESIAS.   I know it. You are a king because of me.

CREON.   You have a certain skill; but you have sold out.

TEIRESIAS.   King, you will drive me to words that—

CREON,   Say them, say them!
Only remember: I will not pay you for them.

TEIRESIAS.   No, you will find them too costly.
CREON.   No doubt. Speak:
    Whatever you say, you will not change my will.
TEIRESIAS.   Then take this, and take it to heart!
    The time is not far off when you shall pay back
    Corpse for corpse, flesh of your own flesh.
    You have thrust the child of this world into living night,
    You have kept from the gods below the child that is theirs:
    The one in a grave before her death, the other,
    Dead, denied the grave. This is your crime:
    And the Furies and the dark gods of Hell
    Are swift with terrible punishment for you.

    Do you want to buy me now, Creon?
                            Not many days,
    And your house will be full of men and women weeping,
    And curses will be hurled at you from far
    Cities grieving for sons unburied, left to rot
    Before the walls of Thebes.

    These are my arrows, Creon: they are all for you.

(To BOY*)*

    But come, child: lead me home.
    Let him waste his fine anger upon younger men.
    Maybe he will learn at last
    To control a wiser tongue in a better head.

(Exit TEIRESIAS.*)*

CHORAGOS.   The old man has gone, King, but his words
    Remain to plague us. I am old, too,
    But I cannot remember that he was ever false.
CREON.   That is true. . . . It troubles me.
    Oh it is hard to give in! but it is worse
    To risk everything for stubborn pride.
CHORAGOS.   Creon: take my advice.
CREON.   What shall I do?
CHORAGOS.   Go quickly: free Antigonê from her vault
    And build a tomb for the body of Polyneicês.
CREON.   You would have me do this?
CHORAGOS.   Creon, yes!
    And it must be done at once: God moves
    Swiftly to cancel the folly of stubborn men.
CREON.   It is hard to deny the heart! But I
    Will do it: I will not fight with destiny.
CHORAGOS.   You must go yourself, you cannot leave it to others.
CREON.   I will go.
        —Bring axes, servants:

Come with me to the tomb. I buried her, I
Will set her free.
           Oh quickly!
My mind misgives—
The laws of the gods are mighty, and a man must serve them
To the last day of his life!

           (Exit CREON.*)*

PÆAN

CHORAGOS.   God of many names   [STROPHE 1]
CHORUS.
                               O Iacchos
                                   son
of Kadmeian Sémelê
                    O born of the Thunder!
Guardian of the West
                 Regent
of Eleusis' plain
                  O Prince of maenad Thebes
and the Dragon Field by rippling Ismenos:
CHORAGOS.   God of many names   [ANTISTROPHE 1]
CHORUS.   the flame of torches
flares on our hills
               the nymphs of Iacchos
dance at the spring of Castalia:
from the vine-close mountain
                     come ah come in ivy:
Evohé evohé! sings through the streets of Thebes
CHORAGOS.   God of many names   [STROPHE 2]
CHORUS.   Iacchos of Thebes
heavenly Child
            of Sémelê bride of the Thunderer!
The shadow of plague is upon us:
                   come
with clement feet
            oh come from Parnasos
down the long slopes
               across the lamenting water
CHORAGOS.   [ANTISTROPHE 2]
Iô Fire! Chorister of the throbbing stars!
O purest among the voices of the night!
Thou son of God, blaze for us!

CHORUS.   Come with choric rapture of circling Maenads
Who cry *Iô Iacche!*
                    God of many names!

ÉXODOS

                                        (Enter MESSENGER, *left.)*

MESSENGER.   Men of the line of Kadmos, you who live
Near Amphion's citadel:
                            I cannot say
Of any condition of human life "This is fixed,
This is clearly good, or bad". Faté raises up,
And Fate casts down the happy and unhappy alike:
No man can foretell his Fate.
                            Take the case of Creon:
Creon was happy once, as I count happiness:
Victorious in battle, sole governor of the land,
Fortunate father of children nobly born.
And now it has all gone from him! Who can say
That a man is still alive when his life's joy fails?
He is a walking dead man. Grant him rich,
Let him live like a king in his great house:
If his pleasure is gone, I would not give
So much as the shadow of smoke for all he owns.
CHORAGOS.   Your words hint at sorrow: what is your news for us?
MESSENGER.   They are dead. The living are guilty of their death.
CHORAGOS.   Who is guilty? Who is dead? Speak!
MESSENGER.   Haimon.
Haimon is dead; and the hand that killed him
Is his own hand.
CHORAGOS.   His father's? or his own?
MESSENGER.   His own, driven mad by the murder his father had done.
CHORAGOS.   Teiresias, Teiresias, how clearly you saw it all!
MESSENGER.   This is my news: you must draw what conclusions you can from it.
CHORAGOS.   But look: Eurydicê, our Queen:
Has she overheard us?

                        (Enter EURYDICE *from the Palace, center.)*

EURYDICE.   I have heard something, friends:
As I was unlocking the gate of Pallas' shrine,
For I needed her help today, I heard a voice
Telling of some new sorrow. And I fainted
There at the temple with all my maidens about me.
But speak again: whatever it is, I can bear it:
Grief and I are no strangers.
MESSENGER.   Dearest Lady,

I will tell you plainly all that I have seen.
I shall not try to comfort you: what is the use,
Since comfort could lie only in what is not true?
The truth is always best.
                  I went with Creon
To the outer plain where Polyneicês was lying,
No friend to pity him, his body shredded by dogs.
We made our prayers in that place to Hecatê
And Pluto, that they would be merciful. And we bathed
The corpse with holy water, and we brought
Fresh-broken branches to burn what was left of it,
And upon the urn we heaped up a towering barrow
Of the earth of his own land.
                  When we were done, we ran
To the vault where Antigonê lay on her couch of stone.
One of the servants had gone ahead,
And while he was yet far off he heard a voice
Grieving within the chamber, and he came back
And told Creon. And as the King went closer,
The air was full of wailing, the words lost,
And he begged us to make all haste. "Am I a prophet?"
He said, weeping, "And must I walk this road,
The saddest of all that I have gone before?
My son's voice calls me on. Oh quickly, quickly!
Look through the crevice there, and tell me
If it is Haimon, or some deception of the gods!"

We obeyed; and in the cavern's farthest corner
We saw her lying:
She had made a noose of her fine linen veil
And hanged herself. Haimon lay beside her,
His arms about her waist, lamenting her,
His love lost under ground, crying out
That his father had stolen her away from him.

When Creon saw him the tears rushed to his eyes
And he called to him: "What have you done, child? Speak to me.
What are you thinking that makes your eyes so strange?
O my son, my son, I come to you on my knees!"
But Haimon spat in his face. He said not a word,
Staring—
              And suddenly drew his sword
And lunged. Creon shrank back, the blade missed; and the boy,
Desperate against himself, drove it half its length
Into his own side, and fell. And as he died
He gathered Antigonê close in his arms again,
Choking, his blood bright red on her white cheek.

And now he lies dead with the dead, and she is his
At last, his bride in the houses of the dead.

(Exit EURYDICE *into the Palace.)*

CHORAGOS.   She has left us without a word. What can this mean?
MESSENGER.   It troubles me, too; yet she knows what is best,
Her grief is too great for public lamentation,
And doubtless she has gone to her chamber to weep
For her dead son, leading her maidens in his dirge.
CHORAGOS.   It may be so: but I fear this deep silence.

(Pause.)

MESSENGER.   I will see what she is doing. I will go in.

(Exit MESSENGER *into the Palace.)*

(Enter CREON *with attendants, bearing*
HAIMON'S *body)*

CHORAGOS.   But here is the King himself: oh look at him,
Bearing his own damnation in his arms.
CREON.   Nothing you say can touch me any more.
My own blind heart has brought me
From darkness to final darkness. Here you see
The father murdering, the murdered son—
And all my civic wisdom!

Haimon my son, so young, so young to die,
I was the fool, not you; and you died for me.
CHORAGOS.   That is the truth; but you were late in learning it.
CREON.   This truth is hard to bear. Surely a god
Has crushed me beneath the hugest weight of heaven,
And driven me headlong a barbaric way
To trample out the thing I held most dear.

The pains that men will take to come to pain!

(Enter MESSENGER *from the Palace.)*

MESSENGER.   The burden you carry in your hands is heavy,
But it is not all: you will find more in your house.
CREON.   What burden worse than this shall I find there?
MESSENGER.   The Queen is dead.
CREON.   O port of death, deaf world,
Is there no pity for me? And you, Angel of evil,
I was dead, and your words are death again.
Is it true, boy? Can it be true?
Is my wife dead? Has death bred death?
MESSENGER.   You can see for yourself.

(The doors are opened, and the body of
EURYDICE *is disclosed within.)*

CREON.   Oh pity!
All true, all true, and more than I can bear!
O my wife, my son!
MESSENGER.   She stood before the altar, and her heart
Welcomed the knife her own hand guided,
And a great cry burst from her lips for Megareus dead,
And for Haimon dead, her sons; and her last breath
Was a curse for their father, the murderer of her sons.
And she fell, and the dark flowed in through her closing eyes.
CREON.   O God, I am sick with fear.
Are there no swords here? Has no one a blow for me?
MESSENGER.   Her curse is upon you for the deaths of both.
CREON.   It is right that it should be. I alone am guilty.
I know it, and I say it. Lead me in,
Quickly, friends.
I have neither life nor substance. Lead me in.
CHORAGOS.   You are right, if there can be right in so much wrong.
The briefest way is best in a world of sorrow.
CREON.   Let it come,
Let death come quickly, and be kind to me.
I would not ever see the sun again.
CHORAGOS.   All that will come when it will; but we, meanwhile,
Have much to do. Leave the future to itself.
CREON.   All my heart was in that prayer!
CHORAGOS.   Then do not pray any more: the sky is deaf.
CREON.   Lead me away. I have been rash and foolish.
I have killed my son and my wife.
I look for comfort; my comfort lies here dead.
Whatever my hands have touched has come to nothing.
Fate has brought all my pride to a thought of dust.

(As CREON *is being led into the house, the*
CHORAGOS *advances and speaks directly to*
the audience.)

CHORAGOS.   There is no happiness where there is no wisdom;
No wisdom but in submission to the gods.
Big words are always punished,
And proud men in old age learn to be wise.

Translated by Dudley Fitts and Robert Fitzgerald

THE ELEPHANT MAN

Bernard Pomerance
(b. 1940)

Biography p. 1093

1884–1890. London. One scene is in Belgium.

Characters

FREDERICK TREVES, a surgeon and teacher
CARR GOMM, administrator of the London Hospital
ROSS, Manager of the Elephant Man
JOHN MERRICK, the Elephant Man
Three PINHEADS, three women freaks whose heads are pointed
BELGIAN POLICEMAN
LONDON POLICEMAN
MAN, at a fairground in Brussels
CONDUCTOR, of Ostend-London boat train
BISHOP WALSHAM HOW
PORTER, at the London Hospital
SNORK, also a porter
MRS. KENDAL, an actress
DUCHESS
COUNTESS
PRINCESS ALEXANDRA
LORD JOHN
NURSE, MISS SANDWICH

SCENE I

HE WILL HAVE 100 GUINEA FEES BEFORE HE'S FORTY

The London Hospital, Whitechapel Rd. Enter GOMM, *enter* TREVES.

TREVES.   Mr. Carr Gomm? Frederick Treves. Your new lecturer in anatomy.
GOMM.   Age thirty-one. Books on Scrofula and Applied Surgical Anatomy—I'm
     happy to see you rising, Mr. Treves. I like to see merit credited, and your
     industry, accomplishment, and skill all do you credit. Ignore the squalor of
     Whitechapel, the general dinginess, neglect and poverty without, and you will
     find a continual medical richesse in the London Hospital. We study and treat

the widest range of diseases and disorders, and are certainly the greatest institution of our kind in the world. The Empire provides unparalleled opportunities for our studies, as places cruel to life are the most revealing scientifically. Add to our reputation by going further, and that'll satisfy. You've bought a house?

TREVES.   On Wimpole Street.

GOMM.   Good. Keep at it, Treves. You'll have an FRS and 100 guinea fees before you're forty. You'll find it is an excellent consolation prize.

TREVES.   Consolation? I don't know what you mean.

GOMM.   I know you don't. You will. *(Exits.)*

TREVES.   A happy childhood in Dorset.

A scientist in an age of science.

In an English age, an Englishman. A teacher and a doctor at the London. Two books published by my thirty-first year. A house. A wife who loves me, and my god, 100 guinea fees before I'm forty.

Consolation for what?

As of the year AD 1884, I, Freddie Treves, have excessive blessings. Or so it seems to me.

(Blackout.)

SCENE II

ART IS AS NOTHING TO NATURE

(Whitechapel Rd. A storefront. A large advertisement of a creature with an elephant's head. ROSS, *his manager.)*

ROSS.   Tuppence only, step in and see: This side of the grave, John Merrick has no hope nor expectation of relief. In every sense his situation is desperate. His physical agony is exceeded only by his mental anguish, a despised creature without consolation. Tuppence only, step in and see! To live with his physical hideousness, incapacitating deformities and unremitting pain is trial enough, but to be exposed to the cruelly lacerating expressions of horror and disgust by all who behold him—is even more difficult to bear. Tuppence only, step in and see! For in order to survive, Merrick forces himself to suffer these humiliations, I repeat, humiliations, in order to survive, thus he exposes himself to crowds who pay to gape and yawp at this freak of nature, the Elephant Man.

(Enter TREVES *who looks at advertisement.)*

ROSS.   See Mother Nature uncorseted and in malignant rage! Tuppence.

TREVES.   This sign's absurd. Half-elephant, half-man is not possible. Is he foreign?

ROSS.   Right, from Leicester. But nothing to fear.

TREVES.   I'm at the London across the road. I would be curious to see him if there is some genuine disorder. If he is a mass of papier-maché and paint however—

ROSS.   Then pay me nothing. Enter, sir. Merrick, stand up. Ya bloody donkey, up, up.

(They go in, then emerge. TREVES *pays.)*

TREVES.   I must examine him further at the hospital. Here is my card. I'm Treves.
I will have a cab pick him up and return him. My card will gain him admit-
tance.

ROSS.   Five bob he's yours for the day.

TREVES.   I wish to examine him in the interests of science, you see.

ROSS.   Sir, I'm Ross. I look out for him, get him his living. Found him in Leicester
workhouse. His own ma put him there age of three. Couldn't bear the sight,
well you can see why. We—he and I—are in business. He is our capital, see.
Go to a bank. Go anywhere. Want to borrow capital, you pay interest. Scientists even. He's good value though. You won't find another like him.

TREVES.   Fair enough. *(He pays.)*

ROSS.   Right. Out here, Merrick. Ya bloody donkey, out!

(Lights fade out.)

SCENE III

WHO HAS SEEN THE LIKE OF THIS?

*(*TREVES *lectures.* MERRICK *contorts himself to approximate projected slides of the
real Merrick.)*

TREVES.   The most striking feature about him was his enormous head. Its circumference was about that of a man's waist. From the brow there projected a huge
bony mass like a loaf, while from the back of his head hung a bag of spongy
fungous-looking skin, the surface of which was comparable to brown cauliflower. On the top of the skull were a few long lank hairs. The osseous growth
on the forehead, at this stage about the size of a tangerine, almost occluded
one eye. From the upper jaw there projected another mass of bone. It protruded from the mouth like a pink stump, turning the upper lip inside out, and
making the mouth a wide slobbering aperture. The nose was merely a lump
of flesh, only recognizable as a nose from its position. The deformities rendered
the face utterly incapable of the expression of any emotion whatsoever. The
back was horrible because from it hung, as far down as the middle of the thigh,
huge sack-like masses of flesh covered by the same loathsome cauliflower stain.
The right arm was of enormous size and shapeless. It suggested but was not
elephantiasis, and was overgrown also with pendant masses of the same cauli-
flower-like skin. The right hand was large and clumsy—a fin or paddle rather
than a hand. No distinction existed between the palm and back, the thumb was
like a radish, the fingers like thick tuberous roots. As a limb it was useless. The
other arm was remarkable by contrast. It was not only normal, but was
moreover a delicately shaped limb covered with a fine skin and provided with
a beautiful hand which any woman might have envied. From the chest hung
a bag of the same repulsive flesh. It was like a dewlap suspended from the neck
of a lizard. The lower limbs had the characters of the deformed arm. They were
unwieldy, dropsical-looking, and grossly mis-shapen. There arose from the

fungous skin growths a very sickening stench which was hard to tolerate. To add a further burden to his trouble, the wretched man when a boy developed hip disease which left him permanently lame, so that he could only walk with a stick. *(To* MERRICK*)* Please. *(*MERRICK *walks.)* He was thus denied all means of escape from his tormentors.

VOICE.   Mr. Treves, you have shown a profound and unknown disorder to us. You have said when he leaves here it is for his exhibition again. I do not think it ought to be permitted. It is a disgrace. It is a pity and a disgrace. It is an indecency in fact. It may be a danger in ways we do not know. Something ought to be done about it.

TREVES.   I am a doctor. What would you have me do?

VOICE.   Well. I know what to do. *I* know.

(Silence. A policeman enters as lights fade out.)

SCENE IV

THIS INDECENCY MAY NOT CONTINUE

(Music. A fair. PINHEADS *huddling together, holding a portrait of Leopold, King of the Congo. Enter* MAN.*)*

MAN.   Now, my pinheaded darlings, your attention please. Every freak in Brussels Fair is doing something to celebrate Leopold's fifth year as King of the Congo. Him. Our King. Our Empire. *(They begin reciting.)* No, don't recite yet, you morons. I'll say when. And when you do, get it *right.* You don't, it's back to the asylum. Know what that means, don't you? They'll cut your heads. They'll spoon out your little brains, replace 'em in the dachshund they were nicked from. *Cut you.* Yeah. Be back with customers. Come see the Queens of the Congo! *(Exits.)*

(Enter MERRICK, ROSS.*)*

MERRICK.   Cosmos? Cosmos?

ROSS.   Congo. Land of darkness. Hoho! *(Sees* PINS.*)* Look at them, lad. It's freer on the continent. Loads of indecency here, no one minds. You won't get coppers sent round to roust you out like London. Reckon in Brussels here's our fortune. You have a little tête-à-tête with this lot while I see the coppers about our license to exhibit. Be right back. *(Exits.)*

MERRICK.   I come from England.

PINS.   Allo!

MERRICK.   At home they chased us. Out of London. Police. Someone complained. They beat me. You have no trouble? No?

PINS.   Allo! Allo!

MERRICK.   Hello. In Belgium we make money. I look forward to it. Happiness, I mean. You pay your police? How is it done?

PINS.   Allo! Allo!

MERRICK.   We do a show together sometime? Yes? I have saved forty-eight pounds. Two shillings. Nine pence. English money. Ross takes care of it.

PINS.   Allo! Allo!

MERRICK.   Little vocabulary problem, eh? Poor things. Looks like they put your noses to the grindstone and forgot to take them away.

(MAN enters.)

MAN.   They're coming.

(People enter to see the girls' act.)

Now.

PINS *(dancing and singing).*

> We are the Queens of the Congo,
> The Beautiful Belgian Empire
> Our niggers are bigger
> Our miners are finer
> Empire, Empire, Congo and power
> Civilizuzu's finest hour
> Admire, perspire, desire, acquire
> Or we'll set you on fire!

MAN.   You cretins! Sorry, they're not ready yet. Out please.

(People exit.)

Get those words right, girls! Or you know what.

(MAN exits. PINS weep.)

MERRICK.   Don't cry. You sang nicely. Don't cry. There there.

(Enter ROSS in grip of two POLICEMEN.)

ROSS.   I was promised a permit. I lined a tour up on that!

POLICEMEN.   This is a brutal, indecent, and immoral display. It is a public indecency, and it is forbidden here.

ROSS.   What about them with their perfect cone heads?

POLICEMEN.   They are ours.

ROSS.   Competition's good for business. Where's your spirit of competition?

POLICEMEN.   Right here. *(Smacks MERRICK.)*

ROSS.   Don't do that, you'll kill him!

POLICEMEN.   Be better off dead. Indecent bastard.

MERRICK.   Don't cry girls. Doesn't hurt.

PINS.   Indecent, indecent, indecent, indecent!!

(POLICEMEN escort MERRICK and ROSS out, i.e., forward. Blackout except spot on MERRICK and ROSS.)

MERRICK.   Ostend will always mean bad memories. Won't it, Ross?

ROSS.   I've decided. I'm sending you back, lad. You're a flop. No, you're a liability. You ain't the moneymaker I figured, so that's it.

MERRICK.   Alone?

ROSS.   Here's a few bob, have a nosh. I'm keeping the rest. For my trouble. I deserve it, I reckon. Invested enough with you. Pick up your stink if I stick around. Stink of failure. Stink of lost years. Just stink, stink, stink, stink, stink.

(Enter CONDUCTOR.)

CONDUCTOR.   This the one?

ROSS.   Just see him to Liverpool St. Station safe, will you? Here's for your trouble.

MERRICK.   Robbed.

CONDUCTOR.   What's he say?

ROSS.   Just makes sounds. Fella's an imbecile.

MERRICK.   Robbed.

ROSS.   Bon voyage, Johnny. His name is Johnny. He knows his name, that's all, though.

CONDUCTOR.   Don't follow him, Johnny. Johnny, come on boat now. Conductor find Johnny place out of sight. Johnny! Johnny! Don't struggle, Johnny. Johnny come on.

MERRICK.   Robbed! Robbed!

(Fadeout on struggle.)

SCENE V

POLICE SIDE WITH IMBECILE AGAINST THE CROWD

(Darkness. Uproar, shouts.)

VOICE.   Liverpool St. Station!

(Enter MERRICK, CONDUCTOR, POLICEMAN.)

POLICEMAN.   We're safe in here. I barred the door.

CONDUCTOR.   They wanted to rip him to pieces. I've never seen anything like it. It was like being Gordon at bleedin' Khartoum.

POLICEMAN.   Got somewhere to go in London, lad? Can't stay here.

CONDUCTOR.   He's an imbecile. He don't understand. Search him.

POLICEMAN.   Got any money?

MERRICK.   Robbed.

POLICEMAN.   What's that?

CONDUCTOR.   He just makes sounds. Frightened sounds is all he makes. Go through his coat.

MERRICK.   Je-sus.

POLICEMAN.   Don't let me go through your coat, I'll turn you over to that lot! Oh, I was joking, don't upset yourself.

MERRICK. Joke? Joke?

POLICEMAN. Sure, croak, croak, croak, croak.

MERRICK. Je-sus.

POLICEMAN. Got a card here. You Johnny Merrick? What's this old card here, Johnny? Someone give you a card?

CONDUCTOR. What's it say?

POLICEMAN. Says Mr. Frederick Treves, Lecturer in Anatomy, the London Hospital.

CONDUCTOR. I'll go see if I can find him, it's not far. *(Exits.)*

POLICEMAN. What's he do, lecture you on your anatomy? People who think right don't look like that then, do they? Yeah, glung, glung, glung, glung.

MERRICK. Jesus. Jesus.

POLICEMAN. Sure, Treves, Treves, Treves, Treves.

(Blackout, then lights go up as CONDUCTOR *leads* TREVES *in.)*

TREVES. What is going on here? Look at that mob, have you no sense of decency. I am Frederick Treves. This is my card.

POLICEMAN. This poor wretch here had it. Arrived from Ostend.

TREVES. Good Lord, Merrick? John Merrick? What has happened to you?

MERRICK. Help me!

(Fadeout.)

SCENE VI

EVEN ON THE NIGER AND CEYLON, NOT THIS

(The London Hospital. MERRICK *in bathtub.* TREVES *outside. Enter* MISS SANDWICH.*)*

TREVES. You are? Miss Sandwich?

SANDWICH. Sandwich. yes.

TREVES. You have had experience in missionary hospitals in the Niger.

SANDWICH. And Ceylon.

TREVES. I may assume you've seen—

SANDWICH. The tropics. Oh those diseases. The many and the awful scourges our Lord sends, yes, sir.

TREVES. I need the help of an experienced nurse, you see.

SANDWICH. Someone to bring him food, take care of the room. Yes, I understand. But it is somehow difficult.

TREVES. Well, I have been let down so far. He really is—that is, the regular sisters —well, it is not part of their job and they will not do it. Be ordinarily kind to Mr. Merrick. Without—well—panicking. He is quite beyond ugly. You understand that? His appearance has terrified them.

SANDWICH. The photographs show a terrible disease.

TREVES. It is a disorder, not a disease; it is in no way contagious though we don't in fact know what it is. I have found however that there is a deep superstition in those I've tried, they actually believe he somehow brought it on himself, this thing, and of course it is not that at all.

SANDWICH.   I am not one who believes it is ourselves who attain grace or bring chastisement to us, sir.

TREVES.   Miss Sandwich, I am hoping not.

SANDWICH.   Let me put your mind to rest. Care for lepers in the East, and you have cared, Mr. Treves. In Africa, I have seen dreadful scourges quite unknown to our more civilized climes. What at home could be worse than a miserable and afflicted rotting black?

TREVES.   I imagine.

SANDWICH.   Appearances do not daunt me.

TREVES.   It is really that that has sent me outside the confines of the London seeking help.

SANDWICH.   "I look unto the hills whence cometh my help." I understand: I think I will be satisfactory.

(Enter PORTER *with tray.)*

PORTER.   His lunch. *(Exits.)*

TREVES.   Perhaps you would be so kind as to accompany me this time. I will introduce you.

SANDWICH.   Allow me to carry the tray.

TREVES.   I will this time. You are ready.

SANDWICH.   I am.

TREVES.   He is bathing to be rid of his odor.

(They enter to MERRICK.*)*

John, this is Miss Sandwich. She—

SANDWICH.   I—*(unable to control herself)* Oh my good God in heaven. *(Bolts room.)*

TREVES *(puts* MERRICK'*s lunch down).*   I am sorry. I thought—

MERRICK.   Thank you for saving the lunch this time.

TREVES.   Excuse me.

(Exits to MISS SANDWICH.*)*

You have let me down, you know. I did everything to warn you and still you let me down.

SANDWICH.   You didn't say.

TREVES.   But I—

SANDWICH.   Didn't! You said—just words!

TREVES.   But the photographs.

SANDWICH.   Just pictures. No one will do this. I am sorry.

(Exits.)

TREVES.   Yes. Well. This is not helping him.

(Fadeout.)

SCENE VII

THE ENGLISH PUBLIC WILL PAY FOR HIM TO BE LIKE US

(The London Hospital. MERRICK *in a bathtub reading.* TREVES, BISHOP HOW *in foreground.)*

BISHOP.   With what fortitude he bears his cross! It is remarkable. He has made the acquaintance of religion and knows sections of the Bible by heart. Once I'd grasped his speech, it became clear he'd certainly had religious instruction at one time.

TREVES.   I believe it was in the workhouse, Dr. How.

BISHOP.   They are awfully good about that sometimes. The psalms he loves, and the book of Job perplexes him, he says, for he cannot see that a just God must cause suffering, as he puts it, merely then to be merciful. Yet that Christ will save him he does not doubt, so he is not resentful.

(Enter GOMM.*)*

GOMM.   Christ had better; be damned if we can.

BISHOP.   Ahem. In any case Dr. Treves, he has a religious nature, further instruction would uplift him and I'd be pleased to provide it. I plan to speak of him from the pulpit this week.

GOMM.   I see our visiting bather has flushed the busy Bishop How from his cruciform lair.

BISHOP.   Speak with Merrick, sir. I have spoken to him of Mercy and Justice. There's a true Christian in the rough.

GOMM.   This makes my news seem banal, yet yes: Frederick, the response to my letter to the *Times* about Merrick has been staggering. The English public has been so generous that Merrick may be supported for life without a penny spent from Hospital funds.

TREVES.   But that is excellent.

BISHOP.   God bless the English public.

GOMM.   Especially for not dismembering him at Liverpool St. Station. Freddie, the London's no home for incurables, this is quite irregular, but for you I permit it—though god knows what you'll do.

BISHOP.   God does know, sir, and Darwin does not.

GOMM.   He'd better, sir; he deformed him.

BISHOP.   I had apprehensions coming here. I find it most fortunate Merrick is in the hands of Dr. Treves, a Christian, sir.

GOMM.   Freddie is a good man and a brilliant doctor, and that is fortunate indeed.

TREVES.   I couldn't have raised the funds though, Doctor.

BISHOP.   Don't let me keep you longer from your duties, Mr. Treves. Yet, Mr. Gomm, consider: is it science, sir, that motivates us when we transport English rule of law to India or Ireland? When good British churchmen leave hearth and home for missionary hardship in Africa, is it science that bears them away?

Sir it is not. It is Christian duty. It is the obligation to bring our light and benefices to benighted man. That motivates us, even as it motivates Treves toward Merrick, sir, to bring salvation where none is. Gordon was a Christian, sir, and died at Khartoum for it. Not for science, sir.

GOMM.   You're telling me, not for science.

BISHOP.   Mr. Treves, I'll visit Merrick weekly if I may.

TREVES.   You will be welcome, sir, I am certain.

BISHOP.   Then good day, sirs. *(Exits.)*

GOMM.   Well, Jesus my boy, now we have the money, what do you plan for Merrick?

TREVES.   Normality as far as is possible.

GOMM.   So he will be like us? Ah. *(Smiles.)*

TREVES.   Is something wrong, Mr. Gomm? With us?

(Fadeout.)

SCENE VIII

MERCY AND JUSTICE ELUDE OUR MINDS AND ACTIONS

(MERRICK in bath. TREVES, GOMM.)

MERRICK.   How long is as long as I like?

TREVES.   You may stay for life. The funds exist.

MERRICK.   Been reading this. About homes for the blind. Wouldn't mind going to one when I have to move.

TREVES.   But you do not have to move; and you're not blind.

MERRICK.   I would prefer it where no one stared at me.

GOMM.   No one will bother you here.

TREVES.   Certainly not. I've given instructions.

(PORTER and SNORK peek in.)

PORTER.   What'd I tell you?

SNORK.   Gawd almighty. Oh. Mr. Treves. Mr. Gomm.

TREVES.   You were told not to do this. I don't understand. You must not lurk about. Surely you have work.

PORTER.   Yes, sir.

TREVES.   Well, it is infuriating. When you are told a thing, you must listen. I won't have you gaping in on my patients. Kindly remember that.

PORTER.   Isn't a patient, sir, is he?

TREVES.   Do not let me find you here again.

PORTER.   Didn't know you were here, sir. We'll be off now.

GOMM.   No, no, Will. Mr. Treves was precisely saying no one would intrude when you intruded.

TREVES.   He is warned now. Merrick does not like it.

GOMM.   He was warned before. On what penalty, Will?

PORTER.   That you'd sack me, sir.

GOMM.   You are sacked, Will. You, his friend, you work here?

SNORK.   Just started last week, sir.

GOMM.   Well, I hope the point is taken now.

PORTER.   Mr. Gomm—I ain't truly sacked, am I?

GOMM.   Will, yes. Truly sacked. You will never be more truly sacked.

PORTER.   It's not me. My wife ain't well. My sister has got to take care of our kids, and of her. Well.

GOMM.   Think of them first next time.

PORTER.   It ain't as if I interfered with his medicine.

GOMM.   That is exactly what it is. You may go.

PORTER.   Just keeping him to look at in private. That's all. Isn't it?

(SNORK and PORTER exit.)

GOMM.   There are priorities, Frederick. The first is discipline. Smooth is the passage to the tight ship's master. Merrick, you are safe from prying now.

TREVES.   Have we nothing to say, John?

MERRICK.   If all that'd stared at me'd been sacked—there'd be whole towns out of work.

TREVES.   I meant, "Thank you, sir."

MERRICK.   "Thank you sir."

TREVES.   We always do say please and thank you, don't we?

MERRICK.   Yes, sir. Thank you.

TREVES.   If we want to properly be like others.

MERRICK.   Yes, sir, I want to.

TREVES.   Then it is for our own good, is it not?

MERRICK.   Yes, sir. Thank you, Mr. Gomm.

GOMM.   Sir, you are welcome. *(Exits.)*

TREVES.   You are happy here, are you not, John?

MERRICK.   Yes.

TREVES.   The baths have rid you of the odor, have they not?

MERRICK.   First chance I had to bathe regular. Ly.

TREVES.   And three meals a day delivered to your room?

MERRICK.   Yes, sir.

TREVES.   This is your Promised Land, is it not? A roof. Food. Protection. Care. Is it not?

MERRICK.   Right, Mr. Treves.

TREVES.   I will bet you don't know what to call this.

MERRICK.   No, sir, I don't know.

TREVES.   You call it, Home.

MERRICK.   Never had a home before.

TREVES.   You have one now. Say it, John: Home.

MERRICK.   Home.

TREVES.   No, no, really say it. I have a home. This is my. Go on.

MERRICK.   I have a home. This is my home. This is my home. I have a home. As long as I like?

TREVES.   That is what home is.

MERRICK.   That is what is home.

TREVES.   If I abide by the rules, I will be happy.

MERRICK.   Yes, sir.

TREVES.   Don't be shy.

MERRICK.   If I abide by the rules I will be happy.

TREVES.   Very good. Why?

MERRICK.   Why what?

TREVES.   Will you be happy?

MERRICK.   Because it is my home?

TREVES.   No, no. Why do rules make you happy?

MERRICK.   I don't know.

TREVES.   Of course you do.

MERRICK.   No, I really don't.

TREVES.   Why does anything make you happy?

MERRICK.   Like what? Like what?

TREVES.   Don't be upset. Rules make us happy because they are for our own good.

MERRICK.   Okay.

TREVES.   Don't be shy, John. You can say it.

MERRICK.   This is my home?

TREVES.   No. About rules making us happy.

MERRICK.   They make us happy because they are for our own good.

TREVES.   Excellent. Now: I am submitting a follow-up paper on you to the London Pathological Society. It would help if you told me what you recall about your first years, John. To fill in gaps.

MERRICK.   To fill in gaps. The workhouse where they put me. They beat you there like a drum. Boom boom: scrape the floor white. Shine the pan, boom boom. It never ends. The floor is always dirty. The pan is always tarnished. There is nothing you can do about it. You are always attacked anyway. Boom boom. Boom boom. Boom boom. Will the children go to the workhouse?

TREVES.   What children?

MERRICK.   The children. The man he sacked.

TREVES.   Of necessity Will will find other employment. You don't want crowds staring at you, do you?

MERRICK.   No.

TREVES.   In your own home you do not have to have crowds staring at you. Or anyone. Do you? In your home?

MERRICK.   No.

TREVES.   Then Mr. Gomm was merciful. You yourself are proof. Is it not so? *(Pause.)* Well? Is it not so?

MERRICK.   If your mercy is so cruel, what do you have for justice?

TREVES.   I am sorry. It is just the way things are.

MERRICK.   Boom boom. Boom boom. Boom boom.

(Fadeout.)

SCENE IX

MOST IMPORTANT ARE WOMEN

(MERRICK *asleep, head on knees.* TREVES, MRS. KENDAL *foreground.*)

TREVES.   You have seen photographs of John Merrick, Mrs. Kendal. You are acquainted with his appearance.

MRS. KENDAL.   He reminds me of an audience I played Cleopatra for in Brighton once. All huge grim head and grimace and utterly unable to clap.

TREVES.   Well. My aim's to lead him to as normal a life as possible. His terror of us all comes from having been held at arm's length from society. I am determined that shall end. For example, he loves to meet people and converse. I am determined he shall. For example, he had never seen the inside of any normal home before. I had him to mine, and what a reward, Mrs. Kendal; his astonishment, his joy at the most ordinary things. Most critical I feel, however, are women. I will explain. They have always shown the greatest fear and loathing of him. While he adores them of course.

MRS. KENDAL.   Ah. He is intelligent.

TREVES.   I am convinced they are the key to retrieving him from his exclusion. Though, I must warn you, women are not quite real to him—more creatures of his imagination.

MRS. KENDAL.   Then he is already like other men, Mr. Treves.

TREVES.   So I thought, an actress could help. I mean, unlike most women, you won't give in, you are trained to hide your true feelings and assume others.

MRS. KENDAL.   You mean unlike most women I am famous for it, that is really all.

TREVES.   Well. In any case. If you could enter the room and smile and wish him good morning. And when you leave, shake his hand, the left one is usable, and really quite beautiful, and say, "I am very pleased to have made your acquaintance, Mr. Merrick."

MRS. KENDAL.   Shall we try it? Left hand out please. *(Suddenly radiant)* I am *very* pleased to have made your acquaintance Mr. Merrick. I am very *pleased* to have made your acquaintance Mr. Merrick. I am very pleased to have made your *acquaintance* Mr. Merrick. I *am* very pleased to have made *your* acquaintance Mr. Merrick. Yes. That one.

TREVES.   By god, they are all splendid. Merrick will be so pleased. It will be the day he becomes a man like other men.

MRS. KENDAL.   Speaking of that, Mr. Treves.

TREVES.   Frederick, please.

MRS. KENDAL.   Freddie, may I commit an indiscretion?

TREVES.   Yes?

MRS. KENDAL.   I could not but help noticing from the photographs that—well—of the unafflicted parts—ah, how shall I put it? *(Points to photograph.)*

TREVES.   Oh. I see! I quite. Understand. No, no, no, it is quite normal.

MRS. KENDAL.   I thought as much.

TREVES.   Medically speaking, uhm, you see the papillomatous extrusions which disfigure him, uhm, seem to correspond quite regularly to the osseous deformities, that is, excuse me, there is a link between the bone disorder and the skin growths, though for the life of me I have not discovered what it is or why it is, but in any case this—part—it would be therefore unlikely to be afflicted because well, that is, well, there's no bone in it. None at all. I mean.

MRS. KENDAL.   Well. Learn a little every day don't we?

TREVES.   I am horribly embarrassed.

MRS. KENDAL.   Are you? Then he must be lonely indeed.

(Fadeout.)

SCENE X

WHEN THE ILLUSION ENDS HE MUST KILL HIMSELF

(MERRICK *sketching. Enter* TREVES, MRS. KENDAL.)

TREVES.   He is making sketches for a model of St. Phillip's church. He wants someday to make a model, you see. John, my boy, this is Mrs. Kendal. She would very much like to make your acquaintance.

MRS. KENDAL.   Good morning Mr. Merrick.

TREVES.   I will see to a few matters. I will be back soon. *(Exits.)*

MERRICK.   I planned so many things to say. I forget them. You are so beautiful.

MRS. KENDAL.   How charming, Mr. Merrick.

MERRICK.   Well. Really that was what I planned to say. That I forgot what I planned to say. I couldn't think of anything else I was so excited.

MRS. KENDAL.   Real charm is always planned, don't you think?

MERRICK.   Well. I do not know why I look like this, Mrs. Kendal. My mother was so beautiful. She was knocked down by an elephant in a circus while she was pregnant. Something must have happened, don't you think?

MRS. KENDAL.   It may well have.

MERRICK.   It may well have. But sometimes I think my head is so big because it is so full of dreams. Because it is. Do you know what happens when dreams cannot get out?

MRS. KENDAL.   Why, no.

MERRICK.   I don't either. Something must. *(Silence.)* Well. You are a famous actress.

MRS. KENDAL.   I am not unknown.

MERRICK.   You must display yourself for your living then. Like I did.

MRS. KENDAL.   That is not myself, Mr. Merrick. That is an illusion. This is myself.

MERRICK.   This is myself too.

MRS. KENDAL.   Frederick says you like to read. So: books.

MERRICK.   I am reading *Romeo and Juliet* now.

MRS. KENDAL.   Ah. Juliet. What a love story. I adore love stories.

MERRICK.   I like love stories best too. If I had been Romeo, guess what.

MRS. KENDAL.   What?

MERRICK.   I would not have held the mirror to her breath.

MRS. KENDAL.   You mean the scene where Juliet appears to be dead and he holds a mirror to her breath and sees—

MERRICK.   Nothing. How does it feel when he kills himself because he just sees nothing?

MRS. KENDAL.   Well. My experience as Juliet has been—particularly with an actor I will not name—that while I'm laying there dead dead dead, and he is lamenting excessively, I get to thinking that if this slab of ham does not part from the hamhock of his life toute suite, I am going to scream, pop off the tomb, and plunge a dagger into his scene-stealing heart. Romeos are very undependable.

MERRICK.   Because he does not care for Juliet.

MRS. KENDAL.   Not care?

MERRICK.   Does he take her pulse? Does he get a doctor? Does he make sure? No. He kills himself. The illusion fools him because he does not care for her. He only cares about himself. If I had been Romeo, we would have got away.

MRS. KENDAL.   But then there would be no play, Mr. Merrick.

MERRICK.   If he did not love her, why should there be a play? Looking in a mirror and seeing nothing. That is not love. It was all an illusion. When the illusion ended he had to kill himself.

MRS. KENDAL.   Why. That is extraordinary.

MERRICK.   Before I spoke with people, I did not think of all these things because there was no one to bother to think them for. Now things just come out of my mouth which are true.

(TREVES *enters.*)

TREVES.   You are famous, John. We are in the papers. Look. They have written up my report to the Pathological Society. Look—it is a kind of apotheosis for you.

MRS. KENDAL.   Frederick, I feel Mr. Merrick would benefit by even more company than you provide; in fact by being acquainted with the best, and they with him. I shall make it my task if you'll permit. As you know, I am a friend of nearly everyone, and I do pretty well as I please and what pleases me is this task, I think.

TREVES.   By god, Mrs. Kendal, you are splendid.

MRS. KENDAL.   Mr. Merrick I must go now. I should like to return if I may. And so that we may without delay teach you about society, I would like to bring my good friend Dorothy Lady Neville. She would be most pleased if she could meet you. Let me tell her yes?

(MERRICK *nods yes.*)

Then until next time. I'm sure your church model will surprise us all. Mr. Merrick, it has been a very great pleasure to make your acquaintance.

TREVES.   John. Your hand. She wishes to shake your hand.

MERRICK.   Thank you for coming.

MRS. KENDAL.   But it was my pleasure. Thank you. (*Exits, accompanied by* TREVES.)

TREVES.   What a wonderful success. Do you know he's never shook a woman's hand before?

(As lights fade MERRICK *sobs soundlessly, uncontrollably.)*

SCENE XI

HE DOES IT WITH JUST ONE HAND

(Music. MERRICK *working on model of St. Phillip's church. Enter* DUCHESS. *At side* TREVES *ticks off a gift list.)*

MERRICK.   Your grace.

DUCHESS.   How nicely the model is coming along, Mr. Merrick. I've come to say Happy Christmas, and that I hope you will enjoy this ring and remember your friend by it.

MERRICK.   Your grace, thank you.

DUCHESS.   I am very pleased to have made your acquaintance. *(Exits.)*

(Enter COUNTESS.)

COUNTESS.   Please accept these silver-backed brushes and comb for Christmas, Mr. Merrick.

MERRICK.   With many thanks, Countess.

COUNTESS.   I am very pleased to have made your acquaintance. *(Exits.)*

(Enter LORD JOHN.)

LORD JOHN.   Here's the silver-topped walking stick, Merrick. Make you a regular Piccadilly exquisite. Keep up the good work. Self-help is the best help. Example to us all.

MERRICK.   Thank you, Lord John.

LORD JOHN.   Very pleased to have made your acquaintance. *(Exits.)*

(Enter TREVES *and* PRINCESS ALEXANDRA.)

TREVES.   Her Royal Highness Princess Alexandra.

PRINCESS.   The happiest of Christmases, Mr. Merrick.

TREVES.   Her Royal Highness has brought you a signed photograph of herself.

MERRICK.   I am honored, your Royal Highness. It is the treasure of my possessions. I have written to His Royal Highness the Prince of Wales to thank him for the pheasants and woodcock he sent.

PRINCESS.   You are a credit to Mr. Treves, Mr. Merrick. Mr. Treves, you are a credit to medicine, to England, and to Christendom. I am so very pleased to have made your acquaintance.

*(*PRINCESS, TREVES *exit. Enter* MRS. KENDAL.)

MRS. KENDAL.   Good news, John. Bertie says we may use the Royal Box whenever I like. Mrs. Keppel says it gives a unique perspective. And for Christmas, ivory-handled razors and toothbrush.

(Enter TREVES.*)*

TREVES.   And a cigarette case, my boy, full of cigarettes!

MERRICK.   Thank you. Very much.

MRS. KENDAL.   Look Freddie, look. The model of St. Phillip's.

TREVES.   It is remarkable, I know.

MERRICK.   And I do it with just one hand, they all say.

MRS. KENDAL.   You are an artist, John Merrick, an artist.

MERRICK.   I did not begin to build at first. Not till I saw what St. Phillip's really was. It is not stone and steel and glass; it is an imitation of grace flying up and up from the mud. So I make my imitation of an imitation. But even in that is heaven to me, Mrs. Kendal.

TREVES.   That thought's got a good line, John. Plato believed this was all a world of illusion and that artists made illusions of illusions of heaven.

MERRICK.   You mean we are all just copies? Of originals?

TREVES.   That's it.

MERRICK.   Who made the copies?

TREVES.   God. The Demi-urge.

MERRICK *(goes back to work)*. He should have used both hands shouldn't he?

(Music. Puts another piece on St. Phillip's. Fadeout.)

SCENE XII

WHO DOES HE REMIND YOU OF?

*(*TREVES, MRS. KENDAL.*)*

TREVES.   Why all those toilet articles, tell me? He is much too deformed to use any of them.

MRS. KENDAL.   Props of course. To make himself. As I make me.

TREVES.   You? You think of yourself.

MRS. KENDAL.   Well. He is gentle, almost feminine. Cheerful, honest within limits, a serious artist in his way. He is almost like me.

(Enter BISHOP HOW.*)*

BISHOP.   He is religious and devout. He knows salvation must radiate to us or all is lost, which it's certainly not.

(Enter GOMM.*)*

GOMM.   He seems practical, like me. He has seen enough of daily evil to be thankful for small goods that come his way. He knows what side his bread is buttered on, and counts his blessings for it. Like me.

(Enter DUCHESS.*)*

DUCHESS.   I can speak with him of anything. For I know he is discreet. Like me.

(All exit except TREVES.*)*

TREVES.   How odd. I think him curious, compassionate, concerned about the world, well, rather like myself, Freddie Treves, 1889 AD.

(Enter MRS. KENDAL.*)*

MRS. KENDAL.   Of course he is rather odd. And hurt. And helpless not to show the struggling. And so am I.

(Enter GOMM.*)*

GOMM.   He knows I use him to raise money for the London, I am certain. He understands I would be derelict if I didn't. He is wary of any promise, yet he fits in well. Like me.

(Enter BISHOP HOW.*)*

BISHOP.   I as a seminarist had many of the same doubts. Struggling as he does. And hope they may be overcome.

(Enter PRINCESS ALEXANDRA.*)*

PRINCESS.   When my husband His Royal Highness Edward Prince of Wales asked Dr. Treves to be his personal surgeon, he said, "Dear Freddie, if you can put up with the Elephant bloke, you can surely put up with me."

(All exit, except TREVES. *Enter* LORD JOHN.*)*

LORD JOHN.   See him out of fashion, Freddie. As he sees me. Social contacts critical. Oh—by the way—ignore the bloody papers; all lies. *(Exits.)*

TREVES.   Merrick visibly worse than 86–87. That, as he rises higher in the consolations of society, he gets visibly more grotesque is proof definitive he is like me. Like his condition, which I make no sense of, I make no sense of mine.

(Spot on MERRICK *placing another piece on St. Phillip's. Fadeout.)*

SCENE XIII

ANXIETIES OF THE SWAMP

*(*MERRICK, *in spot, strains to listen:* TREVES, LORD JOHN *outside.)*

TREVES.   But the papers are saying you broke the contracts. They are saying you've lost the money.

LORD JOHN.   Freddie, if I were such a scoundrel, how would I dare face investors like yourself. Broken contracts! I never considered them actual contracts—just preliminary things, get the old deal under way. An actual contract's something between gentlemen; and this attack on me shows they are no gentlemen. Now I'm only here to say the company remains a terribly attractive proposition. Don't you think? To recapitalize—if you could spare another—ah.

(Enter GOMM.*)*

Mr. Gomm. How good to see you. Just remarking how splendidly Merrick thrives
here, thanks to you and Freddie.

GOMM.   Lord John. Allow me: I must take Frederick from you. Keep him at work.
It's in his contract. Wouldn't want him breaking it. Sort of thing makes the
world fly apart, isn't it?

LORD JOHN.   Yes. Well. Of course, mmm.

GOMM.   Sorry to hear you're so pressed. Expect we'll see less of you around the
London now?

LORD JOHN.   Of course, I, actually—ah! Overdue actually. Appointment in the
City. Freddie. Mr. Gomm. *(Exits.)*

TREVES.   He plain fooled me. He was kind to Merrick.

GOMM.   You have risen fast and easily, my boy. You've forgot how to protect
yourself. Break now.

TREVES.   It does not seem right somehow.

GOMM.   The man's a moral swamp. Is that not clear yet? Is he attractive? Deceit
often is. Friendly? Swindlers can be. Another loan? Not another cent. It may
be your money, Freddie; but I will not tolerate laboring like a navvy that the
London should represent honest charitable and compassionate science, and
have titled swindlers mucking up the pitch. He has succeeded in destroying
himself so rabidly, you ought not doubt an instant it was his real aim all along.
He broke the contracts, gambled the money away, lied, and like an infant in
his mess, gurgles and wants to do it again. Never mind details, don't want to
know. Break and be glad. Don't hesitate. Today. One-man moral swamp.
Don't be sucked in.

(Enter MRS. KENDAL.*)*

MRS. KENDAL.   Have you seen the papers?

TREVES.   Yes.

GOMM.   Yes, yes. A great pity. Freddie: today. *(Exits.)*

MRS. KENDAL.   Freddie?

TREVES.   He has used us. I shall be all right. Come.

*(*MRS. KENDAL, TREVES *enter to* MERRICK.*)*

John: I shall not be able to stay this visit. I must, well, unravel a few things. Nurse
Ireland and Snork are—?

MERRICK.   Friendly and respectful, Frederick.

TREVES.   I'll look in in a few days.

MERRICK.   Did I do something wrong?

MRS. KENDAL.   No.

TREVES.   This is a hospital. Not a marketplace. Don't forget it, ever. Sorry. Not
you. Me. *(Exits.)*

MRS. KENDAL.   Well. Shall we weave today? Don't you think weaving might be
fun? So many things are fun. Most men really can't enjoy them. Their loss,
isn't it? I like little activities which engage me; there's something ancient in
it, I don't know. Before all this. Would you like to try? John?

MERRICK.   Frederick said I may stay here for life.

MRS. KENDAL.   And so you shall.

MERRICK.   If he is in trouble?

MRS. KENDAL.   Frederick is your protector, John.

MERRICK.   If he is in trouble? *(He picks up small photograph.)*

MRS. KENDAL.   Who is that? Ah, is it not your mother? She is pretty, isn't she?

MERRICK.   Will Frederick keep his word with me, his contract, Mrs. Kendal? If he is in trouble.

MRS. KENDAL.   What? Contract? Did you say?

MERRICK.   And will you?

MRS. KENDAL.   I? What? Will I?

*(*MERRICK *silent. Puts another piece on model. Fadeout.)*

SCENE XIV

ART IS PERMITTED BUT NATURE FORBIDDEN

(Rain. MERRICK *working.* MRS. KENDAL*.)*

MERRICK.   The Prince has a mistress. *(Silence.)* The Irishman had one. Everyone seems to. Or a wife. Some have both. I have concluded I need a mistress. It is bad enough not to sleep like others.

MRS. KENDAL.   Sitting up, you mean. Couldn't be very restful.

MERRICK.   I have to. Too heavy to lay down. My head. But to sleep alone; that is worst of all.

MRS. KENDAL.   The artist expresses his love through his works. That is civilization.

MERRICK.   Are you very shocked?

MRS. KENDAL.   Why should I be?

MERRICK.   Others would be.

MRS. KENDAL.   I am not others.

MERRICK.   I suppose it is so hopeless.

MRS. KENDAL.   Nothing is hopeless. However it is unlikely.

MERRICK.   I thought you might have a few ideas.

MRS. KENDAL.   I can guess who has ideas here.

MERRICK.   You don't know something. I have never even seen a naked woman.

MRS. KENDAL.   Surely in all the fairs you worked.

MERRICK.   I mean a real woman.

MRS. KENDAL.   Is one more real than another?

MERRICK.   I mean like the ones in the theater. The opera.

MRS. KENDAL.   Surely you can't mean they are more real.

MERRICK.   In the audience. A woman not worn out early. Not deformed by awful life. A lady. Someone kept up. Respectful of herself. You don't know what fairgrounds are like, Mrs. Kendal.

MRS. KENDAL.   You mean someone like Princess Alexandra?

MERRICK.   Not so old.

MRS. KENDAL.   Ah. Like Dorothy.

MERRICK.   She does not look happy. No.

MRS. KENDAL.   Lady Ellen?

MERRICK.   Too thin.

MRS. KENDAL.   Then who?

MERRICK.   Certain women. They have a kind of ripeness. They seem to stop at a perfect point.

MRS. KENDAL.   My dear she doesn't exist.

MERRICK.   That is probably why I never saw her.

MRS. KENDAL.   What would your friend Bishop How say of all this I wonder?

MERRICK.   He says I should put these things out of my mind.

MRS. KENDAL.   Is that the best he can suggest?

MERRICK.   I put them out of my mind. They reappeared, snap.

MRS. KENDAL.   What about Frederick?

MERRICK.   He would be appalled if I told him.

MRS. KENDAL.   I am flattered. Too little trust has maimed my life. But that is another story.

MERRICK.   What a rain. Are we going to read this afternoon?

MRS. KENDAL.   Yes. Some women are lucky to look well, that is all. It is a rather arbitrary gift; it has no really good use, though it has uses, I will say that. Anyway it does not signify very much.

MERRICK.   To me it does.

MRS. KENDAL.   Well. You are mistaken.

MERRICK.   What are we going to read?

MRS. KENDAL.   Trust is very important you know. I trust you.

MERRICK.   Thank you very much. I have a book of Thomas Hardy's here. He is a friend of Frederick's. Shall we read that?

MRS. KENDAL.   Turn around a moment. Don't look.

MERRICK.   Is this a game?

MRS. KENDAL.   I would not call it a game. A surprise. *(She begins undressing.)*

MERRICK.   What kind of a surprise?

MRS. KENDAL.   I saw photographs of you. Before I met you. You didn't know that, did you?

MERRICK.   The ones from the first time, in '84? No, I didn't.

MRS. KENDAL.   I felt it was—unjust. I don't know why. I cannot say my sense of justice is my most highly developed characteristic. You may turn around again. Well. A little funny, isn't it?

MERRICK.   It is the most beautiful sight I have ever seen. Ever.

MRS. KENDAL.   If you tell anyone, I shall not see you again, we shall not read, we shall not talk, we shall do nothing. Wait. *(Undoes her hair.)* There. No illusions. Now. Well? What is there to say? "I am extremely pleased to have made your acquaintance?"

(Enter TREVES.*)*

TREVES.   For God's sakes. What is going on here? What is going on?

MRS. KENDAL.   For a moment, Paradise, Freddie. *(She begins dressing.)*

TREVES.   But—have you no sense of decency? Woman, dress yourself quickly.

(Silence. MERRICK *goes to put another piece on St. Phillip's.)*

Are you not ashamed? Do you know what you are? Don't you know what is forbidden?

(Fadeout.)

SCENE XV

INGRATITUDE

(ROSS in MERRICK's room.)

ROSS.   I come actually to ask your forgiveness.

MERRICK.   I found a good home, Ross. I forgave you.

ROSS.   I was hoping we could work out a deal. Something new maybe.

MERRICK.   No.

ROSS.   See, I was counting on it. That you were kindhearted. Like myself. Some things don't change. Got to put your money on the things that don't, I figure. I figure from what I read about you, you don't change. Dukes, Ladies coming to see you. Ask myself why? Figure it's same as always was. Makes 'em feel good about themselves by comparison. Them things don't change. There but for the grace of. So I figure you're selling the same service as always. To better clientele. Difference now is you ain't charging for it.

MERRICK.   You make me sound like a whore.

ROSS.   You are. I am. They are. Most are. No disgrace, John. Disgrace is to be a stupid whore. Give it for free. Not capitalize on the interest in you. Not to have a manager then is stupid.

MERRICK.   You see this church. I am building it. The people who visit are friends. Not clients. I am not a dog walking on its hind legs.

ROSS.   I was thinking. Charge these people. Pleasure of the Elephant Man's company. Something. Right spirit is everything. Do it in the right spirit, they'd pay happily. I'd take ten percent. I'd be okay with ten percent.

MERRICK.   Bad luck's made you daft.

ROSS.   I helped you, John. Discovered you. Was that daft? No. Only daftness was being at a goldmine without a shovel. Without proper connections. Like Treves has. What's daft? Ross sows, Treves harvests? It's not fair, is it John? When you think about it. I do think about it. Because I'm old. Got something in my throat. You may have noticed. Something in my lung here too. Something in my belly I guess too. I'm not a heap of health, am I? But I'd do well with ten percent. I don't need more than ten percent. Ten percent'd give me a future slightly better'n a cobblestone. This lot would pay, if you charged in the right spirit. I don't ask much.

MERRICK.   They're the cream, Ross. They know it. Man like you tries to make them pay, they'll walk away.

ROSS.   I'm talking about doing it in the right spirit.

MERRICK.   They are my friends. I'd lose everything. For you. Ross, you lived your life. You robbed me of forty-eight pounds, nine shillings, tuppence. You left me to die. Be satisfied Ross. You've had enough. You kept me like an animal in darkness. You come back and want to rob me again. Will you not be satisfied? Now I am a man like others, you want me to return?

ROSS. Had a woman yet?

MERRICK. Is that what makes a man?

ROSS. In my time it'd do for a start.

MERRICK. Not what makes this one. Yet I am like others.

ROSS. Then I'm condemned. I got no energy to try nothing new. I may as well go to the dosshouse straight. Die there anyway. Between filthy dosshouse rags. Nothing in the belly but acid. I don't like pain, John. The future gives pain sense. Without a future—*(Pauses.)* Five percent? John?

MERRICK. I'm sorry, Ross. It's just the way things are.

ROSS. By god. Then I am lost.

(Fadeout.)

SCENE XVI

NO RELIABLE GENERAL ANESTHETIC HAS APPEARED YET

(TREVES, *reading, makes notes.* MERRICK *works.*)

MERRICK. Frederick—do you believe in heaven? Hell? What about Christ? What about God? I believe in heaven. The Bible promises in heaven the crooked shall be made straight.

TREVES. So did the rack, my boy. So do we all.

MERRICK. You don't believe?

TREVES. I will settle for a reliable general anesthetic at this point. Actually, though—I had a patient once. A woman. Operated on her for—a woman's thing. Used ether to anesthetize. Tricky stuff. Didn't come out of it. Pulse stopped, no vital signs, absolutely moribund. Just a big white dead mackerel. Five minutes later, she fretted back to existence, like a lost explorer with a great scoop of the undiscovered.

MERRICK. She saw heaven?

TREVES. Well. I quote her: it was neither heavenly nor hellish. Rather like perambulating in a London fog. People drifted by, but no one spoke. London, mind you. Hell's probably the provinces. She was shocked it wasn't more exotic. But allowed as how had she stayed, and got used to the familiar, so to speak, it did have hints of becoming a kind of bliss. She fled.

MERRICK. If you do not believe—why did you send Mrs. Kendal away?

TREVES. Don't forget. It saved you once. My interference. You know well enough —it was not proper.

MERRICK. How can you tell? If you do not believe?

TREVES. There are still standards we abide by.

MERRICK. They make us happy because they are for our own good.

TREVES. Well. Not always.

MERRICK. Oh.

TREVES.   Look, if you are angry, just say so.

MERRICK.   Whose standards are they?

TREVES.   I am not in the mood for this chipping away at the edges, John.

MERRICK.   That do not always make us happy because they are not always for our own good?

TREVES.   Everyone's. Well. Mine. Everyone's.

MERRICK.   That woman's, that Juliet?

TREVES.   Juliet?

MERRICK.   Who died, then came back.

TREVES.   Oh. I see. Yes. Her standards too.

MERRICK.   So.

TREVES.   So what?

MERRICK.   Did you see her? Naked?

TREVES.   When I was operating. Of course—

MERRICK.   Oh.

TREVES.   Oh what?

MERRICK.   Is it okay to see them naked if you cut them up afterwards?

TREVES.   Good Lord. I'm a surgeon. That is science.

MERRICK.   She died. Mrs. Kendal didn't.

TREVES.   Well, she came back too.

MERRICK.   And Mrs. Kendal didn't. If you mean that.

TREVES.   I am trying to read about anesthetics. There is simply no comparison.

MERRICK.   Oh.

TREVES.   Science is a different thing. This woman came to me to be. I mean, it is not, well, love, you know.

MERRICK.   Is that why you're looking for an anesthetic.

TREVES.   It would be a boon to surgery.

MERRICK.   Because you don't love them.

TREVES.   Love's got nothing to do with surgery.

MERRICK.   Do you lose many patients?

TREVES.   I—some.

MERRICK.   Oh.

TREVES.   Oh what? What does it matter? Don't you see? If I love, if any surgeon loves her or any patient or not, what does it matter? And what conceivable difference to you?

MERRICK.   Because it is your standards we abide by.

TREVES.   For God's sakes. If you are angry, just say it. I won't turn you out. Say it: I am angry. Go on. I am angry. I am angry! I am angry!

MERRICK.   I believe in heaven.

TREVES.   And it is not okay. If they undress if you cut them up. As you put it. Makes me sound like Jack the, Jack the Ripper.

MERRICK.   No. You worry about anesthetics.

TREVES.   Are you having me on?

MERRICK.   You are merciful. I myself am proof. Is it not so? *(Pauses.)* Well? Is it not so?

TREVES.   Well. I. About Mrs. Kendal—perhaps I was wrong. I, these days that is, I seem to. Lose my head. Taking too much on perhaps. I do not know— what is in me these days.

MERRICK.   Will she come back? Mrs. Kendal?

TREVES.   I will talk to her again.

MERRICK.   But—will she?

TREVES.   No. I don't think so.

MERRICK.   Oh.

TREVES.   There are other things involved. Very. That is. Other things.

MERRICK.   Well. Other things. I want to walk now. Think. Other things. *(Begins to exit. Pauses.)* Why? Why won't she?

(Silence. MERRICK *exits.)*

TREVES.   Because I don't want her here when you die. *(He slumps in chair.)*

(Fadeout.)

SCENE XVII

CRUELTY IS AS NOTHING TO KINDNESS

*(*TREVES *asleep in chair dreams the following:* MERRICK *and* GOMM *dressed as* ROSS *in foreground.)*

MERRICK.   If he is merely papier maché and paint, a swindler and a fake—

GOMM.   No, no, a genuine Dorset dreamer in a moral swamp. Look—he has so forgot how to protect himself he's gone to sleep.

MERRICK.   I must examine him. I would not keep him for long, Mr. Gomm.

GOMM.   It would be an inconvenience, Mr. Merrick. He is a mainstay of our institution.

MERRICK.   Exactly that brought him to my attention. I am Merrick. Here is my card. I am with the mutations cross the road.

GOMM.   Frederick, stand up. You must understand. He is very very valuable. We have invested a great deal in him. He is personal surgeon to the Prince of Wales.

MERRICK.   But I only wish to examine him. I had not of course dreamed of changing him.

GOMM.   But he is a gentleman and a good man.

MERRICK.   Therefore exemplary for study as a cruel or deviant one would not be.

GOMM.   Oh very well. Have him back for breakfast time or you feed him. Frederick, stand up. Up you bloody donkey, up!

*(*TREVES, *still asleep, stands up. Fadeout.)*

SCENE XVIII

WE ARE DEALING WITH AN EPIDEMIC

*(*TREVES *asleep.* MERRICK *at lecturn.)*

MERRICK.   The most striking feature about him, note, is the terrifyingly normal head. This allowed him to lie down normally, and therefore to dream in the exclusive personal manner, without the weight of others' dreams accumulating to break his neck. From the brow projected a normal vision of benevolent enlightenment, what we believe to be a kind of self-mesmerized state. The mouth, deformed by satisfaction at being at the hub of the best of existent worlds, was rendered therefore utterly incapable of self-critical speech, thus of the ability to change. The heart showed signs of worry at this unchanging yet untenable state. The back was horribly stiff from being kept against a wall to face the discontent of a world ordered for his convenience. The surgeon's hands were well-developed and strong, capable of the most delicate carvings-up, for others' own good. Due also to the normal head, the right arm was of enormous power; but, so incapable of the distinction between the assertion of authority and the charitable act of giving, that it was often to be found disgustingly beating others—for their own good. The left arm was slighter and fairer, and may be seen in typical position, hand covering the genitals which were treated as a sullen colony in constant need of restriction, governance, punishment. For their own good. To add a further burden to his trouble, the wretched man when a boy developed a disabling spiritual duality, therefore was unable to feel what others feel, nor reach harmony with them. Please. (TREVES *shrugs.*) He would thus be denied all means of escape from those he had tormented.

(PINS *enter.*)

FIRST PIN.   Mr. Merrick. You have shown a profound and unknown disorder to us. You have said when he leaves here, it is for his prior life again. I do not think it ought to be permitted. It is a disgrace. It is a pity and a disgrace. It is an indecency in fact. It may be a danger in ways we do not know. Something ought to be done about it.

MERRICK.   We hope in twenty years we will understand enough to put an end to this affliction.

FIRST PIN.   Twenty years! Sir, that is unacceptable!

MERRICK.   Had we caught it early, it might have been different. But his condition has already spread both East and West. The truth is, I am afraid, we are dealing with an epidemic.

(MERRICK *puts another piece on St. Phillip's.* PINS *exit.* TREVES *starts awake. Fadeout.*)

SCENE XIX

THEY CANNOT MAKE OUT WHAT HE IS SAYING

(MERRICK, BISHOP HOW *in background.* BISHOP *gestures,* MERRICK *on knees.* TREVES *foreground. Enter* GOMM.)

GOMM.   Still beavering away for Christ?

TREVES.   Yes.

GOMM.   I got your report. He doesn't know, does he?

TREVES.   The Bishop?

GOMM.   I meant Merrick.

TREVES.   No.

GOMM.   I shall be sorry when he dies.

TREVES.   It will not be unexpected anyway.

GOMM.   He's brought the hospital quite a lot of good repute. Quite a lot of contributions too, for that matter. In fact, I like him; never regretted letting him stay on. Though I didn't imagine he'd last this long.

TREVES.   His heart won't sustain him much longer. It may even give out when he gets off his bloody knees with that bloody man.

GOMM.   What is it, Freddie? What has gone sour for you?

TREVES.   It is just—it is the overarc of things, quite inescapable that as he's achieved greater and greater normality, his condition's edged him closer to the grave. So—a parable of growing up? To become more normal is to die? More accepted to worsen? He—it is just a mockery of everything we live by.

GOMM.   Sorry, Freddie. Didn't catch that one.

TREVES.   Nothing has gone sour. I do not know.

GOMM.   Cheer up, man. You are knighted. Your clients will be kings. Nothing succeeds my boy like success. *(Exits.)*

*(*BISHOP *comes from* MERRICK's *room.)*

BISHOP.   I find my sessions with him utterly moving, Mr. Treves. He struggles so. I suggested he might like to be confirmed; he leaped at it like a man lost in a desert to an oasis.

TREVES.   He is very excited to do what others do if he thinks it is what others do.

BISHOP.   Do you cast doubt, sir, on his faith?

TREVES.   No, sir, I do not. Yet he makes all of us think he is deeply like ourselves. And yet we're not like each other. I conclude that we have polished him like a mirror, and shout hallelujah when he reflects us to the inch. I have grown sorry for it.

BISHOP.   I cannot make out what you're saying. Is something troubling you, Mr. Treves?

TREVES.   Corsets. How about corsets? Here is a pamphlet I've written due mostly to the grotesque ailments I've seen caused by corsets. Fashion overrules me, of course. My patients do not unstrap themselves of corsets. Some cannot— you know, I have so little time in the week, I spend Sundays in the poor-wards; to keep up with work. Work being twenty-year-old women who look an abused fifty with worn-outedness; young men with appalling industrial conditions I turn out as soon as possible to return to their labors. Happily most of my patients are not poor. They are middle class. They overeat and drink so grossly, they destroy nature in themselves and all around them so fervidly, they will not last. Higher up, sir, above this middle class, I confront these same— deformities—bulged out by unlimited resources and the ruthlessness of privilege into the most scandalous dissipation yoked to the grossest ignorance and constraint. I counsel against it where I can. I am ignored of course. Then, what, sir, could be troubling me? I am an extremely successful Englishman in a successful and respected England which informs me daily by the way it lives that it wants to die. I am in despair in fact. Science, observation, practice, deduction, having led me to these conclusions, can no longer serve as consolation. I apparently see things others don't.

BISHOP.   I do wish I understood you better, sir. But as for consolation, there is in Christ's church consolation.

TREVES.   I am sure we were not born for mere consolation.

BISHOP.   But look at Mr. Merrick's happy example.

TREVES.   Oh yes. You'd like my garden too. My dog, my wife, my daughter, pruned, cropped, pollarded and somewhat stupefied. Very happy examples, all of them. Well. Is it all we know how to finally do with—whatever? Nature? Is it? Rob it? No, not really, not nature I mean. Ourselves really. Myself really. Robbed, that is. You do see of course, can't figure out, really, what else to do with them? Can we? *(Laughs.)*

BISHOP.   It is not exactly clear, sir.

TREVES.   I am an awfully good gardener. Is that clear? By god I take such good care of anything, anything you, we, are convinced—are you not convinced, him I mean, is not very dangerously human? I mean how could he be? After what we've given him? What you like, sir, is that he is so grateful for patrons, so greedy to be patronized, and no demands, no rights, no hopes; past perverted, present false, future nil. What better could you ask? He puts up with all of it. Of course I do mean taken when I say given, as in what, what, what we have given him, but. You knew that. I'll bet. Because. I. I. I. I—

BISHOP.   Do you mean Charity? I cannot tell what you are saying.

TREVES.   Help me. *(Weeps.)*

(BISHOP consoles him.)

MERRICK *(rises, puts last piece on St. Phillip's).* It is done.

(Fadeout.)

SCENE XX

THE WEIGHT OF DREAMS

(MERRICK alone, looking at model. Enter SNORK with lunch.)

SNORK.   Lunch, Mr. Merrick. I'll set it up. Maybe you'd like a walk after lunch. April's doing wonders for the gardens.

(A funeral procession passes slowly by.)

My mate Will, his sister died yesterday. Twenty-eight she was. Imagine that. Wife was sick, his sister nursed her. Was a real bloom that girl. Now wife okay, sister just ups and dies. It's all so—what's that word? Forgot it. It means chance-y. Well. Forgot it. Chance-y'll do. Have a good lunch. *(Exits.)*

(MERRICK eats a little, breathes on model, polishes it, goes to bed, arms on knees, head on arms, the position in which he must sleep.)

MERRICK.   Chancey? *(Sleeps.)*

(Enter PINHEADS *singing.)*

PINS. We are the Queens of the Cosmos
         Beautiful darkness' empire
         Darkness darkness, light's true flower,
         Here is eternity's finest hour
         Sleep like others you learn to admire
         Be like your mother, be like your sire.

(They straighten MERRICK *out to normal sleep position. His head tilts over too far. His arms fly up clawing the air. He dies. As light fades,* SNORK *enters.)*

SNORK.   I remember it, Mr. Merrick. The word is "arbitrary." Arbitrary. It's all so—oh. Hey! Hey! The Elephant Man is dead!

(Fadeout.)

SCENE XXI

FINAL REPORT TO THE INVESTORS

(GOMM *reading,* TREVES *listening.)*

GOMM.   "To the Editor of the *Times.* Sir; In November, 1886, you were kind enough to insert in the *Times* a letter from me drawing attention to the case of Joseph Merrick—"

TREVES.   John. John Merrick.

GOMM.   Well. "—known as the Elephant Man. It was one of singular and exceptional misfortune" et cetera et cetera ". . . debarred from earning his livelihood in any other way than being exhibited to the gaze of the curious. This having been rightly interfered with by the police . . ." et cetera et cetera, "with great difficulty he succeeded somehow or other in getting to the door of the London Hospital where through the kindness of one of our surgeons he was sheltered for a time." And then . . . and then . . . and . . . ah. "While deterred by common humanity from evicting him again into the open street, I wrote to you and from that moment all difficulty vanished; the sympathy of many was aroused, and although no other fitting refuge was offered, a sufficient sum was placed at my disposal, apart from the funds of the hospital, to maintain him for what did not promise to be a prolonged life. As—"

TREVES.   I forgot. The coroner said it was death by asphyxiation. The weight of the head crushed the windpipe.

GOMM.   Well. I go on to say about how he spent his time here, that all attempted to alleviate his misery, that he was visited by the highest in the land et cetera, et cetera, that in general he joined our lives as best he could, and: "In spite of all this indulgence, he was quiet and unassuming, grateful for all that was done for him, and conformed readily to the restrictions which were necessary." Will that do so far, do you think?

TREVES.   Should think it would.

GOMM.   Wouldn't add anything else, would you?

TREVES.   Well. He was highly intelligent. He had an acute sensibility; and worst for him, a romantic imagination. No, no. Never mind. I am really not certain of any of it. *(Exits.)*

GOMM.   "I have given these details thinking that those who sent money to use for his support would like to know how their charity was used. Last Friday afternoon, though apparently in his usual health, he quietly passed away in his sleep. I have left in my hands a small balance of the money for his support, and this I now propose, after paying certain gratuities, to hand over to the general funds of the hospital. This course I believe will be consonant with the wishes of the contributors.

"It was the courtesy of the *Times* in inserting my letter in 1886 that procured for this afflicted man a comfortable protection during the last years of a previously wretched existence, and I desire to take this opportunity of thankfully acknowledging it.

"I am sir, your obedient servant,

F. C. Carr Gomm

"House Committee Room, London Hospital."

15 April 1890.

*(*TREVES *reenters.)*

TREVES.   I did think of one small thing.

GOMM.   It's too late, I'm afraid. It is done. *(Smiles.)*

(Hold before fadeout.)

HUMAN RELATIONSHIPS

TOPICS FOR SHORT PAPERS, JOURNALS, OR DISCUSSION

1. Contrast a failed relationship in this section with one of the more successful ones. (Some examples of failed relationships are in Thurber's, Poe's, and Wilhelm's stories, and in the ballad "Frankie and Johnny"; some successful ones appear in poems by Browning, Shakespeare, Bradstreet, Donne, and Kumin. It might be useful to pick both your examples from the same category of relationships—marriage, parent-child relationships, or relationships between lovers.

2. Some characters are trying to escape from stultifying or meaningless relationships. Identify their method of escape and whether or not it was successful. (Examples appear in the stories of Cather, Chopin, and Lessing, and in Eliot's poem "The Love Song of J. Alfred Prufrock.")

3. Some of the selections show successful relationships between unlikely individuals: between a woman's disembodied brain and a male pilot in "The Ship Who Sang"; between a grossly disfigured man and a beautiful actress in *The Elephant Man*. To what ingredients do you attribute the success of these relationships? Explain. Support your discussion with details from the readings.

4. Some believe the sonnets of Shakespeare were written to a young man. Also, Walt Whitman's poems in "Choices and Conflicts" and Amy Lowell's "Two Speak Together" were written to members of the same sex. Affection between two men appears in "A Diamond Guitar" and "Nine Lives." Can you find indications in the poems and stories that the love relationships are homosexual ones? Are these expressions of love also universal—able to be applied to any kind of love relationship?

LONGER PAPER OR RESEARCH PROJECT

5. Bernard Pomerance's play *The Elephant Man* was a success both on the stage and as a film in spite of its physically repugnant protagonist. Using library resources, check on the medical history of neurofibromatosis, the disease afflicting Merrick. Frederick Treves, the doctor involved, himself wrote on the subject, and recent articles are available that explain the contemporary treatment of this condition. Contrast the different ways in which the medical reports and Pomerance's play would be likely to affect readers' attitudes and feelings. Explore devices of language and form, and use quotations from your sources to support your points.

CREATIVE PROJECT

6. Write a series of love poems. Read the selection "On Reading Poetry: Limericks to Lyrics" (pp. 1014–1027) for suggestions about the form your poems can take. (Sonnets, ballads, and lyrics, for example, have traditionally been among the common forms for love poetry in English.)

Builders—Red and Green Ball, 1979, by Jacob Lawrence. (Courtesy of Francine Seders Gallery, Seattle.)

CHOICES AND CONFLICTS

THE ROAD NOT TAKEN

Two roads diverged in a yellow wood,
And sorry I could not travel both
And be one traveller, long I stood
And looked down one as far as I could
To where it bent in the undergrowth;

Then took the other, as just as fair,
And having perhaps the better claim,
Because it was grassy and wanted wear;
Though as for that the passing there
Had worn them really about the same,

And both that morning equally lay
In leaves no step had trodden black.
Oh, I kept the first for another day!
Yet knowing how way leads on to way,
I doubted if I should ever come back.

I shall be telling this with a sigh
Somewhere ages and ages hence:
Two roads diverged in a wood, and I—
I took the one less travelled by,
And that has made all the difference.

Robert Frost

As the epigraph suggests, choosing a road, where roads diverge, is the theme of this section. The choices and conflicts that drive characters into dilemmas often frustrate their lives, but they also provide opportunities. Cast in conventional meter and built on one basic, striking image, Robert Frost's poem "The Road Not Taken" is deceptively simple; it raises profound questions about how life should be lived and understood. The poet makes a choice and realizes he has lost an opportunity, but in the end, this introspection strengthens his position. He took the "less traveled," the unconventional, the difficult way, and "that has made all the difference." The stories, poems, and plays that follow illustrate how essential *choosing* is to being human, and how we define ourselves in the act of making choices.

The section begins with a story derived from a myth, the "dream of evil omen" of Young Goodman Brown in Nathaniel Hawthorne's story of the demands and guilts and temptations of the Puritan conscience. As the young Puritan traverses a dark forest, he seems to journey toward a hidden part of his own soul. The witches' Sabbath, common in New England folklore, suggests the theme of the darkness at the center of human existence—a persistent theme in human imagination, from the Greek myths about Hades to the film "Apocalypse Now" and the existential dilemma faced by Jean-Paul Sartre's characters in *No Exit.* Life is absurd, say the existentialists, but one must make meaningful choices to live an authentic life. Sartre's characters, who have led lives of self-deception, find that "Hell is other people."

These characters allowed their choices to be controlled by circumstances, or blame their choices on circumstances beyond their control. Like the old woman in Sherwood Anderson's "Death in the Woods," or Claude McKay's "The Harlem Dancer," some of these characters seem passive or resigned. Others act but are doomed to failure. Miss Emily in William Faulkner's "A Rose for Emily" is reduced to murdering her beloved to ward off the cruel fate of spinsterhood, but her action does not free her. Like the lime sprinkled by well-meaning townsmen to mask the smell of the decaying corpse, it merely covers up the evidence. Truman Capote's elderly convict, Mr. Schaeffer, seduced by the magic of Tico Feo's guitar, makes a desperate but ill-fated leap toward freedom. Circumstances conspire against these characters; they seldom have a real chance to escape their fate.

Those in the next group do make conscious choices. The "New England Nun," Louisa Ellis, chooses her cultivated, solitary existence over marriage. Emily Dickinson's poems echo a similar choice on the part of the poet. They are "letters to the world" from one who willingly retired from it. The "wild" Indian, Johnny Eagle, chooses to jump the Colorado River on his bike in William Kotzwinkle's "Follow the Eagle," although he knows he will most likely be smashed on the rocks. Roberta Silman's protagonist in "Company" escapes the pressure of working in a large city hospital and the blandness of her personal life by peopling her travels with the likes of Donne, Rilke, and a handsome young hitchhiker. The rhetoric of the 1960s would hark back to Thoreau's phrase to say that characters such as these marched to "a different drummer." Sometimes, as in the case of Julia, this characteristic is praised and labeled individualism; sometimes it is ridiculed, its possessors like Miniver Cheevy cast as freaks. Their unconventional life-styles often grow to become subjects for literature.

Characters who use their strengths to influence others fall into a final category. The choices they make become even more important than they. Lillian Hellman's Julia grows from privilege to heroism in combatting Fascism, and her friend Lilly struggles to record her tangle of feelings about Julia and about herself. Other characters such as the young black musician in James Baldwin's "Sonny's Blues" translate torment into art.

In these selections, writers dramatize choices and conflicts through their fictional characters or personae. We, the readers, must guard, though, against identifying the fictional character too closely with the writer. Henry James declared in an essay that if a writer wrote only from experience, our fiction would be merely a collection of reports or case studies. The writer, says James, does not have to experience everything he or she writes about, but should be "one on whom nothing is lost." Such writers can magically transmute the details and experiences of their own lives, those of others, and bits of information picked up here and there, into enduring literature. A study of different choices and conflicts in fiction represents, therefore, not merely a record of life, but something truer and finer: a distillation of experience, a vicarious emotion, a guide to living. In this section, literature shows some of the ways humanity in all times has faced the existential dilemma and lived, or failed to live, authentic lives.

Fiction

YOUNG GOODMAN BROWN

Nathaniel Hawthorne
(1804–1864)

Biography p. 1075

Young Goodman Brown came forth at sunset into the street of Salem village; but put his head back, after crossing the threshold, to exchange a parting kiss with his young wife. And Faith, as the wife was aptly named, thrust her own pretty head into the street, letting the wind play with the pink ribbons of her cap while she called to Goodman Brown.

"Dearest heart," whispered she, softly and rather sadly, when her lips were close to his ear, "prithee put off your journey until sunrise and sleep in your own bed to-night. A lone woman is troubled with such dreams and such thoughts that she's afeard of herself sometimes. Pray tarry with me this night, dear husband, of all nights in the year."

"My love and my Faith," replied young Goodman Brown, "of all nights in the year, this one night must I tarry away from thee. My journey, as thou callest it, forth and back again, must needs be done 'twixt now and sunrise. What, my sweet, pretty wife, dost thou doubt me already, and we but three months married?"

"Then God bless you!" said Faith, with the pink ribbons; "and may you find all well when you come back."

"Amen!" cried Goodman Brown. "Say thy prayers, dear Faith, and go to bed at dusk, and no harm will come to thee."

So they parted; and the young man pursued his way until, being about to turn the corner by the meeting house, he looked back and saw the head of Faith still peeping after him with a melancholy air, in spite of her pink ribbons.

"Poor little Faith!" thought he, for his heart smote him. "What a wretch am I to leave her on such an errand! She talks of dreams, too. Methought as she spoke there was trouble in her face, as if a dream had warned her what work is to be done to-night. But no, no; 'twould kill her to think it. Well, she's a blessed angel on earth; and after this one night I'll cling to her skirts and follow her to heaven."

With this excellent resolve for the future, Goodman Brown felt himself justified in making more haste on his present evil purpose. He had taken a dreary road, darkened by all the gloomiest trees of the forest, which barely stood aside to let the narrow path creep through, and closed immediately behind. It was all as lonely as could be; and there is this peculiarity in such a solitude, that the traveller knows not who may be concealed by the innumerable trunks and the thick boughs overhead; so that with lonely footsteps he may yet be passing through an unseen multitude.

"There may be a devilish Indian behind every tree," said Goodman Brown to himself; and he glanced fearfully behind him as he added, "What if the devil himself should be at my very elbow!"

His head being turned back, he passed a crook of the road, and, looking forward again, beheld the figure of a man, in grave and decent attire, seated at the foot of an old tree. He arose at Goodman Brown's approach and walked onward side by side with him.

"You are late, Goodman Brown," said he. "The clock of the Old South was striking as I came through Boston; and that is full fifteen minutes agone."

"Faith kept me back a while," replied the young man, with a tremor in his voice, caused by the sudden appearance of his companion, though not wholly unexpected.

It was now deep dusk in the forest, and deepest in that part of it where these two were journeying. As nearly as could be discerned, the second traveller was about fifty years old, apparently in the same rank of life as Goodman Brown, and bearing a considerable resemblance to him, though perhaps more in expression than features. Still they might have been taken for father and son. And yet, though the elder person was as simply clad as the younger and as simple in manner too, he had an indescribable air of one who knew the world, and who would not have felt abashed at the governor's dinner table or in King William's court, were it possible that his affairs should call him thither. But the only thing about him that could be fixed upon as remarkable was his staff, which bore the likeness of a great black snake, so curiously wrought that it might almost be seen to twist and wriggle itself like a living serpent. This, of course, must have been an ocular deception, assisted by the uncertain light.

"Come, Goodman Brown," cried his fellow-traveller, "this is a dull place for the beginning of a journey. Take my staff, if you are so soon weary."

"Friend," said the other, exchanging his slow pace for a full stop, "having kept covenant by meeting thee here, it is my purpose now to return whence I came. I have scruples touching the matter thou wot'st of."

"Sayest thou so?" replied he of the serpent, smiling apart. "Let us walk on, nevertheless, reasoning as we go; and if I convince thee not thou shalt turn back. We are but a little way in the forest yet."

"Too far! too far!" exclaimed the goodman, unconsciously resuming his walk. "My father never went into the woods on such an errand, nor his father before him. We have been a race of honest men and good Christians since the days of the martyrs; and shall I be the first of the name of Brown that ever took this path and kept—"

"Such company, thou wouldst say," observed the elder person, interpreting his pause. "Well said, Goodman Brown! I have been as well acquainted with your family as with ever a one among the Puritans; and that's no trifle to say. I helped your grandfather, the constable, when he lashed the Quaker woman so smartly through the streets of Salem; and it was I that brought your father a pitch-pine knot, kindled at my own hearth, to set fire to an Indian village, in King Philip's war. They were my good friends, both; and many a pleasant walk have we had along this path, and returned merrily after midnight. I would fain be friends with you for their sake."

"If it be as thou sayest," replied Goodman Brown, "I marvel they never spoke of these matters; or, verily, I marvel not, seeing that the least rumour of the sort would have driven them from New England. We are a people of prayer, and good words to boot, and abide no such wickedness."

"Wickedness or not," said the traveller with the twisted staff, "I have a very general acquaintance here in New England. The deacons of many a church have drunk the communion wine with me; the select men of divers towns make me their chairman; and a majority of the Great and General Court are firm supporters of my interest. The governor and I, too——But these are state secrets."

"Can this be so?" cried Goodman Brown, with a stare of amazement at his undisturbed companion. "Howbeit, I have nothing to do with the governor and council; they have their own ways, and are no rule for a simple husbandman like me. But were I to go on with thee, how should I meet the eye of that good old man, our minister, at Salem village? O, his voice would make me tremble both Sabbath day and lecture day."

Thus far the elder traveller had listened with due gravity; but now burst into a fit of irrepressible mirth, shaking himself so violently that his snakelike staff actually seemed to wriggle in sympathy.

"Ha! ha! ha!" shouted he again and again; then composing himself. "Well, go on, Goodman Brown, go on; but, prithee, don't kill me with laughing."

"Well, then, to end the matter at once," said Goodman Brown, considerably nettled, "there is my wife, Faith. It would break her dear little heart; and I'd rather break my own."

"Nay, if that be the case," answered the other, "e'en go thy ways, Goodman Brown. I would not for twenty old women like the one hobbling before us that Faith should come to any harm."

As he spoke, he pointed his staff at a female figure on the path, in whom Goodman Brown recognized a very pious and exemplary dame, who had taught him his catechism in youth, and was still his moral and spiritual adviser, jointly with the minister and Deacon Gookin.

"A marvel, truly, that Goody Cloyse should be so far in the wilderness at nightfall," said he. "But, with your leave, friend, I shall take a cut through the woods until we have left this Christian woman behind. Being a stranger to you, she might ask whom I was consorting with and whither I was going."

"Be it so," said his fellow-traveller. "Betake you to the woods, and let me keep the path."

Accordingly the young man turned aside, but took care to watch his companion, who advanced softly along the road until he had come within a staff's length of the old dame. She, meanwhile, was making the best of her way, with singular speed for so aged a woman, and mumbling some indistinct words—a prayer, doubtless—as she went. The traveller put forth his staff and touched her withered neck with what seemed the serpent's tail.

"The devil!" screamed the pious old lady.

"Then Goody Cloyse knows her old friend?" observed the traveller, confronting her and leaning on his writhing stick.

"Ah, forsooth' and it is your worship indeed?" cried the good dame. "Yea, truly is it, and in the very image of my old gossip, Goodman Brown, the grandfather of the silly fellow that now is. But—would your worship believe it?—my broomstick hath strangely disappeared, stolen, as I suspect, by that unhanged witch, Goody Cory, and that, too, when I was all anointed with the juice of smallage, and cinquefoil and wolf's bane—"

"Mingled with fine wheat and the fat of a new-born babe," said the shape of old Goodman Brown.

"Ah, your worship knows the recipe," cried the old lady, cackling aloud. "So, as I was saying, being all ready for the meeting, and no horse to ride on, I made up my mind to foot it; for they tell me there is a nice young man to be taken into communion tonight. But now your good worship will lend me your arm, and we shall be there in a twinkling."

"That can hardly be," answered her friend. "I may not spare you my arm, Goody Cloyse; but here is my staff, if you will."

So saying, he threw it down at her feet, where, perhaps, it assumed life, being one of the rods which its owner had formerly lent to the Egyptian magi. Of this fact, however, Goodman Brown could not take cognizance. He had cast up his eyes in astonishment, and, looking down again, beheld neither Goody Cloyse nor the serpentine staff, but his fellow-traveller alone, who waited for him as calmly as if nothing had happened.

"That old woman taught me my catechism," said the young man; and there was a world of meaning in this simple comment.

They continued to walk onward, while the elder traveller exhorted his companion to make good speed and persevere in the path, discoursing so aptly that his arguments seemed rather to spring up in the bosom of his auditor than to be suggested by himself. As they went, he plucked a branch of maple to serve for a walking stick, and began to strip it of the twigs and little boughs, which were wet with evening dew. The moment his fingers touched them they became strangely withered and dried up as with a week's sunshine. Thus the pair proceeded, at a good free pace, until suddenly, in a gloomy hollow of the road, Goodman Brown sat himself down on the stump of a tree, and refused to go any farther.

"Friend," said he, stubbornly, "my mind is made up. Not another step will I budge on this errand. What if a wretched old woman do choose to go to the devil when I thought she was going to heaven: is that any reason why I should quit my dear Faith and go after her?"

"You will think better of this by and by," said his acquaintance, composedly. "Sit here and rest yourself a while; and when you feel like moving again, there is my staff to help you along."

Without more words, he threw his companion the maple stick, and was as speedily out of sight as if he had vanished into the deepening gloom. The young man sat a few moments by the roadside, applauding himself greatly, and thinking with how clear a conscience he should meet the minister in his morning walk, nor shrink from the eye of good old Deacon Gookin. And what calm sleep would be his that very night, which was to have been spent so wickedly, but so purely and sweetly now, in the arms of Faith! Amidst these pleasant and praiseworthy meditations, Goodman Brown heard the tramp of horses along the road, and deemed it advisable to conceal himself within the verge of the forest, conscious of the guilty purpose that had brought him thither, though now so happily turned from it.

On came the hoof tramps and the voices of the riders, two grave old voices, conversing soberly as they drew near. These mingled sounds appeared to pass along the road, within a few yards of the young man's hiding-place; but, owing doubtless to the depth of the gloom at that particular spot, neither the travellers nor their steeds were visible. Though their figures brushed the small boughs by the wayside, it could not be seen that they intercepted, even for a moment, the faint gleam from the strip of bright sky athwart which they must have passed. Goodman Brown alternately crouched and stood on tiptoe, pulling aside the branches and thrusting forth his head as far as he durst without discerning so much as a shadow. It vexed him the more, because he could have sworn, were such a thing possible, that he recognised the voices of the minister and Deacon Gookin, jogging along quietly, as they were wont to do, when bound to some ordination or ecclesiastical council. While yet within hearing, one of the riders stopped to pluck a switch.

"Of the two, reverend sir," said the voice like the deacon's, "I had rather miss an ordination dinner than to-night's meeting. They tell me that some of our community are to be here from Falmouth and beyond, and others from Connecticut and Rhode Island, besides several of the Indian powwows, who, after their fashion, know almost as much deviltry as the best of us. Moreover, there is a goodly young woman to be taken into communion."

"Mighty well, Deacon Gookin!" replied the solemn old tones of the minister. "Spur up, or we shall be late. Nothing can be done, you know, until I get on the ground."

The hoofs clattered again; and the voices, talking up strangely in the empty air, passed on through the forest, where no church had ever been gathered or solitary Christian prayed. Whither, then, could these holy men be journeying so deep into the heathen wilderness? Young Goodman Brown caught hold of a tree for support, being ready to sink down on the ground, faint and overburdened with the heavy sickness of his heart. He looked up to the sky, doubting whether there really was a heaven above him. Yet there was the blue arch, and the stars brightening in it.

"With heaven above and Faith below, I will yet stand firm against the devil!" cried Goodman Brown.

While he still gazed upward into the deep arch of the firmament and had lifted his hands to pray, a cloud, though no wind was stirring, hurried across the zenith and hid the brightening stars. The blue sky was still visible except directly overhead, where this black mass of cloud was sweeping swiftly northward. Aloft in the air, as if from the depths of the cloud, came a confused and doubtful sound of voices. Once the listener fancied that he could distinguish the accents of townspeople of his own, men and women, both pious and ungodly, many of whom he had met at the communion table, and had seen others rioting at the tavern. The next moment so indistinct were the sounds, he doubted whether he had heard aught but the murmur of the old forest, whispering without a wind. Then came a stronger swell of those familiar tones, heard daily in the sunshine at Salem village, but never until now from a cloud of night. There was one voice, of a young woman, uttering lamentations yet with an uncertain sorrow, and entreating for some favour, which, perhaps, it would grieve her to obtain; and all the unseen multitude, both saints and sinners, seemed to encourage her onward.

"Faith!" shouted Goodman Brown, in a voice of agony and desperation; and the echoes of the forest mocked him, crying, "Faith! Faith!" as if bewildered wretches were seeking her all through the wilderness.

The cry of grief, rage, and terror, was yet piercing the night, when the unhappy husband held his breath for a response. There was a scream, drowned immediately in a louder murmur of voices, fading into far-off laughter, as the dark cloud swept away, leaving the clear and silent sky above Goodman Brown. But something fluttered lightly down through the air and caught on the branch of a tree. The young man seized it, and beheld a pink ribbon.

"My Faith is gone!" cried he, after one stupefied moment. "There is no good on earth; and sin is but a name. Come, devil; for to thee is this world given."

And, maddened with despair, so that he laughed loud and long, did Goodman Brown grasp his staff and set forth again, at such a rate that he seemed to fly along the forest path rather than to walk or run. The road grew wilder and drearier and more faintly traced, and vanished at length, leaving him in the heart of the dark wilderness, still rushing onward with the instinct that guides mortal man to evil. The whole forest was peopled with frightful sounds—the creaking of the trees, the howling of wild beasts, and the yell of Indians; while sometimes the wind tolled like a distant church bell, and sometimes gave a broad roar around the traveller, as if all Nature were laughing him to scorn. But he was himself the chief horror of the scene, and shrank not from its other horrors.

"Ha! ha! ha!" roared Goodman Brown when the wind laughed at him. "Let us hear which will laugh loudest. Think not to frighten me with your deviltry. Come witch, come wizard, come Indian powwow, come devil himself, and here comes Goodman Brown. You may as well fear him as he fear you."

In truth, all through the haunted forest there could be nothing more frightful than the figure of Goodman Brown. On he flew among the black pines, brandishing his staff with frenzied gestures, now giving vent to an inspiration of horrid blasphemy, and now shouting forth such laughter as set all the echoes of the forest laughing like demons around him. The fiend in his own shape is less hideous than when he rages in the breast of man. Thus sped the demoniac on his course, until, quivering among the trees, he saw a red light before him, as when the felled trunks and branches of a clearing have been set on fire, and throw up their lurid blaze against the sky, at the hour of midnight. He paused, in a lull of the tempest that had driven him onward, and heard the swell of what seemed a hymn, rolling solemnly from a distance with the weight of many voices. He knew the tune; it was a familiar one in the choir of the village meeting house. The verse died heavily away, and was lengthened by a chorus, not of human voices, but of all the sounds of the benighted wilderness pealing in awful harmony together. Goodman Brown cried out; and his cry was lost to his own ear by its unison with the cry of the desert.

In the interval of silence he stole forward until the light glared full upon his eyes. At an extremity of an open space, hemmed in by the dark wall of the forest, arose a rock, bearing some rude, natural resemblance either to an altar or a pulpit, and surrounded by four blazing pines, their tops aflame, their stems untouched, like candles at an evening meeting. The mass of foliage that had overgrown the summit of the rock was all on fire, blazing high into the night, and fitfully illuminating the whole field. Each pendent twig and leafy festoon was in a blaze. As the red light arose and fell, a numerous congregation alternately shone forth, then disappeared in shadow, and again grew, as it were, out of the darkness, peopling the heart of the solitary woods at once.

"A grave and dark-clad company," quoth Goodman Brown.

In truth they were such. Among them, quivering to and fro between gloom and splendour, appeared faces that would be seen next day at the council board of the province, and others which, Sabbath after Sabbath, looked devoutly heavenward, and benignantly over the crowded pews, from the holiest pulpits in the land. Some affirm that the lady of the governor was there. At least there were high dames well known to her, and wives of honoured husbands, and widows, a great multitude, and ancient maidens, all of excellent repute, and fair young girls, who trembled lest their mothers should espy them. Either the sudden gleams of light flashing over the obscure field bedazzled Goodman Brown, or he recognised a score of the church members of Salem village famous for their especial sanctity. Good old Deacon Gookin had arrived, and waited at the skirts of that venerable saint, his revered pastor. But, irreverently consorting with these grave, reputable, and pious people, these elders of the church, these chaste dames and dewy virgins, there were men of dissolute lives, and women of spotted fame, wretches given over to all mean and filthy vice, and suspected even of horrid crimes. It was strange to see that the good shrank not from the wicked, nor were the sinners abashed by the saints. Scattered also among their palefaced enemies were the Indian priests, or powwows, who had often scared their native forest with more hideous incantations than any known to English witchcraft.

"But where is Faith?" thought Goodman Brown; and, as hope came into his heart, he trembled.

Another verse of the hymn arose, a slow and mournful strain, such as the pious love, but joined to words which expressed all that our nature can conceive of sin, and darkly hinted at far more. Unfathomable to mere mortals is the lore of fiends. Verse after verse was sung; and still the chorus of the desert swelled between like the deepest tone of a mighty organ; and with the final peal of that dreadful anthem there came a sound, as if the roaring wind, the rushing streams, the howling beasts, and every other voice of the unconverted wilderness were mingling and according with the voice of guilty man in homage to the prince of all. The four blazing pines threw up a loftier flame, and obscurely discovered shapes and visages of horror on the smoke wreaths above the impious assembly. At the same moment the fire on the rock shot redly forth and formed a glowing arch above its base, where now appeared a figure. With reverence be it spoken, the figure bore no slight similitude, both in garb and manner, to some grave divine of the New England churches.

"Bring forth the converts!" cried a voice that echoed through the field and rolled into the forest.

At the word, Goodman Brown stepped forth from the shadow of the trees and approached the congregation, with whom he felt a loathful brotherhood by the sympathy of all that was wicked in his heart. He could have well nigh sworn that the shape of his own dead father beckoned him to advance, looking downward from a smoke wreath, while a woman, with dim features of despair, threw out her hand to warn him back. Was it his mother? But he had no power to retreat one step, nor to resist, even in thought, when the minister and good old Deacon Gookin seized his arms and led him to the blazing rock. Thither came also the slender form of a veiled female, led between Goody Cloyse, that pious teacher of the catechism, and Martha Carrier, who had received the devil's promise to be queen of hell. A rampant hag was she. And there stood the proselytes beneath the canopy of fire.

"Welcome, my children," said the dark figure, "to the communion of your race. Ye have found thus young your nature and your destiny. My children, look behind you!"

They turned; and flashing forth, as it were, in a sheet of flame, the fiend worshippers were seen; the smile of welcome gleamed darkly on every visage.

"There," resumed the sable form, "are all whom ye have reverenced from youth. Ye deemed them holier than yourselves, and shrank from your own sin, contrasting it with their lives of righteousness and prayerful aspirations heavenward. Yet here are they all in my worshipping assembly. This night it shall be granted you to know their secret deeds; how hoary-bearded elders of the church have whispered wanton words to the young maids of their households; how many a woman, eager for widows' weeds, has given her husband a drink at bedtime and let him sleep his last sleep in her bosom; how beardless youths have made haste to inherit their father's wealth; and how fair damsels—blush not, sweet ones—have dug little graves in the garden, and bidden me, the sole guest, to an infant's funeral. By the sympathy of your human hearts for sin ye shall scent out all the places—whether in church, bed-chamber, street, field, or forest—where crime has been committed, and shall exult to behold the whole earth one stain of guilt, one mighty blood spot. Far more than this. It shall be yours to penetrate, in every bosom, the deep mystery of sin, the fountain of all wicked arts, and which inexhaustibly supplies more evil impulses than human power—than my power at its utmost—can make manifest in deeds. And now, my children, look upon each other."

They did so; and, by the blaze of the hell-kindled torches, the wretched man beheld his Faith, and the wife her husband, trembling before that unhallowed altar.

"Lo, there ye stand, my children," said the figure, in a deep and solemn tone, almost sad with its despairing awfulness, as if his once angelic nature could yet mourn for our miserable race. "Depending upon one another's hearts, ye had still hoped that virtue were not all a dream. Now are ye deceived. Evil is the nature of mankind. Evil must be your only happiness. Welcome again, my children, to the communion of your race."

"Welcome," repeated the fiend worshippers, in one cry of despair and triumph.

And there they stood, the only pair, as it seemed, who were yet hesitating on the verge of wickedness in this dark world. A basin was hollowed, naturally, in the rock. Did it contain water, reddened by the lurid light? or was it blood? or, perchance, a liquid flame? Herein did the shape of evil dip his hand and prepare to lay the mark of baptism upon their foreheads, that they might be partakers of the mystery of sin, more conscious of the secret guilt of others, both in deed and thought, than they could now be of their own. The husband cast one look at his pale wife, and Faith at him. What polluted wretches would the next glance show them to each other, shuddering alike at what they disclosed and what they saw!

"Faith! Faith!" cried the husband, "look up to heaven, and resist the wicked one."

Whether Faith obeyed, he knew not. Hardly had he spoken when he found himself amid calm night and solitude, listening to a roar of the wind which died heavily away through the forest. He staggered against the rock, and felt it chill and damp; while a hanging twig, that had been all on fire, besprinkled his cheek with the coldest dew.

The next morning young Goodman Brown came slowly into the street of Salem village, staring around him like a bewildered man. The good old minister was taking a walk along the graveyard to get an appetite for breakfast and meditate his sermon, and bestowed a blessing, as he passed, on Goodman Brown. He shrank from the venerable saint as if to avoid an anathema. Old Deacon Gookin was at domestic worship, and the holy words of his prayer were heard through the open window. "What God doth the wizard pray to?" quoth Goodman Brown. Goody Cloyse, that excellent old Christian, stood in the early sunshine at her own lattice, catechizing a little girl who had brought her a pint of morning's milk. Goodman Brown snatched away the child as from the grasp of the fiend himself. Turning the corner by the meeting house, he spied the head of Faith, with the pink ribbons, gazing anxiously forth, and bursting into such joy at sight of him that she skipped along the street, and almost kissed her husband before the whole village. But Goodman Brown looked sternly and sadly into her face, and passed on without a greeting.

Had Goodman Brown fallen asleep in the forest and only dreamed a wild dream of a witch meeting?

Be it so, if you will; but, alas! it was a dream of evil omen for young Goodman Brown. A stern, a sad, a darkly meditative, a distrustful, if not a desperate man, did he become from the night of that fearful dream. On the Sabbath day, when the congregation were singing a holy psalm, he could not listen, because an anthem of sin rushed loudly upon his ear and drowned all the blessed strain. When the minister spoke from the pulpit, with power and fervid eloquence, and with his hand on the open Bible, of the sacred truths of our religion, and of saint-like lives and triumphant deaths, and of future bliss or misery unutterable, then did Goodman Brown turn pale, dreading lest the roof should thunder down upon the grey blasphemer and his hearers. Often, awaking suddenly at midnight, he shrank from the bosom of Faith; and at morning or eventide, when the family knelt down at prayer, he scowled, and muttered to himself, and gazed sternly at his wife, and turned away. And when he had lived long, and was borne to his grave, a hoary corpse, followed by Faith, an aged woman, and children and grandchildren, a goodly procession, besides neighbors not a few, they carved no hopeful verse upon his tombstone; for his dying hour was gloom.

DEATH IN THE WOODS

Sherwood Anderson
(1876–1941)

Biography p. 1060

She was an old woman and lived on a farm near the town in which I lived. All country and small-town people have seen such old women, but no one knows much about them. Such an old woman comes into town driving an old worn-out horse or she comes afoot carrying a basket. She may own a few hens and have eggs to sell. She brings them in a basket and takes them to a grocer. There she trades them in. She gets some salt pork and some beans. Then she gets a pound or two of sugar and some flour.

Afterwards she goes to the butcher's and asks for some dog-meat. She may spend ten or fifteen cents, but when she does she asks for something. Formerly the butchers gave liver to any one who wanted to carry it away. In our family we were always having it. Once one of my brothers got a whole cow's liver at the slaughter-house near the fairgrounds in our town. We had it until we were sick of it. It never cost a cent. I have hated the thought of it ever since.

The old farm woman got some liver and a soup-bone. She never visited with any one, and as soon as she got what she wanted she lit out for home. It made quite a load for such an old body. No one gave her a lift. People drive right down a road and never notice an old woman like that.

There was such an old woman who used to come into town past our house one Summer and Fall when I was a young boy and was sick with what was called inflammatory rheumatism. She went home later carrying a heavy pack on her back. Two or three large gaunt-looking dogs followed at her heels.

The old woman was nothing special. She was one of the nameless ones that hardly any one knows, but she got into my thoughts. I have just suddenly now, after all these years, remembered her and what happened. It is a story. Her name was Grimes, and she lived with her husband and son in a small unpainted house on the bank of a small creek four miles from town.

The husband and son were a tough lot. Although the son was but twenty-one, he had already served a term in jail. It was whispered about that the woman's husband stole horses and ran them off to some other county. Now and then, when a horse turned up missing, the man had also disappeared. No one ever caught him. Once, when I was loafing at Tom Whitehead's livery-barn, the man came there and sat on the bench in front. Two or three other men were there, but no one spoke to him. He sat for a few minutes and then got up and went away. When he was leaving he turned around and stared at the men. There was a look of defiance in his eyes. "Well, I have tried to be friendly. You don't want to talk to me. It has been so wherever I have gone in this town. If, some day, one of your fine horses turns up missing, well, then what?" He did not say anything actually. "I'd like to bust one of you on the jaw," was about what his eyes said. I remember how the look in his eyes made me shiver.

The old man belonged to a family that had had money once. His name was Jake Grimes. It all comes back clearly now. His father, John Grimes, had owned a sawmill when the country was new, and had made money. Then he got to drinking and running after women. When he died there wasn't much left.

Jake blew in the rest. Pretty soon there wasn't any more lumber to cut and his land was nearly all gone.

He got his wife off a German farmer, for whom he went to work one June day in the wheat harvest. She was a young thing then and scared to death. You see, the farmer was up to something with the girl—she was, I think, a bound girl and his wife had her suspicions. She took it out on the girl when the man wasn't around. Then, when the wife had to go off to town for supplies, the farmer got after her. She told young Jake that nothing really ever happened, but he didn't know whether to believe it or not.

He got her pretty easy himself, the first time he was out with her. He wouldn't have married her if the German farmer hadn't tried to tell him where to get off. He got her to go riding with him in his buggy one night when he was threshing on the place, and then he came for her the next Sunday night.

She managed to get out of the house without her employer's seeing, but when she was getting into the buggy he showed up. It was almost dark, and he just popped up suddenly at the horse's head. He grabbed the horse by the bridle and Jake got out his buggy-whip.

They had it out all right! The German was a tough one. Maybe he didn't care whether his wife knew or not. Jake hit him over the face and shoulders with the buggy-whip, but the horse got to acting up and he had to get out.

Then the two men went for it. The girl didn't see it. The horse started to run away and went nearly a mile down the road before the girl got him stopped. Then she managed to tie him to a tree beside the road. (I wonder how I know all this. It must have stuck in my mind from small-town tales when I was a boy.) Jake found her there after he got through with the German. She was huddled up in the buggy seat, crying, scared to death. She told Jake a lot of stuff, how the German had tried to get her, how he chased her once into the barn, how another time, when they happened to be alone in the house together, he tore her dress open clear down the front. The German, she said, might have got her that time if he hadn't heard his old woman drive in at the gate. She had been off to town for supplies. Well, she would be putting the horse in the barn. The German managed to sneak off to the fields without his wife seeing. He told the girl he would kill her if she told. What could she do? She told a lie about ripping her dress in the barn when she was feeding the stock. I remember now that she was a bound girl and did not know where her father and mother were. Maybe she did not have any father. You know what I mean.

Such bound children were often enough cruelly treated. They were children who had no parents, slaves really. There were very few orphan homes then. They were legally bound into some home. It was a matter of pure luck how it came out.

II

She married Jake and had a son and daughter, but the daughter died.

Then she settled down to feed stock. That was her job. At the German's place she had cooked the food for the German and his wife. The wife was a strong woman with big hips and worked most of the time in the fields with her husband. She fed them and fed the cows in the barn, fed the pigs, the horses and the chickens. Every moment of every day, as a young girl, was spent feeding something.

Then she married Jake Grimes and he had to be fed. She was a slight thing, and when she had been married for three or four years, and after the two children were born, her slender shoulders became stooped.

Jake always had a lot of big dogs around the house, that stood near the unused sawmill near the creek. He was always trading horses when he wasn't stealing something and had a lot of poor bony ones about. Also he kept three or four pigs and a cow. They were all pastured in the few acres left of the Grimes place and Jake did little enough work.

He went into debt for a threshing outfit and ran it for several years, but it did not pay. People did not trust him. They were afraid he would steal the grain at night. He had to go a long way off to get work and it cost too much to get there. In the Winter he hunted and cut a little firewood, to be sold in some nearby town. When the son grew up he was just like the father. They got drunk together. If there wasn't anything to eat in the house when they came home the old man gave his old woman a cut over the head. She had a few chickens of her own and had to kill one of them in a hurry. When they were all killed she wouldn't have any eggs to sell when she went to town, and then what would she do?

She had to scheme all her life about getting things fed, getting the pigs fed so they would grow fat and could be butchered in the Fall. When they were butchered her husband took most of the meat off to town and sold it. If he did not do it first the boy did. They fought sometimes and when they fought the old woman stood aside trembling.

She had got the habit of silence anyway—that was fixed. Sometimes, when she began to look old—she wasn't forty yet—and when the husband and son were both off, trading horses or drinking or hunting or stealing, she went around the house and the barnyard muttering to herself.

How was she going to get everything fed?—that was her problem. The dogs had to be fed. There wasn't enough hay in the barn for the horses and the cow. If she didn't feed the chickens how could they lay eggs? Without eggs to sell how could she get things in town, things she had to have to keep the life of the farm going? Thank heaven, she did not have to feed her husband—in a certain way. That hadn't lasted long after their marriage and after the babies came. Where he went on his long trips she did not know. Sometimes he was gone from home for weeks, and after the boy grew up they went off together.

They left everything at home for her to manage and she had no money. She knew no one. No one ever talked to her in town. When it was Winter she had to gather sticks of wood for her fire, had to try to keep the stock fed with very little grain.

The stock in the barn cried to her hungrily, the dogs followed her about. In the Winter the hens laid few enough eggs. They huddled in the corners of the barn and she kept watching them. If a hen lays an egg in the barn in the Winter and you do not find it, it freezes and breaks.

One day in Winter the old woman went off to town with a few eggs and the dogs followed her. She did not get started until nearly three o'clock and the snow was heavy. She hadn't been feeling very well for several days and so she went muttering along, scantily clad, her shoulders stooped. She had an old grain bag in which she carried her eggs, tucked away down in the bottom. There weren't many of them, but in Winter the price of eggs is up. She would get a little meat in exchange for the eggs, some salt pork, a little sugar, and some coffee perhaps. It might be the butcher would give her a piece of liver.

When she had got to town and was trading in her eggs the dogs lay by the door outside. She did pretty well, got the things she needed, more than she had hoped. Then she went to the butcher and he gave her some liver and some dog-meat.

It was the first time any one had spoken to her in a friendly way for a long time. The butcher was alone in his shop when she came in and was annoyed by the thought of such a sick-looking old woman out on such a day. It was bitter cold and the snow, that had let up during the afternoon, was falling again. The butcher said something about her husband and her son, swore at them, and the old woman stared at him, a look of mild surprise in her eyes as he talked. He said that if either the husband or the son were going to get any of the liver or the heavy bones with scraps of meat hanging to them that he had put into the grain bag, he'd see him starve first.

Starve, eh? Well, things had to be fed. Men had to be fed, and the horses that weren't any good but maybe could be traded off, and the poor thin cow that hadn't given any milk for three months.

Horses, cows, pigs, dogs, men.

III

The old woman had to get back before darkness came if she could. The dogs followed at her heels, sniffing at the heavy grain bag she had fastened on her back. When she got to the edge of town she stopped by a fence and tied the bag on her back with a piece of rope she had carried in her dress-pocket for just that purpose. That was an easier way to carry it. Her arms ached. It was hard when she had to crawl over fences and once she fell over and landed in the snow. The dogs went frisking about. She had to struggle to get to her feet again, but she made it. The point of climbing over the fences was that there was a short cut over a hill and through a woods. She might have gone around by the road, but it was a mile farther that way. She was afraid she couldn't make it. And then, besides, the stock had to be fed. There was a little hay left and a little corn. Perhaps her husband and son would bring some home when they came. They had driven off in the only buggy the Grimes family had, a rickety thing, a rickety horse hitched to the buggy, two other rickety horses led by halters. They were going to trade horses, get a little money if they could. They might come home drunk. It would be well to have something in the house when they came back.

The son had an affair on with a woman at the county seat, fifteen miles away. She was a rough enough woman, a tough one. Once, in the Summer, the son had brought her to the house. Both she and the son had been drinking. Jake Grimes was away and the son and his woman ordered the old woman about like a servant. She didn't mind much; she was used to it. Whatever happened she never said anything. That was her way of getting along. She had managed that way when she was a young girl at the German's and ever since she had married Jake. That time her son brought his woman to the house they stayed all night, sleeping together just as though they were married.

It hadn't shocked the old woman, not much. She had got past being shocked early in life.

With the pack on her back she went painfully along across an open field, wading in the deep snow, and got into the woods.

There was a path, but it was hard to follow. Just beyond the top of the hill, where the woods was thickets, there was a small clearing. Had some one once thought of building a house there? The clearing was as large as a building lot in town, large enough for a house and a garden. The path ran along the side of the clearing, and when she got there the old woman sat down to rest at the foot of a tree.

It was a foolish thing to do. When she got herself placed, the pack against the tree's trunk, it was nice, but what about getting up again? She worried about that for a moment and then quietly closed her eyes.

She must have slept for a time. When you are about so cold you can't get any colder. The afternoon grew a little warmer and the snow came thicker than ever. Then after a time the weather cleared. The moon even came out.

There were four Grimes dogs that had followed Mrs. Grimes into town, all tall gaunt fellows. Such men as Jake Grimes and his son always keep just such dogs. They kick and abuse them, but they stay. The Grimes dogs, in order to keep from starving, had to do a lot of foraging for themselves, and they had been at it while the old woman slept with her back to the tree at the side of the clearing. They had been chasing rabbits in the woods and in adjoining fields and in their ranging had picked up three other farm dogs.

After a time all the dogs came back to the clearing. They were excited about something. Such nights, cold and clear and with a moon, do things to dogs. It may be that some old instinct, come down from the time when they were wolves and ranged the woods in packs on Winter nights, comes back into them.

The dogs in the clearing, before the old woman, had caught two or three rabbits and their immediate hunger had been satisfied. They began to play, running in circles in the clearing. Round and round they ran, each dog's nose at the tail of the next dog. In the clearing, under the snow-laden trees and under the wintry moon they made a strange picture, running thus silently, in a circle their running had beaten in the soft snow. The dogs made no sound. They ran around and around in the circle.

It may have been that the old woman saw them doing that before she died. She may have awakened once or twice and looked at the strange sight with dim old eyes.

She wouldn't be very cold now, just drowsy. Life hangs on a long time. Perhaps the old woman was out of her head. She may have dreamed of her girlhood, at the German's, and before that, when she was a child and before her mother lit out and left her.

Her dreams couldn't have been very pleasant. Not many pleasant things had happened to her. Now and then one of the Grimes dogs left the running circle and came to stand before her. The dog thrust his face close to her face. His red tongue was hanging out.

The running of the dogs may have been a kind of death ceremony. It may have been that the primitive instinct of the wolf, having been aroused in the dogs by the night and the running, made them somehow afraid.

"Now we are no longer wolves. We are dogs, the servants of men. Keep alive, man! When man dies we become wolves again."

When one of the dogs came to where the old woman sat with her back against the tree and thrust his nose close to her face he seemed satisfied and went back to run with the pack. All the Grimes dogs did it at some time during the evening, before she died. I knew all about it afterward, when I grew to be a man, because once in a woods in Illinois, on another Winter night, I saw a pack of dogs act just like that. The dogs were waiting for me to die as they had waited for the old woman that night when I was a child, but when it happened to me I was a young man and had no intention whatever of dying.

The old woman died softly and quietly. When she was dead and when one of the Grimes dogs had come to her and had found her dead all the dogs stopped running.

They gathered about her.

Well, she was dead now. She had fed the Grimes dogs when she was alive, what about now?

There was the pack on her back, the grain bag containing the piece of salt pork, the liver the butcher had given her, the dog-meat, the soup bones. The butcher in town, having been suddenly overcome with a feeling of pity, had loaded her grain bag heavily. It had been a big haul for the old woman.

It was a big haul for the dogs now.

IV

One of the Grimes dogs sprang suddenly out from among the others and began worrying the pack on the old woman's back. Had the dogs really been wolves that one would have been the leader of the pack. What he did, all the others did.

All of them sank their teeth into the grain bag the old woman had fastened with ropes to her back.

They dragged the old woman's body out into the open clearing. The worn-out dress was quickly torn from her shoulders. When she was found, a day or two later, the dress had been torn from her body clear to the hips, but the dogs had not touched her body. They had got the meat out of the grain bag, that was all. Her body was frozen stiff when it was found, and the shoulders were so narrow and the body so slight that in death it looked like the body of some charming young girl.

Such things happened in towns of the Middle West, on farms near town, when I was a boy. A hunter out after rabbits found the old woman's body and did not touch it. Something, the beaten round path in the little snow-covered clearing, the silence of the place, the place where the dogs had worried the body trying to pull the grain bag away or tear it open—something startled the man and he hurried off to town.

I was in Main street with one of my brothers who was town newsboy and who was taking the afternoon papers to the stores. It was almost night.

The hunter came into a grocery and told his story. Then he went to the hardware-shop and into a drugstore. Men began to gather on the sidewalks. Then they started out along the road to the place in the woods.

My brother should have gone on about his business of distributing papers but he didn't. Every one was going to the woods. The undertaker went and the town marshal. Several men got on a dray and rode out to where the path left the road and went into the woods, but the horses weren't very sharply shod and slid about on the slippery roads. They made no better time than those of us who walked.

The town marshal was a large man whose leg had been injured in the Civil War. He carried a heavy cane and limped rapidly along the road. My brother and I followed at his heels, and as we went other men and boys joined the crowd.

It had grown dark by the time we got to where the old woman had left the road but the moon had come out. The marshal was thinking there might have been a murder. He kept asking the hunter questions. The hunter went along with his gun across his shoulders, a dog following at his heels. It isn't often a rabbit hunter has a chance to be so conspicuous. He was taking full advantage of it, leading the procession with the town marshal. "I didn't see any wounds. She was a beautiful young girl. Her face was buried in the snow. No, I didn't know her." As a matter of fact, the hunter had not looked closely at the body. He had been frightened. She might have been murdered and some one might spring out from behind a tree and murder him. In a woods, in the late afternoon, when the trees are all bare and there is white snow on the ground, when all is silent, something creepy steals over the mind and body. If something strange or uncanny has happened in the neighborhood all you think about is getting away from there as fast as you can.

The crowd of men and boys had got to where the old woman had crossed the field and went, following the marshal and the hunter, up the slight incline and into the woods.

My brother and I were silent. He had his bundle of papers in a bag slung across his shoulder. When he got back to town he would have to go on distributing his papers before he went home to supper. If I went along, as he had no doubt already determined I should, we would both be late. Either mother or our older sister would have to warm our supper.

Well, we would have something to tell. A boy did not get such a chance very often. It was lucky we just happened to go into the grocery when the hunter came in. The hunter was a country fellow. Neither of us had ever seen him before.

Now the crowd of men and boys had got to the clearing. Darkness comes quickly on such Winter nights, but the full moon made everything clear. My brother and I stood near the tree, beneath which the old woman had died.

She did not look old, lying there in that light, frozen and still. One of the men turned her over in the snow and I saw everything. My body trembled with some strange mystical feeling and so did my brother's. It might have been the cold.

Neither of us had ever seen a woman's body before. It may have been the snow, clinging to the frozen flesh, that made it look so white and lovely, so like marble. No woman had come with the party from town; but one of the men, he was the town blacksmith, took off his overcoat and spread it over her. Then he gathered her into his arms and started off to town, all the others following silently. At that time no one knew who she was.

V

I had seen everything, had seen the oval in the snow, like a miniature race-track, where the dogs had run, had seen how the men were mystified, had seen the white bare young-looking shoulders, had heard the whispered comments of the men.

The men were simply mystified. They took the body to the undertaker's, and when the blacksmith, the hunter, the marshal and several others had got inside they closed the door. If father had been there perhaps he could have got in, but we boys couldn't.

I went with my brother to distribute the rest of his papers and when we got home it was my brother who told the story.

I kept silent and went to bed early. It may have been I was not satisfied with the way he told it.

Later, in the town, I must have heard other fragments of the old woman's story. She was recognized the next day and there was an investigation.

The husband and son were found somewhere and brought to town and there was an attempt to connect them with the woman's death, but it did not work. They had perfect enough alibis.

However, the town was against them. They had to get out. Where they went I never heard.

I remember only the picture there in the forest, the men standing about, the naked girlish-looking figure, face down in the snow, the tracks made by the running dogs and the clear cold Winter sky above. White fragments of clouds were drifting across the sky. They went racing across the little open space among the trees.

The scene in the forest had become for me, without my knowing it, the foundation for the real story I am now trying to tell. The fragments, you see, had to be picked up slowly, long afterwards.

Things happened. When I was a young man I worked on the farm of a German. The hired-girl was afraid of her employer. The farmer's wife hated her.

I saw things at that place. Once later, I had a half-uncanny, mystical adventure with dogs in an Illinois forest on a clear, moon-lit Winter night. When I was a schoolboy, and on a Summer day, I went with a boy friend out along a creek some miles from town and came to the house where the old woman had lived. No one had lived in the house since her death. The doors were broken from the hinges; the window lights were all broken. As the boy and I stood in the road outside, two dogs, just roving farm dogs no doubt, came running around the corner of the house. The dogs were tall, gaunt fellows and came down to the fence and glared through at us, standing in the road.

The whole thing, the story of the old woman's death, was to me as I grew older like music heard from far off. The notes had to be picked up slowly one at a time. Something had to be understood.

The woman who died was one destined to feed animal life. Anyway, that is all she ever did. She was feeding animal life before she was born, as a child, as a young woman working on the farm of the German, after she married, when she grew old and when she died. She fed animal life in cows, in chickens, in pigs, in horses, in dogs, in men. Her daughter had died in childhood and with her one son she had no articulate relations. On the night when she died she was hurrying homeward, bearing on her body food for animal life.

She died in the clearing in the woods and even after her death continued feeding animal life.

You see it is likely that, when my brother told the story, that night when we got home and my mother and sister sat listening, I did not think he got the point. He was too young and so was I. A thing so complete has its own beauty.

I shall not try to emphasize the point. I am only explaining why I was dissatisfied then and have been ever since. I speak of that only that you may understand why I have been impelled to try to tell the simple story over again.

A NEW ENGLAND NUN

Mary E. Wilkins Freeman

(1852–1930)

Biography p. 1073

It was late in the afternoon, and the light was waning. There was a difference in look of the tree shadows out in the yard. Somewhere in the distance cows were lowing and a little bell was tinkling; now and then a farm-wagon tilted by, and the dust flew; some blue-shirted laborers with shovels over their shoulders plodded past; little swarms of flies were dancing up and down before the peoples' faces in the soft air. There seemed to be a gentle stir arising over everything for the mere sake of subsidence—a very premonition of rest and hush and night.

This soft diurnal commotion was over Louisa Ellis also. She had been peacefully sewing at her sitting-room window all the afternoon. Now she quilted her needle carefully into her work, which she folded precisely, and laid in a basket with her thimble and thread and scissors. Louisa Ellis could not remember that ever in her life she had mislaid one of these little feminine appurtenances, which had become, from long use and constant association, a very part of her personality.

Louisa tied a green apron round her waist, and got out a flat straw hat with a green ribbon. Then she went into the garden with a little blue crockery bowl, to pick some currants for her tea. After the currants were picked she sat on the back door-step and stemmed them, collecting the stems carefully in her apron, and afterwards throwing them into the hen-coop. She looked sharply at the grass beside the step to see if any had fallen there.

Louisa was slow and still in her movements; it took her a long time to prepare her tea; but when ready it was set forth with as much grace as if she had been a veritable guest to her own self. The little square table stood exactly in the centre of the kitchen, and was covered with a starched linen cloth whose border pattern of flowers glistened. Louisa had a damask napkin on her tea-tray, where were arranged a cut-glass tumbler full of teaspoons, a silver cream-pitcher, a china sugar-bowl, and one pink china cup and saucer. Louisa used china every day—something which none of her neighbors did. They whispered about it among themselves. Their daily tables were laid with common crockery, their sets of best china stayed in the parlor closet, and Louisa Ellis was no richer nor better bred than they. Still she would use the china. She had for her supper a glass dish full of sugared currants, a plate of little cakes, and one of light white biscuits. Also a leaf or two of lettuce, which she cut up daintily. Louisa was very fond of lettuce, which she raised to perfection in her little garden. She ate quite heartily, though in a delicate, pecking way; it seemed almost surprising that any considerable bulk of the food should vanish.

After tea she filled a plate with nicely baked thin corn-cakes, and carried them out into the back-yard.

"Caesar!" she called. "Caesar! Caesar!"

There was a little rush, and the clank of a chain, and a large yellow-and-white dog appeared at the door of his tiny hut, which was half hidden among the tall grasses and flowers. Louisa patted him and gave him the corn-cakes. Then she returned to the house and washed the tea-things, polishing the china carefully. The twilight had deepened; the chorus of the frogs floated in at the open window wonderfully loud and shrill, and once in a while a long sharp drone from a tree-toad pierced it. Louisa took off her green gingham apron, disclosing a shorter one of pink and white print. She lighted her lamp, and sat down again with her sewing.

In about half an hour Joe Dagget came. She heard his heavy step on the walk, and rose and took off her pink and white apron. Under that was still another—white linen with a little cambric edging on the bottom; that was Louisa's company apron. She never wore it without her calico sewing apron over it unless she had a guest. She had barely folded the pink and white one with methodical haste and laid it in a table-drawer when the door opened and Joe Dagget entered.

He seemed to fill up the whole room. A little yellow canary that had been asleep in his green cage at the south window woke up and fluttered wildly, beating his little yellow wings against the wires. He always did so when Joe Dagget came into the room.

"Good-evening," said Louisa. She extended her hand with a kind of solemn cordiality.

"Good-evening, Louisa," returned the man, in a loud voice.

She placed a chair for him, and they sat facing each other, with the table between them. He sat bolt-upright, toeing out his heavy feet squarely, glancing with a good-humored uneasiness around the room. She sat gently erect, folding her slender hands in her white-linen lap.

"Been a pleasant day," remarked Dagget.

"Real pleasant," Louisa assented, softly. "Have you been haying?" she asked, after a little while.

"Yes, I've been haying all day, down in the ten-acre lot. Pretty hot work."

"It must be."

"Yes, it's pretty hot work in the sun."

"Is your mother well to-day?"

"Yes, mother's pretty well."

"I suppose Lily Dyer's with her now?"

Dagget colored. "Yes, she's with her," he answered, slowly.

He was not very young, but there was a boyish look about his large face. Louisa was not quite as old as he, her face was fairer and smoother, but she gave people the impression of being older.

"I suppose she's a good deal of help to your mother," she said, further.

"I guess she is; I don't know how mother'd get along without her," said Dagget, with a sort of embarrassed warmth.

"She looks like a real capable girl. She's pretty-looking too," remarked Louisa.

"Yes, she is pretty fair-looking."

Presently Dagget began fingering the books on the table. There was a square red autograph album, and a Young Lady's Gift-Book which had belonged to Louisa's mother. He took them up one after the other and opened them; then laid them down again, the album on the Gift-Book.

Louisa kept eying them with mild uneasiness. Finally she rose and changed the position of the books, putting the album underneath. That was the way they had been arranged in the first place.

Dagget gave an awkward little laugh. "Now what difference did it make which book was on top?" said he.

Louisa looked at him with a deprecating smile. "I always keep them that way," murmured she.

"You do beat everything," said Dagget, trying to laugh again. His large face was flushed.

He remained about an hour longer, then rose to take leave. Going out, he stumbled over a rug, and trying to recover himself, hit Louisa's work-basket on the table, and knocked it on the floor.

He looked at Louisa, then at the rolling spools; he ducked himself awkwardly toward them but she stopped him. "Never mind," said she; "I'll pick them up after you're gone."

She spoke with a mild stiffness. Either she was a little disturbed, or his nervousness affected her, and made her seem constrained in her effort to reassure him.

When Joe Dagget was outside he drew in the sweet evening air with a sigh, and felt much as an innocent and perfectly well-intentioned bear might after his exit from a china shop.

Louisa, on her part, felt much as the kind-hearted, long-suffering owner of the china shop might have done after the exit of the bear.

She tied on the pink, then the green apron, picked up all the scattered treasures and replaced them in her work-basket, and straightened the rug. Then she set the lamp on the floor, and began sharply examining the carpet. She even rubbed her fingers over it, and looked at them.

"He's tracked in a good deal of dust," she murmured. "I thought he must have." Louisa got a dust-pan and brush, and swept Joe Dagget's track carefully.

If he could have known it, it would have increased his perplexity and uneasiness, although it would not have disturbed his loyalty in the least. He came twice a week to see Louisa Ellis, and every time, sitting there in her delicately sweet room, he felt as if surrounded by a hedge of lace. He was afraid to stir lest he should put a clumsy foot or hand through the fairy web, and he had always the consciousness that Louisa was watching fearfully lest he should.

Still the lace and Louisa commanded perforce his perfect respect and patience and loyalty. They were to be married in a month, after a singular courtship which had lasted for a matter of fifteen years. For fourteen out of the fifteen years the two had not once seen each other, and they had seldom exchanged letters. Joe had been all those years in Australia, where he had gone to make his fortune, and where he had stayed until he made it. He would have stayed fifty years if it had taken so long, and come home feeble and tottering, or never come home at all, to marry Louisa.

But the fortune had been made in the fourteen years, and he had come home now to marry the woman who had been patiently and unquestioningly waiting for him all that time.

Shortly after they were engaged he had announced to Louisa his determination to strike out into new fields, and secure a competency before they should be married. She had listened and assented with the sweet serenity which never failed her, not even when her lover set forth on that long and uncertain journey. Joe, buoyed up as he was by his sturdy determination, broke down a little at the last, but Louisa kissed him with a mild blush, and said good-by.

"It won't be for long," poor Joe had said, huskily; but it was for fourteen years.

In that length of time much had happened. Louisa's mother and brother had died, and she was all alone in the world. But the greatest happening of all—a subtle happening which both were too simple to understand—Louisa's feet had turned into a path, smooth maybe under a calm, serene sky, but so straight and unswerving that it could only meet a check at her grave, and so narrow there was no room for any one at her side.

Louisa's first emotion when Joe Dagget came home (he had not apprised her of his coming) was consternation, although she would not admit it to herself, and he never dreamed of it. Fifteen years ago she had been in love with him—at least she considered herself to be. Just at that time, gently acquiescing with and falling into the natural drift of girlhood, she had seen marriage ahead as a reasonable feature and a probable desirability of life. She had listened with calm docility to her mother's views upon the subject. Her mother was remarkable for her cool sense and sweet, even temperament. She talked wisely to her daughter when Joe Dagget presented himself, and Louisa accepted him with no hesitation. He was the first lover she had ever had.

She had been faithful to him all these years. She had never dreamed of the possibility of marrying anyone else. Her life, especially for the last seven years, had been full of a pleasant peace, she had never felt discontented nor impatient over her lover's absence; still she had always looked forward to his return and their marriage as the inevitable conclusion of things. However, she had fallen into a way of placing it so far in the future that it was almost equal to placing it over the boundaries of another life.

When Joe came she had been expecting him, and expecting to be married for fourteen years, but she was as much surprised and taken aback as if she had never thought of it.

Joe's consternation came later. He eyed Louisa with an instant confirmation of his old admiration. She had changed but little. She still kept her pretty manner and soft grace, and was, he considered, every whit as attractive as ever. As for himself, his stent was done; he had turned his face away from fortune-seeking, and the old winds of romance whistled as loud and sweet as ever through his ears. All the song which he had been wont to hear in them was Louisa; he had for a long time a loyal belief that he heard it still, but finally it seemed to him that although the winds sang always that one song, it had another name. But for Louisa the wind had never more than murmured; now it had gone down, and everything was still. She listened for a little while with half-wistful attention; then she turned quietly away and went to work on her wedding-clothes.

Joe had made some extensive and quite magnificent alterations in his house. It was the old homestead; the newly-married couple would live there, for Joe could not desert his mother, who refused to leave her old home. So Louisa must leave hers. Every morning, rising and going about among her neat maidenly possessions, she felt as one looking her last upon the faces of dear friends. It was true that in a measure she could take them with her, but, robbed of their old environments, they would appear in such new guises that they would almost cease to be themselves. Then there were some peculiar features of her happy solitary life which she would probably be obliged to relinquish altogether. Sterner tasks than these graceful but half-needless ones would probably devolve upon her. There would be a large house to care for; there would be company to entertain; there would be Joe's rigorous and feeble old mother to wait upon; and it would be contrary to all thrifty village traditions for her to keep more than one servant. Louisa had a little still, and she used to occupy herself pleasantly in summer weather with distilling the sweet and aromatic essences from roses and peppermint and spearmint. By-and-by her still must be laid away. Her store of essences was already considerable, and there would be no time for her to distil for the mere pleasure of it. Then Joe's mother would think it foolishness; she had already hinted her opinion in the matter. Louisa dearly loved to sew a linen seam, not always for use, but for the simple, mild pleasure which she took in it. She would have been loath to confess how more than once she had ripped a seam for the mere delight of sewing it together again. Sitting at her window during long sweet afternoons, drawing her needle gently through the dainty fabric, she was peace itself. But there was small chance of such foolish comfort in the future. Joe's mother, domineering, shrewd old matron that she was even in her old age, and very likely even Joe himself, with his honest masculine rudeness, would laugh and frown down all these pretty but senseless old maiden ways.

Louisa had almost the enthusiasm of an artist over the mere order and cleanliness of her solitary home. She had throbs of genuine triumph at the sight of the window-panes which she had polished until they shone like jewels. She gloated gently over her orderly bureau-drawers, with their exquisitely folded contents redolent with lavender and sweet clover and very purity. Could she be sure of the endurance of even this? She had visions, so startling that she half repudiated them as indelicate, of coarse masculine belongings strewn about in endless litter; of dust and disorder arising necessarily from a coarse masculine presence in the midst of all this delicate harmony.

Among her forebodings of disturbance, not the least was with regard to Caesar. Caesar was a veritable hermit of a dog. For the greater part of his life he had dwelt in his secluded hut, shut out from the society of his kind and all innocent canine joys. Never had Caesar since his early youth watched at a woodchuck's hole; never had he known the delights of a stray bone at a neighbor's kitchen door. And it was all on account of a sin committed when hardly out of his puppyhood. No one knew the possible depth of remorse of which this mild-visaged, altogether innocent-looking old dog might be capable; but whether or not he had encountered remorse, he had encountered a full measure of righteous retribution. Old Caesar seldom lifted up his voice in a growl or a bark; he was fat and sleepy; there were yellow rings which looked like spectacles around his dim old eyes; but there was a neighbor who bore on his hand the imprint of several of Caesar's sharp white youthful teeth, and for that he had lived at the end of a chain, all alone in a little hut, for fourteen years. The neighbor, who was choleric and smarting with the pain of his wound, had demanded either Caesar's death or complete ostracism. So Louisa's brother, to whom the dog had belonged, had built him his little kennel and tied him up. It was now fourteen years since, in a flood of youthful spirits, he had inflicted that memorable bite, and with the exception of short excursions, always at the end of the chain, under the strict guardianship of his master or Louisa, the old dog had remained a close prisoner. It is doubtful if, with his limited ambition, he took much pride in the fact, but it is certain that he was possessed of considerable cheap fame. He was regarded by all the children in the village and by many adults as a very monster of ferocity. St. George's dragon could hardly have surpassed in evil repute Louisa Ellis's old yellow dog. Mothers charged their children with solemn emphasis not to go too near to him, and the children listened and believed greedily, with a fascinated appetite for terror, and ran by Louisa's house stealthily, with many sidelong and backward glances at the terrible dog. If perchance he sounded a hoarse bark, there was a panic. Wayfarers chancing into Louisa's yard eyed him with respect, and inquired if the chain were stout. Caesar at large might have seemed a very ordinary dog, and excited no comment whatever; chained, his reputation overshadowed him, so that he lost his own proper outlines and looked darkly vague and enormous. Joe Dagget, however, with his good-humored sense and shrewdness, saw him as he was. He strode valiantly up to him and patted him on the head, in spite of Louisa's soft clamor of warning, and even attempted to set him loose. Louisa grew so alarmed that he desisted, but kept announcing his opinion in the matter quite forcibly at intervals. "There ain't a better-natured dog in town," he would say, "and it's downright cruel to keep him tied up there. Some day I'm going to take him out."

Louisa had very little hope that he would not, one of these days, when their interests and possessions should be more completely fused in one. She pictured to herself Caesar on the rampage through the quiet and unguarded village. She saw innocent children bleeding in his path. She was herself very fond of the old dog, because he had belonged to her dead brother, and he was always very gentle with her; still she had great faith in his ferocity. She always warned people not to go too near him. She fed him on ascetic fare of corn-mush and cakes, and never fired his dangerous temper with a heating and sanguinary diet of flesh and bones. Louisa looked at the old dog munching his simple fare, and thought of her approaching marriage and trembled. Still, no anticipation of disorder and confusion in lieu of sweet peace and harmony, no forebodings of Caesar on the rampage, no wild fluttering of her little yellow canary, were sufficient to turn her a hair's-breadth. Joe Dagget had been fond of her and working for her all these years. It was not for her, whatever came to pass, to prove untrue and break his heart. She put the exquisite little stitches into her wedding-garments, and the time went on until it was only a week before her wedding-day. It was a Tuesday evening, and the wedding was to be a week from Wednesday.

There was a full moon that night. About nine o'clock Louisa strolled down the road a little way. There were harvest-fields on either hand, bordered by low stone walls. Luxuriant clumps of bushes grew beside the wall, and trees—wild cherry and old apple-trees—at intervals. Presently Louisa sat down on the wall and looked about her with mildly sorrowful reflectiveness. Tall shrubs of blueberry and meadow-sweet, all woven together and tangled with blackberry vines and horsebriers, shut her in on either side. She had a little clear space between them. Opposite her, on the other side of the road, was a spreading tree; the moon shone between its boughs, and the leaves twinkled like silver. The road was bespread with a beautiful shifting dapple of silver and shadow; the air was full of a mysterious sweetness. "I wonder if it's wild grapes?" murmured Louisa. She sat there some time. She was just thinking of rising, when she heard footsteps and low voices, and remained quiet. It was a lonely place, and she felt a little timid. She thought she would keep still in the shadow and let the persons, whoever they might be, pass her.

But just before they reached her the voices ceased, and the footsteps. She understood that their owners had also found seats upon the stone wall. She was wondering if she could not steal away unobserved, when the voice broke the stillness. It was Joe Dagget's. She sat still and listened.

The voice was announced by a loud sigh, which was as familiar as itself. "Well," said Dagget, "you've made up your mind, then, I suppose?"

"Yes," returned another voice; "I'm going day after to-morrow."

"That's Lily Dyer," thought Louisa to herself. The voice embodied itself in her mind. She saw a girl tall and full-figured, with a firm, fair face, looking fairer and firmer in the moonlight, her strong yellow hair braided in a close knot. A girl full of a calm rustic strength and bloom, with a masterful way which might have beseemed a princess. Lily Dyer was a favorite with the village folk; she had just the qualities to arouse the admiration. She was good and handsome and smart. Louisa had often heard her praises sounded.

"Well," said Joe Dagget, "I ain't got a word to say."

"I don't know what you could say," returned Lily Dyer.

"Not a word to say," repeated Joe, drawing out the words heavily. Then there was a silence. "I ain't sorry," he began at last, "that that happened yesterday—that we kind of let on how we felt to each other. I guess it's just as well we knew. Of course I can't do anything any different. I'm going right on an' get married next week. I ain't going back on a woman that's waited for me fourteen years, an' break her heart."

"If you should jilt her to-morrow, I wouldn't have you," spoke up the girl, with sudden vehemence.

"Well, I ain't going to give you the chance," said he; "but I don't believe you would, either."

"You'd see I wouldn't. Honor's honor, an' right's right. An' I'd never think anything of any man that went against 'em for me or any other girl; you'd find that out, Joe Dagget."

"Well, you'll find out fast enough that I ain't going against 'em for you or any other girl," returned he. Their voices sounded almost as if they were angry with each other. Louisa was listening eagerly.

"I'm sorry you feel as if you must go away," said Joe, "but I don't know but it's best."

"Of course it's best. I hope you and I have got common-sense."

"Well, I suppose you're right." Suddenly Joe's voice got an undertone of tenderness. "Say, Lily," said he, "I'll get along well enough myself, but I can't bear to think— You don't suppose you're going to fret much over it?"

"I guess you'll find out I sha'n't fret much over a married man."

"Well, I hope you won't—I hope you won't, Lily. God knows I do. And—I hope —one of these days—you'll—come across somebody else—"

"I don't see any reason why I shouldn't." Suddenly her tone changed. She spoke in a sweet, clear voice, so loud that she could have been heard across the street. "No, Joe Dagget," said she, "I'll never marry any other man as long as I live. I've got good sense, an' I ain't going to break my heart nor make a fool of myself; but I'm never going to be married, you can be sure of that. I ain't that sort of girl to feel this way twice."

Louisa heard an exclamation and a soft commotion behind the bushes; then Lily spoke again—the voice sounded as if she had risen. "This must be put a stop to," said she. "We've stayed here long enough. I'm going home."

Louisa sat there in a daze, listening to their retreating steps. After a while she got up and slunk softly home herself. The next day she did her housework methodically;

that was as much a matter of course as breathing; but she did not sew on her wedding-clothes. She sat at her window and meditated. In the evening Joe came. Louisa Ellis had never known that she had any diplomacy in her, but when she came to look for it that night she found it, although meek of its kind, among her little feminine weapons. Even now she could hardly believe that she had heard aright, and she would not do Joe a terrible injury should she break her troth-plight. She wanted to sound him without betraying too soon her own inclinations in the matter. She did it successfully, and they finally came to an understanding; but it was a difficult thing, for he was as afraid of betraying himself as she.

She never mentioned Lily Dyer. She simply said that while she had no cause of complaint against him, she had lived so long in one way that she shrank from making a change.

"Well, I never shrank, Louisa," said Dagget. "I'm going to be honest enough to say that I think maybe it's better this way; but if you'd wanted to keep on, I'd have stuck to you till my dying day. I hope you know that."

"Yes, I do," said she.

That night she and Joe parted more tenderly than they had done for a long time. Standing in the door, holding each other's hands, a last great wave of regretful memory swept over them.

"Well, this ain't the way we've thought it was all going to end, is it, Louisa?" said Joe.

She shook her head. There was a little quiver on her placid face.

"You let me know if there's ever anything I can do for you," said he. "I ain't ever going to forget you, Louisa." Then he kissed her, and went down the path.

Louisa, all alone by herself that night, wept a little, she hardly knew why; but the next morning, on waking, she felt like a queen who, after fearing lest her domain be wrested away from her, sees it firmly insured in her possession.

Now the tall weeds and grasses might cluster around Caesar's little hermit hut, the snow might fall on its roof year in and year out, but he never would go on a rampage through the unguarded village. Now the little canary might turn itself into a peaceful yellow ball night after night, and have no need to wake and flutter with wild terror against its bars. Louisa could sew linen seams, and distil roses, and dust and polish and fold away in lavender, as long as she listed. That afternoon she sat with her needle-work at the window, and felt fairly stepped in peace. Lily Dyer, tall and erect and blooming, went past; but she felt no qualm. If Louisa Ellis had sold her birthright she did not know it, the taste of the pottage was so delicious, and had been her sole satisfaction for so long. Serenity and placid narrowness had become to her as the birthright itself. She gazed ahead through a long reach of future days strung together like pearls in a rosary, every one like the others, and all smooth and flawless and innocent, and her heart went up in thankfulness. Outside was the fervid summer afternoon; the air was filled with the sounds of the busy harvest of men and birds and bees; there were halloos, metallic clatterings, sweet calls, and long hummings. Louisa sat, prayerfully numbering her days, like an uncloistered nun.

A ROSE FOR EMILY

William Faulkner
(1897–1962)

Biography p. 1071

I

When Miss Emily Grierson died, our whole town went to her funeral: the men through a sort of respectful affection for a fallen monument, the women mostly out of curiosity to see the inside of her house, which no one save an old manservant—a combined gardener and cook—had seen in at least ten years.

It was a big, squarish frame house that had once been white, decorated with cupolas and spires and scrolled balconies in the heavily lightsome style of the seventies, set on what had once been our most select street. But garages and cotton gins had encroached and obliterated even the august names of that neighborhood; only Miss Emily's house was left, lifting its stubborn and coquettish decay above the cotton wagons and the gasoline pumps—an eyesore among eyesores. And now Miss Emily had gone to join the representatives of those august names where they lay in the cedar-bemused cemetery among the ranked and anonymous graves of Union and Confederate soldiers who fell at the battle of Jefferson.

Alive, Miss Emily had been a tradition, a duty, and a care; a sort of hereditary obligation upon the town, dating from that day in 1894 when Colonel Sartoris, the mayor—he who fathered the edict that no Negro woman should appear on the streets without an apron—remitted her taxes, the dispensation dating from the death of her father on into perpetuity. Not that Miss Emily would have accepted charity. Colonel Sartoris invented an involved tale to the effect that Miss Emily's father had loaned money to the town, which the town, as a matter of business, preferred this way of repaying. Only a man of Colonel Sartoris' generation and thought could have invented it, and only a woman could have believed it.

When the next generation, with its more modern ideas, became mayors and aldermen, this arrangement created some little dissatisfaction. On the first of the year they mailed her a tax notice. February came, and there was no reply. They wrote her a formal letter, asking her to call at the sheriff's office at her convenience. A week later the mayor wrote her himself, offering to call or to send his car for her, and received in reply a note on paper of an archaic shape, in a thin, flowing calligraphy in faded ink, to the effect that she no longer went out at all. The tax notice was also enclosed, without comment.

They called a special meeting of the Board of Aldermen. A deputation waited upon her, knocked at the door through which no visitor had passed since she ceased giving china-painting lessons eight or ten years earlier. They were admitted by the old Negro into a dim hall from which a stairway mounted into still more shadow. It smelled of dust and disuse—a close, dank smell. The Negro led them into the parlor. It was furnished in heavy, leather-covered furniture. When the Negro opened the blinds of one window, they could see that the leather was cracked; and when they sat down, a faint dust rose sluggishly about their thighs, spinning with slow mutes in the single sun-ray. On a tarnished gilt easel before the fireplace stood a crayon portrait of Miss Emily's father.

They rose when she entered—a small, fat woman in black, with a thin gold chain descending to her waist and vanishing into her belt, leaning on an ebony cane with a tarnished gold head. Her skeleton was small and spare; perhaps that was why what would have been merely plumpness in another was obesity in her. She looked bloated, like a body long submerged in motionless water, and of that pallid hue. Her eyes, lost in the fatty ridges of her face, looked like two small pieces of coal pressed into a lump of dough as they moved from one face to another while the visitors stated their errand.

She did not ask them to sit. She just stood in the door and listened quietly until the spokesman came to a stumbling halt. Then they could hear the invisible watch ticking at the end of the gold chain.

Her voice was dry and cold. "I have no taxes in Jefferson. Colonel Sartoris explained it to me. Perhaps one of you can gain access to the city records and satisfy yourselves."

"But we have. We are the city authorities, Miss Emily. Didn't you get a notice from the sheriff, signed by him?"

"I received a paper, yes," Miss Emily said. "Perhaps he considers himself the sheriff . . . I have no taxes in Jefferson."

"But there is nothing on the books to show that, you see. We must go by the—"

"See Colonel Sartoris. I have no taxes in Jefferson."

"But, Miss Emily—"

"See Colonel Sartoris." (Colonel Sartoris had been dead almost ten years.) "I have no taxes in Jefferson. Tobe!" The Negro appeared. "Show these gentlemen out."

II

So she vanquished them, horse and foot, just as she had vanquished their fathers thirty years before about the smell. That was two years after her father's death and a short time after her sweetheart—the one we believed would marry her—had deserted her. After her father's death she went out very little; after her sweetheart went away, people hardly saw her at all. A few of the ladies had the temerity to call, but were not received, and the only sign of life about the place was the Negro man—a young man then—going in and out with a market basket.

"Just as if a man—any man—could keep a kitchen properly," the ladies said; so they were not surprised when the smell developed. It was another link between the gross, teeming world and the high and mighty Griersons.

A neighbor, a woman, complained to the mayor, Judge Stevens, eighty years old. "But what will you have me do about it, madam?" he said.

"Why, send her word to stop it," the woman said. "Isn't there a law?"

"I'm sure that won't be necessary," Judge Stevens said. "It's probably just a snake or a rat that nigger of hers killed in the yard. I'll speak to him about it."

The next day he received two more complaints, one from a man who came in diffident deprecation. "We really must do something about it, Judge. I'd be the last one in the world to bother Miss Emily, but we've got to do something." That night the Board of Aldermen met—three graybeards and one younger man, a member of the rising generation.

"It's simple enough," he said. "Send her word to have her place cleaned up. Give her a certain time to do it in, and if she don't . . ."

"Dammit, sir," Judge Stevens said, "will you accuse a lady to her face of smelling bad?"

So the next night, after midnight, four men crossed Miss Emily's lawn and slunk about the house like burglars, sniffing along the base of the brickwork and at the cellar openings while one of them performed a regular sowing motion with his hand out of a sack slung from his shoulder. They broke open the cellar door and sprinkled lime there, and in all the outbuildings. As they recrossed the lawn, a window that had been dark was lighted and Miss Emily sat in it, the light behind her, and her upright torso motionless as that of an idol. They crept quietly across the lawn and into the shadow of the locusts that lined the street. After a week or two the smell went away.

That was when people had begun to feel really sorry for her. People in our town, remembering how old lady Wyatt, her great-aunt, had gone completely crazy at last, believed that the Griersons held themselves a little too high for what they really were. None of the young men were quite good enough for Miss Emily and such. We had long thought of them as a tableau, Miss Emily a slender figure in white in the background, her father a spraddled silhouette in the foreground, his back to her and clutching a horsewhip, the two of them framed by the back-flung front door. So when she got to be thirty and was still single, we were not pleased exactly, but vindicated; even with insanity in the family she wouldn't have turned down all of her chances if they had really materialized.

When her father died, it got about that the house was all that was left to her; and in a way, people were glad. At last they could pity Miss Emily. Being left alone, and a pauper, she had become humanized. Now she too would know the old thrill and the old despair of a penny more or less.

The day after his death all the ladies prepared to call at the house and offer condolence and aid, as is our custom. Miss Emily met them at the door, dressed as usual and with no trace of grief on her face. She told them that her father was not dead. She did that for three days, with the ministers calling on her, and the doctors, trying to persuade her to let them dispose of the body. Just as they were about to resort to law and force, she broke down, and they buried her father quickly.

We did not say she was crazy then. We believed she had to do that. We remembered all the young men her father had driven away, and we knew that with nothing left, she would have to cling to that which had robbed her, as people will.

III

She was sick for a long time. When we saw her again, her hair was cut short, making her look like a girl, with a vague resemblance to those angels in colored church windows—sort of tragic and serene.

The town had just let the contracts for paving the sidewalks, and in the summer after her father's death they began the work. The construction company came with niggers and mules and machinery, and a foreman named Homer Barron, a Yankee —a big, dark, ready man, with a big voice and eyes lighter than his face. The little boys would follow in groups to hear him cuss the niggers, and the niggers singing in time to the rise and fall of the picks. Pretty soon he knew everybody in town. Whenever you heard a lot of laughing anywhere about the square, Homer Barron would be in the center of the group. Presently we began to see him and Miss Emily on Sunday afternoons driving in the yellow-wheeled buggy and the matched team of bays from the livery stable.

At first we were glad that Miss Emily would have an interest, because the ladies all said, "Of course a Grierson would not think seriously of a Northerner, a day laborer." But there were still others, older people, who said that even grief could not cause a real lady to forget *noblesse oblige*— without calling it *noblesse oblige*. They just said, "Poor Emily. Her kinsfolk should come to her." She had some kin in Alabama; but years ago her father had fallen out with them over the estate of old lady Wyatt, the crazy woman, and there was no communication between the two families. They had not even been represented at the funeral.

And as soon as the old people said, "Poor Emily," the whispering began. "Do you suppose it's really so?" they said to one another. "Of course it is. What else could . . ." This behind their hands; rustling of craned silk and satin behind jalousies closed upon the sun of Sunday afternoon as the thin, swift clop-clop-clop of the matched team passed: "Poor Emily."

She carried her head high enough—even when we believed that she was fallen. It was as if she demanded more than ever the recognition of her dignity as the last Grierson; as if it had wanted that touch of earthiness to reaffirm her impervious-ness. Like when she bought the rat poison, the arsenic. That was over a year after they had begun to say "Poor Emily," and while the two female cousins were visit-ing her.

"I want some poison," she said to the druggist. She was over thirty then, still a slight woman, though thinner than usual, with cold, haughty black eyes in a face the flesh of which was strained across the temples and about the eye-sockets as you imagine a lighthouse-keeper's face ought to look. "I want some poison," she said.

"Yes, Miss Emily. What kind? For rats and such? I'd recom—"

"I want the best you have. I don't care what kind."

The druggist named several. "They'll kill anything up to an elephant. But what you want is—"

"Arsenic," Miss Emily said. "Is that a good one?"

"Is . . . arsenic? Yes, ma'am. But what you want—"

"I want arsenic."

The druggist looked down at her. She looked back at him, erect, her face like a strained flag. "Why, of course," the druggist said. "If that's what you want. But the law requires you to tell what you are going to use it for."

Miss Emily just stared at him, her head tilted back in order to look him eye for eye, until he looked away and went and got the arsenic and wrapped it up. The Negro delivery boy brought her the package; the druggist didn't come back. When she opened the package at home there was written on the box, under the skull and bones: "For rats."

IV

So the next day we all said, "She will kill herself"; and we said it would be the best thing. When she had first begun to be seen with Homer Barron, we had said, "She will marry him." Then we said, "She will persuade him yet," because Homer himself had remarked—he liked men, and it was known that he drank with the younger men in the Elks' Club—that he was not a marrying man. Later we said, "Poor Emily" behind the jalousies as they passed on Sunday afternoon in the glittering buggy, Miss Emily with her head high and Homer Barron with his hat cocked and a cigar in his teeth, reins and whip in a yellow glove.

Then some of the ladies began to say that it was a disgrace to the town and a bad example to the young people. The men did not want to interfere, but at last the ladies forced the Baptist minister—Miss Emily's people were Episcopal—to call upon her. He would never divulge what happened during the interview, but he refused to go back again. The next Sunday they again drove about the streets, and the following day the minister's wife wrote to Miss Emily's relations in Alabama.

So she had blood-kin under her roof again and we sat back to watch developments. At first nothing happened. Then we were sure that they were to be married. We learned that Miss Emily had been to the jeweler's and ordered a man's toilet set in silver, with the letters H.B. on each piece. Two days later we learned that she had bought a complete outfit of men's clothing, including a nightshirt, and we said, "They are married." We were really glad. We were glad because the two female cousins were even more Grierson than Miss Emily had ever been.

So we were not surprised when Homer Barron—the streets had been finished some time since—was gone. We were a little disappointed that there was not a public blowing-off, but we believed that he had gone on to prepare for Miss Emily's coming, or to give her a chance to get rid of the cousins. (By that time it was a cabal, and we were all Miss Emily's allies to help circumvent the cousins.) Sure enough, after another week they departed. And, as we had expected all along, within three days Homer Barron was back in town. A neighbor saw the Negro man admit him at the kitchen door at dusk one evening.

And that was the last we saw of Homer Barron. And of Miss Emily for some time. The Negro man went in and out with the market basket, but the front door remained closed. Now and then we would see her at a window for a moment, as the men did that night when they sprinkled the lime, but for almost six months she did not appear on the streets. Then we knew that this was to be expected too; as if that quality of her father which had thwarted her woman's life so many times had been too virulent and too furious to die.

When we next saw Miss Emily, she had grown fat and her hair was turning gray. During the next few years it grew grayer and grayer until it attained an even pepper-and-salt iron-gray, when it ceased turning. Up to the day of her death at seventy-four it was still that vigorous iron-gray, like the hair of an active man.

From that time on her front door remained closed, save for a period of six or seven years, when she was about forty, during which she gave lessons in china-painting. She fitted up a studio in one of the downstairs rooms, where the daughters and grand-daughters of Colonel Sartoris' contemporaries were sent to her with the same regularity and in the same spirit that they were sent to church on Sundays with a twenty-five-cent piece for the collection plate. Meanwhile her taxes had been remitted.

Then the new generation became the backbone and the spirit of the town, and the painting pupils grew up and fell away and did not send their children to her with boxes of color and tedious brushes and pictures cut from the ladies' magazines. The front door closed upon the last one and remained closed for good. When the town got free postal delivery, Miss Emily alone refused to let them fasten the metal numbers above her door and attach a mailbox to it. She would not listen to them.

Daily, monthly, yearly we watched the Negro grow grayer and more stooped, going in and out with the market basket. Each December we sent her a tax notice, which would be returned by the post office a week later, unclaimed. Now and then we would see her in one of the downstairs windows—she had evidently shut up the top floor of the house—like the carven torso of an idol in a niche, looking or not looking at us, we could never tell which. Thus she passed from generation to generation—dear, inescapable, impervious, tranquil, and perverse.

And so she died. Fell ill in the house filled with dust and shadows, with only a doddering Negro man to wait on her. We did not even know she was sick; we had long since given up trying to get any information from the Negro. He talked to no one, probably not even to her, for his voice had grown harsh and rusty, as if from disuse.

She died in one of the downstairs rooms, in a heavy walnut bed with a curtain, her gray head propped on a pillow yellow and moldy with age and lack of sunlight.

V

The Negro met the first of the ladies at the front door and let them in, with their hushed, sibilant voices and their quick, curious glances, and then he disappeared. He walked right through the house and out the back and was not seen again.

The two female cousins came at once. They held the funeral on the second day, with the town coming to look at Miss Emily beneath a mass of bought flowers, with the crayon face of her father musing profoundly above the bier and the ladies sibilant and macabre; and the very old men—some in their brushed Confederate uniforms—on the porch and the lawn, talking of Miss Emily as if she had been a contemporary of theirs, believing that they had danced with her and courted her perhaps, confusing time with its mathematical progression, as the old do, to whom all the past is not a diminishing road but, instead, a huge meadow which no winter ever quite touches, divided from them now by the narrow bottle-neck of the most recent decade of years.

Already we knew that there was one room in that region above stairs which no one had seen in forty years, and which would have to be forced. They waited until Miss Emily was decently in the ground before they opened it.

The violence of breaking down the door seemed to fill this room with pervading dust. A thin, acrid pall as of the tomb seemed to lie everywhere upon this room decked and furnished as for a bridal: upon the valance curtains of faded rose color, upon the rose-shaded lights, upon the dressing table, upon the delicate array of crystal and the man's toilet things backed with tarnished silver, silver so tarnished that the monogram was obscured. Among them lay a collar and tie, as if they had just been removed, which, lifted, left upon the surface a pale crescent in the dust. Upon a chair hung the suit, carefully folded; beneath it the two mute shoes and the discarded socks.

The man himself lay in the bed.

For a long while we just stood there, looking down at the profound and fleshless grin. The body had apparently once lain in the attitude of an embrace, but now the long sleep that outlasts love, that conquers even the grimace of love, had cuckolded him. What was left of him, rotted beneath what was left of the nightshirt, had become inextricable from the bed in which he lay; and upon him and upon the pillow beside him lay that even coating of the patient and biding dust.

Then we noticed that in the second pillow was the indentation of a head. One of us lifted something from it, and leaning forward, that faint and invisible dust dry and acrid in the nostrils, we saw a long strand of iron-gray hair.

SONNY'S BLUES

James Baldwin
(b. 1924)

Biography p. 1060

I read about it in the paper, in the subway, on my way to work. I read it, and I couldn't believe it, and I read it again. Then perhaps I just stared at it, at the newsprint spelling out his name, spelling out the story. I stared at it in the swinging lights of the subway car, and in the faces and bodies of the people, and in my own face, trapped in the darkness which roared outside.

It was not to be believed and I kept telling myself that, as I walked from the subway station to the high school. And at the same time I couldn't doubt it. I was scared, scared for Sonny. He became real to me again. A great block of ice got settled in my belly and kept melting there slowly all day long, while I taught my classes algebra. It was a special kind of ice. It kept melting, sending trickles of ice water all up and down my veins, but it never got less. Sometimes it hardened and seemed to expand until I felt my guts were going to come spilling out or that I was going to choke or scream. This would always be at a moment when I was remembering some specific thing Sonny had once said or done.

When he was about as old as the boys in my classes his face had been bright and open, there was a lot of copper in it; and he'd had wonderfully direct brown eyes, and great gentleness and privacy. I wondered what he looked like now. He had been picked up, the evening before, in a raid on an apartment downtown, for peddling and using heroin.

I couldn't believe it: but what I mean by that is that I couldn't find any room for it anywhere inside me. I had kept it outside me for a long time. I hadn't wanted to know. I had had suspicions, but I didn't name them, I kept putting them away. I told myself that Sonny was wild, but he wasn't crazy. And he'd always been a good boy, he hadn't ever turned hard or evil or disrespectful, the way kids can, so quick, so quick, especially in Harlem. I didn't want to believe that I'd ever see my brother going down, coming to nothing, all that light in his face gone out, in the condition I'd already seen so many others. Yet it had happened and here I was, talking about algebra to a lot of boys who might, every one of them for all I knew, be popping off needles every time they went to the head. Maybe it did more for them than algebra could.

I was sure that the first time Sonny had ever had horse, he couldn't have been much older than these boys were now. These boys, now, were living as we'd been living then, they were growing up with a rush and their heads bumped abruptly against the low ceiling of their actual possibilities. They were filled with rage. All they really knew were two darknesses, the darkness of their lives, which was now closing in on them, and the darkness of the movies, which had blinded them to that other darkness, and in which they now, vindictively, dreamed, at once more together than they were at any other time, and more alone.

When the last bell rang, the last class ended, I let out my breath. It seemed I'd been holding it for all that time. My clothes were wet—I may have looked as though I'd been sitting in a steam bath, all dressed up, all afternoon. I sat alone in the classroom a long time. I listened to the boys outside, downstairs, shouting and cursing and laughing. Their laughter struck me for perhaps the first time. It was not the joyous laughter which—God knows why—one associates with children. It was mocking and insular, its intent was to denigrate. It was disenchanted, and in this, also, lay the authority of their curses. Perhaps I was listening to them because I was thinking about my brother and in them I heard my brother. And myself.

One boy was whistling a tune, at once very complicated and very simple, it seemed to be pouring out of him as though he were a bird, and it sounded very cool and moving through all that harsh, bright air, only just holding its own through all those other sounds.

I stood up and walked over to the window and looked down into the courtyard. It was the beginning of the spring and the sap was rising in the boys. A teacher passed through them every now and again, quickly, as though he or she couldn't wait to get out of that courtyard, to get those boys out of their sight and off their minds. I started collecting my stuff. I thought I'd better get home and talk to Isabel.

The courtyard was almost deserted by the time I got downstairs. I saw this boy standing in the shadow of a doorway, looking just like Sonny. I almost called his name. Then I saw that it wasn't Sonny, but somebody we used to know, a boy from around our block. He'd been Sonny's friend. He'd never been mine, having been too young for me, and, anyway, I'd never liked him. And now, even though he was a grown-up man, he still hung around that block, still spent hours on the street corners, was always high and raggy. I used to run into him from time to time and he'd often work around to asking me for a quarter or fifty cents. He always had some real good excuse, too, and I always gave it to him, I don't know why.

But now, abruptly, I hated him. I couldn't stand the way he looked at me, partly like a dog, partly like a cunning child. I wanted to ask him what the hell he was doing in the school courtyard.

He sort of shuffled over to me, and he said, "I see you got the papers. So you already know about it."

"You mean about Sonny? Yes, I already know about it. How come they didn't get you?"

He grinned. It made him repulsive and it also brought to mind what he'd looked like as a kid. "I wasn't there. I stay away from them people."

"Good for you." I offered him a cigarette and I watched him through the smoke. "You come all the way down here just to tell me about Sonny?"

"That's right." He was sort of shaking his head and his eyes looked strange, as though they were about to cross. The bright sun deadened his damp dark brown skin and it made his eyes look yellow and showed up the dirt in his kinked hair. He smelled funky. I moved a little away from him and I said, "Well, thanks. But I already know about it and I got to get home."

"I'll walk you a little ways," he said. We started walking. There were a couple of kids still loitering in the courtyard and one of them said goodnight to me and looked strangely at the boy beside me.

"What're you going to do?" he asked me. "I mean, about Sonny?"

"Look. I haven't seen Sonny for over a year, I'm not sure I'm going to do anything. Anyway, what the hell *can* I do?"

"That's right," he said quickly, "ain't nothing you can do. Can't much help old Sonny no more, I guess."

It was what I was thinking and so it seemed to me he had no right to say it.

"I'm surprised at Sonny, though," he went on—he had a funny way of talking, he looked straight ahead as though he were talking to himself—"I thought Sonny was a smart boy, I thought he was too smart to get hung."

"I guess he thought so too," I said sharply, "and that's how he got hung. And now about you? You're pretty goddamn smart, I bet."

Then he looked directly at me, just for a minute. "I ain't smart," he said. "If I was smart, I'd have reached for a pistol a long time ago."

"Look. Don't tell *me* your sad story, if it was up to me, I'd give you one." Then I felt guilty— guilty, probably, for never having supposed that the poor bastard *had* a story of his own, much less a sad one, and I asked, quickly, "What's going to happen to him now?"

He didn't answer this. He was off by himself some place. "Funny thing," he said, and from his tone we might have been discussing the quickest way to get to Brooklyn, "when I saw the papers this morning, the first thing I asked myself was if I had anything to do with it. I felt sort of responsible."

I began to listen more carefully. The subway station was on the corner, just before us, and I stopped. He stopped, too. We were in front of a bar and he ducked slightly, peering in, but whoever he was looking for didn't seem to be there. The juke box was blasting away with something black and bouncy and I half watched the barmaid as she danced her way from the juke box to her place behind the bar. And I watched her face as she laughingly responded to something someone said to her, still keeping time to the music. When she smiled one saw the little girl, one sensed the doomed, still-struggling woman beneath the battered face of the semi-whore.

"I never *give* Sonny nothing," the boy said finally, "but a long time ago I come to school high and Sonny asked me how it felt." He paused, I couldn't bear to watch him, I watched the barmaid, and I listened to the music which seemed to be causing the pavement to shake. "I told him it felt great." The music stopped, the barmaid paused and watched the juke box until the music began again. "It did."

All this was carrying me some place I didn't want to go. I certainly didn't want to know how it felt. It filled everything, the people, the houses, the music, the dark, quicksilver barmaid, with menace, and this menace was their reality.

"What's going to happen to him now?" I asked again.

"They'll send him away some place and they'll try to cure him." He shook his head. "Maybe he'll even think he's kicked the habit. Then they'll let him loose"—he gestured, throwing his cigarette into the gutter. "That's all."

"What do you mean, that's *all?*"

But I knew what he meant.

"I *mean,* that's *all.*" He turned his head and looked at me, pulling down the corners of his mouth. "Don't you know what I mean?" he asked, softly.

"How the hell *would* I know what you mean?" I almost whispered it, I don't know why.

"That's right," he said to the air, "how would *he* know what I mean?" He turned toward me again, patient and calm, and yet I somehow felt him shaking, shaking as though he were going to fall apart. I felt that ice in my guts again, the dread I'd felt all afternoon; and again I watched the barmaid, moving about the bar, washing glasses, and singing. "Listen. They'll let him out and then it'll just start all over again. That's what I mean."

"You mean—they'll let him out. And then he'll just start working his way back in again. You mean he'll never kick the habit. Is that what you mean?"

"That's right," he said, cheerfully. "*You* see what I mean."

"Tell me," I said at last, "why does he want to die? He must want to die, he's killing himself, why does he want to die?"

He looked at me in surprise. He licked his lips. "He don't want to die. He wants to live. Don't nobody want to die, ever."

Then I wanted to ask him—too many things. He could not have answered, or if he had, I could not have borne the answers. I started walking. "Well, I guess it's none of my business."

"It's going to be rough on old Sonny," he said. We reached the subway station. "This is your station?" he asked. I nodded. I took one step down. "Damn!" he said, suddenly. I looked up at him. He grinned again. "Damn it if I didn't leave all my money home. You ain't got a dollar on you, have you? Just for a couple of days, is all."

All at once something inside gave and threatened to come pouring out of me. I didn't hate him any more. I felt that in another moment I'd start crying like a child.

"Sure," I said. "Don't sweat." I looked in my wallet and didn't have a dollar, I only had a five. "Here," I said. "That hold you?"

He didn't look at it—he didn't want to look at it. A terrible, closed look came over his face, as though he were keeping the number on the bill a secret from him and me. "Thanks," he said, and now he was dying to see me go. "Don't worry about Sonny. Maybe I'll write him or something."

"Sure," I said. "You do that. So long."

"Be seeing you," he said. I went on down the steps.

And I didn't write Sonny or send him anything for a long time. When I finally did, it was just after my little girl died, he wrote me back a letter which made me feel like a bastard.

Here's what he said:

Dear brother,

You don't know how much I needed to hear from you. I wanted to write you many a time but I dug how much I must have hurt you and so I didn't write. But now I feel like a man who's been trying to climb up out of some deep, real deep and funky hole and just saw the sun up there, outside. I got to get outside.

I can't tell you much about how I got here. I mean I don't know how to tell you. I guess I was afraid of something or I was trying to escape from something and you know I have never been very strong in the head (smile). I'm glad Mama and Daddy are dead and can't see what's happened to their son and I swear if I'd known what I was doing I would never have hurt you so, you and a lot of other fine people who were nice to me and who believed in me.

I don't want you to think it had anything to do with me being a musician. It's more than that. Or maybe less than that. I can't get anything straight in my head down here and I try not to think about what's going to happen to me when I get outside again. Sometime I think I'm going to flip and *never* get outside and sometime I think I'll come straight back. I tell you one thing, though, I'd rather blow my brains out than go through this again. But that's what they all say, so they tell me. If I tell you when I'm coming to New York and if you could meet me, I sure would appreciate it. Give my love to Isabel and the kids and I was sure sorry to hear about little Gracie. I wish I could be like Mama and say the Lord's will be done, but I don't know it seems to me that trouble is the one thing that never does get stopped and I don't know what good it does to blame it on the Lord. But maybe it does some good if you believe it.

Your brother,
Sonny

Then I kept in constant touch with him and I sent him whatever I could and I went to meet him when he came back to New York. When I saw him many things I thought I had forgotten came flooding back to me. This was because I had begun, finally, to wonder about Sonny, about the life that Sonny lived inside. This life, whatever it was, had made him older and thinner and it had deepened the distant stillness in which he had always moved. He looked very unlike my baby brother. Yet, when he smiled, when we shook hands, the baby brother I'd never known looked out from the depths of his private life, like an animal waiting to be coaxed into the light.

"How you been keeping?" he asked me.

"All right. And you?"

"Just fine." He was smiling all over his face. "It's good to see you again."

"It's good to see you."

The seven years' difference in our ages lay between us like a chasm: I wondered if these years would ever operate between us as a bridge. I was remembering, and it made it hard to catch my breath, that I had been there when he was born; and I had heard the first words he had ever spoken. When he started to walk, he walked from our mother straight to me. I caught him just before he fell when he took the first steps he ever took in this world.

"How's Isabel?"

"Just fine. She's dying to see you."

"And the boys?"

"They're fine, too. They're anxious to see their uncle."

"Oh, come on. You know they don't remember me."

"Are you kidding? Of course they remember you."

He grinned again. We got into a taxi. We had a lot to say to each other, far too much to know how to begin.

As the taxi began to move, I asked, "You still want to go to India?"

He laughed. "You still remember that. Hell, no. This place is Indian enough for me."

"It used to belong to them," I said.

And he laughed again. "They damn sure knew what they were doing when they got rid of it."

Years ago, when he was around fourteen, he'd been all hipped on the idea of going to India. He read books about people sitting on rocks, naked, in all kinds of weather, but mostly bad, naturally, and walking barefoot through hot coals and arriving at wisdom. I used to say that it sounded to me as though they were getting away from wisdom as fast as they could. I think he sort of looked down on me for that.

"Do you mind," he asked, "if we have the driver drive alongside the park? On the west side—I haven't seen the city in so long."

"Of course not," I said. I was afraid that I might sound as though I were humoring him, but I hoped he wouldn't take it that way.

So we drove along, between the green of the park and the stony, lifeless elegance of hotels and apartment buildings, toward the vivid, killing streets of our childhood. These streets hadn't changed, though housing projects jutted up out of them now like rocks in the middle of a boiling sea. Most of the houses in which we had grown up had vanished, as had the stores from which we had stolen, the basements in which we had first tried sex, the rooftops from which we had hurled tin cans and bricks. But houses exactly like the houses of our past yet dominated the landscape, boys exactly like the boys we once had been found themselves smothering in these houses, came down into the streets for light and air and found themselves encircled by disaster. Some escaped the trap, most didn't. Those who got out always left something of themselves behind, as some animals amputate a leg and leave it in the trap. It might be said, perhaps, that I had escaped, after all, I was a school teacher; or that Sonny had, he hadn't lived in Harlem for years. Yet, as the cab moved uptown through streets which seemed, with a rush, to darken with dark people, and as I covertly studied Sonny's face, it came to me that what we both were seeking through our separate cab windows was that part of ourselves which had been left behind. It's always at the hour of trouble and confrontation that the missing member aches.

We hit 110th Street and started rolling up Lenox Avenue. And I'd known this avenue all my life, but it seemed to me again, as it had seemed on the day I'd first heard about Sonny's trouble, filled with a hidden menace which was its very breath of life.

"We almost there," said Sonny.

"Almost." We were both too nervous to say anything more.

We live in a housing project. It hasn't been up long. A few days after it was up it seemed uninhabitably new, now, of course, it's already rundown. It looks like a parody of the good, clean, faceless life—God knows the people who live in it do their best to make it a parody. The beat-looking grass lying around isn't enough to make their lives green, the hedges will never hold out the streets, and they know it. The big windows fool no one, they aren't big enough to make space out of no space. They don't bother with the windows, they watch the TV screen instead. The playground is most popular with the children who don't play at jacks, or skip rope, or roller skate, or swing, and they can be found in it after dark. We moved in partly because it's not too far from where I teach, and partly for the kids; but it's really just like the houses in which Sonny and I grew up. The same things happen, they'll have the same things to remember. The moment Sonny and I started into the house I had the feeling that I was simply bringing him back into the danger he had almost died trying to escape.

Sonny has never been talkative. So I don't know why I was sure he'd be dying to talk to me when supper was over the first night. Everything went fine, the oldest boy remembered him, and the youngest boy liked him, and Sonny had remembered to bring something for each of them; and Isabel, who is really much nicer than I am, more open and giving, had gone to a lot of trouble about dinner and was genuinely glad to see him. And she's always been able to tease Sonny in a way that I haven't. It was nice to see her face so vivid again and to hear her laugh and watch her make Sonny laugh. She wasn't, or, anyway, she didn't seem to be, at all uneasy or embarrassed. She chatted as though there were no subject which had to be avoided and she got Sonny past his first, faint stiffness. And thank God she was there, for I was filled with the icy dread again. Everything I did seemed awkward to me, and everything I said sounded freighted with hidden meaning. I was trying to remember everything I'd heard about dope addiction and I couldn't help watching Sonny for signs. I wasn't doing it out of malice. I was trying to find out something about my brother. I was dying to hear him tell me he was safe.

"Safe!" my father grunted, whenever Mama suggested trying to move to a neighborhood which might be safer for children. "Safe, hell! Ain't no place safe for kids, nor nobody."

He always went on like this, but he wasn't, ever, really as bad as he sounded, not even on weekends, when he got drunk. As a matter of fact, he was always on the lookout for "something a little better," but he died before he found it. He died suddenly, during a drunken weekend in the middle of the war, when Sonny was fifteen. He and Sonny hadn't ever got on too well. And this was partly because Sonny was the apple of his father's eye. It was because he loved Sonny so much and was frightened for him, that he was always fighting with him. It doesn't do any good to fight with Sonny. Sonny just moves back, inside himself, where he can't be reached. But the principal reason that they never hit it off is that they were so much alike. Daddy was big and rough and loud-talking, just the opposite of Sonny, but they both had—that same privacy.

Mama tried to tell me something about this, just after Daddy died. I was home on leave from the army.

This was the last time I ever saw my mother alive. Just the same, this picture gets all mixed up in my mind with pictures I had of her when she was younger. The way I always see her is the way she used to be on a Sunday afternoon, say, when the old folks were talking after the big Sunday dinner. I always see her wearing pale blue. She'd be sitting on the sofa. And my father would be sitting in the easy chair, not far from her. And the living room would be full of church folks and relatives. There they sit, in chairs all around the living room, and the night is creeping up outside, but nobody knows it yet. You can see the darkness growing against the windowpanes and you hear the street noises every now and again, or maybe the jangling beat of a tambourine from one of the churches close by, but it's real quiet in the room. For a moment nobody's talking, but every face looks darkening, like the sky outside. And my mother rocks a little from the waist, and my father's eyes are closed. Everyone is looking at something a child can't see. For a minute they've forgotten the children. Maybe a kid is lying on the rug, half asleep. Maybe somebody's got a kid in his lap and is absent-mindedly stroking the kid's head. Maybe there's a kid, quiet and big-eyed, curled up in a big chair in the corner. The silence, the darkness coming, and the darkness in the faces frightens the child obscurely. He hopes that the hand which strokes his forehead will never stop—will never die. He hopes that there will never come a time when the old folks won't be sitting around the living room, talking about where they've come from, and what they've seen, and what's happened to them and their kinfolk.

But something deep and watchful in the child knows that this is bound to end, is already ending. In a moment someone will get up and turn on the light. Then the old folks will remember the children and they won't talk any more that day. And when light fills the room, the child is filled with darkness. He knows that every time this happens he's moved just a little closer to that darkness outside. The darkness outside is what the old folks have been talking about. It's what they've come from. It's what they endure. The child knows that they won't talk any more because if he knows too much about what's happened to *them,* he'll know too much too soon, about what's going to happen to *him.*

The last time I talked to my mother, I remember I was restless. I wanted to get out and see Isabel. We weren't married then and we had a lot to straighten out between us.

There Mama sat, in black, by the window. She was humming an old church song, *Lord, you brought me from a long ways off.* Sonny was out somewhere. Mama kept watching the streets.

"I don't know," she said, "if I'll ever see you again, after you go off from here. But I hope you'll remember the things I tried to teach you."

"Don't talk like that," I said, and smiled. "You'll be here a long time yet."

She smiled, too, but she said nothing. She was quiet for a long time. And I said, "Mama, don't you worry about nothing. I'll be writing all the time, and you be getting the checks. . . ."

"I want to talk to you about your brother," she said, suddenly. "If anything happens to me he ain't going to have nobody to look out for him."

"Mama," I said, "ain't nothing going to happen to you *or* Sonny. Sonny's all right. He's a good boy and he's got good sense."

"It ain't a question of his being a good boy," Mama said, "nor of his having good sense. It ain't only the bad ones, nor yet the dumb ones that gets sucked under." She stopped, looking at me. "Your Daddy once had a brother," she said, and she smiled in a way that made me feel she was in pain. "You didn't never know that, did you?"

"No," I said, "I never knew that," and I watched her face.

"Oh, yes," she said, "your Daddy had a brother." She looked out of the window again. "I know you never saw your Daddy cry. But *I* did—many a time, through all these years."

I asked her, "What happened to his brother? How come nobody's ever talked about him?"

This was the first time I ever saw my mother look old.

"His brother got killed," she said, "when he was just a little younger than you are now. I knew him. He was a fine boy. He was maybe a little full of the devil, but he didn't mean nobody no harm."

Then she stopped and the room was silent, exactly as it had sometimes been on those Sunday afternoons. Mama kept looking out into the streets.

"He used to have a job in the mill," she said, "and, like all young folks, he just liked to perform on Saturday nights. Saturday nights, him and your father would drift around to different place, go to dances and things like that, or just sit around with people they knew, and your father's brother would sing, he had a fine voice, and play along with himself on his guitar. Well, this particular Saturday night, him and your father was coming home from some place, and they were both a little drunk and there was a moon that night, it was bright like day. Your father's brother was feeling kind of good, and he was whistling to himself, and he had his guitar slung over his shoulder. They was coming down a hill and beneath them was a road that turned off from the highway. Well, your father's brother, being always kind of frisky, decided to run down this hill, and he did, with that guitar banging and clanging behind him, and he ran across the road, and he was making water behind a tree. And your father was sort of amused at him and he was still coming down the hill, kind of slow. Then he heard a car motor and that same minute his brother stepped from behind the tree, into the road, in the moonlight. And he started to cross the road. And your father started to run down the hill, he says he don't know why. This car was full of white men. They was all drunk, and when they seen your father's brother they let out a great whoop and holler and they aimed the car straight at him. They was having fun, they just wanted to scare him, the way they do sometimes, you know. But they was drunk. And I guess the boy, being drunk, too, and scared, kind of lost his head. By the time he jumped it was too late. Your father says he heard his brother scream when the car rolled over him, and he heard the wood of that guitar when it give, and he heard them strings go flying, and he heard them white men shouting, and the car kept on a-going and it ain't stopped till this day. And, time your father got down the hill, his brother weren't nothing but blood and pulp."

Tears were gleaming on my mother's face. There wasn't anything I could say.

"He never mentioned it," she said, "because I never let him mention it before you children. Your Daddy was like a crazy man that night and for many a night thereafter. He says he never in his life seen anything as dark as that road after the lights of that car had gone away. Weren't nothing, weren't nobody on that road, just your Daddy and his brother and that busted guitar. Oh, yes. Your Daddy never did really get right again. Till the day he died he weren't sure but that every white man he saw was the man that killed his brother."

She stopped and took out her handkerchief and dried her eyes and looked at me.

"I ain't telling you all this," she said, "to make you scared or bitter or to make you hate nobody. I'm telling you this because you got a brother. And the world ain't changed."

I guess I didn't want to believe this. I guess she saw this in my face. She turned away from me, toward the window again, searching those streets.

"But I praise my Redeemer," she said at last, "that He called your Daddy home before me. I ain't saying it to throw no flowers at myself, but, I declare, it keeps me from feeling too cast down to know I helped your father get safely through this world. Your father always acted like he was the roughest, strongest man on earth. And everybody took him to be like that. But if he hadn't had *me* there—to see his tears!"

She was crying again. Still, I couldn't move. I said, "Lord, Lord, Mama, I didn't know it was like that."

"Oh, honey," she said, "there's a lot that you don't know. But you are going to find it out." She stood up from the window and came over to me. "You got to hold on to your brother," she said, "and don't let him fall, no matter what it looks like is happening to him and no matter how evil you gets with him. You going to be evil with him many a time. But don't you forget what I told you, you hear?"

"I won't forget," I said. "Don't you worry, I won't forget. I won't let nothing happen to Sonny."

My mother smiled as though she were amused at something she saw in my face. Then, "You may not be able to stop nothing from happening. But you got to let him know you's *there.*"

Two days later I was married, and then I was gone. And I had a lot of things on my mind and I pretty well forgot my promise to Mama until I got shipped home on a special furlough for her funeral.

And, after the funeral, with just Sonny and me alone in the empty kitchen, I tried to find out something about him.

"What do you want to do?" I asked him.

"I'm going to be a musician," he said.

For he had graduated, in the time I had been away, from dancing to the juke box to finding out who was playing what, and what they were doing with it, and he had bought himself a set of drums.

"You mean, you want to be a drummer?" I somehow had the feeling that being a drummer might be all right for other people but not for my brother Sonny.

"I don't think," he said, looking at me very gravely, "that I'll ever be a good drummer. But I think I can play a piano."

I frowned. I'd never played the role of the older brother quite so seriously before, had scarcely ever, in fact, *asked* Sonny a damn thing. I sensed myself in the presence of something I didn't really know how to handle, didn't understand. So I made my frown a little deeper as I asked: "What kind of musician do you want to be?"

He grinned. "How many kinds do you think there are?"

"Be *serious,*" I said.

He laughed, throwing his head back, and then looked at me. "I *am* serious."

"Well, then, for Christ's sake, stop kidding around and answer a serious question. I mean, do you want to be a concert pianist, you want to play classical music and all that, or—or what?" Long before I finished he was laughing again. "For Christ's *sake,* Sonny!"

He sobered, but with difficulty. "I'm sorry. But you sound so—*scared!*" and he was off again.

"Well, you may think it's funny now, baby, but it's not going to be so funny when you have to make your living at it, let me tell you *that.*" I was furious because I knew he was laughing at me and I didn't know why.

"No," he said, very sober now, and afraid, perhaps, that he'd hurt me, "I don't want to be a classical pianist. That isn't what interests me. I mean"—he paused, looking hard at me, as though his eyes would help me to understand, and then gestured helplessly, as though perhaps his hand would help—"I mean, I'll have a lot of studying to do, and I'll have to study *everything,* but, I mean, I want to play *with*— jazz musicians." He stopped. "I want to play jazz," he said.

Well, the word had never before sounded as heavy, as real, as it sounded that afternoon in Sonny's mouth. I just looked at him and I was probably frowning a real frown by this time. I simply couldn't see why on earth he'd want to spend his time hanging around nightclubs, clowning around on bandstands, while people pushed each other around a dance floor. It seemed—beneath him, somehow. I had never thought about it before, had never been forced to, but I suppose I had always put jazz musicians in a class with what Daddy called "goodtime people."

"Are you *serious?*"

"Hell, *yes,* I'm serious."

He looked more helpless than ever, and annoyed, and deeply hurt.

I suggested, helpfully: "You mean—like Louis Armstrong?"

His face closed as though I'd struck him. "No. I'm not talking about none of that old-time, down home crap."

"Well, look, Sonny, I'm sorry, don't get mad. I just don't altogether get it, that's all. Name somebody—you know, a jazz musician you admire."

"Bird."

"Who?"

"Bird! Charlie Parker! Don't they teach you nothing in the goddamn army?"

I lit a cigarette. I was surprised and then a little amused to discover that I was trembling. "I've been out of touch," I said. "You'll have to be patient with me. Now. Who's this Parker character?"

"He's just one of the greatest jazz musicians alive," said Sonny, sullenly, his hands in his pockets, his back to me. "Maybe *the* greatest," he added, bitterly, "that's probably why *you* never heard of him."

"All right," I said, "I'm ignorant. I'm sorry. I'll go out and buy all the cat's records right away, all right?"

"It don't," said Sonny, with dignity, "make any difference to me. I don't care what you listen to. Don't do me no favors."

I was beginning to realize that I'd never seen him so upset before. With another part of my mind I was thinking that this would probably turn out to be one of those things kids go through and that I shouldn't make it seem important by pushing it too hard. Still, I didn't think it would do any harm to ask: "Doesn't all this take a lot of time? Can you make a living at it?"

He turned back to me and half leaned, half sat, on the kitchen table. "Everything takes time," he said, "and—well, yes, sure, I can make a living at it. But what I don't seem to be able to make you understand is that it's the only thing I want to do."

"Well, Sonny," I said, gently, "you know people can't always do exactly what they *want* to do—"

"*No,* I don't know that," said Sonny, surprising me. "I think people *ought* to do what they want to do, what else are they alive for?"

"You getting to be a big boy," I said desperately, "it's time you started thinking about your future."

"I'm thinking about my future," said Sonny, grimly. "I think about it all the time."

I gave up. I decided, if he didn't change his mind, that we could always talk about it later. "In the meantime," I said, "you got to finish school." We had already decided that he'd have to move in with Isabel and her folks. I knew this wasn't the ideal arrangement because Isabel's folks are inclined to be dicty and they hadn't especially wanted Isabel to marry me. But I didn't know what else to do. "And we have to get you fixed up at Isabel's."

There was a long silence. He moved from the kitchen table to the window. "That's a terrible idea. You know it yourself."

"Do you have a *better* idea?"

He just walked up and down the kitchen for a minute. He was as tall as I was. He had started to shave. I suddenly had the feeling that I didn't know him at all.

He stopped at the kitchen table and picked up my cigarettes. Looking at me with a kind of mocking, amused defiance, he put one between his lips. "You mind?"

"You smoking already?"

He lit the cigarette and nodded, watching me through the smoke. "I just wanted to see if I'd have the courage to smoke in front of you." He grinned and blew a great cloud of smoke to the ceiling. "It was easy." He looked at my face. "Come on, now. I bet you was smoking at my age, tell the truth."

I didn't say anything but the truth was on my face, and he laughed. But now there was something very strained in his laugh. "Sure. And I bet that ain't all you was doing."

He was frightening me a little. "Cut the crap," I said. "We already decided that you was going to go and live at Isabel's. Now what's got into you all of a sudden?"

"*You* decided it," he pointed out. "*I* didn't decide nothing." He stopped in front of me, leaning against the stove, arms loosely folded. "Look, brother. I don't want to stay in Harlem no more, I really don't." He was very earnest. He looked at me, then over toward the kitchen window. There was something in his eyes I'd never seen before, some thoughtfulness, some worry all his own. He rubbed the muscle of one arm. "It's time I was getting out of here."

"Where do you want to *go*, Sonny?"

"I want to join the army. Or the navy, I don't care. If I say I'm old enough, they'll believe me."

Then I got mad. It was because I was so scared. "You must be crazy. You goddamn fool, what the hell do you want to go and join the *army* for?"

"I just told you. To get out of Harlem."

"Sonny, you haven't even finished *school*. And if you really want to be a musician, how do you expect to study if you're in the *army*?"

He looked at me, trapped, and in anguish. "There's ways. I might be able to work out some kind of deal. Anyway, I'll have the G.I. Bill when I come out."

"*If* you come out." We stared at each other. "Sonny, please. Be reasonable. I know the setup is far from perfect. But we got to do the best we can."

"I ain't learning nothing in school," he said. "Even when I go." He turned away from me and opened the window and threw his cigarette out into the narrow alley. I watched his back. "At least, I ain't learning nothing you'd want me to learn." He slammed the window so hard I thought the glass would fly out, and turned back to me. "And I'm sick of the stink of these garbage cans!"

"Sonny," I said, "I know how you feel. But if you don't finish school now, you're going to be sorry later that you didn't." I grabbed him by the shoulders. "And you only got another year. It ain't so bad. And I'll come back and I swear I'll help you do *whatever* you want to do. Just try to put up with it till I come back. Will you please do that? For me?"

He didn't answer and he wouldn't look at me.

"Sonny. You hear me?"

He pulled away. "I hear you. But you never hear anything *I* say."

I didn't know what to say to that. He looked out of the window and then back at me. "OK," he said, and sighed. "I'll try."

Then I said, trying to cheer him up a little, "They got a piano at Isabel's. You can practice on it."

And as a matter of fact, it did cheer him up for a minute. "That's right," he said to himself. "I forgot that." His face relaxed a little. But the worry, the thoughtfulness, played on it still, the way shadows play on a face which is staring into the fire.

But I thought I'd never hear the end of that piano. At first, Isabel would write me, saying how nice it was that Sonny was so serious about his music and how, as soon as he came in from school, or wherever he had been when he was supposed to be at school, he went straight to that piano and stayed there until suppertime. And, after supper, he went back to that piano and stayed there until everybody went to bed. He was at the piano all day Saturday and all day Sunday. Then he bought a record player and started playing records. He'd play one record over and over again, all day long sometimes, and he'd improvise along with it on the piano. Or he'd play one section of the record, one chord, one change, one progression, then he'd do it, on the piano. Then back to the record. Then back to the piano.

Well, I really don't know how they stood it. Isabel finally confessed that it wasn't like living with a person at all, it was like living with sound. And the sound didn't make any sense to her, didn't make any sense to any of them—naturally. They began, in a way, to be afflicted by this presence that was living in their home. It was as though Sonny were some sort of god, or monster. He moved in an atmosphere which wasn't like theirs at all. They fed him and he ate, he washed himself, he walked in and out of their door; he certainly wasn't nasty or unpleasant or rude, Sonny isn't any of those things; but it was as though he were all wrapped up in some cloud, some fire, some vision all his own; and there wasn't any way to reach him.

At the same time, he wasn't really a man yet, he was still a child, and they had to watch out for him in all kinds of ways. They certainly couldn't throw him out. Neither did they dare to make a great scene about that piano because even they dimly sensed, as I sensed, from so many thousands of miles away, that Sonny was at that piano playing for his life.

But he hadn't been going to school. One day a letter came from the school board and Isabel's mother got it—there had, apparently, been other letters but Sonny had torn them up. This day, when Sonny came in, Isabel's mother showed him the letter and asked him where he'd been spending his time. And she finally got it out of him that he'd been down in Greenwich Village, with musicians and other characters, in a white girl's apartment. And this scared her and she started to scream at him and what came up, once she began—though she denies it to this day—was what sacrifices they were making to give Sonny a decent home and how little he appreciated it.

Sonny didn't play the piano that day. By evening, Isabel's mother had calmed down but then there was the old man to deal with, and Isabel herself. Isabel says she did her best to be calm but she broke down and started crying. She says she just watched Sonny's face. She could tell, by watching him, what was happening with him. And what was happening was that they penetrated his cloud, they had reached him. Even if their fingers had been a thousand times more gentle than human fingers ever are, he could hardly help feeling that they had stripped him naked and were spitting on that nakedness. For he also had to see that his presence, that music, which was life or death to him, had been torture for them and that they had endured it, not at all for his sake, but only for mine. And Sonny couldn't take that. He can take it a little better today than he could then but he's still not very good at it and, frankly, I don't know anybody who is.

The silence of the next few days must have been louder than the sound of all the music ever played since time began. One morning, before she went to work, Isabel was in his room for something and she suddenly realized that all of his records were gone. And she knew for certain that he was gone. And he was. He went as far as the navy would carry him. He finally sent me a postcard from some place in Greece and that was the first I knew that Sonny was still alive. I didn't see him any more until we were both back in New York and the war had long been over.

He was a man by then, of course, but I wasn't willing to see it. He came by the house from time to time, but we fought almost every time we met. I didn't like the way he carried himself, loose and dreamlike all the time, and I didn't like his friends, and his music seemed to be merely an excuse for the life he led. It sounded just that weird and disordered.

Then we had a fight, a pretty awful fight, and I didn't see him for months. By and by I looked him up, where he was living, in a furnished room in the Village, and I tried to make it up. But there were lots of other people in the room and Sonny just lay on his bed, and he wouldn't come downstairs with me, and he treated these other people as though they were his family and I weren't. So I got mad and then he got mad, and then I told him that he might just as well be dead as live the way he was living. Then he stood up and he told me not to worry about him any more in life, that he *was* dead as far as I was concerned. Then he pushed me to the door and the other people looked on as though nothing were happening, and he slammed the door behind me. I stood in the hallway, staring at the door. I heard somebody laugh in the room and then the tears came to my eyes. I started down the steps, whistling to keep from crying, I kept whistling to myself, *You going to need me, baby, one of these cold, rainy days.*

I read about Sonny's trouble in the spring. Little Grace died in the fall. She was a beautiful little girl. But she only lived a little over two years. She died of polio and she suffered. She had a slight fever for a couple of days, but it didn't seem like anything and we just kept her in bed. And we would certainly have called the doctor, but the fever dropped, she seemed to be all right. So we thought it had just been a cold. Then, one day, she was up, playing, Isabel was in the kitchen fixing lunch for the two boys when they'd come in from school, and she heard Grace fall down in the living room. When you have a lot of children you don't always start running when one of them falls, unless they start screaming or something. And, this time, Grace was quiet. Yet, Isabel says that when she heard that *thump* and then that silence, something happened in her to make her afraid. And she ran to the living room and there was little Grace on the floor, all twisted up, and the reason she hadn't screamed was that she couldn't get her breath. And when she did scream, it was the worst sound, Isabel says, that she'd ever heard in all her life, and she still hears it sometimes in her dreams. Isabel will sometimes wake me up with a low, moaning, strangled sound and I have to be quick to awaken her and hold her to me and where Isabel is weeping against me seems a mortal wound.

I think I may have written Sonny the very day that little Grace was buried. I was sitting in the living room in the dark, by myself, and I suddenly thought of Sonny. My trouble made his real.

One Saturday afternoon, when Sonny had been living with us, or, anyway, been in our house, for nearly two weeks, I found myself wandering aimlessly about the living room, drinking from a can of beer, and trying to work up the courage to search Sonny's room. He was out, he was usually out whenever I was home, and Isabel had taken the children to see their grandparents. Suddenly I was standing still in front of the living room window, watching Seventh Avenue. The idea of searching Sonny's room made me still. I scarcely dared to admit to myself what I'd been searching for. I didn't know what I'd do if I found it. Or if I didn't.

On the sidewalk across from me, near the entrance to a barbecue joint, some people were holding an old-fashioned revival meeting. The barbecue cook, wearing a dirty white apron, his conked hair reddish and metallic in the pale sun, and a cigarette between his lips, stood in the doorway, watching them. Kids and older people paused in their errands and stood there, along with some older men and a couple of very tough-looking women who watched everything that happened on the avenue, as though they owned it, or were maybe owned by it. Well, they were watching this, too. The revival was being carried on by three sisters in black, and a brother. All they had were their voices and their Bibles and a tambourine. The brother was testifying and while he testified two of the sisters stood together, seeming to say, amen, and the third sister walked around with the tambourine outstretched and a couple of people dropped coins into it. Then the brother's testimony ended and the sister who had been taking up the collection dumped the coins into her palm and transferred them to the pocket of her long black robe. Then she raised both hands, striking the tambourine against the air, and then against one hand, and she started to sing. And the two other sisters and the brother joined in.

It was strange, suddenly, to watch, though I had been seeing these street meetings all my life. So, of course, had everybody else down there. Yet, they paused and watched and listened and I stood still at the window. *"Tis the old ship of Zion,"* they sang, and the sister with the tambourine kept a steady, jangling beat, *"it has rescued many a thousand!"* Not a soul under the sound of their voices was hearing this song for the first time, not one of them had been rescued. Nor had they seen much in the way of rescue work being done around them. Neither did they especially believe in the holiness of the three sisters and the brother, they knew too much about them, knew where they lived, and how. The woman with the tambourine, whose voice dominated the air, whose face was bright with joy, was divided by very little from the woman who stood watching her, a cigarette between her heavy, chapped lips, her hair a cuckoo's nest, her face scarred and swollen from many beatings, and her black eyes glittering like coal. Perhaps they both knew this, which was why, when, as rarely, they addressed each other, they addressed each other as Sister. As the singing filled the air the watching, listening faces underwent a change, the eyes focusing on something within; the music seemed to soothe a poison out of them; and time seemed, nearly, to fall away from the sullen, belligerent, battered faces, as though they were fleeing back to their first condition, while dreaming of their last. The barbecue cook half shook his head and smiled, and dropped his cigarette and disapeared into his joint. A man fumbled in his pockets for change and stood holding it in his hand impatiently, as though he had just remembered a pressing appointment further up the avenue. He looked furious. Then I saw Sonny, standing on the edge of the crowd. He was carrying a wide, flat notebook with a green cover, and it made him look, from where I was standing, almost like a school-boy. The coppery sun brought out the copper in his skin, he was very faintly smiling, standing very still. Then the singing stopped, the tambourine turned into a collection plate again. The furious man dropped in his coins and vanished, so did a couple of the women, and Sonny dropped some change in the plate, looking directly at the woman with a little smile. He started across the avenue, toward the house. He has a slow, loping walk, something like the way the Harlem hipsters walk, only he's imposed on this his own half-beat. I had never really noticed it before.

I stayed at the window, both relieved and apprehensive. As Sonny disappeared from my sight, they began singing again. And they were still singing when his key turned in the lock.

"Hey," he said.

"Hey, yourself. You want some beer?"

"No. Well, maybe." But he came up to the window and stood beside me, looking out. "What a warm voice," he said.

They were singing *If I could only hear my mother pray again!*

"Yes," I said, "and she can sure beat that tambourine."

"But what a terrible song," he said, and laughed. He dropped his notebook on the sofa and disappeared into the kitchen. "Where's Isabel and the kids?"

"I think they went to see their grandparents. You hungry?"

"No." He came back into the living room with his can of beer. "You want to come some place with me tonight?"

I sensed, I don't know how, that I couldn't possibly say no. "Sure. Where?"

He sat down on the sofa and picked up his notebook and started leafing through it. "I'm going to sit in with some fellows in a joint in the Village."

"You mean, you're going to play, tonight?"

"That's right." He took a swallow of his beer and moved back to the window. He gave me a sidelong look. "If you can stand it."

"I'll try," I said.

He smiled to himself and we both watched as the meeting across the way broke up. The three sisters and the brother, heads bowed, were singing *God be with you till we meet again.* The faces around them were very quiet. Then the song ended. The small crowd dispersed. We watched the three women and the lone man walk slowly up the avenue.

"When she was singing before," said Sonny, abruptly, "her voice reminded me for a minute of what heroin feels like sometimes—when it's in your veins. It makes you feel sort of warm and cool at the same time. And distant. And—and sure." He sipped his beer, very deliberately not looking at me. I watched his face. "It makes you feel —in control. Sometimes you've got to have that feeling."

"Do you?" I sat down slowly in the easy chair.

"Sometimes." He went to the sofa and picked up his notebook again. "Some people do."

"In order," I asked, "to play?" And my voice was very ugly, full of contempt and anger.

"Well"—he looked at me with great, troubled eyes, as though, in fact, he hoped his eyes would tell me things he could never otherwise say—"they *think* so. And *if* they think so—!"

"And what do *you* think?" I asked.

He sat on the sofa and put his can of beer on the floor. "I don't know," he said, and I couldn't be sure if he were answering my question or pursuing his thoughts. His face didn't tell me. "It's not so much to *play*. It's to *stand* it, to be able to make it at all. On any level," He frowned and smiled: "In order to keep from shaking to pieces."

"But these friends of yours," I said, "they seem to shake themselves to pieces pretty goddamn fast."

"Maybe." He played with the notebook. And something told me that I should curb my tongue, that Sonny was doing his best to talk, that I should listen. "But of course you only know the ones that've gone to pieces. Some don't—or at least they haven't *yet* and that's just about all *any* of us can say." He paused. "And then there are some who just live, really, in hell, and they know it and they see what's happening and they go right on. I don't know." He sighed, dropped the notebook, folded his arms. "Some guys, you can tell from the way they play, they on something *all* the time. And you can see that, well, it makes something real for them. But of course," he picked up his beer from the floor and sipped it and put the can down again, "they *want* to, too, you've got to see that. Even some of them that say they don't—*some,* not all."

"And what about you?" I asked—I couldn't help it. "What about you? Do *you* want to?"

He stood up and walked to the window and remained silent for a long time. Then he sighed. "Me," he said. Then: "While I was downstairs before, on my way here, listening to that woman sing, it struck me all of a sudden how much suffering she must have had to go through—to sing like that. It's *repulsive* to think you have to suffer that much."

I said: "But there's no way not to suffer—is there, Sonny?"

"I believe not," he said and smiled, "but that's never stopped anyone from trying." He looked at me. "Has it?" I realized, with this mocking look, that there stood between us, forever, beyond the power of time or forgiveness, the fact that I had held silence—so long!—when he had needed human speech to help him. He turned back to the window. "No, there's no way not to suffer. But you try all kinds of ways to keep from drowning in it, to keep on top of it, and to make it seem—well, like *you*. Like you did something, all right, and now you're suffering for it. You know?" I said nothing. "Well you know," he said, impatiently, "why *do* people suffer? Maybe it's better to do something to give it a reason, *any* reason."

"But we just agreed," I said, "that there's no way not to suffer. Isn't it better, then, just to—take it?"

"But nobody just takes it," Sonny cried, "that's what I'm telling you! *Everybody* tries not to. You're just hung up on the *way* some people try—it's not *your* way!"

The hair on my face began to itch, my face felt wet. "That's not true," I said, "that's not true. I don't give a damn what other people do. I don't even care how they suffer. I just care how *you* suffer." And he looked at me. "Please believe me," I said. "I don't want to see you—die—trying not to suffer."

"I won't," he said, flatly, "die trying not to suffer. At least, not any faster than anybody else."

"But there's no need," I said, trying to laugh, "is there? in killing yourself."

I wanted to say more, but I couldn't. I wanted to talk about will power and how life could be—well, beautiful. I wanted to say that it was all within; but was it? or, rather, wasn't that exactly the trouble? And I wanted to promise that I would never fail him again. But it would all have sounded—empty words and lies.

So I made the promise to myself and prayed that I would keep it.

"It's terrible sometimes, inside," he said, "that's what's the trouble. You walk these streets, black and funky and cold, and there's not really a living ass to talk to, and there's nothing shaking, and there's no way of getting it out—that storm inside. You can't talk it and you can't make love with it, and when you finally try to get with it and play it, you realize *nobody's* listening. So *you've* got to listen. You got to find a way to listen."

And then he walked away from the window and sat on the sofa again, as though all the wind had suddenly been knocked out of him. "Sometimes you'll do *anything* to play, even cut your mother's throat." He laughed and looked at me. "Or your brother's." Then he sobered. "Or your own." Then: "Don't worry. I'm all right now and I think I'll *be* all right. But I can't forget—where I've been. I don't mean just the physical place I've been, I mean where I've *been*. And *what* I've been."

"What have you been, Sonny?" I asked.

He smiled—but sat sideways on the sofa, his elbow resting on the back, his fingers playing with his mouth and chin, not looking at me. "I've been something I didn't recognize, didn't know I could be. Didn't know anybody could be." He stopped, looking inward, looking helplessly young, looking old. "I'm not talking about it now because I feel *guilty* or anything like that—maybe it would be better if I did, I don't know. Anyway, I can't really talk about it. Not to you, not to anybody," and now he turned and faced me. "Sometimes, you know, and it was actually when I was most *out* of the world, I felt that I was in it, that I was *with* it, really, and I could play or I didn't really have to *play,* it just came out of me, it was there. And I don't know how I played, thinking about it now, but I know I did awful things, those times, sometimes, to people. Or it wasn't that I *did* anything to them—it was that they weren't real." He picked up the beer can; it was empty; he rolled it between his palms: "And other times—well, I needed a fix, I needed to find a place to lean, I needed to clear a space to *listen*—and I couldn't find it, and I—went crazy, I did terrible things to *me,* I was terrible *for* me." He began pressing the beer can between his hands, I watched the metal begin to give. It glittered, as he played with it, like a knife, and I was afraid he would cut himself, but I said nothing. "Oh well. I can never tell you. I was all by myself at the bottom of something, stinking and sweating and crying and shaking, and I smelled it, you know? *my* stink, and I thought I'd die if I couldn't get away from it and yet, all the same, I knew that everything I was doing was just locking me in with it. And I didn't know," he paused, still flattening the beer can, "I didn't know, I still *don't* know, something kept telling me that maybe it was good to smell your own stink, but I didn't think that *that* was what I'd been trying to do—and—who can stand it?" and he abruptly dropped the ruined beer can, looking at me with a small, still smile, and then rose, walking to the window as though it were the lodestone rock. I watched his face, he watched the avenue. "I couldn't tell you when Mama died—but the reason I wanted to leave Harlem so bad was to get away from drugs. And then, when I ran away, that's what I was running from—really. When

I came back, nothing had changed, *I* hadn't changed, I was just—older." And he stopped, drumming with his fingers on the windowpane. The sun had vanished, soon darkness would fall. I watched his face. "It can come again," he said, almost as though speaking to himself. Then he turned to me. "It can come again," he repeated. "I just want you to know that."

"All right," I said, at last. "So it can come again, All right."

He smiled, but the smile was sorrowful. "I had to try to tell you," he said.

"Yes," I said. "I understand that."

"You're my brother," he said, looking straight at me, and not smiling at all.

"Yes," I repeated, "yes. I understand that."

He turned back to the window, looking out. "All that hatred down there," he said, "all that hatred and misery and love. It's a wonder it doesn't blow the avenue apart."

We went to the only nightclub on a short, dark street, downtown. We squeezed through the narrow, chattering, jam-packed bar to the entrance of the big room, where the bandstand was. And we stood there for a moment, for the lights were very dim in this room and we couldn't see. Then, "Hello, boy," said a voice and an enormous black man, much older than Sonny or myself, erupted out of all that atmospheric lighting and put an arm around Sonny's shoulder. "I been sitting right here," he said, "waiting for you."

He had a big voice, too, and heads in the darkness turned toward us.

Sonny grinned and pulled a little away, and said, "Creole, this is my brother. I told you about him."

Creole shook my hand. "I'm glad to meet you, son," he said, and it was clear that he was glad to meet me *there,* for Sonny's sake. And he smiled, "You got a real musician in *your* family," and he took his arm from Sonny's shoulder and slapped him, lightly, affectionately, with the back of his hand.

"Well. Now I've heard it all," said a voice behind us. This was another musician, and a friend of Sonny's, a coal-black, cheerful-looking man, built close to the ground. He immediately began confiding to me, at the top of his lungs, the most terrible things about Sonny, his teeth gleaming like a lighthouse and his laugh coming up out of him like the beginning of an earthquake. And it turned out that everyone at the bar knew Sonny, or almost everyone; some were musicians, working there, or nearby, or not working, some were simply hangers-on, and some were there to hear Sonny play. I was introduced to all of them and they were all very polite to me. Yet, it was clear that, for them, I was only Sonny's brother. Here, I was in Sonny's world. Or, rather: his kingdom. Here, it was not even a question that his veins bore royal blood.

They were going to play soon and Creole installed me, by myself, at a table in a dark corner. Then I watched them, Creole, and the little black man, and Sonny, and the others, while they horsed around, standing just below the bandstand. The light from the bandstand spilled just a little short of them and, watching them laughing and gesturing and moving about, I had the feeling that they, nevertheless, were being most careful not to step into that circle of light too suddenly: that if they moved into the light too suddenly, without thinking, they would perish in flame. Then, while I watched, one of them, the small, black man, moved into the light and crossed the bandstand and started fooling around with his drums. Then—being funny and being, also, extremely ceremonious—Creole took Sonny by the arm and led him to the piano.

A woman's voice called Sonny's name and a few hands started clapping. And Sonny, also being funny and being ceremonious, and so touched, I think, that he could have cried, but neither hiding it nor showing it, riding it like a man, grinned, and put both hands to his heart and bowed from the waist.

Creole then went to the bass fiddle and a lean, very bright skinned brown man jumped up on the bandstand and picked up his horn. So there they were, and the atmosphere on the bandstand and in the room began to change and tighten. Someone stepped up to the microphone and announced them. Then there were all kinds of murmurs. Some people at the bar shushed others. The waitress ran around, frantically getting in the last orders, guys and chicks got closer to each other, and the lights on the bandstand, on the quartet, turned to a kind of indigo. Then they all looked different there. Creole looked about him for the last time, as though he were making certain that all his chickens were in the coop, and then he—jumped and struck the fiddle. And there they were.

All I know about music is that not many people ever really hear it. And even then, on the rare occasions when something opens within, and the music enters, what we mainly hear, or hear corroborated, are personal, private, vanishing evocations. But the man who creates the music is hearing something else, is dealing with the roar rising from the void and imposing order on it as it hits the air. What is evoked in him, then, is of another order, more terrible because it has no words, and triumphant, too, for that same reason. And his triumph, when he triumphs, is ours. I just watched Sonny's face. His face was troubled, he was working hard, but he wasn't with it. And I had the feeling that, in a way, everyone on the bandstand was waiting for him, both waiting for him and pushing him along. But as I began to watch Creole, I realized that it was Creole who held them all back. He had them on a short rein. Up there, keeping the beat with his whole body, wailing on the fiddle, with his eyes half closed, he was listening to everything, but he was listening to Sonny. He was having a dialogue with Sonny. He wanted Sonny to leave the shoreline and strike out for the deep water. He was Sonny's witness that deep water and drowning were not the same thing—he had been there, and he knew. And he wanted Sonny to know. He was waiting for Sonny to do the things on the keys which would let Creole know that Sonny was in the water.

And, while Creole listened, Sonny moved, deep within, exactly like someone in torment. I had never before thought of how awful the relationship must be between the musician and his instrument. He has to fill it, this instrument, with the breath of life, his own. He has to make it do what he wants it to do. And a piano is just a piano. It's made out of so much wood and wires and little hammers and big ones, and ivory. While there's only so much you can do with it, the only way to find this out is to try; to try and make it do everything.

And Sonny hadn't been near a piano for over a year. And he wasn't on much better terms with his life, not the life that stretched before him now. He and the piano stammered, started one way, got scared, stopped; started another way, panicked, marked time, started again; then seemed to have found a direction, panicked again, got stuck. And the face I saw on Sonny I'd never seen before. Everything had been burned out of it, and, at the same time, things usually hidden were being burned in, by the fire and fury of the battle which was occurring in him up there.

Yet, watching Creole's face as they neared the end of the first set, I had the feeling that something had happened, something I hadn't heard. Then they finished, there was scattered applause, and then, without an instant's warning, Creole started into something else, it was almost sardonic, it was *Am I Blue*. And, as though he commanded, Sonny began to play. Something began to happen. And Creole let out the reins. The dry, low, black man said something awful on the drums, Creole answered, and the drums talked back. Then the horn insisted, sweet and high, slightly detached perhaps, and Creole listened, commenting now and then, dry, and driving, beautiful and calm and old. Then they all came together again, and Sonny was part of the family again. I could tell this from his face. He seemed to have found, right there beneath his fingers, a damn brand-new piano. It seemed that he couldn't get over it. Then, for a while, just being happy with Sonny, they seemed to be agreeing with him that brand-new pianos certainly were a gas.

Then Creole stepped forward to remind them that what they were playing was the blues. He hit something in all of them, he hit something in me, myself, and the music tightened and deepened, apprehension began to beat the air. Creole began to tell us what the blues were all about. They were not about anything very new. He and his boys up there were keeping it new, at the risk of ruin, destruction, madness, and death, in order to find new ways to make us listen. For, while the tale of how we suffer, and how we are delighted, and how we may triumph is never new, it always must be heard. There isn't any other tale to tell, it's the only light we've got in all this darkness.

And this tale, according to that face, that body, those strong hands on those strings, has another aspect in every country, and a new depth in every generation. Listen, Creole seemed to be saying, listen. Now these are Sonny's blues. He made the little black man on the drums know it, and the bright, brown man on the horn. Creole wasn't trying any longer to get Sonny in the water. He was wishing him Godspeed. Then he stepped back, very slowly, filling the air with the immense suggestion that Sonny speak for himself.

Then they all gathered around Sonny and Sonny played. Every now and again one of them seemed to say, amen. Sonny's fingers filled the air with life, his life. But that life contained so many others. And Sonny went all the way back he really began with the spare, flat statement of the opening phrase of the song. Then he began to make it his. It was very beautiful because it wasn't hurried and it was no longer a lament. I seemed to hear with what burning he had made it his, with what burning we had yet to make it ours, how we could cease lamenting. Freedom lurked around us and I understood, at last, that he could help us to be free if we would listen, that he would never be free until we did. Yet, there was no battle in his face now. I heard what he had gone through, and would continue to go through until he came to rest in earth. He had made it his: that long line, of which we knew only Mama and Daddy. And he was giving it back, as everything must be given back, so that, passing through death, it can live forever. I saw my mother's face again, and felt, for the first time, how the stones of the road she had walked on must have bruised her feet. I saw the moonlit road where my father's brother died. And it brought something else back to me, and carried me past it, I saw my little girl again and felt Isabel's tears again, and I felt my own tears begin to rise. And I was yet aware that this was only a moment, that the world waited outside, as hungry as a tiger, and that trouble stretched above us, longer than the sky.

Then it was over. Creole and Sonny let out their breath, both soaking wet, and grinning. There was a lot of applause and some of it was real. In the dark, the girl came by and I asked her to take drinks to the bandstand. There was a long pause, while they talked up there in the indigo light and after awhile I saw the girl put a Scotch and milk on top of the piano for Sonny. He didn't seem to notice it, but just before they started playing again, he sipped from it and looked toward me, and nodded. Then he put it back on top of the piano. For me, then, as they began to play again, it glowed and shook above my brother's head like the very cup of trembling.

A DIAMOND GUITAR

Truman Capote
(1924–1984)

Biography p. 1065

The nearest town to the prison farm is twenty miles away. Many forests of pine trees stand between the farm and the town, and it is in these forests that the convicts work; they tap for turpentine. The prison itself is in a forest. You will find it there at the end of a red rutted road, barbed wire sprawling like a vine over its walls. Inside, there live one hundred and nine white men, ninety-seven Negroes and one Chinese. There are two sleep houses—great green wooden buildings with tarpaper roofs. The white men occupy one, the Negroes and the Chinese the other. In each sleep house there is one large pot-bellied stove, but the winters are cold here, and at night with the pines waving frostily and a freezing light falling from the moon the men, stretched on their iron cots, lie awake with the fire colors of the stove playing in their eyes.

The men whose cots are nearest the stove are the important men—those who are looked up to or feared. Mr. Schaeffer is one of these. Mr. Schaeffer—for that is what he is called, a mark of special respect—is a lanky, pulled-out man. He has reddish, silvering hair, and his face is attenuated, religious; there is no flesh to him; you can see the workings of his bones, and his eyes are a poor, dull color. He can read and he can write, he can add a column of figures. When another man receives a letter, he brings it to Mr. Schaeffer. Most of these letters are sad and complaining; very often Mr. Schaeffer improvises more cheerful messages and does not read what is written on the page. In the sleep house there are two other men who can read. Even so, one of them brings his letters to Mr. Schaeffer, who obliges by never reading the truth. Mr. Schaeffer himself does not receive mail, not even at Christmas; he seems to have no friends beyond the prison, and actually he has none there—that is, no particular friend. This was not always true.

One winter Sunday some winters ago Mr. Schaeffer was sitting on the steps of the sleep house carving a doll. He is quite talented at this. His dolls are carved in separate sections, then put together with bits of spring wire; the arms and legs move, the head rolls. When he has finished a dozen or so of these dolls, the Captain of the farm takes them into town, and there they are sold in a general store. In this way Mr. Schaeffer earns money for candy and tobacco.

That Sunday, as he sat cutting out the fingers for a little hand, a truck pulled into the prison yard. A young boy, handcuffed to the Captain of the farm, climbed out of the truck and stood blinking at the ghostly winter sun. Mr. Schaeffer only glanced at him. He was then a man of fifty, and seventeen of those years he'd lived at the farm. The arrival of a new prisoner could not arouse him. Sunday is a free day at the farm, and other men who were moping around the yard crowded down to the truck. Afterward, Pick Axe and Goober stopped by to speak with Mr. Schaeffer.

Pick Axe said, "He's a foreigner, the new one is. From Cuba. But with yellow hair."

"A knifer, Cap'n says," said Goober, who was a knifer himself. "Cut up a sailor in Mobile."

"Two sailors," said Pick Axe. "But just a café fight. He didn't hurt them boys none."

"To cut off a man's ear? You call that not hurtin' him? They give him two years, Cap'n says."

Pick Axe said, "He's got a guitar with jewels all over it."

It was getting too dark to work. Mr. Schaeffer fitted the pieces of his doll together and, holding its little hands, set it on his knee. He rolled a cigarette; the pines were blue in the sundown light, and the smoke from his cigarette lingered in the cold, darkening air. He could see the Captain coming across the yard. The new prisoner, a blond young boy, lagged a pace behind. He was carrying a guitar studded with glass diamonds that cast a starry twinkle, and his new uniform was too big for him; it looked like a Halloween suit.

"Somebody for you, Schaeffer," said the Captain, pausing on the steps of the sleep house. The Captain was not a hard man; occasionally he invited Mr. Schaeffer into his office, and they would talk together about things they had read in the newspaper. "Tico Feo," he said as though it were the name of a bird or a song, "this is Mr. Schaeffer. Do like him, and you'll do right."

Mr. Schaeffer glanced up at the boy and smiled. He smiled at him longer than he meant to, for the boy had eyes like strips of sky—blue as the winter evening—and his hair was as gold as the Captain's teeth. He had a fun-loving face, nimble, clever; and, looking at him, Mr. Schaeffer thought of holidays and good times.

"Is like my baby sister," said Tico Feo, touching Mr. Schaeffer's doll. His voice with its Cuban accent was soft and sweet as a banana. "She sit on my knee also."

Mr. Schaeffer was suddenly shy. Bowing to the Captain, he walked off into the shadows of the yard. He stood there whispering the names of the evening stars as they opened in flower above him. The stars were his pleasure, but tonight they did not comfort him; they did not make him remember that what happens to us on earth is lost in the endless shine of eternity. Gazing at them—the stars—he thought of the jeweled guitar and its worldly glitter.

It could be said of Mr. Schaeffer that in his life he'd done only one really bad thing: he'd killed a man. The circumstances of that deed are unimportant, except to say that the man deserved to die and that for it Mr. Schaeffer was sentenced to ninety-nine years and a day. For a long while—for many years, in fact—he had not thought of how it was before he came to the farm. His memory of those times was like a house where no one lives and where the furniture has rotted away. But tonight it was as if lamps had been lighted through all the gloomy dead rooms. It had begun to happen when he saw Tico Feo coming through the dusk with his splendid guitar. Until that moment he had not been lonesome. Now, recognizing his loneliness, he felt alive. He had not wanted to be alive. To be alive was to remember brown rivers where the fish run, and sunlight on a lady's hair.

Mr. Schaeffer hung his head. The glare of the stars had made his eyes water.

The sleep house usually is a glum place, stale with the smell of men and stark in the light of two unshaded electric bulbs. But with the advent of Tico Feo it was as though a tropic occurrence had happened in the cold room, for when Mr. Schaeffer returned from his observance of the stars he came upon a savage and garish scene.

Sitting cross-legged on a cot, Tico Feo was picking at his guitar with long swaying fingers and singing a song that sounded as jolly as jingling coins. Though the song was in Spanish, some of the men tried to sing it with him, and Pick Axe and Goober were dancing together. Charlie and Wink were dancing too, but separately. It was nice to hear the men laughing, and when Tico Feo finally put aside his guitar, Mr. Schaeffer was among those who congratulated him.

"You deserve such a fine guitar," he said.

"Is diamond guitar," said Tico Feo, drawing his hand over its vaudeville dazzle. "Once I have a one with rubies. But that one is stole. In Havana my sister work in a, how you say, where make guitar; is how I have this one."

Mr. Schaeffer asked him if he had many sisters, and Tico Feo, grinning, held up four fingers. Then, his blue eyes narrowing greedily, he said, "Please, Mister, you give me doll for my two little sister?"

The next evening Mr. Schaeffer brought him the dolls. After that he was Tico Feo's best friend and they were always together. At all times they considered each other.

Tico Feo was eighteen years old and for two years had worked on a freighter in the Caribbean. As a child he'd gone to school with nuns, and he wore a gold crucifix around his neck. He had a rosary too. The rosary he kept wrapped in a green silk scarf that also held three other treasures: a bottle of Evening in Paris cologne, a pocket mirror and a Rand McNally map of the world. These and the guitar were his only possessions, and he would not allow anyone to touch them. Perhaps he prized his map the most. At night, before the lights were turned off, he would shake out his map and show Mr. Schaeffer the places he'd been—Galveston, Miami, New Orleans, Mobile, Cuba, Haiti, Jamaica, Puerto Rico, the Virgin Islands—and the places he wanted to go to. He wanted to go almost everywhere, especially Madrid, especially the North Pole. This both charmed and frightened Mr. Schaeffer. It hurt him to think of Tico Feo on the seas and in far places. He sometimes looked defensively at his friend and thought, "You are just a lazy dreamer."

It is true that Tico Feo was a lazy fellow. After that first evening he had to be urged even to play his guitar. At daybreak when the guard came to rouse the men, which he did by banging a hammer on the stove, Tico Feo would whimper like a child. Sometimes he pretended to be ill, moaned and rubbed his stomach; but he never got away with this, for the Captain would send him out to work with the rest of the men. He and Mr. Schaeffer were put together on a highway gang. It was hard work, digging at frozen clay and carrying croker sacks filled with broken stone. The guard had always to be shouting at Tico Feo, for he spent most of the time trying to lean on things.

Each noon, when the dinner buckets were passed around, the two friends sat together. There were some good things in Mr. Schaeffer's bucket, as he could afford apples and candy bars from the town. He liked giving these things to his friend, for his friend enjoyed them so much, and he thought, "You are growing; it will be a long time until you are a grown man."

Not all the men liked Tico Feo. Because they were jealous, or for more subtle reasons, some of them told ugly stories about him. Tico Feo himself seemed unaware of this. When the men gathered around him, and he played his guitar and sang his songs, you could see that he felt he was loved. Most of the men did feel a love for him; they waited for and depended upon the hour between supper and lights out.

"Tico, play your box," they would say. They did not notice that afterward there was a deeper sadness than there had ever been. Sleep jumped beyond them like a jack rabbit, and their eyes lingered ponderingly on the firelight that creaked behind the grating of the stove. Mr. Schaeffer was the only one who understood their troubled feeling, for he felt it too. It was that his friend had revived the brown rivers where the fish run, and ladies with sunlight in their hair.

Soon Tico Feo was allowed the honor of having a bed near the stove and next to Mr. Schaeffer. Mr. Schaeffer had always known that his friend was a terrible liar. He did not listen for the truth in Tico Feo's tales of adventure, of conquests and encounters with famous people. Rather, he took pleasure in them as plain stories, such as you would read in a magazine, and it warmed him to hear his friend's tropic voice whispering in the dark.

Except that they did not combine their bodies or think to do so, though such things were not unknown at the farm, they were as lovers. Of the seasons, spring is the most shattering: stalks thrusting through the earth's winter-stiffened crust, young leaves cracking out on old left-to-die branches, the falling-asleep wind cruising through all the newborn green. And with Mr. Schaeffer it was the same, a breaking up, a flexing of muscles that had hardened.

It was late January. The friends were sitting on the steps of the sleep house, each with a cigarette in his hand. A moon thin and yellow as a piece of lemon rind curved above them, and under its light, threads of ground frost glistened like silver snail trials. For many days Tico Feo had been drawn into himself—silent as a robber waiting in the shadows. It was no good to say to him, "Tico, play your box." He would only look at you with smooth, under-ether eyes.

"Tell a story," said Mr. Schaeffer, who felt nervous and helpless when he could not reach his friend. "Tell about when you went to the race track in Miami."

"I not ever go to no race track," said Tico Feo, thereby admitting to his wildest lie, one involving hundreds of dollars and a meeting with Bing Crosby. He did not seem to care. He produced a comb and pulled it sulkily through his hair. A few days before this comb had been the cause of a fierce quarrel. One of the men, Wink, claimed that Tico Feo had stolen the comb from him, to which the accused replied by spitting in his face. They had wrestled around until Mr. Schaeffer and another man got them separated. "Is my comb. You tell him!" Tico Feo had demanded of Mr. Schaeffer. But Mr. Schaeffer with quiet firmness had said no, it was not his friend's comb—an answer that seemed to defeat all concerned. "Aw," said Wink, "if he wants it so much, Christ's sake, let the sonofabitch keep it." And later, in a puzzled, uncertain voice, Tico Feo had said, "I thought you was my friend." "I am," Mr. Schaeffer had thought, though he said nothing.

"I not go to no race track, and what I said about the widow woman, that is not true also." He puffed up his cigarette to a furious glow and looked at Mr. Schaeffer with a speculating expression. "Say, you have money, Mister?"

"Maybe twenty dollars," said Mr. Schaeffer hesitantly, afraid of where this was leading.

"Not so good, twenty dollar," Tico said, but without disappointment. "No important, we work our way. In Mobile I have my friend Frederico. He will put us on a boat. There will not be trouble," and it was as though he were saying that the weather had turned colder.

There was a squeezing in Mr. Schaeffer's heart; he could not speak.

"Nobody here can run to catch Tico. He run the fastest."

"Shotguns run faster," said Mr. Schaeffer in a voice hardly alive. "I'm too old," he said, with the knowledge of age churning like nausea inside him.

Tico Feo was not listening. "Then, the world. The world, *el mundo,* my friend." Standing up, he quivered like a young horse; everything seemed to draw close to him —the moon, the callings of screech owls. His breath came quickly and turned to smoke in the air. "Should we go to Madrid? Maybe someone teach me to bullfight. You think so, Mister?"

Mr. Schaeffer was not listening either. "I'm too old," he said. "I'm too damned old."

For the next several weeks Tico Feo kept after him—the world, *el mundo,* my friend; and he wanted to hide. He would shut himself in the toilet and hold his head. Nevertheless, he was excited, tantalized. What if it could come true, the race with Tico across the forests and to the sea? And he imagined himself on a boat, he who had never seen the sea, whose whole life had been land-rooted. During this time one of the convicts died, and in the yard you could hear the coffin being made. As each nail thudded into place, Mr. Schaeffer thought, "This is for me, it is mine."

Tico Feo himself was never in better spirits; he sauntered about with a dancer's snappy, gigolo grace, and had a joke for everyone. In the sleep house after supper his fingers popped at the guitar like firecrackers. He taught the men to cry *olé,* and some of them sailed their caps through the air.

When work on the road was finished, Mr. Schaeffer and Tico Feo were moved back into the forests. On Valentine Day's they ate their lunch under a pine tree. Mr. Schaeffer had ordered a dozen oranges from the town and he peeled them slowly, the skins unraveling in a spiral; the juicier slices he gave to his friend, who was proud of how far he could spit the seeds—a good ten feet.

It was a cold beautiful day, scraps of sunlight blew about them like butterflies, and Mr. Schaeffer, who liked working with the trees, felt dim and happy. Then Tico Feo said, "That one, he no could catch a fly in his mouth." He meant Armstrong, a hog-jowled man sitting with a shotgun propped between his legs. He was the youngest of the guards and new at the farm.

"I don't know," said Mr. Schaeffer. He'd watched Armstrong and noticed that, like many people who are both heavy and vain, the new guard moved with a skimming lightness. "He might could fool you."

"I fool him, maybe," said Tico Feo, and spit an orange seed in Armstrong's direction. The guard scowled at him, then blew a whistle. It was the signal for work to begin.

Sometime during the afternoon the two friends came together again; that is, they were nailing turpentine buckets onto trees that stood next to each other. At a distance below them a shallow bouncing creek branched through the woods. "In water no smell," said Tico Feo meticulously, as though remembering something he'd heard. "We run in the water; until dark we climb a tree. Yes, Mister?"

Mr. Schaeffer went on hammering, but his hand was shaking, and the hammer came down on his thumb. He looked around dazedly at his friend. His face showed no reflection of pain, and he did not put the thumb in his mouth, the way a man ordinarily might.

Tico Feo's blue eyes seemed to swell like bubbles, and when in a voice quieter than the wind sounds in the pinetops he said, "Tomorrow," these eyes were all that Mr. Schaeffer could see.

"Tomorrow, Mister?"

"Tomorrow," said Mr. Schaeffer.

The first colors of morning fell upon the walls of the sleep house, and Mr. Schaeffer, who had rested little, knew that Tico Feo was awake too. With the weary eyes of a crocodile he observed the movements of his friend in the next cot. Tico Feo was unknotting the scarf that contained his treasures. First he took the pocket mirror. Its jellyfish light trembled on his face. For a while he admired himself with serious delight, and combed and slicked his hair as though he were preparing to step out to a party. Then he hung the rosary about his neck. The cologne he never opened, nor the map. The last thing he did was to tune his guitar. While the other men were dressing, he sat on the edge of his cot and tuned the guitar. It was strange, for he must have known he would never play it again.

Bird shrills followed the men through the smoky morning woods. They walked single file, fifteen men to a group, and a guard bringing up the rear of each line. Mr. Schaeffer was sweating as though it were a hot day, and he could not keep in marching step with his friend, who walked ahead, snapping his fingers and whistling at the birds.

A signal had been set. Tico Feo was to call, "Time out," and pretend to go behind a tree. But Mr. Schaeffer did not know when it would happen.

The guard named Armstrong blew a whistle, and his men dropped from the line and separated to their various stations. Mr. Schaeffer, though going about his work as best he could, took care always to be in a position where he could keep an eye on both Tico Feo and the guard. Armstrong sat on a stump, a chew of tobacco lopsiding his face, and his gun pointing into the sun. He had the tricky eyes of a cardsharp; you could not really tell where he was looking.

Once another man gave the signal. Although Mr. Schaeffer had known at once that it was not the voice of his friend, panic had pulled at his throat like a rope. As the morning wore on there was such a drumming in his ears he was afraid he would not hear the signal when it came.

The sun climbed to the center of the sky. "He is just a lazy dreamer. It will never happen," thought Mr. Schaeffer, daring a moment to believe this. But "First we eat," said Tico Feo with a practical air as they set their dinner pails on the bank above the creek. They ate in silence, almost as though each bore the other a grudge, but at the end of it Mr. Schaeffer felt his friend's hand close over his own and hold it with a tender pressure.

"Mister Armstrong, time out . . ."

Near the creek Mr. Schaeffer had seen a sweet gum tree, and he was thinking it would soon be spring and the sweet gum ready to chew. A razory stone ripped open the palm of his hand as he slid off the slippery embankment into the water. He straightened up and began to run; his legs were long, he kept almost abreast of Tico Feo, and icy geysers sprayed around them. Back and forth through the woods the shouts of men boomed hollowly like voices in a cavern, and there were three shots, all highflying, as though the guard were shooting at a cloud of geese.

Mr. Schaeffer did not see the log that lay across the creek. He thought he was still running, and his legs thrashed about him; it was as though he were a turtle stranded on its back.

While he struggled there, it seemed to him that the face of his friend, suspended above him, was part of the white winter sky—it was so distant, judging. It hung there but an instant, like a hummingbird, yet in that time he'd seen that Tico Feo had not wanted him to make it, had never thought he would, and he remembered once thinking that it would be a long time before his friend was a grown man. When they found him, he was still lying in the ankle-deep water as though it were a summer afternoon and he were idly floating on the stream.

Since then three winters have gone by, and each has been said to be the coldest, the longest. Two recent months of rain washed deeper ruts in the clay road leading to the farm, and it is harder than ever to get there, harder to leave. A pair of searchlights has been added to the walls, and they burn there through the night like the eyes of a giant owl. Otherwise, there have not been many changes. Mr. Schaeffer, for instance, looks much the same, except that there is a thicker frost of white in his hair, and as the result of a broken ankle he walks with a limp. It was the Captain himself who said that Mr. Schaeffer had broken his ankle attempting to capture Tico Feo. There was even a picture of Mr. Schaeffer in the newspaper, and under it this caption: "Tried to Prevent Escape." At the time he was deeply mortified, not because he knew the other men were laughing, but because he thought of Tico Feo seeing it. But he cut it out of the paper anyway, and keeps it in an envelope along with several clippings pertaining to his friend: a spinster woman told the authorities he'd entered her home and kissed her, twice he was reported seen in the Mobile vicinity, finally it was believed that he had left the country.

No one has ever disputed Mr. Schaeffer's claim to the guitar. Several months ago a new prisoner was moved into the sleep house. He was said to be a fine player, and Mr. Schaeffer was persuaded to lend him the guitar. But all the man's tunes came out sour, for it was as though Tico Feo, tuning his guitar that last morning, had put a curse upon it. Now it lies under Mr. Schaeffer's cot, where its glass diamonds are turning yellow; in the night his hand sometimes searches it out, and his fingers drift across the strings: then, the world.

FOLLOW THE EAGLE

William Kotzwinkle

(b. 1932)

Biography p. 1081

Johnny Eagle climbed onto his 750-cubic-centimeter Arupa motorcycle and roared out of the Navaho Indian Reservation, followed by the Mexican, Domingo, on a rattling Japanese cycle stolen from a Colorado U law student.

Up the morning highway they rode toward the Colorado River, half-drunk and full-crazy in the sunlight, Eagle's slouch hat brim bent in the wind, Domingo's long black moustaches trailing in the air.

Yes, thought Eagle, wheeling easy over the flat land, yes indeed. And they came to Navaho Canyon where they shut down their bikes. Mist from the winding river far below rose up through the scarred plateau and the air was still.

Eagle and Domingo wheeled their bikes slowly to the edge of the Canyon. Domingo got off and threw a stone across the gorge. It struck the far wall, bounced, echoed, fell away in silence.

"Long way to the other side, man," he said, looking at Eagle.

Eagle said nothing, sat on his bike, staring across the gaping crack in the earth.

Domingo threw another stone, which cleared the gap, kicking up a little cloud of dust on top of the other cliff. "How fast you got to go—hunnert, hunnert twenty-five?"

Eagle spit into the canyon and tromped the starter of his bike.

"When you goin', man?" shouted Domingo over the roar.

"Tomorrow!"

That night was a party for Johnny Eagle on the Reservation. He danced with Red Wing in the long house, pressed her up against a corner. Medicine Man came by, gave Eagle a cougar tooth. "I been talkin' to it, Eagle," he said.

"Thanks, man," said Eagle and he put it around his neck and took Red Wing back to his shack, held her on the falling porch in the moonlight, looked at the moon over her shoulder.

She lay on his broken bed, hair undone on his ragged pillow, her buckskin jacket on the floor. Through the open window came music from the party, guitar strings and a drum head and Domingo singing

Uncle John have everything he need

"Don't go tomorrow," said Red Wing, unbuttoning Eagle's cowboy shirt.

"Gitchimanito is watching' out for me, baby," said Eagle, and he mounted her, riding bareback, up the draw, slow, to the drumbeat. His eyes were closed but he saw her tears, like silver beads, and he rode faster and shot his arrow through the moon.

"Oh, Johnny," she moaned, quivering beneath him, "don't go," and he felt her falling away, down the waving darkness.

They lay, looking out through the window. He hung the cat's tooth around her neck. "Stay with me," she said, holding him till dawn, and he rose up while she was sleeping. The Reservation was grey, the shacks crouching in the dawn light.

Eagle shook Domingo out of his filthy bed. The Mexican crawled across the floor, looking for his sombrero, and they walked across the camp to the garage where the pickup truck was stowed with Eagle's bike.

Eagle pulled the cycle off the kickstand and they rolled it up a wooden ramp into the back of the truck, then slid the ramp in the truck, roped it down, and drove quietly off the Reservation.

They went down the empty highway, Domingo at the wheel, Eagle slouched in the corner by the door. "Why you doin' this, man?" asked the Mexican, not looking at Eagle.

Eagle's hat was over his eyes. He slept a little, nodding with the bounces in and out of a dream. His head dropped against the cold window. The truck was stopped.

Eagle stepped down onto the silent mesa. My legs shakin', he thought and went round to the back of the truck, where Domingo was letting down the ramp. Eagle touched the cold handlebars of the bike and stopped shaking. They wheeled the cycle to the ground.

"I know a chick," said Domingo. They pushed the ramp to the edge of the canyon. "—with a fantastic ass—" They faced the ramp to the misty hole, bracing it with cinder blocks. "She live down in Ensenada, man, whattya say we go down there?"

Eagle climbed onto the bike, turned over the motor, breaking the morning stillness. He circled slowly, making bigger circles until the motor was running strong, then drove over to Domingo at the edge of the ramp.

"*Buena suerte, amigo!*" shouted the Mexican over the roaring engine.

"On the other side!" called Eagle, and drove away from the ramp, fifty, a hundred, two, three, four hundred yards. He turned, lined the bike up with the ramp. A white chicken fluttered in his stomach. Domingo waved his black hat.

In neutral, Eagle gunned the big Arupa engine, once, twice, and engaging first gear spun out toward the ramp.

The sun was rising, the speedometer climbing as he shifted into second gear, fifty, sixty, seventy, eighty miles an hour. Eagle burned across the table land toward Navaho Canyon, into third gear, ninety, a hundred, had jumped twelve cars on this bike, had no job, saw Domingo from the corner of his eye, was going one twenty-five and that was it as he hit the ramp and sailed his ass off into space.

The cycle whined above the mist, floating like a thunder clap, and Johnny Eagle in his slouch hat rode lightly as an arrow, airborne in the glory of the moment as a sunbeam struck him in his arc of triumph, then his sunset came upon him and he saw the flaw in his life story, *one fifty, man, not one twenty-five,* as the far cliff for which he hungered came no closer, seemed to mock him through the mist, was impossible, always had been, and his slouch hat blew away.

Don't go, Johnny.

He strained to lift his falling horse, to carry her above the morning, to fly with her between his legs, rupturing several muscles in his passion and then as he fell for certain just clung sadly with the morning rising up his asshole, poor balls groaning Johnny Eagle, falling down Navaho Canyon, the geological formations quite apparent as the mist was clearing from the rock.

"SO LONG, MAN!" he shouted, with quite a way to go, falling like a regular comet, smoke and fire out the tailpipe as the bike turned slowly over, plunging through the hollow entry. Jesus Christ my blood is boiling there goes the engine.

He fell quietly, hissing through the mist, dreaming it was still dawn on Red Wing's red-brown thighs.

Johnny, don't go. O.K. babe I'll stay here.

But he saw the real rocks rushing past him.

I uster dance. Neck down in the fender. She held me in my screwloose, Johnny Eagle, be my old man, babe I'm crazy and mus' go to Gitchegumee.

Down in Ensenada man

Domingo falling to the barroom laughing with his knife blade bloody, my look at that terra cotter there like faces in the Canyon, Sheriff you kin let us out now, won't do no harm. There goes my shoes man where am I.

A fantastic

Water like rock. Thousand fist pound my brain out. Crack me, shell me, awful snot death crap death hunnert bucks that bike death cost me black death o no Colorado do not take me.

Yes I took you Johnny Eagle

Wham the arrow crossed the morning. I am shot from out my body whoooooooooooooooo the endless sunrise.

Some time later a fledgling eagle was hatched by an old white-headed fierce-beaked queen of the Canyon. She pushed the little eagle into space where he learned to soar, crying *kyreeeee,* high above the morning, turning in the mist upon the wind.

And Domingo, riding down to Ensenada, to see the girl in Ensenada, crossed the border singing

> *He saw Aunt Mary comin' an'*
> *He duck back in the alley*

NINE LIVES

Ursula K. Le Guin

(b. 1929)

Biography p. 1083

She was alive inside but dead outside, her face a black and dun net of wrinkles, tumors, cracks. She was bald and blind. The tremors that crossed Libra's face were mere quiverings of corruption. Underneath, in the black corridors, the halls beneath the skin, there were crepitations in darkness, ferments, chemical nightmares that went on for centuries. "O the damned flatulent planet," Pugh murmured as the dome shook and a boil burst a kilometer to the southwest, spraying silver pus across the sunset. The sun had been setting for the last two days. "I'll be glad to see a human face."

"Thanks," said Martin.

"Yours is human to be sure," said Pugh, "but I've seen it so long I can't see it."

Radvid signals cluttered the communicator which Martin was operating, faded, returned as face and voice. The face filled the screen, the nose of an Assyrian king, the eyes of a samurai, skin bronze, eyes the color of iron: young, magnificent. "Is that what human beings look like?" said Pugh with awe. "I'd forgotten."

"Shut up, Owen, we're on."

"Libra Exploratory Mission Base, come in please, this is *Paserine* launch."

"Libra here. Beam fixed. Come on down, launch."

"Expulsion in seven E-seconds. Hold on." The screen blanked and sparkled.

"Do they all look like that? Martin, you and I are uglier men than I thought."

"Shut up, Owen. . . ."

For twenty-two minutes Martin followed the landing craft down by signal and then through the cleared dome they saw it, small star in the blood-colored east, sinking. It came down neat and quiet, Libra's thin atmosphere carrying little sound. Pugh and Martin closed the headpieces of their imsuits, zipped out of the dome air-locks, and ran with soaring strides, Nijinsky and Nureyev, toward the boat. Three equipment modules came floating down at four-minute intervals from each other and hundred-meter intervals east of the boat. "Come on out," Martin said on his suit radio, "we're waiting at the door."

"Come on in, the methane's fine," said Pugh.

The hatch opened. The young man they had seen on the screen came out with one athletic twist and leaped down onto the shaky dust and clinkers of Libra. Martin shook his hand, but Pugh was staring at the hatch, from which another young man emerged with the same neat twist and jump, followed by a young woman who emerged with the same neat twist, ornamented by a wriggle, and the jump. They were all tall, with bronze skin, black hair, high-bridged noses, epicanthic fold, the same face. They all had the same face. The fourth was emerging from the hatch with a neat twist and jump. "Martin bach," said Pugh, "we've got a clone."

"Right," said one of them, "we're a tenclone. John Chow's the name. You're Lieutenant Martin?"

"I'm Owen Pugh."

"Alvaro Guillen Martin," said Martin, formal, bowing slightly. Another girl was out, the same beautiful face; Martin stared at her and his eye rolled like a nervous pony's. Evidently he had never given any thought to cloning and was suffering technological shock. "Steady," Pugh said in the Argentine dialect, "it's only excess twins." He stood close by Martin's elbow. He was glad himself of the contact.

It is hard to meet a stranger. Even the greatest extravert meeting even the meekest stranger knows a certain dread, though he may not know he knows it. Will he make a fool of me wreck my image of myself invade me destroy me change me? Will he be different from me? Yes, that he will. There's the terrible thing: the strangeness of the stranger.

After two years on a dead planet, and the last half year isolated as a team of two, oneself and one other, after that it's even harder to meet a stranger, however welcome he may be. You're out of the habit of difference, you've lost the touch; and so the fear revives, the primitive anxiety, the old dread.

The clone, five males and five females, had got done in a couple of minutes what a man might have got done in twenty: greeted Pugh and Martin, had a glance at Libra, unloaded the boat, made ready to go. They went, and the dome filled with them, a hive of golden bees. They hummed and buzzed quietly, filled up all silences, all spaces with a honey-brown swarm of human presence. Martin looked bewildered at the long-limbed girls, and they smiled at him, three at once. Their smile was gentler than that of the boys, but no less radiantly self-possessed.

"Self-possessed," Owen Pugh murmured to his friend, "that's it. Think of it, to be oneself ten times over. Nine seconds for every motion, nine ayes on every vote. It would be glorious." But Martin was asleep. And the John Chows had all gone to sleep at once. The dome was filled with their quiet breathing. They were young, they didn't snore. Martin sighed and snored, his Hershey-bar-colored face relaxed in the dim afterglow of Libra's primary, set at last. Pugh had cleared the dome and stars looked in, Sol among them, a great company of lights, a clone of splendors. Pugh slept and dreamed of a one-eyed giant who chased him through the shaking halls of Hell.

From his sleeping bag Pugh watched the clone's awakening. They all got up within one minute except for one pair, a boy and a girl, who lay snugly tangled and still sleeping in one bag. As Pugh saw this there was a shock like one of Libra's earthquakes inside him, a very deep tremor. He was not aware of this and in fact thought he was pleased at the sight; there was no other such comfort on this dead hollow world. More power to them, who made love. One of the others stepped on the pair. They woke and the girl sat up flushed and sleepy, with bare golden breasts. One of her sisters murmured something to her; she shot a glance at Pugh and disappeared in the sleeping bag; from another direction came a fierce stare, from still another direction a voice: "Christ, we're used to having a room to ourselves. Hope you don't mind, Captain Pugh."

"It's a pleasure," Pugh said half truthfully. He had to stand up then wearing only the shorts he slept in, and he felt like a plucked rooster, all white scrawn and pimples. He had seldom envied Martin's compact brownness so much. The United Kingdom had come through the Great Famines well, losing less than half its population: a record achieved by rigorous food control. Black marketeers and hoarders had been executed. Crumbs had been shared. Where in richer lands most had died and a few had thrived, in Britain fewer died and none throve. They all got lean. Their sons were lean, their grandsons lean, small, brittle-boned, easily infected. When civilization became a matter of standing in lines, the British had kept queue, and so had replaced the survival of the fittest with the survival of the fair-minded. Owen Pugh was a scrawny little man. All the same, he was there.

At the moment he wished he wasn't.

At breakfast a John said, "Now if you'll brief us, Captain Pugh—"

"Owen, then."

"Owen, we can work out our schedule. Anything new on the mine since your last report to your Mission? We saw your reports when *Passerine* was orbiting Planet V, where they are now."

Martin did not answer, though the mine was his discovery and project, and Pugh had to do his best. It was hard to talk to them. The same faces, each with the same expression of intelligent interest, all leaned toward him across the table at almost the same angle. They all nodded together.

Over the Exploitation Corps insigne on their tunics each had a nameband, first name John and last name Chow of course, but the middle names different. The men were Aleph, Kaph, Yod, Gimel, and Samedh; the women Sadhe, Daleth, Zayin, Beth, and Resh. Pugh tried to use the names but gave it up at once; he could not even tell sometimes which one had spoken, for all the voices were alike.

Martin buttered and chewed his toast, and finally interrupted: "You're a team. Is that it?"

"Right," said two Johns.

"God, what a team! I hadn't seen the point. How much do you each know what the others are thinking?"

"Not at all, properly speaking," replied one of the girls, Zayin. The others watched her with the proprietary, approving look they had. "No ESP, nothing fancy. But we think alike. We have exactly the same equipment. Given the same stimulus, the same problem, we're likely to be coming up with the same reactions and solutions at the same time. Explanations are easy—don't even have to make them, usually. We seldom misunderstand each other. It does facilitate our working as a team."

"Christ yes," said Martin. "Pugh and I have spent seven hours out of ten for six months misunderstanding each other. Like most people. What about emergencies, are you as good at meeting the unexpected problem as a nor . . . an unrelated team?"

"Statistics so far indicate that we are," Zayin answered readily. Clones must be trained, Pugh thought, to meet questions, to reassure and reason. All they said had the slightly bland and stilted quality of answers furnished to the Public. "We can't brainstorm as singletons can, we as a team don't profit from the interplay of varied minds; but we have a compensatory advantage. Clones are drawn from the best human material, individuals of IIQ ninety-ninth percentile, Genetic Constitution alpha double A, and so on. We have more to draw on than most individuals do."

"And it's multiplied by a factor of ten. Who is—who was John Chow?"

"A genius surely," Pugh said politely. His interest in cloning was not so new and avid as Martin's.

"Leonardo Complex type," said Yod. "Biomath, also a cellist and an undersea hunter, and interested in structural engineering problems and so on. Died before he'd worked out his major theories."

"Then you each represent a different facet of his mind, his talents?"

"No," said Zayin, shaking her head in time with several others. "We share the basic equipment and tendencies, of course, but we're all engineers in Planetary Exploitation. A later clone can be trained to develop other aspects of the basic equipment. It's all training; the genetic substance is identical. We *are* John Chow. But we are differently trained."

Martin looked shell-shocked. "How old are you?"

"Twenty-three."

"You say he died young—had they taken germ cells from him beforehand or something?"

Gimel took over: "He died at twenty-four in an air car crash. They couldn't save the brain, so they took some intestinal cells and cultured them for cloning. Reproductive cells aren't used for cloning, since they have only half the chromosomes. Intestinal cells happen to be easy to despecialize and reprogram for total growth."

"All chips off the old block," Martin said valiantly. "But how can . . . some of you be women . . . ?"

Beth took over: "It's easy to program half the clonal mass back to the female. Just delete the male gene from half the cells and they revert to the basic, that is, the female. It's trickier to go the other way, have to hook in artificial Y chromosomes. So they mostly clone from males, since clones function best bisexually."

Gimel again: "They've worked these matters of technique and function out carefully. The taxpayer wants the best for his money, and of course clones are expensive. With the cell manipulations, and the incubation in Ngama Placentae, and the maintenance and training of the foster-parent groups, we end up costing about three million apiece."

"For your next generation," Martin said, still struggling, "I suppose you . . . you breed?"

"We females are sterile," said Beth with perfect equanimity. "You remember that the Y chromosome was deleted from our original cell. The males can interbreed with approved singletons, if they want to. But to get John Chow again as often as they want, they just reclone a cell from this clone."

Martin gave up the struggle. He nodded and chewed cold toast. "Well," said one of the Johns, and all changed mood, like a flock of starlings that change course in one wingflick, following a leader so fast that no eye can see which leads. They were ready to go. "How about a look at the mine? Then we'll unload the equipment. Some nice new models in the roboats; you'll want to see them. Right?" Had Pugh or Martin not agreed they might have found it hard to say so. The Johns were polite but unanimous; their decisions carried. Pugh, Commander of Libra Base 2, felt a qualm. Could he boss around this superman/woman-entity-of-ten? and a genius at that? He stuck close to Martin as they suited for outside. Neither said anything.

Four apiece in the three large airjets, they slipped off north from the dome, over Libra's dun rugose skin, in starlight.

"Desolate," one said.

It was a boy and girl with Pugh and Martin. Pugh wondered if these were the two that had shared a sleeping bag last night. No doubt they wouldn't mind if he asked them. Sex must be as handy as breathing to them. Did you two breathe last night?

"Yes," he said, "it is desolate."

"This is our first time off, except training on Luna." The girl's voice was definitely a bit higher and softer.

"How did you take the big hop?"

"They doped us. I wanted to experience it." That was the boy; he sounded wistful. They seemed to have more personality, only two at a time. Did repetition of the individual negate individuality?

"Don't worry," said Martin, steering the sled, "you can't experience no-time because it isn't there."

"I'd just like to once," one of them said. "So we'd know."

The Mountains of Merioneth showed leprotic in starlight to the east, a plume of freezing gas trailed silvery from a vent-hole to the west, and the sled tilted groundward. The twins braced for the stop at one moment, each with a slight protective gesture to the other. Your skin is my skin, Pugh thought, but literally, no metaphor. What would it be like, then, to have someone as close to you as that? Always to be answered when you spoke; never to be in pain alone. Love your neighbor as you love yourself. . . . That hard old problem was solved. The neighbor was the self: the love was perfect.

And here was Hellmouth, the mine.

Pugh was the Exploratory Mission's E.T. geologist, and Martin his technician and cartographer; but when in the course of a local survey Martin had discovered the U-mine, Pugh had given him full credit, as well as the onus of prospecting the lode and planning the Exploitation Team's job. These kids had been sent out from Earth years before Martin's reports got there and had not known what their job would be until they got here. The Exploitation Corps simply sent out teams regularly and blindly as a dandelion sends out its seed, knowing there would be a job for them on Libra or the next planet out or one they hadn't even heard about yet. The government wanted uranium too urgently to wait while reports drifted home across the lightyears. The stuff was like gold, old-fashioned but essential, worth mining extraterrestrially and shipping interstellar. Worth its weight in people, Pugh thought sourly, watching the tall young men and women go one by one, glimmering in starlight, into the black hole Martin had named Hellmouth.

As they went in their homeostatic forehead-lamps brightened. Twelve nodding gleams ran along the moist, wrinkled walls. Pugh heard Martin's radiation counter peeping twenty to the dozen up ahead. "Here's the drop-off," said Martin's voice in the suit intercom, drowning out the peeping and the dead silence that was around them. "We're in a side-fissure, this is the main vertical vent in front of us." The black void gaped, its far side not visible in the headlamp beams. "Last vulcanism seems to have been a couple of thousand years ago. Nearest fault is twenty-eight kilos east, in the Trench. This area seems to be as safe seismically as anything in the area. The big basalt-flow overhead stabilizes all these substructures, so long as it remains stable itself. Your central lode is thirty-six meters down and runs in a series of five bubble caverns northeast. It is a lode, a pipe of very high-grade ore. You saw the percentage figures, right? Extraction's going to be no problem. All you've got to do is get the bubbles topside."

"Take off the lid and let 'em float up." A chuckle. Voices began to talk, but they were all the same voice and the suit radio gave them no location in space. "Open the thing right up.—Safer that way.—But it's a solid basalt roof, how thick, ten meters here?—Three to twenty, the report said.—Blow good ore all over the lot.—Use this access we're in, straighten it a bit and run slider rails for the robos.—Import burros. —Have we got enough propping material?—What's your estimate of total payload mass, Martin?"

"Say over five million kilos and under eight."

"Transport will be here in ten E-months.—It'll have to go pure. No, they'll have the mass problem in NAFAL shipping licked by now, remember it's been sixteen years since we left Earth last Tuesday.—Right, they'll send the whole lot back and purify it in Earth orbit.—Shall we go down, Martin?"

"Go on. I've been down."

The first one—Aleph? (Heb., the ox, the leader)—swung onto the ladder and down; the rest followed. Pugh and Martin stood at the chasm's edge. Pugh set his intercom to exchange only with Martin's suit, and noticed Martin doing the same. It was a bit wearing, this listening to one person think aloud in ten voices, or was it one voice speaking the thoughts of ten minds?

"A great gut," Pugh said, looking down into the black pit, its veined and warted walls catching stray gleams of headlamps far below. "A cow's bowel. A bloody great constipated intestine."

Martin's counter peeped like a lost chicken. They stood inside the dead but epileptic planet, breathing oxygen from tanks, wearing suits impermeable to corrosives and harmful radiations, resistant to a 200-degree range of temperatures, tear-proof, and as shock-resistant as possible given the soft vulnerable stuff inside.

"Next hop," Martin said, "I'd like to find a planet that has nothing whatever to exploit."

"You found this."

"Keep me home next time."

Pugh was pleased. He had hoped Martin would want to go on working with him, but neither of them was used to talking much about their feelings, and he had hesitated to ask. "I'll try that," he said.

"I hate this place. I like caves, you know. It's why I came in here. Just spelunking. But this one's a bitch. Mean. You can't ever let down in here. I guess this lot can handle it, though. They know their stuff."

"Wave of the future, whatever," said Pugh.

The wave of the future came swarming up the ladder, swept Martin to the entrance, gabbled at and around him: "Have we got enough material for supports?—If we convert one of the extractor servos to anneal, yes.—Sufficient if we miniblast?—Kaph can calculate stress." Pugh had switched his intercom back to receive them; he looked at them, so many thoughts jabbering in an eager mind, and at Martin standing silent among them, and at Hellmouth and the wrinkled plain. "Settled! How does that strike you as a preliminary schedule, Martin?"

"It's your baby," Martin said.

Within five E-days the Johns had all their material and equipment unloaded and operating and were starting to open up the mine. They worked with total efficiency.

Pugh was fascinated and frightened by their effectiveness, their confidence, their independence. He was no use to them at all. A clone, he thought, might indeed be the first truly stable, self-reliant human being. Once adult it would need nobody's help. It would be sufficient to itself physically, sexually, emotionally, intellectually. Whatever he did, any member of it would always receive the support and approval of his peers, his other selves. Nobody else was needed.

Two of the clone stayed in the dome doing calculations and paperwork, with frequent sled trips to the mine for measurements and tests. They were the mathematicians of the clone, Zayin and Kaph. That is, as Zayin explained, all ten had had thorough mathematical training from age three to twenty-one, but from twenty-one to twenty-three she and Kaph had gone on with math while the others intensified study in other specialties, geology, mining, engineering, electronic engineering, equipment robotics, applied atomics, and so on. "Kaph and I feel," she said, "that we're the element of the clone closest to what John Chow was in his singleton lifetime. But of course he was principally in biomath, and they didn't take us far in that."

"They needed us most in this field," Kaph said, with the patriotic priggishness they sometimes evinced.

Pugh and Martin soon could distinguish this pair from the others, Zayin by gestalt, Kaph only by a discolored left fourth fingernail, got from an ill-aimed hammer at the age of six. No doubt there were many such differences, physical and psychological, among them; nature might be identical, nurture could not be. But the differences were hard to find. And part of the difficulty was that they never really talked to Pugh and Martin. They joked with them, were polite, got along fine. They gave nothing. It was nothing one could complain about; they were very pleasant, they had the standardized American friendliness. "Do you come from Ireland, Owen?"

"Nobody comes from Ireland, Zayin."

"There are lots of Irish-Americans."

"To be sure, but no more Irish. A couple of thousand in all the island, the last I knew. They didn't go in for birth control, you know, so the food ran out. By the Third Famine there were no Irish left at all but the priesthood, and they all celibate, or nearly all."

Zayin and Kaph smiled stiffly. They had no experience of either bigotry or irony. "What are you then, ethnically?" Kaph asked, and Pugh replied, "A Welshman."

"Is it Welsh that you and Martin speak together?"

None of your business, Pugh thought, but said, "No, it's his dialect, not mine: Argentinean. A descendant of Spanish."

"You learned it for private communication?"

"Whom had we here to be private from? It's just that sometimes a man likes to speak his native language."

"Ours is English," Kaph said unsympathetically. Why should they have sympathy? That's one of the things you give because you need it back.

"Is Wells quaint?" asked Zayin.

"Wells? Oh, Wales, it's called. Yes, Wales is quaint." Pugh switched on his rockcutter, which prevented further conversation by a synapse-destroying whine, and while it whined he turned his back and said a profane word in Welsh.

That night he used the Argentine dialect for private communication. "Do they pair off in the same couples or change every night?"

Martin looked surprised. A prudish expression, unsuited to his features, appeared for a moment. It faded. He too was curious. "I think it's random."

"Don't whisper, man, it sounds dirty. I think they rotate."

"On a schedule?"

"So nobody gets omitted."

Martin gave a vulgar laugh and smothered it. "What about us? Aren't we omitted?"

"That doesn't occur to them."

"What if I proposition one of the girls?"

"She'd tell the others and they'd decide as a group."

"I am not a bull," Martin said, his dark, heavy face heating up. "I will not be judged—"

"Down, down, *machismo*," said Pugh. "Do you mean to proposition one?"

Martin shrugged, sullen. "Let 'em have their incest."

"Incest is it, or masturbation?"

"I don't care, if they'd do it out of earshot!"

The clone's early attempts at modesty had soon worn off, unmotivated by any deep defensiveness of self or awareness of others. Pugh and Martin were daily deeper swamped under the intimacies of its constant emotional-sexual-mental interchange: swamped yet excluded.

"Two months to go," Martin said one evening.

"To what?" snapped Pugh. He was edgy lately, and Martin's sullenness got on his nerves.

"To relief."

In sixty days the full crew of their Exploratory Mission were due back from their survey of the other planets of the system. Pugh was aware of this.

"Crossing off the days on your calendar?" he jeered.

"Pull yourself together, Owen."

"What do you mean?"

"What I say."

They parted in contempt and resentment.

Pugh came in after a day alone on the Pampas, a vast lava plain the nearest edge of which was two hours south by jet. He was tired but refreshed by solitude. They were not supposed to take long trips alone but lately had often done so. Martin stooped under bright lights, drawing one of his elegant masterly charts. This one was of the whole face of Libra, the cancerous face. The dome was otherwise empty, seeming dim and large as it had before the clone came. "Where's the golden horde?"

Martin grunted ignorance, cross-hatching. He straightened his back to glance round at the sun, which squatted feebly like a great red toad on the eastern plain, and at the clock, which said 18:45. "Some big quakes today," he said, returning to his map. "Feel them down there? Lots of crates were falling around. Take a look at the seismo."

The needle jigged and wavered on the roll. It never stopped dancing here. The roll had recorded five quakes of major intensity back in midafternoon; twice the needle had hopped off the roll. The attached computer had been activated to emit a slip reading, "Epicenter 61'·N by 42' 4' E."

"Not in the Trench this time."

"I thought it felt a bit different from usual. Sharper."

"In Base One I used to lie awake all night feeling the ground jump. Queer how you get used to things."

"Go spla if you didn't. What's for dinner?"

"I thought you'd have cooked it."

"Waiting for the clone."

Feeling put upon, Pugh got out a dozen dinnerboxes, stuck two in the Instobake, pulled them out. "All right, here's dinner."

"Been thinking," Martin said, coming to table. "What if some clone cloned itself? Illegally. Made a thousand duplicates—ten thousand. Whole army. They could make a tidy power grab, couldn't they?"

"But how many millions did this lot cost to rear? Artificial placentae and all that. It would be hard to keep secret, unless they had a planet to themselves. . . . Back before the Famines when Earth had national governments, they talked about that: clone your best soldiers, have whole regiments of them. But the food ran out before they could play that game."

They talked amicably, as they used to do.

"Funny," Martin said, chewing. "They left early this morning, didn't they?"

"All but Kaph and Zayin. They thought they'd get the first payload above ground today. What's up?"

"They weren't back for lunch."

"They won't starve, to be sure."

"They left at seven."

"So they did." Then Pugh saw it. The air tanks held eight hours' supply.

"Kaph and Zayin carried out spare cans when they left. Or they've got a heap out there."

"They did, but they brought the whole lot in to recharge." Martin stood up, pointing to one of the stacks of stuff that cut the dome into rooms and alleys.

"There's an alarm signal on every imsuit."

"It's not automatic."

Pugh was tired and still hungry. "Sit down and eat, man. That lot can look after themselves."

Martin sat down but did not eat. "There was a big quake, Owen. The first one. Big enough it scared me."

After a pause Pugh sighed and said, "All right."

Unenthusiastically, they got out the two-man sled that was always left for them and headed it north. The long sunrise covered everything in poisonous red jello. The horizontal light and shadow made it hard to see, raised walls of fake iron ahead of them which they slid through, turned the convex plain beyond Hellmouth into a great dimple full of bloody water. Around the tunnel entrance a wilderness of machinery stood, cranes and cables and servos and wheels and diggers and robocarts and sliders and control huts, all slanting and bulking incoherently in the red light. Martin jumped from the sled, ran into the mine. He came out again, to Pugh. "Oh God, Owen, it's down," he said. Pugh went in and saw, five meters from the entrance, the shiny moist, black wall that ended the tunnel. Newly exposed to air, it looked organic, like visceral tissue. The tunnel entrance, enlarged by blasting and double-tracked for robocarts, seemed unchanged until he noticed thousands of tiny spiderweb cracks in the walls. The floor was wet with some sluggish fluid.

"They were inside," Martin said.

"They may be still. They surely had extra air cans—"

"Look, Owen, look at the basalt flow, at the roof, don't you see what the quake did, look at it."

The low hump of land that roofed the caves still had the unreal look of an optical illusion. It had reversed itself, sunk down, leaving a vast dimple or pit. When Pugh walked on it he saw that it too was cracked with many tiny fissures. From some a whitish gas was seeping, so that the sunlight on the surface of the gas pool was shafted as if by the waters of a dim red lake.

"The mine's not on the fault. There's no fault here!"

Pugh came back to him quickly. "No, there's no fault, Martin—Look, they surely weren't all inside together."

Martin followed him and searched among the wrecked machines dully, then actively. He spotted the airsled. It had come down heading south, and stuck at an angle in a pothole of colloidal dust. It had carried two riders. One was half sunk in the dust, but his suit meters registered normal functioning; the other hung strapped onto the tilted sled. Her imsuit had burst open on the broken legs, and the body was frozen hard as any rock. That was all they found. As both regulation and custom demanded, they cremated the dead at once with the laser guns they carried by regulation and had never used before. Pugh, knowing he was going to be sick, wrestled the survivor onto the two-man sled and sent Martin off to the dome with him. Then he vomited and flushed the waste out of his suit, and finding one four-man sled undamaged, followed after Martin, shaking as if the cold of Libra had got through to him.

The survivor was Kaph. He was in deep shock. They found a swelling on the occiput that might mean concussion, but no fracture was visible.

Pugh brought two glasses of food concentrate and two chasers of aquavit. "Come on," he said. Martin obeyed, drinking off the tonic. They sat down on crates near the cot and sipped the aquavit.

Kaph lay immobile, face like beeswax, hair bright black to the shoulders, lips stiffly parted for faintly gasping breaths.

"It must have been the first shock, the big one," Martin said. "It must have slid the whole structure sideways. Till it fell in on itself. There must be gas layers in the lateral rocks, like those formations in the Thirty-first Quadrant. But there wasn't any sign—" As he spoke the world slid out from under them. Things leaped and clattered, hopped and jigged, shouted Ha! Ha! Ha! "It was like this at fourteen hours," said Reason shakily in Martin's voice, amidst the unfastening and ruin of the world. But Unreason sat up, as the tumult lessened and things ceased dancing, and screamed aloud.

Pugh leaped across his spilt aquavit and held Kaph down. The muscular body flailed him off. Martin pinned the shoulders down. Kaph screamed, struggled, choked; his face blackened. "Oxy," Pugh said, and his hand found the right needle in the medical kit as if by homing instinct; while Martin held the mask he struck the needle home to the vagus nerve, restoring Kaph to life.

"Didn't know you knew that stunt," Martin said, breathing hard.

"The Lazarus Jab, my father was a doctor. It doesn't often work," Pugh said. "I want that drink I spilled. Is the quake over? I can't tell."

"Aftershocks. It's not just you shivering."

"Why did he suffocate?"

"I don't know, Owen. Look in the book."

Kaph was breathing normally and his color was restored; only the lips were still darkened. They poured a new shot of courage and sat down by him again with their medical guide. "Nothing about cyanosis or asphyxiation under 'Shock' or 'Concussion.' He can't have breathed in anything with his suit on. I don't know. We'd get as much good out of *Mother Mog's Home Herbalist*. . . . 'Anal Hemorrhoids,' fy!" Pugh pitched the book to a crate table. It fell short, because either Pugh or the table was still unsteady.

"Why didn't he signal?"

"Sorry?"

"The eight inside the mine never had time. But he and the girl must have been outside. Maybe she was in the entrance and got hit by the first slide. He must have been outside, in the control hut maybe. He ran in, pulled her out, strapped her onto the sled, started for the dome. And all that time never pushed the panic button in his imsuit. Why not?"

"Well, he'd had that whack on his head. I doubt he ever realized the girl was dead. He wasn't in his senses. But if he had been I don't know if he'd have thought to signal us. They looked to one another for help."

Martin's face was like an Indian mask, grooves at the mouth corners, eyes of dull coal. "That's so. What must he have felt, then, when the quake came and he was outside, alone—"

In answer Kaph screamed.

He came off the cot in the heaving convulsions of one suffocating, knocked Pugh tight down with his flailing arm, staggered into a stack of crates and fell to the floor, lips blue, eyes white. Martin dragged him back onto the cot and gave him a whiff of oxygen, then knelt by Pugh, who was sitting up, and wiped at his cut cheekbone. "Owen, are you all right, are you going to be all right, Owen?"

"I think I am," Pugh said. "Why are you rubbing that on my face?"

It was a short length of computer tape, now spotted with Pugh's blood. Martin dropped it. "Thought it was a towel. You clipped your cheek on that box there."

"Is he out of it?"

"Seems to be."

They stared down at Kaph lying stiff, his teeth a white line inside dark parted lips.

"Like epilepsy. Brain damage maybe?"

"What about shooting him full of meprobamate?"

Pugh shook his head. "I don't know what's in that shot I already gave him for shock. Don't want to overdose him."

"Maybe he'll sleep it off now."

"I'd like to myself. Between him and the earthquake I can't seem to keep on my feet."

"You got a nasty crack there. Go on, I'll sit up a while."

Pugh cleaned his cut cheek and pulled off his shirt, then paused.

"Is there anything we ought to have done—have tried to do—"

"They're all dead," Martin said heavily, gently.

Pugh lay down on top of his sleeping bag and one instant later was wakened by a hideous, sucking, struggling noise. He staggered up, found the needle, tried three times to jab it in correctly and failed, began to massage over Kaph's heart. "Mouth-to-mouth," he said, and Martin obeyed. Presently Kaph drew a harsh breath, his heartbeat steadied, his rigid muscles began to relax.

"How long did I sleep?"

"Half an hour."

They stood up sweating. The ground shuddered, the fabric of the dome sagged and swayed. Libra was dancing her awful polka again, her *Totentanz*. The sun, though rising, seemed to have grown larger and redder; gas and dust must have been stirred up in the feeble atmosphere.

"What's wrong with him, Owen?"

"I think he's dying with them."

"Them—But they're all dead, I tell you."

"Nine of them. They're all dead, they were crushed or suffocated. They were all him, he is all of them. They died, and now he's dying their deaths one by one."

"Oh, pity of God," said Martin.

The next time was much the same. The fifth time was worse, for Kaph fought and raved, trying to speak but getting no words out, as if his mouth were stopped with rocks or clay. After that the attacks grew weaker, but so did he. The eighth seizure came at about four-thirty; Pugh and Martin worked till five-thirty doing all they could to keep life in the body that slid without protest into death. They kept him, but Martin said, "The next will finish him." And it did; but Pugh breathed his own breath into the inert lungs, until he himself passed out.

He woke. The dome was opaqued and no light on. He listened and heard the breathing of two sleeping men. He slept, and nothing woke him till hunger did.

The sun was well up over the dark plains, and the planet had stopped dancing. Kaph lay asleep. Pugh and Martin drank tea and looked at him with proprietary triumph.

When he woke Martin went to him: "How do you feel, old man?" There was no answer. Pugh took Martin's place and looked into the brown, dull eyes that gazed toward but not into his own. Like Martin he quickly turned away. He heated food concentrate and brought it to Kaph. "Come on, drink."

He could see the muscles in Kaph's throat tighten. "Let me die," the young man said.

"You're not dying."

Kaph spoke with clarity and precision: "I am nine-tenths dead. There is not enough of me left alive."

That precision convinced Pugh, and he fought the conviction. "No," he said, peremptory. "They are dead. The others. Your brothers and sisters. You're not them, you're alive. You are John Chow. Your life is in your own hands."

The young man lay still, looking into a darkness that was not there.

Martin and Pugh took turns taking the Exploitation hauler and a spare set of robos over to Hellmouth to salvage equipment and protect it from Libra's sinister atmosphere, for the value of the stuff was, literally, astronomical. It was slow work for one man at a time, but they were unwilling to leave Kaph by himself. The one left in the dome did paperwork, while Kaph sat or lay and stared into his darkness and never spoke. The days went by, silent.

The radio spat and spoke: the Mission calling from the ship. "We'll be down on Libra in five weeks, Owen. Thirty-four E-days nine hours I make it as of now. How's tricks in the old dome?"

"Not good, chief. The Exploit team were killed, all but one of them, in the mine. Earthquake. Six days ago."

The radio crackled and sang starsong. Sixteen seconds' lag each way; the ship was out around Planet II now. "Killed, all but one? You and Martin were unhurt?"

"We're all right, chief."

Thirty-two seconds.

"Passerine left an Exploit team out here with us. I may put them on the Hellmouth project then, instead of the Quadrant Seven project. We'll settle that when we come down. In any case you and Martin will be relieved at Dome Two. Hold tight. Anything else?"

"Nothing else."

Thirty-two seconds.

"Right then. So long, Owen."

Kaph had heard all this, and later on Pugh said to him, "The chief may ask you to stay here with the other Exploit team. You know the ropes here." Knowing the exigencies of Far Out life, he wanted to warn the young man. Kaph made no answer. Since he had said, "There is not enough of me left alive," he had not spoken a word.

"Owen," Martin said on suit intercom, "he's spla. Insane. Psycho."

"He's doing very well for a man who's died nine times."

"Well? Like a turned-off android is well? The only emotion he has left is hate. Look at his eyes."

"That's not hate, Martin. Listen, it's true that he has, in a sense, been dead. I cannot imagine what he feels. But it's not hatred. He can't even see us. It's too dark."

"Throats have been cut in the dark. He hates us because we're not Aleph and Yod and Zayin."

"Maybe. But I think he's alone. He doesn't see us or hear us, that's the truth. He never had to see anyone else before. He never was alone before. He had himself to see, talk with, live with, nine other selves all his life. He doesn't know how you go it alone. He must learn. Give him time."

Martin shook his heavy head. "Spla," he said. "Just remember when you're alone with him that he could break your neck one-handed."

"He could do that," said Pugh, a short, soft-voiced man with a scarred cheekbone; he smiled. They were just outside the dome airlock, programming one of the servos to repair a damaged hauler. They could see Kaph sitting inside the great half-egg of the dome like a fly in amber.

"Hand me the insert pack there. What makes you think he'll get any better?"

"He has a strong personality, to be sure."

"Strong? Crippled. Nine-tenths dead, as he put it."

"But he's not dead. He's a live man: John Kaph Chow. He had a jolly queer upbringing, but after all every boy has got to break free of his family. He will do it."

"I can't see it."

"Think a bit, Martin bach. What's this cloning for? To repair the human race.

We're in a bad way. Look at me. My IIQ and GC are half this John Chow's. Yet they wanted me so badly for the Far Out Service that when I volunteered they took me and fitted me out with an artificial lung and corrected my myopia. Now if there were enough good sound lads about would they be taking one-lunged short-sighted Welshmen?"

"Didn't know you had an artificial lung."

"I do then. Not tin, you know. Human, grown in a tank from a bit of somebody; cloned, if you like. That's how they make replacement organs, the same general idea as cloning, but bits and pieces instead of whole people. It's my own lung now, whatever. But what I am saying is this, there are too many like me these days and not enough like John Chow. They're trying to raise the level of the human genetic pool, which is a mucky little puddle since the population crash. So then if a man is cloned, he's a strong and clever man. It's only logic, to be sure."

Martin grunted; the servo began to hum.

Kaph had been eating little; he had trouble swallowing his food, choking on it, so that he would give up trying after a few bites. He had lost eight or ten kilos. After three weeks or so, however, his appetite began to pick up, and one day he began to look through the clone's possessions, the sleeping bags, kits, papers which Pugh had stacked neatly in a far angle of a packing-crate alley. He sorted, destroyed a heap of papers and oddments, made a small packet of what remained, then relapsed into his walking coma.

Two days later he spoke. Pugh was trying to correct a flutter in the tape-player and failing; Martin had the jet out, checking their maps of the Pampas. "Hell and damnation!" Pugh said, and Kaph said in a toneless voice, "Do you want me to do that?"

Pugh jumped, controlled himself, and gave the machine to Kaph. The young man took it apart, put it back together, and left it on the table.

"Put on a tape," Pugh said with careful casualness, busy at another table.

Kaph put on the topmost tape, a chorale. He lay down on his cot. The sound of a hundred human voices singing together filled the dome. He lay still, his face blank.

In the next days he took over several routine jobs, unasked. He undertook nothing that wanted initiative, and if asked to do anything he made no response at all.

"He's doing well," Pugh said in the dialect of Argentina.

"He's not. He's turning himself into a machine. Does what he's programmed to do, no reaction to anything else. He's worse off than when he didn't function at all. He's not human any more."

Pugh sighed. "Well, good night," he said in English. "Good night, Kaph."

"Good night," Martin said; Kaph did not.

Next morning at breakfast Kaph reached across Martin's plate for the toast. "Why don't you ask for it?" Martin said with the geniality of repressed exasperation. "I can pass it."

"I can reach it," Kaph said in his flat voice.

"Yes, but look. Asking to pass things, saying good night or hello, they're not important, but all the same when somebody says something a person ought to answer. . . ."

The young man looked indifferently in Martin's direction; his eyes still did not seem to see clear through to the person he looked toward. "Why should I answer?"

"Because somebody has said something to you."

"Why?"

Martin shrugged and laughed. Pugh jumped up and turned on the rock-cutter. Later on he said, "Lay off that, please, Martin."

"Manners are essential in small isolated crews, some kind of manners, whatever you work out together. He's been taught that, everybody in Far Out knows it. Why does he deliberately flout it?"

"Do you tell yourself good night?"

"So?"

"Don't you see Kaph's never known anyone but himself?"

Martin brooded and then broke out. "Then by God this cloning business is all wrong. It won't do. What are a lot of duplicate geniuses going to do for us when they don't even know we exist?"

Pugh nodded. "It might be wiser to separate the clones and bring them up with others. But they make such a grand team this way."

"Do they? I don't know. If this lot had been ten average inefficient E.T. engineers, would they all have got killed? What if, when the quake came and things started caving in, what if all those kids ran the same way, farther into the mine, maybe, to save the one who was farthest in? Even Kaph was outside and went in. . . . It's hypothetical. But I keep thinking, out of ten ordinary confused guys, more might have got out."

"I don't know. It's true that identical twins tend to die at about the same time, even when they have never seen each other. Identity and death, it is very strange. . . ."

The days went on, the red sun crawled across the dark sky, Kaph did not speak when spoken to, Pugh and Martin snapped at each other more frequently each day. Pugh complained of Martin's snoring. Offended, Martin moved his cot clear across the dome and also ceased speaking to Pugh for some while. Pugh whistled Welsh dirges until Martin complained, and then Pugh stopped speaking for a while.

The day before the Mission ship was due, Martin announced he was going over to Merioneth.

"I thought at least you'd be giving me a hand with the computer to finish the rock analyses," Pugh said, aggrieved.

"Kaph can do that. I want one more look at the Trench. Have fun," Martin added in dialect, and laughed, and left.

"What is that language?"

"Argentinean. I told you that once, didn't I?"

"I don't know." After a while the young man added, "I have forgotten a lot of things, I think."

"It wasn't important, to be sure," Pugh said gently, realizing all at once how important this conversation was. "Will you give me a hand running the computer, Kaph?"

He nodded.

Pugh had left a lot of loose ends, and the job took them all day. Kaph was a good co-worker, quick and systematic, much more so than Pugh himself. His flat voice, now that he was talking again, got on the nerves; but it didn't matter, there was only this one day left to get through and then the ship would come, the old crew, comrades and friends.

During tea break Kaph said, "What will happen if the Explore ship crashes?"

"They'd be killed."

"To you, I mean."

"To us? We'd radio SOS signals and live on half rations till the rescue cruiser from Area Three Base came. Four and a half E-years away it is. We have life support here for three men for, let's see, maybe between four and five years. A bit tight, it would be."

"Would they send a cruiser for three men?"

"They would."

Kaph said no more.

"Enough cheerful speculations," Pugh said cheerfully, rising to get back to work. He slipped sideways and the chair avoided his hand; he did a sort of half-pirouette and fetched up hard against the dome hide. "My goodness," he said, reverting to his native idiom, "what is it?"

"Quake," said Kaph.

The teacups bounced on the table with a plastic cackle, a litter of papers slid off a box, the skin of the dome swelled and sagged. Underfoot there was a huge noise, half sound, half shaking, a subsonic boom.

Kaph sat unmoved. An earthquake does not frighten a man who died in an earthquake.

Pugh, white-faced, wiry black hair sticking out, a frightened man, said, "Martin is in the Trench."

"What trench?"

"The big fault line. The epicenter for the local quakes. Look at the seismograph." Pugh struggled with the stuck door of a still-jittering locker.

"Where are you going?"

"After him."

"Martin took the jet. Sleds aren't safe to use during quakes. They go out of control."

"For God's sake man, shut up."

Kaph stood up, speaking in a flat voice as usual. "It's unnecessary to go out after him now. It's taking an unnecessary risk."

"If his alarm goes off, radio me," Pugh said, shut the head-piece of his suit, and ran to the lock. As he went out Libra picked up her ragged skirts and danced a belly dance from under his feet clear to the red horizon.

Inside the dome, Kaph saw the sled go up, tremble like a meteor in the dull red daylight, and vanish to the northeast. The hide of the dome quivered, the earth coughed. A vent south of the dome belched up a slow-flowing bile of black gas.

A bell shrilled and a red light flashed on the central control board. The sign under the light read Suit 2 and scribbled under that, A. G. M. Kaph did not turn the signal off. He tried to radio Martin, then Pugh, but got no reply from either.

When the aftershocks decreased he went back to work and finished up Pugh's job. It took him about two hours. Every half hour he tried to contact Suit 1 and got no reply, then Suit 2 and got no reply. The red light had stopped flashing after an hour.

It was dinnertime. Kaph cooked dinner for one and ate it. He lay down on his cot.

The aftershocks had ceased except for faint rolling tremors at long intervals. The sun hung in the west, oblate, pale red, immense. It did not sink visibly. There was no sound at all.

Kaph got up and began to walk about the messy, half-packed-up, overcrowded, empty dome. The silence continued. He went to the player and put on the first tape that came to hand. It was pure music, electronic, without harmonies, without voices. It ended. The silence continued.

Pugh's uniform tunic, one button missing, hung over a stack of rock samples. Kaph stared at it a while.

The silence continued.

The child's dream: There is no one else alive in the world but me. In all the world.

Low, north of the dome, a meteor flickered.

Kaph's mouth opened as if he were trying to say something, but no sound came. He went hastily to the north wall and peered out into the gelatinous red light.

The little star came in and sank. Two figures blurred the airlock. Kaph stood close beside the lock as they came in. Martin's imsuit was covered with some kind of dust so that he looked raddled and warty like the surface of Libra. Pugh had him by the arm.

"Is he hurt?"

Pugh shucked his suit, helped Martin peel off his. "Shaken up," he said, curt.

"A piece of cliff fell onto the jet," Martin said, sitting down at the table and waving his arms. "Not while I was in it though. I was parked, see, and poking about that carbon-dust area when I felt things humping. So I went out onto a nice bit of early igneous I'd noticed from above, good footing and out from under the cliffs. Then I saw this bit of the planet fall off onto the flyer, quite a sight it was, and after a while it occurred to me the spare aircans were in the flyer, so I leaned on the panic button. But I didn't get any radio reception, that's always happening here during quakes, so I didn't know if the signal was getting through either. And things went on jumping around and pieces of the cliff coming off. Little rocks flying around, and so dusty you couldn't see a meter ahead. I was really beginning to wonder what I'd do for breathing in the small hours, you know, when I saw old Owen buzzing up the Trench in all that dust and junk like a big ugly bat—"

"Want to eat?" said Pugh.

"Of course I want to eat. How'd you come through the quake here, Kaph? No damage? It wasn't a big one actually, was it, what's the seismo say? My trouble was I was in the middle of it. Old Epicenter Alvaro. Felt like Richter fifteen there—total destruction of planet—"

"Sit down," Pugh said. "Eat."

After Martin had eaten a little his spate of talk ran dry. He very soon went off to his cot, still in the remote angle where he had removed it when Pugh complained of his snoring. "Good night, you one-lunged Welshman," he said across the dome.

"Good night."

There was no more out of Martin. Pugh opaqued the dome, turned the lamp down to a yellow glow less than a candle's light, and sat doing nothing, saying nothing, withdrawn.

The silence continued.

"I finished the computations."

Pugh nodded thanks.

"The signal from Martin came through, but I couldn't contact you or him."

Pugh said with effort, "I should not have gone. He had two hours of air left even with only one can. He might have been heading home when I left. This way we were all out of touch with one another. I was scared."

The silence came back, punctuated now by Martin's long, soft snores.

"Do you love Martin?"

Pugh looked up with angry eyes: "Martin is my friend. We've worked together, he's a good man." He stopped. After a while he said, "Yes, I love him. Why did you ask that?"

Kaph said nothing, but he looked at the other man. His face was changed, as if he were glimpsing something he had not seen before; his voice too was changed. "How can you . . . How do you . . . ."

But Pugh could not tell him. "I don't know," he said, "it's practice, partly. I don't know. We're each of us alone, to be sure. What can you do but hold your hand out in the dark?"

Kaph's strange gaze dropped, burned out by its own intensity.

"I'm tired," Pugh said. "That was ugly, looking for him in all that black dust and muck, and mouths opening and shutting in the ground. . . . I'm going to bed. The ship will be transmitting to us by six or so." He stood up and stretched.

"It's a clone," Kaph said. "The other Exploit Team they're bringing with them."

"Is it then?"

"A twelveclone. They came out with us on the *Passerine.*"

Kaph sat in the small yellow aura of the lamp seeming to look past it at what he feared: the new clone, the multiple self of which he was not part. A lost piece of a broken set, a fragment, inexpert at solitude, not knowing even how you go about giving love to another individual, now he must face the absolute, closed self-sufficiency of the clone of twelve; that was a lot to ask of the poor fellow, to be sure. Pugh put a hand on his shoulder in passing. "The chief won't ask you to stay here with a clone. You can go home. Or since you're Far Out maybe you'll come on farther out with us. We could use you. No hurry deciding. You'll make out all right."

Pugh's quiet voice trailed off. He stood unbuttoning his coat, stooped a little with fatigue. Kaph looked at him and saw the thing he had never seen before, saw him: Owen Pugh, the other, the stranger who held his hand out in the dark.

"Good night," Pugh mumbled, crawling into his sleeping bag and half asleep already, so that he did not hear Kaph reply after a pause, repeating, across darkness, benediction.

COMPANY

Roberta Silman

(b. 1934)

Biography p. 1100

When all the cousins in my family got together, it was me they locked in the closet. Or used as the patient when they played doctor. Or ran away and left me counting alone in the yard, hiding my eyes, eagerly anticipating where I would look for them until, finally, I realized that they had once again abandoned me. Lips quivering, I would find my Aunt Beadie. "Don't cry, Mona," she'd say softly as she stroked my hair. And then she'd lift single strands toward the light, trying to discover why my hair didn't shine like the other cousins' hair.

"Children can be very cruel," she always said. "It will be better when you're grown."

When I went to college—a good eastern girls' college, on scholarship, of course— there was one blissful night that first fall. About twenty girls in the scholarship dorm (they had us all in one house just in case we tried to forget we were poorer than the others) sat on the floor in my room and listened to my records of Dvořák's chamber music after the house meeting.

A few weeks later they elected me house president. Was I proud! Even after I discovered that I was the janitor. "She's president of her house at that fancy college they sent her to," Aunt Beadie bragged.

But even smart plain people need company. So if it isn't real company, if you're smart like I am, you make up company. There's no need to die for lack of someone to talk to.

You wouldn't believe what interesting friends I have. Once Virginia Woolf stepped into the car. It was a little awkward; she's very tall and I have a Datsun. But she managed, cape and all, and she hugged that beautiful mauve cape to herself and she stared at me with her marvelous sunken eyes and as we drove we talked. The usual, at first—the road, the fall colors (it was October), a bunch of geese flying south, the bearded philosophers in the sky (they looked like sheep to me, but why argue?). And then I said, "Virginia, with all your troubles, why didn't you ever visit Freud? Surely one of your friends could have gotten you an appointment." After all, sometimes the famous don't like to use their names—they prefer their friends. She sighed. I looked at her out of the corner of my eye, a little afraid I might have offended her. But she is, basically, despite the cape, very down-to-earth. "I was sure if I went to Freud I would never write again. The writing and the insanity were interlocked." She made it sound so simple that I didn't pursue it, though I'm sure she would have liked to be a better wife to Leonard.

Virginia comes back, though after that first time, never alone. Either with her sister Vanessa, or Leonard, or Bunny Garnett, once with Eliot. That was almost disastrous. He's so shy, and I was working so hard to get something, anything, out of his thin lips that I almost wrapped the car around a telephone pole.

At one time or another half of the people who are buried in Westminster Abbey have been in my car. And many who aren't buried there. I took a lot of English Lit at college, though I was a history major. My mother thought I would be another Mommsen. But who wants historians these days—not with the history we're making. So I took my master's in social work, finally succumbed to an afro (Aunt Beadie still says, feebly now—her shiny-haired kids put her in a home—"If only you had brushed it more as a child, Mona"), and I'm head of the social workers in one of those big New York hospitals. All day long I try to help people who have babies with birth defects, sisters with muscular dystrophy, brothers with heart trouble, parents with cancer. Not exactly the life I dreamed for myself. But at least there's money for the Datsun and weekends out of town. Every other weekend, there I am, on some parkway out of New York—to Vermont in the fall, to the Jersey shore in summer, or to Martha's Vineyard, Newport, Nantucket. In the winter it's the cities: Washington, Philadelphia, Boston—there are so many interesting places.

Kafka likes Philadelphia. He likes the quiet old Federal houses, and we have spent days in the Franklin Institute. Once I took him to Washington; he was fascinated by that wonderful pendulum they have in the Smithsonian. "I have finally seen time," he said when he saw it, but he won't go back. It was too noisy for him, the traffic frightened him, the crowds and lines depressed him. Even in Rock Creek Park, which is one of the most beautiful spots in the East, he seemed uncomfortable. "Look at her eyes!" I pointed to those incredible blue eyes of Mohini, the white tigress, stalking her cage. Kafka looked to please me, but he was miserable. "I could have written that lonely tigress," he murmured as we drove home. To divert him I started to talk about my job, but he said quickly, "Tell me something pleasant, Mona, please, just *happy* things."

When *Herzog* was published I had a definite sense of déjà vu. The people were different, but I had been doing it for years, and not just letters. Why write to someone if you can talk to him? Isn't that what the telephone ad says?

Today I am alone. Chekhov had to mulch his roses for winter, Henry James gets carsick on long trips, Napoleon had a stomachache, Bill Shakespeare had another date. Donne was free, but he's such dour company lately, I decided to pass. Occasionally I need to collect my thoughts a little. And it's pouring and there's a rainbow of leaves falling from the trees which, when they land, make the road slick. I need all my wits about me driving today. The slight element of danger in a slick road is exciting, though. Danger, no matter how slight, does make people feel adventurous, and with my hands on the wheel, I feel like those little boys who *vroom vroom* near the hospital all day long, imitating the ambulance call and the police whistle.

Vroom! Vroom! Now I'm in Vermont. I like crossing borders. New possibilities. So far I've been in thirty-six of the fifty states. I have a big wall map at home and I color in the states after I've been there. Sometimes I plan my vacations to see how many more states I can knock off. Once I drove my parents back to Florida just to color in more states. They didn't know that, of course. "You're such a good daughter, Mona," my mother crooned when we said good-bye. I am the only child, and they had high hopes for me, but this time I didn't get the usual lecture about finding a man and settling down and getting married like all your cousins are. Omission is sometimes bliss.

Jeesus Christ! I slam on the brake. I almost killed him! What an idiot to stand practically in the middle of the road wearing an orange jacket when everything else around is orange. He's young, probably in his early twenties, and wearing a pack. He throws it onto the back seat and then sits down beside me. He smells of wet wool and not too many baths recently.

"You're lucky you have all your toes," I say. Did I mention that he has a lovely dark beard? Fine and black and silky, and yes, almost shiny.

I almost never pick up hitchhikers because the car is usually occupied by my friends. But it is pouring and I practically killed him and, as I said before, I am alone. So why not? He doesn't look like the mugging type.

"I'm Louis," he says, "and you are very sweet to pick me up. It is raining very hard." He smiles a toothy smile, almost a caricature of a smile because he has such large, even teeth. He's glad to be in a dry place, that's clear.

"Are you from Paree?" He nods.

"Where are you going?"

"To Canada. I have a cousin north of Montreal. I'm going to stay there till Christmas and then I'll go home."

"Do you go to the university?"

"No, I am graduated, have graduated," he corrected himself. He speaks English slowly, but you can tell that he is getting the feel of the language.

"Where are you going?" He starts unfolding his map.

"Oh, I'm just out for a ride. No place in particular. Just out to see the leaves. But it rained instead."

"Yes." He smiles and gestures at the falling leaves with his skinny palms upward. "What is your name?"

"Mona."

"What do you do?" I can see he is making a guess in his head, and I wonder what I look like to him, but I can't exactly ask.

"Social work—in a big New York hospital. Help people face their lives." He nods.

"My cousin is an anesthetist in l'Hôpital de la Gare in Paris."

"Your cousin is a lot luckier than I," I say, but he doesn't get it.

Still, he's nice. And observant. And it's so good to smell an actual man in the car.

Maybe it was the smell that did it. Who knows? Who knows what makes people act the way I did? Because suddenly, after we had been riding for about half an hour, I wanted desperately to go to bed with him.

"Could you do me a favor?" I asked. His hand sought the window handle and he started opening it a little to get the fog off the windshield.

"Well, yes, that, too. But something else."

He raised his eyebrows.

"Could you go with me to a motel? Could you"—my palms were so sweaty they almost slipped off the wheel—"Could you sleep with me? It won't take long." I needn't have added that, because I could see, thank God, that he wasn't repelled. Just a little surprised. Well, maybe a lot surprised. So was I. But my surprise didn't make me take it back or try to make a joke of it or pretend I had had a moment of madness. The offer was still good, and as he paused before he answered, I could see that he was sizing me up.

Now although I'm not as good-looking as my cousin, who was freshman queen at Penn State, I'm not all that bad either. Plain, not really homely. I have sallow, slightly yellow skin that no amount of makeup can help, and going-gray dirty blond hair, but my figure is tidy and I do have a bust. A married doctor once lived with me off and on for about two years. I finally had to end that because the landlord was getting angry. He never wiped his feet when he came into the hall. It began to get under my skin, too. After he left the apartment I always had to vacuum. Where he found so much mud in New York I'll never know! The landlord was right; he had gotten to be boring anyhow.

Louis took his time. I didn't mind. There is something nice about having a real, actually substantial man looking at you. Kind of like Bishop Berkeley's question: Are you a woman if there is no one to see you as one? Well, Louis made me feel very womanly, and the more he looked the more I felt.

Finally he said, "Sure." That Americanese was perfect. I pulled into the nearest motel.

"My son would like to dry off and take a bath," I said to the clerk and pointed to Louis, who was still sitting in the car.

"You mean you're not staying for the night?"

"No, I'm sorry. We have to be on our way. My mother's dying in Montreal. But my son had to change a flat tire and got soaked to the skin. With one member of the family dying I don't want to take any chances."

She gave me the room for half price.

Actually, I didn't feel like so much of a liar. As soon as the door closed, Louis asked if I wouldn't mind if he took a bath first. I said, "Of course not, take your time."

While Louis was in the bath I undressed slowly and got into bed naked and had an argument with Bill Shakespeare, who had gotten stood up and wanted to join me now.

"I already have a date," I told him in as harsh a whisper as I could muster, because Shakespeare is probably my favorite person in all of history.

Bill stroked his beard and looked at me kindly. "Enjoy it. You don't get a chance like this often," he said, and left quietly.

I lay there and looked around. It was the usual depressing motel room—avocado rug, green-flowered chair, and light green walls that reminded me of the hospital. Near the door was a large stain on the ceiling. I got out of bed and walked closer to it. The ceiling had been patched but it was just a matter of time before the leak would start again. When Louis came out of the bathroom with a towel wrapped around his waist I showed it to him. He smiled and went back into the bathroom and came out with a bucket that had obviously seen some use.

Louis's beard was not unlike Shakespeare's, and as we made love he whispered in French. Though I couldn't understand him, his tone was right. Everything would have been lovely if the leak hadn't begun about halfway through. *Plink, plonk. Plink, plonk.* The steady sound made me want to cry, but I tried not to show it. I guess I succeeded, because Louis looked very pleased with himself and promptly fell asleep in my arms. When he woke up we made love again, and although the water was still dripping I had gotten used to it. That time everything was better.

When I began to get dressed I noticed that a spider had begun to make a web in my underpants. My stomach was in a rage of hunger. I looked at my watch. We had been there four hours. But what better way to spend a rainy autumn afternoon in New England? We ate a little bread and jam from Louis's pack and then left.

"That must have been some bath," the clerk said when I returned the key. I could see in the mirror behind her that I no longer looked as if I had a dying mother. My sallow face was flushed.

"There's a leak in the ceiling of that room," I said brusquely, and ran to the car.

We had coffee and cereal and pancakes in a place up the road that served breakfast food all day. Louis didn't talk much; he kept looking at me with a puzzled expression.

"What's the matter?"

His voice was tinged with regret. "No one will believe me that this happened."

"Why do you have to tell anyone?" I said quietly. I hated to be laughed at over coffee cups.

"Because I'm not sure it will be real unless I tell anyone." He smiled his gorgeous smile. I nodded. That, at least, I understood.

"It's real if it's in your mind." I put my hand on his as he paused between pancakes. "Believe me. I know."

Back in the Datsun we rode peacefully. The weather was beginning to clear; there was going to be a sunset that would make everyone who saw it forget how much it had rained. From the vent on my side of the car I could feel the air getting crisper.

"Could you do me a favor?" I asked.

He spoke quickly: "I have to tell you, Mona, that my cousin in Montreal is a girl." I slowed down. All I had wanted was for him to open the window.

But he was uncomfortable. In Paris older women do live with younger men; maybe he thought I wanted to take him home. In a few minutes there was a picnic area on our side of the road, and I dropped him off.

Soon Shakespeare slid onto the seat next to me and we watched the sunset together in front of one of my favorite inns in all of New England. Then I had a long, leisurely dinner, and George Eliot and Henry Lewes stopped by for a nightcap, and I slept like a baby that night.

The first fifteen minutes at work Monday morning were filled with the usual resistance to the smell of the hospital. In short, I pressed my lips together while taking deep breaths through my nose to fight off nausea. By nine-twenty I felt as if I had been living there forever.

The waiting room to my office was filled. Criss-cross lines of suffering on the people's faces made me feel as if I were surrounded by a dozen pieces of human graph paper. And no matter what I did, arranged, or said, I couldn't help them. I was nothing more than Sisyphus in a white coat, a name tag, and a run beginning in my left stocking. Quickly I passed my puzzled secretary and all those resigned yet still hopeful pairs of eyes. I had to take a walk. If I didn't move my legs a little, I thought I would suffocate.

Emily Brontë joined me in the hall, and we closed our eyes and walked rapidly down the newly tiled corridors. We pretended we were striding along the moors. "Remember, Mona, how many died of tuberculosis then," she said. "And what good work they're doing here now."

"But it smells of death and dying. Why should good work smell of death?" I replied.

"The smell does defeat one," she admitted, and disappeared.

As I was going back to my office, my doctor friend stopped me. "Hi, Mona, how are you?" We're still friends. I don't believe in grudges. "Don't whine, Mona, and hold no grudges. They're dead ends," Aunt Beadie always said. She was right. Even history teaches you that.

"I'm fine," I said. "The foliage in Vermont was beautiful on Sunday after the rain. And I met a nice young man from Paris." Of course he didn't believe me. "And you?"

"The same." His mouth turned down a little at the corners; he expected some comfort, but I wasn't in the mood. I simply waited.

When he saw no sympathy forthcoming, he straightened his mouth briskly.

"Listen, Mona, you saved me a call. There are complicated problems in Room 201. The patient's wife had a heart attack over the weekend and is in Intensive Care. And in 117 there's a boy who was in a motorcycle accident. He'll be a vegetable. His parents are devastated. He was a Merit Scholar at Harvard," he added in a low, confidential voice. Obviously it was Harvard that impressed him. Whenever we talked, he never failed to remind me why I was relieved to see him leave my apartment for the last time.

"I know you'll see someone from both of those families today. Try to get back to me after four." He squeezed my elbow, either for Harvard or for old times, I suppose, and I headed back to the office.

It was a ghastly morning. One of the worst I've ever had. The stone gets heavier as we get older. By noon I was dripping wet—I perspire when I have to watch people cry. Before I went out for lunch I changed my bra and blouse and then picked up a sandwich and coffee and headed toward Central Park. It was a school holiday and they had closed the park to traffic, so as I ate I watched the bicyclers. They looked happy; I began to feel a little better.

Then Rilke came along and sat beside me. Now there's a man. I wished I had combed my hair. We chatted quietly and then, because the sun seemed to be having one last burst of energy before the fall really closed in, we moved to another bench and arranged ourselves so the sun could warm our faces. Saturday's storm had knocked so many of the leaves off the trees. I started to mourn the lost leaves, but then Rilke said, "They'll come back, Mona." He covered my hand with his. "It is so good not to be alone in autumn," he murmured.

After a bit a breeze came up, and although I protested, Rilke insisted on taking off his cape. Tenderly he spread it over my shoulders, and we sat there contentedly until it was time for me to get back to work.

Memoir

JULIA

Lillian Hellman
(1906–1984)

Biography p. 1076

I have here changed most of the names. I don't know that it matters anymore, but I believe the heavy girl on the train still lives in Cologne and I am not sure that even now the Germans like their premature anti-Nazis. More important, Julia's mother is still living and so, perhaps, is Julia's daughter. Almost certainly, the daughter's father lives in San Francisco.

In 1937, after I had written *The Children's Hour* and *Days to Come,* I had an invitation to attend a theatre festival in Moscow. Whenever in the past I wrote about that journey, I omitted the story of my trip through Berlin because I did not feel able to write about Julia.

Dorothy Parker and her husband, Alan Campbell, were going to Europe that same August, and so we crossed together on the old *Normandie,* a pleasant trip even though Campbell, and his pretend-good-natured feminine jibes, had always made me uneasy.

When we reached Paris I was still undecided about going on to Moscow. I stayed around, happy to meet Gerald and Sara Murphy for the first time, Hemingway, who came up from Spain, and James Lardner, Ring Lardner's son, who was soon to enlist in the International Brigade and to lose his life in Spain a few months later.

I liked the Murphys. I was always to like and be interested in them, but they were not for me what they had been to an older generation. They were, possibly, all that Calvin Tomkins says in his biography: they had style, Gerald had wit, Sara grace and shrewdness, and that summer, soon after they had lost both their sons, they had a sweet dignity. But through the many years I was to see them after that I came to believe they were not as bonny as others thought them, or without troubles with each other, and long before the end—the end of my knowing them, I mean, a few years before Gerald died, when they saw very few of their old friends—I came to think that too much of their lives had been based on style. Style is mighty pleasant for those who benefit from it, but maybe not always rewarding for those who make and live by its necessarily strict rules.

There were many other people that summer in Paris, famous and rich, who invited Dottie for dinners and country lunches and the tennis she didn't play and the pools she didn't swim in. It gave me pleasure then, and forever after, that people courted her. I was amused at her excessive good manners, a kind of put-on, often there to hide contempt and dislike for those who flattered her at the very minute she begged for the flattery. When she had enough to drink the good manners got so good they got silly, but then the words came funny and sharp to show herself, and me, I think, that nobody could buy her. She was wrong: they could and did buy her for years. But they only bought a limited ticket to her life and in the end she died on her own road.

It was a new world for me. I had been courted around New York and Hollywood, as is everybody who has been a success in the theatre and young enough not to have been too much on display. But my invitations were second-class stuff compared to Dottie's admirers that month in Paris. I had a fine time, one of the best of my life. But one day, after a heavy night's drinking, I didn't anymore. I was a child of the Depression, a kind of Puritan Socialist, I guess—although to give it a name is to give it a sharper outline than it had—and I was full of the strong feelings the early Roosevelt period brought to many people. Dottie had the same strong feelings about something we all thought of as society and the future, but the difference between us was more than generational—she was long accustomed to much I didn't want. It was true that she always turned against the famous and the rich who attracted her, but I never liked them well enough to bother that much.

I had several times that month spoken on the phone with my beloved childhood friend Julia, who was studying medicine in Vienna, and so the morning after the heavy drinking I called Julia to say I would come to Vienna the next day en route to Moscow. But that same night, very late, she called back.

She said, "I have something important for you to do. Maybe you'll do it, maybe you can't. But please stay in Paris for a few days and a friend will come to see you. If things work as I hope, you'll decide to go straight to Moscow by way of Berlin and I'll meet you on your way back."

When I said I didn't understand, who was the friend, why Berlin, she said, "I can't answer questions. Get a German visa tomorrow. You'll make your own choice, but don't talk about it now."

It would not have occurred to me to ignore what Julia told me to do because that's the way it had always been between us. So I went around the next morning to the German consulate for a visa. The consul said they'd give me a traveling permit, but would not allow me to stay in Berlin overnight, and the Russian consul said that wasn't unusual for people en route to Moscow.

I waited for two days and was about to call Julia again on the day of the morning I went down for an early breakfast in the dining room of the Hotel Meurice. (I had been avoiding Dottie and Alan, all invitations, and was troubled and annoyed by two snippy, suspicious notes from Alan about what was I up to, why was I locked in my room?) The concierge said the gentleman on the bench was waiting for me. A tall middle-aged man got up from the bench and said, "Madame Hellman? I come to deliver your tickets and to talk with you about your plans. Miss Julia asked me to call with the travel folders."

We went into the dining room, and when I asked him what he would like he said, in German, "Do you think I can have an egg, hot milk, a roll? I cannot pay for them."

When the waiter moved away, the tall man said, "You must not understand German again. I made a mistake."

I said I didn't understand enough German to worry anybody, but he didn't answer me and took to reading the travel folders until the food came. Then he ate very fast, smiling as he did it, as if he were remembering something pleasant from a long ago past. When he finished, he handed me a note. The note said, "This is my friend, Johann. He will tell you. But *I* tell you, don't push yourself. If you can't you can't, no dishonor. Whatever, I will meet you soon. Love, Julia."

Mr. Johann said, "I thank you for fine breakfast. Could we walk now in Tuileries?"

As we entered the gardens he asked me how much I knew about Benjamin Franklin, was I an expert? I said I knew almost nothing. He said he admired Franklin and perhaps someday I could find him a nice photograph of Franklin in America. He sat down suddenly on a bench and mopped his forehead on this cool, damp day.

"Have you procured a German visa?"

"A traveling visa. I cannot stay overnight. I can only change stations in Berlin for Moscow."

"Would you carry for us fifty thousand dollars? We think, we do not guarantee, you will be without trouble. You will be taking the money to enable us to bribe out many already in prison, many who soon will be. We are a small group, valuable workers against Hitler. We are of no common belief or religion. The people who will meet you for the money, if your consent is given, were once small publishers. We are of Catholic, Communist, many beliefs. Julia has said that I must remind you for her that you are afraid of being afraid, and so will do what sometimes you cannot do, and that could be dangerous to you and to us."

I took to fiddling with things in my pocketbook, lit a cigarette, fiddled some more. He sat back as if he were very tired, and stretched.

After a while I said, "Let's go and have a drink."

He said, "I repeat. We think all will go well, but much could go wrong. Julia says I must tell you that, but that if we should not hear from you by the time of Warsaw, Julia will use her family with the American ambassador there through Uncle John."

"I know her family. There was a time she didn't believe in them much."

"She said you would note that. And so to tell you that her Uncle John is now governor. He does not like her but did not refuse her money for his career. And that her mother's last divorce has made her mother dependent on Julia as well."

I laughed at this picture of Julia controlling members of her very rich family. I don't think we had seen each other more than ten or twelve times since we were eighteen years old and so the years had evidently brought changes I didn't know about. Julia had left college, gone to Oxford, moved on to medical school in Vienna, had become a patient-pupil of Freud's. We had once, in the last ten years, spent a Christmas holiday together, and one summer, off Massachusetts, we had sailed for a month on her small boat, but in the many letters we had written in those years neither of us knew much more than the bare terms of each other's life, nothing of the daily stuff that is the real truth, the importance.

I knew, for example, that she had become, maybe always was, a Socialist, and lived by it, in a one-room apartment in a slum district of Vienna, sharing her great fortune with whoever needed it. She allowed herself very little, wanted very little. Oddly, gifts to me did not come into the denial: they were many and extravagant. Through the years, whenever she saw anything I might like, it was sent to me: old Wedgwood pieces, a Toulouse-Lautrec drawing, a fur-lined coat we saw together in Paris, a set of Balzac that she put in a rare Empire desk, and a wonderful set of Georgian jewelry, I think the last thing she could have had time to buy.

I said to the gray man, "Could I think it over for a few hours? That's what Julia meant."

He said, "Do not think hard. It is best not to be too prepared for matters of this kind. I will be at the station tomorrow morning. If you agree to carry the money, you will say hello to me. If you have decided it is not right for you, pass by me. Do not worry whichever is decided by you." He held out his hand, bowed, and moved away from me across the gardens.

I spent the day in and around Sainte-Chapelle, tried to eat lunch and dinner, couldn't, and went back to the hotel to pack only after I was sure Dottie and Alan would have gone to dinner with the Murphys. I left a note for them saying I was leaving early in the morning and would find them again after Moscow. I knew I had spent the whole day in a mess of indecision. Now I lay down, determined that I would not sleep until I had taken stock of myself. But decisions, particularly important ones, have always made me sleepy, perhaps because I know that I will have to make them by instinct, and thinking things out is only what other people tell me I should do. In any case, I slept through the night and rose only in time to hurry for the early morning train.

I was not pleased to find Dottie and Alan in the lobby, waiting to take me to the station. My protests were so firm and so awkward that Alan, who had a remarkable nose for deception, asked if I had a reason for not wanting them to come with me. When he went to get a taxi, I said to Dottie, "Sorry if I sounded rude. Alan makes me nervous."

She smiled, "Dear Lilly, you'd be a psychotic if he didn't."

At the railroad station I urged them to leave me when my baggage was carried on, but something had excited Alan: perhaps my nervousness; certainly not his claim that they had never before known anybody who was en route to Moscow. He was full of bad jokes about what I must not say to Russian actors, how to smuggle out caviar, and all the junk people like Alan say when they want to say something else.

I saw the gray man come down the platform. As he came near us Alan said, "Isn't that the man I saw you with in the Tuileries yesterday?" And as I turned to say something to Alan, God knows what it would have been, the gray man went past me and was moving back into the station.

I ran toward him. "Mr. Johann. Please, Mr. Johann." As he turned, I lost my head and screamed, "Please don't go away. *Please.*"

He stood still for what seemed like a long time, frowning. Then he moved slowly back toward me, as if he were coming with caution, hesitation.

Then I remembered: I said, "I only wanted to say hello. Hello to you, Mr. Johann, hello."

"Hello, Madame Hellman."

Alan had come to stand near us. Some warning had to be made. "This is Mr. Campbell and Miss Parker there. Mr. Campbell says he saw us yesterday and now he will ask me who you are and say that he didn't know we knew each other so well that you would come all this way to say goodbye to me."

Mr. Johann said, without hesitation, "I wish I could say that was true. But I have come to search for my nephew who is en route to Poland. He is not in his coach, he is late, as is his habit. His name is W. Franz, car 4, second class, and if I do not find him I would be most grateful if you say to him I came." He lifted his hat. "I am most glad, Madame Hellman, that we had this chance to say hello."

"Oh, yes," I said, "indeed. Hello. Hello."

When he was gone, Alan said, "What funny talk. You're talking like a foreigner."

"Sorry," I said, "sorry not to speak as well as you do in Virginia."

Dottie laughed, I kissed her and jumped for the train. I was nervous and went in the wrong direction. By the time a conductor told me where my compartment was, the train had left the station. On the connecting platform, before I reached my coach, a young man was standing holding a valise and packages. He said, "I am W. Franz, nephew, car 4, second class. This is a birthday present from Miss Julia." He handed me a box of candy and a hatbox marked "Madame Pauline." Then he bowed and moved off.

I carried the boxes to my compartment, where two young women were sitting on the left bench. One girl was small and thin and carried a cane. The other was a big-boned woman of about twenty-eight, in a heavy coat, wrapped tight against this mild day. I smiled at them, they nodded, and I sat down. I put my packages next to me and only then noticed that there was a note pasted on the hatbox. I was frightened of it, thought about taking it to the ladies' room, decided that would look suspicious, and opened it. I had a good memory in those days for poems, for what people said, for the looks of things, but it has long since been blurred by time. But I still remember every word of that note: "At the border, leave the candy box on the seat. Open this box and wear the hat. There is no thanks for what you will do for them. No thanks from me either. But there is the love I have for you. Julia."

I sat for a long time holding the note. I was in a state that I have known since I was old enough to know myself, and that to this day frightens me and makes me unable even to move my hands. I do not mean to be foolishly modest about my intelligence: it is often high, but I have known since childhood that faced with a certain kind of simple problem, I sometimes make it so complex that there is no way out. I simply do not see what another mind grasps immediately. I was there now. Julia had not told me where to open the hatbox. To take it into the corridor or toilet might make the two ladies opposite me suspicious. And so I sat doing nothing for a long time until I realized that I didn't know when we crossed the border—a few minutes or a few hours. A decision had to be made but I could not make it.

Childhood is less clear to me than to many people: when it ended I turned my face away from it for no reason that I know about, certainly without the usual reason of unhappy memories. For many years that worried me, but then I discovered that the tales of former children are seldom to be trusted. Some people supply too many past victories or pleasures with which to comfort themselves, and other people cling to pains, real and imagined, to excuse what they have become.

I think I have always known about my memory: I know when it is to be trusted and when some dream or fantasy entered on the life, and the dream, the need of dream, led to distortion of what happened. And so I knew early that the rampage angers of an only child were distorted nightmares of reality. But I trust absolutely what I remember about Julia.

Now, so many years later, I could climb the steps without a light, move in the night through the crowded rooms of her grandparents' great Fifth Avenue house with the endless chic-shabby rooms, their walls covered with pictures, their tables crowded with objects whose value I didn't know. True, I cannot remember anything said or done in that house except for the first night I was allowed to sleep there. Julia and I were both twelve years old that New Year's Eve night, sitting at a late dinner, with courses of fish and meats, and sherbets in between to change the tastes, "clear the palate" is what her grandmother said, with watered wine for us, and red and white wine and champagne for the two old people. (Were they old? I don't know: they were her grandparents.) I cannot remember any talk at the table, but after dinner we were allowed to go with them to the music room. A servant had already set the phonograph for "So Sheep May Safely Graze," and all four of us listened until Julia rose, kissed the hand of her grandmother, the brow of her grandfather, and left the room, motioning for me to follow. It was an odd ritual, the whole thing, I thought, the life of the very rich, and beyond my understanding.

Each New Year's Eve of my life has brought back the memory of that night. Julia and I lay in twin beds and she recited odds and ends of poetry—every once in a while she would stop and ask me to recite, but I didn't know anything—Dante in Italian, Heine in German, and even though I could not understand either language, the sounds were so lovely that I felt a sweet sadness as if much was ahead in the world, much that was going to be fine and fulfilling if I could ever find my way. I did recite Mother Goose and she did Donne's "Julia," and laughed with pleasure "at his tribute to me." I was ashamed to ask if it was a joke.

Very late she turned her head away for sleep, but I said, "More, Julia, please. Do you know more?" And she turned on the light again and recited from Ovid and Catullus, names to me without countries.

I don't know when I stopped listening to look at the lovely face propped against the pillow—the lamp throwing fine lights on the thick dark hair. I cannot say now that I knew or had ever used the words gentle or delicate or strong, but I did think that night that it was the most beautiful face I had ever seen. In later years I never thought about how she looked, although when we were grown other people often said she was a "strange beauty," she "looked like nobody else," and one show-off said a "Burne-Jones face" when, of course, her face had nothing to do with Burne-Jones or fake spirituality.

There were many years, almost twenty, between that New Year's Eve and the train moving into Germany. In those years, and the years after Julia's death, I have had plenty of time to think about the love I had for her, too strong and too complicated to be defined as only the sexual yearnings of one girl for another. And yet certainly that was there. I don't know, I never cared, and it is now an aimless guessing game. It doesn't prove much that we never kissed each other; even when I leaned down in a London funeral parlor to kiss the battered face that had been so hideously put back together, it was not the awful scars that worried me: because I had never kissed her I thought perhaps she would not want it and so I touched the face instead.

A few years after that childhood New Year's Eve, I was moved to a public school. (My father was having a bad time and couldn't afford to pay for me anymore.) But Julia and I saw each other almost every day and every Saturday night I still slept in her grandparents' house. But, in time, our lives did change: Julia began to travel all summer and in winter holidays, and when she returned all my questions about the beauties of Europe would be shrugged off with badly photographed snapshots of things that interested her: two blind children in Cairo—she explained that the filth carried by flies caused the blindness; people drinking from sewers in Teheran; no St. Mark's but the miserable hovel of a gondolier in Venice; no news of the glories of Vatican art but stories about the poverty of Trastevere.

Once she returned with a framed photograph of a beautiful woman who was her mother and an Englishman who was her mother's husband. I asked her what she felt about seeing her mother—in all the years I had never heard her mention her mother —and she stared at me and said that her mother owned a "very fancy castle" and the new husband poured drinks for all the titles who liked the free stuff, but there was also mention of Evelyn Waugh and H. G. Wells and Nancy Cunard, and when I wanted news of them she said she didn't know anything about them, they'd said hello to her and that she had only wanted to get out of the way and go to her room.

"But I didn't have a *room,*" she said. "Everybody has a suite, and there are fourteen servants somewhere below the earth, and only some of them have a window in the cell my mother calls their room, and there's only one stinking bath for all of them. My mother learns fast, wherever she is. She does not offend the host country."

Once, when we were about sixteen, we went with her grandparents at Easter time to their Adirondacks lodge, as large and shabby as was every place they lived in. Both old people drank a good deal—I think they always had, but I had only begun to notice it—and napped after every meal. But they stayed awake late into the night doing intricate picture puzzles imported from France, on two tables, and gave each other large checks for the one who finished first.

I don't remember that Julia asked their permission for our camping trips—several times we stayed away for weekends—on or near Lake Champlain. It wasn't proper camping, although we carried blankets and clean socks and dry shoes and canned food. We walked a great deal, often I fished for trout, and once, climbing a high hill, Julia threw a net over a rabbit, running with a grace and speed I had never before seen in a girl, and she showed me how to skin the rabbit. We cooked it that night wrapped in bacon and it is still among the best things I ever ate, maybe because *Robinson Crusoe* is one of the best books I ever read. Even now, seeing any island, I am busy with that rabbit and fantasies of how I would make do alone, without shelter or tools.

When we walked or fished we seldom did it side by side: that was her choice and I admired it because I believed she was thinking stuff I couldn't understand and mustn't interfere with, and maybe because I knew even then she didn't want to be side by side with anybody.

At night, wrapped in our blankets, the fire between us, we would talk. More accurately, I would ask questions and she would talk: she was one of the few people I have ever met who could give information without giving a lecture. How young it sounds now that although I had heard the name of Freud, I never knew exactly what he wrote until she told me; that Karl Marx and Engels became men with theories, instead of that one sentence in my school book which mentioned the Manifesto. But we also talked like all young people, of possible beaux and husbands and babies, and heredity versus environment, and can romantic love last, mixing stuff like that in speeches made only for the pleasure of girls on the edge of growing up.

One night, when we had been silent for a long time because she was leaning on an elbow, close to the fire, reading a German grammar, I laughed at the sounds coming from her mouth as she repeated the sentences.

She said, "No, you don't understand. People are either teachers or students. You are a student."

"Am I a good one?"

"When you find what you want, you will be very good."

I reached out and touched her hand. "I love you, Julia." She stared at me and took my hand to her face.

It was in our nineteenth year that she went away to Oxford. The second year she was there I went to visit her. There are women who reach a perfect time of life, when the face will never again be as good, the body never as graceful or as powerful. It had happened that year to Julia, but she was no more conscious of it than she had been of being a beautiful child. Her clothes were ugly now, loose, tacky, and the shoes looked as if they had been stolen from an old man. Nobody came to her rooms because, as one smitten young Indian gentleman told me, she never asked anybody. She was invited everywhere in Oxford and in London, but the only names I remember her speaking of with respect were J. D. Bernal and J. B. S. Haldane. Once or twice we went up to the theatre in London, but she would sigh halfway through and say she had no feeling for the theatre, only Shakespeare on the page, and sometimes not even then.

The following year she wrote to tell me that she was leaving England for medical school in Vienna, with the probably vain hope that Freud would someday accept her as a student.

I wrote a number of letters that year, but the only time I heard from Julia was a cable on my birthday, followed by the Toulouse-Lautrec drawing that hangs today in my house. I was pleased that she thought I knew the excellence of Toulouse-Lautrec, because I didn't, and had to be told about him by a fellow student who used to buy me hamburgers in order, I think, to tell me about his homosexual experiences. (He was a very decorated hero during the Second World War and was killed a week before it ended.)

A few months later I had a letter from Anne-Marie Travers, a girl whom Julia and I had both known in school, but I knew better because we had gone to the same dreadful summer camp. Anne-Marie was an intelligent girl, flirtatious, good-mannered with that kind of outward early-learned passive quality that in women so often hides anger. Now, it seemed, she was in or near Vienna and her unexpected letter— I don't think we had seen each other for four or five years—said she had bumped into Julia on the street and been "snubbed," had heard from people that Julia was leading a strange life, very political, pretending not to be rich and living in the Floridsdorf district, the Socialist working-class "slums." Julia ranked second in the medical school, she had been told, the first candidate being an American also but of a German inheritance, a very remarkable boy from San Francisco, handsome in the Norwegian way, she, Anne-Marie, didn't like. It took knowing Anne-Marie to realize that German and Norwegian used in the same sentence was a combination of put-down and admiration. Anne-Marie added that her brother Sammy had recently tried to kill himself, and was I still torn between being a writer or an architect? There was something strange about the letter, some reason, some tone I didn't understand, didn't like. Then I forgot it for a month or so until her brother Sammy rang to ask me for dinner, saying that he had been living in Elba and thinking of me. He said it again at dinner, having had four whiskeys with beer chasers, and asked me if I was a virgin. This was not like Sammy, who had no interest in me, and I sensed something was to follow. At about four in the morning when we were sitting in Small's in Harlem, and there had been many more whiskeys and beers, he asked me why I had got a divorce, why hadn't I married his older brother Eliot, whose rich Detroit wife had lost all her money in the Depression, and so Eliot was again open to bids and would be right for me, although he himself thought Eliot a handsome bore. He said he rather liked his sister Anne-Marie, because he had slept with her when she was sixteen and he was eighteen. Then, perhaps because I made a sound, he said who the hell was I to talk, everybody knew about Julia and me.

It is one of the strange American changes in custom that the drunks of my day often hit each other, but never in the kind of bar fight that so often happens now with knives. In those days somebody hit somebody, and when that was finished one of them offered his hand and it would have been unheard of to refuse. (James Thurber had once thrown a glass of whiskey at me in the famous Tony's speakeasy, Hammett had pushed Thurber against a wall, Thurber had picked up a glass from another table and, in an attempt to throw it at Dash, missed and hit the waiter who was Tony's cousin. Tony called the police, saying over and over again that he had had enough of Thurber through the years. Almost everybody agreed with Tony, but when the police came we were shocked and went down to the police station to say nothing had happened except a drunken accident of a broken glass; and while I don't think Thurber liked me afterward, I don't think he had liked me before. In any case, none of us ever mentioned it again.) And so, at that minute at the table at Small's, there seemed to me nothing odd about what I did. I leaned across the table, slapped Sammy in the face, got up, turned over the table, and went home. The next day a girl called me to say that Sammy couldn't remember what he had said but he was sorry, anyway, and a large amount of flowers arrived that evening. The girl called again a few days later: I said there were no hard feelings, but Sammy was a bigger dope at twenty-five than he had been at seventeen. She said she'd tell him that.

I wrote to Anne-Marie saying that whatever Julia thought or did was bound to be interesting, and that I didn't want to hear attacks on her beliefs or her life. My letter was returned, unopened or resealed, and it was to be another year before I knew why.

Not long after, I had a letter from Julia suggesting that I come to Vienna for a visit, that Freud had accepted her, that there were things I ought to learn about "the holocaust that is on its way." I wrote back that I was living with Hammett, didn't want to leave, but would come maybe next year. Subsequent letters from her talked of Hitler, Jews, radicals, Mussolini. We wrote a great deal that year, 1933–1934, and I told her that I was trying to write a play, hadn't much hope about it, but that Hammett was pulling me along. I asked her if she liked *The Children's Hour* as a title and was hurt when she forgot the question in her next letter, which was angry with news of the armed political groups in Austria, the threat of Hitler, "the criminal guilt of the English and French in not recognizing the dangers of Fascism, German style, the other one is a peacock." There was much in her letter I didn't understand, although all of us by that time knew that the Nazis would affect our lives.

I could not write a history of those years as it seemed to us then. Or, more accurately, I could not write my own: I have no records and I do not know when I understood what. I know that Hitler—Mussolini might have escaped our notice as no more than a big-talking man in silly uniforms—had shaken many of us into radicalism, or something we called radicalism, and that our raw, new convictions would, in time, bring schisms and ugly fights. But in the early Thirties I don't believe the people I knew had done much more than sign protests, listen to the shocking stories of the few German émigrés who had come to New York or Hollywood, and given money to one cause or another. We were disturbed by the anti-Semitism that was an old story in Germany and some of us had sense enough to see it as more than that. Many people thought of it as not much more than the ignorant rantings of a house painter and his low-down friends, who would certainly be rejected by the Germans, who were for my generation an "advanced," "cultivated" people.

But by 1935 or 1936 what had been only half understood, unsettling, distant stories turned horror-tragic and new assessments had to be made fast of what one believed and what one was going to do about it. The rebels of the Twenties, the generation before mine, now seemed rebels only in the Scott Fitzgerald sense: they had wasted their blood, blind to the future they could have smelled if the odor of booze hadn't been so strong. Scott knew this about himself, and understandably resented those old friends who had turned into the new radicals. But the 1920's rebels had always seemed strange to me: without charity I thought most of them were no more than a classy lot of brilliant comics, performing at low fees for the society rich. The new radicalism was what I had always been looking for.

In 1934, Hammett and I rented a charming house on Long Island and were throwing around the money from *The Thin Man.* It had been a year of heavy drinking for both of us: I drank almost as much as Hammett and our constant guests, but I was younger than most of them and didn't like myself when I drank. In any case, work on *The Children's Hour* was going bad and Hammett, who had a pleasant nature, had resolved on a new, lighter drinking program: nothing but sherry, port and beer. He was never drunker, never ate less, and was in a teasing, irritable mood. I wanted to get away from all of it. Hammett gave me the money to go to Europe.

Because I planned to stay away for a long time to finish the play, the money had to last as long as possible. I went directly to Paris, to the small and inexpensive Hotel Jacob, and decided to see nobody. Once a day I went for a walk, twice a day I ate in working-class restaurants, struggling through French newspapers or magazines. They didn't teach me much but I did know about the formation of the Popular Front. There had been, there were to be, Fascist riots in Paris that year. Like most Americans, now and then, political troubles in Europe seemed far away from my life and certainly far away from a play about a little girl who ruined the lives of two women in a New England private school.

But after a month of nobody, I was lonely and tired of work. I telephoned Julia —we had talked several times my first weeks in Paris—to say I'd like to come to Vienna for a few days. She said that wasn't a good idea at the minute, nor a good idea to talk on a telephone that was tapped, but she'd meet me and would send a message saying where and when. I think that was the first time I ever knew a telephone could be listened in on, a life could and would be spied on. I was impressed and amused.

I waited but no word came from Julia. Then, two weeks after my phone call, the newspaper headlines said that Austrian government troops, aided by local Nazis, had bombarded the Karl Marx Hof in the Floridsdorf district of Vienna. Socialist workers, who owned the district, had defended it, and two hundred of them had been killed. I read the news in a little restaurant called the Fourth Republic, and in the middle of my dinner ran back to the hotel for my address book. But Julia's address said nothing about the Karl Marx Hof or the Floridsdorf and so I went to bed telling myself not to imagine things. At five o'clock in the morning I had a telephone call from a man who said his name was Von Zimmer, he was calling from Vienna, Julia was in a hospital.

I have no memory of the trip to Vienna, no memory of a city I was never to see again, no memory of the name of the hospital, nor how I got to it or in what language. But I remember everything after that. It was a small hospital in a mean section of town. There were about forty people in the ward. Julia's bed was the first behind the door. The right side of her face was entirely in bandages, carried around the head and on to most of the left side, leaving only the left eye and the mouth exposed. Her right arm was lying outside the bed cover, her right leg was lying on an unseen platform. There were two or three people in uniform in the room, but most of the aides were in street clothes and it was a young boy, twelve or thirteen, who brought me a stool and said to Julia, in German, "Your friend has come," as he turned her head so that she could see me with her left eye. Neither the eye nor the hand moved as she looked at me and neither of us spoke. I have no loss of memory about that first visit: there was nothing to remember. After a while, she raised her right arm toward the center of the room and I saw the boy, who was carrying a pail, speak to a nurse. The nurse came to the bed and moved Julia's head away from me and told me she thought I should come back the next day. As I went past the desk, the young boy met me in the hall and told me to ask for a room at the Hotel Sacher. There was another note at the desk of the hotel, a place so much too expensive for me that I was about to take my bags and find another. The note said that the reservation had been made at the Sacher because I would be safe there, and that was best for Julia. It was signed John Von Zimmer.

I went back to the hospital later that evening and, as I got off the trolley car, I saw what I had not seen in the morning. The district was heavily ringed with police, and men in some other uniform. The hospital said I couldn't go into the ward, the patient was asleep after the operation. When I asked what operation, they asked how was I related to the patient, but my German, and much else, had given out. I tried to find out if the hospital desk knew John Von Zimmer's address, but they said they had never heard of him.

I was refused at the hospital the next day and the next. Three days later a handsome, pregnant lady, in a poor coat too small for her, took me into the ward. The same young boy brought me the same stool, and gently turned Julia's head toward me. Her right leg was no longer on a platform and that made me think everything was better. This time, after a few minutes, she raised her right arm and touched my hand. I stared at her hand: it had always been too large even for this tall girl, too blunt, too heavy, ugly. She took the hand away, as if she knew what I thought, and I reached back for it. We sat for a while that way and then she pointed to her mouth, meaning that she couldn't speak because of the bandages. Then she raised her hand to the window, pointed out, and made a pushing movement with her hand.

I said, "I don't know what you mean," and realized they were the first words I had spoken to her in years. She made the motion again and then shut her eye as if she couldn't go on. After a while I fell asleep on the stool with my head against the wall. Toward afternoon a nurse came and said I had to leave. Julia's bed had been wheeled out and I think the nurse was telling me that she was being "treated."

For the three days and nights I had been in Vienna I had gone nowhere, not even for a walk, only once a day to a cheap restaurant a block from the hospital where the old man who ran it talked in English and said he had once lived in Pittsburgh. I don't believe I understood where I was, or what had happened in this city, or why, and that I was too frightened of what I didn't understand to be anything more than quiet. (Fear has always made me unable to talk or to move much, almost drowsy.) I thought constantly about how to find the man called Von Zimmer, but it seemed to me each day that he would certainly come to me. On the fourth night, about ten o'clock, I had nothing more to read, was too restless and nervous for bed, and so I took the long walk back to the restaurant near the hospital. When I got there it was closed and so I walked again until it was long past midnight, thinking how little I knew about Julia's life, how seldom we had met in the last years, how little I knew of what was happening to her now.

When I got back to the hotel the young boy from the hospital ward was standing across the street. I saw him immediately and stood waiting for him. He handed me a folded slip of paper. Then he bowed and moved away.

In the lobby of the hotel, the note, written in a weak, thin handwriting, said, "Something else is needed. They will take me tomorrow to another place. Go back to Paris *fast* and leave your address at the Sacher. Love, Julia."

I was back in Paris before I remembered that when we were kids, doing our Latin together, we would take turns translating and then correcting. Often one of us would say to the other, "Something else is needed"; we said it so often that it got to be a family joke.

I waited in Paris for a month, but no word ever came. A German friend made a telephone call for me to the hospital in Vienna, but they said they didn't know Julia's name, had no record of her ever having been there. My German friend telephoned the university twice to ask for John Von Zimmer, but once somebody said he no longer was enrolled and once they had no information about his address.

And so I went back to New York, finished *The Children's Hour,* and three nights after it was a success I telephoned Julia's grandmother. I think the old lady was drunk —she often had been when we were young—because it took a long time to explain who I was, and then she said what difference did it make who I was, she didn't know anything about Julia, neither did the Morgan Bank, who had been transmitting huge sums of money to her all over Europe, and she thought Julia was plain crazy.

About a year later I had a letter from Julia, but it is lost now and while I am sure of what it said, I am not sure how it was said by a woman who wrote what had become almost foreign English and was telling me something she evidently thought I already knew. The letter had to do with Nazism and Germany, the necessity of a Socialist revolution throughout the world, that she had had a baby, and the baby seemed to like being called Lilly, but then she was a baby who liked almost everything. She said she had no address, but I should send letters to Paris, to 16 Rue de l'Université, in care of apartment 3. I wrote immediately to thank her about Lilly, then two more times, and finally had a postcard from her with a Zurich stamp.

I can no longer remember how long after that Anne-Marie telephoned to ask me for dinner. I think I was about to say yes when Anne-Marie told me that a friend of hers had seen Julia, that Julia was doing something called anti-Fascist work, very dangerous, and throwing away her money, did I know about the baby and wasn't that nutty, a poor unwanted illegitimate child? I said I was leaving town and couldn't have dinner. Anne-Marie said that was too bad because they didn't often visit New York, but happened to be here on the opening night of *Days to Come* and had to say, frankly, that *they* hadn't liked my play. I said that wasn't illegal, not many people had liked it, and then there was more talk about Julia, something about her leg that I didn't understand, and Anne-Marie said that she wanted me to meet her husband, who, as I certainly knew, had been a colleague of Julia's in medical school in Vienna and was now a surgeon, very successful, in San Francisco. She said he was brilliant and a real beauty. I have never liked women who talk about how men look—"so attractive" was a constant phrase of my time—and to hide my irritation I said I knew she had married but I didn't know his name. She said his name was John Von Zimmer. I am sure she heard me take a deep breath because she laughed and said the next time they came to New York she would call me, and why didn't I ever see Sammy, her brother, who was always trying to commit suicide. I was never to see Sammy again, but certainly he never committed suicide because I read about him in Suzy's society column a few months ago.

In all the years that followed I only once again saw Anne-Marie, with John Von Zimmer, in 1970, when I was teaching in Berkeley. They were in a San Francisco restaurant with six or seven other stylish-looking people, and Anne-Marie kissed me and bubbled and we exchanged addresses. Von Zimmer was silent as he stared at a wall behind my head. Neither Anne-Marie nor I did the telephoning that we said we would do the next day, but I did want very much to see Von Zimmer: I had an old question to ask, and so a few days after the meeting in the restaurant I walked around to his office. But, standing near the great Victorian house, I changed my mind. I am glad now that I didn't ask the question that almost certainly would never have been answered.

But on that day in 1937, on the train moving toward the German border, I sat looking at the hatbox. The big girl was now reading the *Frankfurter Zeitung,* the thin girl had done nothing with the book that was lying on her lap. I suppose it was the announcement of the first lunch sitting that made me look up from the past, pick up my coat, and then put it down again.

The thin girl said, "Nice coat. Warm? Of what fur?"

"It's sealskin. Yes, it's warm."

She said, pointing to the hatbox, "Your hat is also fur?"

I started to say I didn't know, realized how paralyzed I had been, knew it couldn't continue, and opened the box. I took out a high, fluffy, hat of gray fox as both ladies murmured their admiration. I sat staring at it until the heavy girl said, "Put on. Nice with coat."

I suppose part of my worry, although I hadn't even got there yet, was what to do with the knitted cap I was wearing. I took it off and rose to fix the fur hat in the long mirror between the windows. The top and sides of the hat were heavy and when I put my hand inside I felt a deep seam in the lining with heavy wads below and around the seam. It was uncomfortable and so I started to take it off when I remembered that the note said I should wear the hat.

Somewhere during my hesitations the heavy girl said she was going to lunch, could she bring me a sandwich? I said I'd rather go to lunch but I didn't know when we crossed the border, and immediately realized I had made a silly and possibly dangerous remark. The thin girl said we wouldn't be crossing until late afternoon—she had unpacked a small box and was eating a piece of meat—and if I was worried about my baggage she was staying in the compartment because she couldn't afford the prices in the dining car. The heavy girl said she couldn't afford them either, but the doctor had said she must have hot meals and a glass of wine with her medicine. So I went off with her to the dining car, leaving my coat thrown over the candy box. We sat at a table with two other people and she told me that she had been studying in Paris, had "contracted" a lung ailment, and was going home to Cologne. She said she didn't know what would happen to her Ph.D. dissertation because the lung ailment had affected her bones. She talked in a disjointed stream of words for the benefit, I thought, of the two men who sat next to us, but even when they left, the chatter went on as her head turned to watch everybody in a nervous tic between sentences. I was glad to be finished with lunch, so worried was I about the candy box, but it was there, untouched, when we got back to our compartment. The thin girl was asleep, but she woke up as we came in and said something in German to the heavy girl about a crowded train, and called her Louisa. It was the first indication I had that they knew each other, and I sat silent for a long time wondering why that made me uneasy. Then I told myself that if everything went on making me nervous, I'd be in a bad fix by the time it came to be nervous.

For the next few hours, the three of us dozed or read until the thin girl tapped me on the knee and said we would be crossing the border in five or ten minutes. I suppose everybody comes to fear in a different way, but I have always grown very hot or very cold, and neither has anything to do with the weather. Now, waiting, I was very hot. As the train pulled to a standstill, I got up to go outside—people were already leaving the train to pass through a check gate, and men were coming on the train to inspect baggage in the cars ahead of us—without my coat or my new hat. I was almost out the compartment door when the thin girl said, "You will need your coat and hat. It is of a windiness."

"Thank you. But I'm not cold."

Her voice changed sharply, "You will have need of your coat. Your hat is nice on your head."

I didn't ask questions because the tone in which she spoke was the answer. I turned back, put the coat around my shoulders, put on the hat that felt even heavier now with the wads of something that filled the lining, and let both girls go past me as I adjusted it in the mirror. Coming out on the platform, they were ahead of me, separated from me by several people who had come from other compartments. The heavy girl moved on. The thin girl dropped her purse and, as she picked it up, stepped to one side and moved directly behind me. We said nothing as we waited in line to reach the two uniformed men at the check gate. As the man in front of me was having his passport examined, the thin girl said, "If you have a temporary travel-through visa, it might take many minutes more than others. But that is nothing. Do not worry."

It didn't take many minutes more than others. I went through as fast as anybody else, turned in a neat line with the other travelers, went back to the train. The thin girl was directly behind me, but as we got to the steps of the train, she said, "Please," and pushed me aside to climb in first. When we reached our compartment, the fat girl was in her seat listening to two customs men in the compartment next to ours as they had some kind of good-natured discussion with a man who was opening his luggage.

The thin girl said, "They are taking great time with the luggage." As she spoke, she leaned over and picked up my candy box. She took off the ribbon and said, "Thank you. I am hungry for a chocolate. Most kind."

I said, "Please, please," and knew I was never meant for this kind of thing. "I am carrying it to a friend for a gift. Please do not open it." As the customs men came into our compartment, the thin girl was chewing on a candy, the box open on her lap. I did not know much about the next few minutes except that all baggage was dragged down from the racks, that my baggage took longer than the baggage of my companions. I remember the heavy girl chatting away, and something being said about my traveling visa, and how I was going to a theatre festival because I was a playwright. (It was two days later before I realized I had never mentioned the Moscow theatre festival or anything about myself.) And the name Hellman came into the conversation I could only half understand. One of the customs men said, "Jew," and the heavy girl said certainly the name was not always of a Jew and gave examples of people and places I couldn't follow. Then the men thanked us, replaced everything neatly, and bowed themselves out the door.

Somewhere in the next hours I stopped being hot or cold and was not to be frightened again that day. The thin girl had neatly retied my candy box, but I don't think any of us spoke again until the train pulled into the station. When the porters came on for the baggage, I told myself that now I should be nervous, that if the money had been discovered at the border gate nothing much could have happened because I was still close to France. Now was the time, therefore, for caution, intelligence, reasonable fears. But it wasn't the time, and I laughed at that side of me that so often panics at a moment of no consequence, so often grows listless and sleepy near danger.

But there was to be no danger that day. The thin girl was right behind me on the long walk toward the station gate, people kissing and shaking hands all along the way. A man and a woman of about fifty came toward me, the woman holding out her arms and saying in English, "Lillian, how good it is to see you. How naughty of you not to stay more than a few hours, but even that will give us time for a nice visit—" as the thin girl, very close to me now, said, "Give her the candy box."

I said, "I am so glad to see you again. I have brought you a small gift, gifts—" but the box was now out of my hands and I was being moved toward the gate. Long before we reached the gate the woman and the thin girl had disappeared.

The man said, "Go through the gate. Ask the man at the gate if there is a restaurant near the station. If he says Albert's go to it. If he gives you another name, go to that one, look at it, and turn back to Albert's, which is directly opposite the door you are facing." As I asked the official at the gate about a restaurant, the man went past me. The official said please to step to one side, he was busy, would take care of me in a minute. I didn't like being in the station so I crossed the street to Albert's. I went through a revolving door and was so shocked at the sight of Julia at a table that I stopped at the door. She half rose, called softly, and I went toward her with tears that I couldn't stop because I saw two crutches lying next to her and now knew what I had never wanted to know before. Half out of her seat, holding to the table, she said, "Fine, fine. I have ordered caviar for us to celebrate, Albert had to send for it, it won't be long."

She held my hand for several minutes, and said, "Fine. Everything has gone fine. Nothing will happen now. Let's eat and drink and see each other. So many years."

I said, "How long have we got? How far is the other station, the one where I get the train to Moscow?"

"You have two hours, but we haven't that long together because you have to be followed to the station and the ones who follow you must have time to find the man who will be with you on the train until Warsaw in the morning."

I said, "You look like nobody else. You are more beautiful now."

She said, "Stop crying about my leg. It was amputated and the false leg is clumsily made so I am coming to New York in the next few months, as soon as I can, and get a good one. Lilly, don't cry for me. *Stop the tears.* We must finish the work now. Take off the hat the way you would if it was too hot for this place. Comb your hair, and put the hat on the seat between us."

Her coat was open, and the minute I put the hat on the bench she pinned it deep inside her coat with a safety pin that was ready for it.

She said, "Now I am going to the toilet. If the waiter tries to help me up, wave him aside and come with me. The toilet locks. If anybody should try to open it, knock on the door and call to me, but I don't think that will happen."

She got up, picked up one of the crutches, and waved me to the other arm. She spoke in German to a man I guess was Albert as we moved down the long room. She pulled the crutch too quickly into the toilet door, it caught at a wrong angle, and she made a gesture with the crutch, tearing at it in irritation.

When she came out of the toilet, she smiled at me. As we walked back to the table, she spoke in a loud voice, saying something in German about the toilet and then, in English, "I forget you don't know German. I was saying that German public toilets are always clean, much cleaner than ours, particularly under the new regime. The bastards, the murderers."

Caviar and wine were on the table when we sat down again and she was cheerful with the waiter. When he had gone away she said, "Ah, Lilly. Fine, fine. Nothing will happen now. But it is your right to know that it is my money you brought in and we can save five hundred, and maybe, if we can bargain right, a thousand people with it. So believe that you have been better than a good friend to me, you have done something important."

"Jews?"

"About half. And political people. Socialists, Communists, plain old Catholic dissenters. Jews aren't the only people who have suffered here." She sighed. "That's enough of that. We can only do today what we can do today and today you did it for us. Do you need something stronger than wine?"

I said I didn't and she said to talk fast now, there wasn't much time, to tell her as much as possible. I told her about my divorce, about the years with Hammett. She said she had read *The Children's Hour,* she was pleased with me, and what was I going to do next?

I said, "I did it. A second play, a failure. Tell me about your baby."

"She's fat and handsome. I've got over minding that she looks like my mother."

"I want very much to see her."

"You will," she said, "I'll bring her when I come home for the new leg and she can live with you, if you like."

I said, meaning no harm, "Couldn't I see her now?"

"Are you crazy? Do you think I would bring her here? Isn't it enough I took chances with your safety? I will pay for that tonight and tomorrow and . . ." Then she smiled. "The baby lives in Mulhouse, with some nice folks. I see her that way whenever I cross the border. Maybe, when I come back for the leg, I'll leave her with you. She shouldn't be in Europe. It ain't for babies now."

"I haven't a house or even an apartment of any permanence," I said, "but I'll get one if you bring the baby."

"Sure. But it wouldn't matter. You'd be good to her." Then she laughed. "Are you as angry a woman as you were a child?"

"I think so," I said. "I try not to be, but there it is."

"Why do you try not to be?"

"If you lived around me, you wouldn't ask."

"I've always liked your anger," she said, "trusted it."

"You're the only one, then, who has."

"Don't let people talk you out of it. It may be uncomfortable for them, but it's valuable to you. It's what made you bring the money in today. Yes, I'll leave the baby with you. Its father won't disturb you, he wants nothing to do with the baby or with me. He's O.K. Just an ordinary climber. I don't know why I did it, Freud told me not to, but I don't care. The baby's good."

She smiled and patted my hand. "Someday I will take you to meet Freud. What am I saying? I will probably never see him again—I have only so much longer to last in Europe. The crutches make me too noticeable. The man who will take care of you has just come into the street. Do you see him outside the window? Get up and go now. Walk across the street, get a taxi, take it to Bahnhof 200. Another man will be waiting there. He will make sure you get safely on the train and will stay with you until Warsaw tomorrow morning. He is in car A, compartment 13. Let me see your ticket."

I gave it to her. "I think that will be in the car to your left." She laughed. "*Left,* Lilly, *left.* Have you ever learned to tell left from right, south from north?"

"No. I don't want to leave you. The train doesn't go for over an hour. I want to stay with you a few more minutes."

"No," she said. "Something could still go wrong and we must have time to get help if that should happen. I'll be coming to New York in a few months. Write from Moscow to American Express in Paris. I have stuff picked up every few weeks." She took my hand and raised it to her lips. "My beloved friend."

Then she pushed me and I was on my feet. When I got to the door I turned and must have taken a step back because she shook her head and moved her face to look at another part of the room.

I did not see the man who followed me to the station. I did not see the other man on the train, although several times a youngish man passed my compartment and the same man took the vacant chair next to me at dinner, but didn't speak to me at all.

When I went back to my compartment from dinner the conductor asked if I wanted my two small valises put in the corridor for examination when we crossed the German-Polish border so that I wouldn't be awakened. I told him I had a wardrobe trunk in the baggage car, handed him the key for the customs people, and went to sleep on the first sleeping pill of my life, which may be why I didn't wake up until just before we pulled into the Warsaw station at seven in the morning. There was bustle in the station as I raised the curtain to look out. Standing below my window was the young man who had sat next to me at dinner. He made a gesture with his hand, but I didn't understand and shook my head. Then he looked around and pointed to his right. I shook my head again, bewildered, and he moved away from the window. In a minute there was a knock on my door and I rose to open it. An English accent said through the crack, "Good morning. Wanted to say goodbye to you, have a happy trip." And then, very, very softly, "Your trunk was removed by the Germans. You are in no danger because you are across the border. Do nothing for a few hours and then ask the Polish conductor about the trunk. Don't return from Moscow through Germany, travel another way." In a loud voice he said, "My best regards to your family," and disappeared.

For two hours I sat in bed, doubtful, frightened of the next move, worried about the loss of clothes in my trunk. When I got dressed, I asked the Polish conductor if the German conductor had left my trunk key with him. He was upset when he told me the German customs people had removed the trunk, that often happened, but he was sure it would be sent on to me in Moscow after a few days, nothing unusual, the German swine often did it now.

The trunk did arrive in Moscow two weeks later. The lining was in shreds, the drawers were broken, but only a camera was missing and four or five books. I did not know then, and I do not know now, whether the trunk had anything to do with Julia because I was not to see Germany for thirty years and I was never to speak with Julia again.

I wrote to her from Moscow, again from Prague on my way back to Paris, and after I had returned to New York from Spain during the Civil War. Three or four months later I had a card with a Geneva postmark. It said, says, "Good girl to go to Spain. Did it convince you? We'll talk about that when I return to New York in March."

But March and April came and went and there was no word from Julia. I telephoned her grandmother, but I should have known better. The old lady said they hadn't heard from Julia in two years and why did I keep worrying her? I said I had seen Julia in October and she hung up the phone. Somewhere about that time I saw a magazine picture of Julia's mother, who had just married again, an Argentine, but I saw no reason for remembering his name.

On May 23, 1938, I had a cable, dated London two days before and sent to the wrong address. It said, "Julia has been killed stop please advise Moore's funeral home Whitechapel Road London what disposition stop my sorrow for you for all of us." It was signed John Watson but had no address.

It is never possible for me to cry at the time when it could do me some good, so, instead, I got very drunk for two days and don't remember anything about them. The third morning I went around to Julia's grandmother's house and was told by the butler, who came out on the street as if I were a danger to the house, that the old people were on a world cruise and wouldn't be back for eight weeks. I asked the name of the boat, was asked for my credentials, and by the time we batted all that around,

I was screaming that their granddaughter was dead and that he and they could go fuck themselves. I was so sick that night that Dash, who never wanted me to go anywhere because he never wanted to, said he thought I should go to London right away.

I have no diary notes of that trip and now only the memory of standing over a body with a restored face that didn't hide the knife wound that ran down the left side. The funeral man explained that he had tried to cover the face slash but I should see the wounds on the body if I wanted to see a mess that couldn't be covered. I left the place and stood on the street for a while. When I went back in the funeral man handed me a note over the lunch he was eating. The note said, "Dear Miss Hellman. We have counted on your coming but perhaps it is not possible for you, so I will send a carbon of this to your New York address. None of us knows what disposition her family wishes to make, where they want what should be a hero's funeral. It is your right to know that the Nazis found her in Frankfurt, in the apartment of a colleague. We got her to London in the hope of saving her. Sorry that I cannot be here to help you. It is better that I take my sorrow for this wonderful woman into action and perhaps revenge. Yours, John Watson, who speaks here for many others. Salud."

I went away that day and toward evening telephoned the funeral man to ask if he had an address for John Watson. He said he had never heard the name John Watson, he had picked up the body at the house of a Dr. Chester Lowe at 30 Downshire Hill. When I got there it was a house that had been made into apartments, but there was no Dr. Lowe on the name plates, and for the first time it occurred to me that my investigations could be bad for people who were themselves in danger.

So I brought the body home with me on the old *De Grasse* and tried this time to reach Julia's mother. The same butler told me that he couldn't give me her mother's address, although he knew the mother had been informed of the death. I had the body cremated and the ashes are still where they were that day so long ago.

I should, of course, have gone to Mulhouse before I came home from London, but I didn't, didn't even think about it in those awful days in London or on the boat. After the cremation, I wrote to Julia's grandmother, told her about the baby and that I knew nothing more than that she lived with a family in Mulhouse, but Mulhouse couldn't be so big that they would have trouble finding an American child. I had no answer. I guess I knew I wouldn't, and so I wrote another letter, this time nasty, and got an answer from a fancy name in a fancy law firm saying that everything would be done "in this strange case" about a child only I believed existed and I would be kept informed of any "doubtful results."

In the next few months, I found I dreamed every night about Julia, who was almost always the age when I first met her. Hammett said I looked awful and if it worried me that much why didn't I find a lawyer or a detective in Mulhouse. William Wyler, the movie director, with whom I had made two pictures, had been born in Mulhouse and his family still owned a department store there. It is too long ago for me to be accurate about when and how he got me the name of a lawyer in Mulhouse, but he did, and after a while the lawyer wrote that the investigation was proving difficult, but he thought, in the end, they would certainly find the baby if she was still there.

Three months later the war broke out and I never heard again from anybody in Western Europe until I arrived in London from Russia in March 1944. My second day there—my reason for being there was to do a documentary film for the British government about people on the docksides during the V–2 bombings—I realized I was somewhere in the neighborhood of the funeral parlor. I found it, but it had been bombed to pieces.

Nothing is left of all this except that sometime in the early 1950's, I was sitting on a stone wall at a Long Island picnic at Ruth and Marshall Field's. A man next to me was talking about a man called Onassis—the first time I had heard his name—and a lawsuit by the U.S. government against Onassis, and when he was finished with that he turned to me and said, "My father was the lawyer to whom you wrote about Julia. I am Julia's third cousin."

After a while I said, "Yes."

He said, "My father died last year."

"Your father never wrote to me again."

He said, "You see, I'm not a lawyer, I'm a banker."

I said, "Whatever happened to her family?"

"The grandparents are dead. Julia senior lives in Argentina—"

"The bastards," I said, "all of them."

He smiled at me. "They are my cousins."

"Did they ever find the baby they didn't want to find? I don't care who you are."

"I never knew anything about a baby," he said.

I said, "I don't believe you," got off the stone fence, left a note for Ruthie saying I didn't feel well, and drove home.

Poetry

Emily Dickinson
(1830–1886)

Biography p. 1069

288

I'm Nobody! Who are you?
Are you—Nobody—too?
Then there's a pair of us!
Dont tell! they'd banish us—you know!

How dreary—to be—Somebody!   5
How public—like a Frog—

To tell your name—the livelong June—
To an admiring Bog!

324

Some keep the Sabbath going to Church—
I keep it, staying at Home—
With a Bobolink for a Chorister—
And an Orchard, for a Dome—

Some keep the Sabbath in Surplice—   5
I just wear my Wings—
And instead of tolling the Bell, for Church,
Our little Sexton—sings.

God preaches, a noted Clergyman—
And the sermon is never long,
So instead of getting to Heaven, at last—   10
I'm going, all along.

303

The Soul selects her own Society—
Then—shuts the Door—
To her divine Majority—
Present no more—

Unmoved—she notes the Chariots—pausing—   5
At her low Gate—
Unmoved—an Emperor be kneeling
Upon her Mat—

I've known her—from an ample nation—
Choose One—   10
Then—close the Valves of her attention—
Like Stone—

640

I cannot live with You—
It would be Life—
And Life is over there—
Behind the Shelf

The Sexton keeps the Key to—   5
Putting up
Our Life—His Porcelain—
Like a Cup—

Discarded of the Housewife—
Quaint—or Broke—   10
A newer Sevres pleases—
Old Ones crack—

I could not die—with You—
For One must wait
To shut the Other's Gaze down—   15
You—could not—

And I—Could I stand by
And see You—freeze—
Without my Right of Frost—
Death's privilege?   20

Nor could I rise—with You—
Because Your Face
Would put out Jesus'—
That New Grace

Glow plain—and foreign 25
On my homesick Eye—
Except that You than He
Shone closer by—

They'd judge Us—How—
For You—served Heaven—You know, 30
Or sought to—
I could not—

Because You saturated Sight—
And I had no more Eyes
For sordid excellence 35
As Paradise

And were You lost, I would be—
Though My Name
Rang loudest
On the Heavenly fame— 40

And were You—saved—
And I—condemned to be
Where You were not—
That self—were Hell to Me—

So We must meet apart— 45
You there—I—here—
With just the Door ajar
That Oceans are—and Prayer—
And that White Sustenance—
Despair— 50

1732

My life closed twice before its close;
It yet remains to see
If Immortality unveil
A third event to me,

So huge, so hopeless to conceive 5
As these that twice befel.
Parting is all we know of heaven,
And all we need of hell.

Walt Whitman
(1819–1892)

Biography p. 1106

Biography p. 1106

WHEN I HEARD AT THE CLOSE OF THE DAY

When I heard at the close of the day how my name had been
    receiv'd with plaudits in the capitol, still it was not a happy
    night for me that follow'd,
And else when I carous'd, or when my plans were accomplish'd,
    still I was not happy,
But the day when I rose at dawn from the bed of perfect health,
    refresh'd, singing, inhaling the ripe breath of autumn,
When I saw the full moon in the west grow pale and disappear
    in the morning light,
When I wander'd alone over the beach, and undressing bathed,
    laughing with the cool waters, and saw the sun rise,   5
And when I thought how my dear friend my lover was on his
    way coming, O then I was happy,
O then each breath tasted sweeter, and all that day my food
    nourish'd me more, and the beautiful day pass'd well,
And the next came with equal joy, and with the next at evening
    came my friend,
And that night while all was still I heard the waters roll slowly
    continually up the shores,
I heard the hissing rustle of the liquid and sands as directed to
    me whispering to congratulate me,   10
For the one I love most lay sleeping by me under the same cover
    in the cool night,
In the stillness in the autumn moonbeams his face was inclined
    toward me,
And his arm lay lightly around my breast—and that night I was
    happy.

WE TWO BOYS TOGETHER CLINGING

We two boys together clinging,
One the other never leaving,
Up and down the roads going, North and South excursions
    making,
Power enjoying, elbows stretching, fingers clutching,
Arm'd and fearless, eating, drinking, sleeping, loving,   5

No law less than ourselves owning, sailing, soldiering, thieving,
threatening,
Misers, menials, priests alarming, air breathing, water drinking,
on the turf or the sea-beach dancing,
Cities wrenching, ease scorning, statutes mocking, feebleness
chasing,
Fulfilling our foray.

O YOU WHOM I OFTEN AND SILENTLY COME

O you whom I often and silently come where you are that I may
be with you,
As I walk by your side or sit near, or remain in the same room
with you,
Little you know the subtle electric fire that for your sake is
playing within me.

POEM OF REMEMBRANCES FOR A GIRL OR A BOY OF THESE STATES

You just maturing youth! You male or female!
Remember the organic compact of These States,
Remember the pledge of the Old Thirteen thenceforward to the
rights, life, liberty, equality of man,
Remember what was promulged by the founders, ratified by The
States, signed in black and white by the Commissioners, and
read by Washington at the head of the army,
Remember the purposes of the founders,—Remember
Washington;   5
Remember the copious humanity streaming from every direction
toward America;

Remember the hospitality that belongs to nations and men;
(Cursed be nation, woman, man, without hospitality!)
Remember, government is to subserve individuals,
Not any, not the President, is to have one jot more than you or
me,
Not any habitan of America is to have one jot less than you or
me.   10

Anticipate when the thirty or fifty millions, are to become the hundred or
two hundred millions, of equal freedmen and freewomen, amicably
joined.

Recall ages—One age is but a part—ages are but a part;
Recall the angers, bickerings, delusions, superstitions, of the idea
  of caste,
Recall the bloody cruelties and crimes.

Anticipate the best women; 15
I say an unnumbered new race of hardy and well-defined women
  are to spread through all These States,
I say a girl fit for These States must be free, capable, dauntless,
  just the same as a boy.

Anticipate your own life—retract with merciless power,
Shirk nothing—retract in time—Do you see those errors,
  diseases, weaknesses, lies, thefts?
Do you see that lost character?—Do you see decay,
  consumption, rum-drinking, dropsy, fever, mortal cancer or
  inflammation? 20
Do you see death, and the approach of death?

Edwin Arlington Robinson
(1869–1935)

Biography p. 1095

MINIVER CHEEVY

Miniver Cheevy, child of scorn,
  Grew lean while he assailed the seasons;
He wept that he was ever born,
  And he had reasons.

Miniver loved the days of old 5
  When swords were bright and steeds were prancing;
The vision of a warrior bold
  Would set him dancing.

Miniver sighed for what was not,
  And dreamed, and rested from his labors; 10
He dreamed of Thebes and Camelot,
  And Priam's neighbors.

Miniver mourned the ripe renown
  That made so many a name so fragrant;

He mourned Romance, now on the town,   15
    And Art, a vagrant.

Miniver loved the Medici,
    Albeit he had never seen one;
He would have sinned incessantly   20
    Could he have been one.

Miniver cursed the commonplace
    And eyed a khaki suit with loathing;
He missed the mediæval grace
    Of iron clothing.

Miniver scorned the gold he sought,   25
    But sore annoyed was he without it;
Miniver thought, and thought, and thought,
    And thought about it.

Miniver Cheevy, born too late,
    Scratched his head and kept on thinking;   30
Miniver coughed, and called it fate,
    And kept on drinking.

RICHARD CORY

Whenever Richard Cory went down town,
We people on the pavement looked at him:
He was a gentleman from sole to crown,
Clean favored, and imperially slim.

And he was always quietly arrayed,   5
And he was always human when he talked;
But still he fluttered pulses when he said,
"Good-morning," and he glittered when he walked.

And he was rich—yes, richer than a king—
And admirably schooled in every grace: 10
In fine, we thought that he was everything
To make us wish that we were in his place.

So on we worked, and waited for the light,
And went without the meat, and cursed the bread;
And Richard Cory, one calm summer night, 15
Went home and put a bullet through his head.

HAMLET'S SOLILOQUY

William Shakespeare
(1564–1616)

Biography p. 1098

To be, or not to be: that is the question:
Whether 'tis nobler in the mind to suffer
The slings and arrows of outrageous fortune,
Or to take arms against a sea of troubles,
And by opposing end them? To die: to sleep;   5
No more; and, by a sleep to say we end
The heart-ache and the thousand natural shocks
That flesh is heir to, 'tis a consummation
Devoutly to be wish'd. To die, to sleep;
To sleep: perchance to dream: ay, there's the rub;   10
For in that sleep of death what dreams may come
When we have shuffled off this mortal coil,
Must give us pause. There's the respect
That makes calamity of so long life;
For who would bear the whips and scorns of time,   15
The oppressor's wrong, the proud man's contumely,
The pangs of dispriz'd love, the law's delay,
The insolence of office, and the spurns
That patient merit of the unworthy takes,
When he himself might his quietus make   20
With a bare bodkin? who would fardels bear,
To grunt and sweat under a weary life,
But that the dread of something after death,
The undiscover'd country from whose bourn
No traveller returns, puzzles the will,   25
And makes us rather bear those ills we have
Than fly to others that we know not of?
Thus conscience does make cowards of us all;
And thus the native hue of resolution
Is sicklied o'er with the pale cast of thought,   30
And enterprises of great pith and moment
With this regard their currents turn awry,
And lose the name of action.

HOME BURIAL

Robert Frost

(1874–1963)

Biography p. 1073

He saw her from the bottom of the stairs
Before she saw him. She was starting down,
Looking back over her shoulder at some fear.
She took a doubtful step and then undid it
To raise herself and look again. He spoke   5
Advancing toward her: "What is it you see
From up there always—for I want to know."
She turned and sank upon her skirts at that,
And her face changed from terrified to dull.
He said to gain time: "What is it you see?"   10
Mounting until she cowered under him.
"I will find out now—you must tell me, dear."
She, in her place, refused him any help
With the least stiffening of her neck and silence.
She let him look, sure that he wouldn't see,   15
Blind creature; and a while he didn't see.
But at last he murmured, "Oh," and again, "Oh."

"What is it—what?" she said.
                 "Just that I see."

"You don't," she challenged. "Tell me what it is."

"The wonder is I didn't see at once.   20
I never noticed it from here before.
I must be wonted to it—that's the reason.
The little graveyard where my people are!
So small the window frames the whole of it.
Not so much larger than a bedroom, is it?   25
There are three stones of slate and one of marble,
Broad-shouldered little slabs there in the sunlight
On the sidehill. We haven't to mind *those*.
But I understand: it is not the stones,
But the child's mound————"

             "Don't, don't, don't, don't," she cried. 30

She withdrew shrinking from beneath his arm
That rested on the banister, and slid downstairs;

And turned on him with such a daunting look,
He said twice over before he knew himself:
"Can't a man speak of his own child he's lost?"   35

"Not you! Oh, where's my hat? Oh, I don't need it!
I must get out of here. I must get air.
I don't know rightly whether any man can."

"Amy! Don't go to someone else this time.
Listen to me. I won't come down the stairs."   40
He sat and fixed his chin between his fists.
"There's something I should like to ask you, dear."

"You don't know how to ask it."
                              "Help me, then."

Her fingers moved the latch for all reply.

"My words are nearly always an offence.   45
I don't know how to speak of anything
So as to please you. But I might be taught
I should suppose. I can't say I see how.
A man must partly give up being a man
With women-folk. We could have some arrangement   50
By which I'd bind myself to keep hands off
Anything special you're a-mind to name.
Though I don't like such things 'twixt those that love.
Two that don't love can't live together without them.
But two that do can't live together with them."   55
She moved the latch a little. "Don't—don't go.
Don't carry it to someone else this time.
Tell me about it if it's something human.
Let me into your grief. I'm not so much
Unlike other folks as your standing there   60
Apart would make me out. Give me my chance.
I do think, though, you overdo it a little.
What was it brought you up to think it the thing
To take your mother-loss of a first child
So inconsolably—in the face of love.   65
You'd think his memory might be satisfied————"

"There you go sneering now!"

                              "I'm not, I'm not!
You make me angry. I'll come down to you.

God, what a woman! And it's come to this,
A man can't speak of his own child that's dead."   70

"You can't because you don't know how.
If you had any feelings, you that dug
With your own hand—how could you?—his little grave;
I saw you from that very window there,
Making the gravel leap and leap in air,   75
Leap up, like that, and land so lightly
And roll back down the mound beside the hole.
I thought, Who is that man? I didn't know you.
And I crept down the stairs and up the stairs
To look again, and still your spade kept lifting.   80
Then you came in. I heard your rumbling voice
Out in the kitchen, and I don't know why,
But I went near to see with my own eyes.
You could sit there with the stains on your shoes
Of the fresh earth from your own baby's grave   85
And talk about your everyday concerns.
You had stood the spade up against the wall
Outside there in the entry, for I saw it."

"I shall laugh the worst laugh I ever laughed.
I'm cursed. God, if I don't believe I'm cursed."   90

"I can repeat the very words you were saying.
'Three foggy mornings and one rainy day
Will rot the best birch fence a man can build.'
Think of it, talk like that at such a time!
What had how long it takes a birch to rot   95
To do with what was in the darkened parlour?
You *couldn't* care! The nearest friends can go
With anyone to death, comes so far short
They might as well not try to go at all.
No, from the time when one is sick to death,   100
One is alone, and he dies more alone.
Friends make pretence of following to the grave,
But before one is in it, their minds are turned
And making the best of their way back to life
And living people, and things they understand.   105
But the world's evil. I won't have grief so
If I can change it. Oh, I won't, I won't!"

"There, you have said it all and you feel better.
You won't go now. You're crying. Close the door.
The heart's gone out of it: why keep it up?   110
Amy! There's someone coming down the road!"

"*You*—oh, you think the talk is all. I must go—
Somewhere out of this house. How can I make you————"
"If—you—do!" She was opening the door wider.
"Where do you mean to go? First tell me that.   115
I'll follow and bring you back by force. I *will!*—"

Amy Lowell
(1874–1925)

Biography p. 1085

PATTERNS

I walk down the garden paths,
And all the daffodils
Are blowing, and the bright blue squills.
I walk down the patterned garden-paths
In my stiff, brocaded gown.   5
With my powdered hair and jewelled fan,
I too am a rare
Pattern. As I wander down
The garden paths.

My dress is richly figured,   10
And the train
Makes a pink and silver stain
On the gravel, and the thrift
Of the borders.
Just a plate of current fashion,   15
Tripping by in high-heeled, ribboned shoes.
Not a softness anywhere about me,
Only whalebone and brocade.
And I sink on a seat in the shade
Of a lime tree. For my passion   20
Wars against the stiff brocade.
The daffodils and squills
Flutter in the breeze
As they please.
And I weep;   25
For the lime-tree is in blossom
And one small flower has dropped upon my bosom.

And the plashing of waterdrops
In the marble fountain
Comes down the garden-paths.   30
The dripping never stops.
Underneath my stiffened gown
Is the softness of a woman bathing in a marble basin,
A basin in the midst of hedges grown
So thick, she cannot see her lover hiding,   35
But she guesses he is near,
And the sliding of the water
Seems the stroking of a dear
Hand upon her.
What is Summer in a fine brocaded gown!   40
I should like to see it lying in a heap upon the ground.
All the pink and silver crumpled up on the ground.

I would be the pink and silver as I ran along the paths,
And he would stumble after,
Bewildered by my laughter.   45
I should see the sun flashing from his sword-hilt and the buckles on his shoes.
I would choose
To lead him in a maze along the patterned paths,
A bright and laughing maze for my heavy-booted lover,
Till he caught me in the shade,   50
And the buttons of his waistcoat bruised my body as he clasped me,
Aching, melting, unafraid.
With the shadows of the leaves and the sundrops,
And the plopping of the waterdrops,
All about us in the open afternoon—   55
I am very like to swoon
With the weight of this brocade,
For the sun sifts through the shade.

Underneath the fallen blossom
In my bosom,   60
Is a letter I have hid.
It was brought to me this morning by a rider from the Duke.
"Madam, we regret to inform you that Lord Hartwell
Died in action Thursday se'nnight."
As I read it in the white, morning sunlight,   65
The letters squirmed like snakes.
"Any answer, Madam," said my footman.
"No," I told him.
"See that the messenger takes some refreshment.
No, no answer."   70
And I walked into the garden,
Up and down the patterned paths,
In my stiff, correct brocade.
The blue and yellow flowers stood up proudly in the sun,
Each one.   75

I stood upright too,
Held rigid to the pattern
By the stiffness of my gown.
Up and down I walked,
Up and down.   80

In a month he would have been my husband.
In a month, here, underneath this lime,
We would have broke the pattern;
He for me, and I for him,
He as Colonel, I as Lady,   85
On this shady seat.
He had a whim
That sunlight carried blessing.
And I answered, "It shall be as you have said."
Now he is dead.   90

In Summer and in Winter I shall walk
Up and down
The patterned garden-paths
In my stiff, brocaded gown.
The squills and daffodils   95
Will give place to pillared roses, and to asters, and to snow.
I shall go
Up and down,
In my gown.
Gorgeously arrayed,   100
Boned and stayed.
And the softness of my body will be guarded from embrace
By each button, hook, and lace.
For the man who should loose me is dead,
Fighting with the Duke in Flanders,   105
In a pattern called a war.
Christ! What are patterns for?

A DECADE

When you came, you were like red wine and honey,
And the taste of you burnt my mouth with its sweetness.
Now you are like morning bread,
Smooth and pleasant.
I hardly taste you at all for I know your savour,   5
But I am completely nourished.

OPAL

You are ice and fire,
The touch of you burns my hands like snow.
You are cold and flame.
You are the crimson of amaryllis,
The silver of moon-touched magnolias.   5
When I am with you,
My heart is a frozen pond
Gleaming with agitated torches.

THE LESSON OF THE MOTH

Don Marquis
(1878–1937)

Biography p. 1088

i was talking to a moth
the other evening
he was trying to break into
an electric light bulb
and fry himself on the wires   5

why do you fellows
pull this stunt i asked him
because it is the conventional
thing for moths or why
if that had been an uncovered   10
candle instead of an electric
light bulb you would
now be a small unsightly cinder
have you no sense

plenty of it he answered   15
but at times we get tired
of using it
we get bored with the routine
and crave beauty
and excitement   20
fire is beautiful
and we know that if we get
too close it will kill us

but what does that matter
it is better to be happy   25
for a moment
and be burned up with beauty
than to live a long time
and be bored all the while
so we wad all our life up   30
into one little roll
and then we shoot the roll
that is what life is for

it is better to be a part of beauty
for one instant and then cease to   35
exist than to exist forever
and never be a part of beauty
our attitude toward life
is come easy go easy
we are like human beings   40
used to be before they became
too civilized to enjoy themselves

and before i could argue him
out of his philosophy
he went and immolated himself   45
on a patent cigar lighter
i do not agree with him
myself i would rather have
half the happiness and twice
the longevity   50

but at the same time i wish
there was something i wanted
as badly as he wanted to fry himself
                                        archy

THE HARLEM DANCER

Claude McKay

(1890–1948)

Biography p. 1087

Applauding youths laughed with young prostitutes
And watched her perfect, half-clothed body sway;
Her voice was like the sound of blended flutes
Blown by black players upon a picnic day.
She sang and danced on gracefully and calm,   5
The light gauze hanging loose about her form;
To me she seemed a proudly-swaying palm
Grown lovelier for passing through a storm.
Upon her swarthy neck black shiny curls
Luxuriant fell; and tossing coins in praise,   10
The wine-flushed, bold-eyed boys, and even the girls,
Devoured her shape with eager, passionate gaze;
But looking at her falsely-smiling face,
I knew her self was not in that strange place.

HER KIND

Anne Sexton

(1928–1974)

Biography p. 1098

I have gone out, a possessed witch,
haunting the black air, braver at night;
dreaming evil, I have done my hitch
over the plain houses, light by light:
lonely thing, twelve-fingered, out of mind.   5
A woman like that is not a woman, quite.
I have been her kind.

I have found the warm caves in the woods,
filled them with skillets, carvings, shelves,
closets, silks, innumerable goods;   10
fixed the suppers for the worms and the elves:

whining, rearranging the disaligned.
A woman like that is misunderstood.
I have been her kind.

I have ridden in your cart, driver,   15
waved my nude arms at villages going by,
learning the last bright routes, survivor
where your flames still bite my thigh
and my ribs crack where your wheels wind.
A woman like that is not ashamed to die.   20
I have been her kind.

TO JULIA DE BURGOS

Julia de Burgos
(1914–1953)

Biography p. 1069

The word is out that I am your enemy
    that in my poetry I am giving you away.

    They lie, Julia de Burgos. They lie, Julia de Burgos.
That voice that rises in my poems is not yours: it is my voice;
you are the covering and I the essence;   5
and between us lies the deepest chasm.

    You are the frigid doll of social falsehood,
and I, the virile sparkle of human truth.

    You are honey of courtly hypocrisy, not I;
I bare my heart in all my poems.   10

    You are selfish, like your world, not I;
I gamble everything to be what I am.

    You are but the grave lady, ladylike;
not I; I am life, and strength, and I am woman.

    You belong to your husband, your master, not I;   15
I belong to no one or to everyone, because to all, to all
I give myself in pure feelings and in my thoughts.

You curl your hair, and paint your face, not I;
I am curled by the wind, painted by the sun.

You are lady of the house, resigned and meek,   20
tied to the prejudices of men, not I;
I am Rocinante, running headlong,
smelling the horizons of the justice of God.

Translated by María Arrillaga

UNDERWEAR

Lawrence Ferlinghetti
(b. 1919)

Biography p. 1072

I didn't get much sleep last night
thinking about underwear
Have you ever stopped to consider
underwear in the abstract
When you really dig into it   5
some shocking problems are raised
Underwear is something
we all have to deal with
Everyone wears
some kind of underwear   10
Even Indians
wear underwear
Even Cubans
wear underwear
The Pope wears underwear I hope   15
Underwear is worn by Negroes
The Governor of Louisiana
wears underwear
I saw him on TV
He must have had tight underwear   20
He squirmed a lot
Underwear can really get you in a bind
Negroes often wear
white underwear
which may lead to trouble   25
You have seen the underwear ads
for men and women

so alike but so different
Women's underwear holds things up
Men's underwear holds things down   30
Underwear is one thing
men and women have in common
Underwear is all we have between us
You have seen the three-color pictures
with crotches encircled   35
to show the areas of extra strength
and three-way stretch
promising full freedom of action
Don't be deceived
It's all based on the two-party system   40
which doesn't allow much freedom of choice
the way things are set up
America in its Underwear
struggles thru the night
Underwear controls everything in the end   45
Take foundation garments for instance
They are really fascist forms
of underground government
making people believe
something but the truth   50
telling you what you can or can't do
Did you ever try to get around a girdle
Perhaps Non-Violent Action
is the only answer
Did Gandhi wear a girdle?   55
Did Lady Macbeth wear a girdle?
Was that why Macbeth murdered sleep?
And that spot she was always rubbing—
Was it really in her underwear?
Modern anglosaxon ladies   60
must have huge guilt complexes
always washing and washing and washing
Out damned spot—rub don't blot—
Underwear with spots very suspicious
Underwear with bulges very shocking   65
Underwear on clothesline a great flag of freedom
Someone has escaped his Underwear
May be naked somewhere
Help!
But don't worry   70
Everybody's still hung up in it
There won't be no real revolution
And poetry still the underwear of the soul
And underwear still covering
a multitude of faults   75
in the geological sense—
strange sedimentary stones; inscrutable cracks!
And that only the beginning

For does not the body stay alive
after death   80
and still need its underwear
or outgrow it
some organs said to reach full maturity
only after the head stops holding them back?
If I were you I'd keep aside   85
an oversize pair of winter underwear
Do not go naked into that good night
And in the meantime
keep calm and warm and dry
No use stirring ourselves up prematurely   90
'over Nothing'
Move forward with dignity
hand in vest
Don't get emotional
And death shall have no dominion   95
There's plenty of time my darling
Are we not still young and easy
Don't shout

Stevie Smith

(1902–1971)

Biography p. 1101

NOT WAVING BUT DROWNING

Nobody heard him, the dead man,
But still he lay moaning:
I was much further out than you thought
And not waving but drowning.

Poor chap, he always loved larking   5
And now he's dead
It must have been too cold for him his heart gave way,
They said.

Oh, no no no, it was too cold always
(Still the dead one lay moaning)   10
I was much too far out all my life
And not waving but drowning.

THE FROG PRINCE

I am a frog
I live under a spell
I live at the bottom
Of a green well

And here I must wait   5
Until a maiden places me
On her royal pillow
And kisses me
In her father's palace.

The story is familiar   10
Everybody knows it well
But do other enchanted people feel as nervous
As I do? The stories do not tell,

Ask if they will be happier
When the changes come   15
As already they are fairly happy
In a frog's doom?

I have been a frog now
For a hundred years
And in all this time   20
I have not shed many tears,

I am happy, I like the life,
Can swim for many a mile
(When I have hopped to the river)
And am for ever agile.   25

And the quietness,
Yes, I like to be quiet
I am habituated
To a quiet life,

But always when I think these thoughts   30
As I sit in my well
Another thought comes to me and says:
It is part of the spell

To be happy
To work up contentment   35
To make much of being a frog
To fear disenchantment

Says, It will be *heavenly*
To be set free,
Cries, *Heavenly* the girl who disenchants   40
And the royal times, *heavenly,*
And I think it will be.

Come then, royal girl and royal times,
Come quickly,
I can be happy until you come   45
But I cannot be heavenly,
Only disenchanted people
Can be heavenly.

INCIDENT

(For Eric Walrond)
Countee Cullen
(1903–1946)

Biography p. 1068

Once riding in old Baltimore,
    Heart-filled, head-filled with glee,
I saw a Baltimorean
    Keep looking straight at me.

Now I was eight and very small,   5
    And he was no whit bigger,
And so I smiled, but he poked out
    His tongue, and called me, "Nigger."

I saw the whole of Baltimore
    From May until December;   10
Of all the things that happened there
    That's all that I remember.

THE CHIMNEY SWEEPER

William Blake

(1757–1827)

Biography p. 1062

When my mother died I was very young,
And my father sold me while yet my tongue,
Could scarcely cry weep weep weep weep.
So your chimneys I sweep & in soot I sleep.

Theres little Tom Dacre, who cried when his head   5
That curl'd like a lambs back, was shav'd, so I said,
Hush Tom never mind it, for when your head's bare,
You know that the soot cannot spoil your white hair.

And so he was quiet, & that very night,
As Tom was a sleeping he had such a sight,   10
That thousands of sweepers Dick, Joe, Ned & Jack
Were all of them lock'd up in coffins of black,

And by came an Angel who had a bright key,
And he open'd the coffins & set them all free.
Then down a green plain leaping laughing they run   15
And wash in a river and shine in the Sun.

Then naked & white, all their bags left behind,
They rise upon clouds, and sport in the wind.
And the Angel told Tom, if he'd be a good boy,
He'd have God for his father & never want joy.   20

And so Tom awoke and we rose in the dark
And got with our bags & our brushes to work.
Tho' the morning was cold, Tom was happy & warm.
So if all do their duty, they need not fear harm.

NOTES FROM A SLAVE SHIP

Edward Field

(b. 1924)

Biography p. 1072

It is necessary to wait until the boss's eyes are on you
Then simply put your work aside,
Slip a fresh piece of paper in the typewriter,
And start to write a poem.

Let their eyes boggle at your impudence;   5
The time for a poem is the moment of assertion,
The moment when you say I exist—
Nobody can buy my time absolutely.

Nobody can buy me even if I say, Yes I sell.
There I am sailing down the river,   10
Quite happy about the view of the passing towns,
When I find that I have jumped overboard.

There is always a long swim to freedom.
The worst of it is the terrible exhaustion
Alone in the water in the darkness,   15
The shore a fading memory and the direction lost.

WE REAL COOL

The Pool Players.
Seven at the Golden Shovel.

Gwendolyn Brooks

(b. 1917)

Biography p. 1063

We real cool. We
Left school. We

Lurk late. We
Strike straight. We

Sing sin. We 5
Thin gin. We

Jazz June. We
Die soon.

PIED BEAUTY

Gerard Manley Hopkins
(1844–1889)

Biography p. 1077

Glory be to God for dappled things—
  For skies of couple-colour as a brinded cow;
    For rose-moles all in stipple upon trout that swim;
Fresh-firecoal chestnut-falls; finches' wings;
  Landscape plotted and pieced—fold, fallow, and plough; 5
  And áll trádes, their gear and tackle and trim.
All things counter, original, spare, strange;
  Whatever is fickle, freckled (who knows how?)
    With swift, slow; sweet, sour; adazzle, dim;
He fathers-forth whose beauty is past change: 10
                Praise him.

Drama

NOAH

From the Wakefield Mystery Plays

Characters

NOAH	1ST SON	1ST SON'S WIFE
GOD	2ND SON	2ND SON'S WIFE
NOAH'S WIFE	3RD SON	3RD SON'S WIFE

NOAH.   To mighty God I pray, maker of all that is,
Three persons, no gainsay, one God in endless bliss,
Thou made both night and day, beast, fowl, and fish,
All creatures in thy sway, wrought thou at thy wish,
    As well thou might;   5
The sun, the moon, heaven's tent,
Thou made; the firmament,
The stars also full fervent,
    To shine thou made full bright.

Angels thou made all even, all orders to bless,   10
To have the bliss in heaven, this did thou more and less,
Now laid thereto the leaven, which fermented faithlessness,
Marvels seven times seven than I can well express;
    And why?
Of all angels in brightness,   15
God gave Lucifer most lightness,
Who priding in his rightness,
    By God himself sat high.

He thought himself as worthy as he that him made,
In brightness and beauty, him God had to degrade,—   20
Put him in low degree, swiftly from sun to shade,
Him and his company, howling in hell were laid,
    For ever.
They shall never get away
Hence until doomsday,   25
But burn in bale for ay,
And never dissever.

Soon after, that gracious Lord in his likeness made man,
That place to be restored, even as he began,
By the trinity in accord, Adam and Eve, that woman,   30
To multiply without discord he gave them space and span
  In paradise to both.
He gave in his command,
On the tree of life to lay no hand;
But yet the false fiend   35
  Made him with man wroth;

Enticed man to gluttony, stirred him to sin in pride;
But in paradise surely, may no sin abide,
And therefore man full hastily was sternly thrust outside,
In woe and wandering for to be, with all pains plied   40
  Without ruth;
First on earth and then in hell
Fiercely with the fiends to dwell,
But to those no harm befell
  Who trusted in his truth.   45

Oil of mercy through his might he promised, as is said,
To all that strove with right in peace his paths to tread,
But now before his sight all people without dread,
For most part day and night, in word and deed they spread
  Their sin full bold;   50
Some in pride, anger, and envy,
Some in covetousness and gluttony,
Some in sloth and lechery,
  In ways manifold.

Therefore I dread lest God on us take vengeance,   55
For sin escapes the rod, without repentance;
Six hundred years and odd has been my existence,
Daily on earth to plod, with great grievance
  Each way;
And now I am old   60
Sick, sorry and cold,
As muck upon mould,
  I wither away.

But yet I cry for mercy and call;
Noah, thy servant, am I, Lord over all!   65
Therefore me and my fry shall with me fall;
Save from villainy and bring to thy hall
  In heaven;
And keep me from sin
This world within;   70

Mankind's comely king,
I pray morn and even.

(GOD *appears above.*)

GOD.   Since I have made each thing that may live and stand,
    Duke, emperor, and king with my own hand,
    To live to their liking by sea and by land,   75
    Every man to my bidding should come at command
        Full fervent;
    That made man such a creature,
    Fairest of favour,
    Man must heed me as a lover,   80
        With reason and repent.

Methought I showed man love when I made him to be
    All angels above, like to the trinity;
    And now in great reproof full low lies he,
    On earth no jot aloof from sins which displease me   85
        Most of all;
    Vengeance will I take,
    On earth for sin's sake,
    My grimness thus will wake
        Both great and small.   90

I repent full sore that ever made I man,
    By me he sets no store, and I am his sovereign;
    I will destroy therefore both beast, man and woman,
    All shall perish less and more that so spurned my plan,
        And ill have done.   95
    In earth I see right nought
    But sin so dearly bought;
    Of those that well have wrought
        Find I but one.

Therefore shall I undo all people that are here,   100
    With floods that shall subdue the land both far and near,
    I have good cause thereto for now no men me fear,
    As I say shall I do, the sword of vengeance rear,
        And make an end—
    Of all that bears life,   105
    Save Noah and his wife,
    They offered no strife,
        Nor me did offend.

To him in great joy hastily will I go,
    Noah shall I not destroy, but warn him of his woe.   110
    Men on earth their sin enjoy, raging to and fro,

Ever ill themselves employ, each the other's foe,
    With evil intent;
All shall I lay low
With floodings that shall flow,   115
I shall work them woe,
    That will not repent.

Noah, my friend, I tell thee, saved be thou by thy zeal,
But build a ship directly, of nail and board full well.
Thou ever showed thy loyalty to me as true as steel,   120
Still be obedient to me and friendship shalt thou feel
    My power provide.
Of length thy ship shall be
Three hundred cubits, warn I thee,
Of height even thirty,   125
    Of fifty cubits wide.

Anoint thy ship with pitch and tar without, also within,
The water to debar from flowing in;
Look no man it mar; three cabin rows begin,
Thou must use many a spar before this work thou win   130
    To end fully.
Make in thy ship also,
Of parlours even a row
And places more to stow
    The beasts that there must be.   135

One cubit in height a window shall thou make;
A side door to fit tight, fashion without mistake;
With thee shall no man fight, nor harm thee for my sake,
When all is done aright; thy wife see that thou take
    Into the ship with thee;   140
Thy sons of good fame,
Ham, Japhet, and Shem,
On board must remain,
    With their wives three.

For all shall be destroyed, that lives on land, but ye,   145
With floods that fill the void, and falling in plenty;
The heavens shall be employed to rain incessantly,
When days seven have cloyed, it shall last days forty,
    Without fail.
Take in thy ship also   150
Two beasts of each kind, so,
Male and female, see they go,
    Before thou raise thy sail.

So thou may thee avail when all these things are wrought,
Stuff thy ship with victual for hunger that ye lack nought;   155
For beasts, fowl, and cattle keep them in your thought
For them is my counsel, that some succour be sought,
    Uppermost;
They must have corn and hay,
And meat enough alway;   160
Do now, as I thee say,
    In the name of the holy ghost.

NOAH.   Ah! Benedicite! What art thou thus,
That tells before what shall be? Thou art full marvellous!
Tell me for charity thy name so gracious.   165
GOD.   My name is of dignity and also full glorious
    To know.
I am God most mighty,
One God in trinity,
Made thee and each man to be;   170
    Love to me thou should show.

NOAH.   I thank thee, Lord, so dear, that would vouchsafe
Thus low to appear to a simple knave;
Bless us, Lord, here for charity I it crave,
The better may we steer the ship that we have,   175
    Certain.
GOD.   Noah, to thee and to thy fry
My blessing grant I;
Ye shall work and multiply,
    And fill the earth again,   180
When all these floods are past and fully gone away.
NOAH.   Lord, homeward will I fast in haste as that I may;

(*Exit* GOD.)

My wife will I ask what she will say,
And I am all aghast lest there be some fray
    Between us both;   185
For she is full tetchy,
For little oft angry,
If anything wrong be,
    Soon is she wroth.

(*He goes to his wife.*)

God speed thee, wife, how fare ye?   190
WIFE.   Now, as ever might I thrive, the worse to see thee;
Tell me, on your life, where thus long could thou be?
To death may we drive, because of thee,
    Alack.

When work weary we sink,   195
Thou dost what thou think,
Yet of meat and drink
    Have we great lack.

NOAH.   Wife, we are hard pressed with tidings new.
WIFE.   But thou ought to be dressed in stafford blue;   200
For thou art always depressed, be it false or true;
God knows I am oppressed, and that may I rue,
    Full ill;
All I hear is thy crow,
From even till morrow,   205
Screeching ever of sorrow;
    God send thee once thy fill.

We women may harry all ill husbands;
I have one, by Mary! That loosed me of my bands;
If he twits I must tarry, however so it stands,   210
And seem to be full sorry, wringing both my hands
    For dread.
But in a little while,
What with game and guile,
I shall smite and smile   215
    And pay him back instead.

NOAH.   Hush! Hold thy tongue, ramshit, or I shall thee still.
WIFE.   As I thrive, if thou smite, I shall pay back with skill.
NOAH.   We shall see who is right, have at thee, Gill!
Upon the bone shall it bite!
WIFE.   Ah, by Mary! Thou smitest ill!   220
    But I suppose
I shall not in thy debt
Leave this place yet!
This strap is what you get
    To tie up thy hose!   225

NOAH.   Ah! Wilt thou so? Mary, that is mine.
WIFE.   Have thou three for two, I swear, by God divine,
NOAH.   I shall requite each blow, your skin will bear my sign.
WIFE.   Out upon thee, ho!
              Thou can both bite and whine
For all thou art worth.   230
For though she will strike,
Her shrieks my ears spike,
There is not her like
    On all this earth.

WIFE.   But I will keep charity in this to-do   235
    Here shall no man tarry thee; I pray thee go to!
    Full well may we miss thee, as peace is our due;
    To spin will I address me.
NOAH.   Farewell, then, to you;
      But wife,
    Pray for me busily,   240
    Till again I come to thee.
WIFE.   Even as thou prayst for me,
      As ever might I thrive.

NOAH.   I tarry full long, to my work I must go;
    My gear take along and watch the work grow;   245
    I may go all wrong, in truth, I it know;
    If God's help is not strong I may sit in sorrow,
      I ken;
    Now assay will I
    Something of carpentry,   250
    In nomine patris, et filii,
      Et spiritus sancti, Amen.

To begin with this tree, my bones will I bend,
I trust that the trinity succour will send;
The work prospers fairly to a fitting end;   255
Now blessed be he that this did commend.
    Lo, here the length,
Three hundred cubits evenly,
Of breadth lo is it fifty,
The height is even thirty   260
    Cubits full strength.

Now my gown will I cast and work in my coat,
Make will I the mast to set in the boat,
Ah! My back breaks fast! This is a sorry note!
It is wonder that I last, so weak that I dote,   265
    Behold,
To begin this affair!
My bones are so bare,
No wonder they despair,
    For I am full old.   270

The top and the sail both will I make,
The helm and the castle also will I take,
To drive in each a nail without a mistake,
This way will never fail, that dare I undertake
    Right soon.   275
This was a noble plan,

These nails so swiftly ran
Through more or less the span
    Of these boards each one.

Window and door even as he said   280
Three cabins more, they are well made,
Pitch and tar full sure upon them have been laid,
This will ever endure, I count myself well paid;
    And why?
It is better wrought   285
Than I could have thought;
Him, that made all of nought,
    I thank only.

Now will I hie me despite the ill weather
My wife and my family, to bring even hither.   290
Listen here carefully, wife, and consider,
Hence must we flee all together
    Right fast.
WIFE.   Why, sir, what ails you?
Who is it assails you?   295
To flee it avails you,
    Yet ye be aghast.

NOAH.   The yarn on the reel is otherwise, dame.
WIFE.   Tell me more and less, else ye be to blame.
NOAH.   He can cure our distress, blessed be his name.   300
Our dole he will redress to shield us from shame
    And said,
All this world about
With fierce floods so stout,
That shall run in a rout,   305
    Shall be overspread.

He said all shall be slain save only we,
Our bairns shall remain and their wives three;
A ship he bad me ordain to save our company,
Therefore with all our main that Lord thank we,   310
    Saviour of our blood;
Get along fast, go thither.
WIFE.   I know not whither,
I daze and I dither,
For fear of that flood.   315

NOAH.   Be not afraid, have done, truss up our gear,
Lest we be undone, without more fear.
1ST SON.   Full soon it shall be done, brothers help me here.

2ND SON.   My part I shall not shun, no matter how severe,
    My brother.   320
3RD SON.   Without any yelp
  With my might shall I help.
WIFE.   I've a blow for each whelp,
  If you help not your mother.

NOAH.   Now are we there, as we should be;   325
  Go, get in our gear, cattle and company,
  Into this vessel here, my children free.
WIFE.   Shut up was I never, so God save me,
  In such an oyster as this.
  In faith I cannot find   330
  Which is before, which is behind;
  Shall we here be confined,
    Noah, as have thou bliss?

NOAH.   Dame, peace and still, we must abide grace;
  Therefore, wife, with good will, come into this place.   335
WIFE.   Sir, for Jack nor for Gill, will I turn my face,
  Till I have on this hill, spun a space
    On my distaff;
  Woe to him who moves me,
  Now will I down set me,   340
  And let no man prevent me,
    For him will I strafe.

NOAH.   Behold in the heaven, the cataracts all
  That are open full even, both great and small
  And the planets seven, left have their stall,   345
  The thunder downdriven, and lightnings now fall
    Full stout,
  On halls and bowers,
  Castles and towers;
  Full sharp are these showers,   350
    That deluge about.

Therefore, wife have done, come in the ship fast.
WIFE.   Patch your shoes and run, the better they will last.
1ST WIFE.   Come, good mother, come, for all is overcast,
  Both the moon and the sun.
2ND WIFE.   And many winds blast   355
    Full sharp;
  These floods may drown our kin,
  Therefore, mother, come in.
WIFE.   In faith, still will I spin;
  All in vain ye carp.   360

3RD WIFE.   If ye like, ye may spin, mother, in the ship.
NOAH.   Ye be twice bidden in, dame, in all friendship.
WIFE.   Whether I lose or I win, in faith, thy fellowship,
 Set I not at a pin, this spindle will I slip
  Upon this hill.   365
 Ere one foot I stir.
NOAH.   By Peter, but ye err;
 Without further spur
  Come in if ye will.
WIFE.   Yea, the water nighs so near that I sit not dry, 370
 Into the ship for fear quickly will I hie
 For dread that I drown here.
NOAH.   Dame, but surely,
 Paid ye have full dear, ye stayed so long by,
  Out of the ship.
WIFE.   I will not at thy bidding,   375
 Go from door to dunghill gadding.
NOAH.   In faith and for your long tarrying,
 Ye shall taste of the whip.
WIFE.   Spare me not, I pray thee, do even as thou think,
 These great words shall not flay me.
NOAH.   Abide dame and drink, 380
 For beaten shalt thou be with this staff till thou stink;
 Are these strokes good, say ye.
WIFE.   What say ye? Go sink!
NOAH.   Now quake!
 Cry me mercy, I say!
WIFE.   To that say I nay.   385
NOAH.   If not, by this day,
 Thy head shall I break.

WIFE.   Lord, I were at ease and heartily hale
 With a pottage of pease and my widow's kale;
 For thy soul it would please me to pay penny bail, 390
 So would more than these I see in this dale,
  Of the wives that here stir,
 For the dance they are led,
 Wish their husbands were dead,
 For, as ever eat I bread,   395
  So, would I our sire were.

NOAH.   Ye men that have wives, while they are young,
 If ye love your lives, chastise their tongue:
 Methinks my heart rives, both liver and lung,
 To see such a strife, wedded men among;   400
  But I,

As have I bliss,
Shall chastise this.
WIFE.   Yet may ye miss,
     Nichol needy!   405

NOAH.   I shall make thee still as stone, beginner of blunder!
     I shall beat thee, back and bone, and break all in sunder.

(They fight.)

WIFE.   Out, alas, I am overthrown! Out upon thee, man's wonder!
NOAH.   See how she can groan, and I lie under;
     But wife,   410
Haste we, without ado,
For my back is near in two.
WIFE.   And I am beaten so blue
     And wish for no more strife.

(They enter the Ark.)

1ST SON.   Ah! Why fare ye thus? father and mother, both!   415
2ND SON.   Your spite would scarce free us from such sin as wroth.
3RD SON.   These scenes are so hideous, I swear on my oath.
NOAH.   We will do as ye bid us, and that with no sloth.
     Sons dear!
At the helm now I am bent   420
To steer the ship as is meant.
WIFE.   I see in the firmament
     The seven stars here.

NOAH.   This is a great flood, wife, take heed.
WIFE.   So methought as I stood we are in great need;   425
That these waves be withstood.
NOAH.   Now God help us, we plead!
As thou art helmsman good, and best may succeed
     Of all;
Rule us in this race,
Thy word we embrace.   430
WIFE.   This is a parlous case:
     Help God, when we call.

NOAH.   To the tiller, wife, see, and I shall assay
The deepness of the sea where we sail, if I may.
WIFE.   That shall I do full wisely, now go thy way,   435
For upon this flood have we fared many a day,
     In pain.

(NOAH lowers a plummet.)

NOAH.   Now the water will I sound:
     Ah! It is far to the ground;
     This labour I have found   440
          Brings little gain.

     Above the hills is seen the water risen of late
     Of cubits full fifteen, but in no higher state
     These waves of water green will spill with former spate,
     Rain forty days has been, it will therefore abate   445
          Its zeal.

(NOAH *again lowers the plummet.*)

     Again it is best,
     The water to test;
     Now I am impressed,
          It has waned a great deal.   450

     Now have the storms ceased and cataracts quit,
     Both the most and the least.
WIFE.   Methinks, by my wit,
     The sun shines in the east, lo, is not yond it?
     We should have a good feast when these floods flit
          So stormy.   455
NOAH.   We have been here, all we,
     Three hundred days and fifty.
WIFE.   Yea, look, now wanes the sea;
          Lord, well are we.

NOAH.   The third time will I try in what depth we steer.   460
WIFE.   Too long will you ply, lay in thy line there.
NOAH.   With my hand touch I the ground even here.
WIFE.   Therefore be we spry and have merry cheer;
          But husband,
     What hills may there be?   465
NOAH.   Of Armenia's country.
WIFE.   Now blessed be he
          That brings us to land!

NOAH.   The tops of the hills I see, many at a sight,
     Nothing prevents me the sky is so bright.   470
WIFE.   Tokens of mercy these are full right.
NOAH.   Dame, now counsel me what bird best might
          Go forth,
     With flight of wing
     And bring without tarrying   475

Of mercy some tokening
    Either by south or north?

For this is the first day of the tenth moon.
WIFE.   The raven durst I lay will come again soon;
As fast as thou may, cast him forth, have done,   480
He may come back today and dispel before noon
    Our dismay.
NOAH.   I will loose to the blue
Sky, doves one or two:
Go your way, do,   485
    God send you some prey.

Now have these fowl flown to separate countries;
Let our prayers be known, kneeling on our knees,
To him that is alone worthiest of dignities,
That he may not postpone their coming back to please   490
    Us with a sign.
WIFE.   Land they should be gaining,
The water so is waning.
NOAH.   Thank we that God reigning,
    That made both me and mine.   495

It is a wondrous thing most certainly,
They are so long tarrying, the fowls that we
Cast out in the morning.
WIFE.   Sir, it may be
They bide something to bring.
NOAH.   The raven is hungry
    Alway;   500
He is without any reason,
If he find any carrion,
No matter the season,
    He will not away.

The dove is more gentle, to her trust is due,   505
Like to the turtle to death she is true.
WIFE.   Hence but a little she comes now, look you!
She brings in her bill some tidings new.
    Behold!
It is of an olive tree   510
A branch, it seems to me.
NOAH.   Yea sooth, verily,
    Right so is it called.

Dove, bird full blest, fair might thee befall,
Thou art true to thy quest, as stone in the wall;   515
Thou wert trusted as best to return to thy hall.

WIFE.   A true token to attest we shall be saved all:
          For why?
     The depth, since she has come,
     Of the water by that plumb,   520
     Hast fallen a fathom
          And more, say I.

1ST SON.   These floods are gone, father, behold.
2ND SON.   There is left right none, and that be ye bold.
3RD SON.   As still as a stone, our ship has firm hold,   525
NOAH.   On land here has run; God's grace is untold;
          My children dear,
     Shem, Japhet, and Ham,
     With glee and with game,
     Go we in God's name,   530
          No longer abide here.

WIFE.   Here have we been, Noah, long enough, now,
     With grief as is seen and full furrowed brow.
NOAH.   Behold on this green, neither cart nor plough
     Is left on the scene, neither tree nor bough,   535
          Nor other thing,
     But all is away:
     Many castles, I say
     Great towns of array,   540
          Flit in this flooding.

WIFE.   These floods put in fright all this world so wide,
     Which moved with great might the sea and the tide.
NOAH.   But death was the plight of the proudest in pride,
     Each person in sight that ever was spied,
          With sin,   545
     All are they slain,
     And put to great pain.
WIFE.   From thence again
     May they never win.

NOAH.   Win? No, indeed, save God turn his face,   550
     Forgive their misdeed, and admit them to grace;
     As he may hardship heed, I pray him in this space,
     In heaven to hear our need, and put us in a place,
          That we,
     With his saints in sight,   555
     And his angels bright,
     May come to his light:
          Amen for charity.

NO EXIT

Jean-Paul Sartre

(1905–1980)

Biography p. 1097

CHARACTERS

VALET
GARCIN
ESTELLE
INEZ

Huis Clos (No Exit) was presented for the first time at the Théâtre du Vieux-Colombier, Paris, in May 1944.

SCENE: *A drawing-room in Second Empire style. A massive bronze ornament stands on the mantelpiece.*

GARCIN *(enters, accompanied by the* ROOM-VALET, *and glances around him).* Hm! So here we are?

VALET.   Yes, Mr. Garcin.

GARCIN.   And this is what it looks like?

VALET.   Yes.

GARCIN.   Second Empire furniture, I observe. . . . Well, well, I dare say one gets used to it in time.

VALET.   Some do. Some don't.

GARCIN.   Are all the other rooms like this one?

VALET.   How could they be? We cater for all sorts: Chinamen and Indians, for instance. What use would they have for a Second Empire chair?

GARCIN.   And what use do you suppose *I* have for one? Do you know who I was? . . . Oh, well, it's no great matter. And, to tell the truth, I had quite a habit of living among furniture that I didn't relish, and in false positions. I'd even come to like it. A false position in a Louis-Philippe dining-room—you know the style?—well, that had its points, you know. Bogus in bogus, so to speak.

VALET.   And you'll find that living in a Second Empire drawing-room has its points.

GARCIN.   Really? . . . Yes, yes, I dare say. . . . *(He takes another look around.)* Still, I certainly didn't expect—this! You know what they tell us down there?

VALET.   What about?

GARCIN.   About *(makes a sweeping gesture)* this—er—residence.

VALET.   Really, sir, how could you believe such cock-and-bull stories? Told by people who'd never set foot here. For, of course, if they had—

GARCIN.   Quite so. *(Both laugh. Abruptly the laugh dies from* GARCIN's *face.)* But, I say, where are the instruments of torture?

VALET.   The what?

GARCIN.   The racks and red-hot pincers and all the other paraphernalia?

VALET.   Ah, you must have your little joke, sir!

GARCIN.   My little joke? Oh, I see. No, I wasn't joking. *(A short silence. He strolls around the room.)* No mirrors, I notice. No windows. Only to be expected. And nothing breakable. *(Bursts out angrily.)* But, damn it all, they might have left me my toothbrush!

VALET.   That's good! So you haven't yet got over your—what-do-you-call-it?—sense of human dignity? Excuse me smiling.

GARCIN *(thumping ragefully the arm of an armchair).*   I'll ask you to be more polite. I quite realize the position I'm in, but I won't tolerate . . .

VALET.   Sorry, sir. No offense meant. But all our guests ask me the same questions. Silly questions, if you'll pardon me saying so. Where's the torture-chamber? That's the first thing they ask, all of them. They don't bother their heads about the bathroom requisites, that I can assure you. But after a bit, when they've got their nerve back, they start in about their toothbrushes and what-not. Good heavens, Mr. Garcin, can't you use your brains? What, I ask you, would be the point of brushing your teeth?

GARCIN *(more calmly).*   Yes, of course you're right. *(He looks around again.)* And why should one want to see oneself in a looking-glass? But that bronze contraption on the mantelpiece, that's another story. I suppose there will be times when I stare my eyes out at it. Stare my eyes out—see what I mean? . . . All right, let's put our cards on the table. I assure you I'm quite conscious of my position. Shall I tell you what it feels like? A man's drowning, choking, sinking by inches, till only his eyes are just above water. And what does he see? A bronze atrocity by—what's the fellow's name?—Barbedienne. A collector's piece. As in a nightmare. That's their idea, isn't it? . . . No, I suppose you're under orders not to answer questions; and I won't insist. But don't forget, my man, I've a good notion of what's coming to me, so don't you boast you've caught me off my guard. I'm facing the situation, facing it. *(He starts pacing the room again.)* So that's that; no toothbrush. And no bed, either. One never sleeps, I take it?

VALET.   That's so.

GARCIN.   Just as I expected. *Why* should one sleep? A sort of drowsiness steals on you, tickles you behind the ears, and you feel your eyes closing—but why sleep? You lie down on the sofa and—in a flash, sleep flies away. Miles and miles away. So you rub your eyes, get up, and it starts all over again.

VALET.   Romantic, that's what you are.

GARCIN.   Will you keep quiet, please! . . . I won't make a scene, I shan't be sorry for myself, I'll face the situation, as I said just now. Face it fairly and squarely. I won't have it springing at me from behind, before I've time to size it up. And you call that being "romantic"! . . . So it comes to this; one doesn't need rest. Why bother about sleep if one isn't sleepy? That stands to reason, doesn't it?

Wait a minute, there's a snag somewhere; something disagreeable. Why, now, should it be disagreeable? . . . Ah, I see; it's life without a break.

VALET.   What do you mean by that?

GARCIN.   What do I mean? *(Eyes the* VALET *suspiciously.)* I thought as much. That's why there's something so beastly, so damn bad-mannered, in the way you stare at me. They're paralyzed.

VALET.   What are you talking about?

GARCIN.   Your eyelids. We move ours up and down. Blinking, we call it. It's like a small black shutter that clicks down and makes a break. Everything goes black; one's eyes are moistened. You can't imagine how restful, refreshing, it is. Four thousand little rests per hour. Four thousand little respites—just think! . . . So that's the idea. I'm to live without eyelids. Don't act the fool, you know what I mean. No eyelids, no sleep; it follows, doesn't it? I shall never sleep again. But then—how shall I endure my own company? Try to understand. You see, I'm fond of teasing, it's a second nature with me—and I'm used to teasing myself. Plaguing myself, if you prefer; I don't tease nicely. But I can't go on doing that without a break. Down there I had my nights. I slept. I always had good nights. By way of compensation, I suppose. And happy little dreams. There was a green field. Just an ordinary field. I used to stroll in it. . . . Is it daytime now?

VALET.   Can't you see? The lights are on.

GARCIN.   Ah yes, I've got it. It's *your* daytime. And outside?

VALET.   Outside?

GARCIN.   Damn it, you know what I mean. Beyond that wall.

VALET.   There's a passage.

GARCIN.   And at the end of the passage?

VALET.   There's more rooms, more passages, and stairs.

GARCIN.   And what lies beyond them?

VALET.   That's all.

GARCIN.   But surely you have a day off sometimes. Where do you go?

VALET.   To my uncle's place. He's the head valet here. He has a room on the third floor.

GARCIN.   I should have guessed as much. Where's the light-switch?

VALET.   There isn't any.

GARCIN.   What? Can't one turn off the light?

VALET.   Oh, the management can cut off the current if they want to. But I can't remember their having done so on this floor. We have all the electricity we want.

GARCIN.   So one has to live with one's eyes open all the time?

VALET.   To *live,* did you say?

GARCIN.   Don't let's quibble over words. With one's eyes open. Forever. Always broad daylight in my eyes—and in my head. *(Short silence.)* And suppose I took that contraption on the mantelpiece and dropped it on the lamp—wouldn't it go out?

VALET.   You can't move it. It's too heavy.

GARCIN *(seizing the bronze ornament and trying to lift it).*   You're right. It's too heavy.

(A short silence follows.)

VALET. Very well, sir, if you don't need me any more, I'll be off.

GARCIN. What? You're going? *(The* VALET *goes up to the door.)* Wait. *(*VALET *looks round.)* That's a bell, isn't it? *(*VALET *nods.)* And if I ring, you're bound to come?

VALET. Well, yes, that's so—in a way. But you can never be sure about that bell. There's something wrong with the wiring, and it doesn't always work. *(*GARCIN *goes to the bell-push and presses the button. A bell purrs outside.)*

GARCIN. It's working all right.

VALET *(looking surprised).* So it is. *(He, too, presses the button.)* But I shouldn't count on it too much if I were you. It's—capricious. Well, I really must go now. *(*GARCIN *makes a gesture to detain him.)* Yes, sir?

GARCIN. No, never mind. *(He goes to the mantelpiece and picks up a paper-knife.)* What's this?

VALET. Can't you see? An ordinary paper-knife.

GARCIN. Are there books here?

VALET. No.

GARCIN. Then what's the use of this? *(*VALET *shrugs his shoulders.)* Very well. You can go. *(*VALET *goes out.)*

*(*GARCIN *is by himself. He goes to the bronze ornament and strokes it reflectively. He sits down; then gets up, goes to the bell-push, and presses the button. The bell remains silent. He tries two or three times, without success. Then he tries to open the door, also without success. He calls the* VALET *several times, but gets no result. He beats the door with his fists, still calling. Suddenly he grows calm and sits down again. At the same moment the door opens and* INEZ *enters, followed by the* VALET.*)*

VALET. Did you call, sir?

GARCIN *(on the point of answering "Yes"—but then his eyes fall on* INEZ*).* No.

VALET *(turning to* INEZ*).* This is your room, madam. *(*INEZ *says nothing.)* If there's any information you require—? *(*INEZ *still keeps silent, and the* VALET *looks slightly huffed.)* Most of our guests have quite a lot to ask me. But I won't insist. Anyhow, as regards the toothbrush, and the electric bell, and that thing on the mantelshelf, this gentleman can tell you anything you want to know as well as I could. We've had a little chat, him and me. *(*VALET *goes out.)* *(*GARCIN *refrains from looking at* INEZ, *who is inspecting the room. Abruptly she turns to* GARCIN.*)*

INEZ. Where's Florence? *(*GARCIN *does not reply.)* Didn't you hear? I asked you about Florence. Where is she?

GARCIN. I haven't an idea.

INEZ. Ah, that's the way it works, is it? Torture by separation. Well, as far as I'm concerned, you won't get anywhere. Florence was a tiresome little fool, and I shan't miss her in the least.

GARCIN. I beg your pardon. Who do you suppose I am?

INEZ. You? Why, the torturer, of course.

GARCIN *(looks startled, then bursts out laughing).* Well, that's a good one! Too comic for words. I the torturer! So you came in, had a look at me, and thought

I was—er—one of the staff. Of course, it's that silly fellow's fault; he should have introduced us. A torturer indeed! I'm Joseph Garcin, journalist and man of letters by profession. And as we're both in the same boat, so to speak, might I ask you, Mrs.—?

INEZ *(testily).* Not "Mrs." I'm unmarried.

GARCIN. Right. That's a start, anyway. Well, now that we've broken the ice, do you *really* think I look like a torturer? And, by the way, how does one recognize torturers when one sees them? Evidently you've ideas on the subject.

INEZ. They look frightened.

GARCIN. Frightened! But how ridiculous! Of whom should they be frightened? Of their victims?

INEZ. Laugh away, but I know what I'm talking about. I've often watched my face in the glass.

GARCIN. In the glass? *(He looks around him.)* How beastly of them! They've removed everything in the least resembling a glass. *(Short silence.)* Anyhow, I can assure you I'm not frightened. Not that I take my position lightly; I realize its gravity only too well. But I'm not afraid.

INEZ *(shrugging her shoulders).* That's your affair. *(Silence.)* Must you be here all the time, or do you take a stroll outside, now and then?

GARCIN. The door's locked.

INEZ. Oh! . . . That's too bad.

GARCIN. I can quite understand that it bores you having me here. And I, too— well, quite frankly, I'd rather be alone. I want to think things out, you know; to set my life in order, and one does that better by oneself. But I'm sure we'll manage to pull along together somehow. I'm no talker, I don't move much; in fact I'm a peaceful sort of fellow. Only, if I may venture on a suggestion, we should make a point of being extremely courteous to each other. That will ease the situation for us both.

INEZ. I'm not polite.

GARCIN. Then I must be polite for two.

(A longish silence. GARCIN *is sitting on a sofa, while* INEZ *paces up and down the room.)*

INEZ *(fixing her eyes on him).* Your mouth!

GARCIN *(as if waking from a dream).* I beg your pardon.

INEZ. Can't you keep your mouth still? You keep twisting it about all the time. It's grotesque.

GARCIN. So sorry. I wasn't aware of it.

INEZ. That's just what I reproach you with. *(*GARCIN*'s mouth twitches.)* There you are! You talk about politeness, and you don't even try to control your face. Remember you're not alone; you've no right to inflict the sight of your fear on me.

GARCIN *(getting up and going towards her).* How about you? Aren't you afraid?

INEZ. What would be the use? There was some point in being afraid *before;* while one still had hope.

GARCIN *(in a low voice).* There's no more hope—but it's still "before." We haven't yet begun to suffer.

INEZ.   That's so. *(A short silence.)* Well? What's going to happen?

GARCIN.   I don't know. I'm waiting.

(Silence again. GARCIN *sits down and* INEZ *resumes her pacing up and down the room.* GARCIN's *mouth twitches; after a glance at* INEZ *he buries his face in his hands. Enter* ESTELLE *with the* VALET. ESTELLE *looks at* GARCIN, *whose face is still hidden by his hands.)*

ESTELLE *(to* GARCIN*).*   No! Don't look up. I know what you're hiding with your hands. I know you've no face left. *(*GARCIN *removes his hands.)* What! *(A short pause. Then, in a tone of surprise)* But I don't know you!

GARCIN.   I'm not the torturer, madam.

ESTELLE.   I never thought you were. I—I thought someone was trying to play a rather nasty trick on me. *(To the* VALET*)* Is anyone else coming?

VALET.   No, madam. No one else is coming.

ESTELLE.   Oh! Then we're to stay by ourselves, the three of us, this gentleman, this lady, and myself. *(She starts laughing.)*

GARCIN *(angrily).*   There's nothing to laugh about.

ESTELLE *(still laughing).*   It's those sofas. They're so hideous. And just look how they've been arranged. It makes me think of New Year's Day—when I used to visit that boring old aunt of mine, Aunt Mary. Her house is full of horrors like that. . . . I suppose each of us has a sofa of his own. Is that one mine? *(To the* VALET*)* But you can't expect me to sit on that one. It would be too horrible for words. I'm in pale blue and it's vivid green.

INEZ.   Would you prefer mine?

ESTELLE.   That claret-colored one, you mean? That's very sweet of you, but really —no, I don't think it'd be so much better. What's the good of worrying, anyhow? We've got to take what comes to us, and I'll stick to the green one. *(Pauses.)* The only one which might do, at a pinch, is that gentleman's. *(Another pause.)*

INEZ.   Did you hear, Mr. Garcin?

GARCIN *(with a slight start).*   Oh—the sofa, you mean. So sorry. *(He rises.)* Please take it, madam.

ESTELLE.   Thanks. *(She takes off her coat and drops it on the sofa. A short silence.)* Well, as we're to live together, I suppose we'd better introduce ourselves. My name's Rigault. Estelle Rigault. *(*GARCIN *bows and is going to announce his name, but* INEZ *steps in front of him.)*

INEZ.   And I'm Inez Serrano. Very pleased to meet you.

GARCIN *(bowing again).*   Joseph Garcin.

VALET.   Do you require me any longer?

ESTELLE.   No, you can go. I'll ring when I want you. *(Exit* VALET, *with polite bows to everyone.)*

INEZ.   You're very pretty. I wish we'd had some flowers to welcome you with.

ESTELLE.   Flowers? Yes, I loved flowers. Only they'd fade so quickly here, wouldn't they? It's so stuffy. Oh, well, the great thing is to keep as cheerful as we can, don't you agree? Of course, you, too, are—

INEZ.   Yes. Last week. What about you?

ESTELLE.   I'm—quite recent. Yesterday. As a matter of fact, the ceremony's not quite over. *(Her tone is natural enough, but she seems to be seeing what she describes.)* The wind's blowing my sister's veil all over the place. She's trying her best to cry. Come, dear! Make another effort. That's better. Two tears, two little tears are twinkling under the black veil. Oh dear! What a sight Olga looks this morning! She's holding my sister's arm, helping her along. She's not crying, and I don't blame her; tears always mess one's face up, don't they? Olga was my bosom friend, you know.

INEZ.   Did you suffer much?

ESTELLE.   No. I was only half conscious, mostly.

INEZ.   What was it?

ESTELLE.   Pneumonia. *(In the same tone as before)* It's over now, they're leaving the cemetery. Good-by. Good-by. Quite a crowd they are. My husband's stayed at home. Prostrated with grief, poor man. *(To* INEZ*)* How about you?

INEZ.   The gas stove.

ESTELLE.   And you, Mr. Garcin?

GARCIN.   Twelve bullets through my chest. *(*ESTELLE *makes a horrified gesture.)* Sorry! I fear I'm not good company among the dead.

ESTELLE.   Please, please don't use that word. It's so—so crude. In terribly bad taste, really. It doesn't mean much, anyhow. Somehow I feel we've never been so much alive as now. If we've absolutely got to mention this—this state of things, I suggest we call ourselves—wait!—absentees. Have you been—been absent for long?

GARCIN.   About a month.

ESTELLE.   Where do you come from?

GARCIN.   From Rio.

ESTELLE.   I'm from Paris. Have you anyone left down there?

GARCIN.   Yes, my wife. *(In the same tone as* ESTELLE *has been using)* She's waiting at the entrance of the barracks. She comes there every day. But they won't let her in. Now she's trying to peep between the bars. She doesn't yet know I'm—absent, but she suspects it. Now she's going away. She's wearing her black dress. So much the better, she won't need to change. She isn't crying, but she never did cry, anyhow. It's a bright sunny day and she's like a black shadow creeping down the empty street. Those big tragic eyes of hers—with that martyred look they always had. Oh, how she got on my nerves!

(A short silence. GARCIN *sits on the central sofa and buries his head in his hands.)*

INEZ.   Estelle!

ESTELLE.   Please, Mr. Garcin!

GARCIN.   What is it?

ESTELLE.   You're sitting on my sofa.

GARCIN.   I beg your pardon. *(He gets up.)*

ESTELLE.   You looked so—so far away. Sorry I disturbed you.

GARCIN.   I was setting my life in order. *(*INEZ *starts laughing.)* You may laugh, but you'd do better to follow my example.

INEZ.   No need. My life's in perfect order. It tidied itself up nicely of its own accord. So I needn't bother about it now.

GARCIN.   Really? You imagine it's so simple as that. *(He runs his hand over his forehead.)* Whew! How hot it is here! Do you mind if—? *(He begins taking off his coat.)*

ESTELLE.   How dare you! *(More gently)* No, please don't. I loathe men in their shirt-sleeves.

GARCIN *(putting on his coat again).*   All right. *(A short pause.)* Of course, I used to spend my nights in the newspaper office, and it was a regular Black Hole, so we never kept our coats on. Stiflingly hot it could be. *(Short pause. In the same tone as previously)* Stifling, that it *is.* It's night now.

ESTELLE.   That's so. Olga's undressing; it must be after midnight. How quickly the time passes, on earth!

INEZ.   Yes, after midnight. They've sealed up my room. It's dark, pitch-dark, and empty.

GARCIN.   They've slung their coats on the backs of the chairs and rolled up their shirt-sleeves above the elbow. The air stinks of men and cigar-smoke. *(A short silence.)* I used to like living among men in their shirt-sleeves.

ESTELLE *(aggressively).*   Well, in that case our tastes differ. That's all it proves. *(Turning to* INEZ*)* What about you? Do you like men in their shirt-sleeves?

INEZ.   Oh, I don't care much for men any way.

ESTELLE *(looking at the other two with a puzzled air).*   Really I can't imagine why they put us three together. It doesn't make sense.

INEZ *(stifling a laugh).*   What's that you said?

ESTELLE.   I'm looking at you two and thinking that we're going to live together . . . . It's so absurd. I expected to meet old friends, or relatives.

INEZ.   Yes, a charming old friend—with a hole in the middle of his face.

ESTELLE.   Yes, him too. He danced the tango so divinely. Like a professional. . . . But why, why should we of all people be put together?

GARCIN.   A pure fluke, I should say. They lodge folks as they can, in the order of their coming. *(To* INEZ*)* Why are you laughing?

INEZ.   Because you amuse me, with your "flukes." As if they left anything to chance! But I suppose you've got to reassure yourself somehow.

ESTELLE *(hesitantly).*   I wonder, now. Don't you think we may have met each other at some time in our lives?

INEZ.   Never. I shouldn't have forgotten you.

ESTELLE.   Or perhaps we have friends in common. I wonder if you know the Dubois-Seymours?

INEZ.   Not likely.

ESTELLE.   But *everyone* went to their parties.

INEZ.   What's their job?

ESTELLE.   Oh, they don't do anything. But they have a lovely house in the country, and hosts of people visit them.

INEZ.   I didn't. I was a post-office clerk.

ESTELLE *(recoiling a little).*   Ah, yes. . . . Of course, in that case—*(A pause.)* And you, Mr. Garcin?

GARCIN.   We've never met. I always lived in Rio.

ESTELLE.   Then you must be right. It's mere chance that has brought us together.

INEZ.   Mere chance? Then it's by chance this room is furnished as we see it. It's an accident that the sofa on the right is a livid green, and that one on the left's wine-red. Mere chance? Well, just try to shift the sofas and you'll see the difference quick enough. And that statue on the mantelpiece, do you think it's there by accident? And what about the heat here? How about that? *(A short silence.)* I tell you they've thought it all out. Down to the last detail. Nothing was left to chance. This room was all set for us.

ESTELLE.   But really! Everything here's so hideous; all in angles, so uncomfortable. I always loathed angles.

INEZ *(shrugging her shoulders).*   And do you think *I* lived in a Second Empire drawing-room?

ESTELLE.   So it was all fixed up beforehand?

INEZ.   Yes. And they've put us together deliberately.

ESTELLE.   Then it's not mere chance that *you* precisely are sitting opposite *me?* But what can be the idea behind it?

INEZ.   Ask me another! I only know they're waiting.

ESTELLE.   I never could bear the idea of anyone's expecting something from me. It always made me want to do just the opposite.

INEZ.   Well, do it. Do it if you can. You don't even know what they expect.

ESTELLE *(stamping her foot).*   It's outrageous! So something's coming to me from you two? *(She eyes each in turn.)* Something nasty, I suppose. There are some faces that tell me everything at once. Yours don't convey anything.

GARCIN *(turning abruptly towards* INEZ*).*   Look here! Why are we together? You've given us quite enough hints, you may as well come out with it.

INEZ *(in a surprised tone).*   But I know nothing, absolutely nothing about it. I'm as much in the dark as you are.

GARCIN.   We've *got* to know. *(Ponders for a while.)*

INEZ.   If only each of us had the guts to tell—

GARCIN.   Tell what?

INEZ.   Estelle!

ESTELLE.   Yes?

INEZ.   What have you done? I mean, why have they sent you here?

ESTELLE *(quickly).*   That's just it. I haven't a notion, not the foggiest. In fact, I'm wondering if there hasn't been some ghastly mistake. *(To* INEZ*)* Don't smile. Just think of the number of people who—who become absentees every day. There must be thousands and thousands, and probably they're sorted out by —by understrappers, you know what I mean. Stupid employees who don't know their job. So they're bound to make mistakes sometimes. . . . Do stop smiling. *(To* GARCIN*)* Why don't you speak? If they made a mistake in my case, they may have done the same about you. *(To* INEZ*)* And you, too. Anyhow, isn't it better to think we've got here by mistake?

INEZ.   Is that all you have to tell us?

ESTELLE.   What else should I tell? I've nothing to hide. I lost my parents when I was a kid, and I had my young brother to bring up. We were terribly poor and when an old friend of my people asked me to marry him I said yes. He was very well off, and quite nice. My brother was a very delicate child and needed all sorts of attention, so really that was the right thing for me to do, don't you agree? My husband was old enough to be my father, but for six years we had a happy married life. Then two years ago I met the man I was fated to love. We knew it the moment we set eyes on each other. He asked me to run away with him, and I refused. Then I got pneumonia and it finished me. That's the whole story. No doubt, by certain standards, I did wrong to sacrifice my youth to a man nearly three times my age. *(To* GARCIN*)* Do *you* think that could be called a sin?

GARCIN.   Certainly not. *(A short silence.)* And now, tell me, do you think it's a crime to stand by one's principles?

ESTELLE.   Of course not. Surely no one could blame a man for that!

GARCIN.   Wait a bit! I ran a pacifist newspaper. Then war broke out. What was I to do? Everyone was watching me, wondering: "Will he dare?" Well, I dared. I folded my arms and they shot me. Had I done anything wrong?

ESTELLE *(laying her hand on his arm).*   Wrong? On the contrary. You were—

INEZ *(breaks in ironically).*   —a hero! And how about your wife, Mr. Garcin?

GARCIN.   That's simple. I'd rescued her from—from the gutter.

ESTELLE *(to* INEZ*).*   You see! You see!

INEZ.   Yes, I see. *(A pause.)* Look here! What's the point of play-acting, trying to throw dust in each other's eyes? We're all tarred with the same brush.

ESTELLE *(indignantly).*   How dare you!

INEZ.   Yes, we are criminals—murderers—all three of us. We're in hell, my pets; they never make mistakes, and people aren't damned for nothing.

ESTELLE.   Stop! For heaven's sake—

INEZ.   In hell! Damned souls—that's us, all three!

ESTELLE.   Keep quiet! I forbid you to use such disgusting words.

INEZ.   A damned soul—that's you, my little plaster saint. And ditto our friend there, the noble pacifist. We've had our hour of pleasure, haven't we? There have been people who burned their lives out for our sakes—and we chuckled over it. So now we have to pay the reckoning.

GARCIN *(raising his fist).*   Will you keep your mouth shut, damn it!

INEZ *(confronting him fearlessly, but with a look of vast surprise).*   Well, well! *(A pause.)* Ah, I understand now. I know why they've put us three together.

GARCIN.   I advise you to—to think twice before you say any more.

INEZ.   Wait! You'll see how simple it is. Childishly simple. Obviously there aren't any physical torments—you agree, don't you? And yet we're in hell. And no one else will come here. We'll stay in this room together, the three of us, for ever and ever. . . . In short, there's someone absent here, the official torturer.

GARCIN *(sotto voce).*   I'd noticed that.

INEZ.   It's obvious what they're after—an economy of man-power—or devil-power, if you prefer. The same idea as in the cafeteria, where customers serve themselves.

ESTELLE.   What ever do you mean?

INEZ.   I mean that each of us will act as torturer of the two others.

(There is a short silence while they digest this information.)

GARCIN *(gently).*   No, I shall never be your torturer. I wish neither of you any harm, and I've no concern with you. None at all. So the solution's easy enough; each of us stays put in his or her corner and takes no notice of the others. You here, you here, and I there. Like soldiers at our posts. Also, we mustn't speak.

Not one word. That won't be difficult; each of us has plenty of material for self-communings. I think I could stay ten thousand years with only my thoughts for company.

ESTELLE. Have *I* got to keep silent, too?

GARCIN. Yes. And that way we—we'll work out our salvation. Looking into ourselves, never raising our heads. Agreed?

INEZ. Agreed.

ESTELLE *(after some hesitation).* I agree.

GARCIN. Then—good-by.

(He goes to his sofa and buries his head in his hands. There is a long silence; then INEZ *begins singing to herself.)*

INEZ *(singing).*

> What a crowd in Whitefriars Lane!
> They've set trestles in a row,
> With a scaffold and the knife,
> And a pail of bran below.
> Come, good folks, to Whitefriars Lane,
> Come to see the merry show!

> The headsman rose at crack of dawn,
> He'd a long day's work in hand,
> Chopping heads off generals,
> Priests and peers and admirals,
> All the highest in the land.
> What a crowd in Whitefriars Lane!

> See them standing in a line,
> Ladies all dressed up so fine.
> But their heads have got to go,
> Heads and hats roll down below.
> Come, good folks, to Whitefriars Lane,
> Come to see the merry show!

(Meanwhile ESTELLE *has been plying her powder-puff and lipstick. She looks round for a mirror, fumbles in her bag, then turns towards* GARCIN.*)*

ESTELLE. Excuse me, have you a glass? *(GARCIN does not answer.)* Any sort of glass, a pocket-mirror will do. *(GARCIN remains silent.)* Even if you won't speak to me, you might lend me a glass. *(His head still buried in his hands,* GARCIN *ignores her.)*

INEZ *(eagerly).* Don't worry. I've a glass in my bag. *(She opens her bag. Angrily)* It's gone! They must have taken it from me at the entrance.

ESTELLE. How tiresome!

(A short silence. ESTELLE *shuts her eyes and sways, as if about to faint.* INEZ *runs forward and holds her up.)*

INEZ.   What's the matter?

ESTELLE *(opens her eyes and smiles).*   I feel so queer. *(She pats herself.)* Don't you ever get taken that way? When I can't see myself I begin to wonder if I really and truly exist. I pat myself just to make sure, but it doesn't help much.

INEZ.   You're lucky. I'm always conscious of myself—in my mind. Painfully conscious.

ESTELLE.   Ah yes, in your mind. But everything that goes on in one's head is so vague, isn't it? It makes one want to sleep. *(She is silent for a while.)* I've six big mirrors in my bedroom. There they are. I can see them. But they don't see me. They're reflecting the carpet, the settee, the window—but how empty it is, a glass in which I'm absent! When I talked to people I always made sure there was one near by in which I could see myself. I watched myself talking. And somehow it kept me alert, seeing myself as the others saw me. . . . Oh dear! My lipstick! I'm sure I've put it on all crooked. No, I can't do without a looking-glass for ever and ever, I simply can't.

INEZ.   Suppose I try to be your glass? Come and pay me a visit, dear. Here's a place for you on my sofa.

ESTELLE.   But—*(Points to* GARCIN.*)*

INEZ.   Oh, he doesn't count.

ESTELLE.   But we're going to—to hurt each other. You said it yourself.

INEZ.   Do I look as if I wanted to hurt you?

ESTELLE.   One never can tell.

INEZ.   Much more likely *you'll* hurt *me.* Still, what does it matter? If I've got to suffer, it may as well be at your hands, your pretty hands. Sit down. Come closer. Closer. Look into my eyes. What do you see?

ESTELLE.   Oh, I'm there! But so tiny I can't see myself properly.

INEZ.   But *I* can. Every inch of you. Now ask me questions. I'll be as candid as any looking-glass.

*(*ESTELLE *seems rather embarrassed and turns to* GARCIN, *as if appealing to him for help.)*

ESTELLE.   Please, Mr. Garcin. Sure our chatter isn't boring you?

*(*GARCIN *makes no reply.)*

INEZ.   Don't worry about him. As I said, he doesn't count. We're by ourselves. . . . Ask away.

ESTELLE.   Are my lips all right?

INEZ.   Show! No, they're a bit smudgy.

ESTELLE.   I thought as much. Luckily *(throws a quick glance at* GARCIN*)* no one's seen me. I'll try again.

INEZ.   That's better. No. Follow the line of your lips. Wait! I'll guide your hand. There. That's quite good.

ESTELLE.   As good as when I came in?

INEZ.   Far better. Crueler. Your mouth looks quite diabolical that way.

ESTELLE.   Good gracious! And you say you like it! How maddening, not being able to see for myself! You're quite sure, Miss Serrano, that it's all right now?

INEZ.   Won't you call me Inez?

ESTELLE.   Are you sure it looks all right?

INEZ.   You're lovely, Estelle.

ESTELLE.   But how can I rely upon your taste? Is it the same as *my* taste? Oh, how sickening it all is, enough to drive one crazy!

INEZ.   I *have* your taste, my dear, because I like you so much. Look at me. No, straight. Now smile. I'm not so ugly, either. Am I not nicer than your glass?

ESTELLE.   Oh, I don't know. You scare me rather. My reflection in the glass never did that; of course, I knew it so well. Like something I had tamed. . . . I'm going to smile, and my smile will sink down into your pupils, and heaven knows what it will become.

INEZ.   And why shouldn't you "tame" *me? (The women gaze at each other,* ESTELLE *with a sort of fearful fascination.)* Listen! I want you to call me Inez. We must be great friends.

ESTELLE.   I don't make friends with women very easily.

INEZ.   Not with postal clerks, you mean? Hullo, what's that—that nasty red spot at the bottom of your cheek? A pimple?

ESTELLE.   A pimple? Oh, how simply foul! Where?

INEZ.   There. . . . You know the way they catch larks—with a mirror? I'm your lark-mirror, my dear, and you can't escape me. . . . There isn't any pimple, not a trace of one. So what about it? Suppose the mirror started telling lies? Or suppose I covered my eyes—as he is doing—and refused to look at you, all that loveliness of yours would be wasted on the desert air. No, don't be afraid, I can't help looking at you, I shan't turn my eyes away. And I'll be nice to you, ever so nice. Only you must be nice to me, too.

(A short silence.)

ESTELLE.   Are you really—attracted by me?

INEZ.   Very much indeed.

(Another short silence.)

ESTELLE *(indicating* GARCIN *by a slight movement of her head).*   But I wish he'd notice me, too.

INEZ.   Of course! Because he's a Man! *(To* GARCIN*)* You've won. (GARCIN *says nothing.)* But look at her, damn it! *(Still no reply from* GARCIN.*)* Don't pretend. You haven't missed a word of what we've said.

GARCIN.   Quite so; not a word. I stuck my fingers in my ears, but your voices thudded in my brain. Silly chatter. Now will you leave me in peace, you two? I'm not interested in you.

INEZ.   Not in me, perhaps—but how about this child? Aren't you interested in her? Oh, I saw through your game; you got on your high horse just to impress her.

GARCIN.   I asked you to leave me in peace. There's someone talking about me in the newspaper office and I want to listen. And, if it'll make you any happier, let me tell you that I've no use for the "child," as you call her.

ESTELLE.   Thanks.

GARCIN.   Oh, I didn't mean it rudely.

ESTELLE.   You cad!

(They confront each other in silence for some moments.)

GARCIN.   So that's that. *(Pause.)* You know I begged you not to speak.

ESTELLE.   It's *her* fault; she started. I didn't ask anything of her and she came and offered me her—her glass.

INEZ.   So you say. But all the time you were making up to him, trying every trick to catch his attention.

ESTELLE.   Well, why shouldn't I?

GARCIN.   You're crazy, both of you. Don't you see where this is leading us? For pity's sake, keep your mouths shut. *(Pause.)* Now let's all sit down again quite quietly; we'll look at the floor and each must try to forget the others are there.

(A longish silence. GARCIN *sits down. The women return hesitantly to their places. Suddenly* INEZ *swings round on him.)*

INEZ.   To forget about the others? How utterly absurd! I *feel* you there, in every pore. Your silence clamors in my ears. You can nail up your mouth, cut your tongue out—but you can't prevent your *being there.* Can you stop your thoughts? I hear them ticking away like a clock, tick-tock, tick-tock, and I'm certain you hear mine. It's all very well skulking on your sofa, but you're everywhere, and every sound comes to me soiled, because you've intercepted it on its way. Why, you've even stolen my face; you know it and I don't! And what about her, about Estelle? You've stolen her from me, too; if she and I were alone do you suppose she'd treat me as she does? No, take your hands from your face, I won't leave you in peace—that would suit your book too well. You'd go on sitting there, in a sort of trance, like a yogi, and even if I didn't see her I'd feel it in my bones—that she was making every sound, even the rustle of her dress, for your benefit, throwing you smiles you didn't see. . . . Well, I won't stand for that, I prefer to choose my hell; I prefer to look you in the eyes and fight it out face to face.

GARCIN.   Have it your own way. I suppose we were bound to come to this; they knew what they were about, and we're easy game. If they'd put me in a room with men—men can keep their mouths shut. But it's no use wanting the impossible. *(He goes to* ESTELLE *and lightly fondles her neck.)* So I attract you, little girl? It seems you were making eyes at me?

ESTELLE.   Don't touch me.

GARCIN.   Why not? We might, anyhow, be natural. . . . Do you know, I used to be mad about women? And some were fond of me. So we may as well stop posing, we've nothing to lose. Why trouble about politeness, and decorum, and the rest of it? We're between ourselves. And presently we shall be naked as— as new-born babes.

ESTELLE.   Oh, let me be!

GARCIN.   As new-born babes. Well, I'd warned you, anyhow. I asked so little of you, nothing but peace and a little silence. I'd put my fingers in my ears. Gomez was spouting away as usual, standing in the center of the room, with all the pressmen listening. In their shirt-sleeves. I tried to hear, but it wasn't too easy. Things on earth move so quickly, you know. Couldn't you have held your tongues? Now it's over, he's stopped talking, and what he thinks of me has gone back into his head. Well, we've got to see it through somehow. . . . Naked as we were born. So much the better; I want to know whom I have to deal with.

INEZ. You know already. There's nothing more to learn.

GARCIN. You're wrong. So long as each of us hasn't made a clean breast of it— why they've damned him or her—we know nothing. Nothing that counts. You, young lady, you shall begin. Why? Tell us why. If you are frank, if we bring our specters into the open, it may save us from disaster. So—out with it! Why?

ESTELLE. I tell you I haven't a notion. They wouldn't tell me why.

GARCIN. That's so. They wouldn't tell me, either. But I've a pretty good idea. . . . Perhaps you're shy of speaking first? Right. I'll lead off. *(A short silence.)* I'm not a very estimable person.

INEZ. No need to tell us that. We know you were a deserter.

GARCIN. Let that be. It's only a side-issue. I'm here because I treated my wife abominably. That's all. For five years. Naturally, she's suffering still. There she is: the moment I mention her, I see her. It's Gomez who interests me, and it's she I see. Where's Gomez got to? For five years. There! They've given her back my things; she's sitting by the window, with my coat on her knees. The coat with the twelve bullet-holes. The blood's like rust; a brown ring round each hole. It's quite a museum-piece, that coat; scarred with history. And I used to wear it, fancy! . . . Now, can't you shed a tear, my love? Surely you'll squeeze one out—at last? No? You can't manage it? . . . Night after night I came home blind drunk, stinking of wine and women. She'd sat up for me, of course. But she never cried, never uttered a word of reproach. Only her eyes spoke. Big, tragic eyes. I don't regret anything. I must pay the price, but I shan't whine. . . . It's snowing in the street. Won't you cry, confound you? That woman was a born martyr, you know; a victim by vocation.

INEZ *(almost tenderly)*. Why did you hurt her like that?

GARCIN. It was so easy. A word was enough to make her flinch. Like a sensitive-plant. But never, never a reproach. I'm fond of teasing. I watched and waited. But no, not a tear, not a protest. I'd picked her up out of the gutter, you understand. . . . Now she's stroking the coat. Her eyes are shut and she's feeling with her fingers for the bullet-holes. What are you after? What do you expect? I tell you I regret nothing. The truth is, she admired me too much. Does that mean anything to you?

INEZ. No. Nobody admired *me*.

GARCIN. So much the better. So much the better for you. I suppose all this strikes you as very vague. Well, here's something you can get your teeth into. I brought a half-caste girl to stay in our house. My wife slept upstairs; she must have heard—everything. She was an early riser and, as I and the girl stayed in bed late, she served us our morning coffee.

INEZ. You brute!

GARCIN. Yes, a brute, if you like. But a well-beloved brute. *(A far-away look comes to his eyes.)* No, it's nothing. Only Gomez, and he's not talking about *me*. . . . What were you saying? Yes, a brute. Certainly. Else why should I be here? *(To* INEZ*)* Your turn.

INEZ. Well, I was what some people down there called "a damned bitch."
Damned already. So it's no surprise, being here.

GARCIN. Is that all you have to say?

INEZ. No. There was that affair with Florence. A dead men's tale. With three
corpses to it. He to start with; then she and I. So there's no one left, I've
nothing to worry about; it was a clean sweep. Only that room. I see it now
and then. Empty, with the doors locked. . . . No, they've just unlocked them.
"To Let." It's to let; there's a notice on the door. That's—too ridiculous.

GARCIN. Three. Three deaths, you said?

INEZ. Three.

GARCIN. One man and two women?

INEZ. Yes.

GARCIN. Well, well. *(A pause.)* Did he kill himself?

INEZ. He? No, he hadn't the guts for that. Still, he'd every reason; we led him
a dog's life. As a matter of fact, he was run over by a tram. A silly sort of end.
. . . I was living with them; he was my cousin.

GARCIN. Was Florence fair?

INEZ. Fair? *(Glances at* ESTELLE.*)* You know, I don't regret a thing; still, I'm not
so very keen on telling you the story.

GARCIN. That's all right. . . . So you got sick of him?

INEZ. Quite gradually. All sorts of little things got on my nerves. For instance,
he made a noise when he was drinking—a sort of gurgle. Trifles like that. He
was rather pathetic really. Vulnerable. Why are you smiling?

GARCIN. Because I, anyhow, am *not* vulnerable.

INEZ. Don't be too sure. . . . I crept inside her skin, she saw the world through
my eyes. When she left him, I had her on my hands. We shared a bed-sitting-
room at the other end of the town.

GARCIN. And then?

INEZ. Then that tram did its job. I used to remind her every day: "Yes, my pet,
we killed him between us." *(A pause.)* I'm rather cruel, really.

GARCIN. So am I.

INEZ. No, you're not cruel. It's something else.

GARCIN. What?

INEZ. I'll tell you later. When I say I'm cruel, I mean I can't get on without
making people suffer. Like a live coal. A live coal in others' hearts. When I'm
alone I flicker out. For six months I flamed away in her heart, till there was
nothing but a cinder. One night she got up and turned on the gas while I was
asleep. Then she crept back into bed. So now you know.

GARCIN. Well! Well!

INEZ. Yes? What's in your mind?

GARCIN. Nothing. Only that it's not a pretty story.

INEZ. Obviously. But what matter?

GARCIN. As you say, what matter? *(To* ESTELLE*)* Your turn. What have you
done?

ESTELLE.   As I told you, I haven't a notion. I rack my brain, but it's no use.

GARCIN. Right. Then we'll give you a hand. That fellow with the smashed face,
who was he?

ESTELLE. Who—who do you mean?

INEZ. You know quite well. The man you were so scared of seeing when you came in.

ESTELLE. Oh, him! A friend of mine.

GARCIN. Why were you afraid of him?

ESTELLE. That's my business, Mr. Garcin.

INEZ. Did he shoot himself on your account?

ESTELLE. Of course not. How absurd you are!

GARCIN. Then why should you have been so scared? He blew his brains out, didn't he? That's how his face got smashed.

ESTELLE. Don't! Please don't go on.

GARCIN. Because of you. Because of you.

INEZ. He shot himself because of you.

ESTELLE. Leave me alone! It's—it's not fair, bullying me like that. I want to go! I want to go! *(She runs to the door and shakes it.)*

GARCIN. Go if you can. Personally, I ask for nothing better. Unfortunately, the door's locked.

(ESTELLE presses the bell-push, but the bell does not ring. INEZ and GARCIN laugh. ESTELLE swings round on them, her back to the door.)

ESTELLE *(in a muffled voice).* You're hateful, both of you.

INEZ. Hateful? Yes, that's the word. Now get on with it. That fellow who killed himself on your account—you were his mistress, eh?

GARCIN. Of course she was. And he wanted to have her to himself alone. That's so, isn't it?

INEZ. He danced the tango like a professional, but he was poor as a church mouse —that's right, isn't it? *(A short silence.)*

GARCIN. Was he poor or not? Give a straight answer.

ESTELLE. Yes, he was poor.

GARCIN. And then you had your reputation to keep up. One day he came and implored you to run away with him, and you laughed in his face.

INEZ. That's it. You laughed at him. And so he killed himself.

ESTELLE. Did you use to look at Florence in that way?

INEZ. Yes. *(A short pause, then ESTELLE bursts out laughing.)*

ESTELLE. You've got it all wrong, you two. *(She stiffens her shoulders, still leaning against the door, and faces them. Her voice grows shrill, truculent.)* He wanted me to have a baby. So there!

GARCIN. And you didn't want one?

ESTELLE. I certainly didn't. But the baby came, worse luck. I went to Switzerland for five months. No one knew anything. It was a girl. Roger was with me when she was born. It pleased him no end, having a daughter. It didn't please *me!*

GARCIN. And then?

ESTELLE. There was a balcony overlooking the lake. I brought a big stone. He could see what I was up to and he kept on shouting: "Estelle, for God's sake, don't!" I hated him then. He saw it all. He was leaning over the balcony and he saw the rings spreading on the water—

GARCIN. Yes? And then?

ESTELLE.   That's all. I came back to Paris—and he did as he wished.

GARCIN.   You mean he blew his brains out?

ESTELLE.   It was absurd of him, really; my husband never suspected anything. *(A pause.)* Oh, how I loathe you! *(She sobs tearlessly.)*

GARCIN.   Nothing doing. Tears don't flow in this place.

ESTELLE.   I'm a coward. A coward! *(Pause.)* If you knew how I hate you!

INEZ *(taking her in her arms).*   Poor child! *(To* GARCIN*)* So the hearing's over. But there's no need to look like a hanging judge.

GARCIN.   A hanging judge? *(He glances around him.)* I'd give a lot to be able to see myself in a glass. *(Pause.)* How hot it is! *(Unthinkingly he takes off his coat.)* Oh, sorry! *(He starts putting it on again.)*

ESTELLE.   Don't bother. You can stay in your shirtsleeves. As things are—

GARCIN.   Just so. *(He drops his coat on the sofa.)* You mustn't be angry with me, Estelle.

ESTELLE.   I'm not angry with you.

INEZ.   And what about me? Are you angry with me?

ESTELLE.   Yes.

(A short silence.)

INEZ.   Well, Mr. Garcin, now you have us in the nude all right. Do you understand things any better for that?

GARCIN.   I wonder. Yes, perhaps a trifle better. *(Timidly)* And now suppose we start trying to help each other.

INEZ.   I don't need help.

GARCIN.   Inez, they've laid their snare damned cunningly—like a cobweb. If you make any movement, if you raise your hand to fan yourself, Estelle and I feel a little tug. Alone, none of us can save himself or herself; we're linked together inextricably. So you can take your choice. *(A pause.)* Hullo? What's happening?

INEZ.   They've let it. The windows are wide open, a man is sitting on my bed. *My* bed, if you please! They've let it, let it! Step in, step in, make yourself at home, you brute! Ah, there's a woman, too. She's going up to him, putting her hands on his shoulders. . . . Damn it, why don't they turn the lights on? It's getting dark. Now he's going to kiss her. But that's my room, *my* room! Pitch-dark now. I can't see anything, but I hear them whispering, whispering. Is he going to make love to her on *my* bed? What's that she said? That it's noon and the sun is shining? I must be going blind. *(A pause.)* Blacked out. I can't see or hear a thing. So I'm done with the earth, it seems. No more alibis for me! *(She shudders.)* I feel so empty, desiccated—really dead at last. All of me's here, in this room. *(A pause.)* What were you saying? Something about helping me, wasn't it?

GARCIN.   Yes.

INEZ.   Helping me to do what?

GARCIN.   To defeat their devilish tricks.

INEZ.   And what do you expect me to do, in return?

GARCIN.   To help *me.* It only needs a little effort, Inez; just a spark of human feeling.

INEZ.   Human feeling. That's beyond my range. I'm rotten to the core.

GARCIN.   And how about me? *(A pause.)* All the same, suppose we try?

INEZ.   It's no use. I'm all dried up. I can't give and I can't receive. How could *I* help you? A dead twig, ready for the burning. *(She falls silent, gazing at* ESTELLE, *who has buried her head in her hands.)* Florence was fair, a natural blonde.

GARCIN.   Do you realize that this young woman's fated to be your torturer?

INEZ.   Perhaps I've guessed it.

GARCIN.   It's through her they'll get you. I, of course, I'm different—aloof. I take no notice of her. Suppose you had a try—

INEZ.   Yes?

GARCIN.   It's a trap. They're watching you, to see if you'll fall into it.

INEZ.   I know. And you're another trap. Do you think they haven't foreknown every word you say? And of course there's a whole nest of pitfalls that we can't see. Everything here's a booby-trap. But what do I care? I'm a pitfall, too. For her, obviously. And perhaps I'll catch her.

GARCIN.   You won't catch anything. We're chasing after each other, round and round in a vicious circle, like the horses on a roundabout. That's part of their plan, of course. . . . Drop it, Inez. Open your hands and let go of everything. Or else you'll bring disaster on all three of us.

INEZ.   Do I look the sort of person who lets go? I know what's coming to me. I'm going to burn, and it's to last forever. Yes, I *know* everything. But do you think I'll let go? I'll catch her, she'll see you through my eyes, as Florence saw that other man. What's the good of trying to enlist my sympathy? I assure you I know everything, and I can't feel sorry even for myself. A trap! Don't I know it, and that I'm in a trap myself, up to the neck, and there's nothing to be done about it? And if it suits their book, so much the better!

GARCIN *(gripping her shoulders).*   Well, *I,* anyhow, can feel sorry for you, too. Look at me, we're naked, naked right through, and I can see into your heart. That's one link between us. Do you think I'd want to hurt you? I don't regret anything, I'm dried up, too. But for you I can still feel pity.

INEZ *(who has let him keep his hands on her shoulders until now, shakes herself loose).* Don't. I hate being pawed about. And keep your pity for yourself. Don't forget, Garcin, that there are traps for you, too, in this room. All nicely set for you. You'd do better to watch your own interests. *(A pause.)* But, if you will leave us in peace, this child and me, I'll see I don't do you any harm.

GARCIN *(gazes at her for a moment, then shrugs his shoulders).*   Very well.

ESTELLE *(raising her head).*   Please, Garcin.

GARCIN.   What do you want of me?

ESTELLE *(rises and goes up to him).*   You can help *me,* anyhow.

GARCIN.   If you want help, apply to her.

(INEZ has come up and is standing behind ESTELLE, but without touching her. During the dialogue that follows she speaks almost in her ear. But ESTELLE keeps her eyes on GARCIN, who observes her without speaking, and she addresses her answers to him, as if it were he who is questioning her.)

ESTELLE.   I implore you, Garcin—you gave me your promise, didn't you? Help me quick. I don't want to be left alone. Olga's taken him to a cabaret.

INEZ.   Taken whom?

ESTELLE.   Peter. . . . Oh, now they're dancing together.

INEZ.   Who's Peter?

ESTELLE.   Such a silly boy. He called me his glancing stream—just fancy! He was terribly in love with me. . . . She's persuaded him to come out with her tonight.

INEZ.   Do you love him?

ESTELLE.   They're sitting down now. She's puffing like a grampus. What a fool the girl is to insist on dancing! But I dare say she does it to reduce. . . . No, of course I don't love him; he's only eighteen, and I'm not a baby-snatcher.

INEZ.   Then why bother about them? What difference can it make?

ESTELLE.   He belonged to me.

INEZ.   Nothing on earth belongs to you any more.

ESTELLE.   I tell you he was mine. All mine.

INEZ.   Yes, he *was* yours—once. But now—Try to make him hear, try to touch him. Olga can touch him, talk to him as much as she likes. That's so, isn't it? She can squeeze his hands, rub herself against him—

ESTELLE.   Yes, look! She's pressing her great fat chest against him, puffing and blowing in his face. But, my poor little lamb, can't you see how ridiculous she is? Why don't you laugh at her? Oh, once I'd have only had to glance at them and she'd have slunk away. Is there really nothing, nothing left of me?

INEZ.   Nothing whatever. Nothing of you's left on earth—not even a shadow. All you own is here. Would you like that paper-knife? Or that ornament on the mantelpiece? That blue sofa's yours. And I, my dear, am yours forever.

ESTELLE.   You mine! That's good! Well, which of you two would dare to call me his glancing stream, his crystal girl? You know too much about me, you know I'm rotten through and through. . . . Peter dear, think of me, fix your thoughts on me, and save me. All the time you're thinking "my glancing stream, my crystal girl," I'm only half here, I'm only half wicked, and half of me is down there with you, clean and bright and crystal-clear as running water. . . . Oh, just look at her face, all scarlet, like a tomato! No, it's absurd, we've laughed at her together, you and I, often and often. . . . What's that tune?—I always loved it. Yes, the *St. Louis Blues.* . . . All right, dance away, dance away. Garcin, I wish you could see her, you'd die of laughing. Only—she'll never know I *see* her. Yes, I see you, Olga, with your hair all anyhow, and you do look a dope, my dear. Oh, now you're treading on his toes. It's a scream! Hurry up! Quicker! Quicker! He's dragging her along, bundling her round and round —it's too ghastly! He always said I was so light, he loved to dance with me. *(She is dancing as she speaks.)* I tell you, Olga, I can see you. No, she doesn't care, she's dancing through my gaze. What's that? What's that you said? "Our poor dear Estelle"? Oh, don't be such a humbug! You didn't even shed a tear at the funeral. . . . And she has the nerve to talk to him about her poor dear friend Estelle! How dare she discuss me with Peter? Now then, keep time. She never could dance and talk at once. Oh, what's that? No, no. Don't tell him. Please, please don't tell him. You can keep him, do what you like with him, but please don't tell him about—that! *(She has stopped dancing.)* All right. You can have him now. Isn't it *foul,* Garcin? She's told him everything, about Roger, my trip to Switzerland, the baby. "Poor Estelle wasn't exactly—" No,

I wasn't exactly—True enough. He's looking grave, shaking his head, but he doesn't seem so very much surprised, not what one would expect. Keep him, then—I won't haggle with you over his long eyelashes, his pretty girlish face. They're yours for the asking. His glancing stream, his crystal. Well, the crystal's shattered into bits. "Poor Estelle!" Dance, dance, dance. On with it. But do keep time. One, two. One, two. How I'd love to go down to earth for just a moment, and dance with him again. *(She dances again for some moments.)* The music's growing fainter. They've turned down the lights, as they do for a tango. Why are they playing so softly? Louder, please. I can't hear. It's so far away, so far away. I—I can't hear a sound. *(She stops dancing.)* All over. It's the end. The earth has left me. *(To* GARCIN*)* Don't turn from me—please. Take me in your arms.

(Behind ESTELLE*'s back,* INEZ *signs to* GARCIN *to move away.)*

INEZ *(commandingly).*   Now then, Garcin!

*(*GARCIN *moves back a step, and, glancing at* ESTELLE, *points to* INEZ.*)*

GARCIN.   It's to her you should say that.

ESTELLE *(clinging to him).*   Don't turn away. You're a man, aren't you, and surely I'm not such a fright as all that! Everyone says I've lovely hair and, after all, a man killed himself on my account. You have to look at something, and there's nothing here to see except the sofas and that awful ornament and the table. Surely I'm better to look at than a lot of stupid furniture. Listen! I've dropped out of their hearts like a little sparrow fallen from its nest. So gather me up, dear, fold me to your heart—and you'll see how nice I can be.

GARCIN *(freeing himself from her, after a short struggle).*   I tell you it's to that lady you should speak.

ESTELLE.   To her? But she doesn't count, she's a woman.

INEZ.   Oh, I don't count? Is that what you think? But, my poor little fallen nestling, you've been sheltering in my heart for ages, though you didn't realize it. Don't be afraid; I'll keep looking at you for ever and ever, without a flutter of my eyelids, and you'll live in my gaze like a mote in a sunbeam.

ESTELLE.   A sunbeam indeed! Don't talk such rubbish! You've tried that trick already, and you should know it doesn't work.

INEZ.   Estelle! My glancing stream! My crystal!

ESTELLE.   *Your* crystal? It's grotesque. Do you think you can fool me with that sort of talk? Everyone knows by now what I did to my baby. The crystal's shattered, but I don't care. I'm just a hollow dummy, all that's left of me is the outside—but it's not for you.

INEZ.   Come to me, Estelle. You shall be whatever you like: a glancing stream, a muddy stream. And deep down in my eyes you'll see yourself just as you want to be.

ESTELLE.   Oh, leave me in peace. You haven't any eyes. Oh, damn it, isn't there anything I can do to get rid of you? I've an idea. *(She spits in* INEZ*'s face.)* There!

INEZ.   Garcin, you shall pay for this.

(A pause. GARCIN *shrugs his shoulders and goes to* ESTELLE.*)*

GARCIN.   So it's a man you need?

ESTELLE.   Not *any* man. You.

GARCIN.   No humbug now. Any man would do your business. As I happen to be here, you want me. Right! *(He grips her shulders.)* Mind, I'm not your sort at all, really; I'm not a young nincompoop and I don't dance the tango.

ESTELLE.   I'll take you as you are. And perhaps I shall change you.

GARCIN.   I doubt it. I shan't pay much attention; I've other things to think about.

ESTELLE.   What things?

GARCIN.   They wouldn't interest you.

ESTELLE.   I'll sit on your sofa and wait for you to take some notice of me. I promise not to bother you at all.

INEZ *(with a shrill laugh).*   That's right, fawn on him, like the silly bitch you are. Grovel and cringe! And he hasn't even good looks to commend him!

ESTELLE *(to* GARCIN*).*   Don't listen to her. She has no eyes, no ears. She's— nothing.

GARCIN.   I'll give you what I can. It doesn't amount to much. I shan't love you; I know you too well.

ESTELLE.   Do you want me, anyhow?

GARCIN.   Yes.

ESTELLE.   I ask no more.

GARCIN.   In that case—*(He bends over her.)*

INEZ.   Estelle! Garcin! You must be going crazy. You're not alone. I'm here too.

GARCIN.   Of course—but what does it matter?

INEZ.   Under my eyes? You couldn't—couldn't do it.

ESTELLE.   Why not? I often undressed with my maid looking on.

INEZ *(gripping* GARCIN*'s arm).*   Let her alone. Don't paw her with your dirty man's hands.

GARCIN *(thrusting her away roughly).*   Take care. I'm no gentleman, and I'd have no compunction about striking a woman.

INEZ.   But you promised me; you promised. I'm only asking you to keep your word.

GARCIN.   Why should I, considering you were the first to break our agreement?

*(*INEZ *turns her back on him and retreats to the far end of the room.)*

INEZ.   Very well, have it your own way. I'm the weaker party, one against two. But don't forget I'm here, and watching. I shan't take my eyes off you, Garcin; when you're kissing her, you'll feel them boring into you. Yes, have it your own way, make love and get it over. We're in hell; my turn will come.

(During the following scene she watches them without speaking.)

GARCIN *(coming back to* ESTELLE *and grasping her shoulders).*   Now then. Your lips. Give me your lips. *(A pause. He bends to kiss her, then abruptly straightens up.)*

ESTELLE *(indignantly).*   Really! *(A pause.)* Didn't I tell you not to pay any attention to her?

GARCIN.   You've got it wrong. *(Short silence.)* It's Gomez; he's back in the press-room. They've shut the windows; it must be winter down there. Six months since I—Well, I warned you I'd be absent-minded sometimes, didn't I? They're shivering, they've kept their coats on. Funny they should feel the cold like that, when I'm feeling so hot. Ah, this time he's talking about me.

ESTELLE.   Is it going to last long? *(Short silence.)* You might at least tell me what he's saying.

GARCIN.   Nothing. Nothing worth repeating. He's a swine, that's all. *(He listens attentively.)* A god-damned bloody swine. *(He turns to* ESTELLE.*)* Let's come back to—to ourselves. Are you going to love me?

ESTELLE *(smiling).*   I wonder now!

GARCIN.   Will you trust me?

ESTELLE.   What a quaint thing to ask! Considering you'll be under my eyes all the time, and I don't think I've much to fear from Inez, so far as you're concerned.

GARCIN.   Obviously. *(A pause. He takes his hands off* ESTELLE*'s shoulders.)* I was thinking of another kind of trust. *(Listens.)* Talk away, talk away, you swine. I'm not there to defend myself. *(To* ESTELLE*)* Estelle, you *must* give me your trust.

ESTELLE.   Oh, what a nuisance you are! I'm giving you my mouth, my arms, my whole body—and everything could be so simple. . . . My trust! I haven't any to give, I'm afraid, and you're making me terribly embarrassed. You must have something pretty ghastly on your conscience to make such a fuss about my trusting you.

GARCIN.   They shot me.

ESTELLE.   I know. Because you refused to fight. Well, why shouldn't you?

GARCIN.   I—I didn't exactly refuse. *(In a far-away voice)* I must say he talks well, he makes out a good case against me, but he never says what I should have done instead. Should I have gone to the general and said: "General, I decline to fight"? A mug's game; they'd have promptly locked me up. But I wanted to show my colors, my true colors, do you understand? I wasn't going to be silenced. *(To* ESTELLE*)* So I—I took the train. . . . They caught me at the frontier.

ESTELLE.   Where were you trying to go?

GARCIN.   To Mexico. I meant to launch a pacifist newspaper down there. *(A short silence.)* Well, why don't you speak?

ESTELLE.   What could I say? You acted quite rightly, as you didn't want to fight. *(*GARCIN *makes a fretful gesture.)* But, darling, how on earth can I guess what you want me to answer?

INEZ.   Can't you guess? Well, *I* can. He wants you to tell him that he bolted like a lion. For "bolt" he did, and that's what's biting him.

GARCIN.   "Bolted," "went away"—we won't quarrel over words.

ESTELLE.   But you *had* to run away. If you'd stayed they'd have sent you to jail, wouldn't they?

GARCIN.   Of course. *(A pause.)* Well, Estelle, am I a coward?

ESTELLE.   How can I say? Don't be so unreasonable, darling. I can't put myself in your skin. You must decide that for yourself.

GARCIN *(wearily).*   I can't decide.

ESTELLE. Anyhow, you must remember. You must have had reasons for acting as you did.

GARCIN. I had.

ESTELLE. Well?

GARCIN. But were they the real reasons?

ESTELLE. You've a twisted mind, that's your trouble. Plaguing yourself over such trifles!

GARCIN. I'd thought it all out, and I wanted to make a stand. But was that my real motive?

INEZ. Exactly. That's the question. Was that your real motive? No doubt you argued it out with yourself, you weighed the pros and cons, you found good reasons for what you did. But fear and hatred and all the dirty little instincts one keeps dark—they're motives too. So carry on, Mr. Garcin, and try to be honest with yourself—for once.

GARCIN. Do I need you to tell me that? Day and night I paced my cell, from the window to the door, from the door to the window. I pried into my heart, I sleuthed myself like a detective. By the end of it I felt as if I'd given my whole life to introspection. But always I harked back to the one thing certain—that I had acted as I did, I'd taken that train to the frontier. But why? Why? Finally I thought: My death will settle it. If I face death courageously, I'll prove I am no coward.

INEZ. And how did you face death?

GARCIN. Miserably. Rottenly. (INEZ *laughs.*) Oh, it was only a physical lapse—that might happen to anyone; I'm not ashamed of it. Only everything's been left in suspense, forever. *(To* ESTELLE*)* Come here, Estelle. Look at me. I want to feel someone looking at me while they're talking about me on earth. . . . I like green eyes.

INEZ. Green eyes! Just hark to him! And you, Estelle, do you like cowards?

ESTELLE. If you knew how little I care! Coward or hero, it's all one—provided he kisses well.

GARCIN. There they are, slumped in their chairs, sucking at their cigars. Bored they look. Half-asleep. They're thinking: "Garcin's a coward." But only vaguely, dreamily. One's got to think of something. "That chap Garcin was a coward." That's what they've decided, those dear friends of mine. In six months' time they'll be saying: "Cowardly as that skunk Garcin." You're lucky, you two; no one on earth is giving you another thought. But I—I'm long in dying.

INEZ. What about your wife, Garcin?

GARCIN. Oh, didn't I tell you? She's dead.

INEZ. Dead?

GARCIN. Yes, she died just now. About two months ago.

INEZ. Of grief?

GARCIN. What else should she die of? So all is for the best, you see; the war's over, my wife's dead, and I've carved out my place in history.

(He gives a choking sob and passes his hand over his face. ESTELLE *catches his arm.)*

ESTELLE.   My poor darling! Look at me. Please look. Touch me. Touch me. *(She takes his hand and puts it on her neck.)* There! Keep your hand there. *(*GARCIN *makes a fretful movement.)* No, don't move. Why trouble what those men are thinking? They'll die off one by one. Forget them. There's only me, now.

GARCIN.   But *they* won't forget *me,* not they! They'll die, but others will come after them to carry on the legend. I've left my fate in their hands.

ESTELLE.   You think too much, that's your trouble.

GARCIN.   What else is there to do now? I was a man of action once. . . . Oh, if only I could be with them again, for just one day—I'd fling their lie in their teeth. But I'm locked out; they're passing judgment on my life without troubling about me, and they're right, because I'm dead. Dead and done with. *(Laughs.)* A back number.

(A short pause.)

ESTELLE *(gently).*   Garcin.

GARCIN.   Still there? Now listen! I want you to do me a service. No, don't shrink away. I know it must seem strange to you, having someone asking you for help; you're not used to that. But if you'll make the effort, if you'll only *will* it hard enough, I dare say we can really love each other. Look at it this way. A thousand of them are proclaiming I'm a coward; but what do numbers matter? If there's someone, just one person, to say quite positively I did not run away, that I'm not the sort who runs away, that I'm brave and decent and the rest of it—well, that one person's faith would save me. Will you have that faith in me? Then I shall love you and cherish you for ever. Estelle—will you?

ESTELLE *(laughing).*   Oh, you dear silly man, do you think I could love a coward?

GARCIN.   But just now you said—

ESTELLE.   I was only teasing you. I like men, my dear, who're real men, with tough skin and strong hands. You haven't a coward's chin, or a coward's mouth, or a coward's voice, or a coward's hair. And it's for your mouth, your hair, your voice, I love you.

GARCIN.   Do you mean this? *Really* mean it?

ESTELLE.   Shall I swear it?

GARCIN.   Then I snap my fingers at them all, those below and those in here. Estelle, we shall climb out of hell. *(*INEZ *gives a shrill laugh. He breaks off and stares at her.)* What's that?

INEZ *(still laughing).*   But she doesn't mean a word of what she says. How can you be such a simpleton? "Estelle, am I a coward?" As if she cared a damn either way.

ESTELLE.   Inez, how dare you? *(To* GARCIN*)* Don't listen to her. If you want me to have faith in you, you must begin by trusting me.

INEZ.   That's right! That's right! Trust away! She wants a man—that far you can trust her—she wants a man's arm round her waist, a man's smell, a man's eyes glowing with desire. And that's all she wants. She'd assure you you were God Almighty if she thought it would give you pleasure.

GARCIN.   Estelle, is this true? Answer me. Is it true?

ESTELLE.   What do you expect me to say? Don't you realize how maddening it is to have to answer questions one can't make head or tail of? *(She stamps her foot.)* You do make things difficult. . . . Anyhow, I'd love you just the same, even if you were a coward. Isn't that enough?

(A short pause.)

GARCIN *(to the two women).*   You disgust me, both of you. *(He goes towards the door.)*

ESTELLE.   What are you up to?

GARCIN.   I'm going.

INEZ *(quickly).*   You won't get far. The door is locked.

GARCIN.   I'll *make* them open it. *(He presses the bell-push. The bell does not ring.)*

ESTELLE.   Please! Please!

INEZ *(to* ESTELLE*).*   Don't worry, my pet. The bell doesn't work.

GARCIN.   I tell you they shall open. *(Drums on the door.)* I can't endure it any longer, I'm through with you both. *(ESTELLE runs to him; he pushes her away.)* Go away. You're even fouler than she. I won't let myself get bogged in your eyes. You're soft and slimy. Ugh! *(Bangs on the door again.)* Like an octopus. Like a quagmire.

ESTELLE.   I beg you, oh, I beg you not to leave me. I'll promise not to speak again, I won't trouble you in any way—but don't go. I daren't be left alone with Inez, now she's shown her claws.

GARCIN.   Look after yourself. I never asked you to come here.

ESTELLE.   Oh, how mean you are! Yes, it's quite true you're a coward.

INEZ *(going up to* ESTELLE*).*   Well, my little sparrow fallen from the nest, I hope you're satisfied now. You spat in my face—playing up to him, of course—and we had a tiff on his account. But he's going, and a good riddance it will be. We two women will have the place to ourselves.

ESTELLE.   You won't gain anything. If that door opens, I'm going, too.

INEZ.   Where?

ESTELLE.   I don't care where. As far from you as I can.

(GARCIN has been drumming on the door while they talk.)

GARCIN.   Open the door! Open, blast you! I'll endure anything, your red-hot tongs and molten lead, your racks and prongs and garrotes—all your fiendish gadgets, everything that burns and flays and tears—I'll put up with any torture you impose. Anything, anything would be better than this agony of mind, this creeping pain that gnaws and fumbles and caresses one and never hurts quite enough. *(He grips the door-knob and rattles it.)* Now will you open? *(The door flies open with a jerk, nearly falling on the floor.)* Ah! *(A long silence.)*

INEZ.   Well, Garcin? You're free to go.

GARCIN *(meditatively).*   Now I wonder why that door opened.

INEZ.   What are you waiting for? Hurry up and go.

GARCIN.   I shall not go.

INEZ.   And you, Estelle? *(ESTELLE does not move.* INEZ *bursts out laughing.)* So what? Which shall it be? Which of the three of us will leave? The barrier's down, why are we waiting? . . . But what a situation! It's a scream! We're—inseparables!

(ESTELLE springs at her from behind.)

ESTELLE.   Inseparables? Garcin, come and lend a hand. Quickly. We'll push her out and slam the door on her. That'll teach her a lesson.

INEZ *(struggling with* ESTELLE*).*   Estelle! I beg you, let me stay. I won't go, I won't go! Not into the passage.

GARCIN.   Let go of her.

ESTELLE.   You're crazy. She hates you.

GARCIN.   It's because of her I'm staying here.

(ESTELLE *releases* INEZ *and stares dumbfoundedly at* GARCIN.*)*

INEZ.   Because of me? *(Pause.)* All right, shut the door. It's ten times hotter here since it opened. *(*GARCIN *goes to the door and shuts it.)* Because of me, you said?

GARCIN.   Yes. *You,* anyhow, know what it means to be a coward.

INEZ.   Yes, I know.

GARCIN.   And you know what wickedness is, and shame, and fear. There were days when you peered into yourself, into the secret places of your heart, and what you saw there made you faint with horror. And then, next day, you didn't know what to make of it, you couldn't interpret the horror you had glimpsed the day before. Yes, you know what evil *costs.* And when you say I'm a coward, you know from experience what that means. Is that so?

INEZ.   Yes.

GARCIN.   So it's you whom I have to convince; you are of my kind. Did you suppose I meant to go? No, I couldn't leave you here, gloating over my defeat, with all those thoughts about me running in your head.

INEZ.   Do you really wish to convince me?

GARCIN.   That's the one and only thing I wish for now. I can't hear them any longer, you know. Probably that means they're through with me. For good and all. The curtain's down, nothing of me is left on earth—not even the name of coward. So, Inez, we're alone. Only you two remain to give a thought to me. She—she doesn't count. It's you who matter; you who hate me. If you'll have faith in me I'm saved.

INEZ.   It won't be easy. Have a look at me. I'm a hard-headed woman.

GARCIN.   I'll give you all the time that's needed.

INEZ.   Yes, we've lots of time in hand. *All* time.

GARCIN *(putting his hands on her shoulders).*   Listen! Each man has an aim in life, a leading motive; that's so, isn't it? Well, I didn't give a damn for wealth, or for love. I aimed at being a real man. A tough, as they say. I staked everything on the same horse. . . . Can one possibly be a coward when one's deliberately courted danger at every turn? And can one judge a life by a single action?

INEZ.   Why not? For thirty years you dreamt you were a hero, and condoned a thousand petty lapses—because a hero, of course, can do no wrong. An easy method, obviously. Then a day came when you were up against it, the red light of real danger—and you took the train to Mexico.

GARCIN.   I "dreamt," you say. It was no dream. When I chose the hardest path, I made my choice deliberately. A man is what he wills himself to be.

INEZ.   Prove it. Prove it was no dream. It's what one does, and nothing else, that shows the stuff one's made of.

GARCIN.   I died too soon. I wasn't allowed time to—to do my deeds.

INEZ.   One always dies too soon—or too late. And yet one's whole life is complete at that moment, with a line drawn neatly under it, ready for the summing up. You are—your life, and nothing else.

GARCIN.   What a poisonous woman you are! With an answer for everything.

INEZ.   Now then! Don't lose heart. It shouldn't be so hard, convincing me. Pull yourself together, man, rake up some arguments. *(GARCIN shrugs his shoulders.)* Ah, wasn't I right when I said you were vulnerable? Now you're going to pay the price, and what a price! You're a coward, Garcin, because I wish it. I wish it—do you hear?—I wish it. And yet, just look at me, see how weak I am, a mere breath on the air, a gaze observing you, a formless thought that thinks you. *(He walks towards her, opening his hands.)* Ah, they're open now, those big hands, those coarse, man's hands! But what do you hope to do? You can't throttle thoughts with hands. So you've no choice, you must convince me, and you're at my mercy.

ESTELLE.   Garcin!

GARCIN.   What?

ESTELLE.   Revenge yourself.

GARCIN.   How?

ESTELLE.   Kiss me, darling—then you'll hear her squeal.

GARCIN.   That's true, Inez. I'm at your mercy, but you're at mine as well.

(He bends over ESTELLE. INEZ gives a little cry.)

INEZ.   Oh, you coward, you weakling, running to women to console you!

ESTELLE.   That's right, Inez. Squeal away.

INEZ.   What a lovely pair you make! If you could see his big paw splayed out on your back, rucking up your skin and creasing the silk. Be careful, though! He's perspiring, his hand will leave a blue stain on your dress.

ESTELLE.   Squeal away, Inez, squeal away! . . . Hug me tight, darling; tighter still —that'll finish her off, and a good thing too!

INEZ.   Yes, Garcin, she's right. Carry on with it, press her to you till you feel your bodies melting into each other; a lump of warm, throbbing flesh. . . . Love's a grand solace, isn't it, my friend? Deep and dark as sleep. But I'll see you don't sleep.

(GARCIN makes a slight movement.)

ESTELLE.   Don't listen to her. Press your lips to my mouth. Oh, I'm yours, yours, yours.

INEZ.   Well, what are you waiting for? Do as you're told. What a lovely scene: coward Garcin holding baby-killer Estelle in his manly arms! Make your stakes, everyone. Will coward Garcin kiss the lady, or won't he dare? What's the betting? I'm watching you, everybody's watching, I'm a crowd all by myself. Do you hear the crowd? Do you hear them muttering, Garcin? Mumbling and muttering. "Coward! Coward! Coward! Coward!"—that's what they're saying. . . . It's no use trying to escape, I'll never let you go. What do you hope to get from her silly lips? Forgetfulness? But I shan't forget you, not I! "It's I you must convince." So come to me. I'm waiting. Come along, now.

. . . Look how obedient he is, like a well-trained dog who comes when his mistress calls. You can't hold him, and you never will.

GARCIN.   Will night never come?

INEZ.   Never.

GARCIN.   You will always see me?

INEZ.   Always.

(GARCIN *moves away from* ESTELLE *and takes some steps across the room. He goes to the bronze ornament.*)

GARCIN.   This bronze. *(Strokes it thoughtfully.)* Yes, now's the moment; I'm looking at this thing on the mantelpiece, and I understand that I'm in hell. I tell you, everything's been thought out beforehand. They knew I'd stand at the fireplace stroking this thing of bronze, with all those eyes intent on me. Devouring me. *(He swings round abruptly.)* What? Only two of you? I thought there were more; many more. *(Laughs.)* So this is hell. I'd never have believed it. You remember all we were told about the torture-chambers, the fire and brimstone, the "burning marl." Old wives' tales! There's no need for redhot pokers. Hell is—other people!

ESTELLE.   My darling! Please—

GARCIN *(thrusting her away).*   No, let me be. She is between us. I cannot love you when she's watching.

ESTELLE.   Right! In that case, I'll stop her watching.

(She picks up the paper-knife from the table, rushes at INEZ, *and stabs her several times.*)

INEZ *(struggling and laughing).*   But, you crazy creature, what do you think you're doing? You know quite well I'm dead.

ESTELLE.   Dead?

(She drops the knife. A pause. INEZ *picks up the knife and jabs herself with it regretfully.*)

INEZ.   Dead! Dead! Dead! Knives, poison, ropes—all useless. It has happened *already,* do you understand? Once and for all. So here we are, forever. *(Laughs.)*

ESTELLE *(with a peal of laughter).*   Forever. My God, how funny! Forever.

GARCIN *(looks at the two women, and joins in the laughter).*   For ever, and ever, and ever.

(They slump onto their respective sofas. A long silence. Their laughter dies away and they gaze at each other.)

GARCIN.   Well, well, let's get on with it. . . .

CURTAIN

THE DARK ROOT OF A SCREAM

Luis Valdéz

(b. 1940)

Biography p. 1105

Characters

LIZARD
CONEJO
GATO
MADRE
DALIA
PRIEST

Setting

The scene is a collage of myth and reality. It forms, in fact, a pyramid with the most real artifacts of barrio *life at the broad base and an abstract mythical-religious peak at the top. The lighting follows the same pyramidal pattern, from bright at the bottom to dark at the top.*

The bottom part of the set consists of two scenes blending into each other. On the right there is a street corner, a brick wall covered with Chicano *writings in* pachuco *script. Three* vatos locos—LIZARD, CONEJO, *and* GATO—*are huddled against the wall. On the left there is an interior scene showing a* velorio, *a wake, in someone's living room.* MADRE, DALIA, *and the* PRIEST *are entering through a curtained doorway. Inside the room is a metallic black coffin draped with an American flag.*

Above these scenes the images blend one into the other to form the upper part of the structure. Some are made of iron and the hard steel of modern civilization—guns, knives, automobile parts; others reveal a less violent, more spiritual origin—molcajetes, rebozos, crucifixes, etc. Finally, the very top of the pyramid is dominated by ancient indio images: conches, jade, the sun stone, feathered serpent heads.

Footnotes from *From the Barrio: A Chicano Anthology.* Luis Omar Salinas and Lillian Faderman. San Francisco: Canfield Press (a Department of Harper & Row, Publishers, Inc., 1973).

I

LIZARD.   Come on, ese, let's toke up.

(CONEJO lights a leno.)

Man, you sure sucking on that thing.

CONEJO *(Holding his breath).*   I awready had a lotta practice wis Indio.

LIZARD.   Every night?

(CONEJO passes the joint to GATO.)

CONEJO.   Sometimes.

LIZARD.   No wonder the vato used to like you so much, ese. I bet you can open your mouth without showing your teeth, huh? Watcha. *(LIZARD does it, sucks his own tongue.)*

CONEJO *(Realizing).*   ¡Toma![1] *(Gives him the finger.)*

LIZARD *(Laughs).*   Chale,[2] man. No te aguites.[3] Indio's dead anyway. *(He gets the leno.)*

GATO *(Holding his breath).*   Heh, Funnybunny, is your carnala[4] going to the wake?

CONEJO.   I don't know.

GATO.   Don't act stupid, ese!

LIZARD.   Take it easy, man! Poor Funnybunny don't know nothing. Besides, you already know she's going to be there. She was Indio's ruca.[5]

II

(The action at the street corner freezes. There is movement at the coffin. The MADRE comes forward, held by DALIA, then the PRIEST.)

PRIEST.   That's it, easy does it, Señora Gonzáles. No sense in getting hysterical about these things.

(The MADRE kneels at the coffin.)

No, not there, madre. You are supposed to sit over there. On the chair.

DALIA.   She'll be all right here.

PRIEST.   Yes, you're right. Of course. Then I guess you and I can sit over here.

(DALIA and the PRIEST sit on the chairs.)

Terrible thing this war. ¡Ojalá que se acabe pronto con la ayuda de Díos! Tú fuiste la prometida de Indio, ¿qué no?[6]

---

[1]Here!
[2]Hell
[3]Don't get mad.
[4]sister
[5]woman
[6]Hope that it ends quickly with the help of God. You were the one promised to Indio, weren't you?

*(*DALIA *looks at him blankly.)*

      Shall I say it in English?

DALIA.   I can speak Spanish, father.

PRIEST.   Entonces puedes contestarme la pregunta, ¿no?[7]

DALIA.   Sí. Indio and I were engaged.

III

(Action freezes at wake. Movement at street corner.)

CONEJO.   Man, it's hard to think of Indio dead, you know?

GATO.   He never done us no favors.

CONEJO.   You don' care he's dead?

GATO *(Shrugs).*   I din' ask him to join the pinche[8] army.

CONEJO.   He din' join. They draft him.

LIZARD.   Símon, it was you that try to join, ese.

GATO.   Órale, but what happen? *(To* CONEJO*)* We walk into that place and tell 'em we want to join up, you know? The púto[9] sergeant laughed at us, man. "You?" he said. "Son, you guys have records longer than your greasy arms. You been shooting too much smack to let you shoot the gooks." Huh! I coulda give it to the cabrón right in the mother! Split his white gavacho belly like a fat pig! Pinche buey.[10]

LIZARD *(Laughs).*   You shoulda cut out his pecker, ese.

IV

(Action freezes at street corner. Movement at the wake. MADRE *makes a choked sound. She is leaning forward, touching the place where the flag sweeps the floor. The* PRIEST *goes forward and sweeps his hand over the same spot. His hand picks up a red stain.)*

MADRE.   Sangre.

PRIEST *(Realization hits him.).*   Oh my God!

MADRE.   ¡Su sangre . . . se está saliendo de la caja! ¡Mijo está vivo! ¡Todavía está vivo![11]

PRIEST.   Now, madre, calm down.

MADRE.   ¡Es su sangre, padre!

PRIEST.   No, señora, creo qué no.[12]

MADRE *(To the coffin).*   ¡Mijito, mijito de mi vida, estás perdiendo tu sangre![13]

---

[7]Then you can answer the question, can't you?

[8]damn

[9]queer

[10]Damn guy.

[11]His blood . . . is coming out of the box! My son is alive! He is still alive!

[12]No, señora, I believe it isn't.

[13]My little son, my little son of my life, you are losing your blood!

PRIEST.　　　Madre, why don't you sit—

MADRE *(Starting to get hysterical).*　　　¡No! ¡No me quiten de mijo! ¡Tengo que verlo! ¡Tengo que verlo![14] *(She tries to open coffin.)*

MADRE.　　　¡Ayyyyyy! ¡Mijo! ¡Mijito de mi alma! ¡Estás muerto y se te está perdiendo la sangre! ¡Ayyyyy, corazón de tu madre, te mataron y nunca te volví a ver! ¡No me dejes, hijo! ¡No dejes a tu madre![15] *(She faints.)*

(PRIEST holds MADRE and with the help of DALIA moves her over to a chair. MADRE is moaning with grief. A medal falls from her hand.)

DALIA.　　　¿Doña Rosa?

PRIEST.　　　¿SEÑNORA? ¡Señora Gonzáles!

DALIA.　　　I'll get some alcohol. *(She goes out.)*

PRIEST *(Looks down at stain on floor).*　　　Bendito sea Dios.[16]

V

CONEJO.　　　You think they gonna open Indio's coffin?

LIZARD.　　　Chale, not a chance. They get him wis a grenade, and I bet you coulda put the pieces in a shoebox. By now he probably look like a rotten enchilada.

CONEJO.　　　I don' like to talk like that.

GATO.　　　You vatos shoulda seen a dead cousin I had once. He was knife in Phoenix, and they ship him out here by train after two weeks, you know? My tia open up the lid to look at him. His hair was black still, but his skin was yellow like pus and the wax in his eyes was melting, and the smell of death was coming through his mouth.

LIZARD.　　　Man, and you look at that? *(Spits)* Smell is right.

GATO.　　　I bet Indio smells like that.

(DALIA returns to the room on the opposite side with a bottle of alcohol and a cloth. She drenches the cloth. The PRIEST takes it.)

PRIEST.　　　Here, madre, smell this.

(The MADRE moans.)

DALIA *(Putting alcohol on the MADRE'S neck).*　　　¿Doña Rosa? Soy yo, señora,[17] Dalia. I think she's waking up.

PRIEST.　　　We'd better clean that up before she—

(MADRE moans in half-conscious grief.)

Ya, madre, no llore. Aquí estoy contigo.[18] Do you have a mop?

(DALIA nods, then looks at the stain on the floor.)

[14]Don't! Don't take me from my son! I have to see him! I have to see him!

[15]My son! My little son of my soul! You're dead and you are losing your blood! Ayyyyy, heart of your mother, they killed you and never again did I see you! Don't leave me, son! Don't leave your mother!

[16]Blessed be God

[17]It's me, señora

[18]There, Mother, don't cry. Here I am with you.

Don't you be silly now. It's not what you think it is.

(MADRE *moans—it is almost a cry.*)

Get the mop.

(DALIA *exits.* PRIEST *prays.*)

Padre nuestro que estás en los cielos, santificado sea tu nombre . . .[19]

VI

GATO *(Passing the cigarette).*   Aquí te va, loco.[20]
LIZARD.   Órale. Dumb-ass vato.
GATO.   Who?
LIZARD.   Indio. I told him not to go in the army.
CONEJO.   He had to go.
LIZARD.   Shit, man. Then what was all this pedo[21] about Chicano power and
        snuffing gavachos? Some Chicano leader he turned out to be.
CONEJO.   If he din't go, they would put him in the pinta.
LIZARD.   Who says? You remember La Mula? He was drafted a couple of years
        ago, and the vato's still on the street. Símon,[22] he just took a little vacation in
        Mexicali, and that was it, man. Indio knew about it, too. If you ask me, that
        vato just like to be out front talking like he was a heavy dude. Now look where
        he's at.
CONEJO.   They give him a Congressional Medal.
LIZARD *(To* GATO*).*   Este vato,[23] man.

VII

(DALIA *has entered and the* PRIEST *mops the stain on the floor. He picks up the
medal.*)

PRIEST.   There, you see? All wiped up. It must have been the dye from the flag.

(*The* MADRE *revives.*)

DALIA.   Señora, ¿cómo se siente?[24]
PRIEST.   You're going to be all right, madre. You fainted. I think you'd better go
        lie down for a while.
DALIA.   Véngase al cuarto para que descanse, señora.[25]

[19]Our Father Who art in Heaven, hallowed be Thy name . . .
[20]Here you go, crazy.
[21]ruckus
[22]Yes
[23]This dude
[24]Señora, how do you feel?
[25]Come to the room so you can rest, señora.

MADRE.   No—

PRIEST.   Vale más que vaya.[26] I'll call you when we start the prayers. Here you dropped this. *(Gives her the medal)* In spite of your grief, you can be very proud of your son. The Congressional Medal of Honor is the highest award his country could give him.

MADRE.   La medalla. Ya van tres.[27]

PRIEST.   ¿Tres?

DALIA.   That's right, father. She has three. One for her oldest boy killed in France, another killed in Korea, and now Indio.

PRIEST.   I didn't know! Madre, you should be taken to see the President. El Presidente, usted debe ir a conocerlo.[28]

MADRE.   Cuauhtemoc, Nezahualcoytl, Quetzalcóatl.

PRIEST.   Perdóname, no entiendo. Otra vez más despacio por favor.[29]

MADRE.   Cuauhtemoc, Nezahualcoytl, Quetzalcóatl.

PRIEST.   I'm sorry. Did you get that? My Spanish isn't bad, but that—

DALIA.   It isn't Spanish, father. Those are the Indian names of her three sons.

(DALIA exits with MADRE.)

PRIEST.   Ah.

VIII

GATO.   Hah! So that's it for Indio, vatos. A medal for your honor and a stinking box. Old chickenshit Gonzáles! Or whatever his name was.

CONEJO.   It was Quetzalcóatl.

LIZARD.   Quetza—what?

CONEJO.   Quetzalcóatl, the feathered serpent.

PRIEST.   Quetzalcóatl Gonzáles. What a name for an American soldier. I wonder what it means? The first part, of course. Everyone knows what Gonzáles means.

CONEJO.   Quetzal means a green bird and cóatl means serpent. Birdserpent. Quetzalcóatl. Feathered-serpent.

LIZARD.   You're fulla shit.

(DALIA re-enters alone.)

IX

PRIEST.   How did Indio come to have a name like that?

CONEJO.   His father name him that.

PRIEST.   Oh yes, his father. How did his father—?

DALIA.   He was a teacher in Mexico.

---

[26]You'd better go.
[27]The medal. That makes three.
[28]The President, you should go meet him.
[29]Pardon me, I don't understand. Another time, this time more slowly, please.

CONEJO.   His name was Mixcóatl—Cloud-serpent.

PRIEST.   I see. A nationalist, eh?

LIZARD.   So what, man? Over here he was a wetback, a farm laborer just like everybody else.

PRIEST.   A political exile, no doubt.

CONEJO.   He knew a lot about Mexican history. Quetzalcóatl used to be a god for the Indians a long time ago.

LIZARD.   Sure, man, the Apaches.

CONEJO.   Chale, indios mexicanos. Like us, we got Aztec blood.

PRIEST.   Is that how Indio learned about the Aztecs? From his father?

DALIA.   Just at first. He died when Indio was eight.

PRIEST.   And left his son misguided. Full of hate.

CONEJO.   Indio used to say a Chicano is an indio with a white man's name.

LIZARD.   Like what?

CONEJO.   Gonzáles.

GATO.   Bullshit, that ain't white.

CONEJO.   It's Spanish. They're white.

GATO.   Who says?

CONEJO.   Indio used to.

X

PRIEST.   That's the only thing that bothers me about this Chicano thing: the racism. Indio was a racist, you know.

DALIA.   Why? Because he taught Chicanos to be proud of what they have—their culture, their heritage?

CONEJO.   Símon, he used to say to be proud of our nonwhite heritage.

LIZARD.   Listen to this vato, ese. What did you say, Funnybunny?

CONEJO.   I don' know. Heritage?

PRIEST.   What heritage is that—human sacrifice?

LIZARD.   Símon.

CONEJO.   Like Quetzalcóatl. He put a stop to human sacrifice.

PRIEST.   I'm sure Indio didn't mean that.

DALIA.   How do you know?

PRIEST.   Because the true facts are not very inspiring at all, Dalia. As a matter of fact, I've studied the subject with a great deal of interest.

GATO.   Big deal.

PRIEST.   The Indians of Mexico practiced ritualistic cannibalism and human sacrifice.

CONEJO.   They used to take these vatos up to a pyramid, you know? Then they put 'em on a big stone—like this, watcha—then wis a big knife—

GATO.   A filero?[30]

PRIEST.   They would tear the living heart out of the bodies of their victims and offer them to their merciless sun god!

[30]knife

LIZARD.   ¡En la madre![31]
GATO.   Who did they sacrifice, ese?
CONEJO.   Oh, sometimes virgins.
LIZARD.   They cut off a chichi to get to the heart, ese.
CONEJO.   Most of the time it was prisoners from the wars.
PRIEST.   They'd have wars especially to capture sacrificial victims.
CONEJO.   They used to call 'em Wars of the Flowers, because nobody was sup-
     posed to get kill. Only take prisoners.
PRIEST.   Some of the captives even considered it an honor to be sacrificed.
CONEJO.   They used to take 'em beans and chocolate to fatten them, you know?
     Then they bring in rucas[32] for 'em and pulque.[33]
LIZARD.   ¿Pulque?
CONEJO.   Pisto.[34]
GATO.   No shit?
CONEJO.   Símon.
PRIEST.   Then after the victims were sufficiently fattened on cactus wine and
     half-naked Indian women, they would be taken to the pyramid of the Sun or
     Moon or Corn God or any of their thousand gods, and there they would
     undergo bloody sacrifice. All in the name of religion.

XI

CONEJO.   And that's the way it was until Quetzalcóatl became the chief. He put
     a stop to all that.
LIZARD.   Nel, he din't.
CONEJO.   Símon. After that he only allowed them to sacrifice monkeys and rocks.
LIZARD.   No more rucas or pisto?
CONEJO.   Chale.[35]
GATO.   Din' I tell you, man? Chickenshit Gonzáles all over again! Pura périca[36]
     and no action.
LIZARD.   So how come this Quetzalcóatl was so hot? He din' do madre.
CONEJO.   That's what you think. He made miracles and change the indio civiliza-
     tion all around.

XII

DALIA.   I don't think you understand what Indio was trying to do, father.
LIZARD.   So what he do?
CONEJO.   He built great pyramids.

[31]Oh, wow!
[32]women
[33]a type of drink
[34]Liquor.
[35]Hell.
[36]Pure talk

DALIA.   He wanted the Raza to be close to God.

CONEJO.   He give the indios corn and fire.

DALIA.   He wanted our people to have enough to eat.

CONEJO.   He show 'em how to make pottery and paint and write books.

DALIA.   He wanted Chicanos to express and educate themselves.

CONEJO.   He teach 'em how to make their own government.

DALIA.   He wanted us to live free and equal.

CONEJO.   He was against all the wars.

DALIA.   He didn't want his carnales to die uselessly.

CONEJO.   He was the God of Civilization.

DALIA.   He was a beautiful nuevo hombre.[37]

CONEJO.   He was a vato de aquellos.[38]

XIII

LIZARD.   ¿Sabes qué?[39] There's only one thing I don't understand, ese. If this Quetzalcóatl was so great, what happen to him?

CONEJO.   The priests got rid of him.

LIZARD.   What priests?

CONEJO.   The Aztec priests. They wanted war and human sacrifice.

DALIA.   Why were you against Indio, father?

PRIEST.   I wasn't against him!

DALIA.   Then why didn't you loan him the church hall for meetings?

PRIEST.   My Dalia, Indio's meetings were violently political. It's not the business of the Church to get involved in such matters.

DALIA.   Some priests do.

PRIEST.   And they must answer to their bishops. Besides, Indio was politically naive.

GATO.   I remember Indio talking all that shit at meetings. He was full of it.

PRIEST.   If you must know, it was some of your own Raza, some Chicanos in the parish, that kept me from loaning Indio the hall. They didn't like what he had to say. What could I do?

DALIA.   You could have done anything, father. You're barrio priest.

LIZARD.   Tell me something, ese. If Quetzalcóatl was a god, how could the priests put him down?

CONEJO.   They call in his brother who was a evil god, Tezcatlípoca. He give 'em a mirror and told them to give it to Quetzalcóatl for a present.

LIZARD.   A mirror?

CONEJO.   Símon, then when Quetzalcóatl see himself in it, he got all scared. Se escamó.[40]

LIZARD.   What did he see?

---

[37]new man
[38]one of those far-out guys
[39]You know what?
[40]He got scared.

CONEJO.   I don't know. But he ask the priests to hide him. So they give him pulque[41] and honey and got him drunk. Then they brought in a ruca for him.

LIZARD.   ¡Hay te llevo! ¿Y se la dejó—?[42]

CONEJO.   Símon, only he wasn' supposed to because he was a god. After that his people turned against him, so he sailed off into the sea on a raft of serpents, telling everybody he was coming back someday.

LIZARD.   ¿Y qué? Did he?

CONEJO.   I don' know.

LIZARD.   ¡Este vato, man! How did you learn all this shit, Funnybunny?

CONEJO *(Shrugs).*   Maybe I'm pendejo[43] like everybody says, but I learn something from Indio. Now he's dead.

XIV

PRIEST.   All I can do now is pray for his immortal soul that God might forgive him.

DALIA.   For what?

PRIEST.   Sus pecados, mujer.[44] Or do you believe he was beyond mortal sin?

GATO.   Chale, man! You vatos got me up to here with Indio. If he was so smart, he wouldn't be lying over at the wake stiff like he is.

PRIEST.   In the final analysis, he was just a boy. Filled with anxiety, uncertainty, fear.

GATO.   All that cuacha[45] he used to say din't mean nothing.

PRIEST.   He came to see me, you know, shortly after he received his draft notice.

GATO.   He rapped against the war, but his time came and he had to go a huevo[46] just like everybody else.

PRIEST.   He was concerned what the barrio would think if he refused induction.

GATO.   If he'd gone to the pinta instead of the army, all the barrio would have said he was chicken.

PRIEST.   He was considering fleeing the country, but he knew he'd never be able to return as a community leader.

GATO.   Big community leader. That draft notice showed him to his face who he was, like a mirror.

PRIEST.   He was caught. He'd been playing at revolución, but the draft letter snapped him back to reality. He wasn't Zapata or Ché Guevara or even Quetzalcóatl, really. He was just Indio—and as Indio, he knew he had no choice, so he went.

GATO.   He tried to play the odds and make it out alive. He lost.

[41]a type of drink
[42]That's really together! And he left her—?
[43]stupid
[44]His sins, women.
[45]bullshit
[46]by force

XV

DALIA.   You're wrong, father. Indio *was* Quetzalcóatl. You just can't see it, because you're racist.

PRIEST *(Pause).*   You hurt me deeply, Dalia. I've always loved your people. I've always felt God had a special place for them.

DALIA.   Where, at the bottom of society?

PRIEST.   This is precisely the kind of talk that turned many of your people against Indio!

DALIA.   He knew that. Our people have loved your God very much. We've brought little things to him—candles, oraciones, devotions—all that we have, even our blood in penance. Or in war. We've loved him because we saw him nailed to a cross, suffering and bleeding like us. Every time we've been cheated, worked like animals, had our lands stolen—we've cried out and prayed to him to help us. ¡Jesucristo! Nothing has happened. But we still go on believing in him like faithful indios.

PRIEST.   Do you still believe in him, Dalia? *(Pause)* Do you?

DALIA.   I don't know. Indio was Quetzalcóatl, and—

PRIEST.   Quetzalcóatl is dead! Remember your commandments? I will not have false Gods before me.

DALIA.   He said he was coming back! *(She weeps.)* Indio!

PRIEST *(Embracing her).*   Padre nuestro, ayudanos a olvidar a este hombre.[47]

XVI

LIZARD.   Yeah, that Indio was one vato I'll never forget.

CONEJO.   A lotta Chicanos learned from him.

GATO.   Who's that, you?

CONEJO.   Nel, lots of raza in the barrio.

GATO.   Oh, símon, I forgot. He was a Chicano leader. Shit, man! What about that last parranda[48] he took after the army call him? Cagó la estaca,[49] man! He was pedo[50] for two weeks and even showed up drunk at a picket line. Then he split with your carnala.[51] I bet your jefitos[52] aren't gonna forget Indio.

PRIEST.   Is your family coming?

(DALIA shakes her head no.)

LIZARD *(To CONEJO).*   How does your sister feel, ese?

GATO.   That depends, man. You mean how she feels or how she *feels.*

CONEJO.   Oh, she's okay, except she cry a lot when Indio was killed.

[47]Our Father, help us to forget this man.
[48]drunken spree
[49]Shitted the stick
[50]drunk
[51]sister
[52]parents

GATO.   Hah! Listen to this vato, man. You're pretty funny, Funnybunny?

CONEJO.   How come?

GATO.   Well, shit, you'd cry too if the vato that was doing it to you got kill.

CONEJO.   Indio was't doing it to her!

GATO.   He took off for a week and din't do nothing, uh? ¡Madera! He did what he wanted, then dumped her off. Ain't that right, Funnybunny?

CONEJO *(Feigning ignorance).*   What?

GATO.   Did Indio pump your carnala?

CONEJO.   Dalia?

GATO.   I don't mean your old lady.

XVII

(MADRE re-enters.)

PRIEST.   ¿Se siente mejor, madre?[53]

MADRE.   Sí, padre, perdóneme.[54]

PRIEST.   No hay que perdonar.[55]

GATO.   WELL?

CONEJO.   I don' know.

GATO.   You're lying, cabrón.[56]

LIZARD.   Aw, get off his case, man! You'd like to pump his sister yourself: I seen the way you go around sniffing up her tail like a dog.

GATO.   Shut up, Lizard.

LIZARD.   You got so much envidia,[57] you wish it was your wake tonight instead of Indio's.

GATO.   Shut up, ese!

LIZARD.   You're licking up Indio's blood.

GATO *(With sinister malevolence).*   Who's going to lick up yours, púto? You want this filero in your guts?

(Pulls out knife; LIZARD *does too.)*

CONEJO.   Eh, man, contrólensela![58] Come on, Lizard.

LIZARD.   Stay outa this, punk.

CONEJO.   Gato, let's go to the wake. It's midnight already.

GATO.   Fuck you, Funnybunny. *(To* LIZARD*)* Some night I'm going to slit your green belly with this.

LIZARD.   ¡Pos pónle, ese![59] Órale, try it. Come on.

(They fight. GATO *kicks the knife out of* LIZARD's *hand, and traps him.)*

[53]Do you feel better, Mother?
[54]Yes, father, forgive me.
[55]There's nothing to forgive.
[56]bastard
[57]envy
[58]cool it
[59]Well, get it on, man!

GATO *(Pause).*   What do you say now, ese?
LIZARD.   Me la pelas.[60]

(GATO pushes LIZARD's face to one side and walks off putting knife away.)

GATO.   Let's go to the fucking wake. *(Exit)*

(CONEJO follows GATO, glancing back at LIZARD, who is still on the ground.)

LIZARD *(Standing up, dusting off).*   Chickenshit!

(He struts off, chuco style, after GATO and CONEJO.)

XVIII

(Prayers start at the wake. PRIEST kneels facing downstage and toward the women, but addressing heaven.)

PRIEST.   Now we will pray.

(All cross themselves.)

En nomine patri, et filio, et spiritu sanctu, amen, amen. Merciful Señor, author of infinite forgiveness, here lies the poor mortal flesh of Quetzalcóatl Gonzáles.
WOMEN *(DALIA and MADRE).*   Bless him, Señor.
PRIEST.   Quetzalcóatl, your humble servant, who was named by his pagan father but who was called Indio by his Catholic madre and all who came to love him.
WOMEN.   Bless him, Señor.
PRIEST.   Quetzalcóatl, your humble—

(GATO, CONEJO, and LIZARD walk in and stand at the door.)

Please, come in. Pray with us.

(LIZARD starts to go; GATO grabs him. CONEJO looks at LIZARD then at DALIA and shrugs his shoulders. As CONEJO tries to kneel beside his sister, GATO edges him to one side. LIZARD then crowds in next to GATO. PRIEST clears his throat.)

PRIEST.   Quetzalcóatl, your humble servant, who was born of the body of woman and died by the hand of man amid the bloody excrement of war.
WOMEN.   Bless him, Señor.
PRIEST *(Whispers to vatos).*   Say "Bless him, Señor." *(Pause)* Go on, say it. The Señor is listening. *(He points heavenward.)*

(CONEJO and LIZARD look up. LIZARD is about to laugh and nudges CONEJO. GATO looks at DALIA, whose head is bowed.)

Come, come, say it!
VATOS *(Clumsily, overlapping one another).*   Bless him, Señor.
PRIEST.   Again.
VATOS *(Still clumsily).*   Bless him, Señor.

[60]You got me.

PRIEST *(Making a face).* Try to follow the women, please. *(Clears throat)* Quet-
zalcóatl, your humble servant, who knew love of God.
ALL *(Clumsily because of boys).* Bless him, Señor.
PRIEST. Quetzalcóatl, your humble servant, who knew love of church.
ALL. Bless him, Señor.

(GATO's hand strokes DALIA's back.)

PRIEST. Quetzalcóatl, your humble servant, who knew love of madre.
ALL. Bless him, Señor.
PRIEST. Quetzalcóatl, your humble servant, who knew love of country.
ALL. Bless him, Señor.

(DALIA shakes off GATO's hand. PRIEST pauses.)

PRIEST. Quetzalcóatl, your humble servant, who knew love of flag.
ALL. Bless him, Señor.
PRIEST. Quetzalcóatl, your humble servant, who knew love of obedience.
ALL. Bless him, Señor.

(GATO's hand comes up again.)

PRIEST *(Intoning rhythmically).* Bless him, Señor. Now he is dead. Quetzalcóatl . . .
WOMEN *(Completing chanted phrases).* Your humble servant.
PRIEST *(Pause).* Well, come on, boys. Where's your catechism? Quetzalcóatl . . .
VATOS *(Clumsily).* Your humble serpent!
PRIEST. WHAT?
VATOS *(Clumsier).* Your humble serpent!
PRIEST. Again!
VATOS *(LIZARD shouts.).* Your humble serpent!

XIX

PRIEST *(Standing).* Serpent! *(Sees GATO fooling with DALIA)* What are you doing?
Have you no respect for the dead? Stop that!
GATO. Stop what?
PRIEST. Get out of here!

(GATO and LIZARD laugh.)

My child, call the police.
GATO *(Grabs DALIA).* No, you don'!
DALIA. Let me go, Gato!
MADRE. ¡Muchachos, por Díos, mijo está muerto y tendido! ¿Cómo pueden hacer
esto?[61]
GATO. AAAH, we're not doing nothing.
MADRE. ¡Padrecito, haz algo![62]

---

[61]Children, for God's sake, my son is dead and lying still! How can you do this?
[62]Dear father do something!

(LIZARD *pulls out a knife casually.*)

PRIEST *(Pause).*   I'm going to get help! *(Rushes out)*

LIZARD.   Heh, man! *(Runs out after the* PRIEST*)*

DALIA.   Conejo, help me!

CONEJO.   Cut it out, Gato.

GATO.   Later for you, punk! *(Pushes* CONEJO *away)*

DALIA *(Almost screaming).*   Let me go, let me go! *(Kicks, scratches* GATO*)*

GATO.   Órale, esa, come off it, man! *(Shoves her aside)* What's all the pedo[63] anyway? We don't come for this! That father shouldn't have tell you to call the pigs.

DALIA.   Get out of here or I will!

GATO.   Órale, and what happen to all the carnalismo?[64] Din't Indio say we gotta unite against the placa?[65]

DALIA.   Somebody oughta kill you!

XX

GATO.   Oh yeah, well who's going to do it? Funnybunny? How about it, Funnybunny? You going to snuff me? Or maybe it's Indio, uh? Símon, the chingón's[66] going to do it. Din't he say he was coming back? Well there he is, ese. He came back. Tell him to get up and snuff me! *(Goes to coffin, bangs on it)* Heh, Indio, it's me, man—Gato! I'm calling you out, ese! I say you're a liar! The Raza's full of shit!

MADRE *(Bloodchilling wail).*   AYYYYYYYYYYYYYY! *(She attacks* GATO.*)*

(DALIA *pulls her away.*)

GATO *(Startled).*   Heh, man, cut that out! *(He backs off.)*

MADRE.   ¿Señor, Señor, cómo puedes permitir ésto, Dios mío?[67] *(She drops to her knees in front of the coffin. Her voice is a despairing whisper.)* ¡Mijo está muerto y estos canallas siguen viviendo![68]

GATO.   Aah, what are you talking, señora? How do you know Indio's in there anyway? You see him? The gavachos send you a stinking coffin; that don't mean Indio's in it.

LIZARD *(Runs in wearing* PRIEST*'s cassock).*   Heh, look what I got! Now I'm a priest like I always want to do it. *(Laughs, blesses* CONEJO*)*

CONEJO.   Where's the father?

LIZARD.   Running down the street in his shorts. *(He glances at* DALIA *and* MADRE.*)* Órale, what are they doing?

[63]ruckus
[64]brotherhood
[65]police
[66]big shot's
[67]God, God, how can you permit this, my God?
[68]My son is dead and these cowards continue to live!

XXI

(They turn toward DALIA *and the* MADRE. *Blood is dripping from flag and coffin again.* CONEJO *goes over to them. The* MADRE *has blood on her hands and is moaning almost inaudibly.)*

CONEJO.   ¡Hijo de la chi—![69] Heh, ese, this thing's dripping blood!
LIZARD.   Blood!
GATO.   You're full of it, Funnybunny.

*(*LIZARD *and* GATO *see for themselves.)*

LIZARD.   It's coming from the flag!
CONEJO.   Chale, it's from the box. Watcha! Let's get out of here, man!
GATO.   Let's open it.
LIZARD.   Open what?
GATO.   The coffin, pendejo.[70]
LIZARD.   'Tás lucas.[71]
GATO.   Funnybunny?
CONEJO.   Screw you, man, I ain't gonna do nothing.
GATO *(To* LIZARD*).*   How about it, ese, you chicken to do it?
LIZARD.   Nel, but you're crazy. This thing's welded together, man!
GATO.   Let's see. *(He pulls off the flag and unsnaps the locks: the coffin snaps open with a thud. The lid is ready to be lifted.)* Okay, which of you vatos is going to help me open it?

XXII

CONEJO.   You really going to do it?
GATO.   What's it look like, punk? Now come and help me.
DALIA.   Don't do it, Conejo! *(She rushes to him.)*
CONEJO.   I'm not doing nothing.
GATO.   Well, Lizard, what you going to do, vato? It's all set. What's the matter? I cut off your machos[72] back on the street? Come on, ese—it's your big leader waiting for you in there. He promise to come back, din't he? Go look at him!
LIZARD.   You go look at him.
GATO.   Chale, that's too easy. I'll do it, if you do it.
DALIA *(Glancing toward the coffin).*   ¡Doña Rosa!

[69]Son of a bitch!
[70]stupid
[71]You're crazy.
[72]manhood

XXIII

(The MADRE *is at the coffin.* DALIA *rushes to her, then* CONEJO, *then* LIZARD. GATO *stays behind. The others are too late.* MADRE *lifts the lid. Everyone gasps, expecting the worst.)*

CONEJO.   It's . . . feathers!

*(*LIZARD *reaches in and pulls out a brilliant headdress of green feathers and a cloak of Aztec design.)*

LIZARD.   Man, this is better than this priest thing! *(He puts the cloak and headdress on.)* How do I look, ese?

GATO *(At loss for what to say).*   See? I tell you it wasn't Indio.

(Drums begin to beat immediately, low and somber and increasingly loud.)

LIZARD.   What's that?

GATO.   Sounds like drums.

(The MADRE *has found something else in the coffin. She cries with horror. Everyone turns to her.)*

GATO.   What?

LIZARD.   Something else in there?

(They approach the coffin and look in. LIZARD, *in his headdress, is at the center of the group. He reaches in and pulls out something, turning around and holding it up before him. Lights dim.)*

LIZARD *(Screams).*   Indio's heart!

(The heart gives out light in the descending darkness.)

(Curtain)

CHOICES AND CONFLICTS

TOPICS FOR SHORT PAPERS, JOURNALS, OR DISCUSSION

1. Take one or more of the selections in this section and discuss the choices the characters made, referring to specific parts of the text. For example:

- Why did Noah beat his wife?
- Why did the narrator in "Company" go to bed in a motel with the French hitchhiker?
- Why did Young Goodman Brown go into the woods? After he met the stranger, why did he not leave when he said he wanted to?
- Why did Louisa of "A New England Nun" finally refuse to marry Joe?
- Why did Johnny Eagle try to traverse Navaho Canyon on his bike?
- Does Kaph decide to go farther out into space with Owen and Martin? Why do you think so?

2. The characters in the plays and stories in this section fall into three sometimes-overlapping categories: those controlled by circumstances, those who make conscious choices of life-style, and those who use their strengths to influence others. Select some characters from this section who illustrate or dramatize one of these categories, and discuss the common thread that ties them together.

LONGER PAPERS OR RESEARCH PROJECTS

3. Read about existentialist philosophy in reference works and source books, and then consider how some selections, notably Sartre's *No Exit,* Kotzwinkle's "Follow the Eagle," and Hellman's "Julia," fit into this twentieth-century view of existence.

4. Several of the works in this section ("Julia," "Company," *Noah,* "Nine Lives," for example) contain a number of academic or obscure references that require explanation for full understanding of the story. Footnote one of the selections, doing relevant research as necessary, or, in the case of "Nine Lives," drawing on your imagination to define or explain terminology, conditions, characters, or events. Your audience should be your classmates, and your aim to help them understand and appreciate the story more completely.

5. An idea that filters through several of the works in this section is how legends are formed and how modern myths are made. Examples of mythmaking in the news today are glamorous public figures, heroes, terrorists, and eccentrics. Look back over the poems, stories, and plays in this section and discuss one or more in which this process occurs. Examples in this section are Lillian Hellman's heroic characterization of Julia, Edwin Arlington Robinson's depiction of the life of ease of Richard Cory, the townspeople's impression of Miss Emily in William Faulkner's story "A Rose for Emily," and Indio from Luis Valdez's play *The Dark Root of a Scream.*

CREATIVE PROJECT

6. Take one of the characters in *The Dark Root of a Scream* or *No Exit,* and on the basis of what the character says about his or her past life, construct a story of some incident in the past or in the future with that character as protagonist, or an autobiography for that character.

Abstraction Blue, 1927, by Georgia O'Keeffe. (The Museum of Modern Art, New York, Acquired through the Helen Acheson Request.)

DREAMS AND REALIZATIONS

THE NEW COLOSSUS

Not like the brazen giant of Greek fame,
With conquering limbs astride from land to land;
Here at our sea-washed, sunset gates shall stand
A mighty woman with a torch, whose flame
Is the imprisoned lightning, and her name
Mother of Exiles. From her beacon-hand
Glows world-wide welcome; her mild eyes command
The air-bridged harbor that twin cities frame.
"Keep, ancient lands, your storied pomp!" cries she
With silent lips. "Give me your tired, your poor,
Your huddled masses yearning to breathe free,
The wretched refuse of your teeming shore,
Send these, the homeless, tempest-tossed to me:
I lift my lamp beside the golden door."

Emma Lazarus

The words carved at the base of the Statue of Liberty in New York Harbor stand as an appropriate epigraph to this final section: "Give me your tired, your poor, Your huddled masses yearning to be free. . . ." In the early years of this century, these words were seen by thousands of immigrants passing by ship into New York Harbor on their way to new lives. The "mighty woman" Liberty who lights her "lamp beside the golden door" has symbolized the American dream for millions. Today, the statue has been renewed and repaired, and immigrants now enter through the impersonal door of an airline terminal. But Emma Lazarus's poem, chosen to be carved on the base of the statue, still inspires those who have chosen the path of change, be they immigrant or not.

Earlier sections of this book define who these people are. They are of all ages; they live in many environments; they are both rich and poor in relationships with other people; and they face dilemmas demanding choices and creating conflicts. The literary works presented in this section involve the most personal aspects of these people: their hopes and their aspirations in the face of sometimes monumental odds. Within this framework, some characters win and some lose; some choose wisely and some poorly. The common denominator is that all of these people struggle in some way to make their dreams come true.

Again, the section begins with a myth, an archetype of the search for dreams—the pilgrimage. A pilgrimage is a difficult journey in quest of an ideal, often religious in motivation and goal, in which the protagonist grows and is purified by trials encountered along the way. In Doris Betts's "The Ugliest Pilgrim," Violet's dream of a cured defect is thwarted, but she achieves something better, for beauty turns out not to hold the highest value for her. The pilgrimage motif fits well into the probing of both dreams and realizations for both immigrants and native Americans who seek something better—sometimes a new land, sometimes a new life, sometimes just a new understanding.

Walt Whitman's words "I hear America singing," echoed by Langston Hughes's poem, "I, Too," perhaps typify the hope and the optimism that inform so many dreams. Even apparently failed dreams, such as Ah Goong's in Maxine Hong Kingston's "The Grandfather of the Sierra Nevada Mountains," become part of building a new country. Stephen Vincent Benét's "By the Waters of Babylon" shows that courage can rebuild a ruined world if humans do not "eat knowledge too fast." A black mother in Ernest J. Gaines's "The Sky Is Gray" teaches her son to be strong, to have pride in himself. Poems such as Marge Piercy's "To Be of Use" and Sylvia Plath's "Mushrooms" have voices that cry out to be heard.

But other works bleakly portray those who have pursued a dream unsuccessfully. Charlotte Perkins Gilman's chilling story "The Yellow Wallpaper," about the beginnings of madness, shows a woman, robbed of choices, slipping into insanity. Tom, Amanda, and Laura in Tennessee Williams's *The Glass Menagerie* each cling desperately to some flicker of hope for better lives which, like Laura's candles, threatens continuously to go out. In *for colored girls who have considered suicide when the rainbow is enuf,* Ntozake Shange puts the thwarted dreams of black women into the form of a choreopoem, combining poetry and dance. Finally, poems such as Abelardo Delgado's "stupid America" tell of dreams of a decent life snuffed out or never realized.

"Things fall apart, the center cannot hold," Yeats says in "The Second Coming."

In spite of this gloomy prophecy, some of the world's meek people, like some of the characters in these selections, may yet inherit the earth. Black, white, oriental, Chicano, and native American writers record their dreams here, as for better or for worse they butt up against actuality. Some stalwart though bumbling characters, like those in Joyce Carol Oates's "Out of Place" or Philip Roth's "Defender of the Faith" may, as Richard Wilbur's poem "Mind" suggests, "correct the cave" in which they live. Martin Luther King's "Dream" of hope and freedom *is* still alive!

Fiction

THE UGLIEST PILGRIM

Doris Betts
(b. 1932)

Biography p. 1061

I sit in the bus station, nipping chocolate peel off a Mounds candy bar with my teeth, then pasting the coconut filling to the roof of my mouth. The lump will dissolve there slowly and seep into me the way dew seeps into flowers.

I like to separate flavors that way. Always I lick the salt off cracker tops before taking my first bite.

Somebody sees me with my suitcase, paper sack, and a ticket in my lap. "You going someplace, Violet?"

Stupid. People in Spruce Pine are dumb and, since I look dumb, say dumb things to me. I turn up my face as if to count those dead flies piled under the light bulb. He walks away—a fat man, could be anybody. I stick out my tongue at his back; the candy oozes down. If I could stop swallowing, it would drip into my lung and I could breathe vanilla.

Whoever it was, he won't glance back. People in Spruce Pine don't like to look at me, full face.

A Greyhound bus pulls in, blows air; the driver stands by the door. He's black-headed, maybe part Cherokee, with heavy shoulders but a weak chest. He thinks well of himself—I can tell that. I open my notebook and copy his name off the metal plate so I can call him by it when he drives me home again. And next week, won't Mr. Wallace Weatherman be surprised to see how well I'm looking!

I choose the front seat behind Mr. Weatherman, settle my bag with the hat in it, then open the lined composition book again. Maybe it's half full of writing. Even the empty pages toward the back have one repeated entry, high, printed off Mama's torn catechism: GLORIFY GOD AND ENJOY HIM FOREVER.

I finish Mr. Weatherman off in my book while he's running his motor and getting us onto the highway. His nose is too broad, his dark eyes too skimpy—nothing in his face I want—but the hair is nice. I write that down, "Black hair?" I'd want it to curl, though, and be soft as a baby's.

Two others are on the bus, a nigger soldier and an old woman whose jaw sticks out like a shelf. There grow, on the backs of her hands, more veins than skin. One fat blue vessel, curling from wrist to knuckle, would be good; so on one page I draw a sample hand and let blood wind across it like a river. I write at the bottom: "Praise God, it is started. May 29, 1969," and turn to a new sheet. The paper's lumpy and I flip back to the thick envelope stuck there with adhesive tape. I can't lose that.

We're driving now at the best speed Mr. Weatherman can make on these winding roads. On my side there is nothing out the bus window but granite rock, jagged and wet in patches. The old lady and the nigger can see red rhododendron on the slope of Roan Mountain. I'd like to own a tight dress that flower color, and breasts to go under it. I write in my notebook, very small, the word "breasts," and turn quickly to another page. AND ENJOY HIM FOREVER.

The soldier bends as if to tie his shoes, but instead zips open a canvas bag and sticks both hands inside. When finally he sits back, one hand is clenched around something hard. He catches me watching. He yawns and scratches his ribs, but the right fist sets very lightly on his knee, and when I turn he drinks something out of its cup and throws his head quickly back like a bird or a chicken. You'd think I could smell it, big as my nose is.

Across the aisle the old lady says, "You going far?" She shows me a set of tan, artificial teeth.

"Oklahoma."

"I never been there. I hear the trees give out." She pauses so I can ask politely where she's headed. "I'm going to Nashville," she finally says. "The country-music capital of the world. My son lives there and works in the cellophane plant."

I draw in my notebook a box and two arrows. I crisscross the box.

"He's got three children not old enough to be in school yet."

I sit very still, adding new boxes, drawing baseballs in some, looking busy for fear she might bring out their pictures from her big straw pocketbook. The funny thing is she's looking past my head, though there's nothing out that window but rock wall sliding by. I mumble, "It's hot in here."

Angrily she says, "I had eight children myself."

My pencil flies to get the boxes stacked, eight-deep, in a pyramid. "Hope you have a nice visit."

"It's not a visit. I maybe will move." She is hypnotized by the stone and the furry moss in its cracks. Her eyes used to be green. Maybe, when young, she was red-haired and Irish. If she'll stop talking, I want to think about trying green eyes with that Cherokee hair. Her lids droop; she looks drowsy. "I am right tired of children," she says and lays her head back on the white rag they button on these seats.

Now that her eyes are covered, I can study that face—china white, and worn thin as tissue so light comes between her bones and shines through her whole head. I picture the light going around and around her skull, like water spinning in a jar. If I could wait to be eighty, even my face might grind down and look softer. But I'm ready, in case the Preacher mentions that. Did Elisha make Naaman bear into old age his leprosy? Didn't Jesus heal the withered hand, even on Sunday, without waiting for the work week to start? And put back the ear of Malchus with a touch? As soon as Job had learned enough, did his boils fall away?

Lord, I have learned enough.

The old lady sleeps while we roll downhill and up again; then we turn so my side of the bus looks over the valley and its thickety woods where, as a girl, I pulled armloads of galax, fern, laurel, and hemlock to have some spending money. I spent it for magazines full of women with permanent waves. Behind us, the nigger shuffles a deck of cards and deals to himself by fives. Draw poker—I could beat him. My papa showed me, long winter days and nights snowed in on the mountain. He said poker would teach me arithmetic. It taught me there are four ways to make a royal flush and, with two players, it's an even chance one of them holds a pair on the deal. And when you try to draw from a pair to four of a kind, discard the kicker; it helps your odds.

The soldier deals smoothly, using his left hand only with his thumb on top. Papa was good at that. He looks up and sees my whole face with its scar, but he keeps his eyes level as if he has seen worse things; and his left hand drops cards evenly and in rhythm. Like a turtle, laying eggs.

I close my eyes and the riffle of his deck rests me to the next main stop where I write in my notebook: "Praise God for Johnson City, Tennessee, and all the state to come. I am on my way."

At Kingsport, Mr. Weatherman calls rest stop and I go straight through the terminal to the ladies' toilet and look hard at my face in the mirror. I must remember to start the Preacher on the scar first of all—the only thing about me that's even on both sides.

Lord! I am so ugly!

Maybe the Preacher will claim he can't heal ugliness. And I'm going to spread my palms by my ears and show him—this is a crippled face! An infirmity! Would he do for a kidney or liver what he withholds from a face? The Preacher once stuttered, I read someplace, and God bothered with that. Why not me? When the Preacher labors to heal the sick in his Tulsa auditorium, he asks us at home to lay our fingers on the television screen and pray for God's healing. He puts forth his own ten fingers and we match them, pad to pad, on that glass. I have tried that, Lord, and the Power was too filtered and thinned down for me.

I touch my hand now to this cold mirror glass, and cover all but my pimpled chin, or wide nose, or a single red-brown eye. And nothing's too bad by itself. But when they're put together?

I've seen the Preacher wrap his hot, blessed hands on a club foot and cry out "HEAL!" in his funny way that sounds like the word "Hell" broken into two pieces. Will he not cry out, too, when he sees this poor, clubbed face? I will be to him as Goliath was to David, a need so giant it will drive God to action.

I comb out my pine-needle hair. I think I would like blond curls and Irish eyes, and I want my mouth so large it will never be done with kissing.

The old lady comes in the toilet and catches me pinching my bent face. She jerks back once, looks sad, then pets me with her twiggy hand. "Listen, honey," she says, "I had looks once. It don't amount to much."

I push right past. Good people have nearly turned me against you, Lord. They open their mouths for the milk of human kindness and boiling oil spews out.

So I'm half running through the terminal and into the café, and I take the first stool and call down the counter, "Tuna-fish sandwich," quick. Living in the mountains, I eat fish every chance I get and wonder what the sea is like. Then I see I've sat down by the nigger soldier. I do not want to meet his gaze, since he's a wonder to me, too. We don't have many black men in the mountains. Mostly they live east in Carolina, on the flatland, and pick cotton and tobacco instead of apples. They seem to me like foreigners. He's absently shuffling cards the way some men twiddle thumbs. On the stool beyond him is a paratrooper, white, and they're talking about what a bitch the army is. Being sent to the same camp has made them friends already.

I roll a dill-pickle slice through my mouth—a wheel, a bitter wheel. Then I start on the sandwich and it's chicken by mistake when I've got chickens all over my back yard.

"Don't bother with the beer," says the black one. "I've got better on the bus." They come to some agreement and deal out cards on the counter.

It's just too much for me. I lean over behind the nigger's back and say to the paratrooper, "I wouldn't play with him." Neither one moves. "He's a mechanic." They look at each other, not at me. "It's a way to cheat on the deal."

The paratrooper sways backward on his stool and stares around out of eyes so blue that I want them, right away, and maybe his pale blond hair. I swallow a crusty half-chewed bite. "One-handed grip; the mechanic's grip. It's the middle finger. He can second-deal and bottom-deal. He can buckle the top card with his thumb and peep."

"I be damn," says the paratrooper.

The nigger spins around and bares his teeth at me, but it's half a grin. "Lady, you want to play?"

I slide my dishes back. "I get mad if I'm cheated."

"And mean when you're mad." He laughs a laugh so deep it makes me retaste that bittersweet chocolate off the candy bar. He offers the deck to cut, so I pull out the center and restack it three ways. A little air blows through his upper teeth. "I'm Grady Fliggins and they call me Flick."

The paratrooper reaches a hand down the counter to shake mine. "Monty Harrill. From near to Raleigh."

"And I'm Violet Karl. Spruce Pine. I'd rather play five-card stud."

By the time the bus rolls on, we've moved to its wider back seat playing serious cards with a fifty-cent ante. My money's sparse, but I'm good and the deck is clean. The old lady settles into my front seat, stiffer than plaster. Sometimes she throws back a hurt look.

Monty, the paratrooper, plays soft. But Flick's so good he doesn't even need to cheat, though I watch him close. He drops out quick when his cards are bad; he makes me bid high to see what he's got; and the few times he bluffs, I'm fooled. He's no talker. Monty, on the other hand, says often, "Whose play is it?" till I know that's his clue phrase for a pair. He lifts his cards close to his nose and gets quiet when planning to bluff. And he'd rather use wild cards but we won't. Ah, but he's pretty, though!

After we've swapped a little money, mostly the paratrooper's, Flick pours us a drink in some cups he stole in Kingsport and asks, "Where'd you learn to play?"

I tell him about growing up on a mountain, high, with Mama dead, and shuffling cards by a kerosene lamp with my papa. When I passed fifteen, we'd drink together, too. Applejack or a beer he made from potato peel.

"And where you headed now?" Monty's windburned in a funny pattern, with pale goggle circles that start high on his cheeks. Maybe it's something paratroopers wear.

"It's a pilgrimage." They lean back with their drinks. "I'm going to see this preacher in Tulsa, the one that heals, and I'm coming home pretty. Isn't that heal-ing?" Their still faces make me nervous. "I'll even trade if he says. . . . I'll take somebody else's weak eyes or deaf ears. I could stand limping a little."

The nigger shakes his black head, snickering.

"I tried to get to Charlotte when he was down there with his eight-pole canvas cathedral tent that seats nearly fifteen thousand people, but I didn't have money then. Now what's so funny?" I think for a minute I am going to have to take out my notebook, and unglue the envelope and read them all the Scripture I have looked up on why I should be healed. Monty looks sad for me, though, and that's worse. "Let the Lord twist loose my foot or give me a cough, so long as I'm healed of my looks while I'm still young enough—" I stop and tip up my plastic cup. Young enough for you, blue-eyed boy, and your brothers.

"Listen," says Flick in a high voice. "Let me go with you and be there for that swapping." He winks one speckled eye.

"I'll not take black skin, no offense." He's offended, though, and lurches across the moving bus and falls into a far seat. "Well, you as much as said you'd swap it off!" I call. "What's wrong if I don't want it any more than you?"

Monty slides closer. "You're not much to look at," he grants, sweeping me up and down till I nearly glow blue from his eyes. Shaking his head, "And what now? Thirty?"

"Twenty-eight. His drink and his cards, and I hurt Flick's feelings. I didn't mean that." I'm scared, too. Maybe, unlike Job, I haven't learned enough. Who ought to be expert in hurt feelings? Me, that's who.

"And you live by yourself?"

I start to say "No, there's men falling all over each other going in and out my door." He sees my face, don't he? It makes me call, "Flick? I'm sorry." Not one movement. "Yes. By myself." Five years now, since Papa had heart failure and fell off the high back porch and rolled downhill in the gravel till the hobblebushes stopped him. I found him past sunset, cut from the rocks but not much blood showing. And what there was, dark, and already jellied.

Monty looks at me carefully before making up his mind to say, "That preacher's a fake. You ever see a doctor agree to what he's done?"

"Might be." I'm smiling. I tongue out the last liquor in my cup. I've thought of all that, but it may be what I believe is stronger than him faking. That he'll be electrified by my trust, the way a magnet can get charged against its will. He might be a lunatic or a dope fiend, and it still not matter.

Monty says, "Flick, you plan to give us another drink?"

"No." He acts like he's going to sleep.

"I just wouldn't count on that preacher too much." Monty cleans his nails with a matchbook corner and sometimes gives me an uneasy look. "Things are mean and ugly in this world—I mean *act* ugly, do ugly, be ugly."

He's wrong. When I leave my house, I can walk for miles and everything's beautiful. Even the rattlesnakes have grace. I don't mind his worried looks, since I'm writing in my notebook how we met and my winnings—a good sign, to earn money on a trip. I like the way army barbers trim his hair. I wish I could touch it.

"Took one furlough in your mountains. Pretty country. Maybe hard to live in? Makes you feel little." He looks toward Flick and says softer, "Makes you feel like the night sky does. So many stars."

"Some of them big as daisies." It's easy to live in, though. Some mornings a deer and I scare up each other in the brush, and his heart stops, and mine stops. Everything stops till he plunges away. The next pulsebeat nearly knocks you down. "Monty, doesn't your hair get lighter in the summers? That might be a good color hair to ask for in Tulsa. Then I could turn colors like the leaves. Spell your last name for me."

He does, and says I sure am funny. Then he spells Grady Fliggins and I write that, too. He's curious about my book, so I flip through and offer to read him parts. Even with his eyes shut, Flick is listening. I read them about my papa's face, a chunky block face, not much different from the Preacher's square one. After Papa died, I wrote that to slow down how fast I was forgetting him. I tell Monty parts of my lists: that you can get yellow dye out of gopherwood and Noah built his ark from that, and maybe it stained the water. That a cow eating snakeroot might give poison milk. I pass him a pressed maypop flower I'm carrying to Tulsa, because the crown of thorns and the crucifixion nails grow in its center, and each piece of the bloom stands for one of the apostles.

"It's a mollypop vine," says Flick out of one corner of his mouth. "And it makes a green ball that pops when you step on it." He stretches. "Deal you some blackjack?"

For no reason, Monty says, "We oughtn't to let her go."

We play blackjack till supper stop and I write in my book, "Praise God for Knoxville and two new friends." I've not had many friends. At school in the valley, I sat in the back rows, reading, a hand spread on my face. I was smart, too; but if you let that show, you had to stand for the class and present different things.

When the driver cuts out the lights, the soldiers give me a whole seat, and a duffelbag for a pillow. I hear them whispering, first about women, then about me; but after a while I don't hear that anymore.

By the time we hit Nashville, the old lady makes the bus wait while she begs me to stop with her. "Harvey won't mind. He's a good boy." She will not even look at Monty and Flick. "You can wash and change clothes and catch a new bus tomorrow."

"I'm in a hurry. Thank you." I have picked a lot of galax to pay for this trip.

"A girl alone. A girl that maybe feels she's got to prove something?" The skin on her neck shivers. "Some people might take advantage."

Maybe when I ride home under my new face, that will be some risk. I shake my head, and as she gets off she whispers something to Mr. Weatherman about looking after me. It's wasted, though, because a new driver takes his place and he looks nearly as bad as I do—oily-faced and toad-shaped, with eyeballs a dingy color and streaked with blood. He's the flatlands driver, I guess, because he leans back and drops one warty hand on the wheel and we go so fast and steady you can hardly tell it.

Since Flick is the tops in cards and we're tired of that, it's Monty's turn to brag on his motorcycle. He talks all across Tennessee till I think I could ride one by hearsay alone, that my wrist knows by itself how far to roll the throttle in. It's a Norton and he rides it in Scrambles and Enduro events, in his leathers, with spare parts and tools glued all over him with black electrician's tape.

"So this bastard tells me, 'Zip up your jacket because when I run over you I want some traction.' "

Flick is playing solitaire. "You couldn't get me on one of them killing things."

"One day I'm coming through Spruce Pine, flat out, throw Violet up behind me! We're going to lean all the way through them mountains. Sliding the right foot and then sliding the left." Monty lays his head back on the seat beside me, rolls it, watches. "How you like that? Take you through creeks and ditches like you was on a skate-board. You can just holler and hang on."

Lots of women have, I bet.

"The Norton's got the best front forks of anybody. It'll nearly roll up a tree trunk and ride down the other side." He demonstrates on the seat back. I keep writing. These are new things, two-stroke and four-stroke, picking your line on a curve, Milwaukee iron. It will all come back to me in the winters, when I reread these pages.

Flick says he rode on a Harley once. "Turned over and got drug. No more."

They argue about what he should have done instead of turning over. Finally Monty drifts off to sleep, his head leaning at me slowly, so I look down on his crisp, light hair. I pat it as easy as a cat would, and it tickles my palm. I'd almost ask them in Tulsa to make me a man if I could have hair like his, and a beard, and feel so different in so many places.

He slides closer in his sleep. One eyebrow wrinkles against my shoulder. Looking our way, Flick smokes a cigarette, then reads some magazine he keeps rolled in his belt. Monty makes a deep noise against my arm as if, while he slept, his throat had cleared itself. I shift and his whole head is on my shoulder now. Its weight makes me breathe shallow.

I rest my eyes. If I should turn, his hair would barely touch my cheek, the scarred one, like a shoebrush. I do turn and it does. For miles he sleeps that way and I almost sleep. Once, when we take a long curve, he rolls against me, and one of his hands drifts up and then drops in my lap. Just there, where the creases are.

I would not want God's Power to turn me, after all, into a man. His breath is so warm. Everywhere, my skin is singing. Praise God for that.

When I get my first look at the Mississippi River, the pencil goes straight into my pocketbook. How much praise would that take?

"Is the sea like this?"

"Not except they're both water," Flick says. He's not mad anymore. "Tell you what, Vi-oh-LETTE. When Monty picks you up on his cycle" ("sickle," he calls it), "you ride down to the beaches—Cherry Grove, O.D., around there. Where they work the big nets in the fall and drag them up on the sand with trucks at each end, and men to their necks in the surf."

"You do that?"

"I know people that do. And afterward they strip and dress by this big fire on the beach."

And they make chowder while this cold wind is blowing! I know that much, without asking. In a big black pot that sits on that whipping fire. I think they might let me sit with them and stir the pot. It's funny how much, right now, I feel like praising all the good things I've never seen, in places I haven't been.

Everybody has to get off the bus and change in Memphis, and most of them wait a long time. I've taken the long way, coming here; but some of Mama's cousins live in Memphis and might rest me overnight. Monty says they plan to stay the night, too, and break the long trip.

"They know you're coming, Violet?" It's Flick says my name that way, in pieces, carefully: Vi-oh-LETTE. Monty is lazier: Viii-lut. They make me feel like more than one.

"I've never even met these cousins. But soon as I call up and tell them who I am and that I'm here . . ."

"We'll stay some hotel tonight and then ride on. Why don't you come with us?"

Monty is carrying my scuffed bag. Flick swings the paper sack. "You know us better than them."

"Kin people," grunts Flick, "can be a bad surprise."

Monty is nodding his head. "Only cousin I had got drunk and drove this tractor over his baby brother. Did it on purpose, too." I see by his face that Monty has made this up, for my sake.

"Your cousins might not even live here anymore. I bet it's been years since you heard from a one."

"We're picking a cheap hotel, in case that's a worry."

I never thought they might have moved. "How cheap?"

When Flick says "Under five," I nod; and my things go right up on their shoulders as I follow them into a Memphis cab. The driver takes for granted I'm Monty's afflicted sister and names a hotel right off. He treats me with pity and good manners.

And the hotel he chooses is cheap, all right, where ratty salesmen with bad territories spend half the night drinking in their rooms. Plastic palm bushes and a worn rug the color of wet cigars. I get Room 210 and they're down the hall in the teens. They stand in my doorway and watch me drop both shoes and walk the bed in bare feet. When Monty opens my window, we can hear some kitchen underneath—a fan, clattering noise, a man's crackly voice singing about the California earthquake.

It scares me, suddenly, to know I can't remember how home sounds. Not one bird call, nor the water over rocks. There's so much you can't save by writing down.

"Smell that grease," says Flick, and shakes his head till his lips flutter. "I'm finding an ice machine. You, Vi-oh-LETTE, come on down in a while."

Monty's got a grin I'll remember if I never write a word. He waves. "Flick and me going to get drunker than my old cousin and put wild things in your book. Going to draw dirty pictures. You come on down and get drunk enough to laugh."

But after a shower, damp in my clean slip, even this bed like a roll of fence wire feels good, and I fall asleep wondering if that rushing noise is a river wind, and how long I can keep it in my mind.

Monty and Flick edge into my dream. Just their voices first, from way downhill. Somewhere in a Shonny Haw thicket. "Just different," Monty is saying. "That's all. Different. Don't make some big thing out of it." He doesn't sound happy. "Nobody else," he says.

Is that Flick singing? No, because the song goes on while his voice says, "Just so . . ." and then some words I don't catch. "It don't hurt"? Or maybe, "You don't hurt"? I hear them climbing my tangled hill, breaking sticks and knocking the little stones loose. I'm trying to call to them which way the path is, but I can't make noise because the Preacher took my voice and put it in a black bag and carried it to a sick little boy in Iowa.

They find the path, anyway. And now they can see my house and me standing little by the steps. I know how it looks from where they are: the wood rained on till the siding's almost silver; and behind the house a wet-weather waterfall that's cut a stream bed downhill and grown pin cherry and bee balm on both sides. The high rock walls by the waterfall are mossy and slick, but I've scraped one place and hammered a mean-looking gray head that leans out of the hillside and stares down the path at whoever comes. I've been here so long by myself that I talk to it sometimes. Right now I'd say, "Look yonder. We've got company at last!" if my voice wasn't gone.

"You can't go by looks," Flick is saying as they climb. He ought to know. Ahead of them, warblers separate and fly out on two sides. Everything moves out of their path if I could just see it—tree frogs and mosquitoes. Maybe the worms drop deeper just before a footstep falls.

"Without the clothes, it's not a hell of a lot improved," says Monty, and I know suddenly they are inside the house with me, inside my very room, and my room today's in Memphis. "There's one thing, though," Monty says, standing over my bed. "Good looks in a woman is almost like a wall. She can use it to shut you outside. You never know what she's like, that's all." He's wearing a T-shirt and his dog tags jingle. "Most of the time I don't even miss knowing that."

And Flick says, disgusted, "I knew that much in grammar school. You sure are slow. It's not the face you screw." If I opened my eyes, I could see him now, behind Monty. He says, "After a while, you don't even notice faces. I always thought, in a crowd, my mother might not pick Daddy out."

"*My* mother could," says Monty. "He was always the one *started* the fight."

I stretch and open my eyes. It's a plain slip, cotton, that I sewed myself and makes me look too white and skinny as a sapling.

"She's waking up."

When I point, Monty hands me the blouse off the doorknob. Flick says they've carried me a soda pop, plus something to spruce it up. They sit stiffly on two hard chairs till I've buttoned on my skirt. I sip the drink, cold but peppery, and prop on the bed with the pillows. "I dreamed you both came where my house is, on the mountain, and it had rained so the waterfall was working. I felt real proud of that."

After two drinks we go down to the noisy restaurant with that smelly grease. And after that, to a picture show. Monty grins widely when the star comes on the screen. The spit on his teeth shines, even in the dark. Seeing what kind of woman he really likes, black-haired as a gypsy and with a juicy mouth, I change all my plans. My eyes, too, must turn up on the ends and when I bend down my breasts must fall forward and push at each other. When the star does that in the picture, the cowboy rubs his mustache low in the front of her neck.

In the darkness, Monty takes my hand and holds it in his swelling lap. To me it seems funny that my hand, brown and crusty from hoeing and chopping, is harder than his. I guess you don't get calluses rolling a motorcycle throttle. He rubs his thumb up and down my middle finger. Oh, I would like to ride fast behind him, spraddle-legged, with my arms wrapped on his belt, and I would lay my face between his sharp shoulder blades.

That night, when I've slept awhile, I hear something brushing the rug in the hall. I slip to my door. It's very dark. I press myself, face first, to the wood. There's breathing on the other side. I feel I get fatter, standing there, that even my own small breasts might now be made to touch. I round both shoulders to see. The movement jars the door and it trembles slightly in its frame.

From the far side, by the hinges, somebody whispers, "Vi-oh-LETTE?"

Now I stand very still. The wood feels cooler on my skin, or else I have grown very warm. Oh, I could love anybody! There is so much of me now, they could line up strangers in the hall and let me hold each one better than he had ever been held before!

Slowly I turn the knob, but Flick's breathing is gone. The corridor's empty. I leave the latch off.

Late in the night, when the noise from the kitchen is over, he comes into my room. I wake when he bumps on a chair, swears, then scrabbles at the footboard.

"Viii-lut?"

I slide up in bed. I'm not ready, not now, but he's here. I spread both arms wide. In the dark he can't tell.

He feels his way onto the bed and he touches my knee and it changes. Stops being just my old knee, under his fingers. I feel the joint heat up and bubble. I push the sheet down.

He comes onto me, whispering something. I reach up to claim him.

One time he stops. He's surprised, I guess, finding he isn't the first. How can I tell him how bad that was? How long ago? The night when the twelfth grade was over and one of them climbed with me all the way home? And he asked. And I thought, *I'm entitled.* Won him a five-dollar bet. Didn't do nothing for me.

But this time I sing out and Monty says, "Shh," in my ear. And he starts over, slow, and makes me whimper one other time. Then he turns sideways to sleep and I try my face there, laid in the nest on his damp back. I reach out my tongue. He is salty and good.

Now there are two things too big for my notebook but praise God! And for the Mississippi, too!

There is no good reason for me to ride with them all the way to Fort Smith, but since Tulsa is not expecting me, we change my ticket. Monty pays the extra. We ride through the fertile plains. The last of May becomes June and the Arkansas sun is blazing. I am stunned by this heat. At home, night means blankets and even on hot afternoons it may rain and start the waterfall. I lie against my seat for miles without a word.

"What's wrong?" Monty keeps asking; but, under the heat, I am happy. Sleepy with happiness, a lizard on a rock. At every stop Monty's off the bus, bringing me more than I can eat or drink, buying me magazines and gum. I tell him and Flick to play two-handed cards, but mostly Flick lectures him in a low voice about something.

I try to stop thinking of Memphis and think back to Tulsa. I went to the Spruce Pine library to look up Tulsa in their encyclopedia. I thought sure it would tell about the Preacher, and on what street he'd built his Hope and Glory Building for his soul crusades. Tulsa was listed in the *Americana,* Volume 27, Trance to Venial Sin. I got so tickled with that I forgot to write down the rest.

Now, in the hot sun, clogged up with trances and venial sins, I dream under the drone of their voices. For some reason I remember that old lady back in Nashville, moved in with Harvey and his wife and their three children. I hope she's happy. I picture her on Harvey's back porch, baked in the sun like me, in a rocker. Snapping beans.

I've left my pencil in the hotel and must borrow one from Flick to write in my book. I put in, slowly, "This is the day which the Lord hath made." But, before Monty, what kind of days was He sending me? I cross out the line. I have this wish to praise, instead of Him, the littlest things. Honeybees, and the wet slugs under their rocks. A gnat in some farmer's eye.

I give up and hand Flick his pencil. He slides toward the aisle and whispers, "You wish you'd stayed in your mountains?"

I shake my head and a piece of my no-color hair falls into the sunlight. Maybe it even shines.

He spits on the pencil point and prints something inside a gum wrapper. "Here's my address. You keep it. Never can tell."

So I tear the paper in half and give him back mine. He reads it a long time before tucking it away, but he won't send a letter till I do—I can tell that. Through all this, Monty stares out the window. Arkansas rolls out ahead of us like a rug.

Monty has not asked for my address, nor how far uphill I live from Spruce Pine, though he could ride his motorcycle up to me, strong as its engine is. For a long time he has been sitting quietly, lighting one cigarette off another. This winter, I've got to learn smoking. How to lift my hand up so every eye will follow it to my smooth cheek.

I put Flick's paper in my pocketbook and there, inside, on a round mirror, my face is waiting in ambush for me. I see the curved scar, neat as ever, swoop from the edge of one nostril in rainbow shape across my cheek, then down toward the ear. For the first time in years, pain boils across my face as it did that day. I close my eyes under that red drowning, and see again Papa's ax head rise off its locust handle and come floating through the air, sideways, like a gliding crow. And it drops down into my face almost daintily, the edge turned just enough to slash loose a flap of skin the way you might slice straight down on the curve of a melon. My papa is yelling, but I am under a red rain and it bears me down. I am lifted and run with through the woodyard and into the barn. Now I am slumped on his chest and the whipped horse is throwing us down the mountainside, and my head is wrapped in something big as a wet quilt. The doctor groans when he winds it off and I faint while he lifts up my flesh like the flap of a pulpy envelope, and sews the white bone out of sight.

Dizzy from the movement of the bus, I snap shut my pocketbook.

Whenever I cry, the first drop quivers there, in the curving scar, and then runs crooked on that track to the ear. I cry straight-down on the other side.

I am glad this bus has a toilet. I go there to cool my eyes with wet paper, and spit up Monty's chocolate and cola.

When I come out, he's standing at the door with his fist up. "You all right, Viii-lut? You worried or something?"

I see he pities me. In my seat again, I plan the speech I will make at Fort Smith and the laugh I will give. "Honey, you're good," I'll say, laughing, "but the others were better." That ought to do it. I am quieter now than Monty is, practicing it in my mind.

It's dark when we hit Fort Smith. Everybody's face looks shadowed and different. Mine better. Monty's strange. We're saying goodbyes very fast. I start my speech twice and he misses it twice.

Then he bends over me and offers his own practiced line that I see he's worked up all across Arkansas, "I plan to be right here, Violet, in this bus station. On Monday. All day. You get off your bus when it comes through. Hear me, Viii-lut? I'll watch for you?"

No. He won't watch. Nor I come. "My schedule won't take me this road going back. Bye, Flick. Lots of good luck to you both."

"Promise me. Like I'm promising."

"Good luck to you, Vi-oh-LETTE." Flick lets his hand fall on my head and it feels as good as anybody's hand.

Monty shoves money at me and I shove it back. "Promise," he says, his voice furious. He tries to kiss me in the hair and I jerk so hard my nose cracks his chin. We stare, blurry-eyed and hurting. He follows Flick down the aisle, calls back, "I'm coming here Monday. See you then, hear? And you get off this bus!"

"No! I won't!"

He yells it twice more. People are staring. He's out of the bus pounding on the steel wall by my seat. I'm not going to look. The seats fill up with strangers and we ride away, nobody talking to anyone else. My nose where I hit it is going to swell—the Preacher will have to throw that in for free. I look back, but he's gone.

The lights in the bus go out again. Outside they bloom thick by the streets, then thinner, then mostly gone as we pass into the countryside. Even in the dark, I can see Oklahoma's mountains are uglier than mine. Knobs and hills, mostly. The bus drives into rain which covers up everything. At home I like that washing sound. We go deeper into the downpour. Perhaps we are under the Arkansas River, after all. It seems I can feel its great weight move over me.

Before daylight, the rain tapers off and here the ground looks dry, even barren. Cattle graze across long fields. In the wind, wheat fields shiver. I can't eat anything all the way to Tulsa. It makes me homesick to see the land grow brighter and flatter and balder. That old lady was right—the trees do give out—and oil towers grow in their place. The glare's in my eyes. I write in my notebook, "Praise God for Tulsa; I am nearly there," but it takes a long time to get the words down.

One day my papa told me how time got slow for him when Mama died. How one week he waded through the creek and it was water, and the next week cold molasses. How he'd lay awake a year between sundown and sunup, and in the morning I'd be a day older and he'd be three hundred and sixty-five.

It works the other way, too. In no time at all, we're into Tulsa without me knowing what we've passed. So many tall buildings. Everybody's running. They rush into taxis before I can get one to wait for me long enough to ask the driver questions. But still I'm speeded to a hotel, and the elevator yanks me to a room quicker than Elijah rode to Heaven. The room's not bad. A Gideon Bible. Inside are lots of dirty words somebody wrote. He must have been feeling bad.

I bathe and dress, trembling from my own speed, and pin on the hat which has traveled all the way from Spruce Pine for this. I feel tired. I go out into the loud streets full of fast cars. Hot metal everywhere. A taxi roars me across town to the Preacher's church.

It looks like a big insurance office, though I can tell where the chapel is by colored glass in the pointed windows. Carved in an arch over the door are the words "HOPE OF GLORY BUILDING." Right away, something in me sinks. All this time I've been hearing it on TV as the Hope *and* Glory Building. You wouldn't think one word could make that much difference.

Inside the door, there's a list of offices and room numbers. I don't see the Preacher's name. Clerks send me down long, tiled halls, past empty air-conditioned offices. One tells me to go up two flights and ask the fat woman, and the fat woman sends me down again. I'm carrying my notebook in a dry hand, feeling as brittle as the maypop flower.

At last I wait an hour to see some assistant—very close to the Preacher, I'm told. His waiting room is chilly, the leatherette chairs worn down to the mesh. I try to remember how much TB and cancer have passed through this very room and been jerked out of people the way Jesus tore out a demon and flung him into a herd of swine. I wonder what he felt like to the swine.

After a long time, the young man calls me into his plain office—wood desk, wood chairs. Shelves of booklets and colored folders. On one wall, a colored picture of Jesus with that fairy ring of light around His head. Across from that, one of His praying hands—rougher than Monty's, smoother than mine.

The young man wears glasses with no rims. In this glare, I am reflected on each lens, Vi-oh-LETTE and Viii-lut. On his desk is a box of postcards of the Hope and Glory Building. *Of* Glory. *Of* Glory.

I am afraid.

I feel behind me for the chair.

The man explains that he is presently in charge. The Preacher's speaking in Tallahassee, his show taped weeks ahead. I never thought of it as a show before. He waits.

I reach inside my notebook where, taped shut, is the thick envelope with everything written down. I knew I could never explain things right. When have I ever been able to tell what I really felt? But it's all in there—my name, my need. The words from the Bible which must argue for me. I did not sit there nights since Papa died, counting my money and studying God's Book, for nothing. Playing solitaire, then going back to search the next page and the next. Stepping outside to rest my eyes on His limitless sky, then back to the Book and the paper, building my case.

He starts to read, turns up his glitter-glass to me once to check how I look, then reads again. His chair must be hard, for he squirms in it, crosses his legs. When he has read every page, he lays the stack down, slowly takes off his glasses, folds them shining into a case. He leaves it open on his desk. Mica shines like that, in the rocks.

Then he looks at me, fully. Oh. He is plain. Almost homely. I nearly expected it. Maybe Samuel was born ugly, so who else would take him but God?

"My child," the man begins, though I'm older than he is, "I understand how you feel. And we will most certainly pray for your spirit. . . ."

I shut my eyes against those two flashing faces on his spectacles. "Never mind my spirit." I see he doesn't really understand. I see he will live a long life, and not marry.

"Our Heavenly Father has purpose in all things."

Stubbornly, "Ask Him to set it aside."

"We must all trust His will."

After all these years, isn't it God's turn to trust mine? Could He not risk a little beauty on me? Just when I'm ready to ask, the sober assistant recites, " 'Favor is deceitful and beauty is vain.' That's in Proverbs."

And I cry, " 'The crooked shall be made straight!' Isaiah said that!" He draws back, as if I had brought the Gideon Bible and struck him with its most disfigured pages. "Jesus healed an impediment in speech. See my impediment! Mud on a blind man's eyes was all He needed! Don't you remember?" But he's read all that. Everything I know on my side lies, written out, under his sweaty hand. Lord, don't let me whine. But I whine, "He healed the ten lepers and only one thanked. Well, I'll thank. I promise. All my life."

He clears his long knotty throat and drones like a bee, " 'By the sadness of the countenance the heart is made better.' Ecclesiastes. Seven. Three."

Oh, that's not fair! I skipped those parts, looking for verses that suited me! And it's wrong, besides.

I get up to leave and he asks will I kneel with him? "Let us pray together for that inner beauty."

No, I will not. I go down that hollow hall and past the echoing rooms. Without his help I find the great auditorium, lit through colored glass, with its cross of white plastic and a pinker Jesus molded onto it. I go straight to the pulpit where the Preacher stands. There is nobody else to plead. I ask Jesus not to listen to everything He hears, but to me only.

Then I tell Him how it feels to be ugly, with nothing to look back at you but a deer or an owl. I read Him my paper, out loud, full of His own words.

"I have been praising you, Lord, but it gets harder every year." Maybe that sounds too strong. I try to ease up my tone before the Amens. Then the chapel is very quiet. For one minute I hear the whir of many wings, but it's only a fan inside an air vent.

I go into the streets of Tulsa, where even the shade from a building is hot. And as I walk to the hotel I'm repeating, over and over, "Praise God for Tulsa in spite of everything."

Maybe I say this aloud, since people are staring. But maybe that's only because they've never seen a girl cry crooked in their streets before.

Monday morning. I have not looked at my face since the pulpit prayer. Who can predict how He might act—with a lightning bolt? Or a melting so slow and tender it could not even be felt?

Now, on the bus, I can touch in my pocketbook the cold mirror glass. Though I cover its surface with prints, I never look down. We ride through the dust and I'm nervous. My pencil is flying: "Be ye therefore perfect as your Heavenly Father is perfect. Praise God for Oklahoma. For Wagoner and Sapulpa and Broken Arrow and every other name on these signs by the road."

Was that the wrong thing to tell Him? My threat that even praise can be withheld? Maybe He's angry. "Praise God for oil towers whether I like them or not." When we pass churches, I copy their names. Praise them all. I want to write, "Bless," but that's *His* job.

We cross the cool Arkansas River. As its damp rises into the bus and touches my face, something wavers there, in the very bottom of each pore; and I clap my rough hands to each cheek. Maybe He's started? How much can He do between here and Fort Smith? If He will?

For I know what will happen. Monty won't come. And I won't stop. That's an end to it.

No, Monty is there. Waiting right now. And I'll go into the bus station on tiptoe and stand behind him. He'll turn, with his blue eyes like lamps. *And he won't know me!* If I'm changed. So I will explain myself to him: how this gypsy hair and this juicy mouth is still Violet Karl. He'll say, "Won't old Flick be surprised?" He'll say, "Where is that place you live? Can I come there?"

But if, while I wait and he turns, he should know me by my old face . . . If he should say my name or show by recognition that my name's rising up now in his eyes like something through water . . . I'll be running by then. To the bus. Straight out that door to the Tennessee bus, saying, "Driver, don't let that man on!" It's a very short stop. We'll be pulling out quick. I don't think he'll follow, anyhow.

I don't even think he will come.

One hundred and thirty-one miles to Fort Smith. I wish I could eat.

I try to think up things to look forward to at home. Maybe the sourwoods are blooming early, and the bees have been laying-by my honey. If it's rained enough, my corn might be in tassel. Wouldn't it be something if God took His own sweet time, and I lived on that slope for years and years, getting prettier all the time? And nobody to know?

It takes nearly years and years to get to Fort Smith. My papa knew things about time. I comb out my hair, not looking once to see what color sheddings are caught in the teeth. There's no need feeling my cheek, since my finger expects that scar. I can feel it on me almost anywhere, by memory. I straighten my skirt and lick my lips till the spit runs out.

And they're waiting. Monty at one door of the terminal and Flick at another.

"Ten minutes," the driver says when the bus is parked, but I wait in my seat till Flick gets restless and walks to the cigarette machine. Then I slip through his entrance door and inside the station. Mirrors shine everywhere. On the vending machines and the weight machines and a full-length one by the phone booth. It's all I can do not to look. I pass the ticket window and there's Monty's back at the other door. My face remembers the shape of it. Seeing him there, how he's made, and the parts of him fitted, makes me forget how I look. And before I can stop, I call out his name.

Right away, turning, he yells to me "*Viii*-lut!"

So I know. I can look, then, in the wide mirror over a jukebox. Tired as I am and unfed, I look worse than I did when I started from home.

He's laughing and talking. "I been waiting here since daylight scared you wouldn't . . ." but by then I've run past the ugly girl in the glass and I race for the bus, for the road, for the mountain.

Behind me, he calls loudly, "Flick!"

I see that one step in my path like a floating dark blade, but I'm faster this time. I twist by him, into the flaming sun and the parking lot. How my breath hurts!

Monty's between me and my bus, but there's time. I circle the cabstand, running hard over the asphalt field, with a pain ticking in my side. He calls me. I plunge through the crowd like a deer through fetterbush. But he's running as hard as he can and he's faster than me. And, oh!

Praise God!

He's catching me!

DEFENDER OF THE FAITH

Philip Roth

(b. 1933)

Biography p. 1096

In May of 1945, only a few weeks after the fighting had ended in Europe, I was rotated back to the States, where I spent the remainder of the war with a training company at Camp Crowder, Missouri. Along with the rest of the Ninth Army, I had been racing across Germany so swiftly during the late winter and spring that when I boarded the plane, I couldn't believe its destination lay to the west. My mind might inform me otherwise, but there was an inertia of the spirit that told me we were flying to a new front, where we would disembark and continue our push eastward—eastward until we'd circled the globe, marching through villages along whose twisting, cobbled streets crowds of the enemy would watch us take possession of what, up till then, they'd considered their own. I had changed enough in two years not to mind the trembling of the old people, the crying of the very young, the uncertainty and fear in the eyes of the once arrogant. I had been fortunate enough to develop an infantry-man's heart, which, like his feet, at first aches and swells but finally grows horny enough for him to travel the weirdest paths without feeling a thing.

Captain Paul Barrett was my C.O. in Camp Crowder. The day I reported for duty, he came out of his office to shake my hand. He was short, gruff, and fiery, and—indoors or out—he wore his polished helmet liner pulled down to his little eyes. In Europe, he had received a battlefield commission and a serious chest wound, and he'd been returned to the States only a few months before. He spoke easily to me, and at the evening formation he introduced me to the troops. "Gentlemen," he said, "Sergeant Thurston, as you know, is no longer with this company. Your new first sergeant is Sergeant Nathan Marx, here. He is a veteran of the European theater, and consequently will expect to find a company of soldiers here, and not a company of *boys.*"

I sat up late in the orderly room that evening, trying half-heartedly to solve the riddle of duty rosters, personnel forms, and morning reports. The Charge of Quarters slept with his mouth open on a mattress on the floor. A trainee stood reading the next day's duty roster, which was posted on the bulletin board just inside the screen door. It was a warm evening, and I could hear radios playing dance music over in the barracks. The trainee, who had been staring at me whenever he thought I wouldn't notice, finally took a step in my direction.

"Hey, Sarge—we having a G.I. party tomorrow night?" he asked. A G.I. party is a barracks cleaning.

"You usually have them on Friday nights?" I asked him.

"Yes," he said, and then he added, mysteriously, "that's the whole thing."

"Then you'll have a G.I. party."

He turned away, and I heard him mumbling. His shoulders were moving, and I wondered if he was crying.

"What's your name, soldier?" I asked.

He turned, not crying at all. Instead, his green-speckled eyes, long and narrow, flashed like fish in the sun. He walked over to me and sat on the edge of my desk. He reached out a hand. "Sheldon," he said.

"Stand on your feet, Sheldon."

Getting off the desk, he said, "Sheldon Grossbart." He smiled at the familiarity into which he'd led me.

"You against cleaning the barracks Friday night, Grossbart?" I said. "Maybe we shouldn't have G.I. parties. Maybe we should get a maid." My tone startled me. I felt I sounded like every top sergeant I had ever known.

"No, Sergeant." He grew serious, but with a seriousness that seemed to be only the stifling of a smile. "It's just—G.I. parties on Friday night, of all nights."

He slipped up onto the corner of the desk again—not quite sitting, but not quite standing, either. He looked at me with those speckled eyes flashing, and then made a gesture with his hand. It was very slight—no more than a movement back and forth of the wrist—and yet it managed to exclude from our affairs everything else in the orderly room, to make the two of us the center of the world. It seemed, in fact, to exclude everything even about the two of us except our hearts.

"Sergeant Thurston was one thing," he whispered, glancing at the sleeping C.Q., "but we thought that with you here things might be a little different."

"We?"

"The Jewish personnel."

"Why?" I asked, harshly. "What's on your mind?" Whether I was still angry at the "Sheldon" business, or now at something else, I hadn't time to tell, but clearly I was angry.

"We thought you—Marx, you know, like Karl Marx. The Marx Brothers. Those guys are all—M-a-r-x. Isn't that how *you* spell it, Sergeant?"

"M-a-r-x."

"Fishbein said—" He stopped. "What I mean to say, Sergeant—" His face and neck were red, and his mouth moved but no words came out. In a moment, he raised himself to attention, gazing down at me. It was as though he had suddenly decided he could expect no more sympathy from me than from Thurston, the reason being that I was of Thurston's faith, and not his. The young man had managed to confuse himself as to what my faith really was, but I felt no desire to straighten him out. Very simply, I didn't like him.

When I did nothing but return his gaze, he spoke, in an altered tone. "You see, Sergeant," he explained to me, "Friday nights, Jews are supposed to go to services."

"Did Sergeant Thurston tell you you couldn't go to them when there was a G.I. party?"

"No."

"Did he say you had to stay and scrub the floors?"

"No, Sergeant."

"Did the Captain say you had to stay and scrub the floors?"

"That isn't it, Sergeant. It's the other guys in the barracks." He leaned toward me. "They think we're goofing off. But we're not. That's when Jews go to services, Friday night. We have to."

"Then go."

"But the other guys make accusations. They have no right."

"That's not the Army's problem, Grossbart. It's a personal problem you'll have to work out yourself."

"But it's un*fair.*"

I got up to leave. "There's nothing I can do about it," I said.

Grossbart stiffened and stood in front of me. "But this is a matter of *religion,* sir."

"Sergeant," I said.

"I mean 'Sergeant,' " he said, almost snarling.

"Look, go see the chaplain. You want to see Captain Barrett, I'll arrange an appointment."

"No, no. I don't want to make trouble, Sergeant. That's the first thing they throw up to you. I just want my rights!"

"Damn it, Grossbart, stop whining. You have your rights. You can stay and scrub floors or you can go to shul—"

The smile swam in again. Spittle gleamed at the corners of his mouth. "You mean church, Sergeant."

"I mean shul, Grossbart!"

I walked past him and went outside. Near me, I heard the scrunching of a guard's boots on gravel. Beyond the lighted windows of the barracks, young men in T shirts and fatigue pants were sitting on their bunks, polishing their rifles. Suddenly there was a light rustling behind me. I turned and saw Grossbart's dark frame fleeing back to the barracks, racing to tell his Jewish friends that they were right—that, like Karl and Harpo, I was one of them.

The next morning, while chatting with Captain Barrett, I recounted the incident of the previous evening. Somehow, in the telling, it must have seemed to the Captain that I was not so much explaining Grossbart's position as defending it. "Marx, I'd fight side by side with a nigger if the fella proved to me he was a man. I pride myself," he said, looking out the window, "that I've got an open mind. Consequently, Sergeant, nobody gets special treatment here, for the good *or* the bad. All a man's got to do is prove himself. A man fires well on the range, I give him a weekend pass. He scores high in P.T., he gets a weekend pass. He *earns* it." He turned from the window and pointed a finger at me. "You're a Jewish fella, am I right, Marx?"

"Yes, sir."

"And I admire you. I admire you because of the ribbons on your chest. I judge a man by what he shows me on the field of battle, Sergeant. It's what he's got *here,* " he said, and then, though I expected he would point to his chest, he jerked a thumb toward the buttons straining to hold his blouse across his belly. "Guts," he said.

"O.K., sir. I only wanted to pass on to you how the men felt."

"Mr. Marx, you're going to be old before your time if you worry about how the men feel. Leave that stuff to the chaplain—that's his business, not yours. Let's us train these fellas to shoot straight. If the Jewish personnel feels the other men are accusing them of goldbricking—well, I just don't know. Seems awful funny that suddenly the Lord is calling so loud in Private Grossman's ear he's just got to run to church."

"Synagogue," I said.

"Synagogue is right, Sergeant. I'll write that down for handy reference. Thank you for stopping by."

That evening, a few minutes before the company gathered outside the orderly room for the chow formation, I called the C.Q., Corporal Robert LaHill, in to see me. LaHill was a dark, burly fellow whose hair curled out of his clothes wherever it could. He had a glaze in his eyes that made one think of caves and dinosaurs. "LaHill," I said, "when you take the formation, remind the men that they're free to attend church services *whenever* they are held, provided they report to the orderly room before they leave the area."

LaHill scratched his wrist, but gave no indication that he'd heard or understood.

"LaHill," I said, *"church.* You remember? Church, priest, Mass, confession."

He curled one lip into a kind of smile; I took it for a signal that for a second he had flickered back up into the human race.

"Jewish personnel who want to attend services this evening are to fall out in front of the orderly room at 1900," I said. Then, as an afterthought, I added, "By order of Captain Barrett."

A little while later, as the day's last light—softer than any I had seen that year—began to drop over Camp Crowder, I heard LaHill's thick, inflectionless voice outside my window: "Give me your ears, troopers. Toppie says for me to tell you that at 1900 hours all Jewish personnel is to fall out in front, here, if they want to attend the Jewish Mass."

At seven o'clock, I looked out the orderly-room window and saw three soldiers in starched khakis standing on the dusty quadrangle. They looked at their watches and fidgeted while they whispered back and forth. It was getting dimmer, and, alone on the otherwise deserted field, they looked tiny. When I opened the door, I heard the noises of the G.I. party coming from the surrounding barracks—bunks being pushed to the walls, faucets pounding water into buckets, brooms whisking at the wooden floors, cleaning the dirt away for Saturday's inspection. Big puffs of cloth moved round and round on the windowpanes. I walked outside, and the moment my foot hit the ground I thought I heard Grossbart call to the others, " 'Ten-*hut!*" Or maybe, when they all three jumped to attention, I imagined I heard the command.

Grossbart stepped forward. "Thank you, sir," he said.

" 'Sergeant,' Grossbart," I reminded him. "You call officers 'sir.' I'm not an officer. You've been in the Army three weeks—you know that."

He turned his palms out at his sides to indicate that, in truth, he and I lived beyond convention. "Thank you, anyway," he said.

"Yes," a tall boy behind him said. "Thanks a lot."

And the third boy whispered, "Thank you," but his mouth barely fluttered, so that he did not alter by more than a lip's movement his posture of attention.

"For what?" I asked.

Grossbart snorted happily. "For the announcement. The Corporal's announcement. It helped. It made it—"

"Fancier." The tall boy finished Grossbart's sentence.

Grossbart smiled. "He means formal, sir. Public," he said to me. "Now it won't seem as though we're just taking off—goldbricking because the work has begun."

"It was by order of Captain Barrett," I said.

"Aaah, but you pull a little weight," Grossbart said. "So we thank you." Then he turned to his companions. "Sergeant Marx, I want you to meet Larry Fishbein."

The tall boy stepped forward and extended his hand. I shook it. "You from New York?" he asked.

"Yes."

"Me, too." He had a cadaverous face that collapsed inward from his cheekbone to his jaw, and when he smiled—as he did at the news of our communal attachment— revealed a mouthful of bad teeth. He was blinking his eyes a good deal, as though he were fighting back tears. "What borough?" he asked.

I turned to Grossbart. "It's five after seven. What time are services?"

"Shul," he said, smiling, "is in ten minutes. I want you to meet Mickey Halpern. This is Nathan Marx, our sergeant."

The third boy hopped forward. "Private Michael Halpern." He saluted.

"Salute officers, Halpern," I said. The boy dropped his hand, and, on its way down, in his nervousness, checked to see if his shirt pockets were buttoned.

"Shall I march them over, sir?" Grossbart asked. "Or are you coming along?"

From behind Grossbart, Fishbein piped up. "Afterward, they're having refreshments. A ladies' auxiliary from St. Louis, the rabbi told us last week."

"The chaplain," Halpern whispered.

"You're welcome to come along," Grossbart said.

To avoid his plea, I looked away, and saw, in the windows of the barracks, a cloud of faces staring out at the four of us. "Hurry along, Grossbart," I said.

"O.K., then," he said. He turned to the others. "Double time, *march!*"

They started off, but ten feet away Grossbart spun around and, running backward, called to me, "Good *shabbus,* sir!" And then the three of them were swallowed into the alien Missouri dusk.

Even after they had disappeared over the parade ground, whose green was now a deep blue, I could hear Grossbart singing the double-time cadence, and as it grew dimmer and dimmer, it suddenly touched a deep memory—as did the slant of the light —and I was remembering the shrill sounds of a Bronx playground where, years ago, beside the Grand Concourse, I had played on long spring evenings such as this. It was a pleasant memory for a young man so far from peace and home, and it brought so many recollections with it that I began to grow exceedingly tender about myself. In fact, I indulged myself in a reverie so strong that I felt as though a hand were reaching down inside me. It had to reach so very far to touch me! It had to reach past those days in the forests of Belgium, and past the dying I'd refused to weep over; past the nights in German farmhouses whose books we'd burned to warm us; past endless stretches when I had shut off all softness I might feel for my fellows, and had managed even to deny myself the posture of a conqueror—the swagger that I, as a Jew, might well have worn as my boots whacked against the rubble of Wesel, Münster, and Braunschweig.

But now one night noise, one rumor of home and time past, and memory plunged down through all I had anesthetized, and came to what I suddenly remembered was myself. So it was not altogether curious that, in search of more of me, I found myself following Grossbart's tracks to Chapel No. 3, where the Jewish services were being held.

I took a seat in the last row, which was empty. Two rows in front of me sat Grossbart, Fishbein, and Halpern, holding little white Dixie cups. Each row of seats was raised higher than the one in front of it, and I could see clearly what was going on. Fishbein was pouring the contents of his cup into Grossbart's, and Grossbart looked mirthful as the liquid made a purple arc between Fishbein's hand and his. In the glaring yellow light, I saw the chaplain standing on the platform at the front; he was chanting the first line of the responsive reading. Grossbart's prayer book remained closed on his lap; he was swishing the cup around. Only Halpern responded to the chant by praying. The fingers of his right hand were spread wide across the cover of his open book. His cap was pulled down low onto his brow, which made it round, like a yarmulke. From time to time, Grossbart wet his lips at the cup's edge; Fishbein, his long yellow face a dying light bulb, looked from here to there, craning forward to catch sight of the faces down the row, then of those in front of him, then behind. He saw me, and his eyelids beat a tattoo. His elbow slid into Grossbart's side, his neck inclined toward his friend, he whispered something, and then, when the congregation next responded to the chant, Grossbart's voice was among the others. Fishbein looked into his book now, too; his lips, however, didn't move.

Finally, it was time to drink the wine. The chaplain smiled down at them as Grossbart swigged his in one long gulp, Halpern sipped, meditating, and Fishbein faked devotion with an empty cup. "As I look down amongst the congregation"—the chaplain grinned at the word—"this night, I see many new faces, and I want to welcome you to Friday-night services here at Camp Crowder. I am Major Leo Ben Ezra, your chaplain." Though an American, the chaplain spoke deliberately—syllable by syllable, almost—as though to communicate, above all, with the lip readers in his audience. "I have only a few words to say before we adjourn to the refreshment room, where the kind ladies of the Temple Sinai, St. Louis, Missouri, have a nice setting for you."

Applause and whistling broke out. After another momentary grin, the chaplain raised his hands, palms out, his eyes flicking upward a moment, as if to remind the troops where they were and Who Else might be in attendance. In the sudden silence that followed, I thought I heard Grossbart cackle, "Let the goyim clean the floors!" Were those the words? I wasn't sure, but Fishbein, grinning, nudged Halpern. Halpern looked dumbly at him, then went back to his prayer book, which had been occupying him all through the rabbi's talk. One hand tugged at the black kinky hair that stuck out under his cap. His lips moved.

The rabbi continued. "It is about the food that I want to speak to you for a moment. I know, I know, I know," he intoned, wearily, "how in the mouths of most of you the *trafe* food tastes like ashes. I know how you gag, some of you, and how your parents suffer to think of their children eating foods unclean and offensive to the palate. What can I tell you? I can only say, close your eyes and swallow as best you can. Eat what you must to live, and throw away the rest. I wish I could help more. For those of you who find this impossible, may I ask that you try and try, but then come to see me in private. If your revulsion is so great, we will have to seek aid from those higher up."

A round of chatter rose and subsided. Then everyone sang "Ain Kelohainu"; after all those years, I discovered I still knew the words. Then, suddenly, the service over, Grossbart was upon me. "Higher up? He means the General?"

"Hey, Shelly," Fishbein said, "he means God." He smacked his face and looked at Halpern. "How high can you go!"

"Sh-h-h!" Grossbart said. "What do you think, Sergeant?"

"I don't know," I said. "You better ask the chaplain."

"I'm going to. I'm making an appointment to see him in private. So is Mickey." Halpern shook his head. "No, no, Sheldon—"

"You have rights, Mickey," Grossbart said. "They can't push us around."

"It's O.K.," said Halpern. "It bothers my mother, not me."

Grossbart looked at me. "Yesterday he threw up. From the hash. It was all ham and God knows what else."

"I have a cold—that was why," Halpern said. He pushed his yarmulke back into a cap.

"What about you, Fishbein?" I asked. "You kosher, too?"

He flushed. "A little. But I'll let it ride. I have a very strong stomach, and I don't eat a lot anyway." I continued to look at him, and he held up his wrist to reinforce what he'd just said; his watch strap was tightened to the last hole, and he pointed that out to me.

"But services are important to you?" I asked him.

He looked at Grossbart. "Sure, sir."

" 'Sergeant.' "

"Not so much at home," said Grossbart, stepping between us, "but away from home it gives one a sense of his Jewishness."

"We have to stick together," Fishbein said.

I started to walk toward the door; Halpern stepped back to make way for me.

"That's what happened in Germany," Grossbart was saying, loud enough for me to hear. "They didn't stick together. They let themselves get pushed around."

I turned. "Look, Grossbart. This is the Army, not summer camp."

He smiled. "So?"

Halpern tried to sneak off, but Grossbart held his arm.

"Grossbart, how old are you?" I asked.

"Nineteen."

"And you?" I said to Fishbein.

"The same. The same month, even."

"And what about him?" I pointed to Halpern, who had by now made it safely to the door.

"Eighteen," Grossbart whispered. "But like he can't tie his shoes or brush his teeth himself. I feel sorry for him."

"I feel sorry for all of us, Grossbart," I said, "but just act like a man. Just don't overdo it."

"Overdo what, sir?"

"The 'sir' business, for one thing. Don't overdo that," I said.

I left him standing there. I passed by Halpern, but he did not look at me. Then I was outside, but, behind, I heard Grossbart call, "Hey, Mickey, my *leben,* come on back. Refreshments!"

"*Leben!*" My grandmother's word for me!

One morning a week later, while I was working at my desk, Captain Barrett shouted for me to come into his office. When I entered, he had his helmet liner squashed down so far on his head that I couldn't even see his eyes. He was on the phone, and when he spoke to me, he cupped one hand over the mouthpiece. "Who the hell is Grossbart?"

"Third platoon, Captain," I said. "A trainee."

"What's all this stink about food? His mother called a goddam congressman about the food." He uncovered the mouthpiece and slid his helmet up until I could see his bottom eyelashes. "Yes, sir," he said into the phone. "Yes, sir. I'm still here, sir. I'm asking Marx, here, right now—"

He covered the mouthpiece again and turned his head back toward me. "Lightfoot Harry's on the phone," he said, between his teeth. "This congressman calls General Lyman, who calls Colonel Sousa, who calls the Major, who calls me. They're just dying to stick this thing on me. Whatsa matter?" He shook the phone at me. "I don't feed the troops? What is this?"

"Sir, Grossbart is strange—" Barrett greeted that with a mockingly indulgent smile. I altered my approach. "Captain, he's a very orthodox Jew, and so he's only allowed to eat certain foods."

"He throws up, the congressman said. Every time he eats something, his mother says, he throws up!"

"He's accustomed to observing the dietary laws, Captain."

"So why's his old lady have to call the White House?"

"Jewish parents, sir—they're apt to be more protective than you expect. I mean, Jews have a very close family life. A boy goes away from home, sometimes the mother is liable to get very upset. Probably the boy mentioned something in a letter, and his mother misinterpreted."

"I'd like to punch him one right in the mouth," the Captain said. "There's a war on, and he wants a silver platter!"

"I don't think the boy's to blame, sir. I'm sure we can straighten it out by just asking him. Jewish parents worry—"

"*All* parents worry, for Christ's sake. But they don't get on their high horse and start pulling strings—"

I interrupted, my voice higher, tighter than before. "The home life, Captain, is very important—but you're right, it may sometimes get out of hand. It's a very wonderful thing, Captain, but because it's so close, this kind of thing . . ."

He didn't listen any longer to my attempt to present both myself and Lightfoot Harry with an explanation for the letter. He turned back to the phone. "Sir?" he said. "Sir—Marx, here, tells me Jews have a tendency to be pushy. He says he thinks we can settle it right here in the company. . . . Yes, sir. . . . I *will* call back, sir, soon as I can." He hung up. "Where are the men, Sergeant?"

"On the range."

With a whack on the top of his helmet, he crushed it down over his eyes again, and charged out of his chair. "We're going for a ride," he said.

The Captain drove, and I sat beside him. It was a hot spring day, and under my newly starched fatigues I felt as though my armpits were melting down onto my sides and chest. The roads were dry, and by the time we reached the firing range, my teeth felt gritty with dust, though my mouth had been shut the whole trip. The Captain slammed the brakes on and told me to get the hell out and find Grossbart.

I found him on his belly, firing wildly at the five-hundred-feet target. Waiting their turns behind him were Halpern and Fishbein. Fishbein, wearing a pair of steel-rimmed G.I. glasses I hadn't seen on him before, had the appearance of an old peddler who would gladly have sold you his rifle and the cartridges that were slung all over him. I stood back by the ammo boxes, waiting for Grossbart to finish spraying the distant targets. Fishbein straggled back to stand near me.

"Hello, Sergeant Marx," he said.

"How are you?" I mumbled.

"Fine, thank you. Sheldon's really a good shot."

"I didn't notice."

"I'm not so good, but I think I'm getting the hang of it now. Sergeant, I don't mean to, you know, ask what I shouldn't—" The boy stopped. He was trying to speak intimately, but the noise of the shooting forced him to shout at me.

"What is it?" I asked. Down the range, I saw Captain Barrett standing up in the jeep, scanning the line for me and Grossbart.

"My parents keep asking and asking where we're going," Fishbein said. "Everybody says the Pacific. I don't care, but my parents—If I could relieve their minds, I think I could concentrate more on my shooting."

"I don't know where, Fishbein. Try to concentrate anyway."

"Sheldon says you might be able to find out."

"I don't know a thing, Fishbein. You just take it easy, and don't let Sheldon—"

"*I'm* taking it easy, Sergeant. It's at home—"

Grossbart had finished on the line, and was dusting his fatigues with one hand. I called to him. "Grossbart, the Captain wants to see you."

He came toward us. His eyes blazed and twinkled. "Hi!"

"Don't point that rifle!" I said.

"I wouldn't shoot you, Sarge." He gave me a smile as wide as a pumpkin, and turned the barrel aside.

"Damn you, Grossbart, this is no joke! Follow me."

I walked ahead of him, and had the awful suspicion that, behind me, Grossbart was *marching,* his rifle on his shoulder, as though he were a one-man detachment. At the jeep, he gave the Captain a rifle salute. "Private Sheldon Grossbart, sir."

"At ease, Grossman." The Captain sat down, slid over into the empty seat, and, crooking a finger, invited Grossbart closer.

"Bart, sir. Sheldon Gross*bart.* It's a common error." Grossbart nodded at me; *I* understood, he indicated. I looked away just as the mess truck pulled up to the range, disgorging a half-dozen K.P.s with rolled-up sleeves. The mess sergeant screamed at them while they set up the chowline equipment.

"Grossbart, your mama wrote some congressman that we don't feed you right. Do you know that?" the Captain said.

"It was my father, sir. He wrote to Representative Franconi that my religion forbids me to eat certain foods."

"What religion is that, Grossbart?"

"Jewish."

" 'Jewish, *sir,* ' " I said to Grossbart.

"Excuse me, sir. Jewish, sir."

"What have you been living on?" the Captain asked. "You've been in the Army a month already. You don't look to me like you're falling to pieces."

"I eat because I have to, sir. But Sergeant Marx will testify to the fact that I don't eat one mouthful more than I need to in order to survive."

"Is that so, Marx?" Barrett asked.

"I've never seen Grossbart eat, sir," I said.

"But you heard the rabbi," Grossbart said. "He told us what to do, and I listened." The Captain looked at me. "Well, Marx?"

"I still don't know what he eats and doesn't eat, sir."

Grossbart raised his arms to plead with me, and it looked for a moment as though he were going to hand me his weapon to hold. "But, Sergeant—"

"Look, Grossbart, just answer the Captain's questions," I said sharply.

Barrett smiled at me, and I resented it. "All right, Grossbart," he said. "What is it you want? The little piece of paper? You want out?"

"No, sir. Only to be allowed to live as a Jew. And for the others, too."

"What others?"

"Fishbein, sir, and Halpern."

"They don't like the way we serve, either?"

"Halpern throws up, sir. I've seen it."

"I thought *you* throw up."

"Just once, sir. I didn't know the sausage was sausage."

"We'll give menus, Grossbart. We'll show training films about the food, so you can identify when we're trying to poison you."

Grossbart did not answer. The men had been organized into two long chow lines. At the tail end of one, I spotted Fishbein—or, rather, his glasses spotted me. They winked sunlight back at me. Halpern stood next to him, patting the inside of his collar with a khaki handkerchief. They moved with the line as it began to edge up toward the food. The mess sergeant was still screaming at the K.P.s. For a moment, I was actually terrified by the thought that somehow the mess sergeant was going to become involved in Grossbart's problem.

"Marx," the Captain said, "you're a Jewish fella—am I right?"

I played straight man. "Yes, sir."

"How long you been in the Army? Tell this boy."

"Three years and two months."

"A year in combat, Grossbart. Twelve goddam months in combat all through Europe. I admire this man." The Captain snapped a wrist against my chest. "Do you hear him peeping about the food? Do you? I want an answer, Grossbart. Yes or no."

"No, sir."

"And why not? He's a Jewish fella."

"Some things are more important to some Jews than other things to other Jews."

Barrett blew up. "Look, Grossbart. Marx, here, is a good man—a goddam hero. When you were in high school, Sergeant Marx was killing Germans. Who does more for the Jews—you, by throwing up over a lousy piece of sausage, a piece of first-cut meat, or Marx, by killing those Nazi bastards? If I was a Jew, Grossbart, I'd kiss this man's feet. He's a goddam hero, and *he* eats what we give him. Why do you have to cause trouble is what I want to know! What is it you're buckin' for—a discharge?"

"No, sir."

"I'm talking to a wall! Sergeant, get him out of my way." Barrett swung himself back into the driver's seat. "I'm going to see the chaplain." The engine roared, the jeep spun around in a whirl of dust, and the Captain was headed back to camp.

For a moment, Grossbart and I stood side by side, watching the jeep. Then he looked at me and said, "I don't want to start trouble. That's the first thing they toss up to us."

When he spoke, I saw that his teeth were white and straight, and the sight of them suddenly made me understand that Grossbart actually did have parents—that once upon a time someone had taken little Sheldon to the dentist. He was their son. Despite all the talk about his parents, it was hard to believe in Grossbart as a child, an heir —as related by blood to anyone, mother, father, or, above all, to me. This realization led me to another.

"What does your father do, Grossbart?" I asked as we started to walk back toward the chow line.

"He's a tailor."

"An American?"

"Now, yes. A son in the Army," he said, jokingly.

"And your mother?" I asked.

He winked. "A *ballabusta*. She practically sleeps with a dustcloth in her hand."

"She's also an immigrant?"

"All she talks is Yiddish, still."

"And your father, too?"

"A little English. 'Clean,' 'Press,' 'Take the pants in.' That's the extent of it. But they're good to me."

"Then, Grossbart—" I reached out and stopped him. He turned toward me, and when our eyes met, his seemed to jump back, to shiver in their sockets. "Grossbart —you were the one who wrote that letter, weren't you?"

It took only a second or two for his eyes to flash happy again. "Yes." He walked on, and I kept pace. "It's what my father *would* have written if he had known how. It was his name, though. *He* signed it. He even mailed it. I sent it home. For the New York postmark."

I was astonished, and he saw it. With complete seriousness, he thrust his right arm in front of me. "Blood is blood, Sergeant," he said, pinching the blue vein in his wrist.

"What the hell *are* you trying to do, Grossbart?" I asked. "I've seen you eat. Do you know that? I told the Captain I don't know what you eat, but I've seen you eat like a hound at chow."

"We work hard, Sergeant. We're in training. For a furnace to work, you've got to feed it coal."

"Why did you say in the letter that you threw up all the time?"

"I was really talking about Mickey there. I was talking *for* him. He would never write, Sergeant, though I pleaded with him. He'll waste away to nothing if I don't help. Sergeant, I used my name—my father's name—but it's Mickey, and Fishbein, too, I'm watching out for."

"You're a regular Messiah, aren't you?"

We were at the chow line now.

"That's a good one, Sergeant," he said, smiling. "But who knows? Who can tell? Maybe you're the Messiah—a little bit. What Mickey says is the Messiah is a collective idea. He went to Yeshiva, Mickey, for a while. He says *together* we're the Messiah. Me a little bit, you a little bit. You should hear that kid talk, Sergeant, when he gets going."

"Me a little bit, you a little bit," I said. "You'd like to believe that, wouldn't you, Grossbart? That would make everything so clean for you."

"It doesn't seem too bad a thing to believe, Sergeant. It only means we should all *give* a little, is all."

I walked off to eat my rations with the other noncoms.

Two days later, a letter addressed to Captain Barrett passed over my desk. It had come through the chain of command—from the office of Congressman Franconi, where it had been received, to General Lyman, to Colonel Sousa, to Major Lamont, now to Captain Barrett. I read it over twice. It was dated May 14, the day Barrett had spoken with Grossbart on the rifle range.

Dear Congressman:
First let me thank you for your interest in behalf of my son, Private Sheldon Gross-bart. Fortunately, I was able to speak with Sheldon on the phone the other night, and I think I've been able to solve our problem. He is, as I mentioned in my last letter, a very religious boy, and it was only with the greatest difficulty that I could persuade him that the religious thing to do—what God Himself would want Sheldon to do—would be to suffer the pangs of religious remorse for the good of his country and all mankind. It took some doing, Congressman, but finally he saw the light. In fact, what he said (and I wrote down the words on a scratch pad so as never to forget), what he said was "I guess you're right, Dad. So many millions of my fellow-Jews gave up their lives to the enemy, the least I can do is live for a while minus a bit of my heritage so as to help end this struggle and regain for all the children of God dignity and humanity." That, Congressman, would make any father proud.
By the way, Sheldon wanted me to know—and to pass on to you—the name of a soldier who helped him reach this decision: SERGEANT NATHAN MARX. Sergeant Marx is a combat veteran who is Sheldon's first sergeant. This man has helped Sheldon over some of the first hurdles he's had to face in the Army, and is in part responsible for Sheldon's changing his mind about the dietary laws. I know Sheldon would appreci-ate any recognition Marx could receive.
Thank you and good luck. I look forward to seeing your name on the next election ballot.

Respectfully,
Samuel E. Grossbart

Attached to the Grossbart communiqué was another, addressed to General Mar-shall Lyman, the post commander, and signed by Representative Charles E. Franconi, of the House of Representatives. The communiqué informed General Lyman that Sergeant Nathan Marx was a credit to the U.S. Army and the Jewish people.

What was Grossbart's motive in recanting? Did he feel he'd gone too far? Was the letter a strategic retreat—a crafty attempt to strengthen what he considered our alliance? Or had he actually changed his mind, via an imaginary dialogue between Grossbart *père* and Grossbart *fils?* I was puzzled, but only for a few days—that is, only until I realized that, whatever his reasons, he had actually decided to disappear from my life; he was going to allow himself to become just another trainee. I saw him at inspection, but he never winked; at chow formations, but he never flashed me a sign.

On Sundays, with the other trainees, he would sit around watching the noncoms' softball team, for which I pitched, but not once did he speak an unnecessary word to me. Fishbein and Halpern retreated, too—at Grossbart's command, I was sure. Apparently he had seen that wisdom lay in turning back before he plunged over into the ugliness of privilege undeserved. Our separation allowed me to forgive him our past encounters, and, finally, to admire him for his good sense.

Meanwhile, free of Grossbart, I grew used to my job and my administrative tasks. I stepped on a scale one day, and discovered I had truly become a noncombatant; I had gained seven pounds. I found patience to get past the first three pages of a book. I thought about the future more and more, and wrote letters to girls I'd known before the war. I even got a few answers. I sent away to Columbia for a Law School catalogue. I continued to follow the war in the Pacific, but it was not my war. I thought I could see the end, and sometimes, at night, I dreamed that I was walking on the streets of Manhattan—Broadway, Third Avenue, 116th Street, where I had lived the three years I attended Columbia. I curled myself around these dreams and I began to be happy.

And then, one Sunday, when everybody was away and I was alone in the orderly room reading a month-old copy of the *Sporting News,* Grossbart reappeared.

"You a baseball fan, Sergeant?"

I looked up. "How are you?"

"Fine," Grossbart said. "They're making a soldier out of me."

"How are Fishbein and Halpern?"

"Coming along," he said. "We've got no training this afternoon. They're at the movies."

"How come you're not with them?"

"I wanted to come over and say hello."

He smiled—a shy, regular-guy smile, as though he and I well knew that our friendship drew its sustenance from unexpected visits, remembered birthdays, and borrowed lawnmowers. At first it offended me, and then the feeling was swallowed by the general uneasiness I felt at the thought that everyone on the post was locked away in a dark movie theater and I was here alone with Grossbart. I folded up my paper.

"Sergeant," he said, "I'd like to ask a favor. It is a favor, and I'm making no bones about it."

He stopped, allowing me to refuse him a hearing—which, of course, forced me into a courtesy I did not intend. "Go ahead."

"Well, actually it's two favors."

I said nothing.

"The first one's about these rumors. Everybody says we're going to the Pacific."

"As I told your friend Fishbein, I don't know," I said. "You'll just have to wait to find out. Like everybody else."

"You think there's a chance of any of us going East?"

"Germany?" I said. "Maybe."

"I meant New York."

"I don't think so, Grossbart. Offhand."

"Thanks for the information, Sergeant," he said.

"It's not information, Grossbart. Just what I surmise."

"It certainly would be good to be near home. My parents—you know." He took a step toward the door and then turned back. "Oh, the other thing. May I ask the other?"

"What is it?"

"The other thing is—I've got relatives in St. Louis, and they say they'll give me a whole Passover dinner if I can get down there. God, Sergeant, that'd mean an awful lot to me."

I stood up. "No passes during basic, Grossbart."

"But we're off from now till Monday morning, Sergeant. I could leave the post and no one would even know."

"I'd know. You'd know."

"But that's all. Just the two of us. Last night, I called my aunt, and you should have heard her. 'Come—come,' she said. 'I got gefilte fish, *chrain*—the works!' Just a day, Sergeant. I'd take the blame if anything happened."

"The Captain isn't here to sign a pass."

"You could sign."

"Look, Grossbart—"

"Sergeant, for two months, practically, I've been eating *trafe* till I want to die."

"I thought you'd made up your mind to live with it. To be minus a little bit of heritage."

He pointed a finger at me. "You!" he said. "That wasn't for you to read."

"I read it. So what?"

"That letter was addressed to a congressman."

"Grossbart, don't feed me any baloney. You *wanted* me to read it."

"Why are you persecuting me, Sergeant?"

"Are you kidding!"

"I've run into this before," he said, "but never from my own!"

"Get out of here, Grossbart! Get the hell out of my sight!"

He did not move. "Ashamed, that's what you are," he said. "So you take it out on the rest of us. They say Hitler himself was half a Jew. Hearing you, I wouldn't doubt it."

"What are you trying to do with me, Grossbart?" I asked him. "What are you after? You want me to give you special privileges, to change the food, to find out about your orders, to give you weekend passes."

"You even talk like a goy!" Grossbart shook his fist. "Is this just a weekend pass I'm asking for? Is a Seder sacred, or not?"

Seder! It suddenly occurred to me that Passover had been celebrated weeks before. I said so.

"That's right," he replied. "Who says no? A month ago—and I was in the field eating hash! And now all I ask is a simple favor. A Jewish boy I thought would understand. My aunt's willing to go out of her way—to make a Seder a month later. . . ." He turned to go, mumbling.

"Come back here!" I called. He stopped and looked at me. "Grossbart, why can't you be like the rest? Why do you have to stick out like a sore thumb?"

"Because I'm a Jew, Sergeant. I *am* different. Better, maybe not. But different."

"This is a war, Grossbart. For the time being *be* the same."

"I refuse."

"What?"

"I refuse. I can't stop being me, that's all there is to it." Tears came to his eyes. "It's a hard thing to be a Jew. But now I understand what Mickey says—it's a harder thing to stay one." He raised a hand sadly toward me. "Look at *you.*"

"Stop crying!"

"Stop this, stop that, stop the other thing! *You* stop, Sergeant. Stop closing your heart to your own!" And, wiping his face with his sleeve, he ran out the door. "The least we can do for one another—the least . . ."

An hour later, looking out of the window, I saw Grossbart headed across the field. He wore a pair of starched khakis and carried a little leather ditty bag. I went out into the heat of the day. It was quiet; not a soul was in sight except, over by the mess hall, four K.P.s sitting around a pan, sloped forward from their waists, gabbing and peeling potatoes in the sun.

"Grossbart!" I called.

He looked toward me and continued walking.

"Grossbart, get over here!"

He turned and came across the field. Finally, he stood before me.

"Where are you going?" I asked.

"St. Louis. I don't care."

"You'll get caught without a pass."

"So I'll get caught without a pass."

"You'll go to the stockade."

"I'm *in* the stockade." He made an about-face and headed off.

I let him go only a step or two. "Come back here," I said, and he followed me into the office, where I typed out a pass and signed the Captain's name, and my own initials after it.

He took the pass and then, a moment later, reached out and grabbed my hand. "Sergeant, you don't know how much this means to me."

"O.K.," I said. "Don't get in any trouble."

"I wish I could show you how much this means to me."

"Don't do me any favors. Don't write any more congressmen for citations."

He smiled. "You're right. I won't. But let me do something."

"Bring me a piece of that gefilte fish. Just get out of here."

"I will!" he said. "With a slice of carrot and a little horseradish. I won't forget."

"All right. Just show your pass at the gate. And don't tell *anybody.*"

"I won't. It's a month late, but a good Yom Tov to you."

"Good Yom Tov, Grossbart," I said.

"You're a good Jew, Sergeant. You like to think you have a hard heart, but underneath you're a fine, decent man. I mean that."

Those last three words touched me more than any words from Grossbart's mouth had the right to. "All right, Grossbart," I said. "Now call me 'sir,' and get the hell out of here."

He ran out the door and was gone. I felt very pleased with myself; it was a great relief to stop fighting Grossbart, and it had cost me nothing. Barrett would never find out, and if he did, I could manage to invent some excuse. For a while, I sat at my desk, comfortable in my decision. Then the screen door flew back and Grossbart burst in again. "Sergeant!" he said. Behind him I saw Fishbein and Halpern, both in starched khakis, both carrying ditty bags like Grossbart's.

"Sergeant, I caught Mickey and Larry coming out of the movies. I almost missed them."

"Grossbart—did I say tell no one?" I said.

"But my aunt said I could bring friends. That I should, in fact."

"*I'm* the Sergeant, Grossbart—not your aunt!"

Grossbart looked at me in disbelief. He pulled Halpern up by his sleeve. "Mickey, tell the Sergeant what this would mean to you."

Halpern looked at me and, shrugging, said, "A lot."

Fishbein stepped forward without prompting. "This would mean a great deal to me and my parents, Sergeant Marx."

"No!" I shouted.

Grossbart was shaking his head. "Sergeant, I could see you denying me, but how you can deny Mickey, a Yeshiva boy—that's beyond me."

"I'm not denying Mickey anything," I said. "You just pushed a little too hard, Grossbart. *You* denied him."

"I'll give him my pass, then," Grossbart said. "I'll give him my aunt's address and a little note. At least let him go."

In a second, he had crammed the pass into Halpern's pants pocket. Halpern looked at me, and so did Fishbein. Grossbart was at the door, pushing it open. "Mickey, bring me a piece of gelfilte fish, at least," he said, and then he was outside again.

The three of us looked at one another, and then I said, "Halpern, hand that pass over."

He took it from his pocket and gave it to me. Fishbein had now moved to the doorway, where he lingered. He stood there for a moment with his mouth slightly open, and then he pointed to himself. "And me?" he asked.

His utter ridiculousness exhausted me. I slumped down in my seat and felt pulses knocking at the back of my eyes. "Fishbein," I said, "you understand I'm not trying to deny you anything, don't you? If it was my Army, I'd serve gefilte fish in the mess hall. I'd sell *kugel* in the PX, honest to God."

Halpern smiled.

"You understand, don't you, Halpern?"

"Yes, Sergeant."

"And you, Fishbein? I don't want enemies. I'm just like you—I want to serve my time and go home. I miss the same things you miss."

"Then, Sergeant," Fishbein said, "why don't you come, too?"

"Where?"

"To St. Louis. To Shelly's aunt. We'll have a regular Seder. Play hide-the-matzoh." He gave me a broad, black-toothed smile.

I saw Grossbart again, on the other side of the screen.

"Pst!" He waved a piece of paper. "Mickey, here's the address. Tell her I couldn't get away."

Halpern did not move. He looked at me, and I saw the shrug moving up his arms into his shoulders again. I took the cover off my typewriter and made out passes for him and Fishbein. "Go," I said. "The three of you."

I thought Halpern was going to kiss my hand.

That afternoon, in a bar in Joplin, I drank beer and listened with half an ear to the Cardinal game. I tried to look squarely at what I'd become involved in, and began to wonder if perhaps the struggle with Grossbart wasn't as much my fault as his. What was I that I had to *muster* generous feelings? Who was I to have been feeling so grudging, so tight-hearted? After all, I wasn't being asked to move the world. Had I a right, then, or a reason, to clamp down on Grossbart, when that meant clamping down on Halpern, too? And Fishbein—that ugly, agreeable soul? Out of the many recollections of my childhood that had tumbled over me these past few days I heard my grandmother's voice: "What are you making a *tsimmes?*" It was what she would ask my mother when, say, I had cut myself while doing something I shouldn't have done, and her daughter was busy bawling me out. I needed a hug and a kiss, and my mother would moralize. But my grandmother knew—mercy overrides justice. I should have known it, too. Who was Nathan Marx to be such a penny pincher with kindness? Surely, I thought, the Messiah himself—if He should ever come—won't niggle over nickels and dimes. God willing, he'll hug and kiss.

The next day, while I was playing softball over on the parade ground, I decided to ask Bob Wright, who was noncom in charge of Classification and Assignment, where he thought our trainees would be sent when their cycle ended, in two weeks. I asked casually, between innings, and he said, "They're pushing them all into the Pacific. Shulman cut the orders on your boys the other day."

The news shocked me, as though I were the father of Halpern, Fishbein, and Grossbart.

That night, I was just sliding into sleep when someone tapped on my door. "Who is it?" I asked.

"Sheldon."

He opened the door and came in. For a moment, I felt his presence without being able to see him. "How was it?" I asked.

He popped into sight in the near-darkness before me. "Great, Sergeant." Then he was sitting on the edge of the bed. I sat up.

"How about you?" he asked. "Have a nice weekend?"

"Yes."

"The others went to sleep." He took a deep, paternal breath. We sat silent for a while, and a homey feeling invaded my ugly little cubicle; the door was locked, the cat was out, the children were safely in bed.

"Sergeant, can I tell you something? Personal?"

I did not answer, and he seemed to know why. "Not about me. About Mickey. Sergeant, I never felt for anybody like I feel for him. Last night I heard Mickey in the bed next to me. He was crying so, it could have broken your heart. Real sobs."

"I'm sorry to hear that."

"I had to talk to him to stop him. He held my hand, Sergeant—he wouldn't let it go. He was almost hysterical. He kept saying if he only knew where we were going. Even if he knew it *was* the Pacific, that would be better than nothing. Just to know."

Long ago, someone had taught Grossbart the sad rule that only lies can get the truth. Not that I couldn't believe in the fact of Halpern's crying; his eyes *always* seemed red-rimmed. But, fact or not, it became a lie when Grossbart uttered it. He was entirely strategic. But then—it came with the force of indictment—so was I!

There are strategies of aggression, but there are strategies of retreat as well. And so, recognizing that I myself had not been without craft and guile, I told him what I knew. "It is the Pacific."

He let out a small gasp, which was not a lie. "I'll tell him. I wish it was otherwise."

"So do I."

He jumped on my words. "You mean you think you could do something? A change, maybe?"

"No, I couldn't do a thing."

"Don't you know anybody over at C. and A.?"

"Grossbart, there's nothing I can do," I said. "If your orders are for the Pacific, then it's the Pacific."

"But Mickey—"

"Mickey, you, me—everybody, Grossbart. There's nothing to be done. Maybe the war'll end before you go. Pray for a miracle."

"But—"

"Good night, Grossbart." I settled back, and was relieved to feel the springs unbend as Grossbart rose to leave. I could see him clearly now; his jaw had dropped, and he looked like a dazed prizefighter. I noticed for the first time a little paper bag in his hand.

"Grossbart." I smiled. "My gift?"

"Oh, yes, Sergeant. Here—from all of us." He handed me the bag. "It's egg roll."

"Egg roll?" I accepted the bag and felt a damp grease spot on the bottom. I opened it, sure that Grossbart was joking.

"We thought you'd probably like it. You know—Chinese egg roll. We thought you'd probably have a taste for—"

"Your aunt served egg roll?"

"She wasn't home."

"Grossbart, she invited you. You told me she invited you and your friends."

"I know," he said. "I just reread the letter. *Next* week."

I got out of bed and walked to the window. "Grossbart," I said. But I was not calling to him.

"What?"

"What are you, Grossbart? Honest to God, what are you?"

I think it was the first time I'd asked him a question for which he didn't have an immediate answer.

"How can you do this to people?" I went on.

"Sergeant, the day away did us all a world of good. Fishbein, you should see him, he *loves* Chinese food."

"But the Seder," I said.

"We took second best, Sergeant."

Rage came charging at me. I didn't sidestep. "Grossbart, you're a liar!" I said. "You're a schemer and a crook. You've got no respect for anything. Nothing at all. Not for me, for the truth—not even for poor Halpern! You use us all—"

"Sergeant, Sergeant, I feel for Mickey. Honest to God, I do. I *love* Mickey. I try—"

"You try! You feel!" I lurched toward him and grabbed his shirt front. I shook him furiously. "Grossbart, get out! Get out and stay the hell away from me. Because if I see you, I'll make your life miserable. *You understand that?*"

"Yes."

I let him free, and when he walked from the room, I wanted to spit on the floor where he had stood. I couldn't stop the fury. It engulfed me, owned me, till it seemed I could only rid myself of it with tears or an act of violence. I snatched from the bed the bag Grossbart had given me and, with all my strength, threw it out the window. And the next morning, as the men policed the area around the barracks, I heard a great cry go up from one of the trainees, who had been anticipating only his morning handful of cigarette butts and candy wrappers. "Egg roll!" he shouted. "Holy Christ, Chinese goddam egg roll!"

A week later, when I read the orders that had come down from C. and A., I couldn't believe my eyes. Every single trainee was to be shipped to Camp Stoneman, California, and from there to the Pacific—every trainee but one. Private Sheldon Grossbart. He was to be sent to Fort Monmouth, New Jersey. I read the mimeographed sheet several times. Dee, Farrell, Fishbein, Fuselli, Fylypowycz, Glinicki, Gromke, Gucwa, Halpern, Hardy, Helebrandt, right down to Anton Zygadlo—all were to be headed West before the month was out. All except Grossbart. He had pulled a string, and I wasn't it.

I lifted the phone and called C. and A.

The voice on the other end said smartly, "Corporal Shulman, sir."

"Let me speak to Sergeant Wright."

"Who is this calling, sir?"

"Sergeant Marx."

And, to my surprise, the voice said, *"Oh!"* Then, "Just a minute, Sergeant."

Shulman's *"Oh!"* stayed with me while I waited for Wright to come to the phone. Why *"Oh!"*? Who was Shulman? And then, so simply, I knew I'd discovered the string that Grossbart had pulled. In fact, I could hear Grossbart the day he'd discovered Shulman in the PX, or in the bowling alley, or maybe even at services. "Glad to meet you. Where you from? Bronx? Me, too. Do you know So-and-So? And So-and-So? Me, too! You work at C. and A.? Really? Hey, how's chances of getting East? Could you do something? Change something? Swindle, cheat, lie? We gotta help each other, you know. If the Jews in Germany . . ."

Bob Wright answered the phone. "How are you, Nate? How's the pitching arm?"

"Good. Bob, I wonder if you could do me a favor." I heard clearly my own words, and they so reminded me of Grossbart that I dropped more easily than I could have imagined into what I had planned. "This may sound crazy, Bob, but I got a kid here on orders to Monmouth who wants them changed. He had a brother killed in Europe, and he's hot to go to the Pacific. Says he'd feel like a coward if he wound up Stateside. I don't know, Bob—can anything be done? Put somebody else in the Monmouth slot?"

"Who?" he asked cagily.

"Anybody. First guy in the alphabet. I don't care. The kid just asked if something could be done."

"What's his name?"

"Grossbart, Sheldon."

Wright didn't answer.

"Yeah," I said. "He's a Jewish kid, so he thought I could help him out. You know."

"I guess I can do something," he finally said. "The Major hasn't been around here for weeks. Temporary duty to the golf course. I'll try, Nate, that's all I can say."

"I'd appreciate it, Bob. See you Sunday." And I hung up, perspiring.

The following day, the corrected orders appeared: Fishbein, Fuselli, Fylypowycz, Glinicki, Gromke, Grossbart, Gucwa, Halpern, Hardy . . . Lucky Private Harley Alton was to go to Fort Monmouth, New Jersey, where, for some reason or other, they wanted an enlisted man with infantry training.

After chow that night, I stopped back at the orderly room to straighten out the guard-duty roster. Grossbart was waiting for me. He spoke first.

"You son of a bitch!"

I sat down at my desk, and while he glared at me, I began to make the necessary alterations in the duty roster.

"What do you have against me?" he cried. "Against my family? Would it kill you for me to be near my father, God knows how many months he has left to him?"

"Why so?"

"His heart," Grossbart said. "He hasn't had enough troubles in a lifetime, you've got to add to them. I curse the day I ever met you, Marx! Shulman told me what happened over there. There's no limit to your anti-Semitism, is there? The damage you've done here isn't enough. You have to make a special phone call! You really want me dead!"

I made the last few notations in the duty roster and got up to leave. "Good night, Grossbart."

"You owe me an explanation!" He stood in my path.

"Sheldon, you're the one who owes explanations."

He scowled. "To *you?*"

"To me, I think so—yes. Mostly to Fishbein and Halpern."

"That's right, twist things around. I owe nobody nothing, I've done all I could do for them. Now I think I've got the right to watch out for myself."

"For each other we have to learn to watch out, Sheldon. You told me yourself."

"You call this watching out for me—what you did?"

"No. For all of us."

I pushed him aside and started for the door. I heard his furious breathing behind me, and it sounded like steam rushing from an engine of terrible strength.

"*You'll* be all right," I said from the door. And, I thought, so would Fishbein and Halpern be all right, even in the Pacific, if only Grossbart continued to see—in the obsequiousness of the one, the soft spirituality of the other—some profit for himself.

I stood outside the orderly room, and I heard Grossbart weeping behind me. Over in the barracks, in the lighted windows, I could see the boys in their T shirts sitting on their bunks talking about their orders, as they'd been doing for the past two days. With a kind of quiet nervousness, they polished shoes, shined belt buckles, squared away underwear, trying as best they could to accept their fate. Behind me, Grossbart swallowed hard, accepting his. And then, resisting with all my will an impulse to turn and seek pardon for my vindictiveness, I accepted my own.

THE SKY IS GRAY

Ernest J. Gaines

(b. 1933)

Biography p. 1074

1

Go'n be coming in a few minutes. Coming round that bend down there full speed. And I'm go'n get out my handkerchief and wave it down, and we go'n get on it and go.

I keep on looking for it, but Mama don't look that way no more. She's looking down the road where we just come from. It's a long old road, and far 's you can see you don't see nothing but gravel. You got dry weeds on both sides, and you got trees on both sides, and fences on both sides, too. And you got cows in the pastures and they standing close together. And when we was coming out here to catch the bus I seen the smoke coming out of the cows's noses.

I look at my mama and I know what she's thinking. I been with mama so much, just me and her, I know what she's thinking all the time. Right now it's home—Auntie and them. She's thinking if they got enough wood—if she left enough there to keep them warm till we get back. She's thinking if it go'n rain and if any of them go'n have to go out in the rain. She's thinking 'bout the hog—if he go'n get out, and if Ty and Val be able to get him back in. She always worry like that when she leaves the house. She don't worry too much if she leave me there with the smaller ones, 'cause she know I'm go'n look after them and look after Auntie and everything else. I'm the oldest and she say I'm the man.

I look at my mama and I love my mama. She's wearing that black coat and that black hat and she's looking sad. I love my mama and I want put my arm round her and tell her. But I'm not supposed to do that. She say that's weakness and that's crybaby stuff, and she don't want no crybaby round her. She don't want you to be scared, either. 'Cause Ty's scared of ghosts and she's always whipping him. I'm scared of the dark, too, but I make 'tend I ain't. I make 'tend I ain't 'cause I'm the oldest, and I got to set a good sample for the rest. I can't ever be scared and I can't ever cry. And that's why I never said nothing 'bout my teeth. It's been hurting me and hurting me close to a month now, but I never said it. I didn't say it 'cause I didn't want act like a crybaby, and 'cause I know we didn't have enough money to go have it pulled. But, Lord, it been hurting me. And look like it wouldn't start till at night when you was trying to get yourself little sleep. Then soon 's you shut your eyes—ummm-ummm, Lord, look like it go right down to your heartstring.

"Hurting, hanh?" Ty'd say.

I'd shake my head, but I wouldn't open my mouth for nothing. You open your mouth and let that wind in, and it almost kill you.

I'd just lay there and listen to them snore. Ty there, right 'side me, and Auntie and Val over by the fireplace. Val younger than me and Ty, and he sleeps with Auntie. Mama sleeps round the other side with Louis and Walker.

I'd just lay there and listen to them, and listen to that wind out there, and listen to that fire in the fireplace. Sometimes it'd stop long enough to let me get little rest. Sometimes it just hurt, hurt, hurt. Lord, have mercy.

2

Auntie knowed it was hurting me. I didn't tell nobody but Ty, 'cause we buddies and he ain't go'n tell nobody. But some kind of way Auntie found out. When she asked me, I told her no, nothing was wrong. But she knowed it all the time. She told me to mash up a piece of aspirin and wrap it in some cotton and jugg it down in that hole. I did it, but it didn't do no good. It stopped for a little while, and started right back again. Auntie wanted to tell Mama, but I told her, "Uh-uh." 'Cause I knowed we didn't have any money, and it just was go'n make her mad again. So Auntie told Monsieur Bayonne, and Monsieur Bayonne came over to the house and told me to kneel down 'side him on the fireplace. He put his finger in his mouth and made the Sign of the Cross on my jaw. The tip of Monsieur Bayonne's finger is some hard, 'cause he's always playing on that guitar. If we sit outside at night we can always hear Monsieur Bayonne playing on his guitar. Sometimes we leave him out there playing on the guitar.

Monsieur Bayonne made the Sign of the Cross over and over on my jaw, but that didn't do no good. Even when he prayed and told me to pray some, too, that tooth still hurt me.

"How you feeling?" he say.

"Same," I say.

He kept on praying and making the Sign of the Cross and I kept on praying, too.

"Still hurting?" he say.

"Yes, sir."

Monsieur Bayonne mashed harder and harder on my jaw. He mashed so hard he almost pushed me over on Ty. But then he stopped.

"What kind of prayers you praying, boy?" he say.

"Baptist," I say.

"Well, I'll be—no wonder that tooth still killing him. I'm going one way and he pulling the other. Boy, don't you know any Catholic prayers?"

"I know 'Hail Mary,' " I say.

"Then you better start saying it."

"Yes, sir."

He started mashing on my jaw again, and I could hear him praying at the same time. And, sure enough, after while it stopped hurting me.

Me and Ty went outside where Monsieur Bayonne's two hounds was and we started playing with them. "Let's go hunting," Ty say. "All right," I say; and we went on back in the pasture. Soon the hounds got on a trail, and me and Ty followed them all 'cross the pasture and then back in the woods, too. And then they cornered this little old rabbit and killed him, and me and Ty made them get back, and we picked up the rabbit and started on back home. But my tooth had started hurting me again. It was hurting me plenty now, but I wouldn't tell Monsieur Bayonne. That night I didn't sleep a bit, and first thing in the morning Auntie told me to go back and let

Monsieur Bayonne pray over me some more. Monsieur Bayonne was in his kitchen making coffee when I got there. Soon 's he seen me he knowed what was wrong.

"All right, kneel down there 'side that stove," he say. "And this time make sure you pray Catholic. I don't know nothing 'bout that Baptist, and I don't want know nothing 'bout him."

3

Last night Mama say, "Tomorrow we going to town."

"It ain't hurting me no more," I say. "I can eat anything on it."

"Tomorrow we going to town," she say.

And after she finished eating, she got up and went to bed. She always go to bed early now. 'Fore Daddy went in the Army, she used to stay up late. All of us sitting out on the gallery or round the fire. But now, look like soon 's she finish eating she go to bed.

This morning when I woke up, her and Auntie was standing 'fore the fireplace. She say: "Enough to get there and get back. Dollar and a half to have it pulled. Twenty-five for me to go, twenty-five for him. Twenty-five for me to come back, twenty-five for him. Fifty cents left. Guess I get little piece of salt meat with that."

"Sure can use it," Auntie say. "White beans and no salt meat ain't white beans."

"I do the best I can," Mama say.

They was quiet after that, and I made 'tend I was still asleep.

"James, hit the floor," Auntie say.

I still made 'tend I was asleep. I didn't want them to know I was listening.

"All right," Auntie say, shaking me by the shoulder. "Come on. Today's the day."

I pushed the cover down to get out, and Ty grabbed it and pulled it back.

"You, too, Ty," Auntie say.

"I ain't getting no teef pulled," Ty say.

"Don't mean it ain't time to get up," Auntie say. "Hit it, Ty."

Ty got up grumbling.

"James, you hurry up and get in your clothes and eat your food," Auntie say. "What time y'all coming back?" she say to Mama.

"That 'leven o'clock bus," Mama say. "Got to get back in that field this evening."

"Get a move on you, James," Auntie say.

I went in the kitchen and washed my face, then I ate my breakfast. I was having bread and syrup. The bread was warm and hard and tasted good. And I tried to make it last a long time.

Ty came back there grumbling and mad at me.

"Got to get up," he say. "I ain't having no teefes pulled. What I got to be getting up for?"

Ty poured some syrup in his pan and got a piece of bread. He didn't wash his hands, neither his face, and I could see that white stuff in his eyes.

"You the one getting your teef pulled," he say. "What I got to get up for. I bet if I was getting a teef pulled, you wouldn't be getting up. Shucks; syrup again. I'm getting tired of this old syrup. Syrup, syrup, syrup. I'm go'n take with the sugar diabetes. I want me some bacon sometime."

"Go out in the field and work and you can have your bacon," Auntie say. She stood in the middle door looking at Ty. "You better be glad you got syrup. Some people ain't got that—hard 's time is."

"Shucks," Ty say. "How can I be strong."

"I don't know too much 'bout your strength," Auntie say; "but I know where you go'n be hot at, you keep that grumbling up. James, get a move on you; your mama waiting."

I ate my last piece of bread and went in the front room. Mama was standing 'fore the fireplace warming her hands. I put on my coat and my cap, and we left the house.

4

I look down there again, but it still ain't coming. I almost say, "It ain't coming yet," but I keep my mouth shut. 'Cause that's something else she don't like. She don't like for you to say something just for nothing. She can see it ain't coming, I can see it ain't coming, so why say it ain't coming. I don't say it, I turn and look at the river that's back of us. It's so cold the smoke's just raising up from the water. I see a bunch of pool-doos not too far out—just on the other side the lilies. I'm wondering if you can eat pool-doos. I ain't too sure, 'cause I ain't never ate none. But I done ate owls and blackbirds, and I done ate redbirds, too. I didn't want kill the redbirds, but she made me kill them. They had two of them back there. One in my trap, one in Ty's trap. Me and Ty was go'n play with them and let them go, but she made me kill them 'cause we needed the food.

"I can't," I say. "I can't."

"Here," she say. "Take it."

"I can't," I say. "I can't. I can't kill him, Mama, please."

"Here," she say. "Take this fork, James."

"Please, Mama, I can't kill him," I say.

I could tell she was go'n hit me. I jerked back, but I didn't jerk back soon enough. "Take it," she say.

I took it and reached in for him, but he kept on hopping to the back.

"I can't, Mama," I say. The water just kept on running down my face. "I can't," I say.

"Get him out of there," she say.

I reached in for him and he kept on hopping to the back. Then I reached in farther, and he pecked me on the hand.

"I can't, Mama," I say.

She slapped me again.

I reached in again, but he kept on hopping out my way. Then he hopped to one side and I reached there. The fork got him on the leg and I heard his leg pop. I pulled my hand out 'cause I had hurt him.

"Give it here," she say, and jerked the fork out my hand.

She reached in and got the little bird right in the neck. I heard the fork go in his neck, and I heard it go in the ground. She brought him out and helt him right in front of me.

"That's one," she say. She shook him off and gived me the fork. "Get the other one."

"I can't, Mama," I say. "I'll do anything, but don't make me do that."

She went to the corner of the fence and broke the biggest switch over there she could find. I knelt 'side the trap, crying.

"Get him out of there," she say.

"I can't, Mama."

She started hitting me 'cross the back. I went down on the ground, crying.

"Get him," she say.

"Octavia?" Auntie say.

'Cause she had come out of the house and she was standing by the tree looking at us.

"Get him out of there," Mama say.

"Octavia," Auntie say, "explain to him. Explain to him. Just don't beat him. Explain to him."

But she hit me and hit me and hit me.

I'm still young—I ain't no more than eight; but I know now; I know why I had to do it. (They was so little, though. They was so little. I 'member how I picked the feathers off them and cleaned them and helt them over the fire. Then we all ate them. Ain't had but a little bitty piece each, but we all had a little bitty piece, and everybody just looked at me 'cause they was so proud.) Suppose she had to go away? That's why I had to do it. Suppose she had to go away like Daddy went away? Then who was go'n look after us? They had to be somebody left to carry on. I didn't know it then, but I know it now. Auntie and Monsieur Bayonne talked to me and made me see.

5

Time I see it I get out my handkerchief and start waving. It's still 'way down there, but I keep waving anyhow. Then it come up and stop and me and Mama get on. Mama tell me go sit in the back while she pay. I do like she say, and the people look at me. When I pass the little sign that say "White" and "Colored," I start looking for a seat. I just see one of them back there, but I don't take it, 'cause I want my mama to sit down herself. She comes in the back and sit down, and I lean on the seat. They got seats in the front, but I know I can't sit there, 'cause I have to sit back of the sign. Anyhow, I don't want sit there if my mama go'n sit back here.

They got a lady sitting 'side my mama and she looks at me and smiles little bit. I smile back, but I don't open my mouth, 'cause the wind'll get in and make that tooth ache. The lady take out a pack of gum and reach me a slice, but I shake my head. The lady just can't understand why a little boy'll turn down gum, and she reach me a slice again. This time I point to my jaw. The lady understands and smiles little bit, and I smile little bit, but I don't open my mouth, though.

They got a girl sitting 'cross from me. She got on a red overcoat and her hair's plaited in one big plait. First, I make 'tend I don't see her over there, but then I start looking at her little bit. She make 'tend she don't see me, either, but I catch her looking that way. She got a cold, and every now and then she h'ist that little handkerchief to her nose. She ought to blow it, but she don't. Must think she's too much a lady or something.

Every time she h'ist that little handkerchief, the lady 'side her say something in her ear. She shakes her head and lays her hands in her lap again. Then I catch her kind of looking where I'm at. I smile at her little bit. But think she'll smile back? Uh-uh. She just turn up her little old nose and turn her head. Well, I show her both of us can turn us head. I turn mine too and look out at the river.

The river is gray. The sky is gray. They have pool-doos on the water. The water is wavy, and the pool-doos go up and down. The bus go round a turn, and you got plenty trees hiding the river. Then the bus go round another turn, and I can see the river again.

I look toward the front where all the white people sitting. Then I look at that little old gal again. I don't look right at her, 'cause I don't want all them people to know I love her. I just look at her little bit, like I'm looking out that window over there. But she knows I'm looking that way, and she kind of look at me, too. The lady sitting 'side her catch her this time, and she leans over and says something in her ear.

"I don't love him nothing," that little old gal says out loud.

Everybody back there hear her mouth, and all of them look at us and laugh.

"I don't love you, either," I say. "So you don't have to turn up your nose, Miss."

"You the one looking," she say.

"I wasn't looking at you," I say. "I was looking out that window, there."

"Out that window, my foot," she say. "I seen you. Everytime I turned round you was looking at me."

"You must of been looking yourself if you seen me all them times," I say.

"Shucks," she say, "I got me all kind of boyfriends."

"I got girlfriends, too," I say.

"Well, I just don't want you getting your hopes up," she say.

I don't say no more to that little old gal 'cause I don't want have to bust her in the mouth. I lean on the seat where Mama sitting, and I don't even look that way no more. When we get to Bayonne, she jugg her little old tongue out at me. I make 'tend I'm go'n hit her, and she duck down 'side her mama. And all the people laugh at us again.

6

Me and Mama get off and start walking in town. Bayonne is a little bitty town. Baton Rouge is a hundred times bigger than Bayonne. I went to Baton Rouge once —me, Ty, Mama, and Daddy. But that was 'way back yonder, 'fore Daddy went in the Army. I wonder when we go'n see him again. I wonder when. Look like he ain't ever coming back home. . . . Even the pavement all cracked in Bayonne. Got grass shooting right out the sidewalk. Got weeds in the ditch, too; just like they got at home.

It's some cold in Bayonne. Look like it's colder than it is home. The wind blows in my face, and I feel that stuff running down my nose. I sniff. Mama says use that handkerchief. I blow my nose and put it back.

We pass a school and I see them white children playing in the yard. Big old red school, and them children just running and playing. Then we pass a café, and I see a bunch of people in there eating. I wish I was in there 'cause I'm cold. Mama tells me keep my eyes in front where they belong.

We pass stores that's got dummies, and we pass another café, and then we pass a shoe shop, and that bald-head man in there fixing on a shoe. I look at him and I butt into that white lady, and Mama jerks me in front and tells me stay there.

We come up to the courthouse, and I see the flag waving there. This flag ain't like the one we got at school. This one here ain't got but a handful of stars. One at school got a big pile of stars—one for every state. We pass it and we turn and there it is— the dentist office. Me and Mama go in, and they got people sitting everywhere you look. They even got a little boy in there younger than me.

Me and Mama sit on that bench, and a white lady come in there and ask me what my name is. Mama tells her and the white lady goes on back. Then I hear somebody hollering in there. Soon 's that little boy hear him hollering, he starts hollering, too. His mama pats him and pats him, trying to make him hush up, but he ain't thinking 'bout his mama.

The man that was hollering in there comes out holding his jaw. He is a big old man and he's wearing overalls and a jumper.

"Got it, hanh?" another man asks him.

The man shakes his head—don't want open his mouth.

"Man, I thought they was killing you in there," the other man says. "Hollering like a pig under a gate."

The man don't say nothing. He just heads for the door, and the other man follows him.

"John Lee," the white lady says. "John Lee Williams."

The little boy juggs his head down in his mama's lap and holler more now. His mama tells him go with the nurse, but he ain't thinking 'bout his mama. His mama tells him again, but he don't even hear her. His mama picks him up and takes him in there, and even when the white lady shuts the door I can still hear little old John Lee.

"I often wonder why the Lord let a child like that suffer," a lady says to my mama. The lady's sitting right in front of us on another bench. She's got on a white dress and a black sweater. She must be a nurse or something herself, I reckon.

"Not us to question," a man says.

"Sometimes I don't know if we shouldn't," the lady says.

"I know definitely we shouldn't," the man says. The man looks like a preacher. He's big and fat and he's got on a black suit. He's got a gold chain, too.

"Why?" the lady says.

"Why anything?" the preacher says.

"Yes," the lady says. "Why anything?"

"Not us to question," the preacher says.

The lady looks at the preacher a little while and looks at Mama again.

"And look like it's the poor who suffers the most," she says. "I don't understand it."

"Best not to even try," the preacher says. "He works in mysterious ways—wonders to perform."

Right then little John Lee bust out hollering, and everybody turn they head to listen.

"He's not a good dentist," the lady says. "Dr. Robillard is much better. But more expensive. That's why most of the colored people come here. The white people go to Dr. Robillard. Y'all from Bayonne?"

"Down the river," my mama says. And that's all she go'n say, 'cause she don't talk much. But the lady keeps on looking at her, and so she says, "Near Morgan."

"I see," the lady says.

7

"That's the trouble with the black people in this country today," somebody else says. This one here's sitting on the same side me and Mama's sitting, and he is kind of sitting in front of that preacher. He looks like a teacher or somebody that goes to college. He's got on a suit, and he's got a book that he's been reading. "We don't question is exactly our problem," he says. "We should question and question and question—question everything."

The preacher just looks at him a long time. He done put a toothpick or something in his mouth, and he just keeps on turning it and turning it. You can see he don't like that boy with that book.

"Maybe you can explain what you mean," he says.

"I said what I meant," the boy says. "Question everything. Every stripe, every star, every word spoken. Everything."

"It 'pears to me that this young lady and I was talking 'bout God, young man," the preacher says.

"Question Him, too," the boy says.

"Wait," the preacher says. "Wait now."

"You heard me right," the boy says. "His existence as well as everything else. Everything."

The preacher just looks across the room at the boy. You can see he's getting madder and madder. But mad or no mad, the boy ain't thinking 'bout him. He looks at that preacher just 's hard 's the preacher looks at him.

"Is this what they coming to?" the preacher says. "Is this what we educating them for?"

"You're not educating me," the boy says. "I wash dishes at night so that I can go to school in the day. So even the words you spoke need questioning."

The preacher just looks at him and shakes his head.

"When I come in this room and seen you there with your book, I said to myself, 'There's an intelligent man.' How wrong a person can be."

"Show me one reason to believe in the existence of a God," the boys says.

"My heart tells me," the preacher says.

" 'My heart tells me,' " the boys says. " 'My heart tells me.' Sure, 'My heart tells me.' And as long as you listen to what your heart tells you, you will have only what the white man gives you and nothing more. Me, I don't listen to my heart. The purpose of the heart is to pump blood throughout the body, and nothing else."

"Who's your paw, boy?" the preacher says.

"Why?"

"Who is he?"

"He's dead."

"And your mom?"

"She's in Charity Hospital with pneumonia. Half killed herself, working for nothing."

"And 'cause he's dead and she's sick, you mad at the world?"

"I'm not mad at the world. I'm questioning the world. I'm questioning it with cold logic, sir. What do words like Freedom, Liberty, God, White, Colored mean? I want to know. That's why *you* are sending us to school, to read and to ask questions. And because we ask these questions, you call us mad. No sir, it is not us who are mad."

"You keep saying 'us'?"

" 'Us.' Yes—us. I'm not alone."

The preacher just shakes his head. Then he looks at everybody in the room—everybody. Some of the people look down at the floor, keep from looking at him. I kind of look 'way myself, but soon 's I know he done turn his head, I look that way again.

"I'm sorry for you," he says to the boy.

"Why?" the boy says. "Why not be sorry for yourself? Why are you so much better off than I am? Why aren't you sorry for these other people in here? Why not be sorry for the lady who had to drag her child into the dentist office? Why not be sorry for the lady sitting on that bench over there? Be sorry for them. Not for me. Some way or the other I'm going to make it."

"No, I'm sorry for you," the preacher says.

"Of course, of course," the boy says, nodding his head. "You're sorry for me because I rock that pillar you're leaning on."

"You can't ever rock the pillar I'm leaning on, young man. It's stronger than anything man can ever do."

"You believe in God because a man told you to believe in God," the boy says. "A white man told you to believe in God. And why? To keep you ignorant so he can keep his feet on your neck."

"So now we the ignorant?" the preacher says.

"Yes," the boy says. "Yes." And he opens his book again.

The preacher just looks at him sitting there. The boy done forgot all about him. Everybody else make 'tend they done forgot the squabble, too.

Then I see that preacher getting up real slow. Preacher's a great big old man and he got to brace himself to get up. He comes over where the boy is sitting. He just stands there a little while looking down at him, but the boy don't raise his head.

"Get up, boy," preacher says.

The boy looks up at him, then he shuts his book real slow and stands up. Preacher just hauls back and hit him in the face. The boy falls back 'gainst the wall, but he straightens himself up and looks right back at that preacher.

"You forgot the other cheek," he says.

The preacher hauls back and hit him again on the other side. But this time the boy braces himself and don't fall.

"That hasn't changed a thing," he says.

The preacher just looks at the boy. The preacher's breathing real hard like he just run up a big hill. The boy sits down and opens his book again.

"I feel sorry for you," the preacher says. "I never felt so sorry for a man before."

The boy makes 'tend he don't even hear that preacher. He keeps on reading his book. The preacher goes back and gets his hat off the chair.

"Excuse me," he says to us. "I'll come back some other time. Y'all, please excuse me."

And he looks at the boy and goes out the room. The boy h'ist his hand up to his mouth one time to wipe 'way some blood. All the rest of the time he keeps on reading. And nobody else in there say a word.

8

Little John Lee and his mama come out the dentist office, and the nurse calls somebody else in. Then little bit later they come out, and the nurse calls another name. But fast 's she calls somebody in there, somebody else comes in the place where we sitting, and the room stays full.

The people coming in now, all of them wearing big coats. One of them says something 'bout sleeting, another one says he hope not. Another one says he think it ain't nothing but rain. 'Cause, he says, rain can get awful cold this time of year.

All round the room they talking. Some of them talking to people right by them, some of them talking to people clear 'cross the room, some of them talking to anybody'll listen. It's a little bitty room, no bigger than us kitchen, and I can see everybody in there. The little old room's full of smoke, 'cause you got two old men smoking pipes over by that side door. I think I feel my tooth thumping me some, and I hold my breath and wait. I wait and wait, but it don't thump me no more. Thank God for that.

I feel like going to sleep, and I lean back 'gainst the wall. But I'm scared to go to sleep. Scared 'cause the nurse might call my name and I won't hear her. And Mama might go to sleep, too, and she'll be mad if neither one of us heard the nurse.

I look up at Mama. I love my mama. I love my mama. And when cotton come I'm go'n get her a new coat. And I ain't go'n get a black one, either. I think I'm go'n get her a red one.

"They got some books over there," I say. "Want read one of them?"

Mama looks at the books, but she don't answer me.

"You got yourself a little man there," the lady says.

Mama don't say nothing to the lady, but she must've smiled, 'cause I seen the lady smiling back. The lady looks at me a little while, like she's feeling sorry for me.

"You sure got that preacher out here in a hurry," she says to that boy.

The boy looks up at her and looks in his book again. When I grow up I want be just like him. I want clothes like that and I want keep a book with me, too.

"You really don't believe in God?" the lady says.

"No," he says.

"But why?" the lady says.

"Because the wind is pink," he says.

"What?" the lady says.

The boy don't answer her no more. He just reads in his book.

"Talking 'bout the wind is pink," that old lady says. She's sitting on the same bench with the boy and she's trying to look in his face. The boy makes 'tend the old lady ain't even there. He just keeps on reading. "Wind is pink," she says again. "Eh, Lord, what children go'n be saying next?"

The lady 'cross from us bust out laughing.

"That's a good one," she says. "The wind is pink. Yes sir, that's a good one."

"Don't you believe the wind is pink?" the boy says. He keeps his head down in the book.

"Course I believe it, honey," the lady says. "Course I do." She looks at us and winks her eye. "And what color is grass, honey?"

"Grass? Grass is black."

She bust out laughing again. The boy looks at her.

"Don't you believe grass is black?" he says.

The lady quits her laughing and looks at him. Everybody else looking at him, too. The place quiet, quiet.

"Grass is green, honey," the lady says. "It was green yesterday, it's green today, and it's go'n be green tomorrow."

"How do you know it's green?"

"I know because I know."

"You don't know it's green," the boy says. "You believe it's green because someone told you it was green. If someone had told you it was black you'd believe it was black."

"It's green," the lady says. "I know green when I see green."

"Prove it's green," the boy says.

"Sure, now," the lady says. "Don't tell me it's coming to that."

"It's coming to just that," the boy says. "Words mean nothing. One means no more than the other."

"That's what it all coming to?" that old lady says. That old lady got on a turban and she got on two sweaters. She got a green sweater under a black sweater. I can see the green sweater 'cause some of the buttons on the other sweater's missing.

"Yes ma'am," the boy says. "Words mean nothing. Action is the only thing. Doing. That's the only thing."

"Other words, you want the Lord to come down here and show Hisself to you?" she says.

"Exactly, ma'am," he says.

"You don't mean that, I'm sure?" she says.

"I do, ma'am," he says.

"Done, Jesus," the old lady says, shaking her head.

"I didn't go 'long with that preacher at first," the other lady says; "but now—I don't know. When a person say the grass is black, he's either a lunatic or something's wrong."

"Prove to me that it's green," the boy says.

"It's green because the people say it's green."

"Those same people say we're citizens of these United States," the boy says.

"I think I'm a citizen," the lady says.

"Citizens have certain rights," the boy says. "Name me one right that you have. One right, granted by the Constitution, that you can exercise in Bayonne."

The lady don't answer him. She just looks at him like she don't know what he's talking 'bout. I know I don't.

"Things changing," she says.

"Things are changing because some black men have begun to think with their brains and not their hearts," the boy says.

"You trying to say these people don't believe in God?"

"I'm sure some of them do. Maybe most of them do. But they don't believe that God is going to touch these white people's hearts and change things tomorrow. Things change through action. By no other way."

Everybody sit quiet and look at the boy. Nobody says a thing. Then the lady 'cross the room from me and Mama just shakes her head.

"Let's hope that not all your generation feel the same way you do," she says.

"Think what you please, it doesn't matter," the boy says. "But it will be men who listen to their heads and not their hearts who will see that your children have a better chance than you had."

"Let's hope they ain't all like you, though," the old lady says. "Done forgot the heart absolutely."

"Yes ma'am, I hope they aren't all like me," the boy says. "Unfortunately, I was born too late to believe in your God. Let's hope that the ones who come after will have your faith—if not in your God, then in something else, something definitely that they can lean on. I haven't anything. For me, the wind is pink, the grass is black."

9

The nurse comes in the room where we all sitting and waiting and says the doctor won't take no more patients till one o'clock this evening. My mama jumps up off the bench and goes up to the white lady.

"Nurse, I have to go back in the field this evening," she says.

"The doctor is treating his last patient now," the nurse says. "One o'clock this evening."

"Can I at least speak to the doctor?" my mama asks.

"I'm his nurse," the lady says.

"My little boy's sick," my mama says. "Right now his tooth almost killing him."

The nurse looks at me. She's trying to make up her mind if to let me come in. I look at her real pitiful. The tooth ain't hurting me at all, but Mama say it is, so I make 'tend for her sake.

"This evening," the nurse says, and goes on back in the office.

"Don't feel 'jected, honey," the lady says to Mama. "I been round them a long time —they take you when they want to. If you was white, that's something else; but we the wrong color."

Mama don't say nothing to the lady, and me and her go outside and stand 'gainst the wall. It's cold out there. I can feel that wind going through my coat. Some of the other people come out of the room and go up the street. Me and Mama stand there a little while and we start walking. I don't know where we going. When we come to the other street we just stand there.

"You don't have to make water, do you?" Mama says.

"No, ma'am," I say.

We go on up the street. Walking real slow. I can tell Mama don't know where she's going. When we come to a store we stand there and look at the dummies. I look at a little boy wearing a brown overcoat. He's got on brown shoes, too. I look at my old shoes and look at his'n again. You wait till summer, I say.

Me and Mama walk away. We come up to another store and we stop and look at them dummies, too. Then we go on again. We pass a café where the white people in there eating. Mama tells me keep my eyes in front where they belong, but I can't help from seeing them people eat. My stomach starts to growling 'cause I'm hungry. When I see people eating, I get hungry; when I see a coat, I get cold.

A man whistles at my mama when we go by a filling station. She makes 'tend she don't even see him. I look back and I feel like hitting him in the mouth. If I was bigger, I say; if I was bigger, you'd see.

We keep on going. I'm getting colder and colder, but I don't say nothing. I feel that stuff running down my nose and I sniff.

"That rag," Mama says.

I get it out and wipe my nose. I'm getting cold all over now—my face, my hands, my feet, everything. We pass another little café, but this'n for white people, too, and we can't go in there, either. So we just walk. I'm so cold now I'm 'bout ready to say it. If I knowed where we was going I wouldn't be so cold, but I don't know where we going. We go, we go, we go. We walk clean out of Bayonne. Then we cross the street and we come back. Same thing I seen when I got off the bus this morning. Same old trees, same old walk, same old weeds, same old cracked pave—same old everything.

I sniff again.

"That rag," Mama says.

I wipe my nose real fast and jugg that handkerchief back in my pocket 'fore my hand gets too cold. I raise my head and I can see David's hardware store. When we come up to it, we go in. I don't know why, but I'm glad.

It's warm in there. It's so warm in there you don't ever want to leave. I look for the heater, and I see it over by them barrels. Three white men standing round the heater talking in Creole. One of them comes over to see what my mama want.

"Got any axe handles?" she says.

Me, Mama and the white man start to the back, but Mama stops me when we come up to the heater. She and the white man go on. I hold my hands over the heater and look at them. They go all the way to the back, and I see the white man pointing to the axe handles 'gainst the wall. Mama takes one of them and shakes it like she's trying to figure how much it weighs. Then she rubs her hand over it from one end to the other end. She turns it over and looks at the other side, then she shakes it again, and shakes her head and puts it back. She gets another one and she does it just like she did the first one, then she shakes her head. Then she gets a brown one and do it that, too. But she don't like this one, either. Then she gets another one, but 'fore she shakes it or anything, she looks at me. Look like she's trying to say something to me, but I don't know what it is. All I know is I done got warm now and I'm feeling right smart better. Mama shakes this axe handle just like she did the others, and shakes her head and says something to the white man. The white man just looks at his pile of axe handles, and when Mama pass him to come to the front, the white man just scratch his head and follows her. She tells me come on and we go on out and start walking again.

We walk and walk, and no time at all I'm cold again. Look like I'm colder now 'cause I can still remember how good it was back there. My stomach growls and I suck it in to keep Mama from hearing it. She's walking right 'side me, and it growls so loud you can hear it a mile. But Mama don't say a word.

10

When we come up to the courthouse, I look at the clock. It's got quarter to twelve. Mean we got another hour and a quarter to be out here in the cold. We go and stand 'side a building. Something hits my cap and I look up at the sky. Sleet's falling.

I look at Mama standing there. I want stand close 'side her, but she don't like that. She say that's crybaby stuff. She say you got to stand for yourself, by yourself.

"Let's go back to that office," she says.

We cross the street. When we get to the dentist office I try to open the door, but I can't. I twist and twist, but I can't. Mama pushes me to the side and she twist the knob, but she can't open the door, either. She turns 'way from the door. I look at her, but I don't move and I don't say nothing. I done seen her like this before and I'm scared of her.

"You hungry?" she says. She says it like she's mad at me, like I'm the cause of everything.

"No, ma'am," I say.

"You want eat and walk back, or you rather don't eat and ride?"

"I ain't hungry," I say.

I ain't just hungry, but I'm cold, too. I'm so hungry and cold I want to cry. And look like I'm getting colder and colder. My feet done got numb. I try to work my toes, but I don't even feel them. Look like I'm go'n die. Look like I'm go'n stand right here and freeze to death. I think 'bout home. I think 'bout Val and Auntie and Ty and Louis and Walker. It's 'bout twelve o'clock and I know they eating dinner now. I can hear Ty making jokes. He done forgot 'bout getting up early this morning and right now he's probably making jokes. Always trying to make somebody laugh. I wish I was right there listening to him. Give anything in the world if I was home round the fire.

"Come on," Mama says.

We start walking again. My feet so numb I can't hardly feel them. We turn the corner and go on back up the street. The clock on the courthouse starts hitting for twelve.

The sleet's coming down plenty now. They hit the pave and bounce like rice. Oh, Lord; oh, Lord, I pray. Don't let me die, don't let me die, don't let me die, Lord.

11

Now I know where we going. We going back of town where the colored people eat. I don't care if I don't eat. I been hungry before. I can stand it. But I can't stand the cold.

I can see we go'n have a long walk. It's 'bout a mile down there. But I don't mind. I know when I get there I'm go'n warm myself. I think I can hold out. My hands numb in my pockets and my feet numb, too, but if I keep moving I can hold out. Just don't stop no more, that's all.

The sky's gray. The sleet keeps on falling. Falling like rain now—plenty, plenty. You can hear it hitting the pave. You can see it bouncing. Sometimes it bounces two times 'fore it settles.

We keep on going. We don't say nothing. We just keep on going, keep on going.

I wonder what Mama's thinking. I hope she ain't mad at me. When summer come I'm go'n pick plenty cotton and get her a coat. I'm go'n get her a red one.

I hope they'd make it summer all the time. I'd be glad if it was summer all the time —but it ain't. We got to have winter, too. Lord, I hate the winter. I guess everybody hate the winter.

I don't sniff this time. I get out my handkerchief and wipe my nose. My hands's so cold I can hardly hold the handkerchief.

I think we getting close, but we ain't there yet. I wonder where everybody is. Can't see a soul but us. Look like we the only two people moving round today. Must be too cold for the rest of the people to move round in.

I can hear my teeth. I hope they don't knock together too hard and make that bad one hurt. Lord, that's all I need, for that bad one to start off.

I hear a church bell somewhere. But today ain't Sunday. They must be ringing for a funeral or something.

I wonder what they doing at home. They must be eating. Monsieur Bayonne might be there with his guitar. One day Ty played with Monsieur Bayonne's guitar and broke one of the strings. Monsieur Bayonne was some mad with Ty. He say Ty wasn't go'n ever 'mount to nothing. Ty can go just like Monsieur Bayonne when he ain't there. Ty can make everybody laugh when he starts to mocking Monsieur Bayonne.

I used to like to be with Mama and Daddy. We used to be happy. But they took him in the Army. Now, nobody happy no more. . . . I be glad when Daddy comes home.

Monsieur Bayonne say it wasn't fair for them to take Daddy and give Mama nothing and give us nothing. Auntie say, "Shhh, Etienne. Don't let them hear you talk like that." Monsieur Bayonne say, "It's God truth. What they giving his children? They have to walk three and a half miles to school hot or cold. That's anything to give for a paw? She's got to work in the field rain or shine just to make ends meet. That's anything to give for a husband?" Auntie say, "Shhh, Etienne, shhh." "Yes, you right," Monsieur Bayonne say. "Best don't say it in front of them now. But one day they go'n find out. One day." "Yes, I suppose so," Auntie say. "Then what, Rose Mary?" Monsieur Bayonne say. "I don't know, Etienne," Auntie say. "All we can do is us job, and leave everything else in His hand . . ."

We getting closer, now. We getting closer. I can even see the railroad tracks.

We cross the tracks, and now I see the café. Just to get in there, I say. Just to get in there. Already I'm starting to feel little better.

12

We go in. Ahh, it's good. I look for the heater; there 'gainst the wall. One of them little brown ones. I just stand there and hold my hands over it. I can't open my hands too wide 'cause they almost froze.

Mama's standing right 'side me. She done unbuttoned her coat. Smoke rises out of the coat, and the coat smells like a wet dog.

I move to the side so Mama can have more room. She opens out her hands and rubs them together. I rub mine together, too, 'cause this keep them from hurting. If you let them warm too fast, they hurt you sure. But if you let them warm just little bit at a time, and you keep rubbing them, they be all right every time.

They got just two more people in the café. A lady back of the counter, and a man on this side the counter. They been watching us ever since we come in.

Mama gets out the handkerchief and count up the money. Both of us know how much money she's got there. Three dollars. No, she ain't got three dollars, 'cause she had to pay us way up here. She ain't got but two dollars and a half left. Dollar and a half to get my tooth pulled, and fifty cents for us to go back on, and fifty cents worth of salt meat.

She stirs the money round with her finger. Most of the money is change 'cause I can hear it rubbing together. She stirs it and stirs it. Then she looks at the door. It's still sleeting. I can hear it hitting 'gainst the wall like rice.

"I ain't hungry, Mama," I say.

"Got to pay them something for they heat," she says.

She takes a quarter out the handkerchief and ties the handkerchief up again. She looks over her shoulder at the people, but she still don't move. I hope she don't spend the money. I don't want her spending it on me. I'm hungry, I'm almost starving I'm so hungry, but I don't want her spending the money on me.

She flips the quarter over like she's thinking. She's must be thinking 'bout us walking back home. Lord, I sure don't want walk home. If I thought it'd do any good to say something, I'd say it. But Mama makes up her own mind 'bout things.

She turns 'way from the heater right fast, like she better hurry up and spend the quarter 'fore she change her mind. I watch her go toward the counter. The man and the lady look at her, too. She tells the lady something and the lady walks away. The man keeps on looking at her. Her back's turned to the man, and she don't even know he's standing there.

The lady puts some cakes and a glass of milk on the counter. Then she pours up a cup of coffee and sets it 'side the other stuff. Mama pays her for the things and comes on back where I'm standing. She tells me sit down at the table 'gainst the wall.

The milk and the cakes's for me; the coffee's for Mama. I eat slow and I look at her. She's looking outside at the sleet. She's looking real sad. I say to myself, I'm go'n make all this up one day. You see, one day, I'm go'n make all this up. I want say it now; I want tell her how I feel right now; but Mama don't like for us to talk like that.

"I can't eat all this," I say.

They ain't got but just three little old cakes there. I'm so hungry right now, the Lord knows I can eat a hundred times three, but I want my mama to have one.

Mama don't even look my way. She knows I'm hungry, she knows I want it. I let it stay there a little while, then I get it and eat it. I eat just on my front teeth, though, 'cause if cake touch that back tooth I know what'll happen. Thank God it ain't hurt me at all today.

After I finish eating I see the man go to the juke box. He drops a nickel in it, then he just stand there a little while looking at the record. Mama tells me keep my eyes in front where they belong. I turn my head like she say, but then I hear the man coming toward us.

"Dance, pretty?" he says.

Mama gets up to dance with him. But 'fore you know it, she done grabbed the little man in the collar and done heaved him 'side the wall. He hit the wall so hard he stop the juke box from playing.

"Some pimp," the lady back of the counter says. "Some pimp."

The little man jumps up off the floor and starts toward my mama. 'Fore you know it, Mama done sprung open her knife and she's waiting for him.

"Come on," she says. "Come on. I'll gut you from your neighbo to your throat. Come on."

I go up to the little man to hit him, but Mama makes me come and stand 'side her. The little man looks at me and Mama and goes on back to the counter.

"Some pimp," the lady back of the counter says. "Some pimp." She starts laughing and pointing at the little man. "Yes sir, you a pimp, all right. Yes sir-ree."

13

"Fasten that coat, let's go," Mama says.

"You don't have to leave," the lady says.

Mama don't answer the lady, and we right out in the cold again. I'm warm right now—my hands, my ears, my feet—but I know this ain't go'n last too long. It done sleet so much now you got ice everywhere you look.

We cross the railroad tracks, and soon's we do, I get cold. That wind goes through this little old coat like it ain't even there. I got on a shirt and a sweater under the coat, but that wind don't pay them no mind. I look up and I can see we got a long way to go. I wonder if we go'n make it 'fore I get too cold.

We cross over to walk on the sidewalk. They got just one sidewalk back here, and it's over there.

After we go just a little piece, I smell bread cooking. I look, then I see a baker shop. When we get closer, I can smell it more better. I shut my eyes and make 'tend I'm eating. But I keep them shut too long and I butt up 'gainst a telephone post. Mama grabs me and see if I'm hurt. I ain't bleeding or nothing and she turns me loose.

I can feel I'm getting colder and colder, and I look up to see how far we still got to go. Uptown is 'way up yonder. A half mile more, I reckon. I try to think of something. They say think and you won't get cold. I think of that poem, "Annabel Lee." I ain't been to school in so long—this bad weather—I reckon they done passed "Annabel Lee" by now. But passed it or not, I'm sure Miss Walker go'n make me recite it when I get there. That woman don't never forget nothing. I ain't never seen nobody like that in my life.

I'm still getting cold. "Annabel Lee" or no "Annabel Lee," I'm still getting cold. But I can see we getting closer. We getting there gradually.

Soon 's we turn the corner, I see a little old white lady up in front of us. She's the only lady on the street. She's all in black and she's got a long black rag over her head.

"Stop," she says.

Me and Mama stop and look at her. She must be crazy to be out in all this bad weather. Ain't got but a few other people out there, and all of them's men.

"Y'all done ate?" she says.

"Just finish," Mama says.

"Y'all must be cold then?" she says.

"We headed for the dentist," Mama says. "We'll warm up when we get there."

"What dentist?" the old lady says. "Mr. Bassett?"

"Yes, ma'am," Mama says.

"Come on in," the old lady says. "I'll telephone him and tell him y'all coming."

Me and Mama follow the old lady in the store. It's a little bitty store, and it don't have much in there. The old lady takes off her head rag and folds it up.

"Helena?" somebody calls from the back.

"Yes, Alnest?" the old lady says.

"Did you see them?"

"They're here. Standing beside me."

"Good. Now you can stay inside."

The old lady looks at Mama. Mama's waiting to hear what she brought us in here for. I'm waiting for that, too.

"I saw y'all each time you went by," she says. "I came out to catch you, but you were gone."

"We went back of town," Mama says.

"Did you eat?"

"Yes, ma'am."

The old lady looks at Mama a long time, like she's thinking Mama might be just saying that. Mama looks right back at her. The old lady looks at me to see what I have to say. I don't say nothing. I sure ain't going 'gainst my mama.

"There's food in the kitchen," she says to Mama. "I've been keeping it warm."

Mama turns right around and starts for the door.

"Just a minute," the old lady says. Mama stops. "The boy'll have to work for it. It isn't free."

"We don't take no handout," Mama says.

"I'm not handing out anything," the old lady says. "I need my garbage moved to the front. Ernest has a bad cold and can't go out there."

"James'll move it for you," Mama says.

"Not unless you eat," the old lady says. "I'm old, but I have my pride, too, you know."

Mama can see she ain't go'n beat this old lady down, so she just shakes her head.

"All right," the old lady says. "Come into the kitchen."

She leads the way with that rag in her hand. The kitchen is a little bitty little old thing, too. The table and the stove just 'bout fill it up. They got a little room to the side. Somebody in there laying 'cross the bed—'cause I can see one of his feet. Must be the person she was talking to: Ernest or Alnest—something like that.

"Sit down," the old lady says to Mama. "Not you," she says to me. "You have to move the cans."

"Helena?" the man says in the other room.

"Yes, Alnest?" the old lady says.

"Are you going out there again?"

"I must show the boy where the garbage is, Alnest," the old lady says.

"Keep that shawl over your head," the old man says.

"You don't have to remind me, Alnest. Come, boy," the old lady says.

We go out in the yard. Little old back yard ain't no bigger than the store or the kitchen. But it can sleet here just like it can sleet in any big back yard. And 'fore you know it, I'm trembling.

"There," the old lady says, pointing to the cans. I pick up one of the cns and set it right back down. The can's so light, I'm go'n see what's inside of it.

"Here," the old lady says. "Leave that can alone."

I look back at her standing there in the door. She's got that black rag wrapped round her shoulders, and she's pointing one of her little old fingers at me.

"Pick it up and carry it to the front," she says. I go by her with the can, and she's looking at me all the time. I'm sure the can's empty. I'm sure she could've carried it herself—maybe both of them at the same time. "Set it on the sidewalk by the door and come back for the other one," she says.

I go and come back, and Mama looks at me when I pass her. I get the other can and take it to the front. It don't feel a bit heavier than that first one. I tell myself I ain't go'n be nobody's fool, and I'm go'n look inside this can to see just what I been hauling. First, I look up the street, then down the street. Nobody coming. Then I look over my shoulder toward the door. That little old lady done slipped up there quiet 's mouse, watching me again. Look like she knowed what I was go'n do.

"Ehh, Lord," she says. "Children, children. Come in here, boy, and go wash your hands."

I follow her in the kitchen. She points toward the bathroom, and I go in there and wash up. Little bitty old bathroom, but it's clean, clean. I don't use any of her towels; I wipe my hands on my pants legs.

When I come back in the kitchen, the old lady done dished up the food. Rice, gravy, meat—and she even got some lettuce and tomato in a saucer. She even got a glass of milk and a piece of cake there, too. It looks so good, I almost start eating 'fore I say my blessing.

"Helena?" the old man says.

"Yes, Alnest?"

"Are they eating?"

"Yes," she says.

"Good," he says. "Now you'll stay inside."

The old lady goes in there where he is and I can hear them talking. I look at Mama. She's eating slow like she's thinking. I wonder what's the matter now. I reckon she's thinking 'bout home.

The old lady comes back in the kitchen.

"I talked to Dr. Bassett's nurse," she says. "Dr. Bassett will take you as soon as you get there."

"Thank you, ma'am," Mama says.

"Perfectly all right," the old lady says. "Which one is it?"

Mama nods toward me. The old lady looks at me real sad. I look sad, too.

"You're not afraid, are you?" she says.

"No, ma'am," I say.

"That's a good boy," the old lady says. "Nothing to be afraid of. Dr. Bassett will not hurt you."

When me and mama get through eating, we thank the old lady again.

"Helena, are they leaving?" the old man says.

"Yes, Alnest."

"Tell them I say good-bye."

"They can hear you, Alnest."

"Good-bye both mother and son," the old man says. "And may God be with you."

Me and Mama tell the old man good-bye, and we follow the old lady in the front room. Mama opens the door to go out, but she stops and comes back in the store.

"You sell salt meat?" she says.

"Yes."

"Give me two bits worth."

"That isn't very much salt meat," the old lady says.

"That's all I have," Mama says.

The old lady goes back of the counter and cuts a big piece off the chunk. Then she wraps it up and puts it in a paper bag.

"Two bits," she says.

"That looks like awful lot of meat for a quarter," Mama says.

"Two bits," the old lady says. "I've been selling salt meat behind this counter twenty-five years. I think I know what I'm doing."

"You got a scale there," Mama says.

"What?" the old lady says.

"Weigh it," Mama says.

"What?" the old lady says. "Are you telling me how to run my business?"

"Thanks very much for the food," Mama says.

"Just a minute," the old lady says.

"James," Mama says to me. I move toward the door.

"Just one minute, I said," the old lady says.

Me and Mama stop again and look at her. The old lady takes the meat out of the bag and unwraps it and cuts 'bout half of it off. Then she wraps it up again and juggs it back in the bag and gives the bag to Mama. Mama lays the quarter on the counter.

"Your kindness will never be forgotten," she says. "James," she says to me.

We go out, and the old lady comes to the door to look at us. After we go a little piece I look back, and she's till there watching us.

The sleet's coming down heavy, heavy now, and I turn up my coat collar to keep my neck warm. My mama tells me turn it right back down.

"You not a bum," she says. "You a man."

THE GRANDFATHER OF THE SIERRA NEVADA MOUNTAINS

Maxine Hong Kingston

(b. 1940)

Biography p. 1081

The trains used to cross the sky. The house jumped and dust shook down from the attic. Sometimes two trains ran parallel going in opposite directions; the railroad men walked on top of the leaning cars, stepped off one train onto the back of the other, and traveled the opposite way. They headed for the caboose while the train moved against their walk, or they walked toward the engine while the train moved out from under their feet. Hoboes ran alongside, caught the ladders, and swung aboard. I would have to learn to ride like that, choose my boxcar, grab a ladder at a run, and fling myself up and sideways into an open door. Elsewhere I would step smoothly off. Bad runaway boys lost their legs trying for such rides. The train craunched past—pistons stroking like elbows and knees, the coal cars dropping coal, cows looking out between the slats of the cattle-cars, the boxcars almost stringing together sentences—Hydro-Cushion, Georgia Flyer, Route of the Eagle—and suddenly sunlight filled the windows again, the slough wide again and waving with tules, for which the city was once named; red-winged blackbirds and squirrels settled. We children ran to the tracks and found the nails we'd placed on them; the wheels had flattened them into knives that sparked.

Once in a while an adult said, "Your grandfather built the railroad." (Or "Your grandfathers built the railroad." Plural and singular are by context.) We children believed that it was that very railroad, those trains, those tracks running past our house; our own giant grandfather had set those very logs into the ground, poured the iron for those very spikes with the big heads and pounded them until the heads spread like that, mere nails to him. He had built the railroad so that trains would thunder over us, on a street that inclined toward us. We lived on a special spot of the earth, Stockton, the only city on the Pacific coast with three railroads—the Santa Fe, Southern Pacific, and Western Pacific. The three railroads intersecting accounted for the flocks of hoboes. The few times that the train stopped, the cows moaned all night, their hooves stumbling crowdedly and banging against the wood.

Grandfather left a railroad for his message: We had to go somewhere difficult. Ride a train. Go somewhere important. In case of danger, the train was to be ready for us.

The railroad men disconnected the rails and took the steel away. They did not come back. Our family dug up the square logs and rolled them downhill home. We collected the spikes too. We used the logs for benches, edged the yard with them, made bases for fences, embedded them in the ground for walkways. The spikes came in handy too, good for paperweights, levers, wedges, chisels. I am glad to know exactly the weight of ties and the size of nails.

Grandfather's picture hangs in the dining room next to an equally large one of

Grandmother, and another one of Guan Goong, God of War and Literature. My grandparents' similarity is in the set of their mouths; they seem to have hauled with their mouths. My mouth also feels the tug and strain of weights in its corners. In the family album, Grandfather wears a greatcoat and Western shoes, but his ankles show. He hasn't shaved either. Maybe he became sloppy after the Japanese soldier bayoneted his head for not giving directions. Or he was born slow and without a sense of direction.

The photographer came to the village regularly and set up a spinet, potted trees, an ornate table stacked with hardbound books of matching size, and a backdrop with a picture of paths curving through gardens into panoramas; he lent his subjects dressy ancient mandarin clothes, Western suits, and hats. An aunt tied the fingers of the lame cousin to a book, the string leading down his sleeve; he looks like he's carrying it. The family hurried from clothes chests to mirrors without explaining to Grandfather, hiding Grandfather. In the family album are group pictures with Grandmother in the middle, the family arranged on either side of her and behind her, second wives at the ends, no Grandfather. Grandmother's earrings, bracelets, and rings are tinted jade green, everything and everybody else black and white, her little feet together neatly, two knobs at the bottom of her gown. My mother, indignant that nobody had readied Grandfather, threw his greatcoat over his nightclothes, shouted, "Wait! Wait!" and encouraged him into the sunlight. "Hurry," she said, and he ran, coat flapping, to be in the picture. She would have slipped him into the group and had the camera catch him like a peeping ghost, but Grandmother chased him away. "What a waste of film," she said. Grandfather always appears alone with white stubble on his chin. He was a thin man with big eyes that looked straight ahead. When we children talked about overcoat men, exhibitionists, we meant Grandfather, Ah Goong, who must have yanked open that greatcoat—no pants.

MaMa was the only person to listen to him, and so he followed her everywhere, and talked and talked. What he liked telling was his journeys to the Gold Mountain. He wasn't smart, yet he traveled there three times. Left to himself, he would have stayed in China to play with babies or stayed in the United States once he got there, but Grandmother forced him to leave both places. "Make money," she said. "Don't stay here eating." "Come home," she said.

Ah Goong sat outside her open door when MaMa worked. (In those days a man did not visit a good woman alone unless married to her.) He saw her at her loom and came running with his chair. He told her that he had found a wondrous country, really gold, and he himself had gotten two bags of it, one of which he had had made into a ring. His wife had given that ring to their son for his wedding ring. "That ring on your finger," he told Mother, "proves that the Gold Mountain exists and that I went there."

Another of his peculiarities was that he heard the crackles, bangs, gunshots that go off when the world lurches; the gears on its axis snap. Listening to a faraway New Year, he had followed the noise and come upon the blasting in the Sierras. (There is a Buddhist instruction that that which is most elusive must, of course, be the very thing to be pursued; listen to the farthest sound.) The Central Pacific hired him on sight; chinamen had a natural talent for explosions. Also there were not enough workingmen to do all the labor of building a new country. Some of the banging came from the war to decide whether or not black people would continue to work for nothing.

Slow as usual, Ah Goong arrived in the spring; the work had begun in January 1863. The demon that hired him pointed up and up, east above the hills of poppies. His first job was to fell a redwood, which was thick enough to divide into three or four beams. His tree's many branches spread out, each limb like a little tree. He circled the tree. How to attack it? No side looked like the side made to be cut, nor did any ground seem the place for it to fall. He axed for almost a day the side he'd decided would hit the ground. Halfway through, imitating the other lumberjacks, he struck the other side of the tree, above the cut, until he had to run away. The tree swayed and slowly dived to earth, creaking and screeching like a green animal. He was so awed, he forgot what he was supposed to yell. Hardly any branches broke; the tree sprang, bounced, pushed at the ground with its arms. The limbs did not wilt and fold; they were a small forest, which he chopped. The trunk lay like a long red torso; sap ran from its cuts like crying blind eyes. At last it stopped fighting. He set the log across sawhorses to be cured over smoke and in the sun.

He joined a team of men who did not ax one another as they took alternate hits. They blew up the stumps with gunpowder. "It was like uprooting a tooth," Ah Goong said. They also packed gunpowder at the roots of a whole tree. Not at the same time as the bang but before that, the tree rose from the ground. It stood, then plunged with a tearing of veins and muscles. It was big enough to carve a house into. The men measured themselves against the upturned white roots, which looked like claws, a sun with claws. A hundred men stood or sat on the trunk. They lifted a wagon on it and took a photograph. The demons also had their photograph taken.

Because these mountains were made out of gold, Ah Goong rushed over to the root hole to look for gold veins and ore. He selected the shiniest rocks to be assayed later in San Francisco. When he drank from the streams and saw a flash, he dived in like a duck; only sometimes did it turn out to be the sun or the water. The very dirt winked with specks.

He made a dollar a day salary. The lucky men gambled, but he was not good at remembering game rules. The work so far was endurable. "I could take it," he said.

The days were sunny and blue, the wind exhilarating, the heights godlike. At night the stars were diamonds, crystals, silver, snow, ice. He had never seen diamonds. He had never seen snow and ice. As spring turned into summer, and he lay under that sky, he saw the order in the stars. He recognized constellations from China. There —not a cloud but the Silver River, and there, on either side of it—Altair and Vega, the Spinning Girl and the Cowboy, far, far apart. He felt his heart breaking of loneliness at so much blue-black space between star and star. The railroad he was building would not lead him to his family. He jumped out of his bedroll. "Look! Look!" other China Men jumped awake. An accident? An avalanche? Injun demons? "The stars," he said. "The stars are here." "Another China Man gone out of his mind," men grumbled. "A sleepwalker." "Go to sleep, sleepwalker." "There. And there," said Ah Goong, two hands pointing. "The Spinning Girl and the Cowboy. Don't you see them?" "Homesick China Man," said the China Men and pulled their blankets over their heads. "Didn't you know they were here? I could have told you they were here. Same as in China. Same moon. Why not same stars?" "Nah. Those are American stars."

Pretending that a little girl was listening, he told himself the story about the Spinning Girl and the Cowboy: A long time ago they had visited earth, where they met, fell in love, and married. Instead of growing used to each other, they remained enchanted their entire lifetimes and beyond. They were too happy. They wanted to be doves or two branches of the same tree. When they returned to live in the sky, they were so engrossed in each other that they neglected their work. The Queen of the Sky scratched a river between them with one stroke of her silver hairpin—the river a galaxy in width. The lovers suffered, but she did devote her time to spinning now, and he herded his cow. The King of the Sky took pity on them and ordered that once each year, they be allowed to meet. On the seventh day of the seventh month (which is not the same as July 7), magpies form a bridge for them to cross to each other. The lovers are together for one night of the year. On their parting, the Spinner cries the heavy summer rains.

Ah Goong's discovery of the two stars gave him something to look forward to besides meals and tea breaks. Every night he located Altair and Vega and gauged how much closer they had come since the night before. During the day he watched the magpies, big black and white birds with round bodies like balls with wings; they were a welcome sight, a promise of meetings. He had found two familiars in the wilderness: magpies and stars. On the meeting day, he did not see any magpies nor hear their chattering jaybird cries. Some black and white birds flew overhead, but they may have been American crows or late magpies on their way. Some men laughed at him, but he was not the only China Man to collect water in pots, bottles, and canteens that day. The water would stay fresh forever and cure anything. In ancient days the tutelary gods of the mountains sprinkled corpses with this water and brought them to life. That night, no women to light candles, burn incense, cook special food, Grandfather watched for the convergence and bowed. He saw the two little stars next to Vega—the couple's children. And bridging the Silver River, surely those were black flapping wings of magpies and translucent-winged angels and faeries. Toward morning, he was awakened by rain, and pulled his blankets into his tent.

The next day, the fantailed orange-beaked magpies returned. Altair and Vega were beginning their journeys apart, another year of spinning and herding. Ah Goong had to find something else to look forward to. The Spinning Girl and the Cowboy met and parted six times before the railroad was finished.

When cliffs, sheer drops under impossible overhangs, ended the road, the workers filled the ravines or built bridges over them. They climbed above the site for tunnel or bridge and lowered one another down in wicker baskets made stronger by the lucky words they had painted on four sides. Ah Goong got to be a basketman because he was thin and light. Some basketmen were fifteen-year-old boys. He rode the basket barefoot, so his boots, the kind to stomp snakes with, would not break through the bottom. The basket swung and twirled, and he saw the world sweep underneath him; it was fun in a way, a cold new feeling of doing what had never been done before. Suspended in the quiet sky, he thought all kinds of crazy thoughts, that if a man didn't want to live any more, he could just cut the ropes or, easier, tilt the basket, dip, and never have to worry again. He could spread his arms and the air would momentarily hold him before he fell past the buzzards, hawks, and eagles, and landed impaled on the tip of a sequoia. This high and he didn't see any gods, no Cowboy, no Spinner. He knelt in the basket though he was not bumping his head against the sky. Through the wickerwork, slivers of depths darted like needles, nothing between him and air but thin rattan. Gusts of wind spun the light basket. "Aiya," said Ah Goong. Winds came up under the basket, bouncing it. Neighboring baskets swung together and parted. He and the man next to him looked at each other's faces. They laughed. They might as well have gone to Malaysia to collect bird nests. Those who had done high work there said it had been worse; the birds screamed and scratched at them. Swinging near the cliff, Ah Goong stood up and grabbed it by a twig. He dug holes, then inserted gunpowder and fuses. He worked neither too fast nor too slow, keeping even with the others. The basketmen signaled one another to light the fuses. He struck match after match and dropped the burnt matches over the sides. At last his fuse caught; he waved, and the men above pulled hand over hand hauling him up, pulleys creaking. The scaffolds stood like a row of gibbets. Gallows trees along a ridge. "Hurry, hurry," he said. Some impatient men clambered up their ropes. Ah Goong ran up the ledge road they'd cleared and watched the explosions, which banged almost synchronously, echoes booming like war. He moved his scaffold to the next section of cliff and went down in the basket again, with bags of dirt, and set the next charge.

This time two men were blown up. One knocked out or killed by the explosion fell silently, the other screaming, his arms and legs struggling. A desire shot out of Ah Goong for an arm long enough to reach down and catch them. Much time passed as they fell like plummets. The shreds of baskets and a cowboy hat skimmed and tacked. The winds that pushed birds off course and against mountains did not carry men. Ah Goong also wished that the conscious man would fall faster and get it over with. His hands gripped the ropes, and it was difficult to let go and get on with the work. "It can't happen twice in a row," the basketmen said the next trip down. "Our chances are very good. The trip after an accident is probably the safest one." They raced to their favorite basket, checked and double-checked the four ropes, yanked the strands, tested the pulleys, oiled them, reminded the pulleymen about the signals, and entered the sky again.

Another time, Ah Goong had been lowered to the bottom of a ravine, which had to be cleared for the base of a trestle, when a man fell, and he saw his face. He had not died of shock before hitting bottom. His hands were grabbing at air. His stomach and groin must have felt the fall all the way down. At night Ah Goong woke up falling, though he slept on the ground, and heard other men call out in their sleep. No warm women tweaked their ears and hugged them. "It was only a falling dream," he reassured himself.

Across a valley, a chain of men working on the next mountain, men like ants changing the face of the world, fell, but it was very far away. Godlike, he watched men whose faces he could not see and whose screams he did not hear roll and bounce and slide like a handful of sprinkled gravel.

After a fall, the buzzards circled the spot and reminded the workers for days that a man was dead down there. The men threw piles of rocks and branches to cover bodies from sight.

The mountainface reshaped, they drove supports for a bridge. Since hammering was less dangerous than the blowing up, the men played a little; they rode the baskets swooping in wide arcs; they twisted the ropes and let them unwind like tops. "Look at me," said Ah Goong, pulled open his pants, and pissed overboard, the wind scattering the drops. "I'm a waterfall," he said. He had sent a part of himself hurtling. On rare windless days he watched his piss fall in a continuous stream from himself almost to the bottom of the valley.

One beautiful day, dangling in the sun above a new valley, not the desire to urinate but sexual desire clutched him so hard he bent over in the basket. He curled up, overcome by beauty and fear, which shot to his penis. He tried to rub himself calm. Suddenly he stood up tall and squirted out into space. "I am fucking the world," he said. The world's vagina was big, big as the sky, big as a valley. He grew a habit: whenever he was lowered in the basket, his blood rushed to his penis, and he fucked the world.

Then it was autumn, and the wind blew so fiercely, the men had to postpone the basketwork. Clouds moved in several directions at once. Men pointed at dust devils, which turned their mouths crooked. There was ceaseless motion; clothes kept moving; hair moved; sleeves puffed out. Nothing stayed still long enough for Ah Goong to figure it out. The wind sucked the breath out of his mouth and blew thoughts from his brains. The food convoys from San Francisco brought tents to replace the ones that whipped away. The baskets from China, which the men saved for high work, carried cowboy jackets, long underwear, Levi pants, boots, earmuffs, leather gloves, flannel shirts, coats. They sewed rabbit fur and deerskin into the linings. They tied the wide brims of their cowboy hats over their ears with mufflers. And still the wind made confusing howls into ears, and it was hard to think.

The days became nights when the crews tunneled inside the mountain, which sheltered them from the wind, but also hid the light and sky. Ah Goong pickaxed the mountain, the dirt filling his nostrils through a cowboy bandanna. He shoveled the dirt into a cart and pushed it to a place that was tall enough for the mule, which hauled it the rest of the way out. He looked forward to cart duty to edge closer to the entrance. Eyes darkened, nose plugged, his windy cough worse, he was to mole a thousand feet and meet others digging from the other side. How much he'd pay now to go swinging in a basket. He might as well have gone to work in a tin mine. Coming out of the tunnel at the end of a shift, he forgot whether it was supposed to be day or night. He blew his nose fifteen times before the mucus cleared again.

The dirt was the easiest part of tunneling. Beneath the soil, they hit granite. Ah Goong struck it with his pickax, and it jarred his bones, chattered his teeth. He swung his sledgehammer against it, and the impact rang in the dome of his skull. The mountain that was millions of years old was locked against them and was not to be broken into. The men teased him, "Let's see you fuck the world now." "Let's see you fuck the Gold Mountain now." But he no longer felt like it. "A man ought to be made of tougher material than flesh," he said. "Skin is too soft. Our bones ought to be filled with iron." He lifted the hammer high, careful that it not pull him backward, and let it fall forward of its own weight against the rock. Nothing happened to that gray wall; he had to slam with strength and will. He hit at the same spot over and over again, the same rock. Some chips and flakes broke off. The granite looked everywhere the same. It had no softer or weaker spots anywhere, the same hard gray. He learned to slide his hand up the handle, lift, slide and swing, a circular motion, hammering, hammering, hammering. He would bite like a rat through that mountain. His eyes couldn't see; his nose couldn't smell; and now his ears were filled with the noise of hammering. This rock is what is real, he thought. This rock is what real is, not clouds or mist, which make mysterious promises, and when you go through them are nothing. When the foreman measured at the end of twenty-four hours of pounding, the rock had given a foot. The hammering went on day and night. The men worked eight hours on and eight hours off. They worked on all eighteen tunnels at once. While Ah Goong slept, he could hear the sledgehammers of other men working in the earth. The steady banging reminded him of holidays and harvests; falling asleep, he heard the women chopping mincemeat and the millstones striking.

The demons in boss suits came into the tunnel occasionally, measured with a yardstick, and shook their heads. "Faster," they said. "Faster. Chinamen too slow. Too slow." "Tell us we're slow," the China Men grumbled. The ones in top tiers of scaffolding let rocks drop, a hammer drop. Ropes tangled around the demons' heads and feet. The cave China Men muttered and flexed, glared out of the corners of their eyes. But usually there was no diversion—one day the same as the next, one hour no different from another—the beating against the same granite.

After tunneling into granite for about three years, Ah Goong understood the immovability of the earth. Men change, men die, weather changes, but a mountain is the same as permanence and time. This mountain would have taken no new shape for centuries, ten thousand centuries, the world a still, still place, time unmoving. He worked in the tunnel so long, he learned to see many colors in black. When he stumbled out, he tried to talk about time. "I felt time," he said. "I saw time. I saw world." He tried again, "I saw what's real. I saw time, and it doesn't move. If we break through the mountain, hollow it, time won't have moved anyway. You translators ought to tell the foreigners that."

Summer came again, but after the first summer, he felt less nostalgia at the meeting of the Spinning Girl and the Cowboy. He now knew men who had been in this country for twenty years and thirty years, and the Cowboy's one year away from his lady was no time at all. His own patience was longer. The stars were meeting and would meet again next year, but he would not have seen his family. He joined the others celebrating Souls' Day, the holiday a week later, the fourteenth day of the seventh month. The supply wagons from San Francisco and Sacramento brought watermelon, meat, fish, crab, pressed duck. "There, ghosts, there you are. Come and get it." They displayed the feast complete for a moment before falling to, eating on the dead's behalf.

In the third year of pounding granite by hand, a demon invented dynamite. The railroad workers were to test it. They had stopped using gunpowder in the tunnels after avalanches, but the demons said that dynamite was more precise. They watched a scientist demon mix nitrate, sulphate, and glycerine, then flick the yellow oil, which exploded off his fingertips. Sitting in a meadow to watch the dynamite detonated in the open, Ah Goong saw the men in front of him leap impossibly high into the air; then he felt a shove as if from a giant's unseen hand—and he fell backward. The boom broke the mountain silence like fear breaking inside stomach and chest and groin. No one had gotten hurt; they stood up laughing and amazed, looking around at how they had fallen, the pattern of the explosion. Dynamite was much more powerful than gunpowder. Ah Goong had felt a nudge, as if something kind were moving him out of harm's way. "All of a sudden I was sitting next to you." "Aiya. If we had been nearer, it would have killed us." "If we were stiff, it would have gone through us." "A fist." "A hand." "We leapt like acrobats." Next time Ah Goong flattened himself on the ground, and the explosion rolled over him.

He never got used to the blasting; a blast always surprised him. Even when he himself set the fuse and watched it burn, anticipated the explosion, the bang—*bahng* in Chinese—when it came, always startled. It cleaned the crazy words, the crackling, and bingbangs out of his brain. It was like New Year's, when every problem and thought was knocked clean out of him by firecrackers, and he could begin fresh. He couldn't worry during an explosion, which jerked every head to attention. Hills flew up in rocks and dirt. Boulders turned over and over. Sparks, fires, debris, rocks, smoke burst up, not at the same time as the boom *(bum)* but before that—the sound a separate occurrence, not useful as a signal.

The terrain changed immediately. Streams were diverted, rock-scapes exposed. Ah Goong found it difficult to remember what land had looked like before an explosion. it was a good thing the dynamite was invented after the Civil War to the east was over.

The dynamite added more accidents and ways of dying, but if it were not used, the railroad would take fifty more years to finish. Nitroglycerine exploded when it was jounced on a horse or dropped. A man who fell with it in his pocket blew himself up into red pieces. Sometimes it combusted merely standing. Human bodies skipped through the air like puppets and made Ah Goong laugh crazily as if the arms and legs would come together again. The smell of burned flesh remained in rocks.

In the tunnels, the men bored holes fifteen to eighteen inches deep with a power drill, stuffed them with hay and dynamite, and imbedded the fuse in sand. Once, for extra pay, Ah Goong ran back in to see why some dynamite had not gone off and hurried back out again; it was just a slow fuse. When the explosion settled, he helped carry two-hundred-, three-hundred-, five-hundred-pound boulders out of the tunnel.

As a boy he had visited a Taoist monastery where there were nine rooms, each a replica of one of the nine hells. Lifesize sculptures of men and women were spitted on turning wheels. Eerie candles under the suffering faces emphasized eyes poked out, tongues pulled, red mouths and eyes, and real hair, eyelashes, and eyebrows. Women were split apart and men dismembered. He could have reached out and touched the sufferers and the implements. He had dug and dynamited his way into one of these hells. "Only here there are eighteen tunnels, not nine, plus all the tracks between them," he said.

One day he came out of the tunnel to find the mountains white, the evergreens and bare trees decorated, white tree sculptures and lace bushes everywhere. The men from snow country called the icicles "ice chopsticks." He sat in his basket and slid down the slopes. The snow covered the gouged land, the broken trees, the tracks, the mud, the campfire ashes, the unburied dead. Streams were stilled in mid-run, the water petrified. That winter he thought it was the task of the human race to quicken the world, blast the freeze, fire it, redden it with blood. He had to change the stupid slowness of one sunrise and one sunset per day. He had to enliven the silent world with sound. "The rock," he tried to tell the others. "The ice." "Time."

The dynamiting loosed blizzards on the men. Ears and toes fell off. Fingers stuck to the cold silver rails. Snowblind men stumbled about with bandannas over their eyes. Ah Goong helped build wood tunnels roofing the track route. Falling ice scrabbled on the roofs. The men stayed under the snow for weeks at a time. Snow-slides covered the entrances to the tunnels, which they had to dig out to enter and exit, white tunnels and black tunnels. Ah Goong looked at his gang and thought, If there is an avalanche, these are the people I'll be trapped with, and wondered which ones would share food. A party of snowbound barbarians had eaten the dead. Cannibals, thought Ah Goong, and looked around. Food was not scarce; the tea man brought whiskey barrels of hot tea, and he warmed his hands and feet, held the teacup to his nose and ears. Someday, he planned, he would buy a chair with metal doors for putting hot coal inside it. The magpies did not abandon him but stayed all winter and searched the snow for food.

The men who died slowly enough to say last words said, "Don't leave me frozen under the snow. Send my body home. Burn it and put the ashes in a tin can. Take the bone jar when you come down the mountain." "When you ride the fire car back to China, tell my descendants to come for me." "Shut up," scolded the hearty men. "We don't want to hear about bone jars and dying." "You're lucky to have a body to bury, not blown to smithereens." "Stupid man to hurt yourself," they bawled out the sick and wounded. How their wives would scold if they brought back deadmen's bones. "Aiya. To be buried here, nowhere." "But this is somewhere," Ah Goong promised. "This is the Gold Mountain. We're marking the land now. The track sections are numbered, and your family will know where we leave you." But he was a crazy man, and they didn't listen to him.

Spring did come, and when the snow melted, it revealed the past year, what had happened, what they had done, where they had worked, the lost tools, the thawing bodies, some standing with tools in hand, the bright rails. "Remember Uncle Long Winded Leong?" "Remember Strong Back Wong?" "Remember Lee Brother?" "And Fong Uncle?" They lost count of the number dead; there is no record of how many died building the railroad. Or maybe it was demons doing the counting and chinamen not worth counting. Whether it was good luck or bad luck, the dead were buried or cairned next to the last section of track they had worked on. "May his ghost not have to toil," they said over graves. (In China a woodcutter ghost chops eternally; people have heard chopping in the snow and in the heat.) "Maybe his ghost will ride the train home." The scientific demons said the transcontinental railroad would connect the West to Cathay. "What if he rides back and forth from Sacramento to New York forever?" "That wouldn't be so bad. I hear the cars will be like houses on wheels." The funerals were short. "No time. No time," said both China Men and demons. The railroad was as straight as they could build it, but no ghosts sat on the tracks; no strange presences haunted the tunnels. The blasts scared ghosts away.

When the Big Dipper pointed east and the China Men detonated nitroglycerine and shot off guns for the New Year, which comes with the spring, these special bangs were not as loud as the daily bangs, not as numerous as the bangs all year. Shouldn't the New Year be the loudest day of all to obliterate the noises of the old year? But to make a bang of that magnitude, they would have to blow up at least a year's supply of dynamite in one blast. They arranged strings of chain reactions in circles and long lines, banging faster and louder to culminate in a big bang. And most importantly, there were random explosions—surprise. Surprise. SURPRISE. They had no dragon, the railroad their dragon.

The demons invented games for working faster, gold coins for miles of track laid, for the heaviest rock, a grand prize for the first team to break through a tunnel. Day shifts raced against night shifts, China Men against Welshmen, China Men against Irishmen, China Men against Injuns and black demons. The fastest races were China Men against China Men, who bet on their own teams. China Men always won because of good teamwork, smart thinking, and the need for the money. Also, they had the most workers to choose teams from. Whenever his team won anything, Ah Goong added to his gold stash. The Central Pacific or Union Pacific won the land on either side of the tracks it built.

One summer day, demon officials and China Man translators went from group to group and announced, "We're raising the pay—thirty-five dollars a month. Because of your excellent work, the Central Pacific Railroad is giving you a four-dollar raise per month." The workers who didn't know better cheered. "What's the catch?" said the smarter men. "You'll have the opportunity to put in more time," said the railroad demons. "Two more hours per shift." Ten-hour shifts inside the tunnels. "It's not ten hours straight," said the demons. "You have time off for tea and meals. Now that you have dynamite, the work isn't so hard." They had been working for three and a half years already, and the track through the Donner Summit was still not done.

The workers discussed the ten-hour shift, swearing their China Man obscenities. "Two extra hours a day—sixty hours a month for four dollars." "Pig catcher demons." "Snakes." "Turtles." "Dead demons." "A human body can't work like that." "The demons don't believe this is a human body. This is a chinaman's body." To bargain, they sent a delegation of English speakers, who were summarily noted as troublemakers, turned away, docked.

The China Men, then, decided to go on strike and demand forty-five dollars a month and the eight-hour shift. They risked going to jail and the Central Pacific keeping the pay it was banking for them. Ah Goong memorized the English, "Forty-five dollars a month—eight-hour shift." He practiced the strike slogan: "Eight hours a day good for white man, all the same good for China Man."

The men wrapped barley and beans in ti leaves, which came from Hawai'i via San Francisco, for celebrating the fifth day of the fifth month (not May but mid-June, the summer solstice). Usually the way the red string is wound and knotted tells what flavors are inside—the salty barley with pickled egg, or beans and pork, or the gelatin pudding. Ah Goong folded it leaves into a cup and packed it with food. One of the literate men slipped in a piece of paper with the strike plan, and Ah Goong tied the bundle with a special pattern of red string. The time and place for the revolution against Kublai Khan had been hidden inside autumn mooncakes. Ah Goong looked from one face to another in admiration. Of course, of course. No China Men, no railroad. They were indispensable labor. Throughout these mountains were brothers and uncles with a common idea, free men, not coolies, calling for fair working conditions. The demons were not suspicious as the China Men went gandying up and down the tracks delivering the bundles tied together like lines of fish. They had exchanged these gifts every year. When the summer solstice cakes came from other camps, the recipients cut them into neat slices by drawing the string through them. The orange jellies, which had a red dye stick inside soaked in lye, fell into a series of sunrises and sunsets. The aged yolks and the barley also looked like suns. The notes gave a Yes strike vote. The yellow flags to ward off the five evils—centipedes, scorpions, snakes, poisonous lizards, and toads—now flew as banners.

The strike began on Tuesday morning, June 25, 1867. The men who were working at that hour walked out of the tunnels and away from the tracks. The ones who were sleeping slept on and rose as late as they pleased. They bathed in streams and shaved their moustaches and wild beards. Some went fishing and hunting. The violinists tuned and played their instruments. The drummers beat theirs at the punchlines of jokes. The gamblers shuffled and played their cards and tiles. The smokers passed their pipes, and the drinkers bet for drinks by making figures with their hands. The cooks made party food. The opera singers' falsettos almost perforated the mountains. The men sang new songs about the railroad. They made up verses and shouted Ho at the good ones, and laughed at the rhymes. Oh, they were madly singing in the mountains. The storytellers told about the rise of new kings. The opium smokers when they roused themselves told their florid images. Ah Goong sifted for gold. All the while the English-speaking China Men, who were being advised by the shrewdest bargainers, were at the demons' headquarters repeating the demand: "Eight hours a day good for white man, all the same good for China Man." They had probably negotiated the demons down to nine-hour shifts by now.

The sounds of hammering continued along the tracks and occasionally there were blasts from the tunnels. The scabby white demons had refused to join the strike. "Eight hours a day good for white man, all the same good for China Man," the China Men explained to them. "Cheap John Chinaman," said the demons, many of whom had red hair. The China Men scowled out of the corners of their eyes.

On the second day, artist demons climbed the mountains to draw the China Men for the newspapers. The men posed bare-chested, their fists clenched, showing off their arms and backs. The artists sketched them as perfect young gods reclining against rocks, wise expressions on their handsome noble-nosed faces, long torsos with lean stomachs, a strong arm extended over a bent knee, long fingers holding a pipe, a rope of hair over a wide shoulder. Other artists drew faeries with antennae for eyebrows and brownies with elvish pigtails; they danced in white socks and black slippers among mushroom rings by moonlight.

Ah Goong acquired another idea that added to his reputation for craziness: The pale, thin Chinese scholars and the rich men fat like Buddhas were less beautiful, less manly than these brown muscular railroad men, of whom he was one. One of ten thousand heroes.

On the third day, in a woods—he would be looking at a deer or a rabbit or an Injun watching him before he knew what he was seeing—a demon dressed in a white suit and tall hat beckoned him. They talked privately in the wilderness. The demon said, "I Citizenship Judge invite you to be U.S. citizen. Only one bag gold." Ah Goong was thrilled. What an honor. He would accept this invitation. Also what advantages, he calculated shrewdly; if he were going to be jailed for this strike, an American would have a trial. The Citizenship Judge unfurled a parchment sealed with gold and ribbon. Ah Goong bought it with one bag of gold. "You vote," said the Citizenship Judge. "You talk in court, buy land, no more chinaman tax." Ah Goong hid the paper on his person so that it would protect him from arrest and lynching. He was already a part of this new country, but now he had it in writing.

The fourth day, the strikers heard that the U. S. Cavalry was riding single file up the tracks to shoot them. They argued whether to engage the Army with dynamite. But the troops did not come. Instead the cowardly demons blockaded the food wagons. No food. Ah Goong listened to the optimistic China Men, who said, "Don't panic. We'll hold out forever. We can hunt. We can last fifty days on water." The complainers said, "Aiya. Only saints can do that. Only magic men and monks who've practiced." The China Men refused to declare a last day for the strike.

The foresighted China Men had cured jerky, fermented wine, dried and strung orange and grapefruit peels, pickled and preserved leftovers. Ah Goong, one of the best hoarders, had set aside extra helpings from each meal. This same quandary, whether to give away food or to appear selfish, had occurred during each of the six famines he had lived through. The foodless men identified themselves. Sure enough, they were the shiftless, piggy, arrogant type who didn't worry enough. The donors scolded them and shamed them the whole while they were handing them food: "So you lived like a grasshopper at our expense." "Fleaman." "You'll be the cause of our not holding out long enough." "Rich man's kid. Too good to hoard." Ah Goong contributed some rice crusts from the bottoms of pans. He kept how much more food he owned a secret, as he kept the secret of his gold. In apology for not contributing richer food, he repeated a Mohist saying that had guided him in China: " 'The superior man does not push humaneness to the point of stupidity.' " He could hear his wife scolding him for feeding strangers. The opium men offered shit and said that it calmed the appetite.

On the fifth and sixth days, Ah Goong organized his possessions and patched his clothes and tent. He forebore repairing carts, picks, ropes, baskets. His work-habituated hands arranged rocks and twigs in designs. He asked a reader to read again his family's letters. His wife sounded like herself except for the polite phrases added professionally at the beginnings and the ends. "Idiot," she said, "why are you taking so long? Are you wasting the money? Are you spending it on girls and gambling and whiskey? Here's my advice to you: Be a little more frugal. Remember how it felt to go hungry. Work hard." He had been an idle man for almost a week. "I need a new dress to wear to weddings. I refuse to go to another banquet in the same old dress. If you weren't such a spendthrift, we could be building the new courtyard where we'll drink wine among the flowers and sit about in silk gowns all day. We'll hire peasants to till the fields. Or lease them to tenants, and buy all our food at market. We'll have clean fingernails and toenails." Other relatives said, "I need a gold watch. Send me the money. Your wife gambles it away and throws parties and doesn't disburse it fairly among us. You might as well come home." It was after one of these letters that he had made a bonus checking on some dud dynamite.

Ah Goong did not spend his money on women. The strikers passed the word that a woman was traveling up the railroad and would be at his camp on the seventh and eighth day of the strike. Some said she was a demoness and some that she was a Chinese and her master a China Man. He pictured a nurse coming to bandage wounds and touch foreheads or a princess surveying her subjects; or perhaps she was a merciful Jesus demoness. But she was a pitiful woman, led on a leash around her waist, not entirely alive. Her owner sold lottery tickets for the use of her. Ah Goong did not buy one. He took out his penis under his blanket or bared it in the woods and thought about nurses and princesses. He also just looked at it, wondering what it was that it was for, what a man was for, what he had to have a penis for.

There was rumor also of an Injun woman called Woman Chief, who led a nomadic fighting tribe from the eastern plains as far as these mountains. She was so powerful that she had four wives and many horses. He never saw her though.

The strike ended on the ninth day. The Central Pacific announced that in its benevolence it was giving the workers a four-dollar raise, not the fourteen dollars they had asked for. And that the shifts in the tunnels would remain eight hours long. "We were planning to give you the four-dollar raise all along," the demons said to diminish the victory. So they got thirty-five dollars a month and the eight-hour shift. They would have won forty-five dollars if the thousand demon workers had joined the strike. Demons would have listened to demons. The China Men went back to work quietly. No use singing and shouting over a compromise and losing nine days' work.

There were two days that Ah Goong did cheer and throw his hat in the air, jumping up and down and screaming Yippee like a cowboy. One: the day his team broke through the tunnel at last. Toward the end they did not dynamite but again used picks and sledgehammers. Through the granite, they heard answering poundings, and answers to their shouts. It was not a mountain before them any more but only a wall with people breaking through from the other side. They worked faster. Forward. Into day. They stuck their arms through the holes and shook hands with men on the other side. Ah Goong saw dirty faces as wondrous as if he were seeing Nu Wo, the creator goddess who repairs cracks in the sky with stone slabs; sometimes she peeks through and human beings see her face. The wall broke. Each team gave the other a gift of half a tunnel, dug. They stepped back and forth where the wall had been. Ah Goong ran and ran, his boots thudding to the very end of the tunnel, looked at the other side of the mountain, and ran back, clear through the entire tunnel. All the way through.

He spent the rest of his time on the railroad laying and bending and hammering the ties and rails. The second day the China Men cheered was when the engine from the West and the one from the East rolled toward one another and touched. The transcontinental railroad was finished. They Yippee'd like madmen. The white demon officials gave speeches. "The Greatest Feat of the Nineteenth Century," they said. "The Greatest Feat in the History of Mankind," they said. "Only Americans could have done it," they said, which is true. Even if Ah Goong had not spent half his gold on Citizenship Papers, he was an American for having built the railroad. A white demon in top hat tap-tapped on the gold spike, and pulled it back out. Then one China Man held the real spike, the steel one, and another hammered it in.

While the demons posed for photographs, the China Men dispersed. It was dangerous to stay. The Driving Out had begun. Ah Goong does not appear in railroad photographs. Scattering, some China Men followed the north star in the constellation Tortoise the Black Warrior to Canada, or they kept the constellation Phoenix ahead of them to South America or the White Tiger west or the Wolf east. Seventy lucky men rode the Union Pacific to Massachusetts for jobs at a shoe factory. Fifteen hundred went to Fou Loy Company in New Orleans and San Francisco, several hundred to plantations in Mississippi, Georgia, and Arkansas, and sugarcane plantations in Louisiana and Cuba. (From the South, they sent word that it was a custom to step off the sidewalk along with the black demons when a white demon walked by.) Seventy went to New Orleans to grade a route for a railroad, then to Pennsylvania to work in a knife factory. The Colorado State Legislature passed a resolution welcoming the railroad China Men to come build the new state. They built railroads in every part of the country—the Alabama and Chattanooga Railroad, the Houston and Texas Railroad, the Southern Pacific, the railroads in Louisiana and Boston, the Pacific Northwest, and Alaska. After the Civil War, China Men banded the nation North and South, East and West, with crisscrossing steel. They were the binding and building ancestors of this place.

Ah Goong would have liked a leisurely walk along the tracks to review his finished handiwork, or to walk east to see the rest of his new country. But instead, Driven Out, he slid down mountains, leapt across valleys and streams, crossed plains, hid sometimes with companions and often alone, and eluded bandits who would hold him up for his railroad pay and shoot him for practice as they shot Injuns and jackrabbits. Detouring and backtracking, his path wound back and forth to his railroad, a familiar silver road in the wilderness. When a train came, he hid against the shaking ground in case a demon with a shotgun was hunting from it. He picked over camps where he had once lived. He was careful to find hidden places to sleep. In China bandits did not normally kill people, the booty the main thing, but here the demons killed for fun and hate. They tied pigtails to horses and dragged chinamen. He decided that he had better head for San Francisco, where he would catch a ship to China.

Perched on hillsides, he watched many sunsets, the place it was setting, the direction he was going. There were fields of grass that he tunneled through, hid in, rolled in, dived and swam in, suddenly jumped up laughing, suddenly stopped. He needed to find a town and human company. The spooky tumbleweeds caught in barbed wire were peering at him, waiting for him; he had to find a town. Towns grew along the tracks as they did along rivers. He sat looking at a town all day, then ducked into it by night.

At the familiar sight of a garden laid out in a Chinese scheme—vegetables in beds, white cabbages, red plants, chives, and coriander for immortality, herbs boxed with boards—he knocked on the back door. The China Man who answered gave him food, the appropriate food for the nearest holiday, talked story, exclaimed at how close their ancestral villages were to each other. They exchanged information on how many others lived how near, which towns had Chinatowns, what size, two or three stores or a block, which towns to avoid. "Do you have a wife?" they asked one another. "Yes. She lives in China. I have been sending money for twenty years now." They exchanged vegetable seeds, slips, and cuttings, and Ah Goong carried letters to another town or China.

Some demons who had never seen the likes of him gave him things and touched him. He also came across lone China Men who were alarmed to have him appear, and, unwelcome, he left quickly; they must have wanted to be the only China Man of that area, the special China Man.

He met miraculous China Men who had produced families out of nowhere—a wife and children, both boys and girls. "Uncle," the children called him, and he wanted to stay to be the uncle of the family. The wife washed his clothes, and he went on his way when they were dry.

On a farm road, he came across an imp child playing in the dirt. It looked at him, and he looked at it. He held out a piece of sugar; he cupped a grassblade between his thumbs and whistled. He sat on the ground with his legs crossed, and the child climbed into the hollow of his arms and legs. "I wish you were my baby," he told it. "My baby." He was very satisfied sitting there under the humming sun with the baby, who was satisfied too, no squirming. "My daughter," he said. "My son." He couldn't tell whether it was a boy or a girl. He touched the baby's fat arm and cheeks, its gold hair, and looked into its blue eyes. He made a wish that it not have to carry a sledgehammer and crawl into the dark. But he would not feel sorry for it; other people must not suffer any more than he did, and he could endure anything. Its mother came walking out into the road. She had her hands above her like a salute. She walked tentatively toward them, held out her hand, smiled, spoke. He did not understand what she said except "Bye-bye." The child waved and said, "Bye-bye," crawled over his legs, and toddled to her. Ah Goong continued on his way in a direction she could not point out to a posse looking for a kidnapper chinaman.

Explosions followed him. He heard screams and went on, saw flames outlining black windows and doors, and went on. He ran in the opposite direction from gunshots and the yell—*eeha awha*—the cowboys made when they herded cattle and sang their savage songs.

Good at hiding, disappearing—decades unaccounted for—he was not working in a mine when forty thousand chinamen were Driven Out of mining. He was not killed or kidnapped in the Los Angeles Massacre, though he gave money toward ransoming those whose toes and fingers, a digit per week, and ears grotesquely rotting or pickled, and scalped queues, were displayed in Chinatowns. Demons believed that the poorer a chinaman looked, the more gold he had buried somewhere, that chinamen stuck together and would always ransom one another. If he got kidnapped, Ah Goong planned, he would whip out his Citizenship Paper and show that he was an American. He was lucky not to be in Colorado when the Denver demons burned all chinamen homes and businesses, nor in Rock Springs, Wyoming, when the miner demons killed twenty-eight or fifty chinamen. The Rock Springs Massacre began in a large coal mine owned by the Union Pacific; the outnumbered chinamen were shot in the back as they ran to Chinatown, which the demons burned. They forced chinamen out into the open and shot them; demon women and children threw the wounded back in the flames. (There was a rumor of a good white lady in Green Springs who hid China Men in the Pacific Hotel and shamed the demons away.) The hunt went on for a month before federal troops came. The count of the dead was inexact because bodies were mutilated and pieces scattered all over the Wyoming Territory. No white miners were indicted, but the government paid $150,000 in reparations to victims' families. There were many family men, then. There were settlers—abiding China Men. And China Women. Ah Goong was running elsewhere during the Drivings Out of Tacoma, Seattle, Oregon City, Albania, and Marysville. The demons of Tacoma packed all its chinamen into boxcars and sent them to Portland, where they were run out of town. China Men returned to Seattle, though, and refused to sell their land and stores but fought until the army came; the demon rioters were tried and acquitted. And when the Boston police imprisoned and beat 234 chinamen, it was 1902, and Ah Goong had already reached San Francisco or China, and perhaps San Francisco again.

In Second City (Sacramento), he spent some of his railroad money at the theater. The main actor's face was painted red with thick black eyebrows and long black beard, and when he strode onto the stage, Ah Goong recognized the hero, Guan Goong; his puppet horse had red nostrils and rolling eyes. Ah Goong's heart leapt to recognize hero and horse in the wilds of America. Guan Goong murdered his enemy—crash! bang! of cymbals and drum—and left his home village—sad, sad flute music. But to the glad clamor of cymbals entered his friends—Liu Pei (pronounced the same as Running Nose) and Chang Fei. In a joyful burst of pink flowers, the three men swore the Peach Garden Oath. Each friend sang an aria to friendship; together they would fight side by side and live and die one for all and all for one. Ah Goong felt as warm as if he were with friends at a party. Then Guan Goong's archenemy, the sly Ts'ao Ts'ao, captured him and two of Liu Pei's wives, the Lady Kan and the Lady Mi. Though Ah Goong knew they were boy actors, he basked in the presence of Chinese ladies. The prisoners traveled to the capital, the soldiers waving horsehair whisks,

signifying horses, the ladies walking between horizontal banners, signifying palan-
quins. All the prisoners were put in one bedroom, but Guan Goong stood all night
outside the door with a lighted candle in his hand, singing an aria about faithfulness.
When the capital was attacked by a common enemy, Guan Goong fought the biggest
man in one-to-one combat, a twirling, jumping sword dance that strengthened the
China Men who watched it. From afar Guan Goong's two partners heard about the
feats of the man with the red face and intelligent horse. The three friends were
reunited and fought until they secured their rightful kingdom.

Ah Goong felt refreshed and inspired. He called out Bravo like the demons in the
audience, who had not seen theater before. Guan Goong, the God of War, also God
of War and Literature, had come to America—Guan Goong, Grandfather Guan,
our own ancestor of writers and fighters, of actors and gamblers, and avenging
executioners who mete out justice. Our own kin. Not a distant ancestor but Grandfather.

In the Big City (San Francisco), a goldsmith convinced Ah Goong to have his gold
made into jewelry, which would organize it into one piece and also delight his wife.
So he handed over a second bag of gold. He got it back as a small ring in a design
he thought up himself, two hands clasping in a handshake. "So small?" he said, but
the goldsmith said that only some of the ore had been true gold.

He got a ship out of San Francisco without being captured near the docks, where
there was a stockade full of jailed chinamen; the demonesses came down from Nob
Hill and took them home to be servants, cooks, and baby-sitters.

Grandmother liked the gold ring very much. The gold was so pure, it squished to
fit her finger. She never washed dishes, so the gold did not wear away. She quickly
spent the railroad money, and Ah Goong said he would go to America again. He had
a Certificate of Return and his Citizenship Paper.

But this time, there was no railroad to sell his strength to. He lived in a basement
that was rumored to connect with tunnels beneath Chinatown. In an underground
arsenal, he held a pistol and said, "I feel the death in it." "The holes for the bullets
were like chambers in a beehive or wasp nest," he said. He was inside the earth when
the San Francisco Earthquake and Fire began. Thunder rumbled from the ground.
Some say he died falling into the cracking earth. It was a miraculous earthquake and
fire. The Hall of Records burned completely. Citizenship Papers burned, Certificates
of Return, Birth Certificates, Residency Certificates, passenger lists, Marriage Certificates—every paper a China Man wanted for citizenship and legality burned in that
fire. An authentic citizen, then, had no more papers than an alien. Any paper a China
Man could not produce had been "burned up in the Fire of 1906." Every China Man
was reborn out of that fire a citizen.

Some say the family went into debt and sent for Ah Goong, who was not making
money; he was a homeless wanderer, a shiftless, dirty, jobless man with matted hair,
ragged clothes, and fleas all over his body. He ate out of garbage cans. He was a louse
eaten by lice. A fleaman. It cost two thousand dollars to bring him back to China,
his oldest sons signing promissory notes for one thousand, his youngest to repay four
hundred to one neighbor and six hundred to another. Maybe he hadn't died in San
Francisco, it was just his papers that burned; it was just that his existence was
outlawed by Chinese Exclusion Acts. The family called him Fleaman. They did not

understand his accomplishments as an American ancestor, a holding, homing ancestor of this place. He'd gotten the legal or illegal papers burned in the San Francisco
Earthquake and Fire; he appeared in America in time to be a citizen and to father
citizens. He had also been seen carrying a child out of the fire, a child of his own in
spite of the laws against marrying. He had built a railroad out of sweat, why not have
an American child out of longing?

THE SOMEBODY

Danny Santiago (Daniel James)

(b. 1913)

Biography p. 1097

This is Chato talking, Chato de Shamrock, from the Eastside in old L.A., and I want you to know this is a big day in my life because today I quit school and went to work as a writer. I write on fences or buildings or anything that comes along. I write my name, not the one I got from my father. I want no part of him. I write Chato, which means Catface, because I have a flat nose like a cat. It's a Mexican word because that's what I am, a Mexican, and I'm not ashamed of it. I like that language too, man. It's way better than English to say what you feel. But German is the best. It's got a real rugged sound, and I'm going to learn to talk it someday.

After Chato I write "de Shamrock." That's the street where I live, and it's the name of the gang I belong to, but the others are all gone now. Their families had to move away, except Gorilla is in jail and Blackie joined the navy because he liked swimming. But I still have our old arsenal. It's buried under the chickens, and I dig it up when I get bored. There's tire irons and chains and pick handles with spikes and two zip guns we made and they shoot real bullets but not very straight. In the good old days nobody cared to tangle with us. But now I'm the only one left.

Well, today started off like any other day. The toilet roars like a hot rod taking off. My father coughs and spits about nineteen times and hollers it's six-thirty. So I holler back I'm quitting school. Things hit me like that—sudden.

"Don't you want to be a lawyer no more," he says in Spanish, "and defend the Mexican people?"

My father thinks he is very funny, and next time I make any plans, he's sure not going to hear about it.

"Don't you want to be a doctor," he says, "and cut off my leg for nothing some-day?"

"*Due beast ine dumb cop,*"[1] I tell him in German, but not very loud.

"How will you support me," he says, "when I retire? Or will you marry a rich old woman that owns a pool hall?"

"I'm checking out of this dump! You'll never see me again!"

I hollered it at him, but already he was in the kitchen making a big noise in his coffee. I could be dead and he wouldn't take me serious. So I laid there and waited for him to go off to work. When I woke up again, it was way past eleven. I can sleep forever these days. So I got out of bed and put on clean jeans and my windbreaker and combed myself very neat, because already I had a feeling this was going to be a big day for me.

I had to wait for breakfast because the baby was sick and throwing up milk on

---

[1] *Due . . . cop.*" "You're an idiot" ("*Du bist ein Dummkopf*").

everything. There is always a baby vomiting in my house. When they're born, everybody comes over and says: "Qué cute!"[2] but nobody passes any comments on the dirty
way babies act. Sometimes my mother asks me to hold one for her but it always cries,
maybe because I squeeze it a little hard when nobody's looking.

When my mother finally served me, I had to hold my breath, she smelled so bad
of babies. I don't care to look at her anymore. Her legs got those dark-blue rivers
running all over them. I kept waiting for her to bawl me out about school, but I guess
she forgot, or something. So I cut out.

Every time I go out my front door I have to cry for what they've done to old
Shamrock Street. It used to be so fine, with solid homes on both sides. Maybe they
needed a little paint here and there but they were cozy. Then the S.P. Railroad bought
up all the land except my father's place, because he was stubborn. They came in with
their wrecking bars and their bulldozers. You could hear those houses scream when
they ripped them down. So now Shamrock Street is just front walks that lead to a hole
in the ground, and piles of busted cement. And Pelón's house and Blackie's are just
stacks of old boards waiting to get hauled away. I hope that never happens to your
street, man.

My first stop was the front gate and there was that sign again, that big S wrapped
around a cross like a snake with rays coming out, which is the mark of the Sierra Street
gang, as everybody knows. I rubbed it off, but tonight they'll put it back again. In
the old days they wouldn't dare to come on our street, but without your gang you're
nobody. And one of these fine days they're going to catch up with me in person and
that will be the end of Chato de Shamrock.

So I cruised on down to Main Street like a ghost in a graveyard. Just to prove I'm
alive, I wrote my name on the fence at the corner. A lot of names you see in public
places are written very sloppy. Not me. I take my time. Like my fifth-grade teacher
used to say, if other people are going to see your work, you owe it to yourself to do
it right. Mrs. Cully was her name and she was real nice, for an Anglo. My other
teachers were all cops, but Mrs. Cully drove me home one time when some guys were
after me. I think she wanted to adopt me but she never said anything about it. I owe
a lot to that lady, and especially my writing. You should see it, man—it's real smooth
and mellow, and curvy like a blond in a bikini. Everybody says so. Except one time
they had me in Juvenile by mistake and some doctor looked at it. He said it proved
I had something wrong with me, some long word. That doctor was crazy, because
I made him show me his writing and it was real ugly like a barbwire fence with little
chickens stuck on the points. You couldn't even read it.

Anyway, I signed myself very clean and neat on that corner. And then I thought,
Why not look for a job someplace? But I was more in the mood to write my name,
so I went into the dime store and helped myself to two boxes of crayons and some
chalk and cruised on down Main, writing all the way. I wondered should I write more
than my name. Should I write "Chato is a fine guy" or "Chato is wanted by the
police"? Things like that. News. But I decided against it. Better to keep them guessing.
Then I crossed over to Forney Playground. It used to be our territory, but now the

[2]*Qué* how

Sierra have taken over there like everyplace else. Just to show them, I wrote on the tennis court and the swimming pool and the gym. I left a fine little trail of Chato de Shamrock in eight colors. Some places I used chalk, which works better on brick or plaster. But crayons are the thing for cement or anything smooth, like in the girls' rest room. On that wall I drew a phone number. I bet a lot of them are going to call that number, but it isn't mine because we don't have a phone in the first place, and in the second place I'm probably never going home again.

I'm telling you, I was pretty famous at the Forney by the time I cut out, and from there I continued my travels till something hit me. You know how you put your name on something and that proves it belongs to you? Things like school books or gym shoes? So I thought, How about that, now? And I put my name on the Triple A Market and on Morrie's Liquor Store and on the Zócalo, which is a beer joint. And then I cruised on up Broadway, getting rich. I took over a barber shop and a furniture store and the Plymouth agency. And the firehouse for laughs, and the phone company so I could call all my girl friends and keep my dimes. And then there I was at Webster and García's Funeral Home with the big white columns. At first I thought that might be bad luck, but then I said, Oh, well, we all got to die sometime. So I signed myself, and now I can eat good and live in style and have a big time all my life, and then kiss you all good-bye and give myself the best funeral in L.A. for free.

And speaking of funerals, along came the Sierra right then, eight or ten of them down the street with that stupid walk which is their trademark. I ducked into the garage and hid behind the hearse. Not that I'm a coward. Getting stomped doesn't bother me, or even shot. What I hate is those blades, man. They're like a piece of ice cutting into your belly. But the Sierra didn't see me and went on by. I couldn't hear what they were saying, but I knew they had me on their mind. So I cut on over to the Boys' Club, where they don't let anybody get you, no matter who you are. To pass the time I shot some baskets and played a little pool and watched the television, but the story was boring, so it came to me: Why not write my name on the screen? Which I did with a squeaky pen. Those cowboys sure looked fine with Chato de Shamrock written all over them. Everybody got a kick out of it. But of course up comes Mr. Calderón and makes me wipe it off. They're always spying on you up there. And he takes me into his office and closes the door.

"Well," he says, "and how is the last of the dinosaurs?"

Meaning that the Shamrocks are as dead as giant lizards.

Then he goes into that voice with the church music in it, and I look out of the window.

"I know it's hard to lose your gang, Chato," he says, "but this is your chance to make new friends and straighten yourself out. Why don't you start coming to Boys' Club more?"

"It's boring here," I tell him.

"What about school?"

"I can't go," I said. "They'll get me."

"The Sierra's forgotten you're alive," he tells me.

"Then how come they put their mark on my house every night?"

"Do they?"

He stares at me very hard. I hate those eyes of his. He thinks he knows everything. And what is he? Just a Mexican like everybody else.

"Maybe you put that mark there yourself," he says. "To make yourself big. Just like you wrote on the television."

"That was my name! I like to write my name!"

"So do dogs," he says. "On every lamppost they come to."

"You're a dog yourself," I told him, but I don't think he heard me. He just went on talking. Brother, how they love to talk up there! But I didn't bother to listen, and when he ran out of gas I left. From now on I'm scratching that Boys' Club off my list.

Out on the street it was getting dark, but I could still follow my trail back toward Broadway. It felt good seeing Chato written everyplace, but at the Zócalo I stopped dead. Around my name there was a big red heart done in lipstick with some initials I didn't recognize. To tell the truth, I didn't know how to feel. In one way I was mad that anyone would fool with my name, especially if it was some guy doing it for laughs. But what guy carries lipstick? And if it was a girl, that could be kind of interesting.

A girl is what it turned out to be. I caught up with her at the telephone company. There she is, standing in the shadows, drawing her heart around my name. And she has a very pretty shape on her, too. I sneak up behind her very quiet, thinking all kinds of crazy things and my blood shooting around so fast it shakes me all over. And then she turns around and it's only Crusader Rabbit. That's what we called her from the television show they had then, on account of her teeth in front.

When she sees me, she takes off down the alley, but in twenty feet I catch her. I grab for the lipstick, but she whips it behind her. I reach around and try to pull her fingers open, but her hand is sweaty and so is mine. And there we are, stuck together all the way down. She twists up against me, kind of giggling. To tell the truth, I don't like to wrestle with girls. They don't fight fair. And then we lost balance and fell against some garbage cans, so I woke up. After that I got the lipstick away from her very easy.

"What right you got to my name?" I tell her. "I never gave you permission."

"You sign yourself real fine," she says.

I knew that already.

"Let's go writing together," she says.

"The Sierra's after me."

"I don't care," she says. "Come on, Chato—you and me can have a lot of fun."

She came up close and giggled that way. She put her hand on my hand that had the lipstick in it. And you know what? I'm ashamed to say I almost told her yes. It would be a change to go writing with a girl. We could talk there in the dark. We could decide on the best places. And her handwriting wasn't too bad either. But then I remembered I had my reputation to think of. Somebody would be sure to see us, and they'd be laughing at me all over the Eastside. So I pulled my hand away and told her off.

"Run along, Crusader," I told her. "I don't want no partners, and especially not you."

"Who are you calling Crusader?" she screamed. "You ugly, squash-nose punk."

She called me everything. And spit at my face but missed. I didn't argue. I just cut out. And when I got to the first sewer I threw away her lipstick. Then I drifted over to the banks at Broadway and Bailey, which is a good spot for writing because a lot of people pass by there.

Well, I hate to brag, but that was the best work I've ever done in all my life. Under the street lamp my name shone like solid gold. I stood to one side and checked the people as they walked past and inspected it. With some you can't tell just how they feel, but with others it rings out like a cash register. There was one man. He got out of his Cadillac to buy a paper and when he saw my name he smiled. He was the age to be my father. I bet he'd give me a job if I asked him. I bet he'd take me to his home and to his office in the morning. Pretty soon I'd be sitting at my own desk and signing my name on letters and checks and things. But I would never buy a Cadillac, man. They burn too much gas.

Later a girl came by. She was around eighteen, I think, with green eyes. Her face was so pretty I didn't dare to look at her shape. Do you want me to go crazy? That girl stopped and really studied my name like she fell in love with it. She wanted to know me, I could tell. She wanted to take my hand and we'd go off together holding hands. We'd go to Beverly Hills and nobody would look at us the wrong way. I almost said "Hi" to that girl and, "How do you like my writing?" But not quite.

So here I am, standing on this corner with my chalk all gone and only one crayon left and it's ugly brown. My fingers are too cold besides. But I don't care because I just had a vision, man. Did they ever turn on the lights for you so you could see the whole world and everything in it? That's how it came to me right now. I don't need to be a movie star or boxing champ to make my name in the world. All I need is plenty of chalk and crayons. And that's easy. L.A. is a big city, man, but give me a couple of months and I'll be famous all over town. Of course they'll try to stop me—the Sierra, the police, and everybody. But I'll be like a ghost, man. I'll be real mysterious, and all they'll know is just my name, signed like I always sign it, CHATO DE SHAMROCK with rays shooting out like from the Holy Cross.

BY THE WATERS OF BABYLON

Stephen Vincent Benét
(1898–1943)

Biography p. 1061

The north and the west and the south are good hunting ground, but it is forbidden to go east. It is forbidden to go to any of the Dead Places except to search for metal and then he who touches the metal must be a priest or the son of a priest. Afterwards, both the man and the metal must be purified. These are the rules and the laws; they are well made. It is forbidden to cross the great river and look upon the place that was the Place of the Gods—this is most strictly forbidden. We do not even say its name though we know its name. It is there that spirits live, and demons—it is there that there are the ashes of the Great Burning. These things are forbidden—they have been forbidden since the beginning of time.

My father is a priest; I am the son of a priest. I have been in the Dead Places near us, with my father—at first, I was afraid. When my father went into the house to search for the metal, I stood by the door and my heart felt small and weak. It was a dead man's house, a spirit house. It did not have the smell of man, though there were old bones in a corner. But it is not fitting that a priest's son should show fear. I looked at the bones in the shadow and kept my voice still.

Then my father came out with the metal—a good, strong piece. He looked at me with both eyes but I had not run away. He gave me the metal to hold—I took it and did not die. So he knew that I was truly his son and would be a priest in my time. That was when I was very young—nevertheless, my brothers would not have done it, though they are good hunters. After that, they gave me the good piece of meat and the warm corner by the fire. My father watched over me—he was glad that I should be a priest. But when I boasted or wept without a reason, he punished me more strictly than my brothers. That was right.

After a time, I myself was allowed to go into the dead houses and search for metal. So I learned the ways of those houses—and if I saw bones, I was no longer afraid. The bones are light and old—sometimes they will fall into dust if you touch them. But that is a great sin.

I was taught the chants and the spells—I was taught how to stop the running of blood from a wound and many secrets. A priest must know many secrets—that was what my father said. If the hunters think we do all things by chants and spells, they may believe so—it does not hurt them. I was taught how to read in the old books and how to make the old writings—that was hard and took a long time. My knowledge made me happy—it was like a fire in my heart. Most of all, I liked to hear of the Old Days and the stories of the gods. I asked myself many questions that I could not answer, but it was good to ask them. At night, I would lie awake and listen to the wind—it seemed to me that it was the voice of the gods as they flew through the air.

We are not ignorant like the Forest People—our women spin wool on the wheel, our priests wear a white robe. We do not eat grubs from the tree, we have not forgotten the old writings, although they are hard to understand. Nevertheless, my knowledge and my lack of knowledge burned in me—I wished to know more. When I was a man at last, I came to my father and said, "It is time for me to go on my journey. Give me your leave."

He looked at me for a long time, stroking his beard, then he said at last, "Yes. It is time." That night, in the house of the priesthood, I asked for and received purification. My body hurt but my spirit was a cool stone. It was my father himself who questioned me about my dreams.

He bade me look into the smoke of the fire and see—I saw and told what I saw. It was what I have always seen—a river, and, beyond it, a great Dead Place and in it the gods walking. I have always thought about that. His eyes were stern when I told him—he was no longer my father but a priest. He said, "This is a strong dream."

"It is mine," I said, while the smoke waved and my head felt light. They were singing the Star song in the outer chamber and it was like the buzzing of bees in my head.

He asked me how the gods were dressed and I told him how they were dressed. We know how they were dressed from the book, but I saw them as if they were before me. When I had finished, he threw the sticks three times and studied them as they fell.

"This is a very strong dream," he said. "It may eat you up."

"I am not afraid," I said and looked at him with both eyes. My voice sounded thin in my ears but that was because of the smoke.

He touched me on the breast and the forehead. He gave me the bow and the three arrows.

"Take them," he said. "It is forbidden to travel east. It is forbidden to cross the river. It is forbidden to go to the Place of the Gods. All these things are forbidden."

"All these things are forbidden," I said, but it was my voice that spoke and not my spirit. He looked at me again.

"My son," he said. "Once I had young dreams. If your dreams do not eat you up, you may be a great priest. If they eat you, you are still my son. Now go on your journey."

I went fasting, as is the law. My body hurt but not my heart. When the dawn came, I was out of sight of the village. I prayed and purified myself, waiting for a sign. The sign was an eagle. It flew east.

Sometimes signs are sent by bad spirits. I waited again on the flat rock, fasting, taking no food. I was very still—I could feel the sky above me and the earth beneath. I waited till the sun was beginning to sink. Then three deer passed in the valley, going east—they did not wind me or see me. There was a white fawn with them—a very great sign.

I followed them, at a distance, waiting for what would happen. My heart was troubled about going east, yet I knew that I must go. My head hummed with my fasting—I did not even see the panther spring upon the white fawn. But, before I knew it, the bow was in my hand. I shouted and the panther lifted his head from the fawn. It is not easy to kill a panther with one arrow but the arrow went through his eye and into his brain. He died as he tried to spring—he rolled over, tearing at the ground. Then I knew I was meant to go east—I knew that was my journey. When the night came, I made my fire and roasted meat.

It is eight suns journey to the east and a man passes by many Dead Places. The Forest People are afraid of them but I am not. Once I made my fire on the edge of a Dead Place at night and, next morning, in the dead house, I found a good knife, little rusted. That was small to what came afterward but it made my heart feel big. Always when I looked for game, it was in front of my arrow, and twice I passed hunting parties of the Forest People without their knowing. So I knew my magic was strong and my journey clean, in spite of the law.

Toward the setting of the eighth sun, I came to the banks of the great river. It was half-a-day's journey after I had left the god-road—we do not use the god-roads now for they are falling apart into great blocks of stone, and the forest is safer going. A long way off, I had seen the water through trees but the trees were thick. At last, I came out upon an open place at the top of a cliff. There was the great river below, like a giant in the sun. It is very long, very wide. It could eat all the streams we know and still be thirsty. Its name is Ou-dis-sun, the Sacred, the Long. No man of my tribe had seen it, not even my father, the priest. It was magic and I prayed.

Then I raised my eyes and looked south. It was there, the Place of the Gods.

How can I tell what it was like—you do not know. It was there, in the red light, and they were too big to be houses. It was there with the red light upon it, mighty and ruined. I knew that in another moment the gods would see me. I covered my eyes with my hands and crept back into the forest.

Surely, that was enough to do, and live. Surely it was enough to spend the night upon the cliff. The Forest People themselves do not come near. Yet, all through the night, I knew that I should have to cross the river and walk in the places of the gods, although the gods ate me up. My magic did not help me at all and yet there was a fire in my bowels, a fire in my mind. When the sun rose, I thought, "My journey has been clean. Now I will go home from my journey." But, even as I thought so, I knew I could not. If I went to the place of the gods, I would surely die, but, if I did not go, I could never be at peace with my spirit again. It is better to lose one's life than one's spirit, if one is a priest and the son of a priest.

Nevertheless, as I made the raft, the tears ran out of my eyes. The Forest People could have killed me without fight, if they had come upon me then, but they did not come. When the raft was made, I said the sayings for the dead and painted myself for death. My heart was cold as a frog and my knees like water, but the burning in my mind would not let me have peace. As I pushed the raft from the shore, I began my death song—I had the right. It was a fine song.

"I am John, son of John," I sang. "My people are the Hill People. They are the men.
I go into the Dead Places but I am not slain.
I take the metal from the Dead Places but I am not blasted.
I travel upon the god-roads and am not afraid. E-yah! I have killed the panther, I have
    killed the fawn!
E-yah! I have come to the great river. No man has come there before.
It is forbidden to go east, but I have gone, forbidden to go on the great river, but I
    am there.
Open your hearts, you spirits, and hear my song.
Now I go to the place of the gods, I shall not return.
My body is painted for death and my limbs weak, but my heart is big as I go to the
    place of the gods!"

All the same, when I came to the Place of the Gods, I was afraid, afraid. The current of the great river is very strong—it gripped my raft with its hands. That was magic, for the river itself is wide and calm. I could feel evil spirits about me, in the bright morning; I could feel their breath on my neck as I was swept down the stream. Never have I been so much alone—I tried to think of my knowledge, but it was a squirrel's heap of winter nuts. There was no strength in my knowledge any more and I felt small and naked as a new-hatched bird—alone upon the great river, the servant of the gods.

Yet, after a while, my eyes were opened and I saw. I saw both banks of the river —I saw that once there had been god-roads across it, though now they were broken and fallen like broken vines. Very great they were, and wonderful and broken— broken in the time of the Great Burning when the fire fell out of the sky. And always the current took me nearer to the Place of the Gods, and the huge ruins rose before my eyes.

I do not know the customs of rivers—we are the People of the Hills. I tried to guide my raft with the pole but it spun around. I thought the river meant to take me past the Place of the Gods and out into the Bitter Water of the legends. I grew angry then —my heart felt strong. I said aloud, "I am a priest and the son of a priest!" The gods heard me—they showed me how to paddle with the pole on one side of the raft. The current changed itself—I drew near to the Place of the Gods.

When I was very near, my raft struck and turned over. I can swim in our lakes— I swam to the shore. There was a great spike of rusted metal sticking out into the river —I hauled myself up upon it and sat there, panting. I had saved my bow and two arrows and the knife I found in the Dead Place but that was all. My raft went whirling downstream toward the Bitter Water. I looked after it, and thought if it had trod me under, at least I would be safely dead. Nevertheless, when I had dried my bow-string and re-strung it, I walked forward to the Place of the Gods.

It felt like ground underfoot; it did not burn me. It is not true what some of the tales say, that the ground there burns forever, for I have been there. Here and there were the marks and stains of the Great Burning, on the ruins, that is true. But they were old marks and old stains. It is not true either, what some of our priests say, that it is an island covered with fogs and enchantments. It is not. It is a great Dead Place —greater than any Dead Place we know. Everywhere in it there are god-roads, though most are cracked and broken. Everywhere there are the ruins of the high towers of the gods.

How shall I tell what I saw? I went carefully, my strung bow in my hand, my skin ready for danger. There should have been the wailings of spirits and the shrieks of demons, but there were not. It was very silent and sunny where I had landed—the wind and the rain and the birds that drop seeds had done their work—the grass grew in the cracks of the broken stone. It is a fair island—no wonder the gods built there. If I had come there, a god, I also would have built.

How shall I tell what I saw? The towers are not all broken—here and there one still stands, like a great tree in a forest, and the birds nest high. But the towers themselves look blind, for the gods are gone. I saw a fish-hawk, catching fish in the river. I saw a little dance of white butterflies over a great heap of broken stones and columns. I went there and looked about me—there was a carved stone with cut letters, broken in half. I can read letters but I could not understand these. They said UB-TREAS. There was also the shattered image of a man or a god. It had been made of white stone and he wore his hair tied back like a woman's. His name was ASHING, as I read on the cracked half of a stone. I thought it wise to pray to ASHING, though I do not know that god.

How shall I tell what I saw? There was no smell of man left, on stone or metal. Nor were there many trees in that wilderness of stone. There are many pigeons, nesting and dropping in the towers—the gods must have loved them, or, perhaps, they used them for sacrifices. There are wild cats that roam the god-roads, green-eyed, unafraid of man. At night they wail like demons but they are not demons. The wild dogs are more dangerous, for they hunt in a pack, but them I did not meet till later. Everywhere there are the carved stones, carved with magical numbers or words.

I went North—I did not try to hide myself. When a god or a demon saw me, then I would die, but meanwhile I was no longer afraid. My hunger for knowledge burned in me—there was so much that I could not understand. After awhile, I knew that my belly was hungry. I could have hunted for my meat, but I did not hunt. It is known that the gods did not hunt as we do—they got their food from enchanted boxes and jars. Sometimes these are still found in the Dead Places—once, when I was a child and foolish, I opened such a jar and tasted it and found the food sweet. But my father found out and punished me for it strictly, for, often, that food is death. Now, though, I had long gone past what was forbidden, and I entered the likeliest towers, looking for the food of the gods.

I found it at last in the ruins of a great temple in the mid-city. A mighty temple it must have been, for the roof was painted like the sky at night with its stars—that much I could see, though the colors were faint and dim. It went down into great caves and tunnels—perhaps they kept their slaves there. But when I started to climb down, I heard the squeaking of rats, so I did not go—rats are unclean, and there must have been many tribes of them, from the squeaking. But near there, I found food, in the heart of a ruin, behind a door that still opened. I ate only the fruits from the jars—they had a very sweet taste. There was drink, too, in bottles of glass—the drink of the gods was strong and made my head swim. After I had eaten and drunk, I slept on the top of a stone, my bow at my side.

When I woke, the sun was low. Looking down from where I lay, I saw a dog sitting on his haunches. His tongue was hanging out of his mouth; he looked as if he were laughing. He was a big dog, with a grey-brown coat, as big as a wolf. I sprang up and shouted at him but he did not move—he just sat there as if he were laughing. I did not like that. When I reached for a stone to throw, he moved swiftly out of the way of the stone. He was not afraid of me; he looked at me as if I were meat. No doubt I could have killed him with an arrow, but I did not know if there were others. Moreover, night was falling.

I looked about me—not far away there was a great, broken god-road, leading North. The towers were high enough, but not so high, and while many of the dead-houses were wrecked, there were some that stood. I went toward this god-road, keeping to the heights of the ruins, while the dog followed. When I had reached the god-road, I saw that there were others behind him. If I had slept later, they would have come upon me asleep and torn out my throat. As it was, they were sure enough of me; they did not hurry. When I went into the dead-house, they kept watch at the entrance—doubtless they thought they would have a fine hunt. But a dog cannot open a door and I knew, from the books, that the gods did not like to live on the ground but on high.

I had just found a door I could open when the dogs decided to rush. Ha! They were surprised when I shut the door in their faces—it was a good door, of strong metal. I could hear their foolish baying beyond it but I did not stop to answer them. I was in darkness—I found stairs and climbed. There were many stairs, turning around till my head was dizzy. At the top was another door—I found the knob and opened it. I was in a long small chamber—on one side of it was a bronze door that could not be opened, for it had no handle. Perhaps there was a magic word to open it but I did not have the word. I turned to the door in the opposite side of the wall. The lock of it was broken and I opened it and went in.

Within, there was a place of great riches. The god who lived there must have been a powerful god. The first room was a small ante-room—I waited there for some time, telling the spirits of the place that I came in peace and not as a robber. When it seemed to me that they had had time to hear me, I went on. Ah, what riches! Few, even, of the windows had been broken—it was all as it had been. The great windows that looked over the city had not been broken at all though they were dusty and streaked with many years. There were coverings on the floors, the colors not greatly faded, and the chairs were soft and deep. There were pictures upon the walls, very strange, very wonderful—I remember one of a bunch of flowers in a jar—if you came close to it, you could see nothing but bits of color, but if you stood away from it, the flowers might have been picked yesterday. It made my heart feel strange to look at this picture— and to look at the figure of a bird, in some hard clay, on a table and see it so like our birds. Everywhere there were books and writings, many in tongues that I could not read. The god who lived there must have been a wise god and full of knowledge. I felt I had right there, as I sought knowledge also.

Nevertheless, it was strange. There was a washing-place but no water—perhaps the gods washed in air. There was a cooking-place but no wood, and though there was a machine to cook food, there was no place to put fire in it. Nor were there candles or lamps—there were things that looked like lamps but they had neither oil nor wick. All these things were magic, but I touched them and lived—the magic had gone out of them. Let me tell one thing to show. In the washing-place, a thing said "Hot" but it was not hot to the touch—another thing said "Cold" but it was not cold. This must have been a strong magic but the magic was gone. I do not understand—they had ways—I wish that I knew.

It was close and dry and dusty in their house of the gods. I have said the magic was gone but that is not true—it had gone from the magic things but it had not gone from the place. I felt the spirits about me, weighing upon me. Nor had I ever slept in a Dead Place before—and yet, tonight, I must sleep there. When I thought of it, my tongue felt dry in my throat, in spite of my wish for knowledge. Almost I would have gone down again and faced the dogs, but I did not.

I had not gone through all the rooms when the darkness fell. When it fell, I went back to the big room looking over the city and made fire. There was a place to make fire and a box with wood in it, though I do not think they cooked there. I wrapped myself in a floor-covering and slept in front of the fire—I was very tired.

Now I tell what is very strong magic. I woke in the midst of the night. When I woke, the fire had gone out and I was cold. It seemed to me that all around me there were whisperings and voices. I closed my eyes to shut them out. Some will say that I slept again, but I do not think that I slept. I could feel the spirits drawing my spirit out of my body as a fish is drawn on a line.

Why should I lie about it? I am a priest and the son of a priest. If there are spirits, as they say, in the small Dead Places near us, what spirits must there not be in that great Place of the Gods? And would not they wish to speak? After such long years? I know that I felt myself drawn as a fish is drawn on a line. I had stepped out of my body—I could see my body asleep in front of the cold fire, but it was not I. I was drawn to look out upon the city of the gods.

It should have been dark, for it was night, but it was not dark. Everywhere there were lights—lines of light—circles and blurs of light—ten thousand torches would not have been the same. The sky itself was alight—you could barely see the stars for the glow in the sky. I thought to myself "This is strong magic" and trembled. There was a roaring in my ears like the rushing of rivers. Then my eyes grew used to the light and my ears to the sound. I knew that I was seeing the city as it had been when the gods were alive.

That was a sight indeed—yes, that was a sight: I could not have seen it in the body —my body would have died. Everywhere went the gods, on foot and in chariots— there were gods beyond number and counting and their chariots blocked the streets. They had turned night to day for their pleasure—they did not sleep with the sun. The noise of their coming and going was the noise of many waters. It was magic what they could do—it was magic what they did.

I looked out of another window—the great vines of their bridges were mended and the god-roads went East and West. Restless, restless, were the gods and always in motion! They burrowed tunnels under rivers—they flew in the air. With unbelievable tools they did giant works—no part of the earth was safe from them, for, if they wished for a thing, they summoned it from the other side of the world. And always, as they labored and rested, as they feasted and made love, there was a drum in their ears— the pulse of the giant city, beating and beating like a man's heart.

Were they happy? What is happiness to the gods? They were great, they were mighty, they were wonderful and terrible. As I looked upon them and their magic, I felt like a child—but a little more, it seemed to me, and they would pull down the moon from the sky. I saw them with wisdom beyond wisdom and knowledge beyond knowledge. And yet not all they did was well done—even I could see that—and yet their wisdom could not but grow until all was peace.

Then I saw their fate come upon them and that was terrible past speech. It came upon them as they walked the streets of their city. I have been in the fights with the Forest People—I have seen men die. But this was not like that. When gods war with gods, they use weapons we do not know. It was fire falling out of the sky and a mist that poisoned. It was the time of the Great Burning and the Destruction. They ran about like ants in the streets of their city—poor gods, poor gods! Then the towers began to fall. A few escaped—yes, a few. The legends tell it. But, even after the city had become a Dead Place, for many years the poison was still in the ground. I saw it happen, I saw the last of them die. It was darkness over the broken city and I wept.

All this, I saw. I saw it as I have told it, though not in the body. When I woke in the morning, I was hungry, but I did not think first of my hunger for my heart was perplexed and confused. I knew the reason for the Dead Places but I did not see why it had happened. It seemed to me it should not have happened, with all the magic they had. I went through the house looking for an answer. There was so much in the house I could not understand—and yet I am a priest and the son of a priest. It was like being on one side of the great river, at night, with no light to show the way.

Then I saw the dead god. He was sitting in his chair, by the window, in a room I had not entered before and, for the first moment, I thought that he was alive. Then I saw the skin on the back of his hand—it was like dry leather. The room was shut, hot and dry—no doubt that had kept him as he was. At first I was afraid to approach him—then the fear left me. He was sitting looking out over the city—he was dressed in the clothes of the gods. His age was neither young nor old—I could not tell his age. But there was wisdom in his face and great sadness. You could see that he would have not run away. He had sat at his window, watching his city die—then he himself had died. But it is better to lose one's life than one's spirit—and you could see from the face that his spirit had not been lost. I knew, that, if I touched him, he would fall into dust—and yet, there was something unconquered in the face.

That is all of my story, for then I knew he was a man—I knew then that they had been men, neither gods nor demons. It is a great knowledge, hard to tell and believe. They were men—they went a dark road, but they were men. I had no fear after that —I had no fear going home, though twice I fought off the dogs and once I was hunted for two days by the Forest People. When I saw my father again, I prayed and was purified. He touched my lips and my breast, he said, "You went away a boy. You come back a man and a priest." I said, "Father, they were men! I have been in the Place of the Gods and seen it! Now slay me, if it is the law—but still I know they were men."

He looked at me out of both eyes. He said, "The law is not always the same shape —you have done what you have done. I could not have done it my time, but you come after me. Tell!"

I told and he listened. After that, I wished to tell all the people but he showed me otherwise. He said, "Truth is a hard deer to hunt. If you eat too much truth at once, you may die of the truth. It was not idly that our fathers forbade the Dead Places." He was right—it is better the truth should come little by little. I have learned that, being a priest. Perhaps, in the old days, they ate knowledge too fast.

Nevertheless, we make a beginning. It is not for the metal alone we go to the Dead Places now—there are the books and the writings. They are hard to learn. And the magic tools are broken—but we can look at them and wonder. At least, we make a beginning. And, when I am chief priest we shall go beyond the great river. We shall go to the Place of the Gods—the place new-york—not one man but a company. We shall look for the images of the gods and find the god ASHING and the others—the gods Licoln and Biltmore and Moses. But they were men who built the city, not gods or demons. They were men. I remember the dead man's face. They were men who were here before us. We must build again.

OUT OF PLACE

Joyce Carol Oates

(b. 1938)

Biography p. 1090

I have this memory: I am waiting in line for a movie. The line is long, noisy, restless, mostly kids my age (I seem to be about thirteen). The movie must be . . . a Western, I think. I can almost see the posters and I think I see a man with a cowboy hat. Good. I do see this man and I see a horse on the poster, it is all becoming clear. A Western. I am a kid, thirteen, but not like the thirteen-year-olds who pass by the hospital here on their way home from school—they are older than I was at that age, everyone seems older. I am nineteen now, I think. I will be twenty in a few weeks and my mother talks about how I will be home, then, in time for my birthday. That gives her pleasure and so I like to hear her talk about it. But my memory is more important: the movie house, yes, and the kids, and I am one of them. We are all jostling together, moving forward in surges, a bunch of us from St. Ann's Junior High. Other kids are there from Clinton, which is a tough school. We are all in line waiting and no one is out of line. I am there, with them. We shuffle up to the ticket window and buy our tickets (50¢) and go inside, running.

There is something pleasant about this memory, but dwelling upon memories is unhealthy. They tell me that. They are afraid I will remember the explosion, and my friend who died, but I have already forgotten these things. There is no secret about it, of course. Everything is open. We were caught in a land mine explosion and some of us were luckier than others, we weren't killed, that's all. I am very lucky to be alive. I am not being sarcastic but quite truthful, because in the end it is only truth you can stand. In camp, and for a while when we fooled around for so long without ever seeing the enemy, then some of the guys were sarcastic—but that went away. Everything falls away except truth and that is what you hang onto.

The truth is that my right leg is gone and that I have some trouble with my "vision." My eyes.

On sunny days we are wheeled outside, so that we can watch the school children playing across the street. The hospital is very clean and white, and there is a kind of patio or terrace or wide walk around the front and sides, where we can sit. Next door, some distance away, is a school that is evidently a grade school. The children play at certain times—ten-fifteen in the morning, at noon, and two in the afternoon. I don't know if they are always the same children. I have trouble with my "vision," it isn't the way it used to be and yet in a way I can't remember what it used to be like. My glasses are heavy and make red marks on my nose, and sometimes my skin is sore around my ears, but that is the only sign that the glasses are new. In a way nothing is new but has always been with me. That is why I am pleased with certain memories, like the memory of the Western movie. Though I do not remember the movie itself, but only waiting in line to get in the theater.

There is a boy named Ed here, a friend of mine. He was hurt at about the same time I was, though in another place. He is about twenty too. His eyes are as good as ever and he can see things I can't; I sometimes ask him to tell me about the playground and the children there. The playground is surrounded by a high wire fence and the children play inside this fence, on their swings and slides and teeter-totters, making a lot of noise. Their voices are very high and shrill. We don't mind the noise, we like it, but sometimes it reminds me of something—I can almost catch the memory but not quite. Cries and screams by themselves are not bad. I mean the sounds are not bad. But if you open your eyes wide you may have latched onto the wrong memory and might see the wrong things—screams that are not happy screams, etc. There was a boy somewhere who was holding onto the hand of his "buddy." ("Buddy" is a word I would not have used before, I don't know where I got it from exactly.) That boy was crying, because the other boy was dead—but I can't quite remember who they were. The memory comes and goes silently. It is nothing to be upset about. The doctor told us all that it is healthier to think about our problems, not to push them back. He is a neat, clean man dressed in white, a very kind man. Sometimes his face looks creased, there are too many wrinkles in it, and he looks like my father—they are about the same age.

I like the way my father calls him *Dr. Pritchard.* You can tell a man's worth by the way my father speaks to him, I know that sounds egotistical but it's true, and my father trusts Dr. Pritchard. It is different when he speaks to someone he doesn't quite trust, oh, for example, certain priests who look too young, too boyish; he hesitates before he calls them *Father.* He hesitates before he says hello to Father Presson, who comes here to see me and hear my confession and all, and then the words "Father Presson" come out a little forced.

"Look at that big kid, by the slide. See?" Ed says nervously.

I think I see him—a short blur of no-color by the slide. "What is he doing?"

"I don't know. I thought he was. . . . No, I don't know," Ed says.

There is hesitation in Ed's voice too. Sometimes he seems not to know what he is saying, whether he should say it. I can hear the distance in his voice, the distance between the school children over there and us up here on the ledge, in the sun. When the children fight we feel nervous and we don't know what to do. Not that they really fight, not exactly. But sometimes the mood of the playground breaks and a new mood comes upon it. It's hard to explain. Ed keeps watching for that though he doesn't want to see it.

Ed has a short, muscular body, and skin that always looks tanned. His hair is black, shaved off close, and his eyebrows of course are black and very thick. He looks hunched up in the wheel chair, about to spring off and run away. His legs just lie there, though, and never move. They are both uninjured. His problem is somewhere else, in his spine—it is a mysterious thing, how a bullet strikes in one place and damages another. We have all learned a lot about the body, here. I think I would like to be a doctor. I think that, to be a doctor like Dr. Pritchard, you must have a great reverence for the body and its springs and wires and tubes, I mean, you must understand how they work together, all together. It is a strange thing. When I tried to talk to my parents about this they acted strange. I told them that Ed and I both would like to be doctors, if things got better.

"Yes," my father said slowly, "the study of medicine is—is—"

"Very beneficial," my mother said.

"Yes, beneficial—"

Then they were silent. I said, "I mean if things get better. I know I couldn't get through medical school, the way I am now."

"I wouldn't be too sure of that," my father said. "You know how they keep discovering all these extraordinary things—"

(My father latches onto special words occasionally. Now it is the word "extraordinary." I don't know where he got it from, from a friend probably. He is a vice-president for a company that makes a certain kind of waxed paper and waxed cardboard.)

"But you will get better," my mother said. "You know that."

I am seized with a feeling of happiness. Not because of what my mother said, maybe it's true and maybe not, I don't know, but because of—the fact of doctors, the fact of the body itself which is such a mystery. I can't explain it. I said, groping for my words, "If this hadn't happened then—then—I guess I'd be just the way I was, I mean, I wouldn't know—what it's like to be like this." But that was a stupid thing to say. Mother began crying again, it was embarrassing. With my glasses off, lying back against the pillow, I could pretend that I didn't notice; so I said, speaking in my new voice which is a little too slow and stumbling, "I mean—there are lots of things that are mysteries—like the way the spine hooks up with things—and the brain—and—and by myself I wouldn't know about these things—"

But it's better to talk about other matters. In my room, away from the other patients, the talk brought to me by my parents and relatives and friends is like a gift from the outside, and it has the quality of the spring days that are here now: sunny and fragrant but very delicate. My visitors' words are like rays of sunlight. It might seem that you could grab hold of them and sit up, but you can't, they're nothing, they don't last—they are gifts, that's all, like the other gifts I have. For instance, my mother says: "Betty is back now. She wants to know when she can see you, but I thought that could wait."

"Oh, is she back?"

"She didn't have a very happy time, you know."

"What's she doing now?"

"Oh, nothing, I don't know. She might go to school."

"Where?"

"A community college, nothing much."

"That's nice."

This conversation is about a cousin of mine who married some jerk and ran away to live in Mexico. But the conversation is not really about her. I don't know what it is about. It is "about" the words themselves. When by mother says, "Betty is back now," that means "Betty-is-back-now" is being talked about, not the girl herself. We hardly know the girl herself. Then we move on to talk about Harold Spender, who is a bachelor friend of my father's. Harold Spender has a funny name and Mother likes him for his name. He is always "spending" too much money. I think he has expensive parties or something, I don't know. But "Harold Spender" is another gift, and I think this gift means: "You see, everything is still the same, your cousin is still a dope and Harold Spender is still with us, spending money. Nothing has changed."

Sometimes when they are here, visiting, and Mother chatters on like that, a terrible door opens in my mind and I can't hear her. It is like waking up at night when you don't know it is night. A door opens and though I know Mother is still talking, I can't hear her. This lasts a few seconds, no more. I go into it and come out of it and no one notices. The door opens by itself, silently, and beyond it everything is black and very quiet, just nothing.

But sometimes I am nervous and feel very sharp. That is a peculiar word, sharp. I mean my body tenses and I seem to be sitting forward and my hands grip the arms of the chair, as if I'm about to throw myself out of it and demand something. Demand something! Ed's voice gets like that too. It gets very thin and demanding and sometimes he begins to cry. It's better to turn away from that, from a boy of twenty crying. I don't know why I get nervous. There is no relationship between what my body feels and what is going on outside, and that is what frightens me.

Dr. Pritchard says there is nothing to be frightened about any longer. Nothing.

He is right, of course. I think it will be nice when I am home again and the regular routine begins. My nervousness will go away and there will not be the strange threat of that door, which opens so silently and invites me in. And Father won't take so much time off from work, and Mother will not chatter so. It will be nice to get back into place and decide what I will do, though there is no hurry about that. When, I was in high school I fooled around too much. It wasn't because of basketball either, that was just an excuse, I wasted time and so did the other kids. I wore trousers the color of bone that were pretty short and tight, and I fooled around with my hair, nothing greasy but pretty long in front, flipped down onto my forehead. Mr. Palisano, the physics teacher, was also the basketball coach and he always said: "Hey, Furlong, what's your hurry? Just what's your hurry?" He had a teasing singsong voice he used only on kids he liked. He was a tall, skinny man, a very intelligent man. "Just what's your hurry?" he said when I handed in my physics problems half-finished, or made a fool of myself in basketball practice. He was happy when I told him I was going into physics, but when I failed the first course I didn't want to go back and tell him —the hell with it. So I switched into math because I had to take math anyway. And then what happened? I don't remember. I was just a kid then, I fooled around too much. The kids at the school—it was a middle-sized school run by Holy Cross fathers, who also run Notre Dame—just fooled around too much, some of them flunked out. I don't think I flunked out. It gives me a headache to think about it—

To think about the kids in my calculus class, that gives me a headache. I don't know why. I can remember my notebook, and the rows of desks, and the blackboard (though it was green), and the bell striking the hour from outside (though it was always a little off), and I think of it all like a bubble with the people still inside. All the kids and me among them, still in the same room, still there. I like to think of that.

But they aren't still there in that room. Everything has moved on. They have moved on to other rooms and I am out here, at this particular hospital. I wonder if I will be able to catch up with them. If I can read, if my eyes get better, I don't see why not. Father talks about me returning. It's no problem with a wheel chair these days, he says, and there is the business about the artificial "limb," etc. I think it will be nice to get back to books and reading and regular assignments.

I am thinking about high school, about the halls and the stairways. Mr. Palisano, and physics class, and the afternoon basketball games. I am thinking about the excitement of those games, which was not quite fear, and about the drive back home, in my car or someone else's. I went out a lot. And one night, coming home from a dance, I saw a car parked and a man fooling around by it so I stopped to help him. "Jesus Christ," he kept saying. He had a flat tire and he was very angry. He kept snuffling and wiping his nose on his shoulder, very angry, saying "Jesus Christ" and other things, other words, not the way the kids said them but in a different way—hard to explain. It made me understand that adults had made up those words, not in play but out of hatred. He was not kidding. The way he said those words frightened me. Fear comes up from the earth, the coldness of the earth, flowing up from your feet up your legs and into your bowels, like the clay of the earth itself, and your heart begins to hammer. . . .

I never told anyone about that night, what a fool I was to stop. What if something had happened to me?

I was ashamed of being such a fool. I always did stupid things, always went out of my way and turned out looking like a fool. Then I'd feel shame and not tell anyone. For instance, I am ashamed about something that happened here in the hospital a few days ago. I think it will be nice when I am home again, back in my room, where these things can't happen. There was myself and Ed and another man, out on the terrace by the side entrance, in the sun, and these kids came along. It was funny because they caught my eye when they drove past in a convertible, and they must have turned into the parking lot and got out. They were visiting someone in the hospital. The girl was carrying a grocery bag that probably had fruit in it or something. She had long dark hair and bangs that fell down to her eyebrows, and she wore sunglasses, and bright blue stretch pants of the kind that have stirrups for the feet to keep them stretched down tight. The boy wore sunglasses too, slacks and a sweater, and sandals without socks. He had the critical, unsurprised look of kids from the big university downtown.

They came up the steps, talking. The girl swung her hair back like a horse, a pony —I mean, the motion reminded me of something like that. She looked over at us and stopped talking, and the boy looked too. They were my age. The girl hesitated but the boy kept on walking fast. He frowned. He seemed embarrassed. The girl came toward me, not quite walking directly toward me, and her mouth moved in an awkward smile. She said, "I know you, don't I? Don't I know you?"

I was very excited. I tried to tell her that with her sunglasses on I couldn't see her well. But when I tried to talk the words came out jumbled. She licked her lips nervously. She said, "Were you in the war? Vietnam?"

I nodded.

She stared at me. It was strange that her face showed nothing, unlike the other faces that are turned toward me all the time. The boy, already at the door, said in an irritated sharp voice: "Come on, we're late." The girl took a vague step backward, the way girls swing slowly away from people—you must have seen them often on sidewalks before ice cream parlors or schools? They stare as if fascinated at one person, while beginning the slow inevitable swing toward another who stands behind them. The boy said, opening the door: "Come on! He deserves it!"

They went inside. And then the shame began, an awful shame. I did not understand this though I thought about it a great deal. Someone came out to help me, a nurse. When I cry most people look away in embarrassment but the nurses show nothing, nothing at all. They boss me around a little. Crying makes me think of someone else crying, a soldier holding another soldier's hand, sitting in some rubble. One soldier is alive and the other dead, the one who is alive is holding the other's hand and crying, like a baby. Like a puppy. A kitten, a baby, something small and helpless, when the crying does no good and is not meant for any good.

I think that my name is Jack Furlong. There was another person named Private Furlong, evidently myself. Now I am back home and I am Jack Furlong again. I can imagine many parts of this city without really seeing them, and what is surprising— and very pleasant—is the way these memories come to me, so unexpected. Lying in bed with no thoughts at all I suddenly find myself thinking of a certain dime store where we hung out, by the comic book racks, many years ago; or I think of a certain playground on the edge of a ravine made by a glacier, many thousands of years ago. I don't know what makes these memories come to me but they exert a kind of tug —on my heart, I suppose. It's very strange. My eyes sometimes fill with tears, but a different kind of tears. I was never good at understanding feelings but now, in the hospital, I have a lot of time for thinking. I think that I am a kind of masterpiece. I mean, a miracle. My body and my brain. It is like a little world inside, or a factory, with everything functioning and the dynamo at the very center—my heart—pumping and pumping with no source of energy behind it. I think about that a lot. What keeps it going? And the eyes. Did you know that the eye is strong, very strong? That the muscles are like steel? Yes. Eyes are very strong, I mean the substance of the eyes is strong. It takes a lot to destroy them.

At last they check me out and bring me home—a happy day. It is good to be back home where everything is peaceful and familiar. When I lived in this house before I did not think about "living" in it, or about the house at all. Now, looking out of my window, I can see the front lawn and the street and the other houses facing us, all ranch houses, and I am aware of being very fortunate. A few kids are outside, racing past on bicycles. It is a spring day, very warm. The houses on the block make a kind of design if you look right. I am tired from all the exertion involved getting me here, and so it is difficult to explain what I mean—a design, a setting. Everything in place. It has not changed and won't change. It is a very pleasant neighborhood, and I think I remember hearing Mother once say that our house had cost $45,000. I had "heard" this remark years ago but never paid any attention to it. Now I keep thinking about it, I don't know why. There is something wonderful about that figure: it means something. Is it secret? It is the very opposite of rubble, yes. There are no screams here, no sudden explosions. Yes, I think that is why it pleases me so. I fall asleep thinking of forty-five thousand dollars.

My birthday. It is a few days later. I have been looking through the books in my room, a history textbook, a calculus textbook, and something called *College Rhetoric.* Those were my books and I can recognize my handwriting in the margins, but I have a hard time reading them now. To get away from the reading I look around—or the door in my mind begins to open slowly, scaring me, and so I wheel myself over to the window to look out. Father has just flown back from Boston. Yes, it is my birthday and I am twenty. We have a wheelchair of our own now, not the hospital's chair but our own. There is a wooden ramp from our side door right into the garage, and when they push me out I have a sudden sensation of panic right in my heart—do they know how to handle me? what if they push me too hard? They are sometimes clumsy and a little rough, accidentally. Whenever Father does something wrong I think at once, not meaning to, *They wouldn't do that at the hospital.*

My uncle and my aunt are coming too. We are going out to Skyway for dinner.

This is a big restaurant and motel near the airport. There is the usual trouble getting me in and out of the car, but Father is getting used to it. My uncle Floyd keeps saying, "Well, it's great to have you back. I mean it. It's just great, it's just wonderful to have you back." My aunt is wearing a hat with big droopy yellow flowers on it, a pretty hat. But something about the flowers makes me think of giant leaves in the jungle, coated with dust and sweat, and the way the air tasted—it made your throat and lungs ache, the dust in the air. Grit. Things were flying in the air. Someone was screaming, "Don't leave me!" A lot of them were screaming that. But my father said, "We'd better hurry, our reservations are for six."

Six is early to eat, I know. They are hurrying up the evening because I get tired so fast. My uncle opens the door and my father wheels me inside, all of it done easily. My father says to a man, "Furlong, for five—" This restaurant is familiar. On one side there is a stairway going down, carpeted in blue, and down there are rooms for —oh, banquets and meetings and things. Ahead of us is a cocktail lounge, very dark. Off to the left, down a corridor lined with paintings (they are by local artists, for sale) is the restaurant we are going to, the Grotto Room. But the man is looking through his ledger. My mother says to my aunt, "I bought that watercolor here, you know, the one over the piano." The women talk about something but my uncle stares at my father and the manager, silent. Something is wrong. The manager looks through his book and his face is red and troubled. Finally he looks up and says, "Yes, all right. Down this way." He leads us down to the Grotto Room.

We are seated. The table is covered with a white tablecloth, a glaring white. A waitress is already at Father's elbow. She looks at us, her eyes darting around the table and lingering no longer on me than on anyone else. I know that my glasses are thick and that my face is not pleasant to look at, not the same face as before. But still she does not look at me more than a second, maybe two seconds. Father orders drinks. It is my birthday. He glances over to the side and I see that someone at the next table, some men and women, are watching us. A woman in red—I think it is red—does something with her napkin, putting it on the table. Father picks up his menu, which is very large. My mother and aunt chatter about something, my mother hands me a menu. At the next table a man stands. He changes places with the woman, and now her back is to our table. I understand this but pretend to notice nothing, look down at the menu with a pleased, surprised expression, because it is better this way. It is better for everyone.

"What do you think you'll order? Everything looks so tempting," she says.

They were in a hurry and the wounded and the dead were stacked together, brought back together in a truck. But not carried at the end of a nylon cord, from a helicopter, not that. This memory comes to me in a flash, then fades. I was driving the truck, I think. Wasn't I? I was on the truck. I did not hover at the end of a line, in a plastic sack. Those were others—I didn't know them, only saw them from a distance. They screamed: "Don't leave me!"

"Lobster," Father says. He speaks with certainty: he is predicting my choice for dinner. "I bet it's lobster, eh?"

"Lobster."

My mother squeezes my arm, pleased that I have given the right answer. "My choice too," she says. "Always have fish on Fridays . . . the old customs . . . I like the old customs, no matter what people say. The Mass in Latin, and . . . and priests who know what their vocations are. . . . How do you want your lobster, dear? Broiled?"

"Yes."

"Or this way—here—the Skyway Lobster?" She leans over to help me with the menu, pointing at the words. There is a film, a gauzy panel between me and the words, and I keep waiting for it to disappear. The faces around the table, the voices . . . the smiling mouths and eyes . . . I keep glancing up at them, waiting for the veil to be yanked away. *He deserves it. Don't leave me!* In the meantime I think I will have the Skyway Lobster.

"You're sure?"

"Yes."

"My own choice also," my mother says. She looks around the table, in triumph, and the faces smile back at her and at me.

THE YELLOW WALLPAPER

Charlotte Perkins Gilman
(1860–1935)

Biography p. 1074

It is very seldom that mere ordinary people like John and myself secure ancestral halls for the summer.

A colonial mansion, a hereditary estate, I would say a haunted house, and reach the height of romantic felicity—but that would be asking too much of fate!

Still I will proudly declare that there is something queer about it.

Else, why should it be let so cheaply? And why have stood so long untenanted?

John laughs at me, of course, but one expects that in marriage.

John is practical in the extreme. He has no patience with faith, an intense horror of superstition, and he scoffs openly at any talk of things not to be felt and seen and put down in figures.

John is a physician, and *perhaps*—(I would not say it to a living soul, of course, but this is dead paper and a great relief to my mind)—*perhaps* that is one reason I do not get well faster.

You see he does not believe I am sick!

And what can one do?

If a physician of high standing, and one's own husband, assures friends and relatives that there is really nothing the matter with one but temporary nervous depression—a slight hysterical tendency—what is one to do?

My brother is also a physician, and also of high standing, and he says the same thing.

So I take phosphates or phosphites—whichever it is, and tonics, and journeys, and air, and exercise, and am absolutely forbidden to "work" until I am well again.

Personally, I disagree with their ideas.

Personally, I believe that congenial work, with excitement and change, would do me good.

But what is one to do?

I did write for a while in spite of them; but it *does* exhaust me a good deal—having to be so sly about it, or else meet with heavy opposition.

I sometimes fancy that in my condition if I had less opposition and more society and stimulus—but John says the very worst thing I can do is to think about my condition, and I confess it always makes me feel bad.

So I will let it alone and talk about the house.

The most beautiful place! It is quite alone, standing well back from the road, quite three miles from the village. It makes me think of English places that you read about, for there are hedges and walls and gates that lock, and lots of separate little houses for the gardeners and people.

There is a *delicious* garden! I never saw such a garden—large and shady, full of box-bordered paths, and lined with long grape-covered arbors with seats under them.

There were greenhouses, too, but they are all broken now.

There was some legal trouble, I believe, something about the heirs and coheirs; anyhow, the place has been empty for years.

That spoils my ghostliness, I am afraid, but I don't care—there is something strange about the house—I can feel it.

I even said so to John one moonlight evening, but he said what I felt was a *draught,* and shut the window.

I get unreasonably angry with John sometimes. I'm sure I never used to be so sensitive. I think it is due to this nervous condition.

But John says if I feel so, I shall neglect proper self-control; so I take pains to control myself—before him, at least, and that makes me very tired.

I don't like our room a bit. I wanted one downstairs that opened on the piazza and had roses all over the window, and such pretty old-fashioned chintz hangings! but John would not hear of it.

He said there was only one window and not room for two beds, and no near room for him if he took another.

He is very careful and loving, and hardly lets me stir without special direction.

I have a schedule prescription for each hour in the day; he takes all care from me, and so I feel basely ungrateful not to value it more.

He said we came here solely on my account, that I was to have perfect rest and all the air I could get. "Your exercise depends on your strength, my dear," said he, "and your food somewhat on your appetite; but air you can absorb all the time." So we took the nursery at the top of the house.

It is a big, airy room, the whole floor nearly, with windows that look all ways, and air and sunshine galore. It was nursery first and then playroom and gymnasium, I should judge; for the windows are barred for little children, and there are rings and things in the walls.

The paint and paper look as if a boys' school had used it. It is stripped off—the paper—in great patches all around the head of my bed, about as far as I can reach, and in a great place on the other side of the room low down. I never saw a worse paper in my life.

One of those sprawling flamboyant patterns committing every artistic sin.

It is dull enough to confuse the eye in following, pronounced enough to constantly irritate and provoke study, and when you follow the lame uncertain curves for a little distance they suddenly commit suicide—plunge off at outrageous angles, destroy themselves in unheard of contradictions.

The color is repellent, almost revolting; a smouldering unclean yellow, strangely faded by the slow-turning sunlight.

It is a dull yet lurid orange in some places, a sickly sulphur tint in others.

No wonder the children hated it! I should hate it myself if I had to live in this room long.

There comes John, and I must put this away,—he hates to have me write a word.

We have been here two weeks, and I haven't felt like writing before, since that first day.

I am sitting by the window now, up in this atrocious nursery, and there is nothing to hinder my writing as much as I please, save lack of strength.

John is away all day, and even some nights when his cases are serious.

I am glad my case is not serious!

But these nervous troubles are dreadfully depressing.

John does not know how much I really suffer. He knows there is no *reason* to suffer, and that satisfies him.

Of course it is only nervousness. It does weigh on me so not to do my duty in any way!

I meant to be such a help to John, such a real rest and comfort, and here I am a comparative burden already!

Nobody would believe what an effort it is to do what little I am able,—to dress and entertain, and order things.

It is fortunate Mary is so good with the baby. Such a dear baby!

And yet I *cannot* be with him, it makes me so nervous.

I suppose John never was nervous in his life. He laughs at me so about this wall-paper!

At first he meant to repaper the room, but afterwards he said that I was letting it get the better of me, and that nothing was worse for a nervous patient than to give way to such fancies.

He said that after the wall-paper was changed it would be the heavy bedstead, and then the barred windows, and then that gate at the head of the stairs, and so on.

"You know the place is doing you good," he said, "and really, dear, I don't care to renovate the house just for a three months' rental."

"Then do let us go downstairs," I said, "there are such pretty rooms there."

Then he took me in his arms and called me a blessed little goose, and said he would go down to the cellar, if I wished, and have it whitewashed into the bargain.

But he is right enough about the beds and windows and things.

It is an airy and comfortable room as any one need wish, and, of course, I would not be so silly as to make him uncomfortable just for a whim.

I'm really getting quite fond of the big room, all but that horrid paper.

Out of one window I can see the garden, those mysterious deepshaded arbors, the riotous old-fashioned flowers, and bushes and gnarly trees.

Out of another I get a lovely view of the bay and a little private wharf belonging to the estate. There is a beautiful shaded lane that runs down there from the house. I always fancy I see people walking in these numerous paths and arbors, but John has cautioned me not to give way to fancy in the least. He says that with my imaginative power and habit of story-making, a nervous weakness like mine is sure to lead to all manner of excited fancies, and that I ought to use my will and good sense to check the tendency. So I try.

I think sometimes that if I were only well enough to write a little it would relieve the press of ideas and rest me.

But I find I get pretty tired when I try.

It is so discouraging not to have any advice and companionship about my work. When I get really well, John says we will ask Cousin Henry and Julia down for a long visit; but he says he would as soon put fireworks in my pillow-case as to let me have those stimulating people about now.

I wish I could get well faster.

But I must not think about that. This paper looks to me as if it *knew* what a vicious influence it had!

There is a recurrent spot where the pattern lolls like a broken neck and two bulbous eyes stare at you upside down.

I get positively angry with the impertinence of it and the everlastingness. Up and down and sideways they crawl, and those absurd, unblinking eyes are everywhere. There is one place where two breadths didn't match, and the eyes go all up and down the line, one a little higher than the other.

I never saw so much expression in an inanimate thing before, and we all know how much expression they have! I used to lie awake as a child and get more entertainment and terror out of blank walls and plain furniture than most children could find in a toy-store.

I remember what a kindly wink the knobs of our big, old bureau used to have, and there was one chair that always seemed like a strong friend.

I used to feel that if any of the other things looked too fierce I could always hop into that chair and be safe.

The furniture in this room is no worse than inharmonious, however, for we had to bring it all from downstairs. I suppose when this was used as a playroom they had to take the nursery things out, and no wonder! I never saw such ravages as the children have made here.

The wall-paper, as I said before, is torn off in spots, and it sticketh closer than a brother—they must have had perseverance as well as hatred.

Then the floor is scratched and gouged and splintered, the plaster itself is dug out here and there, and this great heavy bed which is all we found in the room, looks as if it had been through the wars.

But I don't mind it a bit—only the paper.

There comes John's sister. Such a dear girl as she is, and so careful of me! I must not let her find me writing.

She is a perfect and enthusiastic housekeeper, and hopes for no better profession. I verily believe she thinks it is the writing which made me sick!

But I can write when she is out, and see her a long way off from these windows.

There is one that commands the road, a lovely shaded winding road, and one that just looks off over the country. A lovely country, too, full of great elms and velvet meadows.

This wall-paper has a kind of sub-pattern in a different shade, a particularly irritating one, for you can only see it in certain lights, and not clearly then.

But in the places where it isn't faded and where the sun is just so—I can see a strange, provoking, formless sort of figure, that seems to skulk about behind that silly and conspicuous front design.

There's sister on the stairs!

Well, the Fourth of July is over! The people are all gone and I am tired out. John thought it might do me good to see a little company, so we just had mother and Nellie and the children down for a week.

Of course I didn't do a thing. Jennie sees to everything now.

But it tired me all the same.

John says if I don't pick up faster he shall send me to Weir Mitchell in the fall.

But I don't want to go there at all. I had a friend who was in his hands once, and she says he is just like John and my brother, only more so!

Besides, it is such an undertaking to go so far.

I don't feel as if it was worth while to turn my hand over for anything, and I'm getting dreadfully fretful and querulous.

I cry at nothing, and cry most of the time.

Of course I don't when John is here, or anybody else, but when I am alone.

And I am alone a good deal just now. John is kept in town very often by serious cases, and Jennie is good and lets me alone when I want her to.

So I walk a little in the garden or down that lovely lane, sit on the porch under the roses, and lie down up here a good deal.

I'm getting really fond of the room in spite of the wall-paper. Perhaps *because* of the wall-paper.

It dwells in my mind so!

I lie here on this great immovable bed—it is nailed down, I believe—and follow that pattern about by the hour. It is as good as gymnastics, I assure you. I start, we'll say, at the bottom, down in the corner over there where it has not been touched, and I determine for the thousandth time that I *will* follow that pointless pattern to some sort of a conclusion.

I know a little of the principle of design, and I know this thing was not arranged on any laws of radiation, or alternation, or repetition, or symmetry, or anything else that I ever heard of.

It is repeated, of course, by the breadths, but not otherwise.

Looked at in one way each breadth stands alone, the bloated curves and flourishes —a kind of "debased Romanesque" with *delirium tremens*—go waddling up and down in isolated columns of fatuity.

But, on the other hand, they connect diagonally, and the sprawling outlines run off in great slanting waves of optic horror, like a lot of wallowing seaweeds in full chase.

The whole thing goes horizontally, too, at least it seems so, and I exhaust myself in trying to distinguish the order of its going in that direction.

They have used a horizontal breadth for a frieze, and that adds wonderfully to the confusion.

There is one end of the room where it is almost intact, and there, when the crosslights fade and the low sun shines directly upon it, I can almost fancy radiation after all,—the interminable grotesques seem to form around a common centre and rush off in headlong plunges of equal distraction.

It makes me tired to follow it. I will take a nap I guess.

I don't know why I should write this.

I don't want to.

I don't feel able.

And I know John would think it absurd. But I *must* say what I feel and think in some way—it is such a relief!

But the effort is getting to be greater than the relief.

Half the time now I am awfully lazy, and lie down ever so much.

John says I mustn't lose my strength, and has me take cod liver oil and lots of tonics and things, to say nothing of ale and wine and rare meat.

Dear John! He loves me very dearly, and hates to have me sick. I tried to have a real earnest reasonable talk with him the other day, and tell him how I wish he would let me go and make a visit to Cousin Henry and Julia.

But he said I wasn't able to go, nor able to stand it after I got there; and I did not make out a very good case for myself, for I was crying before I had finished.

It is getting to be a great effort for me to think straight. Just this nervous weakness I suppose.

And dear John gathered me up in his arms, and just carried me upstairs and laid me on the bed, and sat by me and read to me till it tired my head.

He said I was his darling and his comfort and all he had, and that I must take care of myself for his sake, and keep well.

He says no one but myself can help me out of it, that I must use my will and self-control and not let any silly fancies run away with me.

There's one comfort, the baby is well and happy, and does not have to occupy this nursery with the horrid wall-paper.

If we had not used it, that blessed child would have! What a fortunate escape! Why, I wouldn't have a child of mine, an impressionable little thing, live in such a room for worlds.

I never thought of it before, but it is lucky that John kept me here after all, I can stand it so much easier than a baby, you see.

Of course I never mention it to them any more—I am too wise,—but I keep watch of it all the same.

There are things in that paper that nobody knows but me, or ever will.

Behind that outside pattern the dim shapes get clearer every day.

It is always the same shape, only very numerous.

And it is like a woman stooping down and creeping about behind that pattern. I don't like it a bit. I wonder—I begin to think—I wish John would take me away from here!

It is so hard to talk with John about my case, because he is so wise, and because he loves me so.

But I tried it last night.

It was moonlight. The moon shines in all around just as the sun does.

I hate to see it sometimes, it creeps so slowly, and always comes in by one window or another.

John was asleep and I hated to waken him, so I kept still and watched the moonlight on that undulating wall-paper till I felt creepy.

The faint figure behind seemed to shake the pattern, just as if she wanted to get out.

I got up softly and went to feel and see if the paper *did* move, and when I came back John was awake.

"What is it, little girl?" he said. "Don't go walking about like that—you'll get cold."

I thought it was a good time to talk, so I told him that I really was not gaining here, and that I wished he would take me away.

"Why darling!" said he, "our lease will be up in three weeks, and I can't see how to leave before.

"The repairs are not done at home, and I cannot possibly leave town just now. Of course if you were in any danger, I could and would, but you really are better, dear, whether you can see it or not. I am a doctor, dear, and I know. You are gaining flesh and color, your appetite is better, I feel really much easier about you."

"I don't weigh a bit more," said I, "nor as much; and my appetite may be better in the evening when you are here, but it is worse in the morning when you are away!"

"Bless her little heart!" said he with a big hug, "she shall be as sick as she pleases! But now let's improve the shining hours by going to sleep, and talk about it in the morning!"

"And you won't go away?" I asked gloomily.

"Why, how can I, dear? It is only three weeks more and then we will take a nice little trip of a few days while Jennie is getting the house ready. Really dear you are better!"

"Better in body perhaps—" I began, and stopped short, for he sat up straight and looked at me with such a stern, reproachful look that I could not say another word.

"My darling," said he, "I beg of you, for my sake and for our child's sake, as well as for your own, that you will never for one instant let that idea enter your mind! There is nothing so dangerous, so fascinating, to a temperament like yours. It is a false and foolish fancy. Can you not trust me as a physician when I tell you so?"

So of course I said no more on that score, and we went to sleep before long. He thought I was asleep first, but I wasn't, and lay there for hours trying to decide whether that front pattern and the back pattern really did move together or separately.

On a pattern like this, by daylight, there is a lack of sequence, a defiance of law, that is a constant irritant to a normal mind.

The color is hideous enough, and unreliable enough, and infuriating enough, but the pattern is torturing.

You think you have mastered it, but just as you get well underway in following, it turns a back-somersault and there you are. It slaps you in the face, knocks you down, and tramples upon you. It is like a bad dream.

The outside pattern is a florid arabesque, reminding one of a fungus. If you can imagine a toadstool in joints, an interminable string of toadstools, budding and sprouting in endless convolutions—why, that is something like it.

That is, sometimes!

There is one marked peculiarity about this paper, a thing nobody seems to notice but myself, and that is that it changes as the light changes.

When the sun shoots in through the east window—I always watch for that first long, straight ray—it changes so quickly that I never can quite believe it.

That is why I watch it always.

By moonlight—the moon shines in all night when there is a moon—I wouldn't know it was the same paper.

At night in any kind of light, in twilight, candle light, lamplight, and worst of all by moonlight, it becomes bars! The outside pattern I mean, and the woman behind it is as plain as can be.

I didn't realize for a long time what the thing was that showed behind, that dim sub-pattern, but now I am quite sure it is a woman.

By daylight she is subdued, quiet. I fancy it is the pattern that keeps her so still. It is so puzzling. It keeps me quiet by the hour.

I lie down ever so much now. John says it is good for me, and to sleep all I can.

Indeed he started the habit by making me lie down for an hour after each meal.

It is a very bad habit I am convinced, for you see I don't sleep.

And that cultivates deceit, for I don't tell them I'm awake—O no!

The fact is I am getting a little afraid of John.

He seems very queer sometimes, and even Jennie has an inexplicable look.

It strikes me occasionally, just as a scientific hypothesis,—that perhaps it is the paper!

I have watched John when he did not know I was looking, and come into the room suddenly on the most innocent excuses, and I've caught him several times *looking at the paper!* And Jennie too. I caught Jennie with her hand on it once.

She didn't know I was in the room, and when I asked her in a quiet, a very quiet voice, with the most restrained manner possible, what she was doing with the paper —she turned around as if she had been caught stealing, and looked quite angry— asked me why I should frighten her so!

Then she said that the paper stained everything it touched, that she had found yellow smooches on all my clothes and John's, and she wished we would be more careful!

Did not that sound innocent? But I know she was studying that pattern, and I am determined that nobody shall find it out but myself!

Life is very much more exciting now than it used to be. You see I have something more to expect, to look forward to, to watch. I really do eat better, and am more quiet than I was.

John is so pleased to see me improve! He laughed a little the other day, and said I seemed to be flourishing in spite of my wall-paper.

I turned it off with a laugh. I had no intention of telling him it was *because* of the wall-paper—he would make fun of me. He might even want to take me away.

I don't want to leave now until I have found it out. There is a week more, and I think that will be enough.

I'm feeling ever so much better! I don't sleep much at night, for it is so interesting to watch developments; but I sleep a good deal in the daytime.

In the daytime it is tiresome and perplexing.

There are always new shoots on the fungus, and new shades of yellow all over it. I cannot keep count of them, though I have tried conscientiously.

It is the strangest yellow, that wall-paper! It makes me think of all the yellow things I ever saw—not beautiful ones like buttercups, but old foul, bad yellow things.

But there is something else about that paper—the smell! I noticed it the moment we came into the room, but with so much air and sun it was not bad. Now we have had a week of fog and rain, and whether the windows are open or not, the smell is here.

It creeps all over the house.

I find it hovering in the dining-room, skulking in the parlor, hiding in the hall, lying in wait for me on the stairs.

It gets into my hair.

Even when I go to ride, if I turn my head suddenly and surprise it—there is that smell!

Such a peculiar odor, too! I have spent hours in trying to analyze it, to find what it smelled like.

It is not bad—at first, and very gentle, but quite the subtlest, most enduring odor I ever met.

In this damp weather it is awful, I wake up in the night and find it hanging over me.

It used to disturb me at first. I thought seriously of burning the house—to reach the smell.

But now I am used to it. The only thing I can think of that it is like is the *color* of the paper! A yellow smell.

There is a very funny mark on this wall, low down, near the mopboard. A streak that runs round the room. It goes behind every piece of furniture, except the bed, a long, straight, even *smooch,* as if it had been rubbed over and over.

I wonder how it was done and who did it, and what they did it for. Round and round and round—round and round and round—it makes me dizzy!

I really have discovered something at last.

Through watching so much at night, when it changes so, I have finally found out.

The front pattern *does* move—and no wonder! The woman behind shakes it!

Sometimes I think there are a great many women behind, and sometimes only one, and she crawls around fast, and her crawling shakes it all over.

Then in the very bright spots she keeps still, and in the very shady spots she just takes hold of the bars and shakes them hard.

And she is all the time trying to climb through. But nobody could climb through that pattern—it strangles so; I think that is why it has so many heads.

They get through, and then the pattern strangles them off and turns them upside down, and makes their eyes white!

If those heads were covered or taken off it would not be half so bad.

I think that woman gets out in the daytime!

And I'll tell you why—privately—I've seen her!

I can see her out of every one of my windows!

It is the same woman, I know, for she is always creeping, and most women do not creep by daylight.

I see her on that long road under the trees, creeping along, and when a carriage comes she hides under the blackberry vines.

I don't blame her a bit. It must be very humiliating to be caught creeping by daylight!

I always lock the door when I creep by daylight. I can't do it at night, for I know John would suspect something at once.

And John is so queer now, that I don't want to irritate him. I wish he would take another room! Besides, I don't want anybody to get that woman out at night but myself.

I often wonder if I could see her out of all the windows at once.

But, turn as fast as I can, I can only see out of one at one time.

And though I always see her, she *may* be able to creep faster than I can turn!

I have watched her sometimes away off in the open country, creeping as fast as a cloud shadow in a high wind.

If only that top pattern could be gotten off from the under one! I mean to try it, little by little.

I have found out another funny thing, but I shan't tell it this time! It does not do to trust people too much.

There are only two more days to get this paper off, and I believe John is beginning to notice. I don't like the look in his eyes.

And I heard him ask Jennie a lot of professional questions about me. She had a very good report to give.

She said I slept a good deal in the daytime.

John knows I don't sleep very well at night, for all I'm so quiet!

He asked me all sorts of questions, too, and pretended to be very loving and kind.

As if I couldn't see through him!

Still, I don't wonder he acts so, sleeping under this paper for three months.

It only interests me, but I feel sure John and Jennie are secretly affected by it.

Hurrah! This is the last day, but it is enough. John to stay in town over night, and won't be out until this evening.

Jennie wanted to sleep with me—the sly thing! but I told her I should undoubtedly rest better for a night all alone.

That was clever, for really I wasn't alone a bit! As soon as it was moonlight and that poor thing began to crawl and shake the pattern, I got up and ran to help her.

I pulled and she shook, I shook and she pulled, and before morning we had peeled off yards of that paper.

A strip about as high as my head and half around the room.

And then when the sun came and that awful pattern began to laugh at me, I declared I would finish it to-day!

We go away to-morrow, and they are moving all my furniture down again to leave things as they were before.

Jennie looked at the wall in amazement, but I told her merrily that I did it out of pure spite at the vicious thing.

She laughed and said she wouldn't mind doing it herself, but I must not get tired.

How she betrayed herself that time!

But I am here, and no person touches this paper but me,—not *alive!*

She tried to get me out of the room—it was too patent! But I said it was so quiet and empty and clean now that I believed I would lie down again and sleep all I could; and not to wake me even for dinner—I would call when I woke.

So now she is gone, and the servants are gone, and the things are gone, and there is nothing left but that great bedstead nailed down, with the canvas mattress we found on it.

We shall sleep downstairs to-night, and take the boat home to-morrow.

I quite enjoy the room, now it is bare again.

How those children did tear about here!

This bedstead is fairly gnawed!

But I must get to work.

I have locked the door and thrown the key down into the front path.

I don't want to go out, and I don't want to have anybody come in, till John comes.

I want to astonish him.

I've got a rope up here that even Jennie did not find. If that woman does get out, and tries to get away, I can tie her!

But I forgot I could not reach far without anything to stand on!

This bed will *not* move!

I tried to lift and push it until I was lame, and then I got so angry I bit off a little piece at one corner—but it hurt my teeth.

Then I peeled off all the paper I could reach standing on the floor. It sticks horribly and the pattern just enjoys it! All those strangled heads and bulbous eyes and waddling fungus growths just shriek with derision!

I am getting angry enough to do something desperate. To jump out of the window would be admirable exercise, but the bars are too strong even to try.

Besides I wouldn't do it. Of course not. I know well enough that a step like that is improper and might be misconstrued.

I don't like to *look* out of the windows even—there are so many of those creeping women, and they creep so fast.

I wonder if they all come out of that wall-paper as I did?

But I am securely fastened now by my well-hidden rope—you don't get *me* out in the road there!

I suppose I shall have to get back behind the pattern when it comes night, and that is hard!

It is so pleasant to be out in this great room and creep around as I please!

I don't want to go outside. I won't, even if Jennie asks me to.

For outside you have to creep on the ground, and everything is green instead of yellow.

But here I can creep smoothly on the floor, and my shoulder just fits in that long smooch around the wall, so I cannot lose my way.

Why there's John at the door!

It is no use, young man, you can't open it!

How he does call and pound!

Now he's crying for an axe.

It would be a shame to break down that beautiful door!

"John dear!" said I in the gentlest voice, "the key is down by the front steps, under a plantain leaf!"

That silenced him for a few moments.

Then he said—very quietly indeed, "Open the door, my darling!"

"I can't," said I. "The key is down by the front door under a plantain leaf!"

And then I said it again, several times, very gently and slowly, and said it so often that he had to go and see, and he got it of course, and came in. He stopped short by the door.

"What is the matter?" he cried. "For God's sake, what are you doing!"

I kept on creeping just the same, but I looked at him over my shoulder.

"I've got out at last," said I, "in spite of you and Jane. And I've pulled off most of the paper, so you can't put me back!"

Now why should that man have fainted? But he did, and right across my path by the wall, so that I had to creep over him every time!

Poetry

I HEAR AMERICA SINGING

Walt Whitman
(1819–1892)

Biography p. 1106

I hear America singing, the varied carols I hear,
Those of mechanics, each one singing his as it should be blithe
    and strong,
The carpenter singing his as he measures his plank or beam,
The mason singing his as he makes ready for work, or leaves off
    work,
The boatman singing what belongs to him in his boat, the
    deck-hand singing on the steamboat deck,   5
The shoemaker singing as he sits on his bench, the hatter singing
    as he stands,
The wood-cutter's song, the ploughboy's on his way in the
    morning, or at noon intermission or at sundown,
The delicious singing of the mother, or of the young wife at
    work, or of the girl sewing or washing,
Each singing what belongs to him or her and to none else,
The day what belongs to the day—at night the party of young
    fellows, robust, friendly,   10
Singing with open mouths their strong melodious songs.

I, TOO

Langston Hughes
(1902–1967)

Biography p. 1078

I, too, sing America.

I am the darker brother.

They send me to eat in the kitchen
When company comes,
But I laugh,   5
And eat well,
And grow strong.

Tomorrow,
I'll be at the table
When company comes.   10
Nobody'll dare
Say to me,
"Eat in the kitchen,"
Then.

Besides,   15
They'll see how beautiful I am
And be ashamed—

I, too, am America.

WE WEAR THE MASK

Paul Laurence Dunbar
(1872–1906)

Biography p. 1070

We wear the mask that grins and lies,
It hides our cheeks and shades our eyes,—
This debt we pay to human guile;
With torn and bleeding hearts we smile,
And mouth with myriad subtleties.   5

Why should the world be overwise,
In counting all our tears and sighs?
Nay, let them only see us, while
        We wear the mask.

We smile, but, O great Christ, our cries   10
To thee from tortured souls arise.
We sing, but oh the clay is vile
Beneath our feet, and long the mile;
But let the world dream otherwise,
        We wear the mask!   15

OUTCAST

Claude McKay

(1890–1948)

Biography p. 1087

For the dim regions whence my fathers came
My spirit, bondaged by the body, longs.
Words felt, but never heard, my lips would frame;
My soul would sing forgotten jungle songs.
I would go back to darkness and to peace,   5
But the great western world holds me in fee,
And I may never hope for full release
While to its alien gods I bend my knee.
Something in me is lost, forever lost,
Some vital thing has gone out of my heart,   10
And I must walk the way of life a ghost
Among the sons of earth, a thing apart.

For I was born, far from my native clime,
Under the white man's menace, out of time.

NIKKI-ROSA

Nikki Giovanni

(b. 1943)

Biography p. 1074

childhood remembrances are always a drag
if you're Black
you always remember things like living in Woodlawn
with no inside toilet
and if you become famous or something   5
they never talk about how happy you were to have
your mother
all to yourself and
how good the water felt when you got your bath
from one of those   10
big tubs that folk in chicago barbecue in

and somehow when you talk about home
it never gets across how much you
understood their feelings
as the whole family attended meetings about Hollydale   15
and even though you remember
your biographers never understand
your father's pain as he sells his stock
and another dream goes
And though you're poor it isn't poverty that   20
concerns you
and though they fought a lot
it isn't your father's drinking that makes any difference
but only that everybody is together and you
and your sister have happy birthdays and very good   25
Christmasses
and I really hope no white person ever has cause
to write about me
because they never understand
Black love is Black wealth and they'll   30
probably talk about my hard childhood
and never understand that
all the while I was quite happy

KITCHENETTE BUILDING

Gwendolyn Brooks

(b. 1917)

Biography p. 1063

We are things of dry hours and the involuntary plan,
Grayed in, and gray. "Dream" makes a giddy sound, not strong
Like "rent," "feeding a wife," "satisfying a man."

But could a dream send up through onion fumes
Its white and violet, fight with fried potatoes   5
And yesterday's garbage ripening in the hall,
Flutter, or sing an aria down these rooms

Even if we were willing to let it in,
Had time to warm it, keep it very clean,
Anticipate a message, let it begin?   10

We wonder. But not well! not for a minute!
Since Number Five is out of the bathroom now,
We think of lukewarm water, hope to get in it.

IF YOU SAW A NEGRO LADY

June Jordan

(b. 1936)

Biography p. 1080

If you saw a Negro lady
sitting on a Tuesday
near the whirl-sludge doors of
Horn & Hardart on the main drag
of downtown Brooklyn   5

solitary and conspicuous as plain
and neat as walls impossible to
fresco and you watched her self-
conscious features shape about
a Horn & Hardart teaspoon   10
with a pucker from a cartoon

she would not understand
with spine as straight and solid
as her years of bending over floors
allowed   15

skin cleared of interest by a ruthless
soap   nails square and yellowclean
from metal files
sitting in a forty-year-old-flush
of solitude and prickling   20
from the new white cotton blouse
concealing nothing she had ever noticed
even when she bathed and never
hummed a bathtub tune nor knew one

If you saw her square   25
above the dirty
mopped-on antiseptic floors
before the rag-wiped table tops

little finger   broad and stiff
in heavy emulation of a cockney   30

mannerism
would you turn her treat
into surprise
observing

happy birthday   35

I LIKE TO THINK OF HARRIET TUBMAN

Susan Griffin

(b. 1943)

Biography p. 1075

I like to think of Harriet Tubman.
Harriet Tubman who carried a revolver,
who had a scar on her head from a rock thrown
by a slave-master (because she
talked back), and who   5
had a ransom on her head
of thousands of dollars and who
was never caught, and who
had no use for the law
when the law was wrong,   10
who defied the law. I like
to think of her.
I like to think of her especially
when I think of the problem of
feeding children.   15

The legal answer
to the problem of feeding children
is ten free lunches every month,
being equal, in the child's real life,
to eating lunch every other day.   20
Monday but not Tuesday.
I like to think of the President

eating lunch Monday, but not
Tuesday.
And when I think of the President   25
and the law, and the problem of
feeding children, I like to
think of Harriet Tubman
and her revolver.

And then sometimes   30
I think of the President
and other men,
men who practise the law,
who revere the law,
who make the law,   35
who enforce the law,
who live behind
and operate through
and feed themselves
at the expense of   40
starving children
because of the law.

Men who sit in panelled offices
and think about vacations
and tell women   45
whose care it is
to feed children
not to be hysterical
not to be hysterical as in the word
hysterikos, the greek for   50
womb suffering,
not to suffer in their
wombs,
not to care,
not to bother the men   55
because they want to think
of other things
and do not want
to take the women seriously.
I want them   60
to take women seriously.

I want them to think about Harriet Tubman,
and remember,
remember she was beat by a white man
and she lived   65
and she lived to redress her grievances,
and she lived in swamps
and wore the clothes of a man
bringing hundreds of fugitives from
slavery, and was never caught,   70

and led an army,
and won a battle,
and defied the laws
because the laws were wrong, I want men
to take us seriously.   75
I am tired wanting them to think
about right and wrong.
I want them to fear.
I want them to feel fear now
as I have felt suffering in the womb, and   80
I want them
to know
that there is always a time
there is always a time to make right
what is wrong,   85
there is always a time
for retribution
and that time
is beginning.

IN THE GARDEN OF THE HOME GOD
from the Navaho
I

The sacred blue corn-seed I am planting,
In one night it will grow and flourish,
In one night the corn increases,
In the garden of the Home God.

The sacred white corn-seed I am planting,   5
In one day it will grow and ripen,
In one day the corn increases,
In its beauty it increases.

II

With this it grows, with this it grows,
The dark cloud, with this it grows.   10
The dew thereof, with this it grows,
The blue corn, with this it grows.

III

This it eats, this it eats,
The dark cloud,
Its dew   15
The blue corn eats,
This it eats.

This it eats, this it eats,
The dark mist,
Its dew   20
The white corn eats,
This it eats.

IV

The great corn plant is with the bean,
Its rootlets now are with the bean,
Its leaf tips now are with the bean,   25
Its dewdrops now are with the bean,
Its tassel now is with the bean,
Its pollen now is with the bean,
And now its silk is with the bean,
And now its grain is with the bean.   30

The great true plant is with the bean,
Its rootlets now are with the bean,
Its leaf tips now are with the bean,
Its dewdrops now are with the bean,
Its tassel now is with the bean,   35
Its pollen now is with the bean,
And now its silk is with the bean,
And now its grain is with the bean.

V

Truly in the East
The white bean   40
And the great corn plant
Are tied with the white lightning.
Listen! It approaches! [It = rain]
The voice of the bluebird is heard.

Truly in the East   45
The white bean
And the great squash
Are tied with the rainbow.
Listen! It approaches!
The voice of the bluebird is heard.   50

VI

On your farm the cloud is level with the corn,
On your farm the cloud is level with the corn,
On your farm the mist is level with the plant,
On your farm the mist is level with the pollen.

VII

From the East, 55
Through the middle of your field,
Your corn moves. It walks.

From the West,
Through the middle of your field,
Your corn moves. It walks. 60

VIII

The corn grows up.
The waters of the dark clouds drop, drop.
The rain descends.
The waters from the corn leaves drop, drop.
The rain descends. 65
The waters from the plants drop, drop.
The corn grows up.
The waters of the dark mists drop, drop.

IX

From the top of the great corn plant the water gurgles,
I hear it; 70
Around the roots the water foams, I hear it;
Around the roots of the plants it foams, I hear it;
From their tops the water foams, I hear it.

X

Shall I cull this fruit
Of the great corn plant? 75
Shall you break it? Shall I break it?
Shall I break it? Shall you break it?
Shall I? Shall you?

Shall I cull this fruit
Of the great squash vine? 80
Shall you pick it up? Shall I pick it up?
Shall I pick it up? Shall you pick it up?
Shall I? Shall You?

XI

I pulled it with my hand.
The great corn plant I scatter around.   85
I pulled it with my hand.
The standing plants are scattered around.

XII

Since the ancient days, I have planted,
Since the time of the emergence, I have planted,
The great corn plant, I have planted,   90
Its roots, I have planted,
The tips of its leaves, I have planted,
Its dew, I have planted,
Its tassel, I have planted,
Its pollen, I have planted,   95
Its silk, I have planted,
Its seed, I have planted.

Since the ancient days, I have planted,
Since the time of the emergence, I have planted,
The great squash vine, I have planted,   100
Its seed, I have planted,
Its silk, I have planted,
Its pollen, I have planted,
Its tassel, I have planted,
Its dew, I have planted,   105
The tips of its leaves, I have planted,
Its roots, I have planted.

EARTH AND I GAVE YOU TURQUOISE

N. Scott Momaday

(b. 1934)

Biography p. 1089

Earth and I gave you turquoise
when you walked singing
We lived laughing in my house
and told old stories
You grew ill when the owl cried   5
We will meet on Black Mountain

I will bring corn for planting
     and we will make fire
Children will come to your breast
     You will heal my heart   10
I speak your name many times
The wild cane remembers you

My young brother's house is filled
     I go there to sing
We have not spoken of you   15
     but our songs are sad
When Moon Woman goes to you
I will follow her white way

Tonight they dance near Chinle
     by the seven elms   20
There your loom whispered beauty
     They will eat mutton
and drink coffee till morning
You and I will not be there

I saw a crow by Red Rock   25
     standing on one leg
It was the black of your hair
     The years are heavy
I will ride the swiftest horse
You will hear the drumming hooves   30

I AM JOAQUÍN

Rodolfo Gonzales

(b. 1928)

Biography p. 1075

I am Joaquín,
lost in a world of confusion,
caught up in the whirl of a
     gringo society,
confused by the rules,   5
scorned by attitudes,
suppressed by manipulation,
and destroyed by modern society.

My fathers
    have lost the economic battle   10
and won
    the struggle of cultural survival.

And now!
    I must choose
              between   15
    the paradox of
victory of the spirit,
despite physical hunger,
        or
to exist in the grasp   20
of American social neurosis,
sterilization of the soul
    and a full stomach.

Yes,
I have come a long way to nowhere,   25
unwillingly dragged by that
    monstrous, technical,
    industrial giant called
        Progress
and Anglo success. . . .   30

    I look at myself.
     I watch my brothers.
      I shed tears of sorrow.
      I sow seeds of hate.
     I withdraw to the safety within the   35
circle of life—
               MY OWN PEOPLE.

stupid america

Abelardo Delgado

(b. 1931)

Biography p. 1069

stupid america, see that chicano
with a big knife
in his steady hand
he doesn't want to knife you

he wants to sit on a bench 5
and carve christ figures
but you won't let him.
stupid america, hear that chicano
shouting curses on the street
he is a poet 10
without paper and pencil
and since he cannot write
he will explode.
stupid america, remember that chicanito
flunking math and english 15
he is the picasso
of your western states
but he will die
with one thousand masterpieces
hanging only from his mind. 20

AN ELEMENTARY SCHOOL CLASSROOM IN A SLUM

Stephen Spender

(b. 1909)

Biography p. 1102

Far far from gusty waves these children's faces.
Like rootless weeds, the hair torn round their pallor.
The tall girl with her weighed-down head. The paper-
seeming boy, with rat's eyes. The stunted, unlucky heir
Of twisted bones, reciting a father's gnarled disease, 5
His lesson from his desk. At back of the dim class
One unnoted, sweet and young. His eyes live in a dream
Of squirrel's game, in tree room, other than this.

On sour cream walls, donations. Shakespeare's head,
Cloudless at dawn, civilized dome riding all cities. 10
Belled, flowery, Tyrolese valley. Open-handed map
Awarding the world its world. And yet, for these
Children, these windows, not this world, are world,
Where all their future's painted with a fog,
A narrow street sealed in with a lead sky, 15
Far far from rivers, capes, and stars of words.

Surely, Shakespeare is wicked, the map a bad example
With ships and sun and love tempting them to steal—
For lives that slyly turn in their cramped holes
From fog to endless night? On their slag heap, these children   20
Wear skins peeped through by bones and spectacles of steel
With mended glass, like bottle bits on stones.
All of their time and space are foggy slum.
So blot their maps with slums as big as doom.

Unless, governor, teacher, inspector, visitor,   25
This map becomes their window and these windows
That shut upon their lives like catacombs,
Break O break open till they break the town
And show the children to green fields, and make their world
Run azure on gold sands, and let their tongues   30
Run naked into books, the white and green leaves open
History theirs whose language is the sun.

THE UNKNOWN CITIZEN

W. H. Auden

(1907–1973)

Biography p. 1060

*(To JS/07/M/378
This Marble Monument
Is Erected by the State)*

He was found by the Bureau of Statistics to be
One against whom there was no official complaint,
And all the reports on his conduct agree
That, in the modern sense of an old-fashioned word, he was a saint,
For in everything he did he served the Greater Community.   5
Except for the War till the day he retired
He worked in a factory and never got fired,
But satisfied his employers, Fudge Motors Inc.
Yet he wasn't a scab or odd in his views,
For his Union reports that he paid his dues,   10
(Our report on his Union shows it was sound)
And our Social Psychology workers found
That he was popular with his mates and liked a drink.
The Press are convinced that he bought a paper every day
And that his reactions to advertisements were normal in every way.   15
Policies taken out in his name prove that he was fully insured,
And his Health-card shows he was once in hospital but left it cured.

Both Producers Research and High-Grade Living declare
He was fully sensible to the advantages of the Instalment Plan
And had everything necessary to the Modern Man,   20
A phonograph, a radio, a car and a frigidaire.
Our researchers into Public Opinion are content
That he held the proper opinions for the time of year;
When there was peace, he was for peace; when there was war, he went.
He was married and added five children to the population,   25
Which our Eugenist says was the right number for a parent of his generation,
And our teachers report that he never interfered with their education.
Was he free? Was he happy? The question is absurd:
Had anything been wrong, we should certainly have heard.

THE AUTHOR TO HER BOOK

Anne Bradstreet

(1612–1672)

Biography p. 1063

Thou ill-formed offspring of my feeble brain,
Who after birth did'st by my side remain,
Till snatched from thence by friends, less wise than true,
Who thee abroad exposed to public view;
Made thee in rags, halting, to the press to trudge,   5
Where errors were not lessened, all may judge.
At thy return my blushing was not small,
My rambling brat (in print) should mother call;
I cast thee by as one unfit for light,
Thy visage was so irksome in my sight;   10
Yet being mine own, at length affection would
Thy blemishes amend, if so I could:
I washed thy face, but more defects I saw,
And rubbing off a spot, still made a flaw.
I stretched thy joints to make thee even feet,   15
Yet still thou run'st more hobbling than is meet;
In better dress to trim thee was my mind,
But nought save homespun cloth, in the house I find.
In this array, 'mongst vulgars may'st thou roam;
In criticks hands beware thou dost not come;   20
And take thy way where yet thou are not known.
If for thy Father asked, say thou had'st none;
And for thy Mother, she alas is poor,
Which caused her thus to send thee out of door.

EASTER WINGS

George Herbert

(1593–1633)

Biography p. 1077

Lord, who createdst man in wealth and store,
    Though foolishly he lost the same,
        Decaying more and more,
           Till he became
             Most poore: 5
             With thee
           O let me rise
        As larks, harmoniously,
    And sing this day thy victories:
Then shall the fall further the flight in me.   10

My tender age in sorrow did beginne:
And still with sicknesses and shame
    Thou didst so punish sinne,
        That I became
           Most thinne.   15
           With thee
        Let me combine
    And feel this day thy victorie:
For, if I imp my wing on thine,
Affliction shall advance the flight in me.   20

TO BE OF USE

Marge Piercy

(b. 1936)

Biography p. 1092

The people I love the best
jump into work head first
without dallying in the shallows
and swim off with sure strokes almost out of sight.
They seem to become natives of that element,   5

the black sleek heads of seals
bouncing like half-submerged balls.

I love people who harness themselves, an ox to a heavy cart,
who pull like water buffalo, with massive patience,
who strain in the mud and the muck to move things forward,   10
who do what has to be done, again and again.

I want to be with people who submerge
in the task, who go into the fields to harvest
and work in a row and pass the bags along,
who stand in the line and haul in their places,   15
who are not parlor generals and field deserters
but move in a common rhythm
when the food must come in or the fire be put out.

The work of the world is common as mud.
Botched, it smears the hands, crumbles to dust.   20
But the thing worth doing well done
has a shape that satisfies, clean and evident.
Greek amphoras for wine or oil,
Hopi vases that held corn, are put in museums
but you know they were made to be used.   25
The pitcher cries for water to carry
and a person for work that is real.

MUSHROOMS

Sylvia Plath

(1932–1963)

Biography p. 1092

Overnight, very
Whitely, discreetly,
Very quietly

Our toes, our noses
Take hold on the loam,   5
Acquire the air.

Nobody sees us,
Stops us, betrays us;
The small grains make room.

Soft fists insist on   10
Heaving the needles,
The leafy bedding,

Even the paving.
Our hammers, our rams,
Earless and eyeless,   15

Perfectly voiceless,
Widen the crannies,
Shoulder through holes. We

Diet on water,
On crumbs of shadow,   20
Bland-mannered, asking

Little or nothing.
So many of us!
So many of us!

We are shelves, we are   25
Tables, we are meek,
We are edible,

Nudgers and shovers
In spite of ourselves.
Our kind multiplies: 30

We shall by morning
Inherit the earth.
Our foot's in the door.

MIND

Richard Wilbur

(b. 1921)

Biography p. 1107

Mind in its purest play is like some bat
That beats about in caverns all alone,
Contriving by a kind of senseless wit
Not to conclude against a wall of stone.

It has no need to falter or explore;   5
Darkly it knows what obstacles are there,
And so may weave and flitter, dip and soar
In perfect courses through the blackest air.

And has this simile a like perfection?
The mind is like a bat. Precisely. Save   10
That in the very happiest intellection
A graceful error may correct the cave.

THE SECOND COMING

William Butler Yeats

(1865–1939)

Biography p. 1109

Turning and turning in the widening gyre
The falcon cannot hear the falconer;
Things fall apart; the centre cannot hold;
Mere anarchy is loosed upon the world,
The blood-dimmed tide is loosed, and everywhere   5
The ceremony of innocence is drowned;
The best lack all conviction, while the worst
Are full of passionate intensity.

Surely some revelation is at hand;
Surely the Second Coming is at hand.   10
The Second Coming! Hardly are those words out
When a vast image out of *Spiritus Mundi*
Troubles my sight: somewhere in sands of the desert
A shape with lion body and the head of a man,
A gaze blank and pitiless as the sun,   15
Is moving its slow thighs, while all about it
Reel shadows of the indignant desert birds.
The darkness drops again; but now I know
That twenty centuries of stony sleep
Were vexed to nightmare by a rocking cradle,   20
And what rough beast, its hour come round at last,
Slouches towards Bethlehem to be born?

Oration

I HAVE A DREAM

Martin Luther King, Jr.
(1929–1968)

Biography p. 1081

I say to you today, my friends, that in spite of the difficulties and frustrations of the moment I still have a dream. It is a dream deeply rooted in the American dream.

I have a dream that one day this nation will rise up and live out the true meaning of its creed: "We hold these truths to be self-evident; that all men are created equal."

I have a dream that one day on the red hills of Georgia the sons of former slaves and the sons of former slaveowners will be able to sit down together at the table of brotherhood.

I have a dream that one day even the state of Mississippi, a desert state sweltering with the heat of injustice and oppression, will be transformed into an oasis of freedom and justice.

I have a dream that my four little children will one day live in a nation   5
where they will not be judged by the color of their skin but by the content of their character.

I have a dream today.

I have a dream that one day the state of Alabama, whose governor's lips are presently dripping with the words of interposition and nullification, will be transformed into a situation where little black boys and black girls will be able to join hands with little white boys and white girls and walk together as sisters and brothers.

I have a dream today.

I have a dream that one day every valley shall be exalted, every hill and mountain shall be made low, the rough places will be made plain, and the crooked places will be made straight, and the glory of the Lord shall be revealed, and all flesh shall see it together.

This is our hope. This is the faith with which I return to the South. With   10
this faith we will be able to hew out of the mountain of despair a stone of hope. With this faith we will be able to transform the jangling discords of our nation into a beautiful symphony of brotherhood. With this faith we will be able to work together, to pray together, to struggle together, to go to jail together, to stand up for freedom together, knowing that we will be free one day.

This will be the day when all of God's children will be able to sing with new meaning

My country, 'tis of thee
Sweet land of liberty,
   Of thee I sing:
Land where my fathers died,   15
Land of the pilgrims' pride
From every mountain-side
   Let freedom ring.

And if America is to be a great nation this must become true. So let freedom ring from the prodigious hilltops of New Hampshire. Let freedom ring from the mighty mountains of New York. Let freedom ring from the heightening Alleghenies of Pennsylvania!

Let freedom ring from the snowcapped Rockies of Colorado!   20

Let freedom ring from the curvacious peaks of California!

But not only that; let freedom ring from Stone Mountain of Georgia!

Let freedom ring from Lookout Mountain of Tennessee!

Let freedom ring from every hill and molehill of Mississippi. From every mountainside, let freedom ring.

When we let freedom ring, when we let it ring from every village and   25
every hamlet, from every state and every city, we will be able to speed up that day when all of God's children, black men and white men, Jews and Gentiles, Protestants and Catholics, will be able to join hands and sing in the words of the old Negro spiritual, "Free at last! free at last! thank God almighty, we are free at last!"

Drama

FOR COLORED GIRLS WHO HAVE CONSIDERED SUICIDE WHEN THE RAINBOW IS ENUF

Ntozake Shange
(b. 1948)

Biography p. 1099

The stage is in darkness. Harsh music is heard as dim blue lights come up. One after another, seven women run onto the stage from each of the exits. They all freeze in postures of distress. The follow spot picks up the lady in brown. She comes to life and looks around at the other ladies. All of the others are still. She walks over to the lady in red and calls to her. The lady in red makes no response.

  lady in brown
dark phrases of womanhood
of never havin been a girl
half-notes scattered
without rhythm/ no tune
distraught laughter fallin
over a black girl's shoulder
it's funny/ it's hysterical
the melody-less-ness of her dance
don't tell nobody don't tell a soul
she's dancin on beer cans & shingles

this must be the spook house
another song with no singers
lyrics/ no voices
& interrupted solos
unseen performances

are we ghouls?
children of horror?
the joke?

don't tell nobody don't tell a soul
are we animals? have we gone crazy?

i can't hear anythin
but maddening screams
& the soft strains of death
& you promised me
you promised me . . .
somebody/ anybody
sing a black girl's song
bring her out
to know herself
to know you
but sing her rhythms
carin/ struggle/ hard times
sing her song of life
she's been dead so long
closed in silence so long
she doesn't know the sound
of her own voice
her infinite beauty
she's half-notes scattered
without rhythm/ no tune
sing her sighs
sing the song of her possibilities
sing a righteous gospel
the makin of a melody
let her be born
let her be born
& handled warmly.

    lady in brown
i'm outside chicago

    lady in yellow
i'm outside detroit

    lady in purple
i'm outside houston

    lady in red
i'm outside baltimore

    lady in green
i'm outside san francisco

lady in blue
i'm outside manhattan

lady in orange
i'm outside st. louis

lady in brown
& this is for colored girls who have considered suicide
but moved to the ends of their own rainbows.

everyone
mama's little baby likes shortnin, shortnin,
mama's little baby likes shortnin bread
mama's little baby likes shortnin, shortnin,
mama's little baby likes shortnin bread

little sally walker, sittin in a saucer
rise, sally, rise, wipe your weepin eyes
an put your hands on your hips
an let your backbone slip
o, shake it to the east
o, shake it to the west
shake it to the one
that you like the best

lady in purple
you're it

*As the lady in brown tags each of
the other ladies they freeze. When
each one has been tagged the
lady in brown freezes.
Immediately "Dancing in the
Streets" by Martha and the
Vandellas is heard. All of the
ladies start to dance. The lady in
green, the lady in blue, and the
lady in yellow do the pony, the
big boss line, the swim, and the
nose dive. The other ladies dance
in place.*

lady in yellow
it was graduation nite & i waz the only virgin in the crowd
bobby mills martin jerome & sammy yates eddie jones & randi
all cousins
all the prettiest niggers in this factory town
carried me out wit em

in a deep black buick
smellin of thunderbird & ladies in heat
we rambled from camden to mount holly
laughin at the afternoon's speeches
& danglin our tassles from the rear view mirror
climbin different sorta project stairs
movin toward snappin beer cans &
GET IT GET IT THAT'S THE WAY TO DO IT MAMA
all mercer county graduated the same nite
          cosmetology secretarial pre-college autoshop & business
all us movin from mama to what ever waz out there

that nite we raced a big ol truck from the barbeque stand
trying to tell him bout the party at jacqui's
where folks graduated last year waz waitin to hit it wid us
i got drunk & cdnt figure out
whose hand waz on my thigh/ but it didn't matter
cuz these cousins martin eddie sammy jerome & bobby
waz my sweethearts alternately since the seventh grade
& everybody knew i always started cryin if somebody actually
tried to take advantage of me
          at jacqui's
ulinda mason was stickin her mouth all out
while we tumbled out the buick
eddie jones waz her lickin stick
but i knew how to dance
          it got soo hot
vincent ramos puked all in the punch
& harly jumped all in tico's face
cuz he was leavin for the navy in the mornin
hadda kick ass so we'd all remember how bad he waz
seems like sheila & marguerite waz fraid
to get their hair turnin back
so they laid up against the wall
lookin almost sexy
didnt wanna sweat
but me & my fellas   we waz dancin

since 1963 i'd won all kinda contests
wid the cousins at the POLICE ATHLETIC LEAGUE DANCES
all mercer county knew
any kin to martin yates cd turn somersaults
fore smokey robinson cd get a woman excited

The Dells singing "Stay" is heard

we danced   doin nasty ol tricks

*The lady in yellow sings along
with the Dells for a moment. The
lady in orange and the lady in
blue jump up and parody the
lady in yellow and the Dells. The
lady in yellow stares at them.
They sit down.*

doin nasty ol tricks i'd been thinkin since may
cuz graduation nite had to be hot
& i waz the only virgin
so i hadda make like my hips waz inta some business
that way everybody thot whoever was gettin it
was a older man cdnt run the streets wit youngsters
martin slipped his leg round my thigh
the dells bumped "stay"
up & down—up & down the new carver homes
WE WAZ GROWN   WE WAZ FINALLY GROWN

ulinda alla sudden went crazy
went over to eddie cursin & carryin on
tearin his skin wid her nails
the cousins tried to talk sense to her
tried to hold her arms
lissin bitch sammy went on
bobby whispered i shd go wit him
fore they go ta cuttin
fore the police arrived
we teetered silently thru the parkin lot
no un uhuh
we didn't know nothin bout no party
bobby started lookin at me
yeah
he started looking at me real strange
like i waz a woman or somethin/
started talkin real soft
in the backseat of that ol buick
WOW
by daybreak
i just cdnt stop grinnin.

*The Dells singing "Stay" comes
in and all of the ladies except the
lady in blue join in and sing
along.*

    lady in blue
you gave it up in a buick?

lady in yellow
yeh, and honey, it was wonderful.

lady in green
we used to do it all up in the dark
in the corners . . .

lady in blue
some niggah sweating all over you.

lady in red
it was good!

lady in blue
i never did like to grind.

lady in yellow
what other kind of dances are there?

lady in blue
mambo, bomba, merengue

when i waz sixteen i ran off to the south bronx
cuz i waz gonna meet up wit willie colon
& dance all the time
                            mamba bomba merengue
lady in yellow
do you speak spanish?

lady in blue
olà
my papa thot he was puerto rican & we wda been
cept we waz just reglar niggahs wit hints of spanish
so off i made it to this 36 hour marathon dance
con salsa con ricardo
'suggggggggggar' ray on southern blvd
next door to this fotografi place
jammed wit burial weddin & communion relics
next door to la real ideal genuine spanish barber
                up up up up up stairs & stairs & lotsa hallway
wit my colored new jersey self
didn't know what anybody waz saying
cept if dancin waz proof of origin
        i was jibarita herself that nite
& the next day
i kept smilin & right on steppin
if he cd lead i waz ready to dance

if he cdnt lead
i caught this attitude
          i'd seen rosa do
& wd not be bothered
i waz twirlin hippin givin much quik feet
& bein a mute cute colored puerto rican
til saturday afternoon when the disc-jockey say
'SORRY FOLKS WILLIE COLON AINT GONNA MAKE IT TODAY'
& alla my niggah temper came outta control
& i wdnt dance wit nobody
& i talked english loud
& i love you more than i waz mad
uh huh uh huh
more than more than
when i discovered archie shepp & subtle blues
doncha know i wore out the magic of juju
heroically resistin being possessed
oooooooooooooh the sounds
sneakin in under age to slug's
to stare ata real 'artiste'
& every word outta imamu's mouth waz gospel
& if jesus cdnt play a horn like shepp
waznt no need for colored folks to bear no cross at all

& poem is my thank-you for music
& i love you more than poem
more than aureliano buendia loved macondo
more than hector lavoe loved himself
more than the lady loved gardenias
more than celia loves cuba or graciela loves el son
more than the flamingoes shoo-do-n-doo-wah love bein pretty
oyè négro
te amo mas que   te amo mas que
when you play
yr flute

     everyone (very softly)
te amo mas que   te amo mas que

     lady in red
without any assistance or guidance from you
i have loved you assiduously for 8 months 2 wks & a day
i have been stood up four times
i've left 7 packages on yr doorstep
forty poems 2 plants & 3 handmade notecards i left
town so i cd send to you have been no help to me
on my job

you call at 3:00 in the mornin on weekdays
so i cd drive 27 ½ miles cross the bay before i go to work
charmin charmin
but you are of no assistance
i want you to know
this waz an experiment
to see how selfish i cd be
if i wd really carry on to snare a possible lover
if i waz capable of debasin my self for the love of another
if i cd stand not being wanted
when i wanted to be wanted
& i cannot
so
with no further assistance & no guidance from you
i am endin this affair

this note is attached to a plant
i've been waterin since the day i met you
you may water it
yr damn self

    lady in orange
i dont wanna write
in english or spanish
i wanna sing   make you dance
like the bata   dance   scream
twitch hips wit me cuz
i done forgot all abt words
aint got no definitions
i wanna whirl
             with you

                             Music starts, "Che Che Cole" by
                             Willie Colon.
                             Everyone starts to dance.

our whole body
wrapped like a ripe mango
ramblin whippin thru space
on the corner in the park
where the rug useta be
let willie colon take you out
swing your head
push your leg to the moon with me

i'm on the lower east side
in new york city
and i can't   i can't
talk witchu no more

lady in yellow
we gotta dance to keep from cryin

lady in brown
we gotta dance to keep from dyin

lady in red
so come on

lady in brown
come on

lady in purple
come on

lady in orange
hold yr head like it was ruby sapphire
i'm a poet
who writes in english
come to share the worlds witchu

everyone
come to share our worlds witchu
we come here to be dancin
          to be dancin
        to be dancin
      baya

> *There is a sudden light change,*
> *all of the ladies react as if they*
> *had been struck in the face. The*
> *lady in green and the lady in*
> *yellow run out up left, the lady in*
> *orange runs out stage left, the*
> *lady in brown runs out up right.*

lady in blue
a friend is hard to press charges against

lady in red
if you know him
you must have wanted it

lady in purple
a misunderstanding

lady in red
you know
these things happen

lady in blue
are you sure
you didnt suggest

lady in purple
had you been drinkin

lady in red
a rapist is always to be a stranger
to be legitimate
someone you never saw
a man wit obvious problems

lady in purple
pin-ups attached to the insides of his lapels

lady in blue
ticket stubs from porno flicks in his pocket

lady in purple
a lil dick

lady in red
or a strong mother

lady in blue
or just a brutal virgin

lady in red
but if you've been seen in public wit him
danced one dance
kissed him good-bye lightly

lady in purple
wit closed mouth

lady in blue
pressin charges will be as hard
as keepin yr legs closed
while five fools try to run a train on you

lady in red
these men friends of ours

who smile nice
stay employed
and take us out to dinner

   lady in purple
lock the door behind you

   lady in blue
wit fist in face
to fuck

   lady in red
who make elaborate mediterranean dinners
& let the art ensemble carry all ethical burdens
while they invite a coupla friends over to have you
are sufferin from latent rapist bravado
& we are left wit the scars

   lady in blue
bein betrayed by men who know us

   lady in purple
& expect
like the stranger
we always thot waz comin

   lady in blue
that we will submit

   lady in purple
we must have known

   lady in red
women relinquish all personal rights
in the presence of a man
who apparently cd be considered a rapist

   lady in purple
especially if he has been considered a friend

   lady in blue
& is no less worthy of bein beat witin an inch of his life
bein publicly ridiculed
havin two fists shoved up his ass

   lady in red
than the stranger
we always thot it wd be

lady in blue
who never showed up

lady in red
cuz it turns out the nature of rape has changed

lady in blue
we can now meet them in circles we frequent for companionship

lady in purple
we see them at the coffeehouse

lady in blue
wit someone else we know

lady in red
we cd even have em over for dinner
& get raped in our own houses
by invitation
a friend

*The lights change, and the ladies
are all hit by an imaginary slap,
the lady in red runs off up left.*

lady in blue
eyes

lady in purple
mice

lady in blue
womb

lady in blue & lady in purple
nobody

The lady in purple exits up right.

lady in blue
tubes tables white washed windows
grime from age wiped over once
legs spread
anxious
eyes crawling up on me
eyes rollin in my thighs
metal horses gnawin my womb

dead mice fall from my mouth
i really didnt mean to
i really didnt think i cd
just one day off . . .
get offa me alla this blood
bones shattered like soft ice-cream cones

i cdnt have people
lookin at me
pregnant
i cdnt have my friends see this
dyin danglin tween my legs
& i didnt say a thing
not a sigh
or a fast scream
to get
those eyes offa me
get them steel rods outta me
this hurts
this hurts me
& nobody came
cuz nobody knew
once i waz pregnant & shamed of myself.

> *The lady in blue exits stage left.*
>
> *Soft deep music is heard, voices calling "Sechita" come from the wings. The lady in purple enters from up right.*

    lady in purple
once there were quadroon balls/ elegance in st. louis/ laced
mulattoes/ gamblin down the mississippi/ to memphis/ new
orleans n okra crepes near the bayou/ where the pool white trash
wd sing/ moanin/ strange/ liquid tones/ thru the swamps/

> *The lady in green enters from stage right; she is Sechita and for the rest of the poem dances out Sechita's life.*

sechita had heard these things/ she moved
as if she'd known them/ the silver n high-toned laughin/
the violins n marble floors/ sechita pushed the clingin
delta dust wit painted toes/ the patch-work tent waz
poka-dotted/ stale lights snatched at the shadows/ creole
carnival waz playin natchez in ten minutes/ her splendid
red garters/ gin-stained n itchy on her thigh/ blk-diamond

stockings darned wit yellow threads/ an ol starched taffeta
can-can fell abundantly orange/ from her waist round the
splinterin chair/ sechita/ egyptian/ goddess of creativity/
2nd millennium/ threw her heavy hair in a coil over her neck/
sechita/ goddess/ the recordin of history/ spread crimson oil
on her cheeks/ waxed her eyebrows/ n unconsciously slugged
the last hard whiskey in the glass/ the broken mirror she
used to decorate her face/ made her forehead tilt backwards/
her cheeks appear sunken/ her sassy chin only large enuf/
to keep her full lower lip/ from growin into her neck/ sechita/
had learned to make allowances for the distortions/
but the heavy dust of the delta/ left a tinge of grit n
darkness/ on every one of her dresses/ on her arms & her
shoulders/ sechita/ waz anxious to get back to st. louis/
the dirt there didnt crawl from the earth into yr soul/
at least/ in st. louis/ the grime waz store bought
second-hand/ here in natchez/ god seemed to be wipin his
feet in her face/

one of the wrestlers had finally won
tonite/ the mulatto/ raul/ was sposed to hold the boomin
half-caste/ searin eagle/ in a bear hug/ 8 counts/ get
thrown unawares/ fall out the ring/ n then do searin eagle
in for good/ sechita/ cd hear redneck whoops n slappin on
the back/ she gathered her sparsely sequined skirts/ tugged
the waist cincher from under her greyin slips/ n made her face
immobile/ she made her face like nefertiti/ approachin her
own tomb/ she suddenly threw/ her leg full-force/ thru the
canvas curtain/ a deceptive glass stone/ sparkled/ malignant
on her ankle/ her calf waz tauntin in the brazen carnie
lights/ the full moon/ sechita/ goddess/ of love/ egypt/
2nd millennium/ performin the rites/ the conjurin of men/
conjurin the spirit/ in natchez/ the mississippi spewed
a heavy fume of barely movin waters/ sechita's legs slashed
furiously thru the cracker nite/ & gold pieces hittin the
makeshift stage/ her thighs/ they were aimin coins tween her
thighs/ sechita/ egypt/ goddess/ harmony/ kicked viciously
thru the nite/ catchin stars tween her toes.

> *The lady in green exits stage left,*
> *the lady in purple exits into up*
> *stage left.*
>
> *The lady in brown enters from up*
> *stage right.*

    lady in brown
de library waz right down from de trolly tracks

cross from de laundry-mat
thru de big shinin floors & granite pillars
ol st. louis is famous for
i found toussaint
but not til after months uv
cajun katie/ pippi longstockin
christopher robin/ eddie heyward & a pooh bear
in the children's room
only pioneer girls & magic rabbits
& big city white boys
i knew i waznt sposedta
but i ran inta the ADULT READING ROOM
        & came across
          TOUSSAINT
          my first blk man
(i never counted george washington carver
cuz i didnt like peanuts)
            still
TOUSSAINT waz a blk man a negro like my mama say
who refused to be a slave
& he spoke french
& didnt low no white man to tell him nothin
         not napolean
         not maximillien
         not robespierre
TOUSSAINT L'OUVERTURE
waz the beginnin uv reality for me
in the summer contest for
who colored child can read
15 books in three weeks
i won & raved abt TOUSSAINT L'OUVERTURE
at the afternoon ceremony
waz disqualified
         cuz Toussaint
          belonged in the ADULT READING ROOM
           & i cried
& carried dead Toussaint home in the book
he waz dead & livin to me
cuz TOUSSAINT & them
they held the citadel gainst the french
wid the spirits of ol dead africans from outta the ground
TOUSSAINT led they army of zombies
walkin cannon ball shootin spirits to free Haiti
& they waznt slaves no more
           TOUSSAINT L'OUVERTURE
became my secret lover at the age of 8
i entertained him in my bedroom

widda flashlight under my covers
way inta the night/ we discussed strategies
how to remove white girls from my hopscotch games
& etc.
TOUSSAINT
waz layin in bed wit me next to raggedy ann
the night i decided to run away from my
               integrated home
                   integrated street
                     integrated school
1955 waz not a good year for lil blk girls

Toussaint said 'lets go to haiti'
i said 'awright'
& packed some very important things in a brown paper bag
so i wdnt haveta come back
then Toussaint & i took the hodiamont streetcar
to the river
last stop
only 15¢
cuz there waznt nobody cd see Toussaint cept me
& we walked all down thru north st. louis
where the french settlers usedta live
in tiny brick houses all huddled together
wit barely missin windows & shingles uneven
wit colored kids playin & women on low porches sippin beer

i cd talk to Toussaint down by the river
like this waz where we waz gonna stow away
on a boat for new orleans
& catch a creole fishin-rig for port-au-prince
then we waz just gonna read & talk all the time
& eat fried bananas
                  we waz just walkin & skippin past ol drunk men
when dis ol young boy jumped out at me sayin
'HEY GIRL YA BETTAH COME OVAH HEAH N TALK TO ME'
well
i turned to TOUSSAINT (who waz furious)
& i shouted
'ya silly ol boy
ya bettah leave me alone
or TOUSSAINT'S gonna get yr ass'
de silly ol boy came round de corner laughin all in my face
'yellah gal
ya sure must be somebody to know my name so quick'
i waz disgusted
& wanted to get on to haiti

widout some tacky ol boy botherin me
still he kept standin there
kickin milk cartons & bits of brick
tryin to get all in my business
                        i mumbled to L'OUVERTURE 'what shd I do'
finally
i asked this silly ol boy
'WELL WHO ARE YOU?'
he say
'MY NAME IS TOUSSAINT JONES'
well
i looked right at him
those skidded out cordoroy pants
a striped teashirt wid holes in both elbows
a new scab over his left eye
& i said
                        'what's yr name again'
he say
'i'm toussaint jones'
'wow
i am on my way to see
TOUSSAINT L'OUVERTURE in HAITI
are ya any kin to him
he dont take no stuff from no white folks
& they gotta country all they own
& there aint no slaves'
that silly ol boy squinted his face all up
'looka heah girl
i am TOUSSAINT JONES
& i'm right heah lookin at ya
& i dont take no stuff from no white folks
ya dont see none round heah do ya?'
& he sorta pushed out his chest
then he say
'come on   lets go on down to the docks
& look at the boats'
i waz real puzzled goin down to the docks
wit my paper bag & my books
i felt TOUSSAINT L'OUVERTURE sorta leave me
& i waz sad
til i realized
TOUSSAINT JONES waznt too different
from TOUSSAINT L'OUVERTURE
cept the ol one waz in haiti
& this one wid me speakin english & eatin apples
yeah.
toussaint jones waz awright wit me

no tellin what all spirits we cd move
down by the river
st. louis 1955   hey wait.

> *The lady in brown exits stage*
> *right.*
>
> *The lady in red enters from stage*
> *left.*

  lady in red
orange butterflies & aqua sequins
ensconsed tween slight bosoms
silk roses dartin from behind her ears
the passion flower of southwest los angeles
meandered down hoover street
past dark shuttered houses where
women from louisiana shelled peas
round 3:00 & sent their sons
whistlin to the store for fatback & black-eyed peas
she glittered in heat
& seemed to be lookin for rides
when she waznt & absolutely
eyed every man who waznt lame white or noddin out
she let her thigh slip from her skirt
crossin the street
she slowed to be examined
& she never looked back to smile
or acknowledge a sincere 'hey mama'
or to meet the eyes of someone
purposely findin sometin to do in
her direction
                she waz sullen
                & the rhinestones etchin the corners of her mouth
                suggested tears
                fresh kisses that had done no good
she always wore her stomach out
lined with small iridescent feathers
the hairs round her navel seemed to dance
& she didnt let on
she knew
from behind her waist waz aching to be held
the pastel ivy drawn on her shoulders
to be brushed with lips & fingers
smellin of honey & jack daniels
                she waz hot
                a deliberate coquette
                who never did without

what she wanted
& she wanted to be unforgettable
she wanted to be a memory
a wound   to every man
arragant enough to want her
            she waz the wrath
                of women in windows
                    fingerin shades/ ol lace curtains
                        camoflagin despair &
                            stretch marks
so she glittered honestly
delighted she waz desired
& allowed those especially
schemin/ tactful suitors
to experience her body & spirit
tearin/ so easily blendin with theirs/
& they were so happy
& lay on her lime sheets full & wet
from her tongue   she kissed
them reverently   even ankles
edges of beards . . .

The stage goes to darkness except
for a special on the lady in red,
who lies motionless on the floor;
as the lights slowly fade up the
lady in red sits up.

at 4:30 AM
she rose
movin the arms & legs that trapped her
she sighed affirmin the sculptured man
& made herself a bath
of dark musk oil egyptian crystals
& florida water to remove his smell
to wash away the glitter
to watch the butterflies melt into
suds & the rhinestones fall beneath
her buttocks like smooth pebbles
in a missouri creek
layin in water
she became herself
ordinary
brown braided woman
with big legs & full lips
reglar
seriously intendin to finish her
night's work

she quickly walked to her guest
straddled on her pillows & began
    'you'll have to go now/ i've
    a lot of work to do/ & i cant
    with a man around/ here are yr pants/
    there's coffee on the stove/ its been
    very nice/ but i cant see you again/
    you got what you came for/ didnt you'
& she smiled
he wd either mumble curses bout crazy bitches
or sit dumbfounded
while she repeated
    'i cdnt possibly wake up/ with
    a strange man in my bed/ why
    dont you go home'
she cda been slapped upside the head
or verbally challenged
but she never waz
& the ones who fell prey to the
dazzle of hips painted with
orange blossoms & magnolia scented wrists
had wanted no more
than to lay between her sparklin thighs
& had planned on leavin before dawn
& she had been so divine
devastatingly bizarre the way
her mouth fit round
& now she stood a
reglar colored girl
fulla the same malice
livid indifference as a sistah
worn from supportin a wd be hornplayer
or waitin by the window
      & they knew
      & left in a hurry
she wd gather her tinsel &
jewels from the tub
& laugh gayly or vengeful
she stored her silk roses by her bed
& when she finished writin
the account of her exploit in a diary
embroidered with lilies & moonstones
she placed the rose behind her ear
& cried herself to sleep.

          All the lights fade except for a
          special on the lady in red; the
          lady in red exits stage left.

*The lady in blue enters from up
right.*

    lady in blue
i usedta live in the world
then i moved to HARLEM
& my universe is now six blocks

when i walked in the pacific
i imagined waters ancient from accra/ tunis
cleansin me/ feedin me
now my ankles are coated in grey filth
from the puddle neath the hydrant

my oceans were life
what waters i have here sit stagnant
circlin ol men's bodies
shit & broken lil whiskey bottles
left to make me bleed

i usedta live in the world
now i live in harlem & my universe is six blocks
a tunnel with a train
i can ride anywhere
remaining a stranger
     NO MAN YA CANT GO WIT ME/ I DONT EVEN
     KNOW YOU/ NO/ I DONT WANNA KISS YOU/
     YOU AINT BUT 12 YRS OLD/ NO MAN/ PLEASE
     PLEASE PLEASE LEAVE ME ALONE/ TOMORROW/ YEAH/
     NO/ PLEASE/ I CANT USE IT
  i cd stay alone
  a woman in the world
  then i moved to
HARLEM
i come in at dusk
stay close to the curb

*The lady in yellow enters, she's
waiting for a bus.*

round midnite
praying wont no young man
think i'm pretty in a dark mornin

*The lady in purple enters, she's
waiting for a bus.*

wdnt be good
not good at all
to meet a tall short black brown young man fulla his power
in the dark
in my universe of six blocks
straight up brick walls
women hangin outta windows
like ol silk stockings
cats cryin/ children gigglin/ a tavern wit red curtains
bad smells/ kissin ladies smilin & dirt
sidewalks spittin/ men cursing/ playin

*The lady in orange enters, she is
being followed by a man, the
lady in blue becomes that man.*

'I SPENT MORE MONEY YESTERDAY
THAN THE DAY BEFORE & ALL THAT'S MORE N YOU
NIGGAH EVER GOTTA HOLD TO
COME OVER HERE BITCH
CANT YA SEE THIS IS $5'

never mind sister
dont pay him no mind
go go go go go go sister
do yr thing
never mind

i usedta live in the world
really be in the world
free & sweet talkin
good mornin & thank-you & nice day
uh huh
i cant now
i cant be nice to nobody
nice is such a rip-off
reglar beauty & a smile in the street
is just a set-up

i usedta be in the world
a woman in the world
i hadda right to the world
then i moved to harlem
for the set-up
a universe
six blocks of cruelty
piled up on itself
a tunnel
closin

The four ladies on stage freeze,
count 4, then the ladies in blue,
purple, yellow and orange move
to their places for the next poem.

        lady in purple
three of us like a pyramid
three friends
one laugh
one music
one flowered shawl
knotted on each neck
we all saw him at the same time
& he saw us
i felt a quick thump in each one of us
didnt know what to do
we all wanted what waz comin our way
so we split
but he found one
& she loved him

the other two were tickled
& spurned his advances
when the one who loved him waz somewhere else
he wd come to her saying
yr friends love you very much
i have tried
& they keep askin where are you
she smiled
wonderin how long her friends
wd hold out
he waz what they were lookin for
he bided his time
he waited til romance waned
the three of us made up stories
bout usedta & cda been nice
the season waz dry
no men
no quickies
not one dance or eyes unrelentin
one day after another
cept for the one who loved him
he appeared irregularly
expectin graciousness no matter what
she cut fresh strawberries
her friends callt less frequently
went on hunts for passin fancies

she cdnt figure out what waz happenin
then the rose
she left by his pillow
she found on her friends desk
& there waz nothing to say
she said
i wanna tell you
he's been after me
all the time
says he's free & can explain
what's happenin wit you
is nothin to me
& i dont wanna hurt you
but you know i need someone now
& you know
how wonderful he is

her friend cdnt speak or cry
they hugged & went to where he waz
wit another woman
he said good-bye to one
tol the other he wd call
he smiled a lot

she held her head on her lap
the lap of her sisters soakin up tears
each understandin how much love stood between them
how much love between them
love between them
love like sisters

> *Sharp music is heard, each lady
> dances as if catching a disease
> from the lady next to her,
> suddenly they all freeze.*

    lady in orange
ever since i realized there waz someone callt
a colored girl an evil woman a bitch or a nag
i been tryin not to be that & leave bitterness
in somebody else's cup/ come to somebody to love me
without deep & nasty smellin scald from lye or bein
left screamin in a street fulla lunatics/ whisperin
slut bitch bitch niggah/ get outta here wit alla that/
i didnt have any of that for you/ i brought you what joy
i found & i found joy/ honest fingers round my face/ with
dead musicians on 78's from cuba/ or live musicians on five
dollar lp's from chicago/ where i have never been/ & i love

willie colon & arsenio rodriquez/ especially cuz i can make
the music loud enuf/ so there is no me but dance/ & when
i can dance like that/ there's nothin cd hurt me/ but
i get tired & i haveta come offa the floor & then there's
that woman who hurt you/ who you left/ three or four times/
& just went back/ after you put my heart in the bottom of
yr shoe/ you just walked back to where you hurt/ & i didnt
have nothin/ so i went to where somebody had somethin for me/
but he waznt you/ & i waz on the way back from her house
in the bottom of yr shoe/ so this is not a love poem/ cuz there
are only memorial albums available/ & even charlie mingus
wanted desperately to be a pimp/ & i wont be able to see eddie
palmieri for months/ so this is a requium for myself/ cuz i
have died in a real way/ not wid aqua coffins & du-wop cadillacs/
i used to joke abt when i waz messin round/ but a real dead
lovin is here for you now/ cuz i dont know anymore/ how
to avoid my own face wet wit my tears/ cuz i had convinced
myself colored girls had no right to sorrow/ & i lived
& loved that way & kept sorrow on the curb/ allegedly
for you/ but i know i did it for myself/
i cdnt stand it
i cdnt stand bein sorry & colored at the same time
it's so redundant in the modern world

　　lady in purple
i lived wit myths & music waz my ol man & i cd dance
a dance outta time/ a dance wit no partners/ take my
pills & keep right on steppin/ linger in non-english
speakin arms so there waz no possibility of understandin
& you YOU
came sayin i am the niggah/ i am the baddest muthafuckah
out there/
i said yes/ this is who i am waitin for
& to come wit you/ i hadta bring everythin
the dance & the terror
the dead musicians & the hope
& those scars i had hidden wit smiles & good fuckin
lay open
& i dont know i dont know any more tricks
i am really colored & really sad sometimes & you hurt me
more than i ever danced outta/ into oblivion isnt far enuf
to get outta this/ i am ready to die like a lily in the
desert/ & i cdnt let you in on it cuz i didnt know/ here
is what i have/ poems/ big thighs/ lil tits/ &
so much love/ will you take it from me this one time/
please this is for you/ arsenio's tres cleared the way
& makes me pure again/ please please/ this is for you

i want you to love me/ let me love you/ i dont wanna
dance wit ghosts/ snuggle lovers i made up in my drunkenness/
lemme love you just like i am/ a colored girl/ i'm finally bein
real/ no longer symmetrical & impervious to pain

>   *lady in blue*
we deal wit emotion too much
so why dont we go on ahead & be white then/
& make everythin dry & abstract wit no rhythm & no
reelin for sheer sensual pleasure/ yes let's go on
& be white/ we're right in the middle of it/ no use
holdin out/ holdin onto ourselves/ lets think our
way outta feelin/ lets abstract ourselves some families
& maybe maybe tonite/ i'll find a way to make myself
come witout you/ no fingers or other objects just thot
which isnt spiritual evolution cuz its empty & godliness
is plenty is ripe & fertile/ thinkin wont do me a bit of
good tonite/ i need to be loved/ & havent the audacity
to say
where are you/ & dont know who to say it to

>   *lady in yellow*
i've lost it
touch wit reality/ i dont know who's doin it
i thot i waz but i waz so stupid i waz able to be hurt
& that's not real/ not anymore/ i shd be immune/ if i'm
still alive & that's what i waz discussin/ how i am still
alive & my dependency on other livin beins for love
i survive on intimacy & tomorrow/ that's all i've got goin
& the music waz like smack & you knew abt that
& still refused my dance waz not enuf/ & it waz all i had
but bein alive & bein a woman & bein colored is a metaphysical
dilemma/ i havent conquered yet/ do you see the point
my spirit is too ancient to understand the separation of
soul & gender/ my love is too delicate to have thrown
back on my face

> *The ladies in red, green, and*
> *brown enter quietly; in the*
> *background all of the ladies*
> *except the lady in yellow are*
> *frozen; the lady in yellow looks at*
> *them, walks by them, touches*
> *them; they do not move.*

>   *lady in yellow*
my love is too delicate to have thrown back on my face

*The lady in yellow starts to exit
stage right. Just as she gets to the
wings, the lady in brown comes to
life.*

lady in brown
my love is too beautiful to have thrown back on my face

lady in purple
my love is too sanctified to have thrown back on my face

lady in blue
my love is too magic to have thrown back on my face

lady in orange
my love is too saturday nite to have thrown back on my face

lady in red
my love is too complicated to have thrown back on my face

lady in green
my love is too music to have thrown back on my face

everyone
music
music

*The lady in green then breaks
into a dance, the other ladies
follow her lead and soon they are
all dancing and chanting
together.*

lady in green
yank dankka dank dank

everyone
music

lady in green
yank dankka dank dank

everyone
music

lady in green
yank dankka dank dank

everyone (but started by the lady in yellow)
delicate
delicate
delicate

everyone (but started by the lady in brown)
and beautiful
and beautiful
and beautiful

everyone (but started by the lady in purple)
oh sanctified
oh sanctified
oh sanctified

everyone (but started by the lady in blue)
magic
magic
magic

everyone (but started by the lady in orange)
and saturday nite
and saturday nite
and saturday nite

everyone (but started by the lady in red)
and complicated
and complicated
and complicated
and complicated
and complicated
and complicated
and complicated
and complicated

*The dance reaches a climax and
all of the ladies fall out tired, but
full of life and togetherness.*

lady in green
somebody almost walked off wid alla my stuff
not my poems or a dance i gave up in the street
but somebody almost walked off wid alla my stuff
like a kleptomaniac workin hard & forgettin while stealin
this is mine/ this aint yr stuff/
now why dont you put me back & let me hang out in my own self
somebody almost walked off wid alla my stuff
& didnt care enuf to send a note home sayin

i waz late for my solo conversation
or two sizes too small for my own tacky skirts
what can anybody do wit somethin of no value on
a open market/ did you getta dime for my things/
hey man/ where are you goin wid alla my stuff/
this is a woman's trip & i need my stuff/
to ohh & ahh abt/ daddy/ i gotta mainline number
from my own shit/ now wontchu put me back/ & let
me play this duet/ wit this silver ring in my nose/
honest to god/ somebody almost run off wit alla my stuff/
& i didnt bring anythin but the kick & sway of it
the perfect ass for my man & none of it is theirs
this is mine/ ntozake 'her own things'/ that's my name/
now give me my stuff/ i see ya hidin my laugh/ & how i
sit wif my legs open sometimes/ to give my crotch
some sunlight/ & there goes my love my toes my chewed
up finger nails/ niggah/ wif the curls in yr hair/
mr. louisiana hot link/ i want my stuff back/
my rhythms & my voice/ open my mouth/ & let me talk ya
outta/ throwin my shit in the sewar/ this is some delicate
leg & whimsical kiss/ i gotta have to give to my choice/
without you runnin off wit alla my shit/
now you cant have me less i give me away/ & i waz
doin all that/ til ya run off on a good thing/
who is this you left me wit/ some simple bitch
widda bad attitude/ i wants my things/
i want my arm wit the hot iron scar/ & my leg wit the
flea bite/ i want my calloused feet & quik language back
in my mouth/ fried plantains/ pineapple pear juice/
sun-ra & joseph & jules/ i want my own things/ how i lived them/
& give me my memories/ how i waz when i waz there/
you cant have them or do nothin wit them/
stealin my shit from me/ dont make it yrs/ makes it stolen/
somebody almost run off wit alla my stuff/ & i waz standin
there/ lookin at myself/ the whole time
& it waznt a spirit took my stuff/ waz a man whose
ego walked round like Rodan's shadow/ waz a man faster
n my innocence/ waz a lover/ i made too much
room for/ almost run off wit alla my stuff/
& i didnt know i'd give it up so quik/ & the one running wit it/
dont know he got it/ & i'm shoutin this is mine/ & he dont
know he got it/ my stuff is the anonymous ripped off treasure
of the year/ did you know somebody almost got away with me/
me in a plastic bag under their arm/ me
danglin on a string of personal carelessness/ i'm spattered wit
mud & city rain/ & no i didnt get a chance to take a douche/
hey man/ this is not your perogative/ i gotta have me in my

pocket/ to get round like a good woman shd/ & make the poem
in the pot or the chicken in the dance/ what i got to do/
i gotta have my stuff to do it to/
why dont ya find yr own things/ & leave this package
of me for my destiny/ what ya got to get from me/
i'll give it to ya/ yeh/ i'll give it to ya/
round 5:00 in the winter/ when the sky is blue-red/
& Dew City is gettin pressed/ if it's really my stuff/
ya gotta give it to me/ if ya really want it/ i'm
the only one/ can handle it

    lady in blue
that niggah will be back tomorrow, sayin 'i'm sorry'

    lady in yellow
get this, last week my ol man came in sayin, 'i don't know
how she got yr number baby, i'm sorry'

    lady in brown
no this one is it, 'o baby, ya know i waz high, i'm sorry'

    lady in purple
'i'm only human, and inadequacy is what makes us human, &
if we was perfect we wdnt have nothin to strive for, so you
might as well go on and forgive me pretty baby, cause i'm sorry'

    lady in green
'shut up bitch, i told you i waz sorry'

    lady in orange
no this one is it, 'i do ya like i do ya cause i thot
ya could take it, now i'm sorry'

    lady in red
'now i know that ya know i love ya, but i aint ever gonna
love ya like ya want me to love ya, i'm sorry'

    lady in blue
one thing i dont need
is any more apologies
i got sorry greetin me at my front door
you can keep yrs
i dont know what to do wit em
they dont open doors
or bring the sun back
they dont make me happy
or get a mornin paper

didnt nobody stop usin my tears to wash cars
cuz a sorry

i am simply tired
of collectin
   i didnt know
   i was so important toyou'
i'm gonna haveta throw some away
i cant get to the clothes in my closet
for alla the sorries
i'm gonna tack a sign to my door
leave a message by the phone
   'if you called
   to say yr sorry
   call somebody
   else
   i dont use em anymore'
i let sorry/ didnt meanta/ & how cd i know abt that
take a walk down a dark & musty street in brooklyn
i'm gonna do exactly what i want to
& i wont be sorry for none of it
letta sorry soothe yr soul/ i'm gonna soothe mine

you were always inconsistent
doin somethin & then bein sorry
beatin my heart to death
talkin bout you sorry
well
i will not call
i'm not goin to be nice
i will raise my voice
& scream & holler
& break things & race the engine
& tell all yr secrets bout yrself to yr face
& i will list in detail everyone of my wonderful lovers
& their ways
i will play oliver lake
loud
& i wont be sorry for none of it

i loved you on purpose
i was open on purpose
i still crave vulnerability & close talk
& i'm not even sorry bout you bein sorry
you can carry all the guilt & grime ya wanna
just dont give it to me
i cant use another sorry

next time
you should admit
you're mean/ low-down/ triflin/ & no count straight out
steada bein sorry alla the time
enjoy bein yrself

   lady in red
there waz no air/ the sheets made ripples under his
body like crumpled paper napkins in a summer park/ & lil
specks of somethin from tween his toes or the biscuits
from the day before ran in the sweat that tucked the sheet
into his limbs like he waz an ol frozen bundle of chicken/
& he'd get up to make coffee, drink wine, drink water/ he
wished one of his friends who knew where he waz wd come by
with some blow or some shit/ anythin/ there waz no air/
he'd see the spotlights in the alleyways downstairs movin
in the air/ cross his wall over his face/ & get under the
covers & wait for an all clear or til he cd hear traffic
again/

there waznt nothin wrong with him/ there waznt nothin wrong
with him/ he kept tellin crystal/
any niggah wanna kill vietnamese children more n stay home
& raise his own is sicker than a rabid dog/
that's how their thing had been goin since he got back/
crystal just got inta sayin whatta fool niggah beau waz
& always had been/ didnt he go all over uptown sayin the
child waznt his/ waz some no counts bastard/ & any ol city
police cd come & get him if they wanted/ cuz as soon as
the blood type & shit waz together/ everybody wd know that
crystal waz a no good lyin whore/ and this after she'd been
his girl since she waz thirteen/ when he caught her
on the stairway/

he came home crazy as hell/ he tried to get veterans benefits
to go to school & they kept right on puttin him in
remedial classes/ he cdnt read wortha damn/ so beau
cused the teachers of holdin him back & got himself
a gypsy cab to drive/ but his cab kept breakin
down/ & the cops was always messin wit him/ plus not
gettin much bread/

& crystal went & got pregnant again/ beau most beat
her to death when she tol him/ she still gotta scar
under her right tit where he cut her up/ still crystal
went right on & had the baby/ so now beau willie had
two children/ a little girl/ naomi kenya & a boy/ kwame beau
willie brown/ & there waz no air/

how in the hell did he get in this mess anyway/ somebody
went & tol crystal that beau waz spendin alla his money
on the bartendin bitch down at the merry-go-round cafe/
beau sat straight up in the bed/ wrapped up in the sheets
lookin like john the baptist or a huge baby wit stubble
& nuts/ now he hadta get alla that shit outta crystal's
mind/ so she wd let him come home/ crystal had gone &
got a court order saying beau willie brown had no access
to his children/ if he showed his face he waz subject
to arrest/ shit/ she'd been in his ass to marry her
since she waz 14 years old & here when she 22/ she wanna
throw him out cuz he say he'll marry her/ she burst
out laughin/ hollerin whatchu wanna marry me for now/
so i can support yr
ass/ or come sit wit ya when they lock yr behind
up/ cause they gonna come for ya/ ya goddamn lunatic/
they gonna come/ & i'm not gonna have a thing to do
wit it/ o no i wdnt marry yr pitiful black ass for
nothin & she went on to bed/

the next day beau willie came in blasted & got ta swingin
chairs at crystal/ who cdnt figure out what the hell
he waz doin/ til he got ta shoutin bout how she waz gonna
marry him/ & get some more veterans benefits/ & he cd
stop drivin them crazy spics round/ while they tryin
to kill him for $15/ beau waz sweatin terrible/ beatin
on crystal/ & he cdnt do no more with the table n chairs/
so he went to get the high chair/ & lil kwame waz in it/
& beau waz beatin crystal with the high chair & her son/
& some notion got inta him to stop/ and he run out/

crystal most died/ that's why the police wdnt low
beau near where she lived/ & she'd been tellin the kids
their daddy tried to kill her & kwame/ & he just wanted
to marry her/ that's what/ he wanted to marry her/ &
have a family/ but the bitch waz crazy/ beau willie
waz sittin in this hotel in his drawers drinkin
coffee & wine in the heat of the day spillin shit all
over hisself/ laughin/ bout how he waz gonna get crystal
to take him back/ & let him be a man in the house/ & she
wdnt even have to go to work no more/ he got dressed
all up in his ivory shirt & checkered pants to go see
crystal & get this mess all cleared up/
he knocked on the door to crystal's rooms/ & she
didnt answer/ he beat on the door & crystal & naomi
started cryin/ beau gotta shoutin again how he wanted

to marry her/ & waz she always gonna be a whore/ or
did she wanna husband/ & crystal just kept on
screamin for him to leave us alone/ just leave us
alone/ so beau broke the door down/ crystal held
the children in fronta her/ she picked kwame off the
floor/ in her arms/ & she held naomi by her shoulders/
& kept on sayin/ beau willie brown/ get outta here/
the police is gonna come for ya/ ya fool/ get outta here/
do you want the children to see you act the fool again/
you want kwame to brain damage from you throwin him
round/ niggah/ get outta here/ get out & dont show yr
ass again or i'll kill ya/ i swear i'll kill ya/
he reached for naomi/ crystal grabbed the lil girl &
stared at beau willie like he waz a leper or somethin/
dont you touch my children/ muthafucker/ or i'll kill
you/

beau willie jumped back all humble & apologetic/ i'm
sorry/ i dont wanna hurt em/ i just wanna hold em &
get on my way/ i dont wanna cuz you no more trouble/
i wanted to marry you & give ya things
what you gonna give/ a broken jaw/ niggah get outta here/
he ignored crystal's outburst & sat down motionin for
naomi to come to him/ she smiled back at her daddy/
crystal felt naomi givin in & held her tighter/
naomi/ pushed away & ran to her daddy/ cryin/ daddy, daddy
come back daddy/ come back/ but be nice to mommy/
cause mommy loves you/ and ya gotta be nice/
he sat her on his knee/ & played with her ribbons &
they counted fingers & toes/ every so often he
looked over to crystal holdin kwame/ like a statue/
& he'd say/ see crystal/ i can be a good father/
now let me see my son/ & she didnt move/ &
he coaxed her & he coaxed her/ tol her she waz
still a hot lil ol thing & pretty & strong/ didnt
she get right up after that lil ol fight they had
& go back to work/ beau willie oozed kindness &
crystal who had known so lil/ let beau hold kwame/

as soon as crystal let the baby outta her arms/ beau
jumped up a laughin & a gigglin/ a hootin & a hollerin/
awright bitch/ awright bitch/ you gonna marry me/
you gonna marry me . . .
i aint gonna marry ya/ i aint ever gonna marry ya/
for nothin/ you gonna be in the jail/ you gonna be
under the jail for this/ now gimme my kids/ ya give
me back my kids/

he kicked the screen outta the window/ & held the kids
offa the sill/ you gonna marry me/ yeh, i'll marry ya/
anything/ but bring the children back in the house/
he looked from where the kids were hangin from the
fifth story/ at alla the people screamin at him/ &
he started sweatin again/ say to alla the neighbors/
you gonna marry me/

i stood by beau in the window/ with naomi reachin
for me/ & kwame screamin mommy mommy from the fifth
story/ but i cd only whisper/ & he dropped em

     lady in red
i waz missin somethin

     lady in purple
somethin so important

     lady in orange
somethin promised

     lady in blue
a layin on of hands

     lady in green
fingers near my forehead

     lady in yellow
strong

     lady in green
cool

     lady in orange
movin

     lady in purple
makin me whole

     lady in orange
sense

     lady in green
pure

   lady in blue
all the gods comin into me
layin me open to myself

   lady in red
i waz missin somethin

   lady in green
somethin promised

   lady in orange
somethin free

   lady in purple
a layin on of hands

   lady in blue
i know bout/ layin on bodies/ layin outta man
bringin him alla my fleshy self & some of my pleasure
bein taken full eager wet like i get sometimes
i waz missin somethin

   lady in purple
a layin on of hands

   lady in blue
not a man

   lady in yellow
layin on

   lady in purple
not my mama/ holdin me tight/ sayin
i'm always gonna be her girl
not a layin on of bosom & womb
a layin on of hands
the holiness of myself released

   lady in red
i sat up one nite walkin a boardin house
screamin/ cryin/ the ghost of another woman
who waz missin what i waz missin
i wanted to jump up outta my bones
& be done wit myself
leave me alone
& go on in the wind
it waz too much

i fell into a numbness
til the only tree i cd see
took me up in her branches
held me in the breeze
made me dawn dew
that chill at daybreak
the sun wrapped me up swingin rose light everywhere
the sky laid over me like a million men
i waz cold/ i waz burnin up/ a child
& endlessly weavin garments for the moon
wit my tears

i found god in myself
& i loved her/ i loved her fiercely

*All of the ladies repeat to
themselves softly the lines 'i found
god in myself & i loved her.' It
soon becomes a song of joy,
started by the lady in blue. The
ladies sing first to each other,
then gradually to the audience.
After the song peaks the ladies
enter into a closed tight circle.*

    lady in brown
& this is for colored girls who have considered
suicide/ but are movin to the ends of their own
rainbows

THE GLASS MENAGERIE

Tennessee Williams

(1911–1983)

Biography p. 1108

SCENE: *An Alley in St. Louis*

Part I. Preparation for a Gentleman Caller.
Part II. The Gentleman calls.

Time: Now and the Past.

The Characters

AMANDA WINGFIELD (*the mother*)
   A little woman of great but confused vitality clinging frantically to another time and place. Her characterization must be carefully created, not copied from type. She is not paranoiac, but her life is paranoia. There is much to admire in Amanda, and as much to love and pity as there is to laugh at. Certainly she has endurance and a kind of heroism, and though her foolishness makes her unwittingly cruel at times, there is tenderness in her slight person.

LAURA WINGFIELD (*her daughter*)
   Amanda, having failed to establish contact with reality, continues to live vitally in her illusions, but Laura's situation is even graver. A childhood illness has left her crippled, one leg slightly shorter than the other, and held in a brace. This defect need not be more than suggested on the stage. Stemming from this, Laura's separation increases till she is like a piece of her own glass collection, too exquisitely fragile to move from the shelf.

TOM WINGFIELD (*her son*)
   And the narrator of the play. A poet with a job in a warehouse. His nature is not remorseless, but to escape from a trap he has to act without pity.

JIM O'CONNOR (*the gentleman caller*)
   A nice, ordinary, young man.

SCENE ONE

The Wingfield apartment is in the rear of the building, one of those vast hive-like conglomerations of cellular living-units that flower as warty growths in overcrowded urban centers of lower middle-class population and are symptomatic of the impulse of this largest and fundamentally enslaved section of American society to avoid fluidity and differentiation and to exist and function as one interfused mass of automatism.

The apartment faces an alley and is entered by a fire escape, a structure whose name is a touch of accidental poetic truth, for all of these huge buildings are always burning with the slow and implacable fires of human desperation. The fire escape is part of what we see—that is, the landing of it and steps descending from it.

The scene is memory and is therefore nonrealistic. Memory takes a lot of poetic license. It omits some details; others are exaggerated, according to the emotional value of the articles it touches, for memory is seated predominantly in the heart. The interior is therefore rather dim and poetic.

At the rise of the curtain, the audience is faced with the dark, grim rear wall of the Wingfield tenement. This building is flanked on both sides by dark, narrow alleys which run into murky canyons of tangled clotheslines, garbage cans, and the sinister latticework of neighboring fire escapes. It is up and down these side alleys that exterior entrances and exits are made during the play. At the end of Tom's opening commentary, the dark tenement wall slowly becomes transparent and reveals the interior of the ground-floor Wingfield apartment.

Nearest the audience is the living room, which also serves as a sleeping room for Laura, the sofa unfolding to make her bed. Just beyond, separated from the living room by a wide arch or second proscenium with transparent faded portieres (or second curtain), is the dining room. In an old-fashioned whatnot in the living room are seen scores of transparent glass animals. A blown-up photograph of the father hangs on the wall of the living room, to the left of the archway. It is the face of a very handsome young man in a doughboy's First World War cap. He is gallantly smiling, ineluctably smiling, as if to say "I will be smiling forever."

Also hanging on the wall, near the photograph, are a typewriter keyboard chart and a Gregg shorthand diagram. An upright typewriter on a small table stands beneath the charts.

The audience hears and sees the opening scene in the dining room through both the transparent fourth wall of the building and the transparent gauze portieres of the dining-room arch. It is during this revealing scene that the fourth wall slowly ascends, out of sight. This transparent exterior wall is not brought down again until the very end of the play, during Tom's final speech.

The narrator is an undisguised convention of the play. He takes whatever license with dramatic convention is convenient to his purposes.

Tom enters, dressed as a merchant sailor, and strolls across to the fire escape. There he stops and lights a cigarette. He addresses the audience.

TOM.   Yes, I have tricks in my pocket, I have things up my sleeve. But I am the opposite of a stage magician. He gives you illusion that has the appearance of truth. I give you truth in the pleasant disguise of illusion.

To begin with, I turn back time. I reverse it to that quaint period, the thirties, when the huge middle class of America was matriculating in a school for the blind. Their eyes had failed them, or they had failed their eyes, and so they were having their fingers pressed forcibly down on the fiery Braille alphabet of a dissolving economy.

In Spain there was revolution. Here there was only shouting and confusion. In Spain there was Guernica. Here there were disturbances of labor, sometimes pretty violent, in otherwise peaceful cities such as Chicago, Cleveland, Saint Louis . . .

This is the social background of the play.

(Music begins to play.)

The play is memory. Being a memory play, it is dimly lighted, it is sentimental, it is not realistic. In memory everything seems to happen to music. That explains the fiddle in the wings.

I am the narrator of the play, and also a character in it. The other characters are my mother, Amanda, my sister, Laura, and a gentleman caller who appears in the final scenes. He is the most realistic character in the play, being an emissary from a world of reality that we were somehow set apart from. But since I have a poet's weakness for symbols, I am using this character also as a symbol; he is the long delayed but always expected something that we live for.

There is a fifth character in the play who doesn't appear except in this larger-than-life-size photograph over the mantel. This is our father who left us a long time ago. He was a telephone man who fell in love with long distances; he gave up his job with the telephone company and skipped the light fantastic out of town . . .

The last we heard of him was a picture postcard from Mazatlan, on the Pacific coast of Mexico, containing a message of two words: "Hello—Good-bye!" and no address.

I think the rest of the play will explain itself. . . .

(Amanda's voice becomes audible through the portieres.)

(Legend on screen: "Ou sont les neiges.")

(Tom divides the portieres and enters the dining room. Amanda and Laura are seated at a drop-leaf table. Eating is indicated by gestures without food or utensils. Amanda faces the audience. Tom and Laura are seated in profile. The interior has lit up softly and through the scrim we see Amanda and Laura seated at the table.)

AMANDA *(calling).*   Tom?

TOM.   Yes, Mother.

AMANDA.   We can't say grace until you come to the table!

TOM.   Coming, Mother. *(He bows slightly and withdraws, reappearing a few moments later in his place at the table.)*

AMANDA *(to her son).*   Honey, don't *push* with your *fingers.* If you have to push
    with something, the thing to push with is a crust of bread. And chew—chew!
    Animals have secretions in their stomachs which enable them to digest food
    without mastication, but human beings are supposed to chew their food before
    they swallow it down. Eat food leisurely, son, and really enjoy it. A well-
    cooked meal has lots of delicate flavors that have to be held in the mouth for
    appreciation. So chew your food and give your salivary glands a chance to
    function!

*(Tom deliberately lays his imaginary fork down and pushes his chair back from the
table.)*

TOM.   I haven't enjoyed one bite of this dinner because of your constant directions
    on how to eat it. It's you that make me rush through meals with your hawk-like
    attention to every bite I take. Sickening—spoils my appetite—all this discus-
    sion of—animals' secretion—salivary glands—mastication!
AMANDA *(lightly).*   Temperament like a Metropolitan star!

(Tom rises and walks toward the living room.)

    You're not excused from the table.
TOM.   I'm getting a cigarette.
AMANDA.   You smoke too much.

(Laura rises.)

LAURA.   I'll bring in the blanc mange.

(Tom remains standing with his cigarette by the portieres.)

AMANDA *(rising).*   No, sister, no, sister—you be the lady this time and I'll be the
    darky.
LAURA.   I'm already up.
AMANDA.   Resume your seat, little sister—I want you to stay fresh and pretty—
    for gentlemen callers!
LAURA *(sitting down).*   I'm not expecting any gentlemen callers.
AMANDA *(crossing out to the kitchenette, airily).*   Sometimes they come when they
    are least expected! Why, I remember one Sunday afternoon in Blue Moun-
    tain—

(She enters the kitchenette.)

TOM.   I know what's coming!
LAURA.   Yes. But let her tell it.
TOM.   Again?
LAURA.   She loves to tell it.

(Amanda returns with a bowl of dessert.)

AMANDA.   One Sunday afternoon in Blue Mountain—your mother received—
    seventeen!—gentlemen callers! Why, sometimes there weren't chairs enough
    to accommodate them all. We had to send the nigger over to bring in folding
    chairs from the parish house.

TOM (*remaining at the portieres*).   How did you entertain those gentlemen callers?

AMANDA.   I understood the art of conversation!

TOM.   I bet you could talk.

AMANDA.   Girls in those days *knew* how to talk, I can tell you.

TOM.   Yes?

(*Image on screen:* Amanda as a girl on a porch, greeting callers.)

AMANDA.   They knew how to entertain their gentlemen callers. It wasn't enough for a girl to be possessed of a pretty face and a graceful figure—although I wasn't slighted in either respect. She also needed to have a nimble wit and a tongue to meet all occasions.

TOM.   What did you talk about?

AMANDA.   Things of importance going on in the world! Never anything coarse or common or vulgar.

(*She addresses Tom as though he were seated in the vacant chair at the table though he remains by the portieres. He plays this scene as though reading from a script.*)

My callers were gentlemen—all! Among my callers were some of the most prominent young planters of the Mississippi Delta—planters and sons of planters!

(*Tom motions for music and a spot of light on Amanda. Her eyes lift, her face glows, her voice becomes rich and elegiac.*)

(*Screen legend:* "Ou sont les neiges d'antan?")

There was young Champ Laughlin who later became vice-president of the Delta Planters Bank. Hadley Stevenson who was drowned in Moon Lake and left his widow one hundred and fifty thousand in Government bonds. There were the Cutrere brothers, Wesley and Bates. Bates was one of my bright particular beaux! He got in a quarrel with that wild Wainwright boy. They shot it out on the floor of Moon Lake Casino. Bates was shot through the stomach. Died in the ambulance on his way to Memphis. His widow was also well provided-for, came into eight or ten thousand acres, that's all. She married him on the rebound—never loved her—carried my picture on him the night he died! And there was that boy that every girl in the Delta had set her cap for! That beautiful, brilliant young Fitzhugh boy from Greene County!

TOM.   What did he leave his widow?

AMANDA.   He never married! Gracious, you talk as though all of my old admirers had turned up their toes to the daisies!

TOM.   Isn't this the first you've mentioned that still survives?

AMANDA.   That Fitzhugh boy went North and made a fortune—came to be known as the Wolf of Wall Street! He had the Midas touch, whatever he touched turned to gold! And I could have been Mrs. Duncan J. Fitzhugh, mind you! But—I picked your *father!*

LAURA (*rising*).   Mother, let me clear the table.

AMANDA.   No, dear, you go in front and study your typewriter chart. Or practice your shorthand a little. Stay fresh and pretty!—It's almost time for our gentlemen callers to start arriving. *(She flounces girlishly toward the kitchenette.)* How many do you suppose we're going to entertain this afternoon?

(Tom throws down the paper and jumps up with a groan.)

LAURA *(alone in the dining room).*   I don't believe we're going to receive any, Mother.

AMANDA *(reappearing, airily).*   What? No one—not one? You must be joking!

(Laura nervously echoes her laugh. She slips in a fugitive manner through the half-open portieres and draws them gently behind her. A shaft of very clear light is thrown on her face against the faded tapestry of the curtains. Faintly the music of "The Glass Menagerie" is heard as she continues, lightly:)

Not one gentleman caller? It can't be true! There must be a flood, there must have been a tornado!

LAURA.   It isn't a flood, it's not a tornado, Mother. I'm just not popular like you were in Blue Mountain. . . .

(Tom utters another groan. Laura glances at him with a faint, apologetic smile. Her voice catches a little:)

Mother's afraid I'm going to be an old maid.

(The scene dims out with the "Glass Menagerie" music.)

SCENE TWO

On the dark stage the screen is lighted with the image of blue roses. Gradually Laura's figure becomes apparent and the screen goes out. The music subsides.

Laura is seated in the delicate ivory chair at the small clawfoot table. She wears a dress of soft violet material for a kimono—her hair is tied back from her forehead with a ribbon. She is washing and polishing her collection of glass. Amanda appears on the fire escape steps. At the sound of her ascent, Laura catches her breath, thrusts the bowl of ornaments away, and seats herself stiffly before the diagram of the typewriter keyboard as though it held her spellbound. Something has happened to Amanda. It is written in her face as she climbs to the landing: a look that is grim and hopeless and a little absurd. She has on one of those cheap or imitation velvety-looking cloth coats with imitation fur collar. Her hat is five or six years old, one of those dreadful cloche hats that were worn in the late Twenties, and she is clutching an enormous black patent-leather pocketbook with nickel clasps and initials. This is her full-dress outfit, the one she usually wears to the D.A.R. Before entering she looks through the door. She purses her lips, opens her eyes very wide, rolls them upward and shakes her head. Then she slowly lets herself in the door. Seeing her mother's expression Laura touches her lips with a nervous gesture.

LAURA.   Hello, Mother, I was— *(She makes a nervous gesture toward the chart on the wall. Amanda leans against the shut door and stares at Laura with a martyred look.)*

AMANDA.   Deception? Deception? *(She slowly removes her hat and gloves, continuing the sweet suffering stare. She lets the hat and gloves fall on the floor—a bit of acting.)*

LAURA *(shakily).*   How was the D.A.R. meeting?

(Amanda slowly opens her purse and removes a dainty white handkerchief which she shakes out delicately and delicately touches to her lips and nostrils.)

Didn't you go to the D.A.R. meeting, Mother?

AMANDA *(faintly, almost inaudibly).*   —No.—No. *(then more forcibly:)* I did not have the strength—to go to the D.A.R. In fact, I did not have the courage! I wanted to find a hole in the ground and hide myself in it forever! *(She crosses slowly to the wall and removes the diagram of the typewriter keyboard. She holds it in front of her for a second, staring at it sweetly and sorrowfully—then bites her lips and tears it in two pieces.)*

LAURA *(faintly).*   Why did you do that, Mother?

(Amanda repeats the same procedure with the chart of the Gregg Alphabet.)

Why are you—

AMANDA.   Why? Why? How old are you, Laura?

LAURA.   Mother, you know my age.

AMANDA.   I thought that you were an adult; it seems that I was mistaken. *(She crosses slowly to the sofa and sinks down and stares at Laura.)*

LAURA.   Please don't stare at me, Mother.

(Amanda closes her eyes and lowers her head. There is a ten-second pause.)

AMANDA.   What are we going to do, what is going to become of us, what is the future?

(There is another pause.)

LAURA.   Has something happened, Mother?

(Amanda draws a long breath, takes out the handkerchief again, goes through the dabbing process.)

Mother, has—something happened?

AMANDA.   I'll be all right in a minute, I'm just bewildered—*(She hesitates.)*—by life. . . .

LAURA.   Mother, I wish that you would tell me what's happened!

AMANDA.   As you know, I was supposed to be inducted into my office at the D.A.R. this afternoon.

(Screen image: A swarm of typewriters.)

But I stopped off at Rubicam's Business College to speak to your teachers about your having a cold and ask them what progress they thought you were making down there.

LAURA.   Oh. . . .

AMANDA.   I went to the typing instructor and introduced myself as your mother.

She didn't know who you were. "Wingfield," she said, "We don't have any such student enrolled at the school!"

I assured her she did, that you had been going to classes since early in January. "I wonder," she said, "If you could be talking about that terribly shy little girl who dropped out of school after only a few days' attendance?"

"No," I said, "Laura, my daughter, has been going to school every day for the past six weeks!"

"Excuse me," she said. She took the attendance book out and there was your name, unmistakably printed, and all the dates you were absent until they decided that you had dropped out of school.

I still said, "No, there must have been some mistake! There must have been some mix-up in the records!"

And she said, "No—I remember her perfectly now. Her hands shook so that she couldn't hit the right keys! The first time we gave a speed test, she broke down completely—was sick at the stomach and almost had to be carried into the wash room! After that morning she never showed up any more. We phoned the house but never got any answer"—While I was working at Famous–Barr, I suppose, demonstrating those—

(She indicates a brassiere with her hands.)

Oh! I felt so weak I could barely keep on my feet! I had to sit down while they got me a glass of water! Fifty dollars' tuition, all of our plans—my hopes and ambitions for you—just gone up the spout, just gone up the spout like that.

(Laura draws a long breath and gets awkwardly to her feet. She crosses to the victrola and winds it up.)

What are you doing?

LAURA.   Oh! *(She releases the handle and returns to her seat.)*

AMANDA.   Laura, where have you been going when you've gone out pretending that you were going to business college?

LAURA.   I've just been going out walking.

AMANDA.   That's not true.

LAURA.   It is. I just went walking.

AMANDA.   Walking? Walking? In winter? Deliberately courting pneumonia in that light coat? Where did you walk to, Laura?

LAURA.   All sorts of places—mostly in the park.

AMANDA.   Even after you'd started catching that cold?

LAURA.   It was the lesser of two evils, Mother.

(Screen image: Winter scene in a park.*)*

I couldn't go back there. I—threw up—on the floor!

AMANDA.   From half past seven till after five every day you mean to tell me you walked around in the park, because you wanted to make me think that you were still going to Rubicam's Business College?

LAURA.   It wasn't as bad as it sounds. I went inside places to get warmed up.

AMANDA.   Inside where?

LAURA.   I went in the art museum and the bird houses at the Zoo. I visited the penguins every day! Sometimes I did without lunch and went to the movies. Lately I've been spending most of my afternoons in the Jewel Box, that big glass house where they raise the tropical flowers.

AMANDA.   You did all this to deceive me, just for deception? *(Laura looks down.)* Why?

LAURA.   Mother, when you're disappointed, you get that awful suffering look on your face, like the picture of Jesus' mother in the museum!

AMANDA.   Hush!

LAURA.   I couldn't face it.

(There is a pause. A whisper of strings is heard. Legend on screen: "The Crust of Humility."*)*

AMANDA *(hopelessly fingering the huge pocketbook).*   So what are we going to do the rest of our lives? Stay home and watch the parades go by? Amuse ourselves with the glass menagerie, darling? Eternally play those worn-out phonograph records your father left as a painful reminder of him? We won't have a business career—we've given that up because it gave us nervous indigestion! [*She laughs wearily.*] What is there left but dependency all our lives? I know so well what becomes of unmarried women who aren't prepared to occupy a position. I've seen such pitiful cases in the South—barely tolerated spinsters living upon the grudging patronage of sister's husband or brother's wife!—stuck away in some little mousetrap of a room—encouraged by one in-law to visit another—little birdlike women without any nest—eating the crust of humility all their life! Is that the future that we've mapped out for ourselves? I swear it's the only alternative I can think of! [*She pauses.*] It isn't a very pleasant alternative, is it? [*She pauses again.*] Of course—some girls *do* marry.

(Laura twists her hands nervously.)

Haven't you ever liked some boy?

LAURA.   Yes. I liked one once. *(She rises.)* I came across his picture a while ago.

AMANDA *(with some interest).*   He gave you his picture?

LAURA.   No, it's in the yearbook.

AMANDA *(disappointed).*   Oh—a high school boy.

(Screen image: Jim as the high school hero bearing a silver cup.)

LAURA.   Yes. His name was Jim. *(She lifts the heavy annual from the claw-foot table.)* Here he is in *The Pirates of Penzance.*

AMANDA *(absently).*   The what?

LAURA.   The operetta the senior class put on. He had a wonderful voice and we sat across the aisle from each other Mondays, Wednesdays and Fridays in the Aud. Here he is with the silver cup for debating! See his grin?

AMANDA *(absently).*   He must have had a jolly disposition.

LAURA.   He used to call me—Blue Roses.

(Screen image: Blue roses.)

AMANDA.   Why did he call you such a name as that?

LAURA.   When I had that attack of pleurosis—he asked me what was the matter when I came back. I said pleurosis—he thought that I said Blue Roses! So that's what he always called me after that. Whenever he saw me, he'd holler, "Hello, Blue Roses!" I didn't care for the girl that he went out with. Emily Meisenbach. Emily was the best-dressed girl at Soldan. She never struck me, though, as being sincere . . . It says in the Personal Section—they're engaged. That's—six years ago! They must be married by now.

AMANDA.   Girls that aren't cut out for business careers usually wind up married to some nice man. *(She gets up with a spark of revival.)* Sister, that's what you'll do!

(Laura utters a startled, doubtful laugh. She reaches quickly for a piece of glass.)

LAURA.   But, Mother—

AMANDA.   Yes? *(She goes over to the photograph.)*

LAURA *(in a tone of frightened apology).*   I'm—crippled!

AMANDA.   Nonsense! Laura, I've told you never, never to use that word. Why, you're not crippled, you just have a little defect—hardly noticeable, even! When people have some slight disadvantage like that, they cultivate other things to make up for it—develop charm—and vivacity—and—*charm!* That's all you have to do! *(She turns again to the photograph.)* One thing your father had *plenty of*—was *charm!*

(The scene fades out with music.)

SCENE THREE

Legend on screen: "After the fiasco—"

Tom speaks from the fire escape landing.

TOM.   After the fiasco at Rubicam's Business College, the idea of getting a gentleman caller for Laura began to play a more and more important part in Mother's calculations. It became an obsession. Like some archetype of the universal unconscious, the image of the gentleman caller haunted our small apartment. . . .

(Screen image: A young man at the door of a house with flowers.*)*

An evening at home rarely passed without some allusion to this image, this specter, this hope. . . . Even when he wasn't mentioned, his presence hung in Mother's preoccupied look and in my sister's frightened, apologetic manner —hung like a sentence passed upon the Wingfields!

Mother was a woman of action as well as words. She began to take logical steps in the planned direction. Late that Winter and in the early Spring—realizing that extra money would be needed to properly feather the nest and plume the bird—she conducted a vigorous campaign on the telephone, roping in subscribers to one of those magazines for matrons called *The Homemaker's Companion,* the type of journal that features the serialized sublimations of ladies of letters who think in terms of delicate cuplike breasts, slim, tapering waists, rich, creamy thighs, eyes like wood smoke in Autumn, fingers that soothe and caress like strains of music, bodies as powerful as Etruscan sculpture.

(Screen image: The cover of a glamor magazine.*)*

(Amanda enters with the telephone on a long extension cord. She is spotlighted in the dim stage.)

AMANDA.   Ida Scott? This is Amanda Wingfield! We *missed* you at the D.A.R. last Monday! I said to myself: She's probably suffering with that sinus condition! How is that sinus condition?
Horrors! Heaven have mercy!—You're a Christian martyr, yes, that's what your are, a Christian martyr!
Well, I just now happened to notice that your subscription to the *Companion*'s about to expire! Yes, it expires with the next issue, honey!—just when that wonderful new serial by Bessie Mae Hopper is getting off to such an exciting start. Oh, honey, it's something that you can't miss! You remember how *Gone with the Wind* took everybody by storm? You simply couldn't go out if you hadn't read it. All everybody *talked* was Scarlett O'Hara. Well, this is a book that critics already compare to *Gone with the Wind*. It's the *Gone with the Wind* of the post-World-War generation!—What?—Burning?—Oh, honey, don't let them burn, go take a look in the oven and I'll hold the wire! Heavens —I think she's hung up!

(The scene dims out.)

(Legend on screen: "You think I'm in love with Continental shoemakers?"*)*

(Before the lights come up again, the violent voices of Tom and Amanda are heard. They are quarreling behind the portieres. In front of them stands Laura with clenched hands and panicky expression. A clear pool of light is on her figure throughout this scene.)

TOM.   What in Christ's name am I—
AMANDA *(shrilly).*   Don't you use that—
TOM: —supposed to do!
AMANDA: —expression! Not in my—
TOM.   Ohhh!
AMANDA: —presence! Have you gone out of your senses?
TOM.   I have, that's true, *driven* out!
AMANDA.   What is the matter with you, you—big—big—IDIOT!
TOM.   Look!—I've got *no thing,* no single thing—
AMANDA.   Lower your voice!
TOM: —in my life here that I can call my OWN! Everything is—
AMANDA.   Stop that shouting!
TOM.   Yesterday you confiscated my books! You had the nerve to—

AMANDA.   I took that horrible novel back to the library—yes! That hideous book by that insane Mr. Lawrence.

(Tom laughs wildly.)

I cannot control the output of diseased minds or people who cater to them—

(Tom laughs still more wildly.)

BUT I WON'T ALLOW SUCH FILTH BROUGHT INTO MY HOUSE! No, no, no, no, no!
TOM.   House, house! Who pays rent on it, who makes a slave of himself to—
AMANDA *(fairly screeching)*.   Don't you DARE to—
TOM.   No, no, *I* mustn't say things! *I've* got to just—
AMANDA.   Let me tell you—
TOM.   I don't want to hear any more!

(He tears the portieres open. The dining-room area is lit with a turgid smoky red glow. Now we see Amanda; her hair is in metal curlers and she is wearing a very old bathrobe, much too large for her slight figure, a relic of the faithless Mr. Wingfield. The upright typewriter now stands on the drop-leaf table, along with a wild disarray of manuscripts. The quarrel was probably precipitated by Amanda's interruption of Tom's creative labor. A chair lies overthrown on the floor. Their gesticulating shadows are cast on the ceiling by the fiery glow.)

AMANDA.   You *will* hear more, you—
TOM.   No, I won't hear more, I'm going out!
AMANDA.   You come right back in—
TOM.   Out, out, out! Because I'm—
AMANDA.   Come back here, Tom Wingfield! I'm not through talking to you!
TOM.   Oh, go—
LAURA *(desperately)*.—   Tom!
AMANDA.   You're going to listen, and no more insolence from you! I'm at the end of my patience!

(He comes back toward her.)

TOM.   What do you think I'm at? Aren't I supposed to have any patience to reach the end of, Mother? I know, I know. It seems unimportant to you, what I'm *doing*—what I *want* to do—having a little *difference* between them! You don't think that—
AMANDA.   I think you've been doing things that you're ashamed of. That's why you act like this. I don't believe that you go every night to the movies. Nobody goes to the movies night after night. Nobody in their right minds goes to the movies as often as you pretend to. People don't go to the movies at nearly midnight, and movies don't let out at two A.M. Come in stumbling. Muttering to yourself like a maniac! You get three hours' sleep and then go to work. Oh, I can picture the way you're doing down there. Moping, doping, because you're in no condition.
TOM *(wildly)*.   No, I'm in no condition!
AMANDA.   What right have you got to jeopardize your job? Jeopardize the security of us all? How do you think we'd manage if you were—

TOM.   Listen! You think I'm crazy about the *warehouse*? *(He bends fiercely toward her slight figure.)* You think I'm in love with the Continental Shoemakers? You think I want to spend fifty-five *years* down there in that—*celotex interior!* with—*fluorescent—tubes!* Look! I'd rather somebody picked up a crowbar and battered out my brains—than go back mornings! I *go!* Every time you come in yelling that Goddamn *"Rise and Shine!" "Rise and Shine!"* I say to myself, "How *lucky dead* people are!" But I get up. I *go!* For sixty-five dollars a month I give up all that I dream of doing and being *ever!* And you say self—*self's* all I ever think of. Why, listen, if self is what I thought of, Mother, I'd be where he is—GONE! *(He points to his father's picture.)* As far as the system of transportation reaches! *(He starts past her. She grabs his arm.)* Don't grab at me, Mother!

AMANDA.   Where are you going?

TOM.   I'm going to the *movies!*

AMANDA.   I don't believe that lie!

(Tom crouches toward her, overtowering her tiny figure. She backs away, gasping.)

TOM.   I'm going to opium dens! Yes, opium dens, dens of vice and criminals' hangouts, Mother. I've joined the Hogan Gang, I'm a hired assassin, I carry a tommy gun in a violin case! I run a string of cat houses in the Valley! They call me Killer, Killer Wingfield, I'm leading a double-life, a simple, honest warehouse worker by day, by night a dynamic *czar* of the *underworld, Mother.* I go to gambling casinos, I spin away fortunes on the roulette table! I wear a patch over one eye and a false mustache, sometimes I put on green whiskers. On those occasions they call me—*El Diablo!* Oh, I could tell you many things to make you sleepless! My enemies plan to dynamite this place. They're going to blow us all sky-high some night! I'll be glad, very happy, and so will you! You'll go up, up on a broomstick, over Blue Mountain with seventeen gentlemen callers! You ugly—babbling old—*witch.* . . . *(He goes through a series of violent, clumsy movements, seizing his overcoat, lunging to the door, pulling it fiercely open. The women watch him, aghast. His arm catches in the sleeve of the coat as he struggles to pull it on. For a moment he is pinioned by the bulky garment. With an outraged groan he tears the coat off again, splitting the shoulder of it, and hurls it across the room. It strikes against the shelf of Laura's glass collection, and there is a tinkle of shattering glass. Laura cries out as if wounded.)*

(Music.)

(Screen legend: "The Glass Menagerie.")

LAURA *(shrilly).   My glass!*—menagerie. . . . *(She covers her face and turns away.)*

(But Amanda is still stunned and stupefied by the "ugly witch" so that she barely notices this occurrence. Now she recovers her speech.)

AMANDA *(in an awful voice).   I won't speak to you—until you apologize!*

(She crosses through the portieres and draws them together behind her. Tom is left with Laura. Laura clings weakly to the mantel with her face averted. Tom stares

at her stupidly for a moment. Then he crosses to the shelf. He drops awkwardly on his knees to collect the fallen glass, glancing at Laura as if he would speak but couldn't.)

("The Glass Menagerie" music steals in as the scene dims out.)

SCENE FOUR

The interior of the apartment is dark. There is a faint light in the alley. A deep-voiced bell in a church is tolling the hour of five.

    Tom appears at the top of the alley. After each solemn boom of the bell in the tower, he shakes a little noisemaker or rattle as if to express the tiny spasm of man in contrast to the sustained power and dignity of the Almighty. This and the unsteadiness of his advance make it evident that he has been drinking. As he climbs the few steps to the fire escape landing light steals up inside. Laura appears in the front room in a nightdress. She notices that Tom's bed is empty. Tom fishes in his pockets for his door key, removing a motley assortment of articles in the search, including a shower of movie ticket stubs and an empty bottle. At last he finds the key, but just as he is about to insert it, it slips from his fingers. He strikes a match and crouches below the door.

TOM *(bitterly).*   One crack—and it falls through!

(Laura opens the door.)

LAURA.   Tom! Tom, what are you doing?

TOM.   Looking for a door key.

LAURA.   Where have you been all this time?

TOM.   I have been to the movies.

LAURA.   All this time at the movies?

TOM.   There was a very long program. There was a Garbo picture and a Mickey Mouse and a travelogue and a newsreel and a preview of coming attractions. And there was an organ solo and a collection for the Milk Fund—simultaneously—which ended up in a terrible fight between a fat lady and an usher!

LAURA *(innocently).*   Did you have to stay through everything?

TOM.   Of course! And, oh, I forgot! There was a big stage show! The headliner on this stage show was Malvolio the Magician. He performed wonderful tricks, many of them, such as pouring water back and forth between pitchers. First it turned to wine and then it turned to beer and then it turned to whisky. I know it was whisky it finally turned into because he needed somebody to come up out of the audience to help him, and I came up—both shows! It was Kentucky Straight Bourbon. A very generous fellow, he gave souvenirs. *(He pulls from his back pocket a shimmering rainbow-colored scarf.)* He gave me this. This is his magic scarf. You can have it, Laura. You wave it over a canary cage and you get a bowl of goldfish. You wave it over the goldfish bowl and they fly away canaries. . . . But the wonderfullest trick of all was the coffin trick. We nailed him into a coffin and he got out of the coffin without removing one

nail. *(He has come inside.)* There is a trick that would come in handy for me
—get me out of this two-by-four situation! *(He flops onto the bed and starts
removing his shoes.)*

LAURA.   Tom—shhh!

TOM.   What're you shushing me for?

LAURA.   You'll wake up Mother.

TOM.   Goody, goody! Pay 'er back for all those "Rise an' Shines." *(He lies down,
groaning.)* You know it don't take much intelligence to get yourself into a
nailed-up coffin, Laura. But who in hell ever got himself out of one without
removing one nail?

(As if in answer, the father's grinning photograph lights up. The scene dims out.)

*(Immediately following, the church bell is heard striking six. At the sixth stroke the
alarm clock goes off in Amanda's room, and after a few moments we hear her calling:
"Rise and Shine! Rise and Shine! Laura, go tell your brother to rise and shine!")*

TOM *(sitting up slowly).*   I'll rise—but I won't shine.

(The light increases.)

AMANDA.   Laura, tell your brother his coffee is ready.

(Laura slips into the front room.)

LAURA.   Tom!—It's nearly seven. Don't make Mother nervous.

(He stares at her stupidly.)

       (beseechingly:) Tom, speak to Mother this morning. Make up with her, apolo-
       gize, speak to her!

TOM.   She won't to me. It's her that started not speaking.

LAURA.   If you just say you're sorry she'll start speaking.

TOM.   Her not speaking—is that such a tragedy?

LAURA.   Please—please!

AMANDA *(calling from the kitchenette).*   Laura, are you going to do what I asked
       you to do, or do I have to get dressed and go out myself?

LAURA.   Going, going—soon as I get on my coat!

*(She pulls on a shapeless felt hat with a nervous, jerky movement, pleadingly glancing
at Tom. She rushes awkwardly for her coat. The coat is one of Amanda's, inaccu-
rately made-over, the sleeves too short for Laura.)*

       Butter and what else?

AMANDA *(entering from the kitchenette).*   Just butter. Tell them to charge it.

LAURA.   Mother, they make such faces when I do that.

AMANDA.   Sticks and stones can break our bones, but the expression on Mr.
       Garfinkel's face won't harm us! Tell your brother his coffee is getting cold.

LAURA *(at the door).*   Do what I asked you, will you, will you, Tom?

(He looks sullenly away.)

AMANDA.   Laura, go now or just don't go at all!

LAURA *(rushing out).*   Going—going!

(A second later she cries out. Tom springs up and crosses to the door. Tom opens the door.)

TOM.   Laura?

LAURA.   I'm all right. I slipped, but I'm all right.

AMANDA *(peering anxiously after her).*   If anyone breaks a leg on those fire-escape steps, the landlord ought to be sued for every cent he possesses! *(She shuts the door. Now she remembers she isn't speaking to Tom and returns to the other room.)*

(As Tom comes listlessly for his coffee, she turns her back to him and stands rigidly facing the window on the gloomy gray vault of the areaway. Its light on her face with its aged but childish features is cruelly sharp, satirical as a Daumier print.)

(The music of "Ave Maria," is heard softly.)

(Tom glances sheepishly but sullenly at her averted figure and slumps at the table. The coffee is scalding hot; he sips it and gasps and spits it back in the cup. At his gasp, Amanda catches her breath and half turns. Then she catches herself and turns back to the window. Tom blows on his coffee, glancing sidewise at his mother. She clears her throat. Tom clears his. He starts to rise, sinks back down again, scratches his head, clears his throat again. Amanda coughs. Tom raises his cup in both hands to blow on it, his eyes staring over the rim of it at his mother for several moments. Then he slowly sets the cup down and awkwardly and hesitantly rises from the chair.)

TOM *(hoarsely).*   Mother. I—I apologize, Mother.

(Amanda draws a quick, shuddering breath. Her face works grotesquely. She breaks into childlike tears.)

I'm sorry for what I said, for everything that I said, I didn't mean it.

AMANDA *(sobbingly).*   My devotion has made me a witch and so I make myself hateful to my children!

TOM.   *No,* you *don't.*

AMANDA.   I worry so much, don't sleep, it makes me nervous!

TOM *(gently).*   I understand that.

AMANDA.   I've had to put up a solitary battle all these years. But you're my right-hand bower! Don't fall down, don't fail!

TOM *(gently).*   I try, Mother.

AMANDA *(with great enthusiasm).*   Try and you will *succeed!* [*The notion makes her breathless.*] Why, you—you're just *full* of natural endowments! Both of my children—they're *unusual* children! Don't you think I know it? I'm so— *proud!* Happy and—feel I've—so much to be thankful for but—promise me one thing, son!

TOM.   What, Mother?

AMANDA.   Promise, son, you'll—never be a drunkard!

TOM *(turns to her grinning).*   I will never be a drunkard, Mother.

AMANDA.   That's what frightened me so, that you'd be drinking! Eat a bowl of
     Purina!

TOM.   Just coffee, Mother.

AMANDA.   Shredded wheat biscuit?

TOM.   No. No, Mother, just coffee.

AMANDA.   You can't put in a day's work on an empty stomach. You've got ten
     minutes—don't gulp! Drinking too-hot liquids makes cancer of the stomach.
     . . . Put cream in.

TOM.   No, thank you.

AMANDA.   To cool it.

TOM.   No! No, thank you, I want it black.

AMANDA.   I know, but it's not good for you. We have to do all that we can to build
     ourselves up. In these trying times we live in, all that we have to cling to is
     —each other. . . . That's why it's so important to—Tom, I—I sent out your
     sister so I could discuss something with you. If you hadn't spoken I would have
     spoken to you. *(She sits down.)*

TOM *(gently).*   What is it, Mother, that you want to discuss?

AMANDA.   *Laura!*

(Tom puts his cup down slowly.)

(Legend on screen: "Laura." Music: "The Glass Menagerie.")

TOM: —Oh.—Laura . . .

AMANDA *(touching his sleeve).*   You know how Laura is. So quiet but—still water
     runs deep! She notices things and I think she—broods about them.

(Tom looks up.)

     A few days ago I came in and she was crying.

TOM.   What about?

AMANDA.   You.

TOM.   Me?

AMANDA.   She has an idea that you're not happy here.

TOM.   What gave her that idea?

AMANDA.   What gives her any idea? However, you do act strangely. I—I'm not
     criticizing, understand *that!* I know your ambitions do not lie in the ware-
     house, that like everybody in the whole wide world—you've had to—make
     sacrifices, but—Tom—Tom—life's not easy, it calls for—Spartan endurance!
     There's so many things in my heart that I cannot describe to you! I've never
     told you but I—*loved* your father. . . .

TOM *(gently).*   I know that, Mother.

AMANDA.   And you—when I see you taking after his ways! Staying out late—and
     —well, you *had* been drinking the night you were in that—terrifying condi-
     tion! Laura says that you hate the apartment and that you go out nights to get
     away from it! Is that true, Tom?

TOM.   No. You say there's so much in your heart that you can't describe to me.
     That's true of me, too. There's so much in my heart that I can't describe to
     you! So let's respect each other's—

AMANDA.   But, why—*why*, Tom—are you always so *restless?* Where do you *go*
        to, nights?

TOM.   I—go to the movies.

AMANDA.   Why do you go to the movies so much, Tom?

TOM.   I go to the movies because—I like adventure. Adventure is something I
        don't have much of at work, so I go to the movies.

AMANDA.   But, Tom, you go to the movies *entirely* too *much!*

TOM.   I like a lot of adventure.

*(Amanda looks baffled, then hurt. As the familiar inquisition resumes, Tom becomes
hard and impatient again. Amanda slips back into her querulous attitude toward
him.)*

(Image on screen: A sailing vessel with Jolly Roger.*)*

AMANDA.   Most young men find adventure in their careers.

TOM.   Then most young men are not employed in a warehouse.

AMANDA.   The world is full of young men employed in warehouses and offices and
        factories.

TOM.   Do all of them find adventure in their careers?

AMANDA.   They do or they do without it! Not everybody has a craze for adventure.

TOM.   Man is by instinct a lover, a hunter, a fighter, and none of those instincts
        are given much play at the warehouse!

AMANDA.   Man is by instinct! Don't quote instinct to me! Instinct is something
        that people have got away from! It belongs to animals! Christian adults don't
        want it!

TOM.   What do Christian adults want, then, Mother?

AMANDA.   Superior things! Things of the mind and the spirit! Only animals have
        to satisfy instincts! Surely your aims are somewhat higher than theirs! Than
        monkeys—pigs—

TOM.   I reckon they're not.

AMANDA.   You're joking. However, that isn't what I wanted to discuss.

TOM *(rising).*   I haven't much time.

AMANDA *(pushing his shoulders).*   Sit down.

TOM.   You want me to punch in red at the warehouse, Mother?

AMANDA.   You have five minutes. I want to talk about Laura.

(Screen legend: "Plans and Provisions."*)*

TOM.   All right! What about Laura?

AMANDA.   We have to be making some plans and provisions for her. She's older
        than you, two years, and nothing has happened. She just drifts along doing
        nothing. It frightens me terribly how she just drifts along.

TOM.   I guess she's the type that people call home girls.

AMANDA.   There's no such type, and if there is, it's a pity! That is unless the home
        is hers, with a husband!

TOM.   What?

AMANDA.   Oh, I can see the handwriting on the wall as plain as I see the nose
        in front of my face! It's terrifying! More and more you remind me of your

father! He was out all hours without explanation!—Then *left! Good-bye!* And me with the bag to hold. I saw that letter you got from the Merchant Marine. I know what you're dreaming of. I'm not standing here blindfolded. *(She pauses.)* Very well, then. Then *do* it! But not till there's somebody to take your place.

TOM.   What do you mean?

AMANDA.   I mean that as soon as Laura has got somebody to take care of her, married, a home of her own, independent—why, then you'll be free to go wherever you please, on land, on sea, whichever way the wind blows you! But until that time you've got to look out for your sister. I don't say me because I'm old and don't matter! I say for your sister because she's young and dependent.

I put her in business college—a dismal failure! Frightened her so it made her sick at the stomach. I took her over to the Young People's League at the church. Another fiasco. She spoke to nobody, nobody spoke to her. Now all she does is fool with those pieces of glass and play those worn-out records. What kind of a life is that for a girl to lead?

TOM.   What can I do about it?

AMANDA.   Overcome selfishness! Self, self, self is all that you ever think of!

(Tom springs up and crosses to get his coat. It is ugly and bulky. He pulls on a cap with earmuffs.)

Where is your muffler? Put your wool muffler on!

(He snatches it angrily from the closet, tosses it around his neck and pulls both ends tight.)

Tom! I haven't said what I had in mind to ask you.

TOM.   I'm too late to—

AMANDA *(catching his arm—very importunately; then shyly).*   Down at the warehouse, aren't there some—nice young men?

TOM.   No!

AMANDA.   There *must* be—*some* . . .

TOM.   Mother—*(He gestures.)*

AMANDA.   Find out one that's clean-living—doesn't drink and ask him out for sister!

TOM.   What?

AMANDA.   For *sister!* To *meet!* Get *acquainted!*

TOM *(stamping to the door).*   Oh, my *go-osh!*

AMANDA.   Will you?

(He opens the door. She says, imploringly:)

Will you?

(He starts down the fire escape.)

Will you? *Will* you, dear?

TOM *(calling back).*   Yes!

(Amanda closes the door hesitantly and with a troubled but faintly hopeful expression.)

(Screen image: The cover of a glamor magazine.*)*

(The spotlight picks up Amanda at the phone.)

AMANDA.   Ella Cartwright? This is Amanda Wingfield!
     How are you, honey?
     How is that kidney condition?

(There is a five-second pause.)

     Horrors!

(There is another pause.)

     You're a Christian martyr, yes, honey, that's what you are, a Christian martyr!
     Well, I just now happened to notice in my little red book that your subscription
     to the *Companion* has just run out! I knew that you wouldn't want to miss out
     on the wonderful serial starting in this new issue. It's by Bessie Mae Hopper,
     the first thing she's written since *Honeymoon for Three.* Wasn't that a strange
     and interesting story? Well, this one is even lovelier, I believe. It has a sophis-
     ticated, society background. It's all about the horsey set on Long Island!

(The light fades out.)

SCENE FIVE

Legend on the screen: "Annunciation."
  Music is heard as the light slowly comes on.
  *It is early dusk of a Spring evening. Supper has just been finished in the Wingfield
    apartment. Amanda and Laura, in light-colored dresses, are removing dishes
    from the table in the dining room, which is shadowy, their movements formal-
    ized almost as a dance or ritual, their moving forms as pale and silent as moths.
    Tom, in white shirt and trousers, rises from the table and crosses toward the fire
    escape.*

AMANDA *(as he passes her).*   Son, will you do me a favor?
TOM.   What?
AMANDA.   Comb your hair! You look so pretty when your hair is combed!

*(Tom slouches on the sofa with the evening paper. Its enormous headline reads:
"Franco Triumphs.")*

     There is only one respect in which I would like you to emulate your father.
TOM.   What respect is that?
AMANDA.   The care he always took of his appearance. He never allowed himself
     to look untidy.

(He throws down the paper and crosses to the fire escape.)

     Where are you going?

TOM.   I'm going out to smoke.

AMANDA.   You smoke too much. A pack a day at fifteen cents a pack. How much would that amount to in a month? Thirty times fifteen is how much, Tom? Figure it out and you will be astounded at what you could save. Enough to give you a night-school course in accounting at Washington U.! Just think what a wonderful thing that would be for you, son!

(Tom is unmoved by the thought.)

TOM.   I'd rather smoke. *(He steps out on the landing, letting the screen door slam.)*

AMANDA *(sharply).*   I know! That's the tragedy of it. . . . *(Alone, she turns to look at her husband's picture.)*

(Dance music: "The World Is Waiting for the Sunrise!")

TOM *(to the audience).*   Across the alley from us was the Paradise Dance Hall. On evenings in Spring the windows and doors were open and the music came outdoors. Sometimes the lights were turned out except for a large glass sphere that hung from the ceiling. It would turn slowly about and filter the dusk with delicate rainbow colors. Then the orchestra played a waltz or a tango, something that had a slow and sensuous rhythm. Couples would come outside, to the relative privacy of the alley. You could see them kissing behind ash pits and telephone poles. This was the compensation for lives that passed like mine, without any change or adventure. Adventure and change were imminent in this year. They were waiting around the corner for all these kids. Suspended in the mist over Berchtesgaden, caught in the folds of Chamberlain's umbrella. In Spain there was Guernica! But here there was only hot swing music and liquor, dance halls, bars, and movies, and sex that hung in the gloom like a chandelier and flooded the world with brief, deceptive rainbows. . . . All the world was waiting for bombardments!

(Amanda turns from the picture and comes outside.)

AMANDA *(sighing).*   A fire escape landing's a poor excuse for a porch. *(She spreads a newspaper on a step and sits down, gracefully and demurely as if she were settling into a swing on a Mississippi veranda.)* What are you looking at?

TOM.   The moon.

AMANDA.   Is there a moon this evening?

TOM.   It's rising over Garfinkel's Delicatessen.

AMANDA.   So it is! A little silver slipper of a moon. Have you made a wish on it yet?

TOM.   Um-hum.

AMANDA.   What did you wish for?

TOM.   That's a secret.

AMANDA.   A secret, huh? Well, I won't tell mine either. I will be just as mysterious as you.

TOM.   I bet I can guess what yours is.

AMANDA.   Is my head so transparent?

TOM.   You're not a sphinx.

AMANDA.   No, I don't have secrets. I'll tell you what I wished for on the moon.

Success and happiness for my precious children! I wish for that whenever there's a moon, and when there isn't a moon, I wish for it, too.

TOM.   I thought perhaps you wished for a gentleman caller.

AMANDA.   Why do you say that?

TOM.   Don't you remember asking me to fetch one?

AMANDA.   I remember suggesting that it would be nice for your sister if you brought home some nice young man from the warehouse. I think that I've made that suggestion more than once.

TOM.   Yes, you have made it repeatedly.

AMANDA.   Well?

TOM.   We are going to have one.

AMANDA.   *What?*

TOM.   A gentleman caller!

(The annunciation is celebrated with music.)

(Amanda rises.)

(Image on screen: A caller with a bouquet.*)*

AMANDA.   You mean you have asked some nice young man to come over?

TOM.   Yep. I've asked him to dinner.

AMANDA.   You really did?

TOM.   I did!

AMANDA.   You did, and did he—*accept?*

TOM.   He did!

AMANDA.   Well, well—well, well! That's—lovely!

TOM.   I thought that you would be pleased.

AMANDA.   It's definite then?

TOM.   Very definite.

AMANDA.   Soon?

TOM.   Very soon.

AMANDA.   For heaven's sake, stop putting on and tell me some things, will you?

TOM.   What things do you want me to tell you?

AMANDA.   *Naturally* I would like to know when he's *coming!*

TOM.   He's coming tomorrow.

AMANDA.   *Tomorrow?*

TOM.   Yep. Tomorrow.

AMANDA.   But, Tom!

TOM.   Yes, Mother?

AMANDA.   Tomorrow gives me no time!

TOM.   Time for what?

AMANDA.   Preparations! Why didn't you phone me at once, as soon as you asked him, the minute that he accepted? Then, don't you see, I could have been getting ready!

TOM.   You don't have to make any fuss.

AMANDA.   Oh, Tom, Tom, Tom, of course I have to make a fuss! I want things nice, not sloppy! Not thrown together. I'll certainly have to do some fast thinking, won't I?

TOM.   I don't see why you have to think at all.

AMANDA.   You just don't know. We can't have a gentleman caller in a pigsty! All my wedding silver has to be polished, the monogrammed table linen ought to be laundered! The windows have to be washed and fresh curtains put up. And how about clothes? We have to *wear* something, don't we?

TOM.   Mother, this boy is no one to make a fuss over!

AMANDA.   Do you realize he's the first young man we've introduced to your sister? It's terrible, dreadful, disgraceful that poor little sister has never received a single gentleman caller! Tom, come inside! *(She opens the screen door.)*

TOM.   What for?

AMANDA.   I want to ask you some things.

TOM.   If you're going to make such a fuss, I'll call it off, I'll tell him not to come!

AMANDA.   You certainly won't do anything of the kind. Nothing offends people worse than broken engagements. It simply means I'll have to work like a Turk! We won't be brilliant, but we will pass inspection. Come on inside.

(Tom follows her inside, groaning.)

Sit down.

TOM.   Any particular place you would like me to sit?

AMANDA.   Thank heavens I've got that new sofa! I'm also making payments on a floor lamp I'll have sent out! And put the chintz covers on, they'll brighten things up! Of course I'd hoped to have these walls re-papered. . . . What is the young man's name?

TOM.   His name is O'Connor.

AMANDA.   That, of course, means fish—tomorrow is Friday! I'll have that salmon loaf—with Durkee's dressing! What does he do? He works at the warehouse?

TOM.   Of course! How else would I—

AMANDA.   Tom, he—doesn't drink?

TOM.   Why do you ask me that?

AMANDA.   Your father *did!*

TOM.   Don't get started on that!

AMANDA.   He *does* drink, then?

TOM.   Not that I know of!

AMANDA.   Make sure, be certain! The last thing I want for my daughter's a boy who drinks!

TOM.   Aren't you being a little bit premature? Mr. O'Connor has not yet appeared on the scene!

AMANDA.   But will tomorrow. To meet your sister, and what do I know about his character? Nothing! Old maids are better off than wives of drunkards!

TOM.   Oh, my God!

AMANDA.   Be still!

TOM *(leaning forward to whisper).*   Lots of fellows meet girls whom they don't marry!

AMANDA.   Oh, talk sensibly, Tom—and don't be sarcastic! *(She has gotten a hairbrush.)*

TOM.   What are you doing?

AMANDA.   I'm brushing that cowlick down! *(She attacks his hair with the brush.)* What is this young man's position at the warehouse?

TOM *(submitting grimly to the brush and the interrogation).*   This young man's position is that of a shipping clerk, Mother.

AMANDA.   Sounds to me like a fairly responsible job, the sort of a job *you* would be in if you just had more *get-up.* What is his salary? Have you any idea?

TOM.   I would judge it to be approximately eighty-five dollars a month.

AMANDA.   Well—not princely, but—

TOM.   Twenty more than I make.

AMANDA.   Yes, how well I know! But for a family man, eighty-five dollars a month is not much more than you can just get by on. . . .

TOM.   Yes, but Mr. O'Connor is not a family man.

AMANDA.   He might be, mightn't he? Some time in the future?

TOM.   I see. Plans and provisions.

AMANDA.   You are the only young man that I know of who ignores the fact that the future becomes the present, the present the past, and the past turns into everlasting regret if you don't plan for it!

TOM.   I will think that over and see what I can make of it.

AMANDA.   Don't be supercilious with your mother! Tell me some more about this —what do you call him?

TOM.   James D. O'Connor. The D. is for Delaney.

AMANDA.   Irish on *both* sides! *Gracious!* And doesn't drink?

TOM.   Shall I call him up and ask him right this minute?

AMANDA.   The only way to find out about those things is to make discreet inquiries at the proper moment. When I was a girl in Blue Mountain and it was suspected that a young man drank, the girl whose attentions he had been receiving, if any girl *was,* would sometimes speak to the minister of his church, or rather her father would if her father was living, and sort of feel him out on the young man's character. That is the way such things are discreetly handled to keep a young woman from making a tragic mistake!

TOM.   Then how did you happen to make a tragic mistake?

AMANDA.   That innocent look of your father's had everyone fooled! He *smiled*— the world was *enchanted!* No girl can do worse than put herself at the mercy of a handsome appearance! I hope that Mr. O'Connor is not too good-looking.

TOM.   No, he's not too good-looking. He's covered with freckles and hasn't too much of a nose.

AMANDA.   He's not right-down homely, though?

TOM.   Not right-down homely. Just medium homely, I'd say.

AMANDA.   Character's what to look for in a man.

TOM.   That's what I've always said, Mother.

AMANDA.   You've never said anything of the kind and I suspect you would never give it a thought.

TOM.   Don't be so suspicious of me.

AMANDA.   At least I hope he's the type that's up and coming.

TOM.   I think he really goes in for self-improvement.

AMANDA.   What reason have you to think so?

TOM.   He goes to night school.

AMANDA *(beaming).*   Splendid! What does he do, I mean study?

TOM.   Radio engineering and public speaking!

AMANDA.   Then he has visions of being advanced in the world! Any young man who studies public speaking is aiming to have an executive job some day! And radio engineering? A thing for the future! Both of these facts are very illuminating. Those are the sort of things that a mother should know concerning any young man who comes to call on her daughter. Seriously or—not.

TOM.   One little warning. He doesn't know about Laura. I didn't let on that we had dark ulterior motives. I just said, why don't you come and have dinner with us? He said okay and that was the whole conversation.

AMANDA.   I bet it was! You're eloquent as an oyster. However, he'll know about Laura when he gets here. When he sees how lovely and sweet and pretty she is, he'll thank his lucky stars he was asked to dinner.

TOM.   Mother, you mustn't expect too much of Laura.

AMANDA.   What do you mean?

TOM.   Laura seems all those things to you and me because she's ours and we love her. We don't even notice she's crippled any more.

AMANDA.   Don't say crippled! You know that I never allow that word to be used!

TOM.   But face facts, Mother. She is and—that's not all—

AMANDA.   What do you mean "not all"?

TOM.   Laura is very different from other girls.

AMANDA.   I think the difference is all to her advantage.

TOM.   Not quite all—in the eyes of others—strangers—she's terribly shy and lives in a world of her own and those things make her seem a little peculiar to people outside the house.

AMANDA.   Don't say peculiar.

TOM.   Face the facts. She is.

(The dance hall music changes to a tango that has a minor and somewhat ominous tone.)

AMANDA.   In what way is she peculiar—may I ask?

TOM *(gently).*   She lives in a world of her own—a world of little glass ornaments, Mother. . . .

(He gets up. Amanda remains holding the brush, looking at him, troubled.)

       She plays old phonograph records and—that's about all—*(He glances at himself in the mirror and crosses to the door.)*

AMANDA *(sharply).*   Where are you going?

TOM.   I'm going to the movies. *(He goes out the screen door.)*

AMANDA.   Not to the movies, every night to the movies! *(She follows quickly to the screen door.)* I don't believe you always go to the movies!

(He is gone. Amanda looks worriedly after him for a moment. Then vitality and optimism return and she turns from the door, crossing to the portieres.)

       Laura! Laura!

(Laura answers from the kitchenette.)

LAURA.   Yes, Mother.

AMANDA.   Let those dishes go and come in front!

(Laura appears with a dish towel. Amanda speaks to her gaily.)

Laura, come here and make a wish on the moon!

(Screen image: The Moon.*)*

LAURA *(entering).*   Moon—moon?

AMANDA.   A little silver slipper of a moon. Look over your left shoulder, Laura, and make a wish!

(Laura looks faintly puzzled as if called out of sleep. Amanda seizes her shoulders and turns her at an angle by the door.)

Now! Now, darling, *wish!*

LAURA.   What shall I wish for, Mother?

AMANDA *(her voice trembling and her eyes suddenly filling with tears).*   Happiness! Good fortune!

(The sound of the violin rises and the stage dims out.)

SCENE SIX

The light comes up on the fire escape landing. Tom is leaning against the grill, smoking.

(Screen image: The high school hero.*)*

TOM.   And so the following evening I brought Jim home to dinner. I had known Jim slightly in high school. In high school Jim was a hero. He had tremendous Irish good nature and vitality with the scrubbed and polished look of white chinaware. He seemed to move in a continual spotlight. He was a star in basketball, captain of the debating club, president of the senior class and the glee club and he sang the male lead in the annual light operas. He was always running or bounding, never just walking. He seemed always at the point of defeating the law of gravity. He was shooting with such velocity through his adolescence that you would logically expect him to arrive at nothing short of the White House by the time he was thirty. But Jim apparently ran into more interference after his graduation from Soldan. His speed had definitely slowed. Six years after he left high school he was holding a job that wasn't much better than mine.

(Screen image: The Clerk.*)*

He was the only one at the warehouse with whom I was on friendly terms. I was valuable to him as someone who could remember his former glory, who had seen him win basketball games and the silver cup in debating. He knew of my secret practice of retiring to a cabinet of the washroom to work on poems when business was slack in the warehouse. He called me Shakespeare. And while the other boys in the warehouse regarded me with suspicious hostility,

Jim took a humorous attitude toward me. Gradually his attitude affected the others, their hostility wore off and they also began to smile at me as people smile at an oddly fashioned dog who trots across their path at some distance.

I knew that Jim and Laura had known each other at Soldan, and I had heard Laura speak admiringly of his voice. I didn't know if Jim remembered her or not. In high school Laura had been as unobtrusive as Jim had been astonishing. If he did remember Laura, it was not as my sister, for when I asked him to dinner, he grinned and said, "You know, Shakespeare, I never thought of you as having folks!"

He was about to discover that I did. . . .

(Legend on screen: "The accent of a coming foot."*)*

(The light dims out on Tom and comes up in the Wingfield living room—a delicate lemony light. It is about five on a Friday evening of late Spring which comes "scattering poems in the sky.")

(Amanda has worked like a Turk in preparation for the gentleman caller. The results are astonishing. The new floor lamp with its rose silk shade is in place, a colored paper lantern conceals the broken light fixture in the ceiling, new billowing white curtains are at the windows, chintz covers are on the chairs and sofa, a pair of new sofa pillows make their initial appearance. Open boxes and tissue paper are scattered on the floor.)

(Laura stands in the middle of the room with lifted arms while Amanda crouches before her, adjusting the hem of a new dress, devout and ritualistic. The dress is colored and designed by memory. The arrangement of Laura's hair is changed; it is softer and more becoming. A fragile, unearthly prettiness has come out in Laura: she is like a piece of translucent glass touched by light, given a momentary radiance, not actual, not lasting.)

AMANDA *(impatiently).*   Why are you trembling?

LAURA.   Mother, you've made me so nervous!

AMANDA.   How have I made you nervous?

LAURA.   By all this fuss! You make it seem so important!

AMANDA.   I don't understand you, Laura. You couldn't be satisfied with just sitting home, and yet whenever I try to arrange something for you, you seem to resist it. *(She gets up.)* Now take a look at yourself. No, wait! Wait just a moment—I have an idea!

LAURA.   What is it now?

(Amanda produces two powder puffs which she wraps in handkerchiefs and stuffs in Laura's bosom.)

LAURA.   Mother, what are you doing?

AMANDA.   They call them "Gay Deceivers"!

LAURA.   I won't wear them!

AMANDA.   You will!

LAURA.   Why should I?

AMANDA.   Because, to be painfully honest, your chest is flat.

LAURA.   You make it seem like we were setting a trap.
AMANDA.   All pretty girls are a trap, a pretty trap, and men expect them to be.

(Legend on screen: "A pretty trap." *)*

Now look at yourself, young lady. This is the prettiest you will ever be! *(She stands back to admire Laura.)* I've got to fix myself now! You're going to be surprised by your mother's appearance!

(Amanda crosses through the portieres, humming gaily. Laura moves slowly to the long mirror and stares solemnly at herself. A wind blows the white curtains inward in a slow, graceful motion and with a faint, sorrowful sighing.)

AMANDA *(from somewhere behind the portieres).*   It isn't dark enough yet.

(Laura turns slowly before the mirror with a troubled look.)

(Legend on screen: "This is my sister: Celebrate her with strings!" *Music plays.)*

AMANDA *(laughing, still not visible).*   I'm going to show you something. I'm going to make a spectacular appearance!
LAURA.   What is it, Mother?
AMANDA.   Possess your soul in patience—you will see! Something I've resurrected from that old trunk! Styles haven't changed so terribly much after all. . . . *(She parts the portieres.)* Now just look at your mother! *(She wears a girlish frock of yellowed voile with a blue silk sash. She carries a bunch of jonquils—the legend of her youth is nearly revived. Now she speaks feverishly:)* This is the dress in which I led the cotillion. Won the cakewalk twice at Sunset Hill, wore one Spring to the Governor's Ball in Jackson! See how I sashayed around the ballroom, Laura? *(She raises her skirt and does a mincing step around the room.)* I wore it on Sundays for my gentlemen callers! I had it on the day I met your father. . . . I had malaria fever all that Spring. The change of climate from East Tennessee to the Delta—weakened resistance. I had a little tempera-ture all the time—not enough to be serious—just enough to make me restless and giddy! Invitations poured in—parties all over the Delta! "Stay in bed," said Mother, "You have fever!"—but I just wouldn't. I took quinine but kept on going, going! Evenings, dances! Afternoons, long, long rides! Picnics—lovely! So lovely, that country in May—all lacy with dogwood, literally flooded with jonquils! That was the Spring I had the craze for jonquils. Jonquils became an absolute obsession. Mother said, "Honey, there's no more room for jonquils." And still I kept on bringing in more jonquils. Whenever, wherever I saw them, I'd say, "Stop! Stop! I see jonquils!" I made the young men help me gather the jonquils! It was a joke, Amanda and her jonquils. Finally there were no more vases to hold them, every available space was filled with jonquils. No vases to hold them? All right, I'll hold them myself! And then I—*(She stops in front of the picture. Music plays.)* met your father! Malaria fever and jonquils and then—this—boy. . . . *(She switches on the rose-colored lamp.)* I hope they get here before it starts to rain. *(She crosses the room and places the jonquils in a bowl on the table.)* I gave your brother a little extra change so he and Mr. O'Connor could take the service car home.

LAURA *(with an altered look).*   What did you say his name was?
AMANDA.   O'Connor.
LAURA.   What is his first name?
AMANDA.   I don't remember. Oh, yes, I do. It was—Jim!

(Laura sways slightly and catches hold of a chair.)

(Legend on screen: "Not Jim!")

LAURA *(faintly).*   Not—Jim!
AMANDA.   Yes, that was it, it was Jim! I've never known a Jim that wasn't nice!

(The music becomes ominous.)

LAURA.   Are you sure his name is Jim O'Connor?
AMANDA.   Yes. Why?
LAURA.   Is he the one that Tom used to know in high school?
AMANDA.   He didn't say so. I think he just got to know him at the warehouse.
LAURA.   There was a Jim O'Connor we both knew in high school—*(then, with effort)* If that is the one that Tom is bringing to dinner—you'll have to excuse me, I won't come to the table.
AMANDA.   What sort of nonsense is this?
LAURA.   You asked me once if I'd ever liked a boy. Don't you remember I showed you this boy's picture?
AMANDA.   You mean the boy you showed me in the yearbook?
LAURA.   Yes, that boy.
AMANDA.   Laura, Laura, were you in love with that boy?
LAURA.   I don't know, Mother. All I know is I couldn't sit at the table if it was him!
AMANDA.   It won't be him! It isn't the least bit likely. But whether it is or not, you will come to the table. You will not be excused.
LAURA.   I'll have to be, Mother.
AMANDA.   I don't intend to humor your silliness, Laura. I've had too much from you and your brother, both! So just sit down and compose yourself till they come. Tom has forgotten his key so you'll have to let them in, when they arrive.
LAURA *(panicky).*   Oh, Mother—*you* answer the door!
AMANDA *(lightly).*   I'll be in the kitchen—busy!
LAURA.   Oh, Mother, please answer the door, don't make me do it!
AMANDA *(crossing into the kitchenette).*   I've got to fix the dressing for the salmon. Fuss, fuss—silliness!—over a gentleman caller!

(The door swings shut. Laura is left alone.)

(Legend on screen: "Terror!")

(She utters a low moan and turns off the lamp—sits stiffly on the edge of the sofa, knotting her fingers together.)

(Legend on screen: "The Opening of a Door!")

(Tom and Jim appear on the fire escape steps and climb to the landing. Hearing their

approach, Laura rises with a panicky gesture. She retreats to the portieres. The doorbell rings. Laura catches her breath and touches her throat. Low drums sound.)

AMANDA *(calling).* Laura, sweetheart! The door!

(Laura stares at it without moving.)

JIM. I think we just beat the rain.

TOM. Uh-huh. *(He rings again, nervously. Jim whistles and fishes for a cigarette.)*

AMANDA *(very, very gaily).* Laura, that is your brother and Mr. O'Connor! Will you let them in, darling?

(Laura crosses toward the kitchenette door.)

LAURA *(breathlessly).* Mother—you go to the door!

Amanda steps out of the kitchenette and stares furiously at Laura. She points imperiously at the door.)

LAURA. Please, please!

AMANDA *(in a fierce whisper).* What is the matter with you, you silly thing?

LAURA *(desperately).* Please, you answer it, *please!*

AMANDA. I told you I wasn't going to humor you, Laura. Why have you chosen this moment to lose your mind?

LAURA. Please, please, please, you go!

AMANDA. You'll have to go to the door because I can't!

LAURA *(despairingly).* I can't either!

AMANDA. *Why?*

LAURA. I'm *sick!*

AMANDA. I'm sick, too—of your nonsense! Why can't you and your brother be normal people? Fantastic whims and behavior!

(Tom gives a long ring.)

  Preposterous goings on! Can you give me one reason—*(She calls out lyrically.) Coming! Just one second!*—why you should be afraid to open a door? Now you answer it, Laura!

LAURA. Oh, oh, oh . . . *(She returns through the portieres, darts to the victrola, winds it frantically and turns it on.)*

AMANDA. Laura Wingfield, you march right to that door!

LAURA. *Yes—yes, Mother!*

(A faraway, scratchy rendition of "Dardanella" softens the air and gives her strength to move through it. She slips to the door and draws it cautiously open. Tom enters with the caller, Jim O'Connor.)

TOM. Laura, this is Jim. Jim, this is my sister, Laura.

JIM *(stepping inside).* I didn't know that Shakespeare had a sister!

LAURA *(retreating, stiff and trembling, from the door).* How—how do you do?

JIM *(heartily, extending his hand).* Okay!

(Laura touches it hesitantly with hers.)

JIM.		Your hand's *cold,* Laura!

LAURA.		Yes, well—I've been playing the victrola. . . .

JIM.		Must have been playing classical music on it! You ought to play a little hot swing music to warm you up!

LAURA.		Excuse me—I haven't finished playing the victrola. . . . *(She turns awkwardly and hurries into the front room. She pauses a second by the victrola. Then she catches her breath and darts through the portieres like a frightened deer.)*

JIM *(grinning).*		What was the matter?

TOM.		Oh—with Laura? Laura is—terribly shy.

JIM.		Shy, huh? It's unusual to meet a shy girl nowadays. I don't believe you ever mentioned you had a sister.

TOM.		Well, now you know. I have one. Here is the *Post Dispatch.* You want a piece of it?

JIM.		Uh-huh.

TOM.		What piece? The comics?

JIM.		Sports! *(He glances at it.)* Ole Dizzy Dean is on his bad behavior.

TOM *(uninterested).*		Yeah? [*He lights a cigarette and goes over to the fire-escape door.*]

JIM.		Where are *you* going?

TOM.		I'm going out on the terrace.

JIM *(going after him).*		You know, Shakespeare—I'm going to sell you a bill of goods!

TOM.		What goods?

JIM.		A course I'm taking.

TOM.		Huh?

JIM.		In public speaking! You and me, we're not the warehouse type.

TOM.		Thanks—that's good news. But what has public speaking got to do with it?

JIM.		It fits you for—executive positions!

TOM.		Awww.

JIM.		I tell you it's done a helluva lot for me.

(Image on screen: Executive at his desk.*)*

TOM.		In what respect?

JIM.		In every! Ask yourself what is the difference between you an' me and men in the office down front? Brains?—No!—Ability?—No! Then what? Just one little thing—

TOM.		What is that one little thing?

JIM.		Primarily it amounts to—social poise! Being able to square up to people and hold your own on any social level!

AMANDA *(from the kitchenette).*		Tom?

TOM.		Yes, Mother?

AMANDA.		Is that you and Mr. O'Connor?

TOM.		Yes, Mother.

AMANDA.		Well, you just make yourselves comfortable in there.

TOM.		Yes, Mother.

AMANDA.		Ask Mr. O'Connor if he would like to wash his hands.

JIM.		Aw, no—no—thank you—I took care of that at the warehouse. Tom—

TOM.   Yes?

JIM.   Mr. Mendoza was speaking to me about you.

TOM.   Favorably?

JIM.   What do you think?

TOM.   Well—

JIM.   You're going to be out of a job if you don't wake up.

TOM.   I am waking up—

JIM.   You show no signs.

TOM.   The signs are interior.

(Image on screen: The sailing vessel with the Jolly Roger again.*)*

TOM.   I'm planning to change. *(He leans over the fire-escape rail, speaking with quiet exhilaration. The incandescent marquees and signs of the first-run movie houses light his face from across the alley. He looks like a voyager.)* I'm right at the point of committing myself to a future that doesn't include the warehouse and Mr. Mendoza or even a night-school course in public speaking.

JIM.   What are you gassing about?

TOM.   I'm tired of the movies.

JIM.   Movies!

TOM.   Yes, movies! Look at them—*(A wave toward the marvels of Grand Avenue.)* All of those glamorous people—having adventures—hogging it all, gobbling the whole thing up! You know what happens? People go to the *movies* instead of *moving!* Hollywood characters are supposed to have all the adventures for everybody in America, while everybody in America sits in a dark room and watches them have them! Yes, until there's a war. That's when adventure becomes available to the masses! *Everyone's* dish, not only Gable's! Then the people in the dark room come out of the dark room to have some adventures themselves—goody, goody! It's our turn now, to go to the South Sea Island —to make a safari—to be exotic, far-off! But I'm not patient. I don't want to wait till then. I'm tired of the *movies* and I am *about* to *move!*

JIM *(incredulously).*   Move?

TOM.   Yes.

JIM.   When?

TOM.   Soon!

JIM.   Where? Where?

(The music seems to answer the question, while Tom thinks it over. He searches in his pockets.)

TOM.   I'm starting to boil inside. I know I seem dreamy, but inside—well, I'm boiling! Whenever I pick up a shoe, I shudder a little thinking how short life is and what I am doing! Whatever that means, I know it doesn't mean shoes —except as something to wear on a traveler's feet! [*He finds what he has been searching for in his pockets and holds out a paper to Jim.*] Look—

JIM.   What?

TOM.   I'm a member.

JIM *(reading).*   The Union of Merchant Seamen.

TOM.   I paid my dues this month, instead of the light bill.

JIM.   You will regret it when they turn the lights off.

TOM.   I won't be here.

JIM.   How about your mother?

TOM.   I'm like my father. The bastard son of a bastard! Did you notice how he's grinning in his picture in there? And he's been absent going on sixteen years!

JIM.   You're just talking, you drip. How does your mother feel about it?

TOM.   Shhh! Here comes Mother! Mother is not acquainted with my plans!

AMANDA *(coming through the portieres).*   Where are you all?

TOM.   On the terrace, Mother.

[*They start inside. She advances to them. Tom is distinctly shocked at her appearance. Even Jim blinks a little. He is making his first contact with girlish Southern vivacity and in spite of the night-school course in public speaking is somewhat thrown off the beam by the unexpected outlay of social charm. Certain responses are attempted by Jim but are swept aside by Amanda's gay laughter and chatter. Tom is embarrassed but after the first shock Jim reacts very warmly. He grins and chuckles, is altogether won over.)*

(Image on screen: Amanda as a girl.*)*

AMANDA *(coyly smiling, shaking her girlish ringlets).*   Well, well, well, so this is Mr. O'Connor. Introductions entirely unnecessary. I've heard so much about you from my boy. I finally said to him, Tom—good gracious!—why don't you bring this paragon to supper? I'd like to meet this nice young man at the warehouse!—instead of just hearing him sing your praises so much! I don't know why my son is so stand-offish—that's not Southern behavior!

Let's sit down and—I think we could stand a little more air in here! Tom, leave the door open. I felt a nice fresh breeze a moment ago. Where has it gone to? Mmm, so warm already! And not quite summer, even. We're going to burn up when summer really gets started. However, we're having—we're having a very light supper. I think light things are better fo' this time of year. The same as light clothes are. Light clothes an' light food are what warm weather calls fo'. You know our blood gets so thick during th' winter—it takes a while fo' us to *adjust* ou'selves!—when the season changes. . . . It's come so quick this year. I wasn't prepared. All of a sudden—heavens! Already summer! I ran to the trunk an' pulled out this light dress—terribly old! Historical almost! But feels so good—so good an' co-ol, y' know. . . .

TOM.   Mother—

AMANDA.   Yes, honey?

TOM.   How about—supper?

AMANDA.   Honey, you go ask Sister if supper is ready! You know that Sister is in full charge of supper! Tell her you hungry boys are waiting for it. *(to Jim)* Have you met Laura?

JIM.   She—

AMANDA.   Let you in? Oh, good, you've met already! It's rare for a girl as sweet an' pretty as Laura to be domestic! But Laura is, thank heavens, not only pretty but also very domestic. I'm not at all. I never was a bit. I never could make a thing but angel-food cake. Well, in the South we had so many servants. Gone,

gone, gone. All vestige of gracious living! Gone completely! I wasn't prepared for what the future brought me. All of my gentlemen callers were sons of planters and so of course I assumed that I would be married to one and raise my family on a large piece of land with plenty of servants. But man proposes —and woman accepts the proposal! To vary that old, old saying a little bit— I married no planter! I married a man who worked for the telephone company! That gallantly smiling gentleman over there! *(She points to the picture.)* A telephone man who—fell in love with long-distance! Now he travels and I don't even know where! But what am I going on for about my—tribulations? Tell me yours—I hope you don't have any! Tom?

TOM *(returning).*   Yes, Mother?

AMANDA.   Is supper nearly ready?

TOM.   It looks to me like supper is on the table.

AMANDA.   Let me look— *(She rises prettily and looks through the portieres.)* Oh, lovely! But where is Sister?

TOM.   Laura is not feeling well and she says that she thinks she'd better not come to the table.

AMANDA.   What? Nonsense! Laura? Oh, Laura!

LAURA *(from the kitchenette, faintly).*   Yes, Mother.

AMANDA.   You really must come to the table. We won't be seated until you come to the table! Come in, Mr. O'Connor. You sit over there, and I'll. . . . Laura? Laura Wingfield! You're keeping us waiting, honey! We can't say grace until you come to the table!

(The kitchenette door is pushed weakly open and Laura comes in. She is obviously quite faint, her lips trembling, her eyes wide and staring. She moves unsteadily toward the table.)

(Screen legend: "Terror!")

(Outside a summer storm is coming on abruptly. The white curtains billow inward at the windows and there is a sorrowful murmur from the deep blue dusk.)

(Laura suddenly stumbles; she catches at a chair with a faint moan.)

TOM.   Laura!

AMANDA.   Laura!

(There is a clap of thunder.)

(Screen legend: "Ah!")

     (despairingly) Why, Laura, you *are* ill, darling! Tom, help your sister into the living room, dear! Sit in the living room, Laura—rest on the sofa. Well! *(to Jim as Tom helps his sister to the sofa in the living room)* Standing over the hot stove made her ill! I told her that it was just too warm this evening, but—

(Tom comes back to the table.)

     Is Laura all right now?

TOM.   Yes.

AMANDA.   What *is* that? Rain? A nice cool rain has come up! *(She gives Jim a frightened look.)* I think we may—have grace—now . . .

(Tom looks at her stupidly.) Tom, honey—you say grace!

TOM.   Oh . . . "For these and all thy mercies—"

(They bow their heads, Amanda stealing a nervous glance at Jim. In the living room Laura, stretched on the sofa, clenches her hand to her lips, to hold back a shuddering sob.)

God's Holy Name be praised—

(The scene dims out.)

SCENE SEVEN

It is half an hour later. Dinner is just being finished in the dining room, Laura is still huddled upon the sofa, her feet drawn under her, her head resting on a pale blue pillow, her eyes wide and mysteriously watchful. The new floor lamp with its shade of rose-colored silk gives a soft, becoming light to her face, bringing out the fragile, unearthly prettiness which usually escapes attention. From outside there is a steady murmur of rain, but it is slackening and soon stops; the air outside becomes pale and luminous as the moon breaks through the clouds. A moment after the curtain rises, the lights in both rooms flicker and go out.

JIM.   Hey, there, Mr. Light Bulb!

(Amanda laughs nervously.)

(Legend on screen: "Suspension of a public service.")

AMANDA.   Where was Moses when the lights went out? Ha-ha. Do you know the answer to that one, Mr. O'Connor?

JIM.   No, Ma'am, what's the answer?

AMANDA.   In the dark!

(Jim laughs appreciatively.)

Everybody sit still. I'll light the candles. Isn't it lucky we have them on the table? Where's a match? Which of you gentlemen can provide a match?

JIM.   Here.

AMANDA.   Thank you, Sir.

JIM.   Not at all, Ma'am!

AMANDA *(as she lights the candles).*   I guess the fuse has burnt out. Mr. O'Connor, can you tell a burnt-out fuse? I know I can't and Tom is a total loss when it comes to mechanics.

(They rise from the table and go into the kitchenette, from where their voices are heard.)

Oh, be careful you don't bump into something. We don't want our gentleman caller to break his neck. Now wouldn't that be a fine howdy-do?

JIM.   Ha-ha! Where is the fuse-box?

AMANDA.   Right here next to the stove. Can you see anything?

JIM.   Just a minute.

AMANDA.   Isn't electricity a mysterious thing? Wasn't it Benjamin Franklin who tied a key to a kite? We live in such a mysterious universe, don't we? Some people say that science clears up all the mysteries for us. In my opinion it only creates more! Have you found it yet?

JIM.   No, Ma'am. All these fuses look okay to me.

AMANDA.   Tom!

TOM.   Yes, Mother?

AMANDA.   That light bill I gave you several days ago. The one I told you we got the notices about?

(Legend on screen: "Ha!")

TOM.   Oh—yeah.

AMANDA.   You didn't neglect to pay it by any chance?

TOM.   Why, I—

AMANDA.   Didn't! I might have known it!

JIM.   Shakespeare probably wrote a poem on that light bill, Mrs. Wingfield.

AMANDA.   I might have known better than to trust him with it! There's such a high price for negligence in this world!

JIM.   Maybe the poem will win a ten-dollar prize.

AMANDA.   We'll just have to spend the remainder of the evening in the nineteenth century, before Mr. Edison made the Mazda lamp!

JIM.   Candlelight is my favorite kind of light.

AMANDA.   That shows you're romantic! But that's no excuse for Tom. Well, we got through dinner. Very considerate of them to let us get through dinner before they plunged us into everlasting darkness, wasn't it, Mr. O'Connor?

JIM.   Ha-ha!

AMANDA.   Tom, as a penalty for your carelessness you can help me with the dishes.

JIM.   Let me give you a hand.

AMANDA.   Indeed you will not!

JIM.   I ought to be good for something.

AMANDA.   Good for something? *(Her tone is rhapsodic.) You?* Why, Mr. O'Connor, nobody, *nobody's* given me this much entertainment in years—as you have!

JIM.   Aw, now, Mrs. Wingfield!

AMANDA.   I'm not exaggerating, not one bit! But Sister is all by her lonesome. You go keep her company in the parlor! I'll give you this lovely old candelabrum that used to be on the altar at the Church of the Heavenly Rest. It was melted a little out of shape when the church burnt down. Lightning struck it one Spring. Gypsy Jones was holding a revival at the time and he intimated that the church was destroyed because the Episcopalians gave card parties.

JIM.   Ha-ha.

AMANDA.　　And how about you coaxing Sister to drink a little wine? I think it would be good for her! Can you carry both at once?

JIM.　　Sure. I'm Superman!

AMANDA.　　Now, Thomas, get into this apron!

(Jim comes into the dining room, carrying the candelabrum, its candles lighted, in one hand and a glass of wine in the other. The door of the kitchenette swings closed on Amanda's gay laughter; the flickering light approaches the portieres. Laura sits up nervously as Jim enters. She can hardly speak from the almost intolerable strain of being alone with a stranger.)

(Screen legend: "I don't suppose you remember me at all!")

(At first, before Jim's warmth overcomes her paralyzing shyness, Laura's voice is thin and breathless, as though she had just run up a steep flight of stairs. Jim's attitude is gently humorous. While the incident is apparently unimportant, it is to Laura the climax of her secret life.)

JIM.　　Hello there, Laura.

LAURA *(faintly)*.　　Hello.

(She clears her throat.)

JIM.　　How are you feeling now? Better?

LAURA.　　Yes. Yes, thank you.

JIM.　　This is for you. A little dandelion wine. *(He extends the glass toward her with extravagant gallantry.)*

LAURA.　　Thank you.

JIM.　　Drink it—but don't get drunk!

(He laughs heartily. Laura takes the glass uncertainly; she laughs shyly.)

　　Where shall I set the candles?

LAURA.　　Oh—oh, anywhere . . .

JIM.　　How about here on the floor? Any objections?

LAURA.　　No.

JIM.　　I'll spread a newspaper under to catch the drippings. I like to sit on the floor. Mind if I do?

LAURA.　　Oh, no.

JIM.　　Give me a pillow?

LAURA.　　What?

JIM.　　A pillow!

LAURA.　　Oh . . . *(She hands him one quickly.)*

JIM.　　How about you? Don't you like to sit on the floor?

LAURA.　　Oh—yes.

JIM.　　Why don't you, then?

LAURA.　　I—will.

JIM.　　Take a pillow! *(Laura does. She sits on the floor on the other side of the candelabrum. Jim crosses his legs and smiles engagingly at her.)* I can't hardly see you sitting way over there.

LAURA.　　I can—see you.

JIM.   I know, but that's not fair, I'm in the limelight.

(Laura moves her pillow closer.)

> Good! Now I can see you! Comfortable?

LAURA.   Yes.

JIM.   So am I. Comfortable as a cow! Will you have some gum?

LAURA.   No, thank you.

JIM.   I think that I will indulge, with your permission. *(He musingly unwraps a stick of gum and holds it up.)* Think of the fortune made by the guy that invented the first piece of chewing gum. Amazing, huh? The Wrigley Building is one of the sights of Chicago—I saw it when I went up to the Century of Progress. Did you take in the Century of Progress?

LAURA.   No, I didn't.

JIM.   Well, it was quite a wonderful exposition. What impressed me most was the Hall of Science. Gives you an idea of what the future will be in America, even more wonderful than the present time is! *(There is a pause. Jim smiles at her.)* Your brother tells me you're shy. Is that right, Laura?

LAURA.   I—don't know.

JIM.   I judge you to be an old-fashioned type of girl. Well, I think that's a pretty good type to be. Hope you don't think I'm being too personal—do you?

LAURA *(hastily, out of embarrassment).*   I believe I *will* take a piece of gum, if you —don't mind. *(clearing her throat)* Mr. O'Connor, have you—kept up with your singing?

JIM.   Singing? Me?

LAURA.   Yes. I remember what a beautiful voice you had.

JIM.   When did you hear me sing?

(Laura does not answer, and in the long pause which follows a man's voice is heard singing offstage.)

VOICE.

> O blow, ye winds, heigh-ho,
> A-roving I will go!
> I'm off to my love
> With a boxing glove—
> Ten thousand miles away!

JIM.   You say you've heard me sing?

LAURA.   Oh, yes! Yes, very often . . . I—don't suppose—you remember me—at all?

JIM *(smiling doubtfully).*   You know I have an idea I've seen you before. I had that idea soon as you opened the door. It seemed almost like I was about to remember your name. But the name that I started to call you—wasn't a name! And so I stopped myself before I said it.

LAURA.   Wasn't it—Blue Roses?

JIM *(springing up, grinning).*   Blue Roses! My gosh, yes—Blue Roses! That's what I had on my tongue when you opened the door! Isn't it funny what tricks your memory plays? I didn't connect you with high school somehow or other. But that's where it was; it was high school. I didn't even know you were Shakespeare's sister! Gosh, I'm sorry.

LAURA.   I didn't expect you to. You—barely knew me!

JIM.   But we did have a speaking acquaintance, huh?

LAURA.   Yes, we—spoke to each other.

JIM.   When did you recognize me?

LAURA.   Oh, right away!

JIM.   Soon as I came in the door?

LAURA.   When I heard your name I thought it was probably you. I knew that Tom used to know you a little in high school. So when you came in the door—well, then I was—sure.

JIM.   Why didn't you *say* something, then?

LAURA *(breathlessly).*   I didn't know what to say, I was—too surprised!

JIM.   For goodness' sakes! You know, this sure is funny!

LAURA.   Yes! Yes, isn't it, though . . .

JIM.   Didn't we have a class in something together?

LAURA.   Yes, we did.

JIM.   What class was that?

LAURA.   It was—singing—chorus!

JIM.   Aw!

LAURA.   I sat across the aisle from you in the Aud.

JIM.   Aw.

LAURA.   Mondays, Wednesdays, and Fridays.

JIM.   Now I remember—you always came in late.

LAURA.   Yes, it was so hard for me, getting upstairs. I had that brace on my leg —it clumped so loud!

JIM.   I never heard any clumping.

LAURA *(wincing at the recollection).*   To me it sounded like—thunder!

JIM.   Well, well, well, I never even noticed.

LAURA.   And everybody was seated before I came in. I had to walk in front of all those people. My seat was in the back row. I had to go clumping all the way up the aisle with everyone watching!

JIM.   You shouldn't have been self-conscious.

LAURA.   I know, but I was. It was always such a relief when the singing started.

JIM.   Aw, yes, I've placed you now! I used to call you Blue Roses. How was it that I got started calling you that?

LAURA.   I was out of school a little while with pleurosis. When I came back you asked me what was the matter. I said I had pleurosis—you thought I said *Blue Roses.* That's what you always called me after that!

JIM.   I hope you didn't mind.

LAURA.   Oh, no—I liked it. You see, I wasn't acquainted with many—people. . . .

JIM.   As I remember you sort of stuck by yourself.

LAURA.   I—I—never have had much luck at—making friends.

JIM.   I don't see why you wouldn't.

LAURA.   Well, I—started out badly.

JIM.   You mean being—

LAURA.   Yes, it sort of—stood between me—

JIM.   You shouldn't have let it!

LAURA.   I know, but it did, and—

JIM.   You were shy with people!

LAURA.   I tried not to be but never could—

JIM.   Overcome it?

LAURA.   No, I—I never could!

JIM.   I guess being shy is something you have to work out of kind of gradually.

LAURA *(sorrowfully)*.   Yes—I guess it—

JIM.   Takes time!

LAURA.   Yes—

JIM.   People are not so dreadful when you know them. That's what you have to remember! And everybody has problems, not just you, but practically everybody has got some problems. You think of yourself as having the only problems, as being the only one who is disappointed. But just look around you and you will see lots of people as disappointed as you are. For instance, I hoped when I was going to high school that I would be further along at this time, six years later, than I am now. You remember that wonderful write-up I had in *The Torch?*

LAURA.   Yes! *(She rises and crosses to the table.)*

JIM.   It said I was bound to succeed in anything I went into!

(Laura returns with the high school year book.)

Holy Jeez! *The Torch!*

(He accepts it reverently. They smile across the book with mutual wonder. Laura crouches beside him and they begin to turn the pages. Laura's shyness is dissolving in his warmth.)

LAURA.   Here you are in *The Pirates of Penzance!*

JIM *(wistfully)*.   I sang the baritone lead in that operetta.

LAURA *(raptly)*.   So—*beautifully!*

JIM *(protesting)*.   Aw—

LAURA.   Yes, yes—beautifully—beautifully!

JIM.   You heard me?

LAURA.   All three times!

JIM.   No!

LAURA.   Yes!

JIM.   All three performances?

LAURA *(looking down)*.   Yes.

JIM.   Why?

LAURA.   I—wanted to ask you to—autograph my program. *(She takes the program from the back of the year book and shows it to him.)*

JIM.   Why didn't you ask me to?

LAURA.   You were always surrounded by your own friends so much that I never had a chance to.

JIM.   You should have just—

LAURA.   Well, I—thought you might think I was—

JIM.   Thought I might think you was—what?

LAURA.   Oh—

JIM *(with reflective relish).*   I was beleaguered by females in those days.

LAURA.   You were terribly popular!

JIM.   Yeah—

LAURA.   You had such a—friendly way—

JIM.   I was spoiled in high school.

LAURA.   Everybody—liked you!

JIM.   Including you?

LAURA.   I—yes, I—did, too— *(She gently closes the book in her lap.)*

JIM.   Well, well, well! Give me that program, Laura.

(She hands it to him. He signs it with a flourish.)

There you are—better late than never!

LAURA.   Oh, I—what a—surprise!

JIM.   My signature isn't worth very much right now. But some day—maybe—it will increase in value! Being disappointed is one thing and being discouraged is something else. I am disappointed but I am not discouraged. I'm twenty-three years old. How old are you?

LAURA.   I'll be twenty-four in June.

JIM.   That's not old age!

LAURA.   No, but—

JIM.   You finished high school?

LAURA *(with difficulty).*   I didn't go back.

JIM.   You mean you dropped out?

LAURA.   I made bad grades in my final examinations. *(She rises and replaces the book and the program on the table. Her voice is strained.)* How is—Emily Meisenbach getting along?

JIM.   Oh, that kraut-head!

LAURA.   Why do you call her that?

JIM.   That's what she was.

LAURA.   You're not still—going with her?

JIM.   I never see her.

LAURA.   It said in the "Personal" section that you were—engaged!

JIM.   I know, but I wasn't impressed by that—propaganda!

LAURA.   It wasn't—the truth?

JIM.   Only in Emily's optimistic opinion!

LAURA.   Oh—

(Legend: "What have you done since high school?")

(Jim lights a cigarette and leans indolently back on his elbows smiling at Laura with a warmth and charm which lights her inwardly with altar candles. She remains by the table, picks up a piece from the glass menagerie collection, and turns it in her hands to cover her tumult.)

JIM *(after several reflective puffs on his cigarette).*   What have you done since high school?

(She seems not to hear him.)

Huh?

(Laura looks up.)

I said what have you done since high school, Laura?

LAURA.   Nothing much.

JIM.   You must have been doing something these six long years.

LAURA.   Yes.

JIM.   Well, then, such as what?

LAURA.   I took a business course at business college—

JIM.   How did that work out?

LAURA.   Well, not very—well—I had to drop out, it gave me—indigestion—

(Jim laughs gently.)

JIM.   What are you doing now?

LAURA.   I don't do anything—much. Oh, please don't think I sit around doing nothing! My glass collection takes up a good deal of time. Glass is something you have to take good care of.

JIM.   What did you say—about glass?

LAURA.   Collection I said—I have one— *(She clears her throat and turns away again, acutely shy.)*

JIM *(abruptly).*   You know what I judge to be the trouble with you? Inferiority complex! Know what that is? That's what they call it when someone low-rates himself! I understand it because I had it, too. Although my case was not so aggravated as yours seems to be. I had it until I took up public speaking, developed my voice, and learned that I had an aptitude for science. Before that time I never thought of myself as being outstanding in any way whatsoever! Now I've never made a regular study of it, but I have a friend who says I can analyze people better than doctors that make a profession of it. I don't claim that to be necessarily true, but I can sure guess a person's psychology, Laura! *(He takes out his gum.)* Excuse me, Laura. I always take it out when the flavor is gone. I'll use this scrap of paper to wrap it in. I know how it is to get it stuck on a shoe. *(He wraps the gum in paper and puts it in his pocket.)* Yep—that's what I judge to be your principal trouble. A lack of confidence in yourself as a person. You don't have the proper amount of faith in yourself. I'm basing that fact on a number of your remarks and also on certain observations I've made. For instance that clumping you thought was so awful in high school. You say that you even dreaded to walk into class. You see what you did? You dropped out of school, you gave up an education because of a clump, which as far as I know was practically non-existent! A little physical defect is what you have. Hardly noticeable even! Magnified thousands of times by imagination! You know what my strong advice to you is? Think of yourself as *superior* in some way!

LAURA.   In what way would I think?

JIM.   Why, man alive, Laura! Just look about you a little, what do you see? A world full of common people! All of 'em born and all of 'em going to die! Which of

them has one-tenth of your good points! Or mine! Or anyone else's, as far as
that goes—gosh! Everybody excels in some one thing. Some in many! *(He
unconsciously glances at himself in the mirror.)* All you've got to do is discover
in *what!* Take me, for instance. *(He adjusts his tie at the mirror.)* My interest
happens to lie in electro-dynamics. I'm taking a course in radio engineering
at night school, Laura, on top of a fairly responsible job at the warehouse. I'm
taking that course and studying public speaking.

LAURA.   Ohhhh.

JIM.   Because I believe in the future of television! *(turning his back to her.)* I wish
to be ready to go up right along with it. Therefore I'm planning to get in on
the ground floor. In fact I've already made the right connections and all that
remains is for the industry itself to get under way! Full steam—*(His eyes are
starry.) Knowledge—*Zzzzzp! *Money—*Zzzzzzp!—*Power!* That's the cycle democracy is built on!

*(His attitude is convincingly dynamic. Laura stares at him, even her shyness eclipsed
in her absolute wonder. He suddenly grins.)*

I guess you think I think a lot of myself!

LAURA.   No—o-o-o, I—

JIM.   Now how about you? Isn't there something you take more interest in than
anything else?

LAURA.   Well, I do—as I said—have my—glass collection—

(A peal of girlish laughter rings from the kitchenette.)

JIM.   I'm not right sure I know what you're talking about. What kind of glass is
it?

LAURA.   Little articles of it, they're ornaments mostly! Most of them are little
animals made out of glass, the tiniest little animals in the world. Mother calls
them a glass menagerie! Here's an example of one, if you'd like to see it! This
one is one of the oldest. It's nearly thirteen.

(Music: "The Glass Menagerie.")

(He stretches out his hand.)

Oh, be careful—if you breathe, it breaks!

JIM.   I'd better not take it. I'm pretty clumsy with things.

LAURA.   Go on, I trust you with him! *(She places the piece in his palm.)* There now
—you're holding him gently! Hold him over the light, he loves the light! You
see how the light shines through him?

JIM.   It sure does shine!

LAURA.   I shouldn't be partial, but he is my favorite one.

JIM.   What kind of a thing is this one supposed to be?

LAURA.   Haven't you noticed the single horn on his forehead?

JIM.   A unicorn, huh?

LAURA.   Mmmm-hmmm!

JIM.   Unicorns—aren't they extinct in the modern world?

LAURA.   I know!

JIM.   Poor little fellow, he must feel sort of lonesome.

LAURA (*smiling*).   Well, if he does, he doesn't complain about it. He stays on a shelf with some horses that don't have horns and all of them seem to get along nicely together.

JIM.   How do you know?

LAURA (*lightly*).   I haven't heard any arguments among them!

JIM (*grinning*).   No arguments, huh? Well, that's a pretty good sign! Where shall I set him?

LAURA.   Put him on the table. They all like a change of scenery once in a while!

JIM.   Well, well, well, well—(*He places the glass piece on the table, then raises his arms and stretches.*) Look how big my shadow is when I stretch!

LAURA.   Oh, oh, yes—it stretches across the ceiling!

JIM (*crossing to the door*).   I think it's stopped raining. (*He opens the fire-escape door and the background music changes to a dance tune.*) Where does the music come from?

LAURA.   From the Paradise Dance Hall across the alley.

JIM.   How about cutting the rug a little, Miss Wingfield?

LAURA.   Oh, I—

JIM.   Or is your program filled up? Let me have a look at it. (*He grasps an imaginary card.*) Why, every dance is taken! I'll just have to scratch some out.

(*Waltz music:* "La Golondrina.")

      Ahhh, a waltz! (*He executes some sweeping turns by himself, then holds his arms toward Laura.*)

LAURA (*breathlessly*).   I—can't dance!

JIM.   There you go, that inferiority stuff!

LAURA.   I've never danced in my life!

JIM.   Come on, try!

LAURA.   Oh, but I'd step on you!

JIM.   I'm not made out of glass.

LAURA.   How—how—how do we start?

JIM.   Just leave it to me. You hold your arms out a little.

LAURA.   Like this?

JIM (*taking her in his arms*).   A little bit higher. Right. Now don't tighten up, that's the main thing about it—relax.

LAURA (*laughing breathlessly*).   It's hard not to.

JIM.   Okay.

LAURA.   I'm afraid you can't budge me.

JIM.   What do you bet I can't? (*He swings her into motion.*)

LAURA.   Goodness, yes, you can!

JIM.   Let yourself go, now, Laura, just let yourself go.

LAURA.   I'm—

JIM.   Come on!

LAURA.   —trying!

JIM.   Not so stiff—easy does it!

LAURA.   I know but I'm—

JIM.   Loosen th' backbone! There now, that's a lot better.

LAURA.   Am I?

JIM.   Lots, lots better! *(He moves her about the room in a clumsy waltz.)*
LAURA.   Oh, my!
JIM.   Ha-ha!
LAURA.   Oh, my goodness!
JIM.   Ha-ha-ha!

(They suddenly bump into the table, and the glass piece on it falls to the floor. Jim stops the dance.)

What did we hit on?
LAURA.   Table.
JIM.   Did something fall off it? I think—
LAURA.   Yes.
JIM.   I hope that it wasn't the little glass horse with the horn!
LAURA.   Yes. *(She stoops to pick it up.)*
JIM.   Aw, aw, aw. Is it broken?
LAURA.   Now it is just like all the other horses.
JIM.   It's lost its—
LAURA.   Horn! It doesn't matter. Maybe it's a blessing in disguise.
JIM.   You'll never forgive me. I bet that that was your favorite piece of glass.
LAURA.   I don't have favorites much. It's no tragedy, Freckles. Glass breaks so easily. No matter how careful you are. The traffic jars the shelves and things fall off them.
JIM.   Still I'm awfully sorry that I was the cause.
LAURA *(smiling)*.   I'll just imagine he had an operation. The horn was removed to make him feel less—freakish!

(They both laugh.)

Now he will feel more at home with the other horses, the ones that don't have horns. . . .
JIM.   Ha-ha, that's very funny! *(Suddenly he is serious.)* I'm glad to see that you have a sense of humor. You know—you're—well—very different! Surprisingly different from anyone else I know! *(His voice becomes soft and hesitant with a genuine feeling.)* Do you mind me telling you that?

(Laura is abashed beyond speech.)

I mean it in a nice way—

(Laura nods shyly, looking away.)

You make me feel sort of—I don't know how to put it! I'm usually pretty good at expressing things, but—this is something that I don't know how to say!

(Laura touches her throat and clears it—turns the broken unicorn in her hands. His voice becomes softer.)

Has anyone ever told you that you were pretty?

(There is a pause, and the music rises slightly. Laura looks up slowly, with wonder, and shakes her head.)

Well, you are! In a very different way from anyone else. And all the nicer because of the difference, too.

(His voice becomes low and husky. Laura turns away, nearly faint with the novelty of her emotions.)

I wish that you were my sister. I'd teach you to have some confidence in yourself. The different people are not like other people, but being different is nothing to be ashamed of. Because other people are not such wonderful people. They're one hundred times one thousand. You're one times one! They walk all over the earth. You just stay here. They're common as—weeds, but—you —well, you're—*Blue Roses!*

(Image on screen: Blue Roses.*)*

(The music changes.)

LAURA. But blue is wrong for—roses. . . .
JIM. It's right for you! You're—pretty!
LAURA. In what respect am I pretty?
JIM. In all respects—believe me! Your eyes—your hair—are pretty! Your hands are pretty! *(He catches hold of her hand.)* You think I'm making this up because I'm invited to dinner and have to be nice. Oh, I could do that! I could put on an act for you, Laura, and say lots of things without being very sincere. But this time I am. I'm talking to you sincerely. I happened to notice you had this inferiority complex that keeps you from feeling comfortable with people. Somebody needs to build your confidence up and make you proud instead of shy and turning away and—blushing. Somebody—ought to—*kiss* you, Laura!

(His hand slips slowly up her arm to her shoulder as the music swells tumultuously. He suddenly turns her about and kisses her on the lips. When he releases her, Laura sinks on the sofa with a bright, dazed look. Jim backs away and fishes in his pocket for a cigarette.)

(Legend on screen: "A souvenir."*)*

Stumblejohn!

(He lights the cigarette, avoiding her look. There is a peal of girlish laughter from Amanda in the kitchenette. Laura slowly raises and opens her hand. It still contains the little broken glass animal. She looks at it with a tender, bewildered expression.)

Stumblejohn! I shouldn't have done that—that was way off the beam. You don't smoke, do you?

(She looks up, smiling, not hearing the question. He sits beside her rather gingerly. She looks at him speechlessly—waiting. He coughs decorously and moves a little farther aside as he considers the situation and senses her feelings, dimly, with perturbation. He speaks gently.)

Would you—care for a—mint?

(She doesn't seem to hear him but her look grows brighter even.)

Peppermint? Life Saver? My pocket's a regular drug store—wherever I go.
. . . *(He pops a mint in his mouth. Then he gulps and decides to make a clean
breast of it. He speaks slowly and gingerly.)* Laura, you know, if I had a sister
like you, I'd do the same thing as Tom. I'd bring out fellows and—introduce
her to them. The right type of boys—of a type to—appreciate her. Only—well
—he made a mistake about me. Maybe I've got no call to be saying this. That
may not have been the idea in having me over. But what if it was? There's
nothing wrong about that. The only trouble is that in my case—I'm not in a
situation to—do the right thing. I can't take down your number and say I'll
phone. I can't call up next week and—ask for a date. I thought I had better
explain the situation in case you—misunderstood it and—I hurt your feelings. . . .

*(There is a pause. Slowly, very slowly, Laura's look changes, her eyes returning slowly
from his to the glass figure in her palm. Amanda utters another gay laugh in the
kitchenette.)*

LAURA *(faintly).*   You—won't—call again?

JIM.   No, Laura, I can't. *(He rises from the sofa.)* As I was just explaining, I've
—got strings on me. Laura, I've—been going steady! I go out all the time with
a girl named Betty. She's a home-girl like you, and Catholic, and Irish, and
in a great many ways we—get along fine. I met her last summer on a moonlight
boat trip up the river to Alton, on the *Majestic.* Well—right away from the
start it was—love!

(Legend. Love!)

*(Laura sways slightly forward and grips the arm of the sofa. He fails to notice, now
enrapt in his own comfortable being.)*

Being in love has made a new man of me!

*(Leaning stiffly forward, clutching the arm of the sofa, Laura struggles visibly with
her storm. But Jim is oblivious; she is a long way off.)*

The power of love is really pretty tremendous! Love is something that—
changes the whole world, Laura!

(The storm abates a little and Laura leans back. He notices her again.)

It happened that Betty's aunt took sick, she got a wire and had to go to
Centralia. So Tom—when he asked me to dinner—I naturally just accepted
the invitation, not knowing that you—that he—that I—*(He stops awkwardly.)*
Huh—I'm a stumblejohn!

*(He flops back on the sofa. The holy candles on the altar of Laura's face have been
snuffed out. There is a look of almost infinite desolation. Jim glances at her uneasily.)*

I wish that you would—say something.

*(She bites her lip which was trembling and then bravely smiles. She opens her hand
again on the broken glass figure. Then she gently takes his hand and raises it level*

with her own. She carefully places the unicorn in the palm of his hand, then pushes his fingers closed upon it.)

What are you—doing that for? You want me to have him? Laura?

(She nods.)

What for?

LAURA.   A—souvenir. . . .

(She rises unsteadily and crouches beside the victrola to wind it up.)

(Legend on screen: "Things have a way of turning out so badly!" *Or image:* "Gentleman caller waving goodbye—gaily.")

(At this moment Amanda rushes brightly back into the living room. She bears a pitcher of fruit punch in an old-fashioned cut-glass pitcher, and a plate of macaroons. The plate has a gold border and poppies painted on it.)

AMANDA.   Well, well, well! Isn't the air delightful after the shower? I've made you children a little liquid refreshment.

(She turns gaily to Jim.) Jim, do you know that song about lemonade?
"Lemonade, lemonade
Made in the shade and stirred with a spade—
Good enough for any old maid!"

JIM *(uneasily).*   Ha-ha! No—I never heard it.

AMANDA.   Why, Laura! You look so serious!

JIM.   We were having a serious conversation.

AMANDA.   Good! Now you're better acquainted!

JIM *(uncertainly).*   Ha-ha! Yes.

AMANDA.   You modern young people are much more serious-minded than my generation. I was so gay as a girl!

JIM.   You haven't changed, Mrs. Wingfield.

AMANDA.   Tonight I'm rejuvenated! The gaiety of the occasion, Mr. O'Connor! *(She tosses her head with a peal of laughter, spilling some lemonade.)* Oooo! I'm baptizing myself!

JIM.   Here—let me—

AMANDA *(setting the pitcher down).*   There now. I discovered we had some maraschino cherries. I dumped them in, juice and all!

JIM.   You shouldn't have gone to that trouble, Mrs. Wingfield.

AMANDA.   Trouble, trouble? Why, it was loads of fun! Didn't you hear me cutting up in the kitchen? I bet your ears were burning! I told Tom how outdone with him I was for keeping you to himself so long a time! He should have brought you over much, much sooner! Well, now that you've found your way, I want you to be a very frequent caller! Not just occasional but all the time. Oh, we're going to have a lot of gay times together! I see them coming! Mmm, just breathe that air! So fresh, and the moon's so pretty! I'll skip back out—I know where my place is when young folks are having a—serious conversation!

JIM.   Oh, don't go out, Mrs. Wingfield. The fact of the matter is I've got to be going.

AMANDA.   Going, now? You're joking! Why, it's only the shank of the evening, Mr. O'Connor!

JIM.   Well, you know how it is.

AMANDA.   You mean you're a young workingman and have to keep workingmen's hours. We'll let you off early tonight. But only on the condition that next time you stay later. What's the best night for you? Isn't Saturday night the best night for you workingmen?

JIM.   I have a couple of time-clocks to punch, Mrs. Wingfield. One at morning, another one at night!

AMANDA.   My, but you *are* ambitious! You work at night, too?

JIM.   No, Ma'am, not work but—Betty!

(He crosses deliberately to pick up his hat. The band at the Paradise Dance Hall goes into a tender waltz.)

AMANDA.   Betty? Betty? Who's—Betty!

(There is an ominous cracking sound in the sky.)

JIM.   Oh, just a girl. The girl I go steady with!

(He smiles charmingly. The sky falls.)

(Legend: "The Sky Falls.")

AMANDA *(a long-drawn exhalation)*.   Ohhhh . . . Is it a serious romance, Mr. O'Connor?

JIM.   We're going to be married the second Sunday in June.

AMANDA.   Ohhhh—how nice! Tom didn't mention that you were engaged to be married.

JIM.   The cat's not out of the bag at the warehouse yet. You know how they are. They call you Romeo and stuff like that. *(He stops at the oval mirror to put on his hat. He carefully shapes the brim and the crown to give a discreetly dashing effect.)* It's been a wonderful evening, Mrs. Wingfield. I guess this is what they mean by Southern hospitality.

AMANDA.   It really wasn't anything at all.

JIM.   I hope it don't seem like I'm rushing off. But I promised Betty I'd pick her up at the Wabash depot, an' by the time I get my jalopy down there her train'll be in. Some women are pretty upset if you keep 'em waiting.

AMANDA.   Yes, I know—the tyranny of women! *(She extends her hand.)* Goodbye, Mr. O'Connor. I wish you luck—and happiness—and success! All three of them, and so does Laura! Don't you, Laura?

LAURA.   Yes!

JIM *(taking Laura's hand)*.   Goodbye, Laura. I'm certainly going to treasure that souvenir. And don't you forget the good advice I gave you. *(He raises his voice to a cheery shout.)* So long, Shakespeare! Thanks again, ladies. Good night!

(He grins and ducks jauntily out. Still bravely grimacing, Amanda closes the door on the gentleman caller. Then she turns back to the room with a puzzled expression.

She and Laura don't dare to face each other. Laura crouches beside the victrola to wind it.)

AMANDA *(faintly).*   Things have a way of turning out so badly. I don't believe that I would play the victrola. Well, well—well! Our gentleman caller was engaged to be married! *(She raises her voice.)* Tom!

TOM *(from the kitchenette).*   Yes, Mother?

AMANDA.   Come in here a minute. I want to tell you something awfully funny.

TOM *(entering with a macaroon and a glass of the lemonade).*   Has the gentleman caller gotten away already?

AMANDA.   The gentleman caller has made an early departure. What a wonderful joke you played on us!

TOM.   How do you mean?

AMANDA.   You didn't mention that he was engaged to be married.

TOM.   Jim? Engaged?

AMANDA.   That's what he just informed us.

TOM.   I'll be jiggered! I didn't know about that.

AMANDA.   That seems very peculiar.

TOM.   What's peculiar about it?

AMANDA.   Didn't you call him your best friend down at the warehouse?

TOM.   He is, but how did I know?

AMANDA.   It seems extremely peculiar that you wouldn't know your best friend was going to be married!

TOM.   The warehouse is where I work, not where I know things about people!

AMANDA.   You don't know things anywhere! You live in a dream; you manufacture illusions!

(He crosses to the door.)

Where are you going?

TOM.   I'm going to the movies.

AMANDA.   That's right, now that you've had us make such fools of ourselves. The effort, the preparations, all the expense! The new floor lamp, the rug, the clothes for Laura! All for what? To entertain some other girl's fiancé! Go to the movies, go! Don't think about us, a mother deserted, an unmarried sister who's crippled and has no job! Don't let anything interfere with your selfish pleasure! Just go, go, go—to the movies!

TOM.   All right, I will! The more you shout about my selfishness to me the quicker I'll go, and I won't go to the movies!

AMANDA.   Go, then! Go to the moon—you selfish dreamer!

(Tom smashes his glass on the floor. He plunges out on the fire escape, slamming the door. Laura screams in fright. The dance-hall music becomes louder, Tom stands on the fire escape, gripping the rail. The moon breaks through the storm clouds, illuminating his face.)

(Legend on screen: "And so goodbye . . .")

(Tom's closing speech is timed with what is happening inside the house. We see, as though through soundproof glass, that Amanda appears to be making a comforting

speech to Laura, who is huddled upon the sofa. Now that we cannot hear the mother's speech, her silliness is gone and she has dignity and tragic beauty. Laura's hair hides her face until, at the end of the speech, she lifts her head to smile at her mother. Amanda's gestures are slow and graceful, almost dance-like, as she comforts her daughter. At the end of her speech she glances a moment at the father's picture— then withdraws through the portieres. At the close of Tom's speech, Laura blows out the candles, ending the play.)

TOM.   I didn't go to the moon, I went much further—for time is the longest distance between two places. Not long after that I was fired for writing a poem on the lid of a shoe-box. I left Saint Louis. I descended the steps of this fire-escape for a last time and followed, from then on, in my father's footsteps, attempting to find in motion what was lost in space. I traveled around a great deal. The cities swept about me like dead leaves, leaves that were brightly colored but torn away from the branches. I would have stopped, but I was pursued by something. It always came upon me unawares, taking me altogether by surprise. Perhaps it was a familiar bit of music. Perhaps it was only a piece of transparent glass. Perhaps I am walking along a street at night, in some strange city, before I have found companions. I pass the lighted window of a shop where perfume is sold. The window is filled with pieces of colored glass, tiny transparent bottles in delicate colors, like bits of a shattered rainbow. Then all at once my sister touches my shoulder. I turn around and look into her eyes. Oh, Laura, Laura, I tried to leave you behind me, but I am more faithful than I intended to be! I reach for a cigarette, I cross the street, I run into the movies or a bar, I buy a drink, I speak to the nearest stranger— anything that can blow your candles out!

(Laura bends over the candles.)

     For nowadays the world is lit by lightning! Blow out your candles, Laura— and so goodbye. . . .

(She blows the candles out.)

DREAMS AND REALIZATIONS

TOPICS FOR SHORT PAPERS, JOURNALS, OR DISCUSSION

1. Some of the protagonists in the stories in this section show honesty and integrity in adjusting to the loss, thwarting, or possible diminution of their dreams. Examples are Violet in "The Ugliest Pilgrim," Sergeant Marx in "Defender of the Faith," and Jack, the Vietnam veteran in "Out of Place." In a short essay, develop this idea.

2. Some characters in this section made choices and others had choices thrust upon them. Show how you would deal with the dilemmas encountered by the protagonists in "The Yellow Wallpaper," "The Sky Is Gray" or *The Glass Menagerie.*

3. The theme of pretending to be someone else is prevalent in this section, for example in "Defender of the Faith" or the poem "We Wear the Mask." Analyze some of the characters in these selections to see why they pretend to be what they are not, to achieve their dreams by "wearing a mask."

LONGER PAPERS OR RESEARCH PROJECTS

4. Some of the stories, plays, or poems of this final section relate to the epigraph, Lazarus's "The New Colossus," in describing America as a nation of immigrants. The last five lines of her poem are inscribed on the base of the Statue of Liberty. Visit the statue, if possible, or research in your library the construction of the statue, the great periods of immigration into the United States, the museums on Liberty Island and on nearby Ellis Island that depict this heritage. Relate some of the selections in "Dreams and Realizations" to some of the ethnic groups that passed by the statue on their way to a new life in America.

5. Some people have failed in achieving the dream of success and fulfillment. Others seem to have no dream at all. Using examples from this section, discuss why these characters have not realized their dreams. Analyze some of the problems they have encountered and the means, if any, they have taken to solve them.

CREATIVE PROJECT

6. If you were to write a "memory play" like *The Glass Menagerie* about your family's past, what incidents would you choose? How would you portray them using some of the impressionistic, nonrealistic, or nonphotographic techniques Williams employs in his play? Create a summary-outline of a possible script for your play. Who knows—it may be the beginning for you of realizing a dream!

APPENDIXES

ON READING FICTION: PEELING THE ONION

STORY-TELLING, OLD AND NEW

Fiction is story-telling in one form or another, and story-telling is both the oldest and the most enduring kind of literature. We all love what Henry James called a "loose, baggy monster" of a story, as evidenced by the interest in the "soaps" or the "mini-series." Historically, the earliest kinds of stories are handed down orally, often based on legends. Each section of this book purposely begins with a fictional piece incorporating something slightly supernatural—a myth, legend, fable, or allegory— or a story containing, at least in part, elements of one of these. Myths and legends emerge from prehistory about the same time as human language does, so in an anthology stretching across the centuries it is appropriate to include these ancient elements in their modern settings.

Early prose writing up to the eighteenth century tended to be directed toward instruction—sermons or histories, government documents or meditations, heroic tales or homilies for the teaching of young and old. Writers of fancy, imagination, and spirituality wrote in verse. In Shakespeare's *King Lear* (page 93), almost all of the speeches are in verse. Exceptions are those of down-to-earth, low-life, or insane characters, such as Edgar in the part of Poor Tom, the Fool, and the mad king. Ribald jokes belong in prose; expressions of love in verse. While some critics credit Cervantes with becoming the father of the modern novel when *Don Quixote* was published in 1605, throughout most of the eighteenth and early nineteenth centuries, fiction pretended to be fact. Novels were often cast in the form of letters, usually written by the heroines while undergoing hair-raising adventures at peril of life and limb.

The short story we know today dates from the nineteenth century, when a demand for shorter fiction created a market for the literary magazine. At that time, writers like Washington Irving and Nathaniel Hawthorne wrapped their fictional accounts in frame stories, as if they were actually "found in the papers of" someone. Edgar Allan Poe spiced up short fiction by creating the detective story; he also heightened to its excruciating extremes of horror the "gothic" tale already popularized by the longer romances.

The late nineteenth and early twentieth centuries turned from this romantic fiction —unreal and emotional—to the common speech, ordinary characters, and true-to-life settings of *realism*. Mary E. Wilkins Freeman's "A New England Nun" (p. 609) exemplifies realism. Going further with this style, *naturalism* took its cue from scientific experimentation and often placed its characters in a sordid or violent setting to observe them dispassionately. Stephen Crane's famous novel *The Red Badge of Courage* illustrates this approach. His "The Bride Comes to Yellow Sky" (p. 216) shares some of these elements, as does William Kotzwinkle's "Follow the Eagle" (p. 653). Fiction today, in both short stories and novels, contains all of the elements discussed above, and more besides. The realism and naturalism of the late nineteenth and early twentieth centuries made their mark; yet romantic tales, even fantasies, blend with realism in contemporary fiction. Experimental fiction, such as that of Kurt Vonnegut and John Barth, still pushes ahead in search of new sensations, new insights, new forms, and new truths.

HOW TO READ A STORY

The fiction we present in this book consists of short or longer stories meant to be read rather than heard (though the electronic age makes it easier to listen to or see dramatized fiction). Reading a story is like peeling an onion. If this kitchen metaphor seems crude, think about it! As you look at a work of literature—a story, play, or poem —you see a hard outer layer that you can describe in words. You can say the onion's color is yellow, or white, or purple; its diameter one or three inches; its shape round or oval or bumpy. Likewise, you can say that Stephen Crane's "The Bride Comes to Yellow Sky" (p. 216) narrates the tale of the journey of the town's marshal and his new wife back to the small western town, Yellow Sky, to confront the townspeople, especially the town badman, Scratchy Wilson. This summary or paraphrase offers only a superficial version of the story. To get to the next layer of meaning, you must "peel the onion."

When the onion sheds its peel, another layer reveals itself—much like the outer layer, but more pungent, smoother, juicier. To continue the example, you can apply the peeling technique to Stephen Crane's story with good effect. Instead of a detailed summary of the plot line or the action, you can *analyze* elements of the story to find that the action falls into four chapters. As in a filmscript, Crane swiftly switches from one locale to another as if saying: "meanwhile, back in Yellow Sky. . . ." This device depends on the point of view of an omniscient narrator (one who knows all) who, like a film editor, can make leaps in time and space. Thus the story gains depth, throwing into relief some of the author's careful detailing, such as the New York manufactured clothing the characters wear, the presence of a "drummer" or traveling salesman in the Weary Gentleman Saloon during the attempted shoot-up, and even the frantic leaps of the lazy dog, surprised by gunfire.

You find then that the second layer of "The Bride" is Crane's examination of the changing lives of the Yellow Sky residents due to the coming of the railroad with its salesmen and goods from the East as well as the social changes that accompany them. The Marshal, Jack Potter, quits his stereotyped role of bandit-chasing, and, without consulting the town, goes to San Antonio to get married. When he brings his wife back to the town, you see that a family is to be established; ordinary work is to replace gunfights in the streets. To describe this layer, the psychological one, you use more abstract words ("family" and "work" rather than "the bride" or "Jack Potter") than you did when you simply summarized plot and action at the most superficial layer.

Further exploration has to be done in any work of fiction that has stood the test of time and multiple readings. Peel away the next layer of the onion, and the specifics (characters' names, exact locations, details) fade as you formulate a *theme,* a focus that may relate to your own life, or to humanity more generally. In the case of "The Bride Comes to Yellow Sky," the title offers a clue to the story's theme. An irony hovers in these happy-sounding words. The bride is neither conventionally beautiful nor young, but she represents something: the New West of families and prosperity, not the Old West of badmen and gunfights. Another clue to meaning appears in the first sentence: "The great Pullman was whirling onward with such dignity of motion that a glance from the window seemed simply to prove that the plains of Texas were pouring Eastward." *Literally,* "pouring Eastward" suggests the speed of the train, while *figuratively* the plains pour toward the sophisticated East, with its salesmen and its taste for elegance. Importation of "brides" means that the Old West of legend is vanishing, and this is a main theme for the story. Expert onion-peelers may go one layer further, to an even more universal theme: marriage and its stabilizing influence on primitive vigilante society.

You might try the onion method on other short stories in this anthology, but do not go too far: you might ruin the onion (and the story) by overpeeling it. The presence of some mystery, something yet to be solved, seems to be one of the marks of worthwhile literature, and not all details will fit into tidy patterns. Also, close scrutiny of fiction may, like the onion, make you cry. Good works of fiction disturb or rough up the mind, leaving a residue on the consciousness. You "peel the onion," then, to discover the core of what you are reading, to find more than pleasure or distraction. You might read to learn more about human nature, to experience others' emotions vicariously, without their sufferings, or simply to think deeply. If, in analyzing a thoughtful piece of fiction, you look for both pattern and purpose, you will enjoy your reading more and enrich the ways in which you can express your reactions to it.

FORMS OF FICTION

Since literary analysis demands a more formal vocabulary than we have been using so far, the following discussion of literary terms equips you with some basic tools to assist in reading and writing about literature.

We have been discussing a short story, "The Bride Comes to Yellow Sky." A *short story* is just that, short. It is a brief narrative developing one clear incident or plot rather than the many interlocking ones of a novel. Most of the fictional pieces in this anthology are short stories. A novel is not only longer, but may include complex, interweaving plots and many characters. A *novel* is an extended fictional prose narrative, describing the ordinary world with believable characters who use ordinary speech. An example of a novel is *Moby Dick* by Herman Melville.

In addition to this category based on length and complexity, we use other terms in discussing genres of fiction. The word *genre,* a French term meaning "kind" or "type," can refer to short story, play, poem, or novel, or to other categories of fiction such as *romance, confession, myth, legend, fable,* or *satire.*

A *romance* is an extravagant, imaginative work of fiction (short story or novel) dealing with a supernatural or unreal world. Edgar Allan Poe's "The Fall of the House of Usher" (p. 421) fulfills the definition of a romance: its setting appears exotic (the ruined manor on the gloomy fell), its characters act extravagantly, and its events occur as if motivated supernaturally. Ursula Le Guin's "Nine Lives" (p. 661), considered science fiction, is a good example of a romance because it deals with an unreal world. Within that world, though, it shares realistic characteristics with the novel; the characters' motivations are human, not supernatural.

Confession is a literary type beloved of popular checkout-line magazines. Confessions often include personal narrative, usually highly romantic and not reflecting a real world. "The Yellow Wallpaper," by Charlotte Perkins Gilman (p. 885) sounds like confessional literature; its psychological realism, though, is impressive. The narrator at first reports her surroundings realistically; then her perceptions shift and warp with her worsening mental state. The wallpaper itself, at first merely ugly, becomes threatening and damaging, and eventually destroys her.

A *myth* is a tale, usually about gods or heroes, which often attempts to explain some basic truth. Washington Irving's "Rip Van Winkle" (p. 4) uses the recurring myth of the long, enchanted sleep, while Doris Betts's "The Ugliest Pilgrim" (p. 792) transplants the traditional quest myth to a traveling bus and a mundane bus depot. A *legend,* a more traditional folktale containing supernatural elements, builds around some real person, place, or object. That legendary figure of the Old West, the badman, figures ironically in "The Bride Comes to Yellow Sky" (p. 216). "Noah" (page 740) retells a Bible story in dramatic form for the instruction and delight of medieval audiences. Often in short format, *fables* frequently employ animals as characters to illustrate human nature, sometimes cynically or comically. "The Unicorn in the Garden," by James Thurber (p. 366), places a legendary animal in a modern fable.

As in the medieval morality play (see "On Reading Drama," p. 1028), ideas or abstract qualities become personified in *allegory.* The author uses these personifications to make statements about moral issues or values. Hawthorne's "Young Goodman Brown" (page 592) includes elements of allegory. The young man's name is "Goodman" Brown; his wife is called "Faith." Their names stand for qualities connected with the story's examination of the Puritan idea of sin.

BASIC ELEMENTS OF FICTION

Atmosphere and Setting

The *setting* of a story is the physical background against which the action takes place. The *atmosphere,* in contrast, expresses the tone of a literary work—not just the setting but the emotional aura that permeates the work. Modern fiction, like older tales, makes much of these paired characteristics, and adept writers often choose evocative settings to highlight plot and character and add symbolic value to their work. The opening lines of Steinbeck's "The Chrysanthemums" (p. 224) reproduce in terms of landscape an atmosphere of futile striving in the face of frustration. The impact of Ursula Le Guin's "Nine Lives" (p. 661) partly derives from the forbidding, hostile atmosphere of the planet Libra where the clones go to work in the uranium mine. Setting is the place itself—the planet—while atmosphere is the emotional quality that place inspires, what it feels like to be there.

Plot and Structure

The most familiar element of fiction is *plot.* Plot is a planned series of interrelated actions progressing through the struggle of opposing forces to a climax or a denouement. Essentially, it is what happens in a story. Plot is one aspect of the "skin of the onion," the first layer. However, plot also contributes very importantly to the establishment and elaboration of the theme of a work. The *climax* of a well-plotted story is the high point towards which the action rises; the *denouement* (from the French, meaning "un-knotting") puts in order or works out all the strands of the story to a resolution. Nineteenth-century stories arrived at a denouement—and often went beyond, to an explanation of what all the characters became in later life, as in Hawthorne's "Young Goodman Brown" (p. 592). Modern stories often stop short of the denouement, leaving the characters standing poised over the brink. The ending of Kotzwinkle's story "Follow the Eagle" (p. 653) is a good example of such a device.

In addition to plot, works of fiction always have some kind of *structure.* The structure of a literary work is the planned framework, the way the parts of the story are arranged—the outline, the chapters in a novel, the acts in a play. The plot of "Rip Van Winkle" concerns the actions leading to and following Rip's long sleep; the structure consists of the short chapters of the story's organization. The plot is the meat; the structure the skeleton.

Characters: Flat and Round

An author's fleshing out of imagined characters is called *characterization*. The author who wants to create believable personalities does so through description, action, and dialogue. In old-fashioned melodrama and modern soap operas we speak of the "hero" and the "villain"; however, these simple concepts often do not fit the short story and the novel. Instead, we speak of the main character as the *protagonist*, the person who has the problem to solve. In opposition, we find the *antagonist*—the one who creates that problem or in some way forces it into the open. In "A Rose for Emily" (p. 617) the protagonist is Miss Emily Grierson, while the antagonist is the town itself as it tries to solve her mystery.

Some characters are never fully developed in a story; they show only one side, like a cut-out paper doll. We call these *flat characters*. Rip Van Winkle's termagant wife (p. 4) and Wangero, the trendy city daughter in Alice Walker's "Everyday Use" (p. 243), are both flat characters. They neither change nor develop in the story; they remain stereotyped. *Round characters,* on the other hand, present many faces to us; we feel we know them through several phases of growth and can see them from all angles. Not stereotyped, they grow and develop and remain real to us beyond the pages of the story. Phoenix, the brave old grandmother in Eudora Welty's story "A Worn Path" (p. 52), is such a person; she has a life of her own. Though we do not know everything about her, we feel that there are other important aspects of her life not included in the story. Other round characters are Violet, "the ugliest pilgrim" (p. 792); Mrs. Turpin, "the old wart hog" (p. 440); and Chee, the native American (p. 480).

Point of View

In the last section of this book, "Writing About Literature," we discuss the dangers of what is called "the biographical fallacy" (p. 1047): assuming that the narrator of the story is the author. Only in autobiography would this be true. The term *point of view* refers to the vantage point of the narrator, and not to the life of the author or the opinion of the reader. The point of view of a story indicates the distance the author plans to keep from the materials of the story. Sometimes it can be very close, with the writer using the *first person:* "I." A first-person narrative may be told by a mere reporter of the story, or by a participant in it. For example, in Sherwood Anderson's "Death in the Woods" (p. 601), a mature man remembers events of his boyhood and strings them together into a narrative that calls on both memory and experience. However, the "I" form holds a danger for the reader; sometimes it is tempting to confuse the author with the narrator. In some cases a young, inexperienced, or mentally confused narrator reports what he or she sees or thinks, but does not fully understand; we call this a *naive narrator*. Stephen Vincent Benét's young traveler in "By the Waters of Babylon" tells his tale in a naive fashion, but implications emerge in his holocaust story that he himself only begins to understand.

Third-person narrative is more common than first-person narrative. Often a writer will use a *third-person subjective,* or *limited third-person* point of view, telling a story in the third person (using "he," "she," or "it") but actually chronicling events seen only through the eyes of one of the characters. Limited third-person point of view appears in Isaac Bashevis Singer's "The Spinoza of Market Street" (p. 41), where we come to understand, in subtle detail, the thoughts of an old Jewish scholar living in a European ghetto, though the story is told in the third person. In much of the third-person narrative the author withdraws, and an unidentified narrator uses "he," "she," or "it" to report objectively. A good example of this device appears in Hawthorne's "Young Goodman Brown" (p. 592). Though there are few authors whose personal attitudes are not somehow expressed or implied in what they write, we call this type the *self-effacing author.* The author cannot strictly be said to intrude at all into the story, though Hawthorne's feelings of guilt at the excesses of his Puritan ancestors shows in "Young Goodman Brown" as in other stories and novels he wrote about the Massachusetts Bay Colony.

In contrast, sometimes the author becomes very much an influence, if not a manipulator of the action. The *third-person omniscient* author of "Angelina Sando-val" (p. 35) reveals his presence as a camera eye, looking at all aspects and all the personages in the Sandoval family—revealing things no one person could know. As an author becomes more intrusive, even in subtle ways, he or she chooses scenes, or omits them, to achieve certain effects. So an author exerts more or less control over the events of a story. The most impersonal-seeming "camera eye" reflects a mind with particular interests and biases.

Like the narrator, the author may decide to be as much an integral part of the story as any active protagonist. The third-person omniscient point of view gives the author the greatest freedom to choose one character's thoughts and then another's, picking this vantage point or that from which to observe the action. When the writer pleases, he or she can stop in the midst of a narrative to address the reader in an almost conspiratorial tone. This technique probably stemmed from the earlier attempt to present fiction as truth, occasionally taking the form of a *frame story* convincingly quoting a manuscript found in someone's papers. Washington Irving stated that he found the "Rip Van Winkle" sketch in the papers of Diedrich Knickerbocker, an entirely fictional character. In discussing these "true" characters, the reader, thus, could be addressed as an ally, though sometimes in a patronizing fashion. Then the writer could shift back to the limited third-person view, and, like an essayist or journalist, vanish as a separate voice from the reader's consciousness.

Though plot and character at times seem the more important elements of a piece of fiction, awareness of the author's point of view is essential, just as awareness of camera angles is vital in understanding film or video. Where the author stands—and thus how the reader can perceive the plot, action, and characters of a story—largely forms our impression and evaluation of a work of fiction.

STYLE IN FICTION

Style is what makes a work the author's own original production. Style depends on subtleties such as word emphasis, sentence shape, and paragraph structure. Charlotte Perkins Gilman, for example, uses short, breathless sentences and one-sentence para-graphs to convey the hasty, surreptitious writing and the deteriorating mind of her protagonist in "The Yellow Wallpaper" (p. 885); William Kotzwinkle impressionistically depicts the last confused thoughts of Eagle as he and his cycle plunge into the canyon (p. 655): "Wham the arrow crossed the morning. I am shot from out my body whoooooooooooooo the endless sunrise."

The skilled writer knows that various kinds of sentences achieve different effects. For example, if the statement is to be direct, plain, and simple, a simple sentence might be appropriate. "Let him keep her where she belongs. It's his own fault," thinks Wilson, the hunter, of Mr. and Mrs. Macomber's relationship. The *cumulative sentence* with its modifiers puts first things first, with the trimmings at the end of the sentence. The subteen protagonist in Toni Cade Bambara's "Raymond's Run" speaks this way: "I much rather just knock you down and take my chances, even if I am a little girl with skinny arms and a squeaky voice, which is how I got the name Squeaky" (p. 23). Squeaky sounds youthful in her trailing-off sentence, yet decisive in putting subject and strong verbs up front.

In contrast, a leisurely *periodic sentence* keeps its suspense until the end, holding our interest while it suggests heavy rationality. Old-fashioned stories like "Rip Van Winkle" abound in these sentences. The last sentence in Irving's story offers a good example:

> Even to this day they never hear a thunderstorm of a summer afternoon about the Kaatskill, but they say Hendrick Hudson and his crew are at their game of ninepins; and it is a common wish of all hen-pecked husbands in the neighborhood, when life hangs heavy on their hands, that they might have a quieting draught out of Rip Van Winkle's flagon (p. 13).

Interruptions, subordination, fragments, strings of words with either standard punctuation or a series of coordinators, such as *and, but,* or *so,* can depict agonized emotion, puzzlement, or other human feelings. The worried, distracted stream of consciousness of the mother in Tillie Olsen's "I Stand Here Ironing" expresses her desperate concern over her daughter:

> Let her be. So all that is in her will not bloom—but in how many does it? There is still enough left to live by. Only help her to believe—help make it so there is cause for her to believe that she is more than this dress on the ironing board, helpless before the iron (p. 34).

Sentence variety, dashes, repetition, false starts all make the passage sound authentic. *Stream-of-consciousness*—getting into the innermost thoughts of a character—gives depth to the writing of Olsen as well as such authors as William Faulkner, James Joyce, and Virginia Woolf.

Writers also assume various tones—almost separate voices—in what they write. Mimicry, or parody, is a particularly noticeable voice. A *parody* imitates a well-known work or style—usually satirically or comically. Lewis Carroll parodies the heroic ballad in "Jabberwocky" (p. 73). The author's attitude may be tongue-in-cheek, as Thurber's is in "The Unicorn in the Garden" (p. 366), or it may be completely serious and factual. Objectivity belongs more in science and mathematics textbooks than in fiction, where authors' attitudes differ. Hemingway speaks in an understated voice, while Poe is subjective and emotional. Betts's protagonist Violet is simple and sensitive, while Eudora Welty's down-home characters capture the flavor of rural America. One writer's tone, even one story's individual voice, would not be suitable for another one. The aged Phoenix in "A Worn Path" (p. 52) should not turn into a college professor when she speaks. Abrupt shifts like that would jar your willingness to accept the story. A false tone can shatter the illusion, making you less willing to listen.

Good writers try to incorporate suitability, simplicity, and taste into their style. Jonathan Swift's "proper words in their proper places" is a good maxim to remember. Sometimes the right word is a four-letter one, as when a character hammers a thumb. At other times the right words fall into elegant periodic sentences, when leisure permits that formation. This combination of words, sentences, rhythms, tone, or point of view can enthrall or bore you, helping the work to endure for generations or consigning it to be thrown unceremoniously into the trash with the onion peels.

ON READING POETRY: LIMERICKS TO LYRICS

> There once was a baker named Fred
> Who checked out his checkbook and said
> "My funds are so low
> Guess I'll knead some more dough
> That's the best way I know to raise bread!"

. . .

> Last week a bright fellow named Kirk
> Was promoted to head soda jerk.
> Now his pay comes on Mondays,
> He spends it on sundaes,
> And never gets fed up with work!

Remember these laundered limericks from the valentines you sent when you were young? Their peculiar form, the limerick, is often thought to be "subliterary"; that is, not highbrow enough to pay attention to. Although no one knows where limericks began (in Ireland, possibly), people have been enjoying and writing them for a long time. Perhaps the limerick can help us come up with a definition of poetry.

A limerick fulfills the first important qualification of poetry, or indeed of any literary genre: it has a subject. The writer must have something to say. In the case of a limerick, the subject can be anything, preferably something nonserious or bawdy. The well-known limerick that follows won a contest to produce the best "clean" limerick.

> There was a young lady from Niger
> Who smiled as she rode on a tiger
> They returned from the ride
> With the lady inside
> And the smile on the face of the tiger.

The subject of the limerick, then, can be anything, but its outstanding characteristic remains its form: once you hear it, you will never forget its peculiar rhythm. The first, second, and fifth lines of most limericks contain three stressed syllables. The third and fourth lines have only two stressed syllables. The dominant rhythmic (or *metric*) pattern in a limerick is *anapestic*—two short beats and a long—"ditty-*dum.*" (Refer to "A Note on Scansion," on page 1023, for a fuller explanation of poetic meters.) The first of the two rhymes in a limerick depends on a proper name, often an outrageous one. In addition, limericks, especially bawdy ones, include puns or double meanings.

There was a young fellow named Weir,	(8 syllables)
Who hadn't an atom of fear;	(8 syllables)
He indulged a desire	(6 syllables)
To touch a live wire—	(5 syllables)
Most any last line will do here.	(8 syllables)

Word has come down from the Dean
That by use of the teaching machine
Old Oedipus Rex
Could have learned about sex
Without ever disturbing the Queen.

Scan the limericks above. By *scanning* we mean marking down the rhythm, the short beats (˘) and the longs (/), so that you have, for the last limerick, a pattern like this:

/ ˘ ˘ / ˘ ˘ /	(a)
˘ ˘ / ˘ ˘ / ˘ ˘ /	(a)
˘ / ˘ ˘ /	(b)
˘ ˘ / ˘ ˘ /	(b)
˘ ˘ / ˘ ˘ / ˘ ˘ /	(a)

Once you have that down, then mark the rhyme scheme, letting a different letter stand for each rhyming sound. In this case, the rhyme scheme is a relatively easy one: *aabba.* Now you have a model for a limerick of your own. You might even want to try one beginning with a sentence such as this: "There once was a dum-duh named num-duh/ Who . . . ."

WHAT IS A POEM?

Once you have made the breakthrough by writing limericks, you are well on the way to constructing a definition of poetry. This playing with language, letting words have more than one meaning (like the puns in the limericks), especially characterizes poetry. Poetry usually contains sharply condensed language, a boiling down of meaning, as compared to the usually straight statements of prose. Poetry is the liqueur of writing, the distillation of speech. The word "poet" itself derives from the Greek *poietes* and means something like "a mover and a shaker"—someone who makes things, a creator. Poetry—like a garden, a building, or a symphony—is the product of this creativity. It takes the form of a pattern of spoken or written ideas in concentrated, imaginative, and rhythmical language. Poetry often contains rhyme and specific meter (a fixed rhythmic pattern), but not necessarily.

The following short selections all seem to fall within the definition of poetry: patterned, concentrated, imaginative:

> And hence no force, however great
> Can draw a cord, however fine
> Into a horizontal line
> Which shall be absolutely straight.

> Western Wind, when wilt thou blow,
> The small rain down can rain?
> Christ! if my love were in my arms,
> And I in my bed again!

> Twas brillig, and the slithy toves
> Did gyre and gimble in the wabe;
> All mimsy were the borogoves
> And the mome raths outgrabe.

These three quatrains (four-line verses) each have two familiar characteristics of poetry: rhyme, and rhythm or "beat." They could be sung; this puts them in the ancient company of lyrics, originally sung to the music of a plucked stringed instrument called a lyre. Looking at each word and concept of the first quatrain with care, however, you might notice that it fails the test of concentrated meaning. Each word means exactly what it says and no more. This quatrain is not a poem; it is a physics theorem, lacking the wealth of connotation a poem has.

The second quatrain, "Western Wind," consisting of a question and an exclamation, is one of the oldest poems in our language, dating at least from the Crusades. Some small archaic touches suggest its age, but what soldier, sailor, or prisoner today has not cried out from the heart for home, bed, and beloved! The details, wind and rain, establish the mood of chill and loneliness. The sad query "When will I ever get home to my love?" wrings from that misery the exclamation "Christ!" It is a poem, primarily because it appeals to our emotions; the physics theorem, useful though it may be, cannot.

"Jabberwocky" (page 23), by Lewis Carroll, is the source of the third quatrain. Although it is nonsense verse, if you listen to the whole poem read aloud you can actually attempt to tell its story. Like most ballads, this one seems to tell of a dramatic, possibly bloody, incident. It has a regular rhythm (iambic tetrameter) and a rhyme scheme (abab). But the words are neologisms (words made up for the occasion). Some of them ("chortled," "galumphing," "burbled")—see *onomatopoeia* (p. 1021), have since come into our language. But most of the verse *is* nonsense, though it teeters on the edge of making sense. It is still a poem, however, since it appeals to our emotions through our sense of humor; a poem does not have to be completely logical.

TYPES OF POEMS

The first necessity, as we have seen, to make a poem, is to have something to say (a theme or subject). The next is to have a form in which to say it. This form can be conventional, like the limerick or the ballad, or it can be an original pattern created by the poet. Inventive human beings have tried many forms and types in their quest to compose poetry. They can be grouped into two general categories: lyric and narrative. The following section identifies some of the forms the poet might choose.

Lyric Forms

Lyric poetry is what we often think of when considering poetry: short, musical poems, full of emotion. Set to the music of a lyre in ancient Greece, lyrics are now often set to the electric guitar, but the bond between poetry and music remains strong. In twenty years, perhaps, Billy Joel's "The Stranger" and "Uptown Girl" will be in poetry anthologies, the way the Beatles' lyrics and those by Paul Simon and Leonard Cohen appear in this collection.

A lyric poem of grief at the death of a loved one is called an *elegy*. The Theodore Roethke poem "Elegy for Jane" (p. 524) poignantly expresses a teacher's feelings on the death of a student. "Do Not Go Gentle into That Good Night," by Dylan Thomas (p. 85), while not strictly an elegy, reflects the poet's emotion at the anticipation of his father's death.

Written to honor some great event or some outstanding hero, an *ode* is a poem on some high theme. The great odes used as scene transitions in *Antigone* (p. 528, for example), still exemplify some of the world's most noble poetry, even in translation. They are, incidentally, translated by a modern poet, Robert Fitzgerald. In spite of their 2500 years, they touch on universal themes we can all relate to: war, love, death, humanity.

The *pastoral* is another kind of lyric poem, little used today. Its name suggests its purpose: to celebrate nature. The "shepherds" of the pastoral are idealistic and lovely; they do not smell of sweat and sheep. Christopher Marlowe's "The Passionate Shepherd to His Love" (p. 496) gives a prettified view of an ideal love, and an attempted seduction that does not deal with realities. Sir Walter Ralegh offered a wry answer in "The Nymph's Reply to the Shepherd" (p. 497). Shakespeare lampooned the "ideal woman" of the pastorals in his sonnet that begins "My mistress' eyes are nothing like the sun" (p. 502).

A *sonnet* is a lyric poem of fourteen lines, traditionally in the rhythmic pattern known as iambic pentameter (˘ / ˘ / ˘ / ˘ / ˘ /). The fourteen-line form tells a story or sets a problem in the first eight or twelve lines, then usually solves it in the last six lines or in a closing *couplet* (the last two lines). Fascinated by the challenge of the strictures imposed by the sonnet's form, many poets have experimented with it. For example, at the suggestion of her therapist, Anne Sexton watched a television program on the sonnet. Though she had written poetry before, this program prompted her to write many sonnets during her career as poet. Many poets do not stop at a single sonnet; they write a sequence of them that tells a story. Two of these series are Elizabeth Barrett Browning's "Sonnets from the Portuguese" (see Sonnet 43, p. 502) and Anne Sexton's "Angels" (see "Angel of Beach Houses and Picnics," p. 503).

Various kinds of sonnets exist. Three of the most common types are the following:

The *Italian* or *Petrarchan* sonnet (named for Petrarch, the thirteenth-century Italian who developed it) has five rhyming sounds in a specific pattern: *abba abba cde cde*. For an example, look at Louise Labé's Sonnet #8 (p. 500).

The *Spenserian* sonnet was named for the sixteenth-century English poet Edmund Spenser. His "Amoretti," a sonnet series written about 1595, used five rhymes, four of them linked: *abab bcbc cdcd ee.* John Donne's "Death Be Not Proud" (p. 85) is a Spenserian sonnet.

The *Shakespearean* or English sonnet, named for William Shakespeare, uses seven rhymes in three quatrains and ends in a rhymed couplet *(abab cdcd efef gg).* This rhymed couplet or tag rhyme at the end, like the punch line of a joke, wraps up the solution of the problem posed in the three quatrains. An example of this kind of sonnet is Shakespeare's #116:

Let me not to the marriage of true minds	(a)
Admit impediments. Love is not love	(b)
Which alters when it alteration finds,	(a)
Or bends with the remover to remove:	(b)
Oh no! It is an ever fixed mark	(c)
That looks on tempests and is never shaken;	(d)
It is the star to every wandering bark,	(c)
Whose worth's unknown, although his height be taken.	(d)
Love's not Time's fool, though rosy lips and cheeks	(e)
Within his bending sickle's compass come;	(f)
Love alters not with his brief hours and weeks,	(e)
But bears it out even to the edge of doom.	(f)
If this be error, and upon me proved,	(g)
I never writ, nor no man ever loved.	(g)

Narrative Forms

Narrative poems tell stories. Throughout history, long *epic poems* such as Homer's *Odyssey,* the Anglo-Saxon *Beowulf,* and the Icelandic sagas extolled a country's history or a national hero. Writing about his poem "The Raven," Edgar Allan Poe said that he thought the best poem was no longer than one hundred lines. Whether or not his statement was influential, very long epic poems have become rare today.

The familiar *ballad* is a shorter poem from a very old tradition, dealing with one dramatic incident, usually tragic or at least bloody. The ballad tells a short, simple tale in simple verse. Many ballads were handed down orally. Many versions of "Barbara Allan" (p. 489), for example, have traveled from England to America, where some are still sung by Appalachian folk-singers. "Barbara Allan" is a tragic tale of unrequited love; another ballad, "Frankie and Johnnie" (p. 493) gives a modern twist to the same theme. A very old ballad, "Sir Patrick Spens" (p. 490), tells the tragic story of double-dealing and treachery in the voyage from the Firth of Forth in Scotland to bring back the Norwegian Princess Margaret in about 1285.

Most plays written before the eighteenth century were in verse; the tradition continues today in short *dramatic monologues.* The poet has one or more characters speaking in the poem. Robert Browning perfected the short dramatic monologue style in the nineteenth century. One of his best and most powerful is "My Last Duchess" (p. 510). In the poem the Duke talks about his late wife's portrait to an envoy arranging his next marriage. Only the Duke speaks; we see the staging (the palace, the portrait, the envoy) only through the Duke's monologue. The Duke's words suggest how and why he got rid of Duchess No. 1; they simultaneously reveal her character and his own. T. S. Eliot's "The Love Song of J. Alfred Prufrock" (p. 512), in addition to illustrating in its complexity many of the poetic devices we have discussed here, is essentially a dramatic monologue, with one speaker expressing his emotions and describing his actions, as in a one-person play.

Old, New, and Strange Forms

Haiku, a Japanese form dating from the thirteenth century, uses three lines of five, seven, and five syllables to make a seventeen-syllable poem.

The Crystal Spring

In my scooping hands	(5 syllables)
The leaves of the oak-tree move	(7 syllables)
In the crystal spring.	(5 syllables)
—Soin	

Without rhyme or rhythm, haiku creates a picture, an image, a mood, or a contrast meant to evoke emotion. Nature and the seasons are frequent subjects. The haiku distills Japanese thought and culture into a poem based on what Kenneth Yasuda calls "readiness for an experience for its own sake," rather than for the connotations it suggests. "The Mississippi River" is another haiku written in English by a Japanese:

> Under the low grey
> Winter skies water pushes
> Water on its way.
> —Kenneth Yasuda

Abandoning the traditional seventeen-syllable form, Ezra Pound wrote a famous haiku-like poem on the Paris subway, the Metro:

> The apparition of these faces in the crowd;
> Petals on a wet, black bough.

Look at e. e. cummings's puzzler:

> l(a
>
> le
> af
> fa
>
> ll
>
> s)
> one
> l
>
> iness

This poem cannot fit into most discussions on poetry, because its value depends on its graphic or typographic aspect, not on its language. This *concrete poetry,* as it is known, depends on concrete things, like shape, print, paper, or film, rather than on words alone. Egyptian hieroglyphics and Japanese picture-writing suggest that poets experimented with this kind of poetry in ancient times. Later, William Blake integrated his etchings and poems into one art form that included both. One example of shaped verse is George Herbert's "Easter Wings" (p. 912), which appears in wing shape. Poems today can be shaped like swans or popsicles, and the cummings poem above takes the form of a leaf falling through air to show loneliness. The concrete poem "Epithalamium," by Pedro Xisto, has a title longer than itself. "Epithalamium" means "a marriage poem," and once you see the poem, you can instantly appreciate the title.

DEVICES OF SOUND

Repetition of Sounds

Most people expect poetry to have some kind of rhyme. In fact, we started this discussion with the rhyme scheme of the limerick. However, English poetry did not use rhyme until about 1400, when Renaissance Italian poetry influenced poets like Chaucer and later the sonneteers like Wyatt, Surrey, Spenser, Sydney, and Shakespeare. Romance languages such as French and Spanish, however, have many rhymes, since many words sound alike because of their endings. While we might search madly for a word to rhyme with "orange," or "cucumber," for instance, we would not have that problem in the Latin languages.

English (and thus American) verse often depends on other kinds of sounds distributed throughout a poem. Old English poetry, such as *Beowulf,* was typically sung or chanted to the tune of a harp. Four chords were struck for each line, but the intervening number of syllables varied as in real speech and as in modern folk songs. Three of these four heavy thumps in a line had the same initial sound. This sound pattern, known as *alliteration,* repeats two or more initial letters or sounds, usually consonants. Other poems besides those of ancient Britain rely on this attention-getting device. Shapiro's "Auto Wreck" (p. 525) uses alliteration in phrases like "soft silver bell," "tight as tourniquets," "we speak through sickly smiles." Even modern advertising like the J. C. Penney ad that claims "wit meets whimsey" in "sizzling stripes" exploits this poetic device. Richard Wilbur has revived the *Beowulf* pattern in a modern poem, "Junk" (p. 295). Ezra Pound, W. H. Auden, and others have also reinvented Old English poems. A device similar to alliteration is *assonance,* the repetition of *vowel* sounds *within* words. Alliteration rivets our attention by repetition; assonance, instead of waking us by the thumping of the consonants, lulls us by the vowel sounds. Thus it is more subtle, more lyrical. Dylan Thomas manipulates assonance this way throughout "Fern Hill" (p. 70). In line 12, "In the sun that is young once only," the "u" of "sun" shifts to "young," "once," and "only," with the sound going from the back of the throat to the front of the mouth.

Refrain and Repetition

Often today, poetry seems something we make our own only after much study. Consider, though, how in primitive times poetry and dance were familiar arts. The Cro-Magnon man, coming home from a big hunt, would bring back heroic tales along with his kill. Out of the darkness of the cave came the old men, the nursing mothers with their babies, some lazy pre-teens, all eager to hear the account of the hunt. The hunters would build up the comforting fire and act out their hunt rhythmically. Someone would pound on a hollow log or would whistle; when the punch-line "and then the sabre-toothed tiger roared" came again, the rest of the group would take it up. It became the chorus—the refrain, the part everybody knows of the ballad or popular song today. In "Frankie and Johnnie" (p. 493), an early twentieth-century ballad, the third line of each verse repeats itself, with changes that show the development of the dramatic incident. This is called *incremental repetition.* Each time a slight change occurs so that the first chorus, "He was her man, but he done her wrong," becomes in the end "He was my man, and I done him wrong." Frankie shoots Johnny and hangs for it. An older ballad with incremental repetition is "Barbara Allan" (p. 489) where "Fell in love with Barbara Allan" changes gradually to "cried 'Woe to Barbara Allan!' "

In addition to repeating whole lines, words or phrases may be repeated to achieve a special effect—drowsiness, sensuality, suspense—whatever the poet intends. Dylan Thomas in "Fern Hill," and above all, Walt Whitman, make effective use of repetition.

Imitation of Sounds

Primitive people probably began to talk by trying to imitate natural sounds—the buzzing of the fly, the hissing of a snake, the crack of a bone—and we still use these sounds (as we have in this sentence). Using words in this way to imitate or represent natural sounds is the poetic device *onomatopoeia. Crunch, tinkle, sizzle, bang,* and *crash* are all familiar examples. Emily Dickinson's poem about death, #465, "I heard a fly buzz when I died," uses onomatopoeia in the word "buzz," as well as in words like "stumbled" and "heaves."

Similarity of Sounds: Rhyme

The simplest kind of rhyme is the direct echoing of sounds: "moon, June, croon, dune, tune." Many subtleties radiate from that. Rhymes will not always have exactly matching perfection—and in fact should not have. As in nature, infinite variety charms and inspires. The simplest rhyme exists in two adjacent lines: rhymed couplets.

> Listen my children and you shall hear
> Of the midnight ride of Paul Revere.
>
> —Henry Wadsworth Longfellow

Three lines can also rhyme in triplets as in Robert Herrick's "Upon Julia's Clothes":

> Whenas in silks my Julia goes
> Then, then (methinks) how sweetly flows
> The liquefaction of her clothes.
>
> Next, when I cast mine eyes and see
> That brave vibration each way free,
> O how that glittering taketh me!

A longer poem that rhymes throughout in couplets is Andrew Marvell's "To His Coy Mistress" (p. 505). The couplets following one another remind us of the theme: time, with its tick-tock beat. The logic of the couplets suggests a syllogism: if *A* equals *B* then *C* is also true. *A* does not equal *B*, however, therefore let us make love before it is too late! Even more common, especially in popular song or ballad, are quatrains: four lines, alternately rhyming. The "Richard Cory" poem by Edwin Arlington Robinson (p. 706) uses alternate rhymes in quatrains, rhyming *abab cdcd efef ghgh*. All of these devices of sound emphasize the oral quality of poetry, through both repetition of sounds to hold the listener's attention, and memory devices to help the reciter (the scop of Anglo-Saxon England, the troubadour of Medieval France, or the more modern ballad singer or rock star) to remember many verses.

Much poetry depends on other devices than end rhyme. *Blank verse* is anything but blank: it has been the favorite British/American form since alliterative verse passed from fashion before the Renaissance. It has form (iambic pentameter) but no rhyme (except to get attention at highly emotional moments). Once all serious plays, like Shakespeare's *King Lear* (p. 93), were written in blank verse, although the comic actors, like the Fool, still spoke in prose. Some plays and many poems (such as Robert Frost's "Birches," p. 274), continue to be written in blank verse.

Free verse is sometimes wrongly said to have no form. Like all poetry, it has a form, one chosen by the poet and followed consistently throughout the poem. The form may be very subtle, as in the simple arrangement of parts on the page. The effect of Lawrence Ferlinghetti's "the pennycandystore beyond the El" (p. 69), or e. e. cummings' "leaf" (p. 1019) depends on this kind of typography. Free verse might also resemble a more "regular" poem. For example, Karl Shapiro's "Auto Wreck" (p. 525) is cast in four verses of irregular length but somewhat even lines (three or four beats per line). "Auto Wreck" has no rhyme scheme but does contain metaphors, similes, and enough sound effects like assonance and alliteration to make it recognizably poetry. The four verses move progressively from description to abstract speculation about human fate, a case of "peeling the onion" through four layers to a universal truth.

A NOTE ON SCANSION

If poetry is language arranged in various attention-getting ways to appeal to our senses and our emotions, one of these ways is through *meter,* the pattern of stressed and unstressed syllables in lines of poetry. *Scansion* means marking down, by symbols, this pattern. A unit of this pattern of stress and unstress is known as a *foot.* A metrical foot can have two or three syllables. The most common foot is *iambic,* with two syllables, the stress on the second (˘ /). Five of these feet in a line is called *pentameter,* giving us the most common line in English-language poetry, *iambic pentameter.* An example:

A book of verses underneath the bough
A jug of wine, a loaf of bread—and thou
Beside me singing in the wilderness—
Oh, wilderness were paradise enow!
˘ / ˘ / ˘ / ˘ / ˘ /
˘ / ˘ / ˘ / ˘ / ˘ /
˘ / ˘ / ˘ / ˘ / ˘ /
˘ / ˘ / ˘ / ˘ / ˘ /

From the "Rubaiyat of Omar Khayyam"

Table of Meters

FOOT FORM

iamb (/ ˘) basic English speech pattern, hence most poetry; star example: Shakespeare.

trochee (˘ /) Poe, "The Raven": "Once upon a midnight dreary, while I pondered weak and weary"
/ ˘ / ˘ / ˘ / ˘ / ˘ / ˘ / ˘ / ˘

anapest (˘ ˘ /) Byron, "The Destruction of the Sennacherib":

The Assyrian came down like a wolf on the fold
And his cohorts were gleaming in purple and gold,
˘ ˘ / ˘ ˘ / ˘ ˘ / ˘ ˘ /
˘ ˘ / ˘ ˘ / ˘ ˘ / ˘ ˘ /

dactyl (/ ˘ ˘) Natural to Greek language: *An it gon e* (˘ / ˘ ˘); found in English in the limerick.

LINE LENGTH

monometer—one foot (rare)

dimeter—two feet (rare)
Stevie Smith, "The Frog Prince" (p. 720)

> I am a frog
> I live under a spell
> I live at the bottom
> Of a green well.
> / ˘ ˘ /
> ˘ ˘ / ˘ ˘ /
> ˘ / ˘ ˘ / ˘
> / ˘ ˘ /

trimeter—three feet
Theodore Roethke, "My Papa's Waltz":

> The whiskey on your breath
> Could make a small boy dizzy:
> But I hung on like death:
> Such waltzing was not easy.
> ˘ / ˘ / ˘ /
> ˘ / ˘ / ˘ / ˘
> ˘ / ˘ / ˘ /
> ˘ / ˘ / ˘ / ˘

tetrameter—four feet
Andrew Marvell, "To His Coy Mistress" (p. 505):

> Had we but world enough and time
> This coyness, lady, were no crime.
> ˘ / ˘ / ˘ / ˘ /
> ˘ / ˘ / ˘ / ˘ /

pentameter—five feet
many parts of Shakespeare's plays, sonnets:

> The quality of mercy is not strained.
> It droppeth as the gentle rain from heaven.
> ˘ / ˘ / ˘ / ˘ / ˘ /
> ˘ / ˘ / ˘ / ˘ / ˘ /

hexameter—six feet (sometimes called "Alexandrines")—Dowson, "Cynara":

> Last night, ah, yesternight, betwixt her lips and mine,
> There fell thy shadow, Cynara, thy breath was shed
> Upon my soul between the kisses and the wine.
> ˘ / ˘ / ˘ / ˘ / ˘ / ˘ /

˘ / ˘ / ˘ / ˘ / ˘ / ˘ /
˘ / ˘ / ˘ / ˘ / ˘ / ˘ /

Also some modern "Blues," like Bessie Smith's "Empty Bed Blues":

When my bed gets empty, makes me feel awful mean and blue
Cause my springs gettin' rusty, sleepin' single the way I do.

heptameter—seven feet

"Fourteeners," usually broken in two to form a ballad stanza, as in "Sir Patrick Spens" (p. 490):

The King sits in Dumfermline town,
Drinking the blude-red wine;
O whare will I get a skeely skipper,
To sail this new ship of mine?
˘ / ˘ / ˘ / ˘ /
˘ / ˘ / ˘ /
˘ / ˘ ˘ / ˘ / ˘ /˘
˘ / ˘ / ˘ ˘ /

—or as a hymn form (4:3:4:3), like some of Emily Dickinson's poems (p. 285):

A narrow fellow in the grass
Occasionally rides—
You may have met him—
did you not
His notice sudden is—
˘ / ˘ / ˘ / ˘ /
˘ / ˘ / ˘ /
˘ / ˘ / ˘˘
/ ˘ /
˘ / ˘ / ˘ /

octameter—eight feet

Poe, "The Raven":

Once upon a midnight dreary, while I
     pondered, weak and weary
Over many a quaint and curious volume of
     forgotten lore,
/ ˘ / ˘ / ˘ / ˘ / ˘ / ˘ / ˘ / ˘
/ ˘ / ˘ / ˘ / ˘ / ˘ / ˘ / ˘ /

FIGURES OF SPEECH

In the last section we discussed the sounds of poetry. In this section we will discuss the sense of poetry, its intellectual quality, the ideas that can be perceived when we read it or hear it recited.

A *figure of speech* is an expression in which words are used in a nonliteral sense to present a figure or picture. In poetry, words mean what they actually say, of course, but like a pebble thrown into the lake, they create ever-widening circles of meaning, further connotations. The phrase "like a pebble thrown into the lake" is a figure of speech; it goes beyond ordinary language to explain its meaning. To use scientific words to explain the phenomenon would take many more words and probably express the thought less clearly. The figure used here is a *simile:* a direct or stated comparison between unrelated things, using "like" or "as." Many similies occur in Karl Shapiro's poem "Auto Wreck": "like an artery," "like convalescents," "tight as tourniquets."

Another kind of poetic comparison is the *metaphor,* an implied comparison without "like" or "as." In a metaphor, one thing is likened to another by being spoken of as if it were that thing: "All the world's a stage" or "Fred's a pig." These are metaphors —the world is not a stage, and Fred is not literally a pig. In Frost's "The Road Not Taken" (p. 589), one metaphor sustains the entire poem: "roads" stand for different choices of some kind. A *symbol* is a specific object that stands for an abstract idea (a dove is a symbol of peace); in a metaphor this distinction is not so clear-cut. In "The Road Not Taken" the two roads (physical objects) stand for abstract ideas, choices, as well as actual roads. In Carl Sandburg's "Grass" (p. 290), the grass stands for itself (it covers the buried soldiers' bodies); it also stands for an abstract idea (forgetfulness, perhaps). Sylvia Plath used the "mushrooms" in her poem (p. 913) to stand for oppressed people (females?) who will overcome one day by pushing softly through.

Personification—giving human characteristics to ideas, animals, or inanimate objects—is another way of making comparisons through poetic language. We employ this device all the time in ordinary speech: "The factory had three hundred hands," "the lip of the cup," "the bed legs." An interesting example of personification occurs in Anne Bradstreet's "The Author to Her Book" (p. 911), where she writes of her first published poems as if they were fractious children needing their language emended and their errors corrected.

Imagery is a loose term covering words that appeal to your senses to help your imagination feel, taste, touch, hear, or smell. They present an instantaneous picture like a slide flashed on the screen for a split second. "Auto Wreck" has many of these little flash pictures: the wrecked cars, "husks of locusts," beside the highway, the ambulance lights flashing. William Butler Yeats's "The Lake Isle of Innisfree" (p. 282) creates a peaceful pastoral picture with its "bee-loud glade," its "nine bean rows." The Japanese form of *haiku* (discussed on p. 1019) depends on instant, clear imagery in a small compass.

Poetic diction plays with words sometimes by *understatement*—saying less than it means, implying much more. The understatement of W. H. Auden's "The Unknown Citizen" (p. 910) is based on the bitter irony of a hollow civilization that prides itself on dedicating a monument to a pitifully average man. The opposite of understatement is *hyperbole,* exaggeration for effect, as in "I've told you millions of times not to use sentence fragments." *Paradox* is a seeming contradiction, saying two opposite things at the same time and making them perfectly understood in a new, meaningful way. Paul Simon's "The Sound of Silence" (p. 303), even in its title illustrates paradox; how can silence have a sound? Yet we all know it does. The paradox forces us to feel the essence of silence more acutely. We are all acquainted with the paradoxical phrases

People talking without speaking
People hearing without listening,

which make us think about ordinary failures of communication in a new way.

VALUE

What is a poem worth? Of what value is a butterfly . . . or a baby? How can you say that Walt Whitman is "greater" than Carl Sandburg, or that John Donne is "better" than Rod McCuen? The question, as Auden said about the "Unknown Citizen," is absurd. At least, it is unanswerable. We can, however, set up touchstones of works we like and do not like, and measure other books and poems against these. The question of "greater" or "better" may boil down to three kinds of yardsticks to measure values:

1. *Scope:* that is, depth of meaning. Each exploration reveals more layers of meaning or applications to our own lives.
2. *Timelessness:* that is, lasting interest and solace to a variety of readers in widely differing times and places. We find paperback editions of poets in ordinary bookstores; we can see plays based on poems (like the 1983 hit *Cats,* based on T. S. Eliot poems), or see people reading Shakespeare on the subway, so we know poetry can last. What makes it last seems to be its capacity to speak to many different generations in many different circumstances.
3. *Style:* that is, the way a work is written—the fresh and varied word choices, the flexible and surprising sentences, the sharp and shrewd grammar, that make it memorable. A work with scope and style will ring in the ear, pop into the mind when we are high or low, and give comfort and direction to our lives. It may well be timeless.

A young musician once said in a discussion about the value of creative work, "You must absolutely love what you're doing or it won't communicate." Muriel Rukeyser's poem below asserts that poetry can communicate even beyond death. The poems in our anthology that have passed the tests of scope, timelessness, and style must have sprung from some of that love, or they would not be communicating to us, at the end of the twentieth century, as we read them once again.

Then

When I am dead, even then,
I will still love you, I will wait in these poems.
When I am dead, even then
I am still listening to you.
I will still be making poems for you
out of silence;
silence will be falling into that silence,
it is building music.

Muriel Rukeyser

ON READING DRAMA:
THE PLAYERS, THE PLAYHOUSE, AND THE PLAY

While Michael Douglas, Don Jackson, and Luke Skywalker are dashing characters who send Hollywood box office profits soaring, few of us consider the works in which they appear great drama. However, along with Broadway musicals, dinner theaters, and Sunday school plays, their performances are rooted in the same dramatic traditions as those of the Greek kings, Shakespearean heroes, and troubled souls of Tennessee Williams's plays. No matter what the century or how simple the form, people have acted out stories to entertain and instruct others. Such action distinguishes drama from poetry and fiction.

A HISTORY OF DRAMATIC CONVENTIONS

Dramatic urges have always been a part of human history. Early tribes marked great battles or events by acting them out around campfires. Royal entertainments and village fairs often included mimes dancing and acting. For the first dramatic productions on record, we turn to the Greeks. Understanding the dramatic conventions important to a culture helps us see drama as a living echo of its time rather than as a dusty curio.

Greek Drama

Greek drama was a form of religious worship, originating in the processions and ceremonies of the worship of Dionysus, god of fertility and wine. Perhaps initially a chorus of worshippers chanted hymns to Dionysus at the festivals held four times a year. Later, Thespis, the legendary creator of the drama, set aside one member of the choral group to act out the role of the main character of the play, thus establishing dialogue.

Two kinds of plays developed in Greece: comedy and tragedy. The word "tragedy" comes from Greek words meaning "goat-song," probably from the sacrificial goat of the earliest festivals; comedy came from "merrymaking." Actors wore stylized masks to enable their emotional qualities to project to the highest seats in the ampitheater. Today we still use the sad and happy faces of these masks as familiar dramatic symbols.

By the fifth century B.C., the Golden Age of Greece, the Greeks held an annual dramatic competition as part of the spring Dionysian festival. Four days of this Great Dionysia were devoted to plays, attended by huge crowds of up to 15,000 people. On three of these days, the audience viewed sets of three tragedies (like Sophocles' *Oedipus Rex, Oedipus at Colonus,* and *Antigone*), followed by a satiric comedy to relieve the tension. The other day of the festival was devoted to comedy. Prizes rewarded the best actor and best team of writer and producer. We know the identity of three of these tragedeans, Aeschylus, Sophocles, and Euripedes, because they won fame at these competitions.

Greek plays and Greek theaters would seem primitive to a Star Wars generation that can zoom convincingly in and out of hyper-space at will. However, the ruins of these theaters today possess grandeur, and plays are still performed there. Greek theaters were round, open-air amphitheaters, frequently large enough to seat thousands of people. To take advantage of natural light, performances were held during the day. The audience sat on tiered seats facing a raised stage on which rested a small building called a *skene*. Actors entered from the *skene,* and the play's visible action occurred in front of it. The front of the *skene* often represented a palace. Action destined for other settings took place offstage, eliminating the need for scene changes. The audience learned of these events from the characters' speeches. In Sophocles' *Antigone* (p. 528), messengers inform the people (represented by the chorus) that Antigone has committed suicide and that Haimon, in grief, has killed himself after trying to slay his father. Eurydice, Creon's wife, overhears this news and quietly goes to her chamber to take her own life. When the grief-stricken Creon returns carrying the body of Haimon, a messenger emerges from the palace to deliver to Creon the news of his wife's death. Although Greek plots frequently contained such dread events, the audience did not see them. The pleasure of *witnessing* the bloody violence of murders, hangings, and stabbings was to be saved for the tastes of later centuries.

Greek actors did not share the fame of a modern Meryl Streep or Robert Redford. Their audiences were more apt to honor the playwright than the actor. Actors were the messengers of Dionysus; the god supposedly took possession of their souls. The rules of the competition defined their roles. Early Greek plays had only one speaking actor; Aeschylus added another and Sophocles still another, totaling three by the time of *Antigone*. A *chorus,* a group of actors onstage, often formed a collective character, commenting on the play's action or speaking to the heroes in the voice of the people. In *Antigone,* this chorus is a group of the wise old men of Thebes. Actors did not wear costumes, although tragic heroes wore elevated foot gear and large masks that could amplify their voices. Their larger-than-life size underscored their importance, and perhaps more practically, helped a large audience to see and to hear them.

Greek plays, as a part of the yearly festival, were profoundly religious, and the plays' ethical messages overshadowed the actual stories. Playwrights created drama from familiar myths, so Greek audiences knew the plots and characters beforehand. The power of the play lay, thus, in this message. In *Antigone,* Creon's disregard of divine law—loyalty to family and the gods—nurtured by an enormous pride brings on the horrifying disaster which overtakes him.

Aristotle, Greek philosopher and critic, summed up the nature of Greek tragedy in his *Poetics.* "Tragedy," he wrote, "is the imitation of an action that is serious, complete, and of a certain magnitude . . . in the form of action, not of narrative; through pity and fear effecting the proper purgation of these emotions." In other words, tragedy purifies the audience as well as the characters in the play. Exhausted by the dramatic experience, the audience should feel both compassion for the plight of the hero and terror at human inability to control fate. Aristotle's term for this purging of emotion was *catharsis.*

The message of Greek tragedy was powerful partly because it was conveyed through the fall of a noble person, someone "of high estate." Noble birth made the fall of the Greek hero so much greater and so much more terrifying than that of a common person. The folly of an ordinary person might affect that individual and his or her family; the fall of a king, however, could bring ruin to a society. The tragic hero, usually a great king or queen, suffers from a *tragic flaw,* referred to by Aristotle as an "error or frailty." Antigone, noble in suffering, acts on her beliefs though she knows that doing so will lead to her own death. We admire her, and Sophocles named the play for her, yet we are aware of her tragic flaw, unbending pride. Creon, a king recently come to rule, draws undue pride from his power; this blindness leads to his undoing. Tragically, he learns wisdom too late. In the end, the audience feels both compassion for his suffering and terror at the inevitability of his actions and their fearful consequences.

Greek drama flourished for about two hundred years. After the Romans conquered the Greeks in the first century B.C., they imitated Greek plays. Gradually though, Roman drama became little more than spectacle. The barbarians who followed the Romans after A.D. 476 were interested in neither Greek nor Roman theater, and formal drama disappeared for centuries.

Drama of the Middle Ages

Again religious worship brought formal drama back into the civilized world. In the twelfth and thirteenth centuries, Roman Catholic priests sometimes acted out parts of the mass to teach religion to uneducated people. Such spectacle was especially common during liturgical holidays. For an Easter celebration, for instance, the clergy might enact a vignette of Mary at the tomb; during the Christmas mass, they could be shepherds at the manger. The little plays were popular, and gradually they were expanded and moved to the church courtyards. Eventually, the crowds and the plays grew less religious and more rowdy, and a frustrated clergy gave them over to the people.

Workmen's guilds then produced the plays and competed with each other with ornate presentations. The Bakers' Guild, for instance, might do the Last Supper; fishermen might do the Flood. They were serious about their task, paying quality actors and fining those who neglected to attend rehearsals. The guilds mounted their plays on large, flatbed wagons called *pageant wagons* equipped with stage props like bags of blood and huge vats of water. Guild members drove these wagons from place to place, stopping at prearranged spots where crowds of people would gather. The wagons, moving in sequence, would bring to the waiting group all of the plays in a *cycle.* A cycle, a group of short plays, formed one long story, usually from Creation to the Last Judgment. Although guilds performed cycles throughout Europe, the plays were especially important in England. There, four cycles, each dramatizing essentially the same stories in different ways, developed in the cities of York, Towneley, Chester, and Wakefield. This book contains the Wakefield *Noah* (p. 726), but other cycles would have had *Noah* plays based on the same biblical story with differing characters and actions. For example, in the Wakefield *Noah,* the ornery Mrs. Noah refuses to come aboard the ark until she and her husband have beaten each other "back and bone." In the Chester cycle, the reason for her reluctance to enter the ark is that she does not want to come unless her "gossips" (her friends) can come, too.

The guilds secularized the plays, making their characters resemble English peasants rather than holy men of the Bible. These characters wore English clothing rather than

biblical robes; they also spoke English rather than church Latin. Bawdy humor mixed
with simple piety produced stock comic characters such as bumpkin shepherds and
shrewish women like Noah's wife. Much of the entertainment in the Noah play
emerges from Mrs. Noah's tart tongue.

Two other types of plays gradually developed along with these cycles of *mystery*
plays based on stories from the Old and New Testaments. The *miracle play* depicted
a saint's life or the story of a miracle. The *morality play* taught lessons by creating
characters out of vices and virtues. In one familiar morality play, *Everyman,* the
characters bear names such as Good Deeds, Death, and Discretion.

Elizabethan Theater

By the reign of Queen Elizabeth I in the sixteenth century, moving wagons had
given way to fixed stages. In 1576 Richard Burbage built the first actual London
playhouse which he called The Theatre. The Theatre was round like the bear-baiting
and bull-baiting gardens the English loved. Like the Greek theaters, the Burbage
playhouse depended on natural light and was open to the sky. The Theatre stood three
stories high with balconies or galleries on each side, similar to the inn yards where
traveling players had long acted out plays. The stage jutted into the center of the
theater, making it visible from three sides. No curtain divided spectators from actors;
in fact, wealthier patrons could sit on the stage itself, almost becoming a part of the
action. Most of the audience sat in the galleries, although the ordinary people, the
"groundlings," crammed into the "pit" on the ground in front of the stage. This rabble
demanded the slapstick comedy found in even the most serious of Elizabethan tragedies. As you can see from reading or seeing a Shakespearean play like *King Lear*
(p. 93), the stage had little scenery. A chair or a bush was brought on the stage
for a scene and then taken away. Words painted scenes more than actual props.
Tempest-tossed language rather than the actual howling gales of wind machines
created the fierce storm in *Lear.*

Acting also matured. Actors belonged to professional acting companies under the
patronage of a nobleman. Ten to fourteen men and boys made up a company. Young
boys acted out the female roles, and all actors regularly played more than one part.
Actors learned their craft as apprentices in a repertory theater such as Shakespeare's
Globe Theater. They needed strong voices, fencing and dancing skills, and musical
talent. Actors wore elaborate and colorful clothing of their own time rather than
costumes dictated by the historic time of the play.

The new theater left behind the simple tales of Bible stories and vices and virtues
and became a showplace for more sophisticated drama. Like the Greeks, Elizabethan
audiences already knew the plots of many of the plays they viewed; Shakespeare, for
example, reworked plays by other playwrights to create *King Lear.* Dramatic power
lay as much in the psychological depth of the playwright's script as in delivery,
character, and language. Cast in iambic pentameter (see pp. 1023 and 1024), the
Elizabethan dramatic line rose well above the simple rhymes of medieval plays.
Shakespeare wrote comedies, tragedies, and history plays with complicated major and
minor plots. For example, not one but two tragedies emerge in *King Lear*—that of
Lear and that of Gloucester. The two plots crisscross and mirror one another in the
tortured relationships between each parent and his children. Goneril, Regan, and
Edmund personify the power of evil working against the forces of good represented

by Cordelia and Edgar. Elizabethan plots also contain visible violence, for Elizabethan audiences loved blood and gore. Incidents such as the gouging out of Gloucester's eyes in *Lear* were common in tragedies of the time.

Renaissance means rebirth. Historically, the term applies to the rebirth of classical learning at the end of the Middle Ages. Greek and Latin learning rediscovered by the Renaissance found its way into sixteenth-century plays. Most of these plays had five acts and delved deeply into the psychology of the human spirit, enriching the powerful notion of the tragic hero with the Christian concept of free will. Whereas Creon's fate was decreed by the gods, Lear, Macbeth, and Othello condemn themselves by their own free will. Their own blunders rather than fate lead them to destruction. They sin and suffer deeply for that sin, producing *catharsis* or purgation. Lear invites his own downfall by giving up his kingly responsibilities while wishing still to be treated as a king. He suffers mightily before he is redeemed.

Sixteenth-century playwrights also grappled with universal themes. In Lear's foolish division of his kingdom, for instance, Elizabethans would fear the horrifying attack against the natural order. Disorder in the royal family would mean disorder in the state and, symbolically, disorder in the universe. The *macrocosm* (the universe) and the *microcosm* (the smaller world of the individual) parallel one another; the universe reflects Lear's problem in the violence of the storm. The storm that rages through the middle section of the play is both a frightening natural phenomenon and a hideous, cataclysmic purging of Lear's madness.

Modern Theater

Elizabethan theater was ill-fated. When the Puritans beheaded King Charles in the mid-seventeenth century, they closed the theaters because they thought drama sinful. When the theaters reopened in 1660, they were different places. A closed, rectangular building using artificial light replaced the round, open-air theater. Women played female roles, and movable scenery filled stages that no longer jutted into the theater. A *proscenium arch* separating actors from audience created the stage as we know it. The stage now seemed like an open box into which the audience could peer, or like a painting on a framed canvas. Eventually a curtain concealed the stage from the audience, and the technological advances of later centuries would work miracles with stage lighting, scenery, and sound effects.

Stages better equipped to present reality through set changes and scenery encouraged the development of different kinds of comedies and tragedies. The France of Louis XIV was entertained by the witty comedies, classic tragedies, and sumptuous pageants of Molière (born Jean-Baptiste Poquelin), Jean Racine, and Pierre Corneille. Likewise, eighteenth-century England found much to enjoy in the reflection of their society shown in a *comedy of manners* such as *The School for Scandal* by Richard Brinsley Sheridan.

Eventually, with the rise of a comfortable middle class in the nineteenth century, the classic style was replaced by *realism*. Playwrights like Henrik Ibsen in Norway, George Bernard Shaw in England, and Anton Chekhov in Russia wrote "social problem" plays criticizing the lifestyle and values of the middle class. Heroes were ordinary middle-class men and women such as Dr. Stockmann of Ibsen's *An Enemy of the People* (p. 306). These characters were comfortable professionals with pleasant homes, positions, and families. Stockmann's downfall occurs in an ordinary life. No one defies the gods; no kings fall. In *An Enemy of the People* Stockmann incurs the wrath of his town by insisting on declaring the town's mineral springs unhealthy. The theme of Ibsen's play is often thought to be the "tyranny of the majority," a theme that would have suited neither the Greek nor the Renaissance mind, since such a tyranny would never occur to them.

The domestic tragedies or slice-of-life dramas of Thornton Wilder, Arthur Miller, and Tennessee Williams gradually joined these social problem plays. The protagonists of these plays were anti-heroes or non-heroes, ordinary men and women with ordinary life problems. The Wingfields, for instance, in *The Glass Menagerie* (p. 955), live on the fringe of society; they are poor, romantic dreamers trapped by their poverty. They try to escape by going to business college, joining the Merchant Marine, hoping for a gentleman caller. They are people much like us, and their tragedies are in many ways ours.

In the past forty years, drama has stretched well beyond those realistic plays into the *theater of the absurd.* Many plays of the theater of the absurd emerge from the existentialist philosophy of their authors and are essentially plays of ideas. Existentialist playwrights stress the absurdity of the universe. However, to live a valid or authentic life an individual must create coherence out of absurdity by making ethical choices. Existentialism is an organic part of Jean Paul Sartre's one-act play, *No Exit* (p. 740), not merely a guiding abstraction. The psychological motivations of Garcin, Inez, and Estelle are unimportant. The situation, the absence of choice, is all. Sartre makes his characters painfully aware that they *are* the choices they have made during their lives, and that in this context, "Hell is other people."

More recent absurdists such as Eugene Ionesco and Edward Albee, using very few props, bare stages, or no stages at all, go beyond Sartre to dramatize an existential vision of life. Characters in trash cans, dialogue without words—anything is possible in the absurdist's dramatic vision. Edward Albee's play *The Sandbox* (p. 87) illustrates absurdist drama. It is black comedy, humorous but bitter in its unmasking of hypocrisy. Other contemporary playwrights such as Ntozake Shange in *for colored girls who have considered suicide when the rainbow is enuf* (p. 918), Luis Valdez in *The Dark Root of a Scream* (p. 769), and Bernard Pomerance in *The Elephant Man* (p. 557) vary between absurdist and traditional themes to present the dramatic ideas central to their work. Shange uses song and dance; Valdez creates stereotypes like those in a morality play; Pomerance organizes scenes similar to those of a Greek tragedy. Modern playwrights simultaneously build on and react to the twenty-five centuries of dramatic tradition which preceded them. The vibrancy and versatility of modern theater are perhaps best illustrated by the fact that the modern stage exhibits almost as many old plays as new ones.

THE ELEMENTS OF DRAMA

Several of the key elements that make up a work of fiction do double duty in drama as well. When you read a play or watch a dramatic performance, you ask some of the same questions about plot, character, language, and theme that you would if you were reading fiction. To those concerns, however, you add others relating to spectacle: music, sound, costume, make-up, lighting, scenery, and props. These elements that appeal to the eye and the ear elevate dramatic prose above mere storytelling. They make analyzing drama both easier and harder to do than reading fiction or poetry.

If you must read rather than witness the plays you will study in this course, compensate for the missing sound and spectacle by playing the role of director. Create the characters, gestures, lighting, scenery, and sound effects in your head, and then "peel the onion" (see pp. 1008–1009) to discover the layers of meaning hidden in the play.

Plot

Plot is a sequence of events. A damsel is in distress; the hero appears; the villain is vanquished. Dramatic action moves beyond the fictional. It must capture visible action—movements that the audience can see and hear; a character's inner turmoil will rarely sustain good drama unless the audience can share it in some way. Novelists divide their stories into chapters; playwrights break up dramatic action into *acts.* Modern plays usually have three acts; Renaissance plays frequently had five. *Scenes,* smaller frames of action set in one place like a living room or a forest, sometimes further subdivide the acts of a play. On occasion, a play might have several plots. A *major plot* captures the main action, the fate of the damsel in distress. The *minor plot* or *subplot,* perhaps the story of the main character's crippled brother in need of a life-saving operation, injects another storyline, sometimes parallel to the major plot. The trials of Lear and Gloucester intertwine in this way in *King Lear.* Two of Lear's daughters abuse and abandon him; Gloucester's evil son Edmund seeks revenge upon his father for his bastardy. Both plots pit father against child while Gloucester's literal blindness parallels Lear's spiritual blindness.

Playwrights rely on several devices to tell a story in dramatic form. Occasionally, a narrator or one of the characters delivers a *prologue* to introduce the play. For instance, Tom Wingfield, dressed as a member of the Merchant Marine, begins *The Glass Menagerie* (p. 955) with a prologue. In it he describes the play as a "memory play," suggesting he will take the audience back in time. The dramatic structure of the play itself may be best illustrated by a pyramidal scheme devised by the nineteenth-century German author and critic Gustav Freytag.

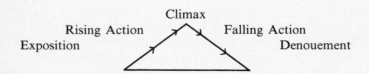

Climax
Rising Action   Falling Action
Exposition   Denouement

Exposition fills in details to build up background information for the audience. In *King Lear* (p. 93), for instance, Scene 1 of Act I shows Lear at the peak of his pride, laying the groundwork for his own tragedy by disowning Cordelia and dividing his kingdom between his other two daughters, Goneril and Regan. Scene 2 weaves the origins of the minor plot, showing Gloucester making the same mistake as Lear, mistaking Edmund for the good son and Edgar for the evil one. Working from this base, Shakespeare builds the play through *rising action,* depicting in successive scenes Lear's irresponsible folly in presuming he could have power without responsibility. His wild behavior soon alienates his daughters and they soon alienate him; he accuses them of ingratitude and takes refuge on the heath. The rising action leads to a *climax* or turning point of the play in the wild storm of Act III. Both Lear and Gloucester suffer a *reversal;* both are purged of their folly, Lear through his wild wandering in the storm and Gloucester through the horrible means of his blindness. The *falling action* of the play—the gathering of forces, the feuding of Goneril and Regan—leads to the *denouement* or final unraveling of the plot. Cordelia is defeated and hanged, and Lear dies.

Other refinements of plot are also possible. The playwright may use *foreshadowing* to hint at action to come. Tennessee Williams, for example, laces *The Glass Menagerie* (p. 955) with references to a gentleman caller, leading up to the pathetic scene in which the real gentleman caller appears. Playwrights also depend on *irony* to ripen a plot. *Irony of situation* sets up a discrepancy between a character's expectations and reality. Creon's triumph in *Antigone* (p. 528), for instance, turns to gall when his stubborn pride destroys his wife and his son. Amanda Wingfield's long-wished-for gentleman caller for Laura turns out to be engaged to another girl. *Dramatic irony* shows the difference between what the audience knows and what the character knows. The audience knows Oedipus is guilty long before he does; the audience also knows that Tom Wingfield will abandon his family long before Amanda and Laura do.

Character

Dramatic characters are fictional characters who, when dramatized, talk and walk in a way that characters in fictional tales cannot. Even before we begin to read or see the play, we know something more about dramatic characters than we know about fictional ones. The *Dramatis Personae,* the list of characters at the beginning of the play, enumerates and often briefly describes the characters before the play begins.

Dramatists use many of the same techniques to create characters as do writers of fiction. They draw battle lines between antagonists and protagonists and create round and flat characters (see "On Reading Fiction," p. 1011). Playwrights, however, have a distinct advantage over fiction writers. Their characters are made flesh and blood by an actor who interprets that character with voice, gesture, movement, and visible emotion. Playwrights and directors also have several techniques not available to their fictional counterparts. In a play, *dialogue*—what people say—is more than words printed on a page; it is people actually talking and gesturing. A southern accent, a lisp, or a Tennessee twang will color in a character's personality, as will a quiver, a clenched fist, or a raised eyebrow. In a play a character may at times share brief private thoughts with the audience by making a comment, known as an *aside,* unheard by other actors. For instance, Grandma in *The Sandbox* (p. 87), speaks only non-words ("Ahhhhhh! Ah-haaaaaa! Graaaaaa!") to Mommy and Daddy. However, she regularly pauses to explain the injustice of her plight to the audience with real words. A similar tactic is the *soliloquy,* in which a character steps to the side of the stage to think out loud. Hamlet's "To be or not to be" speech (p. 707) is Hamlet baring his soul while maintaining the illusion that only the audience can hear him.

Theme

A play's *theme* is its underlying idea or central view. The theme is often revealed by questions raised about the play's moral or social significance. Why should we bother to read it or see it? What idea connects the anguished segments of Ntozake Shange's *for colored girls who have considered suicide when the rainbow is enuf?*

(p. 918). Why would Shange record sketches of the life of the black woman through music, poetry, and dance, if an audience watching it could find no meaning in her effort? The dramatist offers a view of humanity, often documenting issues troublesome to a particular generation or century. Fifth-century Athenians would be concerned with the power of the divine law over that of man. Shakespearean Englishmen would watch with terror a king or queen giving up the crown. Modern audiences experience mixed shock and despair at the bleak comments on humankind offered by plays such as *No Exit* (p. 740), *Elephant Man* (p. 557), and *The Sandbox* (p. 87). They would understand, and to varying degrees share, Sartre's vision that "Hell is other people," Albee's disgust at the treatment of the elderly, and Pomerance's repugnance at the self-serving people surrounding John Merrick. The theme is the heart of the drama, the playwright's voice echoing from a distant inner circle.

Language

Because dramatists usually intend their plays to be seen and heard, reading a play is a doubly difficult task: the reader must imagine the gestures, the inflections, and the actions that might accompany the words. Furthermore, while dramatic language must be believable as human speech, it may also contain the same type of metaphoric language that so often enriches poetry (see pp. 1025–1026) or the symbolism found in fiction and poetry.

In past eras, the conventional language of drama was poetry. Medieval plays, for instance, use rhymed verse to raise the drama above ordinary speech. Noah and his wife quarrel in rhyme:

NOAH: I shall make thee still as stone, beginner of blunder!
      I shall beat thee, back and bone, and break all in sunder.

(They fight.)

WIFE: Out, alas, I am overthrown! Out upon thee, man's wonder!

Elizabethan playwrights commonly wrote dialogue in blank verse—unrhymed iambic pentameter (see p. 1023). Lear cries, for instance, with the dead Cordelia in his arms:

> Howl, howl, howl, howl! O! you are men of stones;
> Had I your tongues and eye, I'd use them so
> That heaven's vaults should crack. She's gone for ever.
> I know when one is dead, and when one lives;
> She's dead as earth. Lend me a looking-glass;
> If that her breath will mist or stain the stone,
> Why, then she lives.

The eighteenth-century favored formality, wit, and restrained emotion in its dramatic presentations. Since the nineteenth century, however, playwrights have preferred to create more realistic dialogue, more believable speech. In an era when salesmen and postal clerks can be heroes, they talk like salesmen and postal clerks. Albee's Grandma says,

Honestly! What a way to treat an old woman! Drag her out of the house . . . stick her in a car . . . bring her out here from the city . . . dump her in a pile of sand . . . and leave her out here to set.

Setting and Staging

Setting is place, and staging is a specific realization of setting. Depending on their century and their culture, dramatists have dealt with setting differently, sometimes emphasizing it and sometimes ignoring it. The Greeks and Elizabethans—with little technology at their disposal—relied primarily on language to paint the details of time and place. The nineteenth century brought technological development and realistic drama to staging. Electricity increased the possibilities for believable on-stage spectacle. Whereas the Greeks might merely have suggested Creon's palace by hanging some painted screens in front of the *skene,* a modern version of *Antigone* could build a real palace complete with mossy stone walls, armed guards, and sounds of creaky battlements, and devise lighting that could suggest night or day. Poetic language originally evoked the wildness of Lear's storm, but a modern production of *Lear* could pelt the anguished face of the actor with rain and have wind whip convincingly through his tattered rags.

Television and film productions can seek out realistic and evocative backdrops for classic plays. George Tzavellas's 1962 film of *Antigone,* shot in Greece, showed real temples, rocks, and sea in the clear light of native land. A BBC Shakespeare series produced in the 1980s depends on ancient English castles, moors, and forests to set off plays like *Macbeth* and *King Lear.* The fact that these plays are filmed and televised does not deny the plays' authenticity. The new media should give life to the old familiar plays and bring them to the people the way the festival of Dionysus, the pageant wagon, the Globe Theatre, or the London and Broadway stages did in the past.

ON WRITING ABOUT LITERATURE

Rock concerts, radio stations, and television screens are rarely places where we seek great literature. For noble ideas and masterworks, we look to grand stages and great books. This clear but unfortunate distinction that we generally make between an everyday world and our academic lives stiffens our responses to literature. Swapping opinions about songs or late-night television with car-pool mates or in a laundromat is routine; actually writing literary criticism seems ominous. But parallels exist between Van Halen's songs and Emily Dickinson's poetry, between the people on "Diff'rent Strokes" and traditional characters like Rip Van Winkle or King Lear. In liking a rock song or in grumbling about a sitcom, you are taking the first steps in the more academic process of reacting to literature. Your responses to popular print and film media give you some beginning experience in literary analysis. In either case, you form a critical opinion based on something you have seen, heard, or read. Writing about literature may demand a more structured form than discussing quiz shows, but both require an exercise in critical judgment.

FIRST STEPS

Reading

Before you write about literature, you must read it—and think about it. Read with a pencil or highlighter in hand. As you read, underline or color over words or images that hint at character, plot, or theme. In this passage from Hawthorne's "Young Goodman Brown" (p. 592), for instance, notice how just a few phrases seem to deserve special note.

"Poor little Faith!" thought he, for his heart smote him. "What a wretch am I, to leave her on such an errand! *She talks of dreams, too.* Methought, as she spoke, there was *trouble in her face, as if a dream had warned her* what work is to be done to-night. But no, no! 't would kill her to think it. Well; *she's a blessed angel on earth and after this one night, I'll cling to her skirts and follow her to Heaven.*"

Like stones in a stream that let you step from one bank to the other, these words and phrases marking Faith's prophetic dreams and the fainthearted promises of the sinner may eventually form a bridge from the simple elements of plot to the more subtle elements of theme and style. They will call up reactions that may eventually mature into critical responses.

Before trying to write about a piece of literature, however, look over the section on reading fiction, drama, or poetry. Each genre has its own form, some of its own techniques, and its own vocabulary. Fiction works through plot, character, setting, theme, and point of view. Drama adds techniques such as extended dialogue and stage effects. Poetry depends on images, rhyme schemes, and meter. If you are comfortable with the terminology, you can write about different types of literary works with critical precision.

Finding a Direction

After you have read the story or poem or seen the play, your next task is to define a direction for your thoughts about it. Often your instructor will do that for you with a specific assignment: discuss the character of Jeff in Arna Bontemps's story "A Summer Tragedy" (p. 58); talk about symbols in Stephen Crane's "The Bride Comes to Yellow Sky" (p. 216). At other times you must shape your own reactions. In either case, your written response generally takes the form of *analysis* or *explication.*

Like the dissection of a frog in a biology class, literary *analysis* takes a work apart, distinguishing between the pieces—characters, setting, theme, plot—and drawing some conclusions from them. You could take a close look at a short story like "Paul's Case" (p. 454), for instance, to see how Willa Cather carefully creates a character who refuses to fit in his world. At another time you could analyze Ibsen's *An Enemy of the People* to see how the play becomes a comment on mob psychology.

Explication, on the other hand, demands a different kind of scrutiny, probing a poem or perhaps a passage from a play or a piece of fiction line by line—even word by word. Here, for example, are the first few lines of e. e. cummings's oddly shaped poem "In Just- spring":

> in Just-
> spring   when the world is mud-
> luscious the little
> lame balloonman
> whistles   far   and wee

To explicate this part of the poem, you would look at one line after another, tackling, as they appear, questions such as:

—Why does cummings capitalize "Just"?

—Why does he leave a space between "spring" and "when"?

—What does that rich image of "mud-luscious" mean and why is the word separated on two lines?

—Who is the little lame balloonman, and why does he whistle "far   and wee" instead of "far and wide"?

Explication is detailed explanation, answering specific questions posed by language, rhythm, form, or style.

GETTING READY TO WRITE

Focusing Your Thoughts

You have probably written a number of nonliterary essays, perhaps directed at social or political issues. The basic writing principles that you used to focus and support opinions about topics like "U.S. Reaction to Terrorism" or "The Leasing of Federal Wilderness Lands" will serve you in your efforts to record your responses to a short story or a poem. Writing about literature is no mysterious craft. The familiar instructions apply: select a topic, consider it, form an opinion, focus it, develop it, and press the whole into a concrete, well-developed shape.

The Thesis

Often after you have read a story, play, or poem, your head is awhirl with ideas and reactions. This character was so evil; that action was contrived; this plot was tragic enough to make you cry. These responses are conclusions based on facts presented by the author. Class discussions revolve around these kinds of opinions. Just as these perceptions focus oral responses, they also direct written ones. In an essay, they take on the familiar form of the *thesis,* the heart of the essay. The *thesis statement* is the sentence that expresses a writer's analytical opinion, directing the paragraphs that follow to explain and support it.

A good thesis will not be too ambitious or unwieldy. You cannot do justice to a broad and debatable issue such as nuclear disarmament in five hundred words. Likewise, you cannot discuss every aspect of a poem, play, or story in that space. What you can do, though, is seize on an angle, an opinion, a thesis or "argumentative edge." The wealth of meaning found in Edward Albee's play *The Sandbox* (p. 87) may be too great to exhaust in one essay, but choosing one aspect of the play—the way in which "Mommy" represents crass, unfeeling America—might be workable. Discussing all facets of language, style, and meaning in Andrew Marvell's poem "To His Coy Mistress" (p. 505) or William Kotzwinkle's story "Follow the Eagle" (p. 653) would overburden one essay. Analyzing some aspect of either—the *carpe diem* or "seize the day" theme of the one or the existential dilemma of the other— might be more manageable.

Properly narrowed, a good thesis usually begins as an idea or an opinion, roughly stated. It is a generalization, not a *fact*. Factual sentences such as the two that follow, for instance, cannot work as thesis statements:

Tennessee Williams wrote *The Glass Menagerie*.

Tom, Laura, and Amanda are characters in *The Glass Menagerie*.

Authorship and character names are facts not subject to anyone's opinion. The sentences above supply information; they do not focus or direct a discussion. On the other hand, a collection of facts could lead to an opinion or generalization which might become a thesis. You may come away from *The Glass Menagerie* feeling depressed by the bleakness of the three pathetic lives Williams creates yet struck by the survival tactics each employs. That impression could take the form of this thesis:

Tom, Laura, and Amanda have each slipped into a kind of surface madness to preserve their sanity.

If after reading the play you feel that Williams uses too many symbols in a self-conscious way, you might reflect that conclusion in this thesis:

Williams relies so heavily on symbols in *The Glass Menagerie* that the play seems contrived.

Perhaps your reader will have a different opinion, but no matter. A thesis statement expresses your opinion, your conclusion, your stand as thinker and writer. Its message is "This is my reasoned opinion"; the paragraphs that follow will attempt to support it, to show how you arrived at it, and—ideally—to convince your reader that your opinion is sound.

Gathering Evidence

If the Bears or the Dolphins lost fifteen out of sixteen games in a season, few of their fans would defend them as good football teams. The facts would suggest the contrary. An opinion, about football or anything else, is not worth much if it is not grounded in facts. Unless you have examples of graft, proving the mayor corrupt would be difficult. Without actual figures, only guesswork determines whether a Ford, Buick, or Toyota gets better gas mileage.

Specific detail is as much a key to proving a point about literature as it is to proving a point about cars. Like all valid generalizations, those you deduce about plot, character, or theme must spring from facts found in the story, play, or poem. A conclusion such as "The girl is beautiful" presumes a collection of observed facts: clear skin, red hair, green eyes, Roman nose. The concept of beauty changes with the viewer; the need for specific support does not. The same holds true for literary opinions. As you read the work, you gathered evidence by underlining passages. The gut instincts that guided your marking pencil earlier helped form initial impressions. Now, in review, the specifics—like the pretty girl's red hair and green eyes—are visible at a glance. Perhaps the main character seems wooden; the dialogue sounds phony; the plot raises suspense; the theme appears trite. But be careful. Just as a straight nose in itself will not make a pretty face, neither will one tiny, tucked-away symbol make a play symbolic. Enough evidence must be found to make the thesis work. A good piece of literary criticism, no matter what its form, will have a clear, focused thought supported by specific detail. If you cannot find enough evidence to support your initial thesis, you may have to modify it in light of the evidence you have found.

STRUCTURING THE EVIDENCE

Assignments to write about literature commonly take one of two forms—the journal entry or the essay. The form you choose may depend on your instructor's wishes, but both draw strength from careful, critical reading and thinking.

The Journal

A journal entry generally records less formal responses to literature. At times a journal is almost a diary of personal reactions; in other instances, it can be a more careful study. Journals have more flexibility in form and content than essays, but they grow from the same thoughtful reaction. They have to be more than plot summaries or lists of likes and dislikes. Personal responses such as "I liked 'A Rose for Emily' " or "I liked 'A Rose for Emily' because Emily reminded me of my aunt" are not enough. Although journal entries are more spontaneous, they should still develop a point. Just as you would need facts to complain intelligently about the Social Security System, you need concrete support to show why you find Sylvia Plath's poetry too confessional or Nikki Giovanni's delightful.

Keeping a journal should become an enjoyable pastime rather than a burden or chore. Whenever possible, write in your journal soon after reading or at times when a thought strikes you. Delay sometimes leaves only the husk of an idea that, after the lapse of time, makes little sense. Do not put off the task of writing in your journal until the last second, leaving just enough time to jot down a few vague sentences. Entries emerging from one night's effort usually sound that way.

The following suggestions make good journal entries:

1. An *immediate reaction*—negative or positive—to some aspect of a piece of literature such as a striking character, a powerful theme, or an unusual ending
2. A more thoughtful, *delayed reaction,* which matures after a first feeling of shock, anger, or joy
3. A *response defending or attacking a point made by someone else* (teacher, fellow student, critic)
4. An *idea* prompted by an *in-class comment*
5. A *personal note* struck by character, theme, or plot which has some meaning in your own life
6. Your own *explication or interpretation* of a poem or passage

7. A *comparison/contrast* with some other work
8. A *question* raised by the text.

Reactions like these can help you compile a series of personal yet intellectual responses to the literature you read.

STUDENT SAMPLE

In the following journal entry, a student commented on the "onion theory" offered on pages 1008–1009 as a means of analyzing fiction:

> Your theory is a great one. I had never considered anything like it, in so many words, and it has given me a lot to think about. There are so many things that people read (and hear in music too) that they never really look at past the outside layer. One of the reasons I am taking literature courses is that I'm interested in other people's interpretations and insights into various authors and their writings. I especially liked the part about the tears. When you get very close to something that affects you, it very often brings tears—or anger, or joy. When you reach this layer the thoughts stay with you much longer than something you never looked at past the surface. I also began to apply your theory to people and friendships. Too often you see only the surface layer and never bother to invest the time to "peel back" the outside, discard it, and see a new person altogether different. These "onions" could be used to greatly change the flavor of our lives. But they're no good unless you peel them!

Cecelia Zampelli

THE CRITICAL ESSAY

The essay gives formal shape to your literary reactions. The same structure can be used to discipline your opinions about everything from political candidates to painting a house. Analyzing John Donne's "Death Be Not Proud" is different from analyzing the stock market or the Palestinian issue, but the job of laying out the conclusions on the page is similar. You need an introduction, a body, and a conclusion.

For an example, we could turn again to *The Glass Menagerie*. A critical opinion about this play cited earlier was that Tom, Laura, and Amanda have each slipped into a kind of surface madness to preserve their sanity. The underpinnings for this idea lie in the text. There the specifics of plot, character, and setting suggest how painful it is for each character to confront reality. After scanning the play and noting the passages you have highlighted, you might make a list, a simple working sketch like the following, to test the opinion or thesis. At this point, unless your instructor requests otherwise, your list should be just that—a rough handwritten itemizing of ideas without regard for parallel structure.

Amanda: – –loud/phony vivaciousness
          – –hides behind her southern girlhood on Moon
             Lake/makes a myth out of her past; exaggerated
             southern accent
          – –tells pathetic stories, giggles, wears faded clothes

Tom: – –a sullen dreamer
            – –refuses to worry about unpaid light bills
            – –goes to the movies to escape reality
            – –thinks the Merchant Marine is his ticket out

Laura: – –nervous; as fragile as her glass collection
            – –plays her father's old phonograph records when she is
                nervous
            – –hides in a half light—candles
            – –hypochondriac

Once you have sketched out your ideas, you at least have a grip on your thesis. Lists like these can help test an opinion, to see if it is valid. Hasty conclusions which cannot be supported will show themselves to be just that. This kind of pre-writing forces you to block out concrete support for your idea before you actually write the essay.

There are many ways to convert this working sketch into an essay. Earlier composition courses have no doubt given you the skill to transform ideas into well-structured essays. Many systems exist (thesis first, thesis last, and so forth), and your instructor can advise you which might be most appropriate for your paper. However, whether you use the keyhole (p. 1045) or a less rigid form, remember to pin your thoughts to a thesis, developed then with supporting paragraphs directed by topic sentences. The suggested format (the five-paragraph essay) that follows is a traditional one that ensures tight essay structure. Once the skeleton is in place, you can flesh out the idea with specific support from the work itself. You may find you need more than three body paragraphs to do justice to your material. Do not allow your original plan to become a straight-jacket.

As the format shows, the supports grow into paragraphs that shape the body of the essay. Specific support from the play develops each paragraph in an effort to prove that the thesis is valid. Then a concluding paragraph rounds out the essay's thought, tying up loose ends.

Beginning Your Paper

Whether you are writing about *Hamlet* or New Wave, your essay needs a strong beginning. The introduction is the spot for fireworks; you are trying to get your reader's attention. Before you try to focus your essay, be sure to identify the work you intend to discuss (while you may devise a descriptive title for your essay, do not rely on it to do this for you.) Include phrases such as:

Robert Browning's "My Last Duchess" is . . .

"The Man Who Was Almost a Man" by Richard Wright . . .

**Written early in his career, "We Two Boys Together Clinging" shows
a side of Walt Whitman . . .**

INTRODUCTION

Thesis: (Often the thesis appears as the last sentence of the introductory paragraph)

Because confronting reality would be too painful, Tom, Amanda, and Laura have each slipped into a kind of surface madness to preserve their sanity.

BODY

(Each paragraph should contain a focusing topic sentence and as many specific details, reasons, examples, etc., as needed to prove its point;

Paragraph 1:

(Topic Sentence)

Amanda cultivates a type of forced happiness.

Supports: 1. (Use as many supports as you need to prove your point)
2.
3.
4.

Paragraph 2: (Topic Sentence)

Tom lives in a sullen fantasy world.

Supports: 1.
2.
3.

Paragraph 3: (Topic Sentence)

Laura nervously moves through a fragile world. . .

Supports: 1.
2.
3.

CONCLUSION

All three of Williams's characters in *The Glass Menagerie* avoid reality in order to survive in a hostile world.

If your reader is a classmate or a teacher already familiar with the work, you may need no more than a brief reference to plot. Sometimes the introduction is a good place to include a short plot summary, to emphasize the aspects of plot most pertinent to your main point. (You may want to save a plot summary for a later point in your essay. Insert it wherever it will best help to develop the paper.)

Strategies for beginning an essay are limited only by your imagination. Many of them are variations on the traditional paragraph form known as the *funnel*. The funnel starts with a generalization and works down to the focus or thesis of the essay.

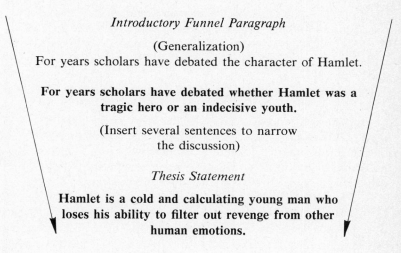

Introductory Funnel Paragraph

(Generalization)
For years scholars have debated the character of Hamlet.

For years scholars have debated whether Hamlet was a tragic hero or an indecisive youth.

(Insert several sentences to narrow the discussion)

Thesis Statement

Hamlet is a cold and calculating young man who loses his ability to filter out revenge from other human emotions.

In a funnel, the last sentence of the paragraph is the thesis; it then acts as a springboard into the rest of the essay.

Unless your instructor specifies otherwise, place the thesis at the end of the introductory paragraph. It will launch your essay clearly and vigorously. In addition to the funnel, you can explore other options such as these to lead down to a focusing thesis.

1. A real or rhetorical **question** which your essay will try to answer:

Did Mrs. Macomber willfully murder her husband?

2. A surprising, troubling, amazing, questionable, or significant **fact** to startle or surprise your reader:

Stephen Crane was dead before he turned thirty.

3. A **quotation** from the work itself, from the author, from a critic, or from some other relevant source.

Of his plays, Tennessee Williams once wrote, "We are all civilized, which means we are all savages at heart."

4. A brief **character sketch** to highlight important character traits:

Born in the city, scrappy, too soon made wise in the ways of the world, Pete, in John Rechy's story "Pete: A Quarter Ahead," . . .

5. A compressed **plot summary** to allow you to move quickly beyond plot:

The actual story line of Sherwood Anderson's "Death in the Woods" is not important: an insignificant young woman grows into an insignificant old woman strained by demands made by men and animals.

6. A brief **narration** or **description** to help illuminate the thesis:

The townspeople break down the door of the upper room in Miss Emily's house. They enter. To their shock and horror they find a long decayed body, the mysterious Homer Barron. Next to the skeleton lies a wisp of iron-grey hair. Now they know the truth . . . sweet, demure Miss Emily was a murderer.

Context will give you other clues to effective beginning tactics: an anecdote, a joke, historical detail, biography. Whichever you pick, remember that the purpose of the introduction is to catch your reader's attention. An introduction should introduce; if it can be made interesting along the way, no one will complain, least of all your reader.

Proving Your Point

The shape of the midsection of the essay depends on the strategy you design to fit your message. Liken the task to the way in which you select strategies to address daily problems: explaining why you were late for work; comparing several calculators before buying one; analyzing what to eat, what to buy, what to wear, what to say. Choosing a strategy to prove a literary point is similar. To write essays previously, you may have relied on rhetorical patterns such as *description, illustration, comparison* or *contrast,* and *causal* or *logical analysis.* Do the same now. Occasionally, you will use one dominant strategy, a contrast, for instance, between some aspect of a short story by Flannery O'Connor and a story by another southern female writer such as Eudora Welty. In another essay, you might describe the character of Angelina Sandoval from the Richard Vasquez story of the same name (p. 35), or Jeff and Jenny from Anna Bontemps's story "A Summer Tragedy" (p. 58). Usually, however, the strategies blend. Discussing Stephen Crane's naturalism requires both an analysis of the influence of environment on his characters and illustration from his novels *The Red Badge of Courage* and *Maggie, Girl of the Streets.* Whatever design you choose, the story, the play, or the poem is still the chief source of information. The details, the examples, the quotations are the mainstay of sound critical commentary.

Tying Up Loose Ends

Knowing when to stop is a virtue; beating the proverbial dead horse can be a trying exercise for both reader and writer. Ending the essay is as important as beginning it. Here, too, you have a choice of several tactics as you try to leave your reader with something to think about.

1. A **summary** of major points to round out your discussion. Be careful, though, because summary is often boring and repetitive.
2. A **final point** in a series of points arranged climactically, giving the last paragraph the strongest proof, the most weight.
3. An **interpretation** or **final evaluation** giving a last impression of details that might be interpreted another way.
4. A concluding **quotation** from the work itself, the author, a critic, or some other relevant source.

Try to clinch the discussion with a brisk, clean ending. The conclusion should not be one meager sentence of summary, nor should it become a soapbox. Bring the essay to a tidy, logical end without raising new issues or blowing old ones out of proportion.

PROBLEMS IN WRITING ABOUT LITERATURE

Emotional Response

Trying to be analytical and logical is difficult, especially when a piece of literature touches you personally. If you are a black person who has felt the sting of prejudice, you may instinctively feel an emotional response to a story like Ann Petry's "Like a Winding Sheet" (p. 236). If you are a woman who feels estranged from her child, you may feel defensive as you read Tillie Olsen's short story "I Stand Here Ironing" (p. 29). Someone with an alcoholic parent or spouse may have a strong personal reaction to Carson McCullers's story "A Domestic Dilemma" (p. 414). No matter what the intrusion from life to art, you must attempt to disassociate your personal reaction from a critical one. Liking or disliking a piece of literature because it speaks to your own life is not an interpretation. Sometimes, however, if kept under control, these personal reactions can help lead you to the more universal, objective significance of the piece.

Biographical Fallacy

Would-be critics sometimes feel the simplest way to resolve the issue of *persona* or author's spokesperson is to put the author into the story, play, or poem—especially if it is told in first person. Sylvia Plath's tormented poems speak of anguish that she may have known, but it would be a mistake to say that the speaker in "Mushrooms" (p. 913) or "For a Fatherless Son" (p. 524) must be Plath herself. A voice speaks in Faulkner's "A Rose for Emily" (p. 617) in first person plural, but Faulkner himself is not the likely speaker. Even when an author uses "I," remember that writers reconstruct experience and hide behind a voice or persona. They need not live through everything they write about. Just as twelve-year-old detectives do not write Nancy Drew and Hardy Boy stories, William Kotzwinkle did not have to smash into the

Colorado River Canyon to write "Follow the Eagle." Of course biographical elements influence writers, but never assume the persona *is* the author.

Influence

Have confidence in the value of your own critical opinions if you have read the work carefully and can support your conclusions. Professional critics do not necessarily have the right answers. They sometimes make mistakes, and they often do not agree. While some critics may see Paul in Willa Cather's "Paul's Case" (p. 454) as a sensitive, romantic hero, others might see him simply as a ragged dreamer who deserves the fate he suffers. Do not depend solely on professional literary critics or let them become stumbling blocks to your own thinking. The professionals read carefully and look to the text to support their opinions. You can do that, too. Literature reflects life and you have a lot of experience in life just from living yours. *Plagiarism* (borrowing the words or ideas of others without giving them credit) becomes a clear danger when you rely too heavily on professional critics. A fresh, thoughtful response of your own, based on close reading, is safer and probably a more valuable kind of reaction.

Paraphrase and Summary

Putting someone else's thoughts into your own words can also create problems. Your criticism should now have greater depth than the book reports you may have prepared in high school. Using other writers' ideas instead of your own can become a way of avoiding your own critical thinking. You also risk treating someone else's ideas as if they were your own.

Brief summaries of plot can be useful to illustrate a point if confined to quick capsules. Rarely, however, will the retelling of a story be a sustained part of a critic's assessment. Your reader will frequently be aware of the story line, so you can mention incidents and scenes as supporting material but dispense with the play-by-play description.

Critical Support: A Reminder

The most important single point to keep in mind as you prepare to write a critical essay is that critics form their opinions based on sound facts. Quotations, details, and examples from the work reinforce conclusions. Each set of facts is unique to the story, play, or poem from which it comes. From these distinctive facts emerge serious analysis and interpretation.

FINDING AND USING RESEARCH TOOLS

Some useful reference sources both in and out of a library can help you learn more about a literary work or its author. We are surrounded by nonacademic sources: literary calendars listing poetry readings and workshops, review sections of books and magazines, theater and book sections of the Sunday papers, public radio and television, and "little magazines." However, in most instances, librarians are your best allies. Sometimes libraries prepare "pathfinders" or guides to help students find out-of-the-ordinary reference materials. Bibliographies can also be helpful, although at times frustrating, if your library does not have the books and articles cited.

If you are seeking information about a work of literature or an author, first look in your library's catalogue on card, fiche, or film. After that try these other library sources:

1. *Literary Handbooks, Guides, and Companions.* These books give biographical information about authors, commentaries on their work, and often a list of relevant books and articles. Some examples are:

Contemporary Authors

Encyclopedia of World Literature in the 20th Century

Oxford and Penguin Companions to American and British Literature

2. *Collected Criticism and Literary Surveys of Authors.* These volumes usually come in series and collect interpretations and criticism of authors' works. Look in the first pages for instructions on how to use the series. Following these directions should dislodge a wealth of information. Some examples of these critical collections are:

Nineteenth Century Literary Criticism

Twentieth Century Literary Criticism

Contemporary Literary Criticism

A Library of Literary Criticism: Modern British Literature

American Writers: A Collection of Literary Biographies

Modern Black Writers

American Women Writers: From Colonial Times to the Present

Critical Survey of Short Fiction

Critical Survey of Long Fiction, English Language Series

Critical Survey of Poetry

A Library of Literary Criticism: Modern American Literature

3. *Indexes and Bibliographies.* For more in-depth information, these sources will refer you to other materials—books or parts of books, journals, or collections of essays. Individual bibliographies, available for most well-known authors, include works about them and editions of their books. Biographical indexes, book review indexes, and bibliographies of literary criticism, as well as the annual bibliographies of the Modern Language Association (MLA), can help for further research. Poetry, short story, and play indexes give locations of individual works in collections or anthologies.

4. *The Stacks.* You might also browse through the library shelves (known as "stacks"). Whether your library arranges books on its shelves with the Library of Congress (LC) system (two letters, followed by numbers and letters) or the Dewey Decimal System (decimals), learn the symbols or call numbers of the areas in which you are interested (for example, in the LC system, PR is the symbol for English literature, PS for American literature). Spend time looking through the shelves. This

old-fashioned way of finding material is sometimes the most practical, since you can browse through the tables of contents and indexes of books you discover there.

MATTERS OF FORM

Writing about literature requires some knowledge of specialized format. Following is a summary of rules for handling titles, quotations, bibliography entries, and citations in literary analysis.

Titles

1. **Capitalize** the first word and all important words in the title of a book, short story, poem, play, newspaper or magazine article, film, etc.

Eve Merriam's "Grandmother's Sampler"

Exception: Respect an author's capitalization if it differs from the traditional:

e. e. cummings's "dominic has a doll"

2. **Italicize** (underline) titles of the following items:
   a. Books (and other long literary works)

Jerzy Kosinski's Being There

John Milton's Paradise Lost

   b. Newspapers

USA Today

   c. Magazines

Time Magazine

   d. Plays

Tennessee Williams's The Glass Menagerie

   e. Films

Gone With the Wind

   f. Television Series

PBS's "Masterpiece Theatre"

3. Surround titles of shorter works with **quotation marks:**
   a. Short Poems

   Lewis Carroll's "Jabberwocky"

   b. Short Stories

   James Baldwin's "Sonny's Blues"

   c. Chapter Titles

   The first chapter heading of Edith Hamilton's *Mythology* is "The Gods."

   d. Song Titles

   Paul Simon's "Sounds of Silence"

   e. Essay Titles

   Ursula Le Guin's essay on the background for her story "Nine Lives" is called "On Theme."

   f. Magazine Articles

   A penetrating glimpse at the power of mythmaking can be found in "The Myth of the American Hero," an article in *American Quarterly.*

Quotations

1. **Double quotation marks** set off direct quotations, words quoted directly from a source:

William Faulkner worried his readers once with this remark: "I breed and train horses. That is what I like to do more than write."

Exception: For quotations that are longer than four typewritten lines, do not use quotation marks but indent five spaces on both sides to set off the quotation:

Intending to honor a poet he respected, Mark Van Doren wrote of e. e. cummings at his death:

> **The nature of life, of love, of death; the glory of the human spirit; the joys and wonders of experience—all these Cummings explores with passion, understanding, humor, and in**

**forms that are in themselves beautifully
wrought and perfectly fitted to their content.**

2. **Single quotation marks** set off a quotation inside another quotation:

**Isaac Bashevis Singer lets his character Dr. Fischelson say ". . . it is
stated in the fourth part of *The Ethics* that 'a free man thinks of
nothing less than of death and his wisdom is a meditation not of
death, but of life.' "**

3. **Punctuation marks** go inside or outside the quotation marks depending on their
type:
   a. A *comma* sets off the beginning of a quotation from the sentence:

Ulysses said, "I must go home."

Exception: Often a colon will introduce a long quotation. (See the Van Doren and
Singer examples just cited.)
   b. *Periods* and *commas* go inside quotation marks:

He whispered, "Amen."

   c. **Question marks** and **exclamation points** go inside the quotation marks if the
quoted material is a question or an exclamation:

The priest muttered, "Can heaven ever forgive me?"

"Twenty bucks!" he shouted.

   d. **Question marks** and **exclamation points** go outside the quotation marks if the
sentence is a question or exclamation but the quotation is not:

Do you know who said, "I have but one life to give for my country"?

How hypocritical of her to say "I'm having a wonderful time"!

   e. **Semicolons** and **colons** go outside quotation marks:

His wife said, "I don't know this man"; his son, too, denied him.

4. **Brackets** let the writer insert an explanatory comment inside a quotation:

"She [Johann's wife] laid a wreath on Voltar's grave."

5. Insert **[sic]** (Latin for "thus") to show you are aware of a misspelling, grammatical
error, etc., in your source.

The student said, "Poe chose to write tales revelant [*sic*] to his life."

6. **Ellipsis** (three dots . . .) shows that something has been omitted from a quotation. Use four dots (. . . .) when the omission comes at the end of a sentence:

> **William Carlos Williams said, "Leaves of Grass! . . . a good title for a book of poems. . . . It is a challenge that still holds good after a century of vigorous life."**

Bibliography Form

When you go beyond your own reading of a piece of literature to explore what others have said about it, you may include references to these critics' comments in your essay. If you do, you will generally be expected to add a *bibliography* (an alphabetized list of all works used) or a *list of works cited* at the end of your discussion. If you use only one source, you can, if your instructor permits, refer informally to the author and title either in the essay or at its end. For several sources, you will need a separate bibliography at the end of the essay with entries alphabetized and in correct bibliographic form.

The type of source determines the form. The sample entries that appear below follow the 1985 documentation format of the Modern Language Association. In all cases, double-space the entries and indent every line after the first. Be careful about internal as well as end punctuation. Use a different format if your instructor requests you to do so.

1. **Books.** You will not need all of this information for each entry. Include only what fits your book's publication facts.

Author (last name first). Title (underlined). Editor or
translator ("Ed." or "Trans." followed by name). Edition
(except for the first edition). Series (if applicable). Number of volumes (in Arabic numbers plus
"vols."). Place of publication: Publisher, date of
publication.

> **Harrison, G. B. *Introducing Shakespeare.* 3rd ed. London: Penguin Books, 1966.**

> **Sophocles. *The Oedipus Cycle.* Trans. Dudley Fitts and Robert Fitzgerald. New York: Harcourt Brace Jovanovich, 1977.**

Exception: If you use more than one work by the same author, do not repeat the author's name in the next entry. Instead, type three hyphens followed by a period. Complete the rest of the entry as shown above.

> **---. *The Shakespearean Mantle.* London: Penguin Books, 1968.**

2. **Magazine Articles.** Again, apply only the information that fits your source. If no author is given, begin at the margin with the title.

Author (last name first). Title of article (in quotation marks). Name of magazine (underlined, with no comma following) date (day, month, and year [without commas] followed by a colon): page numbers (use just the numbers, no "p." or "pp.").

Silman, Roberta. "Company." *Atlantic Monthly* **May 1975: 74–77.**

3. **Newspaper Articles.** Use only the information that applies to your source.

Author (last name first). Title of article (in quotation marks). Name of newspaper (underlined, with no comma following) date (day, month, and year [without commas] followed by a colon): page numbers (section: page [just the number, no "p." or "pp."]).

Sanson, Monique. "Murdering the Bard." *Washington Post* **17 Feb. 1983: B:7.**

Documentation

While you can borrow ideas and language from a source, you are obliged to alert your reader whenever you do this. Formal footnotes or endnotes once routinely performed that function, and if your instructor prefers that you use that more formal process of documentation, you should do so. Otherwise, you may follow this simplified method of citation. The simpler form is particularly appropriate to essay writing. You will want to use such a notation to document information whenever you do the following:

1. Summarize
2. Quote
3. Paraphrase
4. Borrow statistics, charts, or other such data

An exception to this rule occurs when you work with widely known material or information. Labeled *common knowledge,* this kind of information is familiar because it often appears in many sources, making pinpointing an original source difficult. Facts such as birth dates and definitions are examples of material generally considered common knowledge. Such material needs no citation.

Since the bibliography entry gives complete publication information, citations in the text need not do so. Following are several guidelines for documenting in-text information. When you have identified a quotation or a passage you wish to cite, show in parentheses after it the author's last name, a shortened form of the title, and the page number. Omit any or all three of these if the information is already mentioned clearly in the text. Omit the title if you are citing only one work by an author.

1. If the author's name or the title of the work is not cited in your text, include the author's last name. Do not separate author and page number with a comma.

Some say that the images in John Donne's poems which seem obscure to modern readers were not so for the sophisticated audiences who read them (Alvarez 33).

2. If the author's name and/or title is already cited in the text, include only the page number.

> **The critic Alfred Alvarez says that images in John Donne's poems which seem obscure to modern readers were not so for the sophisticated audiences who read them (33).**

> **In *The School of Donne,* Alvarez says that the images in John Donne's poems which seem obscure to modern readers were not so for the sophisticated audiences who read them (33).**

> **The School of Donne shows that the images in John Donne's poems which seem obscure to modern readers were not so for the sophisticated audiences who read them (33).**

3. If you are using more than one source by an author, include a word or two of the title to make it clear which one you mean.

> **Alvarez says that the images in John Donne's poems which seem obscure to modern readers were not so for the sophisticated audiences who read them (*School of Donne* 33).**

4. For a reference to a magazine or newspaper article, use the title of the article, not the title of the magazine or newspaper. If the article appears on only one page, do not include a page number.

> **Alice Walker's book *The Color Purple* seems to have raised critical eyebrows ("Whither Goes Alice").**

Explanatory Notes

Endnotes or footnotes are still used to offer the reader information that supplements the content of an essay. In this type of note, you might define a term, add interesting data, explain a minor point, and so forth. A content footnote of this sort in a discussion of James Joyce's puzzling prose style in *Ulysses,* for instance, might look like this:

> **[9]In 1932, before *Ulysses* appeared in publication, Joyce chuckled to a friend that he had included enough puzzles in it to keep the professors busy for years to come.**

Including this information in the text might interrupt the flow of thought. Content notes are numbered in sequence and appear either as footnotes at the bottom of the page or as endnotes at the end of the paper, before the bibliography.

GENERAL TOPICS FOR WRITING ABOUT LITERATURE

Given below is a list of topics which might inspire ideas of your own when you are set to any of the writing tasks associated with this course. They are not meant to be all-inclusive; they are merely hints at ways that your own writing might go. Each thematic section includes specific questions relating to that section. These topics have been grouped according to the following categories:

Short papers (500 words) or journal entries

Longer papers, or research papers of varying lengths

Creative projects in less traditional form or media

Topics particularly useful for international students

Topics for Short Papers, Journals, or Discussion

1. Choose several lines of poetry, or an entire poem, from any of the poems in this book. Memorize them; recite them in class; and tell, in your Journal, why you chose this particular poem.

2. Compare the points of view in two stories or poems. Refer to the discussion on "point of view" in the "On Reading Fiction" section of this book.

3. Compare two characters from different stories or plays you have read here. Pick two characters who have something in common: two women, two violent individuals, two lovers, two black men, etc.

4. Write a review of a play you have not studied in class but have seen in a local theatre. Write it as though you were a reporter for a local newspaper.

5. Find a review of one of the plays you have seen or one of the films you have viewed as part of this class. Xerox the review or reviews and write a paper on why you agree or disagree with the reviewer.

6. Write a review of one of the American Short Story films on Public Television (many of these are available in libraries; the series is often repeated on TV).

7. Some of the selections in this anthology work with more than one theme. Choose one of these stories from one section and explain how it could fit into another section of the book. For example, "The Yellow Wallpaper" could have been placed into either section 3, "Human Relationships," or Section 4, "Choices and Conflicts."

Longer Papers or Research Projects

1. Pick out three to five poems from a section which you think illustrate its theme particularly well (or select some which illustrate a theme of your own). How does each one relate to the theme? Analyze the poems on the basis of the discussion under "Value" in the section "On Reading Poetry" on page 1027.

2. Choose the author of one of the stories, plays, or poems you have read this term which have made a deep impression on you. Look up that author in the appropriate reference works in your library. Make a short bibliography of the writer's most important works, list a few recent or important biographies of the writer, works of criticism of the writer's work. Read something else by the writer, other than what appears in this book. Summarize your findings in a fact sheet to be distributed to your classmates. In a five minute talk, tell your classmates informally about what you found

and recommend to them, persuasively, some reading by or about the author you have chosen.

3. Each section of this book begins with a story based on myth. For example: in "The Bride Comes to Yellow Sky," it is the myth of the Old West; in "The Ugliest Pilgrim" it is the quest or pilgrimage, as in Chaucer's *Canterbury Tales;* in "Rip Van Winkle," it is the enchanted sleep; in "Young Goodman Brown" it is witchcraft; and in "The Unicorn in the Garden" it is the magic animal. Research the original myths that inspire one or several of the stories and relate them to the plots and characters.

4. One of the reasons we have included biographies of authors in this book is so that we can look at the facts of their lives beside their fictional output and discuss whether a really great writer needs to experience everything he or she writes about. Many writers like di Donato seem to write well about their own lives, or lives that touch theirs strongly, while others, like Henry James or Stephen Crane, seem able to imaginatively recreate lives nothing at all like their own. That extra gift of imaginative insight makes the difference between a competent, or even a vivid writer, and a truly great one—a Shakespeare, a Crane, a Cather, or a Hemingway. Pick out some stories, poems, or plays in this book that seem to you to be "truly great" by this yardstick and some that seem merely competent. Explain your choices. Compare your lists with those of your fellow-students in class. Then see if there is an element common to most of your lists. Discuss these common elements, possibly in a paper.

Creative Projects

1. Using a Reader's Theater approach, (reading parts, some rehearsal and costume) dramatize *No Exit* or *The Sandbox* in class. Choose a cast from among your class-mates, discuss how you will interpret the roles, and read the play, after some short rehearsals, to the class.

2. Submit a work in another medium: painting, photo essay, slide show, sculpture, music—that relates to one or more of the selections in this anthology, or that illus-trates its themes.

3. Submit to your instructor an original short story, series of poems, short play, or television script you have written recently that relates to the readings you have done in this course or in some way illustrates or exemplifies something you have brought to your own creative work from this course.

4. Imagine that you are in some isolated and dangerous situation—perhaps in jail (through no fault of your own, of course!), or a hostage on a hijacked airplane or in an Embassy. Your captors have told you that you may bring with you, for your amusement and comfort, one item from this anthology. Choose the play, poem, or story you would bring with you and tell why it would be valuable to you in this particular situation of isolation and peril.

For International Students

Note for poetry assignment below: Poetry is the last thing understood about a country's literature. T. S. Eliot said: "It is easier to think in a foreign language than to feel in it. Therefore no art is more stubbornly national than poetry." He also believed that people find the deepest expression of their feelings in the poetry of their own language. Given these ideas, we have developed the following assignment to help international students and recent immigrants bridge the gap. A great variety of students from many countries have successfully participated in this project, among them students from Korea, Lebanon, Pakistan, India, China, Vietnam, Japan, Cambodia, Nigeria, Barbados, Iran, the Phillipines, Uganda, Mali, Russia, Somalia, Iraq, and Germany, all of which have rich literatures. The assignment teaches everyone, including the teacher, many important things about poetry.

1. Choose a poem in your own language. Translate it into English—either into prose, or, if possible, into a poem. Then, in a class session devoted to these presentations, read your poem in your own language, translate it, and then explain briefly to your classmates what poetry is like in your language: its rhyme, rhythm, importance, or anything else you think will interest the class. You may want to write your poem on the board or provide photocopies of it.

2. What is the most famous literary work of your own country? What does that work mean to you personally? Please, do not use translations of articles in your language to fulfill this assignment. Merely tell why the work is considered great, and what it means to you. For example, if you were Spanish, you might choose Cervantes; if Nigerian, Chinua Achebe.

3. Upon your return to your own country you are asked to plan to teach a course such as this one. What readings and authors would you include from American and other literature in English that would best represent American literature to your people?

Biographies
of the Authors

These short biographies are intended to provide students with further information about the writers featured in the anthology, to add depth and enjoyment to their reading, and to supply basic information for some of the writing assignments. Each entry includes a sketch of the author's life, a brief outline of the purpose and scope of the author's works, an indication of the writer's importance, and a list of the writer's most important, easily available works (especially in paperback editions), for further reading. For some authors, especially writers of the past, one or two valuable biographies, and occasional critical works are also included. Other materials of help to the student in search of further information about authors or their works appear on pages 1048–1050 in the section titled "Writing About Literature."

LEONARD ADAMÉ(b. 1947) comes to poetry through rock music, as did John Lennon and Leonard Cohen. Born in the San Joaquin Valley of California, Adamé spent his childhood working in his father's restaurant and on his uncle's farm. He has used his memories of how Mexican-Americans lived then as themes in his songs and poems, especially those collected in *Entrance: Four Chicano Poets* (1975) and *The Chicano Chapbook,* series 3 (1979).

EDWARD ALBEE(b. 1928) is a name long connected with the theater of the absurd (see p. 1033), and many of his early works fall into that category. Albee was adopted as an infant into a wealthy theatrical family and as a boy wrote poetry, fiction, and a three-act play. Albee initially disappointed his family, roaming from one odd job to another. He continued writing but had little dramatic success until 1959 when his first play, *Zoo Story,* was produced first in Berlin and then off Broadway. After *Zoo Story,* Albee wrote four more one act plays: *The Sandbox* (1960), *Fam and Yam* (1960), *The Death of Bessie Smith* (1961), and *The American Dream* (1961). He achieved prominence when his first full-length play, *Who's Afraid of Virginia Woolf* (1962), was nominated for the Pulitzer Prize. His long dramatic career has seen him mature from an angry young man to a mature playwright with a substantial list of plays: *Tiny Alice* (1964), *Malcolm* (1966), *A Delicate Balance* (1966), *Everything in the Garden* (1967), *Box-Mao-Box* (1968), *All Over* (1971), *Seascape*(1974), and *The Lady from Dubuque* (1980). *A Delicate Balance* and *Seascape* finally brought Albee Pulitzer Prizes. His plays can be found in *Selected Plays of Edward Albee* (1981) and *The Plays of Edward Albee* (1981).

SHERWOOD ANDERSON(1876–1941), born in Camden, Ohio, had little formal education. He held a variety of odd jobs before finding success in writing. Anderson worked in advertising, served in the Spanish-American War, and managed a paint factory. In 1919, at 43, he published his first successful book, *Winesburg, Ohio,* a volume of interconnected short stories. Much of Anderson's work, like "Death in the Woods," is semi-autobiographical. His dominant theme is the conflict between basic human nature and the oppressiveness of industrialized society. For a time Anderson joined a group of Chicago writers that included Carl Sandburg, and Theodore Dreiser. After World War I he went to Paris, where he knew Gertrude Stein, Ernest Hemingway, and F. Scott Fitzgerald, and to New Orleans, where he briefly shared an apartment with William Faulkner. He later edited both a Democratic and a Republican newspaper in adjacent Virginia towns. His more than two dozen books include volumes of essays, seven novels, and two plays. *Triumph of the Egg* (1921) and *Death in the Woods* (1933) are among his best-known short story collections. His autobiography, *A Story Teller's Story* (1924), tells of his abrupt decision to become a writer, his development as a writer of the Middle West, and his encouragement of others.

W. H. AUDEN(1907–1973) was born Wystan Hugh Auden in York, England, and was educated at Oxford. He taught school for a while and became associated with the leftist poets of his time, principally Stephen Spender, Christopher Isherwood, Louis MacNeice, and Chester Kallman. Auden's poetry of the twenties and thirties, *Poems* (1928) and *The Orators* (1932), increased his reputation. Like his poet friends, he spoke out on the poverty and unemployment sweeping England during the Depression. He collaborated with MacNeice on a book of prose and verse, *Letters from Iceland,* in 1937. His leftist sympathies also took him to Spain to serve as ambulance driver for the Republicans during the Civil War. In 1939 Auden came to America, adding American influences, such as the songs of the blues singers, to his verse. From this period dates his renewed interest in Protestant Christianity. His book *The Age of Anxiety* (1947) was awarded the Pulitzer Prize. Auden spent time lecturing and teaching in both England and America. Although he had become an American citizen in 1945, he returned to England in 1973 to live in Oxford. Auden edited many anthologies; among the most enduring are *W. H. Auden's Oxford Book of Light Verse* (1979) and *The Viking Book of Aphorisms: A Personal Selection* (1981). His *Collected Poems* were published in 1983.

JAMES BALDWIN(b. 1924) is one of America's best-known black writers. The first of nine children of a stern, storefront minister, Baldwin grew up in Harlem. He began writing in his rebellious teen years and continued after high school. He met Richard Wright in 1944 and, like him, left America to escape its racial injustices. From 1948 to 1957, Baldwin lived in Paris, where he became an explosive voice for black America of the 1950s. When he returned to America in 1957, he plunged into civil rights activities. Baldwin was concerned with more than racial conflict, however. While his works seethe with the outraged sense of justice that became the battle cry of the militants of the 1960s, they rise above social commentary. His novels deal with homosexuality, interracial love, and racial conflict, but these concerns plague both his white and black characters. Baldwin's major fiction includes *Go Tell It on The Mountain* (1953), *Giovanni's Room* (1955), *Another Country* (1962), and *Going to Meet the Man* (1965). In addition, he has written plays, notably *Blues for Mister Charlie* (1964) and *Jimmy's Blues: Selected Poems* (1983). Often considered his finest work, Baldwin's essays and nonfiction include *Notes of a Native Son* (1955), *Nobody Knows My Name* (1961), *Harlem, U.S.A.: The Story of a City Within a City* (1976), *The Devil Finds Work* (1976), and *The Evidence of Things Not Seen* (1985).

TONI CADE BAMBARA (b. 1939) was born and educated in New York City. She has been a social investigator, director of recreation in psychiatry, English instructor, professor of African American Studies and Woman's Studies, and writer-in-residence at several colleges and universities. Bambara examines the life choices available to black women. Her works anthologize and celebrate the black woman's life in song, story, and dance. Her writing includes *The Black Woman: An Anthology* (1970) and two collections of short stories—*Gorilla My Love* (1972) and *The Sea Birds Are Still Alive* (1982). Her recent work includes a novel, *The Salt Eaters* (1980).

STEPHEN VINCENT BENÉT (1898–1943) started writing as a Yale undergraduate. By the time he graduated, he had published two volumes of poetry and his first novel appeared shortly afterwards. Benét's interest in the American scene is evident in his poetry: *Heavens and Earth* (1920), *King David* (1923), *The Ballad of William Sycamore* (1923), and *Tiger Joy* (1924). His growing maturity as a poet showed itself in *John Brown's Body* (1928), a long narrative poem on the Civil War which won the Pulitzer Prize. *Western Star* (1943), his unfinished epic poem on the westward American migration, also won the Pulitzer. Benét's forms were traditional; he relied on the ballad and the well-made short story. He also wrote several novels and the librettos for two one-act folk operas. His short stories appear in *Thirteen O'Clock* (1937), *Tales Before Midnight* (1939), and *Selected Works* (1942). During World War II he wrote *America* (1944), a short history for the Office of War Information.

DORIS BETTS (b. 1932) has emerged from relative obscurity as a North Carolina regional writer and teacher into being a nationally recognized artist. Her strength lies in her skill at drawing abandoned people, caught up with dull work and desperate lives, who can sometimes be redeemed by love. Betts's rural or small-town people become almost emblematic figures as she relates the world of every day to the world of legend. She has been a member of the faculty at the University of North Carolina at Chapel Hill since 1966, has taught at many writers' conferences, and has won many prizes for her fiction. Her short story collections are *The Gentle Insurrection* (1954), *The Astronomer and Other Stories* (1966), and *Beasts of the Southern Wild and Other Stories* (1973). Her novels include *Tall Houses in Winter* (1957), *The Scarlet Thread* (1964), *The River to Pickle Beach* (1972), and *Heading West* (1981).

ELIZABETH BISHOP(1911–1979) was an American poet who spent much of her life in Brazil. Born in 1911 in Worcester, Massachusetts, she lost her parents early and lived with relatives in New England and Canada from the age of five. Bishop earned a B.A. degree from Vassar, where she was influenced by the poet Marianne Moore. Soon after, she went to Brazil on a fellowship and remained there for sixteen years. Starting with a Guggenheim Fellowship in 1946, Bishop won a number of grants and awards for her poetry. She started publishing her poems in 1946 and by 1955 had won a Pulitzer Prize by combining her first two volumes of poetry: *Poems: North and South and a Cold Spring.* Critics praise Bishop for her descriptive eye, the sharpness of her details. As she herself has been a traveler and something of an exile, many of her poems deal with these themes. Other volumes of poetry are *Diary of Helen Morley* (1957), *Questions of Travel* (1965), *Selected Poems* (1967), *The Ballad of the Burglar of Babylon* (1968), and *The Complete Poems,* which won her a National Book Award in 1969. *The Complete Poems, 1927–1979* was published in 1983.

WILLIAM BLAKE (1757–1827) developed a world view through his "prophetic books" and his spiritual poetry. He was at the same time a mystic and a practical man who illustrated some of the landmark books of all time, his own and others', with his superb etchings. Blake was a master engraver, studying at the Royal Academy, then traditionally oriented. Blake, however, experienced visions and visitations, and this influenced all his work, filling it with a unique, far from traditional spirit. His *Songs of Innocence* (1789) and *Songs of Experience* (1794) consist of engraved plates in which poems and illustrations relate closely to each other. Blake's wife, whom he taught both to read and to paint, hand-colored the books. In his "prophetic books," such as *Jerusalem, America,* and *Europe,* Blake developed his mystical religion and his prophesies for the future. He became a political radical like Thomas Paine and Mary Wollstonecraft, though he diverted this radicalism into cosmology rather than into the active politics of his time. In spite of the richness, mysticism, and glorious forms of his poems, paintings, and etchings, Blake died in relative poverty. His works are available today in many editions, notably *The Complete Poetry and Prose of William Blake* (1982).

ARNA BONTEMPS(b. 1902), a black writer of Harlem Renaissance fame, was born in Alexandria, Louisiana, and earned a B.A. degree from Pacific Union College in 1923. He came to New York in the thirties and began to write while he taught school to support himself and his family. His attempt to illustrate the life of the blacks in America has led him to work in almost every genre, writing poetry, fiction, essays, and children's books, and editing several anthologies. Some of his more noted works are *The Story of the Negro* (1948), *The Poetry of the Negro: 1746–1949* (1949), *Chariot in the Sky: A Story of the Jubilee Singer* (1951), *The Book of Negro Folklore* (1958), *100 Years of Negro Freedom (1961)*, and *Any Place But Here (1966)*. A record of the correspondence between Bontemps and Langston Hughes appears in *Arna Bontemps-Langston Hughes Letters, 1925–1967* (1979).

PHILIP BOOTH (b. 1925), professor of English at Syracuse University, spends much of his time in Maine, where he collects subjects for his spare, carefully controlled poems. The Maine coast and other New England settings have inspired poems that have won him critical acclaim, a place in many anthologies, as well as honors and fellowships. Booth has published several volumes of poetry, beginning in 1957 with *Letter from a Distant Land.* Subsequent volumes include *The Islanders* (1961), *Syracuse Poems* (1965), *Weathers and Edges* (1966), *North by East* (1966), *Beyond Our Fears* (1967), *Margins* (1970), *Available Light* (1976), and *Before Sleep* (1980).

ANNE BRADSTREET(1612–1672), author of America's first published book of poetry, was a Massachusetts Bay colonist in 1630. Wife and daughter of Massachusetts Bay governors, she left a comfortable, even scholarly life in Lincolnshire as an eighteen-year-old wife to emigrate to New England with the group led by John Winthrop. Though her health was delicate, she survived the first miserable winter, to bear and raise eight children, and to write *The Tenth Muse* (1650). Her poems, mostly long epics based on history and science, were first published in England by her brother-in-law without her knowledge. She later corrected and prepared a new edition, adding more personal poems; it was published in Boston in 1678, six years after her death. In her old age she wrote meditations and a diary for her children, explaining her feelings about emigrating, about living in the wilderness, about her feminist strivings, and analyzing her doubts about religion. *The Works of Anne Bradstreet* (1981) makes available all of her poems, the spiritual diary, and the meditations. John Berryman brings Bradstreet to life in *Homage to Mistress Bradstreet* (1959).

GWENDOLYN BROOKS(b. 1917) was the first black poet to receive a Pulitzer Prize. She won it for her collection *Annie Allen,* in 1950. Other honors such as Guggenheim Fellowships and the Poet Laureateship of Illinois followed. Her earliest poems, like "Kitchinette Building," were portraits of the black urban poor in Chicago, where she grew up, wrote, and taught. Her later poems showed a marked change in tone; they were tougher and more powerful. *In the Mecca* (1968), *The Bean Eaters* (1974), and *Black Love* (1983) are typical of her later poems: restrained, tough without being bitter. Her distinctive style produces controlled pictures of poverty and racism. Brooks's interest in teaching writing and fostering young poets is reflected in *A Capsule Course in Black Poetry Writing* (1975), *Young Poet's Primer* (1980), and *Very Young Poets* (1983). In 1985–86, Brooks was consultant in Poetry at the Library of Congress.

ELIZABETH BARRETT BROWNING (1806–1861), up to her fortieth

year, was the oldest, invalid daughter of a well-to-do Londoner who insisted on absolute obedience and forbade his children to marry. Elizabeth Barrett, in fragile health, retreated to her bedroom and wrote, publishing five volumes and becoming a well-known "poetess" of her time. Her poetry appealed to the young poet Robert Browning, who finally succeeded in seeing her to express his admiration for her verse. Their poetic friendship ripened into love, and in 1846 they eloped to Italy. The couple lived for fifteen years in Florence, writing and producing their best poetic works, as well as a son, and living happily until Elizabeth's death. In Italy, she produced the famous *Sonnets from the Portuguese* (1850), *Casa Guidi Windows* (1851), and the verse-novel *Aurora Leigh* (1857). Her style developed throughout her life; she used conventional forms like the sonnet but in a new, fresh manner. Overlooked in the romance of her life are the real contributions Elizabeth Barrett Browning made to the causes of freedom in Italy, and women's equality worldwide. Recent scholarship, especially that of Barbara Charlesworth Gelpi and Virginia Steinmetz, has reevaluated Elizabeth Barrett Browning's contribution to literature and to ideas. Christopher Ricks's *The Brownings: Letters and Poetry* (1970) tells their story in their own words better than most of the overly sentimental biographies.

ROBERT BROWNING (1812–1882) was the pampered and adored son of a

wealthy British bank clerk. Until his marriage at age thirty-four, Browning rarely spent time away from his parents' home near London, being tutored more at home than at boarding schools. Influenced by the romantic poet Shelley, Browning became an atheist and a liberal. Stung by negative criticism of his first poem, *Pauline,* published when he was twenty-one, Browning vowed to keep his poetry to himself. He then tried unsuccessfully to write plays, an experience that led him to experiment with the dramatic monologue, at which he excelled. Browning's courtship of Elizabeth Barrett is perhaps the best-known element of his life. When he first met her in 1845, she was a practicing poet, six years older than he, and a semi-invalid with a tyrannical father. They eloped to Italy and stayed there for fifteen years. He is best known for his dramatic monologues, poems such as "My Last Duchess," "The Bishop Orders His Tomb," and "Soliloquy of the Spanish

Cloister." His two most impressive volumes of poetry are *Men and Women,* published in 1855, and *The Ring and the Book,* published in 1868–69. His works are available today in *The Poetical Works of Robert Browning* (1983). *The Brownings' Correspondence* (1984) gives a close view of one of literature's greatest romances.

TRUMAN CAPOTE (1924–1984) started his career in his early twenties as the precocious author of several novels. Originally from the South, he eventually settled in New York City, writing short stories. Although already a widely admired writer, he did not achieve real fame until 1965, when he published *In Cold Blood.* Written in a form he claimed to have invented—the nonfiction novel—this account of a real mass murder, the cold-blooded slaying of the Clutter family in Kansas, was both repelling and fascinating. Some of Capote's critics have doubted the quality of his work, suggesting that his colorful personality and his friendships with "beautiful people" caused his success. However, Capote did show a precise eye and ear for detail. His characters are often unusual, almost freaks, caught in their own pathetic struggles. Capote's novels are *Other Voices, Other Rooms* (1948) and *The Grass Harp* (1951). His story collections include *Breakfast at Tiffany's* (1958), *A Tree of Night and Other Stories* (1949), *A Christmas Memory* (1966), and *Music for Chameleons* (1980). His nonfiction, in addition to *In Cold Blood,* includes *Local Color* (1950) and *The Muses Are Heard* (1956). His *Selected Writings* were published in 1979, and *Three by Truman Capote* appeared in 1985.

LEWIS CARROLL (1832–1898) is the pseudonym by which Charles Lutwidge Dodgson is famous the world over. Raised in the English countryside, Carroll displayed an early talent for writing nonsense verses such as "Jabberwocky." Though he became a distinguished scholar in mathematics at Oxford, Carroll maintained the image of a shy, studious professor, ill-at-ease in large groups, except in the company of children. He composed a hand-written book, "Alice's Adventures Underground" for the children of Dean Liddell of his College at Oxford, whose daughter, Alice, was Carroll's special favorite. The book was published as *Alice in Wonderland* in 1865 with illustrations by Sir John Tenniel; *Through the Looking-Glass* followed in 1871. These two books became childhood favorites and continue so today, though mathematicians and logicians also delight in the logical and mathematical puzzles the books pose. He wrote other books of mathematical and logical games, as well as his most famous mathematical work, *Euclid and His Modern Rivals* (1879). Available today are many editions of the *Alice* books, including *The Annotated Alice: Alice's Adventures in Wonderland and Through the Looking-Glass,* edited by Martin Gardner (1960); and *The Complete Illustrated Works of Lewis Carroll,* edited by Edward Guiliano with the Tenniel illustrations (1982).

WILLA CATHER (1873–1947) came from a late nineteenth-century pioneering family that moved from Virginia to Nebraska when she was a young girl. They lived briefly on a farm before moving to the town of Red Cloud, Nebraska, where she grew up among the European immigrants who would later appear in her fiction. With a degree in journalism from the University of Nebraska, Cather worked as both reporter and English teacher in Pittsburgh and then went to New York as managing editor for *McClure's Magazine.* Cather's career as a published writer began with a collection of poems called *April Twilights* (1903), followed by a book of short stories, *The Troll Garden* (1905). She set her first novel, *Alexander's Bridge* (1912), in England but soon returned to the scenes and characters she knew so well from her youth. *O Pioneers* appeared in 1913, with *The Song of the Lark* following in 1915. *My Antonia* (1918) recalled the lives of the strong, independent hired girls who worked for the middle-class families in Red Cloud. Two short story collections that followed—*Youth and the Bright Medusa* (1920) and *Obscure Destinies* (1932)—were also about life on the prairies. Cather experimented with historical novels rich in spiritual values and produced *Death Comes for the Archbishop* (1927), about a missionary priest in New Mexico, and *Shadows on the Rock* (1931), about seventeenth-century Quebec. The definitive edition of Cather's fiction is *The Novels and Stories of Willa Cather,* 13 vols., 1937–41. A recent biography is Phyllis C. Robinson's *Willa: The Life of Willa Cather* (1983).

JOHN CHEEVER (1912–1982) was an urbane storyteller who gained fame by writing about upper-middle-class America. Cheever's own WASP background matches the tradition he satirized. He was born in Quincy, Massachusetts, and started his writing career at seventeen by publishing sketches entitled "Expelled" in the *New Republic.* Much of Cheever's work has been published first in the *New Yorker.* His characters are generally upper-middle-class people, often transplanted New Yorkers, living in New England. His themes revolve around the dilemmas of these people as they try to find happiness in the modern American suburb. His bored female characters nurse their marital woes while his middle-aged male characters pursue fantasies. Cheever is primarily a short story writer, having written over one hundred of them. His first collection, *The Way Some People Live* (1943), was followed by *The Enormous Radio* (1953), *The Housebreaker of Shady Hill* (1958), and *The World of Apples* (1972). These volumes were collected in *The Stories of John Cheever* (1978). Cheever has written several novels, pursuing similar themes. *The Wapshot Chronicle* (1957) and *The Wapshot Scandal* (1964) wittily detail the deterioration of a fine New England family. Other novels are *Bullet Park* (1969), *Falconer* (1976), and *O What a Paradise It Seems* (1982).

KATE CHOPIN (1851–1904) was first identified with New Orleans regional writing, but she has risen above being merely a "local color" writer. Born in St. Louis of Creole stock, Chopin was raised by a grandmother who taught her independence. Married to a New Orleans cotton factor, she lived the life of a society belle until her husband's business failed and he died. Left with the responsibility of supporting six children, Chopin began to write at the age of thirty-seven, contributing more than a hundred short stories to local and national magazines, including the *Atlantic Monthly, Century,* and *Youth's Companion.* These were later collected as *Bayou Folk* (1894) and *A Night in Acadie* (1897). In 1899 she wrote an unconventional and unappreciated novel, *The Awakening,* about a young married woman's sexual and artistic awakening to a world that did not want her to have that freedom. The book caused such an uproar that Chopin gave up writing fiction. Her blending of local color with psychological insight made her one of the finest writers of her era, though her value was not realized until the early 1960s, when her works were rediscovered. Per E. Seyersted's *Kate Chopin: A Critical Biography* (1969) is a valuable study of her life and work.

LEONARD COHEN (b. 1934), well-known Canadian composer, singer, and writer of fiction, was born in Montreal. Educated at McGill University in Montreal and Columbia University in New York, Cohen now divides his time between these two cities, as well as the Greek island of Hydra. Cohen's songs and poetry emerge from the everyday world. He makes poetry, as some say, out of everyday junk, "the garbage and the flowers" ("Suzanne"). Like the poems of Emily Dickinson, Cohen's poetry is lyrical and deceptively simple. The form he handles best is the ballad—the form of his poem "Suzanne," in this book. His earlier poems are collected in *Selected Poems 1956–1968* (1968). His latest volume of poems is *Book of Mercy* (1984). His songs and poems can be heard on his recordings: *The Songs of Leonard Cohen* (1968), *Songs from a Room* (1969), *Live Songs* (1973), *The Best of Leonard Cohen* (1975), and *Recent Songs* (1979).

JANE COOPER (b. 1924) has become a strong voice for women poets both in her own poetry and in her criticism. Her first book of poems, *The Weather of Six Mornings* (1968), received the Lamont Award of the Academy of American Poets. Her next collection, *Maps and Windows* (1974), included a long essay on what it was like to be a woman poet in the post-World-War-II years. Cooper studied at Oxford and Paris after World War II and wrote at Yaddo and at the MacDowell Colony, sanctuaries for writers and artists. She held a Guggenheim Fellowship and has taught at Sarah Lawrence College. She has written and edited much literary criticism, particularly that concerning women poets: *Extended Outlooks: The Iowa Review Collection of Contemporary Women Writers* (1981), and *Reading Adrienne Rich: Reviews and Re-Visions, 1951–81* (1984). The latest volume of her own poems is *Scaffolding: New and Selected Poems* (1984).

STEPHEN CRANE (1871–1900) packed original and varied experiences into his brief twenty-nine years. His life among artists and slum-dwellers in New York as a newspaper reporter led to his explosive novel *Maggie: A Girl of the Streets* (1893). Later he reported events in the South and the West as far as Mexico and covered the Cuban and Greek wars of independence. Being shipwrecked during the Cuban war led to short stories such as "The Open Boat," while western travels inspired "The Blue Hotel" and "The Bride Comes to Yellow Sky." Although Crane had no first-hand knowledge of the Civil War, his novel *The Red Badge of Courage* (1895) has been acclaimed as one of the truest accounts of the effects of war on the foot soldier. Crane married the madam of a Jacksonville bordello and moved to an old manor house in England, where he joined a circle of writer friends including Henry James and Joseph Conrad. Suffering from tuberculosis, he continued writing until he died in a German spa. Crane combined naturalism (see p. 216) with sensuous detail to produce a unique writing style. A recent collection of his works, *Stephen Crane: Prose and Poetry,* has been issued by the Library of America (1984).

COUNTEE CULLEN (1903–1946), the adopted son of a Methodist minister, grew up in New York City. He was educated there in the public schools, graduated from New York University as a member of Phi Beta Kappa, and then earned an M.A. at Harvard. Cullen taught in the New York City public schools for most of his life. He also worked briefly as assistant editor of *Opportunity: Journal of Negro Life.* Cullen was part of the Harlem Renaissance in the 1920s. His first book of poems, *Color,* won the Harmon Gold Award in 1925. Other books of poems were *Copper Sun* (1927), *The Ballad of the Brown Girl* (1928), *The Black Christ* (1929), *The Medea and Some Poems* (1935), *The Lost Zoo* (1940), *My Nine Lives and How I Lost Them* (1942), and *On These I Stand,* published after his death in 1947. Cullen's one novel, *One Way to Heaven,* was published in 1932. *Caroling Dusk: An Anthology of Verse by Negro Poets* (1955) emphasized his stand that the traditions of English literature, rather than dialect or the idioms of colloquial speech, should govern black poetry.

E. E. CUMMINGS (1894–1962), an innovative American poet, attended Harvard and joined the American Red Cross in World War I. Due to an administrative error, he spent three months in a French jail, an experience that resulted in his novel *The Enormous Room* (1922). Many volumes of poetry followed from 1923 to 1963, as well as three plays and a ballet. cummings was also a painter who exhibited in at least three shows during his lifetime. He lectured at Harvard; his collected lectures are entitled *i: six nonlectures* (1953). cummings is well known for his experiments in orthography, spelling his name without capital letters (e.e. cummings) and arranging poems, like "leaf," in patterns which defied conventional rules of placement on the page. Though his forms were nontraditional, cummings's poems treated the familiar themes of childhood dreams, love, nature, and other universal subjects for poetry. His collected poems can be found in *Poems 1905–1962* (1973).

ABELARDO B. DELGADO (b. 1931) is known as the "poet laureate of Aztlan" (Mexican America). He was born in Mexico but came to live and work in Texas in 1943. There he published volumes of poetry as well as studies of barrio living, migrant workers' children, and the Chicano farmworker. Delgado has been director of the Special Services Program at the University of Texas at El Paso and has worked as a community organizer. Among his books are *The Chicano Movement: Some Not Too Objective Observations* (1971) and a collection, *Chicano: 25 Pieces of a Chicano Mind* (1971). A spoken record, *Abelardo: Philosopher, Poet* (1970), is available. Delgado's latest poems are in *Letters to Louise* (1979) and *La Llorona: an Epic Poem* (1980).

JULIA DE BURGOS (1914–1953) grew up in rural Puerto Rico and became a journalist and teacher. Her *Poema en viento surcos* (Poem in Twenty Furrows) was published in 1938, her *Obra Poetica* (Collected Works) in 1961. She calls the poem selected for this anthology by her own name, addressing herself, "Julia de Burgos," and showing her identification with oppressed people everywhere. Leonard Bernstein set this poem to music in his Bicentennial-commissioned choral work *American Songfest* (1976). In her lifetime, Julia de Burgos was rebellious and radical, alienating conventional local poets, critics, and politicians. She writes about working people in her native island and about its mountains and rivers. She suffered extreme poverty and died of alcoholism in New York City. Her works are available only in Spanish, except for an occasional translation in an anthology such as *The Other Voice: Twentieth-Century Women's Poetry in Translation* (1976).

EMILY DICKINSON (1830–1886) is famous for her reclusive life and her extraordinary poetic output, though she published only a few poems in her lifetime. She was the well-educated daughter of a lawyer/politician, and her life in Amherst, Massachusetts, was by no means as isolated as legend would have it. In 1862 Dickinson approached the well-known editor and writer Thomas Wentworth Higginson with a few poems. They were so different, so modern, so passionate and innovative, that Higginson discouraged their publication, though he kept up a friendship and correspondence with her for the rest of her life. After her death, 1,775 poems were found among her papers, sewed into little booklets. Her brother's mistress, Mabel Loomis Todd, along with Higginson, edited some of her poems, though punctuation, spelling, and even word choice were heavily amended. In 1955 Harvard University became owner of the manuscripts, and Thomas H. Johnson edited the definitive three-volume edition, followed by the *Letters* in 1958. The Johnson edition of the poems is available in a one-volume version.

PIETRO DI DONATO (b. 1911), like his protagonist in the selection from *Christ in Concrete* (1937), is the son of a bricklayer and has worked at that trade

himself. He was born in West Hoboken, New Jersey, amid Italian immigrant workers in the building trades. *Christ in Concrete* won critical praise for its strong portraits of Italian construction workers and their families. The sequel to the novel, *Three Circles of Light* (1960), was not as kindly received by critics, who considered it sentimental and trite. Di Donato won the Overseas Press Club Award in 1978 for his story in *Penthouse* on Aldo Moro, a murdered Italian statesman. He has also written several plays and biographies, among them *The Life of Mother Cabrini* (1960), as well as a collection of short stories, *Naked as an Author* (1971).

JOHN DONNE (1572–1631) was a man of his age and of the violent contrasts it presented. Although raised a Roman Catholic, Donne was later ordained in the Church of England and for the last ten years of his life was Dean of St. Paul's Cathedral in London. As a young man he went to Oxford, studied law, wrote intricate love poems, and had a reputation as a womanizer. Eventually, he imprudently eloped with his employer's niece; for this he was dismissed from his position and briefly imprisoned. With his wife, Anne, he spent years of poverty depending on wealthy patrons and friends to help raise his twelve children. Eventually Donne was sent on diplomatic missions to Europe. He continued to write poetry for his friends, but it was not published until after his death. As a widower in poor health, Donne was given the deanship of St. Paul's, a position that inspired sermons, meditations, and religious poems—most notably, his "Holy Sonnets"—which were well known in his lifetime. It was not until the 1920s and 1930s, however, that people began fully to appreciate Donne's passionate early poetry. Later critics called his poems "metaphysical" because they employ images and metaphors from nature and the new sciences of navigation, geography, and medicine. A useful biography of Donne is *Grace for a Witty Sinner* by Edward Le Comte (1965). Helen Gardner has edited a collection of critical essays, *John Donne* (1965). She has also re-edited the *Divine Poems* (1952) and the *Elegies and the Songs and Sonnets* (1965). A popular edition of Donne's poems is *A Complete Poetry and Selected Prose* (1929), edited by John Hayward.

PAUL LAURENCE DUNBAR (1872–1906) was the most acclaimed black poet of his time. He was born in Dayton, Ohio, the son of a former slave who had fought for the North during the Civil War. Dunbar did well in high school, but after graduation he merely became an elevator operator. Then he began writing poetry and entered a charmed literary career. In 1893, Frederick Douglass invited him to read his poetry at "Negro Day" at the Chicago World's Fair. After Dunbar published two books of poetry, *Oak and Ivy* and *Majors and Minors,* William Dean Howells of *Harper's* encouraged him to do a third collection of poetry, choosing the best poems of the first two collections. This book, *Lyrics of Lowly Life,* came out in 1896 to national acclaim. Dunbar wrote in black dialect and filled his poems with images from the lives of rural southern blacks as well as the black migrant to the city. His poem "We Wear the Mask" is an eloquent statement of the plight of black people living in a white world. When Dunbar died, Booker T. Washington honored him with the title "Poet Laureate of the Negro Race." In all, Dunbar produced six collections of poetry, four novels, and four collections of short stories. A recent edition of his poems is *The Complete Poems of Paul Laurence Dunbar* (1980).

BENJAMIN DURAZO (1951–1971) lived a short life in the San Joaquin Valley of California. He worked there, as he said, having "a hand in making the San Joaquin Valley for its owners." He went on to say, however, that he hoped to "die making the San Joaquin Valley for its workers." Though Durazo's career was short and his poetic output small, he used his poems to make vivid the lives of the fruit-pickers and itinerant workers he intimately knew. This serves as a reminder that one does not have to be famous or even a practicing poet to write a poem worth a reader's time. All of us, even a young grapefruit picker from Madera, have at least one good poem in us.

T. S. ELIOT (1888–1965) was a poet, critic, and powerful literary presence between the first and second world wars. Born in St. Louis, Missouri, but educated in Boston, Eliot studied literature and philosophy at Harvard and edited *The Harvard Advocate.* He went abroad to study and remained in London to become teacher, writer, and banker. In 1917, Eliot published his first book of poems, *Prufrock and Other Observations.* He edited the *Egoist,* founded *The Criterion,* and became a partner in Faber and Faber, an important British publishing house. In 1922 he published *The Waste Land,* a masterpiece that became a model for the modernist poets. Eliot emphasized themes of separateness, isolation, and alienation. He filled his poems with learned allusions. Eliot married a British woman in 1926, became a British citizen in 1927, and later converted to Anglicanism. Poetry such as "Ash Wednesday" (1930) and *Four Quartets* (1936–1943) reflected his spiritual quest. Later in life he occupied himself primarily with verse drama: *Murder in the Cathedral* (1935), *The Family Reunion* (1939), *The Cocktail Party* (1950), *The Confidential Clerk* (1954), and *The Elder Stateman* (1959). In 1948 Eliot received both the Nobel Prize for Literature and the British Order of Merit. His *Complete Poems and Plays, 1909–1950* was published in 1971; *The Waste Land and Other Poems* (1972) is a useful edition. A testimony to Eliot's genteel humor is *Old Possom's Book of Practical Cats* (1939), which inspired the recent musical *Cats.*

WILLIAM FAULKNER (1897–1962) was born near Oxford, Mississippi, to the once aristocratic Falkner family. Although Faulkner was to travel widely in Europe and America, Oxford, Mississippi, remained his home. In his fiction Faulkner created a mythical county, Yoknapatawpha, though his plots, themes, and characters are largely Oxford born. Through his hometown, he portrayed the decaying world of the old South beset by the corrupt materialism of the new. Hinting at his own themes, Faulkner stated, in his Nobel Prize acceptance speech, "the problems of the human heart in conflict with itself . . . alone can make good writing because only that is worth writing about, worth the agony and the sweat." Faulkner's literary production began shortly after 1920 with the publication of his poems in *The Double Dealer* and the *New Orleans Times Picayune.* Although he frequently had to supplement his income with script writing and advising for Warner Brothers, he eventually achieved literary success and was awarded the Nobel Prize in 1950. Among his better known novels are *Soldier's Pay* (1926), *The Sound and the Fury* (1929), *As I Lay Dying* (1930), *Light in August* (1932), *Absalom, Absalom!* (1936), *The Hamlet* (1940), *Intruder in the Dust* (1948), *A Fable* (1954), *The Town* (1957), *The Mansion* (1959), and *The Reivers* (1962).

LAWRENCE FERLINGHETTI (b. 1919) runs the City Lights Bookstore in

San Francisco, holds a doctorate from the Sorbonne, and is a gifted painter and poet. Over the years City Lights has published books of importance such as Allen Ginsberg's *Howl* (1956). Ferlinghetti's arrest on obscenity charges for publishing this book, and his subsequent acquittal, drew attention to the Beat poets of the 1950s. His own poetry owes much of its popularity to his common touch. Language and content grow from Ferlinghetti's responses to everyday life; he translates simple images into strong poetic form. Ferlinghetti also intends his poetry to be read aloud. He has complained, "The printing press has made poetry so silent that we've forgotten the power of poetry as oral message." Ferlinghetti has tried his hand at several literary forms, including a novel, *Her* (1960); several books of poems, including *A Coney Island of the Mind* (1958), *Starting from San Francisco* (1961), and *Endless Life: Selected Poems* (1981); volumes of plays such as *Unfair Arguments with Existence: Seven Plays for a New Theatre* (1963), and *Routines* (1964); and *Literary San Francisco: A Pictorial History from Its Beginnings to the Present Day* (1980).

EDWARD FIELD (b. 1924) is a native New Yorker who was born in Brook-

lyn and attended New York University. He served in the Army Air Force during World War II. Field did not emerge as a serious practicing poet until the early 1960s, and his poetic output has come in spurts. He received the Lamont Poetry Selection Award in 1962 and a Guggenheim Fellowship in 1963. His first book of poems, *Stand Up, Friend, With Me,* appeared in that year. Field has a straightforward style grounded in themes of companionship, love, sexuality, and affection. Because of this, he has sometimes been called a Jewish Walt Whitman. His second collection, *Variety Photoplays,* did not appear until 1967 and contained poems inspired by themes of old movies. Almost a decade passed before Field received any further public notice. In 1975 he won the Shelly Memorial Award for *Sweet Gwendolyn and the Countess,* which was followed by two more books of poems, *A Full*

Heart (1977) and *Stars in My Eyes* (1978), as well as *A Geography of Poets: An Anthology of the New Poetry* (1979).

MARY E. WILKINS FREEMAN(1852–1930), born Mary Eleanor Wilkins in Massachusetts, moved to Vermont, where she graduated from high school. As family members died and left her independent, she became well known as a writer of stories for both children and adults. Her early work drew on the local-color tradition of turn-of-the-century realism, but as her career developed she anticipated many of the themes of the modern novel. She created characters like Louisa of "A New England Nun" who were hard-backed, neurotic survivors of the nation's march towards progress. At the age of forty-nine Freeman married and went to live in Metuchen, New Jersey. Her life was comfortable, although her marriage became less than happy because of her husband's alcoholism. In spite of this trouble and her increasing deafness, she continued to write and receive honors and awards. Throughout her career, her stories were published in magazines and collected into volumes like *A Humble Romance* (1887, 1972) and *A New England Nun* (1891, 1980). She also wrote novels—among them *Pembroke* (1894, 1976) and *Jerome, a Poor Man* (1897)—and a volume of ghost stories, *The Wind in the Rose Bush* (1903, 1972). Freeman treated setting and conflict in a poetic and sensitive manner, and she remains a popular author today. In addition to many reprints of her stories and novels, collected editions like *Selected Stories of Mary E. Wilkins Freeman* (1983) make her available to a wide public.

ROBERT FROST(1874–1963), whose name is almost as famous as New England, was actually born in San Francisco. His father was a newspaperman in California, but his parents' troubled relationship prompted his mother to take him to New England several times before his father's death in 1885. After he and his mother moved back to New England permanently, Frost attended Dartmouth and Harvard but was not interested in formal education. From 1899 to 1911 he was farmer, poet, and teacher in New Hampshire. He received no real poetic notice, however, until he went to England. There, with Ezra Pound's help, he published his first book, *A Boy's Will*, in 1913 and a second, *North of Boston*, in 1915. Frost is best known, perhaps, as the homespun Yankee poet, but the rustic speech of his poetry belies the complex emotions found there. The anguish of his own personal tragedies (the deaths of his wife and three children; his daughter's mental illness) filters through into his poetry. Dubbed the unofficial poet laureate of America by President John F. Kennedy, Robert Frost reached great heights within his craft, making his poetry well known among people who often know no other poet's name. Frost's complete poems can be found in *The Poetry of Robert Frost: The Collected Poems, Complete and Unabridged* (1975). A useful critical appraisal of the poet is *The Road Not Taken: An Introduction to Robert Frost* (1971).

ERNEST J. GAINES (b. 1933) was born in the rural Louisiana that would serve as the setting for most of his fiction. Gaines broke away from his poverty, studying at San Francisco State College and at Stanford, and living and writing in San Francisco. His themes center around breaking away from the past, where the black man, as he says, was pushed into "a position where he is not supposed to be a man." Gaines's style is skillful and artistic, relating the culture of rural blacks with deep humanistic insight. A novel, *Catherine Carmier* (1964, 1981), tells the story of a young man who returns to the South from study in the North and finds he cannot adjust. The work that brought him fame was *The Autobiography of Miss Jane Pittman* (1971), the fictional story of a black woman born in slavery whose perspective on events after the Civil War is told with candor and compassion. *Of Love and Dust* (1967, 1979), *A Long Day in November* (1973), *In My Father's House* (1978), and *Gathering of Old Men* (1983) are among his other works.

CHARLOTTE PERKINS GILMAN (1860–1935) was called "the leading intellectual in the women's movement in the United States" in her time. Gilman authored several important books, among them *Women and Economics* (1898), and edited a magazine, *The Forerunner,* most of whose items she wrote herself. The story she wrote that comes closest to her own dynamic yet troubled life is "The Yellow Wallpaper" (1892). Gilman suffered deep anguish when she questioned conventional roles and fought against attempts to repress her own talent. She tried marriage and motherhood, but the birth of a daughter triggered a breakdown. The leading psychologist for "women's disorders" advised complete rest and no intellectual effort. This regimen nearly pushed her over the brink into insanity. Finally, Gilman separated from her husband and then sent her daughter to be brought up by her husband and his new wife, her best friend. She later married a cousin, happily, and lived a long, productive life as writer and lecturer, involved in West Coast social and political movements. Her career closed when, suffering from inoperable cancer, she took her own life. Some of Gilman's fiction, including "The Yellow Wallpaper," is collected in *The Charlotte Perkins Gilman Reader* (1983). Her autobiography, *The Living of Charlotte Perkins Gilman* (1935), gives a history of the work she did in advocating streamlined and scientific housekeeping, kitchenless homes, day care centers ("baby gardens"), and economic independence for both men and women.

NIKKI GIOVANNI (b. 1943), one of the most popular of today's poets, was a witness in her poetry and prose to the crises of the sixties and the problems of her generation. She was born in Tennessee and raised in Ohio, and received a B.A. in history from Fisk University in 1967. At Fisk she studied writing with John Killens and edited the campus literary magazine. Following graduate work at the University of Pennsylvania, Giovanni returned to Cincinnati, where she established the first Cincinnati Black Festival and the New Theatre. Her earliest poems dealt with black awareness and the need for revolutionary change. Her later verse brings forth more private feelings, the struggle of the individual to relations to others. Today Nikki Giovanni lives in New York and teaches at Livingston College of Rutgers University. She reads her poetry at college campuses throughout the country. Her *Gemini: An Extended Autobiographical Statement on My First Twenty-five Years of Being a Black Poet* (1973, 1980) is just that: poems, sketches, prose essays, all on the theme of self-awareness as a black poet. In addition she has written *Re:Creation* (1970, available as a spoken recording) and compiled *Night Comes Softly: An Anthology of Black Female Voices* (1970). Other volumes of verse are *Cotton Candy on a Rainy Day: Poems* (1980) and *My House: Poems* (1980). *Vacation Time* (1980) and *Spin a Soft Black Song* (1985) are both subtitled "Poems for Children."

RODOLFO GONZALES(b. 1928) is an important contemporary Chicano
writer who uses his work to illustrate the social injustices that keep the Chicano American from sharing the American dream. He is well known nationally as a Chicano activist and for founding the Crusade for Justice in Denver, Colorado. Many of his poems stem from his experiences as teacher and director of a cultural center there. *I Am Joaquín: an epic poem with a chronology of people and events in Mexican and Mexican American History* was published in 1972. A film by that title, *I Am Joaquín,* appeared in 1969.

SUSAN GRIFFIN(b. 1943) describes herself as a radical and a feminist. She
was educated at the University of California at Berkeley and at San Francisco State University, and has worked as waitress, telephone operator, drama teacher, editor *(Ramparts),* and as a teacher in the program Poetry in the Schools. She has received many awards for poetry and a National Endowment for the Arts grant in 1976. Griffin's generation came of age during the McCarthy era, the hippie movement, the civil rights movement, the Vietnam War, and the women's movement, and she has participated in her times through her writing. She is both philosopher and poet, writing about women's experience—her own and that of others—in a style that shows growing consciousness and insight. Her work is represented in many anthologies as well as in her own volumes of poetry and essays: *Dear Sky* (1971), *Le Viol* (1972), *Let Them Be Said* (1973), *Letters* (1973), *The Sink* (1973), *Voices* (a play in poetry, 1974), *Like the Iris of an Eye* (1976), *Woman and Nature: The Roaring Inside Her* (1978), and *Rape: The Power of Consciousness* (1979), *Pornography and Silence* (1981), *Made from This Earth: An Anthology of Writings* (1982), and *Pornography and Silence: Culture's Revenge Against Nature* (1982).

NATHANIEL HAWTHORNE(1804–1864) was an important Romantic
writer of the American literary renaissance of the early nineteenth century. Haw-

thorne's works were influenced by his Puritan heritage and by feelings of guilt for his ancestors' part in condemning witches in the seventeenth-century Salem witch trials. A handsome, personable man, he lived, after attending Bowdoin College in Maine, as a recluse in his mother's house in Salem, collecting material and reading avidly. He emerged from this voluntary seclusion when he married the brilliant Sophia Peabody, a member of an intellectual Boston family. They settled in the "Old Manse" in the literary town of Concord. Hawthorne went to work to support his family, first in the Boston Custom House, then as Surveyor of the Port of Salem. It was there that he garnered material and inspiration for his most famous novel, *The Scarlet Letter* (1850). Other stories and sketches appeared in *Twice Told Tales* (1837) and *Mosses from an Old Manse* (1846). *The Blithedale Romance* (1852) was a novel about the Brook Farm communal living experiment; the history of Salem reappeared in *The House of the Seven Gables* (1851). Hawthorne's novels and tales have been reprinted in the *Library of America* (1983) and in *The Portable Hawthorne* (1983). Critical essays appear in Harry Levin, *The Power of Blackness: Hawthorne, Poe, Melville* (1950) and F. O. Matthiessen, *American Renaissance* (1941).

LILLIAN HELLMAN(1906–1984), considered by many critics to be the best recent American playwright, had a long and distinguished career as author, teacher, and critic. An exponent of liberal causes, she, like her long-time companion Dashiell Hammett, was blackballed during the McCarthy era in the 1950s. She was a chronicler of her time, often cruel and cutting, but clear-eyed. Among the awards Hellman won for her plays and screenplays was The New York Drama Critics Circle Award in 1941 for *Watch on the Rhine* and again in 1960 for *Toys in the Attic*. A screen adaptation in 1941 of her play *The Little Foxes* won her an Academy Award nomination. A Broadway revival of this play in 1981 starred Elizabeth Taylor. Other Hellman plays were *The Children's Hour* (1934, her first success), and *Another Part of the Forest* (1947). She adapted Jean Anouilh's drama about Joan of Arc, *The Lark,* for the American stage in 1955, and Voltaire's *Candide* in 1957, with music by Leonard Bernstein. *Pentimento: A Book of Portraits* (1974) is essentially a memoir—a personal history of an era by a participant, semiautobiographical rather than fictional. An earlier volume of memoirs, *An Unfinished Woman* (1969), is more directly personal. Her last books were *Maybe: A Story* (1980) and *Eating Together: Recipes and Recollections* (1980). She also edited *The Dashiell Hammett Story Omnibus* in 1983.

ERNEST HEMINGWAY(1898–1961) was noted for his spare writing style and his depiction of a code of manly behavior for troubled times. His father, a prosperous physician in Oak Park, Illinois, introduced him to this manly ethic, taking him on hunting and fishing trips in the upper peninsula of Michigan, the setting for some of his short stories. After graduating from high school, Hemingway worked as a reporter for the *Kansas City Star.* Poor eyesight prevented him from joining the Army during World War I, so he volunteered as an ambulance driver on the Italian front. Wounded, hospitalized, and decorated for valor, Hemingway drew valuable material from this experience for his fiction. After the war, Hemingway went to Paris, where he met Gertrude Stein, T. S. Eliot, Ezra Pound, and James Joyce. While there, he published his first book, *Three Stories and Ten Poems* (1923). A collection of short stories and sketches titled *In Our Time* followed in 1925. After the publication of *The Sun Also Rises* (1926), Gertrude Stein called him the spokesman for a lost generation. Hemingway's coverage of the Spanish Civil War in 1927 reemerged as *For Whom the Bell Tolls* in 1940. Other notable Hemingway works are *A Farewell to Arms* (1929), *Death in the Afternoon* (1932), *Green Hills of Africa* (1935), *To Have and Have Not* (1937), *Across the River and into the Trees* (1950), and *The Old Man and the Sea* (1952).

GEORGE HERBERT (1593–1633) came of a noble family and after a short period of aspiration to public office became an Anglican rector. His mother, Magdalen Herbert, was friend and patroness to John Donne, whose poetry and career inspired Herbert. A brilliant scholar, Herbert took great pains with his poetry. His health was never good, and he died young, still troubled as to his choice of a religious career. Just before his death, he sent the manuscript of his most famous collection, *The Temple,* to his publisher, with instructions to print it or burn it, whichever seemed best. Luckily, his publisher printed the work just after Herbert's death. He is one of the finest of the seventeenth-century religious poets, particularly known for the craftsmanship of his short poems, many of them shaped verse.

ROBERT HERRICK (1591–1674) is perhaps the most cavalier of the Cavalier poets. His life, however, was more sedate, since for much of it he was a parish priest at Dean Prior, Devonshire. Herrick was born in London, but after the death of his goldsmith father, he was raised in the country. In 1617, he finished his studies at Cambridge and, falling under the spell of Ben Jonson, began writing lyrical poems that sang the praises of pagan joys. His line "Gather ye rosebuds while ye may" is one of the most famous lines in English poetry and almost defines the *carpe diem* or "seize the day" tradition so celebrated by Jonson and his followers. Eventually, the priest in Herrick brought some of these wild and joyful poetic impulses under control. His subject matter changed from women's beauty and the joy of drinking to the praise of the simple joys of country life. Herrick was not a political man, but when the Puritans deposed King Charles I, he lost his post at Dean Prior. The restoration of Charles II, however, in 1660, took him back to his country parish where he quietly lived out his service and died at age eighty-three. A sampling of Herrick's poetry appears in *Selected Poems* (1980).

GERARD MANLEY HOPKINS (1844–1889), was converted to Roman Catholicism while a student at Oxford, under the influence of John Henry Newman. Hopkins then taught at Newman's Oratory School and in 1868 became a novice of the Society of Jesus. Ordained as a Jesuit in 1877, he taught at Stonyhurst and then became Professor of Greek at Dublin University, a post he held until his death at forty-five from typhoid fever. During his lifetime his poetry was read in manuscript by his friends. One of them, the poet Robert Bridges, collected and published Hopkins's *Poems* in 1918, long after Hopkins's death. Since that time, many editions of his notebooks, correspondence, journals, papers, and poems have appeared, as his fame as a completely "new" poet has increased. Hopkins's language, rhythms, and concepts were odd and passionate, giving his poetry a modern flavor. His grammatical inventions and his "sprung rhythm" make his poetry unique. These rhythms return to patterns in Anglo-Saxon verse, with varied unstressed beats, rather than the steady beat of the iambic. Since Hopkins considered his religious calling a higher one than his art, he abstained from writing when so ordered by his superiors, and destroyed many of his early poems. Peter Milward has written an appraisal of Hopkins, *Landscape and Inscape: Vision and Inspiration in Hopkins' Poetry* (1975). The poetry is available in *Gerard Manley Hopkins: Poetry and Prose* (1976) and *The Major Poems* (1979).

A. E. HOUSMAN (1859–1936) wrote lyrical poems celebrating youth and its quickly fading bloom. Oxford educated, Housman eventually became a professor of Latin, first at University College, London, and then at Cambridge. There he spent the rest of his life quietly, editing the Roman writers and publishing a small volume of poems from time to time. His first collection, *A Shropshire Lad* (1896), made him famous, but he did not publish another book until *Last Poems* in 1922. After his death two more volumes appeared, *More Poems* in 1936 and *Collected Poems* in 1939. Housman's poems, usually in ballad meter, were brief and pessimistic, hinting at tragic loves and urging youth to live and love today, for tomorrow may bring sorrow. Though narrow in scope and small in quantity, Housman's poems remain an expression of lost youth in an earlier, more idyllic age. Recent Housman collections are *The Collected Poems of A. E. Housman* (1971) and *Selected Prose* (1980).

LANGSTON HUGHES(1902–1967), a poet, novelist, satirist, and playwright, was born in Joplin, Mississippi, but as a young man lived and worked in Kansas, Colorado, and Mexico. Hughes attended Columbia College in New York and Lincoln University in Pennsylvania. He was poet, seaman, cook, and busboy until he caught the attention of poet Vachel Lindsay in 1925 in a Washington, D.C., hotel. Hughes's success began with the publication of his first two books of poems, *The Weary Blues* (1926) and *Fine Clothes to the Jew* (1927). After that he wrote at least seven volumes of blues, ballads, and lyrics, as well as opera libretti, songs, novels, short stories, and satire. He drew on his black heritage, interweaving Gospel rhythms, jazz, and blues and building on the folk sources of his people. Much of his work narrated the sufferings of the Negro. His sketches of Jesse B.

Simple, collected in three volumes in 1950, 1961, and 1965, created one of America's classic characters. He also wrote two autobiographies, *The Big Sea* (1940) and *I Wonder As I Wander* (1965). Some of his poetry is collected in *Selected Poems of Langston Hughes* (1981). His connection with another important black writer, Arna Bontemps, is recorded in *Arna Bontemps–Langston Hughes Letters, 1925–1967* (1980).

HENRIK IBSEN(1828–1906) was a Norwegian who became the most influential playwright of the modern theater. In his early years, he studied pharmacy at Gelo University but abandoned that vocation to become director of the Oslo Theatre. He wrote his first play in 1850. Public response to his modern, realistic plays was indifferent, and financial troubles led to his moving to the Continent, where he spent twenty-seven years, mostly in Rome, Dresden, and Munich. While in exile, he achieved recognition with *Brand* (1866) and *Peer Gynt* (1867). His most influential plays, *A Doll's House* (1879) and *Ghosts* (1881), deal with realistic subjects—women's rights and venereal disease. These were followed by *An Enemy of the People* (1882), *Hedda Gabler* (1890), and *The Master Builder* (1892). Ibsen attacked conventional beliefs, and although some of his causes are now outmoded, his critical observations, coupled with masterful playwriting, made his a drama of ideas for all times. *Ibsen,* a biography by Michael Meyer (1971), contains letters, photographs, and discussions of Ibsen's plays and life. A useful edition of his work is *Eight Plays,* a 1982 Modern Library collection translated by Eva LaGallienne.

DAVID IGNATOW(b. 1914) is a contemporary poet whose readings, recordings, and videotapes have brought poetry to millions. The son of Russian immigrant parents, he began his career in New York City during the worst years of the Depression when his future looked bleak. He lasted only a half semester at Brooklyn College and then worked in his father's shop as a pamphlet binder and became a reporter on a WPA newspaper project. His short story "I Can't Stop It" was selected by Edward J. O'Brien for the Honor List in his *Best American Short Stories* annual in 1931. Ignatow's writing seems to reflect his own experiences. He writes about a range of themes of common people: marriage, sex, adolescence. His major collections of poetry are *Poems* (1948), *The Gentle Weight Lifter* (1955), *Say Pardon* (1961), *Figures of the Human* (1964), *Rescue the Dead* (1968), *Facing the Tree* (1978), *Sunlight: A Sequence for My Daughter* (1979), and *Whisper to the Earth* (1981). *David Ignatow: Selected Poems* (1975) gathers his earlier poems.

WASHINGTON IRVING (1783–1859) was the first American to make a living writing fiction. Named for George Washington, he was the last of eleven children of a wealthy New York merchant. As a young man, he lived in New York, studied law, and read Romantic writers like Sir Walter Scott. Irving popularized

history and legend by retelling tales in his own suspenseful style. "Rip Van Winkle" and "The Legend of Sleepy Hollow" are two examples of how effectively Irving could rework historical legend. His travels—following the death of his fiancée —led him to England, France, and Spain, where he stayed seventeen years, writing and serving as a diplomat. After fictionalizing the romantic figures of Moorish Spain, Irving returned home to America, with his reputation established, to write about America and its frontier. Some of Irving's books are *Knickerbocker's History of New York* (1809); *The Sketch Book* (1819–20), from which "Rip Van Winkle" is taken; *The Life and Voyages of Christopher Columbus* (1828); *A Chronicle of the Conquest of Granada* (1829); *The Alhambra* (1832); *A Tour on the Prairies* (1835); *Astoria* (1836); and *Life of Washington* (1855–59). Publication of a Twayne edition of Irving's *Complete Works* began in 1983.

JOSEPHINE JACOBSEN (b. 1908) served as Poetry Consultant to the Library of Congress from 1971 to 1973. Born in Canada, she has traveled widely and maintains an interest in the theater as well, acting with the Vagabond Players in Baltimore, where she now lives. Her poems have appeared in several volumes: *For the Unlost* (1946), *The Human Climate* (1953), *The Animal Inside* (1956), *The Shade-Seller: New and Selected Poems* (1974), and *The Chinese Insomniacs: New Poems* (1981). She has also written volumes of literary and dramatic criticism: *The Instant of Knowing* (1974) and *One Poet's Poetry* (1975). Jacobsen published a collection of short stories, *A Walk with Raschid, and Other Stories,* in 1978.

JUNE JORDAN (b. 1936) is a versatile writer of poetry, history, and novels. She was born in Harlem and studied at Barnard College and the University of Chicago. She has taught college English, worked as a research associate, and helped found and direct the Creative Writing Workshop for Children in Brooklyn. Her poems are usually short and tightly-knit, like haiku. Their themes are love, frustration, rage, and despair about the lost hopes of black people. Her many books of poetry began with *Some Changes* (1971) and continued with *Things That I Do in the Dark* (1977), *Passion: New Poems, 1977–1980* (1980), and most recently *Living Room: New Poems, 1980–1984* (1985). Her history of the Civil Rights movement, *Dry Victories* (1972), shows how the apparent victories of blacks in both Reconstruction and Civil Rights were not real ones.

JOHN KEATS (1795–1821) wrote some of the most memorable Romantic poetry of the early nineteenth century. Eldest son of a London stabler, Keats became a certified apothecary but never practiced that trade. At eighteen he began to write poetry instead. Encouraged by his poet friend Leigh Hunt, Keats matured rapidly as a poet. He wrote "On First Looking into Chapman's Homer" in 1816. In 1817 came "Endymion," a much criticized poem that Keats himself considered childish, and "Hyperion," a more polished and ambitious effort. By 1818 Keats began to experience personal problems. The conservative press attacked his poetry, and his family suffered one misfortune after another. Keats fell in love with Fanny Brawne, but ill health and poverty forbade marriage. By 1819, Keats was at his poetic height. In that year he wrote almost all of the poems for which he is famous: "The Eve of St. Agnes," "La Belle Dame sans Merci," a number of sonnets, and his six great odes. These Romantic poems, rich in imagery and rhythmic variations, lyrically express suffering and ecstasy. Two years later Keats died at age twenty-six in Rome, where he had gone in a vain search for restored health. All of Keats's poetry can be found in a Harvard University Press edition of his *Complete Poems* (1982) and in the Modern Library edition of *Complete Poems of Keats and Shelley* (1983).

MARTIN LUTHER KING, JR. (1929–1968) is a modern tragic hero who led the nonviolent civil rights movement of the 1960s. While a young minister in Montgomery, Alabama, Harvard-educated King became a leader in the bus boycott movement, which sparked the battle for civil rights. His charismatic personality inspired freedom rides and other nonviolent protests. It also prompted the violent reactions to his philosophy which eventually led to his assassination. King's literary style, in the famous "I Have a Dream" speech given at the Lincoln Memorial in Washington in 1963, combines the dynamic preaching qualities of the southern black preacher and the genuine voice of an epic poet. Lerone Bennett, Jr.'s *What Manner of Man: A Biography of Martin Luther King, Jr., 1929–1968,* King's own brief autobiography, *Why We Can't Wait* (1964), and Coretta Scott King's *My Life With Martin Luther King, Jr.* (1969) all give good, factual information about his life.

MAXINE HONG KINGSTON (b. 1940), born Chew Hong to a Chinese laundryman and a midwife, typifies the Oriental American brought up in the close atmosphere of a California Chinatown. This kind of immigrant experience—one that arises out of living in America yet remaining steeped in pre-revolutionary Chinese myth and legend—is recreated in *The Woman Warrior: Memoir of a Girlhood Among Ghosts* (1976) and *China Men* (1980). Kingston described her female ancestors in *The Woman Warrior* and her male ancestors in *China Men.* Both books create a new set of myths and phantoms from her past. *The Woman Warrior* won a National Book Critics Circle Award in 1976.

WILLIAM KOTZWINKLE (b. 1932) became famous when he was chosen to write the book for Stephen Spielberg's movie *E.T.: The Extraterrestrial* (1982). Kotzwinkle was born in Scranton, Pennsylvania, attended Rider College and the University of Pennsylvania, and won a scholarship to the Breadloaf Writers' Con-ference. *E.T.* is not Kotzwinkle's only claim to fame: he has written many books for children and some adult fiction as well. He has already written a sequel to *E.T.,* titled *E.T.: The Book of the Green Planet* (1985). In it, E.T., back home on his Green Planet, misses his earth-friend Elliot, who is now a teenager interested only in girls. Kotzwinkle's collection *Elephant Bangs Train* (1981) includes "Follow the Eagle," the story in this anthology. Among his other books are *Doctor Rat, The Great World Circus, The Leopard's Tooth,* and *Trouble in Bugland: A Collection of Inspector Mantis Mysteries,* all published in 1983; and *Seduction in Berlin* (1985).

MAXINE KUMIN (b. 1925) has taught at Tufts and Radcliffe, has been a scholar in the Radcliffe Institute for Independent Study, and has served as a visiting lecturer at the University of Massachusetts, Columbia, Brandeis, and Princeton. Among the many honors and awards this distinguished poet has received is her appointment as Poetry Consultant to the Library of Congress, 1981–82. Maxine Kumin believes that a poet must be "terribly specific about naming things." Her critics judge her Pulitzer Prize-winning poetry as doing just that. One says she "doesn't miss a speck. Her drive for detail and her compulsion to name recall Thoreau." Her volume of poetry *Up Country* (1972) won the Pulitzer Prize in 1973. Other volumes are *Halfway* (1961), *The Privilege* (1965), *The Nightmare Factory* (1970), *House, Bridge, Fountain, Gate* (1975), *The Retrieval System: Poems* (1978), and *Closing the Ring* (1984). Her novels are *Through Dreams of Love* (1965), *The Passions of Uxport* (1968), *The Abduction* (1971), and *The Designated Heir* (1974). She has also written many juvenile books, some of them with her friend and sister-poet Anne Sexton.

LOUISE LABÉ (1520–1566), an early French poet, has always been somewhat of a mystery. The small volume of her works that exists offers few clues to her life and loves. Neither the date of her birth nor the facts of her life are certain. The quality of her verse, with its rich classical references, suggests she had a fine education. Labé was born in Lyon to a well-to-do mercantile family, married a much older man, and held a salon in her home to which literary people went for intelligent conversation. Her book of sonnets, twenty-four of them, was published in 1555, at the time when Ronsard and DuBellay and other poets of the famous Pléiade were writing poems and critical essays in the language of the people. They influenced English poets like Spenser, Shakespeare, and Donne, who brought this new poetry to England. Labé's poetry develops its analysis of love by contrasts: passion and suffering, nature and solitude, sensual and spiritual ideals. Modern editions of Labé's poetry are *Sonnets* (English/French, 1972), *Love Elegies of the Renaissance: Marot, Louise Labé and Ronsard* (1979), and *Six Sonnets of Louise Labé* (1979).

D. H. LAWRENCE (1885–1930) was the son of a refined mother and a Nottinghamshire coal miner. Influenced by his mother, Lawrence became a teacher and a writer instead of a miner. His first book, *The White Peacock,* appeared in 1906. After his mother's death in 1910, Lawrence wrote *Sons and Lovers* (1912), an autobiographical novel detailing her influence. In 1912 he eloped with Frieda von Richthofen Weekley, sister of the famous "Red Baron" and wife of one of his professors at Nottingham University. The Lawrences had to leave the Cornish coast during World War I because of Frieda's German background. They began wandering in search of health for the tubercular Lawrence. Lawrence's books were often criticized and misunderstood because of their sexuality, though Yeats called *Women in Love* (1916) "a beautiful, enigmatic book." His theme of the opposite forces in life carried through to his poetry, which is less controversial than his fiction. Lawrence felt that modern society favored intellect over instinct; nature was defeated by the mechanical. Lawrence produced a number of other novels. Among them were *The Rainbow* (1915), *The Lost Girl* (1920), set in England and Italy; *Kangaroo* (1923), set in Australia; and *The Plumed Serpent* (1926), set in Mexico. The much talked-of *Lady Chatterley's Lover* (1928) became the subject of a famous suit defining pornography.

EMMA LAZARUS (1849–1887) was born in New York to a wealthy family of Sephardic Jews who had lived in America since the seventeenth century. She published her first volume of verse when she was seventeen and soon after met Ralph Waldo Emerson, whom she considered a mentor. Her second volume appeared in 1871 and a novel, *Alide: An Episode in Goethe's Life,* in 1874. In 1881–82 the assassination of Czar Alexander II of Russia set loose pogroms resulting in huge waves of immigration of Russian Jews to the United States. These events and the sweatshop conditions in New York inspired Emma Lazarus to passionate devotion to Judaism in her poems and prose. Her poem "The New Colossus" is a sonnet she wrote in 1883 for a literary auction to collect funds for the Statue of Liberty in New York Harbor. The poem was later inscribed on the base of the statue, which was the first sight to greet immigrants as they arrived in their new country on passenger steamships. *The Poems of Emma Lazarus* and *Songs of a Semite* were reprinted in 1970, and *Selections* from her poetry and prose in 1976.

URSULA K. LE GUIN (b. 1929) has contributed flair, style, and insight to one of the prime genres of contemporary writing—science fiction. Daughter of an anthropologist and a writer, she is married to a historian and lives in Portland, Oregon. She has received both the Hugo award and the National Book Award. The story "Nine Lives" has been collected with others in *The Wind's Twelve Quarters* (1975). In her essay "On Theme," Le Guin points to her main source for this story as *The Biological Time Bomb* by Gordon Rattray Taylor, which raises the issue of cloning. Le Guin is known for her novels, notably the Earthsea trilogy: *A Wizard of Earthsea* (1968), *The Tombs of Atuan* (1971), and *The Farthest Shore*

(1972); and also titles like *The Dispossessed* (1974), *The Lathe of Heaven* (1971), *The Left Hand of Darkness* (1969), *Rocannon's World* (1966), and *The Compass Rose* (1983). She is also a poet, bringing to her work the fantasy of her novels, discussions of important issues, insights into various cultures and beliefs, and a deep feeling of oneness with the land and its history.

JOHN LENNON (1940–1980) gained a kind of immortality in his short life through his music, his lifestyle, and his tragic assassination. Lennon was born in Liverpool, England, the son of a porter. He attended Liverpool College of Art, but his real love was music. He played with several groups—the Quarrymen, the Moondogs, and the Silver Beatles—before joining the Beatles in 1960. Lennon and Paul McCartney were the lyrical brains of the Beatles, writing and composing songs like "Hey Jude," "Magical Mystery Tour," and "Sgt. Pepper's Lonely Hearts Club Band." In 1970, the Beatles disbanded, and Lennon formed a musical and artistic partnership with his new wife, Yoko Ono. Lennon, perhaps more than any of the other Beatles, participated in the highs and lows of the counterculture: drugs, hallucinations, Asian philosophy. Eventually, these excesses took their toll on his creative output. By the time of his death, however, Lennon had come full circle to a peace and calm that had long eluded him. The range of Lennon's writings is diverse. He wrote a number of humorous accounts such as *In His Own Write* (1964); *A Spaniard in the Works* (1965), from which he adapted a one-act play titled *The Lennon Play* (1968); *My Mummy's Dead* (1971); and *A Canoe for Uncle Kila* (1976).

DORIS LESSING (b. 1919), born of British parents in Persia, has spent most of her life in England. Her extraordinary writing career spans most of the concerns of the twentieth century: racism, feminism, Marxism, madness and alienation, extrasensory perception, mysticism, and the future. Her observation of life as a young girl in South Africa and as a young woman in London led to an interest in politics and to the series of novels titled *Children of Violence: Martha Quest* (1952), *A Proper Marriage* (1954), *A Ripple from the Storm* (1958), *Landlocked* (1956), and *The Four-Gated City* (1969). These novels follow the protagonist, Martha Quest, from her youth in white-dominated South Africa to her adulthood in London. They explore the relationship between the individual and society. *The Golden Notebook* (1962), Lessing's most discussed novel, breaks with conventional form. It consists of four notebooks on four levels of consciousness of a woman writer who is attempting to break a writer's block. Even more feminist in tone are *Briefing for a Descent into Hell* (1971), *The Summer Before the Dark* (1973), and *Memoirs of a Survivor* (1974). Lessing's short stories have been collected in *Stories* (1978). In recent years Lessing has followed the mystic thread in all of her works to its logical conclusion, science fiction, in *The Canopus in Argos Archives* (1979–82).

DENISE LEVERTOV(b. 1923) was born in England and educated at home. She was already a published poet when she married American writer Mitchell Goodman in 1947 and moved to the United States. Influenced by American poets such as Wallace Stevens, Ezra Pound, and William Carlos Williams, Levertov gradually shook free of the more traditional forms of English poetry. She draws on a broad range of themes and imagery, emphasizing the world around her in her poetry. She is a radical in politics and feels that poetry should serve as a voice for her political beliefs. Her first book of poems, *The Double Image,* written while she was still in England, was based on her experience of working in London hospitals during the Second World War. Her second volume, *Here and Now,* was published in 1957. Her latest volumes are *Relearning the Alphabet* (1970), *To Stay Alive* (1971), *Footprints* (1972), and *The Freeing of the Dust* (1973). She has also published *The Jacob's Ladder* and been poetry editor of *The Nation.* Her criticism is collected in *In Her Own Province* (1979) and her poems in *Collected Earlier Poems, 1940–1960* (1979) and *Poems, 1960–1967* (1983).

VACHEL LINDSAY (1879–1931) found the inspiration for his poetry in American life; he absorbed that life by tramping across the country, giving poetry readings in a style once described as "high vaudeville." Lindsay grew up in Illinois where his parents wanted him to become a minister. He studied at Hiram College but left after two years to study art in Chicago and New York. His poem "General William Booth Enters into Heaven" was first published in Harriet Monroe's *Poetry* magazine. That poem was contained in his first book, *General William Booth Enters into Heaven and Other Poems* (1913) and announced his arrival as a new poet with popular distinctive rhythms that returned to the oral tradition. *The Congo and Other Poems* was published in 1914, followed by *The Chinese Nightingale and Other Poems* in 1917. With these poems he had apparently reached his heights. He attempted to support himself by poetry readings and royalties from his books, but his audiences dwindled and his later books were not popular. He committed suicide in 1931. His *Letters* have been collected (1978); *The Poetry of Vachel Lindsay: Complete and with Lindsay's Drawings* was published in 1984, helping toward a reevaluation of the contribution he made to poetry and its popularization in the early years of this century.

AMY LOWELL(1874–1925), American poet, critic, and biographer, is most associated with Imagism, a poetic movement of the early years of this century based on free form and the language of common speech. In her book *Tendencies in Modern American Poetry* (1917, 1971), Lowell discussed the main principles of Imagism: to avoid clichés, to create new rhythms, to allow freedom in choosing subjects, to present clear, concentrated images—in short, to suggest, rather than to make complete statements. In her ten volumes of poetry as well as in her lectures, Amy Lowell spoke as a distinguished American poet and as a fearless innovator in poetic style. Lowell came from an old New England family that included poets, statesmen, wealthy businessmen, and scholars. She lived all her life on the family estate, Sevenels, in Brookline, Massachusetts. Her life-style combined staidness and eccentricity. She was hugely stout, and smoked cigars; Ada Russell, an attractive and warm-hearted actress, was her lifelong companion. Lowell also became friends with such writers as D. H. Lawrence, Edna St. Vincent Millay, Robert Frost, e. e. cummings, and Henry James. Lowell's poems contain many images of gardens and flowers, sensuous images of women's bodies, and unexpectedly shocking endings. Her poetry is available in *Selected Poems of Amy Lowell* (1927, 1971) and *Collected Poetical Works* (1955).

ANNE MCCAFFREY (b. 1926) is a particularly lively example of that phenomenon of modern times, the genuinely creative yet wildly popular author. She was born in Massachusetts, studied singing, married, and had three children, all before starting a writing career. McCaffrey's latest work, *Moreta: Dragonlady of Pern,* approaches best-seller status, and her other books have earned enough royalties for her to buy a horse farm in Ireland, where she lives and writes. The series of "Pern" books that have brought her fame ("The Dragonriders of Pern" trilogy and an assortment of other stories) have hit a happy formula somewhere between pure fantasy and pure science fiction. Her work develops infinite plots and colorful combatants, such as the many-colored dragons, who live in empathy with their human riders.

NORMAN MACCAIG (b. 1910), a Scot, was born in Edinburgh. He likes fishing in the Highlands, music, and languages. He has been a teacher at the Universities of Stirling and Edinburgh and is a fellow of the Royal Society of Literature. His poems and articles have appeared in many journals, and he has edited several volumes of Scottish poetry, reflecting his interest in the inhabitants, human and animal, of the Highlands. In addition, his own poetry has been widely published to much acclaim. He is one of three poets featured in volume 1 of *The Penguin Modern Poets* (1972). Recent volumes of his poems are *The World's Room* (1974), *Trees of Strings* (1977), *Old Maps and New: Selected Poems* (1978), *The Equal Skies* (1980), and *A World of Difference* (1983).

PAUL MCCARTNEY (b. 1942) does not need an introduction; nor does the group he helped make famous—the Beatles. McCartney was born in Liverpool, England. His musical career began early, in Liverpool groups such as the Quarrymen, the Moondogs, and the Silver Beatles. Finally, fame came upon him when he joined Ringo Starr, John Lennon, and George Harrison to form the Beatles in 1962. For eight years, Paul and John were the major song writers for the Beatles. Their songs became touchstones for millions of people, old and young. The Beatles sang of love and happiness, drugs and war. They spoke for a generation. In 1965, the Beatles received the Decorated Order of the British Empire. The group disbanded in 1970, and Paul McCartney formed Wings with his wife Linda Eastman. McCartney won an Academy Award for best original song score with "Let It Be" in 1970, as well as five Grammy Awards with the Beatles. Since the Beatles disbanded, he has won two Grammy Awards by himself, and one with Wings.

CARSON MCCULLERS(1917–1967), born in Columbus, Georgia, wanted to be a musician and attended the Juilliard School of Music until lack of finances ended her studies. She then worked at odd jobs during the day and attended writing seminars at Columbia University at night. Her short story "Wunderkind" was published in *Story Magazine* while she was still a student. She became involved with Brooklyn artists and writers such as Christopher Isherwood, Richard Wright, Benjamin Britten, and Gypsy Rose Lee. In 1939 she married a man named Reeves McCullers, whom she later divorced and remarried. Her husband lapsed into alcoholism and drug addiction and commited suicide in 1953. McCullers herself suffered an attack of rheumatic fever in 1936 as well as several strokes which left her paralyzed on the left side of her body. She typed her novel *Clock Without Hands* (1953) one page a day with one hand for a year. Some of McCullers's other works are *The Heart is a Lonely Hunter* (1940), *Reflections in a Golden Eye* (1941), *The Ballad of the Sad Cafe* (1943), and *Member of the Wedding* (1946). Several of McCullers's books have been made into full length films. Some critics have labeled McCullers a southern Gothic writer because of her grotesque symbols and occasionally bizarre characters. Others see her as a much more complex and sophisticated writer with a poet's eye for detail and a logician's skill at structure. A useful biography of McCullers is Oliver Wendell Evans's *The Ballad of Carson McCullers* (1966).

CLAUDE MCKAY(1890–1948) was a prominent figure in the Harlem Renaissance of the 1920s. He was born in Jamaica and came to America, experiencing all the pain of a black immigrant. His early poetry was conservative, as in *Spring in New Hampshire* (1920), but his contact with the racial prejudice of the period radicalized him. He became a social activist, though he did not express the bitter hatred of some later black writers. In his writing he explored the lives of ordinary black people, like the "Harlem Dancer," and found a theme in their distinctive black culture. *Home to Harlem* (1928), his first novel, became a best-seller. He also wrote an autobiography, *A Long Way from Home* (1937). Collections of his works are available in *The Passion of Claude McKay: Selected Poetry and Prose, 1912–1948* (1973) and *Selected Poems of Claude McKay* (1981).

NAOMI LONG MADGETT(b. 1923) was born in Virginia and became a professor of English at Eastern Michigan University, specializing in Afro-American literature and creative writing. Her poems do not fit the pattern of the new black writers; she uses traditional forms, and her poems resemble more the carefully structured poetry of Countee Cullen. Madgett's published collections of poetry include *Songs to a Phantom Nightingale* (1941), *One and the Many* (1956), *Star by Star* (1965), *Pink Ladies in the Afternoon* (1972), and *Exits and Entrances* (1978).

DON MARQUIS (1878–1937), American journalist and humorist, was known for his columns in the old New York *Sun* and *Tribune* newspapers. Among his best-known humorous and satirical books are *The Old Soak* (1921) and *Archy and Mehitabel* (1927), and their many sequels. In addition, Marquis wrote more serious works, volumes of poetry, drama, and an autobiographical novel, *Sons of the Puritans* (1939). His persona of Archy the Cockroach, who wrote poems by jumping from key to key on Marquis's typewriter in the deserted newspaper office, has become a classic, lasting into the computer age.

ANDREW MARVELL (1621–1678) was born in Yorkshire and educated at Cambridge. He joined the cause of Oliver Cromwell and worked as tutor to Lord Fairfax's daughter at Nun Appleton in Yorkshire. His finest poems, such as "To His Coy Mistress" and "The Garden," come from that period. Later he tutored Cromwell's nephew and wrote "On the Death of Oliver Cromwell." He was John Milton's colleague when Milton was Latin Secretary to the Secretary of State. Marvell opposed the policies of Charles II after the Restoration and was a member of Parliament from Hull. Instead of poetry, in his later years he wrote pamphlets and antigovernment propaganda. A modern collection of Marvell's poems can be found in *Complete Poetry* (1984). Critical essays on Marvell have been edited by Robert Wilcher in *Andrew Marvell* (1985).

EDNA ST. VINCENT MILLAY (1892–1950), born in Maine, was called Vincent after the hospital that had almost miraculously cured an uncle at the time of her birth. Millay won prizes for her early poem "Renascence" and a scholarship to Vassar College. Moving to Greenwich Village, she became a pioneer voice in the liberation of women and exulted in the free life and liberal causes of the Village of the 1920s. She demonstrated for Sacco and Vanzetti and counted Edmund Wilson and John Reed among her friends. She published, in addition to *Renascence* (1917), *A Few Figs and Thistles* (1920), *Second April* (1921), and *The Ballad of the Harp Weaver,* which won the Pulitzer Prize in 1923. In spite of these successes, Millay was chronically poor and ill. In 1923, she met and married Eugen Boissevain, a Dutch businessman who devoted his life to nurturing her creativity. Millay wrote the lyrics for the Deems Taylor opera *The King's Henchman* (1927), followed by several volumes of verse: *The Buck in the Snow* (1928), *Fatal Interview*

(1931), and *Wine from These Grapes* (1934). A growing concern with social issues brought new impetus to her poetry in *Conversation at Midnight* (1937) and *Huntsman What Quarry?* (1939). During World War II, she wrote anti-Fascist poetry and a radio play, *The Murder of Lidice* (1942). Recent publications of Millay's work include *Collected Lyrics of Edna St. Vincent Millay* (1981) and *Letters* (1982).

N. SCOTT MOMADAY(b. 1934) is a writer and scholar who has deliberately returned to his ancestral traditions. He is of Kiowa and Cherokee descent, the son of an artist, Al Momaday, and a writer, Natachee Scott Momaday. He received his Ph.D. from Stanford University and is Professor of English and Comparative Literature at the University of California at Berkeley. He became a post-symbolist poet, like Wallace Stevens, under Yvor Winters at Stanford, and is also known for his prose. Momaday's novel, *House Made of Dawn,* won the Pulitzer Prize for Literature in 1969. His roots in Indian culture remain strong both in prose and poetry. His early poem, "Earth and I Gave You Turquoise" was published in the *New Mexico Review.* Other works are a collection of Kiowa folktales illustrated by his father, *The Way to Rainy Mountain* (1969); *Angle of Geese and Other Poems* (1974); *The Gourd Dancer* (1976); and *The Names: A Memoir* (1976). He wrote the filmscript for Frank Waters's *The Man Who Killed the Deer,* and has published many articles and reviews on Indian subjects. Further information on Momaday can be found in *Four American Indian Masters: N. Scott Momaday, James Welch, Leslie Marmon Silko, and Gerald Vizenor* (1982).

AMADO MURO(1915–1971) wrote stories about the American Southwest. His Spanish name is actually a pseudonym for Chester Seltzer. Seltzer was a journalist who became familiar with the southwestern Hispanic culture from his wanderings there as hobo, field hand, and journalist. He took the name Amado Muro from his wife, a Mexican American, born in Chihuahua, Mexico, and the daughter of a singer–ballad composer. Her family had moved to Paco, Texas, where she was educated and where she eventually met and married Seltzer. When he began writing stories about the Southwest in the 1940s, he took both her name and her biography as his own to lend authenticity to his stories about the barrio. Seltzer's short stories are collected in *The Collected Stories of Amado Muro* (1979).

ALFRED NOYES(1880–1937) was born in England at Wolverhampton, Staffordshire, and educated at Exeter College, Oxford. In 1902, while still at Oxford, he published his first book of poems, *The Loom of Years.* Other volumes followed: *Forty Singing Seamen* (1907) and *Drake* (1908). His *Collected Poems* first appeared in 1910, with later editions in 1920, 1927, and 1950. Noyes went to the United States in 1913 and spent ten years there as professor of English literature at

Princeton. His most notable work was *The Torch Bearers* (1929–30), a trilogy tracing science through the ages. Noyes's early poems were patriotic and reflected his love of the sea. Gradually, after he became a Catholic in 1927, his religious beliefs shaped his poems. His later works include *The Unknown God* (1934), *Voltaire* (1936), *Two Worlds for Memory* (1953), and an autobiography, *The Accusing Ghost* (1957). His *Collected Poems* appeared in 1963.

JOYCE CAROL OATES (b. 1938) has gained prominence as an important novelist and short story writer. She was born in Lockport, New York, near Buffalo, and later used the western counties of New York as the setting for her Eden County. She started school in a one-room schoolhouse and began writing at an early age. Oates majored in English and minored in philosophy at the University of Wisconsin and Syracuse University. She was both Phi Beta Kappa and class valedictorian at her graduation in 1960. Oates's extraordinarily prolific output includes short stories, literary criticism, poetry, and novels, although she is best known for the latter. Her characters are ordinary people surviving in what some critics have called a Gothic world. Her stories contain violence of a commonplace kind: rape, suicide, auto wrecks. Some of Oates's more important works are *With Shuddering Fall* (1964), *A Garden of Earthly Delights* (1967), *Them* (1969), for which she won the National Book Award, *Do with Me What You Will* (1973), *The Goddess and Other Women* (1974), *The Assassins: A Book of Hours* (1975), *Night-Side: Eighteen Tales* (1977), *Son of the Morning* (1978), *Angel of Light* (1981), *Bellefleur* (1981), *A Bloodsmoor Romance* (1982), and *Solstice* (1985).

FLANNERY O'CONNOR (1925–1964) lived in Milledgville, Georgia, with her mother. Her life fits the legend of the southern spinster living in faded elegance. Her family was Roman Catholic with strong religious beliefs. She developed her interest in writing by attending a writers' workshop at the University of Iowa and then returned to Georgia to write. Flannery O'Connor suffered from the rare, incurable syndrome known as lupus, but she continued to write in spite of the fact that she was slowly dying. O'Connor's fiction has both a chilling and a comic quality to it. Her stories are sometimes called Gothic, and her view of humanity is not an optimistic one. Her published output is small compared with that of other writers. She wrote two novels: *Wise Blood* (1952) and *The Violent Bear It Away* (1960). Her two books of short stories have been collected, with additions, in *The Complete Stories* (1971); in 1977 a final collection, *A Good Man Is Hard to Find and Other Stories,* was published. O'Connor's letters, *The Habit of Being,* appeared in 1979.

TILLIE OLSEN (b. 1913) began her writing career late but developed powerfully. A high school dropout in the Depression, she married a printer and worked both in industry and as a typist. She raised four children before beginning a writing career in her forties. Since then she has taught at Amherst, Stanford, M.I.T., and the University of Massachusetts; she has also been a Fellow of the Radcliffe Institute. She has received a number of awards for her work, which includes a short story collection, *Tell Me a Riddle* (1961); a novel, *Yonnondio: From the Thirties* (1974); and *Silences* (1978), a collection of nonfiction. Olsen's short stories appear in many anthologies and magazines such as *Ms.* and *Harper's.* She writes movingly about people who have been denied the right of expression because of their race, sex, or class, and has been instrumental in reviving interest in those whose messages and dreams were not heard in their times. Her most recent work is *Mother to Daughter, Daughter to Mother, Mothers on Mothering: A Daybook and Reader* (1984).

DOROTHY PARKER(1893–1967), like Lillian Hellman, Ernest Hemingway, and Edna St. Vincent Millay, gravitated to Greenwich Village and Paris between the world wars. With her wit and satire, she became part of the group that met at New York's Algonquin Hotel for lunch, drinks, and long conversations. Parker began her career in 1916 on the editorial staff of *Vogue* and later became drama critic for *Vanity Fair.* She contributed to Franklin P. Adams's column "The Conning Tower" in the old *New York World* and started writing for *The New Yorker* when it first appeared. *Enough Rope,* her first book of verse, appeared in 1926, followed by *Sunset Gun* in 1928. Parker was widely quoted and became something of a culture heroine. Some of the short stories in her collection *Laments for Living* (1930) won the O. Henry Prize. Another book of poems, *Death and Taxes* (1931), and another of stories, *After Such Pleasures* (1934), added to her fame. Her collected poems, *Not So Deep as a Well* (1936), and collected stories, *Here Lies* (1939), cemented her reputation. In her later years she wrote Hollywood film scripts. Her short story "Big Blonde" has been made into a film in the PBS American Short Story series. Her stories and poems are available in *The Portable Dorothy Parker* (1973, 1980).

ANN PETRY (b. 1911) has been a pharmacist, reporter, editor, and advertising salesperson. Her main work, however, has been as a writer of fiction for both children and adults. Her novel *The Street* (1946) was the first by a black woman writer to look at black slum-dwellers' problems. Her later novels, *Country Place* (1947) and *The Narrows* (1953), and a short story collection, *Miss Muriel and Other Stories* (1971), show further development in departing from racial themes and using New England towns as well as New York City as locales. Her plots are those of violence, cruelty, and dislocation; her prose style and her character development show her artistry. Her descriptions of tensions between black and white, male and female, labor and bosses, all protest against a society that makes machines out of people. Petry is also the author of *Harriet Tubman, Conductor on the Underground Railroad* (1971).

MARGE PIERCY(b. 1936) lives and writes on Cape Cod, at Wellfleet. She has never considered herself a confessional poet, but wants her poems to "work for others, be useful." Piercy writes poems about the Cape, as well as feminist or political poems. She is the author of many books of poetry, including *The Moon Is Always Female* (1980). Selections from these books appeared in *Circles on the Water* (1982). She has also published many novels: *Small Changes* (1973), *Woman on the Edge of Time* (1976), *The High Cost of Living* (1978), *Vida* (1979), *Braided Lives* (1982), *Going Down Fast* (1984), *Dance the Eagle to Sleep* (1984), and *Fly Away Home* (1984).

JUANITA PLATERO AND SIYOWIN MILLER are two Navaho women, friends and collaborators. They moved to California in 1929 and were encouraged to write by Chief Standing Bear of the Teton Sioux. The two wrote short stories and a novel, *The Winds Erase Your Footprints* (1940). Their themes illustrate the Navahos' difficulties in adjusting their culture to the dominant white one and living amid the two in harmony. "Chee's Daughter" and other stories by these women were published in the 1940s in the magazine *Common Ground*.

SYLVIA PLATH(1932–1963) was a prolific, haunted young poet, whose fame has grown since her suicide in 1963. Brilliant and precocious, Plath won a scholarship to Smith College and a *Mademoiselle Magazine* award, but her mental problems interfered. She tells this part of her life, humorously yet sensitively, in *The Bell Jar,* published the year of her death under a pseudonym and reissued in 1967 under her own name. Plath received a Fulbright Fellowship and went to Cambridge University where she met the poet Ted Hughes. She and Hughes married and had two children and enjoyed some happy years of productive writing. The marriage broke up, however, and Plath spent months alone with her two children, writing furiously in a great burst of creative energy that produced some of her strongest poems. In her lifetime, *The Colossus* (1960) and *The Bell Jar* (1963) were the only volumes published; but their strength made Plath the subject of reviews and articles. *Ariel* (1965), *Crossing the Water* (1971), and *Winter Trees* (1971) confirmed her growing reputation after her death. *The Collected Poems,* edited by Ted Hughes, appeared in 1981. Her correspondence, edited by her mother, Aurelia Schober Plath, was published in 1975 as *Letters Home: Correspondence 1950–1963.* Ted Hughes edited *The Journal of Sylvia Plath,* published in 1982. A short but perceptive critical biography is Eileen Aird's *Sylvia Plath: Her Life and Work* (1973).

PO CHU-I(772–846) lived in China during the T'ang dynasty, a time of great political disorder. Assassinations and revolts made life precarious, yet a rich intellectual life flourished among the elite. Po's life was immersed in public affairs, and he was a friend of most of the important political figures of his time. His *Works* provide knowledge for us about contemporary political and religious events, and his poems reflect this period. In "Old Age" he illustrates the traditional Chinese values attached to old age. Arthur Waley has translated Po Chu-i's poems in his *One Hundred and Seventy Chinese Poems* (1939) and *Chinese Poems* (1946), and has written his biography in *The Life and Times of Po Chu-i* (1949).

EDGAR ALLAN POE (1809–1849), the orphaned son of traveling actors, was taken in by the Allan family of Richmond after his mother's death and father's desertion. Poe was an unstable youth who dropped out of the University of Virginia because of gambling debts and was later dismissed from West Point. He published two long poems, *Al Aaraaf* and *Tamerlane,* as a student and *Poems,* a collection, in 1831. He published no more poetry for fifteen years. Poe earned his living first as a journalist and then as a magazine editor. He turned to sensational fiction, but until he produced his most famous poem, "The Raven," in 1844, he was best known as a magazine critic. His peak years were those when he gained international fame as editor of *Graham's Magazine.* Poe had married his cousin Virginia when she was thirteen, but she died of tuberculosis in poverty in New York in 1847. An alcoholic, Poe alternated between bouts of intense work and periods of drinking and melancholia. He finally died in Baltimore. Poe's stories are collected in *Tales of the Grotesque and Arabesque* (1840) and *Tales* (1845). Stories such as *The Murders in the Rue Morgue* (1841), *The Mystery of Marie Roget* (1842–43), and *The Purloined Letter* (1845) exerted great influence on the tale of horror as a genre, and on the modern detective story. A modern collected edition of Poe can be found in Library of America, *Works,* vol. 1, *Poetry and Tales;* vol. 2, *Essays and Reviews* (1984).

BERNARD POMERANCE (b. 1940), a playwright born in Brooklyn, New York, lives and works in London, and came to fame with *The Elephant Man* (1977). Though his ideas and subject matter are innovative, Pomerance goes back to earlier classical drama, even to Sophocles and Racine, with short scenes carefully constructed around a theme or epigraph used as title. His plays therefore join Shaw's as "closet dramas," those suitable to be read by an individual in a small private room (a closet). Pomerance's early theatrical reputation was made in London, where his first plays were produced at the Foco Novo Theatre, which he founded, and other parts of London's fringe theater of the 1970s. Among these plays were *High in Vietnam, Hot Damn, Hospital, Thanksgiving Before Detroit* (1972), *Foco Novo* (1972), *Someone Else Is Still Someone* (1974), and *A Man's a Man* (an adaptation of a play by Brecht, 1975). These were followed by *The Elephant Man,* a play based on the life of the deformed John Merrick (1862–1890). Produced in London in 1977 and New York in 1979, the play won for Pomerance the New York Drama Critics Circle Award, three Tony Awards, three Obie Awards, and the Outer Circle Award.

KATHERINE ANNE PORTER(1890–1980) was an independent young woman raised by her grandmother in Indian Creek, Texas. Porter hated the restrictions imposed by the Catholic schools she attended and early decided to be a writer. At sixteen she eloped, but both that marriage and the one following ended in divorce. Porter was a nomad, spending time in Mexico, studying art and becoming involved in left-wing politics. Her Mexican experiences would later reappear in some of her work, particularly her only novel, *Ship of Fools* (1962), which traced an ocean voyage from Mexico to Europe in the 1930s before Hitler's rise to power. She also worked for newspapers and traveled widely. Porter wrote her first story in 1922, but her first collection of short stories, *Flowering Judas,* was not published until 1930. She lectured, taught and wrote screen plays from 1948 to 1950. Her short stories, published originally in *Pale Horse, Pale Rider* (1939) and *The Leaning Tower* (1944), are available now in *The Collected Stories of Katherine Anne Porter* (1985). The critical esays in Porter's collection *The Days Before* (1952) have been included in *The Collected Essays and Occasional Writings of Katherine Anne Porter* (1973). Porter investigated the trials of Sacco and Vanzetti in her book *The Never-Ending Wrong* (1977).

SIR WALTER RALEGH (1552–1618) is perhaps best known to Americans as the founder of the ill-fated Roanoke Colony in Virginia. But like many of the English courtiers of his time, Ralegh was a poet and a scholar as well as a soldier of fortune. Much of his prose writing is historical documentation of episodes such as the sinking of the Spanish Armada or the exploration of the new world. His poetry, however, is often light-hearted love verse or lyrical praises of the Queen. Although for much of his career Ralegh was a favorite of Queen Elizabeth and very popular with the British people, he was ultimately beheaded for treason after spending fifteen years as a prisoner in the Tower of London. His collected poems appear in a modern edition: *The Poems of Sir Walter Ralegh* (1985). His *History of the World,* a great influence on Anne Bradstreet and other metaphysical poets, has been reprinted (1971).

JOHN RECHY(b. 1934) is a Mexican-American novelist and translator. In his first novel, *City of Night* (1963), Rechy told about the undersides of New York City in a loosely connected series of episodes. *City of the Night* shocked readers in the 1960s with its frank picture of homosexual life, but its authentic jargon and nightmarish picture of existence are clearly focused and show neither self-pity nor pathos. Rechy's other books are *Numbers* (1967), *This Day's Death* (1969), *The Vampires* (1971), *The Fourth Angel* (1972), and his most recent novel, *Bodies and Souls* (1984). He has been a contributor to anthologies and has been published in magazines like *Evergreen Review* and *Nation.*

JOSÉ RENDONwas born in Laredo, Texas, but was taken to Detroit the same year when his father went looking for work. There, Rendon changed his name to

Joseph, but when he returned to Texas at fourteen he rediscovered his Chicano culture and became José again. He returned to Detroit for a time and then traveled to California, where he worked for the grape boycott. The poem selected here, "Sparkling Alleys," tells about the experiences of the Chicano youth in the city, rather than as migratory laborers on the vast ranches and farms of the West. It is a good example of the poetry being written today by the nonliterary, the young, and the unknown writers of America.

ADRIENNE RICH(b. 1929) has recently been called "a true metaphysical poet, made didactic by force of her politics" (Carol Muske in *The New York Times Book Review,* January 20, 1985). Rich's work has changed immeasurably as she has matured as a poet. Her early poems were formal, well crafted, following the standards set by male poets like Auden and Eliot. By the 1960s, however, her poetic form had become increasingly more jagged and less regular, and the content merged more with her pent-up emotions as woman, housewife, mother, and writer. Some of the earlier poems are included in *The Diamond Cutters and Other Poems* (1955, 1980). By the 1970s, Rich had made a definite commitment to feminism and lesbian separatism. She became the leader of a newly defined female writing, full of "dialectical fire." Her works include a prose work, *Of Woman Born: Motherhood as Experience and Institution* (1976), which expresses Rich's strong feminist philosophy through an examination of the feelings of a woman bearing and raising children as opposed to the myths of motherhood. Recent works include: *Diving into the Wreck* (1973), *The Meaning of Our Love for Women Is What We Have Constantly to Expand* (1977), *The Dream of a Common Language: Poems, 1974–1977* (1978), *On Lies, Secrets, and Silence: Selected Prose, 1966–1978* (1979), and *The Fact of a Doorframe: Poems Selected and New, 1950–1984* (1984).

EDWIN ARLINGTON ROBINSON(1869–1935), heir of the New England tradition, was brought up in the town of Gardiner, Maine, which, as Tilbury Town, became the fictional residence of characters like Miniver Cheevy, Richard Cory, and Mr. Flood. Robinson had to leave Harvard because of lack of funds; he went to New York City, where he printed his first book (*The Torrent and the Night Before,* 1896) at his own expense. A withdrawn and unhappy man, beset by poverty and alcoholism, he nevertheless persisted in writing his poetry, and his output during his life was formidable. His next two books, *Children of the Night* (1897, a revision of his first book) and *Captain Craig* (1902), interested Theodore Roosevelt; Roosevelt helped him get a post in the New York Custom House, and the public began buying his books. His successful volume *The Town Down the River* was published in 1910. The next important collection of his poetry was *The Man Against the Sky* (1916). Then followed an Arthurian trilogy: *Merlin* (1917), *Lancelot* (1920), and *Tristram* (1927). His *Collected Poems* in 1921 won him a Pulitzer Prize. He wrote steadily until he died, with a high reputation and real success in his lifetime. His longer works are little read today, though his incisive character sketches, tight rhymes, and apt ironies still appeal. *The Collected Poems of Edwin Arlington Robinson* (1972) became the standard available edition.

CAROLYN M. RODGERS writes poems about revolution, religion, and human relationships. She treats the controversial, angry themes of black poetry with wit, humor, and even a touch of sassiness. Some of her poems react bitterly to injustice, while others treat love tenderly. One of the most powerful is "Portrait" (in this anthology), honoring her mother for the sacrifices she made to help her get an education, though keeping an awareness of the generation gap. Her collection *How I Got Ovah: New and Selected Poems* (1975) contains other poignant pieces about mothers and children.

THEODORE ROETHKE (1908–1963), one of America's most admired twentieth-century poets, was also an English professor and tennis coach. Another poet, Stanley Kunitz, remembered Roethke as a huge man with a smashing serve. He carried that energy over into his poetry, delving deeply into human feelings. Roethke was educated at the University of Michigan and at Harvard. His first book of poems was *Open House* in 1941. Though his output was small, he won the Pulitzer Prize in 1953 for *The Waking* and the Bollingen Prize in poetry in 1958 for *Words for the Wind*. Though he suffered intermittent bouts of mental illness, he carried on a productive life of teaching at various universities, reading poetry with verve and style, and writing poems ranging from lyrical to mystical. A recent collection of his poems is *The Collected Poems of Theodore Roethke* (1975). A selection of his poems appears in *The Achievement of Theodore Roethke* (1966).

PHILIP ROTH (b. 1933) was born in New Jersey and educated at Bucknell University and the University of Chicago. His first book, *Goodbye Columbus* (1959), containing five short stories and a novella, won the National Book Award. Modern American life, starting with World War II, furnishes subjects for his many comedies of manners. He writes especially well about Jewish-Americans, as in *Letting Go* (1962) and *Portnoy's Complaint* (1969). Others of his novels and satires include *The Breast* (1972), *The Great American Novel* (1973), *My Life as a Man* (1974), *The Professor of Desire* (1977), and *The Ghost Writer* (1979). *Our Gang* (1971) is a satire on the Nixon Administration, while *Reading Myself and Others* (1975) collects some of Roth's essays.

CARL SANDBURG (1878–1967), a people's poet, was born in Illinois of Swedish immigrant parents. At thirteen he left school and did odd jobs until becoming a housepainter apprentice. After attending Lombard College in Galesburg, Illinois,

Sandburg wandered about America working at ordinary jobs—milkman, dishwasher, reporter. In 1912, he moved to Chicago where he worked for the *Chicago Daily News* and began to write poetry about Chicago. Sandburg's poems, like Whitman's, reflected optimism and democracy and drew on the history and the folklore of the land to proclaim his faith in a vital America. Sandburg used midwestern speech rhythms to write a colloquial poetry in spontaneous, free-verse style. In 1916 he published *Chicago Poems,* which was followed by *Cornhuskers* in 1918. *Smoke and Steel* won the Pulitzer Prize in 1920. He published *Slabs of the Sunburnt West* in 1922 and *The People, Yes* in 1936. At about that time, Sandburg also began work on his six-volume biography of Lincoln, whom he saw as the epitome of the common man. *The Prairie Years* (2 volumes) and *The War Years* (1926–39, 4 volumes) won the Pulitzer Prize for history.

DANNY SANTIAGO (DANIEL JAMES) (b. 1913) appeared on the literary scene only recently, apparently as a young Chicano writer, a product of the Los Angeles slum environment so tellingly depicted in "The Somebody." In May 1984, Santiago's first novel, *Famous All Over Town,* was awarded a $5000 prize by the American Academy and Institute of Arts and Letters, but the author remained a mystery to the public; even his editor had not personally met him. Finally the mystery was solved: Danny Santiago is an Anglo—not Hispanic at all! He is Daniel James, born in Kansas City, educated at Andover and Yale, a Hollywood screenwriter before being blacklisted by McCarthy in 1951. After that he and his wife became social workers in East Los Angeles, working there for twenty-five years amid poor Chicanos like those who appear in his stories. He Hispanized his name (Santiago means St. James), not to deceive, but as he says "to write about Mexicans from the inside." Undaunted by his double identity, Santiago is hard at work on a second novel.

JEAN-PAUL SARTRE (1905–1980), philosopher, novelist, and playwright, played a large part in the intellectual life of post-World-War-II France—and the world. He was a teacher in the French provinces and then in Paris before the war, but the world conflict and the Nazi occupation of France shook him profoundly. He meditated a long time on his own system, which he developed in a novel, *Nausea*, in 1938, and in a philosophical work, *Being and Nothingness*, in 1943. He showed the absurdity of expecting convention and tradition to give human beings a feeling of security in a hostile and uncaring world. His play *No Exit*, produced in Paris under the noses of the nearly defeated Germans, first became popular among the Parisians as a statement against the Nazis. Its brilliant dialogue and its exposition of the essential Existentialist position have earned it lasting fame. Also available by Sartre to illuminate the philosophy of Existentialism are *Literature and Existentialism* (1949, 1980), translated by Bernard Frechtman, and a collection, *Between Existentialism and Marxism: Sartre on Philosophy, Politics, Psychology and the Arts* (1983). Valuable for appraisals of his work is Edith G. Kern,

Sartre: A Collection of Critical Essays (1962). Simone de Beauvoir, Sartre's life-long companion, has written since his death *Adieux: A Farewell to Sartre* (1984), translated by Patrick O'Brian.

SUSAN FROMBERG SCHAEFFER (b. 1941) is a versatile practitioner

of the craft of writing, a teacher and exemplar and a voice for women in a shifting society. She is a professor of English at Brooklyn College as well as a full-time writer. She says she hates writing about her life and is "something of a hermit," but her production and influence belie that. She has contributed to journals and reviews such as *Modern Fiction Studies.* Among her books are *The Witch and the Weather Report* (poems, 1972), *Anya: A Novel* (1974), *Granite Lady: Poems* (1974), *Alphabet for the Lost Years* (1976), *Time in Its Flight* (1978), *The Queen of Egypt: Short Fiction* (1980), *The Madness of a Seduced Woman* (1983), and *Mainland* (1985).

ANNE SEXTON(1928–1974) started life like many young girls of her era:

boys, dances, clothes, a youthful marriage, wartime separation, children. Pressures developed into mental illness, but with it came poetry. Inspired by an educational television program on the sonnet, she began writing and joined a poetry workshop where she made friendships with other poets. Her first book, *To Bedlam and Part Way Back* (1960), charted part of her recovery. Maxine Kumin, friend and poet, characterized much of Sexton's poetry as "obsessional expiation" for her feelings and guilts. The largest category of her themes concerns death, though Sexton was not entirely a confessional poet. Many of her poems displayed humor, a wry vision of life. Sexton wrote in open forms, but also in intricate, finely crafted forms like the sonnet series. Erica Jong, another poet friend, called Sexton's poetry "the reincarnation, the regurgitation, the living she is making out of the jaws of death" (*Ms* March 1974: 37). In spite of this, or because of her long love affair with death, Anne Sexton committed suicide in 1974. In total, she published nine books of poetry; one of them, *Live or Die,* won her the Pulitzer Prize in 1966. Her *Collected Poems,* edited by her daughter Linda Gray Sexton, appeared in 1982. Her letters to friends and family, *Anne Sexton: A Self-Portrait in Letters,* edited by Linda Gray Sexton and Lois Ames, was published in 1977.

WILLIAM SHAKESPEARE (1564–1616) has gained more notoriety and

honest fame than almost any other writer. Little is known of his youth. Born in Stratford-upon-Avon, England, the son of a bailiff who became a gentleman, Shakespeare probably attended the Stratford grammar school. He married Anne Hathaway in 1582; she bore him a daughter and a set of twins. By 1592 he appeared in London as an actor and playwright, popular with the people but referred to by Robert Greene as "an upstart crow, beautified with our feathers." While in

London, Shakespeare acted with, wrote plays for, and owned a share in the acting troupe known as the Lord Chamberlain's Men, which built the Globe Theater. He was successful enough to retire eventually to Stratford to live the life of a gentleman. Shakespeare's plays—with their universality, power, and lyricism—need little commentary. He wrote a number of comedies—among them *The Comedy of Errors, Love's Labour's Lost, The Taming of the Shrew, The Merchant of Venice, As You Like It,* and *Twelfth Night.* He wrote ten history plays including *King John;* Parts 1 and 2 of *Henry IV; Henry VI;* and *Richard III.* However, the tragedies render Shakespeare most famous—*Romeo and Juliet, Julius Caesar, Hamlet, Othello, King Lear,* and *Macbeth.* Although Shakespeare is best known for his plays, a number of his dramatic pieces contain songs. He also wrote the sonnets that made familiar his "dark lady." Two members of Shakespeare's acting company, John Heminges and Henry Condell, first collected and published his plays in *The First Folio* in 1623.

NTOZAKE SHANGE (b. 1948) was a privileged middle-class "colored girl," the daughter of a surgeon and a psychiatric social worker. She graduated with honors from Barnard College and received a graduate degree from UCLA. Her family's home was filled with music, literature, and art; her parents' guests were intellectuals and musicians. Feeling that this privileged childhood was "living a lie," Shange changed her name in 1971 from a "slave name," Paulette Williams, to an African one. In Zulu, Ntozake means "she who comes with her own things"; Shange means "she who walks like a lion." Shange also adapted the language of her poetry to the street-talk of plain black women such as the live-in maids of her childhood. She and a group of friends—poets, dancers, musicians—began creating the improvisational works out of which *for colored girls who have considered suicide when the rainbow is enuf* (1975) would grow. She chose the title deliberately: "Colored Girls . . . is a word my grandmother would understand," she stated. She wanted to be very clean and honest in these poems about the brutality that threatens—and even ruins—the lives of these black women. Her other works include a novel, *Sassafras* (1976); prose and poems, *Natural Disasters and Other Festive Occasions* (1979); and a collection of poems, *Nappy Edges* (1978). More recent works are *A Daughter's Geography* (1983), *From Okra to Greens: Poems* (1984), and *Betsy Brown: A Novel* (1985).

KARL SHAPIRO (b. 1913) was born in Baltimore and educated there at Johns Hopkins University. After serving in the Army during the Second World War, he turned to university teaching. Shapiro has edited *Poetry Magazine,* the *Newberry Library Bulletin,* and the *Prairie Schooner,* as well as several poetry texts. He has won a number of poetry prizes, including the Pulitzer, and has written literary criticism, as well as an opera called *The Tenor.* Shapiro's poetry covers a broad range of forms and themes from his early interest in social concerns to a later, more intimate style of poetry. Some of his better-known collections are *Per-*

son, Place and Thing (1942), *Trial of a Poet* (1947), *The Bourgeois Poet* (1964), *Selected Poems* (1968), and *White-Haired Lover* (1968). His *Collected Poems, 1940–1978* (1978) and *Love, War, Art, and God: The Poems of Karl Shapiro* (1984) make his work available. Shapiro assembled some of his critical essays in *The Poetry Wreck: Selected Essays, 1950–1970* (1975).

LESLIE MARMON SILKO (b. 1948), of mixed Laguna Indian, Mexican, and white ancestry, grew up at the Laguna Pueblo reservation, where she now writes and lives. She graduated from the University of New Mexico and studied law for several semesters before turning to writing. She has published *Laguna Woman,* a collection of poems (1974), *Ceremony,* a novel (1977), and *Storyteller* (1981). Her short stories and poems have been anthologized in many books, most recently in *The Third Woman: Minority Women Writers of the United States,* edited by Dexter Fisher (1980). Silko insists that "Storytelling for the Indians is like a natural resource," but she warns against "demeaning literature when you label certain books by saying this is black, this is Native American." Her "Love Poem," chosen for this anthology, reflects her wish to write good poetry, rather than specifically ethnic poetry.

ROBERTA SILMAN (b. 1934) was brought up in a close Jewish family and has a family of her own, though she clearly understands the isolated, individualistic Mona in her story, "Company." Her stories have appeared in *The New Yorker, Atlantic,* and other popular magazines. Silman considers fiction "the history of the world" and as a serious writer feels the need to tell the truth about what she knows and is able to invent. Perhaps Mona, with her vivid inner life, stands for the spirit of the modern writer, making an island of her mind in the midst of the world's pressures. Silman investigates in order to be able to understand: certain kinds of family relationships in the stories in *Blood Relations* (1977); the relations between Jews and Germans in *Boundaries* (novel, 1979). She depicts the feelings of an adopted child in *Somebody Else's Child,* a novel for young people (1979), as well as the fantasizing, self-sufficient Mona in "Company."

PAUL SIMON has been linked as a performing artist for many years with Art Garfunkel. Having known each other since they were ten years old, they began their singing career on *American Bandstand* in 1957, when they were sixteen years old. Simon grew up in Queens and majored in English at Queens College. Briefly he tried high school teaching and then went to England with his guitar to do a series of one night stands. The success he and Garfunkel eventually achieved is history; they made a reputation and a fortune singing and writing tasteful music with lyrics that appealed to the audiences of the late sixties. Such albums as *Sounds of Silence* (1965) and *Bridge over Troubled Water* (1970) became classics before the two went their separate ways. Ocassionally performing with Garfunkel, Simon now lives and works in fashionable comfort in New York City. A recent album is *Hearts and Bones* (1983).

ISAAC BASHEVIS SINGER (b. 1904) was born in Poland and educated in

a rabbinical seminary. Although he has lived in the United States since 1935, Singer continues to write in Yiddish, the language of the Polish *shtetl* people, portraying a vanished world as if it still existed. Singer has been a novelist, children's author, and translator, but he is most famous for his short stories. He has received many honors, including the Nobel Prize for Literature in 1978. His novels include *The Family Moskat* (1950), *The Magician of Lublin* (1960), and *Shosha* (1978). Among his short story collections are *Gimpel the Fool and Other Stories* (1957), *The Spinoza of Market Street and Other Stories* (1961), *The Seance and Other Stories* (1968), *A Crown of Feathers and Other Stories* (1973), *Passions and Other Stories* (1975), and *Old Love* (1979). Singer has also written or collaborated on several plays, including *Yentl,* produced on Broadway in 1974 and made into a film by Barbra Streisand in 1984. Singer's short stories continue to be published by such magazines as *The New Yorker, Harper's,* and *Esquire.* His *Collected Stories of Isaac Bashevis Singer* was published in 1982.

STEVIE SMITH (1902–1971) wrote whimsical, haunting, stream-of-conscious-

ness novels and witty poetry that made her popular in England at poetry readings and on the BBC. Recently, renewed interest in her as a person and a poet has been aroused by the film version of Hugh Whitemore's play *Stevie,* starring Glenda Jackson in the title role. Stevie Smith was born Florence Margaret, but nicknamed, as a teenager, for a famous jockey; the name stuck. She lived from the age of three in a plain, middle-class London suburb, Palmers Green, with her beloved aunt, and worked, until her retirement, as a private secretary for a publisher. Caught up in the publishing world, she traveled and had many friends but always returned to her aunt and Palmers Green. She was one of the growing number of poets who brought poetry to the people by tirelessly reading at colleges, schools, and on BBC poetry programs. In 1969, she won the Queen's Gold Medal for Poetry. Her first volume of poems, *A Good Time Was Had by All* (1937) was followed by seven others. They have been republished in *Collected Poems* (1983). She illustrated her poems with her own charming drawings, so that the books themselves are examples of fine book publishing. Her novels—*Novel on Yellow Paper* (1936), *The Holiday* (1949), and *Over the Frontier* (1949)—have all been reissued in the 1980s. An anthology of her work, *Me Again: Uncollected Writings of Stevie Smith* (1982), and *Stevie Smith: A Selection* (1983) indicate how her popularity has grown recently.

SOPHOCLES (496–406 B.C.) lived a long life that spanned the period known

as the Golden Age of Greece. He is the central figure among the three great Greek tragedians of the Golden Age—the others are Aeschylus and Euripides. He combines Aeschylus' high ethical concerns with Euripides' mastery of human psychology. At sixteen, Sophocles took part in the celebration of the victory at Salamis of 480 B.C., when the Athenians overcame the Persians in a great naval battle. By the end of his life, Sparta had conquered Athens. Sophocles was an immensely popular playwright. He wrote more than 120 plays for the various festivals and competitions. Only seven have survived; among them are the three plays of the Oedipus Cycle: *Oedipus Rex, Oedipus at Colonus,* and *Antigone;* the others are *Ajax, The Women of Trachis, Electra,* and *Philoctetes.* Though Sophocles in his long, honorable life was a member of the establishment of his time, his dramas call into question the values of law, order, religion, and justice of his society. This ambiguity, this questioning, is what has made his dramas live long after the society from which they came. Among the many critical works that give interpretations of his plays are Bernard M. W. Knox's *The Heroic Temper: Studies in Sophoclean Tragedy* (1964) and Robert F. Goheen's *The Imagery of Sophocles' Antigone: A Study of Poetic Language and Structure* (1951). Thomas Marion Woodard has edited *Sophocles: A Collection of Critical Essays* (1966).

STEPHEN SPENDER (b. 1909) grew up in a cultured, academic family in London. His father, Edward H. Spender, was a writer and lecturer, and the young Spender inherited his father's writing talents. He attended University College at Oxford, edited the *Oxford Poetry* anthologies, and published three early books of poems, *Nine Experiments* (1928), *Twenty Poems* (1930), and *Poems* (1933). Like Auden, who took up leftist causes in his early poetry and later mellowed into more personal poetry, Spender gradually became more and more a romanticist and less a social activist. Some of his more prominent later works are *The Still Centre* (1939), *Selected Poems* (1940), *Ruins and Visions* (1941), *Poems of Destruction* (1946), *The Burning Cactus* (1955), and *Engaged in Writing* (1958). His *Collected Poems* appeared in 1985. Also published in 1985 were *The Journals of Stephen Spender, 1939–1983.* He has written numerous critical essays and an autobiography, *World Within World* (1951).

JOHN STEINBECK (1902–1968) made Salinas, in the Monterey Valley of California, the locale of many of his novels and stories. His career was long and uneven; he wrote about the tensions between city and country, men and women, and labor and management. He searched in his many writings for a set of values to avoid dehumanization in a complex society. His studies at Stanford University in marine biology gave him a lifetime interest in biological science, and in his writings he developed a sort of bio-myth to explain human actions and greed. Steinbeck's subjects have generally been poor people, as they are in *Tortilla Flat* (1935), *In Dubious Battle* (1936), *The Grapes of Wrath* (1939), and *Cannery Row* (1945). *The Pastures of Heaven* (1932) and *The Long Valley* (1938) are collections of loosely connected short stories. In his later career Steinbeck worked as a war correspondent in World War II, and as a script-writer for the many films made from his novels. His last works were *The Winter of Our Discontent* (1961), in which the scene shifts from California to his new home, Long Island, and *Travels with Charley* (1962), in which he travels in a van with an aged poodle in search of America. He won the Nobel Prize in 1962 for his distinguished career. His short novels have been collected in *The Short Novels of John Steinbeck* (1981).

WALLACE STEVENS (1879–1955) was both businessman and poet. The

son of an attorney, Stevens was born into a prosperous Reading, Pennsylvania, family. After three years at Harvard, he studied law in New York and then joined the legal staff of the Hartford Accident and Indemnity Company. In 1934 he became a vice president and stayed with the Hartford firm until he retired. Stevens had published some poetry at Harvard and had some of his poems published in the little poetry magazines in New York. He was an intellectual poet who played with classical and biblical allusions and whose themes covered a broad range. His first collection of poems, *Harmonium,* was published in 1923, but to such a poor reception that he almost gave up poetry. He went on to publish six other volumes of poems: *Ideas of Order* (1935), *The Man with the Blue Guitar* (1937), *Parts of a World* (1942), *Transport to Summer* (1947), *The Auroras of Autumn* (1950), and *Collected Poems* (1954). His last collection of poems, *Opus Posthumous,* appeared in 1957. His only book of prose was a collection of essays, *The Necessary Angel: Essays on Reality and the Imagination* (1951). His poems have been collected in *Collected Poems of Wallace Stevens* (1982).

ROBERT LOUIS STEVENSON (1850–1894) spent a quiet childhood in

Edinburgh, where he grew to love Scottish tales and adventures. Though he studied law, he never practiced it, turning instead to journalism. His early essays were collected as *Virginibus Puerisque* (1881) and his short tales as *New Arabian Nights* (1882). Stevenson's travels in search of health and adventure took him to France, where he met Mrs. Fanny Osbourne, whom he subsequently married. His perennially popular *Treasure Island* was published in 1883. Buoyed by its success, he continued writing for children, striking an especially happy chord in *A Child's Garden of Verses* (1885), which recalls the pleasures of his childhood. Two more now-famous Stevenson novels appeared in 1886: *The Strange Case of Dr. Jekyll and Mr. Hyde* and *Kidnapped*. At Saranac Lake in the Adirondacks, where he sought a tuberculosis cure, Stevenson wrote *The Master of Ballantrae* (1889). In declining health, he settled on the island of Samoa, where the appreciative natives called him Tusitala (teller of tales), and where he lies buried. He left an impressive body of work—poetry, stories, essays, novels, letters—which continues to be reevaluated today by critics who no longer think of him as merely a writer for children.

ALFRED, LORD TENNYSON (1809–1892) was probably the most popular poet of the Victorian Age. The fourth son of a disinherited cleric who educated his sons himself, Alfred had already published a book of poems, *Poems by Two Brothers,* with his brother Charles, before he entered Cambridge. "The Apostles," a group of Cambridge undergraduates, encouraged Tennyson to devote his life to writing poetry. Arthur Hallam, the leader of the Apostles, became Tennyson's close friend; his death in 1833 devastated Tennyson, who dedicated the long poem *In Memoriam* (1850) to Hallam. Tennyson began writing poetry in earnest when he was forced to withdraw from Cambridge because his family was in financial straits. Slowly he learned his craft, developing a touch with meter and image. By 1842 his poems were receiving acclaim, and in 1850, when he was barely more than forty years old, he succeeded Wordsworth as poet laureate. Thus financially secure, he married Emily Sellwood, his sweetheart for fourteen years. Tennyson's fame gave him financial security and enough money to buy the secluded life he longed for. In 1884 he received a peerage. When he died in 1892, he was buried in Westminster Abbey. Recent collections of Tennyson's work can be found in *Poems* (1980) and *Selections from Tennyson* (1982).

DYLAN THOMAS (1914–1953) was born in Wales, the son of an English teacher. He spent long summers at an aunt's farm in rural Wales, absorbing the images and rolling speech that later appeared in such poems as "Fern Hill." He left school early and worked as a reporter, then moved to London where he continued to write poetry and book reviews. His first volume of poems appeared in 1934; his second, in 1936, established his reputation. He then married and moved back to Wales. Publication of his books in America made him known there; especially popular was his volume of autobiographical sketches, *Portrait of the Artist as a Young Dog* (1940). During World War II he stayed in London making documentary films and working for the BBC as a writer and commentator on poetry. Other volumes of poetry followed, and his first American poetry-reading tour in 1950 was a success. America took to his rollicking voice, lilting Welsh accent, and charismatic presence. On his fourth American tour he directed his "play for voices," *Under Milk Wood,* and died in New York. His *Collected Poems, 1934–1952,* was published in 1966. His *Collected Stories* appeared in 1984.

JAMES THURBER (1894–1961), American humorist, was born in Columbus, Ohio, in 1894 and attended public schools there. He graduated from Ohio State University and worked as a reporter in Ohio, France, and New York. In 1927 he joined the staff of *The New Yorker* and stayed there until 1933, helping to edit the magazine as well as writing stories and drawing cartoons. Thurber's writings and drawings blend nonsense and wisdom in his characters. He depicts amusing aspects of the tension between men and women, frequently making his point by using dogs and other animals to represent people. Thurber has used many literary forms, all showing a keen satiric sense. His best-known short story is "The Secret

Life of Walter Mitty." In 1933, at age thirty-nine, he wrote a comical autobiography, *My Life and Hard Times. Fables for Our Time,* which contains "A Unicorn in the Garden," appeared in 1940 and *The Thurber Carnival* in 1945. In 1950 Thurber wrote a fairy tale, *The Thirteen Clocks,* and a play, *The Male Animal.* Other well-known Thurber works are *The Thurber Album* (1952), an account of family and friends in the Midwest, and *The Years with Ross* (1959), tales of his years at *The New Yorker. Vintage Thurber: A Collection in Two Volumes of the Best Writings and Drawings of James Thurber* (1983) makes a good selection of his works available in one volume.

LUIS VALDÉZ (b. 1940) founded the Teatro Campesino (Farmworkers' Theater) in 1965 in Delano, California, where he presented short plays called "Actos." The earliest plays were designed to help support the United Farm Workers strike called by Cesar Chavez. Today the theater is no longer directly connected with the union, but both the strike *(huelga)* and the Teatro are parts of what is called "La Causa," the unifying Chicano movement. The "Actos" started as a group entertainment, often improvised. Valdéz collected these skits in *Actos: El Teatro Campesino* (1971). He states that the theater pieces are intended "to inspire the audience to social action, illuminate specific points about social problems, satirize the opposition, show or hint at a solution, and express what people are feeling." In addition to *Actos,* Valdéz has edited *Aztlan: An Anthology of Mexican American Literature* (1972), and published his plays in *The Shrunken Head of Pancho Villa: A Play* (1974) and *Zoot Suit* (1978).

RICHARD VASQUEZ has used his experience in the barrios of his native California to present the lives of the Mexican-Americans of the Southwest both in fiction and documentaries. He was once a construction worker but is now a professional writer who lives near Los Angeles. His novel *Chicano* (1970) is an account of four generations in the life of a family named Sandoval who come to the United States, live through war and poverty, and attempt to rise in status while running into many difficulties. The story "Angelina Sandoval" is taken from that novel. Vasquez has written other works on the Chicanos: *The Giant Killer* (1977), *The Mexican-Americans of Clovis, New Mexico* (1979), and *Another Land* (1982).

ALICE WALKER (b. 1944) won both the 1983 Pulitzer Prize and the American Book Award for her novel *The Color Purple* (1983). She was born in Georgia, the eighth child of sharecropping parents. She spent two years at Spellman College in Atlanta, where she showed great promise, and transferred to graduate from Sarah Lawrence College in 1966. Her writing about black women and the black family has earned her a Merrill Fellowship, a grant from the National Endowment for the Arts, and a Fellowship to the Radcliffe Institute. In addition to *The Color*

Purple, Walker's recent work includes *In Love and Trouble* (1973, 1984), from which the short story "Everyday Use" is taken; *You Can't Keep a Good Woman Down: Stories* (1981); *In Search of Our Mothers' Gardens: Womanist Prose* (1983); and *Horses Make a Landscape Look More Beautiful: Poems* (1984).

EUDORA WELTY(b. 1909) has lived for much of her life in her birthplace, Jackson, Mississippi. She graduated from the University of Wisconsin in 1929 and spent a year at Columbia University studying advertising. She returned to the South in 1931 and held a variety of jobs while beginning to write the short stories for which she would become famous. In 1936 Welty had her first story "Death of a Traveling Salesman" published. Critics sometimes compare Welty's strong sense of southern heritage with that of her neighbor William Faulkner, but she is more interested in the individual than in the social impact of historical movements and patterns. One of Welty's strengths is her ability to evoke a sense of place, to paint pictures with words. Her several collections are *A Curtain of Green* (1941) from which "A Worn Path" comes, *The Wide Net* (1943), *The Golden Apple* (1949), and *The Bride of the Innisfallen* (1954). The *Collected Stories of Eudora Welty* appeared in 1983. Welty has also written several novels, sometimes seen as extended short stories: *The Robber Bridegroom* (1942), *Delta Wedding* (1946), *The Ponder Heart* (1954), *Losing Battles* (1970), and *The Optimist's Daughter* (1972).

RUTH WHITMAN(b. 1922), poet, teacher, and editor, has been connected with the Cambridge Center of Adult Education at Radcliffe College. She has also been an editor with Houghton Mifflin and Harvard University Press, and poetry editor of the magazine *Audience.* She has translated both poets and prose writers, among them Isaac Bashevis Singer. In addition to Yiddish, she translates modern Greek and French poetry. She has received MacDowell Colony Fellowships, poetry awards from the Poetry Society of America, a fellowship to the Radcliffe Institute for Independent Study, and a National Foundation for Jewish Culture grant. Her own poems are collected in *The Passion of Lizzie Borden: New and Selected Poems* (1973) and *Permanent Address: New Poems, 1973–1980* (1980). She has edited *An Anthology of Modern Yiddish Poetry* (1979). Her works on poetry include *Poemmaking: Poets in Classrooms* (1975) and *Becoming a Poet: Source, Process, Practice* (1982).

WALT WHITMAN (1819–1892) was perhaps the major influence on twentieth-century American poetry, though he lived in the nineteenth century. On first reading Whitman's *Leaves of Grass* (1855), Emerson wrote to Whitman, "I greet you at the beginning of a great career." This prophetic letter was sent to an unknown New York newspaperman who had grown up on Long Island and had gone from job to job, career to career, developing the style later to blossom forth in *Leaves of Grass.* This book, the work of his lifetime, was first published in 1855. Whitman saw it through eight editions, adding and shifting material each time, up to his death in 1892. Whitman said his intent in writing poetry was "to put a Person, a human being (myself, in the latter half of the Nineteenth Century, in America) freely, fully, and truly on record." To do this, he elevated common experiences to the stuff of poetry. The Civil War profoundly changed the dapper journalist Whitman. He volunteered as a nurse in hospitals in Washington after he went to Virginia to find his brother, wounded there. "Drum Taps" (1865) captures the pain, suffering, and loneliness of the soldier, and the tempo of wartime Washington, as does his prose volume, *Specimen Days* (1882). His poem "When Lilacs Last in the Dooryard Bloom'd" was a moving elegy on the assassination of President Lincoln, a figure Whitman much admired. *Democratic Vistas,* a look at America's political and literary future, appeared in 1870. After the war, Whitman held a government position until 1873, when a stroke forced him into semiretirement at his brother's house in Camden, New Jersey. Ill-luck plagued him all his life: his family was unstable and neurotic; he was fired from his job because of the explicit sexuality of *Leaves of Grass;* he struggled with frustrated homosexual longings, and with poverty. In spite of all this his boundless optimism and love of the whole of America infused his poetry with a spirit that has made him an outstanding American poet. *The Collected Writings of Walt Whitman,* edited by Gay Wilson Allen and Sculley Bradley, have been appearing since 1961. The latest in the series is his *Notebooks* (1984). *Leaves of Grass* appears in many editions: the useful Comprehensive Reader's Edition, edited by Harold W. Blodgett and Sculley Bradley (1965), includes the whole body of Whitman's poems together with a wide selection from surviving fragments and poems from earlier editions not included in the last edition of Whitman's lifetime, that of 1891–92.

RICHARD WILBUR (b. 1921), born the son of a painter in New York City, grew up in New Jersey. He graduated from Amherst College, where he was probably influenced by Robert Frost, and took a Masters Degree at Harvard. Wilbur became a poet and a teacher after serving in the Second World War. He has taught at Harvard and Wesleyan University and considers himself a "poet-citizen" rather than an alienated artist. He teaches poetry and gives readings to make poetry available to the people, believing that is one way to ensure a place of respect for the art that he loves. Wilbur's first two volumes of poetry, poems written in response to the war, *The Beautiful Changes* (1947) and *Ceremony* (1950), brought him immediate acclaim. Wilbur's poetry is not typical of the modernists. He is a careful craftsman who adheres strictly to meter and form and uses varied forms and fresh images. His subjects can be either intellectual or familiar. In 1956 he won the Pulitzer Prize and the National Book Award for *Things of This World.* Other collections are *The Bestiary* (1955), *Advice to a Prophet* (1961), *The Poems of Richard Wilbur* (1963), and *Walking to Sleep* (1969).

KATE WILHELM(b. 1928) practices the craft of writing science fiction and has won three of the genre's prestigious prizes: the Nebula Award in 1968, and the Hugo and Jupiter awards in 1977. She has directed workshops in science fiction at Michigan State University and elsewhere. Her stories have appeared in many science-fiction magazines and anthologies. Like other science-fiction writers, and those who have turned to the genre from other forms, Wilhelm believes we are living in an "age of cataclysmic changes." She says "my work is an attempt to understand how we got here, why we stay, and what lies ahead if anything does." Often her characters, like Mrs. Bagley, are faced with giving up their humanity, but Wilhelm's main theme in her stories is that it is not worth becoming less than human even to save our lives. Some of Wilhelm's collected short stories and novels are *Where Late the Sweet Birds Sang* (1976), *The Infinity Box* (1976), *Fault Lines* (1976), *The Somerset Dreams and Other Fictions* (1978), *The Mile-Long Spaceship* (1980), *Sense of Shadow* (1981), *Oh, Susannah* (1982), and *Welcome, Chaos* (1983).

TENNESSEE WILLIAMS (1911–1983) was born in Columbus, Mississippi, the son of a traveling shoe salesman who wished for a hardy, all-American boy. Williams, however, was sickly and ill-suited to the rough urban St. Louis environment that became their home. He endured a lonely, isolated childhood there, made bearable by his refined mother and his beloved but high-strung sister, Rose. Williams's biography lies at the core of much of his work. At a young age, he tried to hide from his problems by writing, going to the movies, and devoting himself to his sister. His plays echo themes of sexuality as an intense force in people's lives, the plight of the outsider, and the creation of art from suffering and deprivation. Violent images confront beautiful but fragile ones. Williams's plays include *The Glass Menagerie* (1944), *A Streetcar Named Desire* (1947), *The Rose Tattoo* (1950), *Cat on a Hot Tin Roof* (1955), *Sweet Bird of Youth* (1959), *Baby Doll* (a filmscript), *Period of Adjustment* (1960), and *Night of the Iguana* (1962). Williams's *Memoirs* were published in 1983.

WILLIAM WORDSWORTH (1770–1850) is often considered one of the greatest of English poets, though he wrote his best poems before he was thirty-seven. Wordsworth was born near the Lake District he would later make famous. After studying at Cambridge, he took a walking tour of France and Switzerland, recalled in *The Prelude* (1804–05). On a second journey to France, he fell in love with a Frenchwoman by whom he had a daughter. They were separated by the French Revolution, and he returned to England and set up housekeeping with his sister Dorothy. Wordsworth later married, continued writing, and lived at Rydal Mount amid a growing reputation as a poet. He became Poet Laureate of England in 1843. Wordsworth's impact on the generation of Romantic poets came from the principles that he and Samuel Taylor Coleridge set down in the preface to their *Lyrical Ballads* (1798). Wordsworth's *Poetical Works* are edited by Ernest de

Selincourt and Helen Darbishire (1940–49; rprt 1982). Correspondence between Wordsworth and his sister can be found in *The Letters of William and Dorothy Wordsworth* (6 volumes, 1967). Seon Manley's *Dorothy and William Wordsworth: The Heart of a Circle of Friends* (1974) reprints some of Dorothy Wordsworth's *Journals* as well as some of William's poetry, in an easily read biography.

JAMES WRIGHT (b. 1927)

JAMES WRIGHT (b. 1927) was born in Martins Ferry, Ohio, a place that frequently appears in his poetry. Wright studied with John Crowe Ransom at Kenyon College before falling under the influence of Theodore Roethke at the University of Washington. Wright has lived in Europe and has taught at the University of Minnesota and Hunter College in New York. He refuses to teach creative writing and considers himself a teacher of literature. His first book of poems, *The Green Wall,* was chosen by W. H. Auden in 1957 as the best book submitted to the Yale Series of Younger Poets. In simple language, his poems celebrate the world familiar to him: midwestern landscapes and ordinary people doing ordinary things. Later volumes of poetry are *Saint Judas* (1959), *The Branch Will Not Break* (1963), *Shall We Gather at the River* (1968), *Collected Poems* (1971), for which he won a Pulitzer Prize, *Two Citizens* (1973), and *The Devil's Parole* (1981). His *Collected Poems* and *Collected Prose* both appeared in 1983.

RICHARD WRIGHT (1908–1960)

RICHARD WRIGHT (1908–1960) was a black writer who had pricked the racial consciousness of both white and black Americans. Born near Natchez, Mississippi, into a sharecropper's family, Wright was badly scarred by a poverty that gave seed to his later themes of racial suffering and humiliation. He fled to Memphis and Chicago, where he worked during the Depression in both the Federal Negro Theater (a WPA project) and the Illinois Writers' Project. Wright's fame rests largely on two works: his novel *Native Son* (1940) and his autobiography, *Black Boy* (1945). Wright was active in the Communist party for twelve years, writing and publishing stories and essays and eventually moving to Harlem to edit the *Daily Worker.* In 1946, Wright migrated to Paris, but his work became predictable and he gradually lost touch with those for whom he spoke. Nonetheless, his major works stand as landmarks in America's racial dialogue. His novels include *The Outsider* (1953), *Savage Holiday* (1954), *The Long Dream* (1958), and *Lawd Today* (published after his death). Wright's short story collections were *Uncle Tom's Children* (1938) and *Eight Men,* the source for "The Man Who Was Almost a Man."

WILLIAM BUTLER YEATS (1865–1939)

WILLIAM BUTLER YEATS (1865–1939) was a visionary poet who made up his own intricate system to "give metaphors for poetry." Born near Dublin to Anglo-Irish Protestant parents, Yeats came naturally into the political upheavals that were to produce the Irish Free State and Ireland's continuing political "troubles." In his youth, Yeats loved the actress and Irish patriot Maude Gonne, and through her he became devoted to Irish nationalism and the occult. He joined the Theosophist Society, and many of his poems were influenced by that philosophy. Yeats was greatly interested in Irish national art, and with John Millington Synge and Lady Gregory, directed the Abbey Theatre (founded 1904) where many of his own plays were produced. His wife, Georgie, practiced automatic writing, a mystical experience in which the hand writes without the mind willing it to, helping him with *A Vision* (1925), which expounded his theories of poetry. Yeats lived with his family in Thoor Ballylee, a restored Norman tower, which became a symbol in his later work. He served as a senator in the Irish Free State (1922–28) and won the Nobel Prize for Literature in 1924. He is buried in Drumcliffe, Sligo, as he had requested in "Under Ben Bulben," one of his poems. The definitive edition of his poems is *The Collected Poems of W. B. Yeats* (1956). Among the many critical works about him is Richard Ellman's *Yeats: The Man and the Masks* (1948).

INDEX OF TERMS

absurd, theater of the, 1033
allegory, 1010
alliteration, 1020
analysis, 1008, 1038
anapestic, 1015, 1023
antagonist, 1011
Aristotle's *Poetics,* 1029
aside, 1035
assonance, 1021
atmosphere, 1010

ballad, 1018
bibliography form, 1053
biographical fallacy, 1047
blank verse, 1022

catharsis, 1032
character, 1035
characterization, 1011
chorus, 1029
climax, 1010, 1034
comedy of manners, 1032
concrete poetry, 1020
confession, 1009
couplet, 1017
critical essay, 1042
cumulative sentence, 1013

dactylic, 1023
denouement, 1010
dialogue, 1035
dimeter, 1024
documentation, 1054
dramatic irony, 1035
dramatic language, 1036
dramatic monologues, 1018
dramatic pyramid, 1034
Dramatis Personae, 1035

elegy, 1017
Elizabethan theater, 1031
epic poems, 1018
essay format, 1044
Existentialism, 1033
explication, 1038
exposition, 1034

fables, 1010
falling action, 1035
fiction: On Reading Fiction, 1007
figures of speech, 1025, 1026
first-person point of view, 1031
flat characters, 1011
foreshadowing, 1035
format, 1050–1054
frame story, 1012
free verse, 1022
funnel format, 1045

genre, 1009
Greek drama, 1028
guilds, medieval, 1030

haiku, 1019
heptameter, 1025
hexameter, 1024
hyperbole, 1026

iambic, 1023
imagery, 1026
incremental repetition, 1021

journal entry, 1041

legend, 1010
limerick, 1014
limited third person, 1012
lyric poetry, 1017

macrocosm, microcosm, 1032
metaphor, 1026
meter, 1023
Middle Ages: drama, 1030
miracle play, 1031
modern theater, 1032
monometer, 1024
morality play, 1031
mystery play, 1031
myth, 1009

naive narrator, 1011
narrative poems, 1018

INDEX OF AUTHORS AND TITLES

Acknowledgments (continued from copyright page)

"A Summer Tragedy" reprinted by permission of Dodd, Mead & Company, Inc. from *The Old South* by Arna Bontemps. Copyright 1933 by Arna Bontemps. Copyright renewed 1961 by Arna Bontemps. Copyright © 1973 by Alberta Bontemps, Executrix.

"A Cradle Song" by William Butler Yeats from *Collected Poems of W. B. Yeats.* Copyright 1903, 1906, 1907, 1912, 1916, 1918, 1919, 1924, 1928, 1931, 1933, 1934, 1935, 1940, 1944, 1945, 1946, 1950, 1956, by the Macmillan Company. Copyright 1940, by Georgie Yeats. Reprinted with the permission of A. P. Watt Ltd. on behalf of Michael B. Yeats and Macmillan (London) Ltd.

"First Lesson," from *Letter from a Distant Land,* by Philip Booth. Copyright © 1957 by Philip Booth, copyright renewed © 1985 by Philip Booth. Reprinted by permission of Viking Penguin, Inc.

"dominic has a doll," copyright © 1957 by E. E. Cummings. Reprinted from his volume *Complete Poems 1913–1962* by permission of Harcourt Brace Jovanovich, Inc.

"Euclid" reprinted with permission of Macmillan Publishing Company from *Collected Poems* by Vachel Lindsay. Copyright 1914 by Macmillan Publishing Company, renewed 1942 by Elizabeth C. Lindsay.

"Offspring" from *Pink Ladies in the Afternoon* by Naomi Long Madgett (Detroit: Lotus Press, Inc., 1972). By permission of the author.

"The Pennycandystore Beyond the El" by Lawrence Ferlinghetti, from *A Coney Island of the Mind.* Copyright © 1958 by Lawrence Ferlinghetti.

"Fern Hill" by Dylan Thomas, from *Poems of Dylan Thomas.* Copyright 1945 by the Trustees of the Copyrights of Dylan Thomas, 1952 by Dylan Thomas.

"When I Was One and Twenty" from *A Shropshire Lad*—Authorised Edition—from *The Collected Poems of A. E. Housman.* Copyright 1939, 1940, © 1965 by Holt, Rinehart and Winston. Copyright © 1967, 1968 by Robert E. Symons. Reprinted by permission of Henry Holt and Company, The Society of Authors as literary representatives of the Estate of A. E. Housman, and Jonathan Cape Ltd., publishers of A. E. Housman's *Collected Poems.*

"Sonnet" by Edna St. Vincent Millay. From *Collected Poems,* Harper & Row. Copyright © 1931, 1934, 1958, 1962 by Edna St. Vincent Millay and Norma Millay Ellis. Reprinted by permission.

"Lady Lazarus" (Copyright © 1963 by Ted Hughes) from *The Collected Poems of Sylvia Plath,* edited by Ted Hughes. Reprinted by permission of Harper & Row, Publishers, Inc. and Faber & Faber, London.

"Mr. Flood's Party" reprinted with permission of Macmillan Publishing Company from *Collected Poems* by Edwin Arlington Robinson. Copyright 1921 by Edwin Arlington Robinson, renewed 1949 by Ruth Nivison.

"On Being Sixty" and "Old Age" from *Chinese Poems* by Arthur Waley. Reprinted by permission of Allen & Unwin.

"Castoff Skin" from *The Passion of Lizzie Borden: New and Selected Poems* by Ruth Whitman. Copyright © 1973 by Ruth Whitman. Reprinted by permission of October House.

"The Emperor of Ice Cream," copyright 1923 and renewed 1951 by Wallace Stevens. Reprinted from *The Collected Poems of Wallace Stevens,* by permission of Alfred A. Knopf, Inc.

"Sailing to Byzantium" reprinted with permission of Macmillan Publishing Company from *Collected Poems* by W. B. Yeats. Copyright 1928 by Macmillan Publishing Company, renewed 1956 by Georgie Yeats. Reprinted by permission of A. P. Watt Ltd. on behalf of Michael B. Yeats and Macmillan (London) Ltd.

"Window-Pane with Forms" by Josephine Jacobsen. First published in *Rye Bread,* Scop Publications, Inc., 1977.

"Great Farm," from *Letter from a Distant Land,* by Philip Booth. Copyright © 1955 by Philip Booth, copyright renewed © 1983 by Philip Booth. Reprinted by permission of Viking Penguin, Inc.

"The Lake Isle of Innisfree" by William Butler Yeats from *Collected Poems of W. B. Yeats.* Copyright 1903, 1906, 1907, 1912, 1916, 1918, 1919, 1924, 1928, 1931, 1933, 1934, 1935, 1940, 1944, 1945, 1946, 1950, 1956, by the Macmillan Company. Copyright 1940, by Georgie Yeats. Reprinted with the permission of A. P. Watt Ltd. on behalf of Michael B. Yeats and Macmillan (London) Ltd.

"Grapefields as a Child" by Benjamin Durazo from *From the Barrio: A Chicano Anthology* edited by Louis Omar Salinas and Lillian Faderman. Copyright © 1973 by Luis Omar Salinas and Lillian Faderman. Reprinted by permission of Harper & Row, Publishers, Inc.

"On Sides of Tractor Paths" by Leonard Adamé from *From the Barrio: A Chicano Anthology* edited by Luis Omar Salinas and Lillian Faderman. Copyright © 1973 by Luis Omar Salinas and Lillian Faderman. Reprinted by permission of Harper & Row, Publishers, Inc.

"A Narrow Fellow in the Grass" reprinted by permission of the publishers and the Trustees of Amherst College from *The Poems of Emily Dickinson,* edited by Thomas H. Johnson, Cambridge, Mass.: The Belknap Press of Harvard University Press, Copyright 1951, © 1955, 1979, 1983 by the President and Fellows of Harvard College.

"Snake," from *The Complete Poems of D. H. Lawrence,* edited and with an Introduction and Notes by Vivian de Sola Pinto and F. Warren Roberts. Copyright © 1964, 1971 by Angelo Ravagli and C. M. Weekley, Executors of The Estate of Frieda Lawrence Ravagli. Reprinted by permission of Viking Penguin, Inc.

"The Fish" from *The Complete Poems 1927–1979* by Elizabeth Bishop. Copyright 1940, renewed copyright © 1968 by Elizabeth Bishop. Reprinted by permission of Farrar, Straus and Giroux, Inc.

"Grass" from *Cornhuskers* by Carl Sandburg, copyright 1918 by Holt, Rinehart and Winston, Inc.; renewed 1946 by Carl Sandburg. Reprinted by permission of Harcourt Brace Jovanovich, Inc.

"Chicago" from *Chicago Poems* by Carl Sandburg, copyright 1916 by Holt, Rinehart and Winston, Inc; renewed 1944 by Carl Sandburg. Reprinted by permission of Harcourt Brace Jovanovich, Inc.

"Street Window" from *Cornhuskers* by Carl Sandburg, copyright 1918 by Holt, Rinehart and Winston, Inc; renewed 1946 by Carl Sandburg. Reprinted by permission of Harcourt Brace Jovanovich, Inc.

"Skyscraper" from *Chicago Poems* by Carl Sandburg, copyright 1916 by Holt, Rinehart and Winston, Inc; renewed 1944 by Carl Sandburg. Reprinted by permission of Harcourt Brace Jovanovich, Inc.

"Prayers of Steel" from *Cornhuskers* by Carl Sandburg, copyright 1918 by Holt, Rinehart and Winston, Inc; renewed 1946 by Carl Sandburg. Reprinted by permission of Harcourt Brace Jovanovich, Inc.

"Sparkling Alleys" by Jose Rendon from *From the Barrio: A Chicano Anthology* edited by Luis Omar Salinas and Lillian Faderman. Copyright © 1973 by Luis Omar Salinas and Lillian Faderman. Reprinted by permission of Harper & Row, Publishers, Inc.

"Things" reprinted with permission of Macmillan Publishing Company from *Maps and Windows* by Jane Cooper. Copyright © 1973 by Jane Cooper. Originally appeared in *The American Poetry Review.*

"Junk," copyright © 1961 by Richard Wilbur. Reprinted from his volume *Advice to a Prophet and Other Poems* by permission of Harcourt Brace Jovanovich, Inc.

Sylvia Plath, edited by Ted Hughes. Reprinted by permission of Harper & Row, Publishers, Inc. and Faber & Faber, London.

"Elegy for Jane" copyright 1950 by Theodore Roethke from *The Collected Poems of Theodore Roethke*. Reprinted by permission of Doubleday & Company, Inc.

"Auto Wreck," copyright 1942 and renewed 1970 by Karl Shapiro. Reprinted from *Collected Poems 1940–1978*, by Karl Shapiro, by permission of Random House, Inc.

"since feeling is first" is reprinted from *IS 5* by E. E. Cummings, by permission of Liveright Publishing Corporation. Copyright © 1985 by E. E. Cummings Trust. Copyright © 1926 by Horace Liveright.

The Antigone of Sophocles: An English Version by Dudley Fitts and Robert Fitzgerald, copyright 1939 by Harcourt Brace Jovanovich, Inc.; renewed 1967 by Dudley Fitts and Robert Fitzgerald. Reprinted by permission of the publisher. Caution: All rights, including professional, amateur, motion picture, recitation, lecturing, performance, public reading, radio broadcasting, and television are strictly reserved. Inquiries on all rights should be addressed to Harcourt Brace Jovanovich, Inc., 111 Fifth Avenue, New York, NY 10003.

The Elephant Man reprinted by permission of Grove Press, Inc. Copyright © 1979 by Bernard Pomerance.

"The Road Not Taken" from *The Poetry of Robert Frost* edited by Edward Connery Lathem. Copyright 1916, 1923, 1930, 1939, © 1969 by Holt, Rinehart and Winston. Copyright 1944, 1951, © 1958 by Robert Frost. Copyright © 1967 by Lesley Frost Ballantine. Reprinted by permission of Henry Holt and Company.

"Death in the Woods" reprinted by permission of Harold Ober Associates Incorporated. Copyright 1926 by The American Mercury, Inc. Copyright renewed 1953 by Eleanor Copenhaver Anderson.

"A Rose for Emily," copyright 1930 and renewed 1958 by William Faulkner. Reprinted from *Collected Stories of William Faulkner,* by permission of Random House, Inc.

"Sonny's Blues" by James Baldwin from *Going to Meet the Man.* Copyright © 1948, 1951, 1960, 1965 by James Baldwin. Reprinted by permission of Doubleday & Company, Inc. Copyright 1950 by Truman Capote. Reprinted from *Breakfast at Tiffany's,* by Truman Capote, by permission of Random House, Inc.

"Follow the Eagle" from *Elephant Bangs Train* by William Kotzwinkle. Reprinted by permission of William Kotzwinkle.

"Nine Lives," copyright © 1969, 1975 by Ursula K. LeGuin; an earlier version of this story appeared in *Playboy Magazine;* reprinted by permission of the author and the author's agent, Virginia Kidd.

"Company" from *Blood Relations* by Roberta Silman. Copyright © 1973, 1975, 1976, 1977 by Roberta Silman.

"Julia" from *Pentimento* by Lillian Hellman. Copyright © 1973 by Lillian Hellman.

"I'm Nobody! Who are You?" "Some keep the Sabbath going to Church," "The Soul selects her own Society," "I cannot live with You," and "My life closed twice before its close" reprinted by permission of the publishers and the Trustees of Amherst College from *The Poems of Emily Dickinson,* edited by Thomas H. Johnson, Cambridge, Mass.: The Belknap Press of Harvard University Press, Copyright 1951, © 1955, 1979, 1983 by the President and Fellows of Harvard College.

"We Two Boys Together Clinging," "O You Whom I Often and Silently Come," and "Poem of Remembrances for a Girl or Boy of these States" reprinted by permission of New York University Press from *Walt Whitman: Leaves of Grass, Reader's Comprehensive Edition* edited by Harold W. Blodgett and Scully Bradley. Copyright © 1965 by New York University.

"Home Burial" from *The Poetry of Robert Frost* edited by Edward Connery Lathem. Copyright 1916, 1923, 1930, 1939, © 1969 by Holt, Rinehart and Winston. Copyright

1944, 1951, © 1958 by Robert Frost. Copyright © 1967 by Lesley Frost Ballantine. Reprinted by permission of Henry Holt and Company.

"Patterns," "A Decade," "Opal" from *The Complete Poetical Works of Amy Lowell.* Copyright © 1955 by Houghton Mifflin Company. Copyright © 1983 renewed by Houghton Mifflin Company, Brinton P. Roberts, Esquire and G. D'Angelot Belin, Esquire. Reprinted by permission of Houghton Mifflin Company.

"Lesson of the Moth" from *The Lives and Times of Archy and Mehitabel* by Don Marquis. Copyright 1927, 1930, 1933, 1935, 1950 by Doubleday & Company, Inc. Reprinted by permission of the publisher.

"The Harlem Dancer," copyright 1981 and reprinted with permission of Twayne Publishers, a division of G. K. Hall & Co., Boston.

"Her Kind" from *To Bedlam and Part Way Back* by Anne Sexton. Copyright © 1960 by Anne Sexton. Reprinted by permission of Houghton Mifflin Company.

"Underwear" by Lawrence Ferlinghetti, from *Starting from San Francisco.* Copyright © 1961 by Lawrence Ferlinghetti.

"Not Waving but Drowning" by Stevie Smith, from *Collected Poems.* Copyright © 1972 by Stevie Smith.

"Incident" from *On These I Stand* by Countee Cullen. Copyright 1925 by Harper & Row, Publishers, Inc. Renewed 1953 by Ida M. Cullen. Reprinted by permission of Harper & Row, Publishers, Inc.

"Notes from a Slave Ship" by Edward Field. By permission of the author.

"We Real Cool" reprinted by permission of Gwendolyn Brooks Blakely.

Noah from *The Wakefield Mystery Plays* by Martial Rose. Copyright © 1961 by Martial Rose. Reprinted by permission of Doubleday & Company, Inc.

No Exit from *No Exit and The Flies* by Jean-Paul Sartré, translated by Stuart Gilbert. Copyright 1946 by Stuart Gilbert. Copyright renewed 1974, 1975 by Maris Agnes Mathilde Gilbert. Reprinted by permission of Alfred A. Knopf, Inc. and the Hamish Hamilton, Ltd., London.

The Dark Root of a Scream by Luis Valdez from *From the Barrio: A Chicano Anthology* edited by Luis Omar Salinas and Lillian Faderman. Copyright © 1973 by Luis Omar Salinas and Lillian Faderman. Reprinted by permission of Harper & Row, Publishers, Inc.

"The Ugliest Pilgrim" reprinted by permission of Russell & Volkening, Inc. as agents for the author. Copyright © 1973 by Doris Betts.

"Defender of the Faith" from *Goodbye Columbus* by Philip Roth. Copyright © 1959 by Philip Roth. Reprinted by permission of Houghton Mifflin Company.

"The Sky is Gray" copyright © 1963 by Ernest J. Gaines from *Bloodline.* Reprinted by permission of Doubleday & Company, Inc.

"The Grandfather of the Sierra Nevada Mountains" from *China Men,* by Maxine Hong Kingston. Copyright © 1980 by Maxine Hong Kingston. Reprinted by permission of Alfred A. Knopf, Inc.

"The Somebody" by Danny Santiago. Copyright © 1970 by Danny Santiago. First published in *Redbook* magazine. Reprinted by permission of Brandt & Brandt Literary Agents, Inc.

"By the Waters of Babylon" by Stephen Vincent Benét. From: *The Selected Works of Stephen Vincent Benét.* Holt, Rinehart & Winston, Inc. Copyright, 1937 by Stephen Vincent Benét. Copyright renewed © 1965 by Thomas C. Benét, Stephanie B. Mahin and Rachel Benét Lewis. Reprinted by permissions of Brandt & Brandt Literary Agents, Inc.

"Out of Place" reprinted by permission of the author and her agent Blanche C. Gregory, Inc. Copyright © 1975 by Joyce Carol Oates.

"I Hear America Singing" reprinted by permission of New York University Press from

Walt Whitman: Leaves of Grass, Reader's Comprehensive Edition edited by Harold W. Blodgett and Sculley Bradley. Copyright © 1965 by New York University.

"I, Too," copyright 1926 by Alfred A. Knopf, Inc. and renewed 1954 by Langston Hughes. Reprinted from *Selected Poems of Langston Hughes,* by Langston Hughes, by permission of Alfred A. Knopf, Inc.

"We Wear the Mask" from *The Complete Poems of Paul Laurence Dunbar.* Reprinted by permission of Dodd, Mead & Company, Inc.

"Outcast" by Claude McKay. Copyright 1981 and reprinted with permission of Twayne Publishers, a division of G. K. Hall & Co., Boston.

"Nikki-Rosa" from *Black Feeling, Black Talk, Black Judgment* by Nikki Giovanni. Copyright © 1968, 1970 by Nikki Giovanni. By permission of William Morrow & Company.

"kitchenette building" reprinted by permission of Gwendolyn Brooks Blakely.

"If You Saw a Negro Lady," copyright 1981: June Jordan.

"I Like to Think of Harriet Tubman," © Susan Griffin from *Made from This Earth* (Women's Press, 1984).

"In the Garden of the Home God" reprinted with permission of Macmillan Publishing Company from *Literature of the American Indian,* edited by Thomas E. Sanders and Walter W. Peek. Copyright © 1973, 1976 by Benziger Bruce & Glencoe, Inc.

"Earth and I Gave You Turquoise" from *The Gourd Dancer* by N. Scott Momaday. Copyright © 1975 by N. Scott Momaday.

"I Am Joaquín," copyright Rodolfo Gonzales. Reprinted by permission.

"stupid america" appeared first in *Chicano: 25 Pieces of a Chicano Mind,"* 1969, Barrio Publications, Arvada, Colorado.

"An Elementary School Classroom in a Slum," copyright 1942 and renewed 1970 by Stephen Spender. Reprinted from *Collected Poems 1928–1953,* by Stephen Spender, by permission of Random House, Inc. Reprinted by permission of Faber and Faber Ltd. from *Collected Poems* by Stephen Spender.

"The Unknown Citizen," copyright 1940 and renewed 1968 by W. H. Auden. Reprinted from *W. H. Auden: Collected Poems,* by W. H. Auden, edited by Edward Mendelson, by permission of Random House, Inc. Reprinted by permission of Faber and Faber Ltd. from *Collected Poems* by W. H. Auden edited by Edward Mendelson.

"To Be of Use," copyright © 1969, 1971, 1973 by Marge Piercy. Reprinted from *Circles on the Water,* by Marge Piercy, by permission of Alfred A. Knopf, Inc.

"Mushrooms," copyright © 1960 by Sylvia Plath. Reprinted from *The Colossus and Other Poems* by Sylvia Plath, by permission of Alfred A. Knopf, Inc. and by permission of Faber and Faber, Ltd. London.

"Mind" from *Things of This World,* copyright 1956, 1984 by Richard Wilbur. Reprinted by permission of Harcourt Brace Jovanovich, Inc.

"The Second Coming" reprinted with permission of Macmillan Publishing Company from *Collected Poems* by W. B. Yeats. Copyright 1924 by Macmillan Publishing Company, renewed 1952 by Bertha Georgie Yeats. Reprinted by permission of A. P. Watt Ltd. on behalf of Michael B. Yeats and Macmillan London, Ltd.

"I Have a Dream" reprinted by permission of Joan Daves. From *I Have a Dream.* Copyright © 1963 by Martin Luther King, Jr.

Excerpt from *for colored girls who have considered suicide when the rainbow is enuf* by Ntozake Shange. Reprinted by permission of Macmillan Publishing Company, a division of Macmillan, Inc. Copyright © 1975, 1976 by Ntozake Shange.

From *The Glass Menagerie* by Tennessee Williams. Copyright 1945 by Tennessee Williams and Edwina D. Williams and renewed 1973 by Tennessee Williams. Reprinted by permission of Random House, Inc.

Two limericks, © 1981 Hallmark Cards, Inc. Reprinted by permission.

"There was a young woman from Niger," "There was a young fellow named Weir," and "Word has come from the Dean" reprinted from *Lure of the Limerick* by William Baring-Gould. Copyright © 1967 by William S. Baring-Gould. Used by permission of Clarkson N. Potter.

"The Crystal Spring" and "The Mississippi River" reprinted by permission of Charles F. Tuttle Co., Inc. of Tokyo, Japan.

Ezra Pound, *Personae*. Copyright 1926 by Ezra Pound.

"Then" from *The Gates* by Muriel Rukeyser. Reprinted by permission of International Creative Management, Inc. Copyright © 1976 by Muriel Rukeyser.

"in just-" is reprinted from *Tulips & Chimneys* by E. E. Cummings, by permission of Liveright Publishing Corporation. Copyright © 1923, 1925 and renewed 1951, 1953 by E. E. Cummings. Copyright 1973, 1976 by the trustees for the E. E. Cummings Trust. Copyright © 1973, 1976 by George James Firnage.

"1(a," copyright © 1958 by E. E. Cummings. Reprinted from his volume *Complete Poems 1913–1962* by permission of Harcourt Brace Jovanovich, Inc.

ABOUT
THE AUTHORS

Anne Mills King teaches American Literature, Victorian Literature, Women in Literature, and Composition. She received her B.A. from Skidmore College, her M.A. from American University, and her Ph.D. from the University of Maryland.

Sandra Kurtinitis, the author of *A Brief and Lively No-Nonsense Guide to Writing,* teaches Composition, American Studies, and World Literature. She received her B.A. from Misericordia College, her M.A. from the University of Maryland, and her Ph.D. from George Washington University.

Both authors are Professors of English at Prince George's Community College in Largo, Maryland. Each of the authors has published several articles individually, and together they have edited the recent editions of *Values and Voices.*